Housing Allocation and Homelessness

Third Edition

Housing Allocation and Homelessness

Third Edition

Jan Luba QC
Barrister, Garden Court Chambers

Liz Davies
Barrister, Garden Court Chambers

Published by
Jordan Publishing Limited
21 St Thomas Street
Bristol BS1 6JS

British Library Cataloguing-in-Publication Data

A catalogue record for this book is available from the British Library.

ISBN 978 1 84661 524 5

Typeset by Letterpart Ltd, Reigate, Surrey

Printed in Great Britain by CPI Antony Rowe, Chippenham, Wiltshire

STOP PRESS

The publication of this 3rd edition was held back to await the announcement of the date of commencement of the changes to *homelessness* law made by the Localism Act 2011.

In mid-October 2012 we learned that the commencement date for England would be 9 November 2012 and the text has been amended to reflect that development. The changes will not apply to applicants whose applications for homelessness assistance were made before the commencement date if the local housing authority was under a duty to secure accommodation for them, including any interim duty, and that duty had not ceased by that date.[1] The revised text also now includes reference to the new regulations, dealing with the suitability of private rented accommodation to be offered to some homeless households, which come into force on the same date. The regulations themselves are in Appendix 2.

What we did not have at the time of writing was the text of the supplementary statutory guidance, being issued to local housing authorities in England, explaining the new provisions. That was published just after we had finished writing but the text of the guidance itself is reproduced in full in a new Appendix 4 (Stop Press material).

At about the same time, we learned that the rules for eligibility for both *allocation* and *homelessness* were being revised to take account of developments in European Union law with effect from 8 November 2012. We have been able to incorporate the amendments, which only apply in England, in the text of the regulations reproduced at Appendix 2.

However, again, what we did not have at the time of writing was the text of the non-statutory guidance, being issued to local housing authorities in England, explaining these new eligibility provisions. That guidance is contained in a

---

[1]   In the text of this edition, written before the Commencement Order (containing this transitional provision) was published, we refer to the amendments as simply not applying to those whose applications were made before 9 November 2012. However, there will now be some cases where an application for homelessness assistance was made before that date but in respect of which the local housing authority had no continuing accommodation duty on 9 November. Most commonly, this would arise where the local housing authority initially did not have any reason to believe that a pre-9 November applicant might have a priority need and therefore owed no accommodation duty on that date. In those circumstances, the new rules would apply, even though the application had been made before 9 November. Readers should note the complex transitional provision in the Commencement Order reproduced in Appendix 2.

letter from the Department of Communities & Local Government which was published just after we had finished writing but the text of the letter is reproduced in full in a new Appendix 4 (Stop Press Items).

Readers dealing with allocations and homelessness *in Wales* will need to await news from the Welsh Government as to whether (and if so when) the Localism Act provisions, and the eligibility amendments, will be brought into force in Wales.

Jan Luba QC
Liz Davies

November 2012

PREFACE TO THE THIRD EDITION

There has scarcely been a more depressing time to be writing a book about the topics of homelessness and social housing allocation.

After years of decline in the number of applications for homelessness assistance, the tide has turned and the figures are growing again in both England and Wales. By the second quarter of 2012, more than 4,000 homelessness applications a month were being made to local councils in England alone.

There seems little prospect of any imminent reduction. Indeed, the combined effects of the recent restrictions on housing benefit, the imminent introduction of the so-called 'bedroom tax', and the capping of overall benefits from 2013 all strongly suggest that more and more tenants will be forced to leave their homes and apply for homelessness assistance in the next few years. Any significant increase in mortgage interest rates will additionally tip thousands of struggling homeowners over the brink and into homelessness.

Of course, the necessary consequence of increasing homelessness is the steady growth in demand for short-term crisis accommodation provided by local housing authorities, which are having to continue to operate the homelessness 'safety net' despite many other demands on their own diminished resources. By mid-2012 the number of homeless households placed in temporary accommodation had reached over 51,000.

Hard-stretched local housing authorities have found themselves unable to cope with this pressure. Many have been forced to break the law and place families in bed and breakfast accommodation. Earlier this year the position became so bad that the then Minister of Housing had to write to more than a dozen local housing authorities that were unlawfully breaking the embargo on the use of that sort of accommodation for significant numbers of families.

In the longer term, the aspiration for many low income households is access to correspondingly low-rent social housing. There are now more applicants on social housing waiting lists than the system can possibly ever cope with. Given the very low levels of new build and conversion to provide low-rent social housing, for the majority of applicants there is no real prospect of obtaining a tenancy of social housing for many years, if at all.

Against the background of these social trends, the law itself has been undergoing change. This year, the parts of the Localism Act 2011 that are designed to give greater 'flexibility' for local councils to tackle homelessness and the excess demand for social housing allocation have been brought into force in England. On *homelessness*, local housing authorities will now be released from their obligations to the homeless households owed the highest duty by a 'take-it-or-leave it' offer of private rented accommodation. We deal with the detail in Chapter 17. On *housing allocation,* councils are to be given back a power – scrapped a decade ago – to pick and choose which classes of applicant can and cannot get access to their available social housing. That change will enable a dramatic cull of waiting lists and is reviewed in Chapter 3.

Some readers may be heartened by the fact that the preparation of this edition has required us to deal with the impact of many fewer court decisions than in previous years. Our experience suggests that this is not a consequence of the law having become less contentious or easier to apply. It reflects, rather, the greatly reduced availability of resources with which to take or defend court cases. We do not simply mean that local housing authorities are being driven to settle cases they would otherwise have contested or to abandon appeals that they would otherwise have pursued because of pressures on the public purse – although we have seen much of that. The downward trend is equally a reflection of the fact that diminishing numbers of specialist lawyers assisting the homeless and aspirant social housing tenants are finding it harder and harder to deliver high quality services in the face of reductions in their remuneration from legal aid and the impending curtailment of its scope.

The recent history strongly suggests that in future more disputes will find their way to the respective ombudsmen than to the courts. We make no apology for having given greater emphasis in this edition to the work of those ombudsmen and to the lessons to be learned from the investigations they have undertaken and the reports they have published.

What has driven us to maintain our own commitment to this book is the experience we have had, from up and down the country, of continuing interest and enthusiasm among local authority staff, housing association officers, housing lawyers and housing advice workers who still want – despite all the odds – to 'do the right thing', wherever possible, and ensure that the homeless, and applicants for social housing, achieve at least the minimum rights that legislation confers on them. If our writing helps them in that endeavour, in any way, it will have been worth it.

But this book is not the product of our labours alone. This edition has been ably edited by Julian Roskams of Etica Press. Its production has been efficiently steered by Kate Hather and Tony Hawitt at our publishers, Jordans. Our expert professional colleagues Sue Lukes, Adrian Berry and Desmond Rutledge have all helped us on points of detail. Readers of earlier editions have been kind enough to suggest amendments or additions. The indefatigable Di Acon at Jordans has organised a roadshow enabling us to get this new edition directly into use by frontline workers. Most importantly, our respective partners and our family members have provided endless support during the daunting process of carefully revising a text of this magnitude.

We write this preface at the arrival of another anniversary of the loss of that stalwart of the interests of the homeless, the late Bob Lawrence. Our regret is that, for the reasons we have set out above, he must surely be turning in his grave. He will be all the more sorely missed.

Jan Luba QC
Liz Davies

October 2012

BIOGRAPHICAL NOTES

Jan Luba QC is a barrister practising from Garden Court Chambers in London and a Bencher of the Middle Temple. He was called to the Bar in 1980 and in 2000 was made a Queen's Counsel and Recorder (part-time judge). He specialises in housing law with particular emphasis on housing management law, homelessness, allocation of social housing and housing conditions.

He is the author of *Housing & The Human Rights Act: A Special Bulletin* published by Jordans in October 2000. He is co-author of *Homelessness Act 2002: A Special Bulletin* (Jordans, 2002). He is also the co-author of *Defending Possession Proceedings* (Legal Action Group, 7th edn, 2010), the co-author of *Repairs: Tenants Rights* (Legal Action Group, 4th edn, 2010), and is the co-contributor to the monthly column 'Recent Developments in Housing Law' published in the magazine *Legal Action*.

Jan has considerable experience as a housing law trainer and has written widely on housing allocation and homelessness issues in both the legal and housing press. He is a patron of Croydon Housing Aid Society.

Liz Davies is a barrister practising at Garden Court Chambers, London. She specialises in all types of legal work for tenants, other occupiers and homeless applicants. Before coming to the Bar, she was a solicitor specialising in housing law.

With Jan Luba QC, she is co-author of *Homelessness Act 2002: A Special Bulletin* (Jordans, 2002). She is a contributing author to the *Housing Law Handbook* (Law Society, 2009).

In 2001, she published *Through the Looking Glass* (Verso, 2001), an account of her two years' membership of the Labour Party's National Executive Committee. She is Chair of the Haldane Society of Socialist Lawyers.

CONTENTS

TABLE OF CASES

References are to paragraph numbers.

Housing Allocation and Homelessness

TABLE OF STATUTES

References are to paragraph numbers.

TABLE OF STATUTORY INSTRUMENTS

References are to paragraph numbers.

TABLE OF EUROPEAN UNION LEGISLATION

References are to paragraph numbers.

Part I
ALLOCATION

Chapter 1

ALLOCATION OF SOCIAL HOUSING: AN OVERVIEW

PREFACE TO THIS PART OF THE BOOK

1.1 The first Part of this book is concerned with the allocation of social housing. The topic is not one free of political controversy or legal complexity. As the new President of the UK Supreme Court has so aptly said:

> 'The allocation of social housing is a difficult and potentially controversial matter, which gives rise to very hard choices, at all levels of decision making, whether strategic, policy or specific.'[1]

1.2 The last statutory guidance on the topic issued by the outgoing Labour government expressed this view:

> 'Social rented housing is an asset of great significance to the country, to local communities, to families and to individual people. It provides an essential part of the welfare safety net that supports many of the most vulnerable in our society. It provides a firm foundation, with the security and stability that can help people to overcome disadvantage and to build successful lives for themselves and their families. And it can help to create prosperous, healthy local communities, as part of a balanced housing market.
>
> In any circumstances, the way that social housing is allocated would be a matter of real importance.'[2]

1.3 More recently, the first Minister for Housing in the UK Coalition Government wrote in June 2012 that:

> 'Social housing is of enormous importance – for the millions who live in it now, and the many more who look to it to provide the support they need in future – and the way it is allocated is key to creating communities where people choose to live and are able to prosper.'[3]

1.4 For its part, the Welsh Government has recently written that:

> 'The Welsh Government believes that the allocation of housing can play an important role in broader regeneration, sustainability and inclusion. For example, allocations can make a contribution towards meeting the objectives set out in a local authority's homelessness strategy, housing strategy and community strategy. It recognises that allocation schemes will need to form part of an integrated range of measures and initiatives to address social issues at the local level.'[4]

---

[1] Lord Neuberger in *R (Ahmad) v Newham London Borough Council* [2009] UKHL 14 at [25].

[2] *Fair and flexible: statutory guidance on social housing allocations for local authorities in England* (Department for Communities and Local Government, December 2009) paras 10–11.

[3] Grant Shapps MP in the Ministerial Foreword to *Allocation of accommodation: guidance for local housing authorities in England* (DCLG, June 2012) reproduced in Appendix 1 of this book.

[4] *Code of Guidance for Local Authorities Allocation of Accommodation and Homelessness 2012* (Welsh Government), August 2012, para 1.1, reproduced in the CD Rom with this book.

1.5 Our hope is that this Part of this book will provide clarity where there is currently complexity or confusion. Beyond that, we aim merely to outline areas of controversy without, we hope, adding to them.

USING THIS PART OF THE BOOK

1.6 This Part of this book, comprised of the first six Chapters, deals with the process of distributing tenancies of homes available from social landlords, primarily councils and housing associations. That process is known as the 'allocation of' social housing. For those coming new to this subject, the rest of this opening Chapter introduces the topic and relates some of its history. It contains an outline of the present legal framework for allocation of social housing, the primary statutory regime, the impact of customer choice, the relevance of human rights and some comments about possible future developments relating to housing allocation. Until very recently, the law relating to social housing allocation applied in the same way in both England and Wales. However, that is no longer the case and the text of this Part of this book seeks to explain the differences in the way the law now operates in each of the two countries.

1.7 In both England and Wales the allocation of most social housing is organised through the 'local housing authority'[5] for the area in which the housing is situated. These local housing authorities not only allocate their own stock (if they have any) but also make nominations to local housing associations and other social landlords. Indeed, by 2012 council properties had come to represent less than half of the social housing stock in England and the majority of local housing authorities are no longer social landlords. In this part of this book the term 'private registered provider' or 'registered social landlord' is used to refer to social landlords other than local authorities.[6] These landlords are mainly, but not exclusively, housing associations.

1.8 Each local housing authority has an *allocation scheme* explaining local priorities and procedures. Such schemes are the lynchpins of the social housing allocation system. Readers already involved in the process of distributing social housing, or advising those who seek a new home in social housing, will probably want more detailed information on one or more of the essential stages of the allocation process than this introductory Chapter can offer. The immediately following paragraphs provide an indication of where in the book that information can be found. Readers concerned solely with direct

---

[5] Housing Act ('HA') 1996, s 230.

[6] The term 'private registered provider' is used in England and the term 'registered social landlord' is used in relation to such landlords operating in Wales. Therefore, to embrace all non-local authority social landlords whether operating in England or Wales, the modern statutory language uses the rubric "a private registered provider of social housing or a registered social landlord": eg HA 1996, s 159(4A)(b).

allocations, made by private registered providers or by registered social landlords without nomination by a local housing authority, may wish to go directly to Chapter 6.

1.9 The starting point, for most aspiring applicants for social housing, is to assemble the necessary information about local arrangements for allocation of available social housing and then make an application for consideration under those arrangements. Chapter 2 deals with how applications are made, processed and decided.

1.10 The first hurdle for an applicant is to be accepted as eligible to be considered for allocation of a tenancy of social housing by the local housing authority to which the application has been made. Eligibility, and thus access to the local allocation scheme, is the subject of Chapter 3. Even if an applicant is eligible, they may need to pass an additional hurdle of 'qualifying' for consideration under a local allocation scheme if they apply to a local housing authority in England. Chapter 3 also deals with qualification.

1.11 Among those applicants who are eligible and who qualify, there needs to be a process of sifting or assessment to determine respective priorities between them. That may be as simple as a date-ordered queue or as complex as a sophisticated individual assessment of each applicant's housing need. Every local housing authority will need a scheme for assessment or prioritisation by which it can work out who gets what in respect of available homes. Chapter 4 describes how such schemes are drawn up, how they can be amended, and the parameters within which they must be operated.

1.12 Once an applicant's priority has been identified, the next stage will be to determine whether, and on what terms, to make him or her an offer of a new home in social housing. Local arrangements may enable applicants to try to select homes for themselves, by bidding in response to advertisements ('choice-based letting' or 'CBL'), or may provide for staff to choose applicants for available properties. These processes and arrangements are described in Chapter 5.

1.13 Chapter 6 deals with the discrete question of allocation of social housing by housing associations and other private registered providers of social housing or registered social landlords. Most of their available homes are let as a result of nominations made to them by local housing authorities through operation of the allocation scheme arrangements described in Chapters 2 to 5. But Chapter 6 additionally deals with applications made directly to private registered providers or registered social landlords for the allocation of their homes.

1.14 Readers seeking the primary source materials on social housing allocation, rather than descriptive text, will find that we have gathered in the Appendices and on the CD Rom the essential statutory materials, the statutory Codes of Guidance and other relevant documents.

1.15   The authors are ever anxious to improve and make more accessible the content of this Part (and all parts) of this book. Comments on the content or structure are warmly welcomed, either direct to the authors or through the publishers.

INTRODUCTION

1.16   For the purposes of this Part of this book, 'social housing'[7] is taken to embrace the portfolio of residential accommodation for rent held by local housing authorities and by other providers of social housing (such as housing associations and housing co-operatives). This Part of this book primarily focuses on how landlords in the first category (local housing authorities) allocate the homes that they have available to rent. But it also considers the most numerically significant form of letting by the second category (other registered providers of social housing and registered social landlords) – those lettings arising from nominations made by local housing authorities. Direct allocations of their remaining vacancies by private registered providers or registered social landlords are addressed in Chapter 6 of this book.[8]

1.17   Local housing authorities in many (but not all) areas face a difficult task in the distribution of their available rented homes. Demand for such social housing often far exceeds supply, and the supply of affordable housing has been generally diminishing.[9] Pressure on what remains of the stock is increasing.[10]

1.18   In each local housing authority area, those seeking the allocation of social housing will include, among many others:

(1)   applicants for Housing Act 1996 (HA 1996), Part 7 ('Homelessness') assistance who are in temporary accommodation provided by the local housing authority;[11]

---

[7]   A term now technically defined, for other purposes, by Housing and Regeneration Act 2008, s 68(1).

[8]   See also Chapter 10 of Alder & Handy *Housing Association Law and Practice* (Sweet & Maxwell, 4th edn, 2003) and Robert Latham *Allocating social housing: the registered social landlord context* (2008) October *Legal Action*, p 42.

[9]   There were 1.84m households on local authority waiting lists in England on 1 April 2011, an increase of 4.5% on the number as at 1 April 2010: *Local Authority Housing Statistics, England: 2010–11: Housing Strategy Statistical Appendix and Business Plan Statistical Appendix* (DCLG, November 2011). Yet provisional figures indicate that in England only a total of 39,170 new affordable homes were provided for social rent in 2010/11: *Affordable Housing Supply, England, 2010–11* (DCLG, October 2011). Although that number represents the highest total for several years, it bears no resemblance to the heyday of social housebuilding in which in excess of 100,000 new homes became available each year.

[10]   That pressure is likely to increase further as a result of measures to re-stimulate the exercise by social housing tenants of the right to buy which took effect in England on 1 April 2012: *Reinvigorating Right to Buy and one for one replacement: Information for Local Authorities* (DCLG, March 2012).

[11]   See Chapters 7 and 17.

(2)   people staying with family or friends but needing a home of their own;

(3)   tenants in the private sector who occupy unsuitable accommodation or who want the relative permanence of a secure or assured tenancy in social housing;

(4)   the local housing authority's own tenants who may occupy unsuitable or overcrowded accommodation, or who may need to move for work or family reasons;

(5)   people from outside a local housing authority's own area needing to move into it; and

(6)   rough sleepers.

1.19   All of those people may apply to the local housing authority and ask that they be allocated somewhere suitable and secure to live.

1.20   Local housing authorities can meet some of that demand by selecting applicants for secure or introductory tenancies of properties from their own stock (if they hold any), or by nominating applicants to other local housing authorities or to other social landlords. Each time a local housing authority selects an applicant, or nominates in this way, it has, in legal terms, 'allocated' accommodation.[12]

1.21   How does the local housing authority decide which deserving case gets priority over other deserving cases and therefore who should get the next available property? The answer, in broad terms, is that each local housing authority is free to draw up its own policy on how it will prioritise its applicants, provided that the policy adopted complies with certain statutory requirements and with basic legal principles of fairness and rationality. Before looking in somewhat more detail[13] at the current legal framework (to be found largely in HA 1996, Part 6), the rest of this initial Chapter offers a brief résumé of the relevant recent history of legal regulation in the allocation of social housing and a thumbnail outline of the current law.

HISTORY

Allocation law prior to April 1997

1.22   Before 1 April 1997,[14] local housing authorities could organise the allocation of social housing as they saw fit, subject only to legal principles of rationality and fairness, their statutory duties towards applicants for

---

[12]   Subject to exceptions set out at HA 1996, s159(4A) and (4B) [England] and s 159(5), s 160(2) and (3) [Wales] and in regulations; see **1.37–1.43**.

[13]   In Chapters 2 to 5.

[14]   When HA 1996, Part 6 came into force.

homelessness assistance under what is now HA 1996, Part 7 (Homelessness),[15] and a long-standing statutory obligation to give reasonable preference to certain groups.[16] Provided that they complied with those obligations, the priority accorded to different groups of applicants was left to the discretion of each local housing authority.[17] They also enjoyed a general discretion as to when, and in what circumstances, they would exclude certain applicants from consideration for the allocation of social housing.[18] Commonly, local housing authorities would use this discretion to exclude applicants who were in rent arrears, or who had a history of nuisance behaviour. Many also operated policies suspending applicants from consideration if they refused a certain number of offers of suitable accommodation or for other reasons.

1.23   The decisions of the courts and the Ombudsmen about the operation of social housing allocation before April 1997 are likely now to offer little relevant guidance on the correct application of the current statutory regimes.

Allocation law between April 1997 and January 2003

1.24   From 1 April 1997, HA 1996, Part 6 ('Allocation of Housing Accommodation') as enacted provided a new statutory basis for the allocation of social housing by local housing authorities in England and Wales. The big change was the requirement for local housing authorities to maintain a 'Housing Register' – one list that would contain all the different applicants entitled to be considered for an allocation of social housing, except internal applicants for transfer. Within the list of applicants held on that register, local housing authorities were required to give reasonable preference to particular groups. Importantly, no specific preference was required to be given to applicants entitled to assistance under HA 1996, Part 7 ('Homelessness'), thereby abandoning the explicit statutory duty to that effect which had been contained in the earlier Housing Act 1985.[19] At the same time, HA 1996, Part 7 had introduced the concept that local housing authorities' duties to applicants for assistance under that Part (who had a priority need and had not become homeless intentionally) were simply to provide accommodation for a period of two years.[20] The idea was that applicants for assistance under HA 1996, Part 7

---

[15]   And, was then, Housing Act 1985, Part III, s 65.

[16]   Re-enacted in Housing Act 1985, s 22 and giving reasonable preference to: those occupying insanitary or overcrowded houses; those with large families; those living in unsatisfactory housing conditions; and applicants for homelessness assistance to whom duties were owed.

[17]   Housing Act 1985, s 21 vests the general management of its houses in a local housing authority.

[18]   *R v Canterbury City Council ex p Gillespie* (1986) 19 HLR 7, QBD.

[19]   In its original form HA 1996, s 167(2) had required local housing authorities to give reasonable preference only to: those occupying insanitary or overcrowded housing or otherwise living in unsatisfactory housing conditions; those occupying housing accommodation which was temporary or occupied on insecure terms; families with dependent children; households consisting of or including someone who was expecting a child; households consisting of or including someone with a particular need for settled accommodation on medical or welfare grounds; and households whose social or economic circumstances were such that they had difficulty in securing settled accommodation.

[20]   HA 1996, s 193(2) prior to amendments made by the Homelessness Act 2002.

would be provided with safety-net accommodation and, during those two years, they would either rise to the top of the list of those on the local housing register and be allocated social housing accommodation or would find their own accommodation in the private sector. Homelessness was no longer to be an automatic passport into long-term social housing. Some of that changed with the election of a new government (in May 1997), and from 1 November 1997 the effect of a ministerial order was that homeless people, who were in priority need and had not become homeless intentionally, were included among the groups of people to whom 'reasonable preference' had to be given in the allocation of social housing.[21]

1.25 Subject to those 'reasonable preferences', however, a local housing authority could draw up its own policies as to how to recognise – usually by a points system – the different types of need for an allocation of accommodation among those on the housing register. Local housing authorities could also continue to operate policies excluding certain categories of applicants, provided that they scrutinised each applicant's case individually and fairly.[22] Many local housing authorities therefore continued to operate policies, adopted before 1997, of excluding people with rent arrears and those who had committed acts of nuisance, and of suspending applicants who had refused offers of accommodation.[23] They were also entitled to operate policies excluding applicants from outside their own areas.[24] Local housing authorities were additionally required by statute to exclude asylum seekers and other persons subject to immigration control from their registers.[25]

1.26 The housing register scheme did not apply to existing tenants seeking transfers within the same landlord's stock. As far as those transfers were concerned, local housing authorities retained the broad general discretion to operate any policy they wished, subject to public law considerations of fairness and rationality, and limited statutory requirements to consider housing need.[26] Many local housing authorities operated policies excluding tenants who had a certain level of rent arrears or who were accused of nuisance behaviour, from

---

[21] Allocation of Housing (Reasonable and Additional Preference) Regulations 1997, SI 1997/1902.

[22] *R v Wolverhampton Metropolitan Borough Council ex p Watters* (1997) 29 HLR 931, CA.

[23] See eg *R (Giles) v Fareham Borough Council* [2002] EWHC 2951 (Admin), (2003) 35 HLR 36, Admin Ct (acquiescence in nuisance behaviour) and *R v Southwark London Borough Council ex p Mason* (1999) 32 HLR 88, QBD (refusal of offers). One survey of 74 housing organisations found that 47 had an exclusions policy in place, with a further eight operating a deferral/refusal policy: *Exclusions from the housing register* (Northern Housing Consortium, May 2000).

[24] *R (Conway) v Charnwood Borough Council* [2002] EWHC 43 Admin, (2002) March *Legal Action*, p 16, Admin Ct.

[25] HA 1996, s 161(2).

[26] *R v Newham London Borough Council ex p Watkins* (1993) 26 HLR 434, QBD.

being eligible for a transfer,[27] and suspending from transfer schemes those tenants who had refused an offer of a transfer.[28]

Allocation law between January 2003 and June 2012

1.27 In January 2003, HA 1996, Part 6 ('Allocation of Housing Accommodation') was substantially amended by Homelessness Act 2002, ss 13–16 which applied in the same way in both England and Wales.[29] The concept of a compulsory housing register was abolished and replaced by a requirement to have a comprehensive local housing allocation scheme. The categories of reasonable preference were altered. New codes of statutory guidance were issued: the *Allocation of Accommodation Code of Guidance for local housing authorities* in England;[30] and the *Code of Guidance for local housing authorities on allocation of accommodation and homelessness* for Wales.[31] Local housing authorities were required to have regard to that guidance when making allocation schemes and decisions on allocations.[32] Although barely referred to in the statutory amendments, running through the new approach to allocation of social housing was the concept that applicants should have a choice of accommodation, rather than be the subject of a take-it-or-leave-it allocation.[33]

Allocation law since June 2012

1.28 Since 18 June 2012 the legal position has become significantly more complex. The provisions of HA 1996 Part 6, as amended by the Homelessness Act 2002, remain in force in Wales and continue to operate in the same way that they have done since last significantly amended in 2003 (therefore, largely as described in **1.27**). However, in England, the provisions of HA 1996 Part 6 were substantially modified by the Localism Act 2011, ss 145–147 with effect from 18 June 2012.[34] The two key differences are that local housing authorities in England:

(1)   can now designate classes of applicants who can and cannot qualify for housing allocation under their schemes;[35] and

---

27   *R v Lambeth London Borough Council ex p Njomo* (1996) 28 HLR 737, QBD (rent arrears); *R v Southwark London Borough Council ex p Melak* (1996) 29 HLR 223, QBD (rent arrears); and *R v York City Council ex p Wilson* (1997) June *Legal Action*, p 18, QBD (nuisance).
28   *R v Wandsworth London Borough Council ex p Lawrie and Heshmati* (1997) 30 HLR 153, QBD.
29   In force from 27 January 2003 [Wales] and 31 January 2003 [England].
30   *Allocation of Accommodation: Code of Guidance for local housing authorities* (Office of the Deputy Prime Minister, November 2002). Parts of that Code were subsequently replaced by the further statutory guidance given in *Fair and flexible: statutory guidance on social housing allocations for local authorities in England* (DCLG, December 2009).
31   *Code of Guidance for local housing authorities on allocation of accommodation and homelessness* (National Assembly for Wales, April 2003).
32   HA 1996, s 169(1).
33   See Chapter 5.
34   Localism Act 2011 (Commencement No 6 and Transitional, Savings and Transitory Provisions) Order 2012, SI 2012/1463 art 3.
35   HA 1996, s 160ZA. See **3.140–3.202**.

(2) no longer need to include non-priority transfer applicants in their statutory allocation arrangements.[36]

1.29 This legislative dichotomy in the law of social housing allocation as it applies between each of the two countries has been achieved by the insertion of the words 'in Wales' into many of the substantive sections of HA 1996 Part 6 and the insertion into that Part of whole new sections and new subsections containing the words 'in England'. The law as it presently stands is represented by the amended terms of HA 1996 Part 6 as set out in Appendix 1 to this edition of this book. The effect of the present arrangements is briefly outlined in the rest of this Chapter and is more fully described in Chapters 2–5 of this book.

1.30 As before, separate statutory guidance applies in England and in Wales.[37] In the former, the current guidance is that issued by the Secretary of State for Communities & Local Government in June 2012 and contained in *Allocation of accommodation: guidance for local housing authorities in England* which is referred to throughout this Part of this book as 'the English Code'.[38] In Wales, the current guidance is that issued by the Welsh Government in August 2012 which is referred to throughout this book as 'the Welsh Code'.[39] In both cases, the guidance has been issued in exercise of the powers granted by HA 1996, s 169. The English Code is reproduced in full in the Appendix to this book and on the accompanying CD Rom. The Welsh Code is included on the CD Rom.

1.31 The current English Code is less than half the length of its 2002 predecessor and replaces not only that earlier code but all other previous statutory guidance on housing allocation in England.[40] While this is said to be 'evidence of the Government's commitment to "cutting red tape"'[41] the result is that much of the earlier detailed guidance issued in England is no longer applicable and the fullest exposition of the statutory provisions and their application is to be found in the Welsh Code which now runs to over 250 pages. The Welsh Government has made its Code available online and intends to review and update it in January and/or June of each year.

OVERVIEW OF THE CURRENT STATUTORY SCHEME

1.32 The text of this part of this Chapter necessarily provides only an introductory overview of matters that, as the cross-referencing indicates, are

---

[36] HA 1996, s 159(4A). See **2.57–2.68**.
[37] HA 1996, s 169.
[38] *Allocation of accommodation: guidance for local housing authorities in England* (DCLG, June 2012), reproduced in Appendix 1 to this book.
[39] *Code of guidance for local authorities on Allocation of Accommodation and Homelessness 2012* (Welsh Government, August 2012), reproduced on the CD Rom with this book.
[40] English Code, para 1.2.
[41] English Code, Ministerial Foreword, p 4.

given fuller treatment later in this Part of this book. It aims to do no more than introduce the reader to some of the key features of current provisions for the allocation of social housing.

The present statutory scheme in outline

1.33 HA 1996, Part 6 applies to allocations of social housing both to new applicants for social housing and to some existing local housing authority tenants seeking transfers.[42] The key statutory requirement is that every local housing authority must have adopted a local scheme for allocation of social housing.[43] When making an 'allocation', local housing authorities must comply with both the provisions of HA 1996, Part 6 and with their own local allocation schemes.[44] Provided that the local housing authority has complied with HA 1996, Part 6 in drawing up its allocation scheme, and has treated all its applicants in accordance with the provisions of HA 1996, Part 6, it 'may allocate housing accommodation in such manner as they consider appropriate'.[45] However, the key rule is that an allocation can only be made which is in compliance with the terms of the local housing authority's own adopted allocation scheme.[46]

1.34 Whilst the requirement to keep a housing register has long since been abolished,[47] in practice many local housing authorities have decided to maintain a list of applicants whom they have accepted as eligible and/or qualified for their local allocation scheme, and have decided to organise that list so as to reflect the relative priorities of different applicants under the scheme. Local housing authorities may call that list a 'register', a 'waiting list' or anything else, as they wish.[48]

What does and does not count as an 'allocation'?

'Allocation' defined

1.35 An 'allocation' is defined as occurring when a local housing authority selects a person to be its own secure or introductory tenant, nominates a person to be a secure or introductory tenant elsewhere, or nominates a person to be an assured tenant of another social landlord.[49] The selection or nomination of a

---

[42] HA 1996, s 159 as amended.
[43] HA 1996, s 166A(1) [England] and s 167(1) [Wales].
[44] HA 1996, ss 159(1) and 167(8).
[45] HA 1996, s 159(7).
[46] HA 1996, s166A(14) [England] and s 167(8) [Wales].
[47] Homelessness Act 2002, s 14(1).
[48] The Welsh Government has said: 'The 1996 Act also, somewhat curiously, abolishes any requirement for a local authority to maintain a register of housing applicants. Since it is difficult to imagine any effective administrative procedure that could operate without such a register, this Report assumes that all social landlords will, in practice, continue to maintain a register, or "waiting list", of applicants': *A Review of Welsh Social Landlords' Approaches to Increasing Choice in Letting Accommodation* (Welsh Assembly Government, 2008).
[49] HA 1996, s 159(2).

person for the initial grant of a 'flexible' or 'affordable' tenancy of social housing will also be an 'allocation' because those are simply variants of secure or assured tenancies.[50]

1.36   The process of allocation is essentially one of identifying a person apt to be made an offer of a social housing tenancy. The allocation process does *not* include the actual entry by the applicant into the tenancy agreement for a particular property. That is a housing management function well beyond the scope of HA 1996, Part 6.[51]

Exceptions

1.37   The allocation provisions set out in HA 1996, Part 6 do not apply to each and every situation in which a person may come to be a tenant of social housing.

1.38   The Codes each identify the common situations in which social housing can come to be occupied by a new tenant *without* the statutory provisions engaging at all.[52] Some of these exceptions are the result of express provisions in the HA 1996, Part 6 (and regulations made under them) and others are the result of the term 'allocation' in HA 1996 being narrowly defined as occurring only when an authority nominates or selects a person for a specified type of tenancy.[53] If the tenancy to be granted will not be secure, introductory or assured – for example, because it will be a form of tenancy without security of tenure (such as a 'family intervention tenancy'[54]) – selection or nomination for that tenancy will not count as an allocation.

1.39   The provisions of HA 1996, Part 6 do not apply where someone obtains a tenancy of social housing as a result of:

(1)   the vesting by succession of a periodic secure or introductory tenancy on the death of the tenant;[55] or

(2)   the devolution of a fixed term secure tenancy on the death of the tenant;[56] or

---

50   English Code, para 1.4.
51   *Birmingham City Council v Qasim* [2009] EWCA Civ 1080, [2010] HLR 19, CA at [18]: 'Part VI of the 1996 Act is concerned with, indeed limited to, establishing and then managing priorities between applicants for residential accommodation (which may or may not be owned by the local authority in question) as it becomes available for letting, which effectively is preliminary to, and not part of, the actual letting of such accommodation, which is governed by Part II of the 1985 Act.' per Lord Neuberger MR.
52   English Code, para 1.9; Welsh Code, Annex 1.
53   HA 1996, s 159(2).
54   A form of social housing tenancy created by the Housing and Regeneration Act 2008.
55   HA 1996, s 160(2)(a) and (3)(b).
56   HA 1996, s 160(2)(b).

(3)   the assignment of a secure tenancy as part of a mutual exchange;[57] or

(4)   the assignment of a secure or introductory tenancy to a person who would
       have been qualified to succeed to the tenancy on the tenant's death;[58] or

(5)   the vesting or disposal of a secure or introductory tenancy pursuant to a
       court order made under the specified provisions of three family law
       statutes identified in the Act;[59] or

(6)   an order made under specified provisions of the Civil Partnership
       Act 2004 in relation to a secure or introductory tenancy;[60] or

(7)   a transfer initiated by the landlord of a secure or introductory tenant
       (ie not initiated by the making of an application for a transfer by the
       tenant);[61] or

(8)   in England only, a transfer of a social housing tenant who applied for
       such a transfer, who was previously a secure, introductory or assured
       tenant of social housing, and who the local housing authority was
       satisfied was not in a category qualifying for a 'reasonable preference';[62]
       or

(9)   in England only, the tenancy being granted as part of the surrender and
       re-grant procedure available where two social housing tenants in England
       wish to exchange their homes and one of the tenants holds a flexible
       tenancy or an assured shorthold tenancy.[63]

1.40   In none of these cases will there have been an 'allocation' for HA 1996,
Part 6 purposes.

1.41   In fact, HA 1996, Part 6 need not have expressly excepted most of these
situations at all. In each category, except the last three, an existing tenancy has
been transferred – by court order, vesting or deed – from one tenant to another,
rather than by the local housing authority selecting the tenant from among its
applicants.

1.42   Another situation in which a social housing tenancy may pass to a new
tenant without Part 6 applying, is on the making of a court order under the
Family Law Act 1996, Sch 7, Part II. An order under those provisions moves
the tenancy from the existing tenant to a new tenant by 'virtue of the order and

---

[57]   HA 1996, s 160(2)(c).
[58]   HA 1996, s 160(2)(d) and (3)(c).
[59]   HA 1996, s 160(2)(e)(i)–(iii) and (3)(d)(i)–(iii).
[60]   HA 1996, s 160(2)(e)(iv) and (3)(d)(iv), amended by Civil Partnership Act 2004, s 81 and Sch 8,
       in force from 5 December 2005 (Civil Partnership Act 2004 (Commencement No 2)
       Order 2005, SI 2005/3175).
[61]   HA 1996, s 159(4B)(b) [England] and s 159(5) [Wales].
[62]   HA 1996, s 159(4A) and (4B).
[63]   HA 1996, s 160(1)(da) inserted by Localism Act 2011, s 159(7).

without further assurance'.[64] By the order the tenancy is 'transferred to, and vested in' the new tenant without any intervention by the local housing authority.[65] There is, accordingly, no allocation for HA 1996, Part 6 purposes in such a case even though HA 1996 does not make specific reference to these circumstances.

1.43 HA 1996, Part 6 is also not applicable:

(10) where a tenant or owner-occupier has been displaced from his or her previous accommodation and a local housing authority provides suitable alternative accommodation under the Land Compensation Act 1973, s 39; or

(11) where the local housing authority grants a secure tenancy to a former owner-occupier or a statutory tenant of a defective dwelling-house acquired by the local housing authority (under Housing Act 1985, ss 554–555);[66] or

(12) where a tenancy is to be granted to a person who is currently and lawfully occupying a property held on a family intervention tenancy.[67]

Allocation to current non-tenant occupiers

1.44 Local housing authorities receive many requests for tenancy allocation from non-tenants who are occupying existing local housing authority accommodation and are seeking the grant of a tenancy for that particular property. Such an occupier may have no statutory right to the tenancy, but may have been occupying that accommodation as his or her home for some time and wishes to remain there. Examples would include:

- where one joint tenant has terminated the tenancy, by serving a notice to quit on the landlord, and the other former joint tenant remains in the home;[68] or

- where a tenant has died and the remaining household member has no statutory succession rights, but has lived with the tenant for some time, or was the tenant's carer, or needs to live in the property to care for the tenant's dependants;[69] or

---

64 Family Law Act 1996, Sch 7 para 7(1).
65 Family Law Act 1996, Sch 7 para 7(1).
66 HA 1996, s 160(4); Allocation of Housing (England) Regulations 2002, SI 2002/3264, reg 3; and Allocation of Housing (Wales) Regulations 2003, SI 2003/239 (W 36), reg 3.
67 The Allocation of Housing (England)(Amendment)(Family Intervention Tenancies) Regulations 2008, SI 2008/3015.
68 The factual scenario of *R (Dixon) v Wandsworth London Borough Council* [2007] EWHC 3075 (Admin), (2008) February *Legal Action*, p 40, Admin Ct.
69 The factual scenario of *R (Neville) v Wandsworth London Borough Council* [2009] EWHC 2405

- where a tenant has moved to a care home, and the remaining household member has no right to an assignment of the tenancy but has lived with the tenant for some time.[70]

1.45 An allocation of a new tenancy in those situations *will* be subject to HA 1996, Part 6 and will ultimately be governed by the terms of the local housing authority's allocation scheme. The Welsh Code recommends that local housing authorities set out in their allocation schemes whether they will grant tenancies in these circumstances and, if so, on what basis.[71] Where the property is owned by a private registered provider or registered social landlord the arrangements described in Chapter 6 will apply.

The local allocation scheme

Drawing up and amending the local scheme

1.46 When drawing up its local allocation scheme, or making any significant changes to it, a local housing authority is required to consult the other social landlords with which it has nomination arrangements.[72] The Welsh Code also recommends that local health boards, Supporting People teams, relevant voluntary sector organisations and other recognised referral bodies should be consulted.[73] A usual consultation period of 12 weeks is mentioned in the Welsh Code.[74] A local housing authority should take into account the findings and conclusions of its own local homelessness review and homelessness strategy when settling upon (or amending) an allocation scheme.[75] A local housing authority in England must additionally have regard to the current tenancy strategy it has adopted under Localism Act 2011, s 150.[76] London's local housing authorities must also have regard to the London housing strategy.[77] In Wales, the expectation is that local housing authorities will have regard to their local housing strategies or the strategic housing element of their community strategy.[78]

1.47 Once the local allocation scheme has been adopted, if there is any subsequent alteration reflecting 'a major change of policy' (such as a move towards, or away from, choice-based letting),[79] the local housing authority is

---

(Admin), (2009) December *Legal Action*, p 17, Admin Ct and of *R(Moore) v Wandsworth London Borough Council* [2012] All ER (D) 66 (Jan), (2012) April *Legal Action*, p 46, Admin Ct.

[70] The factual scenario of *R (George) v Hammersmith & Fulham London Borough Council* [2012] EWHC 2369 (Admin), (2012) July *Legal Action*, p 36, Admin Ct.

[71] Welsh Code, para 4.15–4.16 (succession only); and see the further discussion at **4.190–4.194**.

[72] HA 1996, s 166A(13) [England] and s 167(7) [Wales]. For detailed consideration of these requirements, see Chapter 4.

[73] Welsh Code, para 5.18.

[74] Welsh Code, para 5.25.

[75] HA 1996, s 166A(12)(a) [England] and English Code, para 4.2. See also **4.9** and Chapter 7.

[76] HA 1996, s 166A(12)(b).

[77] HA 1996, s 166A(12)(c).

[78] Welsh Code, para 4.6–4.7.

[79] See **1.66–1.73** and **5.7–5.60**.

required to take such steps as it considers reasonable, within a reasonable period of time, to bring that alteration to the attention of those likely to be affected by it.[80] A 'major change of policy' is said by the Codes to include any amendment that would affect the relative priority of a large number of people, or any significant alteration to procedures.[81] In *R (A) v Lambeth London Borough Council*,[82] the Court of Appeal was asked to consider whether a change in the proportions of accommodation to be allocated between different groups of applicants constituted 'a major change of policy'. The court held that the targets governing the distribution of offers between the different groups were not a published part of the allocation scheme and that amending them would not be 'a major change of policy' requiring consultation.[83]

1.48 What exactly the 'reasonable' steps required by HA 1996, s 168(3) should be is not addressed in the English Code, although the Welsh Code recommends that current applicants should normally be informed of major policy changes by personal letter.[84]

Avoiding discrimination

1.49 The allocation scheme must not discriminate, directly or indirectly, on grounds related to the protected characteristics (eg race or sex) to which the relevant provisions of the Equality Act 2010 apply.[85] These requirements are explored in Chapter 4.[86]

1.50 Housing authorities should ensure that, when consulting in relation to allocation schemes, the views of groups which are currently under-represented in social housing are taken into account. Local housing authorities may wish to monitor the operation of their allocation schemes in order to identify and prevent discrimination and to review their schemes if particular groups are shown to be disadvantaged.

Co-operation

1.51 Private registered providers and registered social landlords are required to co-operate with any requests from a local housing authority to offer accommodation to rent, to such extent as is reasonable.[87] Local housing authorities should be working with all local social landlords, other housing providers and voluntary agencies in order to meet housing needs, and also be working with support services (Supporting People teams, health authorities,

---

[80] HA 1996, s 168(3).
[81] English Code, para 5.2; Welsh Code, para 5.17. See also **4.15–4.18**.
[82] *R (A) v Lambeth London Borough Council* [2002] EWCA Civ 1084, (2002) 34 HLR 57, CA.
[83] [2002] EWCA Civ 1084, (2002) 34 HLR 57, CA at [26]–[28] per Collins J.
[84] Welsh Code, paras 5.17.
[85] Equality Act 2010, s 4 and Part 4. Welsh Code, para 4.69.
[86] See **4.195–4.213**.
[87] HA 1996, s 170. See also English Code, para 6.1; Welsh Code, para 1.6.

adult care and children's services departments, police and probation services) to ensure that housing, care and support needs of vulnerable people are met.

Contracting out

1.52 Local housing authorities may not contract out of ultimate responsibility for the local housing allocation scheme.[88] Responsibility for adopting or altering the scheme, the principles of the scheme, consulting other social landlords and ensuring that the allocation scheme is available for inspection by the public cannot be contracted out.[89] Local housing authorities may contract out the functions of:

• making inquiries into an application;

• making decisions as to eligibility or qualification;

• carrying out reviews of decisions;

• making arrangements to secure that advice and information and necessary assistance is available; and

• making the actual allocation decision, arranging the tenancy sign-up, etc.

1.53 The local housing authority remains legally responsible for any acts or omissions of the contractor and for decisions made in its name.[90]

The role of councillors

1.54 Elected members are prohibited from taking part in any decisions on an individual allocation if the accommodation is in their electoral ward or if the person subject to the allocation decision has a sole or main residence in their electoral ward. Elected members can, of course, seek and obtain information on behalf of their constituents, and participate in more general policy decisions that affect their wards.[91]

---

[88] See generally Chapter 21 of this book.
[89] Local Authorities (Contracting out of Allocation of Housing and Homelessness Functions) Order 1996, SI 1996/3205, applying to both England and Wales. See also English Code, paras 6.5–6.11, Welsh Code Annex 9, and this book at **21.32–21.38**.
[90] See **21.2**.
[91] Allocation of Housing (Procedure) Regulations 1997, SI 1997/483, reg 3(2) [England] and Local Housing Authorities (Prescribed Principles for Allocation Schemes) (Wales) Regulations 1997, SI 1997/45, reg 3, Sch 1, para 1. See also English Code, paras 5.8–5.9; Welsh Code, paras 5.28–5.30. A local housing authority's practice of inviting elected councillors to comment at the point of a potential allocation was criticised by the Public Service Ombudsman for Wales as giving the impression that there might be undue influence: *Housing Allocation and Homelessness in Wales: A Special Report by the Local Ombudsman for Wales* (February 2006).

Absolute requirement

1.55 Even those local housing authorities which have transferred the whole of their housing stock, and no longer have any properties to allocate, are required to operate an allocation scheme, because they retain nomination rights to other local housing authorities (and non-local authority social landlords) and the exercise of those nomination rights constitutes an 'allocation'. That remains true even if the local housing authority has contracted out delivery of its allocation functions.[92] However, research has found that several local housing authorities in England, which had transferred their housing stock to private registered providers, perceived themselves as 'retaining no such role'.[93]

Rights to information, advice and assistance[94]

1.56 The local housing authority must publish a summary of its adopted allocation scheme and provide a free copy of that summary to any member of the public who asks for one.[95] The whole scheme must be kept available for inspection by members of the public and a copy must be provided upon payment of a reasonable fee to anyone who asks for one.[96] Many local housing authorities publish their scheme on their websites and in Wales the expectation is that they will all do so.[97] Provision of information about social housing allocation in a variety of different languages suited to the local population is recommended by the Welsh Code.[98]

1.57 Members of the public are entitled to receive advice and information about their right to make an application for an allocation of social housing, and the local housing authority must provide assistance free of charge to any person who is likely to have difficulty in making an application.[99] An applicant for an allocation has the right to general information to enable him or her to assess how the application is likely to be treated, whether housing accommodation appropriate to his or her needs is likely to be made available and, if so, how long it is likely to take.[100] He or she also has the right to request information setting out any facts taken into account when making a decision as to whether to allocate accommodation and has the right to request a review of any decision that he or she is not eligible for an allocation or is not a qualifying person.[101]

---

[92] English Code, para 4.2. Welsh Code, para 5.1.
[93] *Exploring local authority policy and practice on housing allocations* (DCLG, July 2009) para 2.15.
[94] See **2.7–2.31** and **2.45–2.48**.
[95] HA 1996, s 168(1).
[96] HA 1996, s 168(2).
[97] Welsh Code, para 5.26.
[98] Welsh Code, para 4.35.
[99] HA 1996, s 166(1).
[100] HA 1996, s 166A(9)(a) [England] and s 167(4A)(a) [Wales].
[101] HA 1996, s 166A(9)(b) and (c) [England] and s 167(4A)(b), (c) and (d) [Wales].

Eligibility and qualification for allocation[102]

1.58 Local housing authorities *must* exclude from their allocation schemes people who are subject to immigration control and people who are not habitually resident in the Common Travel Area (CTA), or who only have limited rights of residence in the CTA under European Union law, *unless* they have been prescribed as eligible by regulations, or *unless* they are already secure, introductory or (in certain cases) assured tenants.[103]

1.59 Local housing authorities in Wales *may*, but are not required to, choose to exclude people whose own behaviour, or the behaviour of a member of their household, makes them unsuitable to be tenants.[104]

1.60 Local housing authorities in England *may* now designate classes of persons as qualifying or non-qualifying persons for the purposes of their allocation arrangements.[105] In effect, membership of the designated classes will determine whether an applicant is or is not qualified for an allocation by that particular local housing authority. The law in England therefore now reflects the arrangements previously in place between 1997 and 2003 (as described at **1.24–1.26**). This new concept of 'qualifying persons' is explored in Chapter 3.

1.61 In both England and Wales, if an applicant is ineligible by reason of his or her immigration status, he or she cannot be granted a sole tenancy or participate in taking a joint tenancy.[106] In Wales, the same consequences follow if a person has been treated as ineligible by reason of past misconduct.[107] In England, a person who is not a qualifying person cannot take a sole tenancy but could be granted a joint tenancy with a qualifying person.[108]

Prioritising among applicants[109]

1.62 The allocation scheme adopted by a local housing authority must incorporate its arrangements for 'determining priorities' between applicants for social housing.[110] Although each local housing authority is generally free to determine its own system of priorities, every scheme must be framed so as to secure that certain applicants are given a 'reasonable preference'.[111] The classes

---

[102] See Chapter 3.
[103] HA 1996, s 160ZA(1)–(4) [England] and the Allocation of Housing and Homelessness (Eligibility) (England) Regulations 2006, SI 2006/1294, reg 3; HA 1996, s 160A(3) and (4)–(6) [Wales] and Allocation of Housing (Wales) Regulations 2003, SI 2003/239, regs 4–5.
[104] HA 1996, s 160A(7) and (8). For an example of such provisions in operation see *R (Dixon) v Wandsworth London Borough Council* [2008] EWCA Civ 595, (2008) July *Legal Action*, p 22, CA.
[105] HA 1996, s 160ZA(7).
[106] HA 1996, s 160ZA(1) [England] and s 160A(1) [Wales]. English Code, para 3.3.
[107] HA 1996, s 160A(1)(b) and (c).
[108] HA 1996, s 160ZA(6)(b), English Code, para 3.29.
[109] See Chapter 4.
[110] HA 1996, s 166A(1) [England] and s 167(1) [Wales].
[111] HA 1996, s 166A(3) [England] and s 167(2) [Wales].

of people to whom the local housing authority must award 'reasonable preference' within its allocation scheme are:

(1)   people who are homeless within the meaning of HA 1996, Part 7 ('Homelessness');

(2)   people who are owed a duty by any local housing authority under HA 1996, ss 190(2), 193(2) or 195(2) (or the equivalent duties under Housing Act 1985), or who are occupying accommodation provided to them by a local housing authority under HA 1996, s 192(3);

(3)   people who are occupying insanitary or overcrowded housing, or otherwise living in unsatisfactory housing conditions;

(4)   people who need to move on medical or welfare grounds, including grounds relating to a disability;[112] and

(5)   people who need to move to a particular locality in the district of the local housing authority, where failure to meet that need would cause hardship to themselves or to others.[113]

1.63   HA 1996, Part 6 contains a power for these categories to be amended or added-to by secondary legislation.[114] Although some had suggested that the last Labour Government might use its regulation-making powers to add to the categories of those entitled to a reasonable preference in housing allocation (for example, to mention expressly those under-occupying social housing), in July 2009 the Labour Housing Minister indicated that no further change to the categories was proposed by that Government.[115] In its 2010/11 consultation about the reform of social housing, the present UK Coalition Government floated the possibility of extending the categories but, in the light of responses received, decided to leave them unaltered.[116]

1.64   An applicant's circumstances, or the circumstances of his or her household, may satisfy more than one of the categories of reasonable preference. Until 2009 the categories had been treated as additional to each other, so that if an applicant's needs meant that he or she fell into more than one category, the allocation scheme had to ensure that all of those needs were reflected in the applicant's relative priority among those to be considered for

---

[112]   Housing Act 2004, s 223 inserted the words '(including grounds relating to a disability)' into HA 1996, s 167(2) and was brought into force in England from 27 April 2005; *Housing Act 2004 (Commencement No 2) (England) Order 2005*, SI 2005/1120. The provision has yet to be brought into force in Wales and is still not applicable there even though s 167(2) now only has effect in Wales.

[113]   HA 1996, s 166A(3) [England] and s 167(2) [Wales].

[114]   HA 1996, s 166A(7) [England] and s 167(3) [Wales].

[115]   Rt Hon John Healey MP, Minister for Housing and Planning, letter to local housing authorities in England, 31 July 2009.

[116]   *Local decisions: next steps towards a fairer future for social housing: summary of responses to consultation* (DCLG, February 2011) para 8.18.

allocation: this was known as 'cumulative' or 'composite' assessment.[117] But in 2009 the House of Lords decided that the re-casting of HA 1996, Part 6 by the Homelessness Act 2002 had removed any requirement to take a cumulative or composite approach.[118]

1.65 Within the preference categories, the local housing authority may award 'additional preference' to particular individuals, if they have 'urgent housing needs'. In determining the relative degree of preference, it can take into account the applicant's financial resources available to meet his or her housing costs, any behaviour of the applicant or a member of his or her household, any local connection between the applicant and the local housing authority's district, and any other matter it considers relevant. It may therefore decide whether to give the applicant additional priority (so as to put him or her higher on any list) or whether to give a lesser priority (move him or her lower down any list).[119] A local housing authority in Wales is entitled to give an applicant no preference at all if it concludes that his or her behaviour, or that of a member of his or her household, has been the type of behaviour that would have entitled the local housing authority to a possession order had the applicant been a tenant when that behaviour was carried out.[120] Each local housing authority in England must design its allocation scheme so as to give additional preference to former members of the armed forces who are in urgent housing need.[121]

Choice[122]

1.66 When the 1997–2001 Labour government first consulted on amending HA 1996, Part 6, it emphasised that one of its priorities was to offer more choice to applicants for social housing.[123] The aims of allocation policies were expressed as being:

> '... to empower people to make decisions over where they live and exercise choice; help create sustainable communities; and encourage the effective use of the nation's social housing stock.'[124]

and the intention was that applicants:

---

[117] *R (A) v Lambeth London Borough Council, R (Lindsay) v Lambeth London Borough Council* [2002] EWCA Civ 1084, (2002) 34 HLR 51, CA; *R v Islington London Borough Council ex p Reilly and Mannix* (1998) 31 HLR 651, QBD; *R v Tower Hamlets London Borough Council ex p Uddin* (2000) 32 HLR 391, QBD; *R (Cali) v Waltham Forest London Borough Council* [2006] EWHC 302 (Admin), (2007) 39 HLR 1, Admin Ct; and *R (Ahmad) v Newham London Borough Council* [2008] EWCA Civ 140, (2008) April *Legal Action*, p 40, CA.

[118] *R (Ahmad) v Newham London Borough Council* [2009] UKHL 14, HL; English Code, para 4.5. and Welsh Code, paras 4.544–4.558.

[119] HA 1996, s 166A (5) [England] and s 167(2A) [Wales]. See **4.123–4.151.**

[120] HA 1996, s 167(2B), (2C). See **4.155–4.163.**

[121] The Housing Act 1996 (Additional Preference for Former Armed Forces Personnel) (England) Regulations 2012, SI ****/2012 and English Code, para 4.14.

[122] For a full discussion of 'choice' in the modern context of housing allocation see **5.7–5.60.**

[123] *Quality and Choice: A Decent Home for All* (Green Paper, DETR April 2000), which led to the Homelessness Act 2002.

[124] *Quality and Choice: A Decent Home for All*, para 9.1.

'... should have as much opportunity as possible for their views to be taken into account when they are seeking a new home.'

1.67 The 'choice' envisaged was to be:

• a free one (in that applicants should not be penalised for refusing offers);

• as wide as possible, both in respect of the types of tenancy on offer from different landlords and geographically; and

• well-informed.[125]

1.68 The then Labour government received a mixed response to these proposals and respondents' views tended to be influenced by whether they were in areas of high or low demand for affordable housing. Obviously, it was easier to provide applicants with 'choice' in areas of low demand, and respondents from those areas were more enthusiastic than those in areas of high demand for, and a limited supply of, affordable housing. However, the decision was taken to proceed with the proposals.

1.69 In the event, and notwithstanding the expressed policy intentions behind the introduction of the amended HA 1996, Part 6, there was hardly any reference to 'choice' in the statutory provisions as amended by the Homelessness Act 2002, save for a requirement that the local housing authority must include a statement as to its policy on 'choice' within its allocation scheme.[126] HA 1996, Part 6 permits local housing authorities to reserve allocation of particular accommodation in their stock either to a person who makes a specific application for that accommodation or to persons of a particular description. These provisions were the limited statutory vehicles for the then Labour government's policy that local housing authorities should offer 'choice'.[127]

1.70 The Labour government's policy had been that all local housing authorities in England and Wales should be implementing choice-based lettings by 2010.[128] A specific statutory Code of Guidance on Choice-based Letting published in the summer of 2008 was intended, at least in part, to drive forward that policy among local housing authorities in England. That government also commissioned research to explore issues arising from the CBL schemes. The research was not published until after the 2010 target for nationwide adoption of CBL in England had passed.[129] The findings are summarised in Chapter 5 of

---

[125] *Quality and Choice: A Decent Home for All*, para 9.17.
[126] HA 1996, s 166A(2) [England] and s 167(1A) [Wales].
[127] HA 1996, s 166A(6) [England] and s 167(2E) [Wales].
[128] *Sustainable Communities: Homes for All*, paras 5.18–5.21 (ODPM, January 2005).
[129] *Choice-based lettings, potentially disadvantaged groups and accessible housing registers: A guide to positive practice* and *Costs and effectiveness of accessible housing registers in a choice-based lettings context* (DCLG, February 2011).

this book.[130] By 1 April 2011, 87% of local housing authorities in England were participating in choice-based lettings schemes.[131]

1.71 The current UK Coalition Government has placed much less emphasis on encouraging local housing authorities to operate particular types of allocation arrangements in England and more on local flexibility to adopt whatever arrangements are considered best suited to a particular district. The previous statutory guidance on choice-based letting, fully exploring the scope for offering 'choice' to applicants, has been replaced by a single paragraph in the current English Code simply indicating that it is for individual local housing authorities to decide on their own policies about providing choice.[132] This shift of emphasis has not (for the reasons explained at **1.69**) required any significant modification in the statutory provisions. The only marginally relevant change made by the Localism Act 2011 has been the repeal of the requirement to provide details of the arrangements for 'choice' to those applicants owed the main housing duty under HA 1996, Part 7 (Homelessness).[133]

1.72 This non-prescriptive approach is in line with the current UK Coalition Government's national strategic plan for housing in England which was published in November 2011.[134] The emphasis in Chapter 3 of that strategy (*Social and affordable housing reform*) is on locally designed solutions to local problems with local housing authorities being encouraged to take advantage of the opportunities – offered by recent amendments made to HA1996, Part 6 – to design local schemes and allocation arrangements best suited to local circumstances.

1.73 In Wales, the Assembly Government commissioned a project to provide a review of letting systems in use by social housing landlords in Wales, which were either choice-based or in which choice was an important component part. Its report found that, by the end of 2006/07, choice-based lettings had become an increasingly significant feature of the social housing sector in Wales. Eleven local housing authorities and housing associations were letting the whole of their stock through CBL schemes, and an increasing number of housing associations had become partners in local housing authority-led CBL schemes. The report concluded that much work needed to be done and that, in particular, the provision of feedback to applicants was 'the area which requires the greatest improvement in CBL schemes'.[135] The current policy approach to choice-based letting in Wales is that the Welsh Government is not proposing

---

[130] See **5.21**.
[131] *Local Authority Housing Statistics, England: 2010–11: Housing Strategy Statistical Appendix and Business Plan Statistical Appendix* (DCLG, November 2011).
[132] English Code, para 4.3.
[133] Localism Act 2011, ss 148(2) and 149(3), English Code, para 2.7.
[134] *Laying the foundations : A Housing Strategy for England* (DCLG, November 2011).
[135] *A Review of Welsh Social Landlords' Approaches to Increasing Choice in Letting Accommodation* (Welsh Assembly Government, November 2007).

one system for use by all local housing authorities and that the local approach to 'choice' should be informed by local circumstances.[136]

How are the modern allocation schemes operating?

England

1.74 Despite the major legislative changes relating to social housing allocation brought into force in England in 1997, 2003 and 2012 respectively, there has been no recent major national research programme to investigate or monitor the lawfulness or effectiveness of the housing allocation schemes subsequently adopted and operated by the hundreds of local housing authorities across England.

1.75 In 2004/05 an independent survey was conducted of the allocation schemes operated by 12 local housing authorities in the London area.[137] Its conclusions were that:

• local housing authorities were not disclosing all aspects of their allocation procedures in their published allocation schemes as required by HA 1996, Part 6;[138]

• requests for copies of allocation schemes were not being met promptly by many housing authorities and in some cases copies of allocation schemes were only available under threat of litigation;

• there was an urgent need for DCLG to provide further guidance to ensure that local housing authorities comply with their statutory duties; and

• to ensure that social housing is allocated in a fair and transparent manner, targets must be set and outcomes monitored and published.[139]

1.76 In 2007/08, the Department for Communities and Local Government commissioned a small scale review by other independent researchers. Its findings presented only a snapshot of practice across a relatively modest selection of local housing authorities.[140] No larger scale work has been undertaken since.

1.77 However, these limited reports do demonstrate that, despite the wholesale restructuring of housing allocation law made by the successive amendments to HA 1996, Part 6, too many local housing authorities have

---

[136] Welsh Code, para 4.34.
[137] Robert Latham 'Allocating accommodation: reconciling choice and need', published in two parts at (2005) March *Legal Action*, p 16 and (2005) May *Legal Action*, p 15.
[138] HA 1996, s 167(1).
[139] R Latham 'Allocating accommodation: reconciling choice and need' (2005) May *Legal Action*, pp 18–19.
[140] *Exploring local authority policy and practice on housing allocations* (CLG, July 2009).

taken too long to catch up with changes in the modern law of social housing allocation and to devise and implement wholly lawful housing allocation schemes. In England it has been left to inspectors, the courts and the Ombudsmen to turn up instances of poor or unlawful practices which may, in fact, be widespread. For example, an Audit Commission inspection of a major English city council's allocation arrangements found:

> 'the allocation policy and practice ... is poor and lacks clarity, clear policies and procedures and there is no effective mechanism of control or audit to ensure the allocation of homes is done fairly and transparently.'[141]

1.78 Indeed, as recently as March 2009 the Local Government Ombudsman in England identified one local housing authority which had not operated a lawful allocation scheme since September 2002.[142]

Wales

1.79 In Wales, the much smaller number of local housing authorities, which were operating from 1997 to 2012 under essentially the same legal framework as those in England, has been subject to significant scrutiny and that scrutiny has thrown up issues equally relevant to social housing allocation by local housing authorities in England. For example, in February 2006, the Public Services Ombudsman for Wales published a special report containing an examination of how the modern legal structure for social housing allocation was operating in Wales.[143] The report found:

- that a significant number of Welsh local housing authorities had yet to adopt allocation policies that fully complied with the law and took account of the statutory guidance;

- in particular, that the changes introduced by the Homelessness Act 2002 had still not been sufficiently implemented, some three years after those changes had come into force;

- that, as a result, the lawfulness of each allocation decision since January 2003 was potentially questionable;

- that some local housing authorities continued to operate unlawful policies of blanket exclusions;[144] and

- that some local housing authorities were failing to accord preference to the categories of applicants entitled to a reasonable preference.[145]

---

[141] *Nottingham City Homes – Nottingham City Council* (Audit Commission, March 2006).
[142] *Complaint against Medway Council* 08/008/647, 23 March 2009, (2009) May *Legal Action*, p 30.
[143] *Housing Allocation and Homelessness: A Special Report by the Public Services Ombudsman for Wales* (Public Services Ombudsman for Wales, 2006).
[144] See **1.25** and Chapter 3 of this book.
[145] See **1.62–1.65** and **4.28–4.114**.

1.80 Local housing authorities in Wales were asked to take expert legal advice and to review their allocation schemes as a matter of urgency. Some Welsh local housing authorities had already started that process as a result of the Public Services Ombudsman's investigations of individual complaints.

1.81 In response to the Ombudsman's Special Report, and to further letters of complaint being received by the Assembly Government and by Shelter, officials of the Welsh Assembly Government carried out a joint review with Shelter Cymru of the 22 local housing authority allocation schemes in Wales. That review was published in March 2007.[146] It found that all the allocation schemes scrutinised required some level of further review. Issues identified ranged from failure to adopt schemes meeting statutory requirements to the need to clarify or elaborate those schemes which did satisfy the legal basics. The report contained a series of recommendations for both the Welsh Assembly Government and for local housing authorities. The latter included a recommendation that every Welsh local housing authority 'undertake a fundamental review of their allocation schemes to ensure they are compliant with the law, Code of Guidance and good practice and review them annually thereafter'.

1.82 The response of the Welsh Assembly Government was to commit itself to 'undertaking a full review of allocation schemes every three years and to issue strengthened guidance to local housing authorities and housing associations on allocations' and to ensuring that the 'revised guidance addresses the issues raised by the Ombudsman'.[147] While the content of that revised guidance was being formulated, the Chartered Institute for Housing in Wales reported that, at least in respect of the operation of provisions excluding applicants from social housing, 'not all the exclusion policies and procedures examined during the project were legal'.[148]

1.83 In April 2010, in its new National Housing Strategy for Wales, the Welsh Assembly Government identified as a priority the need to 'extend the legal powers available to the National Assembly for Wales so that it is able to do more to help meet housing need'.[149] That bore fruit in an Order made in July 2010 by which the Assembly acquired jurisdiction to make legislation relating to 'the arrangements under which social housing is provided'.[150] However, the power given has yet to be exercised by the Assembly in respect of social housing

---

[146] *Review of Local Authority Allocation Schemes (2006): report by Welsh Assembly Government and Shelter Cymru* (March 2007).

[147] Leighton Andrews AM (National Assembly for Wales, Deputy Minister for Housing) answering WAQ50133 on 4 July 2007 in the Welsh Assembly.

[148] *Am I on the list? Exclusion from and re-inclusion on social housing waiting lists* (CIH Cymru, May 2008).

[149] *Improving Lives and Communities Homes in Wales* para 3.8 (WAG, April 2010).

[150] The National Assembly for Wales (Legislative Competence) (Housing and Local Government) Order 2010, SI 2010/1838, Art 2(2) Matter 11.4.

allocation. In May 2012, in a White Paper on Housing, the Welsh Government announced that a Housing Bill would introduced in the Welsh Assembly in the autumn of 2013.[151]

1.84 Meanwhile, the long-awaited revised statutory guidance on housing allocation in Wales was subject to a consultation exercise in 2011[152] and the final version of new guidance was issued in August 2012.[153]

SOCIAL HOUSING ALLOCATION AND HUMAN RIGHTS

1.85 The only 'human rights' directly enforceable in the courts in England and Wales are those set out in Sch 1 of the Human Rights Act 1998 ('HRA 1998'). As explained later in this book, those rights can be deployed in some circumstances to force public bodies to arrange accommodation for particularly vulnerable individuals.[154] However, none of those rights confers on any person a right to obtain a home in *social* housing.

1.86 This does not mean that the Human Rights Act can be ignored by those concerned in the allocation of social housing. The Equality & Human Rights Commission has included valuable coverage of the interface between the HRA 1998 and social housing allocation in its current guidance for social landlords.[155]

1.87 The most obvious overlap occurs if a local housing authority or other social landlord performs its public, mainly statutory, functions relating to social housing allocation in a discriminatory way. That may trigger the application of HRA 1998, Sch 1 Art 14 which provides that the other rights protected in Sch 1 'shall be secured without discrimination on any ground such as sex, race, colour, language, religion, political or other opinion, national or social origin, association with a national minority, property, birth or other status'.

1.88 Where, as in the UK, a state has provided a statutory system of distribution of social housing, the provisions of Art 14 can outlaw discrimination even in the absence of an explicit human right to such housing.[156]

---

[151] *Homes for Wales A White Paper for Better Lives and Communities* (Welsh Government, May 2012).
[152] *Consultation – summary of responses on the Code of Guidance for Local Authorities on Allocation of Accommodation and Homelessness* (Welsh Government, December 2011).
[153] The Welsh Code.
[154] See **20.90** et seq.
[155] *Human Rights at home: guidance for social housing providers* (EHRC, March 2011) at pp161–9.
[156] 'The Court begins by observing that there is no right under Article 8 of the Convention to be provided with housing (see *Chapman v the United Kingdom* [GC], no. 27238/95, § 99). However, as the Court has previously held with regard to other social benefits (see, for example, *Stec and Others v. the United Kingdom* (dec.) [GC], where a Contracting State decides to provide such

1.89 The point is well illustrated by *Bah v UK*[157] which was a homelessness case.[158] The applicant complained that she had been denied access to social housing because of the nationality and immigration status of her son. The UK government argued that it was reasonable, in the allocation of social housing, to prioritise those who had a fixed and permanent right to be in the UK, or who had a priority need for housing due to dependents who themselves had such a right.

1.90 The European Court of Human Rights rejected the complaint. It held that it is legitimate to put in place criteria according to which a benefit such as social housing can be allocated, when there is insufficient supply available to satisfy demand, so long as such criteria are not arbitrary or discriminatory. Further, that any welfare system, to be workable, may have to use broad categorisations to distinguish between different groups in need, particularly in relation to 'resource-hungry public services'. The Court took the view that social housing is such a public service. It decided that the differential treatment to which the applicant was subject was reasonably and objectively justified by the need to allocate, as fairly as possible, the scarce stock of social housing available in the UK and that it was legitimate, in so allocating, to have regard to the immigration status of those who are in need of housing.

1.91 For obvious reasons, it would be much harder to justify discrimination based on age, sex, race, marital status or most other personal characteristics (see **1.49**).

THE FUTURE FOR SOCIAL HOUSING ALLOCATION

England

1.92 In England, the expectation is that during 2012/13 every local housing authority will reconsider the terms of its housing allocation scheme in the light of the amendments made to HA 1996, Part 6 by the Localism Act 2011 which came into force in June 2012. In the foreword to the current English Code, the then Housing Minister explained that the intention was 'to assist councils to make full use of these new freedoms – and the existing flexibilities within the allocation legislation – to encourage work and mobility, and to tailor their allocation priorities to meet local needs and local circumstances.'[159]

1.93 The prompt to local housing authorities in England to reconsider and revise allocation schemes in 2012/13 comes not only from the need to consider new legislation and guidance from central government but also from the requirements of the social housing regulator.

---

benefits, it must do so in a way that is compliant with Article 14.' *Bah v The United Kingdom* (Application no 56328/07) [2011] ECHR 1448, ECrtHR para [40]. See also **12.25–12.26**.

[157] *Bah v The United Kingdom* (Application no 56328/07) [2011] ECHR 1448, ECrtHR.

[158] See **12.25–12.26**.

[159] English Code, p 4.

1.94   Established by the Housing and Regeneration Act 2008,[160] the regulator, now the Regulation Committee of the Homes & Communities Agency, has power to set standards to be followed by the providers of social housing.[161] Those standards require registered providers of social housing to comply with specified rules about criteria for allocating housing accommodation.[162] The Housing and Regeneration Act 2008 gives the regulator considerable powers of inspection and enforcement to ensure that the standards are complied with.[163]. The regulator issues regulatory standards to social housing providers as directed by the Secretary of State.[164]

1.95   The current regulatory standard for housing allocation (part of a broader Tenancy Standard) provides:[165]

'1 Allocations and mutual exchange

1.1 Registered providers shall let their homes in a fair, transparent and efficient way. They shall take into account the housing needs and aspirations of tenants and potential tenants. They shall demonstrate how their lettings:

- make the best use of available housing
- are compatible with the purpose of the housing
- contribute to local authorities' strategic housing function and sustainable communities

There should be clear application, decision-making and appeals processes.'

1.96   It then sets out the following Specific Expectations

'1 Allocations and mutual exchange

1.1 Registered providers shall co-operate with local authorities' strategic housing function, and their duties to meet identified local housing needs. This includes assistance with local authorities' homelessness duties, and through meeting obligations in nominations agreements.

1.2 Registered providers shall develop and deliver services to address under-occupation and overcrowding in their homes, within the resources available to them. These services should be focused on the needs of their tenants, and will offer choices to them.

---

[160] Housing and Regeneration Act 2008, s 81(1).
[161] HRA 2008, s 193(1).
[162] HRA 2008, s 193(2)(a).
[163] HRA 2008, ss 192–269.
[164] The current directions are set out at Annex A of *Implementing Social Housing reform: Directions to the Social Housing Regulator – Consultation: a summary of responses* (DCLG, November 2011).
[165] *The Regulatory framework for social housing in England from April 2012* (Homes and Communities Agency, March 2012). Those passages of the current regulatory standard dealing with mutual exchange have not been reproduced in the above extract.

1.3 Registered providers' published policies shall include how they have made use of common housing registers, common allocations policies and local letting policies. Registered providers shall clearly set out, and be able to give reasons for, the criteria they use for excluding actual and potential tenants from consideration for allocations, mobility or mutual exchange schemes.

1.4 Registered providers shall develop and deliver allocations processes in a way which supports their effective use by the full range of actual and potential tenants, including those with support needs, those who do not speak English as a first language and others who have difficulties with written English.

1.5 Registered providers shall minimise the time that properties are empty between each letting. When doing this, they shall take into account the circumstances of the tenants who have been offered the properties.

1.6 Registered providers shall record all lettings and sales as required by the Continuous Recording of Lettings (CORE) system.'

1.97 This version of the regulatory standard came into statutory effect on 1 April 2012 and the need to comply with it will act as a further prompt to local housing authorities in England to revise their local allocation schemes in 2012/13.

Wales

1.98 In Wales, the publication of the new Welsh Code in August 2012, should also trigger a review of all local housing authority allocation schemes across that country in 2012/13 even though, for the time being, there has been no further amendment of the underlying statutory regime.[166] Although the National Assembly for Wales now has the power to make new law on social housing allocation, that power has yet to be exercised.[167] However, the Welsh Government has indicated that a Housing Bill may be put before the Assembly in 2013.[168]

1.99 Meanwhile, the regulation of housing associations in Wales, where they are still referred to as 'registered social landlords', is undertaken by the Welsh Ministers. A Housing Regulation Team, which is part of the Welsh Government's Housing Division, undertakes the regulation activity on their behalf. The regulatory standards applicable since December 2011 are the delivery outcomes set by the Welsh Ministers exercising their powers under HA

---

[166] See Welsh Code, para 3.1 alerting readers to possible changes to the statutory instruments dealing with 'eligibility' in Wales.

[167] The National Assembly for Wales (Legislative Competence) (Housing and Local Government) Order 2010 SI 2010/1838 Art 2(2) Matter 11.4.

[168] *Homes for Wales A White Paper for Better Lives and Communities* (Welsh Government, May 2012).

1996, s 33A. In relation to social housing allocation, those outcomes are that housing associations in Wales should be able to state with confidence:[169]

'We let homes in a fair, transparent and effective way.

We can demonstrate that:

- We manage our homes to ensure that they are in demand, maintained, modernised and adapted, as people's needs change.
- We ensure that our adapted homes are available to those who need them.
- We keep empty homes to a minimum to maximise the number of homes available and our revenue.
- We work with other organisations to prevent and alleviate homelessness.
- We ensure that access to our homes is fair and open, and we work with others to ensure routes into our housing are well publicised, easy to understand and simple to use. We give reasonable preference to those in greatest housing need or are homeless, maximising choice and sustaining communities.
- We let homes we are proud of. Our ready to let homes meet resident expectations prior to moving in or as soon as practicable thereafter.'

---

[169] *The Regulatory Framework For Housing Associations Registered in Wales* (Welsh Government, December 2011).

Chapter 2

INFORMATION, APPLICATIONS AND DECISION-MAKING IN RESPECT OF SOCIAL HOUSING ALLOCATION

INTRODUCTION

2.1   Anyone considering applying for an allocation of social housing will want to understand, before applying, how the local allocation scheme works in the local housing authority area of their choice and how their application is likely to be treated. An individual who then submits an application will want to know what is happening to his or her application, and may need advice. He or she will want an early indication, and a realistic one, about the prospects of being allocated a suitable home. When decisions are made on applications, applicants will want to have prompt notification and an explanation for any adverse findings. In short, access to straightforward information is crucial to applicants having confidence in the local housing allocation process.

2.2   Consequently, in the Housing Act 1996 ('HA 1996'), Part 6 ('Allocation of Housing Accommodation') there are specific obligations on local housing authorities to inform members of the public about the content of their allocation schemes, and to provide applicants with advice and information about their individual applications. In addition, local housing authorities are subject to the provisions of the Data Protection Act 1998 and the Freedom of Information Act 2000, which may respectively enable applicants to access records relating to their own applications and information about specific aspects of housing allocation locally.

2.3   HA 1996, Part 6 also makes reasonably detailed provision about the receipt and processing of applications, and the notification of decisions. Some applicants will, inevitably, be dissatisfied with decisions affecting their applications. In some, but not all, of those cases, HA 1996, Part 6 gives applicants the right to request a review of those decisions. An applicant dissatisfied with the result of a review could bring judicial review proceedings to challenge the decision on review or the process by which it was reached. There is no provision within HA 1996, Part 6 for an appeal to the county court.

2.4   For those cases in which reviews are not specifically provided for in HA 1996, Part 6, the local housing authority may provide an extra-statutory review. In any event, legal challenge to an initial decision, a statutory review decision, or an extra-statutory review decision can only be by way of judicial review.

2.5   Additionally, a complaint about the handling of an individual application can be made via the local housing authority's internal complaints procedure, or be raised with its monitoring officer or, ultimately, be pursued with the Local Government Ombudsman (in respect of local housing authorities in England) or the Public Services Ombudsman for Wales.[1] An applicant who is or has become a tenant of social housing could also complain

---

[1]   *Allocation of accommodation: Guidance for local housing authorities in England* (DCLG, June 2012) ['the English Code'] reproduced in Appendix 1 of this book, para 5.19viii and *Code of Guidance for Local Authorities Allocation of Accommodation and Homelessness* (Welsh Government, August 2012) ['the Welsh Code'], reproduced on CD ROM with this book, paras 5.36–5.37.

to the statutory regulator of social housing. In England, that is presently the Regulatory Committee of the Homes and Communities Agency. The complainant can seek redress if it appears that the local housing authority has not complied with the relevant regulator's published national standards (described at the end of Chapter 1).[2] In Wales, the 'regulators' are the Welsh Government and the Welsh Ministers.[3]

2.6   This Chapter reviews, in sequence, the statutory duties upon local housing authorities to inform applicants, to receive and process applications, and to notify decisions on those applications. Readers concerned with applications being made directly to housing associations and other private registered providers or registered social landlords will find assistance in Chapter 6.

INFORMATION

General information and advice about local social housing allocation

2.7   HA 1996, Part 6 requires local housing authorities to ensure that advice and information about the right to apply for accommodation is available free of charge to everyone in their districts.[4] Although HA 1996, Part 6 elsewhere specifically requires the publication of a free summary of the allocation scheme,[5] this general duty to make information and advice available goes much wider than that.

2.8   The information provided by local housing authorities should include information about housing allocation procedures and also potential stock availability. Statutory guidance advises that information should also be available about qualification and prioritisation criteria.[6]

2.9   Local housing authorities may also wish to provide general information about the profile of their stock, including the type, size and location of the housing, whether it is accessible or could be adapted, whether there is access to a shared or private garden, and how old it is. Where stock is in short supply, an indication of how frequently it is likely to become available would also be helpful.

2.10   The Chartered Institute of Housing (CIH) has identified that:

> '...the publication of accessible and free information is vital in enabling people to take responsibility for their own housing solutions. This should additionally

---

2   Housing and Regeneration Act 2008, Part 2 as amended by Localism Act 2011 Sch 17 [England]. See **1.92–1.97**.

3   See **1.98**.

4   HA 1996, s 166(1)(a).

5   HA 1996, s 168(1).

6   English Code, para 5.4.

include information about housing options that exist within a local area. Where local authorities have stock or have nomination rights to partners' stock, it is important how that stock will be used and who is eligible for help is clear to everyone. This will be particularly important in the light of the local variations and additions that government is proposing to allow local authorities to introduce. The variety of local differences mean that clarity of local conditions and eligibility will be even more important to help people navigate local circumstances and make effective and empowered choices for themselves.'[7]

2.11 Care must be taken to ensure that this advice and information is accessible to all. Information should be easy to understand and should be available in translation, where relevant, and in alternative formats (Braille, large print, and audiotapes, etc).[8] Arrangements for access to information and advice will need to take account of the special needs of specific groups of prospective applicants, eg prisoners or travellers.[9] Local housing authorities may wish to make information available using a variety of media, including printed hard copy form, on a website or via the telephone.[10] The former Commission for Racial Equality's Code of Practice on Racial Equality in Housing[11] includes this pertinent example of the care that needs to be taken in preparing information:

> 'A local council (or housing association) fails to make sure that information about its lettings services reaches people from all racial groups; for example, by not advertising the service in outlets which it knows are preferred by ethnic minority residents. This could amount to indirect discrimination' (Example 35).

2.12 Prospective applicants may also have the right to obtain a broader range of information about social housing allocation under the Data Protection Act 1998 and the Freedom of Information Act 2000.[12]

2.13 For some enquirers, the provision of information will suffice. But the statutory duty under HA 1996, s 166(1)(a) also requires that *advice* must be available free of charge. This can be particularly important where the local housing authority has adopted a choice-based letting scheme that requires applicants to be pro-active in securing an allocation. Suitable advice could be provided by the local housing authority itself, a social landlord, or the voluntary sector, and is likely to be most effective if the adviser has appropriate housing related experience and is properly trained to sensitively meet the needs of a diverse client group.

---

[7] *How to ... consider new approaches to allocations and lettings* (CIH, April 2012).
[8] See further Welsh Code, para 1.11.
[9] Welsh Code, paras 4.78–4.81.
[10] Welsh Code, paras 4.74–4.75.
[11] See **4.205**.
[12] English Code, para 5.7 and see **2.30–2.31**.

Information about a particular local allocation scheme

2.14 Each local housing authority is required by HA 1996, Part 6 to publish a summary of its allocation scheme and to make a copy of that summary available free of charge to 'any member of the public who asks for one'.[13] The request for a copy can come from 'any member of the public'. There is no requirement that the person making the request should also be an applicant under the local housing authority's allocation scheme, or even a prospective applicant. Indeed, there is no requirement that the person should have any connection with that particular local housing authority's district. Any member of the public, anywhere in the country, is entitled to receive a free summary of any local housing authority's allocation scheme on request. Obviously, it is this provision that allows advisers to collect summaries of any allocation schemes that might be useful to them in advising members of the public.

2.15 There is no requirement to publish the whole of the allocation scheme, although many local housing authorities do put their full scheme on their website[14] and in Wales the expectation is that all local housing authorities will do so.[15] However, each local housing authority must 'make the scheme available for inspection at their principal office'.[16] The principal office is usually the town hall, or the central address for the housing department. Members of the public do not, however, need to attend the principal office in person in order to see the full scheme. If they ask for a copy (in person, by post, by phone, or by email), and pay any required fee (which can only be a reasonable amount), the local housing authority 'shall provide' a copy of the full scheme.[17] Again, advisers may consider purchasing copies of the allocation schemes operated by the local housing authorities which deal with the majority of their clients, or may simply download them from websites.

2.16 Sadly, not all local housing authorities have readily embraced the statutory requirement to make the full scheme available for purchase on demand. The full scheme, which must cover 'all aspects of the allocation process',[18] will often be a substantial document and there is not infrequently a degree of reticence in supplying copies. One limited exercise in requesting copy schemes from 12 local housing authorities in London produced only four responses within 14 days, five further responses within 28 days, and the remaining three only after complaints to the monitoring officer for each local housing authority and service of a pre-action protocol letter threatening

---

[13]   HA 1996, s 168(1).
[14]   Local housing authority websites are usually at the government's domain name: thus, a typical address would be www.anytown.gov.uk. In preparing the report *Exploring local authority policy and practice on housing allocations* (CLG, July 2009) researchers found that only 71% of local housing authorities surveyed had published the full scheme on their websites. Even among those operating CBL schemes, 15% had not done so.
[15]   Welsh Code, para 5.26.
[16]   HA 1996, s 168(2).
[17]   HA 1996, s 168(2).
[18]   HA 1996, s 166A(1) [England], s 167(1) [Wales].

judicial review proceedings.[19] A good deal of time and legal expense can be wasted when a failure to respond promptly to a request for a copy of the scheme leads to a claim for a mandatory order in judicial review proceedings.[20] Such claims never come to trial, for obvious reasons, but leave local housing authorities with substantial legal costs easily exceeding the expense of supplying a copy of the scheme promptly in response to the initial request.

2.17 The scheme adopted by the local housing authority must not only set out how the authority will prioritise applicants but additionally the *procedure* that it follows in allocating housing.[21] Where the local housing authority has adopted a choice-based letting arrangement, the formal allocation scheme ought to set out the procedures and priorities as they apply not only to the initial consideration of an applicant's application but also to the treatment of any bid made by the applicant for specific accommodation.

2.18 Experience would suggest that there has often been a failure to grasp the significance of the fact that for these purposes 'procedure' includes 'all aspects of the allocation process, including the persons or descriptions of persons by whom decisions are to be taken'.[22] In short, the statutory requirement is that the published scheme deals with both 'how' and 'why' allocations are made. Obviously, the statements as to who does what in the allocation process should reflect actual practice. In one case, an allocation scheme provided that particular decisions would be taken by the area housing manager and the rehousing manager jointly. A decision later taken by one of those officers, acting alone, was outside the terms of the scheme and was unlawful.[23]

2.19 The courts have not taken an altogether consistent line as to how much *detail*, on the prioritisation of applications or the procedures to be followed in processing them, is required in a local allocation scheme. The range of approaches taken by the courts is illustrated by the following examples:

- A scheme which did 'not explain what criteria apply or indicate that they will be applied' was held to be unlawful in that respect.[24]

- An allocation scheme provided for nominations by social services but did not explain what sort of communication from what part of social services would qualify as such a nomination. That was insufficient.[25]

---

[19] Robert Latham 'Allocating accommodation: reconciling choice and need' (2005) March *Legal Action*, p 16 and (2005) May *Legal Action*, p 15.

[20] As in *R (Onuegbu) v Hackney London Borough Council* [2005] EWHC 1277 (Admin), (2005) August *Legal Action*, p 17, Admin Ct.

[21] HA 1996, s 166A(1) [England], s 167(1) [Wales].

[22] HA 1996, s 166A(1) [England], s 167(1) [Wales].

[23] *R (Moore) v Wandsworth London Borough Council* [2012] All ER (D) 66 Jan, (2012) April *Legal Action*, p 46, Admin Ct.

[24] *R (Cali, Abdi and Hassan) v Waltham Forest London Borough Council* [2006] EWHC 302 Admin, [2007] HLR 1, Admin Ct.

[25] *R (Yazar) v Southwark London Borough Council* [2008] EWHC 515 (Admin), (2008) May *Legal Action*, p 46, Admin Ct.

- A scheme enabled an applicant to obtain substantially increased points if he was imminently required to give up accommodation leased from the private sector. It wrongly failed to indicate precisely at what stage the extra points would accrue.[26]

- A local housing authority had adopted targets for achieving allocations to particular classes of applicant. The targets were not part of the procedure of the scheme, so the scheme did not need to be amended each time they were changed.[27]

- On a challenge to the sufficiency of detail in a local housing authority's scheme, in respect of allocation to particular priority groups, a judge said:

  'The scheme must set out all aspects of the allocation process but it is not necessary to do more than ... explain what criteria apply to each group and to indicate that an officer will allocate in accordance with those criteria which may be general.'[28]

- An allocation scheme which was already 'very long and detailed' did not set out the precise criteria under which applicants in medical need were to be admitted to a particular priority category. That level of detail did not need to be added to the scheme.[29]

- A local housing authority operated a policy that, at shortlisting stage, bidders from the same bands would have the presence (or otherwise) of a local connection taken into account. The policy was not initially mentioned in the published allocation scheme but was added on a later revision. The court held that the matter was one of minor detail the omission of which was not unlawful.[30]

2.20 A particular issue has been the extent to which the local allocation scheme must be a comprehensive document, containing all aspects and details of the scheme, or can include material by reference to other documents. Too many allocation schemes simply set out broad policy statements, unlawfully leaving the mechanics to be detailed in unpublished procedure manuals or staff training materials. However, it seems that if the allocation scheme refers to relevant details to be found in another published document, the failure to include that material in the allocation scheme itself may not be unlawful. In one case, the introduction to the published scheme said that it had to be read in connection with the annual and mid-year reports made to the council by the cabinet member with responsibility for housing, which were published on the

---

[26] *R (Lin) v Barnet London Borough Council* [2007] EWCA Civ 132, [2007] HLR 30, CA.

[27] *R (A) v Lambeth London Borough Council* [2002] EWCA Civ 2084, [2002] HLR 57, CA.

[28] *R (Lynch) v Lambeth London Borough Council* [2006] EWHC 2737 (Admin), [2007] HLR 15, Admin Ct. at [51].

[29] *R (Ahmad) v Newham London Borough Council* [2008] EWCA Civ 140, (2008) April *Legal Action*, p 34, CA.

[30] *R (Van Boolen) v Barking & Dagenham London Borough Council* [2009] EWHC 2196 (Admin), (2009) September *Legal Action*, p 34, Admin Ct.

internet. Responding to an assertion that that did not meet the statutory
requirements the judge said '[i]t may be cumbersome to have to look at two
(and possibly more) documents, but it is not unlawful'.[31] In refusing permission
to appeal against that decision, another judge said 'The mere proposition that it
[publication in one place] might be more transparent is not sufficient to
establish unlawfulness'.[32]

Information about applications

2.21 When a person applies for an allocation of social housing, he or she must
be informed by the local housing authority of his or her relevant statutory
rights or the local housing authority must otherwise secure that someone else
informs the applicant of those rights.[33] The relevant rights are:

- the right to request such general information as will enable the applicant
  to assess how his or her application is likely to be treated under the
  scheme, including whether he or she is likely to fall within any of the
  groups entitled to a reasonable preference;[34]

- the right to request such general information as will enable him or her to
  assess whether accommodation appropriate to his or her needs is likely to
  be made available and, if so, how long it is likely to be before an offer is
  made;[35]

- the right (if the application is made to a local housing authority in Wales)
  to be notified in writing of any decision that he or she is *not* to be given
  any reasonable preference that he or she would ordinarily have been
  entitled to receive, and of the reasons for that decision;[36]

- the right to ask the local housing authority to inform him or her of any
  decision about the facts of his or her case which has been, or is likely to
  be, taken into account when considering whether to allocate accommodation;[37]

- the right to request a review of any decision that he or she is *not* to be
  given reasonable preference, any decision as to the facts of his or her case,

[31] *R (Babakandi) v Westminster City Council* [2011] EWHC 1756 (Admin), (2011) August *Legal
Action*, p 40 at [21], Admin Ct.
[32] *R (Babakandi) v Westminster City Council* [2011] EWCA Civ 1397, (2012) January *Legal
Action*, p 21, CA, per Sullivan LJ at [5].
[33] HA 1996, s 166(1A) [England] and s 166(2) [Wales]. The Welsh Code suggests that this duty
should be implemented within the context of 'a constructive housing options approach, so that
applicants will understand their prospects of being rehoused into the accommodation they are
seeking': Welsh Code, para 4.166.
[34] HA 1996, s 166(1A)(9)(a)(i) [England], s 167(4A)(a)(i) [Wales].
[35] HA 1996, s 166(1A)(9)(a)(ii) [England], s 167(4A)(a)(ii) [Wales].
[36] HA 1996, s 167(4A)(b) (Wales only).
[37] HA 1996, s 166(1A)(9)(b) [England], s 167(4A)(c) [Wales].

any decision that he or she is *not* eligible for an allocation, or any decision that he or she is not a qualifying person for an allocation;[38] and

- the right to be informed of a review decision and the grounds for that review decision.[39]

2.22   Such information must be given to *every* applicant and, plainly, the terms of the statutory provision indicate a policy intention that the information is provided when the application is first received, in a written acknowledgement of, or response to, the application or as accompanying information to the acknowledgement or response.

2.23   As is clear from the first two items in the list above, the applicant may request 'general information' which will enable him or her to assess how the application is likely to be treated, whether he or she will be entitled to any preference, whether he or she is likely to receive accommodation and, if so, after what period. There is no time limit specified within which this information must be requested. It follows, therefore, that the applicant may request this information *at any time*, once he or she has made the application. Of all the available information, it is this – a realistic appraisal of the prospects of obtaining a suitable local allocation – that the applicant is most likely to want. Many advisers will have drawn up pro-forma requests for this information, to enclose when writing to the local housing authority about individual applications.

2.24   The statutory Codes of Guidance on social housing allocation do not contain much guidance on what information the applicant could expect to receive, having made their request. Local housing authorities might usefully maintain lists of properties earmarked for special groups (eg properties adapted for disabled use, etc), and make those lists available to relevant applicants. However, only a small number of applicants will benefit from that sort of information.[40]

2.25   For most applicants, the information that they receive in response to such a request should include:

- whether or not they have been accepted as eligible for an allocation;

- whether or not (in England) they qualify for an allocation;

- the type of property they are likely to be allocated;

- the method that will be used in assessing their needs, whether by awarding points or by inclusion in a specific group or band, or otherwise;

---

[38]   HA 1996, s 166(1A)(9)(c) [England], s 167(4A)(d) [Wales].
[39]   HA 1996, s 166(1A)(9)(c) [England], s 167(4A)(d) [Wales]..
[40]   See **4.186–4.188**.

- the number of other applicants with equal or greater priority; and

- an assessment of the likely time that they will have to wait to receive an offer (or to make a successful bid in a choice-based letting scheme), by reference to average waiting time or to the number of lettings of similar properties in the previous year or quarter.

2.26 This sort of information allows the applicant an opportunity to assess his or her realistic (if sometimes depressing) chances of receiving an offer. It may usefully be accompanied by a copy of the free published summary of the particular local housing authority's allocation scheme. In short, the thrust of the statutory provisions is that the local allocations process, and information about it, should be transparent and open:

> '...we want a really open and transparent allocation scheme so that anybody can see what a particular council's scheme is, and can understand why they have been included or excluded and whether it is appropriate for them to appeal.'[41]

2.27 These aspects of HA 1996 Part 6, dealing with the provision of information, make it unnecessary for applicants to rely on the general rights to provision of information by a local housing authority set out in Housing Act 1985, s 106. That section was specifically amended by the Homelessness Act 2002 to disapply its provisions so far as they impose requirements corresponding to those to which such a local housing authority is now subject under HA 1996, s 168.[42]

Information about specific facts

2.28 The applicant has the right to ask the local housing authority to inform him or her of any decision about the facts of his or her case which are likely to be, or have been, taken into account in considering whether to allocate housing accommodation to him or her.[43] This right is supplementary to the right of every applicant to have made available, on request, at all reasonable times and without charge, details of the particulars which he has given to the authority about himself or herself and about his or her family and which the authority has recorded as being relevant to the application for accommodation.[44] These rights to information are only triggered if the applicant requests the information; there is no automatic requirement on the local housing authority to give this information to the applicant as a matter of course. The right first mentioned above is a right to be informed of any decision taken 'about the facts of his [or her] case'.[45] The 'facts' relied upon by the local housing

---

[41]   Andrew Stunnell MP, Under-Secretary of State, House of Commons Public Bill Committee on the Localism Bill, 3 March 2011, col 765.
[42]   Housing Act 1985, s 106(6).
[43]   HA 1996, s 166A(9)(b) [England], s 167(4A)(c) [Wales].
[44]   Housing Act 1985, s 106(5) (earlier disapplied by the Access to Personal Files Act 1987 which has itself now been repealed).
[45]   HA 1996, s 166A(9)(b) [England], s 167(4A)(c) [Wales].

authority in reaching its decision may have come from various sources: from the applicant, but also from housing officers, doctors, schools, other professionals or agencies, or even neighbours.

2.29 The right to be informed about decisions made on factual issues is not limited to the facts which the local housing authority takes into account in determining general issues about whether to allocate accommodation to the applicant, for example, as to his or her eligibility or priority. The wording is sufficiently broad to enable an applicant to ask to be informed about any decisions as whether he or she will be considered for, or why he or she was not considered for, a particular property.

2.30 Local housing authorities are also subject to the information disclosure requirements of the Data Protection Act 1998, giving any individual the right of access to 'personal data' held either on computer or in manual files contained in a 'relevant filing system'.[46] The right of access means that an individual is entitled to know whether the local housing authority is processing any of his or her personal data and, if so, to be told what that data is, the source of the data, why it is being processed and to whom the data is being, or may be, disclosed. To constitute 'personal data', the information must have as its focus the individual involved, rather than the individual simply being mentioned peripherally in relation to some other individual or issue.[47] The data can be withheld where it identifies another person who has not consented to its disclosure, or it is reasonable to withhold it.[48] Local housing authorities may also refuse to supply data which is 'unstructured' and where the costs of supplying the data are disproportionate.[49] Any request for data made under the Data Protection Act 1998 must be in writing and accompanied by a fee. The English Code suggests that, if local housing authorities remain unclear about their obligations and responsibilities under the Data Protection Act 1998 in the context of social housing allocation, they may wish to contact the office of the Information Commissioner.[50]

2.31 Local housing authorities are also subject to the information disclosure provisions of the Freedom of Information Act 2000. An individual is entitled to make a written request to a public authority, which includes a local housing authority, and to be informed by the public authority whether it holds information of the description specified in the request and, if so, to have that information communicated to the individual, unless the information is exempt.[51] 'Personal data' is exempt from disclosure, as it is provided to the public authority in confidence.[52] The Freedom of Information Act 2000 can

---

46 Data Protection Act 1998, s 7. See Welsh Code, para 5.35.
47 *Durant v Financial Services Authority* [2003] EWCA Civ 1746, (2004) *The Times*, January 2, CA.
48 Data Protection Act 1998, s 7(4).
49 Data Protection Act 1998, s 9A.
50 English Code, para 5.7. The website of the Information Commissioner is at www.ico.gov.uk.
51 Freedom of Information Act 2000, s 1; exemptions are at ss 21–44 inclusive.
52 Freedom of Information Act 2000, s 40.

therefore be used to obtain the local housing authority's policies, procedures and other general information about social housing allocation, but not confidential information about a particular application. The duties imposed by the Freedom of Information Act 2000 are *additional* to the duties imposed by HA 1996 to provide information. For example, an applicant may use a request under the Freedom of Information Act 2000 to obtain a list of local housing authority properties in a particular area or throughout a local housing authority's district in order to know what properties *might* become available.[53] However, where a local housing authority was asked to give the addresses of properties owned by a private registered provider operating in its area it was entitled to provide that information in a way that did not allow individual occupiers to be identified.[54]

Confidentiality[55]

2.32 The applicant has the personal right to confidentiality, in that the fact that an application has been made cannot be divulged to any other member of the public without the applicant's consent.[56] Routinely, of course, local housing authorities request consent from applicants so that they can seek information from others, such as doctors or social workers, to help them determine the application. This consent should not, however, be treated as a general consent permitting the local housing authority to inform others, who do not need to know, that an application has been made. In practice, a considerable issue has arisen about the sharing of information between local housing authorities and private registered providers or registered social landlords about applicants nominated to such landlords for housing allocation. Local housing authorities could usefully draw up information sharing protocols to cover such situations, but any sharing of personal information about an applicant can only be achieved by consent[57] and only in compliance with the Data Protection Act 1998. To facilitate the drawing up of information-sharing protocols, the former Housing Corporation published a national standard protocol on sharing information about applicants for re-housing.[58]

---

[53] See *Decision Notice concerning Mid Devon DC* [2006] 4 May, Information Commissioner Ref FS50082890, (2006) July *Legal Action*, p 26 and *Decision Notice concerning Braintree DC* (2006) 4 May, Information Commissioner Ref FS50066606, (2007) March *Legal Action*, p 13.

[54] *Turcotte v Information Commissioner* [2008] 12 June, Information Tribunal Case no EA/2007/0129.

[55] Welsh Code, para 4.168.

[56] HA 1996, s 166(4).

[57] Because even the simple fact that an applicant has applied to the local housing authority cannot be revealed except by consent: HA 1996, s 166(4).

[58] *Access to Housing: Information sharing protocol* (Housing Corporation, November 2007).

APPLICATIONS

Making an application

2.33   Local housing authorities are under no duty to seek out those most in need of any available social housing. Their statutory responsibilities are confined to responding to, and considering, applications made to them by those seeking allocation of any available stock. So, for all those seeking social housing, everything turns on successfully making an application and then pursuing its proper consideration under the terms of the allocation scheme adopted by the local housing authority to which the application is made.

2.34   However, to ensure that the most vulnerable are not disadvantaged in gaining access to what might be available, each local housing authority must ensure that free advice and information is available in its district about the right to make an application for social housing.[59] Each local housing authority must also ensure that free assistance is provided to anyone who is likely to have difficulty in making an application.[60]

2.35   Many of those most in need of social housing will have sought the help of the local housing authority because they were homeless or facing the prospect of homelessness. An application for homelessness assistance (made under HA 1996, Part 7 'Homelessness') does *not* automatically count as an application for an allocation of social housing (under HA 1996, Part 6), and therefore local housing authorities receiving homelessness applications should attempt to ensure that applicants also complete any separate application forms required for their allocation schemes.[61]

2.36   Although the HA 1996 Part 6 does not explicitly say so in terms, everyone has a *right* to make an application to a local housing authority.[62] Any person can apply to *any* local housing authority or, indeed, to *every* local housing authority for an allocation of social housing. Obviously, an applicant is more likely to be allocated accommodation quickly in areas where supply exceeds demand. But applications cannot be restricted or rejected because the local housing authority to which application has been made has little or no vacant housing currently available. The chosen local housing authority may not even own any property to rent, perhaps having disposed of its housing stock, but it must still receive and process applications under its allocation scheme and

---

[59]   HA 1996, s 166(1)(a); see **2.7–2.13**.

[60]   HA 1996, s 166(1)(b); see **2.45–2.48**.

[61]   The *Homelessness Code of Guidance for Local Authorities*, (DCLG, July 2006) [the 'English Homelessness Code'] para 6.7, suggests that an applicant for homelessness assistance is advised of the 'various housing options that might be available', including an application for an allocation of long-term social housing. In one case, a delay of six months between a young applicant approaching a local housing authority for homelessness assistance and him being helped to complete a social housing allocation application compounded a catalogue of maladministration: *Complaint against Dover City Council*, 09 017 510, 31 July 2012, Local Government Ombudsman, (2012) October *Legal Action*, p 36.

[62]   HA 1996, s 166(1), which deals with the provision of information, refers to 'the right to make an application' and the English Code, para 5.4, uses the term 'right to apply for an allocation'.

then 'allocate' by making nominations to local private registered providers or registered social landlords, or to other local housing authorities, under that scheme.[63]

2.37   There is no minimum age restriction on applications and nothing in the statutory scheme suggests that a person who is 'dependent' on another cannot apply.[64]

2.38   There is no national prescribed form for the making of an application. The only requirement, in order to have an application considered, is that the application must be made in accordance with the procedural requirements (if any) set out in the allocation scheme of the local housing authority to which the application is directed.[65] If the scheme requires that a particular application form should be completed, the form should ideally be straightforward to complete but might well also be sufficiently detailed to enable a wide range of information to be obtained from the applicant (eg as to age, religion, sexual orientation, ethnicity, disability, gender and any support needs). The Welsh Code suggests that the forms should be accompanied by guidance notes which are themselves easy to understand and 'in plain language'.[66] Any application form will need to elicit the information necessary to enable the local housing authority not only to decide whether the applicant is eligible for an allocation but also whether the household includes any 'restricted persons'.[67]

2.39   Separate applications must be made to each local housing authority from which the applicant seeks consideration for an allocation. To make the process easier for applicants, local housing authorities and private registered providers or registered social landlords which are collaborating in regional or sub-regional allocation arrangements might usefully have a single application form that can be treated as constituting an application to them all.[68]

2.40   There are no statutory pre-conditions to the making of an application. The local housing authority cannot impose a charge for receiving an application or for its consideration. The applicant need not already have an address in the local housing authority's district, nor satisfy any particular period of residence in the district. Even if the local housing authority believes that the applicant is highly likely to be found to be ineligible for an allocation or (in England) not to qualify, or is likely to be given a very low priority under the local scheme, it must still accept an application from anyone, whether that

---

[63]   HA 1996, s 159(2)(c).
[64]   In contrast to an application for homelessness assistance: see **9.34–9.37**. See also *R v Oldham Metropolitan Borough Council ex p Garlick* [1993] AC 509, HL.
[65]   HA 1996, s 166(3).
[66]   Welsh Code, para 4.163.
[67]   See **4.153–4.154**.
[68]   See **6.54–6.62**.

person is physically in its district or elsewhere, if the application is made in accordance with the relevant procedural requirements (if any) of the local housing authority's scheme.[69]

2.41 Again, so as to ensure that the most vulnerable are not excluded, local housing authorities are advised to ensure that applicants who have no fixed address can make applications.[70]

2.42 Once the application has been made in a form which meets the procedural requirements of the local allocation scheme, the local housing authority is required to consider it.[71] However, some local housing authorities require applicants to 'renew' their applications (essentially by re-applying) at regular intervals. This can work to the disadvantage of those applicants with unsettled accommodation, who are in consequence highly mobile, or those applicants who have difficulties with paperwork or bureaucratic processes. Nevertheless, in one challenge to a scheme for the allocation of local housing authority mobile home pitches for gypsies and travellers, a judge said:[72]

> 'Nor, in my view, is it irrational to require that registration on the list must be renewed. Given the small number of pitches and the intense competition for the few pitches that do become available, it is essential that those on the list have a continuing interest and continue to meet the criteria. Without an effective sift of that nature, the list could well become unmanageable and would retain on it those who either had no serious interest in securing a pitch in Hackney, or who had far inferior claims in terms of connection with Hackney. A policy that neglected that requirement might indeed be vulnerable to a challenge on the grounds of irrationality.
>
> I fully recognise ... that some travellers might well find it burdensome to re-register each year and to keep abreast of any changes in relevant policy, especially those relating to allocation criteria. If a traveller is not able to read and write, as is the case with the claimant, there may be special difficulties in effectively communicating from both sides. However, I am not persuaded that such difficulties, which can potentially lead to unfortunate consequences, vitiate the policy as a whole. The traveller may take appropriate steps to ensure, so far as is practicable, that the person at the c/o address is responsible and is aware of the relevant policy, and is alert to the need for re-registration. The traveller may put in place arrangements by which such person either herself provides the necessary documentation, or takes steps to remind the traveller of what is needed so that the latter can herself take the necessary steps. From the evidence in the case, it is clear that the traveller can attend the Council offices to re-register in person, or to get someone to do that for her, provided the documentation is provided – an extra facility that gives some degree of flexibility to the administrative arrangements.'

---

[69]   HA 1996, s 166(3).
[70]   Welsh Code, para 3.39.
[71]   HA 1996, s 166(3).
[72]   *R (McDonagh) v Hackney London Borough Council* [2012] EWHC 373 (Admin), (2012) April *Legal Action*, p 46, Admin Ct. per Kenneth Parker J at [29]–[30].

Offences in relation to applications

2.43 It is a specific criminal offence for a person knowingly or recklessly to make a statement which is false in a material particular or knowingly to withhold information which the local housing authority reasonably requires the applicant to give, in connection with the exercise of any of a local housing authority's functions under HA 1996, Part 6.[73] A suitable warning to this effect should be included with the information that the applicant receives on, or prior to, making an application. The offence can be committed when making an application or when giving the local housing authority any further information. Guidance suggests that the offence may also be committed during any review proceedings.[74] If the false information actually results in the grant of a *secure* tenancy, it may be possible for the local housing authority to recover possession through the civil courts.[75] Likewise, a private registered provider or registered social landlord that has granted an *assured* tenancy may recover possession in such circumstances by court proceedings.[76]

2.44 Of course, providing false information can also constitute an offence under the general criminal law. Recent prosecutions under the Fraud Act 2006 and/or the Forgery and Counterfeiting Act 1981 have been brought against applicants for housing who have given false information or failed to disclose plainly relevant information. One applicant who failed to disclose that she owned a property which she rented out to tenants was sentenced to immediate imprisonment for eight months.[77]

Assistance in making an application

2.45 As already explained,[78] local housing authorities are required to ensure that free *advice* and *information* about the right to make an application for an allocation of social housing is available to people in their districts.[79] But they are also required to ensure that free *assistance* is provided to anyone in their districts who is likely to have difficulty in making an application.[80] Local housing authorities may provide this assistance directly through their own staff (eg in Housing Advice Centres), or may contract the services out to independent advice agencies or other providers.[81]

2.46 Guidance recommends that the written advice and information available to those needing assistance should be available in a range of formats and

---

[73]   HA 1996, s 171.
[74]   English Code, para 5.11. Welsh Code, para 5.33.
[75]   Housing Act 1985, Sch 2 Ground 5 and English Code, para 5.12.
[76]   Housing Act 1988, Sch 2 Ground 17.
[77]   *Basildon District Council v Rita Limbani,* Basildon Magistrates' Court, 10 August 2012 (2012) October *Legal Action,* p 36.
[78]   See **2.7–2.13**.
[79]   HA 1996, s 166(1)(a).
[80]   HA 1996, s 166(1)(b), English Code, para 5.5, Welsh Code, para 4.164.
[81]   See Chapter 21.

languages, as appropriate to the needs of the area.[82] Those formats should presumably include audio tapes, large print versions or Braille copies, as well as copies in the different languages commonly used in the district.[83] Those likely to need specialist information will obviously also be more likely to need specialist support in making their application for an allocation. The local housing authority will need to have addressed these issues in its equality impact assessments (under the Equality Act 2010) made in relation to the adoption of (or changes to) the allocation scheme.[84]

2.47 Particular issues arise where a local housing authority operates a choice-based letting scheme requiring applicants to bid for advertised properties. Assistance must be made available to those who may need help to bid regularly.[85] The housebound, prisoners, and gypsies (and other travellers) may obviously need special help to make applications, as they will not necessarily have access to the internet or be able to attend at pick-up points to collect free sheets describing available properties. Local housing authorities might usefully consider how to meet the needs of applicants who are deaf, blind or partially sighted, who have learning disabilities or who cannot read English. Obviously, any reasonable adjustment sought by an applicant on account of his or her disability should be made. For example, an applicant who could not read printed material could require that the local housing authority advise him or her by telephone of suitable properties available. In a case in which the re-housing of a housebound disabled tenant depended on her husband and full-time carer checking every week what properties had been advertised under a local housing authority's scheme, the Local Government Ombudsman said that 'it was insensitive to expect someone in [his] position to devote time and energy to bidding for properties'.[86]

2.48 In *Housing and the Disability Equality Duty: A guide to the Disability Equality Duty and Disability Discrimination Act 2005 for the social housing sector* the former Disability Rights Commission suggested that when local housing authorities make impact assessments of choice-based lettings arrangements, they should consider these questions:

- Is advertising accessible?

- Are a property's accessible features advertised?

- Does a mechanism exist to identify the requirements of disabled applicants?

---

[82]   Welsh Code, paras 1.11, 4.35, 4.74 and 4.163.
[83]   Welsh Code, paras 1.11, 4.35, 4.74 and 4.163.
[84]   See **4.207–4.209**.
[85]   Welsh Code, para 4.37.
[86]   *Complaint against Leeds City Council* 05/C/13157, 20 November 2007, (2008) January *Legal Action*, p 37.

- Is there a mechanism to allow extra time for disabled applicants if they need it?

- Is there a mechanism for providing support in making applications?[87]

Processing applications

2.49 When an application has been received, the local housing authority will normally consider, first, whether an applicant is 'eligible' for an allocation of social housing under the terms of the statute and its own allocation scheme.[88] It is important that the local housing authority decides eligibility at the initial application stage, because an applicant permitted to engage with the allocation scheme (eg by being allowed to bid for properties in a choice-based letting scheme) will have a legitimate expectation that he or she will receive full consideration for an allocation. The issue of eligibility may be revisited just prior to any prospective allocation to take account of any changed circumstances since the initial application 'particularly where a substantial amount of time has elapsed since the original application'.[89]

2.50 If the application has been made to a local housing authority in England which has exercised its power to limit the classes of applicants who are 'qualifying persons',[90] such an authority will deal with that application by first considering 'eligibility' and then 'qualification'. Again, it is important that the local housing authority decides on qualification at the initial application stage, because an applicant permitted to engage with the allocation scheme (eg by being allowed to bid for properties in a choice-based letting scheme) will have a legitimate expectation that he or she will receive full consideration for an allocation. The issue of qualification may be revisited just prior to any prospective allocation to take account of any changed circumstances since the initial application 'particularly where a substantial amount of time has elapsed since the original application'.[91]

2.51 If the local housing authority decides that the applicant *is* eligible (and, in England, *is* within a class of qualifying persons), it should then consider:

- whether he or she falls into any of the categories to which it must give reasonable preference;[92]

- whether he or she is entitled to any additional preference;[93]

---

[87] *Housing and the Disability Equality Duty: A guide to the Disability Equality Duty and Disability Discrimination Act 2005 for the social housing sector* (DRC, 2006), p 56.
[88] See Chapter 3.
[89] English Code, para 3.2.
[90] HA 1996, s 160ZA(7) and Chapter 3.
[91] English Code, para 3.26.
[92] HA 1996, s 166A(3) [England], s 167(2) [Wales]. See also **4.57–4.114**.
[93] HA 1996, s 166A(3) [England], s 167(2) [Wales]. See also **4.123–4.134**.

- (if the application is made to a local housing authority in Wales) whether the applicant's behaviour permits the local housing authority to give him or her no preference at all;[94] and

- what increased or reduced priority the applicant is entitled to under the scheme as compared to other applicants.[95]

2.52 There is no statutory deadline or time limit within which the local housing authority must decide these questions once it has received an application, although a commitment to process applications within a particular period might well be made by a local housing authority in its own allocation scheme. If it becomes plain that the application is not being considered at all, the applicant may need to seek a mandatory order in a claim for judicial review. If the application is being considered, but progress is unduly slow, the applicant may wish to make a complaint under the local housing authority's own complaints procedure[96] or, if that proves unsatisfactory, seek the help of the Local Government Ombudsman (in England) or the Public Services Ombudsman (in Wales).[97]

2.53 Where a local housing authority is operating a choice-based letting scheme, it may wish to make only a preliminary assessment of an initial application (in order to avoid spending resources on examining in detail applications from applicants who have no realistic prospect of successfully bidding), and to reserve detailed scrutiny to a later stage (eg when an applicant has bid for, and appears to qualify for, the allocation of a particular property).

2.54 Some local housing authorities, operating choice-based letting schemes, may arrange to review applications in detail *twice*, ie at both the initial application stage and again at the bidding stage. On that model, at the second stage, the application will again be assessed to determine whether the applicant:

- is still eligible; and

- (in England) is still a qualifying person; and

- meets any specific letting criteria for the particular property; and

- still has the appropriate priority for an allocation to be made; and

- that the applicant's household matches any size criteria for the property.

---

94 HA 1996, s 167(2B) and (2C) [Wales only]. See also **4.155–4.163**.
95 HA 1996, s 166A(5) [England], s 167(2A) [Wales]. See also **4.135–4.151**.
96 Information about the local housing authority's own complaints procedure should be supplied to applicants by the local housing authority itself.
97 See **2.107** and more generally www.lgo.gov.uk and www.ombudsman-wales.org.uk.

2.55 Local housing authorities adopting this approach may find that they are required to notify decisions[98] on more than one occasion for each applicant and will need to include the detail of the procedures that will be operated at each stage in their allocation schemes.

2.56 The advice in the English Code relating to double-testing for eligibility and qualification (at the stage of determining the initial application and at the pre-offer stage) does not sit happily with the drafting of the eligibility regulations.[99] At least in terms of transitional provisions, those regulations focus on the position when an applicant's *application* was first made.[100]

Applications from current tenants of social housing (transfers)

2.57 Secure, introductory, or other tenants of social housing applying for transfers to alternative social housing accommodation have the same rights:

- to make applications,

- to have their applications considered,

- to be notified as to their rights to information and review, and

- to protection of the confidentiality of the fact of their application,

as applicants who are not existing social housing tenants.[101] Applications to a local housing authority by current tenants of social housing can be made not only by tenants of that local housing authority but also by tenants of any other social landlord (whether a different local housing authority or a private registered provider or registered social landlord).[102]

2.58 Their applications will initially be treated in the same way as all other applications,[103] *except* that the local housing authority should not make inquiries into their eligibility. That is because secure tenants or introductory tenants, or assured tenants who obtained their current accommodation as a result of an allocation by a local housing authority, are eligible for a further allocation regardless of their immigration or habitual residence status.[104]

2.59 Not all transfers will be handled through the housing allocation scheme arrangements made under HA 1996, Part 6. That Part does not apply *unless* the transfer is tenant-initiated ie the tenant has made the application for a transfer

---

[98] See **2.80–2.84**.

[99] See Chapter 3.

[100] Allocation of Housing and Homelessness (Eligibility) (England) Regulations 2006, SI 2006/1294, reg 8, reproduced in Appendix 2.

[101] Welsh Code, para 4.8.

[102] English Code, para 1.5.

[103] Welsh Code, para 4.9.

[104] HA 1996, s 160ZA(5) [England], s 160A(6) [Wales], English Code, para 3.4 and Welsh Code, para 3.5(i). For 'eligibility' see Chapter 3.

himself or herself.[105] A transfer offered to a tenant at the landlord's initiative, eg as part of a decanting programme, does not count as triggering the provisions of Part 6 at all.[106] In Wales, subject to that exception, all transfer applications made to local housing authorities will be handled through the local allocation scheme. Local housing authorities in Wales have been asked by the Welsh Government to ensure that social housing tenants who are under-occupying get particular assistance when they apply for transfers.[107]

2.60 In England, even if the tenant applies for a transfer himself or herself, the provisions of Part 6 will not apply unless the local housing authority is satisfied that the transfer applicant qualifies for a 'reasonable preference' under HA 1996, s 166A(3).[108] Deciding whether a transfer applicant is within a 'reasonable preference' category is therefore a preliminary issue for local housing authorities in England. If the transfer applicant *does* fall into such a category, he or she will join the allocation process in the usual way and will be dealt with on the same basis as a new applicant.[109]

2.61 The difficulties in deciding on which side of the line a transfer applicant falls are illuminated by the example of a transfer application made by a social housing tenant who has a satisfactory home but is presently 'under-occupying' and seeks a move to something smaller. The current statutory guidance in Wales suggests that under-occupation might be a criterion for admission to the reasonable preference category covering those in 'unsatisfactory housing conditions'.[110] If under-occupation is so treated by a local housing authority in its allocation scheme, the transfer applicant will be embraced by that scheme. However, the current statutory guidance in England omits 'under-occupation' from a list of indicators for that category of reasonable preference.[111] So, if the local housing authority adopts the English guidance in this respect the transfer applicant may fall outside the allocation scheme and into the new no-priority transfer class.

2.62 For *non-priority* transfer applicants, the local housing authority can operate separate arrangements either outside, or alongside, the local allocation scheme. Alternatively, all applicants could be dealt with through one over-arching housing allocation system applying both to Part 6 applicants and non-priority transfer applicants.[112]

2.63 Taking non-priority transfer applicants out of the Part 6 regime was perceived to be a means of facilitating greater social mobility and the statutory guidance accordingly encourages local housing authorities to use this

---

[105] HA 1996, s 159(4B)(b) [England], s 159(5) [Wales].
[106] English Code, para 1.9., Welsh Code, para 4.9.
[107] Welsh Code, para 4.8.
[108] HA 1996, s 159(4B)(c), English Code, para 2.3.
[109] English Code, paras 1.5 and 2.3.
[110] Welsh Code, Annex 3.
[111] English Code, Annex 1 (in contrast to the same list in the 2002 English Code).
[112] English Code, para 1.8.

flexibility, particularly to assist tenants who are presently under-occupying social housing.[113] The UK Government has stated that:

> 'A number of respondents have expressed concern that this will necessitate landlords setting up a separate system to handle transfer requests. This is certainly not the intention of the provision, nor do we believe this will be necessary. ... Local authorities and other landlords may choose to operate a separate transfer list. Alternatively, they may decide to continue to operate a single system covering all applicants, but one which, for example, rewards tenants with a good track record, or gives a degree of priority to tenants who want to move for work. Finally, landlords may decide to make no change at all to the way in which they treat transferring tenants, if they believe this best meets the needs of their local area.'[114]

2.64 When a local housing authority in England has decided that an applicant for a transfer is not in the reasonable preference categories, it will be for the local housing authority to decide what prioritisation arrangements to apply as between that transfer applicant and all others. For example, it would need to decide whether an offer of a transfer should first be made to the transfer applicant who has waited longest or to the one who is under-occupying the largest accommodation.

2.65 Perhaps the even more critical question for the local housing authority will be whether to expose a newly available letting to demand from the applicants on the local allocation scheme or, instead, to offer it to one or more of those on the non-priority transfer list.

2.66 Local housing authorities in England which have exercised their powers to specify classes of applicants qualifying (or not qualifying) for allocation under HA 1996 Part 6,[115] may decide to apply the same or different qualifying criteria to those *transfer* applicants to whom Part 6 applies (ie those in the reasonable preference categories). The statutory guidance suggests that there might be sound policy reasons for applying different (more relaxed) criteria to transfer applicants.[116] In response to an amendment to the Localism Bill,[117] which would have prevented any qualification requirements being applied to transferring tenants, the Government minister said:

> 'We are producing secondary legislation that will outline when local authorities can and cannot prevent people transferring. If there were any evidence that local authorities were disqualifying transferring tenants inappropriately, that would be covered by that secondary legislation, which will not be on hand immediately but is coming.'[118]

---

[113] English Code, paras 1.6–1.7.
[114] *Local decisions: next steps towards a fairer future for social housing – Summary of responses to consultation* (DCLG, February 2012) paras 8.16–8.17.
[115] HA 1996, s 160ZA(7).
[116] English Code, para 3.24.
[117] Which subsequently became Localism Act 2011.
[118] *Hansard*, Lords Debates, 5 September 2011 col 32.

2.67 No such secondary legislation[119] had emerged in relation to transfer applicants by the time this edition of this book was being written.

2.68 Transfer applicants to whom the provisions of HA 1996, Part 6 apply will enjoy the same rights to be notified of decisions on their applications (and to be informed of their rights to request information) as those described above in relation to new applicants.[120]

Procedure for handling applications

2.69 There is no prescribed national code in either England or Wales as to the way in which applications must be processed. The respective national authorities have the reserve power to prescribe by regulations the 'principles' that should govern allocation procedures, but the power has not been used except to limit the role of elected members in allocation of properties (see **1.54**).[121] The procedure being followed will therefore be that set out in the particular local housing authority's own allocation scheme. This must cover all aspects of the allocation process, including the identity (or description) of the staff by whom decisions will be taken.[122] The relevant statutory regulators of social housing in each country will set and enforce national standards for housing allocation in exercise of their respective statutory powers.[123]

2.70 In dealing with an application for allocation of social housing, there is no duty upon the local housing authority to 'make ... inquiries' into the application (in contrast to the position in relation to applications for homelessness assistance).[124] The extent of any processes for investigation of an application will be outlined in the local allocation scheme. It would be perfectly lawful for a local housing authority to confine its consideration of an application to the content of the application form. It does not have to investigate for itself, for example, any further medical or welfare needs that an applicant's household may have. This makes it all the more important that application forms are comprehensive (as well as easy to complete) and that any advice given to a prospective applicant underscores the need to put forward all relevant information at the time the application is made.

2.71 The absence of rigorous statutory control of the process of allocating social housing, and the corresponding flexibility given to local housing authorities, can lead to situations in which both applicants and officials are free to abuse local arrangements for social housing allocation. It is therefore important that local housing authorities not only have detailed procedures, and structures for delegation of decision-making, set out in their allocation schemes but also that these are properly monitored and enforced by the authorities

---

[119] Which would be made under HA 1996, s 160ZA(8).
[120] See **2.80–2.84**.
[121] HA 1996, s 166A(10) [England], s 167(5) [Wales].
[122] HA 1996, s 166A(1) [England], s 167(1) [Wales].
[123] See **1.93** and **1.99**.
[124] HA 1996, s 184(1). See Chapter 10.

themselves. The English Code now advises local housing authorities to consider taking action to minimise the risks of staff fraud and error in allocations, including the vetting of junior staff and the use of senior staff to randomly check and validate decisions on applications.[125] The guidance was drawn in the light of a striking instance of a member of staff having access to, and abusing, the allocation processes in the largest local housing authority in England.[126]

Applications which trigger other responsibilities

2.72 It may be plain, from the terms in which the applicant has completed the local housing authority's application form, that there is a need for other assistance, even before consideration of the application for social housing allocation is completed.

2.73 If the form provides material which gives the local housing authority reason to believe that the applicant may be homeless or threatened with homelessness, it *must* make the enquiries necessary to establish whether it owes the applicant a duty under the homelessness legislation.[127] This is because an application for social housing is an application 'for accommodation', which may trigger the threshold for enquiries into any potential homelessness.[128]

2.74 Likewise, if the local housing authority is also an adult care and children's services authority, the application may trigger responsibilities under community care or child care legislation.[129] For example, if the application reveals that:

(1) the applicant is a 'child in need' under the age of 18,[130] and

(2) she or he is seeking accommodation because the person with parental responsibility is unable to accommodate any longer,

the children's services authority may itself owe a statutory duty to accommodate under the Children Act 1989.[131]

Repeat applications

2.75 In principle, there is nothing to stop an unsuccessful applicant from making a further application at any stage. However, in practice, unless the applicant's circumstances have changed, the decision will be likely to be the

---

[125] English Code, para 5.13.
[126] *Birmingham City Council v Qasim* [2009] EWCA Civ 1080, [2010] HLR 19, CA.
[127] HA 1996, Part 7 ('Homelessness').
[128] HA 1996, ss 183–184. Discussed further in Chapter 10; and see *R (Bilverstone) v Oxford City Council* [2003] EWHC 2434 (Admin), [2003] All ER (D) 170 (Oct), Admin Ct.
[129] *R v Tower Hamlets London Borough Council ex p Bradford* (1997) 29 HLR 756, QBD.
[130] Welsh Code, paras 4.103–4.105.
[131] Children Act 1989, s 20. See also *R (M) v Hammersmith and Fulham London Borough Council* [2008] UKHL 14, [2008] 1 WLR 535, HL, and *R (G) v Southwark London Borough Council* [2009] UKHL 26, [2009] 1 WLR 1299, HL; and see **13.148–13.149** and **20.55–20.84**.

same. Indeed, if an application has been fully considered, fairly and on its merits, a local housing authority is entitled to deal with a later re-application on the same facts by asserting that the matter has already been determined, in the absence of any material change of circumstances.[132]

2.76 HA 1996, Part 6 specifically provides for re-applications in two circumstances:

(1) an applicant who has been treated as ineligible by a local housing authority in Wales on account of his or her conduct can make a fresh application at any time, and the Code suggests that, in such a case it will be for the applicant to show that his or her behaviour or circumstances have changed;[133] and

(2) if a local housing authority in England decides that a person is not qualified for an allocation because he or she does not fall within a category of qualifying persons, that person can re-apply if he or she considers that he or she should be treated as a qualifying person.[134] The Code suggests (wrongly) that on such a re-application it would be for the applicant to show that his or her circumstances have changed.[135] However, it may be that there has been no change of personal circumstances but the local housing authority may have simply changed its qualifying criteria.

DECISION-MAKING

Decisions on applications

2.77 As already noted, there is no statutory time limit within which a decision must be reached or within which the applicant must be notified of the outcome of his or her application for social housing (although any local housing authority may include such a provision in its local scheme). Nor is there a general statutory requirement that all decisions on applications be notified in writing, in any particular form or style (although, as will be seen later, adverse decisions often carry notification requirements). Again, the local allocation scheme might be expected to address such matters.

2.78 For the vast majority of applicants, the outcome of the application will be some form of notification of success. This may be a simple letter indicating that the applicant will in future be considered for an allocation based on the material provided in the application form or, where there is a local choice-based letting system, that the applicant is free to make bids for available properties. What the applicant most probably wants to know, and may not have been

---

[132] *R (George) v Hammersmith & Fulham London Borough Council* [2012] EWHC 2369 (Admin), (2012) June *Legal Action*, p 36.
[133] HA 1996, s 160A(11). Welsh Code, para 3.24.
[134] HA 1996, s 160ZA(11).
[135] English Code, para 3.30.

automatically told, is when, realistically, the application will result in an allocation of social housing (ie selection for the offer of a tenancy of a house or flat). The applicant is entitled to ask for information, in writing, about precisely that: whether housing accommodation is likely to be made available and, if so, how long it is likely to be before it is made available.[136]

2.79 For the minority of applicants, the notification will be that their application has been wholly or partly unsuccessful. The most serious adverse decision that an applicant could receive is that he or she is 'ineligible for an allocation' or (in England) not qualified for allocation.[137] The legal framework for decisions on eligibility or qualification and the obligations when notifying such decisions are discussed in the next Chapter.[138] Other adverse decisions, and the notification obligations attaching to them, are dealt with in this and later Chapters.[139]

Notifying decisions

2.80 Curiously, while every local housing authority must accept applications for social housing made in accordance with its allocation scheme and determine them, there is no express statutory obligation on local housing authorities to give written notification of all decisions and/or to give reasons for them. No doubt these matters were thought so central to good administrative practice as not to require explicit mention in HA 1996, Part 6 because they will be included in the allocation scheme adopted by any reasonable local housing authority.

2.81 However, if a local housing authority decides that an applicant is 'ineligible' for its allocation scheme,[140] or (in England) that he is not a 'qualifying' person,[141] or (in Wales) that he or she is not to be given any preference on the grounds of unacceptable behaviour,[142] those decisions must be notified to the applicant in writing.[143]

2.82 The applicant is also entitled to be given *reasons* for those three types of decisions. The statutory guidance suggests that the notification should give clear grounds for the decision 'based on the relevant facts of the case'[144] and that where a particular applicant may have difficulty understanding the implications of the decision 'it would be good practice to make arrangements for the information to be explained verbally in addition to providing a written notice'.[145]

---

[136] HA 1996, s 166A(9)(a)(ii) [England], s 167(4A)(a)(ii) [Wales]; see **2.21–2.23**.
[137] HA 1996, s160ZA [England], s 160A(9) [Wales].
[138] See Chapter 3.
[139] See **2.80–2.84** and Chapters 3 and 4.
[140] See Chapter 3.
[141] See Chapter 3.
[142] See **4.1551–4.163**.
[143] HA 1996, s 160ZA(9) and s 166A(9)(c) [England], s 160A(9), (10), and s 167(4A)(b) [Wales].
[144] English Code, para 5.16, Welsh Code, para 3.31.
[145] English Code, para 5.16.

2.83 In each of the above cases, the decision must be 'notified' to the applicant, meaning that it should actually be received by him or her.[146] However, in the case of a decision that the applicant is not eligible or not qualified, the decision is additionally treated as having been given to the applicant:

'... if it is made available at the authority's office for a reasonable period for collection by him [or her] or on his [or her] behalf.'[147]

2.84 This treating provision only applies if the applicant does not actually receive the decision notice. If the applicant does receive the decision, any time limits run from the date of receipt, not from a notional date when the applicant could have collected the decision. An attempt to supplement the statutory rubric by the addition of the words 'and the applicant has previously been informed that the notice will be available and how it can be collected' was rejected by the Government because the effect of the additional words 'is really a matter of good administrative practice, and might well be expected of local authorities as a matter of course'.[148]

REVIEWS

Right to a review

2.85 A local housing authority is free to provide in its allocation scheme that all of the decisions it takes on an application for social housing will carry a right to a review by the authority at the applicant's request. However, legislation has specified a minimum requirement that all allocation schemes must be framed so as to provide a right to a review of certain important decisions. Strictly speaking, the review being undertaken is never a statutory review. It is always a review provided for by the allocation scheme and not pursuant to an absolute statutory right. This is not a mere matter of semantics. If, for some reason, a badly-drafted scheme had not been framed so as to include the minimum review rights envisaged by the statute, it would be necessary for an applicant first to apply for a mandatory order (by way of judicial review proceedings) requiring the local housing authority to amend its scheme so as to include the review rights and then, once they were included, that applicant could exercise them.

2.86 HA 1996, Part 6, requires that rights to review of the following categories of decisions made by a local housing authority relating to an applicant are included in any allocation scheme:

---

[146] '"Notify" requires the giving of a notice which imports a degree of formality sufficient to constitute the document, as it will usually be, a notice', per May LJ in *Ali v Birmingham City Council* [2009] EWCA Civ 1279, [2011] HLR 17, CA at [39].

[147] HA 1996, s 160ZA(10) [England], s 160A(10) [Wales].

[148] Andrew Stunnell MP, Under-Secretary of State, House of Commons Public Bill Committee on the Localism Bill, 3 March 2011, col 758.

(1)   a decision that he or she is not eligible for an allocation;[149]

(2)   a decision concerning the facts of his or her case which are likely to be, or have been, taken into account in considering whether to allocate accommodation;[150]

(3)   a decision by a local housing authority in England that he or she is not within a class of persons qualifying for an allocation;[151] and

(4)   a decision by a local housing authority in Wales that he or she is not to be awarded any reasonable preference, to which she or he would otherwise be entitled, on the grounds of unacceptable behaviour.[152]

2.87   The first, third and fourth categories of decisions listed refer to decisions taken under specific statutory provisions, and the applicant will have been notified in writing of those decisions with reasons.

2.88   The second category of decision carrying a right to a review is much more wide-ranging. From the wording, it is reasonable to assume that it includes decisions about:

(1)   the type of property for which an applicant will be considered;

(2)   the extent of the applicant's household to be considered for housing with him or her;[153]

(3)   the applicant's medical condition or other welfare needs;

(4)   other facts used to determine whether the applicant is entitled to a reasonable preference;

(5)   whether the applicant should receive additional preference on the grounds of urgent housing needs or otherwise; and

(6)   determining the applicant's priority, including his or her financial resources, behaviour (or that of his or her family), and local connection where the scheme renders any of these relevant.

2.89   This second category carrying a right to request a review, therefore, opens the door for an applicant to request an internal review, and consequent reconsideration, of nearly all the adverse decisions (if any) that are made on his or her application.

---

[149]   HA 1996, s 160ZA(9)(a) and s 166A(9)(c) [England], s 160A(9) and s 167(4A)(d) [Wales].
[150]   HA 1996, s 166A(9)(b) and (c) [England], s 167(4A)(c) and (d) [Wales].
[151]   HA 1996, s 160ZA(9)(b) and s 166A(9)(c).
[152]   HA 1996, s 167(4A)(b) and (d).
[153]   *R (Ariemuguvbe) v Islington London Borough Council* [2009] EWCA Civ 1218, [2010] HLR 14, CA.

2.90 However, unlike the decisions on eligibility, qualification (in England) or unacceptable behaviour (in Wales), there is no automatic *notification* of the initial decision to the applicant in this second category of decisions. For the applicant even to access his or her right to request a review, he or she must first request the local housing authority to inform him or her of its decision about a particular fact, or set of facts, about his or her case.[154] Only having made that request, and having received the response, can the applicant then sensibly request a review although there is no statutory obligation on the local housing authority to provide reasons when notifying this class of decision.

2.91 As already indicated, the statutory requirements relating to reviews of decisions on applications for social housing allocation represent the legal minimum. There is nothing to prevent a local housing authority from adopting an allocation scheme which allows for a review of additional categories of adverse decisions or of all adverse decisions.

2.92 On the *nature* of the review that needs to be undertaken, it is reasonable to assume that Parliament at least intended reviews of decisions made within HA 1996, Part 6 to have the same function as reviews within HA 1996, Part 5 ('Conduct of Tenants')[155] and Part 7 ('Homelessness'), ie a reconsideration of all the relevant facts and law at the time that the review is decided, not a narrow review confining itself to the legality or fairness of the original decision.[156]

Procedure on review

2.93 There are no statutory provisions governing review procedure in relation to social housing allocation. There are, for example, no statutorily specified time limits within which a review must be requested and no statutorily prescribed form or procedure for making the request for a review. All and any procedural requirements must be set out in the particular allocation scheme under which a review is being pursued.

2.94 Before HA 1996, Part 6 was amended by the Homelessness Act 2002, the right to request a review of decisions under HA 1996, Part 6 was contained in HA 1996, s 164. Regulations made under HA 1996, s 165 required the local housing authority to notify the person concerned that he or she had a right to make written representations and of the procedure involved. The local housing authority was required to notify the applicant of its decision on review within 8 weeks from the request, or any longer period as agreed between the parties in writing.[157] The reviewing officer, if employed by the same local housing authority which had made the original decision, had to be an officer who had

---

154 See **2.28–2.32**.
155 HA 1996, s 129 gives an introductory tenant the right to request a review of his or her landlord's decision to seek an order for possession and the Introductory Tenancy (Review Procedures) Regulations 1997, SI 1997/72 regulate the procedure on review.
156 For a discussion of the scope of reviews in the homelessness context see **19.107–19.114**.
157 *Allocation of Housing and Homelessness (Review Procedures) Regulations* 1999, SI 1999/71, regs 3–5. Reproduced in Appendix 2.

not been involved in that original decision and had to be senior to the original decision-maker.[158] However, HA 1996, ss 164 and 165 were both repealed in January 2003.[159] The Secretary of State and Welsh Ministers are now empowered to make regulations governing 'the procedure to be followed' on housing allocation, which appears, from the wording, to encompass any procedural matters under the allocation scheme, including any procedure relating to requests for review.[160] However, no regulations have been made in exercise of that power.

2.95 In this procedural vacuum, left by an absence of statutory prescription, it will be for every local housing authority to spell out the review procedures in its own allocation scheme. This will inevitably mean different review procedures in almost every part of the country. However, the English Code suggests that review procedures should be clearly set out in allocation schemes, should include 'timescales for each stage of the review process, and must accord with the principles of transparency and fairness'.[161]

2.96 Applicants are, of course, entitled to the benefit of the usual public and administrative law protections of natural justice, procedural fairness etc and to expect high standards of administration from a local housing authority. But one would ordinarily expect more detailed guidance. None was given in the initial statutory guidance issued to local housing authorities in England but the current English Code sets out six general principles of good administrative practice that local housing authorities are expected to apply when making provision for review procedures in their allocation schemes and when undertaking reviews. They are:[162]

'1.   Applicants should be notified of the timescale within which they must request a review. 21 days from the date the applicant is notified of the decision is well-established as a reasonable timescale. A housing authority should retain the discretion to extend this time limit in exceptional circumstances.

2.   Applicants should be notified that the request for review should be made in writing, and that it would also be acceptable for the request to be submitted by a representative on their behalf. Applicants should also be advised of the information which should accompany the request.

3.   Authorities should consider whether to advise that provision can be made for verbal representations, as well as written submissions, to be made.

4.   The review should be carried out by an officer who is senior to the person who made the original decision. Alternatively, authorities may wish to appoint a panel to consider the review. If so, it should not include any person involved in the original decision.

5.   The review should be considered on the basis of the authority's allocation scheme, any legal requirements and all relevant information. This should

---

158   SI 1999/71, reg 2.
159   Homelessness Act 2002, ss 14(1), 18(2), Sch 2.
160   HA 1996, s 166A(10) [England] and s 167(5) [Wales].
161   English Code, para 5.19.
162   English Code, para 5.19.

include information provided by the applicant on any relevant developments since the original decision was made – for instance, the settlement of arrears or establishment of a repayment plan, or departure of a member of the household responsible for anti-social behaviour

6.   Reviews should be completed wherever practicable within a set deadline. Eight weeks is suggested as a reasonable timescale. The applicant should be notified of any extension to this deadline and the reasons for this.'

2.97   In relation to adverse decisions on 'eligibility', or 'no preference' made by local housing authorities in Wales, the Welsh Code recommends that allocation schemes adopt the following as 'fair procedure' in relation to reviews:

- ensuring that notifications of decisions include advice on the right to request a review, the time within which the request must be made, and sources of advice and assistance;

- ensuring that applicants have an opportunity to request further information about any decision about the facts of their case;

- advising applicants that they may request a review by way of an oral hearing or a written submission;

- ensuring that the review is carried out by a person who was not involved in the original decision and, if the reviewer is to be another officer, one senior to the original decision-maker;

- ensuring that the circumstances of the applicant at the time of the review, not just at the time of the original decision, are taken into account;

- if there is not to be a hearing, allowing the applicant to make written representations, and informing the applicant of the date by which those representations must be received, giving the applicant at least five clear days' notice;

- if there is to be a hearing, giving notice to the applicant of the date, time and place no sooner than five days after the request for a hearing (unless the applicant consents to lesser notice);

- ensuring that the reviewer determines the procedure to be adopted for hearings, and that the procedure gives the applicant the right to be heard, to be accompanied, to be represented by a lawyer or other person, to call witnesses to give evidence, to put questions to any witness and to make written representations;

- ensuring that, if a person having been given notice should fail to appear at the hearing, the reviewer has regard to all the circumstances, including any explanation offered for the absence and should be able to proceed with the hearing or give any directions he or she thinks proper for the conduct of a further review;

- ensuring that the reviewer will allow applicants to be able to request a postponement of a hearing, and will grant or refuse the request as the reviewer sees fit;

- ensuring that the reviewer should be able to adjourn the hearing at any time during the hearing on the applicant's application, or if the reviewer otherwise sees fit. If, at a re-scheduled hearing, the identity of the reviewer has changed, the hearing should be a complete re-hearing of the case;

- ensuring that, where more than one person is conducting the review, the review should only proceed in the absence of one of the reviewers if the applicant consents;

- ensuring that the applicant is notified of the decision on the review and, if the decision confirms the original decision, of the reasons for it; and

- ensuring that the applicant is notified of any right to re-apply.[163]

2.98 In the absence of explicit statutory provisions and given a wide variety of locally adopted procedures, it has been left to the courts to scrutinise individual review decisions and review procedures on a case-by-case basis applying traditional administrative law principles (outlined in Chapter 19).[164] The courts have developed some expertise in scrutinising the role of reviewing officers in reviews conducted of decisions made within the introductory tenancy and homelessness regimes of HA 1996,[165] so that the move to judicial scrutiny of review procedures in the housing allocation field has been relatively straightforward (see below).

Notifying review decisions

2.99 Each allocation scheme must be framed in terms that provide for an applicant who has sought a review to be notified of the decision on review and the grounds for it.[166] This requirement is interpreted in the statutory guidance as meaning that there should usually be provision in the allocation scheme for delivery of a written statement of the review decision and of the reasons for it.[167]

---

[163] Welsh Code, para 3.35.
[164] For examples of challenges to internal review arrangements on decisions about social housing allocation see: *R v Tower Hamlets London Borough Council ex p Spencer* (1995) 29 HLR 64, QBD (a challenge brought under Housing Act 1985) and *R v Southwark London Borough Council ex p Mason* (2000) 32 HLR 88, QBD (a challenge to a review panel's decision on the suitability of accommodation offered under the allocation scheme).
[165] HA 1996, Part 5 'Conduct of Tenants' and Part 7 'Homelessness' respectively.
[166] HA 1996, s 166A(9)(c) [England], s 167(4A)(d) [Wales].
[167] English Code, para 5.19viii, Welsh Code, para 3.35.

2.100 In one case, in which the adequacy of the reasons given in a review decision was challenged, despite the decision being set out in a lengthy letter to the applicant, a judge said:[168]

> 'In my view proper, adequate and intelligible reasons are set out in the decision letter. The reasons are stated "in sufficient detail" to enable [the Claimant] to know what conclusion [the decision maker] has reached on the "principal important controversial issues" (*Bolton Metropolitan Borough Council v Secretary of State for the Environment* [1995] 3 PLR 37, 43C, Lord Lloyd; and see *William v Wandsworth LBC* [2006] HLR 42 at para 18). Moreover [the reviewing officer] balanced competing factors and explained why he concluded that some outweighed others.'

Challenges to review decisions and non-reviewable decisions about particular applications

2.101 Any legal challenges to review decisions, or to any decisions about individual applications that do not carry the right to request a review, can only be brought by judicial review, on the grounds that the local housing authority has infringed some requirement of public or administrative law, or has failed to comply with the duty to supply the grounds for the decision.[169]

2.102 Judicial review challenges to allocation decisions tend to fall into two distinct categories:

(1)   challenges to the allocation scheme itself (or to some part of it); and

(2)   challenges to particular decisions made relating to particular applicants.

2.103 This part of this Chapter is concerned only with the latter. Challenges to the contents of allocation schemes are dealt with in Chapter 4.[170] Of course, occasionally, both forms of challenge may be available in a particular case. For an example of a judicial review which, at least initially, involved both forms of challenge see *R (Ahmad) v Newham London Borough Council*.[171]

2.104 As far as individual decisions are concerned, an applicant seeking to challenge such a decision would have to show that it was contrary to the provisions of HA 1996, Part 6, or of the local housing authority's allocation scheme, or that it had been reached by applying an unfair or unlawful procedure, or that it was based on some other mistake of law (or, in some circumstances, a mistake of fact.[172]) In one unsuccessful case, the challenge to

---

[168]   *R (Dixon) v Wandsworth London Borough Council* [2007] EWHC (Admin) 3075, (2008) February *Legal Action*, p 40, Admin Ct. per Deputy Judge Supperstone QC at [26].

[169]   The duty to supply reasons in an allocation case is set out at **2.82** and **2.99**. The classic grounds upon which judicial review claims can be mounted are discussed at **19.242–19.245**.

[170]   See **4.219–4.227**.

[171]   [2008] EWCA Civ 140, [2009] HLR 41, CA (later determined by the House of Lords solely as a challenge to the structure of the allocation scheme at [2009] UKHL 14, [2009] HLR 41, HL).

[172]   *E v Secretary of State for the Home Department* [2004] EWCA Civ 49, [2004] QB 1044, CA.

the decision of a reviewing officer on an issue about eligibility for social housing allocation was described as containing 'the familiar complaints that he had misdirected himself, failed to take into account relevant circumstances, and/or failed to give adequate reasons'.[173] Familiar as they may be, those complaints can sometimes be made out by an applicant in an appropriate case. For example, when considering whether to apply a discretionary provision in an allocation scheme a local housing authority must act fairly by giving an applicant an opportunity to deal with matters likely to be weighed against him or her.[174]

2.105 Claims for judicial review have been particularly successful in relation to decisions on medical needs assessment for the purposes of allocation schemes. In one case, a local housing authority's assessment failed to address issues raised by the applicant's medical advisers and gave insufficient reasons for a refusal to accord the highest medical priority in the local scheme.[175] In another, the medical assessment was based on medical advice commissioned by the local housing authority, but that advice had failed to address particular points and specific materials put forward by the applicant's advisers.[176] In a third case, a local housing authority's decisions were:

> 'insufficiently reasoned as to the criteria applied as to how medical need can or fails to come within the doctrine of reasonable preference and how the evidence has been related to the criteria that are applied.'[177]

2.106 In a fourth case, the medical advisers engaged by the local housing authority had gone beyond their remit and advised as to the relative priority of the applicant to others in housing need. The local housing authority had wrongly taken into account those non-medical opinions and relied upon them.[178]

2.107 Where an applicant is dissatisfied either with the decision (or review decision) on his or her application, or with the procedure followed, but there is no arguable error of law, the applicant should invoke the local housing authority's own internal complaints procedure and, if still dissatisfied, can then complain of maladministration to the Local Government Ombudsman (in England)[179] or the Public Services Ombudsman (in Wales). Dissatisfied

---

[173] *R (Dixon) v Wandsworth London Borough Council* [2008] EWCA Civ 595, (2008) July *Legal Action*, p 22, CA.

[174] *R (Moore) v Wandsworth London Borough Council* [2012] All ER (D) 66 (Jan), (2012) April *Legal Action*, p 46, Admin Ct.

[175] *R (Sawalha) v Westminster City Council* [2008] EWHC 1216 (Admin), (2008) July *Legal Action*, p 22, Admin Ct.

[176] *R (Ghandali) v Ealing London Borough Council* [2006] EWHC 1859 (Admin), [2006] All ER (D) 134 (Jul), Admin Ct.

[177] *R (Ahmad) v Newham London Borough Council* [2007] EWHC 2332 (Admin) at [24], (2007) November *Legal Action*, p 34, Admin Ct – not appealed on this point.

[178] *R (Bauer-Czarnomski) v Ealing London Borough Council* [2010] EWHC 130 (Admin), [2010] All ER (D) 101 (Jan), Admin Ct.

[179] See *Unfair Allocation,* Sanderson, [2007] 124 *Adviser* 35.

applicants for social housing can also seek redress through the intervention of the relevant national regulators of social housing providers.[180]

2.108 Complaints to the Ombudsmen may be pursued by complainants personally or by their legal advisers. The latter will need to consider carefully how such assistance might be remunerated.[181]

2.109 Both the English and Welsh Ombudsmen Services have produced fact-sheets for applicants who may want to complain about housing application matters. The Local Government Ombudsmen (LGO) have identified for applicants the sorts of complaints against a local housing authority that they may investigate:[182]

- It is using an allocation scheme that is not clear or fair
- It has failed to apply the allocation scheme properly or fairly failed to follow the Government's code of guidance on housing allocation
- It did not take relevant information into account in reaching its decision, or took irrelevant information into account
- It failed to give you information you should have (for example, about the priority awarded to your application or how to challenge the priority given to it), or
- It delayed in dealing with your application, changes in your situation, or with an appeal from you about the priority given to your application.

2.110 The LGO have provided a similar indicative list relating to complaints arising from *transfer* applications. The complaints they can look at include:[183]

- delay in processing your application
- losing your application or other documents
- turning down or suspending your application for no good reason
- not assessing your application in line with the council's allocations policy
- making a mistake, such as getting your application date wrong, not giving you the points you should have, or putting you in the wrong band
- failing to take special factors into account, such as overcrowding or medical problems
- not offering accommodation to you, including losing a bid made through a choice-based lettings scheme, or
- unreasonable delay in responding to correspondence.

2.111 Recent investigation reports published by the LGO indicate that significant awards of compensation may be recommended if maladministration has caused injustice to individuals who have applied for the allocation of social housing. For example:

---

[180] See **1.92–1.99**.
[181] See *R (Adams) v Commission for Local Administration in England* [2011] EWHC 2972 (Admin), (2012) January *Legal Action*, p 21, Admin Ct.
[182] *Fact Sheet – H2 Complaints about your housing application* (LGO, January 2012).
[183] *Fact Sheet – H1 Complaints about your housing transfers* (LGO, February 2012).

- A local housing authority tenant who was a permanent wheelchair user experienced difficulty entering and leaving the block in which her flat was located. She applied for a transfer. The local housing authority was repeatedly put on notice of her difficulties and the Fire Brigade told the local housing authority that she was at risk in the event of fire. It awarded her a 'Band B' priority for transfer on medical grounds but it did not refer the transfer application to its Social Welfare Panel until September 2011, even though it had identified this as a possibility in May 2009. The complainant then received Band A priority. The Ombudsman decided that the delay in referring the case to the panel was maladministration and that further maladministration by the local housing authority included: (1) telling a councillor that it had carried out works to the door entry system when that had not been done; and (2) failing to consider a suggestion that it modify the front door to the block. The Ombudsman recommended £2,000 compensation and a backdating of Band A status to May 2009.[184]

- An applicant bid, under a choice-based letting scheme, for the allocation to her of a house advertised by the local housing authority as having three bedrooms and a parlour. Her household comprised herself and three daughters. Two of the daughters were adults and the eldest was severely disabled, requiring a ground floor bedroom. She was the highest ranked bidder with a three-bedroom need but was not offered the property because all three bedrooms were on the upper floor. She had intended to convert the ground floor parlour to a bedroom for her disabled daughter. The property was offered to a family with a four-bed need who used the parlour as a bedroom. The Ombudsman found that the allocation scheme was defective in that: (1) it did not define the term 'children', which had allowed officers to treat the adult daughters as children for the purposes of the scheme; and (2) the scheme defined a three bedroom-plus-parlour house as a four bedroom property but such properties were actually advertised as having three bedrooms. The local housing authority had also failed to consider its obligations under the Disability Discrimination Act 2005[185] and the Human Rights Act 1998. The Ombudsman's recommendations included a review of the wording of the allocation scheme and £4,000 compensation.[186]

2.112 The Public Services Ombudsman for Wales (PSOW) has indicated that, in relation to both new applications and transfer requests, he can look at:[187]

- whether your housing application has been dealt with properly.
- whether the Council or housing association has properly applied its policy to your housing application e.g. are you in the correct band?

---

[184] *Complaint against Ealing London Borough Council*, No. 10015936, 16 February 2012 (2012) April Legal Action, p 46.
[185] See **4.195–4.206.**
[186] *Complaint against Havering London Borough Council*, No 10008622, 12 January 2012, (2012) April Legal Action, p 46.
[187] *Housing Application Factsheet* (PSOW, undated).

- whether the organisation has told you how it has dealt with your housing application e.g. has it sent you a letter detailing any points awarded?
- whether the organisation has delayed dealing with changes in your situation which you have told it about e.g. you have been asked to leave your home.
- why your application may have been suspended e.g. has the Council followed the correct procedure if the reason(s) for suspension is your behaviour?

2.113   The Welsh Code suggests that applicants for local housing authority or housing association accommodation may complain to the PSOW if they consider they have been treated unfairly, or have received a bad service through some failure on the part of the organisation and that local housing authorities and housing associations are 'obliged by law' to inform applicants of their rights to complain to the PSOW.[188]

2.114   Recent investigation reports from the PSOW indicate that significant awards of compensation may be recommended if maladministration has caused injustice to individuals who have applied for the allocation of social housing:

- A middle-aged single disabled man living with his mother (who was a tenant of the local housing authority) made repeated applications for rehousing on the grounds that his accommodation was unsuitable for his disabilities and was in disrepair. The Ombudsman found extensive maladministration including: (1) systemic failures in approach to the rehousing applications; (2) failure to follow relevant legislation, statutory guidance and policies and procedures; and (3) poor record keeping. He recommended a wide-ranging re-training of staff, a review of the local housing authority's policies, systems and procedures, an apology and £1,500 compensation.[189]

- In 2008 a local housing authority had allocated a property to a disabled man which it subsequently said could not be adapted to meet his needs (although it had been fully aware of his needs prior to allocating the property). It advised him to apply for a transfer but he did not wish to move again as his family had become settled. The local housing authority carried out no adaptations for over three years until it reassessed the complainant's needs following the complaint to the Ombudsman's office in 2011. It then agreed to carry out all the adaptations requested. The Ombudsman found maladministration in the allocation process and throughout the request for adaptations at the property. There had been no occupational therapist's (OT) assessment prior to allocation, nor was there a full assessment of the need for adaptations by either an OT or social services for over three years after the complainant had moved in. The local housing authority did not appear to recognise its statutory

---

[188]   Welsh Code, para 5.36.
[189]   *Complaint against Wrexham County Borough Council*, Case No. 201002076, 25 January 2012, (2012) April *Legal Action*, p 46.

social care duties to him, or that his human rights may have been engaged. The Ombudsman made a number of recommendations including an apology and payment of £3,000.[190]

- A private rented sector tenant (Ms A) applied in 2000 for allocation of social housing. She made a number of contacts with the local housing authority over the following years to progress her application and raised issues of overcrowding, disrepair and anti-social behaviour in her current home. Ms A complained to the Ombudsman about the length of time she had been waiting to be offered a property and about how her housing application had been dealt with. Although the local housing authority had accepted that it owed her the main housing duty (HA 1996, s 193)[191] in November 2004, it had mislaid her file, had not progressed her application for four and a half years and had not moved her to temporary accommodation until June 2009. The investigation found serious shortcomings in the way that the homelessness and housing applications had been handled. The local housing authority had repeatedly failed to consider all of the available relevant information in accordance with its allocations policy. This led to Ms A not being offered an available property in September 2005. The investigation also uncovered serious deficiencies in record-keeping. The Ombudsman found systemic maladministration. He recommended an apology to Ms A and her family for the failings and a redress payment of £1,500. He also made a number of recommendations for further action by the local housing authority, including the production of up-to-date written procedures on housing allocations and homelessness and further training for relevant officers.[192]

- A tenant applied for a transfer in 2004 on the grounds that her accommodation was overcrowded. She complained that the local housing authority had failed to deal with her application properly. On investigation, the ombudsman found that: (1) for the period from January 2003 to May 2006 the local housing authority had failed to have a lawful allocation scheme; (2) it had failed to visit the accommodation to assess overcrowding; (3) in making its paper assessment of the overcrowding, it had considered only one of the two overcrowding standards in HA 1985, s 326[193] and had failed to conduct an overcrowding assessment under the Health & Safety Hazards Rating System introduced by HA 2004;[194] (4) it had failed to record receipt of and reply promptly to correspondence; and (5) it had failed to consider whether the accommodation might no longer be 'reasonable to continue to occupy': HA 1996, s 175.[195] The

---

[190] *Complaint against Carmarthenshire County Council*, Case No. 201001198, 22 December 2011, (2012) April *Legal Action*, p 46.

[191] See **17.23**.

[192] *Complaint against Isle of Anglesey County Council*, Case No. 200902138, 29 June 2011, (2011) August *Legal Action*, p 40.

[193] See **4.83**.

[194] See **4.86**.

[195] See **11.75**.

Ombudsman recommended an apology, compensation, staff training and a proper assessment of the complainant's application.[196]

2.115 Sadly, the most common source of dissatisfaction with social housing allocation concerns the length of time that applicants have to wait before being made an offer of accommodation or succeeding in a bidding process in a choice-based letting scheme. Invoking legal remedies, or complaints procedures, rarely cures that grievance where the root cause of it is an excess of demand over supply.

---

[196] *Complaint against Blaenau Gwent CBC*, Case No: 09016302, 24 January 2011, (2011) April *Legal Action*, p 30.

Chapter 3

ELIGIBILITY AND QUALIFICATION FOR ALLOCATION

AN OVERVIEW

3.1   The statutory scheme for social housing allocation contained in Housing Act 1996 ('HA 1996'), Part 6[1] has some features which are common to England and Wales and other features which apply differently in the two countries. This Chapter first explores one of the common features – a restriction on eligibility for an allocation which is primarily based on immigration status – and then addresses, in turn, two aspects in which the statutory allocation arrangements apply differently:

(1)   the ability to exclude applicants from allocation based on criteria of 'qualification', available only to local housing authorities in England; and

(2)   the ability to exclude applicants on the basis that past misconduct has rendered them 'ineligible', now available only to local housing authorities in Wales (but which was available to local housing authorities in both countries until 18 June 2012).

3.2   If an applicant is found to be 'ineligible', the local housing authority is statutorily barred from allocating housing accommodation to him or her.[2] Only an applicant who is found to be a 'qualifying' person by a local housing authority in England will be allocated housing accommodation by that authority.[3]

3.3   In relation to eligibility, a local housing authority in England or Wales *must* decide that people who are subject to immigration control (with limited exceptions), and other people who are to be treated as persons from abroad, are ineligible *unless* either:

(1)   they are currently secure, introductory or, in certain cases, assured tenants of social housing;[4] or

(2)   they fall within one of the exceptional classes prescribed by regulations as being eligible for allocation notwithstanding their immigration or residence status.[5]

---

[1]   Statutory guidance on allocation schemes made under HA 1996 Part 6 is given in *Allocation of Accommodation: Guidance for local housing authorities for England* (Department for Communities & Local Government, June 2012) (the English Code) and in *Code of Guidance for Local Authorities Allocation of Accommodation and Homelessness 2012* (Welsh Government, August 2012) (the Welsh Code). See Appendix 1 of this book for the English Code and see the accompanying CD-ROM for the Welsh Code.

[2]   HA 1996, s 160ZA(1) [England], s 160A(1) [Wales].

[3]   HA 1996, s 160ZA(6)

[4]   HA 1996, ss 159(4B) and 160ZA(5) [England] and 160A(6) [Wales]. English Code, para 3.4, Welsh Code, para 3.5(i).

[5]   HA 1996, s 160ZA(2), (3) and (4) [England], s 160A(3), (4), (5) and (6) [Wales]; Allocation of Housing and Homelessness (Eligibility) (England) Regulations 2006, SI 2006/1294, regs 3–4 as amended; Allocation of Housing (Wales) Regulations 2003, SI 2003/239 (W 36), regs 4–5.

3.4   In relation to 'qualification', the position is subject to much more flexibility. Local housing authorities in England are free to decide for themselves what classes of eligible persons are or are not also qualifying persons.[6] That flexibility is subject to a back-stop in that the Secretary of State can prescribe by regulations that certain classes must be treated as qualifying persons or are not to be so treated.[7] At the date of writing, such regulations had only been made in respect of the treatment of applicants with connections to the armed forces: see **3.195**.

3.5   In relation to 'eligibility' turning on past misconduct, a local housing authority in Wales *may* choose to adopt and apply a rule that applicants who have been guilty of unacceptable behaviour, serious enough to make them unsuitable to be tenants of the local housing authority, are ineligible for an allocation.[8] This is a discretionary power available to all local housing authorities in Wales but they are not obliged to use it.[9] If a local housing authority does choose to use it, considers an applicant's behaviour, and concludes that the behaviour is *not* so serious as to make the applicant unsuitable to be a tenant, but that he or she should be penalised in some way, it could decide that the applicant *is* eligible for an allocation, but that he or she should receive a lower priority than other applicants.[10]

3.6   The various categories of ineligibility and qualification are examined in detail in the remainder of this Chapter.

3.7   If an applicant is found by a local housing authority to be ineligible or not qualified for an allocation, that decision and the reasons for it must be notified to him or her in writing.[11] The applicant is then entitled to request a review of the decision and to be notified of the review decision and the reasons for it.[12] There is no provision for any appeal against the review decision to the county court, so any challenge by legal proceedings could only be by judicial review.[13]

3.8   If an applicant is ineligible for an allocation of accommodation for any reason, he or she must not be allocated a sole tenancy, nor be allocated a joint

---

Statutory guidance in Wales alerts Welsh housing authorities to the possibility that the Welsh regulations may be re-issued: Welsh Code, para 3.1.

[6]   HA 1996, s 160ZA(7).
[7]   HA 1996, s 160ZA(8).
[8]   HA 1996, s 160A(7) and (8); Welsh Code, para 3.20.
[9]   HA 1996, s 160A(2); Welsh Code, para 3.19.
[10]   HA 1996, s 167(2A) and Welsh Code, para 3.25. See **4.144**.
[11]   HA 1996, s 160ZA(9) and (10) [England], s 160A(9) and (10) [Wales].
[12]   HA 1996, s 166A(9)(c) [England], s 167(4A)(d) [Wales].
[13]   For three examples of challenges to eligibility decisions by way of judicial review see *R (McQ) v Bolton Metropolitan Borough Council* [2005] EWHC 1285 (Admin), (2005) August *Legal Action*, p 17, Admin Ct; *R (Dixon) v Wandsworth London Borough Council* [2008] EWCA Civ 595, (2008) July *Legal Action*, p 22, Admin Ct; and *R (M) v Hackney London Borough Council* [2009] EWHC 2255 (Admin), (2009) May *Legal Action*, p 26, Admin Ct.

tenancy with others, under the allocation scheme.[14] So, if a couple apply for an allocation of a property to be let on a joint tenancy and only one of them is eligible, a joint tenancy cannot be granted. The tenancy can only be granted to the eligible applicant in his or her sole name. In respect of 'qualification' the rule is different for applicants to local housing authorities in England. While an allocation may not be made to a non-qualifying person as a sole tenant, a joint tenancy may be granted as long as at least one of the joint tenants is an eligible and qualifying person.[15]

3.9　The eligibility and qualification restrictions apply to *applicants*, not to their dependents or others in the household with whom they seek to be accommodated. However, the previous unacceptable behaviour of a household member may allow a local housing authority in Wales to treat the applicant himself or herself as ineligible.[16]

3.10　If an eligible applicant has ineligible or non-qualifying dependents, their needs must still be taken into account when the local housing authority considers the type and size of accommodation to be allocated.[17] However, a local housing authority is free to take into account the immigration status of family members in deciding whether they form part of an applicant's 'household' at all.[18] If an ineligible household member is a 'restricted person',[19] that fact will not render the otherwise eligible applicant ineligible, but it may affect his or her entitlement to a reasonable preference.[20]

3.11　Ineligible or non-qualifying applicants are not prevented from acquiring a tenancy in cases where the provisions of the HA 1996, Part 6 do not apply, e g where the grant of a tenancy to them does not count as an allocation at all.[21]

---

[14]　HA 1996, s 160ZA(1)(b) [England], s 160A(1) [Wales]. However, once a person has been granted a secure or assured tenancy, that tenancy does not come to an end, nor is the landlord entitled to apply for possession, simply because he or she is ineligible for a grant of a secure or assured tenancy. The landlord can only obtain possession under the grounds for possession at Housing Act 1985, Sch 2 (secure tenants) or Housing Act 1988, Sch 2 (assured tenants), or if the tenant loses his or her security of tenure (*Akinbolu v Hackney London Borough Council* (1997) 29 HLR 259, CA).

[15]　HA 1996, s 160ZA(6)(b), English Code, para 3.29.

[16]　See **3.203–3.251**.

[17]　*R (Kimvono) v Tower Hamlets London Borough Council* (2001) 33 HLR 78, Admin Ct.

[18]　*R (Ariemuguvbe) v Islington London Borough Council* [2009] EWHC 470 (Admin), (2009) April *Legal Action*, p 21, Admin Ct, upheld on appeal in *R (Ariemuguvbe) v Islington London Borough Council* [2009] EWCA Civ 1308, [2010] HLR 14, (2010) January *Legal Action*, p 35, CA.

[19]　HA 1996, s 184(7). See **4.153–4.154** and **10.82–10.85**.

[20]　HA 1996, s 166A(4) [England], s 167(2ZA) [Wales] and **4.153–4.154**.

[21]　HA 1996, s 159(4A) –(5), s160(2), (3) and (4). See also **1.35–1.43**.

INELIGIBILITY ON THE GROUNDS OF IMMIGRATION STATUS (ENGLAND & WALES)

A summary

3.12 The provisions governing ineligibility on the basis of immigration status are tortuous and complicated. The Codes of Guidance[22] each have several annexes to help with the assessment of eligibility.[23]

3.13 The immigration status of an existing secure or introductory tenant, or an assured tenant who was nominated to his or her landlord by a local housing authority, who has applied for an allocation (eg by way of a transfer) is irrelevant.[24] Those applicants are eligible for an allocation irrespective of their immigration status.

3.14 The general rule in HA 1996, Part 6 is that applicants who are 'people from abroad' are not eligible.[25] They fall into two distinct categories.

- those subject to immigration control—
  - they are *not eligible* for assistance
  - *unless* they fall within a class prescribed as 'eligible' in regulations made by the Secretary of State or the Welsh Ministers;[26]

- those not subject to immigration control but who are nevertheless prescribed by regulations as being 'persons from abroad'—
  - they are *not eligible* if they are not habitually resident in the Common Travel Area *unless* they are prescribed as exempt from the habitual residence test; or
  - they are *not eligible* if they are prescribed as ineligible because of their particular rights of residence under European Union law.[27]

3.15 In addition, the details of each of the two sub-categories are different depending on whether an application for an allocation is made to a local housing authority in England or to a local housing authority in Wales.

3.16 The Secretary of State and the Welsh Ministers[28] each have the power to make regulations exempting some people from abroad from the exclusory

---

[22] *Allocation of Accommodation: guidance for local housing authorities in England* (Department for Communities and Local Government, June 2012) (the English Code) (see Appendix 1). *Code of Guidance for Local Authorities Allocation of Accommodation and Homelessness 2012* (Welsh Government, August 2012) (the Welsh Code) (see CD-ROM).
[23] English Code, Annexes 2–4 inclusive; Welsh Code, Annexes 3–6 inclusive.
[24] HA 1996, s 160ZA(5) [England], s 160A(6) [Wales].
[25] HA 1996, s 160ZA(1) [England], s 160A(1)(a) [Wales].
[26] HA 1996, s 160ZA(2) [England], s 160A(3) [Wales].
[27] HA 1996, s 160ZA(4) [England], s 160A(5) [Wales].
[28] This power was exercisable by the National Assembly for Wales until 25 May 2007. On that day (which was the day of the appointment of the First Minister after the May 2007 elections to the National Assembly for Wales), functions previously exercised by the National Assembly

rule.[29] They each also have the power to make regulations excluding people who would otherwise be eligible. Each of these powers has been exercised several times, in both England and Wales.

3.17 For England, the Secretary of State has made the Allocation of Housing and Homelessness (Eligibility) (England) Regulations 2006,[30] which apply to all applications for an allocation of social housing to local housing authorities in England made on or after 1 June 2006.[31] Those Regulations have since been amended by:

- the Allocation of Housing and Homelessness (Eligibility) (England) (Amendment) Regulations 2006;[32]

- the Allocation of Housing and Homelessness (Eligibility) (England) (Miscellaneous Provisions) Regulations 2006;[33]

- the Allocation of Housing and Homelessness (Eligibility) (England) (Amendment No 2) Regulations 2006;[34]

- the Allocation of Housing and Homelessness (Eligibility) (England) (Amendment) Regulations 2009;[35] and

- the Allocation of Housing and Homelessness (Eligibility) (England) (Amendment) Regulations 2012.[36]

---

for Wales were transferred to the Welsh Assembly Government (Government of Wales Act 2006, s 161 and Sch 11, para 30). The Welsh Assembly Government subsequently re-named itself the Welsh Government.

[29] They cannot designate as eligible any person who is excluded from entitlement to housing benefit by the Immigration and Asylum Act 1999, s 115 (HA 1996, s 160ZA(3) [England], s 160A(4) [Wales]). Immigration and Asylum Act 1999, s 115 prescribes that 'a person subject to immigration control' is not eligible for housing benefit unless he or she falls within one of the classes of people prescribed by the Secretary of State. Classes of persons subject to immigration control who are entitled to housing benefit are prescribed in the Social Security (Immigration and Asylum) Consequential Amendment Regulations 2000, SI 2000/636, reg 2 and Sch 1, Part 1 and the Housing Benefit Regulations 2006, SI 2006/213, reg 10(3B).

[30] SI 2006/1294. See Appendix 2 of this book.

[31] Any applications for an allocation of social housing made before 1 June 2006 to local housing authorities in England are determined according to the Homelessness (England) Regulations 2000, SI 2000/701, amended by Allocation of Housing and Homelessness (Amendment) (England) Regulations 2004, SI 2004/1235 and further amended by the Allocation of Housing and Homelessness (Amendment) (England) Regulations 2006, SI 2006/1093.

[32] SI 2006/2007, in force for applications to local housing authorities in England made on or after 25 July 2006.

[33] SI 2006/2527, in force for applications to local housing authorities in England made on or after 9 October 2006.

[34] SI 2006/3340, in force for applications to local housing authorities in England made on or after 1 January 2007.

[35] SI 2009/358, in force for applications to local housing authorities in England made on or after 18 March 2009.

[36] SI 2012/2588 in force for applications to local housing authorities in England made on or after 8 November 2012.

3.18   Appendix 2 of this book contains the text of the Allocation of Housing and Homelessness (Eligibility) (England) Regulations 2006[37] as amended by all of the above Regulations. Guidance is provided at paras 3.2–3.17 and Annexes 2–4 of the English Code.

3.19   In Wales, the National Assembly for Wales[38] made the Allocation of Housing (Wales) Regulations 2003,[39] which apply to all applications for an allocation for social housing made to local housing authorities in Wales on or after 29 January 2003.

3.20   The Welsh Regulations have been amended by:

- the Allocation of Housing (Wales) (Amendment) Regulations 2006, reg 2;[40] and

- the Allocation of Housing and Homelessness (Eligibility) (Wales) Regulations 2009.[41]

3.21   Appendix 3 of this book contains the text of the Allocation of Housing (Wales) Regulations 2003 as amended by both these Regulations. Guidance is provided at paras 3.1–3.19 and Annexes 4–6 of the Welsh Code.

3.22   There will be many applicants whose applications were made before June 2006 (to a local housing authority in England) or even before 29 January 2003 (to a local housing authority in Wales). The question of whether or not they were eligible for an allocation fell to be considered under the Regulations in effect at the date that they made their applications. However, the English Code advises that authorities consider applicants' eligibility at the time of the initial application and again when considering making an allocation to them, particularly where a substantial amount of time has elapsed since the original application. This two-stage checking of eligibility will affect applicants:

- who either made their applications before 1 June 2006 and were eligible under one of the classes in the previous Regulations[42] but do not fall within any of the classes prescribed as eligible in the current Regulations; or

- whose immigration status may have changed since they made their applications.

---

[37]   SI 2006/1294.
[38]   Its functions were acquired by the Welsh Assembly Government on 25 May 2007. See fn 28.
[39]   SI 2003/239 (W 36).
[40]   SI 2006/2645 (W 226).
[41]   SI 2009/393 (W 42).
[42]   For applications to a local housing authority in England before 1 June 2006, the relevant Regulations were the Allocation of Housing (England) Regulations 2002, SI 2002/3264. Those Regulations were amended by the Allocation of Housing and Homelessness (Amendment) (England) Regulations 2006, SI 2006/1093, with effect to applicants whose applications were made between 20 April 2006 and 31 May 2006.

3.23 The Welsh Code does not address the point but it is likely that local housing authorities in Wales will take the same approach of assessing an applicant's eligibility by reference to the Regulations in effect at the date when an allocation is due to be made. For that reason, this Chapter does not deal with the Regulations in effect prior to 1 June 2006 (for applications to local housing authorities in England) or 29 January 2003 (for applications to local housing authorities in Wales.)[43] Reference can be made to the two previous editions of this book if necessary.[44]

3.24 The Regulations in both England and Wales set out classes of persons who are subject to immigration control, but are prescribed as nevertheless eligible. They also set out classes of persons who are not subject to immigration control, but are nevertheless ineligible.

3.25 Each of the two categories of persons from abroad (those subject to immigration control and those not subject to such control) needs careful examination. But first it is necessary to work out which sub-category an applicant is within. That depends on whether or not the applicant is 'subject to immigration control'.

3.26 This part of this Chapter deals with:

- the first sub-category (persons subject to immigration control) as it applies to:
    - local housing authorities in England for applications made on or after 1 June 2006, discussed at **3.38–3.54**; then
    - local housing authorities in Wales, discussed at **3.38–3.40** and **3.55–3.64**; and

- the second sub-category (other persons from abroad) as it applies to:
    - local housing authorities in England for applications made on or after 1 June 2006, discussed at **3.65–3.133**; and then
    - local housing authorities in Wales, discussed at **3.65–3.69** and **3.134–3.136**.

3.27 It concludes with a review of the circumstances of those who would be eligible in only one of either England or Wales, at **3.137–3.139**.

3.28 The starting point, however, for either sub-category is consideration of who is and who is not, in the ordinary course of events, 'a person subject to immigration control'.

---

[43] The relevant Regulations in Wales were the Allocation of Housing (Wales) Regulations 2000, SI 2000/1080 (W.73) revoked by SI 2003/239 reg 6, with effect from 29 January 2003.

[44] Luba and Davies *Housing Allocation and Homelessness* (1st edn, 2006; 2nd edn 2010).

The meaning of 'subject to immigration control'

3.29 There is a special meaning of 'subject to immigration control'. The HA 1996, s 160ZA(3) [England], s 160A(3) [Wales] refer to:

'... a person subject to immigration control within the meaning of the Asylum and Immigration Act 1996.'

3.30 The Asylum and Immigration Act 1996 defines 'a person who is subject to immigration control' as being a person:

'... who under the 1971 Act requires leave to enter or remain in the United Kingdom (whether or not such leave has been given).'[45]

3.31 Tracing that route back to the Immigration Act 1971[46] reveals that:

- British citizens;

- Commonwealth citizens with the right of abode in the UK;

- European Economic Area (EEA) and Swiss nationals exercising certain Treaty rights;[47]

- family members and others exercising rights derived from those EEA or Swiss nationals exercising, or who had previously exercised, certain Treaty rights;[48]

- certain people who are exempt from immigration control under the Immigration Acts (diplomats and their family members based in the UK, and some military personnel); and

- Irish citizens with a Common Travel Area entitlement

---

[45] Asylum and Immigration Act 1996, s 13(2).

[46] Immigration Act 1971, ss 1–3.

[47] Immigration Act 1988, s 7; Immigration (European Economic Area) Regulations 2006, SI 2006/1003, regs 13–15. From 1 June 2002, Swiss nationals have had the same rights to freedom of movement and social security within the EEA as EEA nationals: Immigration (Swiss Free Movement of Persons) (No 3) Regulations 2002, SI 2002/1241. Swiss nationals fall within the definition of 'EEA nationals' at Immigration (European Economic Area) Regulations 2006, SI 2006/1003, reg 2. All references to EEA nationals in this book therefore include Swiss nationals.

[48] Immigration (European Economic Area) Regulations 2006, SI 2006/1003, regs 15A and 15B inserted by Immigration (European Economic Area) (Amendment) Regulations 2012, SI 2012.1547, in force from 16 July 2012 and amended by Immigration (European Economic Area) (Amendment) (No 2) Regulations 2012, SI 2012/2560, in force from 8 November 2012. For those derivative rights, see **12.142–12.161**.

do *not* require leave to enter or remain in the UK and therefore cannot be persons 'subject to immigration control'.[49] Those applicants will be eligible *unless* they fall within the second sub-category of persons prescribed as being 'persons from abroad' and not eligible.[50]

3.32 The legal definition of 'The United Kingdom' and its related parts is given in Box 1.

Box 1

Key Geographic Terms:

England: counties established by Local Government Act 1972, s 1, Greater London area and the Isles of Scilly.[51]

Great Britain: England, Wales, and Scotland.[52]

United Kingdom: England, Wales, Scotland and Northern Ireland.[53]

Common Travel Area (CTA): England, Wales, Scotland, Northern Ireland, Republic of Ireland, Isle of Man, and the Channel Islands.[54]

3.33 Box 2 shows which countries are members of the European Union (EU) and/or members of the wider European Economic Area (EEA).[55] For these purposes, nationals of Iceland, Liechtenstein, Norway and Switzerland have the same rights to enter or reside as nationals of most of the EU member states.[56] Rights for nationals of Bulgaria and Romania ('A2 states')[57] are slightly different from those enjoyed by nationals of other EEA states.[58] We refer throughout this Chapter to nationals of EEA member states, by which we

---

49 Immigration Act 1971, ss 1–3; Immigration Act 1988, s 7; Immigration (European Economic Area) Regulations 2006, SI 2006/1003 as amended. See English Code, paras 3.7–3.9; Welsh Code, para 3.5(vi).
50 HA 1996, s 160ZA(4) [England], s 160A(5) [Wales]; Allocation of Housing and Homelessness (Eligibility) (England) Regulations 2006, SI 2006/1294, reg 4 (as amended) and Allocation of Housing (Wales) Regulations 2003, SI 2003/239 (W 36), reg 5 (as amended).
51 Interpretation Act 1978, s 5 and Sch 1.
52 Union of Scotland Act 1706.
53 Interpretation Act 1978, s 5 and Sch 1.
54 Immigration Act 1971, s 1(3).
55 Croatia is due to accede to the European Union in 2013. Iceland, Montenegro, Serbia, Turkey and the former Yugoslav Republic of Macedonia are 'candidate countries' for accession to the EU. Albania, Bosnia and Herzegovina, and Kosovo are all potential 'candidate countries'. See www.europea.eu/about-eu/countries/index_en.htm for an up-to-date list.
56 Immigration (European Economic Area) Regulations 2006, SI 2006/1003 as amended. See Appendix 2 of this book.
57 See **3.99–3.103**.
58 Rights for nationals of the eight 2004 Accession States ('A8 states') were subject to derogation between 1 May 2004 and 30 April 2011 (Accession (Immigration and Worker Regulations) Regulations 2004, SI 2004/1219. From 1 May 2011, nationals of the A8 member states are to be treated in the same way as nationals of any other EEA member state, save that retained

mean all the EU member states, including the A2 states, plus the three additional EEA member states and Switzerland.

Box 2

The European Union (EU):

Member States:[59] Austria, Belgium, Cyprus, Czech Republic, Denmark, Estonia, Finland, France, Germany, Greece, Hungary, Ireland, Italy, Latvia, Lithuania, Luxembourg, Netherlands, Malta, Poland, Portugal, Slovakia, Slovenia Spain, Sweden and the UK; and

Accession States acceding in 2007 ('A2 states'): Bulgaria and Romania

The European Economic Area (EEA):

All EU States[60] plus Iceland, Liechtenstein and Norway.

Switzerland is not part of the EEA, but its nationals are treated as EEA nationals for these purposes.[61]

3.34 Obviously, the lists given in these boxes will fluctuate from time to time. Annex 4 of the Welsh Code provides useful lists and web site addresses that will help advisers keep up to date.

3.35 If a consideration of these provisions shows that the applicant, even if newly arrived in the UK, does not require leave to enter or remain in the UK, he or she will usually be 'eligible' *unless* rendered ineligible by falling within the second sub-category.[62] For these purposes, it is important to emphasise that a person, usually an EEA national, or a person claiming to exercise rights derived from an EEA national, who does not require leave to enter but who does require leave to remain and does not have it, is a person subject to immigration control.[63] It is only a person who requires neither leave to enter nor leave to remain who is not subject to immigration control. Strangely, a person can be ineligible for an allocation of social housing even if he or she was born in the UK and has never left it, simply because he or she does require leave to enter or

---

worker status is slightly different. The A8 states were the Czech Republic, Estonia, Hungary, Latvia, Lithuania, Poland, Slovakia and Slovenia.

[59] All Member States as at 30 April 2004, plus Cyprus and Malta, who both joined on 1 May 2004 along with the A8 states. Cyprus and Malta were not subject to the derogations that the A8 states were subject to.

[60] The Channel Islands, Isle of Man and Gibraltar are not part of the EEA.

[61] Immigration (European Economic Area) Regulations 2006, SI 2006/1003, reg 2.

[62] See **3.65–3.136**.

[63] *Abdi v Barnet London Borough Council, Ismail v Barnet London Borough Council* [2006] EWCA Civ 383, [2006] HLR 23, CA.

remain in the UK and does not have it.[64] Similarly a person is only an EEA national for these purposes if he or she has actually left his or her country of origin and thus exercised freedom of movement.[65]

3.36 Everyone else is a 'person subject to immigration control' and is *not* eligible for assistance *unless* he or she falls into one of the classes prescribed by the Regulations.[66]

3.37 If there is any uncertainty about an applicant's immigration status, local housing authorities are advised to contact the UK Border Agency (UKBA).[67] The UKBA advises on an applicant's immigration status, but the decision on eligibility is for the local housing authority itself.[68] Before making the inquiry, local housing authorities in Wales are advised to inform the applicant that an inquiry will be made, giving the applicant an opportunity to withdraw the application for social housing, so that no further action will be taken and the UKBA will not be informed of the inquiry.[69] If the applicant is an asylum seeker, the application for help with accommodation will usually be referred to the UKBA for support under Immigration and Asylum Act 1999, Part 6.[70]

Sub-category one: those who are subject to immigration control

3.38 Anyone who requires leave to enter or remain in the UK is a 'person subject to immigration control' and will not be eligible for an allocation unless he or she falls within one of the classes prescribed as eligible in regulations made by the Secretary of State or the Welsh Ministers.[71]

3.39 The Secretary of State and the Welsh Ministers cannot designate as 'eligible' anyone who is excluded from entitlement to housing benefit by the Immigration and Asylum Act 1999, s 115.[72]

3.40 The Secretary of State and the Welsh Ministers have exercised their powers given by HA 1996, s 160ZA(2) [England] and s160A(3) [Wales] to set

---

[64] *Ehiabor v Kensington & Chelsea Royal London Borough Council* [2008] EWCA Civ 1074, [2008] All ER (D) 104 (May), CA.

[65] *McCarthy v SSHD* [2011] EUJECJ C-434/09, [2011] All ER (EC) 729, CJEU.

[66] Allocation of Housing and Homelessness (Eligibility) (England) Regulations 2006, SI 2006/1294, reg 4 as amended; Allocation of Housing (Wales) Regulations, SI 2003/239 (W36), reg 4.

[67] At http://ukba.homeoffice.gov.uk.

[68] English Code, para 3.10.

[69] Welsh Code, para 3.16.

[70] Formerly provided by the National Asylum Support Service (NASS).

[71] HA 1996, s 160ZA(2) [England], s 160A(3) [Wales].

[72] HA 1996, s 160ZA(3) [England], s160A(4) [Wales]. Immigration and Asylum Act 1999, s 115 prescribes that 'a person subject to immigration control' is not eligible for housing benefit unless he or she falls within one of the classes of people prescribed by the Secretary of State. Classes of persons subject to immigration control who are entitled to housing benefit are prescribed in the Social Security (Immigration and Asylum) Consequential Amendment Regulations 2000, SI 2000/636, Sch 1, Part 1 and the Housing Benefit Regulations 2006, SI 2006/213, reg 10(3B).

out classes of persons subject to immigration control who are nevertheless eligible for an allocation of accommodation.

The English rules

3.41 The basic rule is that a 'person subject to immigration control' is *not eligible*. The exceptions to that basic rule are contained in classes set out in Regulations. Regulation 3 of the Allocation of Housing and Homelessness (Eligibility) (England) Regulations 2006[73] prescribes that the following classes of people from abroad are eligible even though they are subject to immigration control:

(1) Class A:[74] a person recorded by the Secretary of State as a refugee and who has leave to enter or remain in the UK.

(2) Class B:[75] a person who has—
  (a) exceptional leave to enter or remain in the UK; and
  (b) whose leave is not subject to conditions requiring him or her to maintain and accommodate himself or herself and any dependants without recourse to public funds.

(3) Class C:[76] a person—
  (a) who is habitually resident in the 'common travel area' (CTA); and
  (b) who has current leave to enter or remain in the UK which is not subject to any limitation or condition; but
  (c) is not someone who has—
    (i) been given leave to enter or remain in the UK upon a written undertaking from a sponsor that he or she will be responsible for maintenance and accommodation; and
    (ii) has been resident in the CTA for less than five years beginning on the date of entry or the date of the undertaking (whichever is the later date); and
    (iii) whose sponsor is still alive.

(4) Class D:[77] a person who has humanitarian protection granted under the Immigration Rules.

3.42 Guidance on the four Classes is given in the English Code, para 3.11.

---

[73] Allocation of Housing and Homelessness (Eligibility) (England) Regulations 2006, SI 2006/1294, reg 3, as amended; see Appendix 2.
[74] SI 2006/1294, reg 3(a). See **3.45–3.46**.
[75] SI 2006/1294, reg 3(b). See **3.47–3.50**.
[76] SI 2006/1294, reg 3(c). See **3.51–3.53**.
[77] SI 2006/1294, reg 3(d), as amended by Allocation of Housing and Homelessness (Miscellaneous Provisions) (England) Regulations 2006, SI 2006/2527, reg 2, for applications for an allocation of social housing made on or after 9 October 2006. For applications made before 9 October 2006, Class D contained 'a person who left the territory of Montserrat after 1 November 1995 because of the effect on that territory of a volcanic eruption.' See **3.54**.

3.43 A number of the Classes contain common terms that are themselves defined by the regulations or by case law. For the meaning of:

- 'Common Travel Area' (CTA), see **3.32**, Box 1;

- 'habitually resident', see **3.76–3.85**;

- 'UK', see **3.32**, Box 1.

3.44 Each class can now be examined in further detail.

Class A:[78] *Refugees*

3.45 If a former asylum seeker is granted refugee status by the Secretary of State, he or she will also have the 'leave to enter or remain in the UK' required for Class A purposes and will be eligible for homelessness assistance, welfare benefits, community care services and for an allocation of social housing according to the same criteria as those applicable to British citizens. Leave might be granted for an indefinite period or limited to five years.

3.46 It is not unusual for someone to be granted refugee status and then apply for his or her family to come to the UK. The family enters the UK with the refugee acting as their sponsor. A refugee is entitled to such family reunion,[79] and so the usual rules regarding maintenance and accommodation (which would normally involve a condition of 'no recourse to public funds') do not apply to a refugee's family members. Thus, those family members will also be eligible persons, because they are entitled to 'refugee' status.[80]

Class B:[81] *Exceptional leave to enter or remain*

3.47 'Exceptional leave to enter or remain' was generally a status granted to asylum-seekers whose claim for full refugee status had not succeeded, but where the Home Office recognised that there were compelling humanitarian and/or compassionate circumstances that required that the applicant should be allowed to stay in the UK. From 1 April 2003, the Home Office has called leave granted in those circumstances 'humanitarian protection' or 'discretionary leave'.[82] Viewed broadly, anyone who has been granted leave when the Secretary

---

[78] Allocation of Housing and Homelessness (Eligibility) (England) Regulations 2006, SI 2006/1294, reg 3(a); English Code, para 3.11(i). For eligibility for homelessness assistance, see **12.76–12.78**.

[79] *Immigration Rules*, HC 395, paras 352A–352F (23 May 1994), as amended.

[80] *R (Jimaali) v Haringey London Borough Council* (2002) November *Legal Action*, p 24, Admin Ct.

[81] Allocation of Housing and Homelessness (Eligibility) (England) Regulations 2006, SI 2006/1294, reg 3(b); English Code, para 3.11(ii).

[82] Letter from the Homelessness Directorate to Chief Executives and Housing Directors of English local housing authorities (ODPM, 25 March 2003).

of State has recognised that he or she does not fully meet the requirements of the Immigration Rules has been treated 'exceptionally' and may be said to have been granted 'exceptional leave'.[83]

3.48 People with exceptional leave to enter or remain will be eligible for an allocation unless that leave is subject to a condition requiring them to maintain and accommodate themselves, and their dependents, without recourse to public funds. The presence or absence of such a condition will be manifest from the document, or stamp, containing the grant of leave.

3.49 Subject to that exception, they will not only be entitled to an allocation of social housing but also to homelessness assistance, welfare benefits and community care services.

3.50 Leave is normally, but not always, granted for a period of three years. If, after the end of that period, the leave is not renewed, the person will no longer be eligible for an allocation, unless he or she falls within one of the other classes. However, once an applicant has been allocated a tenancy of social housing, that tenancy cannot be terminated on the basis that he or she is no longer eligible. The applicant will be entitled to remain in his or her tenancy or to apply for another allocation as an existing secure, introductory or assured tenant.[84]

Class C:[85] A person with current leave to enter or remain in the UK with no condition or limitation and who is habitually resident in the CTA

3.51 The type of leave contemplated by this class is commonly referred to as 'indefinite leave to enter or remain' and cannot be granted subject to conditions.[86] Anyone granted indefinite leave will be eligible if he or she is also habitually resident in the CTA.[87]

3.52 If leave to enter or remain was granted on a written undertaking that a sponsor would be responsible for the applicant's maintenance and accommodation, the applicant will *not* be eligible under this class for an allocation for the five years running from:

---

[83] Since April 2012, the UKBA's policy has to been to grant leave limited for a period of three months to people who have left their partner within two years of arriving in the UK and are considering applying for indefinite leave to remain under the Domestic Violence Immigration Rule. Anyone who has been granted that limited leave is entitled to apply for welfare benefits and should also fall under this Class B and be eligible for an allocation of social housing. They should also be eligible for homelessness assistance (Allocation of Housing and Homelessness (Eligibility) (England) Regulations 2006 (SI 2006/1294), reg 5(1)(b), see **12.79–12.81**.

[84] *Akinbolu v Hackney London Borough Council* (1996) 29 HLR 259, CA; HA 1996, s 160ZA(5) [England], s 160A(6) [Wales].

[85] Allocation of Housing and Homelessness (Eligibility) (England) Regulations 2006, SI 2006/1294, reg 3(c), English Code, para 3.11(iii). For eleigibilty for homelessness assistance, see **12.82–12.84**.

[86] Immigration Act 1971, s 3(1)(b) and (c).

[87] For the meaning of 'habitually resident' see **3.76–3.85**.

- the date of his or her arrival in the UK, or

- the date the sponsorship undertaking was given,

starting from whichever is the later event.

3.53 After those five years, or during the five years if the sponsor (or at least one of several sponsors) has died, an applicant will be eligible under this class (subject to satisfying the test of habitual residence).[88]

Class D:[89] *a person granted humanitarian protection under the immigration rules*

3.54 'Humanitarian protection' is granted to those people whose claims for asylum do not succeed, but who have international protection needs (ie they face a serious risk of the death penalty, unlawful killing, torture, inhuman or degrading treatment or punishment if removed from the UK). The status must be granted pursuant to the Immigration Rules.[90] People with humanitarian protection are entitled to family reunion in the same way as refugees.[91] This class was substituted by the Allocation of Housing and Homelessness (Miscellaneous Provisions) (England) Regulations 2006[92] and is in force for applications for an allocation of social housing made on or after 9 October 2006.[93]

The Welsh rules

3.55 Applications for an allocation made to local housing authorities in Wales are governed by the Allocation of Housing (Wales) Regulations 2003[94] and those Regulations apply to all applications made on or after 29 January 2003. The Welsh Code advises that consideration is currently being given to amending the Allocation of Housing (Wales) Regulations 2003 and that the guidance in the Welsh Code may be revised when the Regulations are amended.[95]

---

[88] See **3.76–3.85**.
[89] Allocation of Housing and Homelessness (Eligibility) (England) Regulations 2006, SI 2006/1294, reg 3(d), as amended by the Allocation of Housing and Homelessness (Miscellaneous Provisions) (England) Regulations 2006, SI 2006/2527 and in force for applications for an allocation of social housing made on or after 9 October 2006. English Code, para 3.11(iv). For eligibility for homelessness assistance, see **12.85**.
[90] See *Immigration Rules,* HC 395, paras 339C–339H (23 May 1994 as amended).
[91] *Immigration Rules,* HC 395, paras 352FA–352FI.
[92] SI 2006/2527.
[93] For applications made between 1 June 2006 and 8 October 2006, Class D contained 'a person who left the territory of Montserrat after 1 November 1995 because of the effect on that territory of a volcanic eruption' (Allocation of Housing and Homelessness (Eligibility) (England) Regulations 2006, SI 2006/1294, as originally enacted. This class of person is discussed in relation to the Welsh rules on eligibility for homelessness assistance (Homelessness (Wales) Regulations 2006, SI 2006/2646 (W 227), reg 3(1)(d)) at **12.102–12.104**.
[94] SI 2003/239 (W 36).
[95] Welsh Code, para 3.1.

3.56 Regulation 4 of the Allocation of Housing (Wales) Regulations 2003[96] prescribes six classes of people who are subject to immigration control and nevertheless are eligible for an allocation (there are five Classes, A–D1, but Class D has two subdivisions).

3.57 Those classes are:

(1) Class A:[97] a person recorded by the Secretary of State as a refugee and who has leave to enter or remain in the UK.

(2) Class B:[98] a person who has—
   (a) exceptional leave to enter or remain in the UK; and
   (b) whose leave is not subject to conditions requiring him or her to maintain and accommodate himself or herself and any dependants without recourse to public funds.

(3) Class C:[99] a person—
   (a) who is habitually resident in the CTA; and
   (b) who has current leave to enter or remain in the UK which is not subject to any limitation or condition; but
   (c) is not someone who has—
      (i) been given leave to enter or remain in the UK upon a written undertaking from a sponsor that he or she will be responsible for maintenance and accommodation; and
      (ii) has been resident in the CTA for less than five years beginning on the date of entry or the date of the undertaking (whichever is the later date); and
      (iii) whose sponsor is still alive.

(4) Class D: a person who is habitually resident in the CTA and who:
      (i)[100] is a national of a state which has ratified the European Convention on Social and Medical Assistance [ECSMA] done at Paris on 11 December 1953 or a state which has ratified the European Social Charter [ESC] done at Turin on 18 October 1961 and is lawfully present in the UK; or
      (ii)[101] before 3 April 2000 was owed a duty by a housing authority under Housing Act 1985, Part 3 or HA 1996, Part 7, which is extant, and who is a national of a state which is a signatory to the ECSMA or a state which is a signatory to the ESC;

---

[96] SI 2003/239 (W 36).
[97] SI 2003/239, reg 4(a). See **3.45–3.46**.
[98] SI 2003/239, reg 4(b). See **3.47–3.50**.
[99] SI 2003/239, reg 4(c). See **3.51–3.53**.
[100] SI 2003/239, reg 4(d)(i). See **3.59–3.61**.
[101] SI 2003/239, reg 4(d)(ii). See **3.62–3.64**.

(5)   Class D1:[102] a person who has humanitarian protection granted under the
Immigration Rules.

3.58   Classes A–C and D1 are identical to Classes A–D in the English
Regulations. For Class A, see **3.46–3.46**.[103] For Class B, see **3.47–3.50**.[104] For
Class C, see **3.51–3.53**.[105] For Class D1, see **3.54**.[106] Classes D(i) and D(ii) are
discussed at **3.59–3.64**.

*Class D(i):[107] a person who is a national of a country that has ratified ECSMA
or ESC and who is lawfully present in the UK and habitually resident in the
CTA*

3.59   To qualify as 'eligible' under this class, an applicant must be:

(1)   a national of one of the ratifying countries to the ECSMA or ESC (see
Box 3); and

(2)   lawfully present in the UK; and

(3)   habitually resident[108] in the CTA.

Box 3

> States which have *ratified* the ECSMA are: Belgium, Denmark, Estonia,
> France, Germany, Greece, Iceland, Ireland, Italy, Luxembourg, Malta,
> Netherlands, Norway, Portugal, Spain, Sweden, Turkey and the UK.[109]
> The same states have also *signed* the ECSMA.
>
> States which have *ratified* the ESC are: Austria, Belgium, Croatia, Cyprus,
> the Czech Republic, Denmark, Finland, France, Germany, Greece,
> Hungary, Iceland, Ireland, Italy, Latvia, Luxembourg, Malta, Nether-
> lands, Norway, Poland, Portugal, Slovakia, Spain, Sweden, Turkey, the
> former Yugoslav Republic of Macedonia and the UK.[110] These states
> plus Liechtenstein, Romania, Slovenia, Switzerland and the Ukraine have
> also *signed* the ESC.

---

[102]   SI 2003/239, reg 4(e), as inserted by Allocation of Housing (Wales) (Amendment)
Regulations 2006, SI 2006/2646, reg2(2)(b), for applications for an allocation of social housing
made on or after 9 October 2006. See **3.54**.
[103]   Welsh Code, para 3.5(vi) (a).
[104]   Welsh Code, para 3.5(vi)(b).
[105]   Welsh Code, para 3.5(vi)(c).
[106]   Welsh Code, para 3.5(vi)(e).
[107]   SI 2003/239, reg 4(d)(i); Welsh Code, para 3.5(vi)(d) and Annex 4. For eligibility for
homelessness assistance, see **12.105–12.108**.
[108]   See **3.76–3.85**.
[109]   For up to date lists, see www.conventions.coe.int.
[110]   For up-to-date lists, see www.conventions.coe.int.

3.60 A comparison with the list of members of the EEA[111] reveals that the beneficiaries of this class are nationals of Croatia,[112] Turkey and the former Yugoslav Republic of Macedonia.

3.61 He or she must also be 'lawfully present in the UK',[113] which means that he or she must have leave to enter and remain in the UK, or not require it. Asylum seekers from ECSMA or ESC countries who have been given 'temporary admission', pending the determination of their claims for asylum, are considered to be 'lawfully present'.[114]

Class D(ii):[115] *a person who is a national of a country that has signed the ECSMA or ESC and before 3 April 2000 was owed a homelessness duty which is still extant and who is habitually resident in the CTA*

3.62 To qualify as eligible under this class, a person must be:

(1)   a national of a state which has signed the ECSMA or ESC;[116] and

(2)   have been owed a homelessness duty before 3 April 2000; and

(3)   still be owed a homelessness duty; and

(4)   be habitually resident in the CTA.

3.63 To fall within this class, an applicant must have been owed a homelessness duty before 3 April 2000 and that duty must not have come to an end. In other words, he or she must have both made an application for homelessness assistance and had that application accepted before 3 April 2000 and must still be continuing to receive homelessness assistance under that duty. The duty will be owed either under HA 1996, Part 7, or under its statutory predecessor (Housing Act 1985, Part 3). The only duty likely to be still extant would be the main housing duty under HA 1996, s 193 (or Housing Act 1985, s 65(2)).

3.64 There is no additional requirement that a person should be lawfully present in the UK in order to qualify for this class. Any national of a country ratifying or signing the ECSMA or ESC could potentially fall within this class, provided he or she fulfilled the other conditions.

---

[111]   See **3.33** and Box 2.
[112]   Croatia is due to accede to the European Union in 2013.
[113]   The UK comprises England, Wales, Scotland and Northern Ireland: Interpretation Act 1978, s 5 and Sch 1. See **3.32** and Box 1.
[114]   *Szoma v Secretary of State for the Department of Work and Pensions* [2005] UKHL 64, [2006] 1 AC 564, HL and *R (YA) v Secretary of State for Health* [2009] EWCA Civ 225, [2010] 1 WLR 279, CA.
[115]   SI 2003/239, reg 4(d)(ii); Welsh Code, para 3.5(vi)(d). For eligibility for homelessness assistance, see **12.109–12.112**.
[116]   For states that have signed the ECSMA or ESC, see **3.60** and Box 3.

Sub-category two: other 'persons from abroad' not subject to immigration control but prescribed as not eligible

3.65   Ordinarily, persons not subject to immigration control would be eligible for an allocation of social housing. However, the Secretary of State and the Welsh Ministers are permitted to make regulations treating some people who are not subject to immigration control as 'persons from abroad' and therefore not eligible for allocation.[117] Both have exercised these powers.

Who is, and who is not, a 'person from abroad'?

3.66   In short summary, persons who are not 'subject to immigration control' comprise:[118]

- British citizens;

- Commonwealth citizens with the right of abode in the UK;

- EEA and Swiss nationals exercising certain treaty rights;[119]

- family members and others exercising rights derived from those EEA or Swiss nationals who are exercising or had previously exercised certain treaty rights;[120]

- certain people exempt from immigration control, such as diplomats, their family members and some military personnel; and

- Irish citizens with a CTA entitlement.

Disqualifying some of those who are not 'persons subject to immigration control'

3.67   In general, the effect of the exercise of the Regulation-making powers in both England and Wales has been to produce a situation in which British citizens and Commonwealth citizens with the right of abode in the UK will only be eligible for an allocation of social housing if they satisfy the 'habitual residence'[121] test, *or* fall into one of the classes of people exempt from the test.[122]

---

[117]   HA 1996, s 160ZA(4) [England], s 160A(5) [Wales].

[118]   Immigration Act 1971, ss 1–3. For more detail, see **3.29–3.37**.

[119]   Immigration (European Economic Area) Regulations 2006 (SI 2006/1003), regs 13–15. See **12.124–12.141**.

[120]   Immigration (European Economic Area) Regulations 2006 (SI 2006/1003), regs 13–15B as amended by Immigration (European Economic Area) (Amendment) Regulations 2012 (SI 2012/1547) amendments in force from 16 July 2012. See **12.124–12.163**.

[121]   See **3.76–3.85**.

[122]   HA 1996, s 160ZA(4) [England], s 160A(5) [Wales]; Allocation of Housing and Homelessness (Eligibility) (England) Regulations 2006, SI 2006/1294, reg 4(1)(a) and (2) as amended; Allocation of Housing (Wales) Regulations 2003, SI 2003/239 (W 36), reg 5(1)(a) and (2).

3.68 For EEA nationals and/or their family members or others with rights derived from the exercise of EU Treaty rights,[123] the situation is more complex. In summary:

- If they do not have any rights of residence pursuant to European Union law, they are 'persons subject to immigration control', and fall within HA 1996, s 160ZA(2) [England] or s 160A(3) [Wales] and the appropriate Regulations, ie the first sub-category of people who are not eligible.[124]

- In England, if their only right to reside is the initial three-month right of residence, because of their status as jobseekers, family members of a jobseeker, a derivative right of residence derived from being the primary carer of a British citizen,[125] or any similar rights of residence derived from Art 20 of the Treaty on the Functioning of the European Union,[126] they will not be eligible.[127]

- If they have a right of residence pursuant to European Union law, they will either:
  - have to satisfy the habitual residence[128] test, or
  - fall into one of the classes of people exempt from that test
  so as to be eligible for an allocation of social housing.[129]

3.69 The various rights of residence available to EEA nationals and their family members are considered at **12.123–12.163**.

---

[123] The general rights of residence for EEA nationals and their family members are considered at **12.123–12.163**.

[124] *Abdi v Barnet London Borough Council, Ismail v Barnet London Borough Council* [2006] EWCA Civ 383, [2006] HLR 23, CA. They are not likely to fall within any of the classes prescribed as eligible by either the English or the Welsh Regulations: Allocation of Housing and Homelessness (Eligibility) (England) Regulations 2006, SI 2006/1294, reg 3 (see **3.41–3.54**); and Allocation of Housing (Wales) Regulations 2003, SI 2003/239 (W 36), reg 5 (see **3.55–3.64**).

[125] SI 2006/1003, reg 15A(4A), inserted by SI 2012/2560 and in force from 8 November 2012. See **12.156–12.159**.

[126] See **12.162–12.163**.

[127] Allocation of Housing and Homelessness (Eligibility) (England) Regulations 2006, SI 2006/1294, reg 4(1)(b) and (c) as amended. In Wales, they are likely to be eligible if they are jobseekers, have a derivative right of residence derived from being the primary carer of a British citizen or another EU right of residence derived from Art 20 of the Treaty on the Functioning of the European Union, and, in any of those cases, also satisfy the habitual residence test: Allocation of Housing (Wales) Regulations 2003, SI 2003/239 (W 36), reg 5(1)(a). Those who are relying on the three-month initial right of residence may find that they are unlikely to satisfy the habitual residence test. See **3.134–3.136**.

[128] For 'habitual residence', see **3.76–3.85**.

[129] Allocation of Housing and Homelessness (Eligibility) (England) Regulations 2006, SI 2006/1294, reg 4(1)(a) and (2). Allocation of Housing (Wales) Regulations 2003, SI 2003/239 (W 36), reg 5(1)(a) and (2).

The English rules

3.70 In the Allocation of Housing and Homelessness (Eligibility) (England) Regulations 2006,[130] in force for applications made on or after 1 June 2006, the Secretary of State exercised the power to treat some people who are not subject to immigration control as 'persons from abroad'.[131] This means that some British citizens, nationals of EEA member states, and others who are exempt from immigration control may nevertheless be denied an allocation on the grounds that they are 'not eligible'. The primary function of these provisions is to confine new allocations of social housing to the ordinary residents of the UK, ie those habitually resident here, and to EEA nationals exercising Treaty rights.

3.71 Allocation of Housing and Homelessness (Eligibility) (England) Regulations 2006, reg 4, establishes three classes of people who are to be treated as 'persons from abroad' and therefore *ineligible* for an allocation despite not being subject to immigration control. They are briefly discussed in the English Code at para 3.12

3.72 The *first class*[132] comprises persons who are 'not habitually resident'[133] in the CTA.[134] But that test of habitual residence does not apply to:

- EEA nationals who are 'workers';[135] or

- EEA nationals who are self-employed;[136] or

- until 1 May 2011, Accession State workers requiring registration and registered in accordance with the Accession Regulations 2004[137] ('A8 nationals');[138] or

---

[130] SI 2006/1294.
[131] For applications for an allocation of social housing made *before* 1 June 2006, the relevant provisions are in reg 5 of the Allocation of Housing (England) Regulations 2002, SI 2002/3264, as substituted by the Allocation of Housing and Homelessness (Amendment) (England) Regulations 2004, SI 2004/1235.
[132] Allocation of Housing and Homelessness (Eligibility) (England) Regulations 2006, SI 2006/1294, reg 4(1)(a).
[133] See **3.76–3.85**.
[134] See **3.32**, Box 1.
[135] Allocation of Housing and Homelessness (Eligibility) (England) Regulations 2006, SI 2006/1294, reg 4(2)(a). See **3.33** and Box 2 for list of EEA countries and **3.88–3.94** for 'worker'.
[136] SI 2006/1294, reg 4(2)(b). See **3.95–3.97**.
[137] Accession (Immigration and Worker Registration) Regulations 2004, SI 2004/1219.
[138] SI 2006/1294, reg 4(2)(c)(i), substituted by Allocation of Housing and Homelessness (Eligibility) (England) (Amendment) (No 2) Regulations 2006, SI 2006/3340, reg 2. See **3.98**. From 1 May 2011, nationals of A8 member states are to be treated the same as nationals of other EEA member states (Accession (Immigration and Worker Registration) (Revocation, Savings and Consequential Provisions) Regulations 2011, SI 2011/544.

- until 1 January 2014, Accession State nationals subject to worker authorisation and authorised in accordance with the Accession Regulations 2006[139] ('A2 nationals');[140] or

- family members of EEA nationals where the EEA national is a worker, a self-employed person, an Accession State worker requiring registration or an Accession State national subject to worker authorisation;[141] or

- EEA nationals who have certain permanent rights to reside in the UK;[142] or

- persons who left the territory of Montserrat after 1 November 1995 because of the effect on that territory of a volcanic eruption;[143] or

- persons who are in the UK as a result of having been deported, expelled or otherwise removed by compulsion of law from another country to the UK;[144] or

- between 25 July 2006 and 31 January 2007 only, people who left Lebanon on or after 12 July 2006 because of the armed conflict there;[145] or

- a person who arrived in Great Britain or after 28 February 2009 but before 18 March 2011 and who immediately before arriving in Great Britain had been resident in Zimbabwe and, before leaving Zimbabwe, had accepted an offer made by Her Majesty's Government to assist that person to settle in the UK.[146]

3.73 The *second class* comprises EEA nationals and their family members whose only right to reside in the UK is derived from their status as jobseekers, as family members of jobseekers, from their initial right to reside in the UK for a period not exceeding three months from a derivative right of residence

---

[139] Accession (Immigration and Worker Authorisation) Regulations 2006, SI 2006/3317.

[140] SI 2006/1294, reg 4(2)(c)(ii), substituted by Allocation of Housing and Homelessness (Eligibility) (England) (Amendment) (No 2) Regulations 2006 SI 2006/3340, reg 2, in force from 1 January 2007 up to and including 31 December 2013 (reg 1(2)(c) Accession (Immigration and Worker Authorisation) Regulations 2006, SI 2006/3317, as amended). See **3.99–3.103**.

[141] SI 2006/1294, reg 4(2)(d). See **3.104–3.106**.

[142] SI 2006/1294, reg 4(2)(e). See **3.107–3.109**.

[143] SI 2006/1294, reg 4(2)(f). See **3.110**.

[144] SI 2006/1294, reg 4(2)(g). See **3.111**.

[145] SI 2006/1294, reg 4(2)(h) inserted by Allocation of Housing and Homelessness (Eligibility) (England) (Amendment) Regulations 2006, SI 2006/2007, reg 2(5): see **3.112–3.113**.

[146] SI 2006/1294, reg 4(2)(i) inserted by the Allocation of Housing and Homelessness (Eligibility) (England) (Amendment) Regulations 2009, SI 2009/358; for applications made on or after 18 March 2009, see **3.114–3.116**. The English Code deals with most of these sub-classes at para 3.14.

derived from being the primary carer of a British citizen or any similar rights of residence derived from Art 20 of the Treaty on the Functioning of the European Union.[147]

3.74 The *third class* comprises EEA nationals and their family members whose only right to reside in the rest of the CTA (Channel Islands, Isle or Man or the Republic of Ireland)[148] is derived from their status as jobseekers, as family members of jobseekers, from their initial right to reside in the UK for a period not exceeding three months, a derivative right of residence derived from being the primary carer of an Irish or British citizen or any similar rights of residence derived from Art 20 of the Treaty on the Functioning of the European Union.[149]

3.75 Each of these classes will be examined in turn.

The first class: not habitually resident[150]

3.76 'Habitual residence' is not a term of reference to someone's immigration status. A person may be a British citizen, but if he or she is not habitually resident in the CTA,[151] he or she will not be eligible. Nor is the term 'habitual residence' defined in either HA 1996 or the Regulations.[152] It is a question of fact for the local housing authority to decide. Happily, there is some guidance in the Code.[153]

3.77 A person who is not habitually resident will also not be entitled to non-contributory social security benefits. If the person is receiving social security benefits, it must follow that the Department for Work and Pensions (DWP) has determined that he or she is habitually resident.[154]

---

[147] SI 2006/1294, reg 4(1)(b) as amended by SI 2012/2588. For 'derivative right of residence derived from being the primary carer of a British citizen', see SI 2006/1003 reg 15A(4A) inserted by SI 2012/2560 and **12.156–12.159**. For rights of residence 'derived from Art 20 of the Treaty on the Functioning of the European Union', see **12.162–12.163**. The inclusion of persons whose only right to reside is that derivative right of residence in SI 2006/1003 reg15A(4A) or a similar right derived from Art 20 applies to applicants whose applications for an allocation were made on or after 8 November 2012 (SI 2012/2588, reg 3). See **3.117–3.128**.

[148] See Box 1 at **3.32**.

[149] Allocation of Housing and Homelessness (Eligibility) (England) Regulations 2006, SI 2006/1294, reg 4(1)(c), as amended by SI 2012/2588. For 'derivative right of residence derived from being the primary carer of an Irish or British citizen', see **12.156–12.159**. For rights of residence 'derived from Art 20 of the Treaty on the Functioning of the European Union', see **12.162–12.163**. The inclusion of persons whose only right to reside is the derivative right of residence derived from being the primary carer of an Irish or British citizen or any similar rights of residence derived from Art 20 applies to applicants whose applications for an allocation were made on or after 8 November 2012 (SI 2012/2588, reg 3). See **3.129–3.133**.

[150] SI 2006/1294, reg 4(1)(a).

[151] See Box 1 at **3.32**.

[152] SI 2006/1294.

[153] English Code, paras 3.16–3.17 and Annex 4.

[154] A person who has a derivative right of residence derived from being the primary carer of a British citizen (SI 2006/1003 reg 15A(4A) inserted by SI 2012/2560 and in force from 8 November 2012) is to be treated as not habitually resident and therefore ineligible for income

3.78 There are two aspects required to be present in order to constitute habitual residence:

(1)   a settled purpose of establishing residence in one of the territories of the CTA; and

(2)   an appreciable period of such residence.

3.79   Whether each aspect is satisfied is a question of fact for the local housing authority to decide. The English Code contains the Secretary of State's advice that normally, if someone has lived in one of the territories of the CTA for two years continuously prior to his or her application for an allocation, he or she is likely to be considered to be habitually resident without further inquiry.[155] However, that should not be taken as meaning that a person cannot be habitually resident if he or she has not lived in one of the territories of the CTA for two years.[156]

3.80   Establishing a 'settled purpose' will obviously involve consideration of an applicant's subjective intentions and motivations. Someone in stable employment may be more likely to be able to establish his or her 'settled purpose' to be habitually resident than someone in transitory employment, or dependent on benefit. However, local housing authorities must be careful not to give too much weight to an applicant's lack of finances and not enough weight to other factors such as the applicant's nationality, ties with the UK, and future intentions.[157]

3.81   What constitutes an 'appreciable period of residence' likewise varies according to the circumstances of each individual's case. If a former British resident returns to the UK after living and working abroad, she or he may be habitually resident from the first day of his or her return.[158] When someone is coming to live in the UK for the first time, there must be an appreciable period of residence before habitual residence is obtained. To determine how long that period of residence should be, local housing authorities should consider all the circumstances, including:

•   whether the person is seeking to bring any family members to the UK;

•   whether he or she has brought his or her personal property and possessions to the UK;

---

support, jobseeker's allowance, state pension credit, housing benefit, council tax benefit and employment and support allowance (Social Security (Habitual Residence) (Amendment) Regulations 2012 in force from 8 November 2012).

[155]   English Code, para 3.17.

[156]   See **12.176** and *R (Paul-Coker) v Southwark London Borough Council* [2006] EWHC 497 (Admin), HLR 32, Admin Ct.

[157]   *Barnet London Borough Council v Shah* [1983] 20AC 309, HL; and *Olokunboro v Croydon London Borough Council* (2003) February *Legal Action*, p 37, Croydon County Court.

[158]   *Swaddling v Adjudication Officer* [1999] All ER (EC) 217, ECJ, and see CIS/1304/1997 and CJSA/5394/1998. English Code Annex 4, paras 7–8.

- whether he or she has done everything necessary to establish a residence before coming;

- whether he or she has a right of abode; and

- what 'durable ties' there are with the CTA.[159]

3.82 There is also some useful guidance in the Administrative Court's decision of *R (Paul-Coker) v Southwark London Borough Council*.[160]

3.83 Some EEA nationals, and their family members, are not exempted from the habitual residence test,[161] nor are they prescribed as 'ineligible' by virtue of falling within the second or third classes.[162] For those people to be eligible, they will have to satisfy the habitual residence test.

3.84 Types of EEA nationals who may be required to satisfy the habitual residence test include:

- an EEA national who has resided in the UK in accordance with the Immigration (European Economic Area) Regulations[163] for a continuous period of five years;[164] or

- a person who is not an EEA national but is a family member of an EEA national, the family member having resided in the UK in accordance with the Immigration (European Economic Area) Regulations for a continuous period of five years;[165] or

- a person who has resided in the UK for a continuous period of five years and was, at the end of that period, a family member of an EEA national who had retained the right of residence;[166] or

- a person who has one of four derivative rights of residence[167] and his or her family members; or

---

[159] *Nessa v Chief Adjudication Officer* [1999] 1 WLR 1937, HL. English Code, Annex 4, para 11.

[160] [2006] EWHC 497 (Admin), [2006] HLR 32, Admin Ct and see **12.176**.

[161] Allocation of Housing and Homelessness (Eligibility) (England) Regulations 2006, SI 2006/1294, reg 4(2): see **3.72** and **3.88–3.119**.

[162] Allocation of Housing and Homelessness (Eligibility) (England) Regulations 2006, SI 2006/1294, reg 4(1)(b) and (c): see **3.117–3.133**.

[163] SI 2006/1003. See Appendix 2 of this book.

[164] Entitled to a permanent right of residence by reg 15(1)(a) of the Immigration (European Economic Area) Regulations 2006, SI 2006/1003. See **12.139** and Appendix 2.

[165] Entitled to a permanent right of residence by reg 15(1)(b) of the Immigration (European Economic Area) Regulations 2006, SI 2006/1003, see **12.139**. For 'family member', see **12.131–12.137**.

[166] Entitled to a permanent right of residence by reg 15(1)(f) of the Immigration (European Economic Area) Regulations 2006, SI 2006/1003, see **12.139**. For 'family member', see **12.131–12.137**. For family member who has retained the right of residence, see reg 10 of the Immigration (European Economic Area) Regulations 2006, SI 2006/1003 and **12.137**.

[167] SI 2006/1003, reg 15A inserted by SI 2012/1547, and amended by SI 2012/2560, see

- potentially, a person who has a right to reside that falls outside the Immigration (European Economic Area) Regulations.[168]

3.85 Given the length of their residence, most of those people should not have any difficulty in satisfying the habitual residence test.

Exemptions from the habitual residence test

3.86 As already noted,[169] the following people are eligible for assistance even if they are not habitually resident:

- an EEA national who is a 'worker';[170] or

- an EEA national who is self-employed;[171] or

- until 1 May 2011, a person who is an Accession State worker requiring registration who is registered in accordance with the Accession Regulations 2004[172] ('an A8 national');[173] or

- until 31 December 2013, a person who is an Accession State national subject to worker authorisation who is authorised in accordance with the Accession Regulations 2006[174] ('an A2 national');[175] or

- a family member of an EEA national who is a worker, a self-employed person, an Accession State worker requiring registration who is registered in accordance with the Accession Regulations 2004[176] or an Accession

---

12.141–12.155 and **12.160–12.161**. A person who has fifth derivative right of residence, derived from being the primary carer of a British citizen (SI 2006/1003, reg 15A(4A) inserted by SI 2012/2560), is prescribed as not eligible for an allocation of social housing (SI 2006/1294 amended by SI 2012/2588 for applications for an allocation made on or after 8 November 2012). See **3.117–3.133**.

[168] See **12.162–12.163** for discussion. It should be noted that a person who has a right of residence derived from Art 20 of the Treaty on the Functioning of the European Union, in a case where the right to reside arises because a British citizen would otherwise be deprived of the genuine enjoyment of the substance of their rights as a European Union citizen is excluded from eligibility (SI 2006/1294, reg 4(1)(b) and (c) as amended by SI 2012/2588 for applicants whose applications for an allocation was made on or after 8 November 2012), see **3.117–3.133**.

[169] See **3.72**.

[170] Allocation of Housing and Homelessness (Eligibility) (England) Regulations 2006, SI 2006/1294, reg 4(2)(a). See **3.88–3.94**.

[171] SI 2006/1294, reg 4(2)(b). See **3.95–3.97**.

[172] Accession (Immigration and Worker Registration) Regulations 2004, SI 2004/1219.

[173] SI 2006/1294, reg 4(2)(c)(i) substituted by Allocation of Housing and Homelessness (Eligibility) (England) (Amendment) (No 2) Regulations 2006, SI 2006/3340, reg 2. See **3.98**.

[174] Accession (Immigration and Worker Authorisation) Regulations 2006, SI 2006/3317.

[175] SI 2006/1294, reg 4(2)(c)(ii) substituted by Allocation of Housing and Homelessness (Eligibility) (England) (Amendment) (No 2) Regulations 2006 SI 2006/3340, reg 2, in force from 1 January 2007. See **3.99–3.103**.

[176] Accession (Immigration and Worker Registration) Regulations 2004, SI 2004/1219.

State national subject to worker authorisation who is authorised in accordance with the Accession Regulations 2006[177];[178] or

- a person who has one of certain permanent rights to reside in the UK;[179] or

- a person who left the territory of Montserrat after 1 November 1995 because of the effect on that territory of a volcanic eruption;[180] or

- a person who is in the UK as a result of having been deported, expelled or otherwise removed by compulsion of law from another country to the UK;[181] or

- between 25 July 2006 and 31 January 2007 only, a person who left Lebanon on or after 12 July 2006 because of the armed conflict there;[182] or

- a person who arrived in Great Britain on or after 28 February 2009 but before 18 March 2011 and who, immediately before arriving in Great Britain, had been resident in Zimbabwe and, before leaving Zimbabwe, had accepted an offer made by Her Majesty's Government to assist that person to settle in the UK.[183]

3.87 Most of these categories refer to those persons exercising rights of freedom of movement enjoyed under European Union law, and to the Immigration (European Economic Area) Regulations 2006,[184] which are the current regulations transposing European Union freedom of movement legislation into domestic law. Each of them will be considered in turn. See **12.123–12.163** for consideration of the different European Union 'rights to reside'.

---

[177] Accession (Immigration and Worker Authorisation) Regulations 2006, SI 2006/3317.

[178] SI 2006/1294, reg 4(2)(d). See **3.104–3.106**.

[179] SI 2006/1294, reg 4(2)(e). See **3.107–3.109**.

[180] SI 2006/1294, reg 4(2)(f). See **3.110**.

[181] SI 2006/1294, reg 4(2)(g). See **3.111**.

[182] SI 2006/1294, reg 4(2)(h), inserted by Allocation of Housing and Homelessness (Eligibility) (England) (Amendment) Regulations 2006, SI 2006/2007, reg 2(5). See **3.112–3.113**.

[183] SI 2006/1294, reg 4(2)(i), inserted by the Allocation of Housing and Homelessness (Eligibility) (England) (Amendment) Regulations 2009, SI 2009/358, for applications made on or after 18 March 2009. See **3.114–3.116**.

[184] SI 2006/1003, in force from 30 April 2006. See Appendix 2 of this book.

EEA nationals who are workers[185]

3.88 In order to qualify as a 'worker' under this provision, the person must first be a national of an EEA Member State.[186] The term 'worker' is not defined in HA 1996 or the regulations and nor is it exhaustively defined in European Union legislation. The Court of Justice of the European Union has emphasised that a narrow approach should *not* be taken:

> '[I]t is settled case law that the concept of worker has a specific Community meaning and must not be interpreted narrowly. It must be defined in accordance with objective criteria which distinguish an employment relationship by reference to the rights and duties of the person concerned. In order to be treated as a worker, a person must pursue an activity which is genuine and effective, to the exclusion of activities on such a small scale as to be regarded as purely marginal and ancillary. The essential feature of an employment relationship is that for a certain period of time a person performs services for and under the direction of another person in return for which he receives remuneration. By contrast, neither the *sui generis* nature of the employment relationship under national law, nor the level of productivity of the person concerned, the origin of the funds from which the remuneration is paid or the limited amount of the remuneration can have any consequence in regard to whether the person is a worker for the purposes of Community law ...'.[187]

3.89 A person will be a 'worker'[188] if he or she:

> 'is actually working in the UK, whether full or part-time. Any genuine and effective work should count, so long as it is not so irregular and/or so limited that it is a purely marginal and ancillary activity'.[189]

3.90 A person may retain the status of a worker and so still be treated as a worker for the purposes of these Regulations[190] if he or she:

---

[185] Allocation of Housing and Homelessness (Eligibility) (England) Regulations 2006, SI 2006/1294, reg 4(2)(a); English Code, Annex 4, paras 13–17. For eligibility for homelessness assistance, see **12.182–12.188**.

[186] See Box 2 at **3.33**.

[187] *Kurz Case C-188/00* [2002] ECR I-10691 at para 32.

[188] Immigration (European Economic Area) Regulations 2006, SI 2006/1003, reg 4(1)(a). 'Worker' is defined by Regulation (EEC) No 1612/68 of the Council of 15 October 1968 on freedom of movement for workers within the Community or Regulation (EEC) No 1251/70 of the Commission of 29 June 1970 on the right of workers to remain in the territory of a Member State after having been employed in that State. English Code, Annex 2, paras 13–16.

[189] *Levin 53/81* [1982] ECR 1035; *Kempf Case 139/85* [1986] ECR 1741; *Raulin Case C-357/89* [1992] ECR 1027.

[190] Immigration (European Economic Area) Regulations 2006, SI 2006/1003, reg 6(2) based on *Scrivner Case 122/84* [1985] ECR 1027. Note that A8 workers requiring registration who had not completed 12 month's registered employment before 1 May 2011 do not retain worker status under this Regulation on account of work done before that date. Any work which he or she does after 1 May 2011 will count for these purposes (Immigration (European Economic Area) Regulations 2006, SI 2006/1003, reg 7A inserted by Accession (Immigration and Worker Registration) (Revocation, Savings and Consequential Provisions) Regulations 2011 (SI 2011/544). Note also that this extended definition of 'worker' does not apply where a person is claiming a derivative right of residence, derived from his or her parent being a worker

- has worked in the UK (at any time and even for a short period) but has become temporarily incapable of work as a result of an illness or accident;[191] or

- has worked in the UK for one year or more before becoming involuntarily unemployed and is registered as a jobseeker;[192] or

- has worked in the UK for less than one year before becoming involuntarily unemployed and is registered as a jobseeker and has been unemployed for no more than six months;[193] or

- has worked in the UK for less than one year before becoming involuntarily unemployed and is registered as a jobseeker and has a genuine chance of being engaged;[194] or

- has worked in the UK (at any time and even for a short period), but has become involuntarily unemployed and has embarked on vocational training;[195] or

- has worked in the UK (at any time and even for a short period) and voluntarily given up work in the UK to take up vocational training related to his or her previous job.[196]

3.91 The Court of Appeal has held, in relation to both workers and self-employed persons,[197] that if someone's illness means that he or she is unlikely to be able to work in the foreseeable future, there are no realistic prospects of him or her being able to return to work and he or she is no longer a worker or a self-employed person.[198]

3.92 Attempts to argue that people who have never worked in the UK are, nevertheless, 'workers' for the purpose of entitlement to jobseeker's allowance and Children Act assistance have failed.[199] A jobseeker who has never worked

---

(SI 2006/1003, reg 15A(3), see **12.152–12.153**). An EEA national who ceases working because of pregnancy does not retain the status of worker (*St Prix v SSWP* [2011] EWCA Civ 806, CA).

[191] SI 2006/1003 Reg 6(2)(a). See English Code, Annex 2, para 17(a).

[192] Immigration (European Economic Area) Regulations 2006, SI 2006/1003, reg 6(2) (b)(i). See English Code, Annex 2, para 17 (b)(i).

[193] SI 2006/1003, reg 6(2)(b)(ii). See English Code, Annex 2, para 17(b)(ii).

[194] SI 2006/1003, reg 6(2)(b)(iii). See English Code, Annex 2, para 17(b)(iii).

[195] *Lair Case 39/86* [1988] ECR 3161; and *Raulin Case C-357/89* [1992] ECR 1027. Immigration (European Economic Area) Regulations 2006, SI 2006/1003, reg 6(2)(c). English Code, Annex 2, para 17(c).

[196] *Raulin Case C-357/89* [1992] ECR 1027. Immigration (European Economic Area) Regulations 2006, SI 2006/1003, reg 6(2)(d). English Code, Annex 2, para 17(d).

[197] See **3.93–3.97**.

[198] *Konodyba v Kensington & Chelsea Royal London Borough Council* [2012] EWCA Civ 982, (2012) September *Legal Action*, p 29, CA.

[199] *Collins v Secretary of State for Work and Pensions, C-138/02*, 23 March 2004, ECJ; and *Ali v SSHD* [2006] EWCA Civ 484, [2006] 3 CMLR 326, [2006] ELR 423, CA.

is not, therefore, a 'worker' and, in any event, is specifically excluded from eligibility because he or she would fall into the second or third classes of people who are not eligible.[200] Students and au pairs, working part-time, have been held by the Court of Appeal and the Court of Justice of the European Union not to be 'workers'.[201]

3.93   The decision as to whether an applicant is or is not a worker is a question of fact for the local housing authority. In *R (Mohamed) v Harrow London Borough Council*,[202] it was held that the local housing authority had not made any errors of law in concluding that a woman who had worked part-time for three months, finishing a year before her application for homelessness assistance, spoke little or no English, had two small children to look after and had not registered with an employment agency was not, and had not retained the status of being, a 'worker'. In *Barry v Southwark London Borough Council*,[203] the local housing authority was wrong to decide that an applicant was not a 'worker' during a two-week period when he was employed by Group 4 Securicor for stewarding duties at the Wimbledon All England Tennis Championships. The work done was of economic value, there were PAYE deductions from his pay and the services provided by him to his employer were real and actual, and not merely marginal and ancillary.[204] In the case of a part-time worker earning a low income, the local housing authority made an error of law when it applied a test of whether the work produced enough income to cover 'reasonable living expenses'. The question of whether work is 'effective' is to be looked at from the view of the value of the work to the employer and not to the employee.[205]

3.94   A2 nationals will not be 'workers' if they are Accession State nationals subject to worker authorisation.[206] If they no longer fall into this class (eg because they have been working for more than 12 months, or because they did not need to register as an Accession State national subject to worker authorisation), they are treated the same as all other EEA nationals who are workers.

---

[200] Allocation of Housing and Homelessness (Eligibility) (England) Regulations 2006, SI 2006/1294, regs 4(1)(b) and 4(1)(c). See **3.117–3.133**.

[201] *Ozturk v Secretary of State for the Home Department* [2006] EWCA Civ 541, [2007] 1 WLR 508, CA, C-294/06, 24 January 2008, ECJ.

[202] [2005] EWHC 3194 (Admin), [2006] HLR 18, Admin Ct.

[203] [2008] EWCA Civ 1440, [2009] HLR 30, CA.

[204] Arden LJ at [23].

[205] *Amin v Brent London Borough Council* (2011) August *Legal Action* p 41, Wandsworth County Court.

[206] See **3.99–3.103**.

EEA nationals who are self-employed persons[207]

3.95 A 'self-employed person' is defined as 'a person who establishes himself in order to pursue activity as a self-employed person in accordance with Art 43 of the Treaty establishing the European Community'.[208]

3.96 Art 43 refers to 'freedom of establishment' which is itself defined as 'the right to take up and pursue activities as self-employed persons and to set up and manage undertakings'. Self-employment is not confined to periods of actual work; a person remains self-employed if he or she is engaged on administrative, marketing or other tasks required to run or promote his or her business.[209]

3.97 A person remains a self-employed person if he or she is temporarily unable to pursue his or her self-employment activity as a result of illness or accident[210] but there must be a likelihood that he or she will be able to work in the foreseeable future.[211]

Accession State workers requiring registration or 'A8 nationals'[212]

3.98 This category is largely academic. From 1 May 2011, nationals of A8 member states are to be treated in the same way as nationals of other EEA member states.[213] The only difference is that a national of an A8 member state cannot rely on periods worked before 1 May 2011 for the purposes of determining whether he or she has retained worker status.[214]

---

[207] Allocation of Housing and Homelessness (Eligibility) (England) Regulations 2006, SI 2006/1294, reg 4(2)(b). English Code, Annex 2, paras 21–24. For eligibility for homelessness assistance, see **12.189–12.190**.

[208] Immigration (European Economic Area) Regulations 2006, SI 2006/1003, reg 4(1)(b). The Treaty referred to is the Treaty of Rome (1957).

[209] *Secretary of State for Work and Pensions v JS (IS)* [2010] UKUT 240 (AAC), (2011) March *Legal Action,* p 21, UT.

[210] SI 2006/1003, reg 6(3). See English Code, Annex 2, para 22.

[211] *Konodyba v Kensington & Chelsea Royal London Borough Council* [2012] EWCA Civ 982, (2012) September *Legal Action,* p 29, CA.

[212] Allocation of Housing and Homelessness (Eligibility) (England) Regulations 2006, SI 2006/1294, reg 4(2)(c), substituted by Allocation of Housing and Homelessness (Eligibility) (England) (Amendment) (No 2) Regulations 2006, SI 2006/3340, reg 2. For eligibility for homelessness assistance, see **12.191**.

[213] Accession (Immigration and Worker Registration) (Revocation, Savings and Consequential Provisions) Regulations 2011, SI 2011/544. Previously an 'Accession State worker requiring registration' was defined in the Accession (Immigration and Worker Registration) Regulations 2004, SI 2004/1219, as a national of one of the A8 countries who was working in the UK at some time between 1 May 2004 and 30 April 2011. Once an Accession State worker requiring registration had legally worked for a period of 12 months without interruption, he or she was no longer an 'Accession State worker requiring registration', and was treated as any other EEA national who is a worker.

[214] Immigration (European Economic Area) Regulations 2006, SI 2006/1003, reg 7A inserted by Accession (Immigration and Worker Registration) (Revocation, Savings and Consequential Provisions) Regulations 2011, SI 2011/544. For 'retained worker status' see **3.90**.

Accession State nationals subject to worker authorisation or 'A2 nationals'[215]

3.99   An 'Accession State national requiring worker authorisation' is defined in the Accession (Immigration and Worker Authorisation) Regulations[216] as a national of one of the A2 countries, ie Bulgaria or Romania.[217]

3.100   An Accession State national subject to worker authorisation and authorised in accordance with the Accession Regulations 2006[218] will be exempt from the habitual residence test and thus eligible for an allocation of social housing during such time as he or she holds an Accession Worker authorisation document and is working in accordance with the conditions set out in that document.[219] The document normally issued is an Accession Worker authorisation card.[220] An A2 national who is a jobseeker will not have any right of residence and will not be eligible for an allocation of social housing.

3.101   After 31 December 2013, A2 nationals are to be treated in the same way as other EEA nationals.[221]

3.102   Not all nationals of Bulgaria or Romania fall within the definition of 'an Accession State national subject to worker authorisation'. They should be treated in the same way as other EEA nationals if they fall into one of these categories:

- a person who, on 31 December 2006, had leave to enter or remain without any restriction on taking employment;[222] or

- a person who has legally (with leave to remain) worked in the UK without interruption for a period of 12 months;[223] or

- a person also holding nationality of another EEA Member State (other than Bulgaria or Romania) or British nationality;[224] or

---

[215] SI 2006/1294, reg 4(2)(c)(ii), substituted by Allocation of Housing and Homelessness (Eligibility) (England) (Amendment) (No 2) Regulations 2006, SI 2006/3340, reg 2, in force from 1 January 2007. See English Code, Annex 3. For eligibility for homelessness assistance, see **12.192–12.196**.

[216] SI 2006/3317, reg 2(1).

[217] See Box 2 at **3.33**.

[218] SI 2006/3317.

[219] SI 2006/3317, reg 6(2). English Code, Annex 2, paras 18–20.

[220] SI 2006/3317, reg 7.

[221] SI 2006/3317, reg 1(2)(c) and reg 6(1) as amended by Accession (Immigration and Worker Authorisation) (Amendment) Regulations 2011, SI 2011/2816.

[222] SI 2006/3317, reg 2(2), as substituted by the Accession (Immigration and Worker Authorisation) (Amendment) Regulations 2007, SI 2007/475, reg 2(2). English Code, Annex 3, para 9.

[223] SI 2006/3317, reg 2(3) and (4). This is the case whether the 12-month period falls wholly before 31 December 2006, partly before and partly after 31 December 2006, or wholly after 31 December 2006.

[224] SI 2006/3317, reg 2(5).

- a spouse or civil partner of a UK national or of a person settled in the UK;[225] or

- a diplomat or family member of a diplomat;[226] or

- a person who has a permanent right of residence pursuant to Immigration (European Economic Union) Regulations 2006, reg 15;[227] or

- a family member of an EEA national who has the right to reside in the UK, other than EEA nationals who are Accession State nationals subject to worker authorisation or are family members of such an Accession State national;[228] or

- a family member of an A2 national who has the right to reside in the UK by virtue of being a self-employed person, or a self-sufficient person or a student;[229] or

- a person who holds a registration certificate to the effect that he or she is a highly skilled person and has unconditional access to the labour market;[230] or

- a person who is in the UK as a student, who holds a registration certificate that includes a statement that he or she is a student who has access to the UK labour market, and who is working not more than 20 hours a week during term time,[231] or is working for no more than four months after the end of his or her course and who holds a registration certificate that includes a statement that he or she may work during that period;[232] or

- a 'posted worker'.[233]

3.103 Any national of Bulgaria or Romania who falls within one of these categories will fall to be treated as any other EEA national would be.

---

[225] SI 2006/3317, reg 2(6).
[226] SI 2006/3317, reg 2(6A).
[227] SI 2006/3317, reg 2(7). See **12.139**.
[228] SI 2006/3317, reg 2(8)(a), as substituted by the Accession (Immigration and Worker Authorisation) (Amendment) Regulations 2007, SI 2007/475, reg 2(2). For 'family member', see **12.131–12.137**. For 'right to reside', see **12.123–12.163**.
[229] SI 2006/3317, reg 2(8)(b), as substituted by the Accession (Immigration and Worker Authorisation) (Amendment) Regulations 2007, SI 2007/475, reg 2(2). For 'family member', see **12.131–12.137**. For 'right to reside', see **12.123–12.163**. For 'self-employed person', see **3.95–3.97**. For student, see **12.178**, footnote 415.
[230] SI 2006/3317, reg 2(9).
[231] He or she may work full-time during vacation (SI 2006/3317, reg 10A(b)).
[232] SI 2006/3317, reg 2(10), (10A) and (10B), as substituted by the Accession (Immigration and Worker Authorisation) (Amendment) Regulations 2007, SI 2007/475, reg 2(2).
[233] SI 2006/3317, reg 2(11) and (13)(a). A 'posted worker' is a worker who, for a limited period, is working in the territory of a different Member State from that where he or she normally works (Directive 96/71/EC, arts 1 and 3).

Family members of certain EEA nationals[234]

3.104 A family member of an EEA national (who is a worker, a self-employed person, an Accession State worker requiring registration, or an Accession State national subject to worker authorisation who is authorised in accordance with the Accession Regulations 2006[235]) is exempt from having to satisfy the habitual residence test.

3.105 The 'family member' need not be a worker, a self-employed person, or an Accession State national subject to worker authorisation. Indeed, he or she need not be economically active at all. Nor need he or she be an EEA national. So long as he or she is a 'family member' of an EEA national (who is a worker, a self-employed person, or an Accession State national subject to worker authorisation), he or she is exempt from the habitual residence test. He or she can apply for an allocation for social housing in his or her own right. There is no need for the EEA worker, self-employed person or Accession State national subject to worker authorisation to be the applicant.

3.106 In some circumstances, there is not even any need for the EEA national to be part of the applicant's household in order for the applicant to be eligible as a 'family member'.[236] For 'family members' see **12.131–12.137**.

EEA nationals and their family members who have certain permanent rights to reside in the UK[237]

3.107 'Permanent right of residence' is defined at reg 15(1) of the Immigration (European Economic Area) Regulations 2006.[238] This exemption from the habitual residence test only applies to three sub-classes of persons who are entitled to a permanent right of residence.[239]

---

[234] Allocation of Housing and Homelessness (Eligibility) (England) Regulations 2006, SI 2006/1294, reg 4(2)(d). English Code Annex 2, paras 34–44. For eligibility for homelessness assistance, see **12.201–12.205**.
[235] SI 2006/3317.
[236] For example, spouses and civil partners remain 'family members' until their marriage or partnership is legally terminated, whether or not they are actually cohabiting with the EEA national. See **12.131**, footnote 294.
[237] Allocation of Housing and Homelessness (Eligibility) (England) Regulations 2006, SI 2006/1294, reg 4(2)(e). English Code, Annex 2, paras 34–44. For eligibility for homelessness assistance, see **12.201–12.205**.
[238] SI 2006/1003. See **12.139**.
[239] For 'permanent right of residence', see **12.139**.

3.108 Those three sub-classes give permanent rights of residence to:

(1) an EEA national who was a worker[240] or self-employed person[241] who has ceased activity;[242]

(2) the family member[243] of such an EEA national;[244] and

(3) a person who was:
- the family member of an EEA national who was a worker or self-employed person; and
- the EEA national has died; and
- the family member had resided with the EEA national immediately before his or her death; and
- either the EEA national had resided in the UK for at least two years immediately before his or her death; or
- the death was the result of an accident at work or an occupational disease.[245]

3.109 There will be other EEA nationals who have a permanent right of residence that is not within these three specified sub-classes.[246] They will have to satisfy the habitual residence test in order to be eligible.[247]

People from Montserrat[248]

3.110 This group of people, who are eligible for an allocation even if they are not habitually resident, are persons who left the territory of Montserrat after 1 November 1995 because of the effect on that territory of a volcanic eruption. They will normally be British citizens or Commonwealth citizens with the right of abode in the UK.[249] Not all people leaving Montserrat are rendered eligible by this provision. It does not apply to those who left on or before 1 November 1995. Nor does it apply to those who left after that date for reasons unconnected with the volcanic eruption. The regulation emphasises the departure location, ie it covers those who were in Montserrat and left after 1 November 1995. It also emphasises the reason for departure: the effect of the volcanic eruption. The person's nationality is not relevant. Most of those

---

[240] For 'worker', see **3.88–3.94**.

[241] For 'self-employed person', see **3.95–3.97**.

[242] Immigration (European Economic Area) Regulations 2006, SI 2006/1003, reg 15(1)(c). See **12.139**. 'Worker or self-employed person who has ceased activity' is defined at SI 2006/1003, reg 5. See Appendix 2.

[243] For 'family member', see **12.131–12.137**.

[244] SI 2006/1003, reg 15(1)(d). See **12.139**.

[245] SI 2006/1003, reg 15(1)(e). See **12.139**.

[246] See **12.139–12.140**.

[247] Allocation of Housing and Homelessness (Eligibility) (England) Regulations 2006, SI 2006/1294, reg 4(1)(a). See **3.76–3.85** for 'habitual residence'.

[248] SI 2006/1294, reg 4(2)(f). English Code, para 3.14(f). For eligibility for homelessness assistance, see **12.206**.

[249] Obviously, to be eligible at all, he or she must not be a 'person subject to immigration control'. See **3.29–3.37** for who is and who is not a 'person subject to immigration control'.

displaced to the UK in consequence of the volcanic eruption will long since have become habitually resident and will not need to rely on this exception to that test.

People who are in the UK as a result of having been deported, expelled or otherwise removed by compulsion of law from another country to the UK[250]

3.111   This group of persons who are eligible even if not habitually resident is probably small. The inclusion of this class brings eligibility for an allocation of social housing into line with eligibility for housing benefit.

A person who left Lebanon on or after 12 July 2006 because of the armed conflict there[251]

3.112   This group of people, who are eligible even if not habitually resident, is self-explanatory. In similar terms to the provision exempting those fleeing the volcanic eruption in Montserrat, it refers to people who are British citizens, or have other rights to enter or remain in the UK, but have not been habitually resident in the CTA.[252] This provision exempts them from complying with the habitual residence test. To fall within this group:

- a person must have left Lebanon, not elsewhere;

- he or she must have left on or after 12 July 2006; and

- his or her reason for leaving Lebanon must have been 'because of the armed conflict there'.

3.113   This provision is only effective for 'the relevant period', which is defined as being between 4pm on 25 July 2006 and 31 January 2007.[253] After 31 January 2007, anyone who has fled Lebanon because of the armed conflict, and had not made his or her application for an allocation during the relevant period, would have to satisfy the habitual residence test.

---

[250]   SI 2006/1294, reg 4(2)(g). English Code, para 3.14(g).
[251]   SI 2006/1294, reg 4(2)(h), inserted by Allocation of Housing and Homelessness (Eligibility) (England) (Amendment) Regulations 2006, SI 2006/2007, reg 2(5) and in force from 4pm on 25 July 2006. For eligibility for homelessness assistance, see **12.208–12.209**.
[252]   See **3.76–3.81** for 'habitual residence' and **3.32**, Box 1 for CTA.
[253]   Allocation of Housing and Homelessness (Eligibility) (England) Regulations 2006, SI 2006/1294, reg 2(4), inserted by Allocation of Housing and Homelessness (Eligibility) (England) (Amendment) Regulations 2006, SI 2006/2007, reg 2(2).

***People who arrived in Great Britain on or after 28 February 2009 but before
18 March 2011 and who immediately before arriving in Great Britain had been
resident in Zimbabwe and, before leaving Zimbabwe, had accepted an offer
made by Her Majesty's Government, to assist them to settle in the UK*[254]**

3.114 This exception applies to British citizens and British subjects with the
right of abode in the UK, who have left Zimbabwe and arrived in Great Britain
between 28 February 2009 and 18 March 2011. They must have left as a result
of having accepted an offer of assistance from the British government. The
government intended to offer assistance only to British citizens and British
nationals who had the right of abode in the UK. They were either aged 70 or
over, or they were vulnerable due to health and social care needs that meant
that they could not look after themselves.[255]

3.115 Their spouses, partners and any dependants could accompany them,
but whether they too would be offered assistance was decided on a case-by-case
basis.

3.116 This exception applies only to applications for an allocation of social
housing made on or after 18 March 2009.[256]

*The second class: EEA nationals with a right to reside in the UK by virtue of
being jobseekers, or family members of a jobseeker, by exercising an initial right
to reside, by having a derivative right to reside in the UK as the primary carer of
a British citizen, or by having a right to reside derived from Art 20 of the
Treaty on the of the European Union*[257]

3.117 Anyone who falls exclusively within this class cannot be eligible for
housing allocation. The habitual residence test is not relevant. If an EEA
national is:

(a)   a jobseeker,[258] or

(b)   a family member[259] of a jobseeker, or

---

[254]   SI 2006/1294, reg 4(2)(i), inserted by the Allocation of Housing and Homelessness (Eligibility)
(England) (Amendment) Regulations 2009, SI 2009/358. For eligibility for homelessness
assistance, see **12.210–12.211**.

[255]   Explanatory Memorandum to the Allocation of Housing and Homelessness (Eligibility)
(England) (Amendment) Regulations 2009, SI 2009/358, para 7.

[256]   Allocation of Housing and Homelessness (Eligibility) (England) (Amendment) Regulations 2009, SI 2009/358, reg 1.

[257]   Allocation of Housing and Homelessness (Eligibility) (England) Regulations 2006,
SI 2006/1294, reg 4(1)(b) as amended by SI 2012/2588. English Code, paras 3.12(ii) and (iii).
For eligibility for homelessness assistance, see **12.212–12.221**.

[258]   See **12.130**.

[259]   See **12.131–12.137**.

(c)	only entitled to remain in the UK by virtue of the initial right to reside for three months,[260] or

(d)	has a derivative right to reside because he or she is the primary carer of a British citizen,[261] or

(e)	has a right to reside derived from Art 20 of the Treaty on the Functioning of the European Union, where the right to reside arises because a British citizen would otherwise be deprived of the genuine enjoyment of the substance of those rights as a European Union citizen,[262]

he or she cannot be eligible.

3.118	This second class operates to ensure that any EEA national, or family member of an EEA national, whose *only* right of residence in the UK is the initial three-month right of residence is not eligible for an allocation of social housing.

3.119	It also excludes jobseekers from an allocation of social housing. EEA nationals who are 'jobseekers' are 'qualified persons'[263] and therefore are entitled to the extended right of residence.[264] A 'jobseeker' is defined as 'a person who enters the UK in order to seek employment and can provide evidence that he is seeking employment and has a genuine chance of being engaged'.[265] If the jobseeker had previously been employed, he or she may still have retained worker status and so be a 'worker' in certain circumstances and therefore potentially eligible.[266]

3.120	If a person has more than one right of residence is because of his or her status as a jobseeker, he or she will not be eligible.

3.121	For applications for an allocation of social housing made on or after 8 November 2012,[267] there are two additional exclusions from eligibility.

---

[260]	See **12.126–12.128**.
[261]	SI 2006/1294, reg 4(1)(b)(iii), inserted by SI 2012/2588 for applications for an allocation made on or after 8 November 2012. For 'derivative right to reside because he or she is the primary carer of a British citizen', see **12.156–12.159**.
[262]	SI 2006/1294, reg 4(1)(b)(iv), inserted by SI 2012/2588 for applications for an allocation made on or after 8 November 2012. For 'a right to reside derived from Art 20 of the Treaty on the Functioning of the European Union, where the right to reside arises because a British citizen would otherwise be deprived of the genuine enjoyment of the substance of those rights as a European Union citizen', see **3.126–3.127** and **12.162–12.163**.
[263]	Immigration (European Economic Area) Regulations SI 2006/1003, reg 6(1)(a). See **12.130**.
[264]	See **12.129–12.138**.
[265]	Immigration (European Economic Area) Regulations 2006, SI 2006/1003, reg 6(1)(a) and (4).
[266]	See **3.90**.
[267]	SI 2012/2588, reg 3.

3.122 A person who is exercising a European Union right of residence that is derived from being the primary carer of a British national is excluded.[268] This derivative right of residence arises where:

- the person is an exempt person;[269] and

- he or she is the primary carer of a British citizen; and

- the British citizen is residing in the UK; and

- the British citizen would be unable to reside in the UK or in another EEA state if the primary carer were required to leave.[270]

3.123 This 'derivative right of residence' was recognised by the Court of Justice of the European Union (CJEU) in the case of *Zambrano v Office national de l'emploi*.[271] The Immigration (European Economic Area) Regulations 2006[272] were subsequently amended so that the right of residence is now contained in domestic legislation. At the same time, however, the Eligibility Regulations were amended so as to exclude people who have this derivative right of residence from eligibility for an allocation of social housing. At the date of writing, the equivalent Regulations in Wales had not been amended and so a person with this derivative right of residence would not be excluded from applying for an allocation to a local housing authority in Wales.[273]

3.124 This derivative right of residence will only apply to people who are not, themselves, nationals of any EEA member state.[274] The British citizen is likely to be a child but could include an adult who requires a primary carer.

3.125 The Immigration (European Economic Area) Regulations 2006, reg 15A now identify *five* derivative rights of residence.[275] A person who has one of the other four derivative rights of residence is not excluded from eligibility for an allocation of social housing.[276]

---

[268] SI 2006/1294, reg 4(1)(b) as amended by SI 2012/2588.

[269] In that the person does not have any other right to reside or right of abode in the UK and does not have indefinite leave to enter or remain in the UK (SI 2006/1003, reg 6(2)(c) inserted by SI 2012/2560 and in force from 8 November 2012). See **12.149**.

[270] SI 2006/1003, reg 15A(4A) inserted by SI 2012/2560 and in force from 8 November 2012. See **12.156–12.159**.

[271] C34/09, [2012] QB 265, CJEU.

[272] SI 2006/1003, see Appendix 2.

[273] Allocation of Housing (Wales) Regulations 2003, SI 2003/239 (W. 36). See **3.134–3.136** and Appendix 3.

[274] Because a national of another EEA member state would normally be entitled to reside in that member state with the British citizen.

[275] SI 2006/1003 as amended. See **12.142–12.161**, Appendix 2.

[276] For all five derivative rights of residence, see **12.142–12.161**.

3.126 A person who has a right derived from Art 20 of the Treaty on the Functioning of the European Union, in a case where the right to reside arises because a British citizen would otherwise be deprived of the genuine enjoyment of the substance of his or her rights as an EU citizen, is also excluded from eligibility.[277] This new provision will exclude anyone who has a right of residence which is not, as yet, identified in the Immigration (European Economic Area) Regulations,[278] but which is subsequently declared by the CJEU. Art 20 of the Treaty on the Functioning of the European Union contains the right of citizens of the EU to move and reside freely within the territories of the EU member states. This provision does not exclude all the rights of EU residence that might, in the future, be recognized in CJEU case-law but simply those that:

- are derived from Art 20 of the Treaty; and

- arise because otherwise a British citizen would be deprived of the genuine enjoyment of the substance of his or her EU Treaty rights.

3.127 The case of *Zambrano v Office national de l'emploi*[279] was one example of a right of residence arising under Art 20 because otherwise an EU citizen would be deprived of the genuine enjoyment of the substance of his or her rights. While the *Zambrano* right of residence has now been incorporated into the derivative rights of residence identified at reg 15A of the Immigration (European Economic Area) Regulations 2006,[280] and anyone who has a derivative right of residence as a result of *Zambrano* is excluded from eligibility, this provision operates so that anyone with a right of residence in similar circumstances that is subsequently recognised by the CJEU is ineligible for an allocation.[281]

3.128 If a person has more than one right of residence, such as being both a jobseeker and being the family member of a worker or self-employed person, then his or her right to reside is not 'only' derived from his or her status as a jobseeker, or the other four provisions in this second class, and he or she will not fall within this second class of persons (not subject to immigration control) who are not eligible for an allocation of social housing.

---

[277] SI 2006/1294, reg 4(1)(b)(iv) inserted by SI 2012/2588 for applicants whose applications for an allocation were made on or after 8 November 2012.

[278] SI 2006/1003, see Appendix 2.

[279] C34/09, [2012] QB 265, CJEU.

[280] 2006/1003 as amended, see **12.156–12.159** and Appendix 2.

[281] There is some debate as to whether or not it is lawful for the UK government to withhold social assistance from persons entitled to EU rights of residence under Art 20. No doubt the courts will be required to grapple with the issue.

The third class: EEA nationals with a right to reside in the rest of the Common Travel Area by virtue of a right equivalent to being jobseekers, family members of a jobseeker, exercising an initial right to reside, by having a derivative right to reside as the primary carer of an Irish or British citizen or by having a right to reside derived from Art 20 of the Treaty on the Functioning of the European Union[282]

3.129   This third class refers to people who have been residing in the Channel Islands, the Isle of Man or the Republic of Ireland. The rest of the CTA is dealt with by the second class.

3.130   For 'jobseeker' see **12.130**. For 'family member' see **12.131–12.137**. For 'initial right to reside' see **12.126–12.128**. For 'Common Travel Area' see **3.32**, Box 1. For 'persons with a right to reside derived from Art 20 of the Treaty on the Functioning of the European Union', see **3.126–3.127**.

3.131   The derivative right to reside referred to in this class is the same as that identified in the Immigration (European Economic Area) Regulations 2006, but is separately identified because those Regulations do not apply to the remainder of the CTA.[283] The derivative right arises as a result of the CJEU's decision in *Zambrano v Office national de l'emploi*.[284] That decision recognised rights of residence which are directly effective in the remainder of the CTA: ie the Channel Islands, Isle of Man and the Republic of Ireland. A person will have this derivative right of residence if he or she is the primary carer of a British citizen residing in the Channels Islands or the Isle of Man, or of an Irish citizen, residing in the Republic of Ireland, and the British or Irish citizen would have to leave that country of residence if his or her primary carer did not have an EU right of residence. The derivative right of residence will be enjoyed by people who are not nationals of any EEA member state.

3.132   The exclusion from eligibility for an allocation for those people exercising this derivative right of residence or other rights of residence derived from Art 20 applies to applications for an allocation made on or after 8 November 2012.[285]

3.133   As with the second class, if a person has more than one right of residence, then his or her right to reside is not 'only' derived from his or her status as a jobseeker, or the other four provisions in this class, and he or she will not fall within this third class of persons (not subject to immigration control) who are not eligible for an allocation of social housing.

---

[282] Allocation of Housing and Homelessness (Eligibility) (England) Regulations 2006, SI 2006/1294, reg 4(1)(c) as amended by SI 2012/2588. English Code, para 3.12(iv). For eligibility for homelessness assistance, see **12.222–12.226**.

[283] SI 2006/1003, see **12.156–12.159**, and Appendix 2.

[284] C34/09, [2012] QB 265, CJEU.

[285] SI 2012/2588, reg 3. At the date of writing, there is no exclusion in the equivalent Welsh Regulations and so a person who has one of those rights of residence could consider making an application for an allocation to a local housing authority in Wales, see **3.134–3.136**.

The Welsh rules

3.134 Applicants to local housing authorities in Wales who have come from abroad will find their applications determined under Allocation of Housing (Wales) Regulations 2003, reg 5.[286] These regulations apply to all applications made on or after 29 January 2003.[287] The Welsh Code advises that consideration is currently being given to amending the Regulations and also to revising the guidance in the Welsh Code.[288]

3.135 The basic rule is that people who are not subject to immigration control but who are not habitually resident in the CTA are not eligible unless they are:

(1)   workers exercising European Economic Area Treaty rights;[289]

(2)   people with a right to reside in the UK pursuant to the Immigration (European Economic Area) Regulations 2000;[290] or

(3)   people who left the territory of Montserrat after 1 November 1995 because of the effect on that territory of a volcanic eruption;[291] or

(4)   a person who arrived in Great Britain between 28 February 2009 and 18 March 2011 and who before arriving had been resident in Zimbabwe and who had accepted an offer made by the UK government to settle in the UK.[292]

3.136 These groups have all been discussed earlier in this Chapter or elsewhere in this book:

---

[286]   Allocation of Housing (Wales) Regulations 2003, SI 2003/239 (W 36) as amended by the Allocation of Housing and Homelessness (Eligibility) (Wales) Regulations 2009, SI 2009/393 (W 42), the latter in force for applications for an allocation of social housing made on or after 20 March 2009. For eligibility for homelessness assistance, see **12.227–12.233**.

[287]   The regulations in force in Wales do not reflect the extended rights given by the European Union Citizens' Rights Directive (Directive on the right of citizens of the Union and their family members to move and reside freely within the territory of the Member States, 2004/38/EC) or, indeed, the Civil Partnership Act 2004. It may be that an applicant to a Welsh local housing authority who would be eligible had he or she applied to a local housing authority in England after 1 June 2006 can argue that the Directive is capable of direct effect, and he or she should be entitled to those extended rights.

[288]   Welsh Code, para 3.1.

[289]   Allocation of Housing (Wales) Regulations 2003, SI 2003/239 (W 36), reg 5(a). See Welsh Code, para 3.5(iii).

[290]   SI 2003/239 (W 36), reg 5(b). Although this provision remains in the text of the Allocation of Housing (Wales) Regulations 2003, reg 5, it was repealed by the Immigration (European Economic Area) Regulations 2006, SI 2006/1003, reg 31 and Sch 3. Welsh Code, para 3.5(iii).

[291]   Allocation of Housing (Wales) Regulations 2003 (W 36), SI 2003/239, reg 5(c). Welsh Code, para 3.5(iv).

[292]   Allocation of Housing (Wales) Regulations 2003, SI 2003/239 (W 36), reg 5(d), inserted by the Allocation of Housing and Homelessness (Eligibility) (Wales) Regulations 2009, SI 2009/393 (W 42), reg 2 and in force for applications to local housing authorities in Wales made on or after 20 March 2009. Welsh Code, para 3.5(v).

- For discussion of 'habitual residence', see **3.76–3.81**.

- For 'worker', see **3.88–3.94**.

- For 'a person with a right to reside', see **12.123–12.163**.[293]

- For 'a person who left the territory of Montserrat', see **3.110**.

- For 'a person who arrived in Great Britain between 28 February 2009 and 18 March 2001 from Zimbabwe and who had accepted an offer made by the UK government to settle in the UK', see **3.114–3.116** A person falling within this last group will be exempt from the habitual residence test if he or she made an application for an allocation of social housing on or after 20 March 2009.

Summary of differences in eligibility as between local housing authorities in England and in Wales

Overview

3.137 People considering making applications for an allocation of social housing may want to consider whether they should direct their applications towards local housing authorities in England and Wales, since the eligibility rules are governed by different Regulations depending on which country the local housing authority is in. Unlike HA 1996, Part 7 ('Homelessness'), there is no procedure within HA 1996, Part 6, for any referral between local housing authorities.[294] As a result, an applicant should direct his or her application for an allocation of social housing towards the local housing authorities in whose districts he or she would wish to live. There is nothing to prevent an applicant making applications to more than one local housing authority.

Applications to local housing authorities in Wales

3.138 The following applicants would be eligible for an allocation of social housing if they apply to local housing authorities in Wales, but would not be eligible if they apply to local housing authorities in England:

- a person who is subject to immigration control and is habitually resident[295] in the CTA[296] and who either:
  - is a national of a state which has ratified the ECSMA or the ESC and is lawfully present in the UK,[297] or

---

[293] For applications made before 30 April 2006, the relevant 'right to reside' is in the Immigration (European Economic Area) Regulations 2000, SI 2000/2326.
[294] See Chapter 15.
[295] See **3.76–3.81**.
[296] See **3.32**, Box 1.
[297] Class D(i). See Allocation of Housing (Wales) Regulations 2003, SI 2003/239 (W 36), reg 4. See **3.59–3.61**.

–   before 3 April 2000 was owed a duty by a local housing authority under Housing Act 1985, Part 3, or HA 1996, Part 7, which is extant and is a national of a state which is a signatory to the ECSMA or ESC;[298] or

• a person who is not subject to immigration control and whose sole right of residence in the CTA is by virtue of being a jobseeker or of being a family member of a jobseeker will be exempt from the habitual residence test;[299] or

• a person who has a derivative right of residence identified in Immigration (European Economic Area) Regulations and who satisfies the habitual residence test;[300] or

• a person who has a right of residence derived from Art 20 of the Treaty on the Functioning of the European Union and who satisfies the habitual residence test.[301]

Applications to local housing authorities in England

3.139   The only group of persons who might be found to be eligible on application to a local housing authority in England, but not on application to a local housing authority in Wales, are persons who are in the UK as a result of their deportation, expulsion or other removal by compulsion of law from another country to the UK. If a person falling within that group applies to a local housing authority in England, he or she will be exempt from the habitual residence test.[302] If he or she applies to a local housing authority in Wales, the habitual residence test will be applied.

QUALIFICATION FOR ALLOCATION (ENGLAND)

Background to the current arrangements

3.140   From 1996 to 2003, each local housing authority in England and Wales was at liberty to exclude from its statutory housing register those classes of applicant it chose to designate as 'non-qualifying persons'.[303] This was a power to exclude for membership of a designated class and was *not* a power to specify the only classes who might be treated as qualifying. Not all local housing

---

[298] Class D(ii). See Allocation of Housing (Wales) Regulations 2003, SI 2003/239 (W 36) and **3.62–3.64**.

[299] SI 2003/239 (W 36), reg 5. See **3.134–3.136**. Such a person would be exempt from the habitual residence test.

[300] SI 2006/1003, reg 15A(4A) inserted by SI 2012/2588, in force from 8 November 2012. See **3.122–3.124** and 12.162–12.163 and Appendix 2.

[301] See **3.126–3.127** and 12.162–12.163.

[302] Allocation of Housing and Homelessness (Eligibility) (England) Regulations, SI 2006/1294, reg 6(2)(g). See **3.111**.

[303] HA 1996, s 161(4) repealed by Homelessness Act 2002, Sch 2. See **1.24–1.26**.

authorities chose to use the power, although some used 'suspension' from the housing register as an equivalent but unlawful alternative. Where it was used, it was often targeted at classes of applicants such as those owing arrears of rent or other debts to the local housing authority or those evicted for anti-social behaviour. Indeed, some local housing authorities adopted a plethora of excluded classes, some of dubious propriety.[304]

3.141 By 2000, the then Government had decided that change was needed. It said:

> 'We do not believe that anyone should be permanently excluded from social housing. We therefore propose to remove the power to impose 'blanket' exclusions from the housing register.'[305]

3.142 Its motivation was a concern that:

> '...some housing authorities have made rather extensive use of this broad power to effectively exclude categories of applicants from access to social housing, regardless of housing need. Examples of groups currently excluded are: applicants with rent arrears (however small) and those who have not resided in the authority's district for a minimum period.'[306]

3.143 Therefore, upon the abolition in January 2003 of the requirement to keep housing registers,[307] HA 1996 was also amended to deprive local housing authorities of the power to exclude 'classes of persons'.[308] However, notwithstanding this change, the practice of excluding classes of applicants continued for many more years, in parts of both England and Wales, even though it had become unlawful.[309]

3.144 HA 1996 Part 6, as amended by the Homelessness Act 2002, left local housing authorities with only a limited power to exclude lawfully *individual* applicants in circumstances falling within a very narrowly drawn set of statutory provisions. As a result, from early 2003 to June 2012, a local housing authority in England or Wales only had the ability to treat an applicant as ineligible for allocation either as a result of his or her immigration status or because of his or her unacceptable behaviour or the behaviour of a member of

---

[304] *Exclusions from the Housing Register* (Northern Housing Consortium, May 2000) and **1.25**.
[305] *Quality and Choice – A Decent Home for All* (Department of Environment, Transport and the Regions, 2000), para 9.8.
[306] *Parliamentary Joint Committee On Human Rights First Report, Appendix: The homelessness bill, Memorandum by the Department for Transport, Local Government and the Regions,* para 3.3.
[307] HA 1996, s 162 repealed by Homelessness Act 2002, Sch 2.
[308] HA 1996, s 161(4) repealed by Homelessness Act 2002, Sch 2.
[309] See *Housing Allocation and Homelessness: A Special Report by the Local Government Ombudsman for Wales* (PSOW, February 2006); *Exclusions in Tyne and Wear: an investigation by Shelter's NEHAC into why applicants are excluded from social rented housing* (Shelter, April 2006), and *Am I on the list? Exclusion from and re-inclusion on social housing waiting lists* (Chartered Institute of Housing Cymru, May 2008).

his or her household.[310] The relevant statutory wording prevented blanket exclusions for misconduct and set a high test.

3.145 Several of the relatively small number of cases in which the conditions for exclusion were treated by local housing authorities as having been fulfilled led to applications for judicial review. Against that background, local housing authorities often preferred to permit access by all applicants to their allocation schemes but then to use other powers to remove or reduce the preferences which certain applicants would otherwise have enjoyed in the local allocation schemes.

3.146 In the result, relatively few applicants were wholly excluded by local housing authorities from allocation schemes and those schemes were perceived to be essentially open access. In consequence, the number of applicants on waiting lists grew steadily from 2003 onwards.[311]

3.147 In 2010, the newly elected UK Coalition Government decided that a change of policy was called for. That policy change, reviewed in the next few paragraphs, led to amendments to HA 1996, Part 6 which have re-introduced the concept of 'qualifying classes' of applicants in England but have left in place the arrangements for individual exclusion of ineligible applicants by local housing authorities in Wales. The remainder of this Chapter deals first with the new position in England before dealing with the position in relation to individual behaviour-related eligibility decisions in Wales.

The policy change

3.148 The May 2010 programme of the incoming UK Coalition Government stated that:

> 'The Government believes that it is time for a fundamental shift of power from Westminster to people. We will promote decentralisation and democratic engagement, and we will end the era of top-down government by giving new powers to local councils, communities, neighbourhoods and individuals.'[312]

3.149 The May 2010 programme of the incoming UK Coalition Government stated that:

In the context of social housing allocation, this approach paralleled calls made during 2010 by some local housing authorities in England, and by some

---

[310] See below.

[311] 'In 1998 waiting list numbers were 1.02 million, and remained below 1.1 million until 2002. The introduction of open waiting lists in 2003 coincided with a steep rise in waiting list numbers, which reached 1.77 million in 2008. In 2009, overall waiting list numbers remained stable at 1.76 million. This represents a 61 per cent rise over 2002 levels.' *Localism Bill: A fairer future for social housing – Impact Assessment* (DCLG, January 2011), p 15.

[312] *Freedom Fairness Responsibility, The coalition – our programme for Government* (Cabinet Office, May 2010), p 11.

housing policy makers, for greater local flexibility in relation to decision-making about access to social housing[313] and for a move away from the open access needs-based approach to allocation to one more attuned to prioritising local circumstances and local residents.[314] The National Housing Federation called for local housing authorities to be 'freed and encouraged to establish local priorities and local lettings plans that reflect what is happening in their areas'.[315]

3.150 The new Government's detailed proposals for change to social housing allocation arrangements in England were issued for consultation in November 2010. The published summary stated that under the proposals:[316]

'Councils will be able to set the rules which decide who qualifies to go on the housing waiting list. At the moment they have to keep 'open' waiting lists, which means that people can get onto any council's waiting list whether they need social housing or not.'

3.151 The main consultation paper suggested that:[317]

'Open waiting lists may be acceptable – should even perhaps be encouraged – where there is low demand for social housing. Where there is not enough housing, even for those who really need it, continuing to operate an open waiting list raises false expectations and is likely to fuel the belief that the allocation system is unfair.'

and that:

'By excluding from the waiting list those who are not likely to be successful in accessing social housing, this should make it easier for local authorities to manage unrealistic expectations. Shorter waiting lists should also be simpler – and as a result cheaper – to administer. We therefore intend to legislate to give back to local authorities the freedom to determine which categories of applicants should qualify to join the waiting list. In this way we will reverse the changes which were introduced by the 2002 Act. We take the view that it should be for local authorities to put in place arrangements which suit the particular needs of their local area.'

3.152 In short, what was envisaged was a return to the pre-2003 position in which local housing authorities in England would once again be able to set their own local criteria for admission to, or exclusion, from their allocation schemes.

---

[313] See, for example, *Allocations and Local Flexibility* (Chartered Institute of Housing, February 2010) and *Allocating social housing: opportunities and challenges* (Chartered Institute of Housing, July 2010).

[314] *Making Housing Affordable: A new vision for housing policy* (Policy Exchange, August 2010).

[315] *Fairer access to social housing: a consultation proposal* (National Housing Federation, August 2010), p 21.

[316] *Local decisions: a fairer future for social housing: A summary* (DCLG, November 2010).

[317] *Local decisions: a fairer future for social housing* (DCLG, November 2010).

3.153 The consultation process ended in January 2011. Around two-thirds of the local housing authorities which responded welcomed the proposed flexibility, or indicated that they would consider setting restrictive qualification criteria.[318] In light of that, the Government resolved to pursue its proposals and to introduce a Localism Bill to 'give local authorities a new power to determine which categories of persons qualify to join their waiting list'.[319]

3.154 During its parliamentary passage, the provisions of the Localism Act 2011 addressing this aspect of social housing allocation received relatively little scrutiny. The Act achieved Royal Assent in November 2011 and the relevant changes to the allocation provisions of the HA 1996, Part 6 were brought into force on 18 June 2012.[320]

3.155 Between January and March 2012 the Government carried out a consultation exercise on the draft of a new statutory Code of Guidance about social housing allocation for local housing authorities in England. Although more than half of the responses to the consultation considered that the draft guidance on the implementation of the new qualification criteria for allocations was sufficiently clear,

> 'a significant minority sought further guidance on framing qualification criteria as they were concerned about the risk of legal challenge. In particular, respondents sought clarification on issues such as:
>
> - How to set qualification criteria around income and assets (eg if the applicant owns their own home in another country)
> - How to prioritise 'good behaviour' when setting qualification criteria
> - How to restrict waiting lists, while promoting mixed and sustainable communities.
>
> A number ... requested clarification on how to ensure their qualification criteria were in line with their duties under the equalities legislation; and the relationship between qualification criteria and reasonable preference categories. In particular, respondents wanted guidance on whether an applicant for social housing who fell into one of the reasonable preference categories was also required to meet the qualification criteria before they could join the housing register.'[321]

3.156 The guidance that was eventually published in June 2012 deals with the new arrangements for 'qualification' in only 13 short paragraphs, underscoring the thrust of the Government's policy of leaving it to local housing authorities to decide how best to apply the statutory provisions in their districts.[322]

---

[318] *Local decisions: next steps towards a fairer future for social housing – Summary of responses to consultation* (DCLG, February 2011), para 4.3.

[319] Ibid, para 8.13.

[320] Localism Act 2011 (Commencement No 6 and Transitional, Savings and Transitory Provisions Order 2012, SI 2012/1463, art 3.

[321] *Allocation of accommodation: guidance for local housing authorities in England Summary of responses to consultation* (DCLG, June 2012), paras 3.21–3.22.

[322] English Code, paras 3.18–3.31.

3.157 In summary, the policy intention behind HA 1996, Part 6 as amended is to provide local housing authorities in England with the power to decide locally, based on local circumstances, which classes of applicants can or cannot access social housing in their districts. The result is that there may be considerable variation between different local housing authorities as to which 'classes' of persons are qualified to apply for social housing or are disqualified. The differences in qualifying classes for allocation schemes, between even neighbouring local housing authorities in England, will be likely to create a patchwork of qualifying criteria.

3.158 The present Government does not know whether, or precisely how, local housing authorities in England will respond to this opportunity to change from open to closed waiting lists by developing their own classes of qualifying and non-qualifying applicants. It has, however, stated that:

> '...it is likely that a growing number of authorities will adopt more restrictive criteria for registration on housing waiting lists. It is not possible to predict the way in which local authorities will respond to these new flexibilities, e.g. in terms of what sort of selective criteria they might adopt. There could be significant local variation. We know, though, that many authorities are keen to give some greater weight to residency criteria. It is also conceivable that a number of authorities may decide to continue to operate open waiting lists, for instance, in areas where it might be thought necessary to stimulate demand for social housing.'[323]

3.159 The only safe predictions are that:

(1)   there is likely to be significant variation between local housing authorities in England; and

(2)   some local housing authorities may still operate a wholly 'open' allocation scheme.

The new arrangements

3.160 With effect from 18 June 2012, the Localism Act 2011 amended HA 1996, Part 6 so as to:

(1)   restore to local housing authorities in England the power that they enjoyed between 1996 and 2003, as described at **1.24–1.26**, to exclude applicants 'by class'; and

(2)   add a new power for such authorities to positively prescribe, by class, the only applicants entitled to be allocated social housing under their allocation schemes.[324]

---

[323] *Localism Bill: A fairer future for social housing – Impact Assessment* (DCLG, January 2011), p 19.
[324] Localism Act 2011, s 146, inserting HA 1996, s 160ZA.

3.161   Qualification for, or disqualification from, admission to a local housing allocation scheme may now be wholly regulated by a local housing authority in England which exercises the power to identify 'classes' of persons who are – and/or who are not – qualifying persons for allocation of housing.[325] The only statutory limit on the exercise of these powers by a local housing authority is that they cannot be used to treat as qualifying persons those who are rendered ineligible by their immigration status.[326]

3.162   The key consequence of this change is that applicants will either be in a class capable of joining the particular local housing allocation scheme or they will not, depending on the classes of person identified by the particular local housing authority. Even if a local housing authority chooses not to use the new power to designate classes who qualify, it may use the new power to identify particular classes who do *not* qualify.

3.163   No transitional provisions were made, when the new arrangements were brought into force, to deal with the situation of those persons who had already successfully made applications to join local allocation schemes before 18 June 2012. The structure of the commencement order suggests that the government may have considered making such provision but changed its mind.[327] In the absence of any such provision, each local housing authority in England that decides to revise its allocation scheme to incorporate qualifying and/or non-qualifying classes will need to spell out whether those classes will be applied only to new applicants or to all applications.[328]

3.164   The scope for the adoption of very restrictive qualifying classes, or designation of very broad non-qualifying classes, is obvious. As a potential restraint on any abuse of these new powers, the Secretary of State has retained a regulation-making power to:

(1)   prescribe classes of persons who are or are not to be treated as qualifying; and

(2)   prescribe criteria which cannot be used by local housing authorities to decide which classes of persons are not qualifying persons.[329]

3.165   The former power has yet to be used but the latter power has already been exercised in respect of applicants who are, or are related to, current or former armed services personnel (see **3.195–3.201**). The present Government has also said that the powers will be used if 'there is evidence that people in housing need are being excluded from social housing without good cause'.[330]

---

[325]   HA 1996, s 160ZA(7).
[326]   HA 1996, ss 160ZA(2) and (4).
[327]   See the Localism Act 2011 (Commencement No 6 and Transitional, Savings and Transitory Provisions) Order 2012, art 6.
[328]   See **4.23–4.24**.
[329]   HA 1996, s 160ZA(8).
[330]   *Local decisions: a fairer future for social housing* (DCLG, November 2010), para 4.11.

3.166 During the passage of the Localism Bill, concern was expressed about the scope of the regulation-making powers and an amendment was moved designed to impose on the Secretary of State a requirement to consult, over a minimum 12-week period, with local housing authorities before any exercise of the power.[331] The Minister opposed the amendment on the basis that it simply reflected 'good administrative practice' which was already observed by the Government. He also declined to give examples of the 'type of scenario' in which the powers might be used on the (incorrect) basis that the precise powers already existed and were simply being re-enacted.[332]

Setting the classes

3.167 All local housing authorities in England are likely to need to amend or re-cast their allocation schemes to reflect their policy choices about the exercise of these new powers to adopt classes of qualifying and non-qualifying applicants.[333] Indeed, if the local housing authority is also a social landlord it will need to comply with the statutory regulator's requirement to 'clearly set out, and be able to give reasons for, the criteria they use for excluding actual and potential tenants from consideration for allocations'.[334]

3.168 The Government has made some projections of the likely cost of the exercise of reviewing and revising local allocation schemes in the light of these changes:

> 'All 326 local authorities are expected to incur a one-off cost from familiarising themselves with the new arrangements, at a cost of between £290,000 in the advantageous scenario and £1.2m in the disadvantageous scenario (central case £770,000).

> Those authorities that decide to adapt their policies and procedures will also face costs; these could amount to as little as £400,000 or as much as £3.7m, depending on how many local authorities adapt their waiting list policies and how much staff time is involved.'[335]

3.169 The projection is that these costs will normally be offset, for those local housing authorities choosing to exercise their discretion to limit waiting lists, by the saved costs of receiving and processing applications which have no prospect of securing an allocation.

3.170 The Secretary of State's view is that the adoption of qualifying criteria would form 'part of an allocation scheme' as distinct from forming part of

---

[331] House of Commons Public Bill Committee of the Localism Bill, Amendment No 223.
[332] *Hansard,* Commons Public Bill Committee of the Localism Bill, col 756, 3 March 2011.
[333] For the process of amending an allocation scheme see Chapter 4.
[334] *The regulatory framework for social housing in England from April 2012* (Homes & Communities Agency, March 2012), p 23.
[335] *Localism Bill: A fairer future for social housing – Impact Assessment* (DCLG, January 2011), p 25.

some pre-scheme policy or procedure.[336] If that is correct, identifying in the allocation scheme the classes who qualify and/or those who do not qualify will be highly likely to amount to a 'major change of policy' to any current allocation scheme. Such a change triggers an obligation to consult housing associations and other private registered providers in the authority's district with which it has nomination arrangements.[337]

3.171 Defining with precision the classes who qualify or do not qualify for social housing allocation will require very careful consideration. The objective will be to produce terminology which is clear, fair and transparent (so that applicants can readily see precisely what classes the local housing authority has adopted) and also be readily applicable with certainty and assurance by local housing authority officers and staff.

3.172 Two specific points will, for practical reasons, need to be addressed:

(1)   whether the description of the class will have a built-in override enabling a designated officer to waive the requirements in particular or exceptional cases; and/or

(2)   whether the description of the class should apply to all allocations or should be limited by reference to either (a) some types of applicants and/or (b) particular parts of the housing stock.

3.173 As to the former, the statutory guidance suggests that there may be exceptional circumstances where it is necessary to dis-apply the generally adopted criteria in the case of individual applicants and it encourages local housing authorities to 'make explicit provision for dealing with exceptional cases within their qualification rules', offering the example of the need to move quickly an intimidated witness.[338] This guidance is no doubt intended to meet one of the criticisms made in respect of the equivalent pre-2003 statutory scheme which:

> '... effectively allows housing authorities to exclude a range of different groups of applicants from social housing, but does not allow them to exclude applicants on an individual basis. The effect is that where an applicant falls within a class of non-qualifying persons (eg persons with rent arrears), the housing authority rejects the application and does not make a balanced decision based on consideration of the particular circumstances of the case (eg weigh the degree of housing need against the severity of the rent arrears).'[339]

---

[336]   English Code, para 4.1.
[337]   HA 1996, s 166A(13).
[338]   English Code, para 3.25.
[339]   *Parliamentary Joint Committee On Human Rights First Report, Appendix: The homelessness bill, Memorandum by the Department for Transport, Local Government and the Regions,* para 6.1.

3.174 As to the latter, the statutory guidance advises that local housing authorities may wish to set different qualifying and non-qualifying classes as between:

(a) new applicants and transferring tenants; and/or

(b) different types of housing stock (for example, in relation to hard to let housing).[340]

3.175 Obviously, in taking the policy decisions about the parameters of qualifying and non-qualifying classes, local housing authorities will need to take account of their general equality duties under the Equality Act 2010[341] and the importance of avoiding provisions which may be directly or indirectly discriminatory.[342] However, beyond stating those obvious propositions, the statutory guidance provides no further assistance.[343] The Local Government Association has identified that 'changes to housing allocation plans that have the net effect of negatively impacting on those with protected characteristics, such as disability race or age, may well be against equality laws, and would be subject to legal challenge' and has encouraged local housing authorities to cross-check their arrangements against its Social Housing Equality Framework.[344] The Chartered Institute of Housing has advised that 'establishing criteria for people to be able to go onto the housing waiting list is not without risk of legal challenge and so housing authorities will need to be mindful of unlawfully discriminating, either directly or indirectly' and that 'full consideration of provisions in the Equality Act 2010 and a comprehensive equality analysis will be required to ensure a fair and accessible approach to allocations'.[345]

3.176 Each local housing authority, when modifying an allocation scheme to introduce new qualifying and non-qualifying classes, must also take account of any relevant content of:[346]

(a) its current homelessness strategy adopted under Homelessness Act 2002, s 1;[347]

(b) its current tenancy strategy adopted under Localism Act 2011, s 150; and

(c) in the case of an authority that is a London borough council, the London Housing Strategy.

---

[340] English Code, para 3.24.
[341] See **4.196**.
[342] See **4.204**.
[343] English Code, para 3.20.
[344] *Councils must consider equality laws when changing services* (LGA Media Release 16 February 2012); *Social Housing Equality Framework* (LGA, 2012).
[345] *Allocation of accommodation: guidance for local authorities in England: Briefing paper* (CIH, July 2012), p 7.
[346] HA 1996, s 166A(12).
[347] See Chapter 7.

3.177 Once the policy decisions on the new classes have been taken, the consultation has been completed, the final wording has been adopted and the new allocation scheme has been published, it will fall to officers of local housing authorities in England to apply the new qualifying and non-qualifying classes to applicants for social housing allocation.

Common classes

3.178 In line with its generally non-prescriptive approach to the new powers, the statutory guidance issued by the Secretary of State does not offer any suggested list of qualifying or non-qualifying classes from which local housing authorities may wish to select.[348]

3.179 The only class directly addressed in the guidance is that of current *homeowners*. The guidance encourages local housing authorities to avoid allocation of social housing to applicants in that class and suggests that the rule should only be departed from in exceptional circumstances e g where an elderly homeowner needs to move into sheltered social housing accommodation.[349] The same class is the only one identified in the National Housing Strategy:

> 'Households who are capable of meeting their own housing needs should not be allocated social housing when so many other families are left on waiting lists. Guidance to local authorities will make it clear that we do not expect social homes to be allocated to people who don't need them (for example those who already own a home that would be suitable for them to use)....'[350]

3.180 Many local housing authorities will also consider framing qualifying or non-qualifying classes by reference to *residence* criteria. Admission to the qualifying class might require a minimum period of residence in an area. Alternatively, a non-qualifying class would exclude those with less than a minimum period of residence. The statutory guidance suggests that where local housing authorities do set residency criteria they may wish to consider at least four exceptional categories to be exempted from the normal residency requirements. They are:

(1) people who are moving into the district to take up work or escape violence;[351]

---

[348] 'We have decided to maintain a light-touch approach, in the spirit of localism, and in order to maximise the opportunities for local authorities to innovate and to think creatively about how social housing can best be used to improve people's lives.' *Allocation of accommodation: guidance for local housing authorities in England: Summary of responses to consultation* (DCLG, June 2012), para 4.2.

[349] English Code, para 3.23. In contrast the Welsh Code advises that local housing authorities are 'expected to consider the housing needs of owner-occupiers in the same way as other applicants', para 3.37.

[350] *Laying the Foundations: A Housing Strategy for England* (HM Government, November 2011), p 22.

[351] English Code, para 3.22.

(2) people who have been placed temporarily outside the local housing authority's district but are children in the care of that authority or are applicants for homelessness assistance and therefore need to return to the local housing authority's own district;[352]

(3) people who are existing tenants of social housing seeking to move to a smaller home or to take up a work opportunity;[353] or

(4) people connected with the armed forces (see **3.195–3.201**).

3.181 Some local housing authorities might be attracted to the possibility of framing their qualifying or non-qualifying classes by reference to criteria which already have statutory definitions and well developed case-law such as:

• 'local connection';[354]

• 'reasonable preference';[355] and

• 'priority need'.[356]

3.182 Local housing authorities could specify that those terms, when used in their allocation schemes, have the same meanings as those used in HA 1996 Parts 6 and 7.

3.183 Others may wish to limit or specify qualifying and non-qualifying classes by reference to other criteria such as:

• age;

• anti-social behaviour;

• community involvement/participation;

• employment;

• housing need (eg homeless households and overcrowded families[357]);

• means (eg excluding those with sufficient financial resources to rent or buy privately[358]);

---

[352] English Code, para 3.22.
[353] English Code, para 3.24.
[354] HA 1996, s 199(1) and see **15.42–15.94**.
[355] HA 1996, s 166A(3) [England] and s 167(2) [Wales], see **4.28–4.114**.
[356] HA 1996, s 189 and see Chapter 13.
[357] The examples given in *Local decisions: a fairer future for social housing: Consultation* (DCLG, November 2010), para 4.9.
[358] The example given in *Local decisions: a fairer future for social housing: Consultation* (DCLG, November 2010), para 4.9.

- local residence (responses to the consultation on the proposals to introduce the new qualification power indicated that many local housing authorities were likely to impose residency requirements as part of their qualification criteria and that the criteria might require applicants to have lived in the area for several years before they qualified for social housing[359]); or

- previous tenant history (eg rent arrears).

3.184 Local housing authorities would need to define in their allocation schemes what these criteria mean and how decisions about them will fall to be taken. One commentator has suggested that making 'housing need' a requirement for qualification could have the adverse effects of (1) generating a large number of reviews of decisions that applicants do not fall within a 'need' category and (2) making it difficult to give those owed a homelessness duty a 'reasonable preference' if their immediate housing need has been met by the provision of suitable temporary accommodation.[360]

Qualification and reasonable preference

3.185 It is not at all clear from the text of the amended statutory scheme in HA 1996, Part 6 whether a local housing authority in England may specify a class of non-qualifying persons which includes (and therefore disqualifies from allocation) a person who would otherwise fall within one of the categories[361] required to be given a reasonable preference in the local allocation scheme.

3.186 The present UK Government had seemingly intended that the June 2012 changes in the statutory regime should not lead to those in the reasonable preference categories losing out:

> 'It is important that those who are vulnerable and in housing need do not lose out under these changes and that they continue to be in the frame for social housing, together with appropriate support as necessary. This applies not just to victims of domestic violence forced to flee their home, or members of the Armed Forces who have to leave their married quarters, but also to those leaving prison with no family to return to. We believe that the statutory duty on local authorities to frame their allocation scheme to give 'reasonable preference' to certain groups, together with local authorities' wider equalities duties, should serve to ensure that local authorities put in place allocation systems which are fair and that those who are vulnerable and in housing need are properly protected.'[362]

3.187 However, on the literal wording of the HA 1996 Part 6, there is the clear potential for local housing authorities to adopt classes which exclude even

---

[359] *Explanatory memorandum to the Allocation of Housing (Qualification Criteria for Armed Forces) (England) Regulations 2012*, para 7.4.

[360] *Localism and allocations: is it yesterday once more?*, Makreth, [2012] 150 *Adviser*, p 20.

[361] HA 1996, s 166A(3).

[362] *Local decisions: a fairer future for social housing: Consultation* (DCLG, November 2010), para 4.11.

those applicants who, if they were permitted to join the allocation scheme, would be entitled to a statutory 'reasonable preference'.[363] That must be the effect of providing that a local housing authority can decide for itself which 'classes of persons are, or are not, qualifying persons'.[364] If a person does not 'qualify' for an allocation it is difficult to understand how they can be expected to be given a 'reasonable preference' in an allocation scheme.

3.188 That approach to the construction of the HA 1996, Part 6 is also consistent with the provisions for the individual ineligibility of applicants on grounds of unacceptable behaviour which previously applied in England and now only apply in Wales (see **3.203–3.251**). An applicant to whom those provisions apply is simply ineligible even though he or she would otherwise fulfill one or more reasonable preference categories.

3.189 The statutory guidance in relation to the new concept of 'qualification' itself uses terminology such as 'excluding'[365] and 'disqualify'[366] to describe the effects of falling within an adopted class of non-qualifying persons. It is hard to understand how someone excluded or disqualified from a scheme can ever be said to be able to achieve a reasonable preference within it.

3.190 On the other hand, if fixing the qualifying and non-qualifying categories is part of the process of framing a local allocation scheme, then the scheme must be framed so as to give an overall priority to those in the reasonable preference categories.[367]

3.191 The present Government's approach is that somehow a balance must be struck between, on the one hand, the exercise of the power to use non-qualification to exclude whole classes of applicants and on the other the need to give certain groups of applicants a reasonable preference:

'We want to provide local authorities with the power to decide who should qualify to be considered for social housing, while retaining a role for government in determining which groups should have priority for social housing through the statutory reasonable preference requirements....'[368]

3.192 However, the statutory guidance, which might have been expected to explain how such a balance could lawfully be struck, offers what appear to be two diametrically opposite approaches in a single paragraph:

'Housing authorities should avoid setting criteria which disqualify groups of people whose members are likely to be accorded reasonable preference for social housing, for example on medical or welfare grounds. However, authorities may

[363] HA 1996, s 166A(3).
[364] HA 1996, s 160ZA(7).
[365] English Code, paras 2.1 and 3.22.
[366] English Code, para 3.21.
[367] HA 1996, s 166A(3), English Code, para 3.20.
[368] *Local decisions: a fairer future for social housing: Consultation* (DCLG, November 2010) para 4.10.

wish to adopt criteria which would disqualify individuals who satisfy the reasonable preference requirements. This could be the case, for example, if applicants are disqualified on a ground of anti-social behaviour.'[369]

3.193   In light of this confusion it must be virtually inevitable that there will be an early legal challenge brought by an applicant who has been told that he or she falls within a non-qualifying class but would otherwise have been given a reasonable preference under a local allocation scheme.

When to consider qualification

3.194   As with the approach to the eligibility of applicants (see **3.252–3.253**), the statutory guidance recommends that local housing authorities should consider whether an applicant qualifies for an allocation both at the time of the initial application and then again when considering making an allocation, particularly where a long time has elapsed since the original application.[370]

Special cases (armed forces)

3.195   From the outset of its policy programme to enable local housing authorities in England to set local qualifying and non-qualifying classes of applicant once again, the present UK Government was keen to ensure that no disadvantage would be suffered by members of the armed forces and their families who were seeking to access social housing.[371]

3.196   However, in responses to consultation about the scope of the changes, it became clear that some local housing authorities would be introducing quite restrictive qualifying and non-qualifying categories which might exclude ex-services personnel. The Secretary of State has therefore used his regulation-making power[372] to make regulations[373] which prescribe that when deciding which classes of persons are not qualifying persons a local housing authority cannot use the criterion that a person must have a local connection to the district of a local housing authority, if that category applies to a person who is a 'relevant person'.[374] The Regulations came into force on 24 August 2012.[375]

---

[369]   English Code, para 3.21.

[370]   English Code, para 3.26.

[371]   Members of the Armed Forces who have to leave their married quarters were singled out for mention in *Local decisions: a fairer future for social housing: Consultation* (DCLG, November 2010), para 4.11.

[372]   HA 1996, s 160ZA(8)(b).

[373]   The Allocation of Housing (Qualification Criteria for Armed Forces) (England) Regulations 2012, SI 2012/1869, reproduced in Appendix 1.

[374]   Regulation 3.

[375]   Regulation 1(2).

3.197 For the purposes of the regulations the following are 'relevant' persons:

(a) members of the armed forces and former service personnel, where the application for social housing is made within five years of discharge; and

(b) bereaved spouses and civil partners of members of the armed forces leaving services family accommodation following the death of their spouse or partner where that death was wholly or partly attributable to military service; and

(c) serving or former members of the reserve forces who need to move because of a serious injury, medical condition or disability wholly or partly attributable to their service.[376]

3.198 The intention is to recognise the special position of:

(1) members of the armed forces (and their families) whose employment requires them to be mobile and who are likely therefore to be particularly disadvantaged by local connection requirements; and

(2) those injured reservists who may need to move to another local housing authority district to access treatment, care or support.[377]

3.199 The UK Government had initially been inclined simply to provide for an armed forces exception to any 'residence' requirements that might be used to frame non-qualifying classes. However, when it became clear from consultation responses that some local housing authorities might require an employment or family membership connection to a district as an aspect of qualification for an allocation, the Government decided to broaden the reach of its draft regulations so as to give exemption from any qualifying rules based on 'local connection'.[378] The regulations use the same definition of local connection as that used elsewhere in housing legislation.[379]

3.200 The net effect is that, in practical terms, if a local housing authority elects to use 'local connection' as a factor for disqualifying applicants from being qualifying persons under its local allocation arrangements, it cannot adopt the same approach in relation to armed forces personnel and the other related categories of 'relevant' persons. Those persons cannot be excluded from being 'qualifying persons' due to the absence of a local connection (although they may, of course, fail to qualify under qualifying classes framed by some other criteria).

---

[376] Regulation 3(3) and English Code, para 3.27.
[377] English Code, para 3.28.
[378] *Explanatory memorandum to the Allocation of Housing (Qualification Criteria for Armed Forces) (England) Regulations 2012*, paras 7.4 and 8.8.
[379] Regulation 3 and HA 1996, s 199, see **15.42–15.94**.

3.201 In responses to the consultation draft of the current English Code, a number of voluntary and community organisations highlighted groups other than the armed forces who may have difficulty in meeting residency requirements and suggested that local housing authorities should be encouraged *not* to disqualify those groups on those grounds. The suggested groups included other occupations where people are required to be mobile, such as the construction or entertainment industries, those escaping from intimidation or violence, or individuals who are leaving care or prison.[380] The Government decided not to extend the special cases beyond the armed forces.

Decisions on qualification

3.202 A decision that an applicant does not fall within a qualifying class or falls within a non-qualifying class must be notified to the applicant in writing with the grounds for that decision.[381] The local housing allocation scheme must provide the applicant with a right to have a review of such a decision and to be notified in writing of the grounds for any review decision.[382] For information on challenging review decisions see Chapter 2.[383]

INELIGIBILITY DUE TO UNACCEPTABLE BEHAVIOUR (WALES)

Introduction

3.203 If a person is eligible for an allocation of social housing, because they are not caught by the provisions relating to immigration status explored in the first part of this Chapter, they would ordinarily be able to be considered alongside all other applicants seeking a social housing allocation. However, from early 1997 to 18 June 2012, the provisions of HA 1996, Part 6, enabled local housing authorities in both England and Wales to decide, on a case-by-case basis, that certain applicants were ineligible for allocation on account of their previous misconduct.

3.204 When HA 1996, Part 6 was amended in June 2012 to allow local housing authorities in England to introduce qualifying classes of applicants, in the manner described in the second part of this Chapter, the specific power to decide that certain individual applicants were ineligible on grounds of past misconduct became redundant and was repealed in relation to England.[384] This may have left a window of opportunity for applicants who were previously the subject of adverse decisions on eligibility for behaviour-related reasons, or for new applicants who would have been found ineligible for such reasons, to apply

---

[380] *Allocation of accommodation: guidance for local housing authorities in England: Summary of responses to consultation*, (DCLG, June 2012), para 3.18.
[381] HA 1996, s 160ZA(9)(b) and see **2.81**.
[382] HA 1996, s 166A(9)(c) and see **2.99**.
[383] See **2.101–2.115**.
[384] English Code, para 2.4.

successfully to local housing authorities in England before those local housing authorities managed to adopt new allocation schemes containing classes of non-qualifying applicants which included classes related to previous misconduct.

3.205 However, the misconduct-related eligibility provisions remain fully in force in Wales and the text which follows deals primarily with their effect on applications made to local housing authorities in Wales. The text[385] may also be of interest in respect of any outstanding issues arising from their use by local housing authorities in England in relation to decisions made before 18 June 2012.

An overview

3.206 A local housing authority in Wales may decide, but is not required to decide, that an applicant is to be treated as ineligible for the allocation of social housing as a result of his or her past unacceptable behaviour, or the behaviour of a member of his or her household.[386] The wording of the statutory provision (HA 1996, s 160A) prevents local housing authorities in Wales from operating blanket exclusions, and requires them to consider, if they are minded to use the ineligibility provision, the behaviour of each applicant, or of a member of his or her household, individually.

3.207 A local housing authority's decision that an applicant is 'ineligible' on behaviour grounds, and thus excluded from consideration for an allocation, requires consideration of two stages:

(1) Does the applicant meet certain statutory conditions? If so,

(2) Should the local housing authority, in the exercise of its discretion, elect to treat the applicant as 'ineligible' as a result of the applicant fulfilling those conditions?[387]

3.208 As far as the *first stage* of the test for ineligibility on behaviour grounds is concerned, there are two statutory conditions:

(1) that the applicant, or a member of his or her household, has been guilty of past unacceptable behaviour of a specified standard (described in the rest of this Chapter as Condition One);[388] and

---

[385] See too the 2002 English Code reproduced in Appendix 1 of the last edition of this book.
[386] HA 1996, s 160A(7)–(8) and Welsh Code, para 3.20.
[387] HA 1996, s 160A(7).
[388] HA 1996, s 160A(7)(a).

(2) that in the circumstances at the time when the application for allocation is considered, the applicant is unsuitable to be a tenant of the local housing authority by reason of that past behaviour (described in the rest of this Chapter as Condition Two).[389]

3.209 At the *second stage* the local housing authority is deciding, in the exercise of an unfettered discretion, whether to treat an applicant who satisfies both of the two statutory conditions as ineligible for its scheme.

3.210 The two statutory conditions of the *first stage* are intended to provide a 'high test'. During the passage of the then Homelessness Bill,[390] the provisions attracted concern, not just from the opposition during Parliamentary debate, but also from the Joint Select Committee on Human Rights. The then UK government justified the provisions as part of its:

'... wider policy on tackling anti-social behaviour and ensuring that the relevant agencies have the means of dealing with it. The test ... is *a high test*, and will ensure that authorities will be able to decline only those applicants whose behaviour would genuinely render them unsuitable to be a tenant. This provision will enable housing authorities to protect the rights of their existing tenants and others to the peaceful enjoyment of their home and neighbourhood'[391] [emphasis added].

3.211 The UK government emphasised that the power to decide that an individual was ineligible for allocation was a discretionary power, that local housing authorities were not required to use it, and that it could only be used in a manner that was compatible with an applicant's Convention rights.[392] Even an applicant who met the *first stage* conditions may not be found ineligible in the exercise of the *second stage* discretion. The UK government referred to the safety net of accommodation available to those excluded from an allocation under the National Assistance Act 1948 and the Children Act 1989,[393] and noted that persons declared ineligible by virtue of their behaviour would still be eligible for housing benefit, and thus able to access private rented accommodation.[394]

3.212 The Joint Select Committee accepted that the UK government's argument was tenable. It remained concerned that those excluded from eligibility by their behaviour might suffer degrading treatment by reason of homelessness affecting their health and welfare, or suffer a failure of respect for

---

[389] HA 1996, s 160A(7)(b).
[390] Subsequently Homelessness Act 2002.
[391] *DTLR memo to the Joint Select Committee on Human Rights,* para 6.3, reproduced in the Appendix to the report of the Joint Committee dated 7 November 2001.
[392] Rights under the European Convention of Human Rights set out in Human Rights Act 1998, Sch 1.
[393] See **20.16–20.48** and **20.55–20.84**.
[394] *DTLR memo to the Joint Select Committee on Human Rights,* reproduced in the Appendix to the report of the Joint Committee dated 7 November 2001.

their home and family life. Despite those concerns, the Joint Select Committee was satisfied that the provision was compatible with Convention rights.[395]

The statutory conditions

Condition One: guilty of unacceptable behaviour

3.213 The first condition is that the local housing authority must be satisfied that the applicant or a member of his household has been guilty of unacceptable behaviour serious enough to make him unsuitable to be a tenant of that authority.[396]

The statutory definition of 'unacceptable behaviour'

3.214 Parliament has particularly specified, in HA 1996, s 160A(8), what standard of behaviour is to be considered bad enough to meet the first condition for ineligibility. 'Unacceptable behaviour' is defined as only that behaviour, by the applicant or by a member of his or her household, which would, if the applicant were a secure tenant of the local housing authority, entitle it to a possession order on any ground in Housing Act 1985, Part 1, Sch 2 (other than Ground 8).[397]

3.215 This rather curious phrasing generates four important preliminary points.

(1) Literal or hypothetical approach

3.216 The test may arise for application either literally or hypothetically, in that the applicant may or may not have been a secure tenant of the local housing authority at the time of the relevant past misconduct. If the applicant, or a relevant member of his or her household, was at that time a secure tenant of the same local housing authority and a possession order was obtained, then the definition can be readily and literally applied.[398] There will be a possession order in existence for the local housing authority to consider. But in many more circumstances the question will be being posed hypothetically. The local housing authority will be asking itself: 'What if the applicant had at that time been one of our secure tenants?' This hypothetical approach will be needed where the applicant was, at the relevant time:

---

[395] The ineligibility provision relating to misconduct has yet to generate any litigation claiming that it is incompatible with the provisions of Human Rights Act 1998, although it has been unsuccessfully contended that a decision that an applicant is not eligible for an allocation engages (and may infringe) the right to respect for a home protected by Human Rights Act 1998, Sch 1, art 8: *R (Dixon) v Wandsworth London Borough Council* [2007] EWHC 3075 (Admin), (2008) February *Legal Action* p 40, Admin Ct. at [28]-[30] and *R (Dixon) v Wandsworth London Borough Council* [2008] EWCA Civ 595, (2008) July *Legal Action*, p 22, CA at [11].

[396] HA 1996, s 160A(7)(a).

[397] HA 1996, s 160A(8).

[398] Welsh Code, para 3.22(i).

- only an introductory or non-secure tenant of the same local housing authority; or

- a secure tenant of the same local housing authority where the tenant lost that tenancy otherwise than in response to a possession order;[399] or

- a secure or other tenant of any other local housing authority; or

- a tenant, of whatever type, of any other landlord; or

- a homeowner; or

- a guest, lodger, or any other form of occupier of a previous home.

3.217 Indeed, Condition Two of the statutory conditions (discussed at **3.243–3.251**) also contains an element that requires either a literal or a hypothetical approach, relating to the identity of the likely future landlord. If the likely future landlord is the local housing authority itself, a literal approach can be taken: 'Is the applicant 'unsuitable' for one of our own tenancies?' But the ineligibility test is also available where a successful applicant could only expect to be nominated to a different landlord (a registered social landlord in Wales or a different local housing authority).[400] In such a case, the test is one of suitability to be the local housing authority's tenant even though there is no prospect or possibility of such a tenancy.

(2) The meaning of 'entitle'

3.218 The second general point to emerge from the definition is the curious use of the word 'entitle' in the phrase 'would ... entitle the authority to a possession order ...'.[401] None of the relevant grounds for possession are mandatory grounds.[402] Instead, all of them require the court to find that 'it is reasonable to make the order' for possession.[403] Strictly speaking, it is impossible to say that any landlord is 'entitled' to possession where possession is sought on a discretionary ground that depends (for the grant of an order) on the exercise of discretion by the court. It has been left to the Code of Guidance to spell out that the intention is that the definition will only catch behaviour so bad that a landlord could properly be said to be 'entitled' to an outright order for possession from the court.[404] This has led a judge to accept that 'the effect

---

[399] In *R (Dixon) v Wandsworth London Borough Council* [2007] EWHC 3075 (Admin), (2008) February *Legal Action* p 40, Admin Ct. and *R (Dixon) v Wandsworth London Borough Council* [2008] EWCA Civ 595, (2008) July *Legal Action* p 22, CA the applicant's secure tenancy was lost when the other joint tenant under his tenancy gave notice to quit.

[400] Because the local housing authority may have disposed of all of its stock to one or several other social landlords.

[401] HA 1996, s 160A(8)(a).

[402] See Housing Act 1985, Sch 2.

[403] Under Housing Act 1985, s 84(2)(a). These grounds are therefore commonly referred to as 'discretionary grounds' for possession.

[404] Welsh Code, para 3.22(ii); and see **3.236–3.239**.

of the provisions is to require the local housing authority to be satisfied that a notional county court judge would probably make an outright order for possession in the circumstances of the case'.[405]

(3) The meaning of 'behaviour'

3.219 The statutory wording is concerned with the 'behaviour' of the applicant, or, where relevant, that of a member of his or her household. Indeed, the terminology used is 'guilty of unacceptable behaviour'.[406] This would naturally be understood to require some past action or activity on that person's part. But in this context it must, at least arguably, also include an applicant's omission, failure to act, passivity or inactivity in circumstances where there has been an expectation of action. Otherwise it would not embrace common cases of 'unacceptable behaviour' such as:

(1)   failing to pay rent or other charges; or

(2)   simple inactive non-compliance with obligations under a tenancy, eg failing to maintain the garden; or

(3)   failing to control the actions of lodgers or visitors.

3.220 Such a wide construction would be consistent with the judicial approach to the term 'guilty of conduct causing or likely to cause a nuisance or annoyance' in a statutory ground for possession.[407] It is rather surprising that, in this context, parliamentary counsel did not adopt the now familiar rubric of 'deliberately does or fails to do anything' to be found in other provisions of HA 1996.[408]

3.221 The statutory emphasis on the behaviour of the applicant (or a member of the applicant's household) was relied upon by the claimant in *R (McQ) v Bolton Metropolitan Borough Council*.[409] He had given up his former home for reasons associated with the anti-social behaviour of third parties with whom he had been involved. He argued that that conduct (being neither his conduct nor that of any member of his household) was irrelevant. The Administrative Court held that the claimant's former association with the third parties – members of a paramilitary organisation in Northern Ireland which had undertaken the anti-social conduct – itself constituted ample factual material to support the decision that *his own* behaviour would have notionally made out the statutory grounds for possession.

---

[405]   *R (Dixon) v Wandsworth London Borough Council* [2007] EWHC 3075 (Admin), (2008) February *Legal Action* p 40, Admin Ct. at [17].

[406]   HA 1996, s 160A(7)(a).

[407]   Housing Act 1985, Sch 2, Ground 2. See also *Kensington and Chelsea Royal London Borough Council v Simmonds* (1997) 29 HLR 507, CA.

[408]   Such as the test of becoming homelessness intentionally in HA 1996, s 191(1). See **14.25–14.162**.

[409]   [2005] EWHC 1285 (Admin), (2005) August *Legal Action*, p 17, Admin Ct.

(4) Household membership

3.222   Plainly, the policy of the legislation, reflected in the wording used, is to avoid the ineligibility control from being circumvented by an application being made in the name of an innocent member of the household rather than by the actual perpetrator of the misconduct. Accordingly, local housing authorities may not only consider the applicant's own behaviour but also that of 'a member of his [or her] household'.[410] HA 1996, Part 6 contains no statutory definition of the term 'household'. It will therefore be for the local housing authority to decide which persons constitute the applicant's household for these purposes. The local housing authority's allocation scheme might set out how membership of a household will be ascertained or may be silent on the issue, leaving the decision to be made by officers on the facts of individual cases interpreting 'household' by reference 'to its ordinary, everyday usage'.[411]

3.223   HA 1996, Part 6 appears to be looking to the *present* household composition. So, an applicant with an unblemished past may find that he or she is rendered ineligible by having formed a common household with a person who brings to that household past misconduct, either the new partner's own misconduct, or that of any other person. As will be seen, the innocent applicant is only saved from any adverse consequence of the new partner's past misconduct if that history is immaterial to the applicant's own present suitability to be a tenant.[412]

3.224   But the statutory provision also engages with the *past* composition of the applicant's household. HA 1996, Part 6, when defining unacceptable behaviour, does so in terms that include past 'behaviour of a member of his [or her] household'.[413] Given that the statutory language is taking attention back to past misbehaviour, it must be capable of being satisfied by the misconduct of a person who was at that time a member of the applicant's household but is no longer. This, it appears, protects against the situation in which an applicant may have temporarily separated from a past member of his or her household to avoid the prospect of ineligibility through misconduct, with every intention of resuming residence together once a tenancy has been allocated. It does mean, however, that an innocent applicant, whose former miscreant household member has permanently departed, may nevertheless still be disqualified. Whilst a safeguard is provided by the requirement that the past misconduct must presently render the applicant unsuitable as a tenant (Condition Two – discussed at **3.243–3.251**), that requirement may well be met, even where the perpetrator is long gone, if it is considered material that the applicant failed to bring to an earlier end the other person's misconduct.

---

[410]   HA 1996, s 160A(7)(a).

[411]   *R (Ariemuguvbe) v Islington London Borough Council* [2009] EWHC 470 (Admin), (2009) April *Legal Action*, p 21 at [14], upheld on appeal in *R (Ariemuguvbe) v Islington London Borough Council* [2009] EWCA 1218, (2010) January *Legal Action*, p 35, CA.

[412]   See **3.10**.

[413]   HA 1996, s 160A(8)(b).

Applying the statutory definition of 'unacceptable behaviour'

3.225 On detailed examination, the definition in HA 1996, s 160A(8) itself breaks down into three constituent questions, each of which the local housing authority needs to address in succession:

(1)   Is one, or are more than one, of the seven relevant grounds for possession made out by the circumstances of the past behaviour?

(2)   If so, would a court consider it reasonable to make an order for possession under Housing Act 1985, s 84 on the basis of that behaviour?

(3)   If so, would a court make an *outright* order for possession?

3.226 The applicant is only guilty of 'unacceptable behaviour' for the purposes of this statutory provision if the local housing authority is able to answer 'Yes' to all three questions. It can be readily envisaged that different local housing authorities may well give different answers to some or all of these questions, even when considering the same set of facts. Indeed, it might be thought common knowledge that a county court judge sitting at one court would certainly evict for a particular level of misconduct which, had the matter been tried before the county court judge at another court, would have resulted in dismissal or adjournment of the possession claim or the making of a suspended or postponed order for possession. Precisely because the making of a possession order does require a discretionary decision, the statutory definition is sensitive to such variables.[414]

3.227 The first step in applying the statutory definition is to be clear as to the wording of the relevant statutory grounds for possession. The current wording of Housing Act 1985, Sch 2, Part 1, Grounds 1–7, is given in Table A.[415]

---

[414]   See **3.236**.
[415]   See also Welsh Code, Annex 10.

Table A
Grounds For Possession Under Housing Act 1985, Sch 2, Part 1

Ground 1	Rent lawfully due from the tenant has not been paid or an obligation of the tenancy has been broken or not performed.
Ground 2	The tenant or a person residing in or visiting the dwelling-house: (1) has been guilty of conduct causing or likely to cause a nuisance or annoyance to a person residing, visiting or otherwise engaging in a lawful activity in the locality; or (2) has been convicted of: (i) using the dwelling-house or allowing it to be used for immoral or illegal purposes; or (ii) an indictable offence committed in, or in the locality of, the dwelling house.[416]
Ground 2A	The dwelling-house was occupied (whether alone or with others) by a married couple, a couple who are civil partners of each other,[417] a couple living together as husband and wife or a couple living together as if they were civil partners[418] and: (a) one or both of the partners is a tenant of the dwelling-house; (b) one partner has left because of violence or threats of violence by the other towards: (i) that partner, or (ii) a member of the family of that partner who was residing with that partner immediately before the partner left; and (c) the court is satisfied that the partner who has left is unlikely to return.

[416] 'Indictable' inserted by Serious Organised Crime and Police Act 2005, s 111 and Sch 7, in force from 1 January 2006 (Serious Organised Crime and Police Act 2005 (Commencement No 4 and Transitory Provision) Order 2005, SI 2005/3495, art 2(1)(m).)

[417] Inserted by Civil Partnership Act 2004, s 81, s 263(2) and Sch 8, in force from 5 December 2005 (Civil Partnership Act 2004 (Commencement No 2) Order 2005, SI 2005/3175.

[418] Inserted by Civil Partnership Act 2004, s 81, s 263(2) and Sch 8, in force from 5 December 2005 (Civil Partnership Act 2004 (Commencement No 2) Order 2005, SI 2005/3175.

Ground 3	The condition of the dwelling-house or of any of the common parts has deteriorated owing to acts of waste by, or the neglect or default of, the tenant or a person residing in the dwelling-house and, in the case of an act of waste by, or the neglect or default of, a person lodging with the tenant or a sub-tenant of his, the tenant has not taken such steps as he ought reasonably to have taken for the removal of the lodger or sub-tenant.
Ground 4	The condition of furniture provided by the landlord for use under the tenancy, or for use in the common parts, has deteriorated owing to ill-treatment by the tenant or a person residing in the dwelling-house and, in the case of ill-treatment by a person lodging with the tenant or a sub-tenant of his, the tenant has not taken such steps as he ought reasonably to have taken for the removal of the lodger or sub-tenant.
Ground 5	The tenant is the person, or one of the persons, to whom the tenancy was granted and the landlord was induced to grant the tenancy by a false statement made knowingly or recklessly by: (a)　the tenant; or (b)　a person acting at the tenant's instigation.
Ground 6	The tenancy was assigned to the tenant, or to a predecessor in title of his who is a member of his family and is residing in the dwelling-house, by an assignment made by virtue of s 92 (assignments by way of exchange) and a premium was paid either in connection with that assignment or the assignment which the tenant or predecessor himself made by virtue of that section. In this paragraph 'premium' means any fine or other like sum and any other pecuniary consideration in addition to rent.
Ground 7	The dwelling-house forms part of, or is within the curtilage of, a building which, or so much of it as is held by the landlord, is held mainly for purposes other than housing purposes and consists mainly of accommodation other than housing accommodation, and:

	(a)	the dwelling-house was let to the tenant or a predecessor in title of his in consequence of the tenant or predecessor being in the employment of the landlord; or of
		– a local authority;
		– a new town corporation;
		– a housing action trust;
		– an urban development corporation; or
		– the governors of an aided school; and
	(b)	the tenant or a person residing in the dwelling-house has been guilty of conduct such that, having regard to the purpose for which the building is used, it would not be right for him to continue in occupation of the dwelling-house.

3.228 In practice, behaviour that falls within either or both of Grounds 1 or 2[419] (arrears, breach of tenancy, and/or nuisance) is likely to be the most common form of 'unacceptable behaviour' considered by local housing authorities. But when considering the applicant's behaviour, or that of a member of his or her household, local housing authorities should take care to ensure that the behaviour would in fact have given rise to a ground for possession by satisfying the precise wording of the statute. For example, the only 'rent' that counts for Ground 1 purposes is 'rent lawfully due', and not unpaid instalments of overpaid housing benefit, or arrears owed by a previous tenant.[420] Likewise, nuisance behaviour or indictable offences committed *away* from the locality of the dwelling house do not fall within Ground 2.[421]

3.229 However, if the applicant's behaviour, or that of a member of his or her household, demonstrably does fall within the precise words of one or more of the grounds for possession, the next question is whether it would have been reasonable for a court to make an order for possession on those facts. The question arises because all of the prescribed grounds are discretionary grounds upon which the landlord must be able to satisfy the court that 'it is reasonable to make' a possession order (of whatever type).[422] The test of reasonableness is a very broad one, and will depend on the individual circumstances of each case. The courts themselves are warned by judicial precedent against applying hard and fast rules.[423] The Welsh Code suggests that in deciding whether it is

---

[419] Housing Act 1985, Sch 2.
[420] *Tickner v Clifton* [1929] 1 KB 207, Div Ct.
[421] At the time the edition was being prepared, the Welsh Government was considering responses to a consultation on a proposal to extend Ground 2 to cover such cases: *Consultation Document A New Mandatory Power of Possession for Anti-Social Behaviour* (Welsh Government, 2011).
[422] Housing Act 1985, s 84(2).
[423] *Cresswell v Hodgson* [1951] 2 KB 92, CA and, more recently, *Whitehouse v Lee* [2009] EWCA Civ 375, [2010] HLR 11CA.

reasonable to make an order a court may consider 'the conduct of both parties and the public interest'[424] and that the court must have regard to the interests and circumstances of the tenant (and of his or her household), the local housing authority and the wider public.[425]

3.230 Where the behaviour consists of allowing 'rent arrears' to accrue, a court hearing possession proceedings would normally consider, on the question of reasonableness:

- the level of the arrears; and

- the reason for the arrears accruing, including the degree of personal culpability for those arrears; and

- any outstanding housing benefit issues; and

- any offers to repay; and

- the tenant's, and his or her household's, personal circumstances.[426]

3.231 If relevant past behaviour was 'nuisance or annoyance', the court hearing a possession claim is required to consider:

- the effect that the nuisance or annoyance has had on persons other than the person against whom the order is sought; and

- any continuing effect the nuisance or annoyance is likely to have on such persons; and

- the effect that the nuisance or annoyance would be likely to have on such persons if the conduct is repeated.[427]

3.232 The court hearing a possession claim based on nuisance behaviour should also consider:

- the tenant's personal circumstances and those of his or her household; and

- the landlord's obligation to its other tenants and to the neighbours; and

---

[424] Welsh Code, Annex 10, p 237.

[425] Welsh Code, para 3.22(i)(b).

[426] *Woodspring District Council v Taylor* (1982) 4 HLR 95, CA; *Second WRVS v Blair* (1987) 19 HLR 104, CA; *Haringey London Borough Council v Stewart* (1991) 23 HLR 557, CA; *Lambeth London Borough Council v Thomas* (1998) 30 HLR 89, CA; and *Brent London Borough Council v Marks* (1999) 31 HLR 343, CA. See also Luba et al *Defending Possession Proceedings* (Legal Action Group, 7th edn, 2010).

[427] Housing Act 1985, s 85A, inserted by Anti-social Behaviour Act 2003, s 16 (with effect from 30 June 2004).

- the degree of personal culpability of the tenant; and

- any factors explaining or mitigating the behaviour (such as a medical condition or a disability); and

- the degree of compliance since notices were served and/or proceedings issued; and

- any assurances as to future conduct; and

- any other relevant circumstances.[428]

3.233 Where the behaviour in question consists of the commission of a serious criminal offence in the dwelling-house or in the locality of the dwelling-house, it would only be in exceptional circumstances that the court would consider that it is not reasonable to make an order for possession[429] (although, in such a case, a court should also consider the possibility that an order for possession, suspended or postponed on conditions, could succeed in controlling the tenant's behaviour).[430]

3.234 In *R (McQ) v Bolton Metropolitan Borough Council*,[431] the applicant argued that the local housing authority's decision on his application had failed to address the question of whether a judge would have found it 'reasonable' to make an order for possession (assuming that a ground for possession based on anti-social behaviour would have been made out). In refusing permission to bring judicial review proceedings, the Administrative Court held that there was only one answer to the question of whether it would have been reasonable to make an order for possession on the facts of the applicant's case, which was that it would have been reasonable.

---

[428] *Cresswell v Hodgson* [1951] 2 KB 92, CA; *Woking Borough Council v Bistram* (1993) 27 HLR 1, CA; *Wandsworth London Borough Council v Hargreaves* (1994) 27 HLR 142, CA; *Kensington and Chelsea Royal London Borough Council v Simmonds* (1996) 29 HLR 507, CA; *West Kent Housing Association v Davies* (1998) 31 HLR 415, CA; *Camden London Borough Council v Gilsenan* (1999) 31 HLR 81 CA; *Croydon London Borough Council v Moody* (1999) 31 HLR 738, CA; *Portsmouth City Council v Bryant* (2000) 32 HLR 906, CA; *Newcastle upon Tyne City Council v Morrison* (2000) 32 HLR 891, CA; *Lambeth London Borough Council v Howard* [2001] EWCA Civ 468, (2001) 33 HLR 636, CA; *North Devon Housing Association v Brazier* [2003] EWHC 574, [2003] 35 HLR 59, QBD; *Manchester City Council v Higgins* [2005] EWCA Civ 1423, [2006] 1 All ER 841, CA; and *North Devon Homes v Batchelor* [2008] EWCA Civ 840, (2008) September *Legal Action*, p 23 are some of the reported cases on whether it would be reasonable to make a possession order in respect of nuisance or other anti-social behaviour. See also Luba et al *Defending Possession Proceedings* (Legal Action Group, 7th edn, 2010).

[429] *Bristol City Council v Mousah* (1997) 30 HLR 32, CA, but see also *North Devon Homes v Batchelor* [2008] EWCA Civ 840, (2008) September *Legal Action*, p 23.

[430] *Norwich City Council v Famuyiwa* [2004] EWCA Civ 1770, (2005) February *Legal Action*, p 34, CA; *Sheffield City Council v Shaw* [2007] EWCA Civ 42, [2007] HLR 25, CA; and *Sandwell Metropolitan Borough Council v Hensley* [2007] EWCA Civ 1425, [2008] HLR 22, CA.

[431] [2005] EWHC 1285 (Admin), (2005) August *Legal Action*, p 17, Admin Ct; and see **3.221**.

3.235   For guidance on the application of the reasonableness requirement as operated in relation to the other five relevant prescribed grounds of possession see the discussion in Luba, Gallagher, McConnell and Madge *Defending Possession Proceedings.*[432]

3.236   The final question for the local housing authority, in applying the 'unacceptable behaviour' limb of the ineligibility test, is whether the court did make (or, in the hypothetical cases, would have made) an outright or a suspended/postponed (conditional) order. HA 1996, Part 6 is silent as to whether suspended or postponed (conditional) possession orders fall within the statutory definition, which refers only to 'a possession order'.[433] However, the Code of Guidance is very clear that only behaviour that would result in an outright order for possession falls within the statute.[434] During the Parliamentary debate on the then Homelessness Bill,[435] the opposition quoted figures for the number of possession actions brought by social landlords in 2000, showing that in 82% of possession cases the social landlord had believed that it was entitled to an outright order for possession, but the court decided that it was not.[436] In response, the Minister gave assurances that only behaviour justifying an outright, rather than a suspended or postponed (conditional), possession order would fall within this section:

> '... the authority would need to be satisfied that, if a possession order were granted, it would not be suspended by the court.'[437]

3.237   If an outright order was in fact granted in relation to the past misconduct, there is, perhaps, little difficulty with this element of the definition. But applying it to hypothetical cases[438] is probably the most difficult part of the local housing authority's decision-making on ineligibility for misbehaviour. Whether an order is made outright, or is suspended or postponed on terms, is a very broad discretionary decision for the court, taking into account all the circumstances as at the date of the decision.[439] It is not sufficient for the local housing authority to conclude that, on the facts as they have emerged, it would have requested that the court make an outright possession order. For the applicant not to be eligible, the local housing authority must be able to conclude that a court *would* in all probability have actually made an outright possession order and *not* a suspended or postponed (conditional) possession order.

---

[432]   *Defending Possession Proceedings* (Legal Action Group, 7th edn, 2010).

[433]   HA 1996, s 160A(8).

[434]   Welsh Code, para 3.22(ii).

[435]   Subsequently the Homelessness Act 2002.

[436]   *Hansard*, HL Deb, vol 629, ser 6, col CWH 48 (10 December 2001) (Baroness Maddock): 150,000 actions were started (the vast majority being for rent arrears); 65% resulted in an order being made; but only 18% resulted in an outright order for possession. For the latest statistics, see footnote 442.

[437]   *Hansard*, HL Deb, vol 629, ser 6, col CWH 51 (10 December 2001) (Lord Falconer).

[438]   See **3.216–3.217**.

[439]   Housing Act 1985, s 85(2).

3.238 Examples of behaviour that may lead to only a suspended or postponed possession (conditional) order are given in the Code:

- modest rent arrears, absence of persistent default, delays in housing benefit, liability for a partner's debts, the applicant was not in control of the household finances or was unaware of the accrual of arrears, the local housing authority failed to provide help and advice;[440] or

- where allegations of nuisance are relatively minor, or the nuisance was caused by a member of the household who has since left, or the court would have been satisfied that a suspended or postponed (conditional) order would be sufficient to control the household's future behaviour.[441]

3.239 Local housing authorities frequently request that courts make outright possession orders, but they are far less successful in obtaining them.[442]

3.240 As far as *rent arrears* are concerned, day-to-day practice in the courts suggests that suspended or postponed (conditional) possession orders are made regularly. Postponed or suspended (conditional) possession orders are not confined to cases of arrears that are the responsibility, but not the fault, of the tenant. In practice, suspended or postponed (conditional) possession orders are made where there are realistic offers by the tenant to repay the arrears, however the arrears accrued.[443]

3.241 In *nuisance cases*, suspended or postponed (conditional) possession orders have been approved by the Court of Appeal where the behaviour appears to have ceased, or where the court considers that a postponed (conditional) possession order should be a sufficient deterrent from future misconduct.[444] Often the principal considerations for the court are whether the tenant has some insight into the nuisance caused to his or her neighbours, and whether the court can accept the tenant's assurances as to future behaviour. The prescribed statutory criteria which apply in a nuisance case and may have driven the court to be satisfied that it was 'reasonable' to order possession do not expressly apply to the stage at which the court is deciding whether the order should be outright, suspended or postponed, but they are intended to remind

---

[440] Welsh Code, para 3.22(ii).
[441] Welsh Code, para 3.22(ii).
[442] In 2011, social landlords commenced 93,632 claims for possession; 41,181, suspended possession orders were made and only 21,920 outright orders for possession. The latter will include claims by registered social landlords under mandatory grounds for possession (HA 1988, s 21, and Sch 2, Ground 8). Overall, outright possession orders were made in about a quarter of the claims for possession, including claims brought under mandatory grounds (*Judicial Statistics 2011*, Ministry of Justice, June 2012, Table 1.2).
[443] *Lambeth London Borough Council v Henry* (1999) 32 HLR 874, CA; and *Taj v Ali (No 2)* (2001) 33 HLR 259, CA.
[444] *Kensington and Chelsea Royal London Borough Council v Simmonds* (1996) 29 HLR 507, CA; *West Kent Housing Association v Davies* (1998) 31 HLR 415, CA; *Portsmouth City Council v Bryant* (2000) 32 HLR 906, CA; *Greenwich London Borough Council v Grogan* (2001) 33 HLR 12, CA; *Gallagher v Castle Vale Housing Action Trust* [2001] EWCA Civ 944, (2001) 33 HLR 72, CA; and *Sheffield City Council v Shaw* [2007] EWCA Civ 42, [2007] HLR 25, CA.

the court that the focus is on the effect that nuisance and annoyance has on others, and it would be appropriate to consider them again at this stage.[445]

3.242   Two cases well illustrate the operation of this element of the statutory conditions for ineligibility on behaviour grounds:

(1)   In *R (Dixon) v Wandsworth London Borough Council*,[446] the applicant had a history of drug-related incidents at his former home. He accepted that a ground for possession would have been made out and that a judge would have found it reasonable to have made a possession order. However, he challenged the decision of the local housing authority – that he was not eligible for an allocation – on the grounds that his conduct would not have led to the making of an outright order, but only to a suspended or postponed (conditional) order. His claim failed. The judge was satisfied that, in reaching the decision that a county court would probably have granted an outright order, the reviewing officer had applied the correct test, had regard to the relevant considerations, made proper findings of fact (in a lengthy decision letter) and had not reached an irrational conclusion. The applicant's renewed application for permission to appeal was rejected by the Court of Appeal, which said:

> 'it was open to the authority to conclude that an outright order was likely to be made on the facts of this case. The applicant had a history of drug abuse for a period of ten years, during which time the flat was raided three times. The raid that resulted in this conviction had caused £1000 worth of damage to the flat itself, and each raid must have been very disturbing for the applicant's neighbours.'[447]

(2)   In *R (M) v Hackney London Borough Council*,[448] the applicant was an elderly council tenant living alone and seeking a transfer. He had a long history of convictions for sexual offences and in 2004 he had been made subject, by consent, to a sexual offences prevention order which recited activities relating to a teenage boy. The local housing authority decided that the events of 2004 were so serious that had possession been sought on the basis of them the court would have granted an outright order. Dismissing a claim for judicial review of that decision, the judge emphasised that the judgment as to whether an outright order would have been made was one for the housing authority not the reviewing court. He said:

---

[445]   Housing Act 1985, s 85A, added by Anti-social Behaviour Act 2003, s 16(1) (with effect from 30 June 2004), *Lambeth London Borough Council v Debrah* [2007] EWCA Civ 1503, (2008) May *Legal Action*, p 44, CA. As to the more general question of whether a conditional or outright order would be made in a nuisance case see *Moat Housing Group-South Ltd v Harris & Hartless* [2005] EWCA 287, [2005] HLR 33, CA; and *Manchester City Council v Higgins* [2005] EWCA Civ 1423, [2006] 1 All ER 841, CA per Ward LJ at [29].

[446]   [2007] EWHC Admin 3075, (2008) February *Legal Action* p 40, Admin Ct.

[447]   [2008] EWCA Civ 595, (2008) July *Legal Action* p 22, CA at [7].

[448]   [2009] EWHC 2255 (Admin), (2009) May *Legal Action*, p 26.

'The Council took the view that the incident of 2004 constituted anti-social behaviour sufficient to justify an outright possession order. In considering that matter I have regard to two background factors. In *Hensley*[449] Gage LJ referred to the need for a council, as a provider of social housing, to make sure that its properties are properly managed and kept free from undesirable activity. It is in my view also necessary to underline the remarks in the judgment of Otton LJ, which I have quoted, that the judicial and administrative functions should not be elided.[450] Admittedly the remarks were in a somewhat different context. But the message to me is clear: it is not for me to allocate Hackney's housing.'[451]

Condition Two: unsuitable to be a tenant

3.243 The second condition necessary to sustain a decision of ineligibility on behaviour grounds is that, at the time that the application for allocation falls to be considered, the applicant is still unsuitable to be a tenant of the local housing authority by reason of past behaviour.[452] It must be noted that the relevant date for applying this test is *not* the date that the application for allocation was made (which will be an earlier, and sometimes considerably earlier, date than the critical date, which is the date on which the local housing authority reaches a decision on eligibility or concludes a review of that decision). Although the test refers to suitability to be a tenant of the housing authority, it may fall to be applied even by a local housing authority that no longer has any housing stock that it could let to tenants.[453]

3.244 In determining whether past behaviour renders the applicant currently 'unsuitable', local housing authorities should consider whether the tenant's behaviour has improved,[454] whether the circumstances that caused the behaviour have changed (eg in the case of nuisance behaviour that was caused by drug or alcohol problems whether the tenant has successfully resolved those problems), whether the member of the household who was responsible for the behaviour remains a member of the applicant's household, and whether it can accept any assurances from the applicant as to future behaviour.[455]

 3.245 If the local housing authority has reason to believe that the past unacceptable behaviour was due to physical, mental or learning difficulties, it should consider whether the applicant could now maintain a tenancy with appropriate care and support. Local housing authorities cannot adopt a

---

[449] *Sandwell Metropolitan Borough Council v Hensley* [2007] EWCA Civ 1425, [2008] HLR 22, CA.

[450] Referring to the judgment of Otton LJ in *City of Bristol v Mousah* (1998) 30 HLR 32 at [40].

[451] Per Cranston J at [36].

[452] HA 1996, s 160A(7)(b). Welsh Code, para 3.22(iii).

[453] See **3.217**.

[454] Welsh Code, para 3.22(iii).

[455] *Hansard*, HL Deb, vol 629, ser 6, col CWH 52, (10 December 2001), the Minister, Lord Falconer, referred to the circumstances as 'all the relevant matters before it. Those will include all the circumstances relevant to the particular applicant, whether health, dependents or other factors'.

blanket approach of treating all applicants who were in the past guilty of nuisance behaviour, or were in substantial rent arrears, as ineligible.[456]

The exercise of the local housing authority's discretion

3.246 Even if the statutory conditions for ineligibility on the basis of past behaviour are made out, the local housing authority must go on to consider whether to exercise its discretion to treat the applicant as ineligible due to that unacceptable behaviour. The word used in the statute is 'may' and not 'shall', making it clear that the local housing authority has such a discretion.[457]

3.247 The local housing authority must take into account, in exercising this discretion, the applicant's particular circumstances, any health needs, any dependents and any other relevant factors.[458] The importance of the discretion is most acutely demonstrated in cases where the applicant meets the statutory conditions for ineligibility by reason of previous default in payment of rent and still has arrears outstanding. The local housing authority must be careful not to automatically bar such applicants but instead must exercise discretion on a case-by-case basis. It is essential to avoid loose language which suggests that a fixed rule rather than a discretion is being exercised, eg 'It is the policy of this Council not to make offers to applicants who owe property related debts'.[459]

3.248 The local housing authority, faced with a case meeting the statutory conditions, could nevertheless decide to accept the applicant as eligible for its allocation scheme, but give him or her no preference (even if she or he would otherwise have been entitled to a statutory reasonable preference).[460] That is because, if the behaviour affects the applicant's suitability to be a tenant but does not meet the strict ineligibility test, it can still be taken into account when deciding what priority the applicant receives within the scheme.[461] The Code reminds local housing authorities that they are not obliged to find that an applicant is ineligible on the grounds of unacceptable behaviour, but could

---

[456] Welsh Code, para 3.22(iii). In *R (Onuegbu) v Hackney London Borough Council* [2005] EWHC 1277 (Admin), (2005) August *Legal Action*, p 17, Admin Ct, Hackney explained its operation of the eligibility test in relation to an existing tenant who had rent arrears. Hackney said that its scheme provided that it would assess the application for a transfer, allow the applicant onto its scheme and give the applicant the points to which he or she would be entitled. However, if the applicant then reached the top of the list, he or she would not be offered accommodation. Instead, the applicant would be by-passed, because of his or her rent arrears, and the accommodation offered to the next applicant on the list.

[457] HA 1996, s 160A(7).

[458] Welsh Code, para 3.23.

[459] That text is taken from a decision letter cited in *R (Joseph) v Newham London Borough Council* [2008] EWHC 1637 (Admin), (2009) September *Legal Action* p 34, Admin Ct. The claimant went on to succeed in the claim for judicial review because the property related debt on which the council was relying was an irrecoverable overpayment of housing benefit: *R (Joseph) v Newham London Borough Council* [2009] EWHC 2983 (Admin), (2010) May *Legal Action* p 23 Admin Ct.

[460] HA 1996, s 167(2B); Welsh Code, para 3.25.

[461] See **4.144**.

instead give the applicant no preference.[462] However, the local housing authority cannot refuse to give any preference at all to an applicant in a category entitled to a reasonable preference except on the same specified grounds as the 'unacceptable behaviour' test of eligibility.[463]

3.249 The Welsh Code sets out detailed policy considerations for local housing authorities to take into account when they are deciding whether or not to treat applicants as ineligible on the grounds of unacceptable behaviour. Starting from the view that 'barriers to social housing should be minimised', the Code recommends that local housing authorities should:

- consider their role as providers of social housing in order to meet housing need in their area;

- develop their own 'unacceptable behaviour' policies specifying the grounds when a person is likely to be thought ineligible;

- ensure that the procedures used are robust;

- try to keep exclusions to a minimum;

- work collaboratively with the police, probation services and other statutory and voluntary agencies to share information; and

- monitor and evaluate their policies and practice.[464]

3.250 The Welsh Code suggests that policies regarding the application of sanctions on the grounds of unacceptable behaviour should:

> 'accommodate the broader Welsh Government policy aims of equality of opportunity, social inclusion and sustainability. Therefore, sanctions to exclude people from social housing should be kept to a minimum and support mechanisms developed to maximise opportunities for people to secure social housing.'[465]

3.251 There has been no systematic national monitoring of the operation of the ineligibility provisions relating to behaviour. It is simply not known how many applicants have been held to fall within the statutory conditions and how many of those have gone on to be excluded from an allocation scheme in the exercise of a local housing authority's discretion. A limited study of local housing authorities in England[466] found that 'considerable staff member discretion is often used in determining appropriate treatment of applicants with rent arrears or believed previously responsible for anti-social behaviour. Whether actions taken are fully recorded and monitored is a question beyond

---

[462] Welsh Code, para 3.25.
[463] HA 1996, s 167(2A), (2B) and (2C); Welsh Code, para 3.26. See also **4.155–4.163**.
[464] Welsh Code, para 3.29.
[465] Welsh Code, para 3.19.
[466] *Exploring local authority policy and practice on housing allocations* (CLG, July 2009).

the scope of this research.'[467] In Wales, 11 local housing authorities participated in a study specifically looking at exclusions from allocation schemes.[468] Of those, eight local housing authorities provided copies of their relevant policies. The researchers found that 'not all the exclusion policies and procedures examined were lawful' and that, during the single year 2006–07, four of those authorities had excluded a total of 129 applicants.

WHEN TO DETERMINE ELIGIBILITY AND QUALIFICATION

3.252 Under HA 1996, Part 6, as originally enacted, the *eligibility* test operated as a control on the admission of an applicant to the local housing register. With the abolition in 2003 of the requirement to keep housing registers, the scheme now works by prohibiting the specific allocation of housing to ineligible applicants. This has led to the practice of testing eligibility twice in respect of any given applicant. First, the eligibility tests are operated when an applicant initially applies for consideration under the particular local allocation scheme. Second, assuming satisfaction of the tests at that stage, they are applied again later when the allocation of a specific property is being contemplated. For an applicant who passed the eligibility test when he or she initially applied, this can mean that changed circumstances might render him or her ineligible just prior to the point at which he or she would have been allocated a property. The English Code advises that a similar approach should be taken in relation to checking at both stages for 'qualification'.[469]

3.253 There are two obvious justifications for this double testing.[470] First, if an applicant is admitted for consideration under the local scheme, she or he will have a reasonable (or 'legitimate') expectation that the local housing authority has satisfied itself that he or she is entitled to be allocated property under that scheme. So it is important that eligibility and/or qualification is tested on initial application. Second, there must be a further check just prior to the later prospective allocation of a specific property, because otherwise the local housing authority may mistakenly infringe the statutory injunction that it 'shall not allocate' to an ineligible person.[471] That may include a person who was initially eligible on application but is not eligible when a specific allocation is about to be made. It is therefore particularly important that when a person from abroad receives an initially favourable decision on eligibility, she or he is informed that any changes to his or her immigration status – or, indeed, changes to the complex statutory rules about eligibility and immigration status – could affect eligibility later for a particular allocation of property.

---

[467] *Exploring local authority policy and practice on housing allocations* (CLG, July 2009), para 4.6.
[468] *Am I on the list? Exclusion from and re-inclusion on social housing waiting lists* (CIH Cymru, May 2008).
[469] English Code, para 3.26 and see **3.194**.
[470] Which is specifically recommended by the Secretary of State in the English Code, para 3.2.
[471] HA 1996, s 160ZA(1) [England], s 160A(1) [Wales].

NOTIFICATION OF DECISIONS AND RIGHTS TO REVIEW

3.254 All applicants who have been found ineligible (whether on grounds of immigration status or of past misconduct) should have the right under the local allocation scheme to written notification of that decision and of the grounds for it.[472] The grounds must be firmly 'based on the relevant facts of the case.'[473] The applicant should also have the right under that scheme to request a review of that decision, and to be informed of the review decision and the grounds on which it was made.[474] The reviewer should reconsider afresh the whole of the information put before him or her, and consider the facts as at the date of the review decision.[475] As to the procedure to be followed on the review, see **2.93–2.98**. The Welsh Code contains extensive guidance as to how a review of a decision on eligibility should be organised and conducted to ensure procedural fairness.[476]

3.255 In relation to a decision that an applicant to a local housing authority in England is not a 'qualifying person' there should be a similar right in the local allocation scheme for that person to be given written notice of the decision and of the grounds for it.[477] It is to be hoped that there will be no return to the practices, adopted in some areas from 1996–2003, of deflecting genuine applicants to local housing authorities at their first point of contact by telling them (in person or over the telephone) that they do not meet the local qualifying conditions or that they fall within a class that does not qualify and therefore should not apply. An applicant dissatisfied with such a decision should have the right to request a review of that decision, and to be informed of the review decision and the grounds on which it was made.[478]

3.256 If the review upholds the original decision in any case relating to eligibility or qualification, there is no mechanism to appeal to the county court and the only available legal challenge to the review decision is by judicial review, alleging an error of law in the review process, in the tests applied by the local housing authority in reaching its decision on review, or in the review decision itself.[479]

3.257 In *R (Dixon) v Wandsworth London Borough Council*[480] the applicant complained that the reviewing officer had failed to give the 'grounds' for the review decision because the notice of the review decision (a lengthy document) gave insufficient reasons. The judge rejected the claim and that decision was

---

[472] HA 1996, s 160ZA(9)(a) [England], s 160A(9) [Wales].
[473] English Code, para 5.16 and Welsh Code, para 3.31.
[474] HA 1996, s166A(9)(c) [England], s 167(4A)(d) [Wales].
[475] English Code, para 5.19v.
[476] Welsh Code, para 3.35.
[477] HA 1996, s 160ZA(9)(b).
[478] HA 1996, s 166A(9)(c).
[479] Further information on reviews is given at **2.85–2.100**.
[480] [2007] EWHC 3075 (Admin), (2008) February *Legal Action* p 40. Admin Ct.

upheld by the Court of Appeal which said that 'the reasons were stated in sufficient detail to enable the applicant to know what conclusion the decision maker had reached on the principal important controversial issues.'[481] In another case, the local housing authority's correspondence relating to a decision on eligibility was described as 'opaque', but a challenge based on inadequate reasons was rejected as the claimant himself was well apprised of the issues being addressed.[482]

RENEWED APPLICATIONS

3.258 The decision reached by a local housing authority on an applicant's eligibility (whether on immigration-related grounds or behaviour-related grounds) or whether he or she is a qualifying person does not bind any other local housing authority to reach the same decision. Disappointed applicants unable to overturn the adverse decision may be advised to apply elsewhere. In England that is particularly true of decisions relating to qualification because every local housing authority in England will have adopted different qualifying classes and criteria.

3.259 Alternatively, the applicant could make a further application to the same local housing authority. Plainly, a person who has been declared ineligible on immigration-related grounds will wish to apply again, as soon as his or her immigration status alters.

3.260 HA 1996, Part 6 expressly envisages that an applicant found to be ineligible by a local housing authority in Wales on behaviour-related eligibility grounds may want to re-apply on the basis that she or he should no longer be treated as ineligible. It provides for the making of 'a fresh application' in such cases.[483] This is no doubt because the two statutory conditions for ineligibility in the behaviour category link:

(1)   past misconduct; and

(2)   present suitability to be a tenant.

3.261 Inevitably, that link will become weaker with the passage of time and with other changes in an applicant's circumstances. The Welsh Code suggests that the burden will be on the applicant to show that his or her circumstances or behaviour have changed.[484]

3.262 An applicant who has received a decision from a local housing authority in England that he or she does not qualify can re-apply if he or she

---

[481]   [2008] EWCA Civ 595, (2008) July *Legal Action* p 22, CA at [9].
[482]   *R (M) v London Borough of Hackney* [2009] EWHC 2255 (Admin), (2009) May *Legal Action*, p 26, Admin Ct.
[483]   HA 1996, s 160A(11).
[484]   Welsh Code, para 3.24.

considers that he or she should be treated as a qualifying person.[485] The most obvious example will be where the initial application was made at the time when the applicant was unemployed and the local qualifying class was 'persons in employment'. The applicant may re-apply as soon as he or she obtains employment. The statutory guidance suggests that on any re-application it would be for the applicant to show that his or her circumstances have changed.[486] However, there is no need for there to have been any change of personal circumstances – the local housing authority may simply have changed its qualifying criteria.

---

[485]   HA 1996, s 160ZA(11).
[486]   English Code, para 3.30.

Chapter 4

ALLOCATION SCHEMES

INTRODUCTION

4.1   Each local housing authority in England and Wales is required by the Housing Act 1996 (HA 1996), Part 6 ('Allocation of Housing Accommodation') to have a scheme for the allocation of social housing.[1] Even if there were no statutory requirement, each local housing authority would, in practice, need to adopt arrangements for the selection of candidates for the grant of available secure or introductory tenancies in its own housing stock (if any) and for the nomination of applicants to local private registered providers or registered social landlords (mainly housing associations). Without an allocation scheme, a local housing authority would not have the essential framework enabling it to determine the relative priorities between applicants for housing, nor a comprehensive statement of the procedure that should be followed when considering such applications and making allocations.[2]

4.2   This Chapter discusses how these local housing allocation schemes must be framed (whether from the outset or by amendment) in order to comply with HA 1996, Part 6 and how they must work to enable a lawful assessment of each applicant's application. The process of actual allocation to those who have had their applications assessed is reviewed in the next Chapter. To make sure that the rules described here are followed, HA 1996, Part 6, states that everything that counts as an 'allocation'[3] must be undertaken in accordance with the local allocation scheme or it will be unlawful.[4] As long as a local housing authority complies with the basic requirements set out in this Chapter, it is allowed to exercise its own discretion in settling on a scheme for determining how it actually makes allocations and to whom.[5]

4.3   The allocation scheme is therefore the essential starting point for answering the question 'Will I be allocated a home?', whether that question is directed at a member of the local housing authority's staff or at a local housing adviser. That is why the schemes must be publicly available for purchase and why each local housing authority must produce a free summary of its own scheme.[6]

---

[1]   Housing Act 1996, s 166A(1) [England], s 167(1) [Wales]. Statutory guidance on allocation schemes is given in *Allocation of Accommodation: Guidance for local housing authorities in England* (Department for Communities & Local Government [DCLG], June 2012) (the English Code) and in *Code of Guidance for local authorities: Allocation of accommodation and homelessness 2012* (Welsh Government, August 2012) (the Welsh Code). See Appendix 1 of this book for the English Code and see the accompanying CD-ROM for the Welsh Code.

[2]   As required by HA 1996, s 166A(1) [England], s 167(1) [Wales].

[3]   For the definition see HA 1996, s 159(2); and see also the discussion at **1.35–1.43** of circumstances in which a person can become a tenant of social housing without an allocation.

[4]   HA 1996, s 166A(14) [England], s 167(8) [Wales].

[5]   HA 1996, s 159(7) (England & Wales), s 166A(11) [England] and s 167(6) [Wales].

[6]   Further detail on access to information about local allocation schemes and individual applications is given at **2.7–2.27**.

ADOPTING OR AMENDING AN ALLOCATION SCHEME

Adopting a scheme

4.4 Most local housing authorities will have long since adopted an allocation scheme, as required by HA 1996, Part 6, as amended. But some new local housing authorities are from time to time created (eg by the moves to establish new unitary authorities in areas with multiple layers of local government). Where such a new local authority is being established, which will be a local housing authority for a district, it will need to formulate and adopt a new allocation scheme. There are two essential statutory pre-requisites before any new local allocation scheme can be adopted.

4.5 The first is that the local housing authority must undertake any impact assessments required under equalities legislation and by the local housing authority's own statements of equality policy.[7]

4.6 The second requirement is one of limited consultation. Before an allocation scheme is adopted, the local housing authority is required to consult every private registered provider (or, in Wales, every registered social landlord) with which it has nomination arrangements. As part of that consultation, it must send those landlords a copy of the draft scheme and give them a reasonable opportunity to comment on the proposals.[8] A reasonable opportunity is identified in the Welsh Code as being a minimum period of 12 weeks.[9]

4.7 These are, of course, the *minimum* statutory prerequisites. A local housing authority drawing up a scheme for the first time might well be expected to undertake a much wider range of measures before finally adopting its scheme. There is no *statutory* requirement to consult any other people or organisations before adopting a scheme, but much might usefully be gained by eliciting the views of local tenants' organisations, housing advice agencies and the like. The Welsh Code advises that any such consultation should be broad based and should use a variety of methods to ensure that it is representative and that it addresses the needs of people with protected characteristics.[10]

4.8 Indeed, local housing authorities may wish to engage with and involve all interested groups and the wider community[11] before they produce their first allocation scheme so that people are given the opportunity to contribute to the development of the allocation priorities. The Chartered Institute of Housing has suggested that 'allocation schemes should be developed in consultation

---

[7]   See **4.195–4.209**.
[8]   HA 1996, s 166A(13) [England] and s 167(7) [Wales].
[9]   Welsh Code, para 5.25. A similar provision originally appeared in the English Code (2002 edn), para 6.6.
[10] Welsh Code, para 4.45. For the 'protected characteristics' see Equality Act 2012, ss 5–12.
[11] Welsh Code, para 2.3.

with local registered providers, partners working in health and the local economy and tenants, residents and communities themselves'.[12]

4.9 A local housing authority should take into account the findings and conclusions of its own homelessness review and strategy when settling upon an allocation scheme and, conversely, the homelessness strategy should take into account the local allocation scheme.[13] Indeed, if a local housing authority in England is preparing an allocation scheme it must have regard to:

(1) its homelessness strategy;

(2) its tenancy strategy;[14] and

(3) (if it is a local housing authority in London) the London housing strategy.[15]

4.10 A local housing authority in Wales should have regard, in drawing up an allocation scheme, to the local housing strategy or the strategic housing element of the local Community Strategy.[16]

4.11 HA 1996, Part 6 prescribes that the new local housing allocation scheme must set out:

(1) how the local housing authority will determine priorities between applicants; and

(2) what procedures it will follow in allocating housing accommodation.[17]

4.12 The degree of detail required in the finished scheme is considered later in this Chapter.[18]

Amending the current local allocation scheme

4.13 There is no statutory obligation on a local housing authority to keep the terms of its allocation scheme under review or to revise it regularly[19] but the Welsh Code suggests that it would be 'good practice' to review allocation policies at least every two years.[20] However, a need or desire to change an allocation scheme may be prompted as a result of a review of an existing

---

[12] *Allocation of accommodation: guidance for local housing authorities in England, Briefing paper* (CIH, July 2012), p 7.
[13] Homelessness Act 2002, s 1(5). Welsh Code, para 4.6. See Chapter 7 of this book.
[14] Adopted in order to comply with Localism Act 2011, s 150.
[15] HA 1996, s 166A(12).
[16] Welsh Code, para 4.7.
[17] HA 1996, s 166A(1) [England], s 167(1) [Wales].
[18] See **4.25–4.27**.
[19] In contrast to the requirements in relation to homelessness strategies set out in Homelessness Act 2002, ss 1–4. See **7.68** and **7.184–7.191**.
[20] Welsh Code, para 5.41.

scheme or by a significant change in legislation (or by any other factor). If a local housing authority proposes to make any significant change to the local allocation scheme, two sets of statutory requirements are triggered.

4.14 First, the local housing authority will need to make any impact assessment necessary to achieve compliance with the requirements of equalities legislation and with its own equality policies.[21]

4.15 Second, if an alteration is to be made which amounts to 'a major change of policy', the local housing authority is required to notify and consult with local private registered providers (or, in Wales, registered social landlords) with which it has nomination arrangements and give them a reasonable opportunity to comment on the proposed changes.[22] A minimum consultation period of 12 weeks is recommended.[23]

4.16 The Welsh Code advises that 'a major change of policy' for these purposes would include any amendment affecting the relative priority of a large number of people being considered for an allocation of social housing, and any significant alteration to allocation procedures.[24] The broadest possible approach might sensibly be taken to involving the local community in consultation on the variation of any allocation scheme.[25] That can obviously best be secured by taking a wide view of what constitutes a 'major change of policy'. In any event, a local housing authority which is also a social landlord will usually also need to comply with the requirements of its own statutory scheme[26] for consulting current tenants and with the statutory regulator's expectations[27] as to consultation with, and participation by, tenants in major changes of policy. The Welsh Code suggests that anyone who is affected by or interested in the way social housing is allocated should be included when consulting on changes to an allocation scheme and local housing authorities in Wales are encouraged to engage with a wide range of stakeholders in the statutory, voluntary and community sectors, as well as applicants and the general public.[28]

---

[21] See **4.195–4.209**.

[22] HA 1996, s 166A(13) [England], s 167(7) [Wales].

[23] Welsh Code, para 5.25. A similar provision originally appeared in the English Code (2002), para 6.6.

[24] Welsh Code, para 5.17. A similar provision originally appeared in the English Code (2002), para 6.3.

[25] Welsh Code, paras 4.45 and 5.19–5.20.

[26] HA 1985, s 105.

[27] *The regulatory framework for social housing in England from April* 2012 (Homes & Communities Agency, March 2012) in its Tenant Involvement and Empowerment Standard requires that 'Registered providers shall ensure that tenants are given a wide range of opportunities to influence and be involved in the formulation of their landlord's housing related policies and strategic priorities'

[28] Welsh Code, paras 4.46, 4.74 and 5.16–5.17.

4.17 But what is 'a major change of policy'? The Court of Appeal in *R (A) v Lambeth London Borough Council*[29] was concerned with Lambeth's decision to change the proportions of allocations ('quotas') made available to different groups within its scheme, so that three of the seven groups would receive no allocations whatsoever. Arguably, this constituted 'a major change of policy', certainly as far as the applicants in those three groups were concerned. The prospects of any of them receiving an allocation had suddenly become 'zero'. The allocation scheme itself did not refer to the quotas of allocations that each group could expect, merely stating 'the effect of preference on each applicant Group is also reviewed, and targets changed if necessary'. The Court of Appeal, whilst holding that other aspects of the scheme were unlawful,[30] held that since the actual proportion of allocations between the different groups was not part of the published scheme, and there was no requirement for it to be published, a change in the proportion did not constitute 'a major change of policy' and there was no need to consult or inform applicants. It follows that 'a major change of policy' must at least be a change relating to the information which is contained, or should be contained, in the published allocation scheme.

4.18 In recent years, the most commonly proposed 'major change of policy' has been a move from officer-led allocations towards the adoption of a choice-based element in a current scheme or by a complete replacement of the existing arrangements with a choice-based letting scheme.

4.19 In the immediate future, all local housing authorities in England can be expected to be undertaking reviews of, and making possible amendments to, their current allocation schemes in the light of the latest statutory guidance[31] and the need to take account of the changes to HA 1996, Part 6 made by the Localism Act 2011 with effect from 18 June 2012. One organisation has even prepared a briefing for its members on how to respond to consultations about amendments to housing allocation schemes which will reflect these changes.[32]

4.20 In Wales, there will be a need to review local allocation schemes to take account of the new national guidance on local housing allocation published in August 2012.[33]

4.21 If an alteration is made which reflects a 'major change of policy', the local housing authority must take such steps as it considers reasonable to bring the effects of the change to the attention of those likely to be affected by it.[34] Most obviously, that will be the pool of actual or prospective applicants and those likely to be advising them. Very little guidance is given in the Codes as to what steps might be considered 'reasonable'. The Welsh Code suggests that a major policy change will require 'each potential applicant to be informed

---

[29]   *R (A) v Lambeth London Borough Council* [2002] EWCA Civ 1084, [2002] HLR 57, CA.
[30]   See **5.44**.
[31]   See the English Code.
[32]   *Allocations Consultation Response: Guidance for Members* (Homeless Link, 2012).
[33]   See the Welsh Code.
[34]   HA 1996, s 168(3) as amended.

personally by letter', leaving unanswered the question as to how a local housing authority can identify potential, as opposed to actual, applicants.[35]

4.22 Plainly, those applicants already being dealt with under the current allocation scheme can be directly written to. However, potential applicants and other members of the public will have to be informed through the usual information mechanisms available to the local housing authority, such as publication on the website, notice in the local newspapers, informing housing advice agencies, etc. Given that some existing tenants of social housing who are seeking transfers will fall within the allocation scheme arrangements, and would therefore be likely to be affected, arguably the local housing authority should inform all social housing tenants and tenants' organisations in its district of any 'major change of policy' to be reflected in the revised allocation scheme.

4.23 One of the most difficult aspects of adopting extensive amendments to a local housing allocation scheme is the need to deal with those applicants who have already been considered and assessed under the old scheme. In the absence of any express provision to the contrary in the newly amended scheme, the assumption would be that the requirements of the amended scheme would apply immediately to all applicants.

4.24 In September 2005 a local housing authority in London changed its housing allocation scheme from being points-based to one using wholly new assessment bands in which priority operated by reference to registration dates. The new scheme did not address how applicants registered on the old scheme would be dealt with under the new one. The Court of Appeal declined to fill that gap, holding that it was 'questionable' on what basis the local housing authority could give any applicant a registration date under the new scheme earlier than the date of the adoption of the new scheme – while also indicating that if any such provision was to be made, it should be published as part of the revised allocation scheme.[36]

ENSURING THAT THE SCHEME IS SUFFICIENTLY DETAILED

4.25 The scheme adopted by the local housing authority must not only set out how the local housing authority will prioritise *between* applicants[37] but additionally the *procedure* that it follows in allocating housing.[38] Where the local housing authority has adopted a choice-based letting arrangement, the formal allocation scheme should set out the procedures and priorities as they apply not only to the initial consideration of an applicant's application but also

---

[35] Welsh Code, para 5.17.
[36] *R (Faarah) v Southwark London Borough Council* [2008] EWCA Civ 807, [2009] HLR 12, CA.
[37] HA 1996, s 166A(1) [England] and s 167(1) [Wales].
[38] HA 1996, s 166A(1) [England] and s 167(1) [Wales].

to how any bid made by the applicant for specific accommodation will be treated. The local approach taken to eligibility and qualification should also be set out in the local allocation scheme.[39]

4.26 Experience would suggest that there has been a failure to grasp the significance of the fact that, for these purposes, 'procedure' includes 'all aspects of the allocation process, including the persons or descriptions of persons by whom decisions are to be taken'.[40] Too many allocation schemes simply set out broad policy statements, unlawfully leaving the mechanics to be detailed in unpublished procedure manuals or staff training materials. In short, the statutory requirement is that the published scheme deals with how, by whom and why allocations are made. As the Welsh Code puts it, it is essential that the scheme reflects all the local housing authority's policies and procedures, including information on whether the decisions are taken by elected members or by officers.[41]

4.27 The courts have not taken an altogether consistent line as to how much detail on the relative priority to be given as between applicants, or the procedures to be followed in processing applications, is required in a local allocation scheme. The range of approaches taken by the courts is illustrated by the examples already given in Chapter 2.[42]

DETERMINING PRIORITY FOR ALLOCATION – REASONABLE PREFERENCE CLASSES

4.28 The primary function (and requirement) of a local allocation scheme is that it sets out the local housing authority's priorities in allocating housing accommodation. It represents the local housing authority's policy choices about discrimination between applicants. It sets out which applicants are to have more priority than others and, where priorities are broadly evenly matched, which applicant is to be preferred. The scheme needs to explain to those operating it, or advising about it, the circumstances in which Applicant A will have greater or lesser preference than Applicant B.

4.29 HA 1996, Part 6 leaves a local housing authority free to adopt its own locally agreed policies and principles, subject to the terms of HA 1996, Part 6 itself (and to any regulations made under HA 1996, Part 6).[43] Of course,

---

[39] English Code, para 4.1.
[40] HA 1996, s 166A(1) [England] and s 167(1) [Wales].
[41] Welsh Code, para 4.4.
[42] See **2.19** and see **4.219–4.227**.
[43] HA 1996, s 166A(11) [England] and s 167(6) [Wales]. The functions exercisable by the Secretary of State in HA 1996 were transferred to the National Assembly for Wales when the National Assembly was set up in 1999 (Government of Wales Act 1998, s 22, Sch 3 and National Assembly for Wales (Transfer of Functions) Order 1999, SI 1999/672). The Government of Wales Act 2006, s 162 and Sch 3 transferred the National Assembly for Wales' functions to the relevant Welsh Ministers.

although the whole process is one of discrimination about access to services, any unlawful discrimination is to be avoided.[44] The most significant constraint on the local housing authority's freedom to select particular applicants is the requirement that the scheme must be framed to give a preference to those groups of applicants set out in HA 1996, Part 6. That requirement is considered below.[45]

Giving a 'reasonable preference'

4.30 In relation to prioritisation between applicants, HA 1996, Part 6, states that every local allocation scheme must be drawn up so as secure a 'reasonable preference' for the groups of people specified in HA 1996, Part 6.[46] Local housing authorities must design and operate schemes that broadly comply with the statutory list. That does not mean that the local allocation scheme must adopt precisely the same text as that given in HA 1996, Part 6. All that is required is that the local scheme does actually give a reasonable preference to applicants falling into one or more of the statutory groups. The statutory list contains five broad groups. Each of the five groups is described and discussed in detail later in the Chapter[47] after a consideration of what the concept of a 'reasonable' preference entails.

How much preference is 'reasonable'?

4.31 HA 1996, Part 6 does not require a local allocation scheme to be framed so as to accord *absolute* preference to those in the listed groups. Local housing authorities need give them only a *'reasonable* preference' in the allocation scheme.[48] The scheme must, in effect, be framed so as to ensure that the groups of applicants represented by the reasonable preference categories are given a head start over those who do not have a reasonable preference. Thus, HA 1996, Part 6 only requires that these groups be given a 'reasonable' preference.[49] It does not require that they should be given absolute priority over everyone else.[50] The language of HA 1996, Part 6 does not address the relative standing of any two or more individual applicants because it only requires a 'reasonable preference' to be given to particular groups of people rather than to specific applicants.[51]

4.32 Just how much preference is reasonable under a particular local scheme is a matter for the exercise of local discretion but 'although there is no

[44]   See **4.195–4.209**.
[45]   See **4.30** et seq.
[46]   HA 1996, s 166A(7) [England] and s 167(3) [Wales] respectively permit the Secretary of State for Communities and Local Government and the Welsh Ministers to specify further groups of people, or to amend or repeal the groups specified in HA 1996, Part 6. Neither the Secretary of State nor the Welsh Ministers have exercised these powers.
[47]   See **4.57–4.114**.
[48]   HA 1996, s 166A(3) [England] and s 167(2) [Wales]; emphasis added by the authors.
[49]   English Code, para 4.5.
[50]   *R (Ahmad) v Newham London Borough Council* [2009] UKHL 14, [2009] HLR 41, HL at [18].
[51]   Ibid at [15] and [18].

requirement to give equal weight to each of the reasonable preference categories, authorities will need to demonstrate that, overall, reasonable preference has been given to all of them'.[52] As the Welsh Code puts it, what is important is that an allocation scheme makes a clear distinction between those applicants who fall within the reasonable preference categories and those who do not.[53]

4.33 HA 1996, Part 6 does not require that people in the reasonable preference groups must be given preference in relation to every property which is let under the scheme. It is the scheme taken as a whole that must give a reasonable preference to the statutory groups. Accordingly, a scheme which enabled a mere 5% of its available properties to be open to bids from transfer applicants who were not in the reasonable preference categories did not fail to give those statutory priority groups a 'reasonable' preference overall.[54] The difficulty is to identify the point at which allocation, to applicants without a reasonable preference, of a higher percentage of properties than 5% would prevent the scheme from giving overall priority to the reasonable preference classes. The Welsh Code suggests that the percentage used by particular local housing authorities is a matter for individual consideration of how to best meet the strategic needs of the area.[55]

4.34 Whatever percentage is adopted, the scheme must still give overall reasonable preference to the statutory classes of people entitled to a reasonable preference. A scheme which gave existing secure tenants seeking a transfer an additional 100 points each, when not all of them were entitled to a reasonable preference, was held to be unlawful because it artificially raised the points threshold to the detriment of applicants who were not existing tenants and were entitled to a statutory preference.[56]

4.35 It may not immediately be apparent from the detail of a particular provision in an allocation scheme that, in a particular case, it is operating consistently with the requirement to accord certain groups their statutory entitlement to a reasonable preference. But as one judge put it:

'It seems to me that whether or not a scheme does afford a reasonable preference to those persons falling within the categories of those to whom reasonable preference ought to be given ... is very much a question of fact and it is to be answered ... in a common sense way. While of course the obligation to give reasonable preference is a continuing one and in that sense is absolute and required to be complied with at all times, it would be wrong to assess whether or

---

[52]   English Code, para 4.5.
[53]   Welsh Code, para 4.56.
[54]   *R (Ahmad) v Newham London Borough Council* [2009] UKHL 14, [2009] HLR 41, HL at [17]–[21].
[55]   Welsh Code, para 4.54.
[56]   *R (Lin) v Barnet London Borough Council* [2006] EWHC 1041 (Admin), [2006] HLR 440, Admin Ct; Barnet London Borough Council successfully appealed to the Court of Appeal (*Lin v Barnet London Borough Council* [2007] EWCA Civ 132, [2007] HLR 30, CA) but not on that point.

not it is being complied with by simply taking a snapshot of the operation of the scheme on a particular day or a particular week ... provided [that] over a reasonable period as a result of monitoring a reasonable preference is shown to all groups, then that is sufficient to comply with [HA 1996, Part 6].

As I say, whether a reasonable preference is shown is very much a factual question to be answered in a common sense way; and, to pick up on [the] proposition that the object of the exercise is to give certain persons a "head start", it seems to me that one answers the question of whether they have been given a head start again by looking at the matter over a reasonable period rather than trying to take a snapshot on some particular day.'[57]

4.36 However, HA 1996, Part 6 prohibits local housing authorities from adopting a scheme which awards *no preference at all* to a person within one of the preference groups unless:

(1) the applicant is ineligible by reason of his or her immigration status or insufficient residence in the UK;[58]

(2) the applicant is not within a qualifying class (or is within a non-qualifying class) as defined by the local housing authority in England to which the application has been made;[59]

(3) a local housing authority in Wales has decided that the applicant is not eligible on account of his or her past behaviour;[60]

(4) a local housing authority in Wales has decided that the applicant is eligible but has been guilty of 'unacceptable behaviour' within the statutory definition of that term;[61] or

(5) the applicant is entitled to a preference solely because she or he is in one of the first two reasonable preference categories and that category is only satisfied because of the presence in the applicant's household of a 'restricted person'.[62]

4.37 Beyond the requirement to frame an allocation scheme to reflect the statutory list of reasonable preference groups, local housing authorities are permitted a good deal of autonomy to decide the procedures and principles they wish to apply locally. HA 1996 Part 6 does, however, offer a steer towards other specific factors. Local housing authorities are, for example, expressly permitted to give 'additional preference' to people with 'urgent housing needs'

---

[57] *R (Babakandi) v Westminster City Council* [2011] EWCA Civ 1397, (2012) January *Legal Action*, p 21 at [3]–[4].
[58] See **3.12–3.139**.
[59] See **3.140–3.202**.
[60] See **3.203–3.251**.
[61] HA 1996, s 167(2B) and (2C); see **4.155–4.163**.
[62] HA 1996, s 166A(4) [England] and s 167(2ZA) [Wales]. English Code, para 4.6. See HA 1996, s 184(7) and **10.38–10.40** for the definition of 'restricted person'.

who fall within any of the reasonable preference categories,[63] and to take account of such an applicant's financial resources, his or her behaviour (good or bad), any local connection with a particular local housing authority's area, or any other matter.[64]

4.38 Provided that their allocation schemes comply with these broad statutory 'reasonable preference' categories, local housing authorities may otherwise decide for themselves on the principles for determining priorities in the local allocation scheme.[65] They will have to decide, for example, how to choose, when they come to allocate accommodation, between applicants who fall into the different 'reasonable preference' categories and also how to organise people within each of those different groups (whether according to their comparative need or according to some other locally adopted criteria). The scheme will also need to address the priority to be given to applicants who are not in the reasonable preference categories at all.

4.39 Prior to 2009 it was thought that local housing authorities had to have provision in their allocation schemes to enable them to make a *cumulative* or *composite assessment* of the whole of each *applicant's* needs.[66] In addition, local housing authorities were expected to make a cumulative or composite assessment of the whole of the applicant's *household's* needs, so that the needs of all of the members of the household were identified and taken into account.[67] This approach needed to be applied to all members of the applicant's household, whether they were eligible for an allocation in their own right or not. Schemes that did not reflect these principles were struck down by the courts.

4.40 However, in 2009 the House of Lords decided that the amendments made to HA 1996, Part 6 by the Homelessness Act 2002 had given local housing authorities even greater flexibility than had previously been thought and that it was *not* necessary for an allocation scheme to provide a mechanism for cumulative or composite assessments or, put another way, for a scheme to

---

[63]   HA 1996, s 166A(3) [England], s 167(2) [Wales]; see **4.123–4.134**.

[64]   HA 1996, s 166A(5) [England], s 167(2A) [Wales]; see **4.135–4.151**.

[65]   HA 1996, s 166A(11) [England], s 167(6) [Wales].

[66]   *R v Islington London Borough Council ex p Reilly and Mannix* (1999) 31 HLR 651, QBD; *R (A) v Lambeth London Borough Council, R (Lindsay) v Lambeth London Borough Council* [2002] EWCA Civ 1084, [2002] HLR 57, CA; *R (Cali) v Waltham Forest London Borough Council* [2006] EWHC 302 (Admin), [2007] HLR 1 at [31], Admin Ct; and *R (Ahmad) v Newham London Borough Council* [2008] EWCA Civ 400, (2008) April *Legal Action*, p 40, CA (subsequently considered and overturned by the House of Lords): see **5.51–5.55**.

[67]   *R v Tower Hamlets London Borough Council ex p Uddin* (1999) 32 HLR 391, QBD.

accord priority by reference to the relative gravity of each applicant's housing needs.[68] While the statutory provisions[69] enabled such an approach to be adopted, they did not require it.[70]

4.41 Indeed, the statutory flexibility given by the terms of HA 1996, Part 6 is such that it would be 'impossible to argue that an authority's allocation scheme is unlawful unless the basis on which it accords priority as between those applicants [in the reasonable preference categories] is irrational'.[71] It follows that, whether the cases decided on the pre-amendment terms of HA 1996, Part 6[72] had been rightly decided or not, they can no longer be relied upon.

4.42 This decision of the House of Lords was strongly welcomed by the Secretary of State at the time and is now reflected in the statutory guidance that 'there is no requirement for housing authorities to frame their scheme to afford greater priority to applicants who fall within more than one reasonable preference category (cumulative preference) over those who have reasonable preference on a single, non-urgent basis'.[73] The Welsh Code suggests that the removal of the requirement to provide for cumulative preference gives local housing authorities scope to develop simpler, more transparent systems of applicant prioritisation.[74]

4.43 Notwithstanding the degree of flexibility thus permitted, local housing authorities must actually identify the criteria for determining priorities within their allocation schemes.[75] A scheme which did not clearly identify and define the criteria for awarding a reasonable preference was held not to comply with the requirements of HA 1996, Part 6.[76] As one judge has also said:

> '... it goes without saying that whatever criteria are adopted must be rational and must be related to the particular policy and housing needs ...'[77]

4.44 Once it has identified whether an applicant falls into one or more of the 'reasonable preference' categories, the local housing authority needs a method enabling it to rank that applicant against other applicants, both those falling within and those outside the preference categories. That ranking may be according to their different housing needs or by reference to any other relevant factors, including – if the scheme makes provision for it – the length of time

---

[68] *R (Ahmad) v Newham London Borough Council* [2009] UKHL 14, [2009] HLR 41, HL; see **5.51–5.55**.

[69] Particularly the closing sentence of HA 1996, s 166A(3) [England] and s 167(2) [Wales] read with the opening words of s 166A(5) [England] and s 167(2A) [Wales].

[70] *R (Ahmad) v Newham London Borough Council* [2009] UKHL 14, [2009] HLR 41, HL at [14].

[71] *R (Ahmad) v Newham London Borough Council* [2009] UKHL 14, [2009] HLR 41, HL at [49].

[72] Most particularly those cases noted at footnote 66 above.

[73] English Code, para 4.5. Welsh Code, para 4.54.

[74] Welsh Code, para 4.57.

[75] HA 1996, s 166A(1) [England], s 167(1) [Wales]; Welsh Code, para 4.56.

[76] *R (Cali) v Waltham Forest London Borough Council* [2006] EWHC 302 (Admin), [2007] HLR 1, CA at [31].

[77] *R (George) v Hammersmith & Fulham London Borough Council* [2012] EWHC 2369 (Admin), (2012) June *Legal Action*, p 36 at [19] per Deputy Judge Catchpole QC.

that the applicant has been waiting for an allocation.[78] An allocation scheme could therefore be based on awarding points to applicants, or grouping applicants into bands.

4.45 Either method should accord some preference to those in the 'reasonable preference' categories. In some allocation schemes, a combination of the two methods is used. The most straightforward scheme of allocation, strict date order for all applicants, simply cannot work in the modern statutory framework, which requires some classes of applicants to be given a reasonable preference over others.

4.46 In a *points-based scheme*, points could be awarded to reflect different categories of need, for example for medical and welfare needs, overcrowding, etc, and further points may reflect the length of time that an applicant has been waiting for accommodation after having been accepted onto the scheme. Some have suggested that points-based systems can be complex, lacking in transparency and difficult to understand. Local housing authorities retaining such schemes have previously been encouraged to consider simplifying them.[79]

4.47 If a *banding system* is adopted, applicants within each band may be prioritised by points and/or by date order, reflecting the degree of their need and/or their waiting time. The now withdrawn English (2009) Code strongly suggested this as a preferred model but the present guidance for England does not express any preference for any particular method of identifying relative priorities.[80]

4.48 Self-evidently, an allocation scheme that placed in the same band or group those applicants who were entitled to 'reasonable preference' and those who were not so entitled, and then treated them equally, would be unlawful.[81] A local housing authority must be able to distinguish between applicants who are entitled to the benefit of the 'reasonable preference' categories and those who are not.[82]

4.49 An emphasis on prioritisation by combinations of 'reasonable preference' and the assessment of a particular household's 'need'[83] can produce bizarre results. An applicant could be ceaselessly moving, yo-yo fashion, up and down the list of those eligible (and/or qualified) for an allocation as his or her own housing circumstances and needs change and as others apply for an allocation.

---

[78] Welsh Code, para 4.58.
[79] English (2009) Code, para 74.
[80] English (2009) Code, paras 70–73.
[81] *R (A) v Lambeth London Borough Council, R (Lindsay) v Lambeth London Borough Council* [2002] EWCA Civ 1084, [2002] HLR 57, CA.
[82] English Code, para 4.5, Welsh Code, para 4.56.
[83] HA 1996, s 166A(3) [England] and s 167(2) [Wales].

4.50   For example, a household with no children may find itself almost at the top of the list of those awaiting a bed-sit or other small unit of accommodation, only to be taken towards the bottom of the list of those waiting for larger accommodation when a child arrives. On this basis, one local housing authority's scheme survived a challenge to its provision that, where the applicants' need had changed, so that they required a two-bedroom rather than a one-bedroom unit, they should be put at the bottom of the two-bedroom property list, and lose their points awarded for the time that they had waited on the one-bedroom property list.[84] Another local housing authority's scheme had the same effect, by re-adjusting a registration date to reflect the date of a move to a new priority band, even when an applicant's housing need had decreased. It was nevertheless lawful.[85] The judge said:

> 'The final resting place of the submissions advanced on behalf of Ms Kabashi was by reference to *Yemlahi*. In the light of *Ahmad*, however, it is no longer tenable to contend that a scheme that provides for the alteration of effective dates when an applicant up-sizes would be rational but which does not provide for such an alteration is rational.'[86]

4.51   Similarly, in any scheme based on housing need, a household provided with temporary accommodation under HA 1996, Part 7 ('Homelessness') may find that the prospects of securing an early allocation under HA 1996, Part 6 actually diminish if the household is moved to a higher standard of self-contained temporary accommodation. In one case considered by the Local Government Ombudsman, a homeless couple rejected temporary accommodation from the local housing authority precisely because its superior quality was such that they would fall into a lower priority category under the allocation scheme if they accepted it.[87]

4.52   In *R (Ahmad) v Newham London Borough Council*[88] the House of Lords was persuaded that a scheme based on banding together those applicants in *any* of the reasonable preference categories and then prioritising between them by reference to waiting-time had the merit of being 'quantifiable, transparent and hard to manipulate',[89] in contrast to schemes for the affording of relative priority by case-by-case assessment of housing need reflected in the awarding of points.

---

[84]   *R (Yemlahi) v Lambeth London Borough Council* [2002] EWHC 1187 (Admin), (2002) August *Legal Action*, p 31, Admin Ct. The court held that either scenario created injustice: if the applicants had been placed towards the top of the list for two-bedroom properties (reflecting their waiting time on the list for one-bedroom properties), those below the applicants who had a longer standing need for two-bedroom properties would rightly feel aggrieved.

[85]   *R (Kabashi) v Redbridge London Borough Council* [2009] EWHC 2984 (Admin), (2010) October *Legal Action* 32, Admin Ct.

[86]   At para [19].

[87]   *Complaint against Hounslow London Borough Council*, 14 April 2009, No 07/A/14215, (2009) June *Legal Action*, p 34.

[88]   *R (Ahmad) v Newham London Borough Council* [2009] UKHL 14, [2009] HLR 41, HL.

[89]   *R (Ahmad) v Newham London Borough Council* [2009] UKHL 14, [2009] HLR 41, HL at [52].

4.53 There is one form of prioritisation not accorded by HA 1996, Part 6, and which does not turn on 'need'. It arises where applicants have been given a 'legitimate expectation' that they will be allocated local housing authority tenancies, or nominated to a private registered provider or registered social landlord.[90]

4.54 The possibility of such an expectation being generated must be provided for in the scheme, so that such applicants receive points or are placed in a specific band in order to take account of those expectations.[91] A 'legitimate expectation' generally arose in this context where homeless applicants, who had been accepted as such under the Housing Act 1985, had also been told that they would be given a local housing authority or housing association tenancy in performance of the homelessness duty. It may also arise where a local housing authority has announced a policy giving carers the right to take over tenancies on the death of tenants for whom they were caring.[92] The local housing authority must make provision for such an eventuality in its allocation scheme in order to achieve the recognition of that expectation. No 'legitimate expectation' argument is likely to be established successfully simply where there has been a failure in communication.[93]

4.55 As already indicated, once the local housing authority has adopted its scheme, it must comply with it. It is unlawful for a local housing authority to allocate accommodation otherwise than in accordance with the scheme.[94]

4.56 The rest of this Chapter is concerned with how a local allocation scheme must be framed to meet the relevant statutory and other legal requirements.

---

[90] The issue of 'legitimate expectation' arises where a person is, contrary to his or her expectations, deprived: '... of some benefit or advantage which either (i) he had in the past been permitted by the decision-maker to enjoy and which he can legitimately expect to be permitted to continue to do until there has been communicated to him some rational grounds for withdrawing it on which he has been given an opportunity to comment; or (ii) he has received assurance from the decision-maker that they will not be withdrawn without giving him first an opportunity of advancing reasons for contending that they should not be withdrawn': *Council of Civil Service Unions v Minister for the Civil Service* [1985] AC 374, HL, at 408, per Lord Diplock. See *R v North and East Devon Health Authority ex p Coughlan* [2001] QB 213, CA, and for a more recent discussion, *R (Bhatt Murphy (a firm)) v The Independent Assessor* [2008] EWCA Civ 755, CA.

[91] *R (Bibi and Al-Nashed) v Newham London Borough Council* [2001] EWCA Civ 495, (2001) 33 HLR 84, CA; *R (Ibrahim) v Redbridge London Borough Council* [2002] EWHC 2756 (Admin), (2003) February *Legal Action*, at p 35, Admin Ct; and *R (Bibi) v Newham London Borough Council* [2003] EWHC 1860 (Admin), (2003) September *Legal Action*, at p 28, Admin Ct.

[92] Or made similar provisions in other cases.

[93] *R (Tout a Tout) v Haringey London Borough Council* [2012] EWHC 873 (Admin), (2012) May *Legal Action* p 34, Admin Ct at [24].

[94] HA 1996, s 166A(14) [England] and s 167(8) [Wales], *R (Amirun Begum) v Tower Hamlets London Borough Council* [2002] EWHC (Admin) 633, (2003) 35 HLR 8, Admin Ct.

The 'reasonable preference' groups

4.57 Five groups of people must be accorded a 'reasonable preference' in housing allocation schemes framed under HA 1996, Part 6. They are:

(1)   people who are 'homeless', within the meaning of HA 1996, Part 7;

(2)   people who are owed a particular statutory duty by any local housing authority under certain provisions of homelessness legislation;[95]

(3)   people occupying insanitary or overcrowded housing or otherwise living in unsatisfactory housing conditions;

(4)   people who need to move on medical or welfare grounds, including grounds relating to a disability;[96] and

(5)   people who need to move to a particular locality in the district of the local housing authority, where failure to meet that need would cause hardship, to themselves or to others.[97]

4.58 The list may be extended or reduced by ministerial regulations without the need for primary legislation.[98] No such regulations have been made since that power was enacted.

4.59 The UK Government has from time to time considered possible additional categories. Some were suggested in a ministerial announcement made in December 2007.[99] But later, in a letter to local housing authorities in 2009, the then Minister for Housing wrote that he did *not* propose to change or add to the categories.[100] The present UK Government floated the possibility of further changes to the five categories in its November 2010 consultation paper but the vast majority of respondents were in favour of the retention of the existing reasonable preference categories, as these were seen to capture those in greatest housing need, protect the most vulnerable, and supported local

---

[95]   HA 1996, s 190(2), s 193(2) and s 195(2); Housing Act 1985, s 65(2) and s 68(2) and people who are occupying accommodation provided for them by any local housing authority under HA 1996, s 192(3). These sections define duties to homeless applicants in priority need (whether they became homeless intentionally or not), duties to applicants threatened with homelessness who have a priority need and are not intentionally threatened with homelessness, and the power to provide accommodation to unintentionally homeless applicants not in priority need. See Chapter 17.

[96]   HA 1996, s 166A(3)(d) [England] and s 167(2)(d) [Wales] prospectively amended by Housing Act 2004, s 223, adding '(including grounds relating to a disability)' but yet to be brought into force in Wales.

[97]   HA 1996, s 166A(3) [England], s 167(2) [Wales].

[98]   HA 1996, s 166A(7) [England], s 167(3) [Wales].

[99]   See **1.63**.

[100]   John Healey MP, letter 31 July 2009.

housing authorities in undertaking their statutory duties.[101] Those who did suggest additional reasonable preference categories proposed:[102]

- under-occupation; or

- a work-related category (with the aim of helping those in low income employment); or

- affordability (for households struggling to rent privately); or

- those leaving supported accommodation; or

- 16- or 17-year-olds with housing need within the meaning of ss 17 and 20 of the Children Act 1989; or

- ex-offenders; or

- key workers; or

- ex-service personnel; or

- carers; or

- older people; or

- people who contribute to the social capital of an area.

4.60 The UK Government's reaction was that, in light of the clear majority response to the consultation, it did not propose to make any changes to the existing reasonable preference categories.[103] The Localism Act 2011 therefore simply re-enacted in England the previous reasonable preference categories. The Minister said: 'I do not think anything here will give rise to anything new, although I accept that the current system is not capable of making everybody happy, because we are dealing with a quantity that is in short supply and under pressure.'[104]

4.61 It must be noted again that HA 1996, Part 6 does not require priority to be given to any *particular* applicant. All that HA 1996, Part 6, stipulates is that 'the scheme shall be framed' so that it gives reasonable preference to the statutory classes.[105] Each of the present five categories entitled to 'reasonable preference' requires detailed and careful consideration.

---

[101] *Local decisions: next steps towards a fairer future for social housing: A Summary of responses to consultation* (DCLG, February 2011), para 4.31.

[102] Ibid, paras 4.39–4.41.

[103] Ibid, para 8.18.

[104] *Hansard,* House of Commons Public Bill Committee on the Localism Bill, 3 March 2011, col 764.

[105] HA 1996, s 166A(3) [England], s 167(2) [Wales].

People who are 'homeless'[106]

4.62 'Homelessness' is a concept defined in HA 1996, Part 7.[107] Under that definition, a person is homeless if he or she has no accommodation available for his or her occupation, in the UK or elsewhere, which he or she is entitled to occupy:

(1)   by virtue of an interest in it; or

(2)   because of an order of a court; or

(3)   by an express or implied licence to occupy; or

(4)   by virtue of an enactment or rule of law giving him or her the right to remain in occupation; or

(5)   by reason of a restriction on the right of another person to obtain possession.[108]

4.63   A person who has somewhere to live is therefore 'homeless' *unless* he or she has at least one of these forms of entitlement to occupy – so a person living in a squat is 'homeless'.

4.64   A person is also homeless if he or she has a right to occupy accommodation but cannot secure entry to it, or it is not available, or it is not reasonable for him or her to continue to occupy it.[109] Accommodation is only regarded as 'available' if it is available to be occupied by all the members of the applicant's family who normally reside with him or her, and also by any other person who might reasonably be expected to reside with him or her.[110] Occupiers of caravans, mobile homes, and houseboats are homeless if they have no place where they are permitted both to place and to reside in their vehicle or vessel.[111]

4.65   To fall within the definition of 'homeless', an applicant need not have made an application for homelessness assistance to any local housing authority, let alone have received a decision on such an application. Indeed, the Welsh Code explicitly states that in no circumstances should allocations practices encourage the view that people have to apply as homeless to the local housing authority in order to obtain a social tenancy.[112] The assessment of whether the applicant is 'homeless' will need to be made by the local housing authority to which the application for an allocation has been directed.[113] A person who has

---

[106]   HA 1996, s 166A(3)(a) [England], s 167(2)(a) [Wales].
[107]   HA 1996, ss 175–177; see Chapter 11 of this book.
[108]   HA 1996, s 175(1).
[109]   HA 1996, s 175(2)(a) and (3).
[110]   HA 1996, s 176.
[111]   HA 1996, s 175(2)(b).
[112]   Welsh Code, para 10.26.
[113]   An applicant for social housing accommodation who gives the local housing authority

already applied to a local housing authority as 'homeless' and has been provided with accommodation in compliance with that local housing authority's duty will obviously have ceased to be 'homeless' (and thus normally falls within the second reasonable preference category – category (2) – which specifically deals with those formerly homeless persons owed housing duties).[114] In one case it was conceded, rightly, that a person provided with interim accommodation by a local housing authority pending the determination of an application for homelessness assistance under HA 1996, Part 7 remained 'homeless' for the purposes of this provision while in that accommodation.[115]

4.66 To obtain a 'reasonable preference' under the 'homeless' category, applicants need not have a 'priority need', a concept relevant only to the assessment of any HA 1996, Part 7 duty.[116] Nor is there any need for the local housing authority to consider whether or not applicants have become homeless intentionally.[117] All homeless people fall within this reasonable preference category[118] – even those who are not entitled to a housing duty under the provisions for homelessness assistance in HA 1996, Part 7 because, for example, they have no priority need.[119]

4.67 Precisely because statutory homelessness duties provide a safety net to pick up and accommodate those who are in priority need and are unintentionally homeless, this first category of 'reasonable preference' works to ensure that all *other* homeless people also secure a reasonable preference in allocation: those other homeless people being fit and healthy individuals, couples without children, those who have become homeless intentionally, etc.

4.68 The policy behind HA 1996, Part 6 is therefore unashamedly to ensure that every allocation scheme is open to, and gives preference to, those who are homeless for any reason and in any circumstances. It is intended to 'include rough sleepers and all others who do not have a home, for whatever reason'.[120]

4.69 Indeed, in Wales, the statutory guidance goes further than a strict reading of HA 1996, Part 6 requires and suggests that local housing authorities define homelessness for these purposes as arising 'where a person lacks

---

sufficient reason to believe that she or he may be homeless must also be dealt with under the homelessness provisions in HA 1996, Part 7. See **9.23–9.27**.

[114] See **4.71–4.79**.
[115] *R (Alam) v Tower Hamlets London Borough Council* [2009] EWHC 44 (Admin), (2009) March *Legal Action*, p 24, Admin Ct.
[116] English Code, para 4.4(a). See Chapter 13 of this book for the definition of 'priority need'.
[117] English Code, para 4.4(a). See Chapter 14 of this book for the definition of 'becoming homeless intentionally'.
[118] Applicants who are 'threatened with homelessness' (defined in HA 1996, s 175(4)) will not fall within the category until they are actually homeless.
[119] *R (Alam) v Tower Hamlets London Borough Council* [2009] EWHC (Admin) 44, (2009) March *Legal Action*, p 24, Admin Ct.
[120] *Hansard,* HL Deb, vol 630, ser 6, col 1013 (15 January 2002), Lord Falconer.

accommodation or where their tenure is not secure'.[121] This approach, unlike the statutory definition, includes persons who are threatened with homelessness and those who have no suitable alternative accommodation, whether they are leaving institutions, required to leave by family or friends or due to relationship breakdown, or facing a possession order.[122] When deciding whether or not a person is 'homeless' for these purposes, Welsh local housing authorities must have regard to the Welsh Code's more generous approach, although it is expressly recognised to be guidance which is 'broader than the legal definition'.[123]

4.70 A person in this first 'reasonable preference' category may, if the local scheme so provides, also obtain 'additional preference' if his or her housing needs are 'urgent'[124] or if he or she also falls into another of the preference categories.[125] A person who would otherwise be in this first 'reasonable preference' category will not in fact be entitled to benefit from it if the only reason he or she comes within it is because regard has been had to a 'restricted person' in determining his or her application.[126] The remaining four categories deal with applicants who already have accommodation.

People who are owed certain homelessness duties[127]

4.71 This category encompasses applicants for an allocation who have already applied to a local housing authority for homelessness assistance and have received a decision that the local housing authority owes them a duty because:

(1)   they are homeless and have a priority need, whether or not they became homeless intentionally;[128] or

(2)   they are threatened with homelessness, have a priority need and did not become threatened with homelessness intentionally.[129]

4.72 Applicants who have been found to be homeless, but not to have a priority need, will only fall within this category if:

---

[121]   Welsh Code, para 8.14.

[122]   Welsh Code, para 8.14, giving examples of people who are within three months of the end of their tenancies, are subject to possession proceedings, or are under the threat of eviction, as people whose tenure is not secure.

[123]   Welsh Code, para 4.18. HA 1996, s 167(2)(a) [Wales] provides that to get within the first category of 'reasonable preference' the person must be homeless 'within the meaning of Part 7'. The Welsh Code can only work on the premise that those embraced by its terms would meet that standard because their present accommodation is not 'reasonable for them to continue to occupy' (HA 1996, s 175(3)).

[124]   See **4.123–4.134**.

[125]   See **4.116**.

[126]   HA 1996, s 166A(4) [England], s 167(2ZA) [Wales]. For more on 'restricted person' see **4.153–4.154**.

[127]   HA 1996, s 166A(3)(b) [England], s 167(2)(b) [Wales].

[128]   Duty owed either under HA 1996, s 190(2) (see **17.182–17.189**) or s 193(2) (see **17.23–17.181**), or under Housing Act 1985, s 65(2).

[129]   Duty owed under HA 1996, s 195(2) (see **17.190–17.195**) or Housing Act 1985, s 68(2).

(1)   they did not become homeless intentionally; and

(2)   a local housing authority has decided to exercise its power to provide accommodation for them.[130]

4.73 By definition, these applicants must have made applications for homelessness assistance, and have received decisions that a duty of the prescribed type is owed to them. The duty need not be owed by the same local housing authority as the local housing authority to which the applicant is applying for an allocation. So an applicant who has applied as homeless to District A, and has been placed by that local housing authority, pursuant to one of the prescribed duties, in District B might wish to apply for an allocation to the local housing authorities for both Districts A and B. He or she will have an entitlement to 'reasonable preference' in both the local housing authorities' schemes.

4.74 It must be noted that the terms of this second category of 'reasonable preference' are very tightly drawn. They certainly do *not* cover all applicants who have applied to a local housing authority as homeless, nor all of those who have benefited from a duty under HA 1996, Part 7 (the homelessness safety net). For example, the following applicants for a housing allocation would fall outside the second of the 'reasonable preference' categories because they are not owed one of the prescribed statutory homelessness duties:

- people provided with interim accommodation[131] (pending a HA 1996, Part 7 decision);

- people provided with accommodation pending a review of an unfavourable decision or pending an appeal;[132]

- people accommodated pending a local connection referral;[133]

- people who are not eligible for homelessness assistance;[134]

- people who are homeless, who are not in priority need and who became homeless intentionally;[135]

- people who are threatened with homelessness and who are not in priority need;[136] and

---

[130]   Under HA 1996, s 192(3). See **17.215–17.222**.
[131]   HA 1996, s 188(1). See **16.12–16.28**. They would still be 'homeless' and entitled to a reasonable preference under the first 'reasonable preference' category: *R (Alam) v Tower Hamlets London Borough Council* [2009] EWHC (Admin) 44, (2009) March *Legal Action*, p 24, Admin Ct.
[132]   HA 1996, ss 188(3) and 204(4). See **16.36–16.48** and **16.49–16.55**.
[133]   HA 1996, s 200(1). See **16.56–16.63**.
[134]   HA 1996, s 185. See Chapter 12.
[135]   HA 1996, s 190(3). See Chapters 13 and 14.
[136]   HA 1996, s 195(5). See **11.29–11.33**.

- people who have become threatened with homelessness intentionally.[137]

4.75 Those persons may, depending on their circumstances, fit into the first category, or into one or more of the third to fifth categories, of those entitled to a 'reasonable preference'.[138]

4.76 Amendments made by the Localism Act 2011 to HA 1996, Part 7 (Homelessness) allow a local housing authority in England to bring to an end the duty owed to an unintentionally homeless person in priority need by the making of an offer of suitable private rented sector accommodation.[139] Several respondents to the UK Government's November 2010 consultation paper on social housing noted that the changes to allow local housing authorities to discharge the main homelessness duty in the private rented sector, without the agreement of the person owed the duty, could have a considerable impact on social housing allocation to those in this preference category.[140] To counter the possibility that some local housing authorities might, in consequence, consider it unnecessary to continue to afford applicants for homelessness assistance a reasonable preference under this category, the English Code says in terms that the category remains in place 'notwithstanding the amendments to Part 7 made by the Localism Act'.[141]

4.77 Of course, the local housing authority is entitled to discriminate (provided it does so lawfully) among those within this reasonable preference category to reflect the particular nature of the homelessness duty owed to the applicant, or the way it is being performed, or the applicant's particular circumstances. For example, an applicant owed the main housing duty (HA 1996, s 193(2))[142] who is accommodated in good quality and stable temporary accommodation may be afforded less preference than a similar applicant owed the same duty whose temporary accommodation will shortly become unavailable (eg because the lease from a private landlord is shortly to expire). In one local housing authority's scheme, applying to those facts, 10 points were awarded during the period that the private sector lease was running and 300 points were awarded shortly before the termination of the lease to enable the household to compete realistically for an allocation at that time. That aspect of the scheme was perfectly lawful.[143]

4.78 The Welsh Code advises that local housing authorities in Wales which have placed homeless households in private sector leased accommodation should review the circumstances of those households at least annually. Those

---

[137] HA 1996, s 195(5). See **14.163–14.173**.
[138] See **4.62–4.70** for the first category and **4.80–4.114** for the third to fifth categories.
[139] Localism Act 2011, ss 148–149. Only for applicants whose applications for homelessness assistance were made on or after 9 November 2012 to a local housing authority in England. For 'private rented sector offer' see **17.109–17.131**.
[140] *Local decisions: next steps towards a fairer future for social housing: Summary of responses to consultation* (DCLG, Feb 2011), para 4.34.
[141] English Code, para 4.7.
[142] See **17.23–17.41**.
[143] *R (Lin) v Barnet London Borough Council* [2007] EWCA Civ 132, [2007] HLR 30, CA.

applicants who wish to move out of the private leased accommodation could be awarded 'full homelessness points' while those content to remain could have such points deferred until the lease expires.[144]

4.79 A person in this second 'reasonable preference' category may, if the local scheme so provides, also obtain 'additional preference' if his or her housing needs are 'urgent'[145] or if he or she also falls into another of the preference categories.[146] A person who would otherwise be in this second 'reasonable preference' category will not in fact be entitled to benefit from it if the only reason he or she comes within it is because regard has been had to a 'restricted person' in determining the application.[147] Further, an applicant who receives 'reasonable preference' by being in this category remains subject to any other rules in the allocation scheme, eg the deferral of an application where suitable offers of accommodation under the allocation scheme have been made but refused.[148]

People occupying insanitary or overcrowded housing or otherwise living in unsatisfactory housing conditions[149]

4.80 Nothing in HA 1996, Part 6 defines the three key adjectives in this 'reasonable preference' category: 'insanitary', 'overcrowded', and 'unsatisfactory'. Nor does HA 1996, Part 6 provide a direct link to the meanings that they have in other legislation, even other housing legislation.

4.81 This means that local housing authorities are largely free to develop, and incorporate into allocation schemes, their own approach to determining the circumstances in which an applicant would fall into this 'reasonable preference' category.

4.82 The general law governing insanitary conditions, overcrowding, and unsatisfactory housing standards is scattered over a number of statutes. The Environmental Protection Act 1990, Part 3 is designed to address unhealthy premises. The rules on overcrowding are set out in the Housing Act 1985, Part 10. The law relating to hazardous housing is contained in the Housing Act 2004, Part 1. These statutory provisions should be taken into account by local housing authorities when drawing up their criteria for admission to this third 'reasonable preference' category.[150] However, local housing authorities

---

[144] Welsh Code, paras 4.29–4.30.

[145] HA 1996, s 166(3) [England], s 167(2) [Wales]. See also **4.123–4.134**.

[146] See **4.85**.

[147] HA 1996, s 166A(4) [England], s 167(2ZA) [Wales]. For 'restricted person' see **4.153–4.154**.

[148] *R (Cranfield-Adams) v Richmond upon Thames London Borough Council* (2012) August *Legal Action*, p 27, Admin Ct.

[149] HA 1996, s 166A(3)(c) [England], s 167(2)(c) [Wales].

[150] See Welsh Code, para 4.19 which also refers to statutory controls on houses in multiple occupation.

could, and many do, adopt a more generous approach than the statutory minimum standards when operating this category.[151]

4.83 Many local housing authorities, for example, will have a broader definition of 'overcrowding' than the statutory definition.[152] Indeed, one judge has said that this reasonable preference category:

> 'must include those who live in unsatisfactory housing conditions but need not necessarily statutorily be overcrowded.'[153]

4.84 When local housing authorities in England were asked in 2012 what criteria they were actually operating to define 'overcrowding' in their allocation schemes, most indicated that they either took into account the statutory standards in the Housing Act 1985 or employed the *bedroom standard* or a variant of the *bedroom standard* (see **4.87**). Where they used a variant of the bedroom standard, this usually involved applying different age limits. A small number employed the Local Housing Allowance size criteria and a handful based the award of priority on whether overcrowding was sufficiently severe to present a category 1 hazard under the Housing Health and Safety Rating System. In addition, some had devised a local definition of overcrowding.[154] From these responses it is clear that there is something of a lottery in England as to whether any particular degree of overcrowding would fall within or outside this reasonable preference category for the purposes of any particular local allocation scheme. As one survey report put it:[155]

> 'In defining "overcrowding" in their allocations policies, authorities used a variety of approaches. Some calibrated their rules according to statutory standards, others to the bedroom standard. There were differences in assumptions as to what could be considered "reasonable" in terms of bedroom sharing by children.'

4.85 The researchers conducting that survey of local housing authorities asked respondents to specify the numbers of households on their list who were 'in the reasonable preference category of overcrowding'. They found that:

> 'On average, these accounted for 18 per cent of all new applicants on authorities' housing registers. However, the proportions cited were wide-ranging – from over half in two authorities to less than one per cent in four others. While the incidence

---

[151] For example, in defining 'overcrowding' in their allocation schemes, local housing authorities have been found to be adopting a wide variety of approaches: *Exploring local authority policy and practice on housing allocations* (CLG, July 2009), para 14.

[152] See Housing Act 1985, ss 325–326.

[153] *R (Ahmad) v Newham London Borough Council* [2007] EWHC 2332 (Admin), (2007) November *Legal Action*, p 38, Admin Ct per Blake J at [64]. This part of the decision was not subject to appeal.

[154] *Allocation of accommodation: guidance for local housing authorities in England: Summary of Responses to consultation* (DCLG, June 2012) paras 3.38–3.39.

[155] *Exploring local authority policy and practice on housing allocations* (DCLG, July 2009) p 7.

of overcrowding is certain to vary from area to area these findings suggest that local definitions of the phenomenon as incorporated within allocations policies may well vary more.'[156]

4.86 In responding to another consultation exercise, a number of local housing authorities in England wrote that they considered that some clarification and updating of the 'overcrowding' category of 'reasonable preference' was necessary. For example, it was felt by some that 'overcrowding' should reflect the modern approach taken in the Housing Health and Safety Rating System contained in Housing Act 2004, Part 1.[157]

4.87 In the event, the current statutory guidance for local housing authorities in England expresses no preference for either the Housing Act 1985 definition or the Housing Act 2004 approach but instead holds out the *bedroom standard* as 'an appropriate measure of overcrowding for allocation purposes'.[158] The Secretary of State's bedroom standard[159] allocates a separate bedroom to each:

- married or cohabiting couple;

- adult aged 21 years or more;

- pair of adolescents aged 10–20 years of the same sex; and

- pair of children aged under 10 years regardless of sex.

4.88 The English Code proposes this standard be adopted 'as a minimum' in considering the framing of the reasonable preference category for 'overcrowded' housing in any particular allocation scheme.[160]

4.89 As to the scope of 'unsatisfactory' housing conditions, the Codes of Guidance each provide a list of suggested criteria, which is said to be for illustrative purposes only, although many local housing authorities will adopt most, or all, of the criteria in their own lists for assessment of unsatisfactory housing conditions.[161] The Codes emphasise that the list is not comprehensive or exhaustive (the English Code also describes its list as simply providing 'possible indicators'[162]) and that there may, in particular, be *local* factors that an individual local housing authority would wish to acknowledge in its allocation scheme.[163]

---

[156] Ibid, para 4.28.
[157] *Local decisions: next steps towards a fairer future for social housing Summary of responses to consultation* (DCLG, Feb 2011), para 4.35.
[158] English Code, para 4.8.
[159] Ibid.
[160] English Code, para 4.8.
[161] English Code, para 4.12 and Annex 1; Welsh Code, Annex 3.
[162] English Code, para 4.12.
[163] English Code, para 4.12 and Annex 1; Welsh Code, para 4.19 and Annex 3.

4.90 'Under-occupation' is included in the illustrative list[164] contained in the Welsh Code but has been omitted from the list in the latest English Code.[165] That omission is probably the result of a desire to encourage local housing authorities in England to treat transfer applicants who are under-occupying as *not* falling within this reasonable preference category as defined in their local allocation schemes. In that way, the provisions of HA 1996, Part 6 will not apply to their transfer applications which can be dealt with outside the normal Part 6 arrangements.[166]

4.91 Whether to include under-occupation as a criteria in assessing 'unsatisfactory housing' remains a matter for each local housing authority, provided it has had regard to the relevant national guidance. All the local housing authorities in England which responded to a consultation exercise conducted in early 2012 reported that they 'give priority in their allocation scheme to social tenants who are under-occupying their property, or are reviewing their allocation scheme in order to do so'.[167] In one case in which a local allocation scheme gave considerable preference to under-occupying applicants, none of the parties 'suggested that the very favourable treatment given to under-occupation transfers is unlawful'.[168] The possibility of enlarging the reasonable preference categories to refer explicitly to under-occupation was floated by the then Minister for Housing in 2007, but in July 2009 a subsequent Minister for Housing announced that it would not be pursued.[169] In a more recent consultation exercise, a new category for 'under-occupation' was the most commonly suggested additional category of reasonable preference[170] but no amendment to the statutory scheme was subsequently made in order to expressly and separately include it.

4.92 Local housing authorities are often keen to transfer their own tenants who want a smaller property, so as to free up the larger property for an allocation. From April 2013 the reduction in housing benefit, for working age tenants of social housing who are under-occupying, will provide a further incentive for transfers to smaller homes. Of course, where such a transfer is at the *landlord's* initiative, there is no 'allocation' at all and the allocation scheme does not apply.[171]

---

[164] Welsh Code, Annex 3.

[165] English Code, Annex 1.

[166] HA 1996, s159(4B)(c) and see **2.57–2.68**.

[167] *Allocation of accommodation: guidance for local housing authorities in England: Summary of Responses to consultation* (DCLG, June 2012) para 3.2.

[168] *R (Ahmad) v Newham London Borough Council* [2009] UKHL 14, [2009] HLR 41, HL at [19]

[169] See **4.59**.

[170] *Local decisions: next steps towards a fairer future for social housing Summary of responses to consultation* (DCLG, February 2011), para 4.39.

[171] HA 1996, s 159(4B) [England] and s 159(5) [Wales]. See **2.59**. This may explain why under-occupation has hitherto *not* attracted such high priority within allocation schemes as might otherwise have been expected: see *Exploring local authority policy and practice on housing allocations* (CLG, July 2009), para 16.

4.93 Neither the statutory minimum definitions nor the illustrative lists contained in the Codes should inhibit advisers from assisting applicants to press for a local housing authority to treat them as within this third 'reasonable preference' category where circumstances suggest that the present home is 'overcrowded', 'insanitary' or otherwise 'unsatisfactory' on the broadest approach to that terminology. Advisers will need to consider the wording adopted in the particular local allocation scheme used to reflect this broad statutory category and do their best to bring their clients within that wording.

4.94 A person in this third 'reasonable preference' category may, if the local scheme so provides, also obtain 'additional preference' if his or her housing needs are 'urgent'[172] or if he or she also falls into another of the 'reasonable preference' categories.[173]

People who need to move on medical or welfare grounds (including grounds relating to a disability)[174]

4.95 This fourth 'reasonable preference' category should be framed in any local housing allocation scheme so as to include any applicant for accommodation whose health or welfare, or that of a member of his or her household, is impaired by remaining in the accommodation currently occupied, and thus there is a 'need to move' elsewhere. For obvious reasons, no 'reasonable preference' must be accorded simply because an applicant *wishes* to move on welfare or medical grounds, for example to a warmer part of the country or to be nearer friends or relatives. The category is designed for those who 'need' to move.

4.96 Again, none of the terms 'medical grounds', 'welfare grounds' or 'grounds relating to a disability' are defined by HA 1996, Part 6. Nor are there any direct links made to the definition of these terms in any other statutes. In the first instance it is for local housing authorities to decide what the categories mean and to apply them when framing an allocation scheme.

4.97 The terms do not relate exclusively to the impact, on health or welfare, of the present accommodation alone, although any detrimental effect caused by the present accommodation would obviously fall within this test. As one judge put it:

> 'the relevant question is whether the current housing conditions are having an adverse effect on the medical condition of the claimant, which itself creates a particular need for her to move.'[175]

---

[172] See **4.123–4.134**.
[173] See **4.116**.
[174] HA 1996, s 166A(3)(d) [England], s 167(2)(d) [Wales].
[175] *R (Ghandali) v Ealing London Borough Council* [2006] EWHC 1859 (Admin), at [34], (2006) September *Legal Action*, p 14, Admin Ct, per Leveson J.

4.98 The detrimental effect on health or welfare could be caused by the location of the present accommodation as much as by the physical conditions of the present accommodation.

4.99 Thus, 'medical grounds' could relate to an adverse impact of the current accommodation on health (such as inaccessible washing and toilet facilities, or dampness having an effect on health) or there may be sound medical grounds for changing location, eg to relocate closer to a particular medical facility or to a carer,[176] or to escape adverse environmental factors in the present location.

4.100 'Welfare grounds' would seem to refer to care and support needs or other social needs that do *not* require medical care or support. Examples given in the Codes are the needs of those leaving care or other vulnerable persons who need a stable base from which to build a secure life, and the needs of vulnerable people who are not able to find their own accommodation.[177] The English Code advises that this category would also include the needs to move of those providing (or intending to provide) care and support to certain children:

> '[t]his would include foster carers, those approved to adopt, or those being assessed for approval to foster or adopt, who need to move to a larger home in order to accommodate a looked after child or a child who was previously looked after by a local authority. It would also include special guardians, holders of a residence order and family and friends carers who are not foster carers but who have taken on the care of a child because the parents are unable to provide care.'[178]

4.101 Specialist advice is obviously helpful when assessing whether the applicant's health or welfare necessitates a move. The Welsh Code recommends that the health or social care professional with direct knowledge of the applicant's condition is contacted by the local housing authority for an opinion on the applicant's health and its impact on the applicant's housing needs.[179] Such a person will usually be the applicant's GP, consultant or social worker.

4.102 The local housing authority must, however, be careful in its treatment of medical advice it receives. It must not delegate its decision about admission to its reasonable preference category to a medical adviser. The adviser advises, the local housing authority makes the decisions. A local housing authority should not confine itself to an assessment by its own medical adviser without first seeking information from the applicant's own doctors or other relevant professionals. When the report from an independent or in-house medical adviser is obtained, the local housing authority should not rely on expressions of opinion or value judgments that it contains and which are beyond the remit of true medical advice.[180]

---

[176] Welsh Code, para 4.107.
[177] English Code, para 4.10; Welsh Code, para 4.21.
[178] English Code, para 4.10.
[179] Welsh Code, para 4.20.
[180] *R (Bauer-Czarnomski) v Ealing London Borough Council* [2010] EWHC 130 (Admin), (2010) March *Legal Action*, p 30, Admin Ct and see **2.105–2.106**.

4.103 After a local housing authority's medical adviser has advised on the evidence available at the time, and the local housing authority has made a decision as to the applicant's entitlement to reasonable preference and priority, if there is then further medical evidence or social work opinion, and/or subsequent events, the medical adviser is under a duty to consider that new information. In a case where the medical adviser's advice was not based on a proper consideration of new evidence and events, the local housing authority's decision not to award the applicant any reasonable preference under this category was quashed and required to be reconsidered.[181]

4.104 The additional words '(including any grounds relating to a disability)' were first introduced into HA 1996, Part 6 in England on 27 April 2005[182] so as to make it clear that those applicants whose need to move relates to a disability (but who are not ill or otherwise in 'medical' need) would fall within this 'reasonable preference' category. However, they have never formed part of the applicable provisions in Wales and were not introduced by the amendments made by the Localism Act 2011.[183] The wording includes those with a learning disability as well as those with a physical disability.[184] Prior to the statutory amendment in England, the view that medical needs should be taken to include those needs relating to a disability was recommended by the then statutory guidance in any event. The Welsh Code provides extensive guidance on issues relating to disability in the context of social housing allocation even though the statutory amendment has not been brought into force in Wales.[185]

4.105 It is plain from the additional wording that the 'disability' referred to is not restricted to a disability of the applicant; it could be the disability of any member of the applicant's household. Alternatively, the wording would be satisfied where a non-disabled applicant needs to move so as to be nearer to a disabled relative or some other disabled person. An argument that a local housing authority's allocation scheme was unlawful because it did not allocate points to reflect 'disability' failed when the points awarded for health needs were shown to have included needs arising from disabilities.[186]

4.106 Local housing authorities may wish to consider whether an applicant's needs could be met by providing aids and adaptations to the current accommodation, enabling them to remain in their present home.

4.107 The Codes provide illustrative lists of different types of 'medical grounds' and 'welfare grounds'.[187] Those illustrations encompass the types of accommodation that may be needed (adapted, improved, sheltered or ground

---

[181] *R (Ghandali) v Ealing London Borough Council* [2006] EWHC 1859 (Admin), (2006) September *Legal Action*, p 14, Admin Ct and see **2.105–2.106**.

[182] The then HA 1996, s 167(2)(d), as amended by Housing Act 2004, s 223.

[183] HA 1996, s 167(2)(d) [Wales].

[184] English Code, para 4.9.

[185] Welsh Code, paras 4.82–4.95.

[186] *R v Lewisham London Borough Council ex p Pinzon* (1999) 2 CCLR 152, QBD.

[187] English Code, Annex 1; Welsh Code, Annex 3.

floor), the type of medical condition that might fall within this criterion (mental illness or disorder, physical or learning disability, chronic or progressive medical conditions), and other types of vulnerability (such as young people at risk, people with behavioural difficulties or those recovering from the effects of violence). The needs of those who provide care, as well as those who receive it, are included in the illustrative lists. The need to be near friends, relatives or medical facilities for medical reasons also appears. The Welsh Code, but not the English Code, includes recovery from alcohol or drug problems as a type of 'medical ground' that could fall within this category.[188] The English Code uses the less specific terminology of 'ability to fend for self restricted for other reasons'.[189]

4.108 The Welsh Code recommends that once accommodation is allocated to a person falling within this category, his or her support and care needs should be assessed and there should be liaison with social services, Supporting People and other agencies providing support.[190]

4.109 A person in this fourth 'reasonable preference' category may, if the local scheme so provides, also obtain 'additional preference' if his or her housing needs are 'urgent',[191] or if he or she also falls into another of the 'reasonable preference' categories.[192]

People who need to move to a particular locality in the local housing authority's district where hardship would be caused if they did not move[193]

4.110 This is the most recently created 'reasonable preference' category and was first introduced in January 2003.[194] The Codes suggest that people may fall within it if they need to move in order to give or receive care, to be able to access specialised medical treatment, or to take up particular education, employment or training opportunities in some particular locality.[195] Some, but not all, of those examples would fall within 'medical or welfare grounds' in the fourth category, but those applicants who overlap are now entitled to be placed in both categories. Again, the emphasis is on 'need' to move, not a desire to move. This fifth category will also be suitable for victims of harassment or violence needing to move to safer areas.

4.111 A particular locality should be identified, which must be within the district of the local housing authority to which application is made. Any need to move outside the district of the local housing authority in which the

---

[188] Welsh Code, Annex 3.
[189] English Code, Annex 1.
[190] Welsh Code, para 4.22.
[191] See **4.123–4.134**.
[192] See **4.116**.
[193] HA 1996, s 166A(3)(e) [England], s 167(2)(e) [Wales].
[194] Homelessness Act 2002, s 16(3).
[195] English Code, para 4.11; Welsh Code, paras 4.24.

applicant presently resides requires either application to the other local housing authority in whose district the specific locality falls, or the use of any reciprocal agreements or nomination rights agreed between the two local housing authorities involved.

4.112 The need to move must be sufficiently great that 'hardship' would otherwise be caused, either to the applicant or to others. HA 1996, Part 6 and the Codes do not define 'hardship', nor the degree of severity required for an applicant to fall within this category. The hardship that might be caused to *the applicant* if he or she is not moved may well be fairly self-evident: deterioration in health, inability to take up education, employment or training opportunities, etc. The hardship that might be caused to *others* includes situations where an applicant needs to move to a particular locality to provide care to a friend or relative already living in that locality. The category is not limited to personal hardship. It may include financial hardship, for example, so as to accord preference to an applicant of limited means who needs to move from a high rent to a low rent district. This will become increasing relevant as changes to welfare benefits limit the maximum benefits certain claimants can receive – whether as a cap on housing costs or as an overall cap of benefit receipts.

4.113 A recent consultation exercise in England provoked a wide range of responses to the question of whether the 'hardship' category should be modified or clarified. The summary of those responses indicated that:[196]

- A few considered that the definition of 'hardship' (or 'welfare') needed to be clarified to explicitly include those who are unable to afford other tenure types as a result of unemployment or low income.

- Others commented that it could be adjusted to reflect prevailing socio-economic circumstances, although it was recognised that this might be more a matter for local housing authorities to take into account when exercising their flexibility to address local priorities.

- A few also commented that the hardship category should be supplemented by 'or danger' to make more explicit the needs of those escaping domestic violence.

4.114 A person in this fifth 'reasonable preference' category may, if the local scheme so provides, also obtain 'additional preference' if his or her housing needs are 'urgent',[197] or if he or she also falls into another of the 'reasonable preference' categories.[198]

---

[196] *Local decisions: next steps towards a fairer future for social housing Summary of responses to consultation* (DCLG, February 2011), para 4.35.
[197] See **4.123–4.134**.
[198] See **4.116**.

Assessment of the right 'reasonable preference' category

4.115 The local housing authority will usually want to take into account the whole of the applicant's needs and circumstances, and the needs and circumstances of those members of his or her household who are included in the applicant's application, to determine which, if any, of the 'reasonable preference' categories applies to the applicant.

4.116 But beyond identifying the relevant 'reasonable preference' categories, HA 1996, Part 6 does not dictate how preferences are to be determined. For example, HA 1996, Part 6 does not address what happens where:

(1)   a single household spans two or more 'reasonable preference' categories; or

(2)   there are several households in a particular 'reasonable preference' category, eligible for a particular allocation; or

(3)   there are two households, each in a different 'reasonable preference' category, eligible for a single allocation.

4.117 HA 1996, Part 6 expressly gives the local housing authority a considerable degree of flexibility in according 'additional preference' or in reducing the extent of the 'reasonable preference' that would otherwise be received.[199] It has fallen to the courts to spell out the limits (if any) on the ways in which an allocation scheme can be framed to enhance or reduce the reasonable preference to which a person in one of the statutory categories may otherwise be entitled.

4.118 Between 1996 and 2009 the courts took a fairly interventionist approach. Allocation schemes faced difficulty in the courts if they were too inflexible to respond to comparative needs, whether within categories, across categories, or where applicants fell within more than one category of 'reasonable preference'.

4.119 For example, once the whole of the relevant household's needs are assessed, it may transpire that it falls into more than one of the statutory categories. Until 2009, it was considered that the applicant's subsequent priority in the allocation scheme must reflect that fact. A scheme, whether it operated by bands, points or a combination of the two, had to be sufficiently flexible for the applicant's composite or cumulative needs to be recognised and for circumstances spanning more than one reasonable preference category to be taken into account.[200] Even for those applicants within the same 'reasonable

---

[199] See **4.123–4.151**.

[200] An allocation scheme which had no mechanism for identifying cumulative need and therefore could not award additional preference for cumulative need was held to be unlawful in *R (Cali) v Waltham Forest London Borough Council* [2006] EWHC 302 (Admin), [2007] HLR 1, Admin Ct.

preference' category, there will be different 'housing needs' between them. Until 2009, it was thought that an allocation scheme must be capable of reflecting that fact. For example, an allocation scheme that only awarded medical points for the member of the applicant's household in most medical need, and which failed to recognise the medical needs of any other member of the same household was held to be unlawful.[201] Another allocation scheme which did not recognise different needs of different members of the household was found to be unlawful and was not saved by a discretion to award more points in exceptionally serious cases.[202] An allocation scheme which was entirely points-based and contained no discretion to award points for any other need not specified in the scheme was unlawful because it wholly fettered the local housing authority's discretion.[203]

4.120 However, in 2009, the House of Lords identified that, beyond requiring a local allocation scheme to be framed so as to accord a reasonable priority to those groups in the 'reasonable preference' categories, HA 1996, Part 6 (as modified in 2003) left it largely to individual local housing authorities to determine how their schemes should deal with applicants in more than one reasonable preference category or how to prioritise between applicants in different categories.[204] A local housing authority could adopt a scheme that enabled it to make fine distinctions between different applicants and then prioritise accordingly, based on individual assessments. Alternatively, the scheme could take a broad brush approach gathering all (or almost all) reasonable preference category applicants into a single band or group and then prioritise between them by date of application or some other simple criterion. The House of Lords was clear that it was not for the courts to become embroiled in the details of prioritisation mechanisms in individual schemes. Subject only to the requirements of rationality and compliance with the terms of the statutory provisions, the arrangements for prioritisation within any particular scheme are a matter for local political judgment by a local housing authority. The English Code accordingly spells out that there is no requirement to give equal weight to each of the reasonable preference categories and no requirement for an allocation scheme to afford greater priority to applicants who fall within more than one reasonable preference category over those who are in a single reasonable preference category.[205] The Welsh Code records that there is no longer any requirement to give more preference to an applicant who falls into more than one reasonable preference category[206] and deals with the impact of the decision in *Ahmad* at some length.[207]

---

[201] *R v Tower Hamlets London Borough Council ex p Uddin* (2000) 32 HLR 391, QBD; and *R (Vatansever) v Southwark London Borough Council* [2001] EWHC 546 (Admin), (2001) October *Legal Action*, p 14, Admin Ct.

[202] *R v Islington London Borough Council ex p Reilly and Mannix* (1999) 31 HLR 651, QBD.

[203] *R v Lambeth London Borough Council ex p Anderson* (2000) February *Legal Action*, at p 25, QBD.

[204] *R (Ahmad) v Newham London Borough Council* [2009] UKHL 14, [2009] HLR 41, HL.

[205] English Code, para 4.5.

[206] Welsh Code, para 4.17.

[207] Welsh Code, paras 4.54–4.58.

4.121 'Need' for housing which brings an applicant within any of the reasonable preference categories must, of course, be assessed objectively by the local housing authority. Schemes which rely upon applicants assessing their own needs have been held to be unlawful in that they run the risk of encouraging applicants to assess themselves as requiring unsuitable accommodation, in the hope of a shorter waiting period for undesirable accommodation.[208]

4.122 Having rehearsed the importance of the relevant statutory categories to be afforded 'reasonable preference', this Chapter will next consider how a local housing allocation scheme can:

(1)   award additional preference; and/or

(2)   reduce preference.

Additional preference

4.123 An allocation scheme *may* be framed so as to give 'additional preference' to particular descriptions of people who are already within the reasonable preference categories.[209] The scheme does not need to contain a provision for this form of enhanced priority but *may* do so. HA 1996, Part 6, simply gives a local housing authority a discretion to provide for 'additional preference'.[210] HA 1996, Part 6 does not define the scope of 'additional preference' or offer illustrations of its application.

4.124 Local housing authorities are advised by the Codes that they should consider whether they have a local need to exercise this discretion and include such provisions in their schemes, taking into account their local circumstances, and presumably the particular circumstances of likely applicants.[211] The local allocation scheme will be formulated as a result of that consideration and individual decisions made according to whatever terms the scheme has adopted. It should be noted that the provision does not enable the allocation scheme to be framed so as to simply afford additional preference to particular applicants. Under this statutory provision the scheme can be framed so as to give additional preference to 'particular descriptions of people' with urgent housing needs who are already within the reasonable preference classes.

4.125 Examples of descriptions of people who may be identified by a local housing authority in its allocation scheme as entitled to additional preference, by having more urgent housing needs than other reasonable preference applicants, are included in both Codes of Guidance.

[208]   *R (A) v Lambeth London Borough Council, R (Lindsay) v Lambeth London Borough Council* [2002] EWCA Civ 1084, [2002] HLR 57, CA and *R (Cali) v Waltham Forest London Borough Council* [2006] EWHC 302 (Admin), [2007] HLR 1, Admin Ct.
[209]   HA 1996, s 166A(3) [England] and s 167(2) [Wales], last sentence in each case.
[210]   HA 1996, s 166A(3) [England] and s 167(2) [Wales].
[211]   English Code, para 4.13; Welsh Code, para 4.26.

4.126 The English Code suggests local housing authorities 'should consider' giving additional preference to three specific groups:[212]

- those who need to move urgently because of a life-threatening illness or sudden disability;

- families in severe overcrowding which poses a serious health hazard; and

- those who are homeless and require urgent re-housing as a result of violence or threats of violence, including intimidated witnesses, and those escaping serious anti-social behaviour or domestic violence.

4.127 The English Code makes no further suggestion as to how 'severe' overcrowding or 'serious' health hazard/anti-social behaviour/domestic violence might be defined in any allocation scheme.

4.128 The Welsh Code gives the following examples of applicants to whom the local housing authority 'should' consider awarding additional preference:[213]

- those forced to leave their homes by actual or threatened violence (including intimidated witnesses);

- those who need to move for urgent medical reasons;

- those who have reasonable prospects of an offer of accommodation within a relatively short period but who suddenly lose their existing homes as a result of a disaster;

- those who are under-occupying and wish to move to smaller premises; and

- certain applicants with connections to the armed forces (see **4.131**).

4.129 Both Codes are clear, however, that these are only examples.[214] The intention is that the local scheme should spell out the sorts of circumstances in which additional preference, and thus priority, will be given in respect of the most urgent housing needs. Thus, the House of Lords has upheld as lawful a scheme which made additional priority (beyond ordinary reasonable preference) available to only a small proportion of applicants and only on satisfaction of 'stringent' and 'very strict' criteria.[215]

4.130 The UK Government has been particularly keen that local housing authorities should frame their schemes to give additional preference to applicants who are within the reasonable preference categories and who also have some connection with the armed forces. As an initial measure, in April

---

[212] English Code, para 4.13.
[213] Welsh Code, para 4.26.
[214] English Code, para 4.13; Welsh Code, para 4.26.
[215] *R (Ahmad) v Newham London Borough Council* [2009] UKHL 14, [2009] HLR 41, HL at [54].

2009, the then Secretary of State for Communities and Local Government issued statutory guidance to local housing authorities in England identifying the following very specific category of applicant who should be embraced by any allocation scheme which has been framed to give 'additional preference' to applicants who are in the 'reasonable preference' groups:[216]

> 'any applicant who needs to move to suitable adapted accommodation because of a serious injury, medical condition or disability which he or she, or a member of their household, has sustained as a result of service in the Armed Forces.'

4.131 The current UK Government has taken this a stage further. Although it declined to adopt the suggestion[217] of making 'ex-service personnel' a free-standing reasonable preference category, it did decide to exercise its regulation-making powers[218] to amend HA 1996, s 166A(3) (England). The amendments 'require' local housing authorities to frame their allocation schemes to give *additional* preference to the following categories of people connected with the military, who fall within at least one of the reasonable preference categories and who have urgent housing needs:[219]

(1)   former members of the armed forces;

(2)   serving members of the armed forces who need to move because of a serious injury, medical condition or disability sustained as a result of their service;

(3)   bereaved spouses and civil partners of members of the armed forces leaving services family accommodation following the death of their spouse or partner; and

(4)   serving or former members of the reserve forces who need to move because of a serious injury, medical condition or disability sustained as a result of their service

4.132 For these purposes 'armed forces' means the regular forces ie the Royal Navy, the Royal Marines, the regular army or the Royal Air Force.[220]

4.133 Despite the amendment, and the English Code's description of it, being very tightly drawn, some local housing authorities mistakenly understood the consultation draft of the regulations to require *all* former members of the

---

[216]   *Communities & Local Government Circular 04/2009*, 9 April 2009 reproduced in Appendix 1 of the last edition of this book.

[217]   *Local decisions: next steps towards a fairer future for social housing Summary of responses to consultation* (DCLG, February 2011), para 4.41 and *Allocation of accommodation: guidance for local housing authorities in England Summary of responses to consultation* (DCLG, June 2012), para 3.45.

[218]   HA 1996, s 166A(7) [England].

[219]   *The Housing Act 1996 (Additional Preference for Former Armed Forces Personnel) (England) Regulations* 2012, SI 2012/****. English Code, para 4.14.

[220]   Armed Forces Act 2006, s 374.

armed forces to be given additional preference, whether or not they were in urgent housing need.[221] As the final version of the regulations makes clear, in fact only a small band of those with military connections are within the prescribed class which is required to be given additional preference in an allocation scheme. Local housing authorities may structure their schemes to give more general priority to those with military connections but will do so under different powers.[222]

4.134 Although there has been no equivalent amending legislation in Wales, the Welsh Code invites local housing authorities to give additional preference to two categories of armed forces applicant:[223]

- any applicant who needs to move to suitable adapted accommodation because of a serious injury, medical condition or disability which he or she, or a member of their household, has sustained as a result of service in the armed forces;

- people needing accommodation as a result of leaving the armed forces and the loss of military accommodation;

and encourages local housing authorities to give 'high priority' to injured or disabled servicemen.[224]

Adding, or reducing, preference for other reasons

4.135 Beyond expressly enabling the local scheme to be framed so that additional preference can be given to some sub-classes of applicants who are already in the reasonable preference categories, it might have been expected that HA 1996, Part 6 would leave local housing authorities free to frame their schemes in such manner as they wished in relation to all other applicants.

4.136 But HA 1996, Part 6 expressly provides a further power to frame an allocation scheme so as to particularly prioritise between applicants who are already within one or more of the 'reasonable preference' categories.[225] Local housing authorities are able to design schemes so as to give additional or reduced prioritisation to people in the reasonable preference categories for any reasons that they choose to set out in those allocation scheme.

4.137 Enhancing priority for those in the reasonable preference categories by reference to the length of time an applicant has been waiting is an increasingly popular method adopted in allocation schemes.[226] The use of waiting time is

---

[221] *Allocation of accommodation: guidance for local housing authorities in England Summary of responses to consultation* (DCLG, June 2012), para 3.45.
[222] See **4.136**.
[223] Welsh Code, para 4.26.
[224] Welsh Code, paras 4.126–4.128.
[225] HA 1996, s 166A(5) [England] and s 167(2A) [Wales].
[226] For example, Welsh Code, para 4.31.

probably the simplest way of determining priorities between those with a similar level of need and its use as a criterion may have benefits of simplicity and transparency.

4.138 HA 1996, Part 6 directs local housing authorities towards three particular factors that they might wish to take into account in framing their schemes so as to enable prioritisation between those in the reasonable preference categories. The three are:

(1)   the *financial resources* available to an applicant or a member of his or her household to meet his or her own housing costs; and/or

(2)   any *behaviour* of the applicant or a member of his or her household which affects his or her suitability to be a tenant; and/or

(3)   any *local connection*[227] which exists between the applicant or a member of his or her household and the local housing authority's district.[228]

4.139   The 'financial resources' category permits local housing authorities to give a higher priority in the allocation scheme to applicants who cannot afford to pay a market rent or to take out a mortgage, and, as the other side of that coin, a lower priority to applicants who are in a better financial position. An on-line survey of local housing authority practice in two English regions found that household income (including, in some cases, equity and/or savings) was taken into account under the allocation policies of most local housing authorities responding to the survey. Troublingly, it also found that in rare cases local housing authorities were using resources as a complete bar to allocation at a time when exclusion for such a reason was unlawful.[229] The English Code suggests[230] that the reference to 'financial resources' includes property ownership and that, in consequence, a scheme may be framed so as to give reduced priority to an applicant who falls within a 'reasonable preference' category if he or she is a home-owner (assuming that the local housing authority has declined to follow its earlier guidance[231] and make home owners a non-qualifying category). That Code also suggests that, if it adopts financial resources as a criterion for reducing preference, a local housing authority could make provision for disregarding any lump sum received by a member of the armed forces as compensation for an injury or disability sustained on active

---

[227]   Within the meaning of HA 1996, s 199. For more on 'local connection' see Chapter 15.

[228]   HA 1996, s 166A(5) [England] and s 167(2A) [Wales]. The Welsh Code refers to 'the applicant's' financial resources and/or local connection and only to members of the applicant's household in relation to behaviour (Welsh Code, para 4.28). However, HA 1996, Part 6 refers to 'a person' in respect of all three categories, and the authors of this book suggest that the proper interpretation is that 'a person' refers both to the applicant and to the members of the applicant's household. Any other interpretation would place undue emphasis on an issue irrelevant to the household's housing needs, ie the question of which household member was listed as 'applicant' on the application form.

[229]   *Exploring local authority policy and practice on housing allocations* (CLG, July 2009), para 12.

[230]   English Code, para 4.16.

[231]   English Code, para 3.23 and see **3.179**.

service.[232] The Welsh Code simply suggests that the power could be used to give less preference to an applicant who is financially able to buy or rent privately.[233]

4.140 The 'behaviour' category permits local housing authorities to include provision in an allocation scheme to reward good behaviour and penalise bad behaviour among those who fall into the reasonable preference categories. During the debate in the House of Lords on this provision, the then Housing Minister, Lord Falconer, contrasted the examples of two applicants: one had

'... a history of persistent but minor rent arrears not caused by any problems with housing benefit and another ... who has demonstrated that he is a model tenant.'[234]

4.141 The latter could be accorded priority over the former. The 'model tenant' example of relevant 'behaviour' has been carried into the statutory guidance for England with the additional example of an applicant who has 'benefited the community'.[235]

4.142 In *R (Osei) v Newham London Borough Council*[236] the local allocation scheme enabled the housing authority to take into account former tenant arrears as an aspect of 'behaviour' when prioritising between applicants who would otherwise qualify for urgent rehousing on domestic violence or other emergency grounds. The court held that such a provision would not be unlawful provided it was applied with a flexibility which allowed for the personal circumstances of an applicant which might justify not taking into account that past behaviour in a particular case. In *R (Joseph) v Newham London Borough Council*[237] the allocation scheme enabled account to be taken of 'property-related debts' and gave the example of housing benefit overpayments. The court held that this did not permit the local housing authority to reduce preference where an overpayment had been outstanding so long that it could not be recovered by any legal process.

4.143 Two examples of 'good' behaviour given in the English Code, as potentially justifying provision for additional preference in an allocation scheme, are where:

(1) the applicant is in a household where at least one member is in work or seeking work;[238] or

(2) the applicant's actions have otherwise directly benefited the community.[239]

---

232 English Code, para 4.25.
233 Welsh Code, para 4.28(a).
234 *Hansard,* HL Deb, vol 630, ser 6, col 1017 (15 January 2002), (Lord Falconer).
235 English Code, para 4.17.
236 *R (Osei) v Newham London Borough Council* [2010] EWHC 368 (Admin), (2010) March *Legal Action*, p 30, Admin Ct.
237 [2009] EWHC 2983 (Admin), (2010) May *Legal Action*, p 23, Admin Ct.
238 English Code, para 4.27.
239 English Code, para 4.17.

4.144 The Welsh Code deals with the 'behaviour' category only in relation to the possibility of reducing priority for previous poor behaviour[240] but reminds local housing authorities in Wales that policies regarding the application of sanctions on the grounds of unacceptable behaviour should accommodate the broader Welsh Government policy aims of equality of opportunity, social inclusion and sustainability.[241]

4.145 The 'local connection' category enables discrimination in the allocation scheme, among those within the reasonable preference categories, in favour of local applicants. 'Local connection' is defined in HA 1996.[242] A local housing authority is entitled, should it so choose, to make provision in its scheme so as to give a higher priority to an applicant who has a local connection with its district (either personally or because a member of his or her household has a local connection). On the face of it, this seems perfectly rational in the distribution of limited resources. In dealing with a challenge to the allocation scheme that Hackney Council operated for the distribution of pitches on its official gypsy and traveller sites, which included a local connection requirement, a judge said:

> 'For my part, I discern no irrationality in the starting point of Hackney's policy that requires a residential connection with the borough, nor in the requirement that residence must be contemporary, in the sense that the traveller can show either continuing physical presence, or that the traveller has retained a c/o address in the borough. It must make sense to afford priority to those who are in fact living in Hackney, or who have lived there and have retained a firm point of contact with Hackney.'[243]

4.146 Local housing authorities are advised in the Welsh Code that they should be careful, when using this provision, to comply with the Equality Act 2010 and not to detract from the overall requirement that the allocation scheme must give an overall preference to those in the reasonable preference categories.[244] Some local housing authorities have operated 'sons and daughters' policies whereby children of local residents are given priority over applicants who have moved into the area more recently. This provision for enhanced priority by reference to local connection permits local housing authorities to operate such policies, provided that they ensure that the local allocation scheme adopted is not contrary to the Equality Act 2010 and, more generally, does not run counter to other equal opportunities considerations.[245]

4.147 Where the allocation scheme gives additional weighting based on local connection, it is likely to result in greater complexity, particularly if the scheme

---

[240] Welsh Code, para 4.28(b).
[241] Welsh Code, para 3.19.
[242] HA 1996, s 166A(5)(c) [England], s 167(2A)(c) [Wales] importing the definition used in HA 1996, s 199(1). For more on 'local connection' see Chapter 15.
[243] *R (McDonagh) v Hackney London Borough Council* [2012] EWHC 373 (Admin), (2012) April *Legal Action*, p 46, Admin Ct.
[244] Welsh Code, paras 3.36 and 4.28(c).
[245] See **4.195–4.209**.

generally uses a banding system to confer priority and it is well recognised that a scheme which attaches particular priority to local connection could disadvantage some applicants. Nevertheless, allocation schemes frequently reflect local political priorities by providing for enhanced priority for local connection cases which are also within the reasonable preference categories. The Codes of Guidance particularly highlight recent changes to the local connection definition which have improved the standing of serving military personnel.[246] In *R (van Boolen) v Barking & Dagenham London Borough Council*[247] the local housing authority's policy was to take account of local connection when there was more than one bidder in the same high priority band shortlisted for a property under its choice-based letting scheme. The bidder in that band with a local connection would normally be preferred to a bidder without such a connection. Although the practice had resulted in the claimant being repeatedly shortlisted, but never successful, her claim that the policy was unlawful was rejected.

4.148 Local housing authorities are reminded by the Codes of Guidance that the three statutory factors that might be included in an allocation scheme to enhance or reduce relative preferences among those entitled to a reasonable preference are not exclusive or exhaustive.[248] Within local housing allocation schemes, local housing authorities may give priority to, or downgrade, other classes of applicant who are otherwise within the 'reasonable preference' categories for reasons not listed in HA 1996, Part 6 provided that they act fairly and in accordance with their policy as reflected in the published scheme. They are also reminded that each application has to be considered on its own merits.[249]

4.149 The scope of the statutory discretion to set priorities among those within the 'reasonable preference' categories is plainly wide but the bottom line is that (save in respect of the circumstances described at **4.152–4.163**) the effect of any reduction in priority must not be to eliminate all preference, with the result that a person in a 'reasonable preference' category is in practice getting *no* preference at all. However, at least one court has recently be prepared to hold that provisions in an allocation scheme enabling the 'deferral' of applications made by those within 'reasonable preference' categories (eg for the refusal of a suitable offer) would not be unlawful.[250]

4.150 Precisely 'how' reasonable preference is enhanced or reduced by the exercise of these powers is a matter for the particular local housing allocation scheme. For example, if an applicant in a reasonable preference category has

---

[246] English Code, para 4.18; Welsh Code, para 4.129. See **15.60** and **15.70**.
[247] *R (van Boolen) v Barking & Dagenham London Borough Council* [2009] EWHC 2196 (Admin), September *Legal Action*, p 34, Admin Ct.
[248] English Code, para 4.15; Welsh Code, para 4.26.
[249] For example, Welsh Code, para 4.26.
[250] *R (Cranfield-Adams) v Richmond upon Thames London Borough Council* (2012) August *Legal Action*, p 27 and as to 'refusals' generally see **5.95–5.97**.

rent arrears his or her priority might be reflected in a reduction in points (in a points-based scheme), a move to a lower band (in a banded scheme) or a date adjustment (in a date-order scheme).

4.151 For many years it was unclear whether the statutory powers would enable an applicant or application to be *suspended* from a scheme or from bidding under a scheme (for example until arrears were cleared or reduced). For the time being, that issue appears to have been resolved in favour of suspension being a lawful exercise of these powers by a case involving Westminster City Council's allocation scheme. Section 10 of that scheme suspended applicants from bidding if they owed more than a week's rent, subject to the possibility of the Director of Housing permitting bidding by an applicant with arrears in exceptional cases. In a challenge to that provision, it was conceded that suspension might be lawful but not where it was triggered by an absolute threshold applied in every case (subject to the exceptional override). That criticism was rejected at trial.[251] However, in rejecting an application for permission to appeal from that decision, the appeal court judge put the matter much more broadly. He said:[252]

'... we are concerned with someone who has been given preference but who has been temporarily suspended from bidding under the choice-based scheme while they have rent arrears. That is lawful within [HA 1996, s167] subsection (2A)(b) ...

As I understand it, there is no quarrel with the proposition that the council may in principle have a scheme which suspends from bidding those who have arrears of rent. The only criticism of this scheme is that the suspension is automatic provided a certain rental arrears threshold is reached; and it is then open to the person who is suspended to seek to persuade the Director of Housing that they ought to be allowed to bid 'in exceptional circumstances'. Again, it seems to me that it cannot possibly be said that the scheme is so irrational as to be unlawful. It is clearly sensible to have a fixed threshold so that not every arrears of rent, however minor, will trigger suspension, but so that everybody knows that if they go over a certain level then they will be suspended. The scheme contains the necessary safety valve to enable those who are in arrears to explain to the Director of Housing that there is some good reason for them being in arrears, for example because they are ill in hospital or whatever. In those circumstances the Director of Housing can then allow bidding to take place 'in exceptional circumstances', and that indeed is precisely what happened in the appellant's case.

... It is plainly sensible to have a clear-cut arrears threshold over which one will not be allowed to bid unless one can persuade the director of housing that there are exceptional circumstances. It seems to me that there is nothing arguably unlawful about that policy.'

---

[251] *R (Babakandi) v Westminster City Council* [2011] EWHC 1756 (Admin), (2011) August *Legal Action*, p 40, Admin Ct. at [23]–[25].

[252] *R (Babakandi) v Westminster City Council* [2011] EWCA Civ 1397, (2012) January *Legal Action*, p 21, CA at [6]–[8].

Removing 'reasonable preference' altogether

4.152 An applicant who falls within one or more of the 'reasonable preference' categories may be deprived of that status and given no preference at all, but only if either:

(1) on an application to a local housing authority in England or Wales, the applicant's household includes a 'restricted person' and the applicant's entitlement to a reasonable preference would not have arisen under the first or second of the statutory reasonable preference categories without the presence of that person;[253] or

(2) a local housing authority in Wales decides that he or she or a member of his or her household has been guilty of unacceptable behaviour'.[254]

The presence of a 'restricted person'

4.153 The first ground for removal of a reasonable preference arises where:[255]

(1) the reasonable preference is made out by satisfaction of the first or second categories for such a preference (homelessness or a specific duty owed to the homeless);[256] and

(2) the application would not have fallen within those categories without the local housing authority having had regard to a 'restricted person' (within the meaning of HA 1996, Part 7).

4.154 Only if, *both* those conditions are fulfilled is the applicant deprived of the reasonable preference to which he or she would otherwise have been entitled. An applicant entitled to a reasonable preference under any of the third to fifth statutory categories retains that preference even if it has been triggered by the needs of a restricted person.[257] A 'restricted person' is defined at HA 1996, s 184(7).[258] This provision illustrates the policy intention that households with 'restricted persons' should be looking to the private rented sector, rather than to social housing, for their long-term accommodation needs.

The 'unacceptable behaviour' test

4.155 Until 18 June 2012, local housing authorities in both England and Wales could remove entirely, on 'unacceptable behaviour' grounds, the reasonable preference of a person otherwise entitled to it. However, since that

---

[253] HA 1996, s 166A(4) [England], s 167(2ZA) [Wales].

[254] HA 1996, s 167(2B) and (2C).

[255] HA 1996, s 166A(4) [England], s 167(2ZA) [Wales].

[256] HA 1996, s 166A(3)(a) and (b) [England], s 167(2)(a) and (b) [Wales]. See **4.62–4.70** for the first category and **4.71–4.79** for the second category.

[257] HA 1996, s 166A(3)(b), (c) and (d) [England], s 167(2)(c), (d) and (e) [Wales]. See **4.80–4.94** for the third category, **4.95–4.109** for the fourth category and **4.110–4.114** for the fifth category.

[258] See **10.39**.

date local housing authorities in England have had the power to adopt classes of persons who do not qualify at all for social housing allocation in their districts. This left the 'removal of preference' power unnecessary – those who would have lost preference on 'unacceptable behaviour' grounds can now been kept out of allocation arrangements altogether. As the then Minister said during the passage of the Localism Act 2011 (which made the change):

> 'Proposed new section 166A of the 1996 Act differs from the existing section 167 in one main respect. Section 167 allows local authorities to give no preference to those guilty of unacceptable behaviour; by inverting that, it is possible that somebody guilty of unacceptable behaviour may be excluded from the list.'[259]

4.156 That has left the power to remove preference altogether on 'unacceptable behaviour' grounds only available to local housing authorities in Wales.

4.157 A local housing authority in Wales may *only* treat an applicant otherwise entitled to a 'reasonable preference' as having no preference when it is satisfied that:

- the applicant, or a member of his or her household, has been guilty of unacceptable behaviour serious enough to make him or her unsuitable to be a tenant of the local housing authority; and

- at the time that the application is being considered and by reason of that behaviour, the applicant deserves not to be treated as a member of a group of people who are given 'reasonable preference'.[260]

4.158 The definition of 'unacceptable behaviour' is the same as that applied in determining eligibility for an allocation in Wales. That is to say:

> '... behaviour of the person concerned which would (if he were a secure tenant of the authority) entitle the housing authority to a possession order under s 84 of the Housing Act 1985 on any ground mentioned in Part I of Schedule 2 to that Act (other than ground 8) or behaviour of a member of his household which would (if he were a person residing with a secure tenant of the authority) entitle the housing authority to such a possession order.'[261]

4.159 Before removing any 'reasonable preference' to which an applicant would otherwise be entitled, a local housing authority in Wales must therefore ask itself:

(1) Would the applicant's behaviour, or that of a member of his or her household, have come within one of the grounds for possession?

---

[259] *Hansard* House of Commons Public Bill Committee on the Localism Bill, 3 March 2011, col 762.

[260] HA 1996, s 167(2B) and (2C). See Welsh Code, paras 3.25–3.26 and 4.32.

[261] HA 1996, s 167(2D) applying HA 1996, s 160(8). For a full discussion see **3.203–3.251**.

(2) Would the court have considered it reasonable to make an order for possession?

(3) Would the order be an outright, not a suspended or postponed, possession order?

4.160 Only after it has considered those three questions and answered them all in the affirmative, may the local housing authority then decide whether, at the time that the application is being considered, the applicant deserves not to be given the reasonable preference to which she or he would otherwise be entitled. The key issue that the local housing authority should consider is whether there has been a change of circumstances since those events that led to the affirmative answers to the three questions identified above.[262]

4.161 If a local housing authority in Wales decides that an applicant should have his or her 'reasonable preference' removed on the grounds of 'unacceptable behaviour', it must notify the applicant in writing of the decision and of the grounds for it. The applicant has the right to request a review of that decision and to be informed of the review decision and of the grounds for it.[263] Any further challenge to the review decision would be by judicial review or by complaint, ultimately to the Public Services Ombudsman for Wales.

4.162 This provision, permitting the removal of preference, operates as an alternative to the power available to a local housing authority in Wales to treat an applicant as wholly ineligible for an allocation by reason of his or her unacceptable behaviour.[264] It may therefore be used in respect of an applicant where the local housing authority in Wales has considered his or her behaviour for the purposes of eligibility and concluded that he or she is eligible but nevertheless considers that the behaviour should deprive him or her of the 'reasonable preference' that would otherwise be accorded.

4.163 Even if an applicant in Wales, with a background of unreasonable behaviour, survives both the eligibility test and the removal of 'reasonable preference' test, he or she may still be accorded a lower preference than others in similar circumstances by being given a lower priority than she or he would otherwise receive.[265]

---

[262] For a fuller discussion of the correct approach to this part of the statutory test, see **3.246–3.251**.

[263] HA 1996, s 167(4A)(b) and (d). See also **2.77–2.99**.

[264] Discussed at **3.203–3.251**. One local housing authority's policy that an applicant in rent arrears would be allowed onto its allocation scheme and entitled to points, but would not receive an offer whilst the arrears continued was an attempt to apply this provision, rather than to hold the applicant ineligible: *R (Onuegbu) v Hackney London Borough Council* [2005] EWHC 1277 (Admin), (2005) August *Legal Action*, p 17, Admin Ct (and see note to **3.245**). That interpretation, however, does not sit easily with the statutory provision which does not allow for suspension but simply a removal of reasonable preference as against other applicants.

[265] In exercise of the power at HA 1996, s 167(2A). See **4.140–4.144**.

PRIORITY FOR OTHER CLASSES OF APPLICANT

4.164 Although HA 1996, Part 6 requires an allocation scheme to be framed so as to give a reasonable preference to the five statutory classes described above, it does not prohibit a local housing authority from also framing its allocation scheme to give preferences or priorities to other groups or classes of applicant reflecting local circumstances. Local housing authorities in England and Wales are free to adopt other priority classes of their own choosing, provided that the overall requirement that the statutory classes receive a reasonable preference in the scheme is not displaced.[266] Indeed, the Secretary of State has positively encouraged local housing authorities in England to 'take advantage of this flexibility'[267] and many are actively doing so.[268] As the Codes put it, local housing authorities are free to prioritise groups of applicants who do not fall into the reasonable preference categories provided that:

(1) they do not dominate the scheme, and

(2) overall, the scheme operates to give reasonable preference to those in the statutory reasonable preference categories over those who are not.[269]

4.165 If this advice is followed and unlawful discrimination is avoided, there is no limit as to the number of categories that may be given preference in a local allocation scheme nor any limit as to the size of the class of prospective or actual applicants each category may embrace.

4.166 By virtue of the fact that local housing authorities are required to have regard to statutory guidance, both codes of guidance are able to identify and promote particular classes of applicant they would wish local housing authorities at least to consider prioritising. The guidance ranges in emphasis from mere suggestion that local housing authorities may like to consider giving one particular group priority to local housing authorities being 'strongly encouraged' or 'urged' to give preference to other suggested groups.[270]

4.167 The English Code particularly singles out for possible priority treatment within local allocation schemes the following groups (to the extent that they do not already fall within the reasonable preference categories adopted in those schemes):

• current and former members of the armed forces and their family members;[271]

---

[266] Welsh Code, para 4.53.
[267] English Code, para 4.19.
[268] See the examples given in *How to ... consider new approaches to allocations and lettings* (Chartered Institute of Housing, April 2012) and *Allocations and Local Flexibility* (Chartered Institute of Housing, March 2010).
[269] English Code, para 4.19; Welsh Code, para 4.27.
[270] Contrast, for example, the language used within English Code, paras 4.22–4.32.
[271] English Code, paras 4.24–4.25.

- applicants who are in work or seeking work or living with others who are in work or seeking work;[272]

- prospective adopters and foster carers;[273] and

- former social housing tenants forced to move into the private sector by housing benefit penalties for under-occupation who later wish to move back to social housing.[274]

4.168 The Welsh Code suggests that priority might be given under allocation schemes to:

- promote job mobility;

- help those who are under-occupying (given the changes in welfare benefits);

- meet the needs of extended families; and

- sustain rural communities.[275]

4.169 Local housing authorities in England and Wales are free to adopt, modify or reject the suggested classes for prioritisation put forward in the statutory guidance provided they can demonstrate that they have at least 'had regard' to the relevant code in making their choices when framing their schemes.[276] Some local housing authorities may share the views of the Chartered Institute of Housing that 'there is very little detail in the new guidance [for England] in ensuring the needs of all communities are taken into account'[277] or the views of those who responded to the consultation on the draft English Code and who, according to the DCLG's Summary of Responses, 'were concerned that the guidance lacked clarity or would have preferred more detailed guidance, and were concerned about the risk of legal challenge, or that this would lead to a wide variety of approaches and inconsistency between local authority areas. In particular, there was a call for more guidance on how to strike an appropriate balance between the reasonable preference requirements, local policy priorities and the Government's policy priorities.'[278]

---

[272] English Code, para 4.27. Some of the difficulties in framing a priority class for this group are set out in *Allocation of accommodation: guidance for local housing authorities in England Summary of responses to consultation* (DCLG, June 2012) paras 3.66–3.77.
[273] English Code, para 4.30–4.32. Some of the issues around affording special priority for this group are set out in *Allocation of accommodation: guidance for local housing authorities in England Summary of responses to consultation* (DCLG, June 2012) paras 3.78–3.87.
[274] English Code, para 4.23.
[275] Welsh Code, paras 4.27 and 4.53.
[276] HA 1996, s 169(1).
[277] *Allocation of accommodation: guidance for local housing authorities in England: A Briefing paper* (CIH, July 2012) p 7.
[278] *Allocation of accommodation: guidance for local housing authorities in England Summary of responses to consultation* (DCLG, June 2012) para 3.90.

PRIORITY FOR PARTICULAR TYPES OF ACCOMMODATION

4.170　An allocation scheme does not need to apply uniformly to the whole of a local housing authority's available housing stock, or to all the available nominations to private registered providers or registered social landlords. HA 1996, Part 6 provides that a scheme may, in effect, identify that specified accommodation is available to be allocated:

(1)　only to those who make specific applications for it; or

(2)　only to a particular group or groups of applicants (whether or not in one of the statutory reasonable preference categories).[279]

4.171　By these means, HA 1996, Part 6 allows the local allocation scheme to be drawn so that, in respect of certain types of accommodation specified in the scheme, the normal 'reasonable preference' categories do not, in effect, apply. Care must be taken in framing these provisions in any local allocation scheme. These two special provisions are still subject to the over-arching requirement that the scheme must be framed so as to secure a reasonable preference for all five of the statutory reasonable preference categories. The position remains that the scheme must be framed so as to ensure that, *overall*, reasonable preference is given to applicants who fall within the reasonable preference categories over those who do not.[280]

4.172　The function of the first special provision – that the scheme may provide for the allocation of particular accommodation to those who specifically apply for it – is to facilitate choice. It enables the adoption of advertising schemes whereby applicants can apply for particular properties which have been advertised as vacant by the housing authority. It is thus the lynch-pin for the concept of choice-based lettings,[281] but it is a rather elliptically expressed way of achieving that object.

4.173　In local allocation schemes not structured on choice-based letting, the type of accommodation most likely to be specifically earmarked for those who make 'a specific application' for it[282] is what is commonly known as 'hard to let' housing in respect of which there is little point in operating the normal allocation scheme, because offers are likely to be refused.[283] Indeed, where there is housing stock of that sort, local housing authorities in England are invited to consider adopting different, less stringent, qualification criteria than they operate for the rest of their stock.[284]

---

[279]　HA 1996, s 166A(6) [England], s 167(2E) [Wales].
[280]　English Code, paras 4.5 and 4.19; Welsh Code, para 4.62.
[281]　See **5.7–5.60**.
[282]　HA 1996, s 166A(6)(a) [England], s 167(2E)(a) [Wales].
[283]　Welsh Code, para 4.66.
[284]　English Code, para 3.24.

4.174 The form of accommodation most likely to be earmarked for 'persons of a particular description' under the second special provision[285] is the stock of purpose-built (or adapted) accommodation designed for use by the disabled[286] or elderly.[287] Inclusion of such a provision in an allocation scheme can ensure that such specialist housing is available to those who most need it. Recently withdrawn statutory guidance for local housing authorities in England had specifically suggested that, where possible, priority be given to any applicant who needed to move to suitable adapted accommodation because of a serious injury, medical condition or disability which he or she, or a member of their household, had sustained as a result of service in the Armed Forces.[288] Both codes of guidance now give particular emphasis to the needs of injured or disabled armed services personnel.[289]

4.175 The use of the power, to make special provision for particular classes of persons, who need not be within a reasonable preference category, can sometimes produce unusual results. For example, a local housing authority may have a surfeit of applicants for general accommodation who fall within one or more 'reasonable preference' categories, but its scheme may have excluded particular accommodation from the general pool and earmarked it for the elderly or disabled. If there is little demand for that earmarked accommodation, an elderly or disabled applicant could receive an offer almost immediately, even if his or her circumstances would otherwise command no reasonable, or other, preference at all under the local allocation scheme. The Welsh Code specifically promotes the use of Accessible Housing registers.[290]

4.176 There is at least one other circumstance in which a local allocation scheme could usefully make provision in respect of allocation of particular properties only for particular applicants. That is, to ensure that property is not allocated to an applicant in a particular locality in the local housing authority's district in which he or she has previously been the perpetrator (or, perhaps, victim) of anti-social behaviour. In *R (Carney) v Bolton-at-Home Ltd*[291] an allocation scheme, which utilised choice-based letting, contained a provision enabling a bypass to be applied to the applicant at the top of the shortlist for any property if the allocation would result in a person previously evicted for anti-social behaviour being rehoused in the same area as that where the behaviour took place, even if the applicant was otherwise eligible and qualified to be allocated any other accommodation. The provision itself was not unlawful and had been lawfully applied in the particular case.

---

[285] HA 1996, s 166A(6)(b) [England], s 167(2E)(b) [Wales].
[286] Welsh Code, paras 4.82–4.95.
[287] Welsh Code, paras 4.99–4.101.
[288] *CLG Circular 04/2009*, para 12. Reproduced in Appendix 1 to the last edition of this book.
[289] English Code, paras 4.24–4.25; Welsh Code, paras 4.121–4.133.
[290] Welsh Code, paras 5.7–5.9.
[291] *R (Carney) v Bolton-at-Home Ltd* [2012] EWHC 2553 (Admin), (2012) November *Legal Action,* p 13, Admin Ct.

LOCAL LETTINGS SCHEMES[292]

4.177 Statutory guidance suggests that the power to make special provision for particular classes of persons, who need not be within a reasonable preference category, in relation to particular housing accommodation provides 'the statutory basis for so-called 'local lettings policies' which may be used to achieve a wide variety of housing management and policy objectives.'[293] Specific attention is given in both Codes of Guidance to suggestions that local housing authorities identify particular types or clusters or locations of housing for particular types of applicants and deal with allocation of them by way of local lettings policies.[294]

4.178 For example, the English Code suggests that local housing authorities in England might:

• set aside a proportion of properties for 'former members of the armed forces' under a local lettings policy;[295] or

• use a local lettings policy to 'ensure that specific properties, or a specified proportion of properties, are allocated to households in particular types of employment where, for example, skills are in short supply';[296] or

• set aside a 'quota of properties each year for people who need to move to larger accommodation in order to foster or adopt a child on the recommendation of children's services'.[297]

4.179 The Welsh Code suggests that local housing authorities in Wales can use local letting policies to address a range of issues including:[298]

• creating more mixed communities;

• dealing with a concentration of deprivation;

• ensuring properties that are particularly suited to being made accessible (eg ground floor flats) are prioritised for those with access needs;

• relocating essential workers such as teachers nurses and police officers within a reasonable travelling distance from their work;

---

[292] See generally, *Exploring local authority policy and practice on housing allocations* (DCLG July 2009) Chapter 5 – *Local lettings policies*.
[293] English Code, para 4.21. Welsh Code, para 4.59.
[294] Welsh Code, paras 4.59–4.65.
[295] English Code, para 4.25.
[296] English Code, para 4.27.
[297] English Code, para 4.31.
[298] Welsh Code, paras 4.60.

- supporting people in work/volunteering or who are seeking work or seeking to take up volunteering opportunities;

- dealing sensitively with lettings in rural areas to sustain communities by giving priority to those with a local connection to the local area;

- taking account of the needs of mobile workers such as those in the armed forces; and

- where the child to adult ratio could be lowered on an estate where there is high child density or, conversely, young single people could be integrated into an estate via this route.

4.180 Providing somewhat more practical guidance, the Chartered Institute of Housing (CIH) has suggested that proposals for local lettings policies should set out the following:[299]

- a clear definition of the objective(s) to be achieved, backed up by clear evidence;

- a method which is likely to achieve the objective(s);

- a potential (equality) impact assessment;

- how the scheme will be monitored and who will be involved;

- mechanisms of reporting and reviewing the scheme;

- how the views of local communities have shaped the scheme; and

- a clear exit strategy.

4.181 Local housing authorities in England seeking an understanding of how local lettings policies and schemes are being operated by others may find that not only in the CIH paper but also in the results of a research survey published by DCLG in July 2009.[300]

4.182 The Welsh Code suggests that any local lettings policies should have clear aims linked to community sustainability and be supported by clear evidence of the need for the approach being taken.[301]

4.183 All local housing authorities are reminded by the statutory guidance that local lettings arrangements must not be used in such a way that there will

---

[299] *Allocations and local flexibility: A Practice brief* (CIH, March 2010).
[300] *Exploring local authority policy and practice on housing allocations* (DCLG, July 2009), Chapter 5.
[301] Welsh Code, para 4.63.

be a failure to meet the requirement to give a reasonable preference to statutorily specified groups. In other words, an allocation scheme may include local lettings policies provided that:

- they do not dominate the scheme; and

- overall, the scheme operates to give reasonable preference to those in the statutory reasonable preference categories over those who are not.[302]

4.184 Beyond local lettings schemes, three specific forms of accommodation may be suitable for special treatment under these statutory powers:

- accommodation with linked support;

- accommodation particularly suited for agricultural workers; and

- accommodation subject to an application from a former tenant or other occupier of it.

4.185 Each of these three suggested categories requires careful consideration.

Accommodation with linked support

4.186 Certain applicants may not only seek accommodation but also have needs for support.[303] Where an applicant's household includes a child who needs accommodation on medical and welfare grounds, local housing authorities are advised to consult with children's services about the appropriate level of priority, what support needs are present, and how those support needs will be met. Where applicants for an allocation are cared for by people who do not live with them, local housing authorities are advised that the applicant will need a spare bedroom (for overnight stays).[304]

4.187 Single parents aged under 18, who are not living with their parents, should be offered semi-independent accommodation with support. A joint assessment of the applicant's housing, care and support needs should be undertaken by the housing and children's services departments, provided that the applicant consents to the involvement of children's services. It would be unusual for a young single parent to be given an independent tenancy, but arrangements should be made for the young parent to move on from supported accommodation as he or she reaches adulthood.[305] Local housing authorities should not be deterred by the legal problems associated with the granting of a tenancy to a minor: children's services authorities may underwrite the tenancy

[302] English Code, para 4.19, Welsh Code, para 4.62.
[303] Welsh Code, paras 4.143–4.146.
[304] Welsh Code, para 4.106.
[305] Welsh Code, paras 4.111–4.119.

agreement, and the tenancy itself can be treated as a trust for land (giving the minor the beneficial interest) or as a contract for a lease.[306]

4.188 Access to the allocation of accommodation with support should also be available for rough sleepers and people at risk of sleeping rough. Many rough sleepers will need support with other problems: mental health, alcohol or drug problems, and basic life skills. Local housing authorities should work with adult care services and Supporting People Teams to provide such support.[307] Where sex offenders are allocated accommodation, there should be joint working with the police, probation services, adult care services, health professionals and other bodies to manage any risk to the community.[308]

Accommodation particularly suited for agricultural workers

4.189 Local housing authorities are required by the Rent (Agriculture) Act 1976 to use their best endeavours to provide accommodation for displaced agricultural workers where they are satisfied that the dwelling house from which the worker is displaced is needed to accommodate another agricultural worker, that the farmer cannot provide suitable alternative accommodation for the displaced worker and that the displaced worker needs to be rehoused in the interests of efficient agriculture.[309] Local housing authorities should include within their allocation schemes a policy statement in respect of the priority that will be accorded to displaced agricultural workers.[310]

Accommodation subject to an application from a former tenant or other current occupier[311]

4.190 The exercise of these statutory powers, to separate from the general allocation provisions certain accommodation which would otherwise be available for letting, might be particularly apt where an applicant seeks the specific allocation of just one property – the home in which he or she is already living. For example, this might arise:

- where the applicant has married an existing tenant and they both seek the grant of a fresh tenancy into their joint names; or

---

[306] Welsh Code, para 4.120, Annex 11; *Kingston upon Thames Royal London Borough Council v Prince* (1999) 31 HLR 794, CA; *Newham London Borough Council v Ria* [2004] EWCA Civ 41, (205) March *Legal Action* 23, CA and *Alexander-David v Hammersmith & Fulham London Borough Council* [2009] EWCA Civ 259, [2009] HLR 39, CA.

[307] Welsh Code, paras 4.86–4.87.

[308] Welsh Code, paras 4.91–4.93. See too the discussion of *R (M) v Hackney London Borough Council* [2009] EWHC 2255 (Admin), (2009) May *Legal Action*, p 26, Admin Ct, noted at **3.242**.

[309] Rent (Agriculture) Act 1976, ss 27–28 and see the leaflet *Agricultural Lettings* (ODPM and Welsh Assembly Government, June 2006).

[310] Welsh Code, paras 4.139–4.141.

[311] See **1.44** for an introduction to this topic.

- where the applicant is a former joint tenant and the joint tenancy has ended; or

- where the applicant is a relation of the previous tenant who has died without there being a right of succession; or

- where the applicant has otherwise occupied the particular property for a considerable time.

4.191   Unless the local housing authority has used the power[312] in HA 1996, Part 6 to identify in its scheme the special treatment of applicants in such cases, distinct from the general allocation provisions, it would be in difficulty in lawfully allocating the specific property to the applicant, given the entitlement of many others to a 'reasonable preference' in allocation. The position will be all the more acute where a scheme provides that 'all' allocations will be by way of choice-based letting. A local housing authority will need to ensure that its scheme is framed sufficiently flexibly to take account of these particular cases.

4.192   For example, when a former joint tenancy has ended, a local housing authority may be asked to decide whether to grant a sole tenancy to the former joint tenant who remains in the property. One of the joint tenants may have terminated the former joint tenancy by service of a notice to quit on the landlord.[313] Local housing authorities need to set out in their allocation schemes the circumstances in which they will exercise their discretion to grant a new sole tenancy in this situation.[314] Of course, if the couple are married, have a civil partnership, or have children, a Family Court has jurisdiction to decide that a joint tenancy should be transferred to a sole tenancy in one of the partners' names and such a transfer made following the court's decision is not subject to the allocation scheme.[315]

4.193   Similarly, when a secure tenant dies, and there is no entitlement to a statutory succession, local housing authorities may consider granting a tenancy to somebody who has been living with the tenant. To do so they must specifically provide for that scenario in their allocation schemes and set out the circumstances that they will take into account in determining applications. For example, local housing authorities might consider granting a tenancy where the applicant is a former household member who was living with the tenant for the

[312]   HA 1996, s 166A(6)(b) [England], s 167(2E)(b) [Wales].
[313]   *Hammersmith and Fulham London Borough Council v Monk* [1992] 1 AC 478, HL.
[314]   *R (Hussey) v Southwark London Borough Council* [2002] EWHC 1142 (Admin), [2002] All ER (D) 332 (May), Admin Ct and *R (Dixon) v Wandsworth London Borough Council* [2007] EWHC 3075 (Admin), (2008) February *Legal Action*, p 40, Admin Ct.
[315]   Transfers made by virtue of Matrimonial Causes Act 1973, s 24; Matrimonial and Family Proceedings Act 1984, s 17(1); Children Act 1989, Sch 1 para 1; and Civil Partnership Act 2004, Part 2, Sch 5 are excluded from counting as allocations by HA 1996, s 160(2)(e) and (3)(d). See also **1.39**.

year prior to the tenant's death, had been providing care for the tenant, or has accepted responsibility for the tenant's dependants, and needs to live with them.[316]

4.194 Although not referred to in the Codes, an applicant for homelessness assistance who has been granted a non-secure tenancy of local housing authority accommodation under the main housing duty at HA 1996, s 193(2)[317] could apply to his or her local housing authority for a secure or introductory tenancy of that property. The local housing authority could only allocate a secure tenancy to the applicant if its allocation scheme made provision for such circumstances.[318]

AVOIDING DISCRIMINATION AND ENHANCING EQUALITY OF OPPORTUNITY IN ALLOCATION SCHEMES

4.195 The statutory guidance on housing allocation reminds local housing authorities that their allocation schemes, and the detailed policies and procedures they contain, should take account of their statutory duties under equalities legislation and should not unlawfully discriminate between applicants.[319] But neither of the Codes gives any detailed practical guidance on what compliance with these requirements means in the context of framing an allocation scheme.

The equality duty

4.196 The most important of the relevant statutory duties imposed by the Equality Act 2010 is the public sector equality duty, requiring that a public authority, such as a local housing authority, must, in the exercise of its functions:

'have due regard to the need to –

(a) eliminate discrimination, harassment, victimisation and any other conduct that is prohibited by or under this Act;

(b) advance equality of opportunity between persons who share a relevant protected characteristic and persons who do not share it;

---

[316] Welsh Code, para 4.16. See *R (Sleith) v Camden London Borough Council* [2003] EWHC 347 (Admin), (2003) May *Legal Action*, p 33, Admin Ct, in respect of which an application for permission to appeal was refused: *R (Sleith) v Camden London Borough Council* [2003] EWCA Civ 347, CA. For a more recent example of this scenario, see *R (Neville) v Wandsworth London Borough Council* [2009] EWHC 2405 (Admin), (2009) December *Legal Action*, p 17, Admin Ct.

[317] See **17.23–17.35**.

[318] HA 1996, s 159(3).

[319] English Code, para 3.20; Welsh Code, paras 2.1 and 4.69–4.75.

(c)   foster good relations between persons who share a relevant protected characteristic and persons who do not share it.'[320]

4.197 Each of these elements is expanded-upon in the various sub-sections of Equality Act 2010, s 149 and comprehensive guidance is offered in *The essential guide to the public sector equality duty*.[321] The 'protected characteristics' mentioned in the duty are age, disability, gender reassignment, marriage and civil partnership, pregnancy and maternity, race, religion or belief, sex, and sexual orientation.[322]

4.198 The importance of the public sector equality duty in the context of housing allocation cannot be overstated. It is given particular emphasis in Wales by supplementary regulations[323] which are referred to in the Welsh Code.[324] The Equality & Human Rights Commission advises that decision-makers in public authorities need to:

- be aware of their responsibilities under the duty
- make sure they have adequate evidence (including from consultation, if appropriate) to enable them to understand the potential effects of their decisions on different people covered by the duty
- consciously and actively consider the relevant matters, in such a way that it influences decision-making
- do this before and at the time a decision is taken, not after the event
- be aware that the duty can't be delegated to third parties who are carrying out functions on their behalf'

and recalls that case law[325] also suggests that it is good practice to document how decisions were reached.[326]

4.199 Regard must obviously be had to the various elements of the duty when taking strategic decisions about, for example, consultation arrangements on changes to allocation schemes and the formulation of their major elements. Local housing authorities should ensure that they consult with a wide range of groups when drawing up or revising their allocation schemes, and particularly engage with those who are currently under-represented in social housing. Translation of the scheme into different languages spoken in the local

---

[320] Equality Act 2010, s 149.
[321] *The essential guide to the public sector equality duty: England (and non-devolved public authorities in Scotland and Wales)* Revised (second) edition (Equality & Human Rights Commission) January 2012. See also *Equality Act 2010: Public sector equality duty – What do I need to know? A quick start guide for public sector organisations* (Home Office, June 2011).
[322] Equality Act 2010, ss 5–12.
[323] Equality Act 2010 (Statutory Duties) (Wales) Regulations 2011, SI 2011/1064 (W. 155).
[324] Welsh Code, para 4.71.
[325] For a recent distillation of the principles applied by the courts in determining whether there has been compliance with the public sector equality duty see *Hunt v North Somerset Council* [2012] EWHC 1928 (Admin), [2012] All ER (D) 295 (Jul), Admin Ct. at [55].
[326] *FAQs on the equality duty: What public authorities need to do on assessing impact on equality under the general equality duty* (EHCR website, August 2012).

community is recommended.[327] The Welsh Code advises that local housing authorities should be particularly sensitive to the housing needs of refugees, gypsies and travelers, people with disabilities, older people, people with mental health problems, and lesbian, gay and bisexual people.[328]

4.200 Having due regard to the elements of the public sector equality duty is not, however, only a requirement in relation to 'strategic' decision-making. It will, in relevant circumstances, also need to infuse and inform decision-making by local housing authorities in individual cases. For example, it must be taken into account when deciding whether a household facing eviction, and containing a person with disabilities, should be allowed to remain in their home or be provided with alternative accommodation.[329] Those parts of a local housing allocation scheme which deal with the procedure on applications, and particularly with the making of decisions on applications, will need to indicate that those taking decisions have been alerted to the need to comply with the duty. In *Barnsley Metropolitan Borough Council v Norton*[330] the local housing authority had failed to consider the public sector equality duty in respect of the eviction (and possible rehousing) of a family which included a disabled person. The Court of Appeal said:

> 'The decision of this appeal may serve to reinforce that which the courts have been saying for some time, calling on public authorities to face up to their obligations under [what is now] section 149 of the 2010 Act. It seems to me that the practical problem needs to be resolved by proper consideration being given by the Council, with the cooperation of the Norton family, to the question where they are to be accommodated in the future, whether under [HA 1996] Part 7 or under Part 6.'[331]

4.201 There is a remarkable dearth of material expressly directed to the way in which local housing authorities might best integrate consideration of the public sector equality duty into their housing functions, such as allocation, even from the Equality & Human Rights Commission (EHRC).

4.202 In relation to the protected characteristic of 'disability', the publication *Housing and the Disability Equality Duty: A guide to the Disability Equality Duty and Disability Discrimination Act 2005 for the social housing sector* from the former Disability Rights Commission (DRC) is still available through the EHRC website and offers considerable advice (and examples of good practice) on drawing-up allocation schemes.[332] The Department of Health (DH) commissioned and published research on the experiences of the disabled in

---

327 Welsh Code, paras 1.11, 4.35, 4.74 and 4.163.
328 Welsh Code, paras 4.69–4.102.
329 *Barnsley Metropolitan Borough Council v Norton* [2011] EWCA Civ 834, [2011] HLR 46, CA.
330 [2011] EWCA Civ 834, [2011] HLR 46, CA.
331 Ibid, para [35].
332 *Housing and the Disability Equality Duty: A guide to the Disability Equality Duty and Disability Discrimination Act 2005 for the social housing sector* (DRC, 2006), pp 54–57.

accessing choice-based letting schemes[333] and associated guides for social landlords establishing such schemes[334] and for people with learning difficulties who try to use them.[335]

4.203 The Local Government Association has identified that 'changes to housing allocation plans that have the net effect of negatively impacting on those with protected characteristics, such as disability, race or age, may well be against equality laws, and would be subject to legal challenge' and has encouraged local housing authorities to cross check their arrangements against its Social Housing Equality Framework.[336] The Chartered Institute of Housing has advised that 'establishing criteria for people to be able to go onto the housing waiting list is not without risk of legal challenge and so housing authorities will need to be mindful of unlawfully discriminating, either directly or indirectly' and that 'full consideration of provisions in the Equality Act 2010 and a comprehensive equality analysis will be required to ensure a fair and accessible approach to allocations'.[337] The Welsh Code repeatedly emphasises the need to 'monitor allocations' to determine whether equal opportunities obligations are being met.[338]

Non-discrimination

4.204 The Equality Act 2010 brought together in a single piece of legislation all the previously disparate statutory measures to eliminate discrimination. The housing allocation scheme must obviously not breach that Act by discriminating, directly or indirectly, on grounds such as race, sex, disability or any other relevant characteristic.[339] Sadly, no specific guidance has been published by the national governments or by the EHRC on how unlawful discrimination might be avoided in framing allocation schemes. One recent case from overseas demonstrates that anti-discrimination measures can still be expected to engage with aspects of allocation schemes. In *Rodriguez v Minister of Housing of Gibraltar*[340] a tenant asked her social landlord to agree to make her long-term same sex partner a joint tenant of her home (so that her partner would be secure in the event of her death). The allocation policy was only to agree to such requests if the couple were married or had children. The landlord claimed that the policy was not discriminatory because a heterosexual childless couple would also have been refused. Alternatively, if there was discrimination,

---

[333] *Choice Based Lettings and People with Learning Disabilities* (DH, February 2008).

[334] *Making Choice Based Lettings work for People with Learning Disabilities: A Guide for Choice-based lettings schemes and landlords* (DH, February 2008).

[335] *Choice Based Lettings: A guide to choosing a home through the council* (DH, February 2008)

[336] *Councils must consider equality laws when changing services* LGA Media Release 16 February 2012.

[337] *Allocation of accommodation: guidance for local authorities in England: Briefing paper* (CIH, July 2012), p 7.

[338] Welsh Code, paras 5.4 and 5.38.

[339] Equality Act 2010, Part 4 addresses discrimination in relation to the letting and management of residential premises.

[340] [2009] UKPC 52, (2009) 28 BHRC 189, PC.

it was justified by the aim to support families and children. The Privy Council held that the policy did discriminate and that there was no rational justification for it.

4.205 The former Commission for Racial Equality's *Code of Practice for Racial Equality in Housing* (of which there were separate versions for England, Scotland and Wales respectively)[341] contained the following examples of potential unlawful discrimination on grounds of 'race' relating to social housing allocation schemes (in the version for England):

> 'A council generally allocates the worst properties to homeless applicants, whereas tenants transferring to housing association accommodation receive better properties. Ethnic minority households are disproportionately represented among those whom the council has a duty to house because they are homeless. This policy would be unlawful direct discrimination, unless the council could show it to be a proportionate means of achieving a legitimate aim. It may also be unlawful under the Housing Act 1996' (Example 30).

> 'A housing association's allocation policy gives priority for lettings to tenants' sons and daughters. If the racial profile of tenants does not reflect the racial profile of people in need of housing in the association's catchment area, the policy could disadvantage prospective tenants from under-represented racial groups and could amount to unlawful indirect discrimination. It would therefore need to be carefully considered, and the justification for the policy tested against any possible discriminatory effects' (Example 31).

> 'A local council (or housing association) fails to make sure that information about its lettings services reaches people from all racial groups; for example, by not advertising the service in outlets which it knows are preferred by ethnic minority residents. This could amount to indirect discrimination' (Example 35).

> 'A CRE inquiry into a major public sector landlord's "choice-based" lettings scheme found that:

> - the city council had not done a race equality impact assessment of the scheme;
> - it had not consulted affected groups and agencies in the community adequately;
> - ethnic monitoring of applications and allocations was poor; and
> - information about the new scheme was not available in relevant languages.

> The CRE concluded that there had been contraventions of the duty to promote race equality, and that these failings should be rectified' (Example 38).

> 'Analysis of a council's housing allocations shows that people from certain racial groups are consistently offered inferior accommodation. This constitutes direct discrimination' (Example 39).

---

[341] Welsh Code, para 4.73. All the versions of the CRE's Code are available on the EHRC website.

4.206 The former statutory guidance in the DRC's publication *Duty to Promote Disability Equality: Statutory Code of Practice England and Wales* also contained a number of examples of unlawful discrimination on the grounds of disability in the housing and social housing area.[342]

Equality impact assessments

4.207 In order to avoid discrimination, and to be best able to demonstrate compliance with the public sector equality duty, when considering any substantial variation of its housing allocation scheme a local housing authority will probably first wish to undertake an equality impact assessment. The Equality Act does not impose a statutory duty on public authorities requiring them to conduct a formal impact assessment when carrying out their functions. At the most, it imposes a duty on a public authority to consider undertaking an impact assessment, along with other means of gathering information, and to consider whether it is appropriate to have one in relation to the function or policy at issue, when it will or might have an impact on the protected characteristics.[343]

4.208 A local housing authority should, for example, ensure that the views of groups which are currently under-represented in social housing are taken into account in any consultation about a revision on its allocation scheme.[344] Indeed, local housing authorities would be well advised to monitor the operation of their current allocation schemes in order to identify and prevent discrimination and to review their schemes if particular groups are shown to be disadvantaged.[345]

4.209 In Wales, the position is made more explicit. The Equality Act 2010 (Statutory Duties) (Wales) Regulations 2011 requires that local housing authority policies should be subject to an equality impact assessment and the impact monitored to help ensure and demonstrate compliance with the objectives of the Equality Act 2010. The Welsh Code suggests that this is done by identifying any potential negative impact on people with protected characteristics and adopting an action plan to mitigate this impact.[346]

Allocation and migration

4.210 Despite the measures local housing authorities are – or should be – taking to involve local communities in setting, or at least understanding, priorities in housing allocation and the need to avoid discrimination and

---

[342] Disability Rights Commission, October 2006. The statutory guidance on gender discrimination is *Gender Equality Duty: Code of Practice for England and Wales* (Equal Opportunities Commission, November 2006). All of these Codes are available on the EHRC website.

[343] *R (Brown) v Secretary of State for Work and Pensions* [2008] EWHC 3158 (Admin) at [89].

[344] Welsh Code, para 4.74.

[345] Welsh Code, para 5.38.

[346] Welsh Code, para 4.71.

inequality, recent surveys have found that many people perceive that the way that social housing is allocated is unfair. A UK Government-commissioned study published in 2009 found that less than a quarter (23%) of the public agreed that the way social housing is allocated is fair.[347]

4.211 A particularly popular misconception has been that the majority of available social housing is allocated to new arrivals from overseas. Research commissioned by the EHRC identified anxieties about housing allocation schemes putting white British families at a disadvantage despite evidence which found that less than 2% of all social housing residents are people who have moved to Britain in the last five years and that nine out of ten people who live in social housing were born in the UK.[348] An earlier study had found that the available data suggests that relatively small numbers of new immigrants and migrants are accessing the social rented sector.[349] The most up-to-date analysis[350] suggests that UK-born and foreign-born people are equally likely to be living in social housing (about 17% of the population in each case). But recent arrivals are much less likely to be in social housing. The overall effect is small but growing: in 2009/10 less than 10% of tenants were non-UK citizens.

4.212 A study published by the Welsh Government found that the net pressures created by migration on access to social housing were not as great as public perceptions of those pressures. It made recommendations on the importance of local housing authorities: raising awareness of allocations amongst local communities; producing allocations schemes which are easy to access and understand; advice for applicants about allocation procedures and allocations; and publishing information about lettings.[351]

4.213 Local housing authorities concerned about local public perceptions about allocations may take some comfort from the latest YouGov survey which has found that the public believes that local links are more important than someone's country of birth when it comes to allocating social housing.[352] Against this background, it is obviously important that local housing authorities provide regular, accurate and generalised information on how social housing is allocated and how waiting lists are managed, working actively to dispel any myths and misconceptions which may arise.[353]

---

[347] *Attitudes to Housing: Findings from the Ipsos MORI Public Affairs Monitor Omnibus Survey (England)* (DCLG, 2009) Chapter 7.

[348] *Social housing allocation and immigrant communities* Jill Rutter and Maria Latorre Migration, Equalities and Citizenship Team, IPPR, 2009.

[349] *New immigrants and migrants in social housing in England* (Local Government Association, 2008).

[350] *Housing and migration May 2012 A UK guide to issues and solutions* (Housing and Migration Network, May 2012) and see *Briefing paper 7.4 – Who is being allocated social housing in London?* (Migration Watch UK, April 2012).

[351] *The effects of recent migration on local authorities' allocation of housing and actions under homelessness legislation* (Welsh Government, 2009).

[352] *Findings of the Metropolitan Migration Foundation Survey on housing and migration* commissioned from YouGov (April 2012).

[353] Welsh Code, para 4.44.

THE ROLE OF 'DISCRETION'

4.214 One of the most difficult tasks in framing an allocation scheme is to determine the extent to which flexibility should be retained, on the part of identified officers of the local housing authority, to depart from the normal rules or to deal with exceptional or unusual cases. Sadly, the judicial guidance is not altogether clear on the extent to which this sort of broad discretion is permissible ie lawful.

4.215 At one extreme it is plain that a scheme cannot lawfully allow so much discretion to depart from the rules that, in reality, there is no scheme other than the exercise of discretion on a case-by-case basis. The examples of allocation schemes which were unlawful in that respect include:

• *R v Islington London Borough Council ex p Reilly & Mannix.*[354] That case was concerned with a points-based system. There was discretion to award as many additional points as were needed to bring a particular household to the head of the queue and to gain the needed priority. The judge said:

> '... the residual discretion is not a satisfactory way of bridging the gap between the outcome of the category-based points calculation and the true assessment of need. It is too vague and uncertain and results in a disproportionately large element of need being subject to assessment on an undefined and unguided discretionary basis.' (at p 666)

• *R (Cali) v London Borough of Waltham Forest.*[355] The local housing authority had adopted a banding scheme and choice-based letting. The published scheme gave unfettered power to a panel of officers to move an applicant from one category to another, depending upon their perceived housing need. Applying *Reilly & Mannix* the judge said:

> 'First, the practice identified appears to be the exercise of a broad discretion to promote a household from one category to another. ... In the absence of published criteria, the mechanism described in the letter depends excessively on discretion ... As in *Reilly & Mannix*, the discretion identified ... is too vague and would result in decisions as to comparative need being taken on 'an undefined and unguided discretionary basis' which could lead to inconsistency and arbitrary results.' [39]

In the second case, the effect of introducing an unlimited discretion was that the published allocation scheme failed to meet the statutory obligation that it must set out the local regime for determining priorities.

4.216 Although both these cases concerned a now-overruled requirement that an allocation scheme must allow for cumulative or composite assessment of

---

[354] [1998] EWHC Admin 912, (1998) 31 HLR 651, QBD.
[355] [2006] EWHC 302 (Admin) [2007] HLR 1, Admin Ct.

need,[356] the cautious approach to schemes which allow unfettered discretion has been echoed in more recent cases. For example, in dealing with a scheme which had an absolute rule that registration dates would be adjusted when an applicant moved between priority bands, a judge said:[357]

> 'This policy also excludes any exercise of a residual discretion to modify the details of the selection scheme. It is clear from *Ahmad* that it is both rational and fair to exclude any residual discretion from being exercised when allocations are known. The court should not second guess the policy decisions taken by a local authority in settling the details of how it will allocate properties within a particular banding.

> Moreover, as Lloyd Jones J explained in *R (Cali and others) v London Borough of Waltham Forest* [2007] HLR 1, it is not appropriate for a scheme to allow for the exercise of a residual discretion to enable the local housing authority to relax a harsh or apparently unfair aspect of a scheme. He pointed out that such a discretion would inevitably be too vague and would give rise to uncertain results to enable it to be operated fairly, speedily and transparently, when rejecting a submission that any rigid rules defining how a scheme is to allocate housing should be capable of being ameliorated by the exercise of residual discretion by the local authority.'

4.217 However, courts appear to have been equally content to uphold as lawful those schemes which have fairly fixed rules but do allow for exceptions to be made in exceptional circumstances. A recent example dealt with a rule in an allocation scheme suspending all applicants from bidding where they owed in excess of one weeks' rent arrears, save where the Director of Housing considered there were exceptional circumstances. No-one suggested that the presence of such discretion rendered the scheme unlawful and an appeal court judge said:[358]

> 'The scheme contains the necessary safety valve to enable those who are in arrears to explain to the Director of Housing that there is some good reason for them being in arrears, for example because they are ill in hospital or whatever. In those circumstances the Director of Housing can then allow bidding to take place "in exceptional circumstances" ...'

4.218 There will no doubt shortly be a challenge to an allocation scheme on the basis that the presence of an untrammeled discretion, even one said to be limited to undefined 'exceptional' circumstances, is unlawful.

---

[356] See **4.118–4.119**.

[357] *R (Kabashi) v Redbridge London Borough Council* [2009] EWHC 2984 (Admin), (2010) October *Legal Action*, p 32, Admin Ct. at [16]–[17].

[358] *R (Babakandi) v Westminster City Council* [2011] EWCA Civ 1397 (2012) January *Legal Action*, p 21, CA at [7].

CHALLENGES TO ALLOCATION SCHEMES

4.219 Ordinarily, an applicant will only be concerned with whether his or her particular application has been correctly considered under the terms of the relevant local housing allocation scheme. In other words, whether decisions have been correctly made on questions of eligibility and qualification and whether the application has been attributed to the right band (in a banding scheme) or accorded the appropriate points (in a points-based scheme). Disputes about these and other case-specific matters can be dealt with by reviews, complaints and litigation.[359]

4.220 But, not infrequently, a particular applicant's case may demonstrate that there is – at least arguably – something wrong with the local allocation scheme more generally. In those circumstances the applicant may need to challenge the legality of the scheme or some part of it. That is normally done by proceedings for judicial review.[360]

4.221 For example, it might be suggested that:

- the scheme has failed to comply with some express statutory requirement of HA 1996, Part 6; or

- it has been adopted or varied without the requisite prior consultation;[361] or

- it fails to set out the local housing authority's policies on priority or procedures for allocation;[362] or

- it has been drafted without regard to the statutory Codes of Guidance – or is contrary to them (without explanation);[363] or

- the scheme is discriminatory in an unlawful respect.[364]

4.222 In short, a housing allocation scheme adopted by a local housing authority must 'be lawfully and fairly operated, for example without unlawful discrimination'.[365]

4.223 Very exceptionally, it may be said that the whole or part of a scheme is irrational in the sense that no reasonable local housing authority could have framed its scheme in that way. Between 1996 and 2008, several schemes

---

[359] See **2.85–2.115** for general information about reviews, complaints and litigation and **3.254–3.257** for challenges to decisions about eligibility and qualification.

[360] For a fuller description of judicial review principles and procedures, see **19.224–19.245**.

[361] See **1.46, 4.6** and **4.15**.

[362] See **2.17–2.19**.

[363] HA 1996, s 169(1).

[364] See **4.204–4.206**.

[365] *R (Ahmad) v Newham London Borough Council* [2009] UKHL 14, [2009] HLR 41, HL at [14].

adopted under HA 1996, Part 6 were described in those terms by the courts. But in 2009 the House of Lords emphasised just how difficult it would be to sustain such a criticism, given the very broad terms in which the statute is now framed since the amendments made to HA 1996, Part 6 by the Homelessness Act 2002. As Lord Neuberger put it:

'once a housing allocation scheme complies with the requirements of section 167 and any other statutory requirements, the courts should be very slow to interfere on the ground of alleged irrationality.'[366]

4.224 Indeed, the judicially approved examples of schemes that might be irrational are extreme:

'one possibility might be a policy which ensured that small families had priority over large ones, or that people coming from outside the borough had priority over those living within it, or that people who had been waiting the shortest time had preference over those waiting the longest.'[367]

4.225 Where, in such a very exceptional case, a scheme or part of a scheme is described as 'irrational', the relevant court will probably do no more than declare that to be the case and leave it to the local housing authority to work out how to revise or amend the scheme to address the particular problem:

'Castigating a scheme as irrational is of little help to anyone unless a rational alternative can be suggested. Sometimes it may be possible to do this. But where the question is one of overall policy, as opposed to individual entitlement, it is very unlikely that judges will have the tools available to make the choices which Parliament has required a housing authority to make.'[368]

4.226 However, shortly after setting out the high hurdle that would need to be surmounted to establish that an allocation scheme was in whole or in part irrational, the House of Lords itself declared unlawful an irrational provision in the allocation scheme adopted by the largest housing authority in England.[369] In that case, the allocation scheme gave greater priority to a person owed a homelessness duty if they had been provided with suitable temporary accommodation than if they had remained in the unsuitable accommodation in which conditions were so bad that they were accepted as being 'homeless'. The Court of Appeal decided that the scheme was, in that respect, unlawful. On a further appeal, the House of Lords held that:[370]

'The council's explanation for this priority is to "assert the premise on which the Allocation Policy is based [namely] that those in greatest need are dealt with first". This bald statement is not enough to justify the priority accorded to those in new temporary accommodation over those left temporarily in their existing

---

[366] [2009] UKHL 14, [2009] HLR 41, HL, at [55].
[367] [2009] UKHL 14, [2009] HLR 41, HL, at [16].
[368] [2009] UKHL 14, [2009] HLR 41, HL, at [22].
[369] *Birmingham City Council v Ali* [2009] UKHL 36, [2009] 1 WLR 1506, HL.
[370] Ibid, para [63].

accommodation. Both groups are in accommodation which is temporary. Indeed, at least on the face of it, if anything, it would appear that the latter group would have the more pressing claim. They are, *ex hypothesi*, in accommodation which has been found to be such that it would not be reasonable for them to continue in occupation. No such finding will necessarily have been made as to the accommodation now occupied by the former group. It may be that the council could have shown that, as a matter of fact, applicants in the former group are normally in worse accommodation than those in the latter group: if so, the priority would be justifiable. It may be, for example, that when the council refer to 'temporary accommodation' they are referring to bed and breakfast hotels or hostels. But no such evidence, not even an opinion to that effect, has been put forward in the evidence. Accordingly, on this, relatively narrow aspect, we would agree with the decision of the Court of Appeal.'

4.227 Despite this departure by the House of Lords from its stricture that allocation schemes should not readily be held unlawful, subsequent challenges have very much manifested a judicial approach of reluctance to intervene. For example:

- An allocation scheme was said to be unlawful because it contained an auto-bid facility for homeless applicants who had not successfully bid during a fixed period of two months. Dismissing the claim, the judge held that:

  > 'It is trite law that the court should be very slow to second-guess the judgments made by [local housing authorities] in the formulation of policies for the allocation of social housing: see, most authoritatively, *R(Ahmad) v London Borough of Newham* ... per Lady Hale at para. 22. I am not prepared to say that the Council's judgment that a two-month bidding period gave persons in the Claimants' position an opportunity to exercise a reasonable degree of choice failed to conform to the requirements of the Code or was otherwise irrational.'[371]

- A scheme for allocating pitches on official local authority gypsy and traveller sites was not irrational, applying the *Ahmad* approach, even though it gave priority to applicants with a local connection and required them to renew applications annually.[372]

- An allocation scheme which automatically suspended applicants with rent arrears of more than a threshold amount was not irrational. It enabled applicants in exceptional circumstances to obtain a lifting of the suspension.[373]

---

[371] *R (Tout a Tout) v Haringey London Borough Council* [2012] EWHC 873 (Admin), (2012) May *Legal Action*, p 34, Admin Ct at [19].

[372] *R (McDonagh) v Hackney London Borough Council* [2012] EWHC 373 (Admin), (2012) April *Legal Action*, p 46, Admin Ct.

[373] *R (Babakandi) v Westminster City Council* [2011] EWHC 1756 (Admin), (2011) August *Legal Action*, p 40, Admin Ct.

- In a scheme adopted by Redbridge London Borough Council which prioritised by combined band and application date, it was not irrational to bring forward an applicant's date when he or she moved to a different priority band. The judge said:

  'It is first to be noted that Redbridge has put forward several reasons why the particular policy that operates to bring forward an effective date when property requirements alter. It is not for the court to assess these reasons since, to do so, it would have to examine all relevant aspects of the Scheme before reaching a conclusion as to whether the overall Scheme was rational or not. This policy also excludes any exercise of a residual discretion to modify the details of the selection scheme. It is clear from *Ahmad* that it is both rational and fair to exclude any residual discretion from being exercised when allocations are known. The court should not second guess the policy decisions taken by a local authority in settling the details of how it will allocate properties within a particular banding.'[374]

---

[374] *R (Kabashi) v Redbridge London Borough Council* [2009] EWHC 2984 (Admin) at [16]–[17], (2010) October *Legal Action*, p 32, Admin Ct.

Chapter 5

BEING ALLOCATED A PROPERTY

INTRODUCTION

5.1 Successfully establishing eligibility and/or qualification for allocation of social housing and securing consideration under a local housing authority's housing allocation scheme are only the first stages in obtaining a rented home from a social landlord. What the applicant will usually want from his or her application is an early opportunity to consider an actual offer of a tenancy of a house or flat.

5.2 Most social landlords experience a regular turnover in their housing stock and need to make rapid and effective arrangements to re-let properties falling vacant (or, more unusually, to fill newly constructed or acquired property available for first letting), not least because rapid re-letting maximises rental receipts. For local housing authorities, the question will be whether to re-let pursuant to an 'allocation' within the terms of the allocation scheme established under Housing Act 1996, Part 6[1] or to grant a tenancy which does not constitute an allocation.[2] For private registered providers or registered social landlords (such as housing associations), the question will be whether to make the property available for nomination of a tenant by the local housing authority (which would then count as an 'allocation' by that local housing authority), or whether to keep it as part of their own pool of properties for re-letting to their existing tenants or to those making applications directly to them.[3]

5.3 If the local housing authority has property which is to be re-let in circumstances which do *not* count as an allocation,[4] for example, by offering a secure or introductory tenancy to an existing secure or introductory tenant whom the local housing authority has invited to move, the local housing authority can make that re-letting free of the legal constraints of its ordinary allocation scheme. Alternatively, the property may be let on a tenancy which is not secure or introductory: for example, it may be used to provide temporary accommodation to a homeless household.[5] Only local housing authority lettings to secure or introductory tenants are controlled by the allocation

---

[1] Statutory guidance on allocation schemes made under HA 1996 Part 6 is given in *Allocation of Accommodation: Guidance for local housing authorities in England* (Department for Communities & Local Government, June 2012) (the English Code) and in *Code of Guidance for local authorities Allocation of Accommodation and Homelessness 2012* (Welsh Government, August 2012) (the Welsh Code). See Appendix 1 of this book for the English Code and see the accompanying CD-ROM for the Welsh Code.
[2] See **1.35–1.43** for a review of the circumstances in which a person may become a tenant of social housing without an allocation.
[3] For a discussion of lettings by private registered providers or registered social landlords see Chapter 6.
[4] Housing Act 1996, ss 159 and 160. See also **1.35–1.43** for other circumstances which do not count as an 'allocation'.
[5] Housing Act 1985, Sch 1, para 4.

scheme requirements. Beyond those requirements a local housing authority's only duty is to select a tenant in the lawful exercise of its general discretion to manage its housing stock.[6]

5.4   If a property, whether owned by a local housing authority or another social landlord, is to be re-let in circumstances which *do* count as an 'allocation', that will trigger the operation of the local allocation scheme arrangements described in this book. To whom, and when, an actual offer of that accommodation will be made depends entirely on the detailed operation of the particular local allocation scheme. The allocation scheme is, however, only a process of selection or sifting among potential candidates for a tenancy, or nomination for a tenancy. Following the selection or nomination, the actual offer and acceptance of the tenancy agreement (or 'grant' of a tenancy) is separate from the process of allocation and will take place after that process has completed.[7] The offer and acceptance of any tenancy will be dictated by rules of contract and by any relevant statutory or regulatory controls on the ability of the local housing authority, private registered provider or registered social landlord to let property.[8]

5.5   Essentially, in a true 'allocation' situation, prospective candidates for any available property will be identified through one of two routes:

(1)   by self-selection, in the sense that candidates for the tenancy will put themselves forward or 'bid' for the property in a choice-based letting scheme; or

(2)   by the local housing authority itself selecting a prospective tenant from among the applicants who fall to be considered under its allocation scheme.

5.6   Which route is available will depend upon whether the particular local housing authority has adopted a choice-based letting element in its allocation scheme. As the last UK government's target, for every local housing authority in England to be operating some form of choice-based letting scheme, was largely achieved, this Chapter first considers those arrangements. The second part of the Chapter covers the alternative, ie selection by the local housing authority. Finally, we review more general points affecting offers and refusals under both routes.

---

[6]   Housing Act 1985, s 21 (see *R v Canterbury City Council ex p Gillespie* (1987) 19 HLR 7, QBD).
[7]   *Birmingham City Council v Qasim* [2009] EWCA Civ 1080, [2010] HLR 19, CA.
[8]   For example, the powers of local housing authorities to let or otherwise dispose of the housing they own are controlled by Housing Act 1985, Part 2.

CHOICE-BASED LETTINGS

The policy background

5.7 In 2000, the then Labour Government issued Green and White Papers on Housing Policy, both entitled *Quality and Choice: A Decent Home for All.*[9] Those Papers emphasised that applicant 'choice' would be a feature of the new allocation regime to be brought in by what became the Homelessness Act 2002. There were a number of rationales behind the concept of introducing customer choice into housing allocation. One was to reduce the number of offers of accommodation that were rejected by applicants. If applicants selected their own property, rather than being offered a property selected by the local housing authority, there were likely to be far fewer refusals. A further, associated, rationale was to increase the numbers of offers accepted by applicants by encouraging applicants to provide as much information as possible on the type and location of accommodation that they would accept, in advance of being offered a property

5.8 In anticipation of the amendments later made to the Housing Act 1996 (HA 1996), Part 6 ('Allocation of social housing') by the Homelessness Act 2002, local housing authorities – and to an initially more limited extent private registered providers and registered social landlords,[10] and combinations of local housing authorities and other social landlords[11] – began exploring the prospects for implementation of allocation schemes based on applicant choice, ie choice-based letting schemes. In 2001, the UK government funded 27 local housing authorities to conduct pilot schemes to test the scope for choice-based lettings.[12] The pilots ended in March 2003, and the evaluation reports were published.[13] Most of the schemes established in the pilot period have continued to operate.

5.9 The 27 English local housing authorities that participated in the pilot scheme between April 2001 and March 2003 were, on the whole, positive about the experience. They found that the number of households registered for social housing had increased in almost all of the areas. Choice-based letting was considered, both by local housing authorities and by the applicants, to be more transparent and the system itself more open and simpler to understand. The system required greater participation from applicants than previously, in that

---

[9] *Quality and Choice: A Decent Home for All* (Green Paper, DETR, April 2000); *Quality and Choice: A Decent Home for All — the Way Forward for Housing* (White Paper, DETR, December 2000).

[10] Early housing association choice-based schemes are described in N Winn *The Big Picture: Choice in Lettings* (Housing Corporation, September 2001).

[11] Such as the scheme in Harborough described in T Brown et al *Allocate or let? Your Choice: Lessons from Harborough Home Search* (Chartered Institute of Housing, 2003) and *Implementing a choice-based lettings system for social housing tenants* (Joseph Rowntree Foundation, Findings, January 2003).

[12] See *How to Choose Choice: Lessons from the first year of the ODPM's CBLs Pilot Schemes* (Office of the Deputy Prime Minister, October 2002).

[13] *Piloting Choice-Based Lettings: An Evaluation* (ODPM, August 2004); and *Applicants' Perspectives on Choice-Based Lettings* (ODPM, March 2004).

they were expected to monitor advertised properties and bid themselves. On the whole, applicants seemed to consider that the benefits were worth the extra effort. There was an overall reduction in the rates of refusal of offers.

5.10 The pilot schemes included areas of high and low demand for social housing. However, in none of those areas, even those of low demand, was a truly 'choice-based' lettings scheme implemented. All of the schemes had a mechanism for prioritising candidate households who were entitled to reasonable preference under HA 1996, Part 6 (and, in particular, for prioritising homeless households), as a failure to do so would have been unlawful. The methods used to prioritise varied. In some areas, particularly those where there was high demand for social housing, local housing authorities used banding systems to give those households with higher needs a higher priority. In areas of lower demand, local housing authorities were more likely to give points for waiting time, and to give households with higher needs 'priority cards', which provided a particular period in which to bid for properties.

5.11 Properties were advertised in local newspapers, in council offices and on the internet. Local housing authorities were advised to identify and support those households who may have difficulty in understanding the system and in making their own bids unassisted. Local housing authorities found that there were fewer households with difficulties than they had expected. It was, however, noticeable, and concerning, that homeless households seemed to bid less frequently than other households. Whether this was because those households were more vulnerable and had more difficulty in accessing or understanding the system, or because they were less anxious to move from their temporary accommodation than existing tenants waiting for transfers, was unclear.

5.12 In 2005, Shelter issued a separate evaluation of the pilot schemes, based on direct contact with eight local housing authorities, information publicly available from others, and the experiences of their own housing advisers and clients.[14] Shelter confirmed that choice-based letting was perceived by both applicants and local housing authority staff as fairer and more transparent, the process was quicker and there were fewer refusals than under previous schemes. However, Shelter discovered 'a disturbing pattern' that homeless applicants were given less choice, and were compelled to bid more often or more quickly for properties than other applicants, resulting in an increasing concentration of previously homeless households in low-demand areas.[15] It was also concerned that most local housing authorities had not allocated extra resources to help vulnerable applicants with the bidding process. Shelter concluded by identifying the difficulties of providing choice, given the lack of social housing available, and warning:

> '... choice is a hollow concept when there is a chronic housing shortage ... given the current lack of available social housing, choice-based letting cannot realise its full potential.'

---

[14] *A Question of Choice: Good practice and issues in choice-based letting*, Shelter, June 2005.
[15] Principally through the use of time-limited priority cards; see **5.10** and **5.32**.

5.13 Based upon the perceived successes of the pilot scheme, and the general policy shift towards 'choice' in the provision of public services,[16] in 2005 the UK government set a target in its 5-year plan[17] for 25% of local housing authorities to adopt some form of choice-based letting scheme by the end of 2005 and for all local housing authorities to be offering choice to applicants by 2010.[18]

5.14 There was then considerable progress towards that target. Housing Investment Programme 2005 returns showed that 100 (out of 354) local housing authorities had adopted choice-based letting schemes by the end of 2005 and that approximately a further 192 planned to do so by 2010.[19] Housing Strategy Statistical Appendix returns for 2007/08 showed that 47% of local housing authorities had implemented choice-based letting and a further 49% had plans to do so. By 1 April 2009 there were 217 local housing authorities participating in choice-based letting schemes. That represented 61% of local housing authorities in England but masked wide regional variations. In London, 91% of local housing authorities had moved to choice-based lettings compared to only 30% of authorities in the North-East.[20] By April 2011, 87% of local authorities in England (283 of 326 local housing authorities) participated in choice-based lettings, an increase from 80% on 1 April 2010.[21] But again there were wide regional variations. In the West Midlands region all local housing authorities had choice-based lettings schemes whereas the lowest proportion (67%) was in the Yorkshire and Humber region.[22]

5.15 A major study of 13 schemes, which had each been operating for over 18 months, was published in October 2006.[23] It found that:

- the significance of 'waiting time' as a factor in allocation had increased compared to pre-choice arrangements;

---

[16] See House of Commons Public Administration Select Committee report, *Choice, Voice and Public Services*, Fourth Report of Session 2004–05, March 2005.

[17] *Sustainable Communities: Homes for All – A Five Year Plan* (ODPM, January 2005); and *Sustainable Communities: Homes for All – A Strategy for Choice Based Lettings* (ODPM, June 2005).

[18] A useful overview of how choice-based lettings schemes worked, and of government policies and targets for their implementation, is given in *'Choice-Based Lettings: A Factsheet'* (ODPM, March 2005).

[19] The pilot arrangements and the subsequently established local choice-based schemes were monitored and analysed at the Centre for Comparative Housing Research at De Montfort University, in association with the Department for Communities and Local Government. See T Brown and N Yates *The Choice is yours! Moving Forward on Choice-based lettings* (De Montfort University, November 2005).

[20] *Local Authority Housing Statistics, England, 2008/2009* (CLG, November 2009), p 8.

[21] Local Authority Housing Statistics, England: 2010/2011: Housing Strategy Statistical Appendix and Business Plan Statistical Appendix (DCLG, November 2011).

[22] Local Authority Housing Statistics, England: 2010/2011: Housing Strategy Statistical Appendix and Business Plan Statistical Appendix (DCLG, November 2011).

[23] *Monitoring the Longer Term Impact of Choice-based lettings* (CLG, October 2006 summarised in Housing Research Summary No 231, (CLG, 2006).

- the vast majority of lettings continued to go to high need applicants;

- many applicants saw bidding as a positive pro-active way of looking for a home, but some who had been bidding unsuccessfully over long periods expressed frustration with the systems and lack of confidence in their fairness;

- while most applicants understood the bidding system, many reported having less understanding of the rules by which bidders were ranked;[24]

- the schemes appeared to have improved rather than damaged the prospects of statutory homeless households;

- in most cases, there had been improvement in tenancy sustainment (measured by the proportion of tenancies lasting more than 12 months); and

- the additional costs of the schemes were more than offset by tenancy management savings (in faster re-lets and lower turnover).

5.16 In 2008, the Department of Health (DH) commissioned and published research on the experiences of the disabled in accessing choice-based letting schemes[25] and associated guides for social landlords establishing such schemes[26] and for people with learning difficulties who try to use them.[27]

5.17 A particularly comprehensive report on the operation of choice-based schemes was commissioned by Wirral Council from Heriot Watt University and was also published in 2008. It examined 26 such schemes operating across the country, although the conclusions and recommendations are primarily expressed by reference to the Wirral Homes scheme.[28]

5.18 A concern with choice-based letting has been the impact on members of black and minority ethnic (BME) communities in areas where choice-based letting has been introduced. In October 2004 the then UK government established an advisory group chaired by Lord Adebowale to explore how the new choice-based letting schemes affected BME groups and to undertake a full Race Equality Impact Assessment of the policy.[29] Unpublished research for the Federation of Black Housing Organisations in 2004 showed that the proportion of BME tenants responding to suitable advertised properties was

---

[24] A point later emphasised by the report's author, Professor Hal Pawson: see 'Choice ranking rules not always fully understood' (2007) *Inside Housing* 15, 7 September 2007.

[25] *Choice Based Lettings and People with Learning Disabilities* (DH, February 2008).

[26] *Making Choice Based Lettings work for People with Learning Disabilities: A Guide for Choice-based lettings schemes and landlords* (DH, February 2008).

[27] *Choice Based Lettings: A guide to choosing a home through the council* (DH, February 2008).

[28] H Pawson et al *Review of Wirralhomes Choice Based Lettings Service* (Incisive Minds Ltd, March 2008) and see 'Spoilt for choice' [2008] *Inside Housing* 23, 25 April 2008.

[29] ODPM *News Release 2004/0237*, 8 October 2004.

small.[30] More recently, similar concerns have been expressed.[31] One study has shown that black and ethnic minorities, and especially those using choice-based letting schemes, are the most likely to end up in deprived neighbourhoods with high concentrations of residents from ethnic minorities.[32]

5.19 The move to choice-based letting was given a significant push in the summer of 2008 by the publication of *Allocation of Accommodation: Choice-based Lettings*[33] – a code of statutory guidance issued by the Secretary of State to local housing authorities in England under the powers given by HA 1996, s 169. That now-repealed code, and the earlier statutory guidance issued to English local housing authorities, had advised that the UK government believed that choice should be provided in housing allocation wherever possible.

5.20 The current Codes of Guidance contains no steer towards choice-based letting, or any other particular mechanism for allocation, preferring to leave the matter entirely to the decision of the local authority.[34]

5.21 The only material that the current UK Coalition Government has published on choice-based letting is two research reports commissioned by the previous government. Those local housing authorities that have already adopted, or are minded to adopt, a choice-based letting aspect in their local allocation schemes may find the two reports useful as they focus on an aspect of choice-based lettings previously under-explored ie their effects on 'accessible housing registers'.[35] The two reports are:

(1) *Choice-based lettings, potentially disadvantaged groups and accessible housing registers: A guide to positive practice.* The guide provides advice on how to set up and operate choice-based letting schemes to ensure that social housing applicants are not disadvantaged by the proactive nature of choice-based lettings and is also available in a shorter, standalone summary format.[36] and

---

[30] 'Choice-based lettings threat to BMEs' (2004) *Inside Housing*, 12 November 2004.
[31] See, for example, T. Soares *Needs Must* (2009) *Inside Housing*, 24 July 2009.
[32] *Choice-based Letting, Ethnicity and Segregation in England*, Manley and van Ham, *Urban Studies* November 2011, p 48.
[33] DCLG, 2008.
[34] See, for example, Welsh Code, para 4.34.
[35] An accessible housing register is 'a list of suitable homes for disabled people with access needs': *Disability Equality Report by the Secretary of State for Communities and Local Government* (DCLG, 2008), p 28. See further on 'accessible housing registers' the Welsh Code at paras 4.84–4.95.
[36] *Choice-based lettings, potentially disadvantaged groups and accessible housing registers: a summary guide to positive practice* and *Choice-based lettings, potentially disadvantaged groups and accessible housing registers: a guide to positive practice.* Delia Lomax and Hal Pawson – Heriot-Watt University, Edinburgh (DCLG, 2011).

(2) *Costs and effectiveness of accessible housing registers in a choice-based lettings context.* This report examines the cost and effectiveness of accessible housing registers in the context of choice-based letting.[37]

The statutory basis for choice-based lettings

5.22 Despite all the relatively recent emphasis on 'choice' in *policy* terms, as already described, there is no *statutory* obligation on local housing authorities to implement choice-based letting schemes. HA 1996, Part 6 merely provides that applicants should be informed of any local policy on offering either:

(1) 'a choice of housing accommodation'; or

(2) 'the opportunity to express preferences' about what is to be allocated to them.

5.23 In either case that must be by way of a statement in the local housing allocation scheme.[38]

5.24 Strictly speaking, this obligation could be met by a simple statement in the allocation scheme to the effect that there is *no* local policy on 'choice' or customer 'preferences'. At a minimum, however, local housing authorities could be expected to allow applicants an opportunity to express a preference for accommodation of a particular type or in a particular location. A simple local policy on expression of preferences is often considered to be an interim measure or a second-best to a full-blown policy on choice.

5.25 There is no statutory duty positively to give effect to applicant choice or preference in HA 1996, Part 6. The position in relation to allocations is no different to that in respect of the statutory duty to provide temporary accommodation for the homeless ie unless the local scheme expressly provides to the contrary, an applicant is not entitled to any choice.[39]

5.26 In summary, therefore, HA 1996, Part 6 simply permits, but does not require, local housing authorities to contain within their allocation schemes any provisions allowing applicants opportunities to state preferences or make choices. For those local housing authorities wishing to adopt choice-based letting, HA 1996, Part 6 expressly enables local allocation schemes to include provision for the allocation of particular units of accommodation in response to specific applications for that accommodation.[40] This is the sole statutory basis for local housing authorities to implement 'choice' by means of enabling applicants to 'bid' for specific properties.

---

[37] *Costs and effectiveness of accessible housing registers in a choice-based lettings context* Colin Jones, Heriot-Watt University and Mark Lordon, Incisive Minds Ltd (DCLG, 2011).
[38] HA 1996, s 166A(2) [England], s 167(1A) [Wales].
[39] *R (Khatun) v Newham London Borough Council* [2004] EWCA Civ 55, (2004) 36 HLR 29, CA.
[40] HA 1996, s 166A(6) [England] and s 167(2E) [Wales], discussed further at **4.170–4.194**.

5.27 In this absence of any legislative compulsion, the direction of travel towards choice-based letting is a matter for local policy choices on methods of housing allocation. All the statutory guidance previously issued in England – which positively promoted choice – has been withdrawn.[41] The content of the present statutory guidance for Wales is dealt with separately below.

England

5.28 Those local housing authorities that have gone down the choice-based letting route have generally arranged for their available properties to be advertised on their websites or in magazines or by emails or texts sent to those eligible to 'bid' for them.

5.29 Such local housing authorities have needed to identify mechanisms for ranking those who bid for advertised properties and most have adopted allocation schemes which attribute to applicants a relative rank or priority as against other prospective bidders. Broadly, either of two alternative systems will be in operation:

(1) a 'banding' system, so that applicants are placed in different bands reflecting their different needs, and, within those bands, applicants are prioritised according to the length of time they have waited; or

(2) a 'pointing' system simply giving those applicants with the most urgent housing needs priority over others with less urgent needs by affording them more points.[42]

5.30 The former may be simpler for applicants to understand and simpler for local housing authorities to operate. One survey found that the adoption of choice-based letting tended to put a greater focus on relative waiting times:

'Waiting time made some contribution to applicant priority in most authorities. As perceived by survey respondents, however, its significance tended to be much greater under CBL than under traditional allocations schemes. Whereas 19 of the 20 CBL authorities considered waiting time to be "quite significant" or "very significant" here, this was true for only seven of the other 32 authorities.'[43]

---

[41] By the latest guidance – *Allocation of Accommodation: Guidance for local housing authorities in England* (DCLG, June 2012) (the English Code) – replacing: (1) *Allocation of Accommodation: Code of Guidance for local housing authorities for England* (Office of the Deputy Prime Minister, November 2002); (2) *Allocation of Accommodation: Choice-based Lettings Code of Guidance for Local Housing Authorities* (CLG, August 2008); and (3) *Fair and flexible: statutory guidance on social housing allocations for local authorities in England* (CLG, December 2009). The English Code is reproduced in Appendix 1.

[42] Whether by a simplified points system or by 'time limited priority cards' which would enable an applicant with the most urgent need to have priority over other applicants for a specified period.

[43] *Exploring local authority policy and practice on housing allocations* (CLG, July 2009), p 7.

5.31 Where available properties are openly advertised, so that applicants can apply for particular properties, the advertising will usually state the level of priority or the waiting time required by the likely successful applicant. The thinking is that providing this information will allow applicants to assess their chances of success, and so to refrain from bidding if they would have no prospect of being allocated the accommodation.

5.32 Some local housing authorities in England have allocation schemes under which 'choice' (ie freedom to bid) is only available to certain classes of applicants for limited periods, most often homeless households. When the period expires, the local housing authority reverts to the officer-led form of allocation described later in this Chapter (sometimes called 'direct lettings').[44] Shelter's evaluation of the pilot choice-based lettings schemes in England, published in June 2005,[45] was highly critical of time-limited choice for those in greatest need, arguing that the effect was to put pressure on those applicants to bid for unpopular properties. Shelter also identified at least two local housing authorities that refused to accept bids from homeless applicants for high-demand properties. Shelter recommended that, if time-limited priority cards were to be used, they should be valid for a long enough period of time (at least 6 months) to allow for a suitable range of properties to become available, and that the applicant's needs should be reviewed at the end of the period.

5.33 In one case, a local housing authority's allocation scheme enabled homeless applicants to bid freely alongside other applicants for social housing for two months before the system would auto-bid for the next available property sufficient for their needs. A challenge to the lawfulness of that arrangement failed. The judge said that he was 'not prepared to say that the Council's judgment that a two-month bidding period gave persons in the Claimants' position an opportunity to exercise a reasonable degree of choice failed to conform to the requirements of the Code or was otherwise irrational.'[46]

Wales

5.34 The present Welsh Code is more equivocal than the now-withdrawn English Codes. In it, the Welsh Government does not recommend any one system of allocation and encourages local housing authorities to determine housing need in, and strategic priorities for, their own areas, after consultation.[47]

---

[44] See **5.61–5.65.**
[45] *A Question of Choice: Good Practice and issues in choice-based letting* (Shelter, June 2005). See also **5.12.**
[46] *R (Tout a Tout) v Haringey London Borough Council* [2012] EWHC 873 (Admin), (2012) May *Legal Action,* p 34, Admin Ct at [19].
[47] Welsh Code, para 4.34.

5.35   The Welsh Code briefly mentions three different approaches:

(1)   choice-based lettings;

(2)   needs-based schemes; and

(3)   hybrid schemes

but the present Code offers no further elaboration of them.[48]

5.36   The Welsh Code simply emphasises that any scheme will, in reality, include both an element of choice and also an attempt to meet need. The difference between the three approaches lies in the balance that each attempts to strike between choice and need.[49]

5.37   In general, the Welsh Code suggests that maintaining common housing lists, rather than separate lists for different groups of applicants, encouraging mobility between different areas and different types of tenure, providing good quality information, making the widest practicable range of options available to applicants and, above all, operating a simple and transparent system should be hallmarks of an allocation scheme.[50]

5.38   The Welsh Government commissioned a project to review choice-based allocation systems in use by social landlords in Wales. The project report identified some 11 choice-based schemes which covered the whole of a social landlord's available stock.[51] The report describes the key features of those schemes, recording a shift away from 'time waiting' to 'housing need' as the main means of prioritising among applicants. It found that the weakest general feature of the schemes was the late provision of feedback on bid outcomes and patchy content of that feedback. In keeping with the theme of the Welsh Code, the report's recommendations are non-prescriptive as to the type of scheme a local housing authority in Wales should adopt.

The issue of balancing choice and need

5.39   It had been thought that the greatest difficulty in operating choice-based schemes would arise in areas where demand most heavily outstripped supply. How, after all, could a local housing authority offer a realistic 'choice' if the statutory scheme requires a reasonable preference to be given to applicants in specified categories of housing need and there is not even enough housing available to meet the needs of those 'priority' applicants?[52] Where choice-based

---

48   Welsh Code, para 5.39.
49   See **5.39**.
50   Welsh Code, paras 4.38–4.46.
51   *A Review of Welsh Social Landlords' Approaches to Increasing Choice in Letting Accommodation* (Welsh Assembly Government, 2008).
52   See R Latham 'Allocating Accommodation: reconciling choice and need', Parts 1 and 2 (2005) March *Legal Action* at p 16 and May *Legal Action* at p 15.

letting has been adopted, the Welsh Code suggests that local housing authorities should provide applicants with details about the properties which have been let (eg what level of priority the successful applicants had, and/or the date they applied for housing). Such feedback is considered to be crucial as it enables applicants to assess their chances of success in subsequent applications.[53]

5.40 Even those responsible for framing policies at national level have found this issue (of balancing 'choice' and 'need') difficult to address. When the first of the modern English Codes of Guidance was published in November 2002, it was accompanied by an undertaking by the then Government to issue further guidance on this question 'towards the end of' 2003.[54] Despite that commitment, it was not until August 2008 that an English Code dealing with choice-based letting was issued, providing that guidance. In the light of subsequent developments in case law on the interpretation of HA 1996, Part 6, some of that Code was in turn replaced by further guidance in yet another English Code in 2009. The unhappy consequence was that any local housing authority in England that was between 2009 and 2012 seeking to review or revise its allocation scheme so as to best address issues of 'choice' and 'need' had to take account of all three Codes.

5.41 However, as already indicated, the present English Code is silent on the question; leaving the matter entirely for individual housing authorities to resolve in the light of local circumstances. Even the helpful House of Commons Library research paper covering the issue has been withdrawn.[55]

The courts' approach

1996–2009

5.42 In the first decade of operation of HA 1996, Part 6, the courts discerned the meeting of housing 'need' as the primary policy driver in the legislation[56] and, from 2000 onwards, had several opportunities to consider the application of that principle in the operation of choice-based letting schemes adopted by particular local housing authorities.

5.43 An early attempt to implement a choice-based lettings scheme, reconciling freedom of choice with providing reasonable preference to those groups falling within the statutory categories by the adoption of broad priority bands, was made by the London Borough of Lambeth.[57]

---

[53] Welsh Code, para 4.42.
[54] Letter by Housing Policy Advisor ODPM to Directors of all local authorities in England (ODPM, November 2002).
[55] *Allocating social housing and 'choice-based' schemes*, Briefing paper SN03858 (December 2010).
[56] See the discussion at **4.39–4.42**. Notwithstanding later developments in the case law, the Government's policy is still one of 'ensuring that priority for social housing goes to those in the greatest need': English Code, para 2.1.
[57] The Lambeth experiment with choice-based letting is well-charted by Cowan and Marsh *From Need to Choice* (2004) 67 MLR 3, p 478.

5.44   The Court of Appeal considered that attempt in the linked cases *R (A) v Lambeth London Borough Council, R (Lindsay) v Lambeth London Borough Council*[58] and concluded that Lambeth had been unsuccessful and had failed to give effect to the statutory scheme properly. Lambeth's bands, recognising different categories of needs, were organised in such a way that applicants who did not fall within any of the reasonable preference categories could have the same priority as those who did. The Court of Appeal also criticised Lambeth's policy of allowing applicants to define their own needs, by specifying the size and location of accommodation they sought (and being encouraged to do so as widely and flexibly as possible), as haphazard and not capable of ensuring that the categories of applicants falling within the statutory 'reasonable preference' groups were given preference. The Court expressed concern that applicants might under-estimate their own needs, in order to stand a greater chance of being allocated accommodation, but that some applicants, such as families with young children, would have fewer chances of being allocated accommodation as they would not find it possible to under-estimate their needs. In reality, the main 'choice' offered by the Lambeth scheme was a freedom to opt for poorer quality or less satisfactory accommodation in the hope of an earlier offer. Having been declared unlawful in July 2002, it was replaced by a new allocation scheme in February 2004.

5.45   Surprisingly few cases then reached the courts in relation to choice-based letting schemes after the introduction of the new allocation regime in January 2003 (ie HA 1996, Part 6 as amended by the Homelessness Act 2002).

5.46   In the London Borough of Newham, where a choice-based scheme had been operating (with amendments) since September 2002, at least two early judicial review applications were launched. The first resulted in an undertaking to amend the scheme in June 2003.[59] The second was again settled on terms that the local housing authority would further amend its allocation scheme.[60] Some of those amendments were later revoked by the local housing authority's Director of Housing, and others were incorporated into a scheme that reached its seventh revision before being upheld as lawful.[61]

5.47   In *R (Najha Al-Juboori) v Ealing London Borough Council*,[62] permission had been granted for a challenge to the local choice-based allocation scheme in a judicial review claim. The trial was adjourned to enable other local housing authorities in London to join the proceedings. By the time it was restored, the claimant had been re-housed and the scheme amended so that no judgment on the merits of the claim was delivered.

---

[58]   *R (A) v Lambeth London Borough Council, R (Lindsay) v Lambeth London Borough Council* [2002] EWCA Civ 1084, (2002) 34 HLR 57, CA.

[59]   *R (Nazma Begum) v Newham London Borough Council CO/566/2003* (unreported) 26 June 2003.

[60]   *R (Heather Phillip) v Newham London Borough Council CO/1731/2004* (unreported) 22 June 2004. See also *Choice scheme revised after challenge* (2004) *Inside Housing*, 30 July, p 71.

[61]   See **5.51–5.54**.

[62]   *R (Najha Al-Juboori) v Ealing London Borough Council* [2002] EWHC 2627 (Admin).

5.48 In *R (Cali) v Waltham Forest London Borough Council*,[63] a choice-based scheme containing a banding system was declared to be unlawful because it did not provide for the identification of a household's cumulative needs and so could not effectively offer additional preference.[64] Nor did it identify, within the published scheme, the criteria by which an applicant qualified for reasonable preference.

5.49 In *R (Lin & Hassan) v Barnet London Borough Council*,[65] a points-based scheme of choice-based letting was held to be unlawful as its provision giving 100 points to its existing tenants, seeking transfers, artificially raised the points threshold (above which a bid might succeed) to the detriment of applicants who were not existing tenants and who were entitled to a statutory preference. That decision was not disturbed on an appeal pursued (for the most part unsuccessfully) by the claimants, who sought to establish that the choice-based scheme gave insufficient opportunity to the homeless to secure long-term housing.[66]

5.50 The central problem identified by the litigation in this period was how to establish a system that was easy to operate and understand, that gave priority to customer choice, but that also took account of the vast range of needs exhibited by applicants and ranked them in a way which gave effect to the perceived statutory purpose that those in the greatest need should be housed first.

2009 onwards

5.51 The legal landscape changed dramatically in March 2009 with the first House of Lords decision on a choice-based letting scheme.[67] Newham had adopted a banding scheme with three bands:

(1)   applicants in reasonable preference categories;

(2)   transfer cases with no reasonable preference;

(3)   non-transfer applicants with no reasonable preferences.[68]

5.52 Unsurprisingly, the vast majority of advertised properties went to bidders from the first band. But within that band applicants were afforded

---

[63]   [2006] EWHC 302 (Admin), [2007] 39 HLR 1, Admin Ct.
[64]   See **4.39–4.42** and **4.118–4.119**.
[65]   [2006] EWHC 1041 (Admin), [2006] HLR 440, Admin Ct. See **4.34**.
[66]   *R (Lin) v Barnet London Borough Council* [2007] EWCA Civ 132, [2007] HLR 30, CA.
[67]   *R (Ahmad) v Newham London Borough Council* [2009] UKHL 14, [2009] HLR 41, HL.
[68]   In common with the schemes of many other authorities, Newham's allocation scheme included a 'top slice' facility enabling a very small number of those in the most acute housing need to obtain a priority higher than the main bandings. Subsequently published research has shown that across local housing authorities which assess housing 'need' among applicants the proportion of the 'top banded' applicants was in most cases under 3% of all applicants: *Exploring local authority policy and practice on housing allocations* (CLG, July 2009), para 10.

relative priority as between one another, not by reference to housing need (in the sense of particular assessments of cumulative or composite need), but by date order. The applicant waiting longest among the highest banded bidders for a particular property would be allocated it. In both the High Court and Court of Appeal the scheme was held unlawful.[69]

5.53 The House of Lords allowed the local housing authority's appeal. It decided that nothing in HA 1996, Part 6, as amended by the Homelessness Act 2002, *required* allocation to those in the greatest need, nor *required* a facility for cumulative or composite assessment of needs. A local housing authority such as Newham, where demand vastly outstripped supply, was entitled to adopt a simple banding scheme which met the statutory obligation to give a reasonable preference to the statutory categories but then prioritised amongst them by waiting time.

5.54 This dramatic change in the judicial perception of HA 1996, Part 6 (as amended) gave new impetus to simplified choice-based banding schemes. For the reasons explained in Chapter 4, many fewer legal challenges to allocation schemes can now be expected. Indeed, in the light of the decision in *R (Ahmad) v Newham London Borough Council*, new guidance on housing allocation was issued in 2009 by the then Secretary of State to local housing authorities in England. The guidance encouraged local housing authorities, including those local housing authorities already operating choice-based letting schemes, to review and revise their schemes to take advantage of perceived new flexibilities.[70] That guidance suggested that freedom from the previously understood *requirement* to take account of the composite or cumulative needs of applicants provided the opportunity for more use of:

> 'the flexibilities local authorities have within the allocation legislation to meet local pressures by:
>
> - adopting local priorities alongside the statutory reasonable preference categories
> - taking into account other factors in prioritising applicants, including waiting time and local connection
> - operating local lettings policies.'[71]

5.55 While the current English Code certainly promotes the use of these flexibilities it offers no guidance on 'banding', 'points' or 'choice'. The Chartered Institute of Housing (CIH) has suggested that the whole emphasis in the Code, on a more managed approach to waiting lists, 'may present challenges to local housing authorities also intending to keep a choice-based

[69] *R (Ahmad) v Newham London Borough Council* [2007] EWHC 2332 (Admin), (2007) November *Legal Action*, p 38, Admin Ct; and *R (Ahmad) v Newham London Borough Council* [2008] EWCA Civ 140, (2008) April *Legal Action*, p 38, CA.
[70] *Fair and flexible: statutory guidance on social housing allocations for local authorities in England* (CLG, December 2009) reproduced in Appendix 1 to the last edition of this book.
[71] Ibid, para 1.

letting scheme'.[72] Those local housing authorities deciding to retain an element of choice, whilst also seeking to address housing need, might find the extended guidance available from the CIH[73] of more assistance than the current English Code.

The effectiveness of choice

5.56 Despite the use of the name 'choice-based letting' to describe the process, the ultimate allocation of any particular property by a local housing authority will lie with the local housing authority itself. Many individuals will have expressed their preference to be allocated a particular property advertised as vacant – it will then be for the local housing authority to select one household from among them (or none of them).[74] Of course, the terms of the local allocation scheme may, and should, spell out precisely how the choice is to be made between them, and by whom. For example, the scheme might specify that the property is to be offered to the candidate with the highest banding, longest waiting time, greatest number of points, or whatever.[75] The scheme may also specify who is to be considered next, if the highest bidder pulls out.

5.57 In this sense, 'choice-based letting' is a misnomer. Almost all the schemes adopted by local housing authorities are, in reality, choice-based *applications* schemes. They simply facilitate the expression of interest by bidders in particular properties available for letting. It does not necessarily follow that the highest ranked bidder at the closing date *will* be allocated the property. For example, most schemes incorporate an element of re-assessment of shortlisted bidders to ensure that they are still eligible or qualified and have maintained their initially awarded degree of priority. That element of re-checking (or evaluating the bids) is not at all uncommon and many schemes retain some form of override enabling the rejection of bids by applicants considered, by officers, to be unsuitable for the particular property. These approaches are all perfectly lawful provided they are spelt out in the published allocation scheme.

5.58 In many avowedly 'choice-based' schemes, not all the available properties are advertised. Some empty homes are often reserved for applicants entitled to or required to accept what schemes may describe as 'direct lets' or 'direct offers'. In some schemes, advertised properties may be withdrawn to be offered outside the allocation scheme or to direct-let cases. In others, properties are offered subject to multiple qualifications as to the type of bid that will be considered. In yet others, bidding preferences expire if not used within a fixed period or on the refusal of offers. In some schemes, provision is made for

---

[72] *Allocation of Accommodation: guidance for housing authorities in England – Briefing paper* (CIH, July 2012), p 7.

[73] *Allocations & Local Flexibility* (CIH, March 2010).

[74] Or, where the property is owned by a private registered provider, registered social landlord or a different local housing authority, to decide which applicant(s) to *nominate* to that landlord.

[75] For example, in *R (van Boolen) v Barking and Dagenham London Borough Council* [2009] EWHC 2196 (Admin) (2009) September *Legal Action*, p 34, Admin Ct. the policy of the local housing authority was to identify the bidders in the highest band and then to give further preference as between them to those applicants with a local connection.

'choice' to be available only for a fixed period and thereafter for bids for appropriate properties to be automatically made on an applicant's behalf.[76]

5.59 It has yet to be seen whether the courts will recognise any enforceable 'legitimate expectation' on the part of the candidate who would be due to receive the offer on the strict terms of the choice-based allocation scheme.[77] Could, for example, the local housing authority withdraw a property, advertised under the choice-based scheme, and offer it to another applicant, or let it in circumstances that do not constitute an 'allocation' after the bid process had closed? What would be the legal effect of mistakenly overlooking the bidder with the highest priority under the scheme, and offering the property, inadvertently, to the next person in the queue of bidding candidates?[78] It is unlikely that a simple failure of communication[79] would give rise to a claim of breach of 'legitimate expectation' but a clear departure from the published scheme may well do so. These issues will no doubt be explored by the courts in the reasonably near future.

5.60 Applicants who believe that they have not been treated appropriately under a choice-based scheme will need to obtain access to the courts very quickly if they are to prevent letting of a property for which they and others have bid. Unless an application for judicial review is launched very quickly and, if necessary, an injunction obtained to prevent the property being let, the disappointed applicant may well find that the claim has become academic[80] or at best is reduced to an attempt to prevent any future departure from the published arrangements.[81]

LOCAL HOUSING AUTHORITY LED ALLOCATION (DIRECT LETS)

5.61 If a local housing authority is not operating a choice-based allocation scheme, all allocation decisions will be made by officers of the local housing

---

[76] The circumstances in *R (Tout a Tout) v Haringey London Borough Council* [2012] EWHC 873 (Admin), (2012) May *Legal Action,* p 34, Admin Ct.

[77] For a discussion of 'legitimate expectation' in an allocation context see *R v Brent London Borough Council ex p Jerke CO/2069/97* (unreported) 8 May 1998, QBD; *R v Lambeth London Borough Council ex p Trabi* (1998) 30 HLR 975, QBD; and *R (Tout a Tout) v Haringey London Borough Council* [2012] EWHC 873 (Admin), (2012) May *Legal Action,* p 39, Admin Ct. See also **4.53** and the notes to that paragraph.

[78] In *Globa v Ukraine* [2012] ECHR 1375, Mr Globa had been at the top of the waiting list for a Town Council apartment. A vacant apartment was wrongly allocated to someone below him on the list. He took court proceedings and obtained a judgment that: the occupiers be evicted; he be allocated the flat; and the occupiers be rehoused. The Town Council failed to comply with the order and enforcement measures failed. The European Court of Human Rights awarded him 5000 euros compensation.

[79] *R (Tout a Tout) v Haringey London Borough Council* [2012] EWHC 873 (Admin). (2012) May *Legal Action,* p 34, Admin Ct at [24].

[80] *R (Fidelis-Auma) v Octavia Housing and Care* [2009] EWHC 2263 (Admin), (2009) November *Legal Action,* p 25, Admin Ct.

[81] *Birmingham City Council v Qasim* [2009] EWCA Civ 1080, [2010] HLR 19, CA at [39].

authority applying the principles set out in the local allocation scheme. Indeed, the scheme must identify the procedure for making actual allocation decisions, including the name or designation of the responsible officer(s).[82]

5.62 Planning for such allocations usually starts well before a specific property becomes available to offer. Once an applicant has been accepted onto the allocation scheme, and the preference to which he or she is entitled has been assessed and accorded, the local housing authority must decide what type of property the applicant should be offered, and whether there is any particular geographic area in which an allocation would or would not be appropriate.

5.63 HA 1996, Part 6 permits local housing authorities to target certain properties to certain groups of applicants.[83] Building on that provision, many have established 'local lettings' policies and schemes within their published allocation schemes.[84] Others have decided to make provision in their allocation schemes for a specific quota of properties to be allocated to particular groups of applicants. The English Code, for example, suggests that local housing authorities might set aside an annual quota of properties for prospective adopters and foster parents[85] or a specified proportion of the stock for workers with skills that are in short supply locally.[86] However, none of these arrangements must be allowed to produce an allocation scheme that fails to give an overall preference to those in the reasonable preference groups.[87]

5.64 Once a property of the requisite description in the appropriate area becomes available for letting, the local housing authority must decide from among the pool of available applicants which of them should first be offered it. This is the most sensitive aspect of allocation and the stage at which greatest transparency will be needed. Many authorities will use 'banding' or 'points' to rank the relative priority of those in the pool of available applicants.[88] How the actual selection is made will fall to be determined by the particular local allocation scheme.

5.65 Some local housing authorities reserve a 'direct letting' function for use by officers in tandem with, or as a variant of, what is otherwise a choice-based letting scheme. It is particularly common for such hybrid schemes to be adopted where applicants, who are being accommodated in temporary accommodation under the homelessness provisions of HA 1996, Part 7, would be reluctant to bid under a choice-based scheme for less desirable properties than the temporary homes they occupy. In one case, a local allocation scheme dealt with that scenario by allowing such applicants a 'free' bidding opportunity for a fixed period but thereafter the scheme 'auto-bid' for any

---

[82] HA 1996, s 166A(1) [England], s 167(1) [Wales].
[83] HA 1996, s 166A(6)(b) [England] and s 167(2E)(b) [Wales].
[84] See **4.177–4.194**.
[85] English Code, para 4.31.
[86] English Code, para 4.27.
[87] English Code, para 4.5.
[88] See **4.46–4.47**.

appropriate properties which applicants were offered if they were the highest ranked bidders. A legal challenge to that arrangement, based on the argument that it was inconsistent with the statutory guidance then in place, failed.[89]

GENERAL POINTS

The offer of accommodation

5.66 Under either of the two routes described earlier in this Chapter, a particular applicant will be identified to be allocated an available property. At that stage the strict 'allocation' process, which involves simple selection or nomination of a candidate, comes to an end.[90] The actual letting will normally be handled by housing management staff of the relevant social landlord (which may be the local housing authority itself) who will sign up the new tenant following the offer and acceptance of a tenancy agreement.

5.67 Once an allocation of particular accommodation has been made, the applicant should be given 'a reasonable period' to consider whether to accept it.[91] 'Reasonable period' is not defined in HA 1996, Part 6, or the Codes. The applicant should be given sufficient time for careful consideration and the length of time provided should depend on the individual circumstances of each applicant. Vulnerable applicants, or applicants who are unfamiliar with the property, are likely to need longer. An applicant who is in hospital or in temporary accommodation such as a hostel or refuge may also need longer, as may those who are working or have childcare commitments.[92]

How many offers?

5.68 The local housing allocation scheme may allow unlimited bids for available properties or the making of an unlimited number of offers by officers to applicants. Alternatively, the scheme may cap the number of bids or offers that may be made. There is no nationally prescribed maximum or minimum number.

5.69 Some local housing authorities have allocation schemes that discriminate among classes of applicant, enabling certain applicants to enjoy a greater number of bids or offers than others. In the past this had been particularly true in relation to households owed housing duties under the homelessness assistance provisions of HA 1996, Part 7, who have often been restricted to limited bids or offers. However, the Welsh Code makes it plain that if it was previously expected that homeless households would be discriminated against in that way, the position has changed. It states in terms that:

---

[89] *R(Tout a Tout) v Haringey London Borough Council* [2012] EWHC 873 (Admin), (2012) May *Legal Action,* p 34, Admin Ct.
[90] *Birmingham City Council v Qasim* [2009] EWCA Civ 1080, [2010] HLR 19, CA.
[91] Welsh Code, paras 4.51–4.52.
[92] Welsh Code, para 4.52.

'It is no longer an expectation that homeless people should be given a single offer of accommodation. Wherever possible, they should receive the same number of offers, or range of choices, as existing tenants or Part 6 applicants (general waiting list applicants).'[93]

5.70 Of course, the Code recognises that a single suitable offer may have the effect of releasing a local housing authority from its homelessness duties.[94]

5.71 The effect of refusal of an offer on an application for social housing allocation is discussed later in this Chapter.[95]

Types of tenancies to be offered

Size and location

5.72 The extent and circumstances of the applicant's household as assessed under the allocation scheme obviously determines the number of bedrooms that the applicant may expect to find in an allocated property.[96] It will be for each local housing authority to frame its own rules in its allocation scheme dealing with the size of property to be offered. Provided that the result is not the allocation of a property which would be statutorily overcrowded, local housing authorities are free to set their own criteria.[97] Some may wish to adopt the 'bedroom standard' promoted by the Secretary of State in England.[98] If a property is being allocated to a working-age applicant who would be under-occupying it, the local housing authority will need to be aware of the housing benefit implications.[99]

5.73 An applicant, or a member of his or her household, may have a medical need for a ground floor property or an accessible bathroom, or an additional bathroom or toilet. The Codes advise that applicants who receive support from a carer, who does not live with them, should have their need for a spare bedroom taken into account wherever possible.[100] In Wales, local housing authorities are reminded that elderly applicants who are awaiting an allocation of accommodation have particular needs.[101] In England, local housing

---

[93] Welsh Code, para 4.47.
[94] See Chapter 17 for a discussion of the effect of a HA 1996 Part 6 offer on homelessness duties.
[95] See **5.95**.
[96] *R v Lewisham London Borough Council ex p Pinzon* (1999) 2 CCLR 152, QBD. This may not be a straightforward task. In *R (Bibi) v Camden London Borough Council* [2004] EWHC 2527 (Admin), [2005] HLR 18, Admin Ct, the local housing authority offered a woman a one-bedroom property, overlooking the fact that she had a joint residence order in respect of her children with her former husband. It was required to reconsider the offer, taking into account that order, as well as the other demands on its housing stock and any potential under-occupancy of the property. For a discussion of 'household' in this context see **3.222–3.223**.
[97] English Code, para 4.22.
[98] See **4.87**.
[99] English Code, para 4.22.
[100] English Code, para 4.29; Welsh Code, paras 4.106–4.108.
[101] Welsh Code, paras 4.99–4.101.

authorities considering applications from those proposing to foster or adopt are encouraged to balance the case for allocation of a larger property against the risk that any placement may fail to materialise or break down.[102]

5.74 When determining the extent and circumstances of the applicant's household, the local housing authority must take all of the members of the household into account, whether they were eligible or qualified for an allocation in their own right or not, unless the local allocation scheme otherwise provides. There is no statutory provision permitting local housing authorities to ignore the needs of members who would not have satisfied the eligibility or qualification test had they been the applicant. The matter is one to be determined by the terms of the local scheme.[103]

5.75 An applicant may need or prefer a property to be in a particular location, or there may be locations that the applicant cannot be placed in, for example, if the applicant has left an area due to violence. However, a local allocation scheme might provide that an applicant will not be made an allocation of property in a locality within the local housing authority's district in which he or she has previously been the perpetrator (or, perhaps, victim) of anti-social behaviour.[104]

Sole or joint tenancy?

5.76 The allocation cannot be made of a property to be held on a joint tenancy where one of the joint tenants is not eligible for an allocation.[105] However, the tenancy could be granted as a sole tenancy to the eligible applicant in those circumstances. There is no similar difficulty if one of the applicants to a local housing authority in England is not in a qualifying class.[106] Such a joint applicant can be included in a joint tenancy.[107]

5.77 Where there are joint applicants, or a partner, friend or live-in carer is included as part of an individual applicant's household, local housing authorities will normally offer joint tenancies so that either person would continue as tenant if the other died.[108] To avoid any unlawful discrimination, same-sex partners should be treated in the same way as heterosexual partners.[109] If prospective tenants ask to be granted a joint tenancy, and are

---

[102] English Code, para 4.30.
[103] See *R (Ariemuguvbe) v Islington London Borough Council* [2009] EWCA Civ 1218, [2010] HLR 14, CA.
[104] *R (Carney) v Bolton-at-Home Ltd* [2012] EWHC 2553 (Admin), (2012) November *Legal Action*, p 13, Admin Ct.
[105] HA 1996, s 160ZA(1)(b) [England] and s 160A(1)(c) [Wales].
[106] English Code, para 3.29.
[107] HA 1996, s 160ZA(6)(b).
[108] *Solihull MBC v Hickin* [2012] UKSC 3. Welsh Code, para 4.12.
[109] See *Rodriguez v Minister of Housing of the Government of Gibraltar* [2009] UKPC 52, (2009) 28 BHRC 189, PC. See also Welsh Code, para 4.14 suggesting that if a sole tenancy is initially granted to a person who later enters into a civil partnership that tenant should be 'entitled' to vary it into a joint tenancy with their new partner.

refused, the local housing authority should give clear, written reasons for the refusal.[110] Applicants with children may prefer to take a tenancy which offers contractual rights of succession to the children because new secure and assured tenancies of social housing no longer carry *statutory* rights of succession by family members, other than partners.[111]

What tenure to offer?

5.78 An allocation of accommodation made under the local allocation scheme may produce the offer of a secure, introductory or assured tenancy.[112] But even within those categories there may variants as to the form of tenancy and security of tenure.

5.79 It has always been possible for local housing authorities to grant *secure* tenancies either on a periodic or fixed term basis. However, since 1 April 2012, it has also been possible to offer a variant of the latter, known as a 'flexible tenancy', which carries a mandatory right to re-possession at the end of the term.[113] As a flexible tenancy is a form of secure tenancy, it can be offered as the result of an allocation.

5.80 *Assured* tenancies of social housing are only allocated through allocation schemes by way of nomination to private registered providers or registered social landlords. Assured tenancies can also be periodic or fixed term. An assured *shorthold* tenancy is a form of assured tenancy carrying a mandatory right to recovery of possession. Such assured shorthold tenancies can be offered by private registered providers or registered social landlords.[114] In practice, if a periodic assured shorthold tenancy is offered as an allocation, it may be intended to fulfill the same function as an introductory tenancy, ie that it should be probationary and cease to be an assured shorthold tenancy (and thus become a fully assured tenancy) after a specified period. Alternatively, the property may be offered by the private registered provider or registered social landlord on a fixed term assured shorthold tenancy, perhaps at an 'affordable' rent, rather than an ordinary 'social housing' rent.[115] In the statutory guidance for local housing authorities in England, the Secretary of State has indicated that he expects both local housing authorities and private registered providers to make 'affordable rent' homes available through the local allocation scheme, in the same way that other rented properties are made available.[116]

---

[110] Welsh Code, paras 4.13.
[111] See the amendments made by Localism Act 2011, ss 1601–61 to the succession provisions of the Housing Act 1985 and Housing Act 1988, applying to tenancies granted on or after 1 April 2012.
[112] HA 1996, s 159(2).
[113] Localism Act 2011, ss 154–155.
[114] HA 1996, s 230; Housing Act 1988, s 1 and ss 19A–20.
[115] See, for England, the regulatory guidance given by the 'Tenancy Standard', para 2 (Tenure), in *The regulatory framework for social housing in England from April 2012* (Homes & Communities Agency, March 2012).
[116] English Code, para 6.4.

5.81 In England, which form of tenancy of social housing is likely to be available in any particular district, whether from the local housing authority or from other social landlords within that district, will be explained in the tenancy strategy published by the local housing authority for that district.[117] The local allocation scheme will have been drawn up having regard to the content of that tenancy strategy.[118]

Furnished or unfurnished?

5.82 The allocation scheme will govern selection or nomination for both furnished and unfurnished properties. Most local housing authority stock is let unfurnished, but a significant proportion of properties designed for the elderly or others with support needs will be partly or wholly furnished. The same general pattern is true of the stock made available by other social landlords for nominations from local housing authorities.

5.83 An applicant cannot insist on the provision of (or removal of) furnishings. However, local housing authorities have very broad powers to furnish and fit out their properties and/or sell or hire furniture to tenants.[119] The economies of scale that can be achieved by a local housing authority in bulk-buying furniture and selling it on to incoming tenants should not be underestimated. The golden rule must be that it is always open to an applicant to ask. A local housing authority which responded to a request with a pronouncement that it never provided furniture would be guilty of unlawfully fettering its discretion, and the relevant decision would be quashed in proceedings for judicial review. The question of whether furniture will be provided in lettings by other social landlords will be subject to the terms of any relevant guidance from national regulatory authorities and the terms of that landlord's own governing instrument (for example, any Articles of Association).

Quality of accommodation offered

5.84 There is no minimum standard of accommodation that a property must achieve before a local housing authority or other social landlord offers a particular unit to an applicant selected or nominated under a local allocation scheme. Indeed, it may be precisely the least desirable properties that are most frequently on offer.

5.85 In contrast to the law relating to homelessness, there is no requirement that the offered property be 'suitable' or 'available for occupation'.[120] Advisers must be careful to ensure that this distinction between offers under HA 1996,

---

[117] Localism Act 2011, s 150.

[118] HA 1996, s 166A(12)(b).

[119] Housing Act 1985, s 10.

[120] See Chapter 18 of this book for 'suitable' and Chapter 14 for the concept of 'available for occupation'.

Parts 6 and 7 is made clear to applicants.[121] Of course there may be an overlap: for example, an allocation under HA 1996, Part 6 may be made to an applicant who is owed a HA 1996, Part 7 duty, perhaps in order to release the local housing authority from that duty. Such an allocation would have to be of a 'suitable' property in order to achieve that effect.[122]

5.86 The principle in operation is 'caveat lessee' or 'let the prospective tenant beware'. It is for the prospective tenant to decide whether he or she wants to accept or reject what is offered, having carefully considered it. Accordingly, a tenant who accepts the property can later have no complaint in law if she or he subsequently finds that it is in a more noisy location or situation than expected,[123] or if there is a pungent smell which the tenant erroneously thought could be removed by cleaning.[124]

5.87 There is no general legal rule that the properties of a local authority landlord or other social landlord must meet minimum standards at the date of letting.[125] The previous statutorily implied term that a property must be 'fit for human habitation' at the date of letting no longer has any practical application as a result of failure to up-rate the rent thresholds that govern its operation.[126] What is left is only the old common law rule that a property let furnished (which is itself unusual in social housing) must be fit for occupation at the date of letting.[127]

5.88 Of course, a new tenant who finds that the property is unsatisfactory for some reason may give it up, by notice to quit or surrender, if he or she has somewhere else to go, or could pursue a complaint about the allocation (to the social landlord and thereafter to an Ombudsman) and/or apply for a transfer to more satisfactory accommodation under the allocation scheme. The new tenant can, of course, additionally expect that any repairing obligations, imposed on the social landlord by the tenancy agreement, will be met within a reasonable time of commencement of the tenancy.

---

[121] *Brent London Borough Council v Sharp* [2003] EWCA Civ 779, [2004] HLR 65, CA.
[122] The applicant is free to *accept* any Part 6 offer (HA 1996, s 193(6)(c)) but an offer which has been *refused* must have been 'suitable' in order to work a discharge of the main housing duty (HA 1996, s 193(7)). See **17.92–17.108**.
[123] *Southwark London Borough Council v Tanner and Mills* [2002] 32 HLR 148, HL.
[124] *Smith v Wrekin Housing Trust* [2004] EWCA Civ 1792, CA. In one case, the Local Government Ombudsman did find the local housing authority guilty of maladministration where it had allocated a property, which the Ombudsman described as 'so filthy it could not be lived in' to an applicant: *Complaint against Nottingham City Council 05/C/2965*, 19 April 2007, (2007) June *Legal Action*, p 37.
[125] *Siney v Dublin Corporation* [1980] IR 400.
[126] Landlord and Tenant Act 1985, s 8(1) and (4), only applicable to properties let on low rents (the threshold is now unrealistically low).
[127] See Luba, Prevatt and Forster *Repairs: Tenants Rights* (LAG, 4th edn, 2010), p 13.

Offers to transfer applicants[128]

5.89   Where the offer is made to an applicant who is already a tenant of the local housing authority or another social landlord, two particular issues arise:

(1)   getting the type of tenancy right; and

(2)   determining the old tenancy.

5.90   If the transferring tenant is currently a secure or assured tenant (but not an assured shorthold tenant), whether under a sole or a joint tenancy, the new tenancy to be offered of any local housing authority property can only be a secure tenancy and not an introductory tenancy, even if the local housing authority normally only offers introductory tenancies to new tenants.[129]

5.91   If the allocation process has resulted in a tenant being nominated to a different social landlord (not currently that tenant's landlord) and has produced an offer of a tenancy from that landlord, the tenancy may be offered as an assured tenancy or assured shorthold tenancy irrespective of the applicant's current form of tenancy. In practice, most private registered providers or registered social landlords will offer a full assured tenancy to an incoming tenant who has been the secure or assured tenant of another social landlord.

5.92   Offering an equivalent form of tenancy to that which a transferring social housing tenant has previously enjoyed has become of more acute importance since the changes to security of tenure and succession made in respect of social housing tenancies in England from 1 April 2012 by the Localism Act 2011. In order to ensure that transferring tenants do not inadvertently lose accrued rights, the social housing regulator for England requires that:

> 'Registered providers shall grant those who were social housing tenants on the day on which section 154 of the Localism Act 2011 comes into force [1 April 2012], and have remained social housing tenants since that date, a tenancy with no less security where they choose to move to another social rented home, whether with the same or another landlord. (This requirement does not apply where tenants choose to move to accommodation let on Affordable Rent terms).'[130]

5.93   It will be important for the local housing authority or other social landlord to ensure that the successful applicant's current tenancy is brought to an end at, or immediately following, the commencement of the new tenancy. Unless (unusually) the tenancy is of the same property, the grant of the new tenancy does *not* automatically determine the old one. The old tenancy will need to be determined by a tenant's notice to quit or by surrender, the latter

---

[128]   For the renewed emphasis on securing tenancy transfers see **2.55–2.68**.
[129]   HA 1996, s 124(2).
[130]   *The regulatory framework for social housing in England from April* 2012 (Homes & Communities Agency, March 2012), p 25.

being most safely achieved by deed. If the landlord and tenant have overlooked the need to determine the old tenancy before the new one commences, it will usually be possible for the old one to be immediately surrendered or subject to a notice to quit, with, perhaps, both parties agreeing to short notice.[131]

5.94 A common issue will be whether any arrears of rent outstanding on the old tenancy can be transferred to the new one. Although the parties can make an agreement as to how those arrears will be cleared, that agreement cannot be enforced in proceedings for possession of the new home in respect of those arrears, unless either:

(1) the parties have agreed that any payments made after the date of transfer will be first applied to meet the old debt, in which case arrears will accrue in the new tenancy unless the tenant makes double payment; or

(2) the parties have agreed that compliance with the arrears agreement will be a term of the new tenancy.[132]

Refusal of offers

5.95 No applicant can be compelled to accept an offer of accommodation made under a HA 1996, Part 6 allocation scheme. Where the offer has been made to a homeless applicant, however, the effect of a refusal may, in narrowly prescribed circumstances, operate to bring a homelessness duty to an end.[133]

5.96 In other cases, the effect (if any) of a refusal will be dealt with in the allocation scheme itself. An applicant who has rejected a property cannot properly be subject to some form of penalty or suspension under an allocation scheme unless a rule to that effect appears in the published scheme and has been properly applied.[134] Indeed, even if such a provision did appear in a published scheme, if the scheme itself was based on a needs-led priority system it would be difficult to impose any sanction unless the refusal itself evidenced a change in assessed need. However, a period of deferral resulting from the refusal of an offer would, it seems, be lawful where such a refusal was a reasonable matter for an allocation scheme to take into account in affording relative priority between applicants.[135]

5.97 If the penalty provision for a refusal is legitimately included, the local housing authority must still ensure that its operation is considered on a

---

[131] See *Hackney London Borough Council v Snowden* (2001) 33 HLR 49, CA and *Ealing Family Housing Association v McKenzie* [2003] EWCA Civ 1602, [2004] HLR 21, CA.

[132] *Notting Hill Housing Trust v Jones* [1999] L&TR 397, CA.

[133] See the discussion in Chapter 17.

[134] *R v Wandsworth London Borough Council ex p Lawrie and Heshmati* (1997) 30 HLR 153, QBD.

[135] *R (Cranfield-Adams) v Richmond upon Thames London Borough Council* (2012) August *Legal Action*, p 27.

case-by-case basis, having regard to the circumstances of each refusal.[136] Indeed, many allocation schemes make provision for 'appeals' against, or 'review' of offers, made under the scheme and a significant proportion of such challenges made are successful.[137] The Welsh Code recommends that the allocation scheme should include rights to a review for those penalised by refusal of an offer.[138] The inclusion or application of a penalty can, of course, be challenged by way of judicial review if the local housing authority is not willing to waive it in any particular case.[139]

---

[136] *R v Gateshead Metropolitan Borough Council ex p Lauder* (1996) 29 HLR 360, QBD and *R v Westminster City Council ex p Hussain* (1999) 31 HLR 645, QBD.
[137] A survey conducted in 2006/07 found that a significant proportion of appeals had been upheld. The average 'appeal success rate' ('success' from an applicant perspective) was 40%: *Exploring local authority policy and practice on housing allocations* (CLG, July 2009), para 2.14.
[138] Welsh Code, para 4.48.
[139] *R (Cranfield-Adams) v Richmond upon Thames London Borough Council* (2012) August *Legal Action*, p 27.

Chapter 6

LETTINGS BY SOCIAL LANDLORDS (OTHER THAN LOCAL HOUSING AUTHORITIES)

DEFINITIONS

6.1   Following recent changes to the relevant statutory provisions in England
and Wales, there are now several different technical descriptions of the major
social landlords that may be involved in the allocation of social housing. They
are:

(1)   *registered providers* of social housing in England,[1] of which there are two
       sub-categories:
       (a)   *public* registered providers ie local housing authority landlords; and
       (b)   *private registered providers* (mainly housing associations).

(2)   social landlords in Wales, of which there are two sub-categories:
       (a)   local housing authority landlords; and
       (b)   *registered social landlords*.[2]

6.2   This Chapter is concerned with lettings by social landlords other than
local housing authority landlords ie by private registered providers in England
and by registered social landlords in Wales. These social landlords now hold
more housing stock for rent than do local housing authorities.[3] Indeed,
significantly more lettings of social housing homes in England are now made
by private registered providers than by local housing authorities.[4]

OVERVIEW[5]

6.3   The stock of social housing for rent in England owned by private
registered providers now exceeds 2 million units. In Wales, there are a further

---

[1]   Registered providers in England, of both categories, are now regulated by the Regulatory
       Committee of the Homes & Communities Agency, following amendments made by the
       Localism Act 2011, Part 7 to the Housing & Regeneration Act 2008 with effect from 1 April
       2012. See **6.87**.
[2]   Registered social landlords in Wales are regulated by Welsh Ministers pursuant to the
       provisions of Housing Act 1996, Part 1. See **1.98**.
[3]   The stock of local housing authority dwellings in England fell from 2.81m on 1 April 2001 to
       1.73m on 1 April 2011: *Local Authority Housing Statistics, England 2010–2011* (Department
       for Communities & Local Government, November 2011).
[4]   In England in 2010/11 there were 147,638 lettings of general needs homes by private registered
       providers and only 111,277 lettings by local housing authorities: *Table 750 General needs social
       lettings made by RSL and LA landlords, 2007/08 to 2010/11, England: household type* (DCLG,
       December 2011). For 2011/12, the figures (based on incomplete returns by local housing
       authorities in England) showed that 72% of lets of social housing were by private registered
       providers and 28% by local housing authorities *Social Housing Lettings & Sales in England,
       2011/12: Continuous Recording (CORE) Data* (DCLG, September 2012). In Wales, a new
       system of data collection on lettings of social housing has been developed following the report
       *Who gets social housing in Wales? – the final report of a project to investigate the desirability of
       collecting and analysing data on social housing lettings and sales in Wales* (Community Housing
       Cymru, March 2009).
[5]   We acknowledge our indebtedness to our professional colleague Robert Latham. His
       stimulating article *Allocating social housing: the registered landlord context* (2008) October
       Legal Action, p 43, provided the inspiration for much of the material in this Chapter.

95,000 homes owned by registered social landlords.[6] That stock is gradually being increased with the development of new housing schemes and the acquisition of more properties through funding channeled to these landlords by the Homes & Communities Agency (in England) and by the Welsh Government. It will increase still further if more local housing authorities transfer their stock of council homes to other social landlords. These social landlords do not face the same prospect of diminution in their rented stock as local housing authorities face (particularly because of the restricted access of their tenants to the statutory 'right-to-buy'). The availability of new or newly converted stock for letting, and the natural incidences of tenant mobility (and mortality) in the existing stock, now combine to provide a greater number of opportunities for letting by these other social landlords than in the local housing authority sector.[7] Against that background, the then Secretary of State advised in 2006 that:

> 'Virtually all provision of new social housing is delivered through RSLs and, under the transfer programme, ownership of a significant proportion of housing authority stock is being transferred from housing authorities to RSLs, subject to tenants' agreement. This means that, increasingly, RSLs will become the main providers of social housing. Consequently, it is essential that housing authorities work closely with RSLs, as well as all other housing providers, in order to meet the housing needs in their district and ensure that the aims and objectives of their homelessness strategy are achieved.'[8]

6.4   However, there is no equivalent in the rest of the social housing sector to the relatively strict and over-arching statutory control on allocations imposed on local housing authorities by HA 1996, Part 6. Each private registered provider or registered social landlord will, within the terms of its own governing legal instrument, be free to let its available homes to such applicants as it pleases (subject to the applicable constraints of the general law – eg as to the prohibition of certain forms of discrimination[9]). There is nothing preventing a private registered provider or registered social landlord from letting, for example, to a person who would not meet the statutory eligibility or qualification requirements[10] for local housing authority accommodation in the same district.

6.5   A private registered provider or registered social landlord may – if it chooses – operate a transfer scheme enabling its existing tenants to seek

---

[6]   *The Housing Associations of Wales: Measuring the Impact* (Welsh Economy Research Unit, October 2008).

[7]   In England, 17% of general needs and 6% of supported housing lettings by private registered providers were recorded as being the first let of a property due to it being newly built, converted, rehabilitated or acquired: *CORE Statistical Release 2010/11* (Tenant Services Authority 2011).

[8]   *English Homelessness Code of Guidance* (CLG, July 2006) (reproduced in Appendix 2 of this book), Annex 5, para 2.

[9]   For a discussion of discrimination in the context of social housing allocation see **4.195–4.209**.

[10]   Described in Chapter 3 of this book.

alternative homes within its stock. Most such landlords take that course.[11] For *non-transfer* applicants, a private registered provider or registered social landlord may operate an 'open list' or 'direct applications' system so that anyone who applies may be considered for a tenancy in its stock, and it may then order or organise that list in such manner as it chooses. It may, additionally or alternatively, make available some part or the majority of its stock to the local housing authority or other social landlords to make nominations of prospective tenants – whom it may then accept or reject as it pleases.[12] It may, if it chooses, advertise its available properties through a choice-based letting scheme. That may be the social landlord's own scheme, a scheme operated jointly with a local housing authority, or even a common scheme[13] shared with other social landlords and local housing authorities.

6.6 The relative freedom enjoyed by private registered providers and registered social landlords is held in check only by the requirements of the national regulatory authorities. In England, the regulator is the Homes & Communities Agency's Regulatory Committee. It has power to set standards to be followed by the providers of social housing.[14] Those standards require registered providers of social housing to comply with specified rules about criteria for allocating housing accommodation.[15] The Housing and Regeneration Act 2008 gives the regulator considerable powers of inspection and enforcement to ensure that the standards are complied with.[16] The regulator issues regulatory standards to social housing providers as directed by the Secretary of State.[17]

6.7 The current regulatory standard for housing allocation (part of a broader Tenancy Standard) provides:[18]

'1 Allocations and mutual exchange

1.1 Registered providers shall let their homes in a fair, transparent and efficient way. They shall take into account the housing needs and aspirations of tenants and potential tenants. They shall demonstrate how their lettings:

- make the best use of available housing
- are compatible with the purpose of the housing
- contribute to local authorities' strategic housing function and sustainable communities

---

[11] See **6.70–6.75**.

[12] For 'nominations' see **6.32–6.53**.

[13] For 'common schemes' see **6.54-6.62**.

[14] HRA 2008, s 193(1).

[15] HRA 2008, s 193(2)(a).

[16] HRA 2008, ss 192–269.

[17] The current directions are set out at Annex A of *Implementing Social Housing reform: Directions to the Social Housing Regulator – Consultation: a summary of responses* (DCLG, November 2011).

[18] *The Regulatory framework for social housing in England from April 2012* (Homes and Communities Agency, March 2012). The passages of the current regulatory standard dealing with mutual exchange have not been reproduced in these extracts.

There should be clear application, decision-making and appeals processes.'

6.8 The regulatory standard then sets out the following Specific Expectations[19]

'1 Allocations and mutual exchange

1.1 Registered providers shall co-operate with local authorities' strategic housing function, and their duties to meet identified local housing needs. This includes assistance with local authorities' homelessness duties, and through meeting obligations in nominations agreements.

1.2 Registered providers shall develop and deliver services to address under-occupation and overcrowding in their homes, within the resources available to them. These services should be focused on the needs of their tenants, and will offer choices to them.

1.3 Registered providers' published policies shall include how they have made use of common housing registers, common allocations policies and local letting policies. Registered providers shall clearly set out, and be able to give reasons for, the criteria they use for excluding actual and potential tenants from consideration for allocations, mobility or mutual exchange schemes.

1.4 Registered providers shall develop and deliver allocations processes in a way which supports their effective use by the full range of actual and potential tenants, including those with support needs, those who do not speak English as a first language and others who have difficulties with written English.

1.5 Registered providers shall minimise the time that properties are empty between each letting. When doing this, they shall take into account the circumstances of the tenants who have been offered the properties.

1.6 Registered providers shall record all lettings and sales as required by the Continuous Recording of Lettings (CORE) system.

1.7 Registered providers shall provide tenants wishing to move with access to clear and relevant advice about their housing options.'

6.9   This version of the regulatory standard came into statutory effect on 1 April 2012.

6.10   In Wales, the regulatory function falls to the Welsh Ministers. A Housing Regulation Team, which is part of the Welsh Government's Housing Division, undertakes the regulation activity on their behalf. The regulatory standards applicable since 2 December 2011 are the delivery outcomes set by the Welsh Ministers in accordance with HA 1996, s 33A as amended by the Housing

---

[19]   Ibid.

(Wales) Measure 2011. In relation to social housing allocation, those outcomes are that housing associations in Wales should be able to state with confidence:[20]

'We let homes in a fair, transparent and effective way.

We can demonstrate that:

- We manage our homes to ensure that they are in demand, maintained, modernised and adapted, as people's needs change.
- We ensure that our adapted homes are available to those who need them.
- We keep empty homes to a minimum to maximise the number of homes available and our revenue.
- We work with other organisations to prevent and alleviate homelessness.
- We ensure that access to our homes is fair and open, and we work with others to ensure routes into our housing are well publicised, easy to understand and simple to use. We give reasonable preference to those in greatest housing need or are homeless, maximising choice and sustaining communities.
- We let homes we are proud of. Our ready to let homes meet resident expectations prior to moving in or as soon as practicable thereafter.'

6.11 The Welsh Code[21] also suggests that registered social landlords are required by such regulation to consult with local housing authorities on their own allocations policies.[22]

6.12 Some of the largest private registered providers and registered social landlords are those that were created specifically to acquire the housing stock of particular local housing authorities in large scale voluntary transfers. Most local housing authorities engaging in such transfers took the opportunity, before transfer of their stock, to entrench the new social landlord's future arrangements for allocation of the transferred stock (and, in some cases, allocation of stock subsequently acquired) through contractual commitments. Those contractual obligations operate as a fetter on the freedom in letting that most other social landlords enjoy.[23]

6.13 A private registered provider's or registered social landlord's responsibility in housing allocation may not necessarily be confined to the letting of *its own* stock. Several have commercially contracted to operate housing allocation services for local housing authorities.[24] Those services are contracted out to them pursuant to the arrangements described in Chapter 21 of this book. Such a social landlord may thus find itself directly allocating some of its own stock, managing allocation of local housing authority stock and also operating the local housing authority's system for nomination of prospective tenants to

---

[20]   *The Regulatory Framework For Housing Associations Registered in Wales* (Welsh Government, December 2011).
[21]   *Code of Guidance for Local Authorities Allocation of Accommodation and Homelessness 2012* (Welsh Government, August 2012) (the Welsh Code).
[22]   Welsh Code, para 5.15.
[23]   For contractual 'nomination agreements' see **6.32–6.36**.
[24]   For contracting out of allocation functions see **6.76–6.77**.

itself.[25] However, even in the case where functions are contracted out to a social landlord which acquired the stock through a large-scale transfer, local housing authorities must remain active participants in allocation arrangements.[26]

DIRECT APPLICATIONS

Duty to maintain a lettings policy

6.14 Most, if not all, private registered providers or registered social landlords retain at least some of their available stock for letting by them to new applicants – those who have directly applied to that social landlord for housing – or to their own current tenants who wish to move within their stock. Lettings to current tenants are dealt with separately later in this Chapter.[27]

6.15 The private registered provider's or registered social landlord's governing body will have adopted a lettings policy relating to direct applications (and other lettings) and there will usually be a procedure guide or manual setting out the way in which housing staff are to implement the policy. In 2011/12, 30% of general needs lettings by private registered providers in England were to direct applicants.[28]

6.16 As Chapters 1–5 of this book have explained, HA 1996, Part 6 requires local housing authorities, but not other social landlords, to incorporate a statement of their policies for selection priorities and lettings procedures into a single local allocation scheme, copies of which must be available on request. A similar, but not precisely the same, statutory obligation is cast on private registered providers and registered social landlords by Housing Act 1985, s 106. That requires any 'landlord authority' (a term defined to embrace private registered providers and registered social landlords)[29] to maintain two sets of rules:

(1) the rules for determining *priority* as between applicants in the allocation of its housing accommodation;[30] and

(2) the rules which it has laid down governing the *procedure* to be followed in allocating its housing accommodation.[31]

---

25 See **6.76–6.77**.

26 One survey found that at least a significant minority of local housing authorities had unlawfully treated a large scale transfer, combined with the contracting out of allocation arrangements, as releasing them from any further concern with the allocation of that housing: *Exploring local authority policy and practice on housing allocations* (DCLG 2009, paras 2.15–2.16).

27 See **6.70–6.75**.

28 *Social Housing Lettings & Sales in England, 2011/12: Continuous Recording (CORE) Data* (DCLG, September 2012), p 5.

29 Housing Act 1985, s 114.

30 HA 1985, s 106(2)(a).

31 HA 1985, s 106(2)(a).

6.17 A private registered provider or registered social landlord is under a statutory duty to publish a summary of the first set of rules but not of the second.[32] Although any applicant can *ask* for a full copy of both sets of rules, there is no statutory duty to make them available at the landlord's offices. Copies need only be sent to the relevant statutory regulator and to any local housing authority in the district of which the social landlord still has stock let on secure tenancies.[33] An applicant could inspect the rules, or take copies of them, at the office of any such local housing authority.[34] All the regulatory guidance, reproduced earlier in this Chapter, emphasises the need for transparency and fairness in fixing the terms of, and operating allocation schemes – although it falls short of requiring the production and publication of a formal lettings policy or allocation scheme.

Guidance on contents of lettings policies

6.18 Guidance on the content of allocation policies has changed significantly in the recent past. In England, the former Housing Corporation ('the Corporation') exercised its statutory powers to give guidance – to what were then simply 'housing associations' – in relation to lettings policies, but the guidance (in contrast to the guidance given to local housing authorities by the Secretary of State under HA 1996, s 169) was modest and often expressed in very general terms. In its Regulatory Code and Guidance[35] the Corporation simply required that lettings policies be framed so as to be 'flexible, non-discriminatory and responsive to demand, while contributing to the need to be inclusive and the need to ensure sustainable communities'.[36] The approach of offering only very limited but generally expressed guidance has been carried over into the approach of the current regulator. Indeed, the full extent of the modern guidance on allocations is that set out in the Homes & Communities Agency's *Regulatory Framework* reproduced earlier in this Chapter.[37]

6.19 In Wales, the statutory guidance previously issued to registered social landlords contained a 'key expectation' that each should have a fair selection policy and should seek to achieve a balance in housing allocation between:

- the needs and preferences of applicants and transferees;

- the need to maximise social inclusion;

- the need to build stable communities; and

---

[32] HA 1985, s 106(1)(a).
[33] HA 1985, s 106(3).
[34] HA 1985, s 106(4).
[35] *The Regulatory Code and Guidance* (Housing Corporation, August 2005), containing housing management guidance given under HA 1996, s 36.
[36] Ibid, para 3.6(a).
[37] Adler and Handy *Housing Association Law and Practice* (4th edn, 2003), para 100-08.

- the need to make best use of a publicly funded resource.[38]

6.20 The modern rubric is contained in the extract from the current regulatory guidance in Wales reproduced earlier in this Chapter but again contains very little by way of detailed guidance. It is, in part, supplemented by provisions in the Welsh Code. The Welsh Government's Housing Association Circular *RSL 003/12* directs registered social landlords in Wales to 'take account' of the Welsh Code when addressing their key delivery outcomes reproduced above.[39] The Welsh Code itself contains some material directed at the allocations policies of registered social landlords in Wales including the suggestions that such landlords:

- should consult local housing authorities before framing their allocation policies;[40]

- should not involve board members in decision making on individual allocations;[41] and

- should monitor their allocation outcomes.[42]

6.21 The generality of the wording in this guidance suggests, as already indicated, that, subject to the constraints of the general law (eg the prohibition of certain forms of discrimination), private registered providers and registered social landlords have a relatively free hand in the arrangements they make for direct applications and in the organisation of what will usually be a waiting list where demand exceeds supply. However, it should not be assumed that demand will always exceed supply in the private registered provider or registered social landlord sector. Many such social landlords offer specialist or niche accommodation designed to meet particular needs, and others hold stock targeted at meeting the housing needs of particular groups. There may not always be sufficient applicants to meet the qualifying conditions for such accommodation.

6.22 In relation to the specific content of direct lettings policies, the guidance from the regulators is different in England and Wales. In Wales, the emphasis is still on the giving of 'reasonable preference' to those who are 'in greatest housing need or are homeless'.[43] But in England, the regulatory guidance suggests that private registered providers need only frame their schemes to 'take

---

[38] Welsh Assembly Government's *Regulatory Code for Housing Associations Registered in Wales,* March 2006, Key expectation 1.3.
[39] *RSL 003/12: Code of Guidance for Local Authorities Allocation of Accommodation and Homelessness August 2012* (Welsh Government, August 2012). Reproduced on the CD Rom provided with this book.
[40] Welsh Code, para 5.15.
[41] Welsh Code, para 5.30.
[42] Welsh Code, para 5.38.
[43] See the extract at **6.10**.

into account the housing needs and aspirations of tenants and potential tenants' leaving much greater scope for a flexible approach.[44]

6.23 The starkest contrast between the guidance offered in England and in Wales respectively relates to the possible exclusion of applicants from direct lettings schemes and, to that extent, the guidance reflects the different statutory arrangements which now allow local housing authorities in England (but not Wales) to set classes of qualifying and non-qualifying persons.

6.24 In England, the old regulatory guidance given by the Housing Corporation was replete with detailed requirements about the terms and operation of those lettings schemes which sought to exclude particular applicants.[45] But the modern regulatory guidance in England simply provides that private registered providers 'shall clearly set out, and be able to give reasons for, the criteria they use for excluding actual and potential tenants from consideration for allocations'.[46] In contrast, in Wales, the regulatory guidance does not contemplate exclusion at all.[47] However, the Welsh Government is in the process of developing regulatory guidance which will require that registered social landlords restrict access to housing only in circumstances which mirror the unacceptable behaviour provisions under HA 1996 Part 6.[48]

6.25 Precisely because private registered providers and registered social landlords operate free from the constraints imposed on local housing authorities by HA 1996, Part 6, they have been able to develop and retain their own particular practices and procedures. It is not uncommon for their lettings policies to provide for the admission of applicants to their allocation schemes but then to permit their suspension on misconduct grounds[49] (or, indeed, any grounds). The former Housing Corporation guidance on suspension was that the meaning and purpose of any suspension period, during which an application for housing is held inactive, should be clearly defined and should last no longer than two years. As the guidance advised, the notion of 'suspension' implies that the applicant will be invited to apply to have his or her application re-activated at a specified time or for specified reasons. The modern regulatory guidance does not even mention *suspension* and certainly does not attempt to restrict its use.

---

[44]   Contrast the wording of the two sets of guidance extracted earlier in this Chapter at **6.7–6.8** and **6.10**.

[45]   See *The Regulatory Code and Guidance* (Housing Corporation, August 2005) para 3.6(e); *Circular 02/07 Tenancy management: Eligibility and evictions* (Housing Corporation, April 2007) and *A charter for housing association applicants and residents* (Housing Corporation, April 2007).

[46]   See the extract at **6.8**.

[47]   See the extract at **6.10**.

[48]   Welsh Code, para 3.28. See **3.203–3.251**.

[49]   In *Complaint against Cymdeithas Tai Eryri* (Public Services Ombudsman for Wales, Ref 201102854, 2012) the registered social landlord had a policy enabling it to suspend a housing application for 'unacceptable behaviour' of a type making the applicant unsuitable to be a tenant but it wrongly used that policy to suspend an applicant for providing misleading information in an application form. The Ombudsman said that if it wished to suspend for that reason, its published policies should be amended to make that clear.

6.26   The modern guidance likewise takes a *laissez faire* approach to allocation schemes adopted by private registered providers or registered social landlords which restrict access only to those with a particular connection or link to an area or district. The old Housing Corporation *Circular 02/07* suggested that:

- housing need should normally override any special consideration of local connection; and

- no applicant should be excluded because he or she did not have a local connection, except in specific circumstances.

6.27   That Circular also addressed the subject of 'local lettings' policies and provided that any such policy should demonstrably and reasonably balance the competing demands of local housing authority nominations, and any other indicator of pressing housing need, against policies promoting balanced communities. The practical issues arising from private registered providers or registered social landlords operating local lettings policies were explored in a Homelessness Action Team discussion paper[50] but nothing emerging from that or from the impact of the old Circular has been carried over into the current guidance.

6.28   In short, it is for each private registered provider or registered social landlord to set its own categories for prioritising applicants and its own arrangements for allocating particular properties. Although, the guidance in Wales has retained a push towards 'maximising choice' for applicants in allocation arrangements, the guidance in England mentions 'choice' only in the context of services designed to address overcrowding and under-occupation.[51]

Information about lettings policies and procedure

6.29   The starting point for any applicant considering a direct application to any particular private registered provider or registered social landlord will be to obtain details of its letting scheme. The obligation of a private registered provider or registered social landlord to have a scheme and make it available is described at **6.14**.

6.30   Although no applicant for a direct letting has a statutory right to make an application, or even to be informed of the outcome, the regulatory guidance suggests at least some basic procedural requirements should be observed. The guidance for England requires that 'clear application, decision-making and appeals processes' are in place and that allocations processes are developed and delivered 'in a way which supports their effective use by the full range of actual and potential tenants, including those with support needs, those who do not speak English as a first language and others who have difficulties with written

---

[50]   Homelessness Action Team discussion paper, *Local lettings policies* (TSA, March 2009).
[51]   Contrast the terms of the guidance reproduced at **6.7–6.8**.

English'.[52] In Wales, the guidance encourages registered social landlords to ensure that routes into social housing 'are well publicised, easy to understand and simple to use.'[53]

Disputes about direct lettings

6.31 A dissatisfied applicant under a direct letting scheme has access to a range of options to press matters beyond any internal review or appeal opportunity that the scheme itself may contain. Disputes may be progressed through complaints procedures, with the relevant social housing regulator, to the Housing Ombudsman or Public Services Ombudsman for Wales and/or through the courts.[54]

NOMINATIONS BY LOCAL HOUSING AUTHORITIES

The legal basis

6.32 HA 1996, Part 6 requires that every private registered provider or registered social landlord will, on request from a local housing authority, 'co-operate to such extent as is reasonable in the circumstances in offering accommodation to people with priority under the authority's allocation scheme.'[55] Although that language (and particularly the reference to a 'request') suggests that co-operation will be sought on a case-by-case basis, this provision is the only statutory underpinning for strategic co-operation between local housing authorities and private registered providers or registered social landlords. Presumably Parliament expected that formal arrangements for day-to-day co-operation between local housing authorities and other social landlords would be set out in individually negotiated agreements. These locally agreed arrangements may be highly informal or, at the other extreme, may be set out in legally binding contractual documents. The latter are more common in the cases of those private registered providers or registered social landlords which have taken a large scale transfer of local housing authority stock. Indeed, the Welsh Code suggests that where a local housing authority has transferred its stock to a registered social landlord it is important that the local housing authority and registered social landlord have a clear nomination agreement and effective arrangements for allocations.[56]

6.33 In practice, most private registered providers and registered social landlords co-operate to the extent of making at least some proportion of their lettings available to applicants who are nominees of local housing authorities.

---

[52]   See **6.7**.
[53]   See the extract at **6.10**.
[54]   See further **6.78–6.87**.
[55]   HA 1996, s 170.
[56]   Welsh Code, para 5.13.

Indeed, in England in 2011/12, more than 50% of general needs lettings by private registered providers were made to local housing authority nominees.[57]

6.34 Arrangements made between a private registered provider or registered social landlord and any particular local housing authority may provide for that local housing authority to nominate applicants for general consideration by that landlord, or for consideration for a particular property, or may involve the private registered provider or registered social landlord providing details of its premises to be advertised as available to nominees under a local housing authority's choice-based letting scheme.

6.35 From the perspective of the local housing authority, nominating an applicant to be an assured tenant of housing accommodation held by a private registered provider or registered social landlord constitutes an 'allocation' of accommodation and is therefore governed by the local allocation scheme adopted by that particular local housing authority.[58] To count as an 'allocation', and therefore to be governed by the allocation scheme, the nomination need not be for the tenancy of a specific property. The statutory concept of nomination covers nominations under any arrangements (whether legally enforceable or not) that require housing accommodation generally, or a specific proportion of stock, to be made available to the local housing authority nominees.[59] Of course, as in the case of the local housing authority's own stock, the letting will not constitute an 'allocation' by the local housing authority if the nominee is a local housing authority's secure or introductory tenant transferring to another social landlord not at his or her initiative but at the initiative of the local housing authority (eg as part of a clearance scheme or some other form of management-driven transfer).[60]

6.36 Save in those cases where the private registered provider or registered social landlord has entered into a contractual commitment to take local housing authority nominations, there is no legal obligation on that landlord to agree to take local housing authority nominations, either generally or for specific properties. The statutory duty is only, on request, to co-operate to such extent as the private registered provider or registered social landlord considers is 'reasonable'.[61]

Guidance on co-operation

6.37 In the absence of any strict legal obligation, the matter of private registered provider or registered social landlord participation in nomination arrangements is simply another issue covered by the current statutory guidance

---

[57]   *Social Housing Lettings & Sales in England, 2011/12: Continuous Recording (CORE) Data* (DCLG, September 2012), p 5.
[58]   HA 1996, s 159(2)(c).
[59]   HA 1996, s 159(4), English Code, para 6.2.
[60]   HA 1996, s 159(4A)–(4B) [England], s 159(5) [Wales]. See **2.59**.
[61]   HA 1996, s 170.

issued by the relevant national regulator.[62] In England, the old regulatory guidance issued by the Housing Corporation was replete with detailed requirements.[63] In contrast, the modern guidance simply requires co-operation with 'local authorities' strategic housing functions, and their duties to meet identified local housing needs. This includes assistance with local authorities' homelessness duties, and through meeting obligations in nominations agreements.'[64] For their part, local housing authorities in England are advised to 'negotiate for the maximum number of lettings that will be required to enable them to discharge their housing functions and which would be reasonable for the' particular private registered provider to deliver.[65]

6.38 Similarly, the present Welsh Code simply provides that registered social landlords in Wales should actively work with local housing authorities to help them fulfil their functions and deliver good housing outcomes, particularly as this is a requirement of the regulatory framework in Wales (see extract reproduced at **6.10**).[66]

Guidance to local housing authorities on co-operation

6.39 The statutory guidance issued to local housing authorities in England and Wales concerning housing allocation contains very little guidance about nominations to private registered providers or registered social landlords, in contrast to the content of the *English Homelessness Code of Guidance* which covers the subject fairly fully,[67] and the ample non-statutory guidance.[68] The current guidance in England simply suggests that nomination agreements should identify:

- the proportion of lettings that will be made available;

- any criteria which the private registered provider has adopted for accepting or rejecting nominees; and

- how any disputes will be resolved.[69]

---

[62] See **6.6**.
[63] *Circular 02/03 Local Authority Nominations* (Housing Corporation, February 2003), and *Regulatory Code of Guidance*, paras 3.6c and 3.6d (Housing Corporation, August 2005) and see *The use of nominations to RSLs by local authorities in Tackling Homelessness: Efficiencies in lettings functions* (Housing Corporation, November 2007).
[64] See the extract set out at **6.8**.
[65] *English Homelessness Code of Guidance* Annex 5, para 13. See Appendix 2 of this book.
[66] Welsh Code, para 1.5.
[67] *English Homelessness Code of Guidance*, Annex 5, passim. See Appendix 2 of this book.
[68] See, for example, *Effective Co-operation in Tackling Homelessness: Nomination Agreements and Exclusion* produced jointly by Communities and Local Government (formerly the ODPM), the Housing Corporation, the National Housing Federation and the Local Government Association in November 2004.
[69] English Code, para 6.3.

6.40 Local housing authorities are encouraged by the same guidance to monitor effective delivery of the nomination agreement 'so they can demonstrate they are meeting their obligations under Part 6'.[70] Those 'obligations' are presumably the obligations to ensure that those in the prescribed categories are actually being afforded the 'reasonable preference' to which HA 1996, Part 6 entitles them.[71]

6.41 In short, the local housing authority needs to be able to check that the private registered provider or registered social landlord is accepting the broad range of nominations made and not itself picking and choosing from among nominated applicants.

6.42 Because most nominations will be made under the auspices of the local housing authority's own allocation scheme, it will be the local housing authority which has ultimate responsibility to the applicant for any difficulties. It may well be that an aggrieved applicant seeks redress against that local housing authority. However, a 'nominated' applicant will also have access to avenues of redress against the private registered provider or registered social landlord, where appropriate.[72]

Information sharing

6.43 Where private registered providers or registered social landlords and local housing authorities are working closely together over social housing allocation, there will inevitably be a need to share information. But information-sharing relating to the particulars of individual applicants requires very careful handling.

6.44 Those who have applied to a local housing authority for accommodation under HA 1996, Part 6 have the statutory assurance that even the simple fact that they have applied will not be shared with others (including private registered providers or registered social landlords) without their consent.[73] It will therefore be essential for the local housing authority to have the written consent of each and every applicant before sharing access to such information with a private registered provider or registered social landlord.

6.45 Against this background, both the former Housing Corporation and previous UK governments have produced publications designed to help local housing authorities and private registered providers or registered social landlords to resolve information-sharing issues.[74]

---

[70] English Code, para 6.3

[71] Chapter 4.

[72] See **6.46–6.53**.

[73] HA 1996, s 166(3). See Chapter 2 of this book.

[74] See, in particular, *Access to Housing: Information Sharing Protocol* (Housing Corporation, November 2007).

Housing Allocation and Homelessness

'Failed' or 'problematic' nominations

6.46 A particular difficulty with the operation of nomination agreements, in practice, has been the rejection of nominated applicants by private registered providers or registered social landlords. This occurs most often where applicants have met the local housing authority's criteria (under the local allocation scheme) for nomination, but do not meet the particular private registered provider's or registered social landlord's letting criteria for the particular property (or, in some cases, for any letting by that social landlord). These have been described as 'failed nominations' or 'problematic nominations'.[75]

6.47 Two common reasons for rejection of nominations have been identified. The first cause is information mismatching, ie the local housing authority and the private registered provider or registered social landlord both hold information about the applicant, but the content differs. For their part, local housing authorities should provide details about nominated households that are clear, comprehensive and up to date, including any available information about vulnerability, support needs and arrangements for support. Failure to get this sort of information sharing right could undermine a nomination process, but getting it right will ensure that there are the best chances of new tenancies being sustained.[76]

6.48 A second common reason for failed nominations is a mismatch between the criteria for nomination adopted by the local housing authority and the criteria for allocation, *after* nomination, adopted by the private registered provider or registered social landlord. All such criteria should, of course, be the subject of consultation and subsequent incorporation into the written nominations agreement between the particular private registered provider or registered social landlord and the local housing authority. If rejection of nominations on these grounds occurs frequently, it may seriously impair a local housing authority's statutory obligations, eg to give a 'reasonable preference' to particular categories of its applicants.[77] The Welsh Code advises that local housing authorities should develop common policies, on restricting access to allocations, with partner registered social landlords to maximise consistency in approach and improve efficiency in nominations procedures.[78]

6.49 To avoid these difficulties it is especially important that local housing authorities enter into robust, clear, and enforceable nomination agreements with those private registered providers or registered social landlords acquiring the whole or parts of their own stock of housing. The non-statutory guidance *Housing Allocation, Homelessness and Stock Transfer – A Guide to Key Issues*[79] set out the policy and operational matters which the nomination agreement

[75] D Cowan et al *Problematic Nominations* (School of Law, Bristol University, December 2007).
[76] See: *Access to Housing: Information Sharing Protocol* (Housing Corporation, November 2007).
[77] For the meaning of 'reasonable preference', see Chapter 4 of this book.
[78] Welsh Code, para 3.29.
[79] *Housing Allocation, Homelessness and Stock Transfer – A Guide to Key Issues* (ODPM, 2004).

between a local housing authority in England and its transfer partner should cover. In Wales, further information is available from the Welsh Government's *Regulatory Framework for Housing Associations Registered in Wales* and the *Welsh Government Housing Transfer Guidelines 2009* for stock transfer.[80]

6.50 More recently, a previous Secretary of State, no doubt mindful of the difficulties occurring in practice, advised local housing authorities in England that in negotiating nomination agreements 'housing authorities should try to ensure that criteria for rejecting nominees are kept to a minimum' and that 'this will be particularly important where the housing authority have transferred their housing stock'.[81] However, the language of this guidance, now withdrawn, was particularly unfortunate, as it suggested that attention was given to the matter not *before* but *after* a local housing authority had transferred its stock. The research that has been conducted on rejected nominations has shown that the phenomenon of large scale stock transfer has not resolved the frequency of disputes between local housing authorities and other social landlords over rejected nominations.[82]

6.51 The particular problems arising from inconsistent criteria are thrown into sharp focus when accommodation made available for local housing authority nominees by a private registered provider or registered social landlord is advertised through the local housing authority's choice-based lettings scheme. The highest ranked bidder for that property will expect to be offered the tenancy if he or she meets the local housing authority's own criteria and will not expect to be denied it for failing to meet the private registered provider's or registered social landlord's criteria, eg because it has wider exclusion criteria than the local housing authority or because it gives particular emphasis to local connection or local lettings policies.[83] In an attempt to avoid such difficulties, the now-withdrawn English CBL Code advised that:

> 'the exclusion policy of each participating RSL should be clearly set out in the published CBL scheme details. In addition, where this is feasible, the exclusion criteria applied by an RSL should be stated in the advertisement of any relevant vacancy, so that applicants are clear about the basis on which the property is offered.'[84]

6.52 In parallel to all the emphasis in the old statutory guidance in England on the negotiating position of local housing authorities, in formulating nomination agreements, the now defunct Housing Corporation, for its part,

[80] See Welsh Code, para 5.13.
[81] *Allocation of Accommodation: Choice Based Lettings: Code of Guidance for Local Housing Authorities* (English CBL Code), para 6.11 and *Fair and flexible: statutory guidance on social housing allocations for local authorities in England* (English 2009 Code), para 97 – both now withdrawn.
[82] D Cowan et al *Problematic Nominations* (School of Law, Bristol University, December 2007).
[83] As to 'legitimate expectation' in the housing allocation context see **4.53**.
[84] English CBL Code, para 6.7. The code was reproduced in the second edition of this book at Appendix 1.

had reminded housing associations of the need to protect their own interests. Its guidance stated that, in order to preserve such a landlord's independence, any nomination agreement must:

- reflect the housing association's own objectives both as set out in its governing instrument and as agreed by the governing body;

- be approved by the governing body;

- be subject to regular and timely review; and

- run for such a term as would enable the parties to exit from it should circumstances or requirements change.[85]

6.53 This advice is mirrored in the current *English Homelessness Code of Guidance* which reminds local housing authorities to:

> 'bear in mind that RSLs are required to retain their independence. They must honour their constitutional obligations under their diverse governing instruments, and will make the final decision on the allocation of their housing, within their regulatory framework.'[86]

Common housing registers

6.54 In line with the general policy shift over recent years towards consumer choice, private registered providers and registered social landlords have been encouraged in the recent past to expose more of their available lettings to wider groups of prospective new tenants – where possible, through advertising and other mechanisms for choice-based letting.[87] The current regulatory guidance in England contains no particular push in that direction and simply provides that the published policies of private registered providers should include information about 'how they have made use of common housing registers, common allocations policies and local letting policies'.[88] The regulatory guidance in Wales speaks simply of 'maximising choice'[89] but the Welsh Code is positively effusive about the advantages of common housing registers.[90]

6.55 The modern impetus for the adoption of 'common' allocation schemes between local housing authorities and other social landlords in England was given in August 2008 by publication of the English CBL Code in which the Secretary of State recommended that all local housing authorities work with

---

[85]   Housing Corporation Circular 02/03, para 4.2.
[86]   *English Homelessness Code of Guidance* (see Appendix 2 of this book) Annex 5, para 9.
[87]   See further, Housing Corporation Good Practice Note 12 *Choice Based Lettings* (Housing Corporation, October 2005).
[88]   See the extract at **6.8**.
[89]   See the extract at **6.10**.
[90]   Welsh Code, para 4.38 and 5.105–5.113.

other social housing partners to provide 'joint choice-based lettings schemes which extend to all or the majority' of local social housing vacancies.[91]

6.56 A 'common housing register' was defined in the English CBL Code as an arrangement under which a local housing authority and another social landlord developed a single list or database of all applicants for housing allocation who had applied to either of them.[92] The intention was that, where the operation of such a register had been agreed, properties would actually thereafter be allocated to those on the common register under a jointly operated choice-based 'common allocation scheme'. The Secretary of State considered that the adoption of common housing registers had advantages:

- for applicants (because a single application form and a single access point obviates the need to register separately);

- for local housing authorities (because the register provides a more reliable assessment of housing need in their districts, providing important information for the development of their housing strategy, and enabling the best use to be made of existing stock);[93] and

- more generally, because the process of negotiating and drawing up such registers can build trust between local housing authority partners and other social landlords.[94]

6.57 The Welsh Code now provides its own list of perceived advantages of common housing registers:

- they provide a single point of access to all social housing in the area;

- they help improve joint working between an authority and housing associations and help in meeting strategic housing objectives;

- they support the development of more strategically planned and integrated lettings schemes in an area;

- they give a better understanding of the pattern of local housing needs; and

- they can reduce void levels.

6.58 However, considerable care is needed in drawing up such schemes. In particular, it needs to be clear whether the register is simply a facility for joint storage of information or rather whether it is a means of enabling common

---

[91] English CBL Code, para 6.1 and English (2009) Code, para 99. Both codes were reproduced in the second edition of this book at Appendix 1.
[92] English CBL Code, para 6.16.
[93] English CBL Code, para 6.17 and English (2009) Code, para 99.
[94] English (2009) Code, para 100.

criteria to be applied in assessing applications (eg to ascertain eligibility and priority). There is a significant distinction between the former, which are true common housing registers, and the latter, which are common allocations policies.[95] As a report on the situation in Wales indicated:

> 'The presence of a common housing register in an authority area is not necessarily a requisite for a common allocations policy. 29% of respondents have common registers but no common allocations policy. However, in the 3 authorities where a common allocations policy is in operation, 2 of the authorities also have a common register operating.'[96]

6.59 In England, private registered providers let 77% of general needs properties via choice-based letting schemes in 2011/12[97] and most of those schemes are likely to have been common allocation schemes or based on common registers. A discussion paper, *Common Housing Registers*, published by the TSA's Homelessness Action Team in May 2009 contains a useful literature review and a consideration of topical issues concerning such registers.[98]

6.60 As already explained,[99] if an applicant on the common register is applying directly for a private registered provider or registered social landlord property, the only eligibility criteria will be those adopted by that social landlord. But if the applicant is going to be a local housing authority nominee for a private registered provider or registered social landlord vacancy, the statutory eligibility or qualification criteria must be met.[100]

6.61 These complications are thrown into even sharper relief when a private registered provider or registered social landlord participates in a common registration scheme with more than one local housing authority or with a number of local housing authorities and other social landlords. Ambitious plans to amalgamate registers and allocations policies to produce common schemes, involving private registered providers or registered social landlords but run by a single central organisation exercising the delegated powers of all participants, have run into difficulties. Previous statutory guidance in England has advised that local housing authorities cannot use their general statutory powers of delegation to operate such common lettings schemes together with other social landlords although 'it would be possible to include within such a scheme [those] vacancies to which a local authority had nomination rights'.[101]

[95] Welsh Code, para 4.40.
[96] Homelessness Strategy Working Group Report: *Housing Association Lettings* (Community Housing Cymru).
[97] *Social Housing Lettings & Sales in England, 2011/12: Continuous Recording (CORE) Data* (DCLG, September 2012), p 6.
[98] Housing Action Team discussion paper: *Common Housing Registers* (TSA, May 2009).
[99] See **6.23–6.25**.
[100] Those terms are explained in Chapter 3.
[101] English CBL Code, para 7.8.

6.62 All social landlords have also been encouraged to participate in *regional* choice-based lettings schemes with other local housing authority and social landlord partners.[102] But where private registered provider or registered social landlord property is advertised through a joint choice-based lettings scheme in which the private registered provider or registered social landlord participates with local housing authorities which each have their own allocation scheme:

(1) the partners in the scheme should be clear as to which local housing authority is the nominating local housing authority; and

(2) there should be clear information available for applicants as to which local housing authority's allocation scheme applies to that property (and therefore how priority will be determined).

Partnership working with local housing authorities[103]

6.63 Much of what has already been written in this Chapter has assumed a degree of partnership working between private registered providers or registered social landlords and local housing authorities as collectively the main providers of social housing.[104] But that assumption has a statutory underpinning. HA 1996, s 170 expressly addresses co-operation between private registered providers or registered social landlords and local housing authorities. It provides that, on request from a local housing authority, such a landlord shall co-operate 'to such extent as is reasonable in the circumstances' in offering accommodation to people with priority under the local housing authority's allocation scheme. It should be noted that this is not restricted to requiring co-operation in respect of offering homes to those in the statutory 'reasonable preference' categories. A local housing authority may also have identified other applicants in its scheme as having 'priority'.[105]

6.64 This duty to co-operate with a local housing authority to a reasonable extent mirrors the duty imposed on private registered providers or registered social landlords to co-operate in assisting a local housing authority in discharging its homelessness functions under HA 1996, s 213(1)(a).[106] Indeed, that duty is subjected to extended treatment in statutory guidance in England under the title *Co-operation between registered social landlords and housing*

---

[102] See, for example, Welsh Code, para 5.11.

[103] The Welsh Code, para 2.4 expressly encourages partnership working between local housing authorities and registered social landlords in order to meet the needs of the local community and maximise the best use of the housing stock available.

[104] See generally *A Framework for Partnership* (published jointly by the Local Government Association, the National Housing Federation and the Housing Corporation, 2006) and, more recently, the Homelessness Action Team discussion paper *Developing Partnerships* (TSA, May 2009).

[105] See Chapter 4 of this book.

[106] Discussed at **18.146–18.147**.

authorities[107] – much of which is directed not only to homelessness functions but also to housing allocations – and has been the subject of detailed research as to its effect in practice.[108]

6.65 The former Housing Corporation guidance dealt with these two duties together, requiring that:

> 'when requested to do so by the local authority and to such an extent as is reasonable in the circumstances, associations provide a proportion of their stock to local authority nominations and temporary accommodation to the homeless.'[109]

6.66 The modern regulatory guidance for England requires private registered providers to co-operate 'with local authorities' strategic functions, and their duties to meet housing need.'[110] The Regulatory Code in Wales contains the 'delivery outcome' that registered social landlords should have a 'strong relationship' with local housing authorities and 'support' them in the delivery of their 'strategic housing' roles.[111] The Welsh Code suggests that registered social landlords should actively work with local housing authorities to help them fulfill their housing functions and deliver good housing outcomes, particularly as this is a requirement of the regulatory framework in Wales.[112]

6.67 The statutory obligation to co-operate over housing allocation arises only 'on request'.[113] A generic request from a local housing authority might cause a private registered provider or registered social landlord to offer nomination arrangements or to negotiate a common housing register or some other joint scheme with the requesting local housing authority. But the request may also be applicant specific. The local housing authority may, for example, owe a duty to accommodate a particular applicant needing accommodation of a particular type held by the private registered provider or registered social landlord and may make a request accordingly. The duty to co-operate is, however, limited to 'such extent as is reasonable in the circumstances'. A reasonable response to such a request might include an invitation to the local housing authority to transfer a unit of its stock to the private registered provider or registered social landlord or to accept a reciprocal nomination in return for the provision of the requested assistance.

6.68 If a private registered provider or registered social landlord does not co-operate in the face of a request from the local housing authority, the local

---

[107] *English Homelessness Code of Guidance*, Annex 5 (CLG, July 2006); see Appendix 2 of this book.

[108] *Tackling Homelessness: Efficiencies in lettings functions* (Housing Corporation, November 2007).

[109] *Regulatory Code of Guidance* (Housing Corporation, August 2005), para 3.6c.

[110] See the extract at **6.8**.

[111] Welsh Government's *Regulatory Framework for Housing Associations Registered in Wales* (2011), p 19.

[112] Welsh Code, para 1.5.

[113] HA 1996, s 170.

housing authority could pursue the matter with the relevant regulator or through the courts (because the statutory duty is mandatory).[114] Alternatively, the individual (if there is one) who is the subject of the request could use the private registered provider's or registered social landlord's complaints procedure or could pursue one of the other means of redress.[115]

6.69   Of course, there are a host of other functions in respect of which private registered providers or registered social landlords and local housing authorities should co-operate. The former Housing Corporation expected housing associations to be able to demonstrate their co-operation with local housing authorities at least:

(1)   in local homelessness reviews;

(2)   in the formulation of local homelessness strategies; and

(3)   in the delivery of local housing authorities' homelessness functions.[116]

CURRENT TENANTS WHO WANT TO MOVE ('TRANSFERS')

6.70   All private registered providers or registered social landlords will have arrangements in place to accommodate the receipt of, and subsequent determination of, requests from existing tenants to move to other homes within that landlord's stock, ie applications from tenants seeking a transfer. Indeed, in 2011/12 in England more than a third of general needs lettings by private registered providers went to applicants who were already tenants of social housing.[117]

6.71   The applicable statutory requirements are minimal. They only oblige the minority of private registered providers or registered social landlords which have *secure* tenants to publish a summary of their transfer rules governing cases where their secure tenants wish to move to other dwelling-houses let under secure tenancies by that landlord.[118] Where that obligation does apply, the private registered provider or registered social landlord must also make a copy

---

[114]   HA 1996, s 170 says '*shall* co-operate' (emphasis added).

[115]   See **6.78–6.87**.

[116]   *Regulatory Code of Guidance,* (Housing Corporation, August 2005) para 3.6b. For more on 'homelessness strategies' and 'homelessness reviews', see Chapter 7. For 'homelessness functions', see **21.21–21.25**.

[117]   *Social Housing Lettings & Sales in England, 2011/12: Continuous Recording (CORE) Data* (DCLG, September 2012), p 8.

[118]   Housing Act 1985, s 106(1). Private registered providers and registered social landlords will usually only have 'secure tenants' if they were letting properties before early 1989 (when Housing Act 1988 introduced the assured tenancy for most housing association lettings).

of the transfer rules available at its principal office for inspection at all reasonable hours, without charge, by members of the public.[119]

6.72 Although the adoption of such transfer arrangements (ie published transfer rules and policies) might be thought in any event to represent sensible housing management for all private registered providers or registered social landlords, the matter has in the past been the subject of statutory guidance. Housing associations were previously directed to ensure that their written lettings policies not only 'take account of the need to give reasonable priority to transfer applicants', but also include arrangements for applications to be made to them from tenants of local housing authorities and other housing associations.[120] The current guidance in England simply specifies that tenants of private registered providers wishing to move should be provided 'with access to clear and relevant advice about their housing options'.[121]

6.73 If all the stock of a particular private registered provider or registered social landlord is ring-fenced for allocation only through a nomination arrangement or a common allocation scheme, some requests for transfers will fail because they would not meet the criteria for allocation under those arrangements or schemes.[122]

6.74 The precise detail of a particular private registered provider's or registered social landlord's internal transfer scheme is not regulated by any statutory parameters or guidance and such landlords have, essentially, a free rein. This is, of course, subject to the constraints of the general law (eg the need to avoid unlawful discrimination) and the requirement to act fairly and in accordance with the particular landlord's own published scheme. The private registered provider or registered social landlord may even differentiate between the criteria it applies to transfer applicants and those applying to direct applicants. For example, the now-withdrawn Housing Corporation Circular 02/07 suggested that a housing association may take a stricter view of the effect of rent arrears on eligibility for allocation if the arrears are owed by its own tenant.[123]

6.75 The published information generally provided by the private registered provider or registered social landlord about its lettings arrangements[124] should be made available to transfer applicants. Complaints by, and redress for, dissatisfied transfer applicants are considered later in this Chapter.[125]

---

[119] Housing Act 1985, s 106(1).

[120] *Regulatory Code of Guidance* (Housing Corporation, August 2005) para 3.6f.

[121] See **6.8**.

[122] See, for an example, the facts of *R (Fidelis-Auma) v Octavia Housing & Care* [2009] EWHC 2263 (Admin), (2009) November *Legal Action*, p 25, Admin Ct.

[123] Circular 02/07: *Tenancy Management: Eligibility and Evictions* (Housing Corporation, April 2007).

[124] See **6.29–6.30**.

[125] See **6.78–6.87**.

PRIVATE REGISTERED PROVIDERS OR REGISTERED SOCIAL LANDLORDS AS LOCAL HOUSING AUTHORITY CONTRACTORS

6.76 There is no reason why a local housing authority should not contract out many of its HA 1996, Part 6 responsibilities for housing allocation to a local private registered provider or registered social landlord. Indeed, many private registered providers or registered social landlords do act as such contractors, particularly following large-scale voluntary transfers of local housing authority stock.

6.77 Chapter 21 of this book deals more fully with both contracting out and stock transfer. The report *Housing allocation, homelessness and stock transfer: A guide to key issues* contains advice for private registered providers, registered social landlords and local housing authorities on all three subjects – stock transfer, contracting-out and housing allocation nominations – in a single publication, but this must now be read with some caution as it has not been revised since 2005.[126]

COMPLAINTS, APPEALS AND LEGAL CHALLENGES

6.78 Before deciding whether or how to dispute a decision made on an application for (or nomination for) a housing allocation by a private registered provider or registered social landlord, an applicant should first obtain such details as she or he can about the particular private registered provider's or registered social landlord's housing allocation scheme.[127] At the same time, she or he should ask the private registered provider or registered social landlord to provide the details of the particulars which she or he has given to the local housing authority about 'himself and his family'[128] and which the private registered provider or registered social landlord has recorded as being relevant to the application for accommodation. The applicant has the statutory right to have that information made available on request at all reasonable times and without charge.[129] Complying with the request will require disclosure of not only the application form but also of any details the private registered provider or registered social landlord has subsequently obtained in its consideration of the application. Most simply, the applicant can ask for and will usually be provided with a copy of the application file. Armed with the file and the copy scheme, the applicant (or an adviser) will usually be able to identify, and draw to the private registered provider's or registered social landlord's attention, any simple error, missing material or other mishap that has occurred in considering the application.

---

[126] *Housing allocation, homelessness and stock transfer: A guide to key issues* (CLG, 2005).
[127] See **6.29–6.30**.
[128] Housing Act 1985, s 106(5).
[129] Housing Act 1985, s 106(5).

6.79 In case any difficulty is not so easily resolved, every private registered provider or registered social landlord is required to have a complaints procedure. The Housing Ombudsman Service publishes a useful leaflet for complainants pursuing a complaint to a private registered provider in England under its complaints procedure: *Making a complaint to your landlord.*[130] The regulatory guidance in England requires that:

> 'Providers shall offer a range of ways for tenants to express a complaint and set out clear service standards for responding to complaints, including complaints about performance against the standards, and details of what to do if they are unhappy with the outcome of a complaint. Providers shall inform tenants how they use complaints to improve their services. Registered providers shall publish information about complaints each year, including their number and nature, and the outcome of the complaints. Providers shall accept complaints made by advocates authorised to act on a tenant's/tenants' behalf.'[131]

6.80 The 'delivery outcome' on complaints required by the regulatory guidance in Wales is that registered social landlords will

> 'make it easy for people to tell us when things go wrong, or to make a complaint, so we can quickly put things right.'[132]

6.81 If the complaints procedure does not resolve the matter, an applicant with a continuing grievance concerning a private registered provider operating in England can press the complaint to the Housing Ombudsman service. The Ombudsman is established by statute[133] and provides a free and independent service. Private registered providers are expected to comply with his recommendations. A leaflet, *Guide to making a complaint to a landlord and to the Housing Ombudsman Service*, and online complaint form are available on the Housing Ombudsman's website. More detailed information on the outcomes of complaints in relation to allocations and transfers is available through an online searchable digest of cases. The Localism Act 2011 will modify other arrangements for complaints to the Housing Ombudsman in England with effect from April 2013 but complaints relating to allocation decisions of private registered providers will still be within his jurisdiction.

6.82 Complaints about registered social landlords operating in Wales can be directed to the Public Services Ombudsman for Wales. A *Housing Application Factsheet* is available on his website. In 2006 he published *Housing Allocations and Homelessness: A Special Report* summarising findings in relation to housing allocation complaints.

---

[130] Available at www.housing-ombudsman.org.uk.

[131] *The regulatory framework for social housing in England from April 2012* (HCA March 2012), p 18.

[132] *The regulatory framework for housing associations registered in Wales* (Welsh Government, December 2011), p 18.

[133] Housing Act 1996, s 51 and Sch 2.

6.83 Although a private registered provider or registered social landlord may operate a system of complaints handling, reviews of decisions or even appeals, there is strictly no right of appeal to the courts or tribunals from any decision of a private registered provider or registered social landlord or of the Ombudsmen.

6.84 The Divisional Court and the Court of Appeal have held that the decision of a private registered provider or registered social landlord in relation to the allocation of social housing can be amenable to judicial review – at least to the extent that, in allocating its housing, the private registered provider or registered social landlord might be described as undertaking a 'public function'.[134] The housing association involved in that case was refused permission to appeal to the Supreme Court. Therefore, unless and until – in some other case – the Supreme Court overrules the decision of the Court of Appeal, a dissatisfied applicant is now able to invoke the jurisdiction of the Administrative Court to review a private registered provider's or registered social landlord's decision-making on a housing allocation application (whether the applicant was seeking a transfer[135] or was a direct applicant or was a nominee or was simply a tenant of that social landlord seeking a mutual exchange[136]). The grounds on which the court will interfere with such a decision are narrowly drawn and are described later in this book.[137]

6.85 The Divisional Court and the Court of Appeal have also decided that the act of a private registered provider or registered social landlord in granting or terminating a tenancy of social housing is, where it is done pursuant to a function of a public nature, an act to which the requirements of the Human Rights Act 1998 ('HRA 1998') apply.[138] HRA 1998 prohibits a public authority from acting in a manner contrary to an individual's Convention rights as set out in the Articles reproduced in HRA 1998, Sch 1.[139] Although no Convention right gives an applicant a right to a home from a private registered provider or registered social landlord, the Convention rights might assist an applicant who has been denied a proper hearing of an application or an appeal by such a landlord (Art 6), who has been denied a transfer and thus is left in an unsatisfactory home let by a private registered provider or registered social landlord (Art 8) or who has been a victim of discrimination in consideration of his or her application (Art 14). Obviously, an applicant seeking to conduct a judicial review or to assert his or her Convention rights against a private registered provider or registered social landlord should be referred for specialist legal advice.

---

[134] *R (Weaver) v London & Quadrant Housing Trust* [2008] EWHC Admin 1377; [2009] 1 All ER 17, Divisional Court, and [2009] EWCA Civ 587, [2009] 4 All ER 865, [2009] HLR 40, CA.

[135] As in *R (Fidelis-Auma) v Octavia Housing & Care* [2009] EWHC 2263 (Admin), (2009) November *Legal Action* p 25, Admin Ct.

[136] As in *R (McIntyre) v Gentoo Group Ltd* [2010] EWHC 5 (Admin), (2010) March *Legal Action* p 28, Admin Ct.

[137] See Chapter 19.

[138] *R (Weaver) v London & Quadrant Housing Trust* [2008] EWHC (Admin) 1377, Divisional Court; [2009] 1 All ER 17, [2009] EWCA Civ 587, [2009] 4 All ER 865, [2009] HLR 40, CA.

[139] HRA 1998, s 6(1).

6.86 Equally obviously, where the applicant considers that there has been unlawful discrimination or an infringement of human rights, the assistance of the Equality and Human Rights Commission can be sought.[140]

6.87 It is theoretically possible for individual complaints to be made to the national regulatory authorities[141] about allocation decisions made by private registered providers or registered social landlords but in practice they will be diverted to the private registered provider's or registered social landlord's complaints procedure or to the relevant Ombudsman. However, where the individual complaint reflects a systemic malfunction by the private registered provider or registered social landlord it may be worthwhile seeking to involve the regulator.

---

[140] At www.equalityhumanrights.com.

[141] In England, the Homes & Communities Agency Regulatory Committee and in Wales, the Housing Regulation team.

Part II

HOMELESSNESS

Chapter 7

LOCAL HOUSING AUTHORITIES' HOMELESSNESS REVIEWS AND STRATEGIES

INTRODUCTION

7.1   This Chapter and the following Chapters of this book deal with 'Homelessness'. Like the statutory scheme for the homeless in the Housing Act 1996 (HA 1996), Part 7 itself, this book's primary focus is on the individual applicant for assistance and the powers and duties of a local housing authority in dealing with the application. However, over recent years, increasing attention has been focused on the need to take a more strategic approach to the problem of homelessness beyond simply operating the safety net mechanism for individual applicants now contained in the HA 1996, Part 7. The steady rise, between 2001 and 2004, in the number of applications for homelessness assistance in all parts of the UK, and the consequent growth in the numbers of households in temporary accommodation, caused the focus of attention to shift towards methods of preventing homelessness and to dealing more effectively with it when it does arise. Central government began encouraging a more proactive rather than reactive approach to the issue of homelessness.

7.2   After 2004, the number of applications for homelessness assistance to local housing authorities in England and Wales fell steadily until 2010.[1] The fall has been attributed to a number of factors including the former UK government's policy of encouraging local housing authorities in England to halve their use of temporary accommodation by the year 2010. Critics have observed that another reason might be that the laudable policy of taking action to prevent homelessness can in practice become 'gate-keeping', in that potential applicants for homelessness assistance are dissuaded from making applications.[2]

7.3   Since mid-2010, the number of applications for homelessness assistance has been increasing in both England and Wales. A recent report from housing charities noted: '[h]ouse building is at its lowest level for decades, households across all tenures report that they struggle to afford their housing, and the average age of a first-time buyer has been forecast to rise to 43. Meanwhile our population is both growing and ageing, millions of people are waiting for social housing, vulnerable people face huge cuts in support and homelessness is rising.'[3]

7.4   This Chapter reviews the consequences of the emphasis on a strategic approach. It considers, in turn, the development of 'homelessness strategies' at national, regional and local level. Most of the focus is upon the latter, particularly as a result of statutory duties imposed on local housing authorities

---

[1]   Statistics from local housing authorities in England are available at: http://www.communities. gov.uk/housing/housingresearch/housingstatistics/housingstatisticsby/homelessnessstatistics/. Statistics from local housing authorities in Wales are available at: http://wales.gov.uk/topics/ statistics/headlines/housing2011/1103231/?lang=en.

[2]   See Chapter 8 of this book.

[3]   *The Housing Report* (Chartered Institute of Housing, National Housing Federation and Shelter, 1st edn, October 2011).

to draw up their own local homelessness strategies.[4] Those duties are considered in particular detail. The next Chapter deals specifically with homelessness prevention.

NATIONAL STRATEGIES

7.5 Policy-making at national level relating to homelessness is undertaken by central government for England, and by the devolved governments of Wales, Scotland and Northern Ireland.[5] The UK government has no single national strategy directed towards the prevention of homelessness or to tackling homelessness when it arises. A useful review of practice, and of policy, across the whole of the United Kingdom in 2009 is contained in *Homelessness in the UK: Problems and Solutions.*[6] In 2011, the Joseph Rowntree Foundation published *Tackling homelessness and exclusion: Understanding complex lives* which drew on research conducted across England, Scotland and Northern Ireland.[7] The research considered both 'visible' homelessness (defined as rough sleeping, use of hostels and similar services, and applications for homelessness assistance) and 'invisible' homelessness such as sofa-surfing. It found a strong overlap between experiences of homelessness and need for other forms of support, with a high correlation between experiences of institutional care, substance misuse and/or street activities such as begging and homelessness. Another UK-wide study, which focused on single homelessness, contains useful reviews of policy developments in the four jurisdictions and on the impact of homelessness strategies.[8]

7.6 The previous UK government recognised homelessness as a factor in social exclusion, and included tackling homelessness within the work of its Social Exclusion Task Force. The UK Coalition Government, which delivers housing and homelessness policy for England, emphasises 'decentralisation' and promoting greater autonomy to councils, including local housing authorities.[9] The UK government published a national housing strategy in November 2011: *Laying the Foundations.*[10]

7.7 In 2012, the Coalition Government's Ministerial Working Group on Homelessness published *Making every contact count: A joint approach to*

---

4   Homelessness Act 2002 (HA 2002), ss 1–4.
5   For government policy in England, see www.communities.gov.uk/housing/homelessness. For Welsh Government policy see: http://wales.gov.uk/topics/housingandcommunity/housing/homelessness/?lang=en. For Scottish Executive policy, see www.scotland.gov.uk/Topics/Built-Environment/Housing/homeless. For Northern Ireland Housing Executive policy, see http://www.nihe.gov.uk/index/corporate/strategies/homelessness_strategy.htm.
6   Fitzpatrick, Quilgars and Please (eds) (Chartered Institute of Housing, 2009).
7   McDonagh (ed) (Joseph Rowntree Foundation, 2011).
8   Jones and Pleace *A Review of Single Homelessness in the UK* (University of York and Crisis, 2010), Chapter 3.
9   *Freedom Fairness Responsibility, The Coalition: Our Programme for Government* (2010).
10   *Laying the Foundations: A Housing Strategy for England* (HM Government, November 2011). See **7.20**.

preventing homelessness.[11] Whilst most of the recommendations were aimed at local housing authorities in England, the document stated that central government action on homelessness in areas such as social security, defence and tackling crime were relevant to other parts of the UK and that central government was committed to working with the devolved administrations in Scotland, Wales and Northern Ireland in tackling homelessness.

7.8   In the absence of a UK-wide strategy, we consider each of the four national strategic plans in turn.

England

7.9   Before considering the current government's policy, it is instructive briefly to review the recent history.

7.10   The former Department for Transport, Local Government and the Regions (DTLR) consulted on the development of a National Homelessness Strategy for England in 2001, but no national strategy emerged from that exercise.[12]

7.11   Between July 2004 and January 2005, the Parliamentary Select Committee on the work of the Office of the Deputy Prime Minister (ODPM)[13] carried out an Inquiry into the effectiveness of implementation of the Homelessness Act 2002 and its report was published in January 2005.[14] Its strong view was that the government should aim to eradicate homelessness, through increasing the stock of social housing, and that government action to reduce the number of homeless households in temporary accommodation had not been effective. It expressed concern that the tests of 'vulnerability' for the purposes of priority need[15] and 'becoming homeless intentionally'[16] were not being fairly or consistently applied by local housing authorities. It recommended that the government issue clear and authoritative guidance on the assessment of vulnerability and on the test for becoming homeless intentionally, and that children's services authorities should be issued with guidance on accepting referrals of families who had been found to have become homeless intentionally. There was concern that many local housing authorities displayed a lack of strategic thinking when it came to dealing with the question of homelessness. Above all, the biggest problem in tackling homelessness was said to be the lack of supply of adequate housing, especially social rented housing.

---

[11]   DCLG, 2012, see **7.21**.
[12]   *A national homelessness strategy: an invitation to comment* (DTLR, 21 September 2001).
[13]   Now the Communities and Local Government Parliamentary Select Committee. The ODPM was the relevant government department with responsibility for housing at the time.
[14]   Select Committee on Office of the Deputy Prime Minister 'Housing, Planning, Local Government and the Regions, Third report of session 2004–2005'.
[15]   See **13.75–13.11**.
[16]   See Chapter 14 of this book.

7.12 In January 2005, the ODPM itself published a national five-year housing strategy, *Sustainable Communities: Homes for All*,[17] and then followed it, in March 2005, with a strategy for tackling homelessness, *Sustainable Communities: settled homes; changing lives*.[18] A Housing Green Paper *Homes for the Future: more affordable, more sustainable* was published in July 2007.[19]

7.13 The 'housing strategy' document emphasised the previous government's commitment to promoting home ownership. The Housing Green Paper published in 2007 contained plans to increase the supply of affordable housing, including homes provided by local housing authorities and private registered providers in England.

7.14 The national 'homelessness strategy' developed the homelessness aspects of these national housing strategy commitments. Its specific aim was to halve the number of households living in temporary accommodation by 2010 (from 101,070 households in March 2005[20]) and it identified as methods to achieve this:

- prevention of homelessness;

- providing support for vulnerable people;

- tackling the wider causes and symptoms of homelessness;

- helping people move away from rough sleeping; and

- providing more settled homes.

7.15 The UK government monitored progress through the release of quarterly statistics, based on returns from all local housing authorities in England. The Homelessness Code of Guidance for Local Authorities published in July 2006 reflected the national strategy's emphasis on prevention.[21]

7.16 Guidance on specific aspects of homelessness prevention,[22] assistance towards specifically identified groups, and briefings on particular aspects of homelessness strategy were also published.[23]

---

[17] ODPM, January 2005.

[18] ODPM, March 2005.

[19] Department for Communities and Local Government, July 2007.

[20] Statutory Homelessness Statistics, First Quarter 2005, England (Communities and Local Government, June 2005).

[21] *Homelessness Code of Guidance for Local Authorities* (Department for Communities and Local Government, Department for Education and Skills, Department of Health, July 2006) (the English Code) at Appendix 2 of this book.

[22] See Chapter 8 of this book.

[23] ODPM, 'Policy Briefing No 2' on housing and domestic violence, September 2002; ODPM 'Policy Briefing No 6' on repeat homelessness, January 2004; ODPM 'Policy Briefing No 7' on the health needs of homeless people, April 2004; CLG 'Policy Briefing No 20' on rough

7.17   DCLG announced in November 2006 that reducing youth homelessness was a particular priority. It set out a series of measures: a commitment to end the use of bed and breakfast for 16- and 17-year-olds by 2010; increased use of family mediation; and a supported lodgings development scheme to provide accommodation for young people.

7.18   By December 2010, the target set by the previous government had been met: the number of households in temporary accommodation was 48,010, just under one half of the March 2005 figure.[24] That figure remained static until it started to rise in September 2011, no doubt as a result of the increased numbers of applications for homelessness assistance.[25] From September 2011 to the date of writing, the figure has continued to rise.[26]

7.19   Shortly after the Coalition Government assumed office in May 2010, the Minister for Housing announced the formation of a cross-government Ministerial Working Group on homelessness. The Minister also changed the methodology used by local housing authorities to count the numbers of people sleeping rough.[27] In July 2011, the Working Group published *Vision to End Rough Sleeping? No Second Night Out Nationwide*.[28]

7.20   In November 2011, the UK Government published *Laying the Foundations: a Housing Strategy for England*.[29] In relation to homelessness duties owed under Housing Act 1996, Part 7 the Government's policy was that contained in the Localism Act 2011: to permit local housing authorities to bring the main housing duty to an end with offers of suitable private rented sector accommodation.[30] The strategy continued the previous government's commitment to implement measures to prevent homelessness.[31] It also committed the Government to 'tackle rough sleeping' through the Ministerial Working Group on Homelessness. A pilot 'No Second Night Out' scheme was run in London and the plan was to roll the scheme out across the country.[32] Funds were to be provided to voluntary and charitable groups to help single homeless people.[33]

7.21   In August 2012, DCLG published *Making every contact count, a joint approach to preventing homelessness*,[34] the second publication of the Ministerial

---

sleeping, September 2007; and CLG 'Policy Briefing No 18' on tackling youth homelessness. See also *No One Left Out – Communities Ending Rough Sleeping* (CLG, November 2006).
[24]   Statutory Homelessness, Fourth Quarter, 2010, England (DCLG, 2011).
[25]   Statutory Homelessness Statistics, July to September 2011, England (DCLG, 2011).
[26]   Statutory Homelessness Statistics: April to June Quarter 2012, England (DCLG, 2012).
[27]   *Evaluating the extent of Rough Sleeping: A New Approach* (DCLG, 2010).
[28]   DCLG, 2011.
[29]   HM Government, November 2011.
[30]   Chapter 3, para 21 of *Laying the Foundations*. See **17.23–17.168** of this book for the main housing duty and **17.109–17.131** for private rented sector offers.
[31]   Chapter 6, para 4 of *Laying the Foundations*. See Chapter 8 of this book.
[32]   **17.64–17.65**.
[33]   Chapter 6, paras 6–12 of *Laying the Foundations*.
[34]   DCLG, 2012.

Working Group on Homelessness. Building on research which found that there are substantial central and local government costs incurred when people are homeless,[35] local housing authorities should adopt a corporate commitment to prevent homelessness. That commitment to prevention should inform all of their various services, and should also be taken up by local voluntary sector and other partners. Housing options prevention advice should be available to anyone, not just to those people wanting to make an application for homelessness assistance. The No Second Night Out model, piloted in London, is to be developed by other local housing authorities. Housing options advice should be geared to making offers of suitable private rented accommodation, and try to prevent mortgage repossessions including through the mortgage rescue scheme. Local housing authorities' homelessness strategies should be reviewed annually. Bed and breakfast accommodation should not be provided to any young person aged 16 or 17, and should only be provided for families in emergency situations and even then for no longer than six weeks.[36] The strategy was criticised by homelessness organisations for lacking teeth, in that there were no provisions by which local housing authorities would be penalised if they failed to implement it.[37]

7.22   The DCLG's progress with the national housing strategy is monitored by a new series of publications *The Housing Report*, co-authored by three housing policy organisations.[38] In its most recent edition, it gave the DCLG a red traffic light, meaning that matters were getting worse, for its progress on homelessness. It said:

> 'The large increase in homeless acceptances and rough sleepers is deeply troubling. Ministers need to respond urgently to this growing problem, which could be exacerbated by further cuts to Housing Benefit in 2013.'[39]

7.23   There is no statutory obligation on any local housing authority in England to have regard to the government's national housing or homelessness strategies, either in formulating its own homelessness strategy or when it comes to the performance of its homelessness functions. However, local housing authorities should ordinarily take government policy into account.

Wales

7.24   When the National Assembly for Wales was formed in 1999, it was given competence to make secondary legislation in the areas of housing and homelessness, but not primary legislation.[40] Those functions were passed to the

---

[35]   *The costs of homelessness, a summary* (DCLG, 2012).
[36]   This latter commitment is, of course, required by the Homelessness (Suitability of Accommodation) (England) Order 2003, SI 2003/3326, see **18.114–18.119**.
[37]   'Homeless strategy report lacks teeth', *Inside Housing*, 17 August 2012.
[38]   Chartered Institute for Housing, National Housing Federation and Shelter, Edition 1, October 2011; Edition 2, May 2012.
[39]   *The Housing Report*, Chartered Institute for Housing, National Housing Federation and Shelter, Edition 2, May 2012.
[40]   Government of Wales Act 1998, s 22.

Welsh Assembly Government in 2006.[41] Following a referendum in March 2011, the National Assembly of Wales acquired the right to pass primary legislation in the areas of housing and homelessness. The Assembly has not yet passed any primary legislation relating to homelessness. From May 2011, the Welsh Assembly Government has been known as the Welsh Government and its functions are exercised by the Welsh Ministers.

7.25 Upon formation, the National Assembly for Wales made a commitment to set up a Homelessness Commission to advise it on how it should be tackling homelessness in Wales. Once established, the Commission undertook an intensive programme of activity over seven months. Its report comprised a major review of the causes of homelessness, with 91 recommendations on how it should be addressed.[42]

7.26 The Welsh Assembly Government then published three national homelessness strategies. The 2003 *National Homelessness Strategy*[43] was based on an overall strategic national housing policy document, *Better Homes for People in Wales – National Housing Strategy for Wales*.[44] The two strategies identified measures to:

- significantly reduce the numbers of long-term homeless households;

- eliminate the need for rough sleeping; and

- promote access to specialist housing advice where this was needed.

7.27 In June 2005, the Welsh Assembly Government commissioned a general review of the housing and homelessness situation in Wales.[45] The report of that review emphasised prevention of homelessness. It analysed the number of applications for homelessness assistance and acceptances and concluded that more preventative work would reduce those numbers. Somewhat controversially, it suggested that too many applications for homelessness assistance were inappropriate, that some local housing authorities were failing to apply homelessness legislation, and therefore they were accepting that a main housing duty was owed to applicants who were not necessarily entitled to it.[46]

---

[41] Government of Wales Act 2006.

[42] The Homelessness Commission report to the Minister for Finance, Local Government and Communities, August 2001.

[43] Welsh Assembly Government, March 2003.

[44] Welsh Assembly Government, July 2001.

[45] Report to the Welsh Assembly Government, *Tackling Homelessness – Key issues for consideration by Welsh Local Authorities* (Tarki Technology Ltd, June 2005). The Welsh Code refers to this report as providing 'practical advice for all local authorities on how they can enhance their prevention approach' (Welsh Code, para 10.6). The Welsh Code also reminds local housing authorities that they should not 'avoid their obligations under Part 7' (Welsh Code, para 10.5). *Code of Guidance for Local Authorities Allocation of Accommodation and Homelessness 2012* (Welsh Government, August 2012) (the Welsh Code), see CD-Rom. For the 'obligations under Part 7', see Chapters 9 and 10 of this book.

[46] For 'main housing duty' owed under HA 1996, s 193(2), see **17.23–17.168**.

7.28 In November 2005, following research which had found that more preventative work would reduce the numbers of applications for homelessness assistance, the Welsh Assembly Government published its second *National Homelessness Strategy for Wales (2006–2008).*[47] It emphasised:

- prevention of homelessness;[48]

- co-operative working between different agencies and local housing authority departments;

- reducing the incidence of repeat homelessness; and

- improving the quality of temporary accommodation.

7.29 A few months later, in February 2006, the Public Services Ombudsman for Wales published an account of practices by local housing authorities' in Wales: *Housing Allocations and Homelessness: A Special Report by the Local Government Ombudsman for Wales.*[49] The Ombudsman summarised his findings:

> 'A significant number of the 22 Welsh local authorities have failed to introduce housing allocation and homelessness policies and procedures that implement in practice the relevant legislative requirements.'

7.30 The current national strategy – *Ten Year Homelessness Plan for Wales 2009–2019* – was published by the Welsh Assembly Government in July 2009. This was more ambitious and far-reaching than the previous plans and demonstrated considerable autonomy from the UK Government. When the Plan was out for consultation, Shelter Cymru called for extra resources to be given to homelessness, which was likely to grow, and for the Welsh Assembly Government to aim for an end to all homelessness by 2019.

7.31 The *Ten Year Homelessness Plan for Wales 2009–2019* aims to reduce homelessness 'to a minimum' by 2019 and to eliminate rough sleeping altogether. It will achieve those goals by preventing homelessness wherever possible, and working across organisational and policy boundaries. The Plan requires prevention services to recognise 'the need for a holistic approach to break cycles of homelessness', so that housing advice services should be providing not only advice on homelessness, and on sustaining existing homes, but also referrals for employment, training, education, financial problems and debt, and health advice. The needs of veterans, young homeless people and care-leavers, former prisoners, those fleeing domestic abuse, asylum seekers and refugees are specifically addressed, as is rural homelessness.

---

[47] *National Homelessness Strategy for Wales (2006–2008)* (Welsh Assembly Government, November 2005).

[48] Stopping short of some of the more controversial analysis in the June 2005 report.

[49] Public Services Ombudsman for Wales, 2006. See **8.75**.

7.32 Greater use of the private rented sector is contemplated. Housing support should try to reduce the number of private rented tenants who lose their homes, advice services should provide early and comprehensive information on accessing private rented accommodation, and local housing authorities should be working with the private rented sector as part of their work to tackle homelessness. Mortgage rescue schemes are to be encouraged, along with more advice available to consumers prior to their taking out mortgages. The Welsh Assembly Government wanted to see improvements in regulation and its enforcement, so that courts would only approve mortgage possession actions when lenders have explored all other options to prevent possession. It also wished to see the development of a protocol between lenders and local housing authorities so that lenders would notify local housing authority homelessness prevention teams of any possession proceedings, allowing the homelessness prevention teams to assist households.

7.33 The Plan concluded that the existing framework of HA 1996, Part 7 'does not allow everyone to receive the level of service that they need to ensure that their housing needs can be met'. It planned to review 'key areas of homelessness legislation and the duties placed on Local Authorities, especially around the area of priority need, intentionality, local connection and the discharge of duty into the private rented sector, consulting widely on specific proposals for amendments to the existing statutory framework'. It wished to ensure that 'everyone can have access to the help that they need, to secure a home that meets their needs and provides a platform from which to address their aspirations'.

7.34 In line with its policy of taking primary responsibility for homelessness policy and legislation in Wales, in 2010, the Welsh Assembly Government started to publish statistics on homelessness applications collected from local housing authorities in Wales.[50] A draft new Code of Guidance was sent out for consultation in summer 2011: *Code of Guidance for Local Authorities on Allocation of Accommodation and Homelessness*.

7.35 The Welsh Government's *Programme for Government 2011–2016* states that it plans to introduce a Housing Bill which may include a new flexible tenure allowing people to move between renting, full and shared ownership and that it is committed to continue to implement the ten-year Homelessness Plan.[51]

7.36 In May 2012, the Welsh Government published *Homes for Wales: A White Paper for Better Lives and Communities*,[52] a consultation on proposals for new legislation and for other action. Attached to the White Paper was a research report: *Impact analysis of existing homelessness legislation in Wales*.[53] The report found strong concerns about how HA 1996, Part 7 is interpreted

---

[50] First release 13 January 2010.
[51] *Programme for Government 2011–2016*, Welsh Government, 2011.
[52] Welsh Government, May 2012.
[53] January 2012, Cardiff University and others.

and applied differently across Wales, particularly in relation to homelessness prevention, priority need and intentionality. The legislation was said not to support prevention activity effectively. There was a consensus that priority need groups should be retained, as should the local connection test, but some concern was expressed that being found to have become homeless intentionally was detrimental to households. There was a lack of suitable accommodation for homeless households and particular applicants, such as prison leavers and those found to have become homeless intentionally, face poor housing outcomes. There was said to be 'some appetite' for making use of a wider range of accommodation, including private rented housing. Housing-related support was perceived to be key to successful housing outcomes.

7.37 The White Paper proposes a 'long-term vision' of 'ending family homelessness by 2019'.[54] It wants to achieve a more flexible housing system, where people can move between social housing, private rented accommodation and home ownership, to suit their needs at different times of their lives. It states that a Housing Bill will be introduced in 2013. Part of the Bill will be aimed at preventing homelessness and improving help available for those who do become homeless. Beyond 2019, the Welsh Government wants to see a future where 'homelessness does not exist'. It will achieve that by building more homes, bringing empty homes and other empty properties back into use, and improving the quality of existing homes. One Chapter deals with prevention of homelessness.[55]

7.38 The White Paper contains plans to legislate to change the definition of 'threatened with homelessness' from 28 days to 56 days,[56] and for there to be a new duty on local housing authorities to take 'all reasonable steps to achieve a suitable housing solution for all households which are homeless or threatened with homelessness'. The idea is that if a person approaches a local housing authority at an early stage, the duty would apply without any assessment of whether the applicant has a priority need, has become homeless intentionally or has a local connection. The focus will be on 'identifying a suitable solution for any individual household'.

7.39 The White Paper supports the UK Government's approach of using the private rented sector in order to bring the main housing duty to end. Somewhat surprisingly, it does not indicate when or indeed whether amendments to HA1996, Part 7, made by the Localism Act 2011 (LA 2011) will be brought into effect in Wales. The White Paper also proposes new primary legislation, which would amend HA 1996, Part 7, so that the main housing duty would come to an end if the applicant consented to an offer of a private rented sector fixed-term tenancy for a shorter period, such as six months or where the offer is of suitable supported accommodation for a minimum term. The new legislation would also permit local housing authorities to decide whether or not to apply

---

[54]   Introduction to the White Paper.
[55]   Chapter 8 of the White Paper. See **8.39–8.40** of this book.
[56]   Para 8.43 of the White Paper. See **11.129–11.133** for 'threatened with homelessness'.

the 'becoming homeless intentionally' test.[57] For households with children, that test is to be abolished altogether. The White Paper proposes that new legislation would also repeal the priority need test, but that it would not be brought into effect until such time as the 'housing solutions approach' (use of private rented sector offers) commands confidence. These are ambitious goals and further emphasise the policy distance between the UK and Welsh Governments.

7.40   In August 2012, the Welsh Government published its *Code of Guidance for Local Authorities Allocation of Accommodation and Homelessness 2012*.[58] The Code is effective from 13 August 2012 and local housing authorities in Wales should have regard to its contents from that date.[59] The Code is provided in an electronic form and can be revised and republished electronically. Users are advised to access the electronic version of the document for the most up-to-date version. In the introduction, the Minister wrote:

> 'We must also continue in our efforts to reduce homelessness, despite the challenges we are currently facing. Following a reduction in homelessness, we have begun to see the impact of the economic downturn and the forthcoming reforms to housing benefit are likely to lead to an increase in households with rent arrears who are likely to experience evictions and homelessness. This revised Code of Guidance provides a range of good practice to assist work to prevent and tackle homelessness, linked to the vision and principles of the Ten Year Homelessness Plan for Wales.'

7.41   The new Code itself contains an ambitious long-term objective: 'to end the need for anyone to sleep rough'.[60] That objective is to be achieved by greater emphasis on homelessness prevention, use of the private rented sector and early intervention with housing advice and information.[61]

7.42   Individual local housing authorities in Wales should take into account both the *Ten Year Homelessness Plan,* the national housing policy document, and the Code of Guidance, when formulating their own homelessness strategies.

Northern Ireland

7.43   Since the restoration of the Northern Ireland Executive in May 2007, policy on housing, including homelessness, has been the responsibility of the Department for Social Development. Statutory responsibility for dealing with homeless people lies with the Northern Ireland Housing Executive. Supervision is conducted by the Northern Ireland Audit Office, which produced a report on service provision for the homeless in March 2002.[62] This was followed in June 2002 by the publication of the report of the Social Development Committee's

---

[57]   See Chapter 14 of this book.
[58]   Welsh Code, see CD-Rom.
[59]   Housing Act 1996, s.182(1).
[60]   Welsh Code, para 8.59.
[61]   Chapters 8 and 10 Welsh Code.
[62]   *Housing The Homeless* (NI Audit Office, 21 March 2002).

Inquiry into Homelessness.[63] The Northern Ireland Housing Executive published its own first Homelessness Strategy in September 2002.[64]

7.44 In July 2007 and after a three-year consultation period, the Department for Social Development published *Including the Homeless, a Strategy to promote the social inclusion of homeless people, and those at risk of becoming homeless, in Northern Ireland.*[65]

7.45 Section 1 of the Housing (Amendment) Act (Northern Ireland) 2010 placed a statutory duty on the Northern Ireland Housing Executive to develop and publish a five year homelessness strategy. In 2011, the Housing Executive consulted on a draft Homelessness Strategy 2011 – 2016,[66] which also contained a review of the 2002 strategy. The Northern Ireland Housing Executive stated that its policies are geared to helping people avoid homelessness, helping them escape from homelessness and supporting people when they get a home.

7.46 In April 2012, the Northern Ireland Housing Executive published its *Homelessness Strategy for Northern Ireland 2012–2017.*[67] This contains similarly ambitious targets to those of the Welsh Government[68] or Scottish Executive[69]: to eliminate long term homelessness and rough sleeping across Northern Ireland by 2020. It plans to do so by placing homelessness prevention at the forefront of service delivery; reducing the length of time that households and individuals experience homelessness by improving access to affordable housing; removing the need to sleep rough; and improving services to vulnerable homeless households and individuals. The strategy is progressed and monitored by the Department for Social Development.

7.47 The number of households presenting as homeless in Northern Ireland increased from 16,426 in 2002/03 to over 20,000 in 2005/06. That number remained static until 2010/11 when 20,158 applicants presented as homeless. Nearly 1.47% of all households in Northern Ireland are homeless (in that they have been accepted as owed a duty by the Executive), a similar percentage to households in Scotland but a significantly greater proportion than in England or Wales.[70]

---

[63] *Second Report on the Inquiry into Housing in Northern Ireland* (Social Development Committee of the Northern Ireland Assembly, June 2002).
[64] *The Homelessness Strategy* (Northern Ireland Housing Executive, September 2002.
[65] Department for Social Development, July 2007.
[66] Northern Ireland Housing Executive, 2011.
[67] Northern Ireland Housing Executive, 2012.
[68] See **7.37–7.41**.
[69] See **7.52**.
[70] *Homelessness Strategy for Northern Ireland 2012–2017* (Northern Ireland Housing Executive, April 2012).

Scotland

7.48 At national policy level, homelessness in Scotland is the responsibility of the Scottish Executive. Soon after devolution in 1999, the Executive established a Homelessness Task Force charged with mapping out a programme to address the issue of homelessness in Scotland.

7.49 The initial report of the Task Force (in April 2000) led in due course to the amendment of the statutory homelessness scheme in Scotland, until then contained in the Housing (Scotland) Act 1987, by the Housing (Scotland) Act 2001.

7.50 The final report of the Task Force, *Homelessness: an action plan for prevention and effective response*,[71] set out a 12-year action programme to eliminate and thereafter prevent homelessness in Scotland. The subsequent Homelessness etc (Scotland) Act 2003 contains radical statutory measures designed to implement the Task Force recommendations. These include the enlargement and eventual abolition of priority need categories, the abolition of the local connection referral arrangements, and an obligation to accommodate all the homeless (including the intentionally homeless).

7.51 In May 2004 the Executive issued a new Code of Guidance on Homelessness: *Guidance on legislation, policies and practices to prevent and resolve homelessness*.[72] The Code of Guidance was updated and re-published in May 2005: *Code of Guidance on homelessness*.[73] An addition to the Code of Guidance was published in June 2009: *Prevention of Homelessness Guidance*.[74]

7.52 The ambitions contained in the Homelessness etc (Scotland) Act 2003 have now been modified into a target that all unintentionally homeless households should have a right to settled accommodation by the end of 2012, generally referred to as 'the 2012 homelessness commitment'.[75]

7.53 The statutory responsibility for providing homelessness services in Scotland falls upon the Scottish local authorities. Delivery of around a quarter of the Task Force recommendations and the 2012 homelessness commitment will depend on their being adopted by the 32 local authorities and then incorporated into the homelessness strategies already prepared by them and submitted to the Executive.

7.54 A joint steering group between the Scottish Executive and the Convention of Scottish Local Authorities (CoSLA) was established to monitor progress in October 2009.

---

[71] February 2002.
[72] Scottish Executive, 2004.
[73] Scottish Executive, 2005.
[74] Scottish Executive, June 2009.
[75] *The 2012 homelessness commitment: a background note from Shelter Scotland* (Shelter Scotland, 2011).

7.55 The Scottish Executive monitors implementation of the target by the publication of homelessness statistics based on returns from local authorities. These statistics show that an increasing number of Scottish local authorities are assessing all applicants for homelessness assistance as having a priority, in other words not applying the priority need test, and therefore meeting the 2012 homelessness commitment. Secondary legislation has also been issued permitting local authorities to use the private rented sector in order to perform accommodation duties to applicants.[76]

7.56 The Executive's Minister has power to reject local homelessness strategies submitted by those local authorities.[77]

REGIONAL STRATEGIES

7.57 In England, steps were initially taken towards the development of regional homelessness strategies. In 2003, Regional Housing Boards were established to develop strategic housing policy for the regions. That role passed to the eight Regional Assemblies in England, plus the Mayor of London, in September 2006. Except for the Greater London Assembly, Regional Assemblies in England were abolished between 2008 and March 2010, and replaced by Local Authorities' Leaders Boards: voluntary associations of council leaders. Following the formation of the Coalition Government, funding to those boards has been withdrawn.

7.58 All of the Regional Assemblies had Regional Housing Strategies. The West Midlands Regional Assembly, the East of England Regional Assembly, the North West Regional Assembly and the East Midlands Regional Assembly also published Regional Homelessness Strategies.

7.59 In London, responsibility for housing and homelessness strategy was given to the Mayor in 2006. The London Boroughs retain the statutory obligation for the delivery of homelessness services under HA 1996, Part 7, and must also publish their own homelessness strategies and reviews. In September 2007, the then Mayor of London published a draft housing strategy for consultation.[78] Five specific aims on homelessness were set out:

- borough homelessness strategies would be expected to demonstrate how targets will be achieved, and how the numbers of rough sleepers, and people waiting for 'move-on' accommodation would be rehoused;

- borough homelessness strategies would be expected to focus on prevention where possible but not to seek to achieve government targets through gate-keeping;

---

[76] Homeless Persons (Provision of Non-permanent Accommodation) (Scotland) Regulations 2010 (Scottish SI 2010/2), in force 25 February 2010.
[77] Housing (Scotland) Act 2001, s 1(6).
[78] *Draft Housing Strategy* (Greater London Assembly, September 2007).

- boroughs would be expected to make greater use of private rented homes to discharge their responsibilities, but only if the homes were offered on a long tenancy from an accredited landlord;

- boroughs would be expected to support temporary to settled schemes, where those schemes provide more settled homes, more affordable rents and social assets; and

- boroughs would be expected to sign up to cross-London protocols to improve the response to homeless people who move across borough boundaries.

7.60   The emphasis in the draft Housing Strategy 2007 was on increasing the supply of affordable housing.

7.61   Following the election of a new Mayor of London in 2008, a London Delivery Board was established by him with the aim of ending rough sleeping by 2012. In February 2009, *Ending rough sleeping – the London Delivery Board* was published.[79] The aim was to be achieved by working with hostels, developing a specialist project for rough sleepers with multiple needs, working with the United Kingdom Border Agency (UKBA) and Jobcentre Plus to help rough sleepers who have no resource to public funds and working with the London boroughs and other providers of services to rough sleepers and hostel users. Progress reports are published annually.

7.62   The Mayor of London's first statutory housing strategy was published in February 2010: *The London Housing Strategy*.[80] In the foreword, the Mayor wrote:

> 'Tackling homelessness and reducing overcrowding are two of my key priorities, with targets to end rough sleeping by 2012 and to halve severe overcrowding among social tenants by 2016.'

7.63   Homelessness was to be tackled by building more homes, including social rented homes, supporting the Government's mortgage rescue scheme so as to prevent homelessness as a result of owners being unable to pay their mortgages, and encouraging the use of private rented properties for homeless applicants. The Strategy also committed itself to the then government's target of halving the number of households in temporary accommodation by the end of 2010. This was to be achieved through increased use of homelessness prevention and partnership work with private registered providers.

7.64   A *Revised London Housing Strategy* was issued for consultation in December 2011.[81] The draft Strategy contains a presumption that local housing authorities should perform their accommodation duties under HA 1996,

---

[79]   February 2009, the Mayor of London.
[80]   February 2010, the Mayor of London.
[81]   *Revised London Housing Strategy* (Mayor of London, December 2011).

Part 7, within their local area, and should maintain an 'appropriate balance' between offers of private rented properties and of social housing. Where private rented sector offers are to be used,[82] the Strategy encourages local housing authorities to offer tenancies for a longer period than the statutory minimum of 12 months and only to use landlords with recognised accreditation. The Mayor proposes to set up a joint monitoring committee to monitor the performance of accommodation duties by local housing authorities under HA 1996, Part 7. The London Delivery Board will continue to monitor rough sleeping and aim to achieve the outcome that no one spends a second night on the streets, through the *No Second Night Out* pilot.[83] As with the 2010 Strategy, the emphasis is on increasing housing supply, including the supply of affordable housing.

7.65 The No Second Night Out strategy, which was piloted in London by ten London boroughs, is now to be applied by local housing authorities in England, which are outside of the London area.[84] The pilot operates a 24-hour assessment hub, which assesses the needs of new rough sleepers and provides them with a single service offer as an alternative to rough sleeping. Rough sleepers are identified by outreach teams on the streets, by housing options teams and by members of the public (who call a 24-hour referral line or can access a website). Over the first six-month period of the pilot, 415 rough sleepers had been helped to move quickly off the streets and into accommodation. Some rough sleepers were helped to return to their original home areas, either elsewhere in the UK or abroad. Rough sleepers helped by the pilot were less likely to return to rough sleeping in London. The accommodation arranged was generally either bed and breakfast or hostel accommodation, with a view then to moving on into private rented sector accommodation.[85]

7.66 From April 2012, the Mayor of London, with the Greater London Assembly, has been responsible for strategic housing in London.[86]

LOCAL HOMELESSNESS STRATEGIES AND REVIEWS

Overview

7.67 The Homelessness Act 2002[87] introduced a statutory duty on local housing authorities to formulate and publish local homelessness strategies. The relevant provisions of the Homelessness Act 2002 came into force on 31 July 2002 for local housing authorities in England and 30 September 2002 for local housing authorities in Wales.

---

[82] See **17.109–17.131** for private rented sector offer.
[83] See **7.19–7.21** and **7.65**.
[84] See **7.19–7.21**.
[85] *No Second Night Out: an evaluation of the first six months of the project* (Broadway, University of York and Crunch Consulting, December 2011).
[86] Greater London Authority Act 1999, s 333A as amended by Localism Act 2011, s 188.
[87] HA 2002 (HA 2002), ss 1–4, see Appendix 2 of this book.

7.68 Local housing authorities were required to publish their first local homelessness strategy within a year, ie by 31 July 2003 for local housing authorities in England and by 30 September 2003 for local housing authorities in Wales. They are required to keep the local strategies under review, and modify them if necessary. At the very least, they must publish new strategies every five years,[88] unless they have been categorised as 'excellent', '4-stars' or '3-stars' local authorities in England, in which case that duty has been disapplied by regulations.[89] This meant that all other local housing authorities had to publish new homelessness strategies by 31 July 2008 in England (30 September 2008 in Wales) and will have to publish their third homelessness strategies by 31 July 2013 [England] or 30 September 2013 [Wales].

7.69 The purpose of preparing a local strategy is to enable local housing authorities to have an accurate picture of the levels of homelessness in their district, and to set out the steps to be taken in order to tackle and prevent homelessness.

7.70 Of course, to devise an effective local strategy, the local housing authority must have access to the raw data on the extent of homelessness in its area and on the current prevention programmes and local initiatives to tackle it. The Homelessness Act 2002, therefore, requires every local housing authority to conduct a 'review' of such matters, in relation to its area, so that the design and content of the local strategy may be undertaken on the best possible information.[90]

7.71 In short, the *review* is meant to paint the picture on homelessness locally and the *strategy* is intended to set out how the problem is to be addressed.

7.72 The fundamental objectives underlying the requirement both for a review and for a strategy are:

(1)   identifying action that can be taken to prevent homelessness;

(2)   providing suitable services and accommodation for people who are, or may become homeless; and

(3)   supporting people who are homeless or potentially homeless and those who were formerly homeless and need support, to prevent them becoming homeless again.[91]

7.73 The Homelessness Act 2002 and the Codes of Guidance all emphasise a multi-agency approach, with co-operation between local housing authorities

---

[88]   HA 2002, s 1(3) and (4).

[89]   Local Authorities' Plans and Strategies (Disapplication) (England) Order 2005, SI 2005/157, art 3, as amended by the Local Authorities' Plans and Strategies (Disapplication) (England) (Amendment) Order 2009, SI 2009/714; English Code, para 1.42.

[90]   HA 2002, s 1(1)(a).

[91]   HA 2002, ss 2(2) and 3(1).

and adult care and children's services, and with consultation and joint working with other public authorities, voluntary organisations and individuals in the undertaking of the review and in the formulation of the strategy.[92]

7.74 The strategies, once produced, should not be filed away to gather dust. Both local housing authorities and the relevant adult care and children's services authorities are required to take the contents of the local homelessness strategy into account when exercising other statutory functions, such as decisions on homelessness and allocation and the performance of duties owed to young people, families with children and other vulnerable people.[93] As this Chapter indicates, the requirement to have regard to them in day-to-day work will enable strategies to be used as legal tools, where appropriate.

7.75 There is no statutory timetable for the undertaking, production or publication of the initial homelessness *review* (or any subsequent reviews). In practice, many local housing authorities published both their initial review and initial strategy documents together or, indeed, incorporated the homelessness review into the first local homelessness strategy. Since the strategy must be based on the findings in the review, it follows that a review should always be carried out first.

7.76 Because the statutory requirement to prepare a homelessness strategy was entirely novel when brought into force in 2003, considerable resources were deployed to assist local housing authorities with the task of formulating their first strategies. The UK government provided additional financial resources to assist local housing authorities in England in drawing up their local reviews and strategies. Substantial written guidance was provided to local housing authorities. This included: *Homelessness Strategies: A Good Practice Handbook*[94] and *Preventing tomorrow's rough sleepers: a good practice handbook*,[95] and they were in turn followed by publication of the Homelessness Codes of Guidance providing more assistance.

7.77 Those representing special interest groups lobbied hard for particular consideration to be given to specific aspects of the homelessness issue. The UK Coalition on Older Homelessness, for example, produced *Local Homelessness Strategies and Older People* in April 2003. The group Health Action at Crisis published *A Checklist on Health for Local Authorities and PCTS working on their Homelessness Strategy* in February 2003. Least well served (it would seem) were the interests of the gypsy and travelling community. The Local

[92] HA 2002, s 1(2) and s 3(2)–(4); English Code, paras 1.39–1.41, Chapter 5 and Annexes 3, 5–6; Welsh Code, paras 8.7, 8.17–8.29. For example of guidance on joint working see *Provision of Accommodation for 16 and 17 year old young people who may be homeless and/or require Accommodation* (April 2010, CLG and Children, Schools and Families) and *Provision of Accommodation for 16 and 17 year old young people who may be homeless* (Welsh Assembly Government, September 2010).
[93] HA 2002, s 1(5) and (6).
[94] Department for Transport, Local Government and the Regions, 13 March 2002.
[95] ODPM, June 2001. See also English Code, para 1.4 and Annex 1.

Government Association (LGA) was subsequently to find that 62% of the initial round of strategies (2003–2008) made no reference to the needs of homeless travellers at all.[96]

7.78 At local level, the individual reviews and strategies are expected to take into account other local authority and national government plans and strategies relevant to addressing the causes of homelessness.[97] From 15 January 2012, the strategies must also take into account the local housing authority's own allocation scheme and tenancy strategy.[98] London borough councils must take into account the current London housing strategy.[99] Joint working with adult care and children's services departments or authorities (in the case of non-unitary authorities) is a statutory requirement,[100] and local housing authorities are encouraged to involve other public authorities, such as health authorities, the police, private registered providers or registered social landlords and private landlords, voluntary organisations and other organisations and individuals.[101]

7.79 By the end of 2003, every local housing authority in England and Wales had complied with the duty to conduct a review and had adopted and published a strategy, and most local housing authorities had repeated that exercise in 2008. Copies of those strategies are relatively easy to obtain. Local housing authorities now maintain websites on which their reviews and strategies may be posted. Initially, copies of most local housing authorities' reviews and strategies were helpfully gathered together and links to them published by Homelessness Link. That exercise does not seem to have been repeated or brought up-to-date. Hard copies of local reviews and strategies are available from individual local housing authorities on request.[102]

7.80 A review of the content or methodology in the many hundreds of local housing authorities' published reviews and strategies is beyond the scope of this book. However, between 2003 and 2008, there were several useful reviews of initial local homelessness strategies.

7.81 In January 2004, Shelter published *The Act in Action, an assessment of homelessness reviews and strategies.*[103] Shelter's conclusion was that:

'… compiling reviews and strategies appears to have produced positive outcomes beyond simply delivering an assessment of homelessness levels and patterns. In a

---

[96]   *Homelessness Strategies: A Survey of Local Authorities, Research Briefing 6.04* (Local Government Association, October 2004), and see now the English Code, para 1.5.

[97]   English Code, paras 1.3–1.4, and Annex 1; Welsh Code, paras 8.6, 8.12, 8.46–8.49, 8.53.

[98]   HA 2002 s 3(7A)(a) and (b) inserted by LA 2011 s 153, in force from 15 January 2012 and applicable to local housing authorities in both England and Wales.

[99]   HA 2002 s 3(7A)(c) inserted by LA 2011 s 153, in force from 15 January 2012. For the current London housing strategy see **7.64–7.65** of this book.

[100] HA 2002, s 1(2) and (6).

[101] English Code, para 1.39 and Chapter 5; Welsh Code, paras 8.23–8.29.

[102] HA 2002, ss 2(3) and 3(9) and see **7.133–7.135** and **7.181–7.183**.

[103] *The Act in Action, an assessment of homelessness reviews and strategies* (Shelter, January 2004).

broader sense, it has enabled authorities to identify gaps in their knowledge (even where these gaps are yet to be tackled), build stronger relationships with other departments and agencies and develop a multi-agency approach not just to homelessness, but also to wider issues.'

7.82 A more detailed national picture was given in *Homelessness strategies – a survey of local authorities* published by the LGA.[104] It contained the troubling finding that only 52% of local housing authorities thought that the exercise of preparing a strategy would help to any extent in determining likely future levels of homelessness in their areas.

7.83 The UK government undertook that its Homelessness Directorate would assess the strategies drawn up, notwithstanding that there is no statutory role for ministerial interference with local strategies such as that contained in the scheme in Scotland.[105] In August 2003 it announced that each local housing authority was required to lodge a copy of its strategy with the Directorate. During the first half of 2004, Housing Quality Network Services carried out an evaluation of those strategies (and consulted a number of local housing authorities in England). A summary of that evaluation was published (*Local Authorities' Homelessness Strategies: Evaluation and Good Practice*)[106] and local housing authorities were encouraged to refer to it in carrying out future local homelessness reviews and drawing up further local strategies.[107] The research considered both homelessness reviews and homelessness strategies.

7.84 The analysis of homelessness *reviews* revealed that:

- most local housing authorities worked well at understanding the causes of, and current levels of, homelessness but few estimated future levels of homelessness;

- the availability of data, particularly about the scale and causes of homelessness for those persons considered to be in 'non-priority groups', was acknowledged as a difficulty;

- the main causes of homelessness were:
  - parents/friends/relatives no longer willing or able to accommodate; or
  - violent relationship breakdown with a partner; or
  - the termination of an assured shorthold tenancy;

---

[104] *Homelessness Strategies: A Survey of Local Authorities, Research Briefing 6.04* (Local Government Association, October 2004).
[105] See **7.56**.
[106] *Local Authorities' Homelessness Strategies: Evaluation and Good Practice* (ODPM, 2003).
[107] English Code, para 1.4.

- all local housing authorities provided some information about the current services available, and most had gone further and mapped advice services provided in other sectors, and accommodation provided by other organisations;

- nine out of ten local housing authorities included prevention of homelessness in their reviews, although some had not taken a wide enough view of prevention;

- four out of five local housing authorities considered all forms of homelessness, although one in five confined themselves to groups who would be in priority need;

- many local housing authorities missed particular client groups;

- the groups most frequently missed were single homeless people and/or rough sleepers, ex-services personnel, black and minority ethnic groups, former asylum seekers and gypsies or travellers;

- the key priority groups most often identified by local housing authorities for particular attention were:
  - young people;
  - women and their children who are victims of domestic violence; and
  - people with drug or alcohol problems;

- although many local housing authorities had consulted widely with other agencies and groups, the involvement of adult care and children's services at a strategic level was considered disappointing and other statutory agencies such as the health and probation service were also hard to engage; and

- local housing authorities had generally found it difficult to engage with, and consult, homeless people and service users.

7.85 When it came to homelessness *strategies*, the evaluation concluded:

- the great majority of strategies were clearly based on findings from the homelessness reviews;

- consultation with service users or other agencies had resulted in a new emphasis on prevention or other new approaches in the strategies;

- local housing authorities had focused on tackling rough sleeping and the use of bed and breakfast accommodation, although a number had failed to identify solutions and a small number had increased, rather than decreased, their use of bed and breakfast accommodation;

- only two in five local housing authorities managed to address the issue of wider links with other agencies and only about half demonstrated corporate or wider commitment in their strategies;

- most local housing authorities included all forms of homelessness within their strategy, but a significant number confined themselves to statutorily homeless groups;

- some local housing authorities engaged with black and minority ethnic communities, but many neglected those issues;

- strategies contained a number of innovative ideas for prevention and support activities;

- district councils were less developed in partnership-working than unitary or metropolitan councils;

- a lack of action planning was a weak point in many strategies; and

- many local housing authorities had not identified resources necessary to implement the whole of their strategy.

7.86 The ODPM issued a policy briefing *Homelessness Strategies: Moving Forward* based on this evaluation.[108] The document recommended that local housing authorities in England bring forward plans for comprehensively reviewing their homelessness strategies. It suggested that they should be:

- ensuring greater involvement from the voluntary sector;

- engaging in more co-operation with other authorities, regions and agencies;

- working with Supporting People authorities; and

- taking a more multi-agency approach.

7.87 Much of the material in the Policy Briefing was taken forward into the content of the July 2006 edition of the English *Code of Guidance for Local Authorities*.

7.88 Following publication of the Code, the CLG published *Preventing Homelessness: A Strategy Health Check*,[109] which will have been used by local housing authorities in preparing their new strategies in 2008. There was no

---

[108] ODPM, November 2004.
[109] CLG, September 2006.

attempt by DCLG to repeat in 2008–2009 its earlier exercise of calling in, for review and evaluation, the individual strategies of local housing authorities in England.

7.89 The remainder of this Chapter will outline the detailed legal duties imposed on local housing authorities in relation to local homelessness reviews and strategies, the powers given to them, and the guidance that has been provided. All statutory references in this Chapter, unlike the rest of this book, are to the Homelessness Act 2002 (and not to the Housing Act 1996) unless specifically stated.

7.90 To avoid confusion, it is necessary to emphasise that a local 'Homelessness Strategy' is not the same thing as a local 'Housing Strategy' nor the local 'tenancy strategy'. The housing strategy is required by the terms of any direction made under the Local Government Act 2003[110] and the tenancy strategy is required by the Localism Act 2011 and must be prepared and published by 15 January 2013.[111] Both strategies are beyond the scope of this book. However, the English Code does suggest that the housing and homelessness strategies may be combined in one document where 'it is consistent to do so'.[112] Indeed, Annex 2 of the English Code lists no fewer than 25 strategies and programmes, in addition to the local housing authority's housing and tenancy strategies, that may address homelessness and which the local homelessness strategy may need to take account of. The Welsh Code recommends that the duty to have a homelessness strategy should be met within the framework of the local housing strategy, so that there should just be one document.[113]

A power or a duty to have local reviews and strategies?

7.91 Strictly speaking, HA 2002 gives power to local housing authorities to carry out homelessness reviews for their districts and to formulate and publish homelessness strategies based on the results of those reviews.[114]

7.92 However, HA 2002 also set out mandatory time-scales for the publication of the first local homelessness strategies and of further strategies thereafter. It thereby converted the *power* to formulate and publish the strategy into a *duty*.[115]

7.93 The intention is that strategies will follow the local homelessness review. Homelessness strategies are defined as being 'based on the results of that

---

[110] Local Government Act 2003, s 87.
[111] LA 2011, s 150, in force 15 January 2012.
[112] English Code, para 1.2.
[113] Welsh Code, para 8.3.
[114] HA 2002, s 1(1).
[115] HA 2002, s 1(3) and (4).

review'.[116] It follows that local housing authorities are under a *duty* both to conduct reviews and to formulate and publish strategies.[117]

A power or a duty to have regard to the local strategy?

7.94 Once the strategy has been published, the local housing authority is under a *duty* to take its content into account when exercising its homelessness functions or, indeed, any of its other statutory functions.[118] The strategy should therefore inform, for example, a local housing authority's allocation policy as well as the decisions on any individual homelessness application.

7.95 In *R (Ho-Sang) v Lewisham London Borough Council*,[119] an applicant for homelessness assistance, who had not been provided with interim accommodation to which she was entitled, brought a test case challenging the local housing authority's routine and systematic practice of turning away applicants without providing interim accommodation. The judicial review claim cited the local housing authority's homelessness review, which had identified the provision of interim accommodation as being a major problem for the local housing authority, and attacked the homelessness strategy, which only made provision for 50 additional units of temporary accommodation. The local housing authority settled the judicial review claim by conceding that the strategy was inadequate and agreeing to take measures to acquire additional units for interim accommodation (in addition to accepting that it owed the claimant a duty to provide interim accommodation which it would perform).

Duty on adult care and children's services to co-operate

7.96 In the case of non-unitary authorities, the adult care and children's services authorities are under a duty to give their local housing authority (or authorities) such assistance as the local housing authority (or authorities) may reasonably require with both the carrying out of the local review and the formulation of the homelessness strategy.[120] Examples of the types of assistance that might be required are given in the Homelessness Codes of Guidance for both England and Wales. They range through:

- providing information to the local housing authority, as part of the review process;

- providing financial assistance so as to prevent homelessness; and

---

[116] HA 2002, s 1(1)(b).
[117] Except for those local housing authorities in England which have been categorised as 'excellent', '4-stars', or '3-stars', see **7.68**.
[118] HA 2002, s 1(5), further discussed at **7.197–7.199**.
[119] *R (Ho-Sang) v Lewisham London Borough Council* (2004) CO/5652/03, (2004) July *Legal Action*, p 19, Admin Ct.
[120] HA 2002, s 1(2).

- providing support with homeless persons' associated needs.[121]

7.97 Once the exercise has been completed and a local homelessness strategy has been drawn up, the adult care and children's services authorities are under a duty to take the homelessness strategy into account when carrying out their functions.[122] This duty may particularly assist young people, or disabled people, who are homeless and also have needs for support or assistance from adult care or children's services authorities or departments.

7.98 In the case of unitary authorities, the same obligations apply to the adult care and children's services departments to provide assistance at the strategy design stage and to take account of the strategy in the performance of their own functions.[123]

Duty on private registered providers and registered social landlords to co-operate

7.99 Private registered providers [England] and registered social landlords [Wales] are under a duty to co-operate with local housing authorities to assist them in performing their functions under HA 1996, Parts 6 and 7, if requested, and so far as is reasonable.[124]

7.100 They would normally expect to be consulted by local housing authorities before homelessness strategies are adopted or modified.[125]

7.101 In England, the *Revised Regulatory Framework for social housing in England from April 2012*, published by the Homes and Communities Agency, requires private registered providers to co-operate with local housing authorities' strategic housing functions and their duties to meet local housing needs and provide assistance in meeting homelessness duties.[126]

7.102 In Wales, the *Regulatory Framework for Housing Associations Registered in Wales*[127] requires registered social landlords to support local housing authorities in the delivery of their strategic housing roles. In addition, the Welsh Government published *Housing Association Circular RSL 003/12*[128] simultaneously with the Welsh Code. That Circular advises that housing associations should take account of the Welsh Code when addressing key

---

[121] English Code, paras 1.6–1.8 and 1.10 and Chapters 5 and 13; Welsh Code, para 8.17–8.18.
[122] HA 2002, s 1(6).
[123] HA 2002, s 1(6); English Code, para 1.6; Welsh Code, para 8.17–8.18.
[124] HA 1996, ss 170 and 213(1).
[125] HA 2002, s 3(8).
[126] *Revised Regulatory Framework for social housing in England from April 2012* (Homes and Communities Agency, 2012).
[127] Welsh Government, December 2011.
[128] Welsh Government, August 2012.

delivery outcomes for the *Regulatory Framework* and are expected to work with local housing authorities and other partners to help them meet housing need in their areas.

7.103 Both governments and the the regulatory bodies for social landlords[129] have encouraged private registered providers and registered social landlords to play a more active role in working with local housing authorities to prevent homelessness and to tackle it.[130] The English Code, Annex 5 contains a full account of the extent to which private registered providers and local housing authorities are expected to co-operate in addressing homelessness. In early 2006, the Housing Corporation consulted on how to encourage private registered providers to help develop local housing authority homelessness strategies. The results of the consultation were published in the then Housing Corporation's *Tackling Homelessness: the Housing Corporation Strategy*.[131] The strategy emphasised that private registered providers must fulfill their statutory duty to work with local housing authorities to tackle homelessness and must entrench prevention of homelessness and tenancy sustainment in their work.

LOCAL HOMELESSNESS REVIEWS[132]

7.104 Since the homelessness strategy must be based on the results of the homelessness review, the review must logically be carried out and concluded first (although in the first round of the exercise in 2003 many local housing authorities published both documents simultaneously, or published their review and strategy within the same document).

7.105 The review is an audit of the local scene in relation to homelessness. It is defined to mean a review of:

(1)   the levels and likely future levels of homelessness in the local housing authority's district;[133]

(2)   the activities which are carried out in the district for the purpose of preventing homelessness, securing accommodation for people who are or may be homeless, or providing support for those people or for formerly homeless people who need support to prevent them becoming homeless again;[134] and

---

[129] In England, the regulatory body is the Homes and Communities Agency. In Wales, it is the Welsh Government.

[130] See, for example, *Effective Co-operation in Tackling Homelessness: Nominations and Exclusions* (ODPM, Housing Corporation, Local Government Association and National Housing Federation, November 2004), and *Homelessness Prevention and Housing Associations – Contributing to Efficiency* (Housing Corporation and Chartered Institute of Housing, April 2006).

[131] Housing Corporation, November 2006.

[132] HA 2002, s 2.

[133] HA 2002, s 2(1)(a).

[134] HA 2002, s 2(1)(b) and (2).

(3)   the resources available to the local housing authority, the adult care and children's services authorities, other public authorities, voluntary organisations and other persons in the district for carrying out these activities.[135]

7.106   Each of those aspects will be considered in turn.

What is meant by 'homelessness' for the purposes of conducting the review?

7.107   To be able to assess current and future levels of homelessness with any accuracy, the review must apply the relevant meaning of 'homelessness'. But there can be different interpretations of that concept. Does it mean the likely numbers of applicants to the local housing authority for HA 1996, Part 7 assistance? Or does it have a more practical interpretation, referring to the likely number of people who will be homeless, whether they seek the help of the local housing authority or not? Does it refer simply to literal street homelessness or does it also include those living in temporary or insecure accommodation?

7.108   The English Code advises local housing authorities that they should 'take account of *all* forms of homelessness within the meaning of [Part 7 of] the 1996 Act'.[136] Local housing authorities in England should not, therefore, consider only those applicants towards whom the main housing duty[137] has been accepted in the past, or would be accepted in the future. They should ensure that homeless people who do not have a priority need, or who are or have become or may become intentionally homeless, also fall within the scope of the review. The Codes specifically refer to 'people sleeping rough', as well as 'those who might be more difficult to identify'.[138] The review should therefore consider those who are likely, in future, to have no accommodation that they are entitled to occupy and also those who do have (or will have) accommodation that is not reasonable for them to continue to occupy.

7.109   The Welsh Code contains a different definition of homelessness drawn up by the Welsh Government –'where a person lacks accommodation or where their tenure is not secure' – and gives examples of the types of people, and the types of accommodation, that would fall within that definition.[139]

7.110   The Welsh approach is much broader than that contained in the English Code, drawing attention to the needs of those in insecure accommodation as well as those who are literally roofless. However, the statutory emphasis (on preventing homelessness, identifying those who might become homeless in the

---

[135]   HA 2002, s 2(1)(c),
[136]   English Code, para 1.13.
[137]   HA 1996, s 193. See **17.23–17.131**.
[138]   For a discussion on the definition of homelessness contained in HA 1996, ss 175–177, see Chapter 11 of this book. See further English Code, paras 1.13–1.18; Welsh Code, para 8.14.
[139]   Welsh Code, para 8.14.

future, and providing support to those who are potentially homeless) should mean that, in practice, local housing authorities in England and Wales are considering the same groups of people when undertaking their reviews.

Current and future levels of homelessness in the local housing authority's district

7.111   The review will need to analyse data on local homelessness in the recent past, on current homelessness, and on likely future homelessness.

7.112   The local housing authority will have its own records and statistics of the number of homelessness applications it has received in the past, and the outcome of those applications. It will also regularly compile returns for the UK and Welsh governments' statistics.[140] However, the review should not be confined to those records of past homelessness alone.

7.113   The local housing authority should take into account any information it possesses (or can find with reasonable diligence) on the local homelessness problem. That will include counts or estimates of the numbers of people sleeping rough and estimates of the numbers of people who are staying with family or friends on a temporary or insecure basis. The local housing authority can also consider its own records of the numbers (and outcomes) of possession proceedings it has brought, and the records held by the local court and by local private registered providers or registered social landlords. Local advice agencies may hold records and statistics on the numbers of clients who seek homelessness or housing advice. Hospitals, prisons, the armed forces, and the National Offender Management Service[141] should all have records of people discharged from their various services who had nowhere to live. Children's services departments or authorities should be asked for their records on homeless families with children, young people leaving care and children in need requiring accommodation. Local hostels and refuges should also be asked for records and statistics.[142] This should provide, in its totality, a fairly accurate picture of both past and current homelessness.

7.114   In order to predict *future* levels of homelessness in the district, the local housing authority will need to identify those groups of people most likely to be at risk of homelessness, the reasons why they might become homeless and the extent to which the supply of affordable accommodation locally is likely to increase or decrease.

7.115   The Codes suggest that young people estranged from their families or leaving care, vulnerable people leaving the armed forces or prison, people exposed to domestic or other violence or abuse, vulnerable people with mental

---

[140]   In England: *Statutory Homelessness Quarterly Statistics* (Department for Communities and Local Government). In Wales, *Homelessness Statistics* (Welsh Government). See also **7.15** [England] and **7.34** [Wales].

[141]   Formerly the Probation Service.

[142]   English Code, para 1.14; Welsh Code, paras 8.56–8.65.

health problems, learning disabilities, age-related problems or ill health, people with drug and alcohol problems, people with debt problems, those suffering harassment or abuse from outside the home, and former asylum seekers given permission to stay in the UK, are likely to be amongst those with a higher risk of homelessness.[143]

7.116 Drawing up a 'profile of those who have experienced homelessness' is recommended in the Codes.[144] Such a profile would consider:

- where the person became homeless;

- why;

- the tenure of accommodation from which he or she became homeless;

- his or her personal characteristics, such as ethnic background;

- any institutional or care background;

- age;

- employment or benefits history;

- any specific vulnerabilities;

- any health or drug needs;

- the overall composition of the household; and

- other elements.

7.117 Local factors that affect the future levels of homelessness should be considered, such as:

- the extent to which affordable accommodation is available;

- property prices;

- rent levels; and

- supply of accommodation in the private rented sector, from private registered providers or registered social landlords and from the local housing authority's own stock.

---

[143] English Code, para 1.15; Welsh Code, para 8.66.
[144] English Code, para 1.16; Welsh Code, paras 8.61–8.65.

7.118   Broader factors such as:

- the extent of redevelopment and regeneration activity;

- unemployment;

- the strength of the local economy;

- the local population and projected trends in demography;

- the level of migration into and out of the district;

- the flow of itinerant populations such as gypsies, travellers and rough sleepers; and

- the numbers of people likely to be homeless on leaving the armed forces, the care system, prison, hospital or UKBA accommodation

are also relevant.[145]

7.119   The identification of the current and future levels of homelessness in the district is therefore a substantial task, involving social and economic mapping and projections. Bare statistics of current or recent applications for homelessness assistance will certainly not suffice.[146]

7.120   The UK government-commissioned evaluation of homelessness strategies in 2003 found that many local housing authorities in England had difficulties in assessing future levels of homelessness. Local housing authorities that tackled the issue well had used: population trends; indicators of needs, demands and aspirations from Housing Needs Surveys; trends in homelessness data; and plans for prevention through, for example, advice to those leaving prison, hospital or care.[147]

Current activities being carried out

7.121   This is the second matter that HA 2002 requires to be considered within the local homelessness review.[148] The required review of activities currently being carried out should not be confined to the activity of the local housing authority's own homeless persons' department or officer(s).

7.122   The current 'activities' to be reviewed are defined as activities for the purposes of:

---

[145]   English Code, para 1.17; Welsh Code, para 8.71.
[146]   Welsh Code, paras 8.70–8.72.
[147]   *Local Authorities' Homelessness Strategies: Evaluation and Good Practice* (ODPM Homelessness Research Summary, Number 1, 2004). See also **7.83–7.85**.
[148]   HA 2002, s 2(1)(b).

(1)   preventing homelessness in the local housing authority's district;

(2)   securing that accommodation is or will be available for people who are currently homeless or may become homeless; and

(3)   providing support for those people and for people who were formerly homeless and need support to prevent them becoming homeless again.[149]

7.123 The Codes recommend that the activities, and resources, of a wide range of public authorities and voluntary organisations be considered,[150] but local housing authorities should not confine themselves to those organisations referred to in the Code. They should be considering:

> '... the activities of *all* the various agencies and organisations, across all sectors, which are providing, or contributing to the provision of accommodation, support or relevant services in the district'[151]

including organisations not traditionally associated with housing support such as education or employment organisations, the Samaritans, the police, and faith groups.[152]

7.124 Activities for the prevention of homelessness, for securing accommodation and for providing support to homeless people (or those likely to become homeless) go much further than simply providing a roof over someone's head.[153] They include the 'activities' of giving advice on the availability of benefits and employment, on debt management and on other financial issues. Local housing authorities and adult care and children's services authorities have statutory powers to provide assistance in the form of rent deposits, rent guarantees and disabled facilities grants for adaptations. The exercise of those powers is a relevant activity. Local charities, or even local businesses, may provide limited financial assistance to the homeless and they too would be relevant 'activities'. The local housing authority should also consider what other 'activities' are being carried out to provide support for the homeless and for those potentially homeless, including support with their other needs, such as health care, education, etc.

7.125 The Welsh Code advises that any gaps in services will need to be highlighted, such as lack of emergency accommodation for couples or for people with dogs.[154]

---

[149]   HA 2002, s 2(2).
[150]   See English Code, Annex 3; Welsh Code, para 8.57.
[151]   English Code, para 1.19.
[152]   As set out in Annex 3 to the English Code.
[153]   Welsh Code, paras 8.37–8.41.
[154]   Welsh Code, para 8.72.

Resources currently available for such activities

7.126 This is the third matter that HA 2002 requires to be considered within the local homelessness review.[155] The local housing authority should obviously consider its own resources, and also those available to the adult care and children's services authorities, other public authorities, voluntary organisations and any other persons. Equally obviously, 'resources' in this context means far more than just the financial resources available to tackle local homelessness. The 2006 edition of the English Code places even more emphasis than earlier editions on the importance that government attaches to a move away from the historic local housing authority role as the potential provider of the resources (and, most particularly, homes) for relieving homelessness and into a more modern role of encouraging and facilitating provision by others. The focus has very much shifted from inviting attention to the resources that might be supplied by the local housing authority itself to those which may be marshalled from others in relation to homelessness. As elsewhere in the current Code, the primary emphasis is on those resources which may be directed to homelessness *prevention* in the first instance.[156] The provisions of the Localism Act 2011 (LA 2011) make it even clearer that the UK Coalition government views the local housing authority as housing enabler rather than as housing provider.[157]

7.127 When it comes to their own resources in relation to prevention, local housing authorities are advised to consider their own infrastructure (staff, administrative costs, etc) and also any resources available to them to provide rent guarantees, or other grants or loans to homeless people or to provide funds or other resources to other organisations working to support homeless people.[158] They should also consider the infrastructure resources available in other public authorities, including the local adult care and children's services authorities, and, again, any ability those other authorities may have to contribute to the prevention of homelessness or give financial help to the homeless.

7.128 The infrastructure provided by voluntary organisations, private registered providers and registered social landlords should be considered, along with resources available from any other relevant organisations (including charitable organisations or philanthropic activities by private businesses).[159]

7.129 Physical resources available for securing accommodation to those actually homeless obviously include the local housing authority's own housing stock and that of private registered providers, registered social landlords and private landlords in the district.[160] The availability of hostel and refuge spaces

---

[155] HA 2002, s 2(1)(c).
[156] See English Code, Chapters 2–5, Annexes 2–7; Welsh Code, paras 8.37–8.41.
[157] In particular, the use of 'private rented sector offers' to bring the main housing duty at HA 1996 s 193(2) to an end: HA 1996 s 193(7AA) as amended by LA 2011 s 148(5). For 'main housing duty', see **17.23–17.168**. For 'private rented sector offer', see **17.109–17.131**.
[158] English Code, para 1.27; Welsh Code, paras 8.37–8.41.
[159] English Code, para 1.27.
[160] English Code, para 1.27; Welsh Code, paras 8.42–8.45.

should also be considered. In the English Code, Chapter 3 is directed entirely to the steps that might be taken to ensure a sufficient supply of accommodation locally.

7.130 The mechanisms available to increase the supply of accommodation should be taken into account. These include:

- securing affordable accommodation through planning conditions;

- future developments by private registered providers or registered social landlords;

- the resources made available by the government to the local housing authority; and

- the extent of new development, self-build homes, shared ownership schemes, etc.[161]

7.131 The local housing authority should consider what initiatives could increase the supply of affordable accommodation. Can the local housing authority increase the proportion of lettings made available by private registered providers or registered social landlords or that of affordable homes obtained through planning conditions, etc?

7.132 Local housing authorities are advised to take all available steps to identify the housing resources that might be available in their districts.[162] This includes taking the opportunity of filling any empty accommodation in the district.[163] Such a 'strategy for minimising empty homes' should be an integral part of the homelessness review and strategy and should include tackling any hard-to-let properties, bringing empty private sector properties back into use and encouraging landlords to let flats over shops. The local housing authority should consider what financial resources are available that could be used to encourage private homeowners to repair empty properties and make them available for letting. The powers to take over and manage empty properties[164] should also be considered. 'Resources' for these purposes also includes the resources available to provide 'support' to homeless people, to those likely to become homeless and to those formerly homeless people who need support to prevent them losing their accommodation.[165] This will embrace the availability of housing benefit and other welfare benefits locally, the provision of easily accessible advice, and accommodation with specific levels of support (for

---

[161] English Code, para 1.28 and Chapter 3; Welsh Code, paras 8.42–8.45. The Welsh Government considers that 'move-on planning' to assist a person to move from temporary to permanent accommodation is of critical importance: Welsh Code, para 8.44.
[162] English Code, para 1.28 and Chapter 3; Welsh Code, para 8.42.
[163] English Code, paras 3.24–3.26.
[164] Given by the Housing Act 2004, ss 132–138.
[165] HA 2002, s 2(2)(c).

elderly people, or substance abusers, young parents, etc).[166] In keeping with the modern policy emphasis on sustainability of new homes for the homeless, the current English Code deals at length with the importance of reviewing resources available locally for 'support', and dedicates a Chapter[167] to how support services may be identified and utilised.

Publication and inspection

7.133   Once the review is completed, the local housing authority is required to ensure that the results of the review can be inspected by any member of the public, free, at its principal office.[168]

7.134   It is also required to provide a copy of those results to any member of the public who requests one. The local housing authority may charge a reasonable fee for copying.[169]

7.135   In practice, many local housing authorities make the whole of their review (and strategy) available on their website. Local libraries may provide free internet access enabling these documents to be read online free of charge.

LOCAL HOMELESSNESS STRATEGIES[170]

Overview

7.136   Once the local housing authority has assembled the raw material and completed its review, it can begin to formulate its strategy (or to reconsider an earlier strategy).

7.137   The required content of the local homelessness strategy is defined in HA 2002.[171] The strategy to be formulated by the local housing authority must be a strategy for:

(1)   the prevention of homelessness in the local housing authority's district;[172]

(2)   the securing of suitable accommodation for those people in the local housing authority's district who are, or may become, homeless;[173] and

---

[166]   English Code, para 1.29 and Chapter 4; Welsh Code, paras 8.40–8.41.

[167]   English Code, Chapter 4.

[168]   HA 2002, s 2(3)(a). Lewisham London Borough Council was found to have acted in breach of the Freedom of Information Act 2000 when it failed to provide, in response to a request, updated information on material originally published in its homelessness review (Information Commissioner's Office Decision Notice FS50092310, 7 August 2006, (2006) October *Legal Action*, p 25).

[169]   HA 2002, s 2(3)(b). See also English Code, para 1.30.

[170]   HA 2002, s 3.

[171]   HA 2002, s 3 as amended by LA 2011 s 153.

[172]   HA 2002, s 3(1)(a).

[173]   HA 2002, s 3(1)(b).

(3)   the provision of satisfactory services to those people in the local housing authority's district who are actually or potentially homeless, including those who used to be homeless and now need support in order to prevent them becoming homeless again.[174]

7.138   The strategy is based on the results of the homelessness review[175] and must identify specific objectives for the local housing authority and specific action as to how the local housing authority aims to achieve those objectives.[176] It must also take into account the local housing authority's current allocation scheme, the local tenancy strategy once published and, for London borough councils, the current London housing strategy.[177]

7.139   A multi-agency approach[178] enables the local housing authority to identify specific objectives and action, not only for itself, but also for the local adult care and children's services authorities or departments.[179] The local housing authority can also identify specific action to be taken by any of the other organisations involved, but only if each organisation agrees to that action being included in the strategy.[180]

7.140   As with the homelessness review,[181] the strategy, once completed, must be made available free for inspection and the public permitted to purchase copies.[182]

7.141   Importantly, both the local housing authority and the local adult care and children's services authorities are required to take the homelessness strategy into account when exercising their statutory functions.[183] Obviously, the local housing authority should take the strategy into account when making decisions on applications for homelessness assistance, or under its allocation scheme. It might also be argued that the local housing authority should take the strategy into account when exercising its housing management functions, for example, in considering whether or not to bring possession proceedings in respect of a property occupied by one of its own tenants.[184]

7.142   The children's services authority or department should take the local housing authority's homelessness strategy into account when exercising its

---

[174]   HA 2002, s 3(1)(c).
[175]   HA 2002, s 1(1)(b).
[176]   HA 2002, s 3(2).
[177]   HA 2002, s 3(7A) inserted by LA 2011, s 153 in force from 15 January 2012.
[178]   See **7.194–7.157**.
[179]   HA 2002, s 3(2)(a) and (b).
[180]   HA 2002, s 3(3) and (4).
[181]   See **7.104–7.135**.
[182]   HA 2002, s 3(9).
[183]   HA 2002, s 1(5) and (6).
[184]   In *Barnsley Metropolitan Borough Council v Norton* [2011] EWCA Civ 834, [2011] HLR 46, CA, the Court of Appeal held that a local housing authority was required to take into its public sector equality duty (now contained at Equality Act 2010, s 149) when considering whether or not to bring possession proceedings against one of its tenants whose household contained a disabled person.

functions under the Children Act 1989, so that assistance can be given to homeless young people or to homeless families with children.[185] The strategy should also be taken into account when the adult care authority or department considers its obligations under community care legislation towards those with mental health needs, drug and alcohol abuse problems, the disabled, and ill or elderly people.[186]

Identification of objectives for the strategy

7.143 The Welsh Code identifies five themes from the Welsh Government's *Ten Year Homelessness Plan*[187] which should be taken into account when planning homelessness services:

- preventing homelessness wherever possible;

- working across organisational and policy boundaries;

- placing the service user at the centre of service delivery;

- ensuring social inclusion and equality of access to services; and

- making the best use of resources.[188]

7.144 The long-term objective of the Welsh Government is to end the need for anyone to sleep rough.[189]

7.145 Sixteen objectives in the *Ten Year Homelessness Plan* are set out that should be taken into account in any strategy adopted by a local housing authority in Wales.[190] These objectives underline the emphasis on prevention of homelessness, providing early advice, working with the private rented sector to expand access to suitable accommodation and a partnership approach to meet the needs of homeless people for other services.

7.146 The Welsh Code further advises that homeless people should be provided with choices, and helped to express their needs and preferences about the nature and location of accommodation offered to them.[191] The strategy should be sensitive to the particular difficulties facing homeless people from disadvantaged groups. The needs of different ethnic groups, lesbian, gay and bisexual people, women, people with disabilities and older homeless people

---

[185] HA 2002 s 1(6).
[186] See Chapter 20 of this book for an outline of some of those powers and duties under which a local authority can provide accommodation.
[187] See **7.30–7.33**.
[188] Welsh Code, para 8.30.
[189] Welsh Code, para 8.59.
[190] Welsh Code, para 8.32.
[191] Welsh Code, para 8.33.

should be particularly addressed.[192] Views of homeless people are crucial in developing a successful strategic approach to homelessness.[193] Local housing authorities should establish a framework for monitoring and evaluating implementation of homelessness planning and should keep their services and the strategy under continuing review.[194]

7.147   The English Code gives examples of the types of specific objectives and actions that might be included in a homelessness strategy for the local housing authority and the adult care and children's services authorities or departments.[195] Annex 6 of the English Code contains examples of the types of specific action that might be expected to be taken by other authorities or organisations.

7.148   Obviously, the strategy must be drawn with relevant consideration of the local housing authority's wider responsibilities in relation to equality and diversity issues. Sadly, in the English Code the advice given on importance of the interface between these issues and the discharge of homelessness functions (including the drawing-up of the strategy) has been set out only in the Introduction,[196] where it is likely to be overlooked.[197]

Consultation and the multi-agency approach

7.149   The local housing authority is required to consult before adopting a homelessness strategy or modifying it.[198] HA 2002 gives the local housing authority a very broad discretion as to which organisations it should consult, being such public or local authorities, voluntary organisations or other persons as it considers appropriate. The English Code offers a list of those with whom a local housing authority in England may wish to consult.[199]

7.150   Adult care and children's services authorities are required to co-operate with the local housing authority to the extent that the local housing authority may reasonably require.[200] Examples of joint working between the local housing authority and children's services include joint assessments of homeless families with children, or young applicants for homelessness assistance,[201] as well as the provision of hostels, support services, family reconciliation schemes, mental health support and drug and alcohol support by adult care services.[202]

---

[192]   Welsh Code, para 8.54.
[193]   Welsh Code, para 8.73.
[194]   Welsh Code, paras 8.75–8.76.
[195]   English Code, Annex 4.
[196]   English Code, Introduction, paras 7–13.
[197]   There is some more detail, and links to useful organisations, at para 8.54 of the Welsh Code.
[198]   HA 2002, s 3(8).
[199]   English Code, para 1.41 and Annex 3.
[200]   HA 2002, s 1(2).
[201]   English Code, para 5.6.
[202]   See English Code, para 5.6 and Annex 6; Welsh Code, para 8.23.

7.151 HA 2002 insists upon a multi-agency approach, reaching far beyond the local housing authority or even other public authorities. The local housing authority is required to consider whether any of the objectives can be achieved through joint action with the adult care or children's services authorities or departments, with other public authorities, with voluntary organisations or with other people whose activities might contribute to their achievement.[203] The strategy should then identify which of those organisations will take what specific action, either individually or in association with other organisations.[204] The strategy should only identify specific action to be taken by other public authorities if those other authorities or organisations consent to their inclusion.[205]

7.152 The other organisations that should be consulted over the contents of the homelessness strategy, and the extent to which the actions within the strategy can be performed by them, fall into two categories:

(1) public authorities (other than the local housing authority and adult care or children's services authority) which have functions that are capable of contributing to the achievement of the objectives of preventing homelessness, securing sufficient accommodation, and securing the satisfactory provision of support;[206] and

(2) any voluntary organisation or other person whose activities are capable of contributing to the achievement of the objectives.[207]

7.153 Examples of such public authorities, voluntary organisations and other people are listed in the Annexes to the Codes.[208]

7.154 Public authorities whose functions may contribute to the objectives of the homelessness strategy include the health authority and other health organisations, the police, the National Offender Management Service[209], the Department for Work and Pensions, the UKBA, the armed forces, education and employment programmes, etc.

7.155 The voluntary organisations and 'other persons' mentioned in the legislation would obviously include housing advice agencies and citizens' advice bureaux, local private registered providers or registered social landlords, private landlords and their representative forums. Casting the net wider, youth action groups, refuges, faith groups, victim support groups, refugee organisations, local businesses and the Samaritans are also suggested. Local housing authorities are advised, in the English Code, to consider 'all the organisations

---

[203] HA 2002, s 3(5) and (3).
[204] HA 2002, s 3(3).
[205] HA 2002, s 3(4).
[206] HA 2002, s 3(3)(a).
[207] HA 2002, s 3(3)(b).
[208] English Code, Annex 3; Welsh Code, para 8.23.
[209] Formerly the Probation Service.

and persons working to prevent and alleviate homelessness in the district', public, private and voluntary.[210] In particular, local housing authorities should be entering into 'constructive partnerships' with local private registered providers or registered social landlords.[211]

7.156 Examples of joint working include multi-agency forums to share information and ideas, and clear protocols and agreements about the referral of clients between services and agencies, so that homeless people are not shuttled between different organisations.[212]

7.157 The UK government-commissioned evaluation of the initial local housing authority homelessness strategies in England[213] noted that the involvement of adult care and children's services at a strategic level tended to be disappointing, and that other statutory agencies, such as health and probation services, were also hard to engage. When those other agencies did play a part, they provided helpful input.

Consulting the homeless

7.158 There is no specific requirement in HA 2002 to consult the former or current users of the local housing authority's services, homeless people, or people who have been or might become homeless. However, the broad discretion given to local housing authorities to consult 'such ... voluntary organisations or other persons as they consider appropriate'[214] certainly permits them to consult both representative forums for the homeless and individual homeless people themselves. The English Code suggests that local housing authorities should consult service users and homeless people.[215] The Welsh Code describes the views of homeless people as 'crucial in developing a successful strategic approach to homelessness' and recommends that they should be consulted on their own views of their situation, their needs, their experiences of services, what services work, what barriers there are and what suggestions they have for improvements.[216]

7.159 Many local housing authorities have taken the opportunity to consult homeless people in their district. Shelter's review of homelessness strategies noted:

'... consultation with users has enabled authorities to identify and distinguish between the needs of different groups and plan for services which meet their

---

[210] English Code, para 1.39.
[211] English Code, para 1.36, and Annex 5; Welsh Code, paras 8.25–8.26.
[212] English Code, para 1.39, and Chapter 5.
[213] *Local Authorities' Homelessness Strategies: Evaluation and Good Practice* (ODPM, 2004). See also **7.83–7.85**.
[214] HA 2002, s 3(8).
[215] English Code, para 1.41 and Annex 3.
[216] Welsh Code, para 8.73. See also *Consulting with Homeless People* (National Assembly for Wales, August 2004).

particular needs, rather than providing a "blanket" approach to the problem of homelessness. Importantly, they have identified the need to adopt a proactive approach to tackling homelessness.'[217]

7.160 The UK government-commissioned evaluation of initial strategies noted that, in general, local housing authorities found it difficult to engage with homeless people and users of homelessness services. Local housing authorities said to have addressed this problem creatively had gone to speak to homeless people on the street, or gone into hostels or day centres to talk with them.[218]

The three matters the strategy must address

7.161   As already indicated,[219] HA 2002 requires a local homelessness strategy to address three essential matters: prevention; provision of accommodation; and support.

7.162   Following consideration and evaluation of the first homelessness strategies in England published in 2003, the opportunity was taken in the 2006 edition of the English Code to expand substantially the advice previously given by government on the content of the strategies. Each of the three essential matters has been addressed with a whole Chapter of the new guidance in Chapters 2, 3 and 4 of the Code respectively. This material was intended significantly to influence the content of the new strategies that local housing authorities in England were required to publish by the summer of 2008.

7.163   The very detailed guidance on the first matter – 'preventing homelessness' – reflects modern policy considerations that are reviewed in a separate Chapter of this book.[220]

7.164   Each of the three essential components of a local homelessness strategy is considered in the following paragraphs.

(1) Prevention of homelessness[221]

7.165   This is the first of the three matters that HA 2002 requires the strategy to address.[222] Any strategy to prevent homelessness will obviously include ensuring that general advice and information on homelessness, housing benefit, occupiers' rights, etc is available, and is both comprehensive and effective.[223]

---

[217]   *The Act in action: an assessment of homelessness reviews and strategies* (Shelter, January 2004). See also **7.81**.

[218]   *Local Authorities' Homelessness Strategies: Evaluation and Good Practice* (ODPM Homelessness Research Summary, Number 1, 2004). See also **7.83–7.85**.

[219]   See **7.137**.

[220]   See Chapter 8 of this book. See also English Code Chapter 2; Welsh Code, paras 8.37–8.41 and Chapter 10.

[221]   English Code, Chapter 2; Welsh Code, paras 8.37–8.41.

[222]   See **7.137**.

[223]   English Code, Chapter 2; Welsh Code, paras 8.37–8.41 and Chapter 10.

The local housing authority has a statutory obligation to ensure that free advice and information on homelessness assistance is available to any person in its district.[224]

7.166 The English Code advises local housing authorities to take into account the good practice on homelessness prevention published by the government in *Homelessness Strategies – A Good Practice Handbook*[225] and *Preventing tomorrow's rough sleepers – A Good Practice Handbook*.[226] But surprisingly little emphasis is given to the comprehensive government publication on the subject: *Homelessness Prevention: A guide to good practice*.[227] It would also be expected that local housing authorities in England should take into account the DCLG quarterly publications on *Homelessness Prevention and Relief*.[228]

7.167 In order to contribute to homelessness prevention by minimising the number of evictions for rent arrears, the local housing authority itself should aim to have an effective arrears collection policy and should ask local private registered providers or registered social landlords to ensure that their arrears policies take into account the homelessness strategy's aims.[229] The objective is that all local social landlords should facilitate access to financial and housing advice. The local housing authority is advised to ensure that its housing benefit service is efficient.[230] The Department for Work and Pensions should be asked by local housing authorities to ensure speedy access to severe hardship payments, social fund loans, and the like. The children's services authority should be asked by the local housing authority to exercise its functions under the Children Act 1989 to give children, or families with children, financial assistance with deposits, rent payments in advance, and/or rent guarantees. Tenants in financial difficulties should be enabled to obtain local advice to help them manage their finances or negotiate with any creditors.

7.168 The extended guidance in the Codes (and, in particular, Chapter 2 of the English Code and Chapter 10 of the Welsh Code) offers local housing authorities a range of advice on homelessness prevention initiatives. For example:

- a significant number of applications for homelessness assistance are made by people who have been asked to leave by their parents, relatives or friends.[231] Action to reduce those numbers can include: ensuring that the accommodation provided to the applicant's family is suitable at the outset

---

[224] Housing Act 1996, s 179(1). See **9.4–9.7**.
[225] DTLR, March 2002.
[226] Rough Sleepers Unit, 2001. See also English Code, paras 1.4 and 5.8.
[227] CLG, June 2006.
[228] See **8.2–8.3**.
[229] English Code, para 2.23 and Annex 5, para 13; Welsh Code, para 10.45.
[230] Welsh Code, para 8.40.
[231] Homelessness statistics in England for January – March 2012 (DCLG), at *Live Table 774* showed 33% of applicants as coming from this group. In Wales, the equivalent group constitutes around 27% of applicants (*National Statistics on Homelessness*, Welsh Government, January–March 2012).

for the needs of all members of the household; operating mediation and reconciliation services;[232] and providing children's services' support for young people;

- mediation schemes can also help with neighbour disputes that might otherwise lead to one of them leaving his or her home and making an application for homelessness assistance; and

- adaptations can ensure that people with disabilities remain in their own homes, rather than having to apply for accommodation from adult care services.

7.169 The UK government-commissioned evaluation of homelessness strategies in England published in 2003 recommended a number of 'good practice ideas' on prevention.[233] They included:[234]

- refocusing the housing allocation arrangements to reflect the main causes of homelessness, so that an assessment of potential homelessness could be undertaken when someone applies for an ordinary housing allocation;

- improving housing advice services so that there are systems to identify a housing problem and provide advice to prevent homelessness, before an application for homelessness assistance is made;

- mediation schemes to prevent the loss of homes resulting from exclusion by parents, relatives or friends;

- family reconciliation work;

- working with private landlords to develop accreditation schemes;

- improving housing benefit systems so that the payment of housing benefit is speeded up;

- tackling domestic violence and trying to prevent repeat applications for homelessness assistance from victims of domestic violence;

- identifying the triggers for repeat homelessness;

- addressing homelessness for ex-prisoners (by work with prison advice services);

---

[232] But see *Robinson v Hammersmith & Fulham London Borough Council* [2006] EWCA Civ 1122, [2007] HLR 7, CA, holding that mediation should not be used to delay inquiries and thus deprive a homeless applicant of a benefit he or she would otherwise have been entitled to. See **8.66, 10.69–10.70** and **13.132–13.130**.
[233] Later contained in *Homelessness Prevention: A Guide to Good Practice* (CLG, June 2006).
[234] *Local Authorities' Homelessness Strategies: Evaluation and Good Practice* (ODPM, 2004). See also **7.83–7.85**.

- addressing the needs of vulnerable tenants at risk from crack dealers;

- reviewing the rent arrears policies of local private registered providers or registered social landlords; and

- providing floating support.

7.170 These, and all other relevant local opportunities to prevent homelessness, should be considered and addressed in each local housing authority's homelessness strategy.

(2) Securing that sufficient accommodation is (and will be) available for people who are (or may become) homeless[235]

7.171 This is the second statutory objective of the local homelessness strategy. Its fulfillment is, of course, primarily the responsibility of the local housing authority itself, but private registered providers, registered social landlords and private landlords should be working with the local housing authority to ensure that the supply of affordable and suitable accommodation is maximised.[236]

7.172 While both Codes of Guidance outline the ways in which accommodation can be secured by local housing authorities in order to meet statutory obligations towards particular homeless applicants for homelessness assistance, the English Code places special emphasis on the role of the local homelessness strategy in enabling a local housing authority to meet likely demand for alternative homes. Chapter 3 of the English Code provides guidance, not only as to how the strategy should address the need to secure an increased supply of new housing (through the distribution of financial aid and by planning measures), but also guidance as to the steps that can be taken to maximise the use of existing housing stock, including:

- maximising use of the private rented sector;

- making best use of existing social housing;

- exercising powers over empty privately-owned property; and

- using housing renewal policies and the disabled facilities grant to maximise use of existing dwellings.

7.173 The Welsh Code advises that local housing authorities should aim to minimise the need for people who are owed a duty under HA 1996, Part 7 to spend time in temporary accommodation and, in particular, that use of bed

---

[235] English Code, Chapter 3; Welsh Code, paras 8.42–8.45.
[236] English Code, Chapter 3.

and breakfast accommodation should be kept to an absolute minimum .[237] Children's services authorities should aim to provide supported accommodation for homeless 16- and 17-year-olds who need a supported environment.[238] The local housing authority should ensure that there is access to women's refuges, night stop shelters and supported accommodation provided by voluntary organisations for those who need it.

7.174 Both Codes advise local housing authorities to consider the extent to which they can increase the supply of affordable accommodation to homeless, or potentially homeless, people. Examples include:

• bidding for government resources;

• attracting private investment;

• maximising the amount of private rented accommodation available;

• using planning powers to increase the amount of affordable social or private housing;

• using their nomination agreements with private registered providers or registered social landlords;[239] and

• using their own allocation schemes to provide for homeless people.[240]

7.175 The UK government-commissioned evaluation of the initial homelessness strategies in England published in 2003 noted that, in practice, the proportion of lettings by private registered providers to homeless households (via the local housing authority) is not always at a significant level.[241]

7.176 Commenting on this second statutory objective, one judge has said:

'Local authorities such as the defendant may reasonably say that, given the reduction in its housing stock and the pressure of numbers of those seeking accommodation, it is well nigh impossible at present to achieve what is set out in [Homelessness Act 2002] s 3(1)(b). However, it is important to note that Parliament has clearly placed an understandable emphasis upon the need for authorities to take measures to try to avoid homelessness.'[242]

---

[237] Welsh Code, para 8.43. Avoiding the use of bed and breakfast for families with children [England] and anyone who has a priority need [Wales] is now a statutory requirement; see 18.114–18.119 [England] and **18.120–18.128**.
[238] See the English Code, Annex 4.
[239] See **6.32–6.69**.
[240] English Code, para 1.22.
[241] *Local Authorities' Homelessness Strategies: Evaluation and Good Practice,* (ODPM, November 2004), para 3.175. See **7.83–7.85**.
[242] *R (Aweys) v Birmingham City Council* [2007] EWHC 52 (Admin), [2007] HLR 27, Admin Ct, at [12], per Collins J. The case subsequently reached the House of Lords, but not on this point.

(3) Providing support for people who are (or were, or may be) homeless[243]

7.177 The 'support' envisaged under this third category of matters that must be embraced by the homelessness strategy falls into two sub-categories:

(1) ongoing support for those who already are, or may soon become, homeless; and

(2) help for formerly homeless people who need support to stay in their new homes.

7.178 People in the *first* sub-category have a greater need for support than the provision of bare advice or minimal services to prevent homelessness. For these purposes, 'support' can include help with a homeless person's drug or alcohol addiction, or mental health problems. Rough sleepers and those in temporary accommodation should be able to have access to primary health care, to employment opportunities and to education.

7.179 The objectives, and the activities to be carried out, in relation to the *second* sub-category are very similar to those within the prevention of homelessness objective.[244] Obviously, advice should be available, both from the statutory sector and the voluntary sector, to enable occupiers – particularly formerly homeless occupiers – to stay in their homes. Sources of financial and other assistance should be identified and made available.

7.180 Both Codes emphasise joint working with any Supporting People teams established by local authorities.[245]

Publication and inspection

7.181 Once the strategy has been completed, the local housing authority is required to make a copy available at its principal office for inspection at all reasonable hours, free, by any member of the public.[246] It must also provide a copy of the strategy to any member of the public who requests one, and can charge a reasonable fee for doing so.[247] These statutory provisions mirror the general requirement on local authorities under the Freedom of Information Act 2000 to provide such information.[248]

7.182 Since the local housing authority and the local adult care and children's services authorities are all required to take the homelessness strategy into

[243] English Code, Chapter 4; Welsh Code, paras 8.46–8.53.
[244] See **7.165–7.170**.
[245] English Code, para 4.5; Welsh Code, paras 8.47–8.48.
[246] HA 2002, s 3(9)(a). See also English Code, para 1.43.
[247] HA 2002, s 3(9)(b). See also English Code, para 1.43.
[248] In force from 1 January 2005.

account in the exercise of their functions,[249] it should be expected that the strategy will be readily available to housing and adult care and children's services staff making decisions related to homelessness or to homeless people.

7.183   In practice, many local housing authorities publish the strategy on their websites.

New strategies

7.184   Local housing authorities in England were required to have published their first statutory homelessness strategies by 31 July 2003[250] and local housing authorities in Wales were required to have published by 30 September 2003.[251] By the end of 2003 all local housing authorities had a first strategy in place.

7.185   But homelessness presents a changing landscape. Local housing authorities can keep up to date with the changing local picture by regularly undertaking the homelessness review function.[252] The power to conduct a statutory homelessness review can be exercised at any time.

7.186   Changing circumstances locally, whether identified by a statutory review or otherwise, may require the local homelessness strategy to be re-visited. There is, accordingly, a general statutory duty to keep the strategy under review and a statutory power to modify it from time to time.[253] Local housing authorities may therefore publish modified strategies at any time. Some anticipated that their initial strategies would stand for three or more years before requiring reconsideration; others revisited their strategies earlier than that.

7.187   Before producing a revised or replacement strategy, the local housing authority may conduct another homelessness review and, in any event, must consult those public and local authorities, voluntary organisations and members of the public whom it considers appropriate to be consulted.[254]

7.188   Any modified or replacement strategy must be made available to the public in the same way as the initial strategy.[255]

7.189   The English Code advises that local housing authorities might consider modifying their strategies at various key stages: after they have transferred their housing stock to private registered providers or registered social landlords; after establishing an Arms Length Management Organisation (ALMO), when

---

[249]   HA 2002, s 1(5) and (6).
[250]   The exemption for 'excellent', '4-stars' and '3-stars' local authorities was not brought into effect until 2005, see footnote 117.
[251]   12 months after the HA 2002 was brought into effect.
[252]   See **7.104–7.135**.
[253]   HA 2002, s 3(6).
[254]   HA 2002, s 3(8).
[255]   See **7.181–7.183**.

new data on homelessness has become available; or when there have been significant changes in the levels or causes of homelessness locally or in homelessness legislation.[256] The Welsh Code advises that any change which is likely significantly to affect homelessness, or how it is tackled, will require modifications to homelessness strategies.[257]

7.190 At a minimum, a new strategy must be published within five years of the publication of the last strategy, although that obligation does not apply to local housing authorities in England designated as 'excellent', '4-stars' or '3-stars'.[258] In effect, therefore, most local housing authorities had updated and published their homelessness strategy by July 2008 (September 2008 for local housing authorities in Wales) and will be planning to do so again by July 2013 (September 2013 in Wales). Again, before a new strategy is adopted, the appropriate organisations should be consulted. Once the new strategy is adopted, it must be published and made available to members of the public.

7.191 The obligation to keep a homelessness strategy under review and to consult upon necessary modifications to it was considered in *R (Calgin) v Enfield London Borough Council*.[259] The local housing authority had adopted a homelessness strategy in October 2003, but in spring 2004 it adopted a policy for out-of-borough placements of some homeless households without modifying the strategy or consulting upon its modification. In a challenge brought by judicial review, it was contended that this rendered both the strategy and the policy unlawful. The court found that, at the time of adoption of the strategy, an earlier version of the out-of-borough policy had been in place and the strategy had made reference to households placed out of the borough. The new policy was being applied only to a small proportion (1%) of homeless households. In those circumstances, it was held that there had been no unlawfulness in the failure to modify the strategy or consult upon proposed modification. The judge said:

> 'Furthermore it cannot be the case that every variation of each specific policy relating to the homeless and directed to implementing the strategy has to be made the subject of a formal amendment to the strategy document. The time and cost would take valuable resources away from front line services. I accept that in theory the adoption of a major new homelessness policy could involve such a shift from the strategy that a reasonable authority would need to reflect it in a modified strategy and go through the consultation mechanism laid down in the Act.'[260]

---

[256] English Code, para 1.44.

[257] Welsh Code, para 8.76.

[258] HA 2002, s 1(4); Local Authorities' Plans and Strategies (Disapplication) (England) Order 2005, SI 2005/157, art 3, as amended by the Local Authorities' Plans and Strategies (Disapplication) (England) (Amendment) Order 2009, SI 2009/714; and English Code, para 1.42.

[259] [2005] EWHC 1716 (Admin), [2006] HLR 4, Admin Ct.

[260] *R (Calgin) v Enfield London Borough Council* [2005] EWHC 1716 (Admin), [2006] HLR 4, Admin Ct, at [50] per Elias J.

WHO SHOULD DRAW UP THE STRATEGIES AND REVIEWS?

7.192 As already emphasised, the drawing up of the local homelessness strategy and homelessness review is a key task for the local housing authority. These documents will inform all decisions taken by local housing authority officers under HA 1996, Part 7, and will also set out the local housing authority's policy commitments, the extent to which it works in partnership with private registered providers, registered social landlords, other statutory agencies, voluntarily organisations, and what present and future users of the homelessness service can expect from that service.

7.193 Elsewhere in this book, we discuss the extent to which local housing authorities are permitted to contract out any of the activities that they carry out under HA 1996, Parts 6 and 7.[261] The Local Authorities (Contracting Out of Allocation of Housing and Homelessness Functions) Order 1996[262] only applies to activities carried out under HA 1996, Parts 6 and 7, and not to activities carried out under HA 2002, ss 1–4.

7.194 By HA 2002, s 1, a local housing authority is under a 'duty' to formulate a homelessness strategy, and that homelessness strategy must be informed by the raw data contained in the homelessness review.[263] There are similar duties imposed by HA 2002 on a local housing authority to arrange for its homelessness strategy and its homelessness review to be available for inspection at all reasonable hours, and to provide a copy of those documents on request on payment of a reasonable charge.[264] Any failure to draw up a homelessness strategy would be a breach of the local housing authority's duty.

7.195 The task of formulating the homelessness review and strategy may be contracted out, in that it might be appropriate for a local housing authority to seek assistance in the formulation of those documents from other organisations, such as staff working for private registered providers, registered social landlords, etc. However, the final content of the homelessness review and strategy should be the local housing authority's decision.

7.196 The Welsh Code states that the Welsh Government strongly recommends that the homelessness agenda 'remains a priority at political level', that an elected councillor should be appointed as 'Homelessness Champion' for that purpose, and that there is a named lead officer, appointed by the Chief Executive, with appropriate authority, who has responsibility for the delivery of homelessness policy and services.[265]

---

[261] See Chapter 21 of this book.
[262] SI 1996/3205. See Appendix 1 of this book.
[263] See **7.136–7.142**.
[264] HA 2002, ss 2(3) and 3(9).
[265] Welsh Code, para 8.20.

USING THE STRATEGIES AND REVIEWS

7.197 The local homelessness *review* document will contain essential data on the local homelessness (and prevention of homelessness) scene. It will therefore be an invaluable source of data for those providing, or planning to provide, housing-related services in a local housing authority's district. It will also help the local housing authority itself in dealing with the exercise of judgment in individual homelessness cases. For example, in assessing whether a person is 'homeless' or 'has become homeless intentionally' a local housing authority may (for limited purposes) have regard to 'general circumstances prevailing in relation to housing in the district'.[266] The local homelessness review should provide an up-to-date snapshot of those 'general circumstances' for easy reference by officers and advisers alike.

7.198 The local homelessness *strategy* document is an essential additional ingredient in the local housing authority's own work in dealing with individual applications for homelessness assistance and/or housing allocation. For this reason, the strategy document will not contain bland statements of policy objectives, but rather 'action plans' with targets and arrangements for monitoring and evaluation of their attainment.[267] The requirement on local housing authorities to 'take their homelessness strategy into account' makes the strategy document, in effect, a local mini-Code of Guidance.[268] Failure to take the strategy into account where it contains material relevant to a particular decision would potentially render that decision unlawful (for failure to have regard to a relevant consideration). The strategy should certainly help officers who are making decisions about the exercise of discretionary powers (for example, whether to accommodate a non-priority unintentionally homeless applicant) to make decisions which fit with local strategic objectives.[269]

7.199 Both documents will, of course, be relied upon by advisers assisting the homeless. They may well contain material which can be referred to when making representations on behalf of a particular applicant or in making a complaint under the local housing authority's complaints procedure. It might be expected that the Local Government Ombudsman[270] will ask to see copies of the current strategy when investigating homelessness complaints. Indeed, as has already been demonstrated, the review and strategy may well provide material which can be deployed (on both sides) in litigation concerning an individual applicant for homelessness assistance or a local housing authority's policies and procedures on services for the homeless.[271]

---

[266] HA 1996, s 177(2). See **11.98–11.100** and **14.136–14.137**.
[267] See, for example, English Code, para 1.40.
[268] HA 2002, s 1(5).
[269] See *R (Seabrook) v Brighton & Hove City Council* (2005) CO/5670/2004, (2005) March *Legal Action*, p 23, Admin Ct.
[270] Public Services Ombudsman in Wales.
[271] See *R (Ho-Sang) v Lewisham London Borough Council* (2004) CO/5652/03, (2004) July *Legal*

Action, p 19, Admin Ct and *R (Calgin) v Enfield London Borough Council* [2005] EWHC 1716 (Admin), [2006] HLR 4, Admin Ct as examples of such an approach in practice. See also **7.191**.

Chapter 8

HOMELESSNESS PREVENTION

INTRODUCTION

8.1   Prevention of homelessness has been at the heart of government policy on homelessness in England since 2002[1] and in Wales since 2003.[2]

8.2   The policy of 'prevention' has been embraced so enthusiastically by some local housing authorities that it has led to criticism that the true policy agenda is the prevention of homelessness *applications* rather than of homelessness itself and to accusations of 'gate-keeping'. Both national governments hope that they have found the right balance between assisting people to remain in their homes, or to find new homes without an intervening period of homelessness, on the one hand, and ensuring that homeless people and potentially homeless people secure the rights given to them in Housing Act 1996 (HA 1996), Part 7, on the other. In England, the publication *Homelessness Prevention: a good practice guide*[3] was intended to help local housing authorities in England get that balance right. The Department for Communities and Local Government (DCLG)[4] subsequently published an evaluation of prevention practices by local housing authorities in England: *Evaluating Homelessness Prevention.*[5]

8.3   In recent years, annual statistics on homelessness prevention and relief from local housing authorities in England have been published by DCLG. These were first described as 'experimental' statistics because they are published outside the homelessness statutory framework, but are now described as 'official statistics'.[6] The most recent statistics available at the date of writing were *Homelessness Prevention and Relief, England, 2011–2012.*[7] They show that homelessness prevention work had assisted around 174,800 cases in England between April 2011 and March 2012. 43% of those cases were individuals or households who had been assisted to remain in their existing homes, and the other 57% were assisted to obtain alternative accommodation. There were a further 24,200 cases of individuals obtaining alternative accommodation as a result of an application for homelessness assistance, even though they had been found not to be owed any accommodation duties under HA 1996, Part 7. Those latter cases are referred to as 'homelessness relief'.[8]

---

[1]   *More than a Roof: a Report into Tackling Homelessness* (Department for Transport, Local Government and the Regions, March 2002).

[2]   *Code of Guidance for Local Authorities on Allocation of Accommodation and Homelessness* (Welsh Assembly Government, April 2003), Chapter 10. The current guidance from the Welsh Government is the *Code of Guidance for Local Authorities on Allocation of Accommodation and Homelessness* 2012 (Welsh Government, August 2012) (the Welsh Code, see CD-Rom). All references to 'the Welsh Code' are to the current Code published in 2012 (see CD-Rom).

[3]   CLG, June 2006. See **8.17–8.20**.

[4]   Formerly Communities and Local Government (CLG) until May 2010.

[5]   Pawson, Netto, Jones, Wager, Fancy and Lomax (CLG, December 2007). See **8.50–8.54**.

[6]   DCLG news-release, 16 August 2012.

[7]   DCLG, August 2012.

[8]   *Homelessness Prevention and Relief: England 2011/2012 Official Statistics* (DCLG, August 2012).

8.4   In the light of the amendments to HA 1996, Part 7, inserted by the Localism Act 2011 (LA 2011),[9] it remains to be seen whether the two national governments, and local housing authorities, will place as much emphasis on prevention of homelessness as they have in recent years. Amendments to HA 1996 s 193 permit local housing authorities in England to make offers of suitable private rented sector tenancies, to bring the main housing duty to an end.[10] If an application for homelessness assistance simply acts as a mechanism for finding the applicant a new assured shorthold tenancy in the private rented sector, there is little incentive for local housing authorities to seek to arrange for assured shorthold tenancies outside of HA 1996, Part 7, through prevention assistance. Of course, local housing authorities may continue to use homelessness prevention to assist those facing homelessness to remain in their own homes. The Welsh *Code of Guidance for Local Authorities Allocation of Accommodation and Homelessness 2012*[11] states: '[t]he Welsh Government has not yet decided to commence the [Localism] Act'[12] and places considerable emphasis on prevention.[13]

A HISTORY OF PREVENTION POLICY

Prevention in England and Wales: 2002–2004

8.5   In *More than a Roof*, the then Department of Transport, Local Government and the Regions (DTLR) emphasised the complex reasons why people may become homeless:

> 'Housing supply is important in preventing homelessness but there are "people" factors in addition to "place" factors that must feature more in the way Government and its partners work. Homelessness is as much a manifestation of social exclusion as it is of housing market failures.'[14]

8.6   *More than a Roof* noted that homelessness should not be considered as a condition only experienced by those people recognised as statutorily homeless, ie those who make applications for homelessness assistance under HA 1996, Part 7, and who are accepted as having a priority need and as having not become homeless intentionally. Nor are the non-statutorily homeless to be confined to the visible category of 'rough sleepers'. The report suggested that research, and the compilation of statistics about the causes of homelessness,

---

[9]   LA 2011, ss 148–149. At the date of writing, the amendments to HA 1996 made by LA 2011, ss 148–149 had not been brought into effect in Wales.

[10]   HA 1996, ss 193(7AA)–(7AC) as amended by LA 2011, s 148(5)–(7) and in force from 9 November 2012. See **17.109–17.131 for 'private rented sector offers'**. 'Private rented sector offers' can be made to applicants for homelessness assistance whose applications were made on or after 9 November 2012 to local housing authorities in England. At the date of writing, the amendments to HA 1996 made by Localism Act 2011, ss 148–149 had not been brought into force in Wales.

[11]   Welsh Government, 2012.

[12]   Welsh Code, para 16.31.

[13]   Welsh Code, Chapter 10, see **7.40–7.41**.

[14]   *More than a Roof: a Report into Tacking Homelessness* (DTLR, March 2002), Chapter 2.

was required. The basic categories used at that time in data recording the causes of homelessness, such as 'excluded by family or friends' or 'loss of assured shorthold tenancy', were to be broken down into more detail. In particular, vulnerable people leaving institutions (such as prison, hospital or care), and young people leaving home were recognised as people who might need positive help with finding homes, if homelessness was to be prevented.

8.7   Local housing authorities were encouraged to adopt a partnership and 'joined-up government' approach, working with other statutory services, particularly adult care and children's services, and with the voluntary sector and other institutions, to tackle the causes of homelessness and the supply of accommodation. Emphasis was laid on helping people to remain in their present homes, or to accomplish a smooth transition between the loss of one home and the acquisition of another. Local housing authorities were to consider strategies to help tenants, particularly those in financial difficulties, sustain their tenancies. Housing benefit services should be improved. Local housing authorities were encouraged to consider landlord-tenant mediation schemes, in the hope of ameliorating any conflicts that could otherwise lead to a tenant's eviction. Homeowners facing mortgage arrears could be given financial help. Increased information and advice services for both tenants and homeowners were recommended.

8.8   *More than a Roof* realistically acknowledged that the causes of homelessness are much wider than the lack of housing supply (although the decline in the number of homes in the social housing sector was acknowledged as one of the reasons). Poverty, unemployment, drug addiction, and mental health problems were all among the complex causes of homelessness. 'Joined-up government', partnership approaches and the DTLR's (then) new scheme of 'Supporting People'[15] could help by providing medical services, support with addiction, education, training and employment schemes.

8.9   The DTLR recommended a twin-track approach of increasing the supply of social housing ('affordable housing'), principally through the then Housing Corporation's funding of housing associations, now referred to as in England as private registered providers and in Wales as registered social landlords, and the increased use of the private rented sector. Rent deposit schemes were to be encouraged, as were 'accredited landlord' schemes.

8.10   Many of the recommendations in *More than a Roof* were already a feature of the Homelessness Bill 2002, making its way through Parliament at the time. The categories of vulnerable people who had a priority need were extended in the Homelessness (Priority Need for Accommodation) (England) Order 2002.[16] The new Homelessness Act 2002 obliged local housing authorities to draw up homelessness reviews and strategies, carrying out the statistical analysis recommended by *More than a Roof* and working with other

---

[15]   After the election of the UK Coalition government, local authorities were no longer required to ring-fence their Supporting People budgets.
[16]   SI 2002/2051, applicable to local housing authorities in England (at Appendix 2). The National

agencies, statutory and voluntary, to deliver advice and information, and services for 'preventing homelessness in their district'.[17] By the end of 2002, prevention was firmly on the agenda in both England and Wales.

Prevention in England: 2004–2012

8.11 In England, the government's national housing strategy, *Sustainable Communities: Homes for All*[18] and its national homelessness strategy, *Sustainable Communities: Settled Homes; Changing Lives*,[19] both published in early 2005, emphasised:

- an increase in use of the private rented sector;

- financial assistance for tenants to remain in their homes;

- mediation schemes between landlords and tenants or, more commonly, family mediation schemes; and

- identification of possible homelessness at an early stage, so as to allow for intervention to prevent homelessness.

8.12 They also set an ambitious target: to halve the then number of homeless households in temporary accommodation by 2010 from a high point in 2004 of 101,000 households. That target was achieved in that the number of homeless households in temporary accommodation in England by the end of 2010 was 48,010.[20]

8.13 Between September and November 2005, the then Office of the Deputy Prime Minister (ODPM)[21] carried out a survey of all local housing authorities in England to assess the progress of their work on prevention. Its findings were published in December 2005 in the ODPM's 13th Policy Briefing, *Homelessness Prevention*.[22] All but one local housing authority ran at least one prevention scheme, most having a range available. The most popular schemes were rent deposit or bond schemes, so that potentially homeless households could be helped to obtain private sector rented accommodation. Mediation schemes were also commonly offered. Other methods of homelessness prevention included providing advice and assistance for money and debt problems, mediating between landlord and tenant and offering existing temporary

---

Assembly for Wales had passed the Homeless Persons (Priority Need) (Wales) Order 2001, SI 2001/607 (W 30) over a year earlier on 27 February 2001 (at Appendix 3). See **13.126–13.211** [England] and **13.212–13.245** [Wales].

[17] Homelessness Act 2002, ss 1–4; see **7.76–7.90**.

[18] ODPM, January 2005 see **7.12–7.13**.

[19] ODPM, March 2005; see **7.14**.

[20] DCLG Live tables on homelessness, Table 777, *Homeless households in temporary accommodation, London and England.*

[21] The government department responsible for housing and homelessness in England between 2003 and 2006.

[22] ODPM Policy Briefing No 13 *Homelessness Prevention*, December 2005.

accommodation to homeless households as an allocation under HA 1996, Part 6, or as a qualifying offer of an assured shorthold tenancy.[23] Choice based lettings, allowing potentially homeless households to bid for and be allocated properties in the social housing sector before they became homeless, also helped reduce the number of homeless acceptances. Local housing authorities were reported to be enthusiastic about prevention, partly because they anticipated budget savings if they reduced the number of households in temporary accommodation.

8.14   The responses of local housing authorities suggested that not all offers of help to prospectively homeless households were enthusiastically received. For example, offers to pay rent deposits were being refused because households found that they could not afford high private sector rents, even with help, or because properties were not available. Offers to assist with family mediation were even more commonly refused. The local housing authorities surveyed displayed a degree of cynicism about the reasons for refusal: a determination to obtain social housing was seen as one of the reasons.

8.15   Investigation reports from the Local Government Ombudsmen added to the general concern that, in their enthusiasm for preventing homelessness, local housing authorities in England might not be allowing homeless people, or, more often, potentially homeless people to make applications for assistance under HA 1996, Part 7.[24] In other words, they were not applying the statutory test at HA 1996, s 183(1):

> 'the following provisions of this Part apply where a person applies to a local housing authority for accommodation, or for assistance in obtaining accommodation, and the authority have reason to believe that he is or may be homeless or threatened with homelessness.'[25]

8.16   The UK government was sufficiently concerned at reports of bad practice for the then Minister for Housing to write to all local housing authorities in England on 12 April 2006 reminding them that 'reductions in homelessness numbers' were to be achieved through more effective help, and not through 'a gate-keeping approach that discourages people from applying for housing assistance'.[26]

---

[23]   See **17.147–17.154** for 'qualifying offers'.

[24]   See, for example, *Complaint against Blackpool Borough Council*, 04/C/373, 18 January 2005 and *Complaint against Barnet London Borough Council*, 04/A/09817, 16 May 2006. More recent Ombudsmen reports are at **8.77–8.78**.

[25]   See **9.80–9.56**.

[26]   Minister for Housing and Planning 'Letter to Chief Housing Officers, English local housing authorities', 12 April 2006.

Homelessness prevention: a guide to good practice

8.17 In June 2006, the UK Government published *Homelessness prevention, a guide to good practice*,[27] bringing together all the various policy initiatives and guidance since the publication of *More than a Roof*.[28]

8.18 The non-statutory *Good Practice Guidance*[29] for local housing authorities in England defined homelessness prevention as 'activities that enable a household to remain in their current home, where appropriate, or that provide options to enable a planned and timely move and help to sustain independent living'.[30] It reviewed the activities undertaken by local housing authorities in England in the area homelessness prevention and found that the six most common prevention practices were:

- provision of housing advice;

- rent deposit schemes;[31]

- family mediation;

- domestic violence victim support;

- assistance for ex-offenders; and

- tenancy sustainable services.

8.19 The Guidance itself concentrated on the same areas. It recommended more use of rent deposit and rent guarantee schemes; mediation schemes; and working closely with local private sector and voluntary sector landlords. Early intervention was recommended where possible. In an example of how prevention work can be used simultaneously with the duties to an applicant for homelessness assistance under HA 1996, Part 7,[32] the Guidance encouraged local housing authorities in England to offer rent deposits and assured shorthold tenancies in order to bring a main housing duty owed to an end.[33] It also suggested that private landlords could be approached to agree that rents

---

[27] CLG, June 2006.

[28] DTLR, 2002.

[29] *Homeless Prevention: a guide to good practice* (CLG, June 2006).

[30] *Homelessness prevention*, para 2.2.

[31] See *R (Raw) v Lambeth London Borough Council* [2010] EWHC 507 (Admin), (2010) May *Legal Action*, p 24, Admin Ct, for the operation of one such rent deposit scheme see **8.73**.

[32] For those duties, see Chapter 17. For some court decisions on the inter-play of prevention activity and duties owed to applicants for homelessness assistance, see **8.66–8.73**.

[33] At the time of publication of the Guidance, assured shorthold tenancies could be offered to applicants who were owed the main housing duty at HA 1996, s 193(2) by way of 'qualifying offers' of accommodation which applicants could refuse without the main housing duty coming to an end (see **17.147–17.154**). Applicants whose applications for homelessness assistance have been made on or after 9 November 2012 to a local housing authority in England can now be made 'private rented sector offers' (HA 1996, s 193(7AA)–(7AC) amended by LA 2011, s 148 (5)–(7)), see **17.109–17.131**. At the date of writing, the

should be set at no higher than housing benefit limits and consideration could be given to making discretionary housing benefit payments available where there is a shortfall between rent and housing benefit limits. Three Chapters contained advice on prevention work with beneficiaries of what were then the new categories of priority need: young people, victims of domestic violence and ex-offenders.[34]

8.20 In July 2006, the new and still current edition of the English Homelessness Code of Guidance was published.[35] This edition of the Code contains a substantial Chapter (Chapter 2) on prevention, together with a very full annex (Annex 7).

Reports and activities following the good practice guidance

8.21 An evaluation of the prevention activities operated by local housing authorities in England was published by Communities and Local Government in December 2007: *Evaluating Homelessness Prevention.*[36]

8.22 In 2008, Communities and Local Government published guidance on specific aspects of prevention: *Prevention of Homelessness – the role of health and social* care,[37] and *Joint Working between Housing and Children's Services, preventing homelessness and tackling its effects on children and young people.*[38]

8.23 In response to the recession, Communities and Local Government introduced a 'mortgage rescue' scheme for use by local housing authorities in England in January 2009 which remains in operation. People who have a priority need[39] and whose household earns less than £60,000 a year are able to apply to their local housing authorities for help. The help comes in the form either of a shared equity loan, whereby a private registered provider pays a proportion of the mortgage in return for a share of the equity, or of an outright purchase by a private registered provider on terms that the homeowner continues to occupy the property as a tenant.[40]

8.24 A *Short Guide from Regional Resource Teams to Local Authorities on how to Prevent Homelessness due to Mortgage and Landlord Repossession* was

---

amendments to HA 1996, Part 7, made by LA 2011, ss 148–149 had not been brought into effect in Wales and so local housing authorities may still make qualifying offers to applicants owed the main housing duty.

[34] Homelessness (Priority Need for Accommodation) (England) Order 2002, SI 2002/2015, arts 3, 4, 5(e) and 6. See Appendix 2 of this book. See **13.126–13.211**.

[35] *Homelessness Code of Guidance for Local Authorities* (Department for Communities and Local Government, Department for Education and Skills, Department of Health, July 2006) (the English Code), see Appendix 2.

[36] Pawson, Netto, Jones, Wager, Fancy and Lomax (CLG, December 2007).

[37] CLG, Department of Health and the Housing Learning and Improvement Network, May 2007.

[38] CLG and Department for Children, Schools and Families, May 2008.

[39] See Chapter 13 of this book.

[40] For some of the potential difficulties in these arrangements, see *Cook v The Mortgage Business plc* [2012] EWCA Civ 17, [2012] 1 WLR 1521, CA.

published in April 2009.[41] The *Guide* contained a recommendation to local housing authorities in England that they should each develop an action plan. Possible components of that action plan might be:

- regular collection and monitoring of local data for mortgage possession claims and court orders in their areas;

- co-ordination of money advice and court advice services so as to reduce the numbers of possession orders being made against borrowers;

- a targeted plan for supporting home-owners and tenants in the private rented sector who have accumulated mortgage or rent arrears;

- publicity of the government help available;

- regular meetings with local private registered providers to agree ways of tackling the risk of increased numbers of applications for homelessness assistance as a result of higher levels of rent arrears;

- meetings with local private landlords to co-ordinate local action to prevent increased numbers of applications for homelessness assistance due to rent arrears, including the setting up of early warning systems with the housing benefit services, a landlord hotline to enable early intervention from the housing options service, support for vulnerable tenants and consideration of direct payments of housing benefit, improving the take-up of housing benefit, ensuring that people can obtain money advice and the possibility of the local housing authority agreeing to pay a proportion of arrears through a homeless prevention fund in some cases; and

- a small hardship fund operated by a local housing authority to pay for finders' fees or small one-off payments to clear or reduce rent or mortgage arrears.

8.25 The mortgage rescue scheme was subject to an interim evaluation in September 2009, and those findings were published in July 2010.[42] DCLG collected and published statistics on the take-up of the Mortgage Rescue Scheme until May 2011. By March 2011 2,621 households had accepted offers of assistance under the scheme. The most recent statistics, now published by the Homes and Communities Agency, show that 820 households were helped under the Mortgage Rescue Scheme between April and September 2011.[43]

---

[41] CLG, 2009. See also HB/CTB Circular A21/2009 (DWP, 2009).
[42] *Evaluation of the Mortgage Rescue Scheme and Home-owners Mortgage Support: Interim Report* (DCLG, July 2010).
[43] *2011/12 Mortgage Rescue Completions – April to September 2011* (Homes and Communities Agency, 2011).

8.26 Home-owners who are receiving welfare benefits may also be eligible for Support for Mortgage Interest (SMI) payments.[44] For claimants receiving job-seekers' allowance, SMI payments are limited to a maximum period of two years. The effectiveness of the SMI scheme was evaluated by the Department for Work and Pensions (DWP) in July 2011.[45] It was noted that the number of repossessions by lenders might increase as the two-year maximum period of help for some claimants had come to a close, although overall the scheme was considered to be successful.

8.27 A scheme for the whole of the UK, 'Homeowners Mortgage Support', involves the Government encouraging lenders to delay some of the monthly interest payments due on a mortgage. The DCLG *Evaluation of the Mortgage Rescue Scheme and Home-owners Mortgage Support: Interim Report*[46] found that the Scheme had only reached 32 borrowers when assistance to up to 42,000 borrowers had been anticipated.[47]

DCLG reports

8.28 In August 2012, DCLG published two reports: *Evidence review of the costs of homelessness*[48] and *Making every contact count: a joint approach to preventing homelessness.*[49] The latter report was the second report of the Ministerial Working Group on Homelessness, set up in 2010 after the election of the UK Coalition Government.[50]

8.29 The *Evidence review of the costs of homelessness* relied upon research studies which found that the DWP, the Department of Health, the Ministry of Justice and local housing authorities all spent considerable resources in dealing with individuals who are homelessness. The estimates of costs incurred ranged from a gross annual cost per person of £24,500 to an overall annual cost of £1 billion spent by DCLG and local housing authorities. This latter figure does not include the amounts spent on additional health or welfare benefits needs as a result of a person being homeless, nor the costs involved in dealing with criminal offences committed as a result of homelessness.

8.30 In order to reduce those costs, the second publication *Making every contact count: a joint approach to preventing homelessness*[51] contains one simple aim: 'to make sure that every contact local agencies make with vulnerable people and families really counts'. It contains recommendations as to how the

---

[44] Support for Mortgage Interest is a UK-wide benefit operated by the DWP and so is available to claimants in England, Wales, Scotland and Northern Ireland.
[45] DWP Research Report, No 740 (DWP, 2011).
[46] DCLG, July 2010, see **8.25**.
[47] More up to date figures are collated by the Homes and Communities Agency, see **8.25**.
[48] DCLG, August 2012.
[49] DCLG, August 2012.
[50] See **7.19–7.22**.
[51] DCLG, August 2012.

UK Government can help local authorities, including local housing authorities, along with the voluntary sector and other 'local agencies' to work together so as to:

- tackle troubled childhoods and adolescence;

- improve health and tackle inequalities in health;

- provide early intervention for drug and alcohol misuse;

- target help on offenders so as to reduce re-offending;

- help homeless individuals to gain confidence, skills and paid employment;

- assist people in debt, through the mortgage rescue scheme, co-ordinated debt advice services and the introduction of universal credit; and

- prevent homelessness in specific communities, such as recent migrants, or former servicemen and women.

8.31 Since 2010, DCLG has made £160 million a year available to local housing authorities in England as a Homelessness Prevention Grant. In September 2012, the then Minister for Housing announced the continuation of this grant, and the amount specifically allocated to each local housing authority in England, for another two years, to early 2015.[52] The Homelessness Prevention Grant is to be used by local housing authorities in England to:

- provide rent deposit schemes;

- provide mediation schemes so as to prevent homelessness upon the breakdown of relationships; and

- fund outreach services to help rough sleepers obtain accommodation.

8.32 The latest figures published by DCLG show that around 43% of people who are potentially homeless and obtained prevention assistance are assisted to remain in their existing homes and around 57% are assisted to obtain alternative accommodation.[53]

Prevention in Wales: 2004–2012

8.33 The Welsh Assembly Government published *The prevention of homelessness: an advice note* in August 2004.[54] The document was aimed at the

---

[52] *Homelessness Prevention Grant – provisional allocation to local authorities 2013/2014 and 2014/2015* (DCLG, September 2012).

[53] *Homelessness Prevention and Relief: England 2011/2012 Official Statistics* (DCLG, August 2012).

[54] Welsh Assembly Government, 2004.

voluntary sector, not at local housing authorities. Drawing on research from elsewhere in the United Kingdom, and from the United States, Germany and Australia, it stressed the importance of early intervention in order to prevent homelessness. It identified six particularly vulnerable groups of people who would benefit from advice tailored to their needs:

- young people;

- households at risk of homelessness through anti-social behaviour;

- those suffering from mental health problems;

- ex-offenders;

- long-term homeless people; and

- drug users.

8.34 The main recommendations were:

- increased use of rent in advance and deposit schemes to access the private rented sector;

- offering mediation between families, neighbours, and landlords and tenants; and

- providing long-term support to assist vulnerable people to maintain tenancies.

8.35 Some critical reports of local housing authority practice in Wales on prevention have emerged, notably the Public Services Ombudsman for Wales' report *Housing Allocations and Homelessness: A Special Report by the Local Government Ombudsman for Wales*.[55]

8.36 The Welsh Assembly Government's *Ten Year Homelessness Plan for 2009–2019*[56] has 'preventing homelessness, wherever possible' as its first of five strategic aims. The aim is to reduce homelessness to a minimum by 2019 and eliminate rough sleeping. It encourages housing advice and early intervention, before an existing home has been lost. In the private rented sector, local housing authorities in Wales should work with private landlords so that those landlords might be encouraged to let to people traditionally seen as vulnerable and 'high risk'. Housing benefit payments should be made quickly, accurately and promptly. There should be more financial and debt advice available. In the social housing sector, there should be more help to assist tenants to sustain their tenancy and possession should only be pursued as a last resort.

---

[55] February 2006. See **7.29** and **8.75**.
[56] Welsh Assembly Government, July 2009. See also **7.31–7.33**.

8.37 The *Ten Year Homelessness Plan for 2009–2019* aims for comprehensive advice and assistance to be available to consumers before they purchase their homes and enter into mortgage commitments. It also suggests improvements in regulation and enforcement, so that the courts only approve possession actions when lenders have explored all other options. It suggests the possibility of regulation for private sale and leaseback schemes, and the development of a protocol between lenders and local housing authorities so that lenders would notify local housing authorities' homelessness prevention teams, presumably in advance of any possession claim being issued.

8.38 In September 2009, the Welsh Assembly Government set up and funded a mortgage rescue scheme, similar to that set up by the UK government.[57] Home-owners who are receiving benefits may also be eligible for Support for Mortgage Interest payments.[58] Some home-owners may benefit from the UK-wide 'Home-owners Mortgage Support'.[59]

8.39 In May 2012, the Welsh Government published *Homes for Wales: A White Paper for Better Lives and Communities*.[60] A Chapter is devoted to the prevention of homelessness. The White Paper states 'access to good advice is the foundation for preventing homelessness'. It contains proposals for legislation so as to extend the definition of 'threatened with homelessness' to a period of 56 rather than 28 days.[61] The aim is that, during that period, the applicant might be assisted to remain in his or her home.[62]

8.40 In addition, the White Paper proposes new legislation to create a new statutory duty to oblige local housing authorities in Wales to take 'all reasonable steps to achieve a suitable housing solution for all households which are homeless or threatened with homelessness'. The duty would be owed to all eligible homeless households,[63] irrespective of any priority need,[64] without any application of the 'becoming homeless intentionally' test[65] or any consideration of local connection or other conditions for referral.[66] The local housing authority would be required to consider what could be done to enable an applicant to sustain his or her existing accommodation or to move to suitable accommodation. If the applicant has nowhere safe to stay, interim accommodation should be secured by local housing authorities while housing

---

[57]   *Guidance to housing associations and local authorities on the mortgage rescue scheme* (Welsh Assembly Government, September 2009). For the UK government funded mortgage rescue scheme, see **8.23–8.25**.

[58]   See **8.26**.

[59]   See **8.27**.

[60]   May 2012, Welsh Government. See **7.36–7.39**.

[61]   See **7.38** and **11.129–11.133** for 'threatened with homelessness'.

[62]   For duties owed to applicants who are threatened with homelessness, see **17.190–17.200**.

[63]   For 'eligible', see Chapter 12 of this book. The White Paper uses the term 'households'. The authors assume that in this context 'households' includes a single applicant without any dependents.

[64]   See Chapter 13 of this book.

[65]   See Chapter 14 of this book.

[66]   See Chapter 15 of this book.

solutions are being considered, regardless of any priority need test.[67] The duty to seek a suitable housing solution will be brought to an end in one of two ways: firstly by the offer a qualifying housing solution and, secondly, if a qualifying housing solution cannot be achieved, through the usual process of making inquiries into whether any duty is owed to the applicant under HA 1996, Part 7.[68]

Prevention in the 2012 Welsh Code of Guidance

8.41   The new Welsh Code of Guidance was published in August 2012.[69] In his introduction, the Welsh Minister for Housing, Regeneration and Heritage writes:

> '[t]his revised Code of Guidance provides a range of good practice to assist work to prevent and tackle homelessness, linked to the vision and principles of the Ten Year Homelessness Plan for Wales'.[70]

8.42   The Welsh Code contains a specific Chapter on 'preventing homelessness'[71] and the Chapter's contents are summarised as placing 'an emphasis on greater use of the private rented sector recognising the pressure on the social housing sector. For many people in housing need the private rented sector may be the only option for finding the housing they want. The development of Private Sector Access agencies and stronger lies with the private rented sector is encouraged.'[72]

8.43   The Welsh Code advises that '[a]ll services working with people vulnerable to homelessness should have prevention as a primary objective'. The 'first option to be considered should be for the client to remain at the current accommodation where suitable',[73] and that, where this is not possible, the client should be assisted to find and retain alternative accommodation, with support if necessary. The Code reminds local housing authorities in Wales that advice and information about homelessness, and the prevention of homelessness, are available free of charge to **any person** in their district regardless of whether they have a local connection'.[74] Where a person may be homeless within 28 days, the Code correctly advises that an application for homelessness assistance should be accepted and that prevention work should continue alongside the statutory inquiries.[75]

---

[67]   For the duty to secure interim accommodation, see **16.12–16.35**.
[68]   See Chapter 17 of this book.
[69]   See CD-Rom.
[70]   Huw Lewis AM, Minister for Housing, Regeneration and Heritage, introduction, Welsh Code.
[71]   Welsh Code, Chapter 10, see **7.40–7.41**.
[72]   Welsh Code, para 7.5.
[73]   Welsh Code, para 10.26.
[74]   Welsh Code, para 10.13, bold emphasis in original. For the duty at HA 1996, s 179 to provide advice and information, see **9.4–9.7**.
[75]   For 'an application for homelessness assistance', see **9.8–9.63**. For 'may be homeless within 28 days', see **11.129–11.133**. For inquiries, see **10.1–10.65**.

8.44 Prevention activities can include advice, joint working with other statutory services and with registered social landlords, financial assistance including the provision of rent deposits or bond, ensuring the efficient delivery of housing benefit and maintaining a homelessness prevention fund for financial assistance to applicants. Such financial assistance is described as 'spend to save policies', thus saving the potential costs of receiving an application for homelessness assistance and performing any of the duties owed under HA 1996, Part 7.[76]

8.45 Family mediation schemes, negotiation with private landlords, and co-operation with the local housing authority's own housing department so as to avoid possession proceedings are all encouraged.

8.46 Use of the private rented sector is described as offering 'the only realistic opportunity of finding the type of property [applicants] need in their preferred location'.[77] Schemes for low-cost home-ownership or for assistance with mortgages or other debts are also encouraged.[78] Particular groups of people who are more likely to be at risk of homelessness are listed, together with measures that could assist them.[79]

8.47 The effectiveness of prevention work should be regularly monitored, so that services can be improved to accord with best practice.[80] Consideration should be given to the risk of recurrent homelessness, and to helping applicants tackle reasons why they might be repeatedly homelessness.[81]

8.48 Local housing authorities in Wales should monitor the effectiveness of their prevention practices. All cases should be recorded and the results considered in order to measure the effectiveness of each aspect of prevention.[82]

8.49 As already noted,[83] the Welsh Government has ambitious plans to create a new statutory duty requiring local housing authorities to take 'all reasonable steps to achieve a suitable housing solution for all households which are homeless or threatened with homelessness'.[84]

---

[76] Welsh Code, paras 10.41–10.42.
[77] Welsh Code, para 10.29.
[78] Welsh Code, paras 10.27–10.28.
[79] Welsh Code, paras 10.43–10.45, 10.49–10.69.
[80] Welsh Code, para 10.73.
[81] Welsh Code, paras 10.46–10.47.
[82] Welsh Code, para 10.73.
[83] See **7.36–7.39**.
[84] *Homes for Wales: A White Paper for Better Lives and Communities* (Welsh Government, May 2012), see Chapter 7, at **7.38**.

EVALUATING HOMELESSNESS PREVENTION

UK government evaluation

8.50 In December 2007, research commissioned by Communities and Local Government was published: *Evaluating Homelessness Prevention.*[85] The authors had studied local housing authorities' homelessness prevention activities launched as a result of their homelessness strategies. They found that homelessness prevention work was increasing amongst local housing authorities. They recommended that, to be effective, prevention should be pro-active rather than reactive and aim at resolving applicants' housing problems. The most widely adopted methods of homelessness prevention were:

- enhanced housing advice;

- rent deposit and similar schemes to increase access to private tenancies;

- family mediation schemes;

- domestic violence victim support; and

- help sustaining tenancies.

8.51 The intended beneficiaries of homelessness prevention work included those people who did not have a priority need, as well as those who were likely to be assessed as being homeless and having a priority need. However, the sharp drop in the numbers of homeless applicants who were found to be owed the main housing duty[86] showed that those who did have a priority need were also likely to receive prevention assistance. Prevention was said to be cost-effective, particularly where households who had a priority need were concerned, and also particularly for Greater London local housing authorities (because there were substantial savings in the cost of temporary accommodation).[87]

8.52 The authors of the report were aware of the criticisms made by housing advisers, and occasionally reiterated in the courts, that homelessness prevention activities can amount to 'gatekeeping' and to an unlawful delay or postponement of inquiries under HA 1996, Part 7. They recommended that local housing authorities should review their procedures and practices to ensure that they are complying with their obligations under HA 1996, Part 7.

8.53 As far as particular areas of homelessness prevention are concerned, enhanced and pro-active housing advice was said to be cost-effective for those

---

[85] Pawson, Netto, Jones, Wager, Fancy and Lomax (CLG, December 2007).
[86] HA 1996, s 193(2). See **17.23–17.168**.
[87] The cost-effectiveness of homelessness prevention work has been emphasised most recently by the two reports published by DCLG in August 2012: *Evidence review of the costs of homelessness* and *Making every contact count: a joint approach to preventing homelessness*, see **7.21** and **8.28–8.30**.

people who would otherwise have made an application for homelessness assistance under HA 1996, Part 7, and be owed the main housing duty. The cost-effectiveness of housing advice to a household that is unlikely to be owed the main housing duty was less clear-cut. Rent deposits and other schemes assisting people to find private tenancies were said to be 'highly cost-effective'. Family mediation schemes were more problematic. For applicants leaving domestic violence, sanctuary schemes had proved effective in preventing homelessness, provided it was recognised that they were not appropriate in every case. Housing advice provided in prison to offenders approaching release was considered effective, but there was a lack of suitable post-release supported and mainstream accommodation for prisoners, and only a few ex-prisoners were likely to be classed as 'vulnerable' and therefore have a priority need.[88]

8.54 The authors concluded that, since the number of applicants for homelessness assistance who were found to be owed the main housing duty had declined substantially since 2003, homelessness prevention was a success, even taking into account the economic stability between 2003 and 2006 and other factors that may influence the numbers of applicants for homelessness assistance. Their principal recommendation was that the outcomes of homelessness prevention should be more carefully monitored, so that their effectiveness can be better assessed.

8.55 In August 2010, DCLG published an evaluation of sanctuary schemes, enabling those at risk of domestic violence to remain in their homes: *The effectiveness of schemes to enable households at risk of domestic violence to remain in their homes.*[89]

Evaluation in Wales

8.56 In 2010 and 2011, the Welsh Government funded 16 short-term projects designed to 'help embed the prevention agenda within the homelessness framework operating in Wales'.[90] Recognising that evaluation was a critical part of the programme, the Welsh Government also set aside additional funding for an independent evaluation of those projects. The results of the evaluation, carried out by Housing + Cymru, were published in October 2011: *Evaluation of one year homelessness prevention projects.*[91] The report contained a number of recommendations for the Welsh Government and for other organisations involved in delivering services for the prevention of homelessness. It found that:

---

[88] The requirement that ex-offenders must also be 'vulnerable' in order to have a priority need applies to applicants to local housing authorities in England only (see **13.196–13.202**) and not to applicants to local housing authorities in Wales (see **13.239–13.245**).

[89] Jons, Bretherton, Bowles & Croucher (DCLG, August 2010).

[90] *Evaluation of one year homelessness prevention projects* (Welsh Government, October 2011), para 1.1.

[91] Welsh Government, October 2011.

- prevention of homelessness projects should be monitored to assess outcomes over the medium and long term, rather than simply the short term;

- some short-term projects limited to one financial year had problems assessing what services could be realistically delivered in that period;

- there was a risk that some projects receiving short-term funding could not be sustained in the longer term; and

- one of the measurements affecting the amount of funding that the Welsh Government gives local housing authorities for the delivery of homelessness services is the number of decisions on applications for homelessness assistance made by a local housing authority in the previous year, and that this 'potentially creates a perverse incentive' for local housing authorities not to invest in homelessness prevention services.[92]

8.57 The report set out five new measures to monitor homelessness prevention, and its authors recommended that those should be adopted by the Welsh Government in place of the government's national performance indicators for local housing authorities in Wales.[93] It contained recommendations for increased investment in homelessness prevention work, in order to achieve benefits and savings for national government and local housing authorities over a longer period.[94] Its authors noted '[s]ometimes, homelessness prevention can be considered from the perspective of preventing people from accessing resources (rationing) as opposed to preventing people becoming homeless.... As more gateway type projects are developed and operated by local authorities, this issue may become more prevalent. The Welsh Government needs to consider whether this is an acceptable outcome, or whether guidance is necessary.'[95]

8.58 Surprisingly, although the Welsh Code of Guidance[96] was published less than a year later, it contains no specific reference to any of these recommendations. As already noted,[97] the Welsh Code does contain advice that local housing authorities and other organisations monitor the effectiveness of their prevention practices, but does not include any guidance as to how that monitoring might be carried out. The Code also notes that the Welsh

---

[92] *Evaluation of one year homelessness prevention projects* (Welsh Government, October 2011), para 4.6.
[93] *Evaluation of one year homelessness prevention projects* (Welsh Government, October 2011), para 4.8 and Appendix 3.
[94] *Evaluation of one year homelessness prevention projects* (Welsh Government, October 2011), para 4.9.
[95] *Evaluation of one year homelessness prevention projects* (Welsh Government, October 2011), para 4.18.
[96] Welsh Code, see CD-Rom.
[97] See **8.41–8.49**.

Government is reviewing the effectiveness of the current national Performance Indicator on homelessness prevention.[98]

Other commentators on homelessness prevention

8.59 Shelter published concerns about the actual practice of prevention operated by local housing authorities in England, whilst supporting the principle. In its *Policy Briefing: Homelessness Prevention*,[99] it commented:

> 'the current policy framework around homelessness prevention contains certain ambiguities and tensions that must be resolved if suitable prevention is to be achieved. These tensions centre around the relationship between homelessness prevention policy and the statutory safety net provided by homelessness legislation.'

8.60 It recommended:

> 'applicants who are entitled to accommodation as a result of a duty being owed to them under HA 1996, Part 7, should be free to decide to accept that accommodation in addition to any other options being offered to them under homelessness prevention services.'

8.61 Shelter criticised the publication *Homelessness Prevention: A Guide to Good Practice*[100] as suggesting a two-stage process for households that are homeless and likely to be owed the main housing duty, so that options and prevention are considered first, with the homelessness duty acting as a 'safeguard'. The target to halve the number of households living in temporary accommodation by 2010, combined with the shortage of social rented housing, created a strong incentive for local housing authorities to pursue homelessness prevention as a means of reducing the number of homelessness acceptances. Shelter urged local housing authorities to review their practices. It was concerned that some of the prevention options only provided a short-term response to long-term housing problems. It recommended that the causes of homelessness should be tackled.

8.62 Alongside this general briefing, Shelter published briefings on particular aspects of homelessness prevention schemes: *Homelessness prevention and the private rented sector*,[101] *Homelessness prevention and sanctuary schemes*,[102] and *Homelessness prevention and mediation*,[103] and its own Good Practice Guide: *Homelessness: Early Identification and Prevention – A Good Practice Guide*.[104]

---

[98] Welsh Code, para 10.73.
[99] Shelter, August 2007.
[100] CLG, June 2006. See **8.17–8.19**.
[101] Shelter, August 2007.
[102] Shelter, August 2007.
[103] Shelter, August 2007.
[104] Shelter, June 2007.

8.63 A barrister who represented the claimants in several legal challenges to the practices operated by Birmingham's City Council Housing Options Services[105] has commented on 'the systematic neglect of homeless people caused by cash-strapped councils'.[106] He identified six examples of 'gate-keeping' rather than prevention:

- failing to take an application for homelessness assistance;

- insisting that the applicant, if an existing council tenant, proceed by making an application for a transfer through the allocation scheme;

- making an appointment for a date in the future for an application for homelessness assistance to be taken and telling the potential applicant to return on that date;

- not accepting that the 'reason to believe' test has been satisfied until written evidence has been produced to prove homelessness or priority need;

- referring an applicant to another organisation; and

- making a negative decision on the same day as the application for assistance.

8.64 Each of these examples – save possibly for the last one – would be a breach of a local housing authority's duties under HA 1996, Part 7, to accept an application for homelessness assistance and to make full inquiries into the application before notifying the applicant of the decision.[107]

8.65 In September 2011, the magazine *Inside Housing* found that a very high proportion of decisions on applications for homelessness assistance were subsequently overturned on review. It quoted solicitors, homelessness charities and legal advisers who were concerned that the poor decision-making was a form of gate-keeping.[108]

Prevention in the courts

8.66 The Court of Appeal first considered a local housing authority's use of prevention – in the particular case, family mediation – alongside its statutory duty to an applicant for homelessness assistance under HA 1996, Part 7, in *Robinson v Hammersmith & Fulham London Borough Council*.[109] A homeless 17-year-old girl, approaching her 18th birthday, had applied to the local housing authority for homelessness assistance, having been excluded from the

[105] See **8.67–8.70**.
[106] 'Out in the cold', Nabi [2010] 104 *Solicitors Journal* Issue 43, p 12.
[107] See Chapters 9 and 10.
[108] *42% of reviews overturned, Inside Housing*, 23 September 2011, p 2.
[109] [2006] EWCA Civ 1122, [2007] HLR 7, CA.

family home by her mother. The local housing authority accepted the application, but postponed making its inquiries into whether or not she was homeless, and whether it owed her a duty,[110] while it attempted to set up mediation between the girl and her mother. The Court of Appeal held that it was not legitimate to use mediation to postpone either the making of inquiries or the taking of a decision. Mediation may be used in order to *perform* any duty that is owed to the applicant under HA 1996, Part 7, but not to prevent the duty arising in the first place.[111]

The Birmingham litigation

8.67 A more general practice came under scrutiny in *R (Aweys) v Birmingham City Council*.[112] Birmingham City Council operated a policy whereby an individual who indicated that he or she might be homeless was required to go through a Home Options Interview so that the local housing authority could consider whether homelessness could be prevented or alternative accommodation provided.

8.68 The Administrative Court judge said:

'the Home Options Scheme ... cannot lawfully be used to defer consideration of a homeless application. All steps taken to avoid homelessness are of course laudable. But any such steps must be taken in parallel to the carrying out of the duty under Pt VII.'[113]

8.69 In 2009, another Administrative Court judge was severely critical of Birmingham City Council's instruction to its housing officers to advise an applicant to return to his or her address, rather than providing interim accommodation, finding that the instruction was unlawful and a breach of the duty at HA 1996, s 188(1).[114]

8.70 In 2010, the Administrative Court considered an instruction from the Interim Head of Housing Needs at Birmingham City Council which stated that an application for homelessness assistance should not be completed in certain

---

[110] See Chapter 17.

[111] If, for example, the mediation had achieved reconciliation between mother and daughter, the local housing authority could have performed any duty owed to the daughter to accommodate her by securing accommodation from the mother, or by providing advice and assistance that secured that the mother's accommodation was available to the daughter (HA 1996, s 206(1)(b) and (c)). See **17.12**.

[112] [2007] EWHC 52 (Admin), [2007] HLR 27, Admin Ct. Birmingham subsequently appealed to the Court of Appeal and to the House of Lords, as *Ali & others v Birmingham City Council* is at [2009] UKHL 36, [2009] 1 WLR 1506, HL. The appeal was not against the first-instance judge's findings in relation to the Home Options Interview.

[113] *R (Aweys) v Birmingham City Council* [2007] EWHC 52 (Admin), [2007] HLR 27 at [25] per Collins J.

[114] *R (Kelly & Mehari) v Birmingham City Council* [2009] EWHC 3240 (Admin), (2010) *Legal Action* January, p 35, Admin Ct. See **16.19**.

cases.[115] The instruction was retracted six months' later. The judge found that the instruction had been unlawful, as were actions taken as a result of it (a point conceded by Birmingham City Council). The judge also found that a blanket 'same day' policy, which required a decision on the application for homelessness assistance on the same day as the application had been made, so that any duty to secure interim accommodation did not arise, would be unlawful. The judge suggested that the council undertook a thorough review of the procedures adopted in homelessness cases.

Other court decisions

8.71 Various court decisions have dealt with what should happen when an applicant has made an application for homelessness assistance and homelessness is resolved by prevention activity. The first case decided that, if the applicant has been assisted to find alternative accommodation, usually in the form of an assured shorthold tenancy, before the conclusion of the statutory inquiries required by HA 1996, s 184(1),[116] the local housing authority can lawfully notify a decision that the applicant is no longer homeless and therefore no duty is owed under HA 1996, Part 7.[117]

8.72 In the second case,[118] the local housing authority had secured accommodation for the applicant after she had made an application for homelessness assistance. It could have then notified her of a decision under HA 1996, s 184(1) that she was not homeless. However, it failed to conclude its statutory inquiries or notify her of any HA 1996 s 184(1) decision. When she was later evicted from that accommodation and made a further application for homelessness assistance, the local housing authority decided that she had become homeless intentionally from that accommodation. That decision was held by a county court judge to be wrong in law. As there had been no HA 1996, s 184(1) decision on her first application for homelessness assistance, the applicant had occupied the accommodation as a result of the local housing authority's duty at HA 1996, s 188(1).[119] An applicant cannot be found to have become homeless intentionally from accommodation occupied under the HA 1996, s 188(1) duty.[120] Had the local housing authority concluded its statutory inquiries on the applicant's first application for homelessness assistance and

---

[115] *R (Khazai & others) v Birmingham City Council* [2010] EWHC 2576 (Admin), *Legal Action*, December p 37, Admin Ct.

[116] See **10.66–10.74**.

[117] *Hanton-Rhouila v Westminster City Council* [2010] EWCA Civ 1334, [2011] HLR 12, CA.

[118] *O'Callaghan v Southwark London Borough Council* (2010) *Legal Action* May p 23, Lambeth County Court.

[119] A duty that only comes to an end when a HA 1996, s 184(1) decision has been notified to the applicant (HA 1996, s 188(3)), see Chapter 16, at **16.12–16.35**.

[120] Because the applicant remains 'homeless' while he or she occupies the accommodation secured under HA 1996, s 188(1), see *R (Alam) v Tower Hamlets London Borough Council* [2009] EWHC 44, (2009) March Legal Action, p 24, Admin Ct, and Chapter 11, at **11.13**. As a person remains 'homeless' according to the definition of HA 1996, ss 175–177 whilst occupying interim accommodation, he or she cannot have become homeless intentionally from that accommodation.

notified her of a HA 1996, s 184(1) decision that she was not homeless, it might have been entitled to find that she had become homeless intentionally when that accommodation subsequently came to an end.

8.73 The operation of a homelessness prevention rent deposit scheme was considered in *R (Raw) v Lambeth London Borough Council*.[121] The local housing authority's published terms and conditions for its rent deposit scheme included 'by agreeing to seek housing through the Letting First Scheme, you understand (and have decided) that you will not be making, or continuing with a homelessness application to Lambeth or to any other local authority'. In correspondence through solicitors, the local housing authority informed one claimant that he would not be prevented from making an application for homelessness assistance. By the time the case was heard in court, the local housing authority had accepted an application for homelessness assistance and had found that it owed the applicant a main housing duty to secure accommodation for him. As a result, the Administrative Court decided not to consider the lawfulness of the rent deposit scheme, since the issue was academic for the applicant. However, the judge did say:

> 'it might well be that a blanket policy of ceasing inquiries in all cases where a [HA 1996] Part VII applicant has been referred to the rent deposit scheme could be construed as such an avoidance of statutory obligation. In short the benefits of the rent deposit scheme, great though they may be, are not equivalent to and may not be an adequate substitute for at any rate the benefits to a [HA 1996] Part VII applicant of the duty to provide interim accommodation under section 188, which benefits may in practice be diminished or undermined in the event of the Council not completing its section 184 inquiries.'[122]

Ombudsmen reports

8.74 The Ombudsmen for both England and Wales have each considered the use of homelessness prevention measures where applicants have made applications for homelessness assistance in accordance with HA 1996, Part 7. They have each said that alternatives to using the homelessness legislation may be considered by local housing authorities but should not be used to set aside the rights and duties conferred by law.[123]

8.75 The Public Services Ombudsman for Wales published *Housing Allocation and Homelessness: A Special Report by the Local Government Ombudsman for Wales*[124] in 2006. The Public Services Ombudsman found that too many local housing authorities were refusing to accept applications for homelessness assistance, failing to conduct inquiries or issue decisions and failing to inform homeless applicants (and applicants to their allocation schemes) of their statutory rights. The findings were particularly ironic, given that a report just

---

[121] [2010] EWHC 507 (Admin), (2010) May *Legal Action*, p 24, Admin Ct.
[122] Stadlen J at [77]. It should be noted that Stadlen J had decided that the claim was academic and these observations were *obiter*.
[123] *Complaint against Nottingham City Council*, 04/C/18012, 12 July 2006.
[124] Public Services Ombudsman for Wales, 2006.

six months earlier had castigated some local housing authorities in Wales for permitting too many homelessness acceptances (by recognition of the main housing duty) and for not implementing the prevention agenda.[125]

8.76 The Local Government Ombudsman was concerned enough about possible avoidance of duties by local housing authorities in England under HA 1996, Part 7, to issue a special focus report in July 2011: *Homelessness: how councils can ensure justice for homeless people.*[126] The Ombudsman found that local housing authorities can cause serious injustice to homeless people by making mistakes in four areas, including in the area of homelessness prevention. The Ombudsman said that, where local housing authorities suggest solutions to people who are potentially homeless, other than the solution of making an application for homelessness assistance, those solutions 'must be appropriate and acceptable to the individual' and 'people must be made aware of their right to make an application if they wish to'.

8.77 Recent finding of maladministration against local housing authorities in England by the Local Government Ombudsman have included:

- a case where the local housing authority had failed to acknowledge that a pregnant applicant was in effect making an application for homelessness assistance when she visited the council office and wrote on a form 'I am homeless now';[127]

- a case where the local housing authority had told an applicant for homelessness assistance that the first available appointment was in 10 days' time. When she attended the appointment, she was not permitted to make an application for homelessness assistance and was told that no temporary accommodation could be made available. The Ombudsman recorded: 'I asked the council to ensure that front-line officers in the H[ousing] A[dvice] C[entre] who deal with people who are homeless understand that, when the statutory criteria are met, a [HA 1996] Part 7 homelessness application should be taken and investigated in tandem with exploring other housing options';[128]

- a case where a man approached the local housing authority with a letter from his mother, with whom he and his family had been living, giving him two week's notice to leave her home. Instead of treating him as threatened with homelessness,[129] the local housing authority told him to start looking for alternative accommodation in the private rented sector and gave him

---

[125] See *Report to the Welsh Assembly Government on Tackling Homelessness – Key issues for consideration by Welsh Local Authorities* (Tarki Technology Ltd, June 2005). See **7.27**.

[126] LGO, July 2011.

[127] *Complaint against Hammersmith & Fulham London Borough Council*, 09 001 262, 21 January 2010, (2010) March *Legal Action*, p 31.

[128] *Complaint against Islington London Borough Council*, 10 013 025, 24 February 2011, (2011) April *Legal Action*, p 31.

[129] HA 1996, s 175(4). See **11.129–11.133**.

details of local landlords and about housing benefit. When his mother's notice had expired, the man and his family returned to the council's offices. They waited six hours and were told that no interim accommodation would be made available for them. They were told to go to the police station. The police were unable to help and the family slept in a car. No decision was made on the application for homelessness assistance until two months later;[130]

- a case where a disabled woman with two children had approached the local housing authority after she had been served with a valid Housing Act 1988, s 21 notice by her landlord, she was told to 'come back when the court had made an order for possession', a possession order was made and she returned to the council offices, she was not provided with accommodation and was later notified of a decision that she was not eligible. It was not until she asked for accommodation pending review that she and her children were provided with accommodation;[131]

- a case where the local housing authority did not take an application for homelessness assistance from a man who had to leave his home following domestic violence, and who said that he suffered from depression and had a history of self-harming, because it did not consider him to have a priority need. The Ombudsman said that was irrelevant: 'the issue was whether [the local housing authority] had reason to believe he was homeless or threatened with homelessness' and 'guidance is clear that steps to prevent homelessness should never replace a statutory assessment'.[132]

8.78 The Public Services Ombudsman for Wales has found both Cardiff City Council[133] and Conwy County Borough Council[134] guilty of maladministration for operating schemes similar to that operated in Birmingham,[135] whereby those approaching the councils for homelessness assistance were seen first by housing advisers and were only in some cases referred for a homelessness assessment.[136] In January 2012, the Public Services Ombudsman for Wales recommended that Wrexham County Borough Council train all its housing staff on the recognition of homelessness and on identification of when

---

[130] *Complaint against Newham London Borough Council*, 11 000 383, 3 March 2012, (2012) May *Legal Action*, p 34.
[131] *Complaint against Southwark London Borough Council*, 10 000 207, 22 May 2012, (2012) August *Legal Action*, p 27.
[132] *Complaint against Hounslow London Borough Council*, 11 008 191, 28 August 2012, (2012) November *Legal Action*, p 14.
[133] *Complaint against Cardiff City Council*, 200600749, 16 April 2008, (2008) June *Legal Action*, p 32.
[134] *Complaint against Conwy County Borough Council*, 200702044, 11 December 2008, (2009) April *Legal Action*, p 22.
[135] See **8.67–8.70**.
[136] See **8.67–8.68**.

inquiries under HA 1996, Part 7 should commence.[137] The local housing authority was required to pay £1,500 compensation to a man who used a wheelchair who had been approaching it since 2007 in an effort to find alternative accommodation.

PREVENTION AND THE REQUIREMENTS OF THE HOUSING ACT 1996, PART 7

8.79 The decisions of the courts and the Ombudsmen discussed in the last section of this Chapter succinctly set out how prevention measures can and cannot lawfully be used in tandem with local housing authorities' statutory duties towards applicants for homelessness assistance under HA 1996, Part 7. Prevention can be used at any stage, but should not be used to avoid or escape the obligations that local housing authorities owe to applicants for homelessness assistance who appear to be, or may be, homeless or threatened with homelessness.[138] Prevention may be used at any time *before* a person in contact with a local housing authority appears to be, or may be, homeless. Once that statutory threshold is achieved, prevention can be used at the same time as the obligations under HA 1996, Part 7 are performed. Those obligations are to make inquiries,[139] notify the applicant of a decision,[140] and provide interim accommodation, if appropriate.[141] The local housing authority cannot refuse to undertake these obligations whilst it provides prevention advice and assistance. If, as a result of advice and assistance provided whilst the local housing authority is carrying out its inquiries, the applicant secures suitable accommodation before the inquiries are concluded, the local housing authority will be entitled to find that the applicant is not homeless and no duty is owed.[142] If the applicant is still homeless (and eligible for assistance), however, a duty will be owed to the applicant, and the local housing authority must perform that duty.

8.80 At that stage, the local housing authority may use the various forms of advice and assistance normally provided under prevention activities in order to perform the duty that it owes to the applicant. Local housing authorities may also bring the main housing duty to an end by making an applicant a private rented sector offer.[143] However, the local housing authority cannot refuse to

---

[137] *Complaint against Wrexham County Borough Council*, Case No: 201002076, 25 January 2012, (2012) April *Legal Action*, p 46.

[138] HA 1996, s 183(1). See **9.8–9.98**. See also English Code, para 2.3; Welsh Code, para 10.5.

[139] HA 1996, s 184(1). See **10.1–10.65**.

[140] HA 1996, s 184(3). See **10.66–10.91**.

[141] HA 1996, s 188(1). See **9.64–9.65** and **16.12–16.35**.

[142] See **11.1–11.128** for definition of 'homeless' and Chapter 17 of this book for duties owed. This is the situation considered by the Administrative Court in *Hanton-Rhouila v Westminster City Council* [2010] EWCA Civ 1334, [2011] HLR 12, CA, see **8.71**.

[143] See **17.109–17.131** for 'private rented sector offers' (HA 1996, s 193(7AA)–(7AC) as amended by LA 2011, s 148(5)–(7)). Private rented sectors offers can be made by local housing authorities in England to applicants for homelessness assistance whose applications were made

perform, or delay performing, any duty that it owes to the applicant whilst the applicant participates in its prevention schemes.

8.81 Local housing authorities may be concerned that an applicant for homelessness assistance will refuse to co-operate with any efforts made to secure accommodation for him or her through the homelessness prevention process. For local housing authorities in England, this concern can be easily resolved by making the applicant who is owed a main housing duty at HA 1996, s 193(2)[144] a private rented sector offer.[145] Provided that this offer is suitable for the needs of the applicant, and all the other requirements at HA 1996, s 193(7AA)–(7AC)[146] have been fulfilled, the main housing duty will be brought to an end whether the applicant accepts or refuses the private rented sector offer.[147] Applicants who are not owed the main housing duty will not have any expectation of any accommodation secured for them by the local housing authority in England for any longer than the short term[148] and so should be more likely to co-operate with efforts to find them accommodation.

8.82 At the date of writing, the amendments to HA 1996 made by LA 2011, ss 148–149 had not been brought into effect in Wales. A local housing authority in Wales may make an applicant who is owed the main housing duty at HA 1996, s 193(2) a qualifying offer of an assured shorthold tenancy, but the main housing duty will only come to an end if the applicant accepts it.[149] The Welsh Code suggests that qualifying offers should be considered 'as an mainstream element in the provision of accommodation for homeless people, including in the discharge of the s 193 duty'.[150] Since there are no adverse consequences for an applicant who is owed the main housing duty if he or she refuses the qualifying offer, the offer can be made more attractive by use of discretionary housing payments to meet any shortfall between the rent and the amount of housing benefit payable. A qualifying offer might also be attractive if it is of accommodation that the applicant is already occupying under the interim

---

on or after 9 November 2012. At the date of writing, the amendments to HA 1996 made by LA 2011, ss 148–149 had not been brought into effect in Wales.

[144] See **17.23–17.168**.

[145] See **17.109–17.131** for 'private rented sector offers' (HA 1996, s 193(7AA)–(7AC) as amended by LA 2011, s 148(5)–(7)). Private rented sectors offers can be made by local housing authorities in England to applicants for homelessness assistance whose applications were made on or after 9 November 2012. At the date of writing, the amendments to HA 1996 made by LA 2011, ss 148–149 had not been brought into effect in Wales.

[146] As amended by LA 2011, s 148 (5)–(7) for applicants whose applications for homelessness assistance were made on or after 9 November 2012 to a local housing authority in England. At the date of writing, the amendments to HA 1996 made by LA 2011, ss 148–149 had not been brought into effect in Wales.

[147] HA 1996, s 193(7AA) as amended by LA 2011, s 148(5) or applicants whose applications for homelessness assistance were made on or after 9 November 2012 to a local housing authority in England. At the date of writing, the amendments to HA 1996 made by LA 2011, ss 148–149 had not been brought into effect in Wales.

[148] For the duties other than main housing duty owed to applicants, see Chapter 17.

[149] HA 1996, s 193(7B)–(7F) prior to amendment by LA 2011, s 148. See Chapter 17, at **17.147–17.154**.

[150] Welsh Code, para 18.27.

accommodation duty at HA 1996, s 188(1)[151] or the main housing duty at HA 1996, s 193(2).[152] However, for local housing authorities in Wales, if an applicant owed the main housing duty refuses a qualifying offer, the main housing duty will continue until one of the other events at HA 1996, s 193(5)–(7) occurs.[153]

---

[151] See **16.12–16.35**.
[152] Welsh Code, paras 18.52–18.54.
[153] See Chapter 17, at **17.23–17.168**.

Chapter 9

ADVISORY SERVICES AND APPLICATIONS FOR HOMELESSNESS ASSISTANCE

INTRODUCTION

9.1   Anyone seeking assistance with homelessness from a local housing authority must take the initiative and approach that local housing authority or its contracted provider of homelessness services. There is no legal duty on local housing authorities in England and Wales to seek out homeless people within their districts in order to offer their services to them. That is as true for those who are 'vulnerable' in housing terms[1] as it is for all the homeless.

9.2   As this Chapter explains, at the point of first contact, a local housing authority has twin responsibilities:

- to ensure that an advice and information service is available in its district for those who want help in preventing or dealing with their homelessness; and

- to receive applications made to it for accommodation (or for assistance in obtaining accommodation).

9.3   This Chapter outlines the statutory requirements relating to advice and information before reviewing the considerable body of law on the treatment of applications.

ADVICE AND INFORMATION

9.4   Each local housing authority must make arrangements so that free advice and information about homelessness and the prevention of homelessness is available to everyone in its district.[2] Beyond that bald requirement, Housing Act 1996 (HA 1996), Part 7, does not specify where, or in what form, or even in what language(s), the free advice and information is to be provided. It is certainly intended that the arrangements should provide 'wide ranging and comprehensive' advice and information.[3] Indeed, the availability of such 'comprehensive' or 'wide-ranging' advice is intended to play an 'important part' in delivering the local housing authority's locally adopted Homelessness Strategy.[4] But beyond that, it is a matter for each local housing authority to determine the format and content of its advice and information arrangements.

9.5   The scope of the advice and information provided should obviously include an outline of what different housing options might be available in the

---

[1]   See Chapter 13.
[2]   Housing Act 1996, s 179(1).
[3]   *Homelessness Code of Guidance for Local Authorities* (Department for Communities and Local Government, Department for Education and Skills, Department of Health, July 2006) (the English Code), para 2.10; *Code of Guidance for Local Authorities allocation of accommodation and homelessness 2012* (Welsh Government, August 2012) (the Welsh Code), paras 9.2 and 9.9–9.12.
[4]   English Code, para 2.9; Welsh Code, para 9.1 and see **7.136–7.191**.

particular district. The advice and information should also try to address some of the common reasons why people may become homeless (such as financial difficulties, delays with housing benefit payments, etc). If advice or information is provided before someone becomes homeless, it is intended that it be specifically targeted to help that person keep his or her home and thus prevent homelessness.[5] The English and Welsh Codes go so far as to suggest that local housing authorities might provide an advocacy service for people facing the loss of their homes as part of the advice service.[6] It is also suggested that advice services should be able to refer people to more specialised advice provision, such as debt counselling, family mediation or counselling services, or for advice on drug or alcohol abuse.[7]

9.6   The advice and information service may either be provided by the local housing authority itself, or the local housing authority may fund or otherwise support other organisations to enable them to provide the advice and information.[8] Whoever provides it, the advice should be available and accessible to everyone in the local housing authority's district, free of charge and of a high standard.[9] The Welsh Code recommends that it should be 'impartial'.[10] The English Code suggests that 'an independent advisory service may help to avoid conflicts of interest'.[11] The English Code identifies, by way of illustration, more than a dozen issues which could be covered by advice on *prevention* of homelessness.[12] Both the English and the Welsh Codes have Chapters on the prevention of homelessness, including identifying some of the groups who are most likely to become homeless and what types of advice might be needed in order to prevent homelessness in common scenarios.[13] In addition, the Welsh Local Government Association has published a *Better Housing Services Toolkit: Housing Advice and Homelessness*[14] which contains useful tools for assessing the effectiveness of housing advice services.

9.7   Both Codes, reflecting the policy emphasis on 'prevention', repeat some of their guidance on appropriate forms of advice and assistance as part of prevention in their Chapter on applications and inquiries.[15] It is important, however, as the Codes acknowledge, that, while local housing authorities may

---

5   English Code, paras 2.11–2.15. See Chapter 8 of this book.
6   English Code, para 2.12; Welsh Code, para 9.10.
7   English Code, para 2.14; Welsh Code, paras 9.2 and 9.11.
8   HA 1996, s 179(2)–(3).
9   English Code, paras 2.9 and 2.17–2.20; Welsh Code, paras 9.1 and 9.9.
10   Welsh Code, para 9.9.
11   English Code, para 2.18.
12   English Code, para 2.12. See **8.20** for the references to the Code and Chapter 8 of this book for prevention generally.
13   English Code, Chapter 2, especially paras 2.9–2.15; Welsh Code, para 9.12 and Chapter 10. See Chapter 8 of this book.
14   Welsh Local Government Association, 2008.
15   English Code, Chapter 6; Welsh Code, Chapter 12. See Chapter 8 of this book.

'suggest alternative solutions in cases of potential homelessness', they 'must not avoid their obligations under Part 7 (especially the duty to make inquiries ...)'.[16]

APPLICATIONS

Applying to a local housing authority

9.8   Local housing authorities are obliged to have arrangements in place so that anyone who wants to make an application for homelessness assistance can do so.[17] In practice, that means that there must be, at the very least, a locally accessible contact point where an applicant can make an application. Usually this will be an office of the local housing authority where applications can be made face to face and, if necessary, in private.[18] There must also be an emergency 24-hour service enabling applications to be made and received day or night.[19] Local housing authorities should publicise the opening hours, address and telephone number of the homelessness service and the 24-hour emergency contact details, translate the information into any 'main languages' in their district, and ensure that interpreters are accessible for less frequently spoken languages.[20] They should ensure that emergency services, such as the police and adult care and children's services, have details of the opening hours and contact numbers.[21] An application need not be directed to any particular department of the local housing authority.[22] A letter giving details of an applicant's homelessness and containing a request for accommodation which is sent, for example, to the local housing authority's own housing or adult care or children's services departments should be sufficient to trigger the duty to make inquiries.

9.9   A local housing authority's practice of requiring an applicant for homelessness assistance to go through a 'home options interview' before the local housing authority accepted that the applicant had made an application and triggered duties under HA 1996, Part 7, was conceded, by that local housing authority, to be unlawful after an applicant had brought a challenge in judicial review proceedings.[23] The judge said:

---

[16]   English Code, para 6.4; Welsh Code, para 12.6. A point subsequently made by Collins J in *R (Aweys) v Birmingham City Council* [2007] EWHC 52 (Admin), [2007] HLR 27, Admin Ct at [17]. See **8.67–8.68** of this book. The case was later considered by the Court of Appeal and the House of Lords (*Ali & others v Birmingham City Council* [2009] UKHL 36, [2009] 1 WLR 1506, HL) but not in relation to that specific point. See also various Local Government Ombudsman decisions in England and decisions of the Public Services Ombudsman for Wales 8.74–8.78. See also **10.1–10.65**.
[17]   HA 1996, s 183(1).
[18]   English Code, para 6.9; Welsh Code, para 12.36.
[19]   *R v Camden London Borough Council ex p Gillan* (1988) 21 HLR 114, QBD; English Code, para 6.8; Welsh Code, para 12.35.
[20]   English Code, para 6.10; Welsh Code, para 12.37.
[21]   English Code, paras 6.8 and 6.9; Welsh Code, para 12.35.
[22]   English Code, para 6.6; Welsh Code, para 12.2.
[23]   *R (Aweys) v Birmingham City Council* [2007] EWHC 52 (Admin), [2007] HLR 27, Admin Ct.

'the Home Options Scheme ... cannot lawfully be used to defer consideration of a homeless application. All steps taken to avoid homelessness are of course laudable. But any such steps must be taken in parallel to the carrying out of the duty under Part [7].'[24]

9.10 The Welsh Code advises '[i]f there is any doubt as to whether or not the applicant may be homeless or threatened with homelessness within 28 days, then the local authority should err on the side of caution and take a homelessness application'.[25]

Applications made to other organisations

9.11 If the local housing authority has contracted out its homelessness services, applications may need to be directed to, or referred to, that contractor.[26] No doubt the contractor will be anxious to demonstrate that its arrangements for receiving applications are at least as wide-ranging and flexible as the arrangements the local housing authority itself would have made.

9.12 Local housing authorities may choose to contract out the delivery of housing advice and information, or, indeed, the administration of part or all of their mainstream homelessness services. If they do, they remain responsible for the acts or omissions of the contractor in the exercise of the local housing authorities' advice and homelessness functions.[27] They cannot contract out:

- their strategic functions of drawing up homelessness strategies and reviews;

- their duty to ensure that housing advice and information is provided free to any person in their district;

- their power to fund voluntary organisations concerned with homelessness; or

- their duty to co-operate with other local housing authorities.[28]

The case was later considered by the House of Lords under the name of *Ali v Birmingham City Council* [2009] UKHL 36, HL, but not in relation to that specific point.

[24] *R (Aweys) v Birmingham City Council* [2007] EWHC 52 (Admin), [2007] HLR 27, Admin Ct at [17] per Collins J. See also *Complaint against Cardiff City Council*, 20060749, 16 April 2008, (2008) June *Legal Action*, p 32, and *Complaint against Conwy County Borough Council*, 200702044, 11 December 2008, (2009) April *Legal Action*, p 22. See also **8.74–8.78**.

[25] Welsh Code, para 12.4.

[26] See **21.21–21.25**.

[27] Local Authorities (Contracting Out of Allocation of Housing and Homelessness Functions) Order 1996, SI 1996/3205, at Appendix 1 of this book. See also English Code, Chapter 21; Welsh Code, Annex 9; and Chapter 21 of this book.

[28] HA 1996, s 179(2) and (3), s 180(1) and s 213. See **21.24**.

9.13 Nor, it would seem, can they contract out of their responsibilities for decisions made on applications for homelessness assistance, the performance of any duties owed and the exercise of any powers.[29]

To which local housing authority can the application be made?

9.14 There are more than 300 local housing authorities in England and Wales. People seeking accommodation or assistance in obtaining accommodation can apply to any local housing authority they choose, as they need not fulfil any residence requirement or other preliminary condition.[30] Indeed, applications can be made consecutively or concurrently to several local housing authorities.[31] As it is not necessary to make an application in person, applications can be directed to widely dispersed local housing authorities.

9.15 The statutory scheme is obviously based on the premise that the applicant will apply to the local housing authority for the area in which he or she wishes to be accommodated. Not surprisingly, therefore, if the local housing authority to which the application is made decides to accept and perform the main housing duty by providing accommodation in its area, the applicant has no redress against that decision, even if he or she would have preferred to have been referred to a different local housing authority for it to perform that duty.[32]

9.16 It is notorious that local housing authorities have different approaches to the strictness with which they apply homelessness legislation. In areas of acute housing shortage, applicants must expect the law to be tightly applied. In areas where there is a surplus of housing accommodation available, applicants may find that their applications receive very little scrutiny and promptly result in the acceptance of the main housing duty.

9.17 Those considering making applications could therefore often benefit from early advice as to the appropriate local housing authority to approach with an application. If their home local housing authority takes a very strict approach to applications, they may be better advised to apply to a more generous local housing authority in the hope that the duty to accommodate them will be promptly accepted and then referred back to their home area.[33]

9.18 Indeed, the adoption of different rules governing priority need[34] and eligibility[35] and different Codes of Guidance for England and Wales may mean that the same applicant will be differently treated if the application is made to a local housing authority in one country rather than the other.

---

[29]   See **21.1–21.2** and **21.23**.
[30]   *R v Slough Borough Council ex p Ealing London Borough Council* [1981] QB 801, CA.
[31]   See **9.47–9.52** and **9.86–9.88**.
[32]   *Hackney London Borough Council v Sareen* [2003] EWCA Civ 351, (2003) 35 HLR 54, CA.
[33]   Under the 'local connection' provisions described in Chapter 15.
[34]   See **13.126–13.211** [England] and **13.212–13.245** [Wales].
[35]   See **12.72–12.97** and **12.164–12.226** [England] and **12.98–12.115** and **12.227–12.233** [Wales].

9.19   There is no eligibility condition or geographic connection required to make an application. The local housing authority cannot therefore turn away homeless applicants who appear to have just arrived in the UK from overseas, nor those who seem to have no local connection with its district (even if they have an obvious and current connection with the district of another local housing authority). The proper course, if an applicant does not appear to have a local connection with the local housing authority's district, is for the local housing authority to make the usual inquiries into:

(1)   whether the applicant is 'eligible' for services under HA 1996, Part 7; and

(2)   if so, whether any duty is owed under HA 1996, Part 7 to the applicant.[36]

9.20   The scope of those latter inquiries may (but does not need to) include considering whether the applicant has a local connection with the local housing authority and, if not, whether he or she has a local connection elsewhere.[37]

9.21   A local housing authority must also accept an application for homelessness assistance made by an applicant who had previously accepted a private rented sector offer,[38] made by a different local housing authority in the first local housing authority's area. If the application is made within two years of acceptance of the private rented sector offer, the special provisions of HA 1996, s 195A will apply.[39]

9.22   The local housing authority must accept the application, secure interim accommodation if required,[40] make inquiries and notify the applicant of its decision as to whether any duty is owed. If the applicant is owed the main housing duty at HA 1996, s 193(2),[41] the local housing authority can then refer the applicant to the local housing authority which made him or her the private rented sector offer.[42]

---

[36]   HA 1996, s 184(1). See Chapter 10 of this book.

[37]   HA 1996, s 184(2). For further discussion of local connection see **15.42–15.115**.

[38]   For 'private rented sector offer' see HA 1996, s 193(7AA) as amended by Localism Act 2011, s 148(5) and **17.109–17.131**. These offers can be made to applicants for homelessness assistance whose applications were made on or after 9 November 2012 to a local housing authority in England. At the date of writing, the amendments to HA 1996 made by LA 2011, ss 148–149 had not been brought into effect in Wales.

[39]   Inserted by LA 2011, s 149(4), see **9.89–9.95** of this book. The special provisions will apply to applicants for homelessness assistance whose applications were made on or after 9 November 2012 to a local housing authority in England. At the date of writing, the amendments to HA 1996 made by LA 2011, ss 148–149 had not been brought into effect in Wales.

[40]   Under its duty at HA 1996, s 188(1A) inserted by LA 2011, s 149(2), which will not require the local housing authority to consider whether or not it has reason to believe that the applicant may have a priority need, see **16.29–16.35** of this book. The special provisions will apply to applicants for homelessness assistance whose applications were made on or after 9 November 2012 to a local housing authority in England. At the date of writing, the amendments to HA 1996 made by LA 2011, ss 148–149 had not been brought into effect in Wales.

[41]   See **17.23–17.168**.

[42]   HA 1996, s 198(2ZA) inserted by LA s 149(6) in force from 9 November 2012. See **15.121–15.131**. These special provisions will apply to applicants for homelessness assistance

Form in which the application is made

9.23 Whenever a person approaches a local housing authority for accommodation, or for assistance in obtaining accommodation, and the local housing authority has reason to believe that he or she may be homeless or threatened with homelessness, then he or she has made a homelessness application.[43]

9.24 Although it may be convenient for a local housing authority to have its own application form for applicants to complete, there is no legal requirement that an application should be in writing or in any specified form.[44] An application could perfectly properly be made in person, by letter, fax, telephone, text or email. So long as the communication seeks accommodation or assistance in obtaining accommodation and sets out an account that gives the local housing authority reason to believe that the person might be homeless or threatened with homelessness, it constitutes an application. As the Codes make clear, there is absolutely no requirement on applicants to specify that they are seeking services under HA 1996, Part 7.[45] Obviously, there is room for possible disagreement as to whether what is said in the course of a conversation constitutes an application. In *R v Cherwell District Council ex p Howkins*,[46] the applicant's solicitor telephoned the local housing authority shortly after it had evicted the applicant (who had been a council tenant) for rent arrears. The judge was quite satisfied that an application for homelessness assistance did not need to be in writing. He said that:

> '... in order to be treated as an application it seems to me that an oral conversation has to be conducted in such a way that it is clear that it amounts to an application.'

9.25 However, on the facts, the conversation had simply been an inquiry by the solicitor as to whether the local housing authority was going to offer temporary accommodation and was not itself an application for any accommodation.

9.26 Local housing authorities should take particular care to identify when someone appears only to be applying for an allocation of social housing, but is actually indicating that he or she might be homeless according to the HA 1996, Part 7 definition.[47] Where the information on an inquiry about the allocation

---

whose applications were made on or after 9 November 2012 to a local housing authority in England. At the date of writing, the amendments to HA 1996 made by LA 2011, ss 148–149 had not been brought into effect in Wales.

[43]   HA 1996, s 183.

[44]   *English Code, para 6.6; R v Chiltern District Council ex p Roberts* (1990) 23 HLR 387, QBD; and *R (Aweys) v Birmingham City Council* [2007] EWHC 52 (Admin), [2007] HLR 27, Admin Ct at [8] per Collins J. The case was later considered by the House of Lords under the name of *Ali v Birmingham City Council* [2009] UKHL 36, [2009] 1 WLR 1506, HL, but not in relation to that specific point.

[45]   English Code, para 6.6; Welsh Code, para 12.2.

[46]   *R v Cherwell District Council ex p Howkins* (unreported) 14 May 1984, QBD.

[47]   See **11.2–11.120** for definition of 'homelessness'.

scheme, or on an application for an allocation, gives the local housing authority 'reason to believe' that the applicant might be homeless, that approach is also an application for homelessness assistance. The courts and the ombudsmen have criticised local housing authorities who have failed to recognise such applications.[48]

9.27 Once an application meeting the above (fairly minimal) requirements is received, the local housing authority cannot ignore it until the applicant has completed the local housing authority's standard application form. It must act upon the application and start to make inquiries.

'Actual' and 'deemed' applications

9.28 The regime for homelessness assistance does not recognise the concept of an implied, constructive or deemed homelessness application. The only application which counts, and triggers the duty to make inquiries, is one actually made.

9.29 This can be a source of frustration for a local housing authority that is seeking to free itself from responsibility for particularly problematic tenants. It is not at all uncommon for tenants, in both the social housing and the private rented sectors, who are facing eviction for rent arrears or persistent anti-social behaviour, to be forewarned that the local housing authority will not accept a responsibility for rehousing them once evicted. If the tenant potentially has a priority need, and chooses to refrain from making a homelessness application until the moment of eviction (or very shortly beforehand), it is likely that the local housing authority will have to provide further accommodation, at least initially (while inquiries are made into the application)[49] and thereafter yet more temporary accommodation (even if the finding is of intentional homelessness).[50]

9.30 For this reason, some local housing authorities have in the past tried to explore a concept of an implied or deemed application made well before the eviction, allowing them to undertake inquiries while the tenants are still in their homes (and awaiting the bailiffs) and thus reducing any temporary accommodation responsibility to an absolute minimum. However, it seems that (very properly) this device has been abandoned.

Who can make an application?

9.31 Anyone can make a request for accommodation or for assistance in obtaining accommodation. If that person does not appear to be homeless or threatened with homelessness, he or she will be entitled to housing advice and information, free of charge, but the local housing authority will owe no further

---

[48] See **9.53–9.55**.
[49] HA 1996, s 188(1). See **16.12–16.28**.
[50] HA 1996, s 190(2)(a). See **17.23–17.168** for the main housing duty and **17.182–17.189** for the short-term accommodation duty.

duty.[51] If the person appears to be homeless or to be threatened with homelessness, the local housing authority must treat the request as an application for homelessness assistance and start to make inquiries.[52]

9.32 There is no eligibility condition or geographic connection required to make an application. The local housing authority cannot therefore turn away homeless applicants who appear to have just arrived in the UK from overseas, nor those who seem to have no local connection with its district (even if they have an obvious and current connection with the district of another local housing authority).[53]

9.33 A person must have *legal capacity* in order to make an application for homeless assistance. Accordingly, those who lack the mental capacity to make an application cannot apply.[54] It is for the local housing authority, in the first instance, to decide whether the applicant has the mental capacity to make an application.[55] There is no right of statutory review or appeal if the application is refused on the basis of lack of capacity. The obvious practical route to achieving a reversal of the local housing authority's decision would be the submission of clear medical evidence that the applicant did have capacity. If the local housing authority persisted in its refusal to accept the application, proceedings for judicial review would need to be brought.[56]

9.34 There is no minimum *age* for applicants (although the Codes wrongly suggest that all applicants must be 'adults' or at least aged 16 or over).[57] In the absence of a statutory minimum age, the House of Lords has, in dealing with an application made by a four-year old, held that applications from 'dependent' children should not be considered.[58] There is no statutory definition of that term.[59] It follows that an application may be made by any child who is no longer 'dependent'. As the House of Lords recognised:

> 'There will obviously be the case from time to time when a child leaves home under the age of 16 and ceases to be dependent on the parents or those with whom he or she was living.'[60]

---

[51]   HA 1996, s 179(1).
[52]   English Code, para 6.12; Welsh Code, para 12.4.
[53]   See Chapter 15 of this book.
[54]   *R v Oldham Metropolitan Borough Council ex p Garlick, R v London Borough of Tower Hamlets ex p Begum* [1993] AC 509, HL. A local authority which has adult care responsibilities would almost certainly have community care duties towards someone who attempted to make an application for homelessness assistance but did not have the capacity to do so. Those community care duties can include the provision of accommodation. See **20.16–20.48**.
[55]   [1993] AC 509 HL at 520, per Lord Griffiths.
[56]   See *R (Halewood) v West Lancashire District Council* (2009) May 2010 *Legal Action*, p 24 where the local housing authority had decided that the claimant lacked capacity. Judicial review proceedings were subsequently compromised when the claimant produced new evidence. See **19.224–19.250** for judicial review.
[57]   English Code, para 6.6; Welsh Code, para 12.2.
[58]   *R v Oldham Metropolitan Borough Council ex p Garlick* [1993] AC 509, HL.
[59]   The guidance given on it by the Codes is discussed at **13.50–13.52**.
[60]   [1993] AC 509, HL at 517, per Lord Griffiths.

9.35   Such an individual can make his or her own application. Applicants need not show a history of independence from their parents or others. Plainly, the very first step that an applicant may have taken to demonstrate that he or she is no longer 'dependent' might be making the application.

9.36   There are occasionally applications made by non-dependent young people under the age of 16,[61] but applications by those aged 16 or 17 are more common. Since 31 July 2002 in England,[62] most 16- and 17-year-olds have been designated as being in priority need.[63] As a result there has been an increase in applications from non-adults in that age group.[64] Guidance suggests that local housing authorities should have arrangements in place so that, when applications for homelessness assistance are received from 16- or 17-year-olds, assessments of their housing, care and support needs are carried out jointly with children's services.[65] Obviously, unless the local housing authority is a unitary authority, the consent of the young person will be required before his or her details are disclosed to the children's services department of a different authority.

9.37   Both the courts and the Ombudsmen have been extremely critical of local authorities passing 16- and 17-year-olds between housing departments and children's services departments, with neither agency accepting a statutory duty to the young person.[66] In one case, the Local Government Ombudsman found two councils guilty of maladministration where a 16-year-old homeless boy spent nine months sleeping in a tent or occasionally on friends' sofas because neither council had complied with its statutory duty to secure accommodation for him.[67]

---

[61]   For an example, see *Kelly v Monklands District Council* (1985) SLT 169, OH.

[62]   1 March 2001 in Wales.

[63]   See **13.127–13.174** [England] and **13.214–13.218** [Wales].

[64]   Homelessness (Priority Need for Accommodation) (England) Order 2002, SI 2002/2051, art 3; Homeless Persons (Priority Need) (Wales) Order 2001, SI 2001/607 (W 30), reg 4. Until 2002, around 3–4,000 applicants in England each year were accepted as homeless and having priority need due to their vulnerability as young people. The number rose to 11,050 in 2003/04 and then fell to 4,070 in 2008/09. It has since fallen even further, to 2,060 in 2011 presumably as a result of more young people being accepted as children in need and accommodated by children's services under the Children Act 1989 duties, see **13.148–13.149** and **20.74–20.80**. Similarly, in Wales in 2004/2005, 970 children were accepted as homeless and having a priority need due to their being aged 16 or 17. The numbers declined from 2005 onwards In 2010/2011, 460 children were accepted as homeless (Welsh Government, National Statistics on Homelessness,Table 2).

[65]   English Code, para 6.19 and paras 12.1–12.17; Welsh Code, para 14.32. *See R (M) v Hammersmith & Fulham London Borough Council* [2008] UKHL 14, [2008] 1 WLR 535, HL, and *R (G) v Southwark London Borough Council* [2009] UKHL 26, [2009] 1 WLR 2399, HL. See *Provision of Accommodation for 16 and 17 year old young people who may be homeless and/or require Accommodation* (April 2010, CLG and Children, Schools and Families) and *Provision of Accommodation for 16 and 17 year old young people who may be homeless* (September 2010, Welsh Assembly Government). See also **13.148–13.174** [England] and **13.214–13.218** [Wales].

[66]   See **13.140–13.142**.

[67]   *LGO Investigation into complaints about Kent County Council 09 017 510 and about Dover District Council 09 017 512*, 31 July 2012, (2012) October *Legal Action*, p 36.

Joint applications

9.38 The law does not recognise an application for accommodation, or for assistance in obtaining accommodation, made by a couple, a family or a household. Applications are made by individuals. HA 1996, Part 7 refers to 'a person' making the application.[68] One judge has said:

> 'I am quite unable to conclude that an application for housing as a homeless person falls to be treated as being made by a family unit. It is, and must be, an application at the instance of an individual. Of course, if that individual is residing with others in a family, that will affect the accommodation he requires, and whether he has priority need, but it does not alter the fact that the application is the application of an individual.'[69]

9.39 Of course, there is nothing to prevent more than one individual in the same household from making an application. Indeed, several applicants from a single household may apply at the same time to the same local housing authority and even on the same application form. This is particularly common where there are two adult heads of household and both choose to apply.

9.40 There is some helpful judicial guidance on how to deal with such jointly made applications:

> 'It seems to me that where the application which is made to the authority is, as here, a joint application, it is a joint application which the authority must determine. If there is no request by one of two joint applicants for his or her case to be treated separately, there is no obligation upon the authority to deal with the application as being other than a joint application. However, in considering the joint application there may be an obligation on the housing authority to consider the separate circumstances of the individuals who are making the joint application.'[70]

9.41 In *Hemans v Windsor and Maidenhead Royal Borough Council,*[71] the application for homelessness assistance had been made by solicitors acting for both husband and wife and had been expressed as a 'joint application'. There was some discussion before the Court of Appeal as to what that meant. One member of the Court of Appeal said:

> 'We were referred to the provision in the Interpretation Act 1978 that, unless the contrary intention appears, the singular includes the plural. In practice, joint homelessness applications are common. It is also common ground that in such cases, the council must look at the circumstances of both or all the applicants. In the vast majority of cases, it will make no practical difference whether technically it is to be regarded as a single application capable only of a single determination or

---

[68]   HA 1996, s 183(1).
[69]   *MacLeod (aka Hynds) v Midlothian District Council* (1986) SLT 54, (1985) November SCOLAG 163, per Lord Ross.
[70]   *R v Wandsworth London Borough Council ex p Lord* (unreported) 8 July 1985, QBD per Woolf J.
[71]   [2011] EWCA Civ 374, [2011] HLR 25, CA.

two applications in a single document. I would leave further discussion of that arcane point until such time as a case may arise where it matters.'[72]

9.42   In practice, this judicial guidance enables local housing authorities to proceed on the basis that there is an identity of interest between the joint applicants unless and until material before the local housing authority indicates that separate consideration of each application is required. Such material could be a disagreement between the joint applicants in the course of interviews with the local housing authority or might be implied from the giving of mutually inconsistent accounts. The safer course must ordinarily be to treat even joint applicants with a degree of separate consideration.

9.43   This sense, in which even supposed joint applications are simply two applications contained in one single form, was emphasised in *Lewis v Brent London Borough Council*.[73] Mr and Mrs Lewis had applied together for homelessness assistance to the local housing authority. However, Mrs Lewis was unable to rely on her husband's circumstances in an appeal against a decision that she had become homeless intentionally. Although they had made a joint application, he was not a party to the appeal and so his – more favourable – circumstances could not be relied upon by her.

9.44   Where more than one individual in a household *could* apply, it may be sensible for one rather than the other to make the application. For example, one may be eligible for HA 1996, Part 7 services and the other not; one may qualify for priority need and the other may not;[74] or one may be more likely to be found to have become homeless intentionally. There may even be an advantage in applicants in similar circumstances making consecutive applications in order to obtain not only the possibility of a second, and more favourable decision, but also to obtain at least a further period in interim accommodation whilst the second application is considered. Where the application is a re-application for homelessness assistance, made within two years of the acceptance of a private rented sector offer to the applicant by a local housing authority in England in order to bring the main housing duty to an end,[75] the special provisions at HA

---

[72]   *Hemans v Windsor and Maidenhead Royal Borough Council* [2011] EWCA Civ 374, [2011] HLR 25, CA per Toulson LJ at [23].

[73]   [2005] EWCA Civ 605, (2005) July *Legal Action*, p 29, CA.

[74]   This is relevant where the form of priority need is that at HA 1996, s 189(1)(d) or one of those listed in the Homelessness (Priority Need for Accommodation) (England) Order 2002, SI 2002/2051 or Homelessness (Priority Need) (Wales) Order 2001, SI 2001/607 because each of those Orders require that the applicant must have the requisite priority need. In the case of priority need acquired under one of the categories at HA 1996, s 189(1)(a)–(c), the applicant has a priority need if either he or she, or a member of his or her household, has the requisite characteristics. See **13.26–13.32**.

[75]   HA 1996, s 193(7AA)–(7AC) as amended by LA 2011, s 148(5)–(7), see **17.109–17.131** for 'private rented sector offer'. Private rented sector offers can be made to applicants for homelessness assistance whose applications were made on or after 9 November 2012 to local housing authorities in England. At the date of writing, the amendments to HA 1996 made by LA 2011, ss 148–149 had not been brought into effect in Wales.

1996, s 195A will only apply if the application is made by the same person who had accepted the private rented sector offer[76] and is made to a local housing authority in England.[77]

9.45   Where the application by one adult member of the household results in the acceptance of the main housing duty, accommodation will be provided for the whole household.[78] What happens, however, if the applying adult rejects that offer and the other household members then make further applications? This occurred in *R v Camden London Borough Council ex p Hersi*.[79] In that case, the new applicant was a 19-year-old daughter of the first applicant, her own mother. After the mother had rejected an offer of accommodation, the local housing authority refused to accept the daughter's application. The Court of Appeal described the daughter as having 'no standing' to apply for homelessness assistance for the whole family (although the reasoning seems to suggest that this was because the younger children of the household were dependent on their mother and not on her). However, in that case Camden accepted (correctly) that had the new application been from another adult member of the household on whom the children *were* dependent, inquiries into that application would need to have been made.

Multiple applications

9.46   There is nothing to prevent someone applying simultaneously to more than one local housing authority. If this happens, each local housing authority will be obliged to carry out its own inquiries, potentially resulting in a wasteful duplication of effort. The Codes suggest that the receiving local housing authorities should agree amongst themselves which one will be responsible for carrying out inquiries.[80] Presumably this is on the basis that the local housing authority which does undertake the inquiries does so both on its own behalf and as agent for (or delegate of) the others.[81] Each local housing authority should then make its own assessment of the results of the inquiries and reach its own decision. It seems implicit in this suggested arrangement, however, that in practice the applicant will withdraw all other applications as soon as one of the local housing authorities accepts that it owes the applicant the main housing duty.

---

[76]   HA 1996, s 195A inserted by LA 2011, s 149(4) and see **9.89–9.95**. These special provisions will apply to applicants for homelessness assistance whose applications were made on or after 9 November 2012 to local housing authorities in England. At the date of writing, the amendments to HA 1996 made by LA 2011, ss 148–149 had not been brought into effect in Wales.

[77]   At the date of writing, the amendments to HA 1996 made by LA 2011, ss 148–149 had not been brought into effect in Wales.

[78]   See **17.28**.

[79]   *R v Camden London Borough Council ex p Hersi* (2001) 33 HLR 577, CA.

[80]   English Code, para 6.7; Welsh Code, para 12.13.

[81]   As permitted by Local Government Act 1972, s 101(1)(b).

Consecutive applications

9.47 As already stated, there is nothing to prevent an applicant applying first to one local housing authority and then to another. When an applicant has previously applied to one local housing authority (the first local housing authority), the second or subsequent local housing authority would normally seek the applicant's consent so that it is free (in the course of making inquiries into the second or subsequent application) to contact the first local housing authority and request information on the application made and on that local housing authority's decision (if any) on that application. The first local housing authority is under a duty to co-operate with any such request.[82]

9.48 The second local housing authority, however, must not rely solely on the first local housing authority's decision in reaching its own decision on the application made to it, although it may take that decision into account. Nor may it merely adopt the first local housing authority's decision. It must make its own independent inquiries and reach an independent decision on the application it has received.[83]

9.49 It may well be that the second local housing authority reaches a different decision from the first local housing authority. For example, it may decide that the applicant *is* owed a main housing duty because he or she is eligible, in priority need and has not become homeless intentionally even if the first local housing authority had decided all (or any) of those matters against the applicant.

9.50 The second local housing authority may also decide that the main housing duty is to be referred to the first local housing authority on the grounds that the conditions for referral at HA 1996, s 198 are satisfied.[84] This can result in the first local housing authority being obliged to receive back and accommodate an applicant to whom it had previously notified an adverse decision.

9.51 A dispute resolution mechanism is available where there is disagreement between two local housing authorities as to which of them the applicant has a local connection with. However, that mechanism does not apply in cases where there is no dispute over the local connection conditions, but where the local housing authority to whom the applicant has been referred does not agree with the referring local housing authority's decision that a duty to accommodate is owed to the applicant. In those circumstances, the first local housing authority cannot refuse to accept the referral unless it can successfully demonstrate, in the usual way, that the local connection conditions are not satisfied.[85]

---

[82] HA 1996, s 213. See also English Code, para 6.20; Welsh Code, para 12.44
[83] English Code, para 6.7; Welsh Code, para 12.13.
[84] For an introduction to the conditions for referral, including local connection, see **15.31–15.41**.
[85] *R v Slough Borough Council ex p Ealing London Borough Council* [1981] QB 801, CA; *R (Bantamagbari) v Westminster City Council and Southwark London Borough Council* [2003] EWHC 1350 (Admin), [2003] All ER (D) 163 (May), Admin Ct.

9.52   If the first local housing authority believes that the second local housing authority has incorrectly reached a decision that the main duty is owed to the applicant, it cannot simply refuse the referral of the duty and wait for the applicant or the second local housing authority to bring legal proceedings.[86] Instead, it must take the initiative and bring judicial review proceedings to demonstrate that the decision-making by the second local housing authority was unlawful. Obviously, the second local housing authority must apply the law correctly when making its inquiries and reaching its decision. If it has not done so, the first local housing authority will succeed in having the decision overturned. In *R v Newham London Borough Council ex p Tower Hamlets London Borough Council*,[87] the Court of Appeal held that Newham had been entitled to accept an application from someone whom Tower Hamlets had previously found to have become homeless intentionally. Newham would have been, had it applied the law correctly, entitled to refer the applicant back to Tower Hamlets under the local connection provisions. However, Newham made an error of law when considering whether the applicant had become homeless intentionally, in that it took into account its own local housing conditions rather than those of Tower Hamlets. Tower Hamlets succeeded in having the Newham decision, and consequently the referral, set aside.

Applications from owners and tenants

9.53   It is not necessary for someone to be physically without a roof over his or her head in order to make an application for accommodation (or for assistance in obtaining accommodation) which requires consideration under HA 1996 Part 7. An applicant cannot be treated as having accommodation unless it is accommodation which it would be reasonable for him or her to continue to occupy.[88] Such an applicant may be a freehold owner, long leaseholder or a tenant who gives the local housing authority some reason to believe that it is no longer reasonable for him or her to continue occupying the present accommodation. The concept of reasonable continued occupation is discussed in detail elsewhere,[89] but obvious examples of those who may be homeless include owners or tenants who might be victims of domestic violence, who cannot afford their accommodation or who experience gross overcrowding or other adverse physical conditions.

9.54   Local housing authorities need particular sensitivity to this type of application where an applicant is an existing tenant of that local housing authority. Local housing authorities should be aware that an application for alternative accommodation from one of their existing tenants might, in reality, be an application for homelessness assistance if the tenant is saying that it is not reasonable for him or her to continue to occupy the existing home.

---

[86]   *R (Bantamagbari) v City of Westminster and Southwark London Borough Council* [2003] EWHC 1350 (Admin), [2003] All ER (D) 163 (May), Admin Ct.
[87]   *R v Newham London Borough Council ex p London Borough of Tower Hamlets* [1991] 1 WLR 1032, CA.
[88]   HA 1996, s 175(3).
[89]   See **11.75–11.120**.

Generally, a local housing authority is entitled to presume that an application for a transfer from one of its existing tenants is exactly that – an application for a transfer – rather than an application under HA 1996, Part 7.[90] However, where, from the circumstances of the application, it is clear that the tenant is saying that it is not reasonable for him or her to continue in occupation, the local housing authority would be in breach of its statutory duty if it treated the application as a simple application for a transfer rather than also as an application for HA 1996, Part 7 assistance.[91] An obvious example, where a tenant apparently seeking a transfer is in fact asserting that his or her existing accommodation is not reasonable to continue to occupy, is where the tenant is complaining that he or she has to be transferred because of violence or harassment.[92] It is not necessary for the applicant to spell out that the application should be considered under HA 1996, Part 7.[93]

9.55 Local housing authorities must take exactly the same approach with applications from those who are not existing local housing authority tenants but who apply for accommodation under the local housing authority's ordinary allocation scheme. A private sector tenant applying for long-term council accommodation (or for nomination to a private registered provider in England or a registered social landlord in Wales) who writes, on his or her application form, that the application must be considered urgently because the present home is grossly overcrowded, unfit for occupation, or is for some other reason no longer suitable to occupy, must likewise be the subject of inquiries under HA 1996, Part 7.[94] Self-evidently that information is sufficient to give the local housing authority reason to believe that the applicant may be homeless. The

---

[90]   *R v Lambeth London Borough Council ex p Pattinson* (1996) 28 HLR 214, QBD.

[91]   *R v Islington London Borough Council ex p B* (1998) 30 HLR 706, QBD. See also *R v Sefton Metropolitan Borough Council ex p Healiss* (1995) 27 HLR 34, QBD; *Complaint against Tower Hamlets London Borough Council*, 91/A/2474 and *Complaint against Hounslow London Borough Council*, 99/A/03731. See also the findings of the Commissioner for Complaints relating to the Northern Ireland Housing Executive, where a tenant whose accommodation was unsuitable because of his disability wrote asking to be assessed as homeless, and no inquiries were made promptly: 200700491, 6 November 2008, (2009) April *Legal Action*, p 22 and Public Services Ombudsman for Wales investigation of a *Complaint against Blaenau Gwent County Borough Council*, 09016302, 24 January 2011, (2011) April *Legal Action*, p 30.

[92]   *Complaint against Hounslow London Borough Council*, 99/A/03731.

[93]   *R (Aweys) v Birmingham City Council* [2007] EWHC 52 (Admin), [2007] HLR 27, Admin Ct, later considered by the House of Lords under the name of *Ali v Birmingham City Council*, [2009] UKHL 36, [2009] 1 WLR 1506, HL, but not in relation to that specific point. In these seven linked cases, tenants were accepted to be homeless because their tenancies were so overcrowded that it was not reasonable for them, and all the members of their households, to continue to occupy. See **11.109–11.11**.

[94]   Public Services Ombudsman for Wales *Complaint against Conwy County Borough Council*, 200702044, 11 December 2008, (2009) April *Legal Action*, p 22. In *Bury Metropolitan Borough Council v Gibbons* [2010] EWCA Civ 327, [2010] HLR 33, CA, Mr Gibbons had completed an application form for Part 6 accommodation in which he stated that he could not afford his rent and had to move out of his home 15 days later when the notice expired. The Court of Appeal held that the Part 6 housing application disclosed information triggering an obligation on the local housing authority to make inquiries and, had it done so, it would have concluded that Mr Gibbons was threatened with homelessness and that it owed him a duty to provide advice and assistance (HA 1996 s 195(2)), see **17.190–17.200**).

applicant does not need to spell out that he or she is applying for consideration under both HA 1996, Part 6[95] and Part 7.

Warnings

9.56 It is a criminal offence for an applicant knowingly or recklessly to make a false statement in order to induce the local housing authority to believe that he or she is entitled to accommodation or assistance with homelessness. It is also a criminal offence for the applicant knowingly to withhold information reasonably required by the local housing authority, or to fail to notify the local housing authority of any change of facts material to his or her case.[96] Local housing authorities are obliged to explain the duty to notify any change of facts, and what that means, to each applicant, in ordinary language, and are encouraged to explain it in a sensitive way, in order to avoid intimidating applicants.[97] Where a person can show that the explanation was not given, or if that there is some other reasonable excuse for non-compliance, no offence will have been committed.[98]

A local housing authority's immediate duties

9.57 As soon as a local housing authority has reason to believe that a person who has made an application may be homeless or threatened with homelessness, it is obliged to make inquiries into whether the person is eligible for assistance and, if so, whether any duty is owed to him or her under the homelessness provisions.[99] The duty to make inquiries cannot be postponed.[100]

9.58 There have been a number of findings of maladministration by the Local Government Ombudsmen against local housing authorities in England which, instead of considering whether applicants were homeless or might be threatened with homelessness, refused to make inquiries, told applicants that they would not be helped (thereby pre-judging the result of inquiries), or told them that they should make their own accommodation arrangements.[101] The Local Government Ombudsmen have indicated that it is essential to good

---

[95] See **2.33–2.76**.
[96] HA 1996, s 214. See also English Code, para 6.11.
[97] HA 1996, s 214(2), English Code, para 6.11.
[98] HA 1996, s 214(3).
[99] HA 1996, ss 183 and 184(1).
[100] *Robinson v Hammersmith & Fulham London Borough Council* [2006] EWCA Civ 1122, [2007] HLR 7, CA.
[101] *Complaint against Hammersmith & Fulham London Borough Council*, 09001262, 21 January 2010, (2010), March *Legal Action*, p 31; *Richmond upon Thames Royal London Borough Council*, 10 009 069, 10 February 2011, (2011) April *Legal Action*, p 30; *Islington London Borough Council*, 10 013 025, 24 February 2011, (2011) April *Legal Action*, p 31; *Hounslow London Borough Council*, 10 019 388, 5 October 2011, (2011) December *Legal Action*, p 29; *Newham London Borough Council*, 11 000 383, 8 March 2012, (2012) May *Legal Action*, p 34; *Southwark London Borough Council*, 10 000 27, 10 004 245 and 11 000 195, 22 May 2012, (2012) August *Legal Action*, p 27; *Kent County Council*, 09 017 510 and *Dover District Council*, 09 017 512, 31 July 2012, (2012) October *Legal Action* p 36; and *Hounslow London Borough Council*, 11 008 191, 28 August 2012, (2012) November *Legal Action*, p 14. See also the

administration that all applicants receive equal treatment, and that their applications are given fair consideration and are properly investigated before decisions are reached.[102] The Public Services Ombudsman for Wales has taken the same approach.[103]

9.59 Indeed, both Ombudsmen have been so concerned, following their analyses of recent complaints, at local housing authorities' failure to comply with their statutory duties, that each one has issued his own report into those failings. In 2006, the Public Services Ombudsman for Wales published *Housing Allocations and Homelessness: A Special Report by the Local Government Ombudsman for Wales*[104] in which he said 'I have found shortcomings in the manner in which some authorities deal with applicants who approach them claiming to be homeless. Recording practices were found to be wanting as well as in some instances the quality of inquires and decision making.'

9.60 In 2011, the Local Government Ombudsmen published *Homelessness: how councils can ensure justice for homeless people Focus Report: learning the lessons from complaints.*[105] In the *Focus Report*, the Ombudsmen said:

> 'complaints to the Local Government Ombudsman suggest that people who face homelessness do not always receive the help that they are entitled to from councils. Other organisations have coined the phrase "gatekeeping" to describe where councils refuse to accept a homelessness application or to provide interim accommodation where there is no legitimate reason . . .We know that councils are currently under pressure with limited resources and increasing numbers of people presenting as homeless. To avoid more people suffering personal injustice councils should always properly apply the law in practice.'[106]

9.61 Given the absolute duty to make inquiries and, in some cases, to secure interim accommodation when an application for homelessness assistance is made, it is essential that local housing authority staff in direct contact with the public are well trained and can recognise and receive applications and ensure that inquiries are put in hand. Far too often, applicants are wrongly turned away by busy or inexperienced reception staff. It is not unknown for applicants to be told:

- 'you need to apply to a different local housing authority'; or

- 'we do not take homelessness applications from our own tenants'; or

---

findings of the Commissioner for *Complaints relating to the Northern Ireland Housing Executive*, 200700491, 6 November 2008, (2009) April *Legal Action*, p 22. See **8.76–8.77**.

[102] *Complaint against Cheltenham Borough Council*, 88/B/1795.

[103] *Complaint against Cardiff City Council*, 20060749, 16 April 2008, (2008) June *Legal Action*, p 32; *Conwy County Borough Council*, 200702044, 11 December 2008, (2009) April *Legal Action*, p 22; and *Complaint against Blaenau Gwent County Borough Council*, 09016302, 24 January 2011, (2011) April *Legal Action*, p 30. See also **8.78**.

[104] (2006) Public Services Ombudsman for Wales. See **8.75**.

[105] (2011) Local Government Ombudsman. See **8.76**.

[106] For prevention and 'gatekeeping', see Chapter 8. For interim accommodation duties, see Chapter 16.

- 'we only help the priority homeless here'.

9.62 All of these responses to an application, and any other similar statements, are wrong in law.

9.63 The Welsh Code informs local housing authorities that a service sampling, or 'mystery shopper', exercise was completed in Wales in 2010 to assess the quality of frontline housing services provided to people who present as homeless. Generally the survey found that much of the advice, information and support provided by local housing authorities was not of a high quality. As a result, the Welsh Code advises that it is essential that housing staff are trained in the requirements of HA 1996, Part 7, and are familiar with the Code and the local housing authority's own policies. Staff should have a sympathetic and caring manner when dealing with applications and it is very important that an accurate and detailed written record is kept of all contacts with applicants. Reception staff can recognise people who may be homeless or threatened with homelessness but unless they are thoroughly trained should not be expected to exercise any informal 'first-screening' of applicants.[107]

The local housing authority's first decision: interim accommodation

9.64 The very first issue that a local housing authority must consider when it has received an application for homelessness assistance is whether it has reason to believe that an applicant *may* be homeless, eligible for assistance and have a priority need. If the local housing authority does have reason to believe that the applicant *may* fall into all of these categories and the application for homelessness assistance cannot be inquired into and concluded that day, it *must* provide accommodation for the applicant and his or her household pending notification of a decision on the application.[108] That duty cannot be postponed.[109] The threshold trigger is very low: the local housing authority

---

[107] Welsh Code, paras 12.32–12.34. The reference to 'any kind of informal "first screening" of applicants' (Welsh Code, para 12.34) is puzzling. As can be seen by the contents of this Chapter, there should be no screening process whatsoever. If a potential applicant meets the criteria at HA 1996, s 183 (see **9.57–9.63**), an application for homelessness assistance has been made and the local housing authority is obliged to make inquiries and to notify the applicant of its decision in writing. See also *Better Housing Services Toolkit: Housing Advice and Homelessness* (Welsh Local Government Association, 2008).

[108] HA 1996, s 188(1). See also English Code, para 6.5; Welsh Code, para 12.14–12.17; and see Chapter 16.

[109] In *R (Ho-Sang) v Lewisham London Borough Council* (2004) CO 5562/03, (2004) July *Legal Action*, p 19, Admin Ct, the local housing authority conceded that it was in breach of its statutory duty by not immediately providing accommodation in those circumstances. In the Local Government Ombudsman's investigation into *Complaint against Waltham Forest London Borough Council*, 21 October 2009, 03/A/15819, (2010) February *Legal Action* p 34, the local housing authority was very severely criticised and ordered to pay compensation and legal costs, where it had failed to provide accommodation to a vulnerable single man who was forced to sleep rough as a result. See also *Complaint against Hammersmith & Fulham London Borough Council*, 09 001 262, 21 January 2010, (2010), March *Legal Action*, p 31; *Complaint against Richmond upon Thames Royal London Borough Council*, 10 009 069, 10 February 2011, (2011)

need only have 'reason to believe' that the applicant 'may be' homeless, 'may be' eligible for assistance and 'may' have a priority need.[110] Both Codes remind local housing authorities that 'having reason to believe' is a lower test than 'being satisfied'.[111] If in doubt, interim accommodation should be provided.

9.65 It was suggested in one case that a local housing authority was encouraging its officers to make decisions on applications for homelessness assistance on the same day as the application was received, so that the duty to secure interim accommodation at HA 1996, s 188(1) would not arise. The judge said:

> '[t]here is no doubt that a blanket "same day" policy, which requires a decision on the homeless application and, in consequence, the interim accommodation all in one day would be unlawful . . ..it would only be "in the most straightforward of cases that a decision can be reached on the same day as the application itself".'[112]

Repeat applications

9.66 There is no bar on someone who has made an earlier application for homelessness assistance, and had that application determined by the local housing authority, from re-applying to the same local housing authority for accommodation (or assistance in obtaining accommodation) at any later time.[113] The local housing authority must accept the application if there is reason to believe the applicant may be homeless or threatened with homelessness.

9.67 Nothing in the legislation cuts down the right to make such repeat applications. Indeed, HA 1996, Part 7 specifically states that even a person

---

April *Legal Action*, p 30; *Complaint against Islington London Borough Council*, 0 013 025, 24 February 2011, (2011), April *Legal Action*, p 31; *Complaint against Hounslow London Borough Council*, 10 019 388, 5 October 2011, (2011), December *Legal Action*, p 29; and *Complaint against Hounslow London Borough Council*, 11 008 191, 28 August 2012 (2012) November *Legal Action*, p 14. The Ombudsman ordered a total of £10,100 to be paid by two councils where a homeless 16 year old had had to sleep for a tent, and occasionally on friends' sofa, for nine months: *Complaints against Kent County Council*, 09 017 510 and *Dover District Council*, 09 017 512, 31 July 2012, (2012) October *Legal Action*, p 36.

[110] *R (Aweys) v Birmingham City Council* [2007] EWHC 52 (Admin), [2007] HLR 27, Admin Ct, at [8]–[9] per Collins J. See also *R (Kelly & Mehari) v Birmingham City Council* [2009] EWHC 3240 (Admin), (2010) January *Legal Action*, p 35, Admin Ct. See **16.12–16.28**.

[111] English Code, para 6.5; Welsh Code, para 12.14.

[112] *R (Khazai & others) v Birmingham City Council* [2010] EWHC 2576 (Admin) (2011) December *Legal Action*, p 37, Admin Ct per Foskett J at [47]. The Welsh Code contains a confusing mix of guidance on this point. Para 12.4 states '[t]here is nothing to stop the local authority undertaking initial investigations immediately and reaching a decision that the applicant is not homeless.' Para 12.9 says '[i]t is not appropriate for the local authority to provide an immediate non-priority decision to the applicant on first contact without having clear evidence of their status.' Presumably the Code contemplates that the issue as to whether an applicant is homeless, or threatened with homelessness, is a simpler question to determine that the question of whether or not he or she has a priority need.

[113] English Code, para 6.27; Welsh Code, para 12.56.

whose previous application resulted in the local housing authority owing him or her the main housing duty can make a fresh application when that duty ends.[114]

9.68 In these circumstances it has been left to the courts to work out sensible limits to protect local housing authorities from having to investigate fully what are essentially repetitive applications. The broad rule established by the courts is that a local housing authority is entitled to preface any inquiries into a repeat application by simply considering whether the factual circumstances have relevantly changed since the previous application.

9.69 If there has been no factual change, the local housing authority is entitled to refuse to entertain the application and to rely on its previous decision (including any previous decision that the local housing authority's duty to the applicant had been discharged). If, however, there has been such a factual change of circumstances, the local housing authority can no longer rely on its previous decision and must make inquiries into the application in the usual way.[115] In *R v Harrow London Borough Council ex p Fahia*,[116] the House of Lords held that there were no administrative short cuts available which would enable a local housing authority to avoid the duty to make at least that level of inquiries into a repeat application.

9.70 The Court of Appeal applied this approach in *Begum v Tower Hamlets London Borough Council*.[117] Unless a repeat application discloses no new facts on the application form, or any new facts that are disclosed are merely fanciful or trivial, the local housing authority must accept the application, make its inquiries, comply with any other statutory duties that might arise (such as securing accommodation) and notify its decision in accordance with HA 1996, Part 7. Both Codes reflect this approach.[118]

9.71 Prior to the decision in *Begum v Tower Hamlets London Borough Council*,[119] most local housing authorities were only prepared to accept repeat applications if there had been a 'material change of circumstances'. There was also a practice of asking repeat applicants if they had obtained and occupied settled accommodation since their earlier applications. The former approach was overruled by *Begum v Tower Hamlets London Borough Council*,[120] and the latter practice is no longer appropriate. Intervening settled accommodation should be treated as one of those changes in factual circumstances which would require a local housing authority to accept and determine a fresh application.

---

[114] HA 1996, s 193(9). See *R (Dumbaya) v Lewisham London Borough Council* [2008] EWHC 1852 (Admin) (2008) September *Legal Action*, p 25, Admin Ct; and *R (Dragic) v Wandsworth London Borough Council* [2012] EWHC 1241 (Admin), (2012) July *Legal Action*, p 42, Admin Ct.

[115] *R v Harrow London Borough Council ex p Fahia* [1998] 1 WLR 1396, HL.

[116] (1998) 30 HLR 1124, HL.

[117] [2005] EWCA Civ 340, [2005] HLR 34, CA.

[118] English Code, para 6.27; Welsh Code, para 12.56.

[119] [2005] EWCA Civ 340, [2005] HLR 34, CA.

[120] [2005] EWCA Civ 340, [2005] HLR 34, CA.

Factual changes

9.72 As explained,[121] the effect of the decisions in *R v London Borough of Harrow ex p Fahia*[122] and *Begum v Tower Hamlets London Borough Council*[123] is that a local housing authority must ask, on a repeat application for homelessness assistance, whether there has been any changes in relevant facts.

9.73 In *R v London Borough of Harrow ex p Fahia*,[124] the applicant had occupied guest house accommodation originally provided by the local housing authority while it was making inquiries into her first application. After the local housing authority had decided that she had become intentionally homeless, she had been permitted by the guest house manager to stay on there. She claimed housing benefit in order to pay the rent. Over a year later, she was asked to leave the guest house and applied again to the local housing authority. The local housing authority's refusal to accept her application was quashed as there had been a relevant change in her factual circumstances. The local housing authority had failed to address itself to whether the loss of the non-settled accommodation was a new or supervening event causing a new incidence of homelessness.

9.74 In *Begum v Tower Hamlets London Borough Council*,[125] the presence of two additional adults in the applicant's accommodation, rendering it overcrowded, was a relevant change of factual circumstances sufficient for the local housing authority to have to accept a further application.[126]

9.75 The Court of Appeal's decision in *Begum v Tower Hamlets London Borough Council*[127] on repeat applications was applied in *R (May) v Birmingham City Council*.[128] In that case, the local housing authority had accepted that it owed a main housing duty to the applicant. It made the applicant an offer of accommodation which she refused. She was at the time living with her grandmother. The local housing authority notified the applicant that it had decided that its main housing duty had come to an end as a result of her refusal of the offer. The applicant continued to live with her grandmother. Ten months later, the grandmother required the applicant and her children to leave and the applicant tried to make a fresh application for homelessness assistance. The local housing authority refused to accept the application stating

---

[121] See **9.66–9.69**.
[122] [1998] 1 WLR 1396, HL.
[123] [2005] EWCA Civ 340, [2005] HLR 34, CA.
[124] *R v London Borough of Harrow ex p Fahia* [1998] 1 WLR 1396, HL.
[125] [2005] EWCA Civ 340, [2005] HLR 34, CA.
[126] See **11.109–11.110**.
[127] [2005] EWCA Civ 340, [2005] HLR 34, CA.
[128] [2012] EWHC 1399 (Admin) (2012) July *Legal Action*, p 41, Admin Ct. See also *R (Daie) v Camden London Borough Council* [2006] EWHC 452 (Admin), (2006) May *Legal Action*, p 34, Admin Ct, where permission was given for an applicant to bring judicial review proceedings where the local housing authority had refused to accept a second application saying that there had been no 'material change of circumstances'. By the time that the judicial review claim came to a full hearing, the local housing authority had not only accepted the second application but had also concluded that the applicant was owed the main housing duty.

that it was not satisfied that there had been a relevant change of circumstances. The judge held that the local housing authority's decision was irrational and that the circumstances of the applicant were not exactly the same as when she had made her first application for homelessness assistance. Accordingly, the local housing authority was obliged to accept a further application for homelessness assistance.[129]

9.76   Case law decided under the old test of material change of circumstances had held that events that *might* have been sufficient to require a local housing authority to entertain a second application included:

- the breakdown of the applicant's marriage;[130]

- the award of Disability Living Allowance for night-time supervision (so that an applicant who originally needed one bedroom now needed two-bedroom accommodation);[131]

- a threat of possession proceedings combined with overcrowded accommodation;[132] and

- where a medical report showed that an applicant's health was poor and deteriorating and contained additional material relevant to the original decision that the applicant had become homeless intentionally (a case said to be unusual on its facts).[133]

9.77   Any of these circumstances would now be instances of changes in relevant facts.

9.78   Changes of circumstances which, on their facts, the courts found, under the old test, were *not* sufficient to give rise to a duty to entertain a second application included:

- the illness and death of a friend who had been providing unsettled accommodation;[134]

---

[129]   It should be noted that the local housing authority had notified the applicant that she was entitled to a review of its decision that there had been no relevant change of circumstances and the applicant had requested a review. This was plainly the wrong procedure since a decision that an application will not be accepted is not one of the decisions of which the applicant has a right to request a review at HA 1996, s 202(1) (see **19.12–19.37**). This was recognised by the applicant's legal representatives, who brought proceedings in judicial review in order to challenge the decision.

[130]   *R v Basingstoke and Deane Borough Council ex p Bassett* (1983) 10 HLR 125, QBD.

[131]   *Ali v Camden London Borough Council* (1998) October *Legal Action*, p 22, Central London County Court.

[132]   *R (Jeylani) v Waltham Forest London Borough Council* [2002] EWHC 487 (Admin), (2002) May *Legal Action*, p 30, Admin Ct.

[133]   *R (Van der Stolk) v Camden London Borough Council* [2002] EWHC 1621 (Admin), (2002) July *Legal Action*, p 26, Admin Ct.

[134]   *R v Brighton Borough Council ex p Harvey* (1997) 30 HLR 670, QBD.

- pregnancy of the applicant;[135]

- the failure of an arrangement made by a prisoner for his sister to pay the rent during his sentence;[136] and

- disrepair to the applicant's home.[137]

9.79 Many of these would now constitute changed factual circumstances requiring the local housing authority to entertain a new application under the modern approach.

9.80 Particular issues may arise where the first application results in the local housing authority accepting a duty to accommodate the applicant, but the applicant refuses the accommodation offered (or refuses the local connection referral then made) and then later makes a repeat application. In general, a local housing authority is entitled to rely on the ending of its duty following a refusal of accommodation.[138] However, if, after the refusal of accommodation (and ending of duty), the factual circumstances change, the local housing authority can no longer rely on the completion of the earlier duty. That was the case in *Begum v Tower Hamlets London Borough Council*,[139] where a homeless applicant unreasonably refused an offer of accommodation. She spent a year in unsettled accommodation, returned to her former home and re-applied to the local housing authority when overcrowding there worsened. The Court of Appeal held that the local housing authority was not entitled to rely on the duty having previously ended, and had to accept the further application in the light of the changed factual situation. The same was the case in *R (May) v Birmingham City Council*.[140]

Abandoned and withdrawn applications

9.81 Having made an application, an individual may decide not to proceed with it or otherwise be unable to proceed with it. Although this must be commonplace, there is no statutory process for the deemed abandonment or withdrawal of applications. In the absence of such provision, local housing authorities will want to make sensible practical arrangements.

9.82 For example, if the applicant dies before a decision is reached on the application, the local housing authority can simply substitute (with that person's consent) another member of the late applicant's household as applicant.[141]

---

[135]   *R v Hackney London Borough Council ex p Ajayi* (1997) 30 HLR 473, QBD.
[136]   *Stewart v Lambeth London Borough Council* [2002] EWCA Civ 753, [2002] HLR 40, CA.
[137]   *R (Campbell) v Enfield London Borough Council* [2001] EWHC 357 (Admin).
[138]   *R v Westminster City Council ex p Chambers* (1982) 6 HLR 24, QBD. See **17.55–17.66**, **17.92–17.108** and **17.119–17.131** [England] and **17.136–17.146** [Wales].
[139]   [2005] EWCA Civ 340, [2005] HLR 34, CA.
[140]   [2012] EWHC 1399 (Admin), (2012) July *Legal Action*, p 41, Admin Ct.
[141]   As was done in *R v Camden London Borough Council ex p Hersi* (2001) 33 HLR 577, CA.

9.83 Likewise, each local housing authority will have its own procedures and policies for allowing applicants to withdraw their own applications.[142]

9.84 More controversial is the question as to whether there are circumstances in which the local housing authority may itself treat an application as withdrawn. The Codes recommend that local housing authorities may wish to consider an application as 'closed' where there has been no contact from the applicant for 3 months or longer and that any further approach after that time may be treated as a fresh application. If the applicant renews contact during the three months, the suggestion is that the local housing authority should resume its original inquiries, and consider all relevant matters, including whether there are any relevant new facts that affect those inquiries.[143]

9.85 That guidance is somewhat at variance with HA 1996, Part 7. The legislation recognises that contact will be lost with at least some applicants, because it makes special provision for notice of decisions on applications to be retained for later collection at the local housing authority's offices.[144] This would suggest that the proper course is for every application to result in a decision even if the decision is that, on the material available to the local housing authority, it is not satisfied that the applicant is homeless or threatened with homelessness. This has the additional advantage of enabling a local housing authority to maintain comprehensive statistics for decisions on all applications (and the time it takes to reach them).

Simultaneous applications to the same local housing authority

9.86 What happens when an applicant has made one application for homelessness assistance and the decision-making process and any legal challenges to decisions made on the application have not yet concluded before another application is made to the same local housing authority? That was the case in *R (Konodyba) v Kensington & Chelsea Royal London Borough Council*[145] where the applicant had been notified of a decision that she was not eligible for assistance, had requested a review which upheld the original decision, had appealed unsuccessfully against the review decision to the County Court and had applied for permission to appeal to the Court of Appeal. In the meantime, she had indicated to the local housing authority that she wished to make a fresh application for homelessness assistance because the legal position regarding eligibility had changed. The local housing authority responded that, while the applicant had an outstanding application for homelessness assistance, which was currently the subject of an application to the Court of Appeal for permission to appeal, she could not make a fresh application and that a local housing authority cannot entertain two applications for homelessness assistance at the same time.

---

[142] English Code, para 6.27; Welsh Code, para 12.50.
[143] English Code, para 6.27; Welsh Code, para 12.50.
[144] HA 1996, ss 184(6) and 203(8).
[145] [2011] EWHC 2653 (Admin), (2011) December *Legal Action*, p 30, Admin Ct.

9.87   The applicant then brought a judicial review claim challenging the local housing authority's refusal to secure interim accommodation[146] for her pending notification of a decision on her asserted new application. At an early stage in the case, a Deputy High Court Judge considered whether the claimant had a strong prima facie claim and found, for a number of reasons, that she did not. There was a discussion as to whether or not an application for homelessness assistance could be made when the previous application was still subject to legal proceedings. The judge said:

'[i]f there is arguably a significant change in the circumstances there would be merit in the authority taking a fresh decision on that basis, particularly if the previous application is out of their hands because it is under appeal. If the fresh application is successful, it might render the appeal otiose and thus avoid the time and expense of the appeal being determined. If it is unsuccessful, why should the applicant be prejudiced by having had to withdraw his appeal which might otherwise have succeeded. On the other hand, how is an authority to decide if a new application is or is not on exactly the same facts as the previous one . . . ..If the further application is accepted on the grounds that it is not on exactly the same facts as the previous one, would the authority have to carry out the same statutory inquiries as in the former application, even on matters where it is not said that there had been any change . . . ..On this approach, and where the first application is under appeal, it could lead to the appeal being pursued on a factual basis which is inconsistent with the facts of any subsequent application.'[147]

9.88   The judge found that it was arguable that the refusal to accept a second application for homelessness assistance in these circumstances was based on a misconstruction of HA 1996, Part 7.[148]

Re-applying within two years of a private rented sector offer

9.89   For applicants who:

- make an application for homelessness assistance to a local housing authority in England on or after 9 November 2012;[149] and

---

[146]   HA 1996, s 188(1). See **16.12–16.28**.

[147]   HHJ Robinson at [53].

[148]   It should be noted that the facts of this case are unusual. The applicant's principal argument – that she was eligible for assistance (see Chapter 12 of this book) – had been rejected by Kensington & Chelsea Royal London Borough Council, an appeal against that review decision was dismissed by a County Court Judge, she was granted permission to appeal the decision of the County Court Judge and in the Court of Appeal abandoned the main point on which she relied. The Court of Appeal dismissed the appeal, treating it as abandoned. On her application to Kensington & Chelsea Royal London Borough Council, she sought to raise the same point on eligibility that she had abandoned before the Court of Appeal. The local housing authority found that she was not eligible; a county court judge dismissed her appeal against that decision and the Court of Appeal decided that she could not rely on a legal point that she had previously had the opportunity to raise and had abandoned (*Konodyba v Royal Borough of Kensington & Chelsea* [2012] EWCA Civ 982, (2012) September *Legal Action*, p 30, CA).

[149]   At the date of writing, the amendments to HA 1996 made by LA 2011, ss 148–149 had not been brought into effect in Wales.

- accept a private rented sector offer which brings the main housing duty to an end;[150] and

- the private rented sector tenancy subsequently comes to an end;

the applicant will have the right to make a further application for homelessness assistance.[151]

9.90 If the application is made within two years of the date of the applicant's acceptance of the private rented sector offer, the applicant will be entitled to the main housing duty, or to the equivalent duty owed to those threatened with homelessness, if the applicant is eligible for assistance, homeless or threatened with homelessness, and did not become homeless intentionally.[152] In other words, the applicant need not still have a priority need in order to be entitled to the main housing duty again.

9.91 This special provision will not apply where an applicant would only be entitled to the main housing duty (or equivalent duty to those threatened with homelessness) again because of the presence in the applicant's household of a restricted person.[153] Where the applicant is homeless because of the presence in his or her household of a restricted person, he or she has to have a priority need in order to be entitled to the main housing duty (or equivalent duty to those threatened with homelessness).

9.92 The special provision only will apply once. Where an applicant has been the beneficiary of this special provision and has subsequently accepted another private rented sector offer, which then comes to an end within two years of the date of acceptance, the applicant must make a fresh application for homelessness assistance and would have to have a priority need in order to be entitled to the main housing duty again (or equivalent duty to those threatened with homelessness).[154]

---

[150] HA 1996, s 193((7AA)–(7AC) as amended by LA 2011, s 148(5)–(7). See **17.109–17.131**. 'Private rented sector offers' can be made to applicants for homelessness assistance whose applications are made on or after 9 November 2012 to local housing authorities in England. At the date of writing, the amendments to HA 1996 made by LA 2011, ss 148–149 had not been brought into effect in Wales.

[151] HA 1996, s 193(9).

[152] HA 1996, s 195A(1) and (3) inserted by LA 2011, s 149(4) and in force from 9 November 2012. These provisions will apply to applicants for homelessness assistance whose applications were made on or after 9 November 2012 to local housing authorities in England. At the date of writing, the amendments to HA 1996 made by LA 2011, ss 148–149 had not been brought into effect in Wales.

[153] HA 1996, s 195A(5) inserted by LA 2011, s 149(4) and in force from 9 November 2012. These provisions will apply to applicants for homelessness assistance whose applications were made on or after 9 November 2012 to local housing authorities in England. At the date of writing, the amendments to HA 1996 made by LA 2011, ss 148–149 had not been brought into effect in Wales. For 'restricted person', see HA 1996, s 184(7) and **10.82–10.85** and **12.32–12.47**.

[154] HA 1996, s 195A(6) inserted by LA 2011, s 149(4) and in force from 9 November 2012. These provisions will apply to applicants for homelessness assistance whose applications were made

9.93 The special provision will not apply to applicants whose applications for homelessness assistance are made more than two years after the date of acceptance of a private rented sector offer. Applicants in that position who may be homeless or threatened with homelessness would have to have a priority need to be entitled to the main housing duty (or equivalent duty to those threatened with homelessness). It should be noted that the date from which the two-year period begins is the date of acceptance of the private rented sector offer, not the date when the tenancy was granted or when the applicant actually moved in.[155]

9.94 An applicant who had accepted a private rented sector offer and subsequently is served with a Housing Act 1988, s 21 notice by his or her landlord should make his or her application for homelessness assistance as soon as he or she is served with the notice. Provided that the notice is valid, he or she will be found to be threatened with homelessness and the duties at HA 1996, s 195 will apply.[156] Once the date for possession in the notice has been reached, and provided that the applicant did not become homeless intentionally, he or she will be homeless and entitled to the main housing duty at HA 1996, s 193(2).[157]

9.95 The immediate duty to secure interim accommodation for the applicant and his or her household will apply if the local housing authority has 'reason to believe' that it might owe the applicant the main housing duty under the special provision 'regardless of whether the applicant has a priority need'.[158]

Challenges to refusals to accept applications

9.96 If a local housing authority refuses to accept an application for homelessness assistance (and therefore declines to undertake inquiries into it) there is no right to any statutory review of that decision, or appeal against it.

---

on or after 9 November 2012 to local housing authorities in England. At the date of writing, the amendments to HA 1996 made by LA 2011, ss 148–149 had not been brought into effect in Wales.

[155] HA 1996, s 195A(1) and (3) inserted by LA 2011, s 149(4) and in force from 9 November 2012. These provisions will apply to applicants for homelessness assistance whose applications were made on or after 9 November 2012 to local housing authorities in England. At the date of writing, the amendments to HA 1996 made by LA 2011, ss 148–149 had not been brought into effect in Wales.

[156] See **17.190–17.200**.

[157] See **17.23–17.168**. If the applicant is found to have become homeless intentionally from the private rented sector accommodation, the special provision exempting the applicant from a priority need does not apply. Accordingly if the applicant does have a priority need, he or she will be entitled to the short-term duty to secure accommodation for those who have become homeless intentionally at HA 1996, s 190(2)(a) (see **17.182–17.189**). If he or she does not have a priority need, the only duty owed will be to provide advice and assistance (HA 1996, s 190(3), see **17.201–17.214**.

[158] HA 1996, s 188(1A) inserted by LA 2011, s 149(2) and in force from 9 November 2012. See **16.29–16.35**. These provisions will apply to applicants for homelessness assistance whose applications were made on or after 9 November 2012 to local housing authorities in England. At the date of writing, the amendments to HA 1996 made by LA 2011, ss 148–149 had not been brought into effect in Wales.

The applicant could lodge a complaint through the local housing authority's complaints procedure, but if a swifter remedy is needed, the applicant should apply for a judicial review[159] and ask for a mandatory order requiring the local housing authority to accept the application and comply with its consequent statutory duties. Judicial review is also the proper course if the applicant is dissatisfied with a local housing authority's decision that it need not accept an application because it is a repeat application and there is no relevant change of facts.[160]

9.97   If the judicial review challenge results in the local housing authority being required to entertain and inquire into the application, then a decision must be reached on it by the local housing authority and notified with reasons. The applicant will then be entitled to seek a review of that decision (and, if necessary, appeal) in the usual way.[161]

9.98   Complaint can also be made to the Ombudsmen that the local housing authority is guilty of maladministration by refusing to accept an application for homelessness assistance. In both England and Wales, Ombudsmen have been so concerned at the number of complaints against local housing authorities in this respect that special reports have been published.[162]

[159] See **19.224–19.250**.
[160] See **9.66–9.80**.
[161] See **19.8–19.223**.
[162] *Homelessness: how councils can ensure justice for homeless people Focus Report: learning the lessons from complaints* (2011) Local Government Ombudsmen; *Housing Allocations and Homelessness: A Special Report by the Local Government Ombudsman for Wales,* (2006) Public Services Ombudsman for Wales. See **8.74–8.78**.

Chapter 10

INQUIRIES AND DECISIONS

INQUIRIES INTO APPLICATIONS

10.1 Once a local housing authority has reason to believe that a person who has made an application for accommodation (or for assistance in obtaining accommodation) may be homeless or threatened with homelessness, it *must* make inquiries sufficient to enable it to answer three questions:

(1)   whether the applicant is 'eligible' for assistance;

(2)   if so, whether any duty under the Housing Act 1996 (HA 1996) Part 7 is owed to the applicant; and

(3)   if so, what duty is owed.[1]

10.2 Separately, the local housing authority has a power, but not a duty, to make inquiries into whether the applicant has a local connection with its district and, if not, whether he or she has a local connection elsewhere.[2] This is an entirely discretionary line of inquiry for the local housing authority; it can choose whether or not to make inquiries into local connection, but if it chooses not to do so, the applicant has no right to a review of that negative decision.[3]

10.3 The trigger for the making of inquiries into the applicant's eligibility and whether any duty is owed to him or her is extremely low.[4] Any information that causes the local housing authority to have reason to believe that the applicant *may* be homeless or *may* be threatened with homelessness is sufficient. An applicant does not need to be applying explicitly for homelessness assistance.

10.4 The scope of the compulsory inquiries may appear to be quite limited. For example, although local housing authorities must inquire into an application to see whether any duty is owed under HA 1996, Part 7, there does not appear to be any obligation to inquire into the application to see whether the applicant could be the beneficiary of the exercise of any *power* that the provisions of HA 1996, Part 7 confer on the local housing authority (eg the power to accommodate the non-priority unintentionally homeless).[5] Likewise, inquiries only need be made to determine 'whether' a duty is owed and, therefore, inquiries need not necessarily be made as to the way in which it is appropriate to perform the duty.

10.5 In practice these artificial statutory limitations are ignored. It is good administration for a local housing authority to direct inquiries not only to the

---

[1]   HA 1996, s 184(1).

[2]   HA 1996, s 184(2).

[3]   *Hackney London Borough Council v Sareen* [2003] EWCA Civ 351, (2003) 35 HLR 54, CA.

[4]   See *R (Aweys) v Birmingham City Council* [2007] EWHC 52 (Admin), [2007] HLR 27, Admin Ct at [8] per Collins J; and see **9.57–9.63**.

[5]   See **17.215–17.222**.

prescribed matters but also to broader questions, such as whether it should exercise its relevant powers and as to how it might best discharge any duties that it finds it owes the applicant.

10.6   In addition, the legal obligation is to inquire into the possible application of *every* relevant duty under HA 1996, Part 7 regarding the applicant's circumstances. That would include, for example, whether the duty to protect the applicant's possessions had been triggered.[6] This minimum requirement should not be overlooked.

10.7   Considerable guidance as to how these inquiries should be carried out is provided in each of the Codes.[7]

The sequence of inquiries

10.8   The process of making inquiries may be undertaken in stages, thus reflecting the statutory scheme. For example, the first statutory inquiry is as to whether the applicant is 'eligible'.[8] If the local housing authority decides that an applicant is not eligible for assistance, it is not required to make any further inquiries. It would be a waste of time and effort if the local housing authority had to embark on detailed inquiries into other matters (eg whether the applicant had become homeless intentionally), because no duty is owed to an applicant who is ineligible for assistance, beyond the duty to notify the applicant of the reasons for that decision. Treating eligibility as a discrete first issue may therefore lead to a saving of time and resources. However, if the applicant may be eligible but the question of eligibility cannot be inquired into and resolved immediately, at least some preliminary further inquiries will be necessary in order for the local housing authority to determine whether the applicant may also be homeless and may have a priority need and thus be the subject of a duty to provide interim accommodation.[9]

10.9   If the local housing authority decides as a result of its inquiries that an applicant is eligible for assistance, it must then inquire into whether it owes him or her a duty under HA 1996, Part 7. In order to resolve that general question, it must first inquire into and decide whether the applicant is homeless or threatened with homelessness. If the applicant is neither homeless nor threatened with homelessness, no further duty will be owed under HA 1996, Part 7. No further inquiries need be made and the applicant will be notified accordingly that no duty is owed and provided with the reasons for that decision.

---

6   HA 1996, s 211. See **17.233–17.284**.
7   *Homelessness Code of Guidance for Local Authorities* (Communities and Local Government, Department for Education and Skills, Department of Health, July 2006) (the English Code), paras 6.1–6.20; *Code of Guidance for Local Authorities Allocation of Accommodation and Homelessness 2012* (Welsh Government, August 2012) (the Welsh Code), paras 12.7–12.12, 12.20–12.31 and 12.41–12.56.
8   HA 1996, s 184(1)(a). See Chapter 12 of this book.
9   HA 1996, s 188(1). English Code, para 6.16; Welsh Code, para 12.9. See also **16.12–16.28**.

10.10 If the applicant is both eligible for assistance and homeless (or threatened with homelessness), the local housing authority will owe the applicant at least some duty under HA 1996, Part 7. The question then arises as to which duty is owed. In order to answer that question, the local housing authority must inquire into and determine two further issues in respect of most applicants:

(1)   whether the applicant has a priority need;[10] and

(2)   whether the applicant became homeless intentionally, or became threatened with homelessness intentionally.[11]

10.11   For most applicants, each of those issues must be the subject of inquiry by the local housing authority in order to determine what duty is owed to the applicant. This requirement to inquire into both matters represents something of a departure from local housing authority practice prior to the Homelessness Act 2002. Before the amendments made by that Act, it was common for local housing authorities to 'slice up'[12] the making of inquiries and to stop if it became plain that the applicant had no priority need for accommodation. Inquiries into whether the applicant has become homeless intentionally are among the most difficult and time-consuming to make. They were to be avoided, if possible, and there was no point in making them if the applicant had no priority need. This practice had been approved by the courts.[13] The new approach requires both matters to be the subject of inquiries in most cases where homelessness, or threatened homelessness, and eligibility are established.[14] To this extent, the old practice of ceasing to make inquiries once an applicant had been found not to have a priority need has gone.[15]

10.12   Where an applicant had made an application for homelessness assistance to a local housing authority in England on or after 9 November 2012 and had accepted a private rented sector offer,[16] if the applicant subsequently makes a further application for homelessness assistance to a local housing

---

[10]   An applicant who had accepted a private rented sector offer following an application for homelessness assistance made to a local housing authority in England on or after 9 November 2012 and who makes a new application for homelessness assistance to a local housing authority in England within two years of the date of acceptance of the offer does not need to have a priority need in order to be entitled to the main housing duty at HA 1996, s 193(2). See HA 1996, s 195A inserted by Localism Act 2011 (LA 2011), s 149(4) and **9.89–9.95**. At the date of writing, the amendments to HA 1996 made by LA 2011, ss 148–149 had not been brought into effect in Wales.

[11]   HA 1996, s 184(1)(b).

[12]   *Crawley Borough Council v B* (2000) 32 HLR 636, CA per Buxton LJ.

[13]   *Crawley Borough Council v B* (2000) 32 HLR 636, CA.

[14]   English Code, para 6.12; Welsh Code, para 12.20.

[15]   Although the Court of Appeal has held that there was no error of law where a local housing authority simply decided that an applicant did not have a priority need and did not make any decision as to whether she had become homeless intentionally: *Gaskin v Norwich City Council* [2007] EWCA Civ 1239, (2008) January *Legal Action*, p 38, CA.

[16]   HA 1996, s 193(7AA)–(7AC) as amended by LA 2011, s 148(5)–(8), in force from 9 November 2012. See **17.190–17.168**.

authority in England within two years of the date of acceptance of that offer, he or she need not have a priority need in order to be entitled to the main housing duty or equivalent duty to those threatened with homelessness.[17] This does not apply where the main housing duty (or equivalent duty) would not be owed were it not for the presence in the applicant's household of a restricted person'.[18] If the applicant in those circumstances does have a priority need, he or she will be entitled to the main housing duty or equivalent duty.[19]

10.13 If the local housing authority decides to exercise its discretionary power to inquire into whether an applicant has a local connection, care must be taken in deciding *when* to make such inquiries. If the applicant is owed anything short of the main housing duty, such inquiries will have been a waste of time and effort (because local connection is only of relevance if the main housing duty is owed).[20] On the other hand, a local housing authority may want to inquire into local connection at the same time as making its other inquiries, where there is a real prospect that the main housing duty might be found to be owed – thus allowing the local housing authority to make a referral of the main housing duty to a different local housing authority as soon as it has been identified that the duty is owed.

10.14 If the main housing duty[21] is owed (or the equivalent duty is owed to an applicant who is threatened with homelessness[22]),the local housing authority must consider whether that duty is only owed as a result of the presence in the applicant's household of a restricted person.[23] It follows that the local housing authority need only make inquiries into whether the applicant's household contains a restricted person if it has already accepted that the main housing duty is owed to the applicant. It also follows that, if the main housing duty

---

[17] HA 1996, s 195A(1) and (3) inserted by LA 2011, s 149(4) applying to applicants for homelessness assistance whose applications were made on or after 9 November 2012 to a local housing authority in England. At the date of writing, the amendments to HA 1996 made by LA 2011, ss 148–149 had not been brought into force in Wales. See **9.89–9.95**.

[18] HA 1996, s 195A(5) inserted by LA 2011, s 149(4) applying to applicants for homelessness assistance whose applications were made on or after 9 November 2012 to a local housing authority in England. At the date of writing, the amendments to HA 1996 made by LA 2011, ss 148–149 had not been brought into force in Wales. For more on this special provision for re-applications, see **9.89–9.95**. For 'restricted person' see HA 1996, s 184(7) at **10.82–10.85** and **12.32–12.47**.

[19] The presence of a restricted person, such as a dependent child or any person who has a priority need under HA 1996, s 189(1), in the household will provide the applicant with a priority need, so the applicant will still be able to show that he or she has a priority need. There may be cases where the presence of the restricted person has resulted in the applicant and his or her household becoming homeless, in which case the applicant would have to have a priority need in order to be entitled to the main housing duty or equivalent duty to those threatened with homelessness. For 'restricted person' see **10.82–10.85** and **12.32–12.47**. For 'priority need, see Chapter 13.

[20] HA 1996, s 198(1). See also English Code, para 6.14; Welsh Code, para 12.11. See **15.19–15.30**.

[21] HA 1996, s 193(2). See **17.23–17.168**.

[22] HA 1996, s 195(2). See **17.190–17.200**.

[23] HA 1996, s 184(3A). See **10.82–10.85** and **12.32–12.47** for definition of restricted person. In force for applications made on or after 2 March 2009.

would be owed whether or not the applicant's household included a restricted person, there is no obligation to make inquiries into the presence of the restricted person.[24]

Burden of proof

10.15   The burden of making inquiries rests on the local housing authority. It is for the local housing authority to make the inquiries necessary to 'satisfy' itself whether the applicant is 'eligible' and then, if satisfied that she or he is eligible, to make the inquiries necessary to satisfy itself whether any duty is owed under HA 1996, Part 7.[25]

10.16   It is not for the applicant to 'prove' his or her case.[26] This point has been reiterated in decisions of the courts and in successive editions of the Codes.[27] The applicant can obviously be asked, or invited, to co-operate with the inquiries and to provide information, but an application cannot be rejected simply because the applicant has not provided some document or other material considered necessary to prove part of his or her case. It follows that the local housing authority cannot suspend inquiries or transfer its responsibilities onto the applicant by such practices as refusing to make a decision unless the applicant obtains a letter from a person with whom he or she recently resided, or a medical report, or a copy of a police or accident report.[28]

10.17   The correct approach was summarised in *R v Gravesham Borough Council ex p Winchester*.[29] The burden lies on local housing authorities to make appropriate inquiries in a caring and sympathetic way. Such inquiries should be pursued rigorously and fairly, but there is no duty to conduct 'CID type inquiries'. Applicants should be given an opportunity to explain matters which local housing authorities consider may weigh substantially against them.[30]

10.18   Very infrequently, an applicant will simply make an application and then refuse to co-operate in the conduct of inquiries, or refuse to provide any but the barest details of himself or herself, or of his or her circumstances. This is not a position that any applicant who was sensibly advised would take, and, if adopted, might suggest that there were issues relating to the applicant's capacity to conduct his or her affairs.[31]

---

[24]   See **17.155–17.168** for the duties owed to restricted cases.

[25]   HA 1996, s 184(1).

[26]   *R v Woodspring Borough Council ex p Walters* (1984) 16 HLR 73, QBD.

[27]   English Code, para 6.15; Welsh Code, para 12.22.

[28]   See, for example, *Complaints against Southwark London Borough Council*, 10 000 207, 10 004 245 and 11 000 195, 22 May 2012, (2012) August *Legal Action* p 27.

[29]   *R v Gravesham Borough Council ex p Winchester* (1986) 18 HLR 207, QBD.

[30]   See **10.25–10.34**. For an example where a decision was quashed because the decision-maker had not obtained the applicant's full account, see *Mondeh v Southwark London Borough Council* (2010) November *Legal Action*, p 19, Lambeth County Court.

[31]   *AB v Leicester City Council* [2009] EWCA Civ 192, CA. For a similar instance of lack of

10.19 At the end of the inquiries there is unlikely to be any remaining doubt or uncertainty as to whether an applicant is 'eligible', or over most of the decisions as to what duties, if any, are owed. The local housing authority will be able to determine whether it is satisfied that the applicant is 'eligible', 'homeless', and has a 'priority need'. However, the burden of proof may be decisive where the issue is whether the applicant has become homeless intentionally. On that matter the legal question is whether the local housing authority is *not* satisfied that the applicant became homeless, or threatened with homelessness, intentionally.[32] Accordingly, on that question, if there is doubt or uncertainty, the issue must be resolved in the applicant's favour.[33]

Scope of inquiries

10.20 The legal obligation on the local housing authority is to make 'such inquiries as are necessary'.[34] But who decides which inquiries are 'necessary'? The courts have repeatedly indicated that it is for the local housing authority to decide what inquiries it considers 'necessary' to undertake. A local housing authority will only err in law if it has failed to make an inquiry that no reasonable local housing authority would have regarded as unnecessary.[35]

10.21 The local housing authority must ensure that it has, in the course of its inquiries, taken all of the applicant's circumstances into account and come to an overall, or composite, view. Whilst inquiries into different aspects, such as medical factors, may be made by different officers of the local housing authority, the final decision should be taken by an officer who has all of the information available.[36]

10.22 Local housing authorities are required by HA 1996, s 182, to take into account the guidance contained in the Codes of Guidance and any other guidance that the Secretary of State (or the Welsh Ministers) issues under that section. For this purpose, local housing authorities need to be able to refer to the current version of the relevant Codes.[37]

---

co-operation in a context of a challenge to a decision of a local authority's adult care services, see *R (WG) v Leicester City Council* [2011] EWHC 189 (Admin), [2011] EWCA Civ 483 and [2011] EWCA Civ 861, CA.

[32] HA 1996, s 193(1); and see **14.19–14.24**.

[33] The Welsh Code advises that if there is any doubt surrounding the factors under consideration, the decision should be given in favour of the applicant: para 12.23.

[34] HA 1996, s 184(1), as explained in *R v Kensington and Chelsea Royal London Borough Council ex p Bayani* (1990) 22 HLR 406, CA.

[35] See *R v Nottingham City Council ex p Costello* (1989) 21 HLR 301, QBD; *R v Kensington and Chelsea Royal London Borough Council ex p Bayani* (1990) 22 HLR 406, CA; and *Cramp v Hastings Borough Council* [2005] EWCA Civ 1005, [2005] HLR 48, CA.

[36] *R v Lewisham London Borough Council ex p Dolan* (1993) 25 HLR 68, QBD.

[37] See *R v Newham London Borough Council ex p Bones* (1993) 25 HLR 357, QBD, where a decision based on an out-of-date edition of the Code was quashed. In *Mondeh v Southwark London Borough Council* (2010) November *Legal Action*, p 19, Lambeth County Court, a review decision was quashed, in part because the reviewing officer had failed to address the Code of Guidance and had failed to give reasons for departing from its guidance.

10.23 In fixing the scope, form and manner of making its inquires, a local housing authority must bear in mind its obligations under equalities legislation. The Equality Act 2010, s 149(1) requires local housing authorities to:

'have due regard to the need to—

(a)   eliminate discrimination, harassment, victimisation and any other conduct that is prohibited by or under this Act;

(b)   advance equality of opportunity between persons who share a relevant protected characteristic[38] and persons who do not share it;

(c)   foster good relations between persons who share a relevant protected characteristic and persons who do not share it.'

10.24 The Court of Appeal has held that decision-makers must therefore take steps to take account of any disability which may be relevant to the decision being considered. This is the case even if the disability is not obvious to the decision-maker. The decision-maker should consider whether there is some feature of the information presented by the applicant which might raise a real possibility that the applicant was disabled.[39] In the case considered by the Court of Appeal, there was some information before the decision-maker which indicated that the applicant and/or his wife might be disabled and that this might be relevant to whether or not they had become homeless intentionally. That was sufficient for there to be real possibility that the applicant's acts and omission had been affected by mental impairment. The point applies to all of the protected characteristics set out in the Equality Act 2010,[40] although it is most obviously likely to arise in relation to disability.

Interviewing the applicant

10.25 A local housing authority is obviously obliged to give the applicant the opportunity to explain his or her circumstances fully. In particular, matters that could lead to a decision against the applicant's interests must be put to him or her for comment before the decision is made.[41] In *Royal Borough of Windsor and Maidenhead v Hemans*,[42] Toulson LJ said: '[i]t is striking that at no time was [the applicant], either directly or through her solicitors, given the opportunity to meet the suggestion, if the review officer really had it in mind, that this account was essentially fictitious.'[43] One county court judge has decided that, where an applicant's credibility is at issue, he or she should be

---

[38]   The protected characteristics are: age, disability, gender re-assignment, marriage and/or civil partnership, race, religion and/or belief, sex, and sexual orientation (Equality Act 2010, ss 5–12).

[39]   *Pieretti v Enfield London Borough Council* [2010] EWCA Civ 1140, [2011] HLR 3, CA considering the statutory predecessor to Equality Act 2010, s 149 which was Disability Discrimination Act 1995, s 49.

[40]   See footnote 38.

[41]   English Code, para 6.15; Welsh Code, para 12.23 which advises that a face to face interview is considered 'best practice'. See also *R v Wyre Borough Council ex p Joyce* (1983) 11 HLR 73, QBD and *R v Dacorum Borough Council ex p Brown* (1989) 21 HLR 405, QBD.

[42]   [2010] EWCA Civ 374, [2011] HLR 25, CA.

[43]   Toulson LJ at [56].

personally interviewed by the officer making the relevant decision, not by another officer.[44] The courts would be unlikely to hold that *every* applicant must be interviewed, but also very likely to find that, in some circumstances, an interview would be essential, particularly where the local housing authority is considering disbelieving the applicant's account.[45] The Codes are premised on there being at least an initial interview on the day of application.[46]

10.26 Generally, the local housing authority will interview the applicant face to face, although there is no reason why the local housing authority should not put questions to the applicant by letter.[47] There is no statutory requirement that the applicant must be interviewed or offered an interview. Whether the applicant should be interviewed is a matter for the local housing authority to decide.[48]

10.27 A local housing authority in England was severely criticised by the Local Government Ombudsman for failing to use interpreters in all of its interviews with a particular applicant.[49] In another case, an applicant with impaired hearing was not provided with sufficient assistance during the inquiries.[50]

10.28 The local housing authority's inquiries and, in particular, any interview of the applicant, should be conducted in a 'caring and sympathetic way'.[51] It is for the local housing authority to decide how it conducts any interview, how long it lasts and what questions are asked. An error of law will only be made out if the style of questioning has the effect of inhibiting the applicant from putting forward his or her case or any facts which might assist the application.[52]

10.29 The local housing authority is not required to accept what the applicant says at face value.[53] If the applicant's response raises a relevant matter of fact that the local housing authority is not prepared simply to accept, the local

---

44 *N v Allerdale Borough Council* (2008) October *Legal Action*, p 38, Carlisle County Court.

45 *R v Hackney London Borough Council ex p Decordova* (1994) 27 HLR 108, QBD; *Burr v Hastings Borough Council* [2008] EWCA Civ 1217, (2009) January *Legal Action*, p 27, CA; and *Royal Borough of Windsor and Maidenhead v Hemans* [2010] EWCA Civ 374, [2011] HLR 25, CA. See also English Code, para 6.15; Welsh Code, para 12.27.

46 English Code, para 6.16; Welsh Code, paras 12.8–12.9 and 12.22–12.23.

47 In *Rowley v Rugby Borough Council* [2007] EWCA Civ 483, [2007] HLR 40, CA, a local housing authority had not made an error of law when it asked the applicant to confirm what it understood to be her version of events on a tear-off slip, and then relied upon that confirmation.

48 *Tetteh v Kingston upon Thames London Borough Council* [2004] EWCA Civ 1775, [2005] HLR 21, CA at [26].

49 *Complaint against Waltham Forest London Borough Council*, 03/A/15819, 9 November 2005.

50 *Complaint against Redbridge London Borough Council*, 07/A/03275, 23 March 2009 (2009) May *Legal Action*, p 26.

51 *R v Gravesham Borough Council ex p Winchester* (1986) 18 HLR 207, QBD.

52 *R v Tower Hamlets London Borough Council ex p Khatun (Shafia)* (1996) 27 HLR 465, CA.

53 *R v Kensington and Chelsea Royal London Borough Council ex p Cunha* (1989) 21 HLR 16, QBD.

housing authority must investigate it.[54] If there is any doubt, and the matter cannot be resolved by further reasonable inquiries, the question should be resolved in the applicant's favour, at least where it relates to whether or not the applicant had become homeless intentionally.[55]

10.30 Statements from third parties containing material contrary to the applicant's case should be put to the applicant for comment before the local housing authority decides whether or not it accepts those statements. Usually this can be achieved by simply showing the applicant the statements. Guidance on the situation which arises where it is important not to disclose the identity of the third party is given in *R v Poole Borough Council ex p Cooper*.[56] It may be that the applicant is able to provide reasons why the adverse information from the third party cannot be relied upon.[57] Adverse medical evidence, whether from the local housing authority's own medical adviser or the applicant's doctor(s), should also be put to the applicant for comment before a decision is reached.[58]

10.31 If the local housing authority is relying on factual information in relation to the applicant's case which conflicts with the applicant's own account, that information should be put to the applicant for comment.[59]

10.32 The local housing authority is entitled to rely upon the applicant's own statement or statements. However, if there is ambiguity or subsequent contradiction of a statement by the applicant, the local housing authority should give the applicant an opportunity to challenge its interpretation of his or her earlier statement.[60]

---

[54] See *R v Tower Hamlets London Borough Council ex p Bibi* (1991) 23 HLR 500, QBD; *R v Northampton Borough Council ex p Clarkson* (1992) 24 HLR 529, QBD; *R v Newham London Borough Council ex p Bones* (1993) 25 HLR 357, QBD; *R v Kensington and Chelsea Royal London Borough Council ex p Silchenstedt* (1996) 29 HLR 728, QBD; and *Forbes v Lambeth London Borough Council* (2000) July *Legal Action*, p 30, Lambeth County Court.

[55] *R v Gravesham Borough Council ex p Winchester* (1986) 18 HLR 207, QBD. See also **10.19**.

[56] (1994) 27 HLR 605, QBD.

[57] See *R v Ealing London Borough Council ex p Chanter* (1992) December *Legal Action*, p 22, QBD, where the applicant's sister had informed the local housing authority that the applicant had left accommodation voluntarily but, had the statement been put to the applicant, she would have told the local housing authority of long-standing hostility between herself and her sister.

[58] *R v Newham London Borough Council ex p Lumley* (2001) 33 HLR 11, QBD, and *Begum (Amirun) v Tower Hamlets London Borough Council* [2002] EWHC 633, (2003) 35 HLR 8, QBD. A careful distinction should be drawn between adverse medical evidence and adverse medical opinion. See **10.50–10.64** for a fuller discussion on the proper conduct of medical inquiries.

[59] See *Lane and Ginda v Islington London Borough Council* (2001) April *Legal Action*, p 21, Clerkenwell County Court, where the local housing authority's failure to put information as to the frequency of lift breakdown to the applicant before deciding that accommodation offered was 'suitable' resulted in the decision being quashed.

[60] *Robinson v Brent London Borough Council* (1999) 31 HLR 1015, CA.

10.33 It is not for the applicant to volunteer matters that may or may not be relevant. It is for the local housing authority, through interview and other inquiries, to identify those relevant matters and then make the necessary inquiries into them.[61]

10.34 Where an interview would not yield more information than is already known to the local housing authority, an interview will not be a necessary part of the duty to make inquiries.[62]

Timescale

10.35 There is no time limit prescribed by HA 1996, Part 7 for the completion of inquiries. The Codes work on the premise that the obligation to inquire is triggered as soon as the applicant gives the local housing authority reason to believe that he or she may be homeless, or may be threatened with homelessness. They encourage local housing authorities to carry out their inquiries 'as quickly as possible'.[63] They suggest that local housing authorities should aim to complete their inquiries and notify the applicant of their decision within 33 working days, counted from the date on which the application was received.[64] Local housing authorities are advised that they should carry out an interview and preliminary assessment on the day that the application is received.[65]

10.36 It is unlawful for a local housing authority to postpone the taking of a decision once it has reached the conclusion of its inquiries (or to extend the inquiry process artificially) simply in order to avoid a duty. Most commonly, this might arise where a 17-year-old makes an application for homelessness assistance shortly before his or her eighteenth birthday.[66]

10.37 If the local housing authority simply fails to progress or complete its inquiries, or fails to notify the decision made on the conclusion of its inquiries to the applicant, the applicant is left in a limbo situation.[67] As no decision has

---

[61] *R v Tower Hamlets London Borough Council ex p Ullah* (1992) 24 HLR 680, QBD.
[62] *Kacar v Enfield London Borough Council* (2001) 33 HLR 64, CA.
[63] English Code, para 6.16; Welsh Code, para 12.27.
[64] English Code, para 6.16 and Welsh Code, para 12.29. Both Codes add that 'in many cases it should be possible for authorities to complete the inquiries significantly earlier'.
[65] English Code, para 6.16; Welsh Code, para 12.27.
[66] *Robinson v Hammersmith & Fulham London Borough Council* [2006] EWCA Civ 1122, [2007] HLR 7, CA and Welsh Code, para 12.30. While 17-year-olds have a priority need by virtue of their age, that is not the position with 18-year-olds: Homelessness (Priority Need for Accommodation) (England) Order 2002, SI 2002/2051, art 3 and Homeless Persons (Priority Need) (Wales) Order 2001, SI 2001/607 (W 30), art 4 and see **13.127–13.174** [England] and **13.214–13.218** [Wales]. In *R (Raw) v Lambeth London Borough Council* [2010] EWHC 507 (Admin), (2011) May *Legal Action*, p 24, Admin Ct, the Judge considered that a practice of deferring or ceasing inquiries where an applicant for homelessness assistance had been referred to a rent deposit scheme would also be an illegitimate approach and an impermissible reason for not performing the duty to inquire. See **8.73**.
[67] If no decision is reached and notified to the applicant, then any accommodation that had been secured for the applicant under the duty at HA 1996, s 188(1), will continue to be occupied

been notified, the applicant does not have the right to request a review of it. Instead, an applicant would need to bring judicial review proceedings for a mandatory order requiring the local housing authority to complete its inquiries and notify its decision by a specified date.[68] Alternatively, the applicant could complain through the local housing authority's complaints procedure and ultimately to the Local Government Ombudsman or Public Services Ombudsman for Wales who can recommend that inquiries be concluded and/or that the applicant should be compensated for delays which amount to maladministration.[69]

The special rules for restricted persons

10.38 Where the applicant's household includes a 'restricted person',[70] there may be additional inquiries to be made and additional notification duties.[71]

10.39 A 'restricted person' is defined as a person:

- who is not eligible for assistance under HA 1996, Part 7;[72] and

- who is subject to immigration control within the meaning of the Asylum and Immigration Act 1996;[73] and either

- does not have leave to enter or remain in the UK; or

---

under that duty (see **16.12–16.28**). In *O'Callaghan) v Southwark London Borough Council* (2010) May *Legal Action*, p 23, Lambeth County Court, the applicant was in that position. She subsequently lost her accommodation. On a further application for homelessness assistance, the local housing authority's decision that she had become homeless intentionally was wrong in law, as she could not have become homeless intentionally from accommodation secured under HA 1996, s 188(1). See **11.13**.

[68] In *R v Lambeth London Borough Council ex p Weir* [2001] EWHC 121 (Admin), (2001) June *Legal Action*, p 26, Admin Ct, the local housing authority was required to notify the applicant within 14 days after a 20-month delay; in *R v Brent London Borough Council ex p Miyanger* (1996) 29 HLR 628, QBD, the local housing authority was required to make a decision within 28 days and notify the applicant within a further 3 days, after the local housing authority had failed to comply with an agreement made 3 months earlier that a decision would be made. See **19.224–19.250** for judicial review.

[69] See, for example, *Complaints against Lambeth London Borough Council*, 07/B/01138 and 07/B/05232, 30 June 2008, (2008) September *Legal Action*, p 25, where £500 was paid for delay causing uncertainty and anxiety, but no serious disadvantage; and the conclusions of the Commissioner for Complaints against Northern Ireland Housing Executive. He recommended £4,000 for a delay of a year (200700491), 6 November 2008, (2009) April *Legal Action*, p 22. The Local Government Ombudsman described a local housing authority's failure to reach a decision in one case as '*clearly unacceptable*' and '*a failure to fulfill its statutory responsibilities*': *Complaint against Hounslow London Borough Council*, 10 019 388, 5 October 2011, (2011) December *Legal Action*, p 29. See also *Complaint against Hounslow London Borough Council*, 11 008 191, 28 August 2012 (2012) November *Legal Action*, p 14 where maladministration was found for, amongst other failings, a delay of approximately three months in reaching a decision. See **19.251–19.258**.

[70] HA 1996, s 184(7). See **10.82–10.85** and **12.32–12.47**.

[71] HA 1996, s 184(3A). See **10.82–10.85**. See Welsh Code, para 13.6.

[72] See Chapter 12 of this book.

[73] See **12.64–12.70**.

- whose leave to enter or remain in the UK is subject to a condition to maintain and accommodate himself or herself, and any dependent, without recourse to public funds.[74]

10.40 It follows that British nationals, some Commonwealth nationals with the right of abode in the UK and most EEA nationals and their family members cannot be restricted persons.[75]

PARTICULAR SITUATIONS

Violence or harassment

10.41 The Codes recommend that inquiries into cases where violence is alleged 'will need careful handling'. Local housing authorities are advised that it is essential that their inquiries do not provoke further violence and are warned against approaching the alleged perpetrator. Information may be sought from the applicant, his or her friends or relatives, from adult care or children's services, or from the police.[76]

10.42 If the violence alleged is *domestic* violence, local housing authorities are reminded that the applicant 'may be in considerable distress'. Any interview should be conducted by an officer who is trained to deal with domestic violence allegations, and the applicant should have the option of requesting an officer of the same sex as him or her.[77] Local housing authorities are advised that applicants alleging domestic violence may not be able to produce independent evidence of the violence. Whilst a local housing authority may seek corroboration, it should not reject the applicant's account merely because there is no evidence of complaints to the police or other agencies.[78] Local housing authorities are reminded that the test to be applied is not whether violence occurred in the past but whether it is probable that there will be violence (or threats of violence that are likely to be carried out) if the applicant continues to occupy his or her home.[79]

---

[74] HA 1996, s 184(7).

[75] See **12.64–12.70**. For applicants to local housing authorities in England whose applications were made on or after 9 November 2012, the only difference between those who are owed a main housing duty because of the presence in his or her household of a restricted person, and other applicants owed the main housing duty, is that the local housing authority is required to bring the main housing duty to an end by a private rented sector offer so far as reasonably practicable, whereas it may, but is not required to, make a private rented sector offer to other applicants (HA 1996, s 193(7AA)–(7AD) amended by LA 2011, s 148(5)–(7)). See **17.159–17.162**. At the date of writing, the amendments to HA 1996 made by LA 2011, ss 148–149 had not been brought into effect in Wales.

[76] English Code, para 6.17; Welsh Code, paras 12.41 and 14.46.

[77] English Code, para 6.17; Welsh Code, paras 12.41 and 13.21.

[78] *Hawa Abdilah Ali v Newham London Borough Council* (2000) November *Legal Action*, p 23, Bow County Court. English Code, paras 6.19 and 8.22.

[79] English Code, paras 6.17–6.18 and 8.18–8.25; Welsh Code, para 13.21. See also *Bond v Leicester City Council* [2001] EWCA Civ 1544, (2002) 34 HLR 6, CA. See further **11.81–11.92**.

10.43 A local housing authority must investigate accounts of violence or harassment given by the applicant when it is making its inquiries into whether accommodation is or was reasonable for the applicant to occupy.[80] A local housing authority cannot refuse to investigate these accounts merely because the applicant had failed to raise them at an earlier stage.[81]

10.44 If the local housing authority is considering disbelieving an applicant because of contradictions or inconsistencies in his or her account, or because of information derived from other sources, those contradictions or inconsistencies should be put to the applicant for explanation.[82]

Financial problems

10.45 If accommodation has been lost as a result of the applicant accruing rent or mortgage arrears, the local housing authority will need to make inquiries into the applicant's financial affairs. Those same issues may also be relevant to the question of whether accommodation currently occupied by the applicant is reasonable for him or her to continue to occupy.[83]

10.46 The local housing authority should examine why the applicant had fallen into arrears and give him or her an opportunity to explain the cause of the arrears, their extent and any arrangements made to repay them.[84] The local housing authority should investigate whether an applicant knew about the availability of housing benefit, whether housing benefit was claimed and if not, why not.[85] In a case where the applicants had not disputed the landlord's claim to possession on the grounds that they were in arrears, but had subsequently argued that the contractual rent was lower than that put forward to the court and therefore they were not in arrears, the local housing authority was not obliged to make inquiries into the actual level of the contractual rent. The court would not have made a possession order if the contractual rent had been the amount stated by the applicants.[86]

10.47 If an applicant gave up his or her accommodation due to financial pressures, the local housing authority must determine the extent of those pressures, eg what debts may have been owed by the applicant and what the arrangements for repayment were. If loans were taken out to support a business

---

[80]   *R v Northampton Borough Council ex p Clarkson* (1992) 24 HLR 529, QBD, where the local housing authority's decision that an applicant had become homeless intentionally was quashed, as it had failed to make inquiries into her account that her brother had sexually harassed her at the accommodation.

[81]   *R v Hackney London Borough Council ex p Decordova* (1994) 27 HLR 108, QBD.

[82]   *R v Camden London Borough Council ex p Mohammed* (1997) 30 HLR 315, QBD.

[83]   Homelessness (Suitability of Accommodation) Order 1996, SI 1996/3204 at Appendix 2. See **11.101** and **18.47–18.48**.

[84]   *R v Wyre Borough Council ex p Joyce* (1983) 11 HLR 73, QBD.

[85]   *R v Tower Hamlets London Borough Council ex p Saber* (1992) 24 HLR 611, QBD.

[86]   *Green v Croydon London Borough Council* [2007] EWCA Civ 1367, [2008] HLR 28, CA. See also *Sheppard v Richmond-upon-Thames Royal London Borough Council* [2012] EWCA Civ 302, (2012) June *Legal Action*, p 38, CA.

venture, it is relevant to inquire into what the applicant knew or ought to have known about the business's prospects.[87] The local housing authority must consider fully whether or not an applicant could have afforded to have remained in his or her accommodation, but need not engage in detailed arithmetical calculations or verification of itemised expenses.[88]

Acquiescence

10.48 In general, if a couple has lost accommodation as a result of the deliberate act or omission of one of them (e g by the one who was the tenant or owner accruing rent or mortgage arrears or engaging in nuisance behaviour), the local housing authority is entitled to assume that the other one acquiesced in that behaviour.[89] However, if there is any suggestion to the contrary, the local housing authority must investigate whether there was such acquiescence in that particular case.[90] Whilst the English Code states 'the applicant will need to demonstrate that he or she was not involved in the acts or omissions that led to homelessness, and did not have control over them'[91] – a reversal of the burden of proof – this is over-stating the lawful approach which can be found in the judgment of Woolf J in *R v North Devon District Council ex p Lewis*:[92]

> 'it would be perfectly proper in the ordinary case for the housing authority to look at the family as a whole and assume, in the absence of material which indicates to the contrary, where the conduct of one member of the family was such that he should be regarded as having become homeless intentionally, that was conduct to which the other members of the family were a party.'[93]

10.49 Where there is material which indicates that the applicant did not acquiesce in the action that rendered the household homeless intentionally, that material must be considered.[94]

Medical conditions

10.50 A local housing authority may need to make inquiries into an applicant's medical condition in order to decide whether he or she has a priority need,[95] whether previous accommodation was reasonable for the

---

[87] *R v Exeter City Council ex p Tranckle* (1993) 26 HLR 244, QBD. See Welsh Code, para 15.9.

[88] *R v Brent London Borough Council ex p Grossett* (1994) 28 HLR 9, CA; and *Bernard v Enfield London Borough Council* [2001] EWCA Civ 1831, (2002) 34 HLR 46, CA. English local housing authorities should have regard to the Secretary of State's *Supplementary Guidance on Intentional Homelessness* (CLG, August 2009): see Appendix 2.

[89] *R v North Devon District Council ex p Lewis* [1981] 1 WLR 328, QBD.

[90] *R v Eastleigh Borough Council ex p Beattie (No 2)* (1984) 17 HLR 168, QBD. See **14.93–14.97**.

[91] English Code, para 11.5; see also Welsh Code, paras 15.4 and 15.7–15.8.

[92] [1981] 1 WLR 328, QBD.

[93] *R v North Devon District Council ex parte Lewis* [1981] 1 WLR 328, QBD at 333.

[94] *R v West Dorset District Council ex parte Phillips* (1984) 17 HLR 336, QBD; and *N v Allerdale Borough Council* (2008) October *Legal Action*, p 38, Carlisle County Court.

[95] See **13.75–13.119**.

applicant to continue to occupy,[96] or whether accommodation currently occupied or offered for occupation is suitable for the applicant's needs.[97]

10.51 Where a medical issue is raised by an applicant, the local housing authority should obtain medical evidence.[98] A local housing authority can obtain the opinion of its own medical adviser, but any decisions on the facts and the overall assessment should each be made by the local housing authority and not delegated to the medical adviser.[99]

10.52 The medical adviser must act fairly in obtaining any relevant information from the applicant's own doctors and in coming to an opinion. Depending on the circumstances, the applicant's medical records should be considered and it may even be necessary for the medical adviser to examine the applicant personally or to discuss the applicant's case with his or her own doctors.[100]

10.53 If the applicant complains that he or she is anxious or depressed, it may be appropriate to obtain specialist psychiatric evidence.[101]

10.54 If there are differences of opinion between the local housing authority's medical advisers and the medical opinion put forward on behalf of the applicant, the local housing authority should request an explanation for those

---

[96]   See **11.75–11.120** and **14.125–14.143**.
[97]   See Chapter 18 of this book.
[98]   *Osmani v Camden London Borough Council* [2004] EWCA Civ 1706, [2005] HLR 22, CA.
[99]   *R v Lambeth London Borough Council ex p Walters* (1994) 26 HLR 170, QBD; *Osmani v Camden London Borough Council* [2004] EWCA Civ 1706, [2005] HLR 22, CA; *Cramp v Hastings Borough Council* [2005] EWCA Civ 1005, [2005] HLR 48, CA; and *Shala v Birmingham City Council* [2007] EWCA Civ 624, [2008] HLR 8, CA. Where an adviser had informed the local housing authority that more evidence was required, and the decision-maker had known that a further report would be produced, it was wrong in law for the local housing authority to make its decision without waiting for that report or obtaining further evidence itself:*Woldeab v Southwark London Borough Council* (2011), November *Legal Action*, p 39, Lambeth County Court. See also Welsh Code, para 14.19.
[100] *R v Lambeth London Borough Council ex p Walters* (1994) 26 HLR 170, QBD; and *Shala v Birmingham City Council* [2007] EWCA Civ 624, [2008] HLR 8, CA. Whether or not a personal examination is required will depend on the particular facts. See *Khelassi v Brent London Borough Council* [2006] EWCA Civ 1825, (2007) February *Legal Action*, p 31, CA (where there had been a personal medical examination); *Shala v Birmingham City Council* [2007] EWCA Civ 624, [2008] HLR 8, CA (where the local housing authority was required to bear in mind that its medical adviser had not examined the applicant); *Wandsworth London Borough Council v Allison* [2008] EWCA Civ 354, (2008) June *Legal Action*, p 33, CA (where a personal examination was not necessary); and *R (Bauer-Czarnomski) v Ealing London Borough Council* [2010] EWHC Admin 130, (2010) March *Legal Action*, p 30, Admin Ct (a judicial review claim relating to an application for an allocation of social housing, see**4.102**).
[101] *R v Brent London Borough Council ex p McManus* (1993) 25 HLR 643, QBD. But see *Wells v Tower Hamlets London Borough Council* [2006] EWCA Civ 755, (2006) September *Legal Action*, p 14, CA, where the local housing authority was entitled to rely on the opinion of its own medical adviser, a GP, who had accepted (but provided a 'gloss' to) the opinion expressed by the applicant's treating psychiatrist.

differences.[102] The local housing authority should also take into account differences in medical expertise when trying to reconcile conflicting medical opinions.[103]

10.55 An adverse medical opinion, including one from the applicant's own doctor(s), should normally be put to the applicant for comment.[104] So too should any medical advice that raises new issues or contentious points.[105]

10.56 Where a local housing authority's policy was to 'encourage persons who have any knowledge of an applicant's medical or social history to attend' the decision-making panel, and the applicant's doctor had expressed a wish to attend, the local housing authority was severely criticised by the Local Government Ombudsman for failing to invite the doctor.[106]

10.57 The final decision (for example, as to whether or not an applicant is vulnerable) is for the local housing authority, not for the medical adviser, but normally the medical adviser should be asked to address the relevant statutory test (such as vulnerability).[107]

10.58 Where the local housing authority has to make decisions on both medical and non-medical aspects, it cannot treat the two aspects entirely separately. It must come to an overall, or composite, assessment of the applicant's circumstances.[108]

10.59 When the local housing authority is assessing whether an applicant is 'vulnerable', and care, health or other support needs are identified in the course of that assessment, the local housing authority should liaise with adult care

---

[102] *R v Kensington and Chelsea Royal London Borough Council ex p Assiter* (1996) September *Legal Action*, p 13, QBD.

[103] *Yemlahi v Lambeth London Borough Council* (2000) August *Legal Action*, p 26, Wandsworth County Court; *Khelassi v Brent London Borough Council* [2006] EWCA Civ 1825, (2007) February *Legal Action*, p 31, CA; and *Shala v Birmingham City Council* [2007] EWCA Civ 624, [2008] HLR 8, CA.

[104] *R v Newham London Borough Council ex p Lumley* (2001) 33 HLR 11, QBD; *Yemlahi v Lambeth London Borough Council* (2000) August *Legal Action*, p 26, Wandsworth County Court; and *R (Amirun Begum) v Tower Hamlets London Borough Council* [2002] EWHC 633 (Admin), (2003) 35 HLR 8, QBD. But see *Wells v Tower Hamlets London Borough Council* [2006] EWCA Civ 755, (2006) September *Legal Action*, p 14, CA, where the applicant's medical evidence had been accepted and the local housing authority's medical adviser had added 'a gloss'. In those circumstances, there was no obligation to put the medical adviser's comments to the applicant.

[105] *Hall v Wandsworth London Borough Council* [2004] EWCA Civ 1740, [2005] HLR 23, CA.

[106] *Complaint against Waltham Forest London Borough Council*, 03/A/15819, 9 November 2005.

[107] *Sicilia v Waltham Forest London Borough Council* (2002) December *Legal Action*, p 21, Bow County Court; *Ryde v Enfield London Borough Council* [2005] EWCA Civ 1281, (2006) January *Legal Action*, p 32, CA. See also, in the context of an application for an allocation of social housing, *R (Bauer-Czarnomski) v Ealing London Borough Council* [2010] EWHC Admin 130, March *Legal Action*, p 30, Admin Ct, where the medical adviser did overstep his remit, see **4.102**.

[108] *R v Lewisham London Borough Council ex p Dolan* (1993) 25 HLR 68, QBD; and *Crossley v City of Westminster* [2006] EWCA Civ 140, [2006] HLR 26, CA.

services and health authorities, where appropriate, as part of its inquiries.[109] It may be necessary to obtain an assessment from the relevant specialist authority. Medical reports obtained as part of an assessment by the Department for Work and Pensions of a person's entitlement for specific welfare benefits may be taken into account, but the local housing authority must bear in mind that assessment of entitlement to benefits is a wholly different exercise from assessment of priority need.[110]

10.60 The Court of Appeal has considered the issue of the use, by local housing authorities, of medical advisers.[111] It has held:

> 'It is entirely right that local authority officers, themselves without any medical expertise, should not be expected to make their own critical evaluation of applicants' medical evidence and should have access to specialist advice about it. What would not be acceptable is seeking out advisers to support a refusal of priority need housing wherever possible.'[112]

10.61 It reminded local housing authorities that it is not the medical advisers but the local housing authorities that have the task of determining whether an applicant has a priority need (or any other medically related question). It is appropriate for medical advisers to be asked to address the specific issue which the local housing authority has to decide, and to furnish material within their professional competence which addresses that issue. It also reminded local housing authorities that, unless their medical adviser has personally examined the applicant, his or her opinion cannot be considered expert evidence of the applicant's condition.[113]

10.62 A later Court of Appeal decision held that the role of a medical adviser is to comment 'on the medical evidence in order to enable the local authority to understand the medical issues and to evaluate for itself the evidence before it as to [the applicant's] medical condition'.[114] In that case, it was not appropriate for the medical adviser to have examined the applicant personally.

10.63 An application to the Court of Appeal for permission to bring a second appeal,[115] on the grounds that those two decisions of the Court of Appeal were inconsistent, was refused. The judge said:

---

[109] English Code, para 10.17; Welsh Code, paras 12.43 and 14.16–14.19.

[110] *Mangion v Lewisham London Borough Council* [2008] EWCA Civ 1642, (2009) January *Legal Action*, p 26, CA; and *Simpson-Lowe v Croydon London Borough Council* [2012] EWCA Civ 131, (2012) April *Legal Action*, p 47, CA.

[111] *Shala v Birmingham City Council* [2007] EWCA Civ 624, [2008] HLR 8, CA.

[112] *Shala v Birmingham City Council* [2007] EWCA Civ 624, [2008] HLR 8, CA at [19] per Sedley LJ.

[113] *Shala v Birmingham City Council* [2007] EWCA Civ 624, [2008] HLR 8, CA at [19]–[22] per Sedley LJ. An attempt to argue that the particular medical adviser's organisation was 'biased in favour of their paymasters' received short shrift from the Court of Appeal in *Harper v Oxford City Council* [2007] EWCA Civ 1169, (2008) January *Legal Action*, p 37, CA.

[114] *Wandsworth London Borough Council v Allison* [2008] EWCA Civ 354, (2008) June *Legal Action*, p 33, CA per Wall LJ at [71].

[115] For 'second appeals', see **19.213–19.223**.

'I do not see any inconsistency between the two decisions in [*Birmingham City Council v*] *Shala* and [*Wandsworth London Borough Council v*] *Allison*. In *Allison* the Court of Appeal helpfully set out the kind of assistance that a local authority's in-house medical adviser can give. In *Shala*, on the other hand, the Court of Appeal pointed out the limitations which exist if the in-house medical adviser instead of assisting the local authority to understand the medical expert seeks to offer conflicting expert opinion.'[116]

10.64 The decision-maker must ensure that he or she takes due steps to take account of any disability (or any other protected characteristic[117]) where some feature of the evidence presented raises a real possibility that the applicant might be disabled and this might be relevant to the issue under consideration.[118]

Overcrowded accommodation

10.65 If an applicant claims that his or her present or previous accommodation is or was overcrowded, and therefore not reasonable for him or her to continue to occupy, the local housing authority must make inquiries to determine whether the accommodation is or was overcrowded and, if so, to what extent.[119] Where there is a dispute as to the size, space or arrangement of the accommodation, inquiries should be made so that the local housing authority can make its own decision on the disputed issues.[120]

DECISIONS ON APPLICATIONS

10.66 Once the local housing authority has completed its inquiries into an application, it is required to notify the applicant of its decision.[121] *Every* application therefore results in notification of a decision.[122] The requirements as to the content of the decision notice are given in HA 1996, s 184, so that the colloquialism 'a section 184 notice' or 'section 184 letter' is commonly used to refer to a local housing authority's notification of a decision on an application. There is no question of applicants being given the result informally in lieu of a written notification. Every applicant, even if she or he is found to be not

---

[116] *Simpson-Lowe v Croydon London Borough Council* [2012] EWCA Civ 131, (2012) April *Legal Action* p 47, CA at [9] per Jackson LJ. See also *Nagi v Birmingham City Council* [2010] EWCA Civ 1391, (2011) January *Legal Action* p 36, CA.

[117] Equality Act 2010, ss 5–12. See **10.23–10.24**.

[118] *Pieretti v Enfield London Borough Council* [2001] EWCA Civ 1104, [2011] HLR 3, CA. See Welsh Code, para 14.18 and **10.23–10.24**.

[119] *R v Tower Hamlets London Borough Council ex p Bibi* (1991) 23 HLR 500, QBD. See **11.109–11.110**.

[120] *R v Kensington and Chelsea Royal London Borough Council ex p Silchenstedt* (1997) 29 HLR 728, QBD.

[121] HA 1996, s 184(3). The Codes recommend that inquiries should be completed as quickly as possible and that applicants are notified within 33 working days: English Code, para 6.16; Welsh Code, paras 12.26–2.31. See **10.35–10.37**.

[122] English Code, paras 6.21–6.25; Welsh Code, paras 12.45–12.48.

eligible or not homeless, is entitled to a written decision. Even those successful in their application obtain a written record of that success.[123]

10.67 The local housing authority is under an obligation, when making its decision, to consider the facts and the law in existence at the date of the decision. This means that any change of circumstances between the date of the application for homelessness assistance and the date of the decision must be taken into account. So, where an applicant for homelessness assistance had obtained an assured shorthold tenancy before the s 184 decision had been made, the local housing authority was entitled to decide that the applicant was not homeless.[124]

10.68 There is one circumstance in which it might be important to distinguish between the date on which the decision was actually made and the date when it was put in writing and 'notified' to the applicant. If either the facts or the law change in an interval between the actual making of the decision and putting it in writing, it will be the facts and law that existed at the date of the actual making of the decision that are relevant, not those existing at the date of the written notification.

10.69 In one case, the local housing authority concluded, on the day before an applicant's eighteenth birthday, that she did not have a priority need. The decision was actually put in writing on the following day. The Court of Appeal held that the decision was made on the day before the birthday, and therefore, applying the facts and law at that date, the local housing authority should have concluded that the applicant had a priority need by reason of her age.[125]

10.70 However, time limits attaching to rights to request a review (and subsequently appeal) run from the date when the written decision is 'notified' to the applicant. This is likely to be a date different from, and later than, either the actual date of the decision, or the date of the written decision.[126]

10.71 There is no statutory time limit within which the decision reached on the application must be notified.[127] HA 1996, Part 7 assumes that notice of the decision will be given by local housing authorities 'on completing their inquiries', which suggests immediately.[128] However, and rather more practically, previous editions of the Code have suggested that written notifications be produced within three working days of the completion of inquiries. The present

---

[123] The Local Government Ombudsman found maladministration when a local housing authority failed to notify the applicant of the decision on his application for homelessness assistance (Local Government Ombudsmen Digest of Cases 2005–2006, D7).

[124] *Hanton-Rhouila v Westminster City Council* [2010] EWCA Civ 1334, [2011] HLR 12, CA. See **8.71**.

[125] *Robinson v Hammersmith & Fulham London Borough Council* [2006] EWCA Civ 1122, [2007] HLR 7, CA. See **13.132–13.139**.

[126] Notification refers to receipt of the decision by the applicant or by his or her agents, not the date on the letter: see **19.38–19.40, 19.59** and **19.115–19.126**.

[127] See **10.35–10.37**.

[128] HA 1996, s 184(3).

English Code reproduces the statutory formula: notification of a decision must be given 'when a housing authority has completed its inquiries'.[129]

10.72 The decision must be put in writing.[130] If any issue has been decided against the applicant's interests, the local housing authority must not only notify that decision but also inform the applicant in writing of the reasons for its decision.[131] The duty to give reasons applies to all decisions that the local housing authority is obliged to make on an application (decisions as to whether the applicant is 'eligible', whether a duty is owed, and, if so, what duty) and to any decision that it chooses to make as to whether the applicant has a local connection.[132] However, to make sense in practice, this obligation is interpreted to mean that any adverse finding on any issue decided in the course of working out what duty is owed must be explained by reasons. Therefore, it is not sufficient for a local housing authority simply to notify a positive decision that the duty owed is the limited duty in HA 1996, s 190. It must explain, with reasons, why the applicant is not owed the highest duty set out in HA 1996, s 193.[133]

10.73 The decision is limited to whether or not the statutory criteria are met and, as a result of those findings, what duty (if any) is owed to the applicant. The local housing authority cannot impose further requirements on an applicant or suggest that a duty is conditional upon the applicant doing something, such as surrendering an existing tenancy.[134]

---

[129] English Code, para 6.21; Welsh Code, para 12.45. A decision which was reached 11 months after the applicant had been interviewed, and where the applicant's circumstances had changed during those 11 months, was held to be 'manifestly' flawed, and the special procedure under Allocation of Housing and Homelessness (Review Procedures) Regulations 1999, SI 1999/71, reg 8(2) should have been implemented: *Lambeth London Borough Council v Johnston* [2008] EWCA Civ 690, [2009] HLR 10, CA. See **19.87–19.101**. See also *Complaints against the London Borough of Lambeth*, 07/B/01138 and 07/B/05232, 30 June 2008, (2008) September *Legal Action*, p 25, where £500 was paid for delay causing uncertainty and anxiety, but no serious disadvantage. £500 was recommended where the local housing authority had failed to offer temporary accommodation and failed to reach a fresh decision after a decision that the applicant was not homeless had been overturned: *Complaint against Hounslow London Borough Council*, 10 019 388, 5 October 2011, (2011) December *Legal Action*, p 29. The Commissioner for Complaints investigating the Northern Ireland Housing Executive has recommended £4,000 for a delay of a year: Complaint 200700491, 6 November 2008, (2009) April *Legal Action*, p 22.

[130] HA 1996, s 184(6).

[131] HA 1996, s 184(3).

[132] HA 1996, s 184(4); where a local housing authority found that an applicant did not have a priority need, but failed to make any decision as to whether or not he was homeless, the Local Government Ombudsman said that the decision was defective: *Complaint against Waltham Forest London Borough Council*, 03/A/15819, 9 November 2005, Annual Digest of Cases 2005/06.

[133] As to the detail required to be given see **10.75–10.81**.

[134] *R (Hammia) v Wandsworth London Borough Council* [2005] EWHC 1127 (Admin), [2005] HLR 45, Admin Ct. However, conditions may attach to the duty to protect the applicant's possessions: see **17.233–17.254**.

10.74 Whether the decision notified by the local housing authority is favourable or unfavourable, the notification letter must inform the applicant of his or her right to request a review and also of the 21-day period within which any request for a review must be made.[135] The Codes advise local housing authorities that the decision letter should also notify applicants about the local housing authority's procedure for conducting reviews.[136]

Reasons

10.75 The Codes recommend that the reasons for the decision are explained clearly and fully and that any assistance that can be made available to the applicant is also clearly set out. If the applicant has difficulty in understanding the decision, the local housing authority should consider arranging for a member of staff to explain the decision in person.[137]

10.76 The reasons given must be proper, intelligible and adequate and relate to the substantive issues raised by the applicant.[138] An applicant is entitled to reasons so that he or she can understand, clearly, why he or she has not succeeded and can properly assess any prospects of challenging that decision.[139] In addition, adequate reasons serve to indicate that:

> '... the decision-maker has gone through the right process of thinking in arriving at its conclusion.'[140]

10.77 Merely reciting the relevant legal formula set out in HA 1996, Part 7, and stating that the applicant does not meet it, will not amount to giving adequate and sufficient reasons.[141] For example, where a local housing authority is satisfied that an applicant has become homeless intentionally, the decision letter should state:

(1) when the local housing authority considers that the applicant became homeless;

(2) why he or she become homeless;

---

[135] HA 1996, s 184(5).

[136] English Code, para 6.22; Welsh Code, para 12.46.

[137] English Code, para 6.23; Welsh Code, para 12.48.

[138] *Re Poyser and Mills' Arbitration* [1964] 2 QB 467, QBD; *Westminster City Council v Great Portland Estates plc* [1985] AC 661, HL; and *South Bucks District Council v Porter (No 2)* [2004] UKHL 33, [2004] 1 WLR 1953, HL.

[139] *R v Croydon London Borough Council ex p Graham* (1993) 26 HLR 286, CA; *R v Camden London Borough Council ex p Mohammed* (1998) 30 HLR 315, QBD; and *Shire v Birmingham City Council* (2003) March *Legal Action*, p 30, Birmingham County Court. Reasons in the s.184 decision also permit the applicant to address them in his or her request for a review: *Connors v Birmingham City Council* (2010) May *Legal Action*, p 25, Birmingham County Court.

[140] *R v Newham London Borough Council ex p Qureshi* (1998) March *Legal Action*, p 14, QBD.

[141] *R v Camden London Borough Council ex p Adair* (1996) 29 HLR 236, QBD; and *R v Islington London Borough Council ex p Trail* (1993) Times, 27 May, QBD.

(3) whether the accommodation lost was 'available' for the applicant's occupation;[142] and

(4) why it would have been be reasonable for the applicant to have continued to occupy the accommodation.[143]

10.78 The deliberate act or omission of the applicant which is said to have caused the homelessness should be identified, even though the findings can be expressed simply and briefly.[144] Where the central issue is whether it would have been reasonable for the applicant to have continued to occupy the previous accommodation, the decision letter should state what factors were considered in deciding that it would have been reasonable to continue to occupy and specifically address the reasons given by the applicant for leaving.[145]

10.79 Where there are medical issues, the decision letter should give reasons for rejecting any medical opinions.[146]

10.80 Where there were contradictory factual accounts put before the local housing authority, and it prefers one account to another, the decision letter should explain that that was the case, and why a particular account was preferred.[147]

10.81 If a decision letter fails to refer to part of the applicant's case, the inference will be that the local housing authority has failed to have regard to that matter.[148]

The special rules for restricted persons

10.82 There is an additional notification duty falling on local housing authorities where the applicant's household includes a restricted person.[149] For applicants to local housing authorities in England whose applications for

---

[142] HA 1996, s 175(1). See **11.17–11.34**.

[143] *R v Gloucester City Council ex p Miles* (1985) 17 HLR 292, CA.

[144] *R v Hillingdon London Borough Council ex p H* (1988) 20 HLR 554, QBD.

[145] *R v Tower Hamlets London Borough Council ex p Monaf* (1988) 20 HLR 529, CA; and *R v Tower Hamlets London Borough Council ex p Ojo* (1991) 23 HLR 488, QBD.

[146] *R v Kensington and Chelsea Royal London Borough Council ex p Campbell* (1995) 28 HLR 160, QBD. In *Al-Kabi v Southwark London Borough Council* (2008) March *Legal Action*, p 21, Lambeth County Court, a decision letter was found to be defective for its failure to mention the medical evidence at all, and no reasons were given for the local housing authority's decision to reject the undisputed medical evidence.

[147] *R v Wandsworth London Borough Council ex p Dodia* (1997) 30 HLR 562, QBD.

[148] *R (Jeylani) v Waltham Forest London Borough Council* [2002] EWHC 487 (Admin), (2002) May *Legal Action*, p 30, Admin Ct.

[149] HA 1996, s 184(3A) and (7), inserted by Housing and Regeneration Act 2008, s 314 and Sch 15. For 'restricted person', see **10.38–10.40** and **12.32–12.47**. This provision applies to applications to local housing authorities in both England and Wales made on or after 2 March 2009.

homelessness assistance are made on or after 9 November 2012,[150] there is no longer such a significant difference between duties owed to applicants who have a 'restricted person' in their household and duties owed to other applicants. The only remaining differences are:

- the additional notification duty;[151]

- a requirement on the local housing authority to bring the main housing duty to an end by making a private rented sector offer, so far as reasonably practicable;[152]

- no requirement on the local housing authority to have notified the applicant of the effect of HA 1996, s 195A;[153] and

- where an applicant is making an application for homelessness assistance within two years of acceptance by him or her of a private rented sector offer,[154] if the main housing duty would only be owed because of the presence of a restricted person in his or her household, he or she must also have a priority need in order to be entitled to that duty.[155]

10.83 The additional notification duty only arises if:

- the local housing authority decides that the applicant is owed the main housing duty[156] or the equivalent duty where the applicant is threatened with homelessness;[157] and

- that duty is only owed to the applicant because of the presence of the restricted person in the applicant's household.[158]

---

[150] HA 1996 amended by LA 2011, ss 148–149. At the date of writing, the amendments to HA 1996 made by LA 2011 had not been brought into effect in Wales.

[151] HA 1996, s 184(3A).

[152] HA 1996, s 193(7AD). See also HA 1996, s 193(4A) and (4B) for the equivalent duty where the applicant is threatened with homelessness.

[153] HA 1996, s 193(7AB)(c) as amended by LA 2011, s 148(6).

[154] 'Private rented sector offer' as defined at HA 1996, s 193(7AA) as amended by LA 2011, s 148(5), for applicants to local housing authorities in England whose applications for homelessness assistance were made on or after 9 November 2012. At the date of writing, the amendments to HA 1996 made by LA 2011, ss 148–149 had not been brought into force in Wales. See **17.109–17.131**.

[155] HA 1996, s 195A(1) and (5) inserted by LA 2011, s 149(4), for applicants to local housing authorities in England whose applications for homelessness assistance were made on or after 9 November 2012. At the date of writing, the amendments to HA 1996 made by LA 2011, ss 148–149 had not been brought into force in Wales. See **9.89–9.95**.

[156] HA 1996, s 193(2). See **17.23–17.168**.

[157] HA 1996, s 195(2). See **17.190–17.200**.

[158] HA 1996, s 184(3A).

10.84 If those two conditions are met, the local housing authority must:

- inform the applicant that the decision that he or she is owed the main housing duty (or equivalent duty) was reached having regard to the restricted person in the applicant's household;

- include the name of the restricted person;

- explain why the person is a restricted person; and

- explain the effect of the modification to the main housing duty, or equivalent duty, as a result of HA 1996, s 193(7AD) or s 195(4A).[159]

10.85 It should be noted that the additional notification duty does not apply in all cases where the applicant's household includes a restricted person. If the main housing duty, or equivalent duty where the applicant is threatened with homelessness, is not owed, the additional notification duty does not apply. Nor does it apply if the main housing duty (or equivalent duty) would have arisen despite the presence in the applicant's household of a restricted person.[160]

Insufficient reasons

10.86 A properly notified decision should give sufficient reasons for the applicant to understand why she or he has been unsuccessful on an issue and to enable the applicant to assess whether to make, and how best to frame, an application for review.

10.87 If the applicant considers that the reasoning given is insufficient to explain the decision, she or he could simply ignore the deficiency and apply for a review.[161] If the reasons given in a subsequent review decision are sufficient, the failure to comply with the requirement to give reasons in the initial decision will generally be cured by the reasons in the review decision (but not always).[162]

10.88 However, where the paucity of reasons in the initial decision means that the applicant cannot make a properly informed assessment as to whether to request a review, or how best to frame a review request, there will be a real need to secure the proper reasons. In the first instance the applicant might simply ask the local housing authority to give, or to supplement, its reasons. If the local housing authority's response does not provide adequate reasons, then the applicant may want to seek a judicial review and a declaration that the obligation to give reasons has not been complied with, in breach of the legal

---

[159] HA 1996, s 184(3A). For the modification to the main housing duty, and equivalent duty, as a result of HA 1996, s 193(7AD) and s 195(4A), see **17.155–17.168** and **17.196–17.200**.

[160] See **10.83**.

[161] See **19.8–19.145**.

[162] *Simpson v Brent London Borough Council* (2000) November *Legal Action*, p 23, Willesden County Court; and *R (Lynch) v Lambeth London Borough Council* [2006] EWHC 2737 (Admin), [2007] HLR 15, Admin Ct.

requirement. The courts will be slow to intervene unless it is clear that the deficiency in the reasons is such as to render any attempt to use the statutory mechanism unfair because the applicant simply does not know what was found against him or her, and what the case is that needs to be met.[163] As a fall-back, to protect against the eventuality that the court may find the reasons adequate, the applicant may want to lodge a formal request for a review within the 21-day time limit and invite the local housing authority to defer the conclusion of the review until the outcome of the judicial review proceedings.

The effect of a decision

10.89   When a local housing authority has concluded its inquiries and notified the applicant as to whether he or she is eligible, whether he or she is owed a duty and, if so, what duty, then (unless the applicant requests a review of the decision) that is normally the end of the matter. If the notification is that a duty is owed, the local housing authority then has to ensure that the duty is performed. The duty cannot be postponed or made conditional upon the applicant complying with certain requirements.[164] The duty to secure interim accommodation for the applicant will cease upon notification of the HA 1996, s 184 decision.[165]

10.90   Once the local housing authority has complied with the relevant statutory duty to provide accommodation or provide advice and assistance, then it has performed its duty. If the duty towards the applicant is the main HA 1996, s 193 duty to provide accommodation, it only comes to an end if one or more of the events set out at HA 1996, s 193(5)–(7F) occur.[166]

10.91   Once the local housing authority has accepted a duty towards the applicant, it cannot subsequently reconsider its decision if the applicant's circumstances change (if, for example, he or she ceases to have a priority need).[167] If the HA 1996, s 184 decision has been obtained by the applicant's fraud or deception, or is the result of a fundamental mistake over the facts prevailing at the date of the decision, the local housing authority may revisit and re-open its decision.[168]

---

[163]   *R v Camden London Borough Council ex p Mohammed* (1998) 30 HLR 315, QBD.

[164]   *R (Hammia) v Wandsworth London Borough Council* [2005] EWHC 1127 (Admin), [2005] HLR 45, Admin Ct.

[165]   HA 1996, s 188(3). See *O'Callaghan v Southwark London Borough Council* (2010) May *Legal Action*, p 23, Lambeth County Court, for the consequences where an applicant is occupying interim accommodation and no HA 1996, s 184 decision is notified. See **8.72**.

[166]   See **17.142–17.168**.

[167]   *R v Brent London Borough Council ex p Sadiq* (2001) 33 HLR 47, QBD, unless the duty is that owed under HA 1996, s 193(2) and the change of circumstances is one of the events set out at HA 1996, s 193(6). See **17.67–17.91**.

[168]   *R v Southwark London Borough Council ex p Dagou* (1995) 28 HLR 72, QBD; *Crawley Borough Council v B* (2000) 32 HLR 636, CA; and *Porteous v West Dorset District Council* [2004] EWCA Civ 244, [2004] HLR 30, CA. For a discussion of the limited circumstances in which s 184 decisions might be withdrawn unilaterally by a local housing authority, see Ian Loveland 'Homelessness reviews: when can local authorities withdraw s 184 decisions?' (2007) March *Legal Action*, p 20.

DECISIONS PENDING THE OUTCOME OF
AN APPLICATION

10.92 Not every decision made by a local housing authority in the course of dealing with an application must be notified to the applicant in writing, let alone with reasons given. In the course of dealing with an application for homelessness assistance, the local housing authority may well take a number of decisions of importance to the applicant. For example:

(1) whether to accept an application for homelessness assistance;[169]

(2) whether to provide interim accommodation pending a decision on the application;

(3) what interim accommodation to provide;

(4) whether to withdraw the interim accommodation, perhaps because the applicant has rejected it;

(5) whether to conduct an interview in the course of inquiries;

(6) which matters to inquire into;

(7) whether to explore local connection issues;

and many more.

10.93 None of these decisions need be put in writing by the local housing authority. None of them give rise to an opportunity for a statutory review. If a local housing authority is asked for a written notification and/or reasons for one of these decisions, it may provide them. On any challenge to the relevant decision (in proceedings brought by judicial review) it would be helpful to the local housing authority to be able to point to a contemporaneous written explanation to the applicant as to why it had reached the decision under challenge.[170]

---

[169] In *R (May) v Birmingham City Council* [2012] EWHC 1399 (Admin), (2012) July *Legal Action* p 41, the local housing authority initially notified the prospective applicant that she had the right to request a review of its decision not to accept a repeat application for homelessness assistance. This was clearly wrong and the prospective applicant successfully challenged the local housing authority through judicial review, rather than through an appeal to the County Court. For 'repeat applications', see **9.66–9.80**. For 'judicial review', see **19.224–19.250**. For 'appeal to the County Court', see **19.146–19.223**.

[170] See *Complaint against Newham London Borough Council*, 11 000 383, 8 March 2012 (2012) May *Legal Action*, p 34, where the Local Government Ombudsman found maladministration and stated: '[i]t is good practice to record reasons for a refusal to provide interim accommodation' (para 50).

INQUIRIES AND DECISIONS AFTER THE INITIAL APPLICATION HAS BEEN DETERMINED

10.94 The decision notified to the applicant on the conclusion of inquiries into his or her application is unlikely to be the last important decision that has to be made by the local housing authority, particularly where the initial decision is that the applicant *is* owed a duty under HA 1996, Part 7.

10.95 Very commonly, having made the initial decision on the application, the local housing authority will have to make a whole series of subsequent decisions in its dealings with the applicant. Even in the relatively simple case, that of a priority need applicant who has been found to have become homeless intentionally, the decision on the application will only be that there is a duty owed under HA 1996, Part 7, and that that duty is the duty contained in HA 1996, s 190 (in summary, to assess housing needs and to provide assistance and short-term accommodation).[171] But later, having conducted the assessment required by HA 1996, s 190(4), the local housing authority must decide exactly what assistance to provide and for how long accommodation should be provided. It must decide which members of the household to accommodate and where to accommodate them. And so on.

10.96 While HA 1996, s 184 gives helpful direction about the content and terms of written decisions on the initial application, HA 1996, Part 7 has little guidance to offer about such subsequent matters which will be the subject of significant decision-making.

10.97 A few specific decisions made after determination of the initial application *are* subject to notification requirements. These include:

(1) a decision to refer an application to another local housing authority under the local connection provisions (because the local housing authority making the referral owes the main housing duty and believes that the conditions for referral may be met);[172]

(2) a decision that the conditions for referral of an application to another local housing authority are actually met;[173] and

(3) a decision that the local housing authority regards its duty under HA 1996, s 193 as ended by operation of HA 1996, s 193(5), (6), (7) or (7AA).[174]

---

[171] See **17.201–17.214**.
[172] HA 1996, s 184(4): a decision which must be notified with reasons. See **15.151–15.154**.
[173] HA 1996, s 200(2): a decision which must be notified with reasons. See **15.151–15.154**.
[174] HA 1996, s 193: a decision which is not required to be notified with reasons, but carries a right to request a review under HA 1996, s 202(1)(b) (*Warsame v Hounslow London Borough Council* (2002) 32 HLR 335, CA). See **17.42–17.47**.

10.98   Beyond that, the questions of how and when local housing authorities conduct inquiries into post-application matters and how, if at all, they must notify decisions on those matters are not directly answered by HA 1996, Part 7.

10.99   It is probably safe to suggest that the proper inference to be drawn from the structure of the statutory provisions on the 'right to request a review'[175] is that, at least in respect of the decisions that are potentially subject to a right of review, the local housing authority must notify (ie put in writing) those decisions.

10.100   For example, the first potentially reviewable decision is a decision as to whether an applicant is 'eligible' for assistance.[176] Where that decision has been made on the initial application, no difficulty arises. The decision must have been the subject of inquiries and must be notified in writing with reasons.[177]

10.101   But the question of eligibility can fall for consideration again at a later stage. There may be a question as to whether an applicant who was found to be eligible on the initial application and was owed the main HA 1996, s 193 duty has since ceased to be eligible, with the effect that that duty has ended.[178] HA 1996, Part 7 imposes no express obligation on a local housing authority to inquire into the applicant's possibly changed circumstances in relation to eligibility, nor any duty to reach a new decision, nor to notify a new decision – let alone with reasons.

10.102   However, the structure of HA 1996, s 202 suggests that all reviewable decisions will have been notified in writing.[179] So, if the proper reading of HA 1996, s 202(1)(a) is that it applies to a decision that an applicant has *ceased* to be eligible, the inference is that that decision must be notified in writing.[180] Although there is no express obligation to give reasons for the decision, it makes good administrative sense for reasons to be given, so that both the applicant and any subsequent reviewing officer can understand why the new decision was made.

10.103   Two further decisions which frequently fall to be made by local housing authorities, *after* the notified HA 1996, s 184 decision on the original application, are:

(1)   whether accommodation offered to an applicant in performance of a HA 1996, Part 7 duty is 'suitable';[181] and

---

[175]   HA 1996, s 202(1). See **19.12–19.37**.
[176]   HA 1996, s 202(1)(a). See also Chapter 12 and **19.13**.
[177]   HA 1996, s 184 (1) and (3).
[178]   HA 1996, s 193(6)(a). See **17.67–17.69**.
[179]   See, in particular, HA 1996, s 202(3). See **19.12–19.40**.
[180]   In *Tower Hamlets London Borough Council v Deugi* [2006] EWCA Civ 509, [2006] HLR 28, CA, May LJ said at [33]: 'Section 193(6)(a) may theoretically not even require a decision, although no doubt the local housing authority in practice needs to communicate its view, and section 202(1)(a) seems to contemplate a decision.'
[181]   See Chapter 18 of this book.

(2) whether the circumstances triggering an end of a duty owed to an applicant are made out.[182]

10.104 The decision as to suitability is not specifically required to be notified in writing, nor is it the subject of any obligation to give reasons. Nor, indeed, is there any express obligation on the local housing authority to make inquiries into the issue of suitability (although, because it is a public authority, it must have regard to all relevant considerations and otherwise comply with the ordinary principles of administrative law). However, where the issue of suitability relates to anything other than HA 1996, s 188 interim accommodation, the applicant has a right to request a review of the local housing authority's assessment of suitability.[183] So again, the necessary inference is that the local housing authority is required to give a written notification of the decision on 'suitability'. Although there is no express obligation to give reasons for the decision, it makes good administrative sense for reasons to be given so that both the applicant (and any subsequent reviewing officer) can understand why the decision has been made.

10.105 The same inference applies to any decision that the duty owed to the applicant has come to an end. The Court of Appeal has decided that a local housing authority's decision that 'has the effect of causing the duty to cease to exist' is a decision which is capable of statutory review.[184] Accordingly, the necessary inference must be that the decision in respect of which there is a right to review is one that must be notified in writing. But again, there is no express obligation on the local housing authority to conduct any inquiries leading up to its decision, nor is there any duty to give reasons for the decision. Although there is no express obligation to give reasons for the decision, it makes good administrative sense for reasons to be given so that both the applicant (and any subsequent reviewing officer) can understand why the new decision has been made.

10.106 For applicants to local housing authorities in England[185] whose applications were made on or after 9 November 2012, if the local housing authority decides that its duty has come to an end as a result of the applicant's refusal of suitable accommodation offered under the main housing duty,[186] or his or her refusal of a final offer of Part 6 accommodation,[187] or his or her refusal of a private rented sector offer,[188] the applicant must first have been notified in writing of the possible consequence of refusal or acceptance and of his or her right to request a review of the suitability of the accommodation.

---

[182] See **17.42–17.168**.
[183] HA 1996, s 202(1)(f). See **19.27–19.37**.
[184] *Warsame v Hounslow London Borough Council* (2000) 32 HLR 335, CA.
[185] At the date of writing, the amendments to HA 1996 made by LA 2011, ss 148–149 had not been brought into effect in Wales.
[186] HA 1996, s 193(5) as amended by LA 2011, s 148(3). See **17.55–17.66**.
[187] HA 1996, s 193(7) as amended by LA 2011, s 148(4). See **17.92–17.108**.
[188] HA 1996, s 193(7AA) as amended by LA 2011, s 148(5). See **17.119–17.131**.

10.107 This still leaves a large number of decisions which will be made by a local housing authority in the course of its dealings with an applicant which are not the subject of any express requirement:

(1)   to make inquiries;

(2)   to notify the decision in writing; or

(3)   to give reasons.

10.108 Those are the decisions in relation to which there is no explicit statutory requirement under HA 1996, s 184 or elsewhere,[189] and no right to a statutory review.[190] Accordingly, these decisions are subject only to the normal constraints of good administration and administrative law. An applicant aggrieved by any such decision could use the complaints procedure, complain to the relevant Ombudsman and/or bring proceedings for judicial review. These options are explored in Chapter 19.[191]

---

[189]   See **10.1**.
[190]   See **19.12–19.37**.
[191]   See **19.224–19.250** and **19.251–19.258**.

Chapter 11

HOMELESS OR THREATENED WITH HOMELESSNESS

INTRODUCTION

11.1 The main statutory duties set out in Part 7 of the Housing Act 1996 (HA 1996) are owed only to those whom a local housing authority is satisfied are either 'homeless' or 'threatened with homelessness'. Each of those terms is very tightly defined by HA 1996, Part 7, so that there is no room for alternative terminology, such as 'rooflessness', or for more colloquial approaches such as whether someone has 'a place to sleep' or 'a home of their own'. As this Chapter demonstrates, the tightness of the legal definitions can produce some surprising results: even the owner of a mansion could, in certain circumstances, be 'homeless' for the purposes of HA 1996, Part 7.

DEFINITION OF 'HOMELESS'

Overview

11.2 The legal definition of 'homeless' is contained in three inter-related sections of HA 1996, Part 7.[1] Taken together, these sections provide that a person is homeless if he or she:

(1) has no accommodation physically available for him or her to occupy in the UK or elsewhere;[2] or

(2) has no accommodation available which he or she is legally entitled to occupy;[3] or

(3) has accommodation which is available and which he or she is entitled to occupy, but cannot secure entry to that accommodation;[4] or

(4) has accommodation available, which he or she is entitled to occupy, but that accommodation consists of a moveable structure and there is no place where the applicant is entitled or permitted both to place and reside in it;[5] or

(5) has accommodation available, which he or she is entitled to occupy and entry can be secured to it, but that accommodation is not reasonable to continue to occupy.[6]

11.3 In practice, the easiest way to apply the statutory definition is to start from the presumption that everyone is homeless. Then to ask whether, on the facts, *all* of the following conditions are satisfied:

---

1. Housing Act 1996, ss 175–178.
2. HA 1996, s 175(1).
3. HA 1996, s 175(1)(a)–(c).
4. HA 1996, s 175(2)(a).
5. HA 1996, s 175(2)(b).
6. HA 1996, s 175(3).

(1)   there is 'Accommodation';[7] and

(2)   it is 'available' for the applicant's occupation;[8] and

(3)   the applicant has some right to occupy it;[9] and

(4)   the applicant can physically enter it;[10] and

(5)   it would be reasonable for the applicant to continue to occupy it.[11]

11.4   Only if *all* of those conditions are fulfilled can the applicant be said not to be 'homeless'. There is an extra condition which must be satisfied if the relevant accommodation is 'a moveable structure'.[12]

11.5   The question for the local housing authority is whether the applicant is homeless at the date of the making of the decision on his or her application. If an applicant for homelessness assistance has obtained accommodation, meeting the conditions described at HA 1996, ss 175–177, after he or she has made the application, but before the making of the decision on that application, he or she will no longer be homeless.[13]

11.6   There is a special deeming provision for applicants who are re-applying for homelessness assistance within two years of acceptance of a private rented sector offer.[14] Applicants in those circumstances who have been served with a valid Housing Act 1988, s 21 notice are to be treated as threatened with homelessness from the date on which the notice is given, and treated as homeless from the date on which the notice expires.[15]

11.7   In the following paragraphs each of the conditions which form the component parts of the statutory definition of 'homeless' are examined in turn.

---

[7]   See **11.8–11.16**.
[8]   See **11.17–11.34**.
[9]   See **11.35–11.67**.
[10]   See **11.68–11.74**.
[11]   See **11.75–11.120**.
[12]   Discussed at **11.70–11.74**.
[13]   *Hanton-Rhouila v Westminster City Council* [2010] EWCA Civ 1334, [2011] HLR 12, CA.
[14]   'Private rented sector offers' are defined at HA 1996 s 193(7AA) as amended by Localism Act 2011 (LA 20011), s 148(5) and can be made to applicants for homelessness assistance whose applications were made on or after 9 November 2012 to local housing authorities in England, see **17.109–17.131**. At the date of writing, the amendments to HA 1996 made by LA 2011, ss 148–149 had not been brought into force in Wales.
[15]   HA 1996, s 195A(2) and (4) inserted by LA 2011 s 149(4) for applicants whose applications were made on or after 9 November 2012 to local housing authorities in England and who accepted a private rented sector offer in performance of the main housing duty owed. These special provisions apply where an applicant makes a subsequent application for homelessness assistance to a local housing authority in England within two years of the date of acceptance of the private rented sector offer. At the date of writing, the amendments to HA 1996 made by LA 2011, ss 148–149 had not been brought into effect in Wales. See **9.89–9.95** and **11.121–11.128**.

The meaning of 'Accommodation'

11.8   The question is not 'Does the applicant have an "address"?'[16] or 'Does he or she have somewhere to stay?' but rather 'Does the applicant have "accommodation"?'.

11.9   HA 1996, Part 7 gives no definition of this term. The standard dictionary definitions refer to 'lodgings or premises'.[17] In practice, ordinary English usage tends to refer to 'Accommodation' as shelter with a degree of permanence.

11.10   It is for the local housing authority to decide whether what it is considering is 'Accommodation'. Houses or flats (or parts of them) are not the only units that the local housing authority can regard as falling within the meaning of 'Accommodation'. In *R v Hillingdon London Borough Council ex p Puhlhofer*,[18] the courts upheld a local housing authority's decision that a modest hotel room in a bed and breakfast guest house occupied by a husband and wife and their two children (later described as a 'single cramped and squalid bedroom')[19] was 'Accommodation'.

11.11   This does not mean that anything pressed into service for sleeping in can constitute 'Accommodation'. Examples not constituting 'Accommodation' canvassed in the case law include 'Diogenes' barrel'[20] and 'a potting shed'.[21] It would be hard to describe a cardboard box in a shop doorway, a factory where a homeless worker was allowed to sleep overnight, or a car used to sleep in as 'Accommodation'. Even though a prison cell is physically capable of accommodating a prisoner, it cannot be treated as 'Accommodation' for the purposes of the definition of 'homeless'.[22]

11.12   From 1982 until 2008, the approach of the courts was that *crisis accommodation* should not fall within the definition of 'Accommodation' for these purposes. This approach was based on a 1982 decision that women's

---

16   *Tickner v Mole Valley District Council* [1980] *LAG Bull* 187, CA.
17   For example, in the *Shorter Oxford English Dictionary*.
18   *R v Hillingdon London Borough Council ex p Puhlhofer* [1986] AC 484, HL.
19   *R v Brent London Borough Council ex p Awua* [1996] 1 AC 55, HL at 68B–D per Lord Hoffmann.
20   *R v Hillingdon London Borough Council ex p Puhlhofer* [1986] AC 484, HL at 517 per Lord Brightman, also referred to in *R v Newham London Borough Council ex p Ojuri (No 2)* (1999) 31 HLR 452, QBD by Collins J. In *Moran v Manchester City Council, Richards v Ipswich Borough Council* [2008] EWCA Civ 378, [2008] HLR 39, CA at [28] Wilson LJ described Lord Brightman's reference to Diogenes' barrel as a phrase 'which, with respect, was neatly apt but has since become hackneyed by repetition'.
21   *R v Hillingdon London Borough Council ex p Puhlhofer* [1986] AC 484, HL at 491 per Ackner LJ (giving judgment in the Court of Appeal).
22   *Stewart v London Borough of Lambeth* [2002] EWCA Civ 753, [2002] HLR 40, CA and *R (B) v Southwark London Borough Council* [2003] EWHC 1678 (Admin), (2004) 36 HLR 3, Admin Ct.

refuges did not fall within the definition.[23] The approach was reviewed, and held to be wrong, by the Court of Appeal in 2008 in *Moran v Manchester City Council, Richards v Ipswich Borough Council*.[24] The House of Lords subsequently considered an appeal in that case and decided that women's refuges were not reasonable for women to continue to occupy indefinitely. As a result, the House of Lords held that there was no need to consider, in reaching its own decision in that case, whether other refuges and hostels, or other forms of shelter such as prison cells or hospital wards, were 'Accommodation' or not.[25]

11.13 For policy reasons, accommodation provided by a local housing authority under the interim duty to accommodate,[26] or under its powers to provide accommodation pending review[27] or pending appeal,[28] is not 'Accommodation' for the purposes of the statutory definition. An applicant is still homeless even if occupying such interim accommodation.[29]

11.14 But some circumstances can generate real issues as to whether the subject matter is 'Accommodation'. For example, is a tent or a beach hut, which a family has been forced to occupy for several weeks, 'Accommodation'?

11.15 These issues on the meaning of 'Accommodation' are brought into sharper focus by the globalisation of the definition of homelessness. Until 1996 the question was whether the applicant had 'Accommodation' in England, Scotland or Wales. Now the question is whether the applicant has 'Accommodation' in the United Kingdom (bringing Northern Ireland within scope)[30] or 'elsewhere', ie anywhere in the world.[31] As a result, the question 'Is it "accommodation"?' must now be applied to a wider range of forms of habitation.

---

[23] *R v Ealing London Borough Council ex p Sidhu* (1982) 2 HLR 41, QBD, applying *Williams v Cynon Valley Borough Council* [1980] LAG Bull 16.

[24] [2008] EWCA Civ 378, [2008] HLR 39, CA.

[25] *Ali & others v Birmingham City Council, Moran v Manchester City Council* [2009] UKHL 36, [2009] 1 WLR 1506, HL at [52] and [56] per Baroness Hale.

[26] HA 1996, s 188(1). See **16.12–16.28**.

[27] HA 1996, s 188(3). See **16.36–16.48**.

[28] HA 1996, s 204(4). See **16.49–16.55**.

[29] *R (Alam) v Tower Hamlets London Borough Council* [2009] EWHC 44, (2009) March *Legal Action*, p 24. In *Ali & others v Birmingham City Council, Moran v Manchester City Council* [2009] UKHL 36, [2009] 1 WLR 1506, HL, Manchester City Council accepted that an applicant remained homeless while occupying interim accommodation provided under HA 1996, s 188(1): see Baroness Hale at [55]. In *O'Callaghan v Southwark London Borough Council* (2010) May *Legal Action*, p 23, Lambeth County Court, an applicant who was occupying interim accommodation secured under the local housing authority's duty at HA 1996, s 188(1) could not have become homeless intentionally when she subsequently lost the accommodation, because she had remained 'homeless' throughout the period of occupation of the accommodation. See **8.72**.

[30] See **12.66** and Box 1.

[31] HA 1996, s 175(1).

11.16 If the local housing authority has decided that the applicant has 'Accommodation', the next inquiry is whether it is 'available for his occupation'.[32]

The meaning of 'available for occupation'

11.17 The local housing authority must consider first whether the accommodation is factually 'available'. If so, the second consideration is whether the accommodation is 'available for' the applicant's occupation and for the occupation of all members of the applicant's household as defined by HA 1996, s 176.

The factual test

11.18 The factual question is the most straightforward: is the particular accommodation 'available' to the applicant as a matter of fact? HA 1996, Part 7, specifically deals with situations where admission to the accommodation is physically barred so that the applicant cannot secure entry to it.[33] But factual 'availability' can embrace broader issues, especially given that the accommodation under consideration might be anywhere in the world. In *Begum v Tower Hamlets London Borough Council*,[34] the accommodation being considered was a room in the applicant's father-in-law's house in Bangladesh. The court was satisfied that if the applicant had said to the local housing authority that she could not get to Bangladesh (eg because of her lack of means) or could not enter that country (eg because of her immigration status) the local housing authority would have had to decide whether the accommodation was in fact 'available' to her:

> 'To hold that it is available to her because it is legally and physically hers to occupy, without regard to the question of whether she has any way of getting there, is not only to take leave of reality; it is to drain the word "available" of any meaning.'[35]

11.19 So, if there is accommodation that the applicant has the right to occupy, but it is not in fact 'available', the applicant is homeless. Those granted refugee status in the UK because they cannot return to their countries of origin may have perfectly good homes in those countries but would be 'homeless' here because their accommodation is not 'available'. Likewise, the issue of whether accommodation is 'available' is raised where:

---

[32] HA 1996, s 175(1).

[33] HA 1996, s 175(2)(a); see **11.68–11.74**.

[34] *Begum v Tower Hamlets London Borough Council* (2000) 32 HLR 445, CA.

[35] *Begum v Tower Hamlets London Borough Council* (2000) 32 HLR 445, CA at 464 per Sedley LJ. It should be noted that the majority of the Court of Appeal in *Begum v Tower Hamlets London Borough Council* said that the issue of whether or not accommodation was reasonable for an applicant to occupy was not relevant where the applicant was not actually occupying the accommodation. That has now been held to be wrong by the Court of Appeal in *Waltham Forest London Borough Council v Maloba* [2008] EWCA Civ 1281, [2008] HLR 26, CA. See **11.73**.

(1)   a person leaves his or her home in search of work, travels to the other end of the country and expends all his or her resources looking for work, leaving him or her unable to return home;

(2)   a person is the subject of a banning order under anti-terrorism legislation preventing him or her from returning to a country (or a part of this country) in which his or her home is situated; or

(3)   a person is prohibited by a court order (such as an anti-social behaviour order (ASBO), injunction, closure notice, closure order, or bail conditions) from entering the premises or geographic area in which his or her home is situated.[36]

11.20 In each of these cases, although the applicant would have accommodation which he or she is legally entitled to occupy, the accommodation would not be 'available' for his or her occupation.

The special statutory definition

11.21 If there is accommodation factually available to the applicant, the next question is whether the special statutory definition of 'available' is met.[37] Accommodation only counts as available if it is available for occupation not only by the applicant but also by those people who normally reside with the applicant as members of his or her family and also by any other person who might reasonably be expected to reside with the applicant.[38]

11.22 In effect, this means that accommodation will only be considered available if it is available to occupy by both the applicant and all of the other members of his or her household to occupy. The purpose of the provision is clear: a person is to be considered homeless *unless* there is accommodation sufficient in its factual and legal capacity to accommodate the applicant's entire household. So the local housing authority first needs to establish the extent of the relevant household and then consider whether there is accommodation available for all those persons to occupy together.[39]

---

[36]   Some of these examples were cited in *Begum v Tower Hamlets London Borough Council* (2000) 32 HLR 445, CA at 464 per Sedley LJ.
[37]   HA 1996, s 176.
[38]   HA 1996, s 176.
[39]   Where a household has to live in separate units of accommodation, the applicant and all members of his or her household (as defined by HA 1996, s 176) will be homeless. In *Sharif v Camden London Borough Council* [2011] EWCA Civ 463, [2011] HLR 32, CA, Etherton LJ said: '[i]t cannot be said, on any ordinary use of language, that persons living in separate self-contained flats, however close, and not sharing any communal area, are residing together' [17]. The local housing authority has been granted permission to appeal this decision to the Supreme Court.

Members of the applicant's household

11.23 Two different groups of people could fall within the applicant's household for these purposes:

(1)   Group One – those who normally reside with the applicant as a member of the applicant's family.[40]

(2)   Group Two – any other persons who might reasonably be expected to reside with the applicant.[41]

Group One: 'normally resides with him as a member of his family'[42]

11.24   To fall within Group One a person must fulfil two conditions:

•   he or she must normally reside with the applicant; and

•   must do so as a member of the applicant's family.

11.25   There is no additional condition that it must be 'reasonable' for that person to reside with the applicant.[43] The local housing authority may or may not think it reasonable for the applicant to be normally residing, as part of one family unit, with a host of relatives, in-laws, or even friends and others. But the local housing authority's opinion is irrelevant. The conditions raise simple factual questions for decision – who is living with the applicant and why – not issues of judgment.

11.26   To fall within the first condition, it is necessary that the person concerned 'resides with' the applicant. Someone who is simply a regular visitor to the applicant's home will not fall within the definition.[44] A very short period of temporary residence with the applicant is also unlikely to suffice, because the person must 'normally' reside with the applicant. Finally, there is no requirement that the person who normally lives with the applicant is literally doing so at the time of the application for homelessness assistance.[45] Children will still 'normally reside' with their mother even if she fled the family home in fear of domestic violence a few days earlier. An elderly frail person unable to return from hospital to his or her normal home will 'normally reside with' those with whom he or she was living before going into hospital.

[40]   HA 1996, s 176(a).
[41]   HA 1996, s 176(b).
[42]   HA 1996, s 176(a).
[43]   *R v Newham London Borough Council ex p Khan and Hussain* (2001) 33 HLR 269, QBD, where the local housing authority's decision that two adult sisters, who both occupied accommodation together along with their husbands and children, did not normally reside together was held to be irrational.
[44]   See further discussion of 'resides with' at **13.53–13.56**.
[45]   *Homelessness Code of Guidance for Local Authorities* (Communities and Local Government, Department for Education and Skills, Department of Health, July 2006) (the English Code), para 8.6, at Appendix 2 of this book.

11.27 The second condition is that the person normally resides with the applicant 'as a member of his [or her] family'.[46] This term is not defined in HA 1996, Part 7. Indeed, a definition of 'family' would not help, as the test is whether the person lived with the applicant 'as' a member of the applicant's family. The question is not whether the other person *is* a member of the applicant's family.

11.28 Limited help is to be found in the Codes of Guidance, which advise that '[t]he phrase "as a member of his [or her] family" will include those with close blood or marital relationships and cohabiting partners (including same sex partners)'.[47]

11.29 However, in the Welsh Code, 'as a member of his [or her] family' is given a broader treatment and the Code advises that the phrase be taken to include foster children, housekeepers, companions and carers as well as those falling within the English Code's definition of relationships through blood, marriage or cohabitation. This advice ignores the phrase 'as a' which suggests a wider test than blood or marital relationship. The correct legal question is 'Does this person normally live with the applicant *as* a member of the applicant's family?' That person may or may not actually *be* a member of the applicant's family.

Group Two: 'any other person who might reasonably be expected to reside with him'[48]

11.30 The second group who may qualify for these purposes as members of the applicant's household (Group Two) contains three potential sub-groups. These comprise:

(1) *any member of the applicant's family not normally residing with him or her, but who might reasonably be expected to reside with the applicant.*

For example, a dependent child who has been living with his or her mother but who is, by arrangement between the separated parents, to begin living with his or her father (the applicant) will fall within this category.[49] As the Codes helpfully emphasise, the question of who the child is to reside with is nowadays more likely to be dealt with by parental agreement than by court order.[50] Another example would be a young married couple who have to live apart, with their respective parents,

---

[46] HA 1996, s 176(a).

[47] English Code, paras 8.5–8.6; *Code of Guidance for Local Authorities Allocation of Accommodation and Homelessness 2012* (Welsh Government, August 2012) (the Welsh Code), para 13.4, see CD-Rom.

[48] HA 1996, s 176(b).

[49] For further examples where the person is a dependent child, see **13.57–13.74**.

[50] English Code, para 8.6; Welsh Code, paras 14.8–14.9 See *Holmes-Moorhouse v Richmond upon Thames Royal London Borough Council* [2009] UKHL 7, [2009] 1 WLR 413, HL for a discussion on 'reside with' in the context of the priority need test. See **13.70–13.74**.

because they have nowhere they can live together.[51] It must be remembered that one purpose of HA 1996, Part 7, is 'bringing families together'.[52]

(2) *someone already normally residing with the applicant (but not as a member of his or her family) who might reasonably be expected to continue to reside with the applicant.*

This might be a lodger, nanny, paid housekeeper, au pair, friend of the family or anyone else who has been living with the applicant but not 'as' a family member. Obviously the fact that the person is already actually residing with the applicant will be a powerful factor when the local housing authority decides whether it is reasonable for him or her to continue to live with the applicant.

(3) *someone who is not a member of the applicant's family and does not normally live with the applicant but who might reasonably be expected to reside with the applicant.*

This sub-group will embrace those who wish to live with the applicant but do not currently do so. The classic example is the prospective carer[53] who wishes to live with and look after the applicant. But the classic example can sometimes cause a local housing authority to believe that the relevant question is whether the applicant needs a companion or carer. That is not the correct approach.[54] The question is simple: 'Is it reasonable to expect this person to reside with the applicant?'

11.31 The Codes give two further examples of those who will fall within the second group of household members (Group Two):

• foster children;[55] and

• companions for elderly or disabled applicants.

11.32 The Codes advise that they might reasonably be expected to reside with an applicant.[56]

Application of the special statutory definition

11.33 Once the local housing authority has identified the total number of people forming the applicant's household (ie the composite of Groups One and Two), it can return to the central task of determining whether the applicant is

---

[51] As was the case in *R v Westminster City Council ex p Chambers* [1982] 6 HLR 24, QBD.

[52] *Din v Wandsworth London Borough Council* [1983] 1 AC 657, HL at 663, per Lord Wilberforce.

[53] *R v Kensington and Chelsea Royal London Borough Council ex p Kassam* (1994) 26 HLR 455, QBD; and *R v Hackney London Borough Council ex p Tonnicodi* (1998) 30 HLR 916, QBD.

[54] *R v Hackney London Borough Council ex p Tonnicodi* (1998) 30 HLR 916, QBD.

[55] Although the correct approach in the authors' view should be that current foster children would fall within Group One, and prospective foster children within Group Two.

[56] English Code, para 8.5; Welsh Code, para 13.4.

'homeless'. The relevant question posed by HA 1996, Part 7 is then whether the accommodation under consideration is available not just for occupation by the applicant but also for occupation by all the members of the applicant's household.[57]

11.34 This is essentially a factual issue about practical and legal availability. If the only accommodation available to a male applicant is a shared room with four other men in a men-only lodging house, he will be homeless if his household now includes a female (for example, a woman he has just married or a wife with whom he has been reunited)[58] and he does not have other accommodation into which he can move. Likewise, if a husband and wife have a home together, but the husband is prevented from returning to it by some legal restriction (such as a court order obtained by a third party) the wife will be 'homeless' on her application to the local housing authority, because her home is no longer available to a member of her family with whom she normally resides.[59]

The meaning of 'entitled to occupy'

11.35 Assuming that the local housing authority is satisfied that there is accommodation[60] available to the applicant and his or her household,[61] the next question is whether the applicant has some sort of right or legal entitlement to occupy the accommodation.[62]

11.36 An applicant will have a relevant entitlement to occupy accommodation only if he or she has the right to occupy by reason of one of the following:

- a legal interest in it;[63] or

- the benefit of an order of a court that he or she is entitled to occupy it;[64] or

- an express or implied licence to occupy it;[65] or

---

57 HA 1996, s 176.
58 As was the case in *R v Hillingdon London Borough Council ex p Islam* [1983] 1 AC 688, HL.
59 A family of three adults given two separate self-contained units of accommodation could not be said to be 'residing together' 'on any ordinary use of language' and so would be homeless: *Sharif v Camden London Borough Council* [2011] EWCA Civ 463, [2011] HLR 32, Etherton LJ [17] and [38]. The local housing authority has been granted permission to appeal against this decision to the Supreme Court.
60 See **11.8–11.16**.
61 See **11.17–11.34**.
62 HA 1996, s 175(1).
63 HA 1996, s 175(1)(a).
64 HA 1996, s 175(1)(a).
65 HA 1996, s 175(1)(b).

- some legal protection preventing the applicant from being evicted from it.[66]

11.37 If an applicant rids himself or herself of the right to occupy his or her only available accommodation (eg by selling owned property or by assigning or ending a lease or tenancy), then he or she will be homeless but is likely to be found to have become homeless intentionally.[67]

11.38 Each of the relevant forms of right to occupy requires close consideration.

'... an interest in it'[68]

11.39 This first alternative is satisfied if the applicant has a legal interest in the accommodation. That might be freehold or leasehold ownership or a tenancy. Unless the applicant enjoys some other right to occupy the accommodation, he or she will become homeless when the legal interest is brought to an end. For example, a joint tenant's legal interest will end on the expiry of a notice to quit given by the other joint tenant.[69]

11.40 However, a legal interest only counts for these purposes if, by virtue of it, the applicant is entitled to occupy the accommodation. It is not sufficient for the local housing authority to establish that the applicant owns the accommodation. He or she may have let or sub-let it to others who are, as a result, the people entitled to occupy it, whereas the applicant is not. The local housing authority could not, in those circumstances, avoid finding that the applicant is homeless by advising him or her to repossess the property let out to tenants. The applicant is 'homeless' now.

'... an order of a court'[70]

11.41 A person may be entitled to occupy accommodation under an order of a court, if, for example, he or she has the protection of a court order granting him or her the right to occupy in family proceedings, or (more unusually) a court has made a declaration that the person has a beneficial interest in the land carrying a right to immediate occupation.[71]

'... express or implied licence to occupy'[72]

11.42 A licence is simply permission to occupy. The person giving the permission is a licensor; the person given the permission is the licensee. An

---

[66]   HA 1996, s 175(1)(c).
[67]   *R v Wandsworth London Borough Council ex p Oteng* (1994) 26 HLR 413, CA. See Chapter 14.
[68]   HA 1996, s 175(1)(a).
[69]   *Fletcher v Brent London Borough Council* [2006] EWCA Civ 960, [2007] HLR 12, CA.
[70]   HA 1996, s 175(1)(a).
[71]   Family Law Act 1996, ss 30–39; Trusts of Land and Appointment of Trustees Act 1996, s 12.
[72]   HA 1996, s 175(1)(b).

express licence arises when permission to occupy is explicitly given verbally or in writing. An implied licence exists when permission to occupy has never been expressly granted but can simply be inferred or assumed (for example, very few parents expressly say to their young children 'you can live with me' – such permission is to be inferred).

11.43 Sometimes, the permission will have been granted in return for the payment of money or provision of services. More often, the licence will be a bare licence, the simple grant of permission to occupy without any money or services paid in return. Examples of licensees given in the Codes are lodgers, employees who have service occupancies (ie accommodation that they occupy in order to do their jobs) and those living with relatives.[73] Precisely because 'licence' simply means 'permission' it can be used to apply to accommodation anywhere in the world without the need to refer to the property laws of the relevant country.

11.44 The task for the local housing authority is to identify whether the applicant 'has' (present tense) an express or implied licence to occupy the relevant accommodation.[74] This means that a licence that an applicant did have in the past, or could get in the future, is quite irrelevant to the question of whether he or she is homeless now. Even if the local housing authority can identify accommodation that the applicant has recently occupied under a licence (which has ended), and where a further licence is being offered, the applicant will still be 'homeless'. So, where a former live-in housekeeper, having lost her employment and the licence to occupy accommodation, had been offered re-employment and a further licence, she was still homeless at the date of her application.[75] Likewise, an applicant who has a licence to occupy a night shelter for one night only is homeless during the day, even if he or she could secure another licence for another night in the same shelter.[76]

11.45 If an applicant occupies accommodation under an express or an implied licence, she or he will normally be entitled to four weeks' written notice to end that licence.[77] If the legal requirement of four weeks' notice does not apply,[78] the notice period will be whatever is stated in any written licence agreement. If there is no such agreement, the licence can be ended by reasonable notice, which can be given verbally. In certain circumstances 'you've

---

[73]   English Code, paras 8.7(ii) and 8.8(ii); Welsh Code, para 13.8.

[74]   HA 1996, s 175(1)(b).

[75]   *R v Kensington and Chelsea Royal London Borough Council ex p Minton* (1988) 20 HLR 648, QBD.

[76]   *R v Waveney District Council ex p Bowers* [1983] QB 238, CA. The decision that the applicant was homeless in these circumstances was made at first instance by Stephen Brown J (as he then was) and was not subject to appeal to the Court of Appeal. The first instance decision is at (1982) The Times, May 25.

[77]   Protection from Eviction Act 1977, s 5.

[78]   There are a wide range of circumstances in which it will not, such as where the licensee shares accommodation with the licensor. See *R v Hammersmith & Fulham London Borough Council ex p O'Sullivan* [1991] EGCS 110, QBD.

got 10 minutes to leave my house' could be sufficient reasonable notice to end a licence. Obviously, during any notice period, the licence will still be in place.

11.46 Once the licence has ended (ie any fixed term, or notice period, has expired), the former licensee will be a trespasser in the accommodation. Some ex-licensees will be protected by the Protection from Eviction Act 1977 from eviction without a court order and will therefore not be immediately homeless (because there is a restriction on the former licensor recovering possession).[79]

11.47 For those licensees who are *not* protected by the Protection from Eviction Act 1977,[80] homelessness will arise immediately the licence ends, even if they do not actually move out. In such cases, the Codes correctly advise local housing authorities that if the licence has been determined, but the occupier remains in occupation as a trespasser, the occupier will be homeless.[81] The Codes give, as examples, the termination of licences to those who have been living with friends or relatives, in hostels or hospitals, or former employees occupying premises under a service occupancy whose contracts of employment have ended.[82] Each of those examples is outside the protection of the Protection from Eviction Act 1977.

11.48 The Court of Appeal has held that, where a secure tenant leaves his or her accommodation, and the landlord subsequently terminates the tenancy by service of a notice to quit, but has refrained from taking possession proceedings, the former tenant becomes a licensee during the 'period of grace' before proceedings are brought.[83] This is a difficult decision to construe. If the tenant was occupying his or her accommodation at the date of expiry of the notice to quit, then the notice would not have determined the tenancy and the tenant would have continued to enjoy security of tenure.[84] If, on the other hand, the tenant had not been occupying his or her accommodation at that date,[85] then he or she was not a residential occupier and was not entitled to the protection offered by the Protection from Eviction Act 1977. In effect, this former tenant was being offered a chance to return to the accommodation, even though the previous tenancy had been terminated and she did not enjoy the protection of the Protection from Eviction Act 1977. It is hard to see how that chance can be construed as a licence.

---

[79] See **11.58–11.67** and **11.102–11.103**.

[80] Protection from Eviction Act 1977, s 3A defines licences and tenancies which are excluded from protection.

[81] English Code, para 8.8; Welsh Code, para 13.8. See also *R v Surrey Heath Borough Council ex p Li* (1984) 16 HLR 79, QBD, where the local housing authority's advice to a former licensee asked to leave service accommodation – that he could remain in occupation until a possession order was obtained – was held to be wrong, and a decision that the applicant was not homeless was quashed.

[82] English Code, para 8.8; Welsh Code, para 13.8.

[83] *Porteous v West Dorset District Council* [2004] EWCA Civ 244, [2004] HLR 30, CA.

[84] Housing Act 1985, ss 81–82 for secure tenancies; Housing Act 1988, ss 1 and 5 for assured tenancies.

[85] As was the case in *Porteous v West Dorset District Council* [2004] EWCA Civ 244, [2004] HLR 30, CA.

11.49 Various Local Government Ombudsman investigations have found maladministration where applicants who did not enjoy protection under the Protection from Eviction Act 1977 were wrongly told that they were not homeless until possession orders were obtained against them.[86]

11.50 One of the most common causes of homelessness is the termination of a licence to occupy the home of a friend or relative with whom the applicant has been staying. Many such applicants apply to local housing authorities reporting simply that they have been 'asked to leave'. Quite properly, the Codes recommend that where someone reports being asked to leave accommodation by family or friends: 'the housing authority will need to consider carefully whether the applicant's licence to occupy has in fact been revoked' (so that the applicant is 'homeless') or whether, instead, the request to leave is merely a warning of an intention to terminate the licence at some future date (in which case the applicant may not be homeless, although he or she may be threatened with homelessness).[87]

11.51 Beyond that, the Codes offer a confusing mix of advice on best practice in such cases. They warn that there may be collusion in order to assist the applicant to obtain housing from the local housing authority. Or there may be genuine difficulties between the guest and host that could be resolved with help. They suggest that local housing authorities should consider providing support, arranging family mediation services, or assisting the applicant to find alternative accommodation. Local housing authorities are reminded that they should be sensitive to the possibility that applicants may be at risk of violence or abuse if they return home.[88] But all this guidance leaves unasked and unanswered the important central question: whether the permission to occupy (ie the licence) has been ended or not ended.[89]

11.52 All too often the resolution of that simple question is deferred (quite improperly) by requiring the friend or relative, who has already told the applicant to leave, to confirm it in writing or by suggesting that a home visit at some later date will be necessary. As indicated above, save in those cases covered by the Protection from Eviction Act 1977, there is no need for notice terminating a licence to be given in writing.[90] If the licence has been

---

[86] See for example *Complaint against Ealing London Borough Council*, 90/A/1038, where the local housing authority was invited to repay to the complainants the legal costs that they had been ordered to pay to their resident landlord by the court in the possession proceedings, having been wrongly told by the local housing authority that they should await a court order.

[87] English Code, para 8.9; Welsh Code, para 13.9.

[88] English Code, paras 8.9–8.12; Welsh Code, paras 13.9–13.11.

[89] In *Abdullah v Westminster City Council* [2011] EWCA Civ 1171, [2012] HLR 5, CA, the local housing authority was not wrong in law to find that an applicant still had an implied licence to occupy where the joint tenants of the property (her mother and her husband) had asked to leave but not taken any steps to enforce that request, and the applicant would have had matrimonial home rights to enforce her right to occupy the property. See also *Complaint against Newham London Borough Council*, 11 000 388, 8 March 2012 (2012) May *Legal Action*, p 34. See **11.111**.

[90] See **11.47**. This is recognised by the Welsh Code, para 13.9.

terminated, the applicant has no home to visit. Worse still, applicants are sometimes told that the local housing authority will not even entertain applications for homelessness assistance without the applicants themselves producing a letter from their former hosts requiring them to leave. This practice is, of course, an unlawful attempt to reverse the burden imposed on the local housing authority to undertake the inquiries itself.[91]

11.53   Sadly, it is often young people asked to leave their parental home (frequently in sudden and traumatic circumstances), who find it most difficult to achieve prompt decisions as to whether they are 'homeless' because their licence has been determined. A person who has been told 'Get out now and never set your foot in this house again' is pretty plainly 'homeless'.

11.54   The English Code contains specific guidance on dealing with 16- and 17-year-olds in this situation.[92] The Secretary of State's view is that generally it is in their best interests to remain in the family home, unless they would be at risk of violence or abuse. The Code warns that turbulent relationships between a 16- or 17-year-old and his or her family are not unusual. There may be temporary disagreements or estrangements, but not always a genuine intention to exclude the child from the family home. Local housing authorities are advised to consider the possibility of family reconciliation, or of the 16- or 17-year-old residing with a member of the wider family. They are advised to be particularly alive to the possibility of collusion when assessing applications from 16- and 17-year-olds.[93] Again, such general guidance can blur the real question: whether the licence to occupy has been ended or not. If it has, the young person is 'homeless'.

11.55   The statutory guidance was considered by the House of Lords in *R (M) v Hammersmith & Fulham London Borough Council*.[94] Giving the leading judgment, Baroness Hale considered the guidance in the English Code. She noted the 'risk of collusion and fabrication' but added that 'any mediation or reconciliation will need careful brokering and housing authorities may wish to seek the assistance of social services in all such cases'.[95]

---

91   See **10.15–10.19**. *R v Woodspring District Council ex p Walters* (1984) 16 HLR 73, QBD is one example, albeit not concerning applicants living with friends or relatives.

92   English Code, paras 8.9–8.13 and paras 12.7–12.11; similar points in the Welsh Code are made in relation to anyone who has been asked to leave accommodation by family or friends, paras 13.9–13.11.

93   English Code, paras 8.9 and 12.10–12.11.

94   [2008] UKHL 14, [2008] 1 WLR 535, HL.

95   *R (M) v Hammersmith & Fulham London Borough Council* [2008] UKHL 14, [2008] 1 WLR 535, HL at [26] and [27], quoting English Code, paras 12.9 and 12.11. See also *R (G) v Southwark London Borough Council* [2009] UKHL 26, [2009] 1 WLR 2399, HL. As a result of these two House of Lords' decisions, the Secretaries of State in England and the Welsh Assembly Government issued guidance to housing and children's services departments: *Provision of Accommodation for 16 and 17 year old young people who may be homeless and/or require Accommodation* (April 2010, CLG and Children, Schools and Families) and *Provision of Accommodation for 16 and 17 year old young people who may be homeless* (September 2010, Welsh Assembly Government), both on CD-Rom. See also **13.127–13.174** [England] and **13.214–13.218** [Wales].

11.56 The Court of Appeal has considered the position of a 17-year-old, approaching her eighteenth birthday, who made an application for homelessness assistance having been asked to leave the family home by her mother.[96] The local housing authority delayed making its decision until the day before her eighteenth birthday and then, unlawfully, decided that she did not have a priority need.[97] The Court of Appeal acknowledged that 'an authority is entitled to have time to check the genuineness of the decision to exclude the child, and indeed the reasons given by the child for being excluded, for example where there may have been collusion'.[98] However, 'it cannot be right that an authority can persuade a family into mediation while a child is 17 and then use the time that the mediation would take to deprive the child of a right that it would have had without mediation.'[99] If the child genuinely has had his or her licence withdrawn, he or she will be homeless.

11.57 In such circumstances it is suggested that the better interpretation of the guidance in the English Code is that local housing authorities should accept that the applicant is homeless and then perform their statutory duty to secure accommodation for the homeless person by achieving a 'reconciliation' under which the applicant can in future live either with his or her parents or with members of the wider family.[100]

'... enactment or rule of law'[101]

11.58 Even if an applicant does not have any legal interest in, or licence to occupy, his or her accommodation, she or he may nevertheless be entitled to live there under an 'enactment' or 'rule of law' permitting his or her occupation or preventing another person from obtaining possession.[102] Such occupation is treated for the purposes of HA 1996, Part 7 as though it was under a right to occupy and may prevent the applicant from being homeless.

11.59 An 'enactment' in this context would normally mean an Act of Parliament. But in HA 1996, Part 7 it is defined to include 'an enactment comprised in subordinate legislation (within the meaning of the Interpretation Act 1978)'.[103] This wide definition brings in orders, rules, regulations, by-laws, schemes, warrants and other instruments made under any Act of Parliament.[104]

---

[96]   *Robinson v Hammersmith & Fulham London Borough Council* [2006] EWCA Civ 1122, [2007] HLR 7, CA.
[97]   See **13.127–13.174** [England] and **13.214–13.218** [Wales].
[98]   *Robinson v Hammersmith & Fulham London Borough Council* [2006] EWCA Civ 1122, [2007] HLR 7, CA at [39] per Waller LJ.
[99]   *Robinson v Hammersmith & Fulham London Borough Council* [2006] EWCA Civ 1122, [2007] HLR 7, CA at [41] per Waller LJ.
[100] English Code, para 12.7; Welsh Code, paras 13.9–13.11. *Robinson v Hammersmith & Fulham London Borough Council* [2006] EWCA Civ 1122, [2007] HLR 7, CA per Waller LJ at [41]. See **13.169–13.173**.
[101] HA 1996, s 175(1)(c).
[102] HA 1996, s 175(1)(c).
[103] HA 1996, s 230.
[104] Interpretation Act 1978, s 21.

So, if any of those give a right to occupy, or inhibit someone else from recovering possession, the applicant may not be homeless.

11.60 A 'rule of law' is not defined in HA 1996, Part 7. In contrast to 'enactment', it probably means a judge-made rule of common law, eg the rule that a licence to occupy may not normally be ended without giving reasonable notice.

11.61 Some Acts of Parliament expressly provide that individuals who are otherwise without rights may remain in possession. The classic example is the Rent Act 1977. Statutory tenants, whose contractual tenancies have ended, enjoy a personal right under the Rent Act 1977 not to be evicted without a court order, and thus fall within this category.[105] The Codes specifically refer to Rent Act statutory tenants because their personal right to remain is created by statute.[106] A statutory tenant remains under the protection of the Rent Act 1977 and the Protection from Eviction Act 1977 not just until a possession order has been obtained against him or her, but until the point of actual eviction by court bailiffs.[107]

11.62 Other Acts of Parliament provide that tenancies cannot be ended without landlords obtaining possession orders. This is the case for introductory, demoted, secure and assured tenants.[108] Even where former tenants remain in occupation as trespassers, they are not 'homeless', because a different form of enactment, the procedural rules of court, restricts them from being ousted other than by a bailiff's warrant. They do not lose the benefit of that enactment until the bailiffs actually turn them out.[109]

11.63 Anyone who is occupying premises where a possession order has been obtained but has not yet been executed will not become 'homeless' until actually evicted by the bailiffs.[110]

---

[105] Rent Act 1977, s 2.

[106] English Code, para 8.7(iii); Welsh Code, para 13.7.

[107] *Haniff v Robinson* [1993] QB 419, CA.

[108] Housing Act 1985, Part 4 governs secure tenants; Housing Act 1988, Part 1 governs assured tenants.

[109] There are complex provisions, which are beyond the scope of this text, governing when tenancies end on or after the making of a possession order. All assured tenants remain tenants until any possession order is executed against them (*Knowsley Housing Trust v White* [2008] UKHL 70, [2009] HLR 17, HL). From 20 May 2009, secure tenants are in the same position (Housing Act 1985, s 82 as amended by Housing and Regeneration Act 2008, s 299 and Sch 11). There were certain 'tolerated trespassers' who had originally been secure tenants until they were subject to outright or suspended possession orders made before 20 May 2009. Most of them became holders of 'replacement tenancies' on 20 May 2009 (Housing and Regeneration Act 2008, Sch 11, Part 2).

[110] *R (Sacupima) v Newham London Borough Council* (2001) 33 HLR 2, CA; if the possession order is to be executed within 28 days, the applicant will be threatened with homelessness. Alternatively, the applicant might be homeless because it is not reasonable for him or her, and his or her household, to continue to occupy the accommodation until the date of the eviction, see **11.102–11.103**.

11.64 It is not possible to set out in this text details of all the primary and secondary legislation giving rights to remain in occupation of accommodation or restricting the rights of others to recover possession. Spouses, civil partners, heterosexual cohabitants and same-sex partners[111] may have rights to remain in their homes under the Family Law Act 1996.[112]

11.65 It must not be assumed that all residential occupiers have the benefit of enactments or rules of law enabling them to remain in occupation or restricting others from recovering possession. True trespassers – squatters who have entered property without authority – have no such rights and are 'homeless' throughout.

11.66 Even in relation to former tenants and licensees, the Protection from Eviction Act 1977 is not comprehensive. There are very many occupiers who are excepted from its protection and will become 'homeless' as soon as their tenancies or licences end. That is precisely because there is no legal right to remain, nor any restriction on their eviction. A comprehensive list of those excluded from the Protection from Eviction Act 1977 is found at s 3A of that Act. It includes those living with resident landlords, occupying holiday lets or subject to licences granted not for money or money's worth.[113]

11.67 There are many people – owners, tenants, former tenants and former licensees – who have no defence to an inevitable possession order, but who do have the benefit of the protection of an enactment or rule of law preventing their eviction. They will not be automatically 'homeless' in that they have accommodation that they are entitled to occupy.[114] However, if the mortgage lender, landlord, former landlord or former licensor is taking steps to obtain a possession order, it may not be reasonable for them to continue in occupation and they may nevertheless be 'homeless'.[115] Where an applicant is re-applying for homelessness assistance, within two years of acceptance of a private rented sector offer[116] and has been served with a valid Housing Act 1988, s 21 notice,

---

[111] The Civil Partnership Act 2004 introduced registration of civil partnerships for same-sex couples, in force from 5 December 2005.

[112] Those matrimonial home rights need not have been exercised. Where a woman was asked to leave by her mother and her husband, who were the joint tenants of the property, she was not homeless because she could bring a claim under s 30 Family Law Act to enforce her right of occupation in the property: *Abdullah v Westminster City Council* [2011] EWCA Civ 1171, [2012] HLR 5, CA. If she had obtained an order under Family Law Act 1996, s 30, she would be not homeless by virtue of HA 1996, s 175(2)(a), see **11.41**. See also footnote 89 for the additional factual background to *Abdullah v Westminster City Council.*

[113] Protection from Eviction Act 1977, s 3A.

[114] Protection from Eviction Act 1977, s 3; HA 1996, s 175(1)(c).

[115] English Code, paras 8.14 and 8.30–8.32a; Welsh Code, paras 13.12–13.13. See **11.102–11.103**.

[116] A 'private rented sector offer' is defined at HA 1996, s 193(7AA) as amended by LA 2011, s 148(5) and can be made to applicants for homelessness assistance whose applications were made on or after 9 November 2012 to local housing authorities in England, see **17.109–17.131**. At the date of writing, the amendments to HA 1996 made by LA 2011, ss 148–149 had not been brought into effect in Wales.

the applicant is deemed to be threatened with homelessness from the date on which the notice was served and deemed to be homeless from the date on which the notice expires.[117]

Can the applicant secure entry to the accommodation?

11.68　Even if there is 'Accommodation'[118] which is 'available'[119] and which the applicant is 'entitled to occupy',[120] he or she will still be homeless if he or she is physically barred from entering the property.[121] The examples given in the Codes are where an occupier has been illegally evicted, or comes home to find his or her accommodation occupied by squatters.[122] But those examples are far from exhaustive. The property may be cut off temporarily by floodwaters or sealed behind a police barrier. An emergency may have rendered it temporarily impossible to enter the property. Whatever the cause, if the applicant physically cannot enter (and has no other accommodation meeting the legal definition) he or she is 'homeless'.

11.69　Even though practical or legal remedies to gain entry at some later stage will usually be available to the applicant, he or she remains homeless until entry can be secured. Local housing authorities cannot, therefore, decide that the applicant is not homeless because he or she has not yet exhausted all legal and practical remedies to secure entry (although they can, of course, give advice on the remedies available). To put it in the language of the English Code:

> '... although legal remedies may be available to the applicant to regain possession of the accommodation, housing authorities cannot refuse to assist while he or she is actually homeless.'[123]

The special rule for mobile homes

11.70　A local housing authority may find that an applicant has 'Accommodation' in the form of a moveable structure (eg a mobile home or towing caravan), or in the form of a vehicle or vessel designed for, or adapted for, human habitation. The latter category includes not only purpose built caravanettes and houseboats but also adapted or converted buses, lorries, vans and boats.

---

[117]　HA 1996, s 195A(2) and (4) inserted by LA 2011, s 149(4) and applicable to applicants for homelessness assistance whose applications were made on or after 9 November 2012 to local housing authorities in England, who accepted private rented sector offers which brought the main housing duty to an end, and who subsequently made a further application for homelessness assistance to a local housing authority in England within two years of the date of acceptance of the private rented sector offer At the date of writing, the amendments to HA 1996 made by LA 2011, ss 148–149 had not been brought into effect in Wales.

[118]　See **11.8–11.16**.

[119]　See **11.17–11.34**.

[120]　See **11.35–11.67**.

[121]　HA 1996, s 175(2).

[122]　English Code, para 8.16; Welsh Code, para 13.14. See also *Nipa Begum v Tower Hamlets London Borough Council* (2000) 32 HLR 445, CA.

[123]　English Code, para 8.16; Welsh Code, para 13.14.

11.71 An applicant who has a right to occupy such accommodation, which is available to him or her, will be homeless unless he or she has a place where he or she is permitted or entitled both to place it and to reside in it. Simply having a place to put or park the mobile home is not enough. The applicant must also be entitled to live in it at that location.

11.72 Typically, a mobile home occupier has a licence to station and live in his or her home on a particular plot or to tie up and live in his or her boat at a particular mooring. The Codes advise that, where an applicant has an itinerant lifestyle, the site or mooring need not be permanent in order to avoid homelessness.[124] But it is quite common for those with mobile homes to have no permission to stay anywhere. Such travellers would obviously be 'homeless', however comfortable their mobile accommodation.

11.73 A person who has a licence to bring his or her mobile home onto a particular piece of land to live in it has an entitlement or permission to 'place it and to reside in it' and would therefore not be homeless.[125] So, a houseboat owner with permission to use and live in the houseboat on a particular waterway is not homeless.[126] If the licence then expires, but no proceedings are brought and he or she continues to occupy the land (or water), he or she may or may not be homeless, depending upon whether it can be inferred from the landowners' inaction that the permission is continuing.[127] If an occupier is required to leave a site, but has another site to go to, he or she will not be homeless.[128] If, on the other hand, an occupier is required to leave and has no alternative provision in place, he or she will be homeless. An occupier who is camping unlawfully, and never had the right or permission to occupy the land, is homeless throughout.[129]

11.74 Local Government Ombudsman investigations have found maladministration where caravan-dwellers were subject to imminent eviction proceedings but the local housing authorities refused to accept them as homeless.[130]

Is the accommodation reasonable for the applicant to occupy?

11.75 If the applicant has 'Accommodation'[131] which is 'available',[132] which he or she is 'entitled to occupy',[133] and to which entry can be secured,[134] that

---

[124] English Code, para 8.17; Welsh Code, para 13.15.
[125] HA 1996, s 175(2)(b).
[126] *R v Hillingdon London Borough Council ex p Bax* (1992) December *Legal Action*, p 21, QBD.
[127] *R (O'Donoghue) v Brighton and Hove City Council* [2003] EWHC (Admin) 129, (2003) April *Legal Action*, p 27, Admin Ct and [2003] EWCA Civ 459, (2003) May *Legal Action*, p 35, CA.
[128] *R v Chiltern District Council ex p Roberts* (1991) 23 HLR 387, QBD.
[129] *Higgs v Brighton and Hove City Council* [2003] EWCA Civ 895, [2004] HLR 2, CA.
[130] For example, *Complaint against Boston Borough Council*, 518/L/85 and *Complaint against East Lindsey District Council*, 88/B/1216.
[131] See **11.8–11.16**.
[132] See **11.17–11.34**.
[133] See **11.35–11.67**.
[134] See **11.68–11.74**.

would, before 1986, have been sufficient to demonstrate that he or she was not homeless. But that approach could and did produce absurd results. It paid no attention to the quality, condition or appropriateness of the accommodation for the applicant and his or her family. The narrowness of the definition was amply demonstrated by the finding in the *Puhlhofer*[135] case that a family of four occupying a small squalid single room in a guest house was not homeless. As a direct response to that decision, in 1986, Parliament enlarged the definition of 'homeless' so that, as well as fulfilling all other parts of the statutory definition, the accommodation in question also has to be 'reasonable' for the applicant to continue to occupy.[136]

11.76 The words 'continue to occupy' refer to Parliament's intention to deal specifically with accommodation that an applicant already 'has', and is therefore occupying, rather than accommodation that the applicant has left.[137] The Court of Appeal has held that the words 'continue to occupy' mean that the question of reasonableness of occupation is relevant to any accommodation that is 'available' to the applicant, whether or not she or he is actually occupying it.[138]

11.77 The words 'continue to occupy' look to occupation over time and suggest an element of looking to the future. This means that accommodation could be considered not to be reasonable to continue to occupy, even though the occupiers could get by in it for a little while longer.[139]

11.78 The words '… shall not be treated as having accommodation unless it is accommodation which would be reasonable for him to continue to occupy' used in HA 1996, s 175(3) might suggest that a local housing authority had to probe, with the applicant, every conceivable aspect of the existing property to establish whether or not it was reasonable to occupy. That would be unworkable. A local housing authority must always consider whether or not the accommodation is affordable for the applicant, as it is required to do so by ministerial order.[140] A local housing authority must also make inquiries into any other material before it that might lead it to conclude that the accommodation would not be reasonable.

11.79 Once a finding has been made that accommodation is not reasonable for an applicant to continue to occupy, the applicant is homeless and, if the other statutory criteria are met, the main housing duty will be owed. The local

---

[135] *R v Hillingdon London Borough Council ex p Puhlhofer* [1986] AC 484, HL.
[136] HA 1996, s 175(3), previously inserted into Housing Act 1985, s 58(2A), by Housing and Planning Act 1986, s 14(2).
[137] *R v Brent London Borough Council ex p Awua* [1996] 1 AC 55, HL at 67 per Lord Hoffmann.
[138] *Waltham Forest London Borough Council v Maloba* [2007] EWCA Civ 1271, [2008] HLR 26, CA, which considered the dicta in *Begum v Tower Hamlets London Borough Council* (2000) 32 HLR 445, CA and held that *Begum* was wrongly decided on this point.
[139] *Ali & others v Birmingham City Council, Moran v Manchester City Council* [2009] UKHL 36, [2009] 1 WLR 1506, HL at [36]–[39], per Baroness Hale.
[140] Homelessness (Suitability of Accommodation) Order 1996, SI 1996/3204; see **11.101** and Appendix 2.

housing authority cannot impose any additional conditions, such as requiring the applicant to terminate his or her tenancy, before performing the duty.[141]

11.80 There are two distinct circumstances in which accommodation will not be reasonable for the applicant to continue to occupy:

(1) where the circumstances are such that HA 1996, Part 7 *deems* the accommodation to be unreasonable to continue to occupy;[142] or

(2) where the circumstances are such that, *as a matter of fact*, the accommodation is not reasonable to continue to occupy.[143]

Deemed unreasonableness

11.81 If it is 'probable' that continued occupation of the accommodation will lead to 'domestic violence or other violence' against the applicant or against a member of the applicant's household,[144] the accommodation is deemed by HA 1996, Part 7 not to be reasonable for the applicant to continue to occupy and the applicant is homeless.[145] The local housing authority's inquiries are simply confined to finding the facts necessary to answer the question of whether such violence is probable.

11.82 This is currently the only circumstance in which accommodation is deemed to be unreasonable to continue to occupy. There is provision within HA 1996, Part 7 for the Secretary of State (or the Welsh Ministers) to specify by order other circumstances in which accommodation should be regarded, as a matter of law, as not reasonable for the applicant to continue to occupy.[146] This power has not yet been exercised.

11.83 For the purposes of the deeming provision, 'violence' means 'violence from another person; or threats of violence from another person which are likely to be carried out'.[147] Although HA 1996, Part 7 refers to 'threats' of violence, this can include a single threat of violence.[148] It is 'domestic violence' if the violence or threats of violence come from 'a person who is associated with the victim'.[149]

---

[141] *R (Hammia) v Wandsworth London Borough Council* [2005] EWHC 1127 (Admin) [2005] HLR 45, Admin Ct. See **10.89–10.91**.

[142] See **11.81–11.92**.

[143] See **11.93–11.120**.

[144] HA 1996, s 177(1)(a) and (b). For this purpose household membership is to be ascertained in the way described at **11.21–11.34**.

[145] HA 1996, s 177(1).

[146] HA 1996, s 177(3)(a).

[147] HA 1996, s 177(1A).

[148] Interpretation Act 1978, s 6(c): '... unless the contrary intention appears ... words in the singular include the plural and words in the plural include the singular.'

[149] HA 1996, s 177(1A).

11.84 The modern approach is to understand 'violence' as a very broad concept. The Codes record the Secretary of State's and Welsh Government's opinions that 'the term "violence" should not be given a restrictive meaning' and that:

> '"domestic violence" should be understood to include threatening behaviour, violence or abuse (psychological, physical, sexual, financial or emotional) between persons who are, or have been, intimate partners, family members or members of the same household, regardless of gender or sexuality.'[150]

11.85 The Supreme Court has held that the term 'domestic violence' should be interpreted in the same sense as it is used in family proceedings: '[d]omestic violence' includes physical violence, threatening or intimidating behaviour and any other form of abuse which, directly or indirectly may give rise to the risk of harm'.[151] It follows that, where it is probable that an applicant would be subject to abuse that may give rise to harm, but would not necessarily be subject to physical violence, she or he will be deemed to be homeless under HA 1996, s 177(1) if that abuse comes from a person who is associated with the victim. The Supreme Court declined to decide whether this extended definition of violence should also apply to people who might be fleeing from violence that was not domestic violence.[152]

11.86 'A person who is associated with the victim' is exhaustively defined in HA 1996, Part 7.[153] If the relationship between the perpetrator and the victim does not fall within the statutory definition, the violence cannot be domestic violence (but will be 'other violence'). The Codes reiterate that the question of whether the violence is 'domestic' or not turns on the relationship between the perpetrator and the victim; not on where the violence took place.[154] The statutory definition of 'associated person' is very widely drawn, so as to include both existing and former spouses or civil partners, heterosexual and same-sex cohabitants, any person who has lived in the same household as the victim, any blood relation or relation by marriage, cohabitation or civil partnership, and any person who shares the parentage of, or parental responsibility for, a child with the victim (including adoptive parents in their relationship to natural parents).[155]

---

[150] English Code, para 8.21; Welsh Code, para 13.20.

[151] *Yemshaw v Hounslow London Borough Council* [2011] UKSC 3, [2011] 1 WLR 433, [2011] HLR 16, SC, Baroness Hale at [28] quoting the Practice Direction (Residence and Contact Orders: Domestic Violence) (No 2) [2009] 1 WLR 251.

[152] *Yemshaw v Hounslow London Borough Council* [2011] UKSC 3, [2011] 1 WLR 433, [2011] HLR 16, SC, Baroness Hale said: '[p]eople who are at risk of intimidating or harmful behaviour from their near neighbours are equally worthy of protection as are those who run the same risk from their relatives. But it may be less likely that they will suffer harm as a result of the abusive behaviour of their neighbours than it is in the domestic context. In practice, the threshold of seriousness may be higher' at [35]. The wording of the two Codes potentially contains the same distinction, both Codes give an extended meaning to 'domestic violence': English Code, para 8.21; Welsh Code, para 13.20.

[153] HA 1996, s 178(1)–(3).

[154] English Code, paras 8.19–8.25; Welsh Code, paras 13.18–13.20.

[155] Civil Partnership Act 2004, s 81 and Sch 8, para 61 amended HA 1996, s 178 to include

11.87 Before the implementation of the Homelessness Act 2002, only 'domestic' violence led to it deeming that it would not be reasonable for an applicant to continue to occupy accommodation. Since the amendment made by the Homelessness Act 2002, which inserted 'or other violence' into the deeming section, it is no longer necessary for local housing authorities to distinguish between domestic or other violence for the purposes of taking a decision on whether an applicant is homeless.[156] Where it is probable that continued occupation of the accommodation will lead to violence or threats of violence that are likely to be carried out against the applicant or a member of his or her household, that accommodation cannot be reasonable for the applicant to continue to occupy, whoever the violence (or threat of it) comes from. However, the distinction between 'domestic' violence and 'other violence' may be relevant if it is probable that the applicant would suffer abuse (rather than physical violence) which, directly or indirectly, gives rise to the risk of harm.[157] The distinction also remains relevant if a local housing authority is considering a referral under the local connection provisions.[158]

11.88 The test is not whether there has been violence in the past, or whether violence will definitely occur in the future. The question for the local housing authority is whether it is 'probable' that continued occupation of the accommodation would lead either to violence, or to threats of violence which are likely to be carried out. The Court of Appeal set aside a local housing authority's decision that an applicant was not homeless because she could have invoked legal remedies in order to prevent a recurrence of domestic violence. The local housing authority had asked itself the wrong question and had taken into account wider considerations (including whether the applicant had acted reasonably) rather than confining itself to the probability of her being subject to violence or threats of violence likely to be carried out if she remained in her accommodation.[159] 'Probable' means 'more likely than not'. 'Likely' in the context of 'threats of violence' includes 'a real or serious possibility'. If, therefore, it is more likely than not that an applicant's continued occupation of his or her home will lead to violence, or to threats of violence where there is a real or serious possibility that those threats will be carried out, the applicant will be homeless.

11.89 Local housing authorities are entitled to advise applicants about any legal or practical remedies (obtaining injunctions, improving security, etc) but

---

references to civil partnerships and same-sex couples living together as though they were civil partners, in force from 5 December 2005. Para 8.20 of the English Code contains an up-to-date list, but wrongly omits relatives of a civil partner or former civil partner (para 8.20(e)). The list in the Welsh Code, para 13.19, contains the same error.

[156] Homelessness Act 2002, s 10. During its passage the Minister specifically referred to racial violence as falling within this provision (*Hansard*, SC, 10 July 2001, Sally Keeble MP).

[157] *Yemshaw v Hounslow London Borough Council* [2011] UKSC 3, [2011] 1 WLR 433, [2011] HLR 16, SC. Such abuse from a person who is associated with the victim would certainly be 'domestic violence' for the purposes of HA 1996, s 177(1). It is less clear whether it would amount to 'violence' with no domestic context. See footnote 152.

[158] See **15.98–15.111**.

[159] *Bond v Leicester City Council* [2002] EWCA Civ 1544, [2002] HLR 6, CA.

should make it clear to applicants that they are not under any obligation to use these remedies.[160] The safety of the applicant and his or her household must be the primary consideration at all stages.[161] Local housing authorities are also advised that the fact that violence has not yet occurred does not mean that it is not likely to occur; and that (particularly in cases of domestic violence) they should not necessarily expect direct evidence of violence to be available from the applicant.[162]

11.90 The definition of 'violence 'and 'threats of violence' as coming 'from another person' means that the risk of self-harm from continued occupation of accommodation does not put an applicant into this deemed unreasonableness category (although any risk of self-harm may be relevant to the broader test of whether the accommodation is reasonable to continue to occupy, as a matter of fact).

11.91 The local housing authority cannot take into account, when determining whether an applicant falls within this deemed unreasonableness category, general housing circumstances prevailing in its district. The local housing authority can only consider the applicant's individual circumstances and that of his or her household.

11.92 Where there is harassment falling short of actual violence, or threats of violence that are likely to be carried out, the accommodation will not be deemed to be unreasonable for the applicant and members of his or her household to continue to occupy, but may be as a matter of fact unreasonable for them to continue to occupy.[163]

Factual unreasonableness

11.93 As a matter of fact, accommodation may not be reasonable for an applicant to continue to occupy. This is a much broader question for a local housing authority to determine than the relatively narrow deemed unreasonableness category. It is always required to consider whether or not the accommodation is 'affordable' for the applicant.[164] It should also take into account any other relevant matters, including all those raised by the applicant. In making its decision as to whether or not the accommodation is reasonable for the applicant to continue to occupy, the local housing authority may, but is not obliged to, have regard to the general housing circumstances prevailing in its district.[165]

---

[160] English Code, paras 18.23–18.24; Welsh Code, para 13.22.
[161] English Code, para 8.24.
[162] English Code, paras 6.17 and 8.22; Welsh Code, paras 13.21–13.26. See Chapter 10, at **10.41–10.44**.
[163] See **11.116**.
[164] HA 1996, s 177(3)(b); Homelessness (Suitability of Accommodation) Order 1996, SI 1996/3204 at Appendix 2.
[165] HA 1996, s 177(2).

11.94 The phrase 'reasonable to continue to occupy' is also used as part of the definition of intentional homelessness.[166] Case law and guidance relating to that part of the definition of intentional homelessness applies to the interpretation of the same phrase in relation to homelessness.

11.95 Both Codes contain the advice that '[t]here is no simple test of reasonableness'.[167] Each case will require an individual assessment involving consideration of the applicant's circumstances and (if the local housing authority elects to have regard to them) the general housing conditions in the district.

11.96 As already noted, a local housing authority must always consider whether the applicant can afford to occupy the accommodation, and should then also consider any other relevant issues, whether raised directly by the applicant or becoming apparent during the local housing authority's inquiries. Examples of matters that might be relevant are given in the Codes, but the scope of the local housing authority's inquiries is not confined to those examples.[168] Any matter that appears to be relevant must be considered. The question of reasonableness is not limited to the characteristics of the accommodation alone; it can include other factors such as whether the applicant has access to employment or to welfare benefits in the place (or country) where the accommodation is located.[169]

11.97 The Court of Appeal has set out a useful list of indicative factors that might be taken into account when considering whether any accommodation is reasonable to continue to occupy.[170] The House of Lords allowed an appeal in that case against the Court of Appeal's decision that women's refuges were accommodation that might be reasonable to continue to occupy, but did not specifically overrule the list.[171] Those factors are:

- the size, type and quality of the available accommodation, including the extent of any need to share its facilities;

- the terms of the agreement by which it is made available;

- the ability to afford it;

- the appropriateness of its location for an applicant and child (if any);

- the extent of its facilities;

---

[166] Discussed at **14.125–14.143**.
[167] English Code, para 8.18; Welsh Code, para 13.17.
[168] English Code, paras 8.26–8.34; Welsh Code, paras 13.27–13.33.
[169] *R v Hammersmith and Fulham London Borough Council ex p Duro-Rama* (1983) 9 HLR 71, QBD; and *R v Gravesham Borough Council ex p Winchester* (1986) 18 HLR 207, QBD.
[170] *Moran v Manchester City Council* [2008] EWCA Civ 378, [2008] HLR 39, CA.
[171] *Ali & others v Birmingham City Council, Moran v Manchester City Council* [2009] UKHL 36, [2009] 1 WLR 1506, HL.

- its appropriateness in the light of any particular characteristics (including as to health);

- the length of time for which the applicant has already occupied it;

- the state of physical and emotional health of the applicant while in occupation of it; and

- the length of time for which, unless accepted as homeless, they might expect to continue to occupy it.[172]

General circumstances prevailing in relation to housing in the local housing authority's district

11.98 The local housing authority may, but is not obliged to, take into account 'the general circumstances prevailing in relation to housing in the district of the local housing authority to whom [the applicant] has applied'.[173] The Codes give two examples of when such a comparison might be appropriate: where the application is based on the physical condition of the property, or on overcrowding.[174] Other circumstances that local housing authorities have lawfully taken into account include the demands for housing in the local housing authority's area,[175] its capacity to absorb and accomodate homeless families,[176] the shortage of supply,[177] and conflicts of lifestyle in multi-occupied homes.[178] A reasonably up-to-date picture of general housing conditions in a local housing authority's district will be available from the local housing authority's own local homelessness review.[179] Local housing authorities should ensure that they are taking into account general housing conditions, rather than applying a narrower test. A decision that compared the applicant's degree of overcrowding only with that of others on the local housing register was overturned because those others were, by definition, in the most housing need.[180]

---

[172] *Moran v Manchester City Council* [2008] EWCA Civ 378, [2008] HLR 39, CA at [49] per Wilson LJ.
[173] HA 1996, s 177(2).
[174] English Code, paras 8.26–8.28; Welsh Code, para 13.27 which adds a third: 'type of accommodation'. See **11.104–11.108** for physical conditions and **11.109–11.110** for overcrowding.
[175] *Noh v Hammersmith & Fulham London Borough Council* [2001] EWCA Civ 905, [2002] HLR 54, CA.
[176] *Noh v Hammersmith & Fulham London Borough Council* [2001] EWCA Civ 905, [2002] HLR 54, CA.
[177] *R v Kensington and Chelsea Royal London Borough Council ex p Moncada* (1997) 29 HLR 289, QBD.
[178] *R v Brent London Borough Council ex p Yusuf* (1997) 29 HLR 48, QBD; *R v Brent London Borough Council ex p Bariise* (1999) 31 HLR 50, CA.
[179] See **7.104–7.135**.
[180] *Chawa v Kensington and Chelsea Royal London Borough Council* (2012) January *Legal Action*, p 21, Central London County Court.

11.99 It is the local housing authority that is in the best position to assess the seriousness of the general conditions relating to housing in its area, and the extent to which an applicant's complaints might take his or her case out of the norm and make it unreasonable to continue in occupation.[181] It follows that applicants who apply to hard-pressed local housing authorities will find that satisfying the local housing authority that accommodation is not reasonable for them to continue to occupy is a harder task than if they had applied to local housing authorities with more accommodation available.[182]

11.100 The following paragraphs deal with the more common situations in which questions arise about factual reasonableness to continue to occupy.

Affordability

11.101 Accommodation is not reasonable for an applicant to continue to occupy if the cost of paying for it would deprive the applicant of the means to provide for 'the ordinary necessities of life'.[183] What constitutes 'the ordinary necessities of life' is a question of fact and can vary according to each applicant's needs.[184] The local housing authority is required to consider the whole of the applicant's financial resources as against the cost of the accommodation, any child support or other payments that the applicant is required to make, and all the applicant's other reasonable living expenses.[185] The guidance in the English Code is also relevant: 'the Secretary of State recommends that housing authorities regard accommodation as not being affordable if the applicant would be left with a residual income which would be less than the level of income support or income-based jobseekers allowance that is applicable in respect of the applicant, or would be applicable if he or she was entitled to claim such benefit'.[186]

---

[181] *R v Brent London Borough Council ex p Bariise* (1999) 31 HLR 50, CA.
[182] See *Harouki v Kensington and Chelsea Royal London Borough Council* [2007] EWCA Civ 1000, [2008] HLR 16, CA for one such example.
[183] *R v Wandsworth London Borough Council ex p Hawthorne* [1994] 1 WLR 1442, CA; and *R v Brent London Borough Council ex p Baruwa* (1997) 29 HLR 915, CA. See English Code, para 8.29; Welsh Code, paras 13.29–13.30. The Welsh Code advises in relation to housing benefit changes: 'households should not be penalised for the loss of accommodation where it was a change in their welfare benefits that led to the accommodation becoming unaffordable. They should be assisted at the earliest point to maintain the accommodation if possible through available resources or provided with assistance to look for alternative accommodation' (para 13.30).
[184] *R v Hillingdon London Borough Council ex p Tinn* (1988) 20 HLR 305, QBD.
[185] Homelessness (Suitability of Accommodation) Order 1996, SI 1996/3204, reg 2.
[186] English Code, para 17.40. When applying this paragraph, local housing authorities should not confine themselves to those specified benefits which only apply to adult claimants, but also consider the level of equivalent benefits paid in respect of the entire household, such as child tax credits: *Eryurekler v Hackney London Borough Council* (2010) May *Legal Action*, p 24, Clerkenwell & Shoreditch County Court.

Imminent or actual possession proceedings

11.102 Where an applicant is entitled to occupy rented accommodation, because no possession order has yet been obtained, but possession proceedings are imminent or have been started, the local housing authority should consider whether in those circumstances it is reasonable for the applicant to continue to occupy until the possession order has been obtained, and executed. Factors that the local housing authority should take into account include: the general cost to the local housing authority of accepting the applicant as 'homeless' at that stage; the position of the tenant; the position of the landlord; the likelihood that the landlord will actually proceed (or continue) with the possession claim; the burden on the courts of unnecessary proceedings where there is no defence to a claim for possession; and the general housing circumstances prevailing in the local housing authority's district.[187] The Codes suggest that it is unlikely to be reasonable for an assured shorthold tenant (who has received a proper statutory notice)[188] to continue to occupy where the local housing authority is satisfied that the landlord intends to seek possession and where there would be no defence to a possession claim.[189] This guidance would also apply to other tenants or licensees faced with imminent possession proceedings to which they have no defence and who would therefore become liable to pay the costs of those proceedings.[190] Case law has stressed that 'it is undesirable that a tenant, or an ex-tenant, in those circumstances should be required to hang on till the bitter end and require a court order'.[191] However, the decision as to the imminence of possession proceedings, and whether or not an applicant would have a defence, is a question of fact for the local housing authority.[192]

11.103 Applicants to local housing authorities in England who are re-applying for homelessness assistance within two years of acceptance of a private rented sector offer[193] and who have been served with a valid HA 1988,

---

[187] English Code, paras 8.32–8.32a; Welsh Code, paras 13.31–13.32.

[188] Complying with Housing Act 1988, s 21.

[189] English Code, para 8.32; Welsh Code, para 13.32. Both Codes dis-apply the advice where the local housing authority is taking steps to persuade the landlord to withdraw the notice or to allow the tenant to continue to occupy the accommodation for a reasonable period.

[190] Such as introductory tenants, demoted tenants, non-secure tenants, occupiers whose former tenancies were determined by notices to quit, and other former common-law tenants.

[191] *R v Croydon London Borough Council ex p Jarvis* (1994) 26 HLR 194, QBD at 205 per Collins J.

[192] *R v Bradford Metropolitan Borough Council ex p Parveen* (1996) 28 HLR 681, QBD. See also *Goddard v Torridge District Council* (1982) January *Legal Action*, p 9; *R v Portsmouth City Council ex p Knight* (1983) 10 HLR 115, QBD; and *R v Surrey Heath Borough Council ex p Li* (1984) 16 HLR 69, QBD. In *Khadija Ali v Bristol City Council* (2007) October *Legal Action*, p 26, Bristol County Court, the review decision was defective because there was no reference to the guidance given in the Code, or any explanation of the reviewing officer's decision to depart from it.

[193] 'Private rented sector offers' are defined at HA 1996 S 193(7AA) as amended by LA 2011, s 148(5) and can be made to applicants for homelessness assistance whose applications were made on or after 9 November 2012 to local housing authorities in England, see **17.109–17.131**. At the date of writing, the amendments to HA 1996 made by LA 2011, ss 148–149 had not been brought into effect in Wales.

s 21 notice will be deemed to be threatened with homelessness from the date when the notice is given, and deemed to be homeless from the date of the expiry of the notice.[194]

Physical conditions

11.104 The English Code suggests that the local housing authority ask itself:

'... whether the condition of the property was so bad in comparison with other accommodation in the district that it would not be reasonable to expect someone to continue to live there.'[195]

11.105 The Welsh Code repeats that proposed test, but also refers to the the question of whether the property is unsuitable for human habitation and to the Health and Safety Rating System.[196] It also draws attention to the particular needs of disabled people, and the needs of children.[197]

11.106 The English Code also refers to 'the physical characteristics of the accommodation' being reasonable for the particular applicant (eg a wheelchair user) to continue to occupy.[198]

11.107 Whether or not a property has adequate fire prevention and escape facilities, in comparison with other properties in the local housing authority's district, is a relevant consideration.[199] A vandalised property was, on the facts of a particular case, found to be not reasonable for the applicant to continue to occupy.[200] A damp beach chalet, which a pregnant applicant had been told would be unsafe for her baby, was held not to be reasonable to continue to occupy, given the clear medical advice.[201]

---

[194] HA 1996, s 195A((2) and (4) inserted by LA 2011, s 149(4) and applicable to applicants for homelessness assistance whose applications were made on or after 9 November 2012 to local housing authorities in England, and who accepted a private rented sector offer which brought the main housing duty to an end, and who subsequently make a further application for homelessness assistance to a local housing in England within two years of the date of acceptance of the private rented sector offer. See **9.89–9.95**. At the date of writing, the amendments to HA 1996 made by LA 2011, ss 148–149 had not been brought into effect in Wales.

[195] English Code, para 8.27.

[196] Housing Act 2004, Part 1.

[197] Welsh Code, para 13.27.

[198] English Code, para 8.34.

[199] *R v Kensington and Chelsea Royal London Borough Council ex p Ben-El-Mabrouk* (1995) 27 HLR 564, CA; and *R v Haringey London Borough Council ex p Flynn* (1995), (1995) June *Legal Action*, p 21, QBD.

[200] *City of Gloucester v Miles* (1985) 17 HLR 292, CA.

[201] *R v Medina Borough Council ex p Dee* (1992) 24 HLR 562, QBD. See also *Bavi v Waltham Forest London Borough Council* [2009] EWCA Civ 551, (2009) August *Legal Action*, p 37, CA, where the local housing authority had properly considered all the relevant defects, including rising dampness, and found that the applicant was not homeless, and *Nagi v Birmingham City Council* [2010] EWCA Civ 1391, (2011) January *Legal Action*, p 36, CA, where a local housing

11.108 Local housing authorities are entitled to compare the physical conditions of the applicant's accommodation with the general physical conditions of housing in their districts.[202]

Overcrowding

11.109 When considering the question of overcrowding, local housing authorities should consider all the different aspects of the statutory overcrowding test at Housing Act 1985, ss 324–326.[203] They must not limit themselves to whether the property is statutorily overcrowded, although that can be a key or contributing factor to their decision on reasonableness.[204] They should also consider any overcrowding that does not amount to statutory overcrowding, any medical needs and any other matters relevant to the impact of overcrowding.[205] The extent to which the accommodation may be a 'hazard', as defined by Housing Act 2004,[206] and the severity of that hazard, should also be relevant.[207]

11.110 Even when accommodation is statutorily overcrowded, a local housing authority may be entitled to find that it is reasonable to continue to occupy, taking into account the general housing circumstances prevailing in its district.[208] However, a decision that an overcrowded property was reasonable to continue to occupy because the overcrowding was a result of the increasing size of the applicant's family was quashed. It was a value judgment that had no place in the statutory scheme. The reason for the overcrowding is simply not relevant to whether or not the property is reasonable to continue to occupy.[209] A local housing authority is entitled to compare the degree of overcrowding with the general housing circumstances prevailing in its district, including the

---

authority was not wrong in law to find that accommodation which had internal stairs and was accessed by a steep slope was reasonable to continue to be occupied by a couple where the wife had epilepsy and a mobility problem.

[202] HA 1996, s 177(2). For examples, see *R v Brent London Borough Council ex parte Yusuf* (1997) 29 HLR 48, QBD; *R v Brent London Borough Council ex p Bariise* (1999) 31 HLR 50, CA; *R (Lynch) v Lambeth London Borough Council* [2006] EWHC 2737 (Admin), [2007] HLR 15, Admin Ct. See **11.98–11.100**.

[203] *Elrify v Westminster City Council* [2007] EWCA Civ 332, [2007] HLR 36, CA.

[204] English Code, para 8.28 and Annex 16; Welsh Code, para 13.27(ii).

[205] *R v Westminster City Council ex p Alouat* (1989) 21 HLR 477, QBD.

[206] Housing Act 2004, ss 1–2.

[207] *Khadija Ali v Bristol City Council* (2007) October *Legal Action*, p 26, Bristol County Court; and see also *Hashi v Birmingham City Council* (2010) November *Legal Action*, p 19, Birmingham County Court, where there had been a total reliance or an over-reliance on the test of statutory overcrowding and a failure to give a rational explanation for rejecting independent advice that there was a Category 1 hazard.

[208] *Harouki v Kensington and Chelsea Royal London Borough Council* [2007] EWCA Civ 1000, [2008] HLR 16, CA, where an applicant was statutorily overcrowded and thus committing an offence (Housing Act 1985, s 327). It should be noted that the extent to which the accommodation might constitute a 'hazard' within the meaning of the Housing Act 2004 was not considered.

[209] *R v Eastleigh Borough Council ex p Beattie (No 1)* (1983) 10 HLR 134, QBD; *R v Eastleigh Borough Council ex p Beattie (No 2)* (1985) 17 HLR 168, QBD; and *R v Tower Hamlets London Borough Council ex p Hoque* (1993) The Times, July 20, QBD.

general degree of overcrowding in its district,[210] but it should ensure that it addresses the particular degree of overcrowding experienced by the applicant. Merely asserting the general prevalence of overcrowding in the district without evidence showing the numbers of households experiencing a similar degree of overcrowding to that experienced by the applicant is not sufficient.[211]

Relationship breakdown

11.111 A local housing authority's decision that it was reasonable for an ex-husband to occupy his former matrimonial home with his ex-wife and her new boyfriend, given the general housing circumstances prevailing in its district, was held not to contain errors of law. Although it was undesirable for a divorced couple to have to live together, the local housing authority was entitled to take into account the shortage of accommodation in its district.[212]

Types of accommodation

11.112 Short-term crisis-type accommodation, such as women's refuges, direct access hostels and night shelters, should not be considered accommodation that is reasonable to continue to occupy in the medium and long term (assuming that such facilities are capable of constituting 'Accommodation' at all).[213]

11.113 The House of Lords has held that women's refuges, in particular, should not be considered reasonable to continue to occupy indefinitely. Baroness Hale said:

> '... a refuge is not simply crisis intervention for a few nights. It is a safe haven in which to find peace and support. But it is not a place to live. There are rules which

---

[210]   *R v Tower Hamlets London Borough Council ex p Monaf* (1988) 20 HLR 529, CA; *R v Tower Hamlets London Borough Council ex p Ojo* (1991) 23 HLR 488, QBD; *R v Tower Hamlets London Borough Council ex p Uddin* (1993) June *Legal Action*, p 15, QBD; *Osei v Southwark London Borough Council* [2007] EWCA Civ 787, [2008] HLR 15, CA; and *Harouki v Kensington and Chelsea Royal London Borough Council* [2007] EWCA Civ 1000, [2008] HLR 16, CA; *Mohamoud v Greenwich London Borough Council* (2003) January *Legal Action*, p 23, Woolwich County Court; *Khadija Ali v Bristol City Council* (2007) October *Legal Action*, p 26, Bristol County Court; and *Chawa v Kensington and Chelsea Royal London Borough Council* (2012) January *Legal Action*, p 21, Central London County Court.

[211]   *Mohamoud v Greenwich London Borough Council* (2003) January *Legal Action*, p 23, Woolwich County Court; and *Khadija Ali v Bristol City Council* (2007) October *Legal Action*, p 26, Bristol County Court.

[212]   *R v Kensington and Chelsea Royal London Borough Council ex p Moncada* (1997) 29 HLR 289, QBD. See also *Abdullah v Westminster City Council* [2011] EWCA Civ 1171, [2012] HLR 5, CA and footnote 89.

[213]   English Code, para 8.34; Welsh Code, paras 13.27(iii)–13.28. The House of Lords, when considering the special position of women's refuges in *Ali & others v Birmingham City Council, Moran v Manchester City Council* [2009] UKHL 36, [2009] 1 WLR 1506, HL, held that since refuges were not reasonable for women to continue to occupy indefinitely, they did not need to decide whether refuges were 'accommodation' within the meaning of HA 1996, s 175. See also **11.8–11.16**.

are necessary for the protection of residents but make it impossible to live a normal family life. It is a place to gather one's strength and one's thoughts and to decide what to do with one's life.'[214]

Tenure

11.114 Accommodation need not be subject to any security of tenure for it to be accommodation which is available to the applicant and reasonable for him or her to continue to occupy. The mere fact that accommodation is temporary will not, in itself, render accommodation not reasonable to continue to occupy.[215] If accommodation is so precarious that the occupier is likely to have to leave within 28 days, then the applicant will in any event be threatened with homelessness.[216]

Former members of the armed forces

11.115 Former members of the armed forces, who were provided with accommodation during their service, are likely to lose that accommodation upon discharge. The Ministry of Defence will usually issue a Certificate of Cessation of Entitlement to Occupy Service Living Accommodation, which contains a date on which entitlement to occupy service quarters will end. The Codes recommend that local housing authorities should accept the date in the Certificate as being the date upon which an applicant becomes homeless, and should not insist upon the Ministry of Defence obtaining possession orders.[217] They add that the 6-month notice period before the date of cessation in the certificate can be used to ensure that service personnel receive advice on housing options available to them. Obviously, if by the date of cessation the advice has not succeeded in providing alternative accommodation, the applicant will be homeless (having been threatened with homelessness in the preceding 28 days) and will be entitled to have his or her application for homelessness assistance determined in accordance with HA 1996, Part 7.

Harassment falling short of violence

11.116 Where there is harassment falling short of actual violence, or threats of violence that are likely to be carried out, the English Code recommends that local housing authorities should 'consider carefully' the question of whether or not it would be reasonable for the applicant and his or her household to continue to occupy. Examples of verbal abuse, damage to property or the risk of intimidation of witnesses in criminal proceedings are given.[218]

---

[214] *Ali & others v Birmingham City Council, Moran v Manchester City Council* [2009] UKHL 36, [2009] 1 WLR 1506, HL at [43].

[215] *R v Brent London Borough Council ex p Awua* [1996] AC 55, HL.

[216] HA 1996, s 175(4); see **11.129–11.131**.

[217] English Code, para 8.33 and Annexes 14 and 15; Welsh Code, para 13.33 and Annex 8.

[218] English Code, para 8.34; the Welsh Code advises '[l]ocal authorities will need to consider the full circumstances of such cases carefully': para 13.26.

Accommodation overseas

11.117 Where the applicant has accommodation available to him or her overseas,[219] the question of whether it is reasonable to occupy the accommodation requires consideration of all relevant matters, including the affordability of the accommodation, its physical condition, etc. The local housing authority should not limit itself to the issue of the accommodation's size and facilities. Any risk of violence to the applicant, the location of the accommodation, the applicant's personal circumstances, financial circumstances and employment prospects are also relevant.[220] If the impact of the local housing authority's decision would or might involve a child or children having to relocate to another country, the local housing authority must carry out a proportionality analysis of the impact of its decision on the Art 8[221] rights of the applicant and any children involved, and must also consider whether relocating would be in the best interests of the child. Those best interests are to be given primacy.[222]

11.118 When considering the location, physical characteristics, etc, of the accommodation abroad, the local housing authority is entitled to take into account the general circumstances prevailing in relation to housing in its own district. The comparison is not with general housing circumstances in the area in which the accommodation is located.[223]

Other circumstances

11.119 It is impossible to set out and examine all of the many factors that may cause accommodation to be, or to have become, unreasonable for an applicant to continue to occupy. For example, one factor recently considered by the Court of Appeal was the location of the accommodation in relation to the

---

[219] See **11.15**.
[220] *R v Hammersmith & Fulham London Borough Council ex p Duro-Rama* (1983) 9 HLR 71, QBD; *R v Camden London Borough Council ex p Aranda* (1998) 30 HLR 76, CA; *R v Kensington and Chelsea Royal London Borough Council ex p Bayani* (1990) 22 HLR 406, CA; *R v Newham London Borough Council ex p Ajayi* (1996) 28 HLR 25, QBD; and *Waltham Forest London Borough Council v Maloba* [2007] EWCA Civ 1291, [2008] HLR 26, CA, where a decision that it was reasonable for a family to occupy accommodation in Uganda, when the husband had lived in the UK for 10 years and had acquired British citizenship, was held to be a decision that no reasonable local housing authority would have come to on those particular facts.
[221] The 'right to respect for his ... family life' at Article 8, Sch 1, Human Rights Act 1998.
[222] *Kumaning v Haringey London Borough Council* (2012) April *Legal Action*, p 47, Central London County Court. The Supreme Court held in *ZH (Tanzania) v Secretary of State for the Home Department* [2011] UKSC 4, [2011] 2 AC 166, SC, that a child's best interests must be given primacy.
[223] *R v Tower Hamlets London Borough Council ex p Monaf* (1988) 20 HLR 529, CA; *R v Newham London Borough Council ex p Tower Hamlets London Borough Council* [1991] 1 WLR 1032, (1991) 23 HLR 62, CA; and *Osei v Southwark London Borough Council* [2007] EWCA Civ 787, [2008] HLR 15, CA.

applicant's place of employment.[224] That is precisely why the local housing authority will have to examine carefully any matter raised by the applicant. Applicants may advance highly subjective reasons for not wanting to continue in occupation of a particular property.[225] The question for the local housing authority is not 'Would it be reasonable for this applicant to leave this property?' but rather 'Would it be reasonable for the applicant to continue in occupation?' Even when faced with what might seem to be compelling personal objections to the applicant continuing to occupy accommodation, a local housing authority may be able to point to general housing conditions in its area to demonstrate that it would be reasonable for the applicant to stay on.

Reasonable for whom?

11.120 When a local housing authority is considering whether accommodation is 'available' for the applicant, HA 1996, Part 7 requires it to consider availability for all others in the applicant's household.[226] In contrast, when considering the reasonableness of continued occupation, the focus is only on the reasonableness of *the applicant* continuing in occupation, and not on whether or not it is reasonable for his or her *household* to continue in occupation. HA 1996, Part 7 expressly addresses the others in the household for the purposes of deemed unreasonableness (violence or threats of violence),[227] but not otherwise. However, this does not mean that, in cases not involving violence, the circumstances of the applicant's household can be ignored. An applicant may very commonly assert that the factor causing the accommodation to be no longer reasonable for his or her occupation is the medical or other situation of a different member of their household. The local housing authority must make inquiries sufficient to determine whether, in view of those matters, the accommodation is not reasonable for the applicant to continue to occupy.

The special position for applicants to local housing authorities in England re-applying within two years of acceptance of a private rented sector offer[228]

11.121 As a result of the amendments to HA 1996, Part 7, made by Localism Act 2011, ss 148–149, local housing authorities in England can make a private

---

[224] *Hemans v Royal Borough of Windsor and Maidenhead* [2011] EWCA Civ 374, [2011] HLR 25, CA.

[225] In *R v Nottingham City Council ex p Costello* (1989) 21 HLR 301, QBD, the issue was whether the accommodation was troubled by poltergeists (either actually or in the applicant's belief) and therefore not reasonable to continue to occupy.

[226] See **11.21–11.34**.

[227] HA 1996, s 177(1).

[228] HA 1996, s 195A inserted by LA 2011, s 149(4) for applicants for homelessness assistance whose applications were made to local housing authorities in England on or after 9 November 2012 and who accepted private rented sector offers which brought the main housing duty to an end. For 'private rented sector offers' (HA 1996, s 193(7AA) as amended by LA 2011, s 148(4)), see **17.109–17.131**. At the date of writing, the amendments to HA 1996 made by LA 2011, ss 148–149 had not been brought into effect in Wales.

rented sector offer to an applicant whose application for homelessness assistance was made on or after 9 November 2012 and who is owed the main housing duty.[229] If the private rented sector offer is suitable for the needs of the applicant and of his or her household,[230] and if the applicant has been informed in writing of the matters set out at HA 1996, s 193(7AB),[231] the main housing duty will come to an end whether the applicant accepts or refuses the private rented sector offer.[232]

11.122 Where an applicant has accepted a private rented sector offer,[233] and subsequently makes a fresh application for homelessness assistance to a local housing authority in England within two years of the date of his or her acceptance of the offer, he or she will be deemed to be threatened with homelessness at the date when a valid Housing Act 1988, s 21 notice was given.[234] He or she will be deemed to be homeless at the date of expiry of the notice.[235]

11.123 To obtain the benefit of this provision, the fresh application must be made within two years of the date of acceptance of the private rented sector offer, not the date when the tenancy is granted or when it actually began.[236]

11.124 An applicant should therefore make his or her new application for homelessness assistance quickly, as soon as the Housing Act 1988, s 21, notice has been given (or even earlier if he or she knows that a notice is to be served). If, at the date of the HA 1996, s 184 decision, the notice has been given, the applicant will be threatened with homelessness and the local housing authority will be subject to a duty to take reasonable steps to secure that the accommodation does not cease to be available for his or her occupation.[237] Those reasonable steps might include negotiating with the landlord for a further assured shorthold tenancy.

---

[229] At the date of writing, the amendments to HA 1996, Part 7, made by LA 2011, ss 148–149 had not been brought into effect in Wales. For 'private rented sector offer', see **17.109–17.131**. For 'main housing duty', see **17.23–17.168**.

[230] HA 1996, s 193(7F), for suitability see Chapter 18.

[231] As amended by LA 2011, s 148(6) for applicants for homelessness assistance whose applications were made to local housing authorities in England on or after 9 November 2012. At the date of writing, the amendments to HA 1996 made by LA 2011, ss 148–149 had not been brought into effect in Wales.

[232] HA 1996, s 193(7AA) as amended by LA 2011, s 148(5), for applicants for homelessness assistance whose applications were made to local housing authorities in England on or after 9 November 2012. At the date of writing, the amendments to HA 1996 made by LA 2011, ss 148–149 had not been brought into effect in Wales. See **17.109–17.131**.

[233] HA 1996, s 193(7AA)–(7AC) amended by LA 2011, s 148(5)–(7) for applicants for homelessness assistance whose applications were made to local housing authorities in England on or after 9 November 2012. At the date of writing, the amendments to HA 1996 made by LA 2011, ss 148–149 had not been brought into effect in Wales.

[234] HA 1996, s 195A(4) inserted by LA 2011, s 149(4).

[235] HA 1996, s 195A(2) inserted by LA 2011, s 149(4).

[236] HA 1996, s 195A(1) inserted by LA 2011, s 149(4).

[237] HA 1996, s 195(2). See **17.190–17.200**.

11.125 If, by the time of the date for possession given in the HA 1988, s 21 notice, the landlord still requires the applicant to leave the accommodation, the applicant will be homeless.[238] It may be that, even then, the local housing authority can perform any duty it owes to the applicant by making arrangements with the landlord for the applicant to remain in the accommodation or even for the landlord to offer another private rented sector offer.[239] However, if the landlord does not agree that the applicant can continue to occupy the accommodation, the local housing authority will have to secure alternative accommodation for the applicant and his or her household (and can, of course, make arrangements for another private rented sector offer to be offered to the applicant by a different landlord).[240]

11.126 For that reason, it is important not to delay the making of an application. If the applicant were to wait to make his or her application until after two years from the date of his or her acceptance of the private rented sector offer had elapsed, this special deeming provision will not apply.[241]

11.127 This special deeming provision does not apply to applicants to whom the main housing duty at HA 1996, s 193(2) is only owed because of the presence in his or her household of a restricted person.[242] Applicants in those circumstances would have to be homeless applying the usual rules and also have a priority need in order to be owed the HA 1996, s 193(2) main housing duty.

11.128 This special deeming provision only applies once. If an applicant in these circumstances accepts a further private rented sector offer and that accommodation subsequently comes to an end within two years of the date of that acceptance, the usual rules governing whether or not the applicant is homeless would apply and the applicant would have to have a priority need in order to be owed the HA 1996, s 193(2) main housing duty.[243]

THREATENED WITH HOMELESSNESS

11.129 If it is likely that an applicant will become homeless (within the extended definition explained in this Chapter) within 28 days, that person is 'threatened with homelessness'.[244] In practice, many homeless applicants are

---

[238] HA 1996, s 195A(2) inserted by LA 2011, s 149(4).

[239] HA 1996, s 193(7AA)–(7AC) amended by LA 2011, s 148(5)–(7). See **17.109–17.131**.

[240] HA 1996, s 193(2) and (7AA)–(7AC) amended by LA 2011, s 148(5)–(7). See **17.23–17.168** for 'main housing duty' and **17.109–17.131** for 'private rented sector offer'.

[241] The applicant will have been advised of the importance of making a further application within two years of the date of his or her acceptance of the private rented sector offer when the offer was first made (HA 1996, s 193(7AB)(c) amended by LA 2011, s 148(6)). This notification provision does not apply to applicants who were restricted cases (HA 1996, s 193(7AB)(c) inserted by LA 2011, s 148(6)).

[242] HA 1996, s 195A(5) inserted by LA 2011, s 149(4). For 'restricted person' see HA 1996, s 184(7) and **10.38–10.40, 10.82–10.85** and **12.32–12.47**.

[243] HA 1996, s 195A(6) inserted by LA 2011, s 149(4).

[244] HA 1996, s 175(4).

likely to be threatened with homelessness rather than being actually homeless when they first make their application to a local housing authority for accommodation or assistance in obtaining accommodation. The Codes advise that local housing authorities should not wait for homelessness to be imminent before providing assistance.[245]

11.130 Where a local housing authority has reason to believe that an applicant 'may be threatened with homelessness', it is subject to the duty to accept the application and make inquiries.[246] If, upon concluding its inquiries, the local housing authority decides that the applicant is threatened with homelessness and that it has a duty towards him or her, that duty may either be:

(1) to take reasonable steps to secure that accommodation does not cease to be available for his or her occupation;[247] or

(2) to provide advice and assistance to help the applicant secure that accommodation does not cease to be available for his or her occupation.[248]

11.131 The Codes advise that advice and assistance might succeed in preventing homelessness.[249] This guidance muddles two distinct occasions when advice and assistance might be provided. When it is provided at an early stage, *before* a local housing authority might have reason to believe that an applicant may be homeless or threatened with homelessness, it is provided as part of the policy aim of homelessness prevention.[250] When advice and assistance is provided *during* the 28 days before the date on which the applicant is to be homeless, it is provided in performance of the local housing authority's duty to take reasonable steps to secure that the accommodation does not cease to be available, or to help the applicant secure that accommodation does not cease to be available.[251] If the advice and assistance does not succeed in retaining the

---

[245] English Code, para 8.3; Welsh Code, para 13.2.
[246] HA 1996, s 184(1). *R v Newham London Borough Council ex p Khan & Hussain* (2001) 33 HLR 269, QBD. See also **9.57–9.63**.
[247] HA 1996, s 195(2) and (9).
[248] HA 1996, s 195(5). In *Bury Metropolitan Borough Council v Gibbons* [2010] EWCA Civ 327, [2010] HLR 33, CA, the local housing authority had failed to recognise that an applicant who had been given a Housing Act 1988, s 21 notice might be threatened with homelessness. It consequently failed to perform the HA 1996, s 195(2) duty to him and specifically failed to advise him that he was entitled to housing benefit and that he was not required to leave until the landlord had obtained a possession order. The landlord subsequently required Mr Gibbons to leave, he made a further application for homelessness assistance and the local housing authority found him to have become homeless intentionally. The decision was quashed as wrong in law because the local housing authority had failed to take into account its own failure to accept the earlier application for homelessness assistance and failure to provide advice and assistance. See **14.50**.
[249] English Code, para 8.3; Welsh Code, para 13.2.
[250] See **8.53–8.54**.
[251] HA 1996, s 195(2), (5) and (9).

accommodation for the applicant, he or she will become homeless and entitled to performance of one of the statutory duties owed to applicants who are found to be homeless.[252]

11.132 There is obviously a wide range of circumstances in which an applicant may face the prospect of homelessness within 28 days. One of the more common arises where an applicant has been informed that a court has issued a warrant for his or her eviction and there are fewer than 28 days left before the date scheduled for execution of the warrant.[253] If an applicant in these circumstances is not homeless, he or she will be threatened with homelessness.

11.133 Where an applicant whose application for homelessness assistance had been made to a local housing authority in England and who had previously accepted a private rented sector offer[254] subsequently makes a fresh application for homelessness assistance to a local housing authority in England within two years of the date of that acceptance and has been served with a valid Housing Act 1988, s 21 notice, he or she is deemed to be threatened with homelessness at the date when the notice is given.[255]

---

[252] HA 1996, ss 190, 192, 193 and 200.

[253] *R (Sacupima) v Newham London Borough Council* (2001) 33 HLR 2, CA.

[254] HA 1996, s 193(7AA)–(7AC) amended by LA 2011, s 148(5)–(7) and applicable to applicants whose application for homelessness assistance was made to a local housing authority in England on or after 9 November 2012. At the date of writing, the amendments to HA 1996 made by LA 2011, ss 148–149 had not been brought into effect in Wales. For 'private rented sector offer', see **17.109–17.131**.

[255] HA 1996, s 195A(4) inserted by LA 2011, s 149(4) and applicable to applicants whose application for homelessness assistance was made to a local housing authority in England on or after 9 November 2012 and who had accepted a private rented sector offer which brought the main housing duty to an end. At the date of writing, the amendments to HA 1996 made by LA 2011, ss 148–149 had not been brought into effect in Wales. For the full effect of this deeming provision, see **9.89–9.95** and **11.121–11.128**.

Chapter 12

ELIGIBILITY FOR ASSISTANCE

INTRODUCTION

12.1 Not everyone qualifies for help from a local housing authority under the homelessness provisions. There is an 'eligibility' test and, because of that, one of the first inquiries that a local housing authority must make of an applicant for assistance is whether he or she is eligible to obtain any help at all.[1]

12.2 As this Chapter will demonstrate, 'eligibility' normally (but not exclusively) depends on the immigration status of the person seeking assistance. For this reason, both those who advise the homeless, and the staff who receive and determine their applications, need a familiarity with the homelessness eligibility rules set out here, and also with the basic rules of UK immigration control.[2] Self-evidently, a system which discriminates between potential service-users on the basis of nationality may lay itself open to a complaint of discrimination. Not surprisingly, the impact of the anti-discrimination provisions of the European Convention on Human Rights, Art 14 on the eligibility test has already been explored in the courts.[3]

12.3 The normal rule is that anyone is able to apply for help to any local housing authority, whatever his or her connection with the district of that particular local housing authority (or even if he or she has no connection with the UK at all). When the homelessness safety net was first brought into law by the Housing (Homeless Persons) Act 1977, it contained no eligibility test at all. Anyone from anywhere could apply.[4] It was left to the courts to identify the first ineligible categories: those who had entered the country unlawfully and those who, having entered lawfully, remained unlawfully in the UK.[5]

12.4 But nowadays the modern statutory regime contains sophisticated exclusion provisions. The general rule, that homelessness assistance is available to all, is preserved. However, the Housing Act 1996 (HA 1996), Part 7, at ss 185 and 186, provides for the exclusion of specific categories of applicants. As a result, eligibility is defined in the negative. A person is *not excluded* from homelessness assistance *unless* caught by the provisions of either HA 1996, s 185 or s 186.[6]

12.5 The largest excluded group comprises those rendered ineligible by HA 1996, s 185, which contains two categories of 'persons from abroad'. They are:

(1) 'persons subject to immigration control'; and

---

[1] Housing Act 1996, s 184(1)(a).

[2] Immigration law is beyond the scope of this book. Standard texts include MacDonald and Toal *MacDonald's Immigration Law and Practice* (8th edn, 2010) and Seddon *Immigration, Nationality and Refugee Law Handbook* (6th edn, 2006).

[3] *R (Morris) v Westminster City Council* [2005] EWCA Civ 1184, [2006] HLR 8, CA; *Bah v UK* App No 56328/07 [2011] ECHR 1448, [2012] HLR 2, ECtHR. See **12.24–12.26**.

[4] *R v Hillingdon London Borough Council ex p Streeting* [1980] 1 WLR 1430, CA.

[5] See *R v Hillingdon London Borough Council ex p Streeting* [1980] 1 WLR 1430, CA at 1434, per Lord Denning MR.

[6] HA 1996, s 183(2).

(2)   'other persons from abroad'.

12.6   Anyone falling within the first category will be excluded from homelessness assistance, *unless* he or she is within one of the classes of persons prescribed as eligible by Regulation.[7] Anyone falling within the second category will be excluded from homelessness assistance if he or she is not habitually resident,[8] unless he or she falls within one of the groups of people prescribed as exempt from the habitual residence test,[9] or falls within the two other classes of people[10] prescribed as excluded within the Regulations.[11]

12.7   The classes of people prescribed as exempt from the overall exclusory provisions are different depending on whether an applicant has applied for homelessness assistance to a local housing authority in England or to a local housing authority in Wales. In England, the current relevant Regulations apply to applications for homelessness assistance made on or after 1 June 2006.[12] In Wales, the current Regulations apply to applications made on or after 9 October 2006.[13] For applications to local housing authorities in England made *before* 1 June 2006 [England] or 9 October 2006 [Wales], the relevant Regulations were considered in previous editions of this book.[14]

12.8   The law relating to the eligibility of EEA nationals is particularly complex and requires understanding not only of the Regulations made under HA 1996, s 185(2) and (3), but also of the immigration status of EEA nationals and their family members. We therefore consider the various rights of residence available to EEA nationals and their family members later in this Chapter.[15]

12.9   In this Chapter, we review the two categories of persons from abroad as defined by HA 1996, s 185 as follows:

•   the meaning of the phrase 'subject to immigration control';[16]

•   'persons subject to immigration control':
  –   the English exemptions to the overall exclusionary rule;[17]

---

[7]   HA 1996, s 185(2); the relevant Regulations are the Allocation of Housing and Homelessness (Eligibility) (England) Regulations 2006, SI 2006/1294 (as amended), reg 5 (at Appendix 2); and the Homelessness (Wales) Regulations 2006, SI 2006/2646 (W 227) (as amended), reg 5 (at Appendix 3). See **12.71–12.97** [England] and **12.98–12.115** [Wales].

[8]   See **12.170–12.179**.

[9]   See **12.180–12.221** [England] and **12. 230–12.232** [Wales].

[10]   See **12.212–12.226** [England] and **12.233** [Wales].

[11]   HA 1996, s 185(3); Allocation of Housing and Homelessness (Eligibility) (England) Regulations 2006, SI 2006/1294 (as amended), reg 6; and the Homelessness (Wales) Regulations 2006, SI 2006/2646 (W 227) (as amended), reg 6.

[12]   Allocation of Housing and Homelessness (Eligibility) (England) Regulations 2006, SI 2006/1294, regs 5 and 6, as amended.

[13]   Homelessness (Wales) Regulation 2006, SI 2006/2646 (W 227), reg 5.

[14]   Luba & Davies (2006, 1st edn; 2010, 2nd edn).

[15]   See **12.123–12.163**.

[16]   See **12.64–12.70**.

[17]   See **12.71–12.97**.

—   the Welsh exemptions to the overall exclusionary rule;[18]

- 'other persons from abroad':[19]
  —   rights to reside for EEA nationals and their family members;[20]
  —   the English classes of people from abroad prescribed as excluded from homelessness assistance;[21]
  —   the English exemptions to the prescribed exclusionary rules;[22]
  —   the Welsh classes of people from abroad prescribed as excluded from homelessness assistance;[23]
  —   the Welsh exemptions to those prescribed exclusionary rules.[24]

12.10   The other provision, HA 1996, s 186, caught the ever-diminishing number of pre-April 2000 asylum seekers who are eligible for homelessness assistance. It will be repealed when the last of those cases passes through the asylum system.[25] It contains additional exclusions from assistance for those asylum-seekers who are eligible.[26] At the date of writing the third edition of this book, any applicant who fell within HA 1996, s 186 would have made his or her application for homelessness assistance over twelve years previously. This edition does not contain commentary on HA 1996, s 186. Readers who might still need that commentary are referred to the first or second editions of this book.[27]

12.11   The Isles of Scilly have their own separate eligibility criteria, also dealt with at the end of this Chapter.[28]

Ineligible for what?

12.12   Those who are 'not eligible' are excluded from almost all the forms of assistance available under HA 1996, Part 7. This is because HA 1996, Part 7 defines 'assistance' to mean:

> '... the benefit of any functions under the following provisions of this Part relating to accommodation or assistance in obtaining accommodation.'[29]

---

[18]   See **12.98–12.115**.
[19]   See **12.116–12.233**.
[20]   See **12.123–12.163**.
[21]   See **12.164–12.179** and **12.212–12.222**.
[22]   See **12.180–12.211**.
[23]   See **12.127–12.129** and **12.233**.
[24]   See **12.190–12.192**.
[25]   See Immigration and Asylum Act 1999, ss 117(5), 169(3) and Sch 16.
[26]   HA 1996, s 185(2); Allocation of Housing and Homelessness (Eligibility) (England) Regulations, SI 2006/1294, reg 5(1)(e), Classes E(i)–(iii) (see **12.86–12.97**); and Homelessness (Wales) Regulations 2006, SI 2006/2646 (W 227), reg 3(1)(f): Class F(i)–(ii), (g): Class G(i)–(iii), (h): Class H(i)–(ii) (see **12.99–12.100**).
[27]   Luba and Davies *Housing Allocation and Homelessness* (2006) and Luba and Davies *Housing Allocation and Homelessness* (2010).
[28]   See **12.241–12.242**.
[29]   HA 1996, s 183(2).

12.13 Someone who is not eligible will not be entitled to the benefit of any of the duties or powers set out from HA 1996, s 188 onwards. However, he or she will still be able to obtain advice and information about homelessness (and about the prevention of homelessness) from the local housing authority, free of charge.[30]

12.14 This very wide definition of the exclusion from assistance under HA 1996, Part 7 makes it all the more important that the provisions of HA 1996, s 185 (and the Regulations made under them) are looked at very carefully to ensure that only those whom HA 1996 deems 'not eligible' are in fact excluded.

Going in and out of eligibility

12.15 Because eligibility is linked to immigration status, which can change, it is possible for an applicant's eligibility also to change.

12.16 The *first crucial date* for determining eligibility is the date on which the local housing authority reaches its decision as to whether the applicant is 'eligible'.[31] If there is then a review of that decision, the critical date becomes the date of the review decision.[32] It would be maladministration and unlawful for a local housing authority deliberately to delay its inquiries in the hope that an applicant's eligibility might change,[33] although it may be sensible in particular circumstances to delay a determination of eligibility if a decision of the immigration authorities is a matter of hours or days away.

12.17 If, at the first crucial date, the applicant is 'eligible', then the appropriate service under HA 1996, Part 7 must be provided. That may even be the main housing duty owed under HA 1996, s 193(2).[34] If, subsequently, the applicant's immigration status changes such that he or she becomes 'not eligible', that does not mean that all services or, more importantly, accommodation can simply be withdrawn.

12.18 If the applicant has been provided with only short-term accommodation (for example, a person who has been found to have become homeless intentionally),[35] the loss of eligibility is irrelevant. Likewise, if the homeless applicant has passed through HA 1996, Part 7 into longer-term social housing

---

[30] HA 1996, ss 179(1) and 183(3). See Chapter 8 and **9.4–9.7**.

[31] Unless the applicant has applied for homelessness assistance before 1 June 2006 (local housing authorities in England) or 9 October 2006 (local housing authorities in Wales), in which case transitional provisions state that his or her eligibility will be determined by the relevant Regulations in force at the date of his or her application (Allocation of Housing and Homelessness (Eligibility) (England) Regulations 2006, SI 2006/1294, reg 8; and Homelessness (Wales) Regulations 2006, SI 2006/2646 (W 227), reg 5).

[32] *Ealing London Borough Council v Surdonja* [2001] QB 97, CA; and *Mohammed v Hammersmith and Fulham London Borough Council* [2001] UKHL 57, [2002] 1 AC 547, HL.

[33] *Robinson v Hammersmith & Fulham London Borough Council* [2006] EWCA Civ 1122, [2007] HLR 7, CA.

[34] See **17.23–17.168**.

[35] HA 1996, s 190(2)(a). See **17.182–17.189**.

allocated under HA 1996, Part 6, or has accepted a private rented sector offer[36] which brought the main housing duty to an end, the change in eligibility is irrelevant to his or her status as a tenant. Where an applicant is making a fresh application for homelessness assistance to a local housing authority in England, within two years of acceptance of a private rented sector offer,[37] he or she would have to be eligible for assistance in order to be entitled to any of the duties under HA 1996, Part 7.[38]

12.19 However, there is one circumstance in which a change in eligibility is very important. If the applicant has the benefit of the HA 1996, s 193(2) main housing duty, that duty comes to an end at the point at which he or she ceases to be eligible.[39] The date when he or she ceases to be eligible is therefore the *second crucial date*. On the strict wording of HA 1996, s 193(6)(a), it would appear that the duty automatically ceases. However, normally a decision that the applicant is no longer eligible should be notified to the applicant in the usual way (providing reasons and notifying him or her of the right to a review).[40]

12.20 Even if an applicant who is owed the main housing duty becomes ineligible on a change in his or her immigration status, this does not mean that he or she is instantly put out onto the streets. The expectation is that public authorities will behave reasonably which (in this context) means that accommodation provision should at least be continued for such time as gives the applicant a fair chance to find somewhere else to live.[41]

---

36   HA 1996, s 193(7AA) as amended by Localism Act 2011, s 148(5). Private rented sector offers can be made to applicants for homelessness assistance whose applications were made on or after 9 November 2012 to local housing authorities in England, see **17.109–17.131**. At the date of writing, the amendments to HA 1996 made by LA 2011, ss 148–149 had not been brought into effect in Wales.

37   HA 1996, s 193(7AA) as amended by LA 2011, s 148(5). Private rented sector offers can be made to applicants for homelessness assistance whose applications were made on or after 9 November 2012 to local housing authorities in England, **17.109–17.131**. At the date of writing, the amendments to HA 1996 made by LA 2011, ss 148–149 had not been brought into effect in Wales.

38   HA 1996, s 195A inserted by LA 2011, s 149 (4). These provisions apply where an applicant to a local housing authority in England made his or her application for homelessness assistance on or after 9 November 2012 and accepted a private rented sector offer so as to bring the main housing duty to an end. If he or she makes a fresh application for homelessness assistance to a local housing authority in England within two years of the date of acceptance of the private rented sector offer, the special provisions at HA 1996, s 195A will apply, see **9.89–9.95**. At the date of writing, the amendments to HA 1996 made by LA 2011, ss 148–149 had not been brought into effect in Wales.

39   HA 1996, s 193(6)(a). See **17.67–17.69**.

40   HA 1996, s 184(3) and (5), discussed at **10.66–10.81**. See *Tower Hamlets London Borough Council v Deugi* [2006] EWCA Civ 159, [2006] HLR 28, CA at [33], where May LJ doubted whether a loss of eligibility required a decision under HA 1996, s 193(6)(a), since the local housing authority had no discretion, but recognised that there may be a dispute over the decision that eligibility has been lost.

41   *R v Secretary of State for the Environment ex p Shelter and the Refugee Council* [1997] COD 49, QBD; and *R v Newham London Borough Council ex p Ojuri (No 5)* (1999) 31 HLR 631, QBD.

12.21 Where an ineligible applicant (or an applicant who becomes ineligible) has children under the age of 18 (or is himself or herself a child), the local housing authority should make arrangements to refer the applicant's case to the relevant children's services authority or department, so that they can consider the exercise of their statutory duties and powers to protect children.[42]

12.22 Any applicant who is found to be ineligible for homelessness assistance (whether on his or her initial application or subsequently while occupying accommodation provided under the main housing duty at HA 1996, s 193(2)) may re-apply for homelessness assistance if his or her circumstances change such that he or she may have become eligible.[43]

Whose eligibility?

12.23 The eligibility test is primarily directed to working out whether the 'applicant' is eligible for, or excluded from, homelessness services. If the applicant is found not to be eligible, that will (subject to any review or appeal) be an end to his or her attempt to obtain homelessness services, even if other members of his or her household are plainly eligible for such services. The proper course in that situation is for the other household member(s) to apply to the local housing authority on behalf of the household.[44]

Disregard of ineligible members of the household

Overview

12.24 Even if an applicant is eligible for assistance, not all of the members of his or her household will necessarily also be eligible. HA 1996 provides, at s 185(4), that, for certain applicants, any member of his or her household who is not eligible for assistance must be disregarded when the local housing authority is considering whether the applicant is homeless or threatened with homelessness, or whether the applicant has a priority need.[45]

12.25 HA 1996, s 185(4) was declared incompatible with the European Convention on Human Rights (ECHR) in 2005 by the Court of Appeal.[46] The reason was because its wording at that date provided for a difference in

---

[42] HA 1996, s 213A; see *R (Badu) v Lambeth London Borough Council* [2005] EWCA Civ 1184, [2006] HLR 8, CA, and see Chapter 20 for the range of statutory powers and duties available to children's services authorities.

[43] Local housing authorities must accept fresh applications where there are 'new facts' that are not merely fanciful or trivial (*Begum v Tower Hamlets London Borough Council* [2005] EWCA Civ 340, [2005] HLR 34, CA; and *R (May) v Birmingham City Council* [2012] EWHC 1399 (Admin), (2012) July *Legal Action*, p 41, Admin Ct): see English Code, para 6.27; Welsh Code para 12.56 and see **9.68–9.80**. Applicants who cease to be owed the main housing duty at HA 1996, s 193(2) may make a fresh application (HA 1996, s 193(9)): see **17.169–17.170**.

[44] Any accommodation duty owed to the new applicant will extend to accommodating everyone else who falls within the definition of 'household' at HA 1996, s 176 (see **11.21–11.34**).

[45] HA 1996, s 185(4).

[46] *R (Morris) v Westminster City Council* [2005] EWCA 1184, [2006] HLR 8, CA.

treatment between applicants on the grounds of national origin or on a combination of one or more of nationality, immigration control, settled residence or social welfare, and that difference in treatment could prevent the applicant and his or her child from being able to enjoy their right to respect for their home and family life (Art 8) and was therefore discriminatory (Art 14). The court found that the difference in treatment was not justified. However, until the government took action to remedy the incompatibility, local housing authorities were required to continue to operate HA 1996, s 185(4).[47] The new rules came into force in both England and Wales on 2 March 2009 and applied to applications for homelessness assistance made on or after that date.[48]

12.26 Some two and a half years after the new rules came into force, the European Court of Human Rights (ECtHR) considered whether the previous rules (and, by implication, the current disregard[49]) violated an applicant's right to respect for his or her private and family life and home (Art 8) and was discriminatory (contrary to Art 14). The ECtHR found that there was differential treatment between applicants who rely for priority need status on people who are in the UK unlawfully or subject to a condition that they do not have recourse to public funds, and those applicants who rely for priority need on people not subject to the same immigration restriction. It found that that differential treatment was reasonably and objectively justified by the need to allocate the scarce stock of social housing available and that it could be legitimate when allocating social housing to have regard to the immigration status of those who are in need of social housing. Accordingly there was no violation of Art 14 taken in conjunction with Art 8.[50]

The rules

12.27 The current rules came into force on 2 March 2009 and apply to applications for homelessness assistance made on or after that date to local housing authorities in England and in Wales. They are found at HA 1996, s 185(4) and (5).[51] Neither Code of Guidance contains any guidance on the subject.[52]

---

[47]　Human Rights Act 1998, s 4(6)(a).

[48]　HA 1996, s 185(4) and (5) as amended and inserted by s 314 and Sch 15 Housing and Regeneration Act 2008.

[49]　See **12.28–12.31**.

[50]　*Bah v UK App No 56328/07* [2011] ECHR 1448, [2012] HLR 2, ECtHR. The current rules are now being challenged by an application to the ECtHR: *Ijaola-Jokesenumi v UK*, App no 45996/11 [2012] ECHR 652, (2012) September *Legal Action*, p 29. See **12.29**.

[51]　As amended by Housing and Regeneration Act 2008, s 314 and Sch 15.

[52]　The English Code was published three years before the amendments came into force. The Welsh Code was published in 2012 but does not deal with the disregard. *Homelessness Code of Guidance for local authorities* (Communities and Local Government, Department for Education and Skills, Department of Health, July 2006) [English Code]: see Appendix 2 of this book. *Code of Guidance for Local Authorities Allocation of Accommodation and Homelessness 2012* (Welsh Government, August 2012) [Welsh Code]: see CD-ROM.

Retaining the disregard where the applicant is a person subject to immigration control

12.28 For applications to local housing authorities made on or after 2 March 2009,[53] this disregard of non-eligible household members *only* applies where the eligible *applicant* is:

- a person subject to immigration control;[54] and

- is eligible as a result of falling within one of the classes of people prescribed as eligible by Regulation;[55] and

- is not a national of an EEA state or of Switzerland.[56]

12.29 If the applicant falls within that statutory test, any ineligible members of his or her household must be disregarded when the local housing authority is considering whether the applicant is homeless or threatened with homelessness, or whether the applicant has a priority need.[57] So, when a local housing authority is considering whether, for example, overcrowded accommodation is reasonable for the applicant and his or her household to continue to occupy for the purpose of deciding whether the applicant is homeless or threatened with homelessness, ineligible members of the household cannot be considered. Even more importantly, if an applicant's children or other family members are all persons from abroad and ineligible for assistance, they cannot provide the applicant with a priority need.[58] This rule is now being challenged by an application to the ECtHR on the grounds that it is incompatible with the right to respect to family life (Art 8) and is discriminatory (Art 14).[59]

12.30 It does not follow, however, that those members of an applicant's household who are not eligible are to be disregarded for all purposes. When it comes to the discharge of the local housing authority's duty by the provision of suitable accommodation, that accommodation must be suitable for the needs of the applicant and his or her household, even if the household includes persons who are not eligible for assistance.

---

[53] The date applies to applications to local housing authorities in both England and Wales (Housing and Regeneration Act 2008, s 314 and Sch 15).

[54] See **12.64–12.70**.

[55] For applications to local housing authorities in England, the classes are Classes A–E at Allocation of Housing and Homelessness (Eligibility) (England) 2006, SI 2006/1294 (as amended), reg 5(1): see **12.71–12.97**. For applications to local housing authorities in Wales, the classes are Classes A–J at Homelessness (Wales) Regulations 2006, SI 2006/2646 (W 227), reg 3(1): see **12.98–12.115**.

[56] HA 1996, s 184(5).

[57] HA 1996, s 185(4), as amended by Housing and Regeneration Act 2008, s 314 and Sch 15, para 4.

[58] *R (Morris) v Westminster City Council* [2005] EWCA 1184, [2006] HLR 8, CA.

[59] *Ijaola-Jokesenumi v UK, App no 45996/11* [2012] ECHR 652, (2012) September *Legal Action*, p 29.

12.31   In addition, local authorities have a range of other statutory duties and powers under which they may provide accommodation, particularly where there are dependent children.[60] If a household is caught by HA 1996, s 185(4), and none of any dependent children or other vulnerable members are eligible and so cannot confer a priority need, local authorities may consider using those other statutory duties and powers in order to provide accommodation. But they may not do so simply with the object of circumventing the restriction in HA 1996, s 185(4).[61]

Disregard abolished where the applicant is not a person subject to immigration control

12.32   The disregard of ineligible household members no longer applies if the applicant is not a person subject to immigration control.[62] The applicant will be entitled to have the whole of his or her household assessed for the purposes of determining whether he or she is homeless and whether he or she has a priority need, irrespective of the immigration status of the people in his or her household.

12.33   However, if there are ineligible members of an applicant's household in those circumstances, the ineligible members are to be known as 'restricted persons' and, in some circumstances, the main housing duty owed to the applicant may be modified as a result of that person's presence in the household.[63] For applications to a local housing authority in England made on or after 9 November 2012, the modifications are less significant than prior to that date, as a result of the amendments to HA 1996, s 193 made by the Localism Act 2011, ss 148–149.[64] At the date of writing, the amendments to HA 1996 made by LA 2011, ss 148–149 had not been brought into effect in Wales.[65]

12.34   A 'restricted person' is defined as a person:

• who is not eligible for assistance under HA 1996, Part 7; and

• who is subject to immigration control within the meaning of the Asylum and Immigration Act 1996;[66] and

---

[60]   See Chapter 20 generally, and **20.55–20.84** for Children Act duties.
[61]   *R (Badu) v Lambeth London Borough Council* [2005] EWCA Civ 1184, [2006] HLR 8, CA; and see Chapter 20 for the range of statutory powers and duties available to local authorities.
[62]   HA 1996, s 185(4) and (5), as amended and inserted by Housing and Regeneration Act 2008, s 314 and Sch 15, para 4. See **12.64–12.70**.
[63]   HA 1996, s 184(7), inserted by Housing and Regeneration Act 2008, s 314 and Sch 15, para 3.
[64]   For the duties owed to 'restricted cases' by local housing authorities in England, see **17.159–17.162**.
[65]   For the duties owed to 'restricted cases' by local housing authorities in Wales, see **17.163–17.168**.
[66]   See **12.64–12.70**.

- either does not have leave to enter or remain in the UK;[67] or

- whose leave to enter or remain in the UK is subject to a condition to maintain and accommodate himself or herself, and any dependents, without recourse to public funds.[68]

12.35 If the applicant is owed the main housing duty,[69] or the equivalent duty owed to those threatened with homelessness,[70] and that duty is only owed to the applicant because of the presence in his or her household of a restricted person, the local housing authority has additional notification duties.[71] It must notify the applicant that the main housing duty, or equivalent duty, is owed on the basis of the restricted person's presence in the applicant's household, must name the restricted person, must explain why that person is a restricted person, and must explain the effects of the modifications to the main housing duty or equivalent duty.[72]

12.36 In those circumstances, the applicant's case becomes known as 'a restricted case'[73] or a 'restricted threatened homelessness case'.[74]

12.37 The mere presence of a restricted person in an applicant's household is not sufficient for the applicant's case to become a restricted case. The applicant's case *only* becomes a restricted case if the presence of the restricted person has either:

- caused the applicant to become homeless or threatened with homelessness;[75] or

- caused the applicant to have a priority need.

---

[67] See **12.64–12.70**.
[68] HA 1996, s 184(7), inserted by Housing and Regeneration Act 2008, s 314 and Sch 15, para 3. For an example of a 'restricted case' and 'restricted person', see *Lekpo-Bozua v Hackney London Borough Council* [2010] EWCA Civ 909, [2010] HLR 46, CA.
[69] HA 1996, s 193(2). See **17.23–17.168**.
[70] HA 1996, s 195(2). See **17.190–17.200**.
[71] HA 1996, s 184(3A), inserted by Housing and Regeneration Act 2008, s 314 and Sch 15, para 3. See **10.38–10.40**.
[72] For the modifications to the main housing duty where the application for homelessness assistance has been made to a local housing authority in England on or after 9 November 2012, see **17.159–17.162**. For the modifications to the main housing duty where the application for homelessness assistance was made to any local housing authority in England before 9 November 2012 or was made on any date after 2 March 2009 to a local housing authority in Wales, see **17.163–17.168**.
[73] HA 1996, s 193(3B), inserted by Housing and Regeneration Act 2008, s 314 and Sch 15, para 5.
[74] HA 1996, s 195(4B), inserted by Housing and Regeneration Act 2008, s 314 and Sch 15, para 6.
[75] If, for example, the presence of the restricted person or persons has brought the level of overcrowding in the applicant's household to such an extent that it is not reasonable for the applicant to continue to occupy (HA 1996, s 175(3)): see **11.109–11.110**. Or where the applicant is homeless because accommodation is not available for the occupation of the applicant and of the restricted person. (HA 1996, s 176): see **11.17–11.34**.

12.38 If the applicant would have been homeless or threatened with homelessness, and/or had a priority need, whether or not he or she had the restricted person in his or her household, his or her case will not be a restricted case.

Duties owed to restricted cases whose applications for homelessness assistance were made to a local housing authority in England before 9 November 2012, or to a local housing authority in Wales before or after 9 November 2012

12.39 Before the coming into force in England of the amendments to HA 1996, Part 7, inserted by LA 2011[76], the main housing duty was modified for restricted cases in two respects:

- there was no obligation on the local housing authority to give the applicant a copy of its statement of the policy in its allocation scheme as to choice;[77] and

- the local housing authority was required, so far as is reasonably practicable, to start to bring the main housing duty to an end by arranging for the applicant to be made a 'private accommodation offer', defined as an assured shorthold tenancy made available by a private landlord for a fixed term of at least 12 months.[78]

12.40 The offer of private accommodation must have been suitable for the needs of the applicant and his or her household.[79] If the applicant accepted or refused the offer, the duty could come to an end.[80] The applicant had the right to request a review of any decision by the local housing authority that the private accommodation was suitable for him or her, and his or her household.[81]

---

[76] LA 2011, ss 148 and 149, which apply to applications for homelessness assistance whose applications were made on or after 9 November 2012 to local housing authorities in England. At the date of writing, the amendments to HA 1996 made by LA 2011, ss 148–149 had not been brought into effect in Wales.

[77] HA 1996, s 193(3A), as amended by Housing and Regeneration Act 2008, s 314 and Sch 15, para 5. This is because the applicant would not be entitled to reasonable preference in a local housing authority's allocation scheme as a result of being owed the main housing duty (HA 1996, s 167(2ZA), inserted by Housing and Regeneration Act 2008, s 314 and Sch 15, para 1. HA 1996, Part 6, was amended by LA 2011, s 147 and the equivalent provisions are now found at HA 1996, s 166A(4) for applications to local housing authorities in England and HA 1996, s 167(2ZA) for applications to local housing authorities in Wales. See **4.153–4.154**.

[78] HA 1996, s 193(7AA)–(7AD), inserted by Housing and Regeneration Act 2008, s 314 and Sch 15, para 5. See **17.165–17.168**.

[79] See Chapter 18.

[80] HA 1996, s 193(7AA)–(7AD), inserted by Housing and Regeneration Act 2008, s 314 and Sch 15, para 5.

[81] HA 1996, s 202(1)(g), inserted by Housing and Regeneration Act 2008, s 314 and Sch 15, para 7.

12.41 Where the applicant was threatened with homelessness, and the duty owed to him or her was the duty to take reasonable steps to secure that accommodation does not cease to be available,[82] that duty was similarly modified in a restricted case.[83]

Duties owed to restricted cases whose applications for homelessness assistance were made to a local housing authority in England on or after 9 November 2012

12.42 Since the amendments to HA 1996, s 193 made by LA 2011, s148, which apply to applications for homelessness assistance made to a local housing authority in England on or after 9 November 2012[84], and permit local housing authorities to bring the main housing duty to an end by making an applicant a private rented sector offer,[85] the distinction between restricted cases and other applicants has become less significant.

12.43 If an applicant is a 'restricted case'[86], the local housing authority is required to bring the main housing duty to an end by making a private rented sector offer, so as is reasonably practicable.[87] Any regulations made by the Secretary of State specifying a minimum period greater than 12 months for a private rented sector offer need not apply to restricted cases,[88] so if, in a Regulation in the future, a longer minimum period is specified for most applicants owed the main housing duty, restricted cases may still be made a private rented sector offer of a 12-month fixed-term tenancy.[89]

12.44 In addition, an applicant who is a restricted case need not have been informed in writing of the effect under HA 1996, s 195A[90] for the local housing authority to be able to bring the main housing duty to an end if the applicant refuses a suitable private rented sector offer.[91] This is because the special

---

[82]   HA 1996, s 195(2). See **17.190–17.200**.
[83]   HA 1996, s 195(3A), (4) and (4A–4B), inserted by Housing and Regeneration Act 2008, s 314 and Sch 15, para 6.
[84]   At the date of writing, the amendments to HA 1996 made by LA 2011, ss 148–149 had not been brought into effect in Wales.
[85]   'Private rented sector offers' are defined at HA 1996, s 193(7AA) as amended by LA 2011, s 148(5) and can be made to applicants for homelessness assistance whose applications were made on or after 9 November 2012 to local housing authorities in England, see **17.109–17.131**.
[86]   HA 1996, s 193(3B), see **12.32–12.38**.
[87]   HA 1996, s 193(7AD).
[88]   HA 1996, s 193(11)(b) inserted by LA 2011, s 148(11).
[89]   The Homelessness (Suitability of Accommodation) (England) Order 2012, SI 2012/2601, does not contain any regulation to increase the length of the minimum term, so at the date of writing, all applicants can be made a private rented sector offer for a minimum term of 12 months. See **17.109–17.131** and **18.51–18.54**.
[90]   Inserted by LA 2011, s 149(4) and applicable where an applicant for homelessness assistance made his or her application to a local housing authority in England on or after 9 November 2012 and accepted a private rented sector offer which brought the main housing duty to an end, and then subsequently makes a fresh application for homelessness assistance to a local housing authority in England within two years of the date of acceptance of the private rented sector offer. See **9.89–9.95**.
[91]   HA 1996, s 193(7AB)(c) amended by LA 2011, s 148(6) and applicable to an applicant for

provisions at HA 1996, s 195A,[92] which provide for the interim accommodation duty at HA 1996, s 188, the main housing duty at HA 1996, s 193 and/or the main duty owed to applicants who are threatened with homelessness at HA 1996, s 195 to be owed regardless of whether the applicant has a priority need,[93] do not apply where the main housing duty or equivalent duty to those threatened with homelessness would not apply without having regard to the presence of a restricted person in the applicant's household.[94]

12.45 The wording of this new subsection is somewhat confusing. It does not state that the applicant is only entitled to the main housing duty if he or she has a priority need as a result of the presence of a restricted person in his or her household (which might be thought to have been Parliament's intention). Instead, it provides that if an applicant is only homeless, or eligible for assistance, or has not become homeless intentionally because of the 'regard to a restricted person', the special provisions do not apply and the applicant must also have a priority need in order to be entitled to the main housing duty, or the equivalent duty owed to those applicants threatened with homelessness. If an applicant would have been homeless, eligible for assistance and have not become homeless intentionally whether or not a restricted person was in his or her household, he or she will still be entitled to the special provisions and to the main housing duty without having to show a priority need. From the wording of the subsection, it appears that it is only if the presence of the restricted person has rendered the applicant homeless,[95] that the applicant would also have to have a priority need in order to be entitled to the main housing duty.

12.46 Even if the applicant is only homeless (or eligible or has not become homeless intentionally) because of the presence in his or her household of a restricted person, he or she will still be entitled to the special provision deeming him or her threatened with homelessness when a Housing Act 1988, s 21 notice is served and homeless from the date on which the notice expires.[96]

---

homelessness assistance whose application was made to a local housing authority in England on or after 9 November 2012. See **17.119–17.131**.

[92] Inserted by LA 2011, s 149(4) and applicable where an applicant for homelessness assistance made his or her application to a local housing authority in England on or after 9 November 2012 and accepted a private rented sector offer which brought the main housing duty to an end, and then subsequently makes a fresh application for homelessness assistance to a local housing authority in England within two years of the date of acceptance of the private rented sector offer. See **9.89–9.95**.

[93] HA 1996, ss 188(1A), 195A(1) and (3).

[94] HA 1996, s 195A(5) inserted by LA 2011, s 149(4) and applicable where an applicant for homelessness assistance made his or her application to a local housing authority in England on or after 9 November 2012 and accepted a private rented sector offer which brought the main housing duty to an end, and then subsequently makes a fresh application for homelessness assistance to a local housing authority in England within two years of the date of acceptance of the private rented sector offer. See **9.89–9.95**.

[95] Perhaps because the arrival of the restricted person has made the accommodation overcrowded and unreasonable to occupy or because his or her presence has resulted in the landlord requiring possession.

[96] HA 1996, s 195A inserted by LA 2011, s 149(4) and applicable where an applicant for homelessness assistance made his or her application to a local housing authority in England on

12.47 If the applicant who makes a further application for homelessness assistance within two years of the date of his or her acceptance of a private rented sector offer is only entitled to the main housing duty because of the presence in his or her household of a restricted person,[97] he or she will again be regarded as a 'restricted case'.[98] The modifications to the main housing duty will apply and the local housing authority will be required, so far as is reasonably practicable, to make a private rented sector offer to the applicant,[99] and will not be required to notify him or her of the special provision at HA 1996, s 195A.[100]

Working out whether the applicant is 'eligible'

12.48 To work out whether either of the two statutory exclusion provisions (HA 1996, ss 185 and 186) apply, it is first necessary to know something of the nationality and immigration status of the applicant. Inquiries need to be made sensitively and without applying any form of discriminatory approach as between different applicants.[101]

12.49 Detailed discussion of an applicant's immigration status is outside the scope of this book, but very helpful guidance in this complex area is provided at Chapter 9 and Annexes 8–13 inclusive of the *Homelessness Code of Guidance for Local Authorities* [England] and Chapter 11 and Annexes 4–6 inclusive of the *Code of Guidance for Local Authorities Allocation of Accommodation and Homelessness 2012* [Wales].

12.50 It should be remembered, however, that for local housing authorities in England, the Code of Guidance was published in July 2006 and does not take account of amendments to the Regulations since then.[102]

12.51 The resolution of any uncertainty about an applicant's immigration or asylum status, or the relevant dates (e g of entry into the UK or application for

---

or after 9 November 2012 and accepted a private rented sector offer which brought the main housing duty to an end, and then subsequently makes a fresh application for homelessness assistance to a local housing authority in England within two years of the date of acceptance of the private rented sector offer. See **9.89–9.95**.

[97] HA 1996, s 193(3B).

[98] HA 1996, s 193(3B).

[99] HA 1996, s 193(7AD).

[100] HA 1996, s 193(7AB)(c) as amended by LA 2011, s 148(6).

[101] English Code, para 9.2: see Appendix 2 of this book. Welsh Code, para 11.2: see the accompanying CD-ROM.

[102] Specifically, the English Code does not deal with: the amendments to the disregard at HA 1996, s 185(4) and (5) (see **12.27–12.31**), 'restricted persons' (see **12.34**), 'restricted cases' (see **12.32–12.33**), 'derivative rights of residence' (see **12.42–12.161**), the concept of EEA rights of residence not contained in domestic Regulations (see **12.162**), the position of A2 nationals (see **12.192–12.196**), the exemptions from the habitual residence for certain people leaving Lebanon (see **12.208–12.209**), and for certain people leaving Zimbabwe (see **12.210–12.221**). Nor does it deal with the exclusions from eligibility at SI 2006/1294, reg 6(1)(b) and (c) as amended by SI 2012/2588, see **12.212–12.1226**.

asylum) may require the help of the UK Border Agency (UKBA).[103] Local housing authorities are advised to contact the UKBA if there is any uncertainty arising from an application, and to inform the applicant that an inquiry will be made before doing so.[104] This allows the applicant an opportunity to withdraw his or her application for homelessness assistance if she or he does not want such an inquiry to be made.

12.52 The UKBA is required to provide local housing authorities, on request, with information about whether a person falls within any particular statutory category (eg within Immigration and Asylum Act 1999, s 115)[105] or any other information required to enable local housing authorities to determine whether applicants are eligible for assistance.[106] Most requests for information are made, and the responses to them given, by telephone. Having regard to the complexity of the subject matter and the importance of accuracy, it may be sensible for a local housing authority receiving complex information from UKBA (particularly if it is going to be used to make or support an adverse eligibility decision) to ask that UKBA provide the information in writing.[107] The UKBA need not provide written confirmation unless the request itself is in writing.[108] A local housing authority is entitled to rely on the UKBA's view of an applicant's current immigration status, and need not make inquiries as to, for example, the possible outcome of a pending appeal.[109] The UKBA may advise on an applicant's immigration status, but the decision on eligibility is for the local housing authority itself.

12.53 If the UKBA does provide information to a local housing authority, it is then under a continuing obligation to notify that local housing authority, in writing, if there are any subsequent applications, decisions or other changes of circumstance affecting the particular applicant's status.[110] This continuing obligation is obviously of crucial importance if the applicant's immigration status is under review (or awaiting an initial decision or subject to an appeal) when the local housing authority makes its first request for information.

---

[103] The English Codes refers to the Home Office Immigration and Nationality Directorate (IND). The UKBA replaced the IND in April 2008.

[104] English Code, para 9.9; Welsh Code, para 11.8.

[105] Which excludes 'persons subject to immigration control' from housing benefit and is referred to at HA 1996, s 185(2A).

[106] HA 1996, s 187(1) and (2).

[107] Contact details for the former Immigration and Nationality Directorate are given in English Code, Annex 8. The up-to-date details are at Welsh Code, Annex 5.

[108] HA 1996, s 187(2).

[109] *Burns v Southwark London Borough Council* [2004] EWHC 1901 (Admin), [2004] All ER (D) 328 (Jul), Admin Ct.

[110] HA 1996, s 187(3). From the wording, it appears that the UKBA is obliged to notify these changes of circumstances in writing, whether or not the information originally provided was provided in writing or verbally.

THE PRIMARY EXCLUSION PROVISION: HOUSING ACT 1996, S 185

Overview

12.54 The governing provision for the main excluded group is HA 1996, s 185(1).[111] It provides that 'a person from abroad who is ineligible for housing assistance' is not eligible for assistance from a local housing authority under the homelessness provisions in HA 1996, Part 7. Working out who is, and who is not, caught by that term is therefore crucial in deciding whether homelessness services can be provided.

12.55 There are two categories of 'persons from abroad' for the purposes of HA 1996, s 185:

(1) those subject to immigration control –
   * they are *not eligible* for assistance
   * *unless* they fall within a class prescribed as 'eligible' in regulations made by the Secretary of State or the Welsh Ministers;[112]

(2) those not subject to immigration control but who are nevertheless prescribed by regulations as being 'persons from abroad' –
   * they are *not eligible* if they are not habitually resident in the Common Travel Area *unless* they are prescribed as exempt from the habitual residence test, or
   * they are *not eligible* if they are prescribed as ineligible because of their particular rights of residence under European Union law.[113]

12.56 As is apparent from the terms of these provisions, the general rule is that people from abroad are excluded. But the Secretary of State and the Welsh Ministers each have the power to make regulations exempting some people from abroad from that exclusory rule.[114] They each also have the power to make regulations excluding people who would otherwise be eligible. Each of these powers has been exercised several times in both England and Wales.

12.57 For England, the Secretary of State has made the Allocation of Housing and Homelessness (Eligibility) (England) Regulations 2006,[115] which

---

[111] *R (Morris) v Westminster City Council* [2005] EWCA Civ 1184, [2006] HLR 8, CA, at [13] and [14] per Sedley LJ.
[112] HA 1996, s 185(2).
[113] HA 1996, s 185(3).
[114] They cannot designate as eligible any person who is excluded from entitlement to housing benefit by the Immigration and Asylum Act 1999, s 115 (HA 1996, s 185(2A)). Immigration and Asylum Act 1999, s 115 prescribes that 'a person subject to immigration control' is not eligible for housing benefit unless he or she falls within one of the classes of people prescribed by the Secretary of State. Classes of persons subject to immigration control who are entitled to housing benefit are prescribed in the Social Security (Immigration and Asylum) Consequential Amendment Regulations 2000, SI 2000/636, reg 2 and Sch 1, Part 1 and the Housing Benefit Regulations 2006, SI 2006/213, regs 10(3B) and 10A.
[115] SI 2006/1294. See Appendix 2 of this book.

apply to all applications for homelessness assistance to local housing authorities in England made on or after 1 June 2006.[116] Those Regulations have since been made amended by:

- the Allocation of Housing and Homelessness (Eligibility) (England) (Amendment) Regulations 2006;[117] and

- the Allocation of Housing and Homelessness (Eligibility) (England) (Miscellaneous Provisions) Regulations 2006;[118] and

- the Allocation of Housing and Homelessness (Eligibility) (England) (Amendment No 2) Regulations 2006;[119] and

- the Allocation of Housing and Homelessness (Eligibility) (England) (Amendment) Regulations 2009;[120]

- the Allocation of Housing and Homelessness (Eligibility) (England) (Amendment) Regulations 2012.[121]

12.58 Appendix 2 of this book contains the text of the Allocation of Housing and Homelessness (Eligibility) (England) Regulations 2006,[122] as amended by all of the above Regulations. Guidance is provided at Chapter 9 and Annexes 8–13 of the English Code.

12.59 In Wales, the National Assembly for Wales[123] made the Homelessness (Wales) Regulations 2006,[124] which apply to all applications for homelessness assistance to local housing authorities in Wales made on or after 9 October 2006.[125]

---

[116] Any applications for homelessness assistance made before 1 June 2006 to local housing authorities in England are determined according to the Homelessness (England) Regulations 2000, SI 2000/701, amended by Allocation of Housing and Homelessness (Amendment) (England) Regulations 2004, SI 2004/1235, and further amended by the Allocation of Housing and Homelessness (Amendment) (England) Regulations 2006, SI 2006/1093. See previous editions of this book.

[117] SI 2006/2007, in force for applications to local housing authorities in England made on or after 25 July 2006.

[118] SI 2006/2527, in force for applications to local housing authorities in England made on or after 9 October 2006.

[119] SI 2006/3340, in force for applications to local housing authorities in England made on or after 1 January 2007.

[120] SI 2009/358, in force for applications to local housing authorities in England made on or after 18 March 2009.

[121] SI 2012/2588, in force for applications to local housing authorities in England made on or after 8 November 2012.

[122] SI 2006/1294.

[123] Its functions were acquired by the Welsh Assembly Government on 25 May 2007; in May 2011 the Welsh Assembly Government was renamed the Welsh Government and the functions are exercised by the Welsh Ministers.

[124] SI 2006/2646 (W 227).

[125] For the relevant regulations in Wales before 9 October 2006, see previous editions of this book.

12.60 The Welsh Regulations have been amended by:

- the Employment and Support Allowance (Consequential Provisions) (No 3) Regulations 2008, para 31;[126] and

- the Allocation of Housing and Homelessness (Eligibility) (Wales) Regulations 2009.

12.61 Appendix 3 of this book contains the text of the Homelessness (Wales) Regulations 2006,[127] as amended by both these Regulations. Guidance is provided at Chapter 11 and Annexes 4–6 of the Welsh Code. The Welsh Code advises that the Welsh Ministers are currently considering whether to amend the Homelessness (Wales) Regulations 2006.[128] If the Regulations are amended, the guidance at Chapter 11 of the Welsh Code will also be reconsidered.

12.62 The Regulations in both England and Wales set out classes of persons who are subject to immigration control but are prescribed as nevertheless eligible. They also set out classes of persons who are not subject to immigration control, but are nevertheless ineligible.

12.63 Each of the two categories of persons from abroad (those subject to immigration control and those not subject to such control) needs careful examination. But first it is necessary to work out which category an applicant is within. That depends on whether or not the applicant is 'subject to immigration control'.

Meaning of 'subject to immigration control'

12.64 The starting point is the special meaning of 'subject to immigration control'. It means 'a person who is subject to immigration control within the meaning of the Asylum and Immigration Act 1996'.[129] The Asylum and Immigration Act 1996 itself states:

'... "person subject to immigration control" means a person who under the 1971 Act requires leave to enter or remain in the United Kingdom (whether or not such leave has been given).'[130]

12.65 Tracing that route back to the Immigration Act 1971[131] reveals that:

- British citizens;

---

[126] SI 2008/1879, in force for applications to local housing authorities in Wales on or after 27 October 2008.
[127] SI 2006/2646 (W 227).
[128] SI 2006/2646 (W 227). Welsh Code para 11.3.
[129] HA 1996, s 185(2).
[130] Asylum and Immigration Act 1996, s 13(2).
[131] Immigration Act 1971, ss 1–3.

- Commonwealth citizens with the right of abode in the UK;

- European Economic Area ('EEA') nationals and Swiss nationals exercising certain Treaty rights[132] (see Box 2 at **12.66**);

- people exercising rights derived from those EEA and Swiss nationals exercising or who had exercised certain Treaty rights;[133]

- certain people who are exempt from immigration control under the Immigration Acts (diplomats and their family members based in the UK, and some military personnel); and

- Irish citizens with a Common Travel Area[134] entitlement.

do *not* require leave to enter or remain in the UK and therefore cannot be 'persons subject to immigration control'.[135] Those applicants will be eligible *unless* they fall within the second category of persons prescribed as being 'persons from abroad' and not eligible.[136]

12.66 The legal definition of the term 'the United Kingdom' and its related parts is given in Box 1.

---

[132] Immigration Act 1988, s 7; Immigration (European Economic Area) Regulations 2006, SI 2006/1003, regs 13–15. From 1 June 2002, Swiss nationals have had the same rights to freedom of movement and social security within the EEA as EEA nationals: and so Swiss nationals fall within the definition of EEA nationals at Immigration (European Economic Area) Regulations 2006, SI 2006/1003, reg 2. All references to 'EEA nationals' in this book include Swiss nationals.

[133] Immigration (European Economic Area) Regulations 2006, SI 2006/1003, Regs 15A and 15B inserted by Immigration (European Economic Area) (Amendment) Regulations 2012, SI 2012/1547, in force from 16 July 2012 and amended by Immigration (European Economic Area) (Amendment) (No 2) Regulations 2012, SI 2012/2560 from 8 November 2012. See **12.141–12.161**.

[134] See Box 1.

[135] English Code, paras 9.7–9.8; Welsh Code paras 11.6–11.7. If an EEA national is not a 'qualifying person', he or she does not have the right to remain without leave, and is therefore a 'person subject to immigration control' and would fall within HA 1996, s 185(2) (*Abdi v Barnet London Borough Council, Ismail v Barnet London Borough Council* [2006] EWCA Civ 383, [2006] HLR 23, CA).

[136] HA 1996, s 185(3) and Allocation of Housing and Homelessness (Eligibility) (England) Regulations 2006, SI 2006/1294, reg 6 as amended, or Homelessness (Wales) Regulations 2006, SI 2006/2646 (W 227), reg 4. See **12.164–12.226** for the position in England and **12.227–12.233** for the position in Wales.

Box 1

Key Geographic Terms:

England: counties established by Local Government Act 1972, s 1, Greater London area and the Isles of Scilly.[137]

Great Britain: England, Wales, and Scotland.[138]

United Kingdom: England, Wales, Scotland and Northern Ireland.[139]

Common Travel Area (CTA): England, Wales, Scotland, Northern Ireland, Republic of Ireland, Isle of Man, and the Channel Islands.[140]

12.67 Box 2 shows which countries are members of the European Union (EU) and/or members of the wider European Economic Area (EEA).[141] For these purposes, nationals of Iceland, Liechtenstein, Norway, and Switzerland have the same rights to enter or reside as nationals of most of the EU Member States.[142] Rights for nationals of Bulgaria and Romania ('the A2 states')[143] are slightly different from those enjoyed by nationals of other EEA states.[144] We refer throughout this Chapter to nationals of EEA Member States, by which we mean all the EU Member States, including the A2 states, plus the three additional EEA Member States and Switzerland.

---

[137] Interpretation Act 1978, s 5 and Sch 1.
[138] Union of Scotland Act 1706.
[139] Interpretation Act 1978, s 5 and Sch 1.
[140] Immigration Act 1971, s 1(3).
[141] Croatia is due to accede to the European Union in 2013. Iceland, Montenegro, Serbia, Turkey and the former Yugoslav Republic of Macedonia are 'candidate countries' for accession to the EU. Albania, Bosnia and Herzegovina, and Kosovo are all potential 'candidate countries'. See www.europa.eu/about-eu/countries/index_en.htm for an up-to-date list.
[142] Immigration (European Economic Area) Regulations 2006, SI 2006/1003, as amended. See Appendix 2 of this book.
[143] See **12.192–12.196**.
[144] Rights for nationals of the eight 2004 Accession States ('A8 states') were subject to derogation between 1 May 2004 and 30 April 2011 (Accession (Immigration and Worker Registration) Regulations 2004, SI 2004/1219). From 1 May 2011 nationals of the A8 member states are to be treated in the same way as nationals of any other EEA member state, save that retained worker status is slightly different. The A8 states were the Czech Republic, Estonia, Hungary, Latvia, Lithuania, Poland, Slovakia and Slovenia. See **12.191**.

Box 2

The European Union (EU):

Member States:[145] Austria, Belgium, Cyprus, Czech Republic, Denmark, Estonia, Finland, France, Germany, Greece, Hungary, Ireland, Italy, Latvia, Lithuania, Luxembourg, Netherlands, Malta, Poland, Portugal, Slovakia, Slovenia, Spain, Sweden and the UK; and

Accession States acceding in 2007 ('A2 states'): Bulgaria and Romania

The European Economic Area (EEA):

All EU States[146] plus Iceland, Liechtenstein and Norway.

Switzerland is not part of the EEA, but its nationals are treated as EEA nationals for these purposes.[147]

12.68   Obviously, the lists given in these boxes will fluctuate from time to time. The most up-to-date list is at Annex 4 of the Welsh Code. Annex 11 of the English Code does not include reference to the A2 countries.

12.69   If a consideration of these provisions shows that the applicant is *not* 'subject to immigration control', because he or she does not require leave to enter or remain in the UK, he or she will usually be 'eligible' *unless* rendered ineligible by falling within the second category. For these purposes, it is important to emphasise that a person, usually an EEA national or a person claiming to exercise rights derived from an EEA national, who does not require leave to enter but who does require leave to remain and does not have it, is a person subject to immigration control.[148] It is only a person who requires neither leave to enter nor leave to remain who is not subject to immigration control. Strangely, a person can be ineligible for homelessness assistance even if he or she was born in the UK and has never left it, simply because he or she does require leave to enter or remain in the UK and does not have it.[149] Similarly a person is only an EEA national if he or she has actually left his or her country of origin and thus exercised freedom of movement.[150]

---

[145]   All member states as at 30 April 2004, plus Cyprus and Malta, who each joined on 1 May 2004 along with the A8 states. Cyprus and Malta were not subject to the derogations that the A8 states were subject to until 1 May 2011.

[146]   The Channel Islands, Isle of Man and Gibraltar are not part of the EEA.

[147]   Immigration (European Economic Area) Regulations 2006, SI 2006/1003, reg 2.

[148]   *Abdi v Barnet London Borough Council, Ismail v Barnet London Borough Council* [2006] EWCA Civ 383, [2006] HLR 23, CA.

[149]   *Ehiabor v Kensington & Chelsea Royal London Borough Council* [2008] EWCA Civ 1074, [2008] All ER (D) 104 (May), CA.

[150]   *McCarthy v SSHD* C-434/09, [2011] All ER (EC) 729, Court of Justice of the European Union (CJEU).

12.70 Everyone else is a 'person subject to immigration control' and is *not* eligible for assistance *unless* he or she falls into one of the classes prescribed by Allocation of Housing and Homelessness (Eligibility) (England) Regulations 2006, reg 5 or by Homelessness (Wales) Regulations 2006, reg 3.[151]

Category One: those who are subject to immigration control

12.71 The starting point is that:

'... a person who is subject to immigration control within the meaning of the Asylum and Immigration Act 1996 is not eligible for housing assistance unless he is of a class prescribed by regulations made by the Secretary of State.'[152]

The English rules

The basic rule

12.72 The basic rule is that 'a person subject to immigration control' is *not eligible*. The exceptions to that basic rule are contained in classes set out in Regulations. Regulation 5 of the Allocation of Housing and Homelessness (Eligibility) (England) Regulations 2006[153] prescribes that the following classes of persons from abroad are eligible even though they are subject to immigration control:

(1) Class A:[154] a person recorded by the Secretary of State as a refugee and who has leave to enter or remain in the UK.

(2) Class B:[155] a person who has:
   (a) exceptional leave to enter or remain in the UK granted outside of the provisions of the Immigration Rules; and
   (b) whose leave is not subject to conditions requiring him or her to maintain and accommodate himself or herself and any dependents without recourse to public funds.

(3) Class C:[156] a person who:
   (a) is habitually resident in the CTA;[157] and
   (b) has current leave to enter or remain in the UK which is not subject to any limitation or condition; but
   (c) is not a person who:

---

[151] SI 2006/1294 [England]; SI 2006/2646 (W 227) [Wales].
[152] HA 1996, s 185(2).
[153] SI 2006/1294. See Appendix 2 of this book.
[154] SI 2006/1294, reg 5(1)(a). See **12.76–12.78**.
[155] SI 2006/1294, reg 5(1)(b). See **12.79–12.81**.
[156] SI 2006/1294, reg 5(1)(c). See **12.82–12.84**.
[157] See Box 1 at **12.66**.

>   (i)   has been given leave to enter or remain in the UK upon a written undertaking from a sponsor that he or she will be responsible for maintenance and accommodation; and
>
>   (ii) has been resident in the CTA for less than 5 years beginning on the date of entry or the date of the undertaking (whichever is the later date); and
>
>   (iii) whose sponsor is still alive.

(4)   Class D:[158] a person who has humanitarian protection granted under the Immigration Rules.

(5)   Class E:[159] a person who is an asylum-seeker[160] whose claim for asylum is recorded by the Secretary of State as having been made before 3 April 2000 and in one of the following circumstances:

    (i)   on arrival in the UK from a country outside the CTA;[161] or

    (ii) within three months from the day on which the Secretary of State made a declaration of upheaval and where the applicant was in Great Britain[162] on the date of the declaration;[163] or

    (iii) on or before 4 February 1996 by an applicant who was on 4 February 1996 entitled to housing benefit under reg 7A of the Housing Benefit (General) Regulations 1987.[164]

12.73 Guidance on the scope of each of these Classes is given in the English Code at paras 9.10–9.12.[165] These classes are individually considered at **12.76–12.97**.

12.74 A number of the Classes contain terms that are defined by the regulations or by case law. For the meaning of:

- 'asylum seeker' see **12.86–12.90**;

- 'Common Travel Area (CTA)' see Box 1 at **12.66**;

- 'habitually resident' see **12.170–12.179**;

---

[158] SI 2006/1294, reg 5(1)(d), as amended by Allocation of Housing and Homelessness (Miscellaneous Provisions) (England) Regulations 2006, SI 2006/2527, reg 2, for applications for homelessness assistance made on or after 9 October 2006. See **12.85**. For applications made before 9 October 2006, Class D contained 'a person who left the territory of Montserrat after 1 November 1995 because of the effect on that territory of a volcanic eruption'.

[159] SI 2006/1294, reg 5(1)(e). See **12.86–12.97**.

[160] See **12.86–12.90**.

[161] See Box 1 at **12.66**.

[162] See Box 1 at **12.66**.

[163] Two declarations of upheaval have been issued: Zaire (on 16 May 1997) and Sierra Leone (on 1 July 1997). See **12.93–12.95**.

[164] SI 1987/1971. See **12.96–12.97**.

[165] Note that the guidance at para 9.10(iv) on Class D is out of date and refers to the former Class D (English Code, para 9.10(iv)).

- 'UK' see Box 1 at **12.66**.

12.75 Even if an applicant is eligible under any of these five Classes, any members of his or her household who are not eligible are to be disregarded for the purposes of deciding whether the applicant is homeless and whether he or she has a priority need.[166]

Exemptions from the basic rule

Class A: refugees[167]

12.76 If a former asylum seeker has been granted refugee status by the Secretary of State, he or she will also have the 'leave to enter or remain in the UK' required for Class A purposes and will be eligible for homelessness assistance, welfare benefits, community care services and for an allocation of social housing according to the same criteria as those applicable to British citizens. Leave may be granted either for an indefinite period or limited for five years.

12.77 It is not unusual for someone to be granted refugee status and then to apply for his or her family to come to the UK. The family enters the UK with the refugee acting as their sponsor. A refugee is entitled to such family reunion,[168] and so the usual rules regarding maintenance and accommodation (which would normally involve a condition of 'no recourse to public funds') do not apply to a refugee's family members. Thus, those family members will also be eligible for homelessness assistance because they are entitled to 'refugee' status.[169]

12.78 Once a former asylum-seeker is granted refugee status, any accommodation which was provided by the UKBA[170] under Immigration and Asylum Act 1999, Part 6 will be withdrawn. If the asylum-seeker was occupying accommodation provided by the UKBA under Immigration and Asylum Act 1999, s 95 (the main duty to provide support to asylum-seekers), he or she will have a local connection with the local housing authority in whose district the UKBA accommodation was situated.[171] This does not preclude the former asylum-seeker from establishing a local connection, or several local connections, elsewhere, whether by residence, family associations, employment or special circumstances. He or she might then have a local connection with more than one local housing authority.

---

[166] HA 1996, s 185(4) in its original form and as amended by Housing and Regeneration Act 2008, s 314 and Sch 15, para 4. See **12.24–12.31**.
[167] Allocation of Housing and Homelessness (Eligibility) (England) Regulations 2006, SI 2006/1294, reg 5(1)(a). English Code, para 9.10(i).
[168] See *Immigration Rules*, HC 395 (23 May 1994 as amended), paras 352A–352F.
[169] *R (Jimaali) v Haringey London Borough Council* (2002) November *Legal Action*, p 24, Admin Ct.
[170] Formerly the National Asylum Support Service or 'NASS'.
[171] HA 1996, s 199(6), as amended. See **15.88–15.94**.

Class B: exceptional leave to enter or remain[172]

12.79 'Exceptional leave to enter or remain' was generally a status granted to asylum-seekers whose claim for full refugee status had not succeeded but where the Home Office recognised that there were compelling humanitarian and/or compassionate circumstances that required that the applicant should be allowed to stay in the UK. From 1 April 2003, the Home Office has called leave granted in those circumstances 'humanitarian protection' or 'discretionary leave'.[173] Viewed broadly, anyone who was granted leave to enter or remain when the Secretary of State has recognised that he or she does not fully meet the requirements of the Immigration Rules has been treated 'exceptionally' and may be said to have been granted 'exceptional leave'.[174] Leave is normally, but not always, granted for a period of three years.

12.80 People with exceptional leave to enter or remain will be eligible for homelessness assistance unless that leave is subject to a condition requiring them to maintain and accommodate themselves (and their dependents) without recourse to public funds. The presence or absence of such a condition will be manifest from the document (or stamp) containing the grant of leave itself.

12.81 Unless they fall within the prohibition of 'no recourse to public funds', they will not only be entitled to homelessness assistance but also to welfare benefits and community care services, and can apply for an allocation of social housing.

Class C: a person with current leave to enter or remain in the UK with no condition or limitation and who is habitually resident in the Common Travel Area[175]

12.82 The type of leave contemplated by this class is commonly referred to as 'indefinite leave to enter or remain' and cannot be granted subject to conditions.[176] Anyone granted indefinite leave to enter or remain will be eligible if he or she is also habitually resident in the CTA.[177]

---

[172] Allocation of Housing and Homelessness (Eligibility) (England) Regulations 2006, SI 2006/1294, reg 5(1)(b). English Code, para 9.10(ii).

[173] Letter from the Homelessness Directorate (Office of the Deputy Prime Minister) to Chief Executives and Housing Directors of English local housing authorities, dated 25 March 2003.

[174] Since April 2012, the UKBA's policy has been to grant leave limited for a period of three months to people who have left their partner within two years of arriving in the UK and are considering applying for indefinite leave to remain under the Domestic Violence Immigration Rule. Anyone who has been granted that limited leave is entitled to apply for welfare benefits and should also fall under this Class B and be eligible for homelessness assistance.

[175] Allocation of Housing and Homelessness (Eligibility) (England) Regulations 2006, SI 2006/1294, reg 5(1)(c). English Code, para 9.10(iii).

[176] Immigration Act 1971, s 3(1)(b) and (c).

[177] For the meaning of 'habitually resident', see **12.170–12.179**. For the 'Common Travel Area', see Box 1 at **12.66**.

12.83 If leave to enter or remain has been granted on the basis of a written undertaking that a sponsor would be responsible for the applicant's maintenance and accommodation, the applicant will *not* be eligible for homeless assistance under Class C for five years running from:

- the date of his or her arrival in the UK; or

- the date the sponsorship undertaking was given;

starting from whichever is the later event.[178]

12.84 After those five years, or if the sponsor (or at least one of several sponsors) dies within the five years,[179] an applicant will be eligible under this class (subject to satisfying the test of habitual residence).[180]

Class D: a person granted humanitarian protection under the Immigration Rules[181]

12.85 'Humanitarian protection' is granted to those people whose claims for asylum do not succeed, but who have international protection needs (ie they face a serious risk of the death penalty, unlawful killing, torture, inhuman or degrading treatment or punishment if removed from the UK). The status must be granted pursuant to the Immigration Rules.[182] People with humanitarian protection are entitled to family reunion in the same way as refugees.[183]

Class E: asylum-seekers (in three specific circumstances)[184]

12.86 An 'asylum-seeker' is defined in the Regulations as:

'... a person who is at least 18 years old, who is in the UK, and who has made a claim for asylum.'[185]

---

[178] SI 2006/1294, reg 5(1)(c)(ii).
[179] SI 2006/1294, reg 5(1)(c)(iii).
[180] See **12.170–12.179**.
[181] Allocation of Housing and Homelessness (Eligibility) (England) Regulations 2006, SI 2006/1294, reg (1)(d), as amended by Allocation of Housing and Homelessness (Miscellaneous Provisions) (England) Regulations 2006, SI 2006/2527, reg 3(2). Paragraph 9. 10(iv) of the English Code is out of date and deals with the former Class D applying to applications made before 9 October 2006. There is reference at English Code, para 9.10(ii) to humanitarian protection.
[182] See *Immigration Rules*, HC 395, paras 339C–339H (23 May 1994, as amended).
[183] *Immigration Rules*, HC 395, paras 352FA–352FI. See **12.77–12.78**.
[184] Allocation of Housing and Homelessness (Eligibility) (England) Regulations 2006, SI 2006/1294, reg 5(1)(e). English Code, paras 9.11–9.12 and Annex 9.
[185] SI 2006/1294, reg 5(2)(a).

12.87 A person ceases to be an asylum-seeker 'when his claim for asylum is recorded by the Secretary of State as having been decided (other than on appeal) or abandoned',[186] unless he or she continues to be eligible for housing benefit.[187]

12.88 A 'claim for asylum' is defined as:

> '... a claim that it would be contrary to the UK's obligations under the Refugee Convention for the claimant to be removed from, or required to leave the UK.'[188]

12.89 The date of a claim for asylum is the date on which it was recorded by the Secretary of State.[189] To fall within Class E, that date must be *before 3 April 2000*. There will be very few people now falling within any of the three parts of Class E. For these few asylum-seekers, there are additional exclusionary rules for those who do fall within Class E made at HA 1996, s 186.[190]

12.90 'Asylum-seekers' who fall into the three different variants of Class E described below must be adult asylum seekers who made their claims for asylum before 3 April 2000 and are still waiting for determination of their applications. All other adult asylum seekers will be the responsibility of the UKBA, which provides support under Immigration and Asylum Act 1999, Part 6. Asylum seekers who are children will be the responsibility of children's authorities.[191]

12.91 Asylum-seekers who are eligible for homelessness assistance as a result of falling within Class E are also eligible for welfare benefits.[192]

Class E(i): claims for asylum made on arrival[193]

12.92 Class E(i) is concerned with those who made an asylum claim 'on arrival' in the UK. The UKBA may have made a decision, when the asylum-seeker first came to its attention, as to whether he or she claimed 'on arrival'. The UKBA has a duty to inform a local housing authority of its decision on that question or any change in that decision.[194]

---

[186] SI 2006/1294, reg 5(2)(d).
[187] SI 2006/1294, reg 5(3).
[188] SI 2006/1294, reg 5(2)(b). The scope would normally include claims for leave to remain based on Art 3 of the European Convention on Human Rights.
[189] SI 2006/1294, reg 5(1)(e).
[190] See the first and second editions of this book.
[191] See **20.74–20.84**.
[192] Because the provision excluding asylum-seekers from certain welfare benefits at Immigration and Asylum Act 1999, s 115 does not apply to those people who sought asylum before 3 April 2000 and whose claims have not yet been determined.
[193] Allocation of Housing and Homelessness (Eligibility) (England) Regulations 2006, SI 2006/1294, reg 5(1)(e)(i). English Code, Annex 9, para 7(i).
[194] HA 1996, s 187. English Code, Annex 9, para 11.

Class E(ii): claims for asylum made within three months of a relevant declaration of upheaval[195]

12.93 The claim for asylum must have been made *after* the declaration of upheaval and have been recorded by the Secretary of State as made within three months of it. Any person who claims asylum within that period, but who had already made a prior claim for asylum in the UK will not fall within this class.

12.94 Two declarations of upheaval have been made by the Secretary of State: Zaire (16 May 1997) and Sierra Leone (1 July 1997). Nationals of Zaire/the Congo must have claimed asylum between 16 May 1997 and 15 August 1997 and nationals of Sierra Leone between 1 July 1997 and 30 September 1997 to fall within this class. Accordingly, the class only currently operates to assist those who sought asylum from those two countries over 15 years ago and who still await final decisions on their claims.

12.95 Note that the individual must have been in 'Great Britain'[196] when the declaration was made. The terms of the class will not be satisfied if on that date he or she was in Northern Ireland or elsewhere in the CTA.[197]

Class E(iii): an asylum-seeker who claimed asylum on or before 4 February 1996 and who was entitled to benefit on 4 February 1996[198]

12.96 This class is largely self-explanatory. For the purposes of this class, the 'benefit' to which the person was entitled must have been Housing Benefit payable under the Housing Benefit (General) Regulations 1987 until 2006 and since then under the Housing Benefit Regulations 2006.[199] The individual must still be an asylum-seeker,[200] ie a person still awaiting final determination of his or her claim for asylum.

12.97 If a person who is subject to immigration control is *not* within any of the Classes A–E described above, and made his or her application for homelessness assistance on or after 1 June 2006, he or she is *not* 'eligible' for homelessness assistance.

---

[195] Allocation of Housing and Homelessness (Eligibility) (England) Regulations 2006, SI 2006/1294, reg 5(1)(e)(ii). English Code, Annex 9, para 7(ii).
[196] 'Great Britain' is defined as England, Scotland and Wales: Union with Scotland Act 1706; see Box 1 at **12.66**.
[197] See Box 1 at **12.66**.
[198] Allocation of Housing and Homelessness (Eligibility) (England) Regulations 2006, SI 2006/1294, reg 5(1)(e)(iii). English Code, Annex 9, para 7(iii).
[199] SI 1987/1971, reg 7A.The current housing benefit regulations are Housing Benefit Regulations 2006, SI 2006/213, in force from 6 March 2006.
[200] As defined at Allocation of Housing and Homelessness (Eligibility) (England) Regulations 2006, SI 2006/1294, reg 5(2)(a). See **12.86–12.91**.

The Welsh rules

The basic rule

12.98 The National Assembly for Wales exercised its power to prescribe classes of people who are subject to immigration control, but are nevertheless eligible, by the Homelessness (Wales) Regulations 2006, as amended.[201] These Regulations apply to applications for homelessness assistance made to local housing authorities in Wales on or after 9 October 2006.[202] At the date of writing, the Welsh Government is considering whether to amend these Regulations.[203]

Exemptions to the basic rule

12.99 Regulation 3 of the Homelessness (Wales) Regulations 2006[204] prescribes that the following Classes of persons from abroad are eligible, even though they are subject to immigration control:

(1)   Class A:[205] a person recorded by the Secretary of State as a refugee within the definition in Art 1 of the Refugee Convention.

(2)   Class B:[206] a person:
    (a)   who has been granted by the Secretary of State exceptional leave to remain in the UK outside the provisions of the Immigration Rules; and
    (b)   whose leave is not subject to a condition requiring that person to maintain and accommodate himself or herself and any dependents, without recourse to public funds.

(3)   Class C:[207] a person who:
    (a)   is habitually resident in the CTA;[208] and
    (b)   has current leave to enter or remain in the UK which is not subject to any limitation or condition; but
    (c)   is not a person who:
        (i)   has been given leave to enter or remain in the UK upon a written undertaking from a sponsor that he or she will be responsible for maintenance and accommodation; and

---

[201]   SI 2006/2646 (W 227), reg 3. Those powers are now exercised by the Welsh Government. See **12.59–12.60** for a list of the amendments to the Homelessness (Wales) Regulation 2006, SI 2006/2646 (W 227).
[202]   Homelessness (Wales) Regulations 2006, SI 2006/2646 (W 227), as amended, reg 5.
[203]   Welsh Code, para 11.9.
[204]   SI 2006/2646 (W 227).
[205]   SI 2006/2646 (W 227), reg 3(1)(a). See Welsh Code, para 11.9(i). See **12.76–12.78**.
[206]   SI 2006/2646 (W 227), reg 3(1)(b). See Welsh Code, para 11.9(ii). See **12.79–12.81**.
[207]   SI 2006/2646 (W 227), reg 3(1)(c). See Welsh Code, para 11.9(iii). See **12.82–12.84**.
[208]   See Box 1 at **12.66**.

(ii) has been resident in the CTA for less than 5 years beginning on the date of entry or the date of undertaking (whichever is the later date); and

(iii) whose sponsor is still alive.

(4) Class D:[209] a person who left the territory of Montserrat after 1 November 1995 because of the effect on that territory of a volcanic eruption.

(5) Class E:[210] a person who is habitually resident[211] in the CTA[212] and who is either:

(a) a national of a state which has ratified the European Convention on Social and Medical Assistance ('ECSMA') or the European Social Charter ('ESC') and is lawfully present in the UK;[213] or

(b) before 3 April 2000 was owed a duty by a local housing authority under Housing Act 1985, Part 3, or HA 1996, Part 7, which is extant and who is a national of a state which is a signatory to the ECSMA or to the ESC.[214]

(6) Class F:[215] a person who is an asylum-seeker and who made a claim for asylum which is recorded by the Secretary of State as having been made on his or her arrival in the UK from a country outside the CTA and which has not been recorded by the Secretary of State as having been either decided (other than on appeal) or abandoned.

(7) Class G:[216] a person who is an asylum-seeker and who was in Great Britain when the Secretary of State made a declaration of upheaval in respect of his or her country, who made a claim for asylum which is recorded by the Secretary of State as having been made within a period of 3 months from the day on which that declaration was made and whose claim for asylum has not been recorded by the Secretary of State as having been either decided (other than on appeal) or abandoned.

---

[209] SI 2006/2646 (W 227), reg 3(1)(d). There is no guidance on this class in the Welsh Code, see English Code, para 9.10(iv). See **12.102–12.104**.

[210] SI 2006/2646 (W 227), reg 3(1)(e). See Welsh Code, paras 11.9(iv) and (v). See **12.105–12.112**.

[211] See **12.170–12.179**.

[212] See Box 1 at **12.66**.

[213] See **12.105–12.108**.

[214] See **12.109–12.112**.

[215] SI 2006/2646 (W 227), reg 3(1)(f). There is no guidance on this Class in the Welsh Code, see English Code, paras 9.11–9.12. See **12.86–12.95**.

[216] SI 2006/2646 (W 227), reg 3(1)(g). There is no guidance on this Class in the Welsh Code; see English Code, Annex 9, para 7(ii). See **12.86–12.91** and **12.93–12.95**.

(8) Class H:[217] a person who is an asylum-seeker and who made a relevant claim for asylum on or before 4 February 1996 and was, on that date, entitled to housing benefit under Housing Benefit (General) Regulations 1987, reg 7A.[218]

(9) Class I:[219] a person who is on income-based jobseeker's allowance or income support (with certain exceptions).

(10) Class J:[220] a person who has humanitarian protection granted under the Immigration Rules.

12.100 Several of these classes are identical to those prescribed as eligible under the English Regulations and are discussed at **12.76–12.97**.

– For Class A, see **12.76–12.78**.

– For Class B, see **12.79–12.81**.

– For Class C, see **12.82–12.84**.

– For Class F, see **12.86–12.92**.

– For Class G, see **12.86–12.91** and **12.93 – 12.95**.

– For Class H, see **12.86–12.91** and **12.96 – 12.97**.

– For Class J, see **12.85**.

– Classes D, Ei, Eii and I are considered in turn.

12.101 Where an applicant is eligible because he or she falls within one of these classes, members of his or her household who are not eligible are to be disregarded for the purposes of deciding whether the applicant is homeless and whether he or she has a priority need.[221]

---

217 SI 2006/2646 (W 227), reg 3(1)(h). There is no guidance on this Class in the Welsh Code, see English Code, Annex 9, para 7(iii). See **12.86–12.91** and **12.96–12.97**.
218 SI 1987/1971.
219 SI 2006/2646 (W 227), reg 3(1)(i). See Welsh Code, para 11.9(vi). See **12.113–12.115**.
220 SI 2006/2646 (W 227), reg 3(1)(j). See Welsh Code, para 11.9(ii). See **12.85**.
221 HA 1996, s 185(4), in its original form and as amended by Housing and Regeneration Act 2008, s 314, and Sch 15, para 4, in force for applications to local housing authorities made on or after 2 March 2009. See **12.24–12.31**.

Class D:*[222] *a person who left the territory of Montserrat after 1 November 1995 because of the effect on that territory of a volcanic eruption

12.102   This class refers to persons who are subject to immigration control and who left Montserrat for this identified reason. A British citizen, or other person who is not 'subject to immigration control',[223] and who had left Montserrat for this identified reason would fall within HA 1996, s 185(3) and be treated as an 'other person from abroad'.[224] He or she will normally be exempt from the habitual residence test.[225]

12.103   Note that not all those leaving Montserrat are rendered eligible by this class. It does not apply to those who left on or before 1 November 1995, nor to those who left after that date for reasons unconnected with the volcanic eruption. The Regulation emphasises the *location* of the departure: those who were living in Montserrat and left after 1 November 1995. It also emphasises the *reason* for departure: because of the effect of the volcanic eruption.

12.104   A person falling within this class does not need to be habitually resident in the CTA. Nor is his or her nationality relevant.

Class Ei:*[226] *a person who is habitually resident in the CTA and who is a national of a state which has ratified the ECSMA or the ESC and is lawfully present in the UK

12.105   To qualify as eligible under this class, an applicant must be:

- a national of one of the ratifying countries to the ECSMA or ESC;[227] and

- lawfully present in the UK;[228] and

- habitually resident in the CTA.[229]

12.106   For 'habitually resident', see **12.170–12.179**.

---

[222]   SI 2006/2646 (W 227), reg 3(1)(d). See English Code, para 9.10(iv) because there is no guidance on this class in the Welsh Code.

[223]   See **12.64–12.70**. British citizens, Commonwealth citizens with a right of abode in the UK, EEA nationals exercising EU Treaty rights, others exercised rights derived from EEA nationals' exercise of EU Treaty and Irish citizens with a CTA entitlement are not subject to immigration control.

[224]   See **12.117**.

[225]   SI 2006/2646 (W 227), reg 4(2)(d). See **12.206**.

[226]   SI 2006/2646 (W 227), reg 3(1)(e)(i); Welsh Code, para 11.9(iv).

[227]   See Box 3.

[228]   See Box 1 at **12.66**.

[229]   See Box 1 at **12.66**.

Box 3

> States which have *ratified* the ECSMA are: Belgium, Denmark, Estonia,
> France, Germany, Greece, Iceland, Ireland, Italy, Luxembourg, Malta,
> Netherlands, Norway, Portugal, Spain, Sweden, Turkey and the UK. The
> same states have also *signed* the ECSMA.
>
> States which have *ratified* the ESC are: Austria, Belgium, Croatia, Cyprus,
> the Czech Republic, Denmark, Finland, France, Germany, Greece,
> Hungary, Iceland, Ireland, Italy, Latvia, Luxembourg, Malta, Nether-
> lands, Norway, Poland, Portugal, Slovakia, Spain, Sweden, Turkey, the
> former Yugoslav Republic of Macedonia and the UK.[230] These states
> plus Liechtenstein, Romania, Slovenia, Switzerland and the Ukraine have
> also *signed* the ESC.

12.107 A comparison with the list of members of the EEA[231] reveals that the
beneficiaries of this class are nationals of Croatia[232], Turkey, and the former
Yugoslav Republic of Macedonia.[233]

12.108 A person falling within this class must also be 'lawfully present in the
UK'. This means that he or she must have leave to enter or remain in the UK,
or not require it. Asylum-seekers from ECSMA or ESC countries who have
been given 'temporary admission', pending the determination of their claims
for asylum, are considered to be 'lawfully present'.[234]

***Class Eii:[235] a person who is habitually resident in the CTA and who before
3 April 2000 was owed a duty by a housing authority under Housing Act 1985,
Part 3, or HA 1996, Part 7, which is extant, and who is a national of a state
which is a signatory to the ECSMA or the ESC***

12.109 To qualify as eligible under this class, an applicant must be:

- habitually resident in the CTA;[236] and

- a national of a state which has signed the ECSMA or ESC;[237] and

- have been owed a homelessness duty before 3 April 2000;[238] and

---

[230] For up-to-date lists, see www.coe.int/t/dghl/monitoring/socialcharter/Presentation/SignatureRatificationIndex_en.asp.
[231] See Box 2 at **12.67**.
[232] Croatia is due to accede to the EU in 2013.
[233] See also Welsh Code, Annex 4.
[234] *Szoma v Secretary of State for the Department of Work and Pensions* [2005] UKHL 64, [2006] 1 AC 546, HL; and *R (YA) v Secretary of State for Health* [2009] EWCA Civ 225, [2010] 1 WLR 279, CA.
[235] SI 2006/2646 (W 227), reg 3(1)(e)(ii); Welsh Code, para 11.9(v).
[236] See Box 1 at **12.66**.
[237] See Box 3 at **12.106**.
[238] See **12.111**.

- still be owed a homelessness duty.[239]

12.110 For 'habitually resident', see **12.170–12.179**. For states that have signed the ECSMA or ESC, see Box 3 at **12.106**. This class can potentially benefit nationals of Croatia, Turkey, the Ukraine and the former Yugoslav Republic of Macedonia.

12.111 To fall within this class, an applicant must have been owed a homelessness duty before 3 April 2000 and that duty must not have come to an end. In other words, he or she must have both made an application for homelessness assistance and had that application accepted before 3 April 2000, and must still be continuing to receive homelessness assistance under that duty. The duty will be owed either under HA 1996, Part 7 or under its statutory predecessor (Housing Act 1985, Part 3). The only duty likely to be still extant would be the main duty under HA 1996, s 193(2) (or Housing Act 1985, s 65(2)).

12.112 There is no additional requirement that a person should be lawfully present in the UK in order to qualify for this class. Any national of a country signing the ECSMA or ESC can fall within this class, provided he or she fulfils the other conditions.

Class I:[240] a person who is on an income-based jobseeker's allowance or in receipt of income support (with certain exceptions)

12.113 The benefit received must be *income-based jobseeker's allowance* (rather than contribution-based jobseeker's allowance) or *income support*.[241]

12.114 If the applicant is receiving benefit only because he or she has limited leave to enter or remain in the UK, given in accordance with the Immigration Rules, and remittances from abroad have been disrupted so that he or she is temporarily without funds, he or she will not be eligible under this class.[242] A person who has been granted leave to enter or remain in the UK exceptionally for the purposes of the provision of means of subsistence,[243] and is only receiving benefit as a result, will also not be eligible.[244]

12.115 This class benefits some EEA nationals, who do not have a right to reside[245] and are therefore 'persons subject to immigration control',[246] provided that they are receiving the appropriate benefit.

---

[239] See **12.111**.
[240] SI 2006/2646 (W 227), reg 3(1)(b); Welsh Code, para 11.9(vi).
[241] For entitlement to these benefits, see *Welfare Benefits and Tax Credits Handbook 2012–2013* (CPAG, 14th edn, 2012).
[242] SI 2006/2646 (W 227), reg 3(1)(b)(i).
[243] Displaced Persons (Temporary Protection) Regulations 2005, SI 2005/1379, reg 3.
[244] SI 2006/2646 (W 227), reg 3(1)(b)(ii).
[245] See **12.123–12.163**.
[246] *Abdi v Barnet London Borough Council, Ismail v Barnet London Borough Council* [2006] EWCA Civ 383, [2006] HLR 23, CA.

Category Two: other 'persons from abroad'

Overview

12.116 Ordinarily, persons not subject to immigration control would be eligible for homelessness assistance. However, the Secretary of State and Welsh Ministers are permitted to make regulations treating some people who are not subject to immigration control as 'persons from abroad' and therefore ineligible for homelessness assistance. Both have exercised these powers.

Who is, and who is not, a 'person from abroad'?

12.117 In short summary, persons who are not 'subject to immigration control' comprise:[247]

- British citizens;

- Commonwealth citizens who have the right of abode in the UK;

- EEA and Swiss nationals exercising certain Treaty rights;

- people exercising rights derived from EEA or Swiss nationals exercising certain Treaty rights;

- certain people exempt from immigration control such as diplomats, their family members and some military personnel; and

- Irish citizens with a CTA[248] entitlement.

Disqualifying some of those who are not 'persons subject to immigration control'

12.118 In general, the effect of the exercise of the regulation-making powers in both England and Wales has been to produce a situation in which British citizens and Commonwealth citizens with the right of abode in the UK will only be eligible for homelessness assistance if they satisfy the 'habitual residence' test, or fall into one of the classes of people exempt from the test.[249]

12.119 For EEA nationals, their family members and any others with rights derived from an EEA national's exercise of EU Treaty rights, the situation is more complex. In summary:

---

[247] Immigration Act 1971, ss 1–3.
[248] See **12.66,** Box 1.
[249] HA 1996, s 185(3); Allocation of Housing and Homelessness (Eligibility) (England) Regulations 2006, SI 2006/1294, reg 6(1)(a) and (2); Homelessness (Wales) Regulations 2006, SI 2006/2646 (W 227), reg 4(1)(a) and (2).

- if they do not have any rights of residence pursuant to European Union law, they are 'persons subject to immigration control', and fall within the first category of ineligible persons at HA 1996, s 185(2) and the appropriate Regulations;[250]

- in England, if their only right to reside is the initial three-month right of residence, because of their status as jobseekers or as family members of jobseekers, a derivative right of residence derived from being the primary carer of a British citizen,[251] or any similar rights of residence derived from Art 20 of the Treaty on the Functioning of the European Union,[252], they will not be eligible;[253]

- if they have a right of residence pursuant to European Union law, they will either:
  - have to satisfy the habitual residence test, or
  - fall into one of the classes of people exempt from that test so as to be eligible for homelessness assistance.[254]

For 'habitual residence', see **12.170–12.179**.

12.120 It is therefore necessary to consider general rights of residence for EEA nationals and their family members[255] before turning to the relevant homelessness rules for local housing authorities in England and in Wales.[256]

12.121 In addition, EEA nationals and those deriving rights from an EEA national may be subject to the restrictions on the provision of accommodation pending review of an initially adverse decision and accommodation pending appeal.[257]

12.122 If an applicant is eligible under these provisions, any ineligible members of his or her household will be taken into account for the purposes of deciding whether the applicant is homeless and whether he or she has a priority need for applications made for homelessness assistance on or after 2 March

---

[250] *Abdi v Barnet London Borough Council, Ismail v Barnet London Borough Council* [2006] EWCA Civ 383, [2006] HLR 23, CA. See **12.69** and **12.123–12.163** for EU rights of residence.

[251] SI 2006/1003, reg 15A(4A), inserted by SI 2012/2560 and in force from 8 November 2012. See **12.156–12.159**.

[252] See paras **12.162–12.163**.

[253] Allocation of Housing and Homelessness (Eligibility) (England) Regulations 2006 SI 2006/1294, reg 6(1)(b) and (c) as amended. See **12.212–12.226**. In Wales, they are likely to be eligible (Homelessness (Wales) Regulations 2006, SI 2006/2646 (W 277), reg 4(1)(a)), but, if their own right of residence is the three- month initial right of residence, theymay find that they become ineligible when the period of three months ends. See **12.227–12.233**.

[254] Allocation of Housing and Homelessness (Eligibility) (England) Regulations 2006, SI 2006/1294, reg 6(1)(a) and (2). Homelessness (Wales) Regulations 2006, SI 2006/2646 (W 227), reg 4(1)(a) and (2).

[255] See **12.123–12.163**.

[256] For the English rules, see **12.164–12.226**. For the Welsh rules, see **12.227–12.233**.

[257] Nationality, Immigration and Asylum Act 2002, s 54 and Sch 3, paras 1(1)(j) and 5. See **16.47, 16.54, 20.46–20.48** and **20.65–20.73**.

2009.[258] However, if the applicant's household contains a 'restricted person',[259] and it is the presence of that restricted person that has resulted in the local housing authority accepting that a main housing duty[260] (or equivalent duty to applicants threatened with homelessness)[261] is owed, the main housing duty is modified.[262]

European Union rights of residence

12.123 The principal rights of residence are those contained in domestic law by the Immigration (European Economic Area) Regulations 2006, regs 13–15A as amended.[263] Those Regulations are derived from the Freedom of Movement in the European Union Directive.[264] The Court of Justice of the European Union (CJEU) has held that European Union Treaties and Regulations can confer rights to residence directly, whether or not those rights are specifically found in domestic law.[265] The specific rights that the CJEU has recently declared have now been given effect in domestic legislation, to some extent, by the Immigration (European Economic Area) (Amendment) Regulations 2012[266] which inserts the concept of derivative rights into the Immigration (European Economic Area) Regulations 2006.[267] However, the principle remains that EU Treaties and EU Regulations can confer rights to residence directly and there may be other rights of residence which have not yet been considered by legislators or by the CJEU.[268] Nationals of EEA member states who have never exercised any right of freedom of movement under EU Treaty rights are not beneficiaries of rights of free movement under EU Directive 2004/38/EC.[269]

---

[258] HA 1996, s 185(4) and (5), inserted by Housing and Regeneration Act 2008, Sch 15, para 4.
[259] Defined at HA 1996, s 184(7), inserted by Housing and Regeneration Act 2008, Sch 15, para 3. See **12.34**.
[260] HA 1996, s 193(2). See **17.23–17.168**.
[261] HA 1996, s 195(2). See **17.190–17.200**.
[262] See **12.32–12.47**.
[263] SI 2006/1003 amended by Immigration (European Economic Area) (Amendment) Regulations 2012, SI 2012/1547 and by Immigration (European Economic Area) (Amendment) (No 2) Regulations 2012, SI 2012/2560.
[264] Directive 2004/38/EC.
[265] *Baumbast & R v Secretary of State for the Home Department* [2002] ECR I-7091, ECJ; *Harrow London Borough Council v Ibrahim* [2010] EUECJ 310-08, [2010] HLR 31, CJEU and *Teixeira v Lambeth London Borough Council* [2010] EUECJ 48008, [2010] HLR 32, CJEU.
[266] SI 2012/1547. And also by SI 2012/2560, in force from 8 November 2012.
[267] SI 2006/1003 as amended. See **12.142–12.161**.
[268] See **12.162–12.163**.
[269] *McCarthy v SSHD* [2011] EUECJ C-434/09, [2011] All ER (EC) 729, CJEU.

The rights of residence in the Immigration (European Economic Area)
Regulations 2006[270]

12.124 These Regulations confer four[271] rights of residence:

- an initial right of residence;[272]

- an extended right of residence;[273]

- a permanent right of residence;[274] and

- a derivative right of residence.[275]

12.125 Each will be examined in turn. Rights of residence will be most easily
apparent where the person has a registration certificate or residence card issued
by the Secretary of State. However, the registration certificate or residence card
is simply confirmation of the person's right, rather than the conferring of a
right of reside. Where there is no residence certificate or residence card, local
housing authorities will have to decide for themselves whether someone has a
right of residence under EU law.[276]

The 'initial right of residence'[277]

12.126 Regulation 13 of the Immigration (European Economic Area)
Regulations 2006[278] gives all EEA nationals and their family members[279] an
initial right of residence in the UK for a period not exceeding three months,
upon condition that each person has a valid identity card issued by an EEA
member state or a valid passport.

---

[270] SI 2006/1003, as amended.
[271] There is an additional provision for continuation of a right of residence where the Secretary of
State has decided that a person who is entitled to a right of residence should be removed from
the UK, or the issue of his or her residence documentation is refused or revoked.
Regulation 15B of SI 2006/1003 as amended by SI 2012/1547 allows for any previous right of
residence to continue whilst the person appeals against the Secretary of State's decision.
[272] SI 2006/1003, reg 13. See **12.126–12.128**.
[273] SI 2006/1003, reg 14. See **12.129–12.138**.
[274] SI 2006/1003, reg 15. See **12.139–12.141**.
[275] SI 2006/1003 as amended by SI 2012/1547, reg 15A and by SI 2012/2560. See **12.142–12.161**.
[276] *Secretary of State for Work and Pensions v Dias* [2011] EUECJ C-325/09, [2011] 3 CMLR 1103,
CJEU. Indeed, the registration certificate or residence card will only prove the holder's right of
residence at the date of issue of the document, SI 2006/1003, reg 2.
[277] SI 2006/1003, reg 13.
[278] SI 2006/1003.
[279] Including 'family member who has retained the right of residence'. 'Family member' is defined
at SI 2006/1003, reg 7 and 'family member who has retained the right of residence' at
SI 2006/1003, reg 10. See **12.131–12.137**.

12.127   There is an exception where the Secretary of State has decided that a person's removal is justified for the purposes of public policy, public security or public health, or where the person has become an unreasonable burden on the social assistance system of the UK.[280]

12.128   Any person whose sole right of residence in the CTA[281] is as a result of this initial right of residence will not be eligible for homelessness assistance in England.[282] In Wales, a person whose sole right of residence is as a result of the initial right of residence would be eligible if the habitual residence test is also satisfied.[283] In practice, it seems unlikely that such a person would be habitually resident.[284]

The 'extended right of residence'[285]

12.129   'Qualified persons' and their family members[286], including family members who have retained the right of residence,[287] are entitled to an 'extended right of residence' in the UK for so long as they remain qualified persons and/or family members of qualified persons.

12.130   'Qualified person' is defined at reg 6 of the Immigration (European Economic Area) Regulations 2006[288] as being a person who is an EEA national and, in the UK, is:

- a job-seeker;[289] or

- a worker;[290] or

- a self-employed person;[291] or

- a self-sufficient person;[292] or

---

[280]   SI 2006/1003, reg 13(3) and (4).
[281]   See Box 1 at **12.66**.
[282]   Allocation of Housing and Homelessness (Eligibility) (England) Regulations 2006, SI 2006/1294, reg 6(1)(b) and (c). See **12.212–12.226**.
[283]   See **12.179–12.179** for 'habitual residence'. Homelessness (Wales) Regulations 2006, SI 2006/2646 (W 277), reg 4(1)(a); see **12.127–12.232**.
[284]   In any event, once the initial three months have expired, if there is no further right of residence, the person will not be treated as habitually resident and will no longer be eligible (Homelessness (Wales) Regulations 2006, SI 2006/2646 (W 277), reg 4(3)). Any outstanding homelessness duties will come to an end (HA 1996, s 193(6)(a)). See **17.67–17.69**.
[285]   SI 2006/1003, reg 14.
[286]   As defined at SI 2006/1003, reg 7. See **12.131–12.173**
[287]   As defined at SI 2006/1003, reg 10. See **12.135–12.137**.
[288]   SI 2006/1003.
[289]   Defined at SI 2006/1003, reg 6(4).
[290]   Defined at SI 2006/1003, regs 4(1)(a) and 6(2). See **12.182–12.188**.
[291]   Defined at SI 2006/1003, regs 4(1)(b) and 6(3). See **12.189–12.190**.
[292]   Defined at SI 2006/1003, reg 4(1)(c). See footnote 415.

* a student.[293]

12.131 'Family members' are defined at reg 7 of the Immigration (European Economic Area) Regulations 2006[294] as:

* the EEA national's spouse or civil partner;[295]

* any direct descendants of the EEA national, or of his or her spouse or civil partner, who are under 21, or who are dependent on the qualifying person, or his or her spouse or civil partner;[296]

* any dependent direct relatives in the ascending line of the EEA national or his or her spouse or civil partner;[297] and

* any extended family member who has been issued with an EEA family permit, a registration certificate or residence card and continues to satisfy the conditions for the issue of the document.[298]

12.132 There are special rules for students.[299]

12.133 'Family members' thus include children who are under 21, dependent children who are 21 or older, dependent parents, parents-in-law, and parents of a qualifying person's civil partner.[300] So long as children aged 21 or over are 'dependent' on the qualifying person, their ages are irrelevant. Children who are not dependent on the qualifying person, but are nevertheless under 21 (for example, an 18-year-old who is working) also fall within the definition.

12.134 Cohabiting partners, whether of the same sex or different sex, do *not* fall within the definition of 'spouse' or 'civil partner'. For cohabiting partners to be 'family members', they must be:

* the partner of an EEA national; and

---

[293] Defined at SI 2006/1003, reg 4(1)(d). See footnote 416.
[294] SI 2006/1003.
[295] Immigration (European Economic Area) Regulations, SI 2006/1003, reg 7(1)(a). A 'spouse' means a person who is formally contracted to a legal marriage (*Netherlands v Reed 59/85* [1986] ECR 1283, ECJ; *R v Secretary of State for the Home Department ex p Monro-Lopez* [2007] Imm AR 11, QBD; and *Diatta v Land Berlin* [1986] 2 CMLR 164, ECJ). 'Civil partnership' is defined at Civil Partnership Act 2004, s 1. In both cases, the emphasis is on the legal condition, not on whether or not the parties continue to live together. A marriage or civil partnership only ends upon death, divorce, annulment, or dissolution of the civil partnership. A party to a marriage of convenience, or to a civil partnership of convenience, is excluded from the definition (Immigration (European Economic Area) Regulations 2006, SI 2006/1003, reg 2(1)).
[296] Immigration (European Economic Area) Regulations, SI 2006/1003, reg 7(1)(b).
[297] SI 2006/1003, reg 7(1)(c).
[298] SI2006/10033, reg 7(1)(d). For 'extended family member', see **12.135–12.137** and fn 301.
[299] SI 2006/1003, reg 7(2) and (4).
[300] The inclusion of the word 'direct' in the Immigration (European Economic Area) Regulations, SI 2006/1003, suggests that 'family members' cannot be grandchildren or grandparents.

- in a 'durable relationship' with him or her; and

- have been issued with an EEA family permit, registration certificate or residence card.[301]

12.135 Other types of relationship could fall within the definition of 'extended family members'.[302] An 'extended family member' is one of the following:

(1) a relative of an EEA national, or of his or her spouse or civil partner:[303]
   (a) who is residing in a country other than the UK and is dependent upon the EEA national or is a member of his or her household; or
   (b) who was residing in a country other than the UK and was dependent upon the EEA national or was a member of his or her household and is accompanying the EEA national to the UK or wishes to join the EEA national in the UK; or
   (c) who was residing in a country other than the UK and was dependent upon the EEA national or was a member of his or her household and who has joined the EEA national in the UK and continues to be dependent upon the EEA national or to be a member of his or her household; or

(2) a relative of an EEA national or of his or her spouse or civil partner and who, on serious health grounds strictly requires the personal care of the EEA national, his or her spouse or civil partner; or

(3) a relative of an EEA national who would meet the requirements in the immigration rules (other than those relating to entry clearance) for indefinite leave to enter or remain in the UK as a dependent relative of the EEA national were the EEA national a person who is present and settled in the UK; or

(4) a cohabiting partner (other than a civil partner) of an EEA national if he or she can prove that he or she is in a 'durable relationship'[304] with the EEA national.[305]

---

[301] 'Partner' falls within the definition of 'extended family members' if the relationship is a 'durable relationship' (Immigration (European Economic Area) Regulations 2006, SI 2006/1003, reg 8(5)). 'Extended family members' are to be counted as 'family members' if they have been issued with an EEA family permit, registration certificate or residence card which has not ceased to be valid and has not been revoked (SI 2006/1003, reg 7(1)(d) and (3)).

[302] SI 2006/1003, reg 8 as amended by Immigration (European Economic Area) (Amendment) Regulations 2011/1247, reg 1(1) and by Immigration (European Economic Area) (Amendment) (No. 2) Regulations 2012, SI 2012/2560, the latter amendment in force from 8 November 2012.

[303] See SI 2006/1003, reg 2(1) for 'spouse' and for 'civil partner'. See also footnote 295.

[304] See SI 2006/1003, reg 2(1) for 'durable partner'. See also footnote 301.

[305] SI 2006/1003, reg 8.

12.136 If an extended family member of a qualified person or of an EEA national has been issued with an EEA family permit, a registration certificate or a residence card, he or she is to be treated as a 'family member' of a qualified person or of an EEA national for so long as he or she continues to fall within the definition of an 'extended family member' and so long as the documentation has not ceased to be valid or been revoked.[306]

12.137 A person who was a family member of a qualified person, or of an EEA national with the permanent right of residence, and who had resided in the UK in accordance with the Regulations for at least a year immediately before the death of the qualified person or of the EEA national with the permanent right of residence, may have 'retained the right of residence'[307] if the qualified person subsequently dies or ceases to reside in the UK. Similarly, if a person was a spouse or civil partner of a qualified person, and they have divorced or terminated the civil partnership, he or she may have 'retained the right of residence'. If that is the case, the surviving person (or former spouse or civil person) may be entitled to the extended right of residence, even though he or she is not a qualifying person.[308]

12.138 Applying the categories of 'qualified persons' and their 'family members' to eligibility for homelessness assistance, in summary:

- if a person has an extended right of residence solely as a result of being a job-seeker, or of being a family member of a job-seeker, he or she will not be eligible in England,[309] but will be eligible in Wales if he or she satisfies the habitual residence test;[310]

- a person who is a worker will be exempt from the habitual residence test in both England and Wales;[311]

- self-employed persons are exempt from the habitual residence test in England,[312] but will have to satisfy it in Wales;[313]

---

[306] Immigration (European Economic Area) Regulations 2006, SI 2006/1003, reg 7(3). Note the differential treatment of EEA nationals who are students at SI 2006/1003, reg 7(4). Para 9.14 of the English Code suggests that extended family members who have been issued with an EEA family permit, registration certificate or residence card which has not ceased to be valid and has not been revoked will not fall within this exception. This does not seem to be a proper construction of the Regulations and is at odds with the guidance at Annex 12, paras 43 and 45 of the English Code.

[307] SI 2006/1003, reg 10. The provisions are complex and care should be taken to apply the exact wording of the Regulation.

[308] SI 2006/1003, reg 14(3).

[309] Allocation of Housing and Homelessness (Eligibility) (England) Regulations 2006, SI 2006/1294, reg 6(1)(b) and (c). See **12.212–12.226**.

[310] Homelessness (Wales) Regulations 2006, SI 2006/2646 (W 277), reg 4(1)(a) See **12.227–12.233**

[311] Allocation of Housing and Homelessness (Eligibility) (England) Regulations 2006, SI 2006/1294, reg 6(1)(a) and (2)(a) [England] (see **12.182–12.188**); Homelessness (Wales) Regulations 2006, SI 2006/2646 (W 277), reg 4(1)(a) and (2)(a) [Wales], see **12.230**.

[312] Allocation of Housing and Homelessness (Eligibility) (England) Regulations 2006, SI 2006/1294, reg 6(1)(a) and (2)(b). See **12.189–12.190** [England] and **12.227–12.232** [Wales].

- family members of workers and self-employed persons are exempt from the habitual residence test in England[314] but will have to satisfy it in Wales;[315]

- self-sufficient persons and students and their family members will be eligible if they satisfy the habitual residence test.[316]

The 'permanent right of residence'[317]

12.139 The permanent right of residence is defined by Immigration (European Economic Union) Regulations 2006, reg 15(1).[318] There are six categories of people who can acquire 'permanent rights of residence':

(1)   an EEA national who has resided in the UK in accordance with the Regulations for a continuous period of five years;[319]

(2)   a family member of an EEA national who is not himself or herself an EEA national but who has resided in the UK with the EEA national in accordance with the Regulations for a continuous period of five years;[320]

(3)   a worker or self-employed person who has ceased activity;[321]

(4)   a family member of a worker or self-employed person who has ceased activity;[322]

---

[313]   Homelessness (Wales) Regulations 2006, SI 2006/2646 (W 277), reg 4(1)(a). See **12.187–12.192**.

[314]   Allocation of Housing and Homelessness (Eligibility) (England) Regulations 2006, SI 2006/1294, reg 6(1)(a) and (2)(d). See **12.197–12.200**.

[315]   Homelessness (Wales) Regulations 2006, SI 2006/2646 (W 277), reg 4(1)(a). See **12.227–12.232**.

[316]   Allocation of Housing and Homelessness (Eligibility) (England) Regulations 2006, SI 2006/1294, reg 6(1)(a) [England]: see **12.170–12.179**; Homelessness (Wales) Regulations 2006, SI 2006/2646 (W 277), reg 4(1)(a) [Wales]: see **12.227–12.232**. However, note that the definitions of each category require that self-sufficient people and students have sufficient resources not to become a burden on the social assistance system on the UK during the period of residence (SI 2006/1003, reg 4(1)(c) and (d)) and so any person who required homelessness assistance may not fall within these definitions. See fn 415 for further discussion of 'self-sufficient'.

[317]   SI 2006/1003, reg 15(1).

[318]   SI 2006/1003.

[319]   SI 2006/1003, reg 15(1)(a). The five-year period can be at any time, including before the Regulations came into force in 2006, provided that at all times during that five-year period the applicant was residing lawfully, in accordance with European Union law (*SSWP v Lassal* [2010] EUECJ C-162/09 [2011] 1 CMLR 972, CJEU). See also *SSWP v Dias* [2011] EUECJ C-325/09, [2011] 3 CMLR 1103, CJEU. However, lawful residence as a result of a derivative right of residence does not constitute residence for these purposes (SI 2006/1003, reg 15(1A)). This point was recognised in case-law before SI 2006/1003 was amended: see *Okafor v SSHD* [2011] EWCA Civ 499, [2011] 1 WLR 3071, CA. For 'derivative right of residence' see **12.142–12.161**.

[320]   SI 2006/1003, reg 15(1)(b).

[321]   SI 2006/1003, reg 15(1)(c). Note that 'worker or self-employed person who has ceased activity' is defined at SI 2006/1003, reg 5.

[322]   SI 2006/1003, reg 15(1)(d).

(5) a person who was the family member of a worker or self-employed person where:
  (a) the worker or self-employed person has died, and
  (b) the family member resided with him or her immediately before his or her death, and
  (c) the worker or self-employed person had resided continuously in the UK for at least the two years immediately before his or her death, or the death was the result of an accident at work or an occupational disease;[323]

(6) a person who:
  (a) has resided in the UK in accordance with the Regulations for a continuous period of five years, and
  (b) was, at the end of that period, a family member who has retained the right of residence.[324]

For 'family member', see **12.131–12.137**.

12.140 Applying these categories of people to the rules governing eligibility for homelessness assistance in *England*, in summary:

- the third, fourth and fifth categories are exempt from the habitual residence test;[325] and

- the first, second and sixth categories would have to satisfy the habitual residence test.[326]

12.141 In *Wales*, any person who has a permanent right of residence would have to satisfy the habitual residence test.[327] Given their length of residence, any of these people would normally be expected to satisfy that test.

The 'derivative right of residence'[328]

12.142 The 'derivative right of residence' has been inserted into the Immigration (European Economic Area) Regulations 2006[329] by the Immigration (European Economic Area) (Amendment) Regulations 2012[330] and subsequently amended by the Immigration (European Economic Area)

---

[323] SI 2006/1003, reg 15(1)(e).
[324] SI 2006/1003, reg 15(1)(f). For 'a family member who has retained the right of residence', see **12.137**.
[325] Allocation of Housing and Homelessness (Eligibility) (England) Regulations 2006, SI 2006/1294, reg 6(1)(a) and (2)(e): see **12.201–12.205**.
[326] SI 2006/1294, reg 6(1)(a). See **12.170–12.179**.
[327] Homelessness (Wales) Regulations 2006, SI 2006/2646 (W 227), reg 4(1)(a). See **12.227–12.232**.
[328] SI 2006/1003, reg 15A inserted by SI 2012/1547 and applicable from 16 July 2012. These derivative rights of residence were declared as EU Treaty rights of residence by the CJEU in various decisions and have now been incorporated into domestic regulation.
[329] SI 2006/1003
[330] SI 2012/1547, in force from 16 July 2012.

(Amendment) (No 2) Regulations 2012.[331] The rights in reg 15A are based on declarations by the CJEU of various EU Treaty rights which were not identified in the original enactment of SI 2006/1003. There are five different derivative rights of residence.[332] It should be noted that these derivative rights can only be exercised in certain circumstances, such as when a child is in education. If the relevant circumstance comes to an end, and the holder of the derivative right of residence has no claim on any other right of residence under the Regulations or EU law, he or she will no longer have any right to reside.

12.143 Residence in the UK as a result of the exercise of a derivative right of residence does not constitute 'residence' for the purpose of acquiring a permanent right of residence.[333]

12.144 None of these derivative rights require the recipient to be a national of an EEA member state. Indeed, the rights will often be exercised by people who are not nationals of the UK or of any other EEA member state.[334]

12.145 These 'derivative' rights of residence identify rights which, among other outcomes, enable former workers and other formerly qualified persons to exercise their right to extended or permanent residence. They provide that a child who is in education because of the exercise of his or her parent's right of residence as a worker derives a right of residence from his or her parent's right.[335] The child's right – whether derived from his or her parent or because the child has his or her own rights as a self-sufficient person – would be meaningless if his or her primary carer could not also enjoy a right of residence and so the first and third rights are derived from the exercise of the child's right.[336] A primary carer's right of residence would also be meaningless if his or her other children, for whom he or she is the primary carer, did not also have a right of residence.[337]

12.146 A derivative right of residence can be withdrawn or cancelled by the Secretary of State on the grounds of that it is conducive to the public good to do so.[338]

12.147 If a person has one of these five derivative rights of residence, he or she will also be eligible for homelessness assistance in both England and in

---

[331] SI 2012/2560 in force 8 November 2012.
[332] SI 2006/1003, reg 15A(2), (3), (4), (4A) and (5).
[333] SI 2006/1003, reg 15(1A) inserted by SI 2012/1547. For permanent right of residence, see **12.139–12.141**.
[334] They might also be exercised by nationals of EEA member states who have no other rights of residence, see **12.123–12.141**. The derivative right of residence identified in SI 2006/1003, reg 15A(4A), 'the Zambrano right of residence', can only be enjoyed by a national of a non-EEA member state. See **12.156–12.159**.
[335] SI 2006/1003, reg 15A(3) inserted by SI 2012/1547. See **12.151–12.153**.
[336] SI 2006/1003, reg 15A(2) and (4) inserted by SI 2012/1547. See **12.149–12.151** and **12.154–12.155**.
[337] SI 2006/1003, reg 15A(5) inserted by SI 2012/1547, see **12.160–12.161**.
[338] SI 2006/1003, reg 15A(9) inserted by SI 2012/1547.

Wales, if he or she is also habitually resident.[339] However, for applications for homelessness assistance made to a local housing authority in England on or after 8 November 2012, a person who has a derivative right of residence identified in reg 15A(4A) of SI 2006/1003 is excluded from eligibility.[340] This derivative right of residence, whose beneficiaries are excluded from eligibility, is an enactment of the CJEU's decision in *Zambrano v Office national de l'emploi*.[341]

12.148 Neither of the Codes give any guidance on any of these derivative rights, or even on the cases decided by the CJEU which gave rise to the Regulation.[342]

A primary carer of an EEA national child who is self-sufficient[343]

12.149 A person will have a derivative right of residence to reside in the UK if he or she is:

- not an exempt person;[344] and

- the primary carer of an EEA national; and

- the EEA national is:
  - under the age of 18; and
  - is residing in the UK as a self-sufficient person; and
  - would be unable to remain in the UK if the primary carer were required to leave.[345]

12.150 The primary carer need not be a national of an EEA member state but the child must be. A 'primary carer' is defined as a direct relative or legal guardian of the child and either has primary responsibility for the child's care or shares responsibility equally with another person who is not an exempt person.[346] 'Responsibility' requires more than a financial contribution towards care.[347]

---

[339] See **12.170–12.179**.
[340] SI 2006/1294, reg 6(1)(b) and (c) as amended by SI 2012/2588. See **12.156–12.159** for derivative right of residence at SI 2006/1003, reg 15(4A).
[341] C34/09, [2012] QB 265, CJEU.
[342] SI 2006/1003, reg 15A inserted by SI 2012/1547.
[343] SI 2006/1003, reg 15A(2) inserted by SI 2012/1547.
[344] 'Exempt person' is defined as a person who has a right to reside in the UK as a result of any other provision of SI 2006/1003, or who has a right of abode in the UK by virtue of s 2 Immigration Act 1971 or who has indefinite leave to enter or remain in the UK or has been exempted from these provisions: SI 2006/1003, reg 15A(6)(c) inserted by SI 2012/2560, in force from 8 November 2012.
[345] SI 2006/1003, reg 15A(2) inserted by SI 2012/1547. For 'self-sufficient person', see SI 2006/1003, reg 4(1)(c) and fn 415. This right was declared by the ECJ in October 2004 in *Chen v UK* (C-200/02, [2005] All ER (EC) 129, ECJ).
[346] SI 2006/1003, Reg 15A(7) as amended.
[347] SI 2006/1003, reg 15A(7) inserted by SI 2012/1547 and amended by SI 2012/2560. See also the

12.151 This right will cease if:

• the person is no longer the primary carer of the child; or

• the child reaches the age of 18; or

• the child is no longer in the UK or is no longer self-sufficient; or

• the child no longer requires the primary carer in order to remain in the UK.

A child in education in the UK who is a child of an EEA national[348]

12.152 A person will have a derivative right of residence to reside in the UK if he or she is:

• not an exempt person;[349] and

• a child of an EEA national; and

• he or she resided in the UK at a time when his or her EEA national parent was residing in the UK as a worker;[350] and

• he or she was in education in the UK at a time when the EEA national parent was in the UK and is still in education in the UK.[351]

12.153 The child not need be himself or herself a national of an EEA member state but one of his or her parents must be. Furthermore, that parent must have resided in the UK as a worker. The child must have been, at some point, in education at a time when his or her parent was in the UK. There is no requirement that the parent should still be in the UK, or should still be a worker.[352] There is no definition of 'child' in the Regulations and so this right does not necessarily cease when the young person turns 18. However, it will cease when he or she ceases to be in education, whether that occurs before or after his or her 18th birthday. 'Education' does not include nursery education.[353]

---

additional defintions regarding shared care at SI 2006/1003, reg 15A(7A) and (7B) inserted by SI 2012/2560 and in force from 8 November 2012.

[348] SI 2006/1003, reg 15A(3) inserted by SI 2012/1547.

[349] See fn 344 (above).

[350] For 'worker', see SI 2006/1003, reg 4(1)(a) and **12.182–12.188**. Note that the extended definition of 'worker' at reg 6(2) does not apply to this regulation (reg 15A(6)(b)). See **12.184–12.185**.

[351] SI 2006/1003, reg 15A(3) inserted by SI 2012/1547.

[352] Indeed it is likely that the parent is either no longer in the UK, or no longer has any EU rights of residence, as otherwise the child would probably be a family member and be entitled to the same right of residence as his or her parent.

[353] SI 2006/1003, Reg 15A(6)(a). This right was declared by the European Court of Justice in *R (Bidar) v Ealing London Borough Council* C209-03, [2005] QB 812, ECJ.

A primary carer of a child in education who is a child of an EEA national[354]

12.154   The primary carer of a child who has the derivative right described at paras 12.152 – 12.153 will also have a derivative right of residence. That right exists where:

- the primary carer is not an exempt person;[355] and

- the child of an EEA national parent was residing in the UK at a time when the parent was residing here as a worker; and

- the child is in education in the UK and was in education at a time when the EEA national parent was in the UK; and

- the child has a primary carer; and

- the child would be unable to continue to be educated in the UK if his or her primary carer were required to leave.[356]

12.155   For 'primary carer', see **12.150**. For 'education', see **12.153**. This right ends when:

- the person ceases to be the child's primary carer; or

- the child ceases to need a primary carer; or

- the child ceases to be in education.[357]

A primary carer of a British citizen residing in the UK where the British citizen would be unable to reside in the UK or another EEA member state if the primary carer were required to leave[358]

12.156   A person will have a derivative right of residence in the UK if he or she is:

- not an exempt person;[359] and

- the primary carer of a British citizen; and

- the British citizen for whom he or she cares is residing in the UK; and

---

[354] SI 2006/1003, reg 15A(4) inserted by SI 2012/1547.
[355] See fn 344 (above).
[356] SI 2006/1003, reg 15A(4) inserted by SI 2012/1547.
[357] This right was declared by the CJEU in several cases: *Baumbast & R v SSHD* [2002] ECR 1-7091, ECJ; *Ibrahim v Harrow London Borough Council* C-310/08, [2010] HLR 31, CJEU; and *Teixeira v Lambeth London Borough Council*, C4-380/08, [2010] HLR 32, CJEU.
[358] SI 2006/1003, reg 15A(4A) inserted by SI 2012/2560 and in force from 8 November 2012.
[359] See fn 344 (above).

- the British citizen would be unable to reside in the UK or in another EEA member state if his or her primary carer were required to leave.[360]

12.157 For 'primary carer', see **12.150**. This derivative right of residence was recognised by CJEU in the case of *Zambrano v Office national de l'emploi*.[361] It has now been identified in domestic legislation, effective from 8 November 2012.

12.158 The beneficiaries of this derivative right of residence will be adults who are not nationals of any EEA member state. They will be entitled to the derivative right of residence for so long as they are a primary carer of a British citizen child or adult who needs a primary carer. The right will cease if:

- the person ceases to be the primary carer of the British citizen; or

- the British citizen no longer requires the primary carer; or

- either the British citizen or his or her primary carer has a right of residence in another EEA member state.

12.159 Importantly, beneficiaries of this derivative right of residence are excluded from eligibility for homelessness assistance in England.[362] The exclusion applies to applications for homelessness assistance made to a local housing authority in England on or after 8 November 2012.[363] At the date of writing, they are not excluded from eligibility if they make applications for homelessness assistance to a local housing authority in Wales.[364] They are also to be treated as not habitually resident and thus excluded from receiving non-contributory benefits.[365] They are also excluded from eligibility for an allocation of social housing in England but not, at the date of writing, excluded from eligibility for an allocation of social housing in Wales.[366]

---

[360] SI 2006/1003, reg 15A(4A) inserted by SI 2012/2560 and in force from 8 November 2012.

[361] C34/9, [2012] QB 265, CJEU.

[362] SI 2006/1294, reg 6(1)(b) and (c) amended by SI 2012/2588, in force from 8 November 2012. See Letter DCLG to Chief Housing Officers of Local Authorities in England, 17 October 2012, at Appendix 4.

[363] SI 2012/2588, reg 3.

[364] See **12.226–12.233**.

[365] Social Security (Habitual Residence) (Amendment) Regulations 2012, SI 2012/2587, in force 8 November 2012. There will be no exclusion prohibiting the person who has this derivative right of residence from working or from receiving contributory benefits. However, if the person is not in or cannot work (not least because of his or her caring responsibilities), has no entitlement to contributory benefits, and the household is destitute, the recourse is likely to be to adult care or children's services for financial and accommodation assistance. See Chapter 20.

[366] SI 2006/1294, reg 4(1)(b) and (c) as amended by SI 2012/2588 [England]. See **3.117–3.133**. For eligibility for an allocation of social housing in Wales, see **3.134–3.136**.

A child whose primary carer is also a primary carer of a EEA national child who is self-sufficient or of a child in education who is a child of an EEA national[367]

12.160 The child of a person who has a derivative right as a primary carer of a child who is an EEA national and is self-sufficient,[368] or of a child in education who is a child of an EEA national,[369] will also have a derivative right of residence so long as:

- the child is not an exempt person;[370] and

- the child entitled to this derivative right is under the age of 18; and

- his or her primary carer is entitled to the derivative right to reside in the UK by virtue of either reg 15A(2)[371] or (4)[372] SI 2006/1003; and

- the child does not have leave to enter or remain in the UK; and

- if the child was required to leave the UK, his or her primary carer would be prevented from residing in the UK.[373]

12.161 For 'primary carer', see **12.150**. For 'a child who is an EEA national and is self-sufficient', see **12.149**. For 'education', see **12.153**. The child entitled to the derivative right does not have to be related by blood or marriage either to his or her primary carer or to the child from whose right to reside the primary carer's right is derived. However, the primary carer must be the primary carer of both children. This right ends when:

- the child reaches the age of 18; or

- the derivative right of residence of the child's primary carer comes to an end;[374] or

- the child acquires leave to enter or remain in the UK or an EEA right of residence; or

- the child no longer requires his or her primary carer.

---

[367] SI 2006/1003, reg 15A(5), inserted by SI 2012/1547.
[368] SI 2006/1003, reg 15A(2). See **12.149–12.151**.
[369] SI 2006/1003, reg 15A(4). See **12.154–12.155**.
[370] See **fn 344**.
[371] A primary carer of an EEA national child who is self-sufficient: see **12.149–12.151**.
[372] A primary carer of a child in education in the UK who is a child of an EEA national: see **12.154–12.155**.
[373] SI 2006/1003, reg 15A(5) inserted by SI 2012/1547.
[374] See **12.151** and **12.155**.

EU rights of residence not contained in domestic Regulations

12.162   There may be rights of residence, that are not specifically identified in
the Immigration (European Economic Area) Regulations 2006 as amended.[375]
Such rights may potentially arise under a variety of provisions including,
additionally, Arts 20, 21 and 56 of the Treaty on the Functioning of the
European Union.[376] For applications for homelessness assistance made to local
housing authorities in England on or after 8 November 2012, a person who has
a right of residence solely deriving from Art 20 of that Treaty, in a case where
the right to reside arises because a British citizen would otherwise be deprived
of the genuine enjoyment of the substance of his or her rights as an EU citizen,
is excluded from eligibility.[377] At the date of writing, there is no equivalent
exclusion from eligibility for an application for homelessness assistance made
to a local housing authority in Wales.[378] He or she is likely to be eligible if he or
she can satisfy the habitual residence test.[379]

12.163   Whether anyone having any other right of residence would be further
required to satisfy the habitual residence test in order to be eligible for
homelessness assistance may depend, among other things, on whether he or she
derives a right from having been formerly economically active in the UK.[380]

The English rules

The basic rule

12.164   In the Allocation of Housing and Homelessness (Eligibility) (England)
Regulations 2006,[381] in force for applications for homelessness assistance made
on or after 1 June 2006, the Secretary of State has exercised the power to treat
some people who are not subject to immigration control as 'persons from
abroad'.[382] This means that some British citizens, nationals of EEA Member
States, and others who are exempt from immigration control may nevertheless
be denied homelessness assistance on the grounds that they are 'not eligible'.

---

[375]   SI 2006/1003 amended by SI 2012/1547 and SI 2012/2560.
[376]   Article 20 on the rights of nationals of EU member states to be EU citizens; Art 21 on the
        rights of EU citizens to move and reside as EU citizens; Art 56 on the freedom to provide and
        receive services.
[377]   SI 2006/1294, reg 6(1)(b)(iv) and (c)(iv) inserted by SI 2012/2588, see Appendix 2. See also
        12.212–12.226. Letter DCLG to Chief Housing Officers of Local Authorities in England, 17
        October 2012, at Appendix 4.
[378]   See **12.227–12.233**.
[379]   For 'habitual residence', see **12.170–12.179**.
[380]   Allocation of Housing and Homelessness (England) Regulations 2006, SI 2006/1294,
        reg 6(1)(a); Homelessness (Wales) Regulations 2006, SI 2006/2646 (W 277), reg 4(1)(a). See
        12.170–12.179 for 'habitual residence'.
[381]   SI 2006/1294, as amended.
[382]   For applications for homelessness assistance made *before* 1 June 2006, the relevant provisions
        are in reg 4 of the Homelessness (England) Regulations 2000, SI 2000/701, as substituted by
        the Allocation of Housing and Homelessness (Amendment) (England) Regulations 2004,
        SI 2004/1235.

The primary function of these provisions is to confine homelessness assistance to the ordinary residents of the UK, ie those habitually resident here, and to EEA nationals exercising Treaty rights.

12.165 Allocation of Housing and Homelessness (Eligibility) (England) Regulations 2006, reg 6 establishes three classes of people who are to be treated as 'persons from abroad' and therefore *ineligible* for housing assistance despite not being subject to immigration control. They are described in the English Code at paras 9.13–9.20 and Annexes 10–13.

12.166 The *first class*[383] comprises persons who are 'not habitually resident'[384] in the CTA.[385] But that test of habitual residence does *not* apply to:

- EEA nationals who are 'workers';[386] or

- EEA nationals who are self-employed;[387] or

- until 1 May 2011, Accession State workers requiring registration who were registered in accordance with the Accession Regulations 2004[388] ('A8 nationals');[389] or

- until 1 January 2014, Accession State nationals subject to worker authorisation who are authorised in accordance with the Accession Regulations 2006[390] ('A2 nationals');[391] or

- family members of EEA nationals where those EEA nationals are workers, self-employed, Accession State workers requiring registration or Accession State nationals subject to worker authorisation;[392] or

---

[383] Allocation of Housing and Homelessness (Eligibility) (England) Regulations 2006, SI 2006/1294, reg 6(1)(a).

[384] See **12.170–12.181**.

[385] See Box 1 at **12.66**.

[386] Allocation of Housing and Homelessness (Eligibility) (England) Regulations 2006, SI 2006/1294, reg 6(2)(a). See Box 2 at **12.67** for list of EEA countries, and **12.182–12.188** for 'worker'.

[387] SI 2006/1294, reg 6(2)(b). See **12.189–12.190**.

[388] Accession (Immigration and Worker Registration) Regulations 2004, SI 2004/1219.

[389] SI 2006/1294, reg 6(2)(c)(i), substituted by Allocation of Housing and Homelessness (Eligibility) (England) (Amendment) (No 2) Regulations 2006, SI 2006/3340, reg 2(4). See **12.191**. From 1 May 2011 nationals of A8 member states are to be treated in the same way as other nationals of other EEA member states (Accession (Immigration and Worker Registration) (Revocation, Savings and Consequential Provisions) Regulations 2011, SI 2011/544).

[390] Accession (Immigration and Worker Authorisation) Regulations 2006, SI 2006/3317.

[391] SI 2006/1294, reg 6(2)(c)(ii), substituted by SI 2006/3340, reg 2, in force from 1 January 2007 up to and including 31 December 2013 (reg 1(2)(c) Accession (Immigration and Worker Authorisation) Regulations 2006 (SI 2006/3317) as amended). See **12.192–12.196**.

[392] SI 2006/1294, reg 6(2)(d). See **12.197–12.200**.

- EEA nationals who have certain permanent rights to reside in the UK;[393] or

- persons who left the territory of Montserrat after 1 November 1995 because of the effect on that territory of a volcanic eruption;[394] or

- persons who are in the UK as a result of having been deported, expelled or otherwise removed by compulsion of law from another country to the UK;[395] or

- between 25 July 2006 and 31 January 2007 only, people who left Lebanon on or after 12 July 2006 because of the armed conflict there;[396] or

- a person who arrived in Great Britain or after 28 February 2009 but before 18 March 2011 and who, immediately before arriving in Great Britain, had been resident in Zimbabwe and, before leaving Zimbabwe, had accepted an offer made by Her Majesty's Government to assist that person to settle in the UK.[397]

12.167 The *second class* comprises EEA nationals and their family members whose only right to reside in the UK is derived from their status as job-seekers, as family members of job-seekers, from their initial right to reside in the UK for a period not exceeding three months, by having a derivative right to reside in the UK as the primary carer of a British citizen, or by having a right to reside derived from Art 20 of the Treaty on the Functioning of the European Union.[398]

12.168 The *third class* comprises EEA nationals and their family members whose only right to reside in the rest of the CTA (Channel Islands, Isle of Man or the Republic of Ireland) is derived from their status as job-seekers, as family members of job-seekers, from their initial right to reside in the UK for a period not exceeding three months, by having a derivative right to reside in the CTA as the primary carer of an Irish or British citizen, or by having a right to reside derived from Art 20 of the Treaty on the Functioning of the European Union.[399]

12.169 Each of the three classes will be examined in turn.

---

[393] SI 2006/1294, reg 6(2)(e). See **12.201–12.205**.
[394] SI 2006/1294, reg 6(2)(f). See **12.206**.
[395] SI 2006/1294, reg 6(2)(g). See **12.207**.
[396] SI 2006/1294, reg 6(2)(h), inserted by Allocation of Housing and Homelessness (Eligibility) (England) (Amendment) Regulations 2006, SI 2006/2007, reg 2(8). See **12.208–12.209**.
[397] SI 2006/1294, reg 6(2)(i), inserted by the Allocation of Housing and Homelessness (Eligibility) (England) (Amendment) Regulations 2009, SI 2009/358, for applications made on or after 18 March 2009. See **12.210–12.211**.
[398] SI 2006/1294, reg 6(1)(b) as amended by SI 2012/2588. See **12.212–12.221**.
[399] SI 2006/1294, reg 6(1)(c) as amended by SI 2012/2588. See **12.222–12.226**.

The first class: not habitually resident[400]

12.170 'Habitual residence' is not a term of reference to someone's immigration status. A person may be a British citizen, but if he or she is not habitually resident in the CTA,[401] he or she will not be eligible. Nor is the term 'habitual residence' defined in either HA 1996 or in the Regulations.[402] It is a question of fact for the local housing authority to decide. Happily, there is some guidance in the English Code of Guidance.[403]

12.171 A person who is not habitually resident will also not be entitled to non-contributory social security benefits. If the person is receiving one of those social security benefits, it must follow that the Department for Work and Pensions (DWP) has determined that he or she is habitually resident.[404]

12.172 There are two aspects required to be present in order to constitute habitual residence:

(1) a settled purpose of establishing residence in one of the territories of the CTA;[405] and

(2) an appreciable period of such residence.

12.173 Whether each aspect is satisfied is a question of fact for the local housing authority to decide. The English Code advises that normally, if someone has lived in one of the territories of the CTA for two years continuously prior to his or her application for homelessness assistance, he or she should be considered to be habitually resident without further inquiry.[406] However, that should not be taken as meaning that a person cannot be habitually resident if he or she has not lived in one of the territories of the CTA for two years. In *R (Paul-Coker) v Southwark London Borough Council*,[407] a number of instances where people had been resident for periods of time that were shorter than two years, but had been sufficient to constitute 'an appreciable period', were cited to the judge. He said: '[i]t is therefore clear that what constitutes an appreciable period of time for these purposes will vary from case to case and will depend on the facts of the individual case'.[408]

---

[400] SI 2006/1294, reg 6(1)(a).
[401] See Box 1 at **12.66**.
[402] SI 2006/1294.
[403] English Code, paras 9.3(i) and 9.15–9.18 and Annex 10.
[404] A person who has a derivative right of residence contained at SI 2006/1003, reg 15A(4A) (the 'Zambrano' right of residence) is treated as not habitually resident for the purposes of entitlement to income support, jobseeker's allowance, state pension credit, housing benefit and council tax benefit (SI 2012/ 2587, in force 8 November 2012). See fn 365 (above).
[405] For 'CTA', see **12.66**, Box 1.
[406] English Code, para 9.16.
[407] [2006] EWHC 497 (Admin), [2006] HLR 32, Admin Ct.
[408] *R (Paul-Coker) v Southwark London Borough Council* [2006] EWHC 497 (Admin), [2006] HLR 32, Admin Ct, Forbes J at [22].

12.174 Establishing a 'settled purpose' will obviously involve consideration of an applicant's subjective intentions and motivations. Someone in stable employment may be more likely to be able to establish his or her 'settled purpose' to be habitually resident than someone in transitory employment, or dependent on benefit. However, local housing authorities must be careful not to give too much weight to an applicant's lack of finances and not enough weight to other factors such as the applicant's nationality, ties with the UK, and future intentions.[409]

12.175 What constitutes an 'appreciable period of residence' likewise varies according to the circumstances of each individual's case. If a former British resident returns to the UK after living and working abroad, she or he may be habitually resident from the first day of his or her return.[410] When someone is coming to live in the UK for the first time, there must be an appreciable period of residence before habitual residence is obtained. To determine how long that period of residence should be in any particular case, local housing authorities should consider all the circumstances, including:

- whether the person is seeking to bring any family members to the CTA;

- whether he or she has brought his or her personal property and possessions to the CTA;

- whether he or she has done everything necessary to establish a residence before coming;

- whether he or she has a right of abode; and

- what 'durable ties' there are with the CTA.[411]

12.176 In *R (Paul-Coker) v Southwark London Borough Council*,[412] a local housing authority was wrong in law to have directed itself that an applicant had to have been resident for six months before she could be considered to be habitually resident. It had also been wrong not to have taken into account that the applicant had, in fact, been resident for seven months, had given birth to a child who was a British national, had spent her formative years in the UK and had returned for extended holidays in the three years preceding her arrival, that she had travelled to the UK on a one-way ticket and had family and friends in the UK. All of those factors should have been considered.

---

[409] *Barnet London Borough Council v Shah* [1983] 2 AC 309, HL; and *Olokunboro v Croydon London Borough Council* (2003) February *Legal Action*, p 37, Croydon County Court.

[410] *Swaddling v Adjudication Officer* [1999] All ER (EC) 217 ECJ; and see CIS/1304/1997 and CJSA/5394/1998; and English Code, para 9.17 and Annex 10, paras 7–8.

[411] *Nessa v Chief Adjudication Officer* [1999] 1 WLR 1937, HL. English Code, Annex 10, paras 9–20.

[412] [2006] EWHC 497 (Admin), [2006] HLR 32, Admin Ct.

12.177 Some EEA nationals, and their family members, are not exempted from the habitual residence test,[413] nor are they prescribed as 'ineligible' by virtue of falling within the second or third classes.[414] For those people to be eligible, they will have to satisfy the habitual residence test.

12.178 Types of EEA nationals who may be required to satisfy the habitual residence test include:

- an EEA national who is a self-sufficient person or a family member of an EEA national who is a self-sufficient person;[415] or

- an EEA national who is a student or a family member of an EEA national who is a student;[416]or

- an EEA national who has resided in the UK in accordance with the Immigration (European Economic Area) Regulations[417] for a continuous period of five years;[418] or

---

[413] Allocation of Housing and Homelessness (Eligibility) (England) Regulations 2006, SI 2006/1294, reg 6(2). See **12.166** and **12.180–12.211**.

[414] SI 2006/1294, reg 6(1)(b) and (c). See **12.212–12.226**.

[415] A 'self-sufficient person' is defined at SI 2006/1003, reg 4(1)(c). Part of that definition is that the person has 'sufficient resources not to become a burden on the social assistance system of the United Kingdom during his period of residence'. The same test applies to any family members of a self-sufficient person (SI 2006/1003, reg 4(2)). However, EU law has made it clear that the test is: 'as long as the beneficiaries of the right of residence do not become an unreasonable burden on the social assistance system of the host Member State they should not be expelled. . . .The host Member State should examine whether it is a case of temporary difficulties and take into account the duration of residence, the personal circumstances and the amount of aid granted in order to consider whether the beneficiary has become an unreasonable burden on its social assistance system and to proceed to his expulsion' (Directive 2004/38/EC(16)). See also para 2.3.1 of *Commission of the European Communities Communication to the European Parliament and the Council on guidance for better transposition and application of Directive 2004/38/EC on the right of citizens of the Union and their family members to move and reside freely within the territory of the Member States,* COM\2009\0313 final and SI 2006/1003, reg 4(4). In other words, a self-sufficient person and/or his or her family member who has a temporary need for homelessness assistance might not be 'an unreasonable burden' on the social assistance system of the UK and so can make an application for homelessness assistance whilst still retaining his or her status as a self-sufficient person, or as a family member of a self-sufficient person and therefore as a qualified person.

[416] 'Student' is defined at SI 2006/1003, reg 4(1)(d) and 'family member' of a student at SI 2006/1003, reg 4((3). Part of the test includes a requirement that the student has assured the Secretary of State that he or she has sufficient resources not to become a burden on the social assistance system of the UK during his or her period of residence (and has provided the same assurance in relation to any family members). As with self-sufficient persons (see **fn 415**) the test is whether or not someone is 'an unreasonable burden' on the social assistance system of the UK and so a student, or any family members of a student, could retain his or her status as a student and a qualified person whilst also having a temporary need for homelessness assistance.

[417] SI 2006/1003. See Appendix 2 of this book.

[418] Entitled to a permanent right of residence by reg 15(1)(a) of the Immigration (European Economic Area) Regulations 2006, SI 2006/1003. See **12.139**(1).

- a person who is not an EEA national but is a family member of an EEA national, the family member having resided in the UK in accordance with the Immigration (European Economic Area) Regulations for a continuous period of five years;[419] or

- a person who has resided in the UK for a continuous period of five years and was, at the end of that period, a family member of an EEA national who had retained the right of residence;[420] or

- a person who has one of four derivative rights of residence[421] and his or her family members;[422] or

- potentially, any person who has a right to reside that falls outside the Immigration (European Economic Area) Regulations.[423]

12.179   Given the length of their residence, few of those people should have any difficulty in satisfying the habitual residence test.

Exemptions from the habitual residence test

12.180   As already noted,[424] the following people are eligible for assistance even if they are *not habitually resident*:

---

[419] Entitled to a permanent right of residence by reg 15(1)(b) of the Immigration (European Economic Area) Regulations 2006, SI 2006/1003. See **12.139(2)**. For 'family member', see **12.131–12.137**.

[420] Entitled to a permanent right of residence by reg 15(1)(f) of the Immigration (European Economic Area) Regulations 2006, SI 2006/1003. See **12.139(6)**. For 'family member', see **12.131–12.137**. For 'family member who has retained the right of residence', see Immigration (European Economic Area) Regulations 2006, SI 2006/1003, reg 10 and **12.137**.

[421] SI 2006/1003, reg 15A inserted by SI 2012/1547, see **12.142–12.161**. The four rights of residence are at SI 2006/1003, reg 15A(2) (see **12.149–12.151**), (3) (see **12.152–12.153**), (4) (see **12.154–12.155**) and (5) (see **12.160–12.161**). People entitled to the fifth derivative right of residence, at SI 2006/1003, reg 15A(4A) are specifically excluded from eligibility for homelessness assistance in England, but not in Wales. See **12.156–12.159** for the derivative right of residence, **12.212–12.226** for exclusion from eligibility in England; **12.227–12.233** for Wales. See also letter DCLG to Chief Housing Officers of Local Authorities in England, 17 October 2012, at Appendix 4. For 'family members' see **12.131–12.137**.

[422] There is an argument that the habitual residence test should not be applied to a child in education in the UK who is the child of an EEA national (SI 2006/1003, reg 15A(3) (see **12.152–12.153**)) or to a person who is the primary carer of a child in education in the UK who is the child of an EEA national (SI 2006/1003, reg 15A(4) (see **12.154–12.155**)). This is because those rights derive from an EEA national who is or has exercised his or her rights of freedom of movement as a worker or self-employed person and the habitual residence test should not be applied to diminish those rights.

[423] See **12.162–12.163**. Unless that right to reside is derived from Art 20 of the Treaty on the Functioning of the European Union and arises because a British citizen would otherwise be deprived of the genuine enjoyment of the substance of his or her rights as an EU citizen (SI 2006/1294, reg 6(1)(b)(iv) and (c) (iv), see **12.212–12.226**). If that is the case, the beneficiary of that right of residence will not be eligible for homelessness assistance in England, but, at the date of writing, may be eligible in Wales. See also letter DCLG to Chief Housing Officers of Local Authorities in England, 17 October 2012, at Appendix 4.

[424] See **12.166**.

- an EEA national who is a 'worker';[425] or

- an EEA national who is self-employed;[426] or

- until 1 May 2011, a person who is an Accession State worker requiring registration who was registered in accordance with the Accession Regulations 2004[427] ('an A8 national');[428] or

- until 1 January 2014, a person who is an Accession State national subject to worker authorisation who is authorised in accordance with the Accession Regulations 2006[429]('an A2 national');[430] or

- a family member of an EEA national who is a worker, a self-employed person, an Accession State worker requiring registration who is registered in accordance with the Accession Regulations 2004,[431] or an Accession State national subject to worker authorisation who is authorised in accordance with the Accession Regulations 2006;[432] or

- a person who has one of certain permanent rights to reside in the UK;[433] or

- a person who left the territory of Montserrat after 1 November 1995 because of the effect on that territory of a volcanic eruption;[434] or

- a person who is in the UK as a result of having been deported, expelled or otherwise removed by compulsion of law from another country to the UK;[435] or

- between 25 July 2006 and 31 January 2007 only, a person who left Lebanon on or after 12 July 2006 because of the armed conflict there;[436] or

---

[425] Allocation of Housing and Homelessness (Eligibility) (England) Regulations 2006, SI 2006/1294, reg 6(2)(a). See **12.182–12.188**.
[426] SI 2006/1294, reg 6(2)(b). See **12.189–12.190**.
[427] Accession (Immigration and Worker Registration) Regulations 2004, SI 2004/1219.
[428] SI 2006/1294, reg 6(2)(c)(i), substituted by Allocation of Housing and Homelessness (Eligibility) (England) (Amendment) (No 2) Regulations 2006, SI 2006/3340, reg 2. See **12.191**.
[429] Accession (Immigration and Worker Authorisation) Regulations 2006, SI 2006/3317.
[430] SI 2006/1294, reg 6(2)(c)(ii), substituted by Allocation of Housing and Homelessness (Eligibility) (England) (Amendment) (No 2) Regulations 2006, SI 2006/3340, reg 2(4), in force from 1 January 2007. See **12.192–12.196**.
[431] SI 2006/1219.
[432] SI 2006/1294, reg 6(2)(d). Accession (Immigration and Worker Registration) Regulations 2006, SI 2006/3317. See **12.197–12.200**.
[433] SI 2006/1294, reg 6(2)(e). See **12.201–12.205**.
[434] SI 2006/1294, reg 6(2)(f). See **12.206**.
[435] SI 2006/1294, reg 6(2)(g). See **12.207**.
[436] SI 2006/1294, reg 6(2)(h), inserted by Allocation of Housing and Homelessness (Eligibility) (England) (Amendment) Regulations 2006, SI 2006/2007, reg 2(8). See **12.208–12.209**.

- a person who arrived in Great Britain on or after 28 February 2009 but before 18 March 2011 and who, immediately before arriving in Great Britain, had been resident in Zimbabwe and, before leaving Zimbabwe, had accepted an offer made by Her Majesty's Government to assist that person to settle in the UK.[437]

12.181 Most of these categories refer to those persons exercising rights of freedom of movement enjoyed under European Union law and contained in the Immigration (European Economic Area) Regulations 2006,[438] which are the current regulations transposing European Union freedom of movement legislation into domestic law. Each of them will be considered in turn. See **12.123–12.163** for consideration of the different European Union 'rights to reside'.

EEA nationals who are workers[439]

12.182 In order to qualify as a 'worker' under this provision, the person must first be a national of an EEA Member State.[440] The term 'worker' is not defined in HA 1996 or regulations and nor is it exhaustively defined in European Union legislation. The Court of Justice of the European Union has emphasised that a narrow approach should *not* be taken:

> '[I]t is settled case law that the concept of worker has a specific Community meaning and must not be interpreted narrowly. It must be defined in accordance with objective criteria which distinguish an employment relationship by reference to the rights and duties of the person concerned. In order to be treated as a worker, a person must pursue an activity which is genuine and effective, to the exclusion of activities on such a small scale as to be regarded as purely marginal and ancillary. The essential feature of an employment relationship is that for a certain period of time a person performs services for and under the direction of another person in return for which he receives remuneration. By contrast, neither the *sui generis* nature of the employment relationship under national law, nor the level of productivity of the person concerned, the origin of the funds from which the remuneration is paid or the limited amount of the remuneration can have any consequence in regard to whether the person is a worker for the purposes of Community law …'[441]

12.183 A person will be a 'worker'[442] if he or she is actually working in the UK, whether full- or part-time. Any genuine and effective work should count, so long as it is not so irregular and/or so limited that it is a purely marginal and ancillary activity.[443]

---

[437] SI 2006/1294, reg 6(2)(i), inserted by Allocation of Housing and Homelessness (Eligibility) (England) (Amendment) Regulations 2009, SI 2009/358, for applications made on or after 18 March 2009. See **12.210–12.211**.

[438] SI 2006/1003, in force from 30 April 2006, as amended. See Appendix 2.

[439] Allocation of Housing and Homelessness (Eligibility) (England) Regulations 2006, SI 2006/1294, reg 6(2)(a). English Code, para 9.14(a), and Annex 12, paras 15–19.

[440] See Box 2 at **12.67**.

[441] *Kurz* [2002] ECR I-10691, para 32.

[442] Immigration (European Economic Area) Regulations 2006, SI 2006/1003, reg 4(a). 'Worker' is

12.184 A person will retain the status of a worker and so still be treated as a worker for the purposes of these Regulations[444] if he or she:

- has worked in the UK (at any time and even for a short period) but has become temporarily incapable of work as a result of an illness or accident;[445] or

- has worked in the UK for one year or more before becoming involuntarily unemployed and is registered as a jobseeker;[446] or

- has worked in the UK for less than one year before becoming involuntarily unemployed and is registered as a jobseeker and has been unemployed for no more than six months;[447] or

- has worked in the UK for less than one year before becoming involuntarily unemployed and is registered as a jobseeker and has a genuine chance of being engaged;[448] or

- has worked in the UK (at any time and even for a short period), but has become involuntarily unemployed and has embarked on vocational training;[449] or

---

defined by Regulation (EEC) No 1612/68 of the Council of 15 October 1968 on freedom of movement for workers within the Community, or Regulation (EEC) No 1251/70 of the Commission of 29 June 1970 on the right of workers to remain in the territory of a member state after having been employed in that State. English Code, Annex 12, paras 15–18.

[443] *Levin 53/81* [1982] ECR 1035; *Kempf Case 139/85* [1986] ECR 1741; *Raulin Case C-357/89* [1992] ECR 1027.

[444] Immigration (European Economic Area) Regulations 2006, SI 2006/100, reg 6(2) based on *Scrivner Case 122/84* [1985] ECR 1027. Note that A8 workers requiring registration who had not completed 12 months' registered employment before 1 May 2011 do not retain worker status under this regulation on account of work done before that date. Any work which he or she does after 1 May 2011 will count for these purposes (Immigration (European Economic Area) Regulations 2006, SI 2006/1003, reg 7A inserted by Accession (Immigration and Worker Registration) (Revocation, Savings and Consequential Provisions) Regulations 2011, SI 2011/544). Note also that this extended definition of 'worker' does not apply where a person is claiming a derivative right of residence, derived from his or her parent being a worker (SI 2006/1003, reg 15A(3) (see **12.152–12.153**)). An EEA national who ceases working because of pregnancy does not retain the status of worker (*St Prix v SSWP* [2011] EWCA Civ 806, CA).

[445] SI 2006/1003, reg 6(2)(a). See English Code, Annex 12 para 19(a).

[446] Immigration (European Economic Area) Regulations 2006, SI 2006/1003, reg 6(2) (b)(i). See English Code, Annex 12, para 19(b).

[447] SI 2006/1003, reg 6(2)(b)(ii). See English Code, Annex 12, para 19(b).

[448] SI 2006/1003, reg 6(2)(b)(iii). See English Code, Annex 12, para 19(b).

[449] *Lair Case 39/86* [1988] ECR 3161; and *Raulin Case C-357/89* [1992] ECR 1027. Immigration (European Economic Area) Regulations 2006, SI 2006/1003, reg 6(2)(c). English Code, Annex 12, para 19(c).

- has worked in the UK (at any time and even for a short period) and voluntarily given up work in the UK to take up vocational training related to his or her previous job.[450]

12.185 The Court of Appeal has held, in relation to both workers and self-employed persons,[451] that if someone's illness means that he or she is unlikely to be able to work in the foreseeable future, there are no realistic prospects of him or her being able to return to work and he or she is no longer a worker or a self-employed person.[452]

12.186 Attempts to argue that people who have never worked in the UK are, nevertheless, 'workers' for the purpose of entitlement to job-seeker's allowance and Children Act assistance have failed.[453] A job-seeker who has never worked is not, therefore a 'worker' and, in any event, is specifically excluded from eligibility because he or she would fall into the second or third classes of people who are not eligible.[454] Students and au pairs, working part-time, have been held by the Court of Appeal and the Court of Justice of the European Union to be 'workers'.[455]

12.187 The question, as to whether an applicant is or is not a worker, is a question of fact for the local housing authority. In *R (Mohamed) v Harrow London Borough Council*,[456] it was held that the local housing authority had not made any errors of law in concluding that a woman who had worked part-time for three months, finishing a year before her application for homelessness assistance, spoke little or no English, had two small children to look after and had not registered with an employment agency was not and had not retained the status of being a 'worker'. In *Barry v Southwark London Borough Council*,[457] the local housing authority was wrong to decide that an applicant was not a 'worker' during a two-week period when he was employed by Group 4 Securicor for stewarding duties at the Wimbledon All England Tennis Championships. The work done was of economic value, there were PAYE deductions from his pay and the services provided by him to his employer were real and actual, and not merely marginal and ancillary.[458] In the case of a part-time worker earning a low income, the local housing authority made an error of law when it applied a test of whether the work produced enough

---

[450] *Raulin Case C-357/89* [1992] ECR 1027. Immigration (European Economic Area) Regulations 2006, SI 2006/1003, reg 6(2)(d). English Code, Annex 12, para 19(d).

[451] See **12.189–12.190** for 'self-employed persons'.

[452] *Konodyba v Kensington & Chelsea Royal London Borough Council* [2012] EWCA Civ 982, (2012) September *Legal Action*, p 29, CA.

[453] *Collins v Secretary of State for Work and Pensions, C-138/02 ECJ, 23 March 2004*; and *Ali v SSHD* [2006] EWCA Civ 484, [2006] 3 CMLR 326, [2006] ELR 423, CA.

[454] Allocation of Housing and Homelessness (Eligibility) (England) Regulations 2006, SI 2006/1294, reg 6(1)(b) and (c). See **12.212–12.226**.

[455] *Ozturk v Secretary of State for the Home Department* [2006] EWCA Civ 541, [2007] 1 WLR 508, CA, C-294/06, judgment 24 January 2008, ECJ.

[456] [2005] EWHC 3194 (Admin), [2006] HLR 18, Admin Ct.

[457] [2008] EWCA Civ 1440, [2009] HLR 30, CA.

[458] Arden LJ at [23].

income to cover 'reasonable living expenses'. The question of whether work is 'effective' is to be looked at from the view of the value of the work to the employer and not to the employee.[459]

12.188 A2 nationals will not be 'workers' if they are Accession State nationals subject to worker authorisation.[460] If they no longer fall into this class, for example because they have been working for more than 12 months, or because they did not need to register as an Accession State national subject to worker authorisation, they are treated the same as all other EEA nationals who are workers.

EEA nationals who are self-employed persons[461]

12.189 A 'self-employed person' is defined as 'a person who establishes himself in order to pursue activity as a self-employed person in accordance with Art 43 of the Treaty establishing the European Community'.[462] Article 43 refers to 'freedom of establishment', which is itself defined as 'the right to take up and pursue activities as self-employed persons and to set up and manage undertakings'. Self-employment is not confined to periods of actual work; a person remains self-employed if he or she is engaged on administrative, marketing or other tasks required to run or promote his or her business.[463]

12.190 A person remains a self-employed person if he or she is temporarily unable to pursue his or her self-employment activity as a result of illness or accident,[464] but there must be a likelihood that he or she will be able to work in the foreseeable future.[465]

'Accession State workers requiring registration' or 'A8 nationals'[466]

12.191 This category is largely academic. From 1 May 2011, nationals of A8 member states are to be treated in the same way as nationals of other EEA member states.[467] The only difference is that a national of an A8 member state

---

[459] *Amin v Brent London Borough Council* (2011) August *Legal Action*, p 41, Wandsworth County Court.
[460] See **12.192–12.196**.
[461] Allocation of Housing and Homelessness (Eligibility) (England) Regulations 2006, SI 2006/1294, reg 6(2)(b). See English Code, para 9.14(b) and Annex 12, paras 26–30.
[462] Immigration (European Economic Area) Regulations 2006, SI 2006/1003, reg 4(1)(b). The Treaty referred to is the Treaty of Rome (1957).
[463] *Secretary of State for Work and Pensions v JS (IS)* [2010] UKUT 240 (AAC), (2011) March *Legal Action*, p 21, UT.
[464] SI 2006/1003, reg 6(3). See English Code, Annex 12, paras 26–30.
[465] *Konodyba v Kensington & Chelsea Royal London Borough Council* [2012] EWCA Civ 982, (2012) September *Legal Action*, p 29, CA.
[466] Allocation of Housing and Homelessness (Eligibility) (England) Regulations 2006, SI 2006/1294, reg 6(2)(c)(i), substituted by Allocation of Housing and Homelessness (Eligibility) (England) (Amendment) (No 2) Regulations 2006, SI 2006/3340, reg 2(4). See English Code, para 9.14(c), Annex 10, paras 20–25 and Annex 13.
[467] Accession (Immigration and Worker Registration) (Revocation, Savings and Consequential Provisions) Regulations 2011, SI 2011/544. Previously an 'Accession State worker requiring registration' was defined in the Accession (Immigration and Worker Registration)

cannot rely on periods worked before 1 May 2011 for the purposes of determining whether he or she has retained worker status.[468]

'Accession State nationals subject to worker authorisation' or 'A2 nationals'[469]

12.192　An 'Accession State national requiring worker authorisation' is defined in the Accession (Immigration and Worker Authorisation) Regulations[470] as a national of one of the A2 countries: ie of Bulgaria or Romania.[471]

12.193　An Accession State national subject to worker authorisation and authorised in accordance with the Accession Regulations 2006[472] will be exempt from the habitual residence test and thus eligible for homelessness assistance during such time as he or she holds an Accession Worker authorisation document and is working in accordance with the conditions set out in that document.[473] The document normally issued is an Accession worker authorisation card.[474] An A2 national who is a job-seeker will not have any right of residence and will not be eligible for homelessness assistance.[475]

12.194　After 31 December 2013, A2 nationals are to be treated in the same way as other EEA nationals.[476]

12.195　Not all nationals of Bulgaria or Romania fall within the definition of 'an Accession State national subject to worker authorisation'. They should be treated in the same way as other EEA nationals if they fall into one of these categories:

Regulations 2004, SI 2004/1219, as a national of one of the A8 countries who was working in the UK at some time between 1 May 2004 and 30 April 2011. Once an Accession State worker requiring registration had legally worked for a period of 12 months without interruption, he or she was no longer an 'Accession State worker requiring registration', and was treated in the same way as any other EEA national who is a worker.

[468]　Immigration (European Economic Area) Regulations 2006, SI 2006/1003, reg 7A inserted by Accession (Immigration and Worker Registration) (Revocation, Savings and Consequential Provisions) Regulations 2011, SI 2011/544. For 'retained worker status' see **12.184**.

[469]　SI 2006/1294, reg 6(2)(c)(ii), substituted by Allocation of Housing and Homelessness (Eligibility) (England) (Amendment) (No 2) Regulations 2006, SI 2006/3340, reg 2(4), in force from 1 January 2007 until 31 December 2013 inclusive.

[470]　SI 2006/3317, reg 2(1).

[471]　See Box 2 at **12.67**.

[472]　Accession (Immigration and Worker Authorisation) Regulations 2006, SI 2006/3317.

[473]　SI 2006/3317, reg 6(2).

[474]　SI 2006/3317, reg 7.

[475]　SI 2006/3317, reg 6(2). He or she will be a 'person subject to immigration control' and therefore fall within the first category of persons from abroad at HA 1996, s 185(2). See **12.119**. He or she is unlikely to fall within Classes A–E of Allocation of Housing and Homelessness (Eligibility) (England) Regulations 2006, SI 2006/1294, reg 5(1) and therefore unlikely to be eligible. See **12.72**. However, an A2 national who holds a registration certificate to the effect that he or she is a highly skilled person and has unconditional access to the labour market and who is looking for work continues to be treated as a 'highly skilled person' and not as a 'job-seeker', see **12.195**.

[476]　SI 2006/3317, reg 1(2)(c) and reg 6(1) as amended by Accession (Immigration and Worker Authorisation) (Amendment) Regulations 2011, SI 2011/2816.

- a person who, on 31 December 2006, had leave to enter or remain without any restriction on taking employment;[477] or

- a person who has legally (with leave to remain) worked in the UK without interruption for a period of 12 months;[478] or

- a person also holding nationality of another EEA Member State (other than Bulgaria or Romania) or British nationality;[479] or

- a spouse or civil partner of a UK national or of a person settled in the UK;[480] or

- a diplomat or family member of a diplomat;[481] or

- a person who has a permanent right of residence pursuant to Immigration (European Economic Area) Regulations 2006, reg 15;[482] or

- a family member of an EEA national who has the right to reside in the UK, other than EEA nationals who are Accession State nationals subject to worker authorisation or are family members of such an Accession State national;[483] or

- a family member of an A2 national who has the right to reside in the UK by virtue of being a self-employed person, or a self-sufficient person or a student;[484] or

- a person who holds a registration certificate to the effect that he or she is a highly skilled person and has unconditional access to the labour market;[485] or

- a person who is in the UK as a student, who holds a registration certificate that includes a statement that he or she is a student who has access to the UK labour market, and who is working not more than 20

---

[477] SI 2006/3317, reg 2(2), as substituted by the Accession (Immigration and Worker Authorisation) (Amendment) Regulations 2007, SI 2007/475, reg 2(2).

[478] SI 2006/3317, reg 2(3) and (4). This is the case whether the 12-month period falls wholly before 31 December 2006, partly before and partly after 31 December 2006, or wholly after 31 December 2006.

[479] SI 2006/3317, reg 2(5).

[480] SI 2006/3317, reg 2(6).

[481] SI 2006/3317, reg 2(6A).

[482] SI 2006/3317, reg 2(7). See **12.139–12.141**.

[483] SI 2006/3317, reg 2(8)(a), as substituted by the Accession (Immigration and Worker Authorisation) (Amendment) Regulations 2007, SI 2007/475, reg 2(2). For 'family member', see **12.131–12.137**. For 'right to reside', see **12.123–12.163**.

[484] SI 2006/3317, reg 2(8)(b), as substituted by the Accession (Immigration and Worker Authorisation) (Amendment) Regulations 2007, SI 2007/475, reg 2(2). For 'family member', see **12.131–12.137**. For 'right to reside', see **12.123–12.163**. For 'self-employed person', see **12.189–12.190**. For 'student', see fn 416.

[485] SI 2006/3317, reg 2(9).

hours a week during term time,[486] or is working for no more than four months after the end of his or her course and who holds a registration certificate that includes a statement that he or she may work during that period;[487] or

- a 'posted worker'.[488]

12.196 Any national of Bulgaria or Romania who falls within one of these categories will fall to be treated as any other EEA national would be.

Family members of certain EEA nationals[489]

12.197 A family member of an EEA national (who is a worker, a self-employed person, or an Accession State national subject to worker authorisation who is authorised in accordance with the Accession Regulations 2006[490]) is exempt from having to satisfy the habitual residence test.

12.198 The 'family member' need not be a worker, a self-employed person, or an Accession State national subject to worker authorisation. Indeed, he or she need not be economically active at all. Nor need he or she be an EEA national. So long as he or she is a 'family member' of an EEA national (who is a worker, a self-employed person, or an Accession State national subject to worker authorisation), he or she is exempt from the habitual residence test. He or she can apply for homelessness assistance in his or her own right. There is no need for the EEA worker, self-employed person, or Accession State national subject to worker authorisation to be the applicant.

12.199 In some circumstances, there is not even any need for the EEA national to be part of the applicant's household in order for the applicant to be eligible as a 'family member'.[491]

12.200 For 'family member', see **12.131–12.137**.

---

[486] He or she may work full-time during vacation (SI 2006/3317, reg 10A(b)).

[487] SI 2006/3317, reg 2(10), (10A) and (10B), as substituted by the Accession (Immigration and Worker Authorisation) (Amendment) Regulations 2007, SI 2007/475, reg 2(2).

[488] SI 2006/3317, reg 2(11) and (13)(a). A 'posted worker' is a worker who, for a limited period, is working in the territory of a different member state from that where he or she normally works (Directive 96/71/EC, Arts 1 and 3).

[489] Allocation of Housing and Homelessness (Eligibility) (England) Regulations 2006, SI 2006/1294, reg 6(2)(d). See English Code, para 9.14(d) and Annex 12, paras 43–50.

[490] SI 2006/3317.

[491] For example, spouses and civil partners remain 'family members' until their marriage or partnership is legally terminated, whether or not they are actually cohabiting with the EEA national. See fn 295.

EEA nationals and their family members who have certain permanent rights to reside in the UK[492]

12.201 'Permanent right of residence' is defined at Immigration (European Economic Area) Regulations 2006, reg 15(1).[493] This exemption from the habitual residence test only applies to three sub-classes of persons who are entitled to a permanent right of residence.

12.202 Those three sub-classes give permanent rights of residence to:

(1) an EEA national who was a worker or self-employed person who has ceased activity;[494]

(2) the family member of such an EEA national;[495] and

(3) a person who was:
- the family member of an EEA national who was a worker or self-employed person; and
- the EEA national has died; and
- the family member had resided with the EEA national immediately before his or her death; and
- either the EEA national had resided in the UK for at least two years immediately before his or her death; or
- the death was the result of an accident at work or an occupational disease.[496]

12.203 'Worker or self-employed person who has ceased activity' is defined at Immigration (European Economic Area) Regulations 2006, reg 5.[497]

12.204 For 'family member', see **12.131–12.137**. For 'worker', see **12.182–12. 188**. For 'self-employed person' see **12.189–12.190**.

12.205 There will be other EEA nationals who have a permanent right of residence that is not within these three specified sub-classes.[498] They will have to satisfy the habitual residence test in order to be eligible.[499]

---

[492] Allocation of Housing and Homelessness (Eligibility) (England) Regulations 2006, SI 2006/1294, reg 6(2)(e). English Code, Annex 12, paras 38–39.
[493] SI 2006/1003. See **12.139–12.141**.
[494] Immigration (European Economic Area) Regulations 2006, SI 2006/1003, reg 15(1)(c). See **12.139**(3).
[495] SI 2006/1003, reg 15(1)(d). See **12.139**(4).
[496] SI 2006/1003, reg 15(1)(e). See **12.139**(5).
[497] SI 2006/1003.
[498] See **12.139–12.141**.
[499] Allocation of Housing and Homelessness (Eligibility) (England) Regulations 2006, SI 2006/1294, reg 6(1)(a). See **12.170–12.179**.

People from Montserrat[500]

12.206 This group of persons, who are eligible even if they are not habitually resident, are persons who left the territory of Montserrat after 1 November 1995 because of the effect on that territory of a volcanic eruption. They will normally be British citizens or Commonwealth citizens with the right of abode in the UK.[501] Not all people leaving Montserrat are rendered eligible by this provision. It does not apply to those who left on or before 1 November 1995. Nor does it apply to those who left after that date for reasons unconnected with the volcanic eruption. The regulation emphasises the departure location, ie it covers those who were in Montserrat and left after 1 November 1995. It also emphasises the reason for departure: the effect of the volcanic eruption. Most of those displaced to the UK in consequence of the volcanic eruption will long since have become habitually resident and will not need to rely on this exception to that test.

People who are in the UK as a result of having been deported, expelled or otherwise removed by compulsion of law from another country to the UK[502]

12.207 This group of persons, who are eligible even if not habitually resident, is probably small. The inclusion of this group brings eligibility for homelessness assistance into line with eligibility for housing benefit.

People who left Lebanon on or after 12 July 2006 because of the armed conflict there[503]

12.208 This group of people, who are eligible even if not habitually resident, is self-explanatory. In similar terms to the provision exempting those fleeing the volcanic eruption in Montserrat, it refers to people who are British citizens, or have other rights to enter or remain in the UK, but who have not been habitually resident in the CTA.[504] This provision exempts them from complying with the habitual residence test. To fall within this group:

- a person must have left Lebanon, not elsewhere;

- he or she must have left on or after 12 July 2006; and

- his or her reason for leaving Lebanon must have been 'because of the armed conflict there'.

---

[500] SI 2006/1294, reg 6(2)(f). English Code, paras 9.19–9.20.
[501] Obviously, to be eligible at all, he or she must not be a 'person subject to immigration control'. See **12.64–12.70** for who is and who is not a 'person subject to immigration control'.
[502] SI 2006/1294, reg 6(2)(g). English Code, para 9.21.
[503] SI 2006/1294, reg 6(2)(h), inserted by Allocation of Housing and Homelessness (Eligibility) (England) (Amendment) Regulations 2006, SI 2006/2007, reg 2(8) and in force from 4pm on 25 July 2006.
[504] See Box 1 at **12.66**.

12.209 This provision was only effective for 'the relevant period', which is defined as being between 4pm on 25 July 2006 and 31 January 2007.[505] After 31 January 2007, anyone who had fled Lebanon because of the armed conflict, and had not made his or her application for homelessness assistance during the relevant period, would have to satisfy the habitual residence test.

People who arrived in Great Britain on or after 28 February 2009 but before 18 March 2011 and who immediately before arriving in Great Britain had been resident in Zimbabwe and, before leaving Zimbabwe, had accepted an offer made by Her Majesty's Government, to assist them to settle in the UK[506]

12.210 This exception applies to British citizens and British subjects with the right of abode in the UK, who have left Zimbabwe and arrived in Great Britain between 28 February 2009 and 18 March 2011.[507] They must have left as a result of having accepted an offer of assistance from the British government. The government intended to offer assistance only to British citizens and British nationals.[508] They were either aged 70 or over, or were vulnerable due to health and social care needs that meant that they were not able to look after themselves.[509] Their spouses, partners and any dependents could accompany them, but whether they too would be offered assistance was to be decided on a case-by-case basis.

12.211 This exception applies only to applications for homelessness assistance made on or after 18 March 2009.[510]

---

[505] Allocation of Housing and Homelessness (Eligibility) (England) Regulations 2006, SI 2006/1294, reg 2(4), inserted by Allocation of Housing and Homelessness (Eligibility) (England) (Amendment) Regulations 2006, SI 2006/2007, reg 2(2).

[506] SI 2006/1294, reg 6(2)(i), inserted by the Allocation of Housing and Homelessness (Eligibility) (England) (Amendment) Regulations 2009, SI 2009/358.

[507] Unlike in the previous case of people who had left Lebanon, there is no time limit within which these applicants must make their applications for homelessness assistance. Anyone who arrived in the UK on or before 18 March 2011 and subsequently makes an application for homelessness assistance, on any date, will be exempt from the habitual residence test if he or she fulfils all of the criteria specified.

[508] The UK government's offers of assistance were to be made both to British citizens and to other British nationals who were leaving Zimbabwe. However, only British citizens and British nationals with the right of abode in the UK fall within the exception to the habitual residence test at SI 2006/1294, reg 6(2)(i).

[509] Explanatory Memorandum to the Allocation of Housing and Homelessness (Eligibility) (England) (Amendment) Regulations 2009, SI 2009/358, para 7.

[510] Allocation of Housing and Homelessness (Eligibility) (England) (Amendment) Regulations 2009, SI 2009/358, reg 1.

The second class: EEA nationals with a right to reside in the UK by virtue of being job-seekers, family members of a job-seeker, by exercising an initial right to reside, by having a derivative right to reside in the UK as the primary carer of a British citizen or by having a right to reside derived from Art 20 of the Treaty on the Functioning of the European Union[511]

12.212 Anyone who falls exclusively within this class cannot be eligible for homelessness assistance. The habitual residence test is not relevant. If an EEA national is:

(a)   a job-seeker;[512] or

(b)   a family member[513] of a job-seeker; or

(c)   only entitled to remain in the UK by virtue of the initial right to reside for three months;[514] or

(d)   has a derivative right to reside because he or she is the primary carer of a British citizen;[515] or

(e)   has a right to reside derived from Art 20 of the Treaty on the Functioning of the European Union, where the right to reside arises because a British citizen would otherwise be deprived of the genuine enjoyment of the substance of those rights as a European Union citizen,[516]

he or she cannot be eligible.[517]

12.213 So, this second class operates to ensure that any EEA national, or family member of an EEA national, whose *only* right of residence in the UK is the initial three-month right of residence is not eligible for homelessness assistance.

12.214 It also excludes job-seekers from homelessness assistance. EEA nationals who are 'job-seekers' are 'qualified persons'[518] and therefore are

---

[511]   Allocation of Housing and Homelessness (Eligibility) (England) Regulations 2006, SI 2006/1294, reg 6(1)(b) amended by SI 2012/2588. English Code, para 9.13(ii) and (iii), Annex 12, paras 9–10 and 12–14.

[512]   See **12.130**.

[513]   See **12.131–12.137**.

[514]   See **12.126–12.128**.

[515]   SI 2006/1003, reg 15A(4A), in force from 8 November 2012, see **12.156–12.159**.

[516]   See **12.162–12.163**.

[517]   SI 2012/1294, reg 6(1)(b) amended by SI 2012/2588, to insert the fourth and fifth categories. Persons falling within the fourth and fifth categories are not eligible if their applications for homelessness assistance were made on or after 8 November 2012 (SI 2012/2588, reg 3). See letter DCLG to Chief Housing Officers of Local Authorities in England, 17 October 2012, at Appendix 4.

[518]   Immigration (European Economic Area) Regulations, SI 2006/1003, reg 6(1)(a).

entitled to the extended right of residence.[519] A 'job-seeker' is defined as 'a person who enters the UK in order to seek employment and can provide evidence that he is seeking employment and has a genuine chance of being engaged'.[520] If a job-seeker had previously been employed, he or she may still be a 'worker' in certain circumstances and is potentially eligible because of the 'worker' status.[521]

12.215   However, if a person's *only* claim to the extended right of residence is because of his or her status as a 'job-seeker', or as a family member of a job-seeker, he or she will not be eligible.

12.216   For 'family member' see **12.131–12.137**. For 'initial right of residence', see **12.124–12.128**.

12.217   For applications for homelessness assistance made on or after 8 November 2012,[522] there are two additional exclusions from eligibility.

12.218   A person who is entitled to a European Union right of residence that is derived from being the primary carer of a British national is excluded.[523] This 'derivative right of residence' was recognised by the CJEU in the case of *Zambrano v Office national de l'emploi*,[524] and is now identified in the Immigration (European Economic Area) Regulations 2006,[525] see **12.156 – 12.158**. At the date of writing, a person entitled to this derivative right is not excluded from eligibility for homelessness assistance in Wales.[526] People entitled to any of the four other derivative rights of residence in reg 15A of the Immigration (European Economic Area) Regulations 2006[527] do not fall within this second class of people excluded from eligibility.

12.219   A person who has a right derived from Art 20 of the Treaty on the Functioning of the European Union, in a case where the right to reside arises because a British citizen would otherwise be deprived of the genuine enjoyment of the substance of his or her rights as an EU citizen, is also excluded from eligibility.[528] This new provision appears to exclude anyone who has a right of residence which is not, as yet, identified in the Immigration (European Economic Area) Regulations,[529] but which is subsequently declared by the CJEU. Article 20 of the Treaty contains the right of nationals of EU member

---

[519]   See **12.129–12.138**.
[520]   Immigration (European Economic Area) Regulations 2006, SI 2006/1003, reg 6(1)(a) and (4). See English Code, Annex 12, paras 12–14.
[521]   SI 2006/1003, reg 6(2)(b). See **12.184–12.185**
[522]   SI 2012/2588, reg 3.
[523]   SI 2006/1294, reg 6(1)(b)(iii) inserted by SI 2012/2588.
[524]   C34/09, [2012] QB 265, CJEU.
[525]   SI 2006/1003, reg 15A(4A) inserted by SI 2012/2560 in force from 8 November 2012.
[526]   See **12.227–12.233**.
[527]   SI 2006/1003 as amended, see **12.142–12.161** and Appendix 2.
[528]   SI 2006/1294, reg 6(1)(b)(iv) inserted by SI 2012/2588 for applications for homelessness assistance made on or after 8 November 2012.
[529]   SI 2006/1003 as amended, see Appendix 2.

states to be citizens of the EU and to move and reside freely within the territories of the EU Member States. This provision does not exclude all the rights of EU residence that might, in the future, be recognised in CJEU case-law but simply those that are:

- derived from Art 20 of the Treaty; and

- arise because otherwise a British citizen would be deprived of the genuine enjoyment of the substance of his or her rights under EU law.

12.220 For rights declared by the CJEU, see **12.162–12.163**.[530]

12.221 If a person has more than one right of residence, such as being both a job-seeker and being the family member of a worker or self-employed person, then his or her right to reside is not 'only' derived from his or her status as a job-seeker, or from any of the other four provisions in this second class, and he or she will not fall within this second class of persons (not subject to immigration control) who are not eligible for homelessness assistance.

The third class: EEA nationals with a right to reside in the rest of the Common Travel Area by virtue of being job-seekers, family members of a job-seeker, exercising an initial right to reside, by a derivative right of residence as the primary carer of an Irish or British citizen, or by a right to reside derived from Art 20 of the Treaty on the Functioning of the European Union[531]

12.222 This third class refers to people who have been residing in the Channel Islands, the Isle of Man or the Republic of Ireland. The rest of the CTA is dealt with by the second class.[532]

12.223 For 'job-seeker', see **12.130**. For 'family member', see **12.131–12.137**. For 'initial right to reside', see **12.126–12.129**. For 'Common Travel Area' see Box 1 at **12.66**. For 'persons with a right to reside derived from Art 20 of the Treaty on the Functioning of the European Union', see **12.162–12.163**.

12.224 The derivative right to reside referred to in this class is not identified in the Immigration (European Economic Area) Regulations 2006.[533] It arises as a result of the CJEU's decision in *Zambrano v Office national de l'emploi*.[534] That decision recognized rights of residence which are directly effective in the remainder of the CTA: ie the Channel Islands, Isle of Man and the Republic of Ireland. A person will have this derivative right of residence if he or she is the primary carer of a British citizen residing in the Channels Islands or the Isle of

---

[530] At the date of writing, DCLG had written to Chief Housing Officers of Local Authorities in England, see letter dated 17 October 2012 at Appendix 4.
[531] Allocation of Housing and Homelessness (Eligibility) (England) Regulations 2006, SI 2006/1294, reg 6(1)(c) as amended by SI 2012/2588. English Code, para 9.13(iv).
[532] See **12.212–12.221**.
[533] SI 2006/1003, see Appendix 2.
[534] C34/09, [2012] QB 265, CJEU.

Man, or of an Irish citizen residing in the Republic of Ireland, and the British or Irish citizen would have to leave those countries and would not be able to reside in any other EU member state if his or her primary carer did not have an EU right of residence.

12.225 The exclusion from eligibility for homelessness assistance for those people exercising the derivative right of residence or other rights of residence derived from Art 20 applies to applications for homelessness assistance made on or after 8 November 2012.[535]

12.226 As with the second class, if a person has more than one right of residence, then his or her right to reside is not 'only' derived from his or her status as a jobseeker, or from the other four provisions in this class, and he or she will not fall within this third class of persons (not subject to immigration control) who are not eligible for homelessness assistance.

The Welsh rules

The basic rules

12.227 The National Assembly for Wales[536] exercised its power to prescribe other classes of persons from abroad who are not persons subject to immigration control but are to be treated as ineligible by the Homelessness (Wales) Regulations 2006.[537] These Regulations apply to applications for homelessness assistance made to local housing authorities in Wales on or after 9 October 2006.[538] There is limited guidance in the Welsh Code at Chapter 11 and Annex 6.[539]

12.228 Regulation 4 of the Homelessness (Wales) Regulations 2006[540] designates two classes of people as not eligible for homelessness assistance, even though they are not persons subject to immigration control. They are:

---

[535] SI 2012/2588, reg 3. At the date of writing, there is no exclusion in the equivalent Welsh Regulations and so a person who has one of those rights of residence could consider making an application for an allocation to a local housing authority in Wales, see **12.227–12.233**. See also letter DCLG Chief Housing Officers to Local Authorities in England, 17 October 2012, at Appendix 4.

[536] The National Assembly for Wales' power to make regulations under HA 1996, Part 7, was transferred to the Welsh Assembly Government on 25 May 2007 (Government of Wales Act 2006, s 161 and Sch 11, para 30), the Welsh Assembly Government subsequently became the Welsh Government in May 2011.

[537] SI 2006/2646 (W 227), reg 3.

[538] Homelessness (Wales) Regulations 2006, SI 2006/2646 (W 227), reg 5.

[539] Welsh Code, Annex 6 contains useful guidance on the habitual residence test, see **12.170–12.179** of this book. However, the remainder of the guidance in the Welsh Code simply contains lists derived from the Regulations and no explanation (see para 11.12, Welsh Code). Reference might usefully be made to the identical categories in the English Regulations and English Code for guidance.

[540] SI 2006/2646 (W 227).

- people not habitually resident in the CTA, subject to exemptions;[541] and

- people whose right to reside in the CTA is derived solely from their status as self-sufficient or retired persons.[542]

The first class: not habitually resident[543]

12.229 For 'habitually resident', see **12.170–12.179** and Welsh Code Annex 6. For 'Common Travel Area', see Box 1 at **12.66**.

Exemptions from the habitual residence test[544]

12.230 Five groups of persons from abroad are not required to satisfy the habitual residence.[545] They are:

- EEA nationals who are workers;[546] and

- until 1 May 2011, a person who is an Accession State worker requiring registration who was registered in accordance with the Accession Regulations 2004[547] ('an A8 national');[548] and

- EEA nationals who have the right to reside in the UK including a person who is an Accession State national subject to worker authorisation who is authorised in accordance with the Accession Regulations 2006;[549] and

- persons who left the territory of Montserrat after 1 November 1995 because of the effect on that territory of a volcanic eruption;[550] and

- for applications made on or after 20 March 2009, persons who arrived in Great Britain on or after 28 February 2009 but before 18 March 2011 and who, immediately before arriving in Great Britain, had been resident in

---

[541] SI 2006/2646 (W 227), reg 4(1)(a). See **12.170–12.179** for habitual residence and **12.230–12.232** for exemptions. See also Welsh Code Annex 6 for guidance on habitual residence.

[542] SI 2006/2646 (W 227), reg 4(1)(b). See **12.123–12.163** for 'right to reside' and Box 1 at **12.66** for 'CTA'.

[543] SI 2006/2646 (W 227), reg 4(1)(a).

[544] SI 2006/2646 (W 227), reg 4(2).

[545] Welsh Code, para 11.12.

[546] SI 2006/2646 (W 227), reg 4(2)(a). For 'worker' see **12.182–12.188**.

[547] Accession (Immigration and Worker Registration) Regulations 2004, SI 2004/1219.

[548] SI 2006/1294, reg 6(2)(c)(i), substituted by Allocation of Housing and Homelessness (Eligibility) (England) (Amendment) (No 2) Regulations 2006, SI 2006/3340, reg 2. See **12.192–12.196**.

[549] Accession (Immigration and Worker Authorisation) Regulations 2006, SI 2006/3317. SI 2006/2646 (W 227), reg 4(2)(c). For 'right to reside', see **12.123–12.163**. For 'a person who is an Accession State national subject to worker authorisation who is authorised in accordance with Accession Regulations 2006', see **12.192–12.196**.

[550] SI 2006/2646 (W 227), reg 4(2)(d), see **12.206**.

Zimbabwe and before leaving Zimbabwe had accepted an offer made by Her Majesty's Government to assist that person to settle in the UK.[551]

12.231 Four of these exemptions are discussed in relation to the English Regulations. For 'worker', see **12.182–12.188**. For 'Accession State worker requiring registration', see **12.191**. For 'person who left the territory of Montserrat', see **12.206**. For 'persons who left Zimbabwe', see **12.210–12.211**.

12.232 The third group of people are exempt from the habitual residence test if they apply to local housing authorities in Wales, but are not all exempt if they are apply to local housing authorities in England. They are EEA nationals and family members of EEA nationals who have the right to reside in the UK.[552] The rights of EEA nationals and their family members to reside are discussed at **12.123–12.163**. Note that if a person does not have a 'right to reside', he or she will not be treated as habitually resident.[553] If the 'right to reside' enjoyed by the EEA national is derived solely from his or her status as a self-sufficient or retired person, he or she will not be eligible (because he or she falls into the second class of people from abroad prescribed as not eligible).[554]

The second class: people whose right to reside in the CTA is derived solely from their status as self-sufficient or retired persons[555]

12.233 The second class of persons who are not eligible for homelessness assistance, even though they are not persons subject to immigration control, comprises those EEA nationals, and their family members, whose right to reside is derived solely from European Community Council Directives 90/364/EEC or 90/365/EEC.[556] These Directives referred to nationals of EEA Member States who are self-sufficient or retired. These Directives were repealed by Directive 2004/38/EC with effect from 30 April 2006.[557] The same rights to reside are now contained in the Directive 2004/38/EC and are transposed into UK domestic law by the Immigration (European Economic Area) Regulations 2006.[558]There are no exceptions to this class. Anyone who falls within this class will be ineligible whether or not he or she is habitually resident.

---

[551] SI 2006/2646 (W 227), reg 4(2)(e), as inserted by Allocation of Housing and Homelessness (Eligibility) (Wales) Regulations 2009, SI 2009/393 (W 42), reg 3. For 'persons who left Zimbabwe', see **12.210–12.211**.

[552] Some EEA nationals and family members who have a right to reside are exempt from the habitual residence test in England (SI 2006/1294, reg 6(2)) but not all of them. See **12.166**.

[553] SI 2006/2646 (W 227), reg 4(3).

[554] SI 2006/2646 (W 227), reg 4(1)(h). See **12.233**.

[555] SI 2006/2646 (W 227), reg 4(1)(b).

[556] SI 2006/2646 (W 277), reg 4(1)(b).

[557] Directive 2004/38/EC, art 38(2).

[558] SI 2006/1003 as amended. Any rights contained in Directive 2004/38/EC which are not transposed into SI 2006/1003 would still apply directly.

SUMMARY OF DIFFERENCES IN ELIGIBILITY AS BETWEEN LOCAL HOUSING AUTHORITIES IN ENGLAND AND IN WALES

Overview

12.234 Since any person is entitled to make an application for homelessness assistance to any local housing authority in England or Wales without having any geographical connection to that local housing authority, applicants and their advisers might consider whether they should direct their applications to a local housing authority in the country where they will be found to be eligible under HA 1996, s 185 and the different Regulations made under this section.

12.235 If the applicant has no local connection with the local housing authority to which he or she applied, and is found to be eligible for assistance, to be homeless, to have a priority need and not to have become homeless intentionally, the local housing authority would be entitled to consider whether the applicant should be referred to another local housing authority under the conditions for referral at HA 1996, s 198(2), or (4).[559] It may be, therefore, that an applicant who is eligible under the Welsh Regulations and who directs his or her application to a local housing authority in Wales, and who has no local connection with the local housing authority in Wales but does have a local connection with a local housing authority in England, will find that he or she is referred to the local housing authority in England for performance of the main housing duty at HA 1996, s 193(2). The local housing authority in England will be required to perform the main housing duty, and secure accommodation for the applicant and his or her household, even though the applicant would not have been eligible for homelessness assistance if he or she had applied directly to the local housing authority in England. The same analysis applies where an applicant who is not eligible under the Welsh Regulations directs his or her application for homelessness assistance to a local housing authority in England.

12.236 Of course, if a duty other than the main housing duty[560] (or the duty at HA 1996, s 195A[561] owed to applicants who are re-applying for homelessness

---

[559] See Chapter 15. The additional condition for referral at HA 1996, s 198(2ZA) was inserted by LA 2011, s 149(6) and applies to applicants who made their applications for homelessness assistance to local housing authorities in England on or after 9 November 2012 and subsequently accepted a private rented sector offer (HA 1996, s 193(7AA) as amended by LA 2011, s 148(4)). At the date of writing, the amendments to HA 1996 made by LA 2011, ss 148–149 had not been brought into effect in Wales. For 'private rented sector offer', see **17.109–17.131**.

[560] Such as the duty to secure accommodation in the short term to applicants who have a priority need but have become homeless intentionally (HA 1996, s 190(2)(a): see **17.182–17.189**) or the duty to provide advice and assistance to the applicant (HA 1996, ss 190(2)(b) and 192(2): see **17.201–17.214**).

[561] Inserted by LA 2011, s 149(4) and applicable to applicants for homelessness assistance who applied to a local housing authority in England on or after 9 November 2012 and accepted a private rented sector offer. At the date of writing, the amendments to HA 1996 Part 7 made by LA 2011, ss 148–149 had not been brought into effect in Wales. See **9.89–9.95**.

assistance within two years of acceptance of a private rented sector offer[562]) is owed to the applicant, the conditions for referral do not apply and that duty must be performed by the local housing authority to which the applicant applied. In addition, there is no obligation on a local housing authority to consider whether the conditions for referral are made out, and an applicant cannot insist on being referred under the conditions for referral.[563]

Applications to local housing authorities in Wales

12.237   The following applicants would be eligible for homelessness assistance if they apply to local housing authorities in Wales, but would not be eligible if they apply to local housing authorities in England:

- a person subject to immigration control who left the territory of Montserrat after 1 November 1995 because of the effect on that territory of a volcanic eruption;[564]

- a person subject to immigration control who is habitually resident in the CTA and who is either:
  - a national of a state which has ratified the ECSMA or the ESC and is lawfully present in the UK;[565] or
  - before 3 April 2000 was owed a duty by a local housing authority under Housing Act 1985, Part 3, or HA 1996, Part 7, which is extant and who is a national of a state which is a signatory to the ECSMA or ESC;[566]

- a person who is subject to immigration control and who is on income-based jobseeker's allowance or income support (with certain exceptions);[567]

- a person who is not subject to immigration control and whose sole right of residence in the CTA[568] is by virtue of being a job-seeker[569] or of being a family member[570] of a job-seeker and who is habitually resident in the CTA;[571]

---

[562] See HA 1996, s 193(7AA)–(7AC) amended by LA 2011, s 148(5)–(7). Private rented sector offers can be made to applicants for homelessness assistance who applied to a local housing authority in England on or after 9 November 2012. At the date of writing, the amendments to HA 1996 Part 7 made by LA 2011, ss 148–149 had not been brought into effect in Wales. See **17.109–17.131**.

[563] *Hackney London Borough Council v Sareen* [2003] EWCA Civ 351, [2003] HLR 54, CA.

[564] Homelessness (Wales) Regulations 2006, SI 2006/2646 (W 227), reg 3(1)(d). See **12.102–12.104**.

[565] SI 2006/2646 (W 227), reg 3(1)(e)(i). See **12.105–12.108**.

[566] SI 2006/2646 (W 227), reg 3(1)(e)(ii). See **12.109–12.112**.

[567] SI 2006/2646 (W 227), reg 3(1)(i). See **12.113–12.115**.

[568] See Box 1 at **12.66**.

[569] See **12.130**.

[570] See **12.131–12.137**.

[571] There is no prescription for this group of people in the Homelessness (Wales) Regulations 2006, SI 2006/2646. It follows that a person will be eligible if he or she satisfies the habitual residence test (SI 2006/2646, reg 4(1)(a)). See **12.229–12.232**. The same could apply to

- a person who has a derivative right of residence identified in Immigration (European Economic Area) Regulations 2006, reg 15A(4A) and who satisfies the habitual residence test;[572] or

- a person who has a right of residence derived from Art 20 of the Treaty on the Functioning of the European Union and who satisfies the habitual residence test.[573]

Applications to local housing authorities in England

12.238 Applicants who are persons subject to immigration control will find that there are no classes of people who are prescribed as eligible for homelessness assistance from local housing authorities in England who are not also prescribed as eligible for homelessness assistance from local housing authorities in Wales. There is therefore no benefit in directing an application specifically to a local housing authority in England rather than to a local housing authority in Wales on issues of eligibility.

12.239 However, applicants who are not persons subject to immigration control but may have difficulty in satisfying the habitual residence test could consider applying to local housing authorities in England if they fall within the following exemptions to the habitual residence test:

- an Accession State national subject to worker authorisation who is authorised in accordance with the Accession Regulations 2006 ('an A2 national');[574] or

- a person who is in the UK as a result of having been deported, expelled or otherwise removed by compulsion of law from another country to the UK.[575]

12.240 These exemptions do not feature in the Welsh Regulations and so, if an application for homelessness assistance was made to a local housing authority in Wales, the habitual residence test would have to be applied.[576] Particular guidance relating to such asylum-seekers is given at paras 9.11–9.12

---

a person whose sole right of residence in the UK is by virtue of exercising an initial right to reside (see **12.126–12.128**), but such a person would be unlikely to satisfy the habitual residence test.

[572] SI 2006/1003, reg 15A(4A) inserted by SI 2012/2588, in force from 8 November 2012. See **12.156–12.159** and Appendix 2.

[573] See **12.162–12.163**.

[574] Allocation of Housing and Homelessness (Eligibility) (England) Regulations 2006, SI 2006/1294, reg 6(2)(c)(ii), substituted by Allocation of Housing and Homelessness (Eligibility) (England) (Amendment) (No 2) Regulations 2006, SI 2006/3340, reg 2(4), in force from 1 January 2007; see **12.192–12.196**. SI 2006/2646 (W 227), reg 4(2)(c). For 'right to reside', see **12.123–12.163**.

[575] Allocation of Housing and Homelessness (Eligibility) (England) Regulations 2006, SI 2006/1294, reg 6(2)(g). See **12.207**.

[576] Homelessness (Wales) Regulations 2006, SI 2006/2646 (W 227), reg 4(1)(a).

and Annex 9 of the English Code.[577] Even if they do fall within any of Classes E(i), (ii) or (iii), HA 1996, s 186 applies an additional test of eligibility for homelessness assistance.

ISLES OF SCILLY

12.241   The Isles of Scilly are administratively part of England,[578] but special measures have been taken to protect the very limited stock of social housing on those islands. HA 1996[579] enables the Secretary of State to make an Order adapting HA 1996, Part 7 in its application to the Isles of Scilly and that power has been used to make special provisions governing eligibility for applicants applying for homelessness assistance there.[580]

12.242   The Order amends HA 1996, ss 183–218, to provide that a person is not eligible for homelessness assistance from the authorities in the Isles of Scilly unless he or she has been resident in the district of the Isles of Scilly for a total period of two years and six months during the period of three years immediately prior to the application.[581] If an applicant is eligible, by virtue of having resided in the Isles of Scilly for that period, he or she is also deemed to have a local connection with the Isles of Scilly.[582]

---

[577]   Welsh Code, Annex 10.
[578]   Interpretation Act 1978, s 5 and Sch 1.
[579]   HA 1996, s 225(1).
[580]   Homelessness (Isles of Scilly) Order 1997, SI 1997/797.
[581]   SI 1997/797, reg 2(2).
[582]   SI 1997/797, reg 2(3). See also **15.209–15.212**.

Chapter 13

PRIORITY NEED

INTRODUCTION

13.1 Once a local housing authority has decided that someone is homeless or threatened with homelessness, and is eligible for assistance, it owes that person a duty. The next question is: What duty does it owe?[1] In order to answer that question, the local housing authority must decide whether the applicant has a 'priority need' for accommodation. That involves the local housing authority applying the tight statutory definition of the term,[2] not making a value judgment.

13.2 The local housing authority should initially consider whether the applicant has a priority need in his or her own right. If not, it should ask whether any person who resides, or might reasonably be expected to reside, with the applicant falls into one of the priority need categories which would confer a priority need on the applicant.

Why it matters

13.3 If the applicant *does not* have a priority need for accommodation, the local housing authority's duty is to assess his or her housing needs and then to provide him or her with advice and assistance in any attempts he or she may make to obtain accommodation to meet those needs.[3] Additionally, if an applicant without priority need has not become homeless intentionally, the local housing authority has a power (but not a duty) to provide accommodation for the applicant and his or her household.[4] Where the non-priority need applicant has not become 'threatened with' homelessness intentionally, there is a parallel power to take reasonable steps to secure that accommodation does not cease to be available for his or her occupation.[5]

13.4 Where an applicant is making a fresh application for homelessness assistance to a local housing authority in England, within two years of acceptance of a private rented sector offer, normally he or she will not need to have a priority need in order to be entitled to the main housing duty at Housing Act 1996 (HA 1996), s 193(2) or to the equivalent duty owed to those threatened with homelessness.[6]

---

[1] Housing Act 1996, s 184(1)(b).

[2] See **13.14–13.19**.

[3] HA 1996, ss 190(3), (4), 192(2) and (4). See **17.201–17.214**.

[4] HA 1996, s 192(3). See **17.215–17.222**.

[5] HA 1996, s 195(9). See **17.215**.

[6] HA 1996, s 195A as inserted by Localism Act 2011, s 149(4) and applicable to applicants for homelessness assistance whose applications were made on or after 9 November 2012 to local housing authorities in England. At the date of writing, the amendments to HA 1996 made by LA 2011, ss 148–149 had not been brought into effect in Wales. See **9.89–9.95**. For 'private rented sector offer', see Chapter 17, at **17.109–17.131**. The exception is where the local housing authority is also satisfied that an applicant is homeless, eligible for assistance and is not satisfied that he or she became homeless intentionally, without having regard to a restricted person (HA 1996, s 195A(5) inserted by LA 2011, s 149(4)). In those cases, the applicant would

13.5 If the applicant *does* have a priority need, he or she will be entitled to accommodation together with his or her household. If that applicant has become homeless intentionally, the accommodation will only be provided for such period as the local housing authority considers will give him or her a reasonable opportunity of securing accommodation.[7] If the applicant has not become homeless intentionally, accommodation must be provided until the duty is discharged by the occurrence of one of the events listed at HA 1996, s 193.[8] Similar duties are owed to applicants who are 'threatened with' homelessness and have a priority need.[9] Again, the extent of the duty owed turns on whether the applicant has become threatened with homelessness intentionally.[10]

When it matters

13.6 There are four stages in the handling of an application for homelessness assistance at which the question of 'priority need' may be significant.

At the application stage

13.7 At the outset of an application for homelessness assistance, the local housing authority must take a preliminary view about priority need. If the local housing authority has reason to believe that the applicant may have a priority need and may also be homeless and eligible, it *must* provide interim accommodation while it works out what duty under HA 1996, Part 7 (if any) the applicant is owed.[11] The threshold for the provision of interim accommodation is very low; any 'reason to believe' that an applicant may have a priority need is sufficient. There have been findings of maladministration against local housing authorities which turned away applicants, telling them to obtain medical evidence, and, as a result, failed to discharge their duty to provide interim accommodation.[12]

---

still have to have a priority need in order to be entitled to the main housing duty or equivalent duty owed to those threatened with homelessness. For 'restricted person', see **12.32–12.47**.

[7]   HA 1996, s 190(2)(a). See **17.182–17.189**.

[8]   HA 1996, s 193(5)–(7F) as amended by LA 2011, s 148(3)–(9), in the case of an applicant for homelessness assistance whose application was made on or after 9 November 2012 to a local housing authority in England; at the date of writing, the amendments to HA 1996 made by LA 2011, ss 148–149 had not been brought into effect in Wales. See **17.54–17.168**.

[9]   HA 1996, s 195(2) and (5)(b). See **17.190–17.200**.

[10] For more on the concepts of becoming homeless (or becoming threatened with homelessness) intentionally, see Chapter 14.

[11] HA 1996, s 188(1). See also *Homelessness Code of Guidance for Local Authorities* (Communities and Local Government, Department for Education and Skills, Department of Health, July 2006) (the English Code), Chapter 7 and para 10.3, at Appendix 2 of this book. *Code of Guidance for Local Authorities Allocation of Accommodation and Homelessness 2012* (Welsh Government, August 2012) (the Welsh Code), paras 12.14–12.17 and 14.5, on CD-Rom. The interim duty is more fully discussed at **16.12–16.28**.

[12] *Complaint against Tunbridge Wells Borough Council*, 89/A/2825; *Complaint against Ealing London Borough Council*, 90/A/2032; *Complaint against Kingston upon Hull City Council*, 90/C/2893; *Complaint against Eastleigh Borough Council*, 06/B/7896; *Complaint against Hammersmith & Fulham London Borough Council*, 09 001 262, 21 January 2010, (2010) March

13.8 On receiving an application, the local housing authority is under a duty to make all necessary inquiries into whether or not the applicant actually has a priority need. That burden rests on the local housing authority; it is not for the applicant to have to prove his or her case. The local housing authority should make its inquiries as quickly as possible and aim to complete them and notify the applicant of the outcome within 33 working days.[13]

The decision stage

13.9 The local housing authority is *not*, at this stage, concerned with whether the applicant had a priority need at the date of *application*, but rather with whether she or he has a priority need at the date of the *decision* as to what HA 1996, Part 7 duty is owed (if any). If there has been a change of circumstances between the making of the application and the date of the decision, the local housing authority must take that change into account. In one case, which reached the Court of Appeal, the applicant had had a priority need at the date of application and for the following six days, but not at the date of the decision.[14]

13.10 The question for the local housing authority is whether, at the date of its decision (or, if a review has been requested, at the date of the review decision) the applicant has a priority need.[15] The local housing authority must not improperly delay making its decision (or concluding its review) in order to see whether the applicant might meanwhile lose an apparent priority need.[16] It is not at all unusual for an applicant to have one form of priority need at the date of application (eg pregnancy) and another at the date of decision or review (eg a dependent child).

The stage after decision

13.11 Once the local housing authority has reached a decision that the applicant has a priority need and has identified what duty it therefore owes to the applicant, that duty will not be displaced by any later change in the applicant's priority need (unless a review has been sought and the change takes place between the original decision and conclusion of the review). The scheme

---

Legal Action, p 31; *Complaint against Richmond upon Thames Royal London Borough Council*, 10 009 069, 10 February 2011, (2011) April *Legal Action*, p 30; *Complaint against Hounslow London Borough Council*, 10 019 388, 5 October 2011 (2011) December *Legal Action*, p 29; and *Complaint against Hounslow London Borough Council*, 11 008 191, 28 August 2012 (2012) November *Legal Action*, p 14.

13 English Code, para 6.16; Welsh Code, para 12.29. See **10.35–10.37**.

14 *R v Kensington and Chelsea Royal London Borough Council ex p Amarfio* (1995) 27 HLR 543, CA.

15 *Mohammed v Hammersmith and Fulham London Borough Council* [2001] UKHL 57, [2002] 1 AC 547, HL.

16 *Robinson v Hammersmith & Fulham London Borough Council* [2006] EWCA Civ 1122, [2007] HLR 7, CA.

of HA 1996, Part 7 does not permit a concluded duty to be re-opened simply because priority need is later lost. Once a duty has been accepted, the duty continues until it is discharged.[17]

13.12 However, the manner in which the local housing authority's duty to the applicant is performed may be affected if priority need is lost. An obvious example would be where the applicant is provided with temporary four-bedroom accommodation because four dependent children who are residing with him or her confer a priority need. If those children all leave, the local housing authority will be entitled to perform its duty by providing smaller accommodation.

On a new application

13.13 If the applicant has been owed the main housing duty[18] and that duty ends, the applicant may apply again.[19] It is quite irrelevant that the applicant had a priority need on his or her earlier application. What is important is whether she or he may have a priority need at the date of the new application and at the date of the decision on that new application.

13.14 If the applicant was not owed the main housing duty on the initial application (because she or he had no priority need) but has now applied again, it will be critically important whether she or he has since acquired a priority need. Subsequently acquiring a priority need may constitute a change of the factual position so that the local housing authority is required to entertain and inquire into the new application.[20]

13.15 An applicant whose earlier application for homelessness assistance was made to a local housing authority in England on or after 9 November 2012,[21] who had accepted a private rented sector offer,[22] and who subsequently makes a fresh application for homelessness assistance to a local housing authority in England within two years of the date of accepting the offer, will generally not need to have a priority need in order to be entitled to the HA 1996, s 193(2) main housing duty again or to the HA 1996, s 195(2) duty owed to those threatened with homelessness. He or she will still have to be homeless, eligible

---

[17] *R v Brent London Borough Council ex p Sadiq* (2001) 33 HLR 47, QBD. English Code, para 10.4; Welsh Code, para 14.6.

[18] HA 1996, s 193(2). See **17.23–17.168**.

[19] HA 1996, s 193(9). See **9.66–9.80** and **17.169–17.170**.

[20] *R (Van der Stolk) v Camden London Borough Council* [2002] EWHC 1261 (Admin), (2002) July *Legal Action*, p 26, Admin Ct.

[21] At the date of writing, the amendments to HA 1996 made by LA 2011, ss 148–149 had not been brought into effect in Wales.

[22] HA 1996, s 193(7AA)–(7AC) as amended by LA 2011, s 148(5)–(7) defines 'private rented sector offers' which can be made to applicants whose applications for homelessness assistance were made to a local housing authority in England on or after 9 November 2012. At the date of writing, the amendments to HA 1996 made by LA 2011, ss 148–149 had not been brought into effect in Wales. See **17.109–17.131**.

for assistance, and the local housing authority not be satisfied that he or she became homeless intentionally in order to be entitled to either of those duties.[23]

13.16 The exception is where a local housing authority in England is only satisfied that the applicant is homeless or eligible for assistance, and is not satisfied that he or she became homeless intentionally, a result of the presence in his or her household of a 'restricted person'.[24] Where that is the case, the applicant will still have to have a priority need in order to be entitled to the main housing duty.[25] Generally, it will be the very presence of the restricted person in the applicant's household that will give the applicant a priority need.

THE STATUTORY SCHEME

13.17 The concept and definition of 'priority need' was first given statutory expression in the Housing (Homeless Persons) Act 1977 and is now found in very similar (but not precisely the same) terms in HA 1996, s 189(1). HA 1996, sets out four different categories. If the applicant falls into any one of the four categories, he or she has a priority need.

13.18 Those categories are:

- a pregnant woman or a person with whom she resides or might reasonably be expected to reside;[26]

- a person with whom dependent children reside or might reasonably be expected to reside;[27]

- a person who is vulnerable as a result of old age, mental illness or mental handicap or physical disability or other special reason, or with whom such a person resides or might reasonably be expected to reside;[28] and

- a person who is homeless or threatened with homelessness as a result of an emergency such as flood, fire or other disaster.[29]

---

[23] HA 1996, s 195A as inserted by LA 2011, s 149(4) and applicable to applicants whose applications for homelessness assistance were made to a local housing authority in England on or after 9 November 2012. At the date of writing, the amendments to HA 1996 made by LA 2011, ss 148–149 had not been brought into effect in Wales. See **9.89–9.95**.
[24] As defined at HA 1996, s 184(7). See **12.32–12.47**.
[25] HA 1996, s 195A(5) inserted by LA 2011, s 149(4) applicable to applicants whose applications for homelessness assistance were made to a local housing authority in England on or after 9 November 2012. At the date of writing, the amendments to HA 1996 made by LA 2011, ss 148–149 had not been brought into effect in Wales. See **9.89–9.95**.
[26] HA 1996, s 189(1)(a). See **13.34–13.37**.
[27] HA 1996, s 189(1)(b). See **13.38–13.74**.
[28] HA 1996, s 189(1)(c). See **13.75–13.119**.
[29] HA 1996, s 189(1)(d). See **13.120–13.125**.

13.19 Each of these four categories is examined in more detail at **13.34–13.125**.

13.20 The Secretary of State and the Welsh Ministers[30] are given powers under HA 1996, Part 7, to specify further categories of priority need and to amend or repeal any part of the four statutory categories.[31] For more than 20 years, the statutory categories remained unchanged. In recent years, however, further categories have been added by both the Secretary of State in England and the National Assembly for Wales.

13.21 In *England*, the Homelessness (Priority Need for Accommodation) (England) Order 2002,[32] made by the Secretary of State, came into force from 31 July 2002. It adds six *additional* categories to those at HA 1996, s 189(1). In summary they cover:

(1) a child aged 16 or 17, subject to exceptions;[33]

(2) a young person under 21, who has been looked after, accommodated or fostered, but who is not a student in full-time education;[34]

(3) a person over 21 who is vulnerable as a result of having been looked after, accommodated or fostered;[35]

(4) a person who is vulnerable as a result of having served in the armed forces;[36]

(5) a person who is vulnerable as a result of having been imprisoned;[37] and

(6) a person who is vulnerable as a result of ceasing to occupy accommodation because of actual or threatened violence.[38]

13.22 Each of these six categories is examined in more detail at **13.126–13.211**.

---

[30] The power was exercised by the National Assembly for Wales until 25 May 2007, when it was transferred to the Welsh Assembly Government (Government of Wales Act 2006, s 161 and Sch 11, para 30). The Welsh Assembly Government has been known as the Welsh Government since May 2011.

[31] HA 1996, s 189(2).

[32] SI 2002/2051. See Appendix 2.

[33] SI 2002/2051, art 3. Since the making of this Order, both case-law and government guidance have directed that a homeless child in these circumstances will often be considered 'a child in need' (Children Act 1989, s 20) so a duty to secure accommodation will be owed by a children's services authority. Most importantly, the guidance emphasises that local housing authorities and children's services authorities should work together and co-operate in order to meet the accommodation and other needs of children and young people. See **13.127–13.174**.

[34] SI 2002/2051, art 4. See **13.175–13.181**.

[35] SI 2002/2051, art 5(1). See **13.182–13.189**.

[36] SI 2002/2051, art 5(2). See **13.182–13.185** and **13.190–13.195**.

[37] SI 2002/2051, art 5(3). See **13.182–13.185** and **13.196–13.202**.

[38] SI 2002/2051, art 6. See **13.182–13.185** and **13.203–13.211**.

13.23 In *Wales*, the Homeless Persons (Priority Need) (Wales) Order 2001,[39] made by the National Assembly for Wales, came into force on 1 March 2001. It adds six *additional* categories to those in HA 1996, s 189(1). In summary, these are:

(1) a young person aged 18, 19 or 20 who has been looked after, accommodated or fostered;[40]

(2) a young person aged 18, 19 or 20 who is at particular risk of sexual or financial exploitation;[41]

(3) a 16- or 17-year-old;[42]

(4) a person who has been subject to domestic violence, or is at risk of domestic violence;[43]

(5) a person who is homeless after leaving the armed forces;[44] and

(6) a former prisoner who is homeless after being released from custody.[45]

13.24 Each of these categories is examined in more detail at **13.212–13.245**.

13.25 Each Code of Guidance has a separate Chapter giving guidance on the priority need categories applicable to local housing authorities in the two countries.[46]

How do the categories work?

13.26 An applicant may acquire a priority need in one of two ways. The statutory categories make the available routes clear.

13.27 In some cases, the applicant will only acquire a priority need if he or she personally meets the qualifying conditions. For example, if priority need arises from homelessness caused by an emergency, it must be the applicant who has been personally rendered homeless by the emergency.

---

[39] SI 2001/607 (W 30). See Appendix 3.
[40] SI 2001/607, art 3(1)(a) and (b). See **13.219–13.227**.
[41] SI 2001/607, art 3(1)(a) and (c). See **13.219–13.227**.
[42] SI 2001/607, art 4. Since the making of this Order, both case law and government guidance have directed that a homeless child in these circumstances will often be considered 'a child in need' (Children Act 1989, s 20) so the duty to secure accommodation will be owed by a children's services authority. Most importantly, the guidance emphasises that local housing authorities and children's services authorities should work together and co-operate in order to meet the accommodation and other needs of children and young people. See **13.214–13.218**.
[43] SI 2001/607, art 5. See **13.228–13.233**.
[44] SI 2001/607, art 6. See **13.234–13.238**.
[45] SI 2001/607, art 7. See **13.239–13.245**.
[46] English Code, Chapter 10; Welsh Code, Chapter 14.

13.28 In other cases, the applicant may acquire priority need as a result of another person's circumstances. When it comes to pregnancy or the main statutory category of vulnerability, the applicant will be in priority need either if he or she personally is in that condition or if it applies to any person with whom the applicant resides or might reasonably be expected to reside.

13.29 If the applicant is a person subject to immigration control[47] who is eligible for assistance[48] and is not a British or EEA national, and if the applicant has (or may have) a priority need only because a person with whom he or she resides, or might reasonably be expected to reside, is pregnant, vulnerable or a dependent child, that person must be 'eligible' for assistance.[49] Otherwise the person is invisible, for the purposes of assessing priority need, to the local housing authority.[50]

13.30 If the applicant has a priority need *only* because of the presence in his or her household of a 'restricted person',[51] the applicant is known as a 'restricted case'.[52] Prior to the amendments to HA 1996 made by the Localism Act 2011 in England,[53] the main housing duty was modified so that the applicant could be made a private accommodation offer[54] in order to bring the main housing duty to an end.[55] This remains the case in Wales.[56]

13.31 Since the amendments to HA 1996 by LA 2011, ss 148 and 149, all applicants whose applications for homelessness assistance were made on or after 9 November 2012 to a local housing authority in England can be made private rented sector offers.[57] However, HA 1996, s 193(7AD) requires a local housing authority to make an applicant who is a restricted case a 'private rented sector offer'[58] 'so far as reasonably practicable'.

---

[47] See **12.64–12.70**.

[48] By virtue of falling within one of Classes A–E at reg 5 of the Allocation of Housing and Homelessness (Eligibility) (England) Regulations 2006, SI 2006/1294 (see **12.71–12.97**), or within one of Classes A–J at reg 3 of the Homelessness (Wales) Regulations 2006, SI 2006/2646 (W 227) (see **12.98–12.115**).

[49] HA 1996, s 185(4) and (5); *Kaya v Haringey London Borough Council* [2001] EWCA Civ 677, [2002] HLR 1, CA.

[50] HA 1996, s 185(4) and (5). See **12.28–12.31**.

[51] As defined at HA 1996, s 184(7); see **12.34**.

[52] HA 1996, s 193(3B).

[53] The amendments came into effect on 9 November 2012.

[54] HA 1996, s 193(7AC) as originally enacted. See **17.165–17.168**.

[55] HA 1996, s 193(7AA)–(7AD) as originally enacted. See **17.163–17.168**.

[56] At the date of writing, the amendments to HA 1996 made by LA 2011, ss 148–149 had not been brought into effect in Wales.

[57] HA 1996, s 193(7AA)–(7AC) amended by LA 2011, s 148(5)–(7) and applicable to applicants whose applications for homelessness assistance were made on or after 9 November 2012 to a local housing authority in England. At the date of writing, the amendments to HA 1996 made by LA 2011, ss 148–149 had not been brought into effect in Wales. See **17.109–17.131**.

[58] HA 1996, s 193(7AA) amended by LA 2011, s 148(5). Private rented sector offers can be made to applicants whose applications for homelessness assistance where made to local housing authorities in England on or after 9 November 2012. At the date of writing, the amendments to HA 1996 made by LA 2011, ss 148–149 had not been brought into effect in Wales.

13.32 Both the English and Welsh Priority Need Orders set out additional categories which refer only to an applicant's own personal circumstances. They do not contain any mechanism whereby another member of the applicant's household who falls within one of those priority need categories could confer priority need upon the applicant.[59] In that situation, the proper course is for the application to be made by any person who does fall within any of those categories. Any housing duty he or she is owed will be met by accommodation being provided to all members of his or her household (including non-priority members).[60] For example, if a childless couple is considering making an application for homelessness assistance, and one of the two is vulnerable as a result of having been in care, having served in the armed forces, or having been imprisoned, it is that person who should be the applicant.

THE STATUTORY CATEGORIES IN HOUSING ACT 1996, S 189(1)

13.33 These categories apply to applicants to local housing authorities in England and in Wales.

Pregnancy[61]

13.34 It is a question of fact whether an applicant, or someone who resides with or might reasonably be expected to reside with him or her, is pregnant at the date of the local housing authority's decision.[62] The length of the pregnancy is not an issue. Nor is the age of the pregnant woman.

13.35 It is for the local housing authority to undertake such sensitive inquiries as it considers necessary to satisfy itself whether a woman is pregnant. It is not for the applicant to prove pregnancy in any particular way (or at all). Obviously, as the Codes advise,[63] the normal confirmation of pregnancy issued by a GP or midwife should be accepted as sufficient evidence of pregnancy.

13.36 If the pregnant woman is not herself the applicant, the applicant will have a priority need if he or she resides with the pregnant woman or might reasonably be expected to reside with her. This would include the non-pregnant partner in a couple who had not previously lived together, but who now, in the

---

[59] Although the Welsh Code goes further and suggests that applicants should be treated as having a priority need if a member of their household falls within one of the categories in the Welsh Order: Welsh Code, para 14.2.

[60] See *R (Ogbeni) v Tower Hamlets London Borough Council* [2008] EWHC 2444 (Admin), (2008) October *Legal Action*, p 37, Admin Ct, where a 17-year-old applicant had a priority need and was entitled to the main housing duty. The local housing authority was required to secure accommodation for both him and his aunt, who had normally resided with him as a member of his family.

[61] HA 1996, s 189(1)(a).

[62] English Code, para 10.5; Welsh Code, para 14.11.

[63] English Code, para 10.5; Welsh Code, para 14.11.

light of the pregnancy, intend to do so. In those circumstances, it is for the local housing authority to determine whether such a couple might reasonably be expected to reside together, although it might be thought manifestly reasonable if the partner is the father of the expected child.[64] Self-evidently, both same sex and different sex couples can fall within this statutory definition.

13.37 If the pregnancy ends *before* the decision is made, there will be no priority need under this category, although local housing authorities are advised to consider whether the woman is vulnerable for some other special reason where there has been a miscarriage or termination.[65] Conversely, if the pregnancy ends *after* the decision has been made, the local housing authority will continue to owe its acknowledged duty towards the applicant, whether or not a child has been born. The safeguard for the local housing authority is the obligation on the applicant to notify any relevant change of circumstance occurring during the assessment process.[66]

Dependent child or children[67]

13.38 Dependent children cannot be applicants for homelessness assistance in their own right.[68] Where an application is made which involves dependent children, the question for the local housing authority is whether the applicant is someone with whom dependent children reside or with whom they might reasonably be expected to reside.

13.39 That question itself breaks down into several parts:

(1) Is there a 'child' or 'children'?

(2) Is that child, or are those children, 'dependent'?

(3) Does the dependent child, or do the dependent children, reside with the applicant?

(4) If not, might that child or those children be reasonably expected to reside with the applicant?

13.40 Advice on this priority need category is set out in the English Code, paras 10.6–10.11 and in the Welsh Code, paras 14.7–14.10.

---

[64] A single man argued that this category discriminated against single men by giving preferential treatment to women who are pregnant. A County Court Judge and subsequently a Court of Appeal judge dismissed the argument. The preferential treatment given to pregnant women is justified by their particular vulnerability while pregnant and by society's need to protect unborn children (*Thorburne v Oxford City Council* [2010] EWCA Civ 957, (2010) October *Legal Action*, p 32, CA).

[65] English Code, para 10.5; Welsh Code, para 14.11.

[66] HA 1996, s 214(2).

[67] HA 1996, s 189(1)(b).

[68] *R v Oldham Metropolitan Borough Council ex p Garlick* [1993] AC 509, HL. See **9.33**.

13.41 It is no part of the statutory requirement that the dependent children are the applicant's children. The Codes make this plain: 'dependent children need not necessarily be the applicant's own children'.[69] However, the Codes do suggest that there must be something in the nature of a parent/child relationship, referring to adoptive, foster or step relationships.[70] Nothing in HA 1996, Part 7, requires a relationship of this nature or any form of relationship between the applicant and the dependent child.

13.42 Confusingly, the Codes also refer to the category as comprising those applicants who '*have* one or more dependent children who normally live with them or who might reasonably be expected to live with them'.[71] The word 'have' in that sentence must refer to the sense that the children physically live with the applicant, rather than to their parentage.

'Children'

13.43 HA 1996, Part 7 does not specify an age at which a child ceases to be a 'child' for the purposes of this priority need category; so there is no statutory maximum age. The critical distinction is not the child's age, but the date at which the child (of whatever age) ceases to be 'dependent'.[72]

13.44 One judge has expressed the view that the word 'child' should be construed in a narrower rather than a broader sense. He suggested that:

'... "children" cannot be taken to refer to children of any age but to those who have not, or perhaps have only just, attained their majority.'[73]

13.45 The Codes of Guidance refer to the phrase 'dependent children' as embracing 'all children under 16', and also:

'... all children aged 16–18 who are in, or are about to begin, full-time education or training or who for other reasons are unable to support themselves and who live at home.'[74]

13.46 This wording suggests that adults aged 18 can be 'children' for the purposes of HA 1996, Part 7.

13.47 In *Miah v Newham London Borough Council*,[75] the Court of Appeal was dealing with a 'child' of 18. It refused the local housing authority permission to appeal against a decision that she was a dependent child. The court accepted

---

[69] English Code, para 10.8; Welsh Code, para 14.7.
[70] English Code, para 10.8; Welsh Code, para 14.7.
[71] English Code, para 10.6; Welsh Code, para 14.7 (emphasis added).
[72] See **13.50–13.52**.
[73] *R v Kensington and Chelsea Royal London Borough Council ex p Amarfio* (1995) 27 HLR 543, CA at 545, per Nourse LJ.
[74] English Code, para 10.7; Welsh Code, para 14.7.
[75] *Miah v Newham London Borough Council* [2001] EWCA Civ 487, (2001) June *Legal Action*, p 25, CA.

that, applying the guidance in the English Code, the words could include children of any age up to the child's nineteenth birthday and would therefore include someone in his or her eighteenth year.

13.48   The fact that the Codes offer no guidance concerning those who have reached their nineteenth birthday does not mean that a person of 19 or older could not be a dependent child.

13.49   It would be an extreme use of language to suggest that a person who had married could simultaneously be a 'dependent child' for the purposes of this priority need provision. The Court of Appeal has decided that a 17-year-old wife was not a 'dependent child' and, as a result, her husband did not fall within this priority need category.[76] The better course, now, would be for the 16- or 17-year-old wife to be the applicant, as she would have a priority need under the Priority Need Orders[77] and the husband would be accommodated with her in performance of the local housing authority's duty to her.

Dependent

13.50   The term 'dependent' is also not defined in HA 1996, Part 7. While it obviously includes financial dependence, local housing authorities are reminded by both the Codes and the case law that children aged 16 or over may be financially independent, but not yet mature enough to live independently from their parents. They will therefore still be 'dependent' for these purposes.[78]

13.51   HA 1996, Part 7 does not say that the dependent child must be dependent on the applicant. On the face of it, the statutory language could be satisfied if a dependent child is living with the applicant, even if the child is wholly dependent on another. An example would be two brothers who live together, the eldest being in full-time employment, and the younger being financially supported by his parents who are abroad but send money. In such a case, the older brother would have a priority need, even though his brother was not financially dependent on him or her. The point is probably academic since, in this and any other similar examples, the younger brother would be likely to have some emotional dependence on his older brother.

13.52   The English Code advises that 'there must be actual dependence on the applicant' although the dependence need not be wholly or exclusively on the applicant, suggesting that a child may be dependent upon more than one

---

[76]   *Hackney London Borough Council v Ekinci* [2001] EWCA Civ 776, (2002) 34 HLR 2, CA.

[77]   Homelessness (Priority Need for Accommodation) (England) Order 2002, SI 2002/2051, art 3 (see **13.127–13.174**) and Homeless Persons (Priority Need) (Wales) Order 2001, SI 2001/607 (W 30), reg 4 (see **13.218–13.218**).

[78]   English Code, para 10.7; Welsh Code, para 14.7; and *R v Kensington and Chelsea Royal London Borough Council ex p Amarfio* (1995) 27 HLR 543, CA.

person.[79] This wording, which was not in the previous edition of the Code, reflects the statutory language originally used in the Housing (Homeless Persons) Act 1977, when the category was defined as 'if he has dependent children who are residing with him or who might reasonably be expected to reside with him'.[80] Indeed, in 1996, a judge decided that this language did require that there be at least some dependency by the child on the applicant.[81] However, that decision does not, strictly speaking, apply to the definition in HA 1996, Part 7, and there is nothing in the case law on HA 1996, Part 7 to suggest that this priority need category can only be met if the child is dependent on the applicant, rather than upon someone else.

'Resides with' the applicant

13.53 The next question for the local housing authority is whether the dependent child actually resides with the applicant. This is a straightforward question of fact. If a child does in fact reside with the applicant, the question of whether or not the child 'might reasonably be expected' to reside with him or her does not arise.[82]

13.54 The word 'reside' would not normally be used to describe a situation in which one person is visiting another, or even staying with them for a short time, such as for a holiday. The English Code of Guidance goes, perhaps, too far in suggesting that there must be:

'... some degree of permanence or regularity, rather than a temporary arrangement whereby the children are merely staying with the applicant for a limited period.'[83]

13.55 Certainly, the English Code is wrong to suggest that the test is whether applicants have children who *'normally* live with them'.[84] Where HA 1996 intends to address a concept of normally living together, it uses the term

---

[79] English Code, para 10.6. The Welsh Code says 'there must be a dependent relationship akin to that of a parent-child', para 14.7.

[80] Housing (Homeless Persons) Act 1977, s 2(1)(a).

[81] *R v Westminster City Council ex p Bishop* (1997) 29 HLR 546, QBD at 551–4. The decision is complicated, because the language considered by the judge was not that in the Housing (Homeless Persons) Act 1977 but instead that in the Housing Act 1985, where the relevant category was said to be 'with whom dependent children reside' – removing 'he has'. However, the Housing Act 1985 was a consolidating Act and so the judge held that the language used was not intended to change the original statutory meaning. HA 1996, which reproduces the language of the Housing Act 1985 (and not the language of the Housing (Homeless Persons) Act 1977) is not a consolidating Act, but replaces the legislative scheme in the Housing Act 1985. The language of HA 1996 is not, therefore, subject to the same construction and can be considered afresh.

[82] *R v Hillingdon London Borough Council ex p Islam* [1983] 1 AC 688, HL (a decision on priority need at first instance and that aspect of the judgment not subject to appeal); *R v Lambeth London Borough Council ex p Ly* (1986) 19 HLR 51, QBD; *R v Lambeth London Borough Council ex p Bodunrin* (1992) 24 HLR 647, QBD; and *Oxford City Council v Bull* [2011] EWCA Civ 609, [2011] HLR 35, [2012] 1 WLR 203, CA.

[83] English Code, para 10.6. There is no similar phrase in the Welsh Code, see paras 14.7–14.10.

[84] English Code, para 10.6 (emphasis added). There is no similar phrase in the Welsh Code.

'normally resides with him'.[85] In the case of this priority need category, the simple question is: 'With whom do the children reside?' – not 'With whom do they normally reside?'.

13.56 Children who are temporarily away from the applicant on holiday or for other purposes would ordinarily be said to 'reside with' the applicant during their absence, not with the person with whom they are staying.[86]

'Reasonably expected to reside' with the applicant

13.57 Even if no dependent child is actually residing with him or her, an applicant will have priority need if at least one dependent child might reasonably be expected to reside with him or her.[87] This covers the situation where the applicant and the dependent child (or children) are not currently living together but might reasonably be expected to live together in future. It will come into play where, for example, children are in the care of children's services or staying with relatives, but would return to live with their parents if the parents obtain accommodation.

13.58 Where children are in the care of a children's services authority (whether voluntarily or under the terms of a care order) and are not currently living with the applicant, local housing authorities are advised that liaison with the children's services authority[88] is essential and that there should be joint consideration before the local housing authority reaches its decision.[89]

13.59 The correct approach to the question of whether it is reasonable to expect a person who does not currently live with an applicant to live with him or her is more fully discussed in Chapter 11.[90]

Separated parents and dependent children

13.60 Most of the difficult decisions on the 'dependent children' priority need category arise where the application is made by one of two parents who are separated. The local housing authority will have to consider three questions:

(1) Is there a child who is dependent ('dependency')?

(2) If so, does the child reside with the applicant ('residence')?

---

[85] HA 1996, s 176(a). See **11.25–11.29**.
[86] *Halonen v Westminster City Council* (1997) September *Legal Action*, p 19, Central London County Court, and *R v Lewisham London Borough Council ex p Creppy* (1992) 24 HLR 121, CA.
[87] HA 1996, s 189(1)(b).
[88] Or children's services department, in the case of a unitary authority.
[89] English Code, para 10.11; Welsh Code, para 14.10.
[90] See **11.30–11.32**.

(3) If not, is the child reasonably expected to reside with the applicant in the future ('future residence')?[91]

Dependency

13.61 As already indicated, HA 1996, Part 7 itself does not require that the child be dependent on the applicant.[92] However, in cases where parents are separated, the expectation will be that the child is at least to some extent dependent on the parent who is applying to the local housing authority for homelessness assistance. Where a local housing authority found on the facts of a particular case that a child was exclusively dependent upon his mother (who received both child benefit and income support for the child) and not the father (who was the applicant), the father's challenge to that decision was dismissed.[93] However, the question for the local housing authority is not whether the child is wholly and exclusively dependent upon the applicant, or upon its other parent,[94] but simply whether the child is dependent. The question of dependency has been described as 'fact-sensitive to a very large degree'.[95]

Residence and co-residence

13.62 When considering whether the child resides with the applicant, the local housing authority should consider all the circumstances, including whether or not a court order has been made in respect of where the child should reside. An issue about where a child resides, or might reasonably be expected to reside, might arise where a child's two parents are separated, or in any other circumstance where more than one adult is involved in bringing up the child, such as different sets of foster parents, adoptive parents, grandparents or other members of the child's family.

Residence orders

13.63 Where a residence order in favour of one of the parents has been made, the Codes advise that the local housing authority should normally follow the provisions of the order and treat the child as residing with the person identified in the order.[96]

13.64 Nowadays, it is not unusual for family courts to make shared residence orders, either after a contested hearing between the parents, or by consent.[97] Shared residence orders can be made even when the child does not divide his or

---

[91]   *R v Port Talbot Borough Council ex p McCarthy* (1990) 23 HLR 207, CA.
[92]   See **13.50–13.52**.
[93]   *R v Westminster City Council ex p Bishop* (1997) 29 HLR 546, QBD and see fn 81.
[94]   *R v Lambeth London Borough Council ex p Vagliviello* (1991) 22 HLR 392, CA.
[95]   *McGrath v Camden London Borough Council* [2007] EWCA Civ 1269, (2008) January *Legal Action*, p 37, CA.
[96]   English Code, para 10.9; Welsh Code, para 14.8.
[97]   Children Act 1989, s 8. As recognised by the House of Lords in *Holmes-Moorhouse v Richmond upon Thames Royal London Borough Council* [2009] UKHL 7, [2009] 1 WLR 413, HL at [7], per Lord Hoffmann.

her time equally between the parents.[98] This is recognised in the current versions of the Codes, which no longer advise that it is exceptional for a child to reside with both parents.[99]

Informal arrangements

13.65 Where no court order has been obtained, the local housing authority cannot just refuse to consider the question of a child's residence until a court makes such an order.[100] The local housing authority must consider all the present circumstances of the case. It is looking to see whether the child resides with the applicant; it is not enough that the child visits the applicant. A court order or parental agreement for staying contact does not make the visiting child resident or co-resident with the applicant, because 'staying access does not equal residence'[101] and 'the staying access will not amount to residence with their father'.[102]

13.66 A child need not live full-time with the applicant in order to 'reside' with him or her. The child may divide his or her time between the two parents. However, there should be 'some regularity' to the arrangement.[103] The possibility that the child may be residing with both of his or her separated parents was previously described by the courts as 'unlikely to be the normal arrangement',[104] as 'a remote possibility', or 'a very rare case'.[105] However, the current edition of the English Code reflects a more modern and flexible approach: 'housing authorities should remember that where parents separate, it will often be in the best interests of the child to maintain a relationship with both parents'.[106]

13.67 Local housing authorities which have considered where a child's 'main' residence is, or which parent has a 'greater' responsibility, have been held to be

---

[98]   See *D v D* [2000] EWCA Civ 3009, [2001] 1 FLR 495, CA.

[99]   English Code, para 10.10; Welsh Code, para 14.8. The 2002 English Code contained similar advice at para 8.10 (Homelessness Code of Guidance for Local Authorities (England) (Department of Health and Office of the Deputy Prime Minister), July 2002) but concluded 'it would only be in very exceptional cases though that a child might be considered to reside with both parents'. This last sentence is omitted from the current guidance at para 10.10 of the English Code. In *Holmes-Moorhouse v Richmond upon Thames Royal London Borough Council* [2009] UKHL 7, [2009] 1 WLR 413, HL at [11], Lord Hoffmann described the paragraph in the 2002 Code as 'muddling in its reasoning' and saying little as to what considerations the local housing authority should take into account.

[100] *R v Ealing London Borough Council ex p Sidhu* (1982) 2 HLR 45, QBD; Welsh Code, para 14.8.

[101] *R v Port Talbot Borough Council ex p McCarthy* (1991) 23 HLR 207, CA at 210, per Butler-Sloss LJ.

[102] *R v Port Talbot Borough Council ex p McCarthy* (1991) 23 HLR 207, CA at 211, per Dillon LJ.

[103] English Code, para 10.10; this phrase is not contained in the Welsh Code, paras 14.8–14.9.

[104] *R v Port Talbot Borough Council ex p McCarthy* (1991) 23 HLR 207, CA at 210, per Butler-Sloss LJ.

[105] *R v Lambeth London Borough Council ex p Vaglivello* (1990) 22 HLR 392, CA at 397, per Purchas LJ.

[106] English Code, para 10.10; see also Welsh Code, paras 14.8–14.9.

wrong in law.[107] But where a local housing authority applied the correct test ('Does the child reside with the applicant?'), its decision that an applicant's children did not reside with him (even though they spent three or four nights each week with him) was not wrong in law.[108]

13.68 In *Oxford City Council v Bull*,[109] three children moved from living with their mother in adequate accommodation to live with their father in a single room. He made an application for homelessness assistance shortly afterwards. The local housing authority accommodated the father and the three children in interim accommodation.[110] It subsequently decided that the children were not residing with their father and that the arrangements in the interim accommodation should not be taken into account. The Court of Appeal held that the local housing authority's decision was wrong in law. The period in interim accommodation constituted 'residence' for the purposes of HA 1996, s 189(1)(b).[111] Accordingly, by the date of the review decision, the children were and had been 'residing with' their father. The interim accommodation was 'where [the children] kept their clothes and possessions. It was their main home, from which they went to school. It is quite true that the children went to stay with their mother regularly, but that does not detract from the fact that they resided at their father's house'.[112]

13.69 It is often very difficult to say whether a child is residing with an applicant (as distinct from visiting), and a sensitive home visit by an officer can provide the local housing authority with much useful information. But even when the facts are established, two officers of the same local housing authority (and, indeed, of different local housing authorities) can legitimately reach different conclusions. For example, in one case[113] a visiting officer found the child with the applicant at his flat and the presence of 'many personal effects, toothbrush and paste, clothing and food' belonging to the child. The visiting officer concluded that this (together with assertions by both the separated parents that the child was residing with the applicant) established that the child was therefore living with the applicant. Her recommendation was reversed by her superior, who took a different view of the facts. The case amply demonstrates why, in this context, an initial adverse decision could usefully be subject to the review procedure[114] in almost all cases. If the initial adverse decision is upheld on review, it may be sensible to apply to a different local housing authority with the prospect of receiving a more favourable decision.

---

[107] *R v Kingswood Borough Council ex p Smith-Morse* [1995] 2 FLR 137, QBD, and *R v Leeds City Council ex p Collier* (1998) June *Legal Action*, p 14, QBD.

[108] *R v Oxford City Council ex p Doyle* (1998) 30 HLR 506, QBD.

[109] [2011] EWCA Civ 609, [2011] HLR 35, [2012] 1 WLR 203, CA.

[110] HA 1988, s 188(1). See **16.12–16.28**.

[111] Relying on *Mohamed v Hammersmith & Fulham London Borough Council* [2011] UKHL 57, [2002]1 AC 547, HL. See **15.54–15.59**.

[112] Jackson LJ at [39]. However, the father had become homeless intentionally because his decision to permit the children to move in with him was his own deliberate conduct which led to his being required to live his previous accommodation. See **14.122**.

[113] *R v Westminster City Council ex p Bishop* (1997) 29 HLR 546, QBD.

[114] Described at **19.8–19.141**.

Future residence

13.70 If the child is not currently residing with the applicant, the local housing authority should next consider whether it is reasonable to expect the child to reside with him or her in the future. This issue will often arise in the context of a child whose parents have separated, but may be relevant if the child is living with foster parents, or there are potential adoptive parents, or other members of the child's family wishes to be involved in the child's up-bringing.

13.71 It may be that there is a genuine arrangement between the separated parents that the child should reside with the applicant once the applicant has suitable accommodation. Again, this is a question of fact for the local housing authority. Its decision notification should show that it has separately considered the questions:

(1) Is the child now residing with the applicant?

(2) If not, is it reasonable to expect the child to reside with the applicant in the future?[115]

13.72 In some cases, family courts have made shared residence orders, either after a contested hearing between the parents, or by consent. What should happen when the parents have a shared residence order but one parent is homeless and has made an application for homelessness assistance to a local housing authority? His or her children do not actually reside with him or her.

13.73 This scenario was considered by the House of Lords in *Holmes-Moorhouse v Richmond upon Thames Royal London Borough Council*.[116] In that case, the Court of Appeal had held that once a family court had decided in contested proceedings that residence should be shared, and had made an order to that effect, the local housing authority could not deny that the children might reasonably be expected to live with the father (who was applying for homelessness assistance) as well as with their mother. The House of Lords overturned the Court of Appeal's decision. It held that when the local housing authority is deciding whether dependent children might reasonably be expected to reside with a homeless parent, the local housing authority is entitled to take into account the fact that housing is a scarce resource, and to have regard to the social purposes of HA 1996, Part 7, to the claims of other homeless applicants and the scale of the local housing authority's own responsibilities. The question for the local housing authority is whether it is reasonably to be expected, in the context of a scheme for housing the homeless, that children who already have a home with one parent should also be able to reside with their other parent. The existence of a shared residence order is relevant, but not a determinative factor. It added that the paramount consideration for family courts, when deciding

---

[115] For an illustration of a judicial challenge prompted by the failure to distinguish these two questions, see *R v Port Talbot Borough Council ex p McCarthy* (1997) 23 HLR 207, CA.

[116] [2009] UKHL 7, [2009] 1 WLR 413, HL.

issues about the upbringing of a child, is the child's welfare under Children Act 1989. A local housing authority should not intervene in family proceedings to argue against a court making a shared residence order, but the family court should not make a shared residence order unless it appears reasonably likely that both parties will have accommodation in which the children can reside.[117]

13.74 In *El Goure v Kensington & Chelsea Royal London Borough Council*,[118] the Court of Appeal held that Lord Hoffmann's reference in *Holmes-Moorhouse v Richmond upon Thames Royal London Borough Council*[119] to it only being reasonable for a child to reside with both his or her separated parents 'in exceptional circumstances' was not intended to provide an additional test and the correct test was 'the statutory test of reasonable expectation of residence'.[120]

Vulnerability[121]

13.75 To meet this category of priority need the relevant person (the applicant or a person with whom the applicant resides or might reasonably be expected to reside) must:

(1)   be currently 'vulnerable'; and

(2)   be vulnerable by reason of one of the prescribed statutory matters.

'Vulnerable'

13.76 The term 'vulnerable' is not defined in HA 1996, Part 7. It has been judicially defined by the Court of Appeal in *R v Camden London Borough Council ex p Pereira*.[122] That definition has been repeatedly followed and applied in later cases and is reproduced in the current Codes.[123] A person is 'vulnerable' if he or she is less able to fend for himself or herself than an ordinary homeless person and so will suffer injury or detriment in circumstances in which the ordinary homeless person would not.

13.77 In its very earliest form, the judicial definition of 'vulnerable' given in 1982 was:

---

[117]   Welsh Code, paras 14.8–14.9 contain guidance on the important case of *Holmes-Moorhouse v Richmond upon Thames Royal London Borough Council* ([2009] UKHL 7, [2009] 1 WLR 413, HL). The English Code was published three years before the case was decided by the House of Lords.

[118]   [2012] EWCA Civ 670, [2012] HLR 36, CA.

[119]   [2009] UKHL 7, [2009] 1 WLR 413, HL.

[120]   Per Mummery LJ at [44].

[121]   HA 1996, s 189(1)(c).

[122]   *R v Camden London Borough Council ex p Pereira* (1999) 31 HLR 317, CA, reconciling the earlier and somewhat contradictory authorities of *R v Waveney District Council ex p Bowers* [1982] 3 WLR 661, CA; *R v Lambeth London Borough Council ex p Carroll* (1987) 20 HLR 142, QBD; and *R v Westminster City Council ex p Ortiz* (1993) 27 HLR 364, CA.

[123]   English Code, para 10.13; Welsh Code, para 14.13.

'... less able to fend for oneself so that injury or detriment would result when a less vulnerable man would be able to cope without harmful effects.'[124]

13.78 The most recent authoritative guidance from the Court of Appeal is contained in the judgment of Auld LJ in *Osmani v Camden London Borough Council*.[125] In *Osmani*, the judicial meaning of 'vulnerable' was put in this way:

> 'the test is a single one of a homeless person's less than normal ability to fend for himself such that he will suffer more harm than would an ordinary homeless person – a 'composite' assessment'.[126]

13.79 Other important points from the same judgment include:

(1)   The test adopted by the judiciary is not a statutory formulation but a judicial guide.

(2)   The test has to be applied in its broad and immediate statutory context, that context being the priorities between different homeless persons within a scheme of social welfare conferring benefits at public expense on those identified as entitled to priority.

(3)   Decisions on identifying those priorities, weighed in the context of local housing authorities' own local burdens and finite resources, are likely to be highly judgmental and it is local housing authorities, not judges, who are best placed to make those decisions.

(4)   Local housing authorities should take care to apply the test on the assumption that the applicant has become, or will become, street homeless, not on any ability to fend for him or herself while still housed.

(5)   In this respect, regard should be had to the particular debilitating effects of depressive disorders and the fragility of those suffering from them if suddenly deprived of the 'prop' of their own home.

(6)   Although local housing authorities should look for, and pay close regard to, medical evidence, it is for the local housing authority to determine whether an applicant is vulnerable.

(7)   Reasons should be given for a decision, and those reasons should be sufficient to enable an applicant to form a view on whether to challenge it by requesting a review (or, in respect of a review decision, by an appeal on

---

[124]   *R v Waveney District Council ex p Bowers* [1982] 3 WLR 661, CA at 122, per Donaldson MR, Waller and Griffiths LJJ.

[125]   [2004] EWCA Civ 1706, [2005] HLR 22, CA at [38], per Auld LJ.

[126]   *Osmani v Camden London Borough Council* [2004] EWCA Civ 1706, [2005] HLR 22, CA at [38.6], per Auld LJ.

a point of law).[127] But decision letters should not be treated as if they were statutes. When looking for reasoning in a letter, it should be read as a whole to get its full sense.[128]

13.80 Some examples of decisions in which the courts have found that the local housing authority's decision-maker either did apply the test correctly or did not apply the test correctly are:

- *Frempomah v Haringey London Borough Council:* where the local housing authority had found 'scarcely any homeless people are on the streets'; this was the wrong test, as Haringey had not considered what would happen if *the applicant* were street homeless;[129]

- *Dostenko v Westminster City Council:* where the applicant was actually street homeless while his request for a review was being considered; he appealed on the ground that the reviewing officer had not taken into account the effects on him of being street homeless. The appeal was dismissed in part because the reviewing officer had not been told that he was street homeless, and permission to bring a second appeal was refused by the Court of Appeal. The Court of Appeal commented that, if there had been a significant deterioration in his ability to cope, he might have been better advised to make a fresh application;[130]

- *Littlejohn v City of Westminster Council:* where Rix LJ, although dismissing the applicant's application for permission to bring a second appeal, said '[i]t may be that a proven ability to obtain accommodation will not prevent an applicant from being found to be vulnerable within the statutory guidelines, if his obtaining of accommodation proves to be illusory because of an inability to maintain that accommodation'.[131]

13.81 The previous edition of the English Code suggested that the judicial definition is also met if it is 'likely' that the person would suffer such injury or detriment.[132] But the Court of Appeal has held that there is no element of likelihood in the definition of vulnerability.[133] The current editions of each Code refer to 'would suffer' rather than 'likely to'.[134]

13.82 The material sense in which the person must be less well able to 'fend' for himself or herself is in coping with his or her actual (or threatened)

---

127 For reviews, see **19.8–19.141**. For appeals on a point of law, see Chapter 19, at **19.146–19.201**.
128 *Osmani v Camden London Borough Council* [2004] EWCA Civ 1706, [2005] HLR 22, CA at [38.7], per Auld LJ, confirmed in *Bellouti v Wandsworth London Borough Council* [2005] EWCA Civ 602, [2005] HLR 46, CA.
129 *Shelter Housing Law Update June 2006, Edmonton County Court.*
130 [2007] EWCA Civ 1325, (2008) February *Legal Action*, p 40, CA.
131 [2007] EWCA Civ 1652, (2008) October *Legal Action*, p 37, CA.
132 *Homelessness Code of Guidance for Local Authorities (England)* (Department of Health and Office of the Deputy Prime Minister, July 2002), para 8.13.
133 *Griffin v City of Westminster* [2004] EWCA Civ 108, [2004] HLR 32, CA.
134 English Code, para 10.13; Welsh Code, para 14.13.

homelessness.[135] It had previously been suggested that being 'able to fend' for himself or herself was a general reference to ability to find or keep accommodation, or to the ability to deal with being homeless.[136] In other words, the relevant 'vulnerability' was thought to be 'vulnerability loosely in housing terms or in the context of housing'[137] and therefore to mean 'vulnerable in the context of a need for housing accommodation'.[138] However, since the decision in the leading 'vulnerability' case of *Pereira* (in which all the earlier judgments were considered and explained or overruled), the test has been narrowed in its application by reference to its strict statutory context of homelessness or threatened homelessness:

> 'It must appear that his inability to fend for himself whilst homeless [or threatened with homelessness] will result in injury or detriment to him which would not be suffered by an ordinary homeless person who was able to cope.'[139]

13.83 Obviously, that test will be satisfied by a person whose circumstances are such that he or she is not able to obtain housing unaided and is thus unable to deal with homelessness in the ordinary way.[140] There need not be actual injury or detriment. An increase in the risk of injury or other harm is itself a 'detriment'. 'Injury or detriment' can include physical injury, a deterioration of a person's mental condition, or the risk of self-harm.[141]

13.84 The difficult exercise required in applying the *Pereira* test has been summed up by one judge who referred to two important, and in part conflicting, interests:

> 'One is the need of local housing authorities to husband their resources and to ensure that only those genuinely entitled are treated as in priority need. The other is the catastrophic consequences of a failure to house someone whose vulnerability

---

[135] *R v Camden London Borough Council ex p Pereira* (1998) 31 HLR 317, CA at 330, per Hobhouse LJ.

[136] *R v Lambeth London Borough Council ex p Carroll* (1988) 20 HLR 142, QBD.

[137] *R v Bath City Council ex p Sangermano* (1984) 17 HLR 94, QBD at 97, per Hodgson J, followed with approval in *R v Wandsworth London Borough Council ex p Banbury* (1986) 19 HLR 76, QBD at 78, by Russell J and in *R v Reigate and Banstead District Council ex p Di Domenico* (1988) 20 HLR 153, QBD at 154, per Mann J.

[138] *R v Kensington and Chelsea Royal London Borough Council ex p Kihara* (1997) 29 HLR 147, CA at 158, per Neill LJ.

[139] *R v Camden London Borough Council ex p Pereira* (1998) 31 HLR 317, CA at 330, per Hobhouse LJ. Note that there is no requirement on local housing authorities to identify precisely the attributes of the normal homeless person with whom the applicant is being compared (*Tetteh v Kingston upon Thames Royal London Borough Council* [2004] EWCA 1775, [2005] HLR 21, CA).

[140] *R v Camden London Borough Council ex p Pereira* (1998) 31 HLR 317, CA at 330, per Hobhouse LJ.

[141] *Griffin v City of Westminster Council* [2004] EWCA Civ 108, CA, [2004] HLR 32, CA; *Gentle v Wandsworth London Borough Council* [2005] EWCA Civ 1377, (2006) January *Legal Action*, p 32, CA; and *Khelassi v Brent London Borough Council* [2006] EWCA Civ 1825, CA.

will make them unable to cope with homelessness – a legal test which itself makes the dubious assumption that homelessness is something fit people can always cope with.'[142]

Making inquiries into whether a person is vulnerable[143]

13.85 Whether a person is 'vulnerable' is a question of fact and degree for the local housing authority to determine. It is not a question that can be delegated to a doctor, nurse, consultant or anyone else.[144]

13.86 A local housing authority will usually need to make inquiries into the applicant's medical condition in order to determine vulnerability. The local housing authority should take account of any medical evidence it receives and may seek its own medical adviser's view. Indeed,

> '... where the applicant claims to be vulnerable for medical reasons or where on making proper inquiries it is apparent to the authorities that such is his claim, it is both proper and necessary ... to take and consider a medical opinion, unless the applicant's condition renders him so obviously vulnerable that that is not necessary.'[145]

13.87 Very often the medical evidence will be helpful in identifying the physical disability, mental handicap or mental illness, but less useful on whether the applicant satisfies the definition of 'vulnerable'. That is a question for a local housing authority, not a doctor. If a view is expressed by a medical expert, that is merely one consideration which may influence the local housing authority's own conclusion, but it is certainly not bound by it.[146] Likewise, the local housing authority's own medical adviser may express a view on 'vulnerability', but the local housing authority should not merely rubber-stamp that view.[147] Where there is competing medical evidence, the evaluation of it is a matter for the local housing authority.[148]

---

[142] *Shala v Birmingham City Council* [2007] EWCA Civ 624, [2008] HLR 8, CA at [24], per Sedley LJ.

[143] See also 10.50–10.64 and English Code para 10.13; Welsh Code para 14.13.

[144] *R v Lambeth London Borough Council ex p Walters* (1994) 26 HLR 170, QBD; *Osmani v Camden London Borough Council* [2004] EWCA Civ 1706, [2005] HLR 22, CA; and *Cramp v Hastings Borough Council* [2005] EWCA Civ 1005, [2005] HLR 48, CA.

[145] *R v Lambeth London Borough Council ex p Carroll* (1988) 20 HLR 142, QBD at 150, per Webster J.

[146] *Chowdhoury v Newham London Borough Council* [2004] EWCA Civ 8, (2004) March *Legal Action*, p 25, CA; *Cramp v Hastings Borough Council* [2005] EWCA Civ 1005, [2005] HLR 48, CA; and *R (Bauer-Czarnomski) v Ealing London Borough Council* [2010] EWHC Admin 130, (2010) March *Legal Action*, p 30, Admin Ct (the latter was in respect of an application for an allocation of social housing, see **4.102**).

[147] *R v Wandsworth London Borough Council ex p Banbury* (1987) 19 HLR 76, QBD; and *R v Lambeth London Borough Council ex p Carroll* (1988) 20 HLR 142, QBD.

[148] *Mehmet v Wandsworth London Borough Council* [2004] EWCA Civ 1560, (2005) January *Legal Action*, p 28, CA.

13.88 In keeping with the general burden on the making of inquiries,[149] it is for the local housing authority to make all necessary inquiries into the person's medical condition, not for the applicant to produce medical evidence. The applicant may, however, be expected to give written consent to the local housing authority's medical advisers to seek medical information or inspect medical records. The local housing authority is under a duty to act fairly in its gathering of, and use of, medical information. That includes a requirement to put adverse medical opinions to the applicant for comment before an initial decision is reached.[150]

13.89 There has been some judicial consideration of the role of medical advisers to local housing authorities. A local housing authority is entitled to obtain its own expert opinion, but care has to be taken not to appear to be using professional medical advisers simply to provide or shore up reasons for a negative decision.[151] Where there is a conflict between medical opinions, the local housing authority must bear in mind the respective qualifications of the experts.[152] The local housing authority's medical adviser has the function of enabling the local housing authority to understand the medical issues and to evaluate for itself the expert evidence from the applicant's medical advisers. In the absence of an examination of the patient, the local housing authority's medical adviser's advice cannot itself constitute expert evidence of an applicant's condition. The local housing authority must take any absence of a personal examination of the applicant into account. If a medical adviser has not personally examined the applicant, he or she could consider discussing the applicant's condition with his or her treating doctors.[153]

13.90 It is for the local housing authority to decide what inquiries are necessary and what weight to give to the various pieces of medical evidence.[154]

---

[149] See **10.15–10.19**.

[150] *Yemlahi v Lambeth London Borough Council* (2000) August *Legal Action*, p 26, Wandsworth County Court; and *Thorne v Winchester City Council* (2000) April *Legal Action*, p 32, CA. There is no requirement that the applicant should always have 'the last word' in respect of medical advice (*Bellouti v Wandsworth London Borough Council* [2005] EWCA Civ 602, [2005] HLR 46, CA).

[151] *Hall v Wandsworth London Borough Council, Carter v Wandsworth London Borough Council* [2004] EWCA Civ 1740, [2005] HLR 23, CA; *Shala v Birmingham City Council* [2007] EWCA Civ 624, [2008] HLR 8, CA.

[152] *R v Newham London Borough Council ex p Lumley* (2001) 33 HLR 11, QBD; *Khelassi v Brent London Borough Council* [2006] EWCA Civ 1825, CA; and *Shala v Birmingham City Council* [2007] EWCA Civ 624, [2008] HLR 8, CA. All of those cases concerned medical evidence from a psychiatrist which had been evaluated by a GP advising the local housing authority.

[153] *Shala v Birmingham City Council* [2007] EWCA Civ 624, [2008] HLR 8, CA at [23], per Sedley LJ. The Court of Appeal made these comments in relation to the use of medical advisers from the organisation, Nowmedical, which is regularly used by local housing authorities. However, the Court of Appeal refused permission to bring a second appeal where the applicant was arguing that advice from Nowmedical should not be relied upon by local housing authorities in any circumstances (*Harper v Oxford City Council* [2007] EWCA Civ 1169, (2008) January *Legal Action*, p 37, CA). A barrister has compiled the various court decisions and other public references to Nowmedical at: http://www.niknicol.co.uk/page6.html.

[154] *Wandsworth London Borough Council v Allison* [2008] EWCA Civ 354, (2008) June *Legal Action*, p 33, CA.

A local housing authority's decision is only susceptible to challenge for failure to make all necessary inquiries if no reasonable local housing authority would have failed to regard certain additional inquiries as necessary.[155] Inquiries by local housing authorities in these 'medical' cases are further considered at **10.50–10.64**.

13.91 Medical reports obtained as part of an assessment by the Department for Work and Pensions of a person's entitlement to specific welfare benefits may be taken into account by the local housing authority, but the local housing authority must bear in mind that assessment of eligibility for benefits is a wholly different exercise from assessment of priority need.[156]

13.92 There will obviously be a close relationship between the issue of vulnerability and a possible disability that the applicant, or a member of the applicant's household, might have. This relationship will require the local housing authority to be alive to equality issues. The local housing authority must always take due steps to consider any disability (or other protected characteristic) that might be relevant.[157] That duty is not confined to circumstances where the disability is 'obvious'. The decision-maker must make inquiries into the issue of disability if some feature of the evidence presented raises a real possibility that the applicant (or a member of his or her household) might be disabled and that disability (or other protected characteristic) is relevant to the decision under consideration.[158]

13.93 Once the local housing authority is satisfied that there is 'vulnerability', the next step is for it to decide on the cause. For there to be priority need, the vulnerability must have arisen as a result of one of the specified statutory causes[159] or, in the case of applications to local housing authorities in England, one of the additional causes set out in the Priority Need Order.[160] If the relevant person is vulnerable, but the cause of the vulnerability cannot be put into one of the specified categories, the relevant person may still be vulnerable for some 'other special reason'.[161]

---

[155] *Cramp v Hastings Borough Council* [2005] EWCA Civ 1005, [2005] HLR 48, CA; and see **10.20–10.24**.

[156] *Mangion v Lewisham London Borough Council* [2008] EWCA Civ 1642, (2009) January *Legal Action*, p 26, CA; and *Simpson-Lowe v Croydon London Borough Council* [2012] EWCA Civ 131, (2012) April *Legal Action*, p 47, CA. See **10.63**.

[157] Equality Act 2010, ss 5–12.

[158] *Pieretti v Enfield London Borough Council* [2010] EWCA Civ 1104, [2011] HLR 3, CA. For 'vulnerable as a result of ... physical disability', see **13.104–13.109**.

[159] HA 1996, s 189(1)(c). See **13.94**.

[160] SI 2002/2051. See **13.95**.

[161] HA 1996, s 189(1)(c). See **13.110–13.119**.

The statutory causes

13.94 A range of potential causes of vulnerability are set out in HA 1996, Part 7[162] including 'old age', 'physical disability' and many others. But a person does not accrue priority need simply by achieving 'old age' or by reason of having a 'physical disability', etc. Neither being 100 years old nor having lost a limb (or even two) automatically qualifies the relevant person as having priority need. The specified statutory causes are relevant only in that they could give rise to a vulnerability that counts for priority need purposes. The test is not whether an applicant, or a member of his or her household, falls within the ambit of one of these causes, but whether he or she is vulnerable and, if so, whether the vulnerability is the result of one of the specified reasons (or the result of some 'other special reason'). The full list (for local housing authorities in both England and Wales) is:

(1) old age;[163]

(2) mental illness;[164]

(3) mental handicap;[165]

(4) physical disability;[166] or

(5) other special reason.[167]

13.95 For applications to local housing authorities in England only,[168] the list also includes:

(6) having been looked after, accommodated or fostered;[169]

(7) having been in the armed forces;[170]

(8) having been imprisoned;[171] or

(9) having been driven from home by actual or threatened violence.[172]

---

[162] And, for local housing authorities in England, in the Homelessness (Priority Need for Accommodation) (England) Order 2002, SI 2002/2051. See **13.95** and **13.182–13.211**.

[163] See **13.97–13.98**.

[164] See **13.99–13.103**.

[165] See **13.99–13.103**.

[166] See **13.104–13.109**.

[167] See **13.110–13.119**.

[168] See **13.126** and **13.182–13.211**.

[169] See **13.186–13.189**.

[170] See **13.190–13.195**.

[171] See **13.196–13.202**.

[172] See **13.203–13.211**.

13.96 The vulnerability need not be *wholly* the result of one of the specified matters listed above. Many vulnerable individuals will have been rendered vulnerable by several causes or by a combination of factors. Some causal factors may be in the list, others not. The statutory test is satisfied if at least one of the listed matters contributes to the vulnerability. So, in one case,[173] the court considered that a man who had been reduced to a state of vulnerability by alcoholism would not normally, by that reason alone, have qualified. But he had suffered a severe head injury a year prior to his application and the medical advice was that this had caused 'some persistent disability made worse by his drinking habits'. The court said that whether the brain injury was described as a 'mental handicap' or 'other special reason', it was 'another important factor' in the applicant's current vulnerability and made the 'whole difference' so as to bring him into the priority need category. In another case, a man who had an addiction to hard drugs, partly as a result of having spent most of his childhood in care, might be 'vulnerable' as a result of the combination of difficulties he suffered from.[174]

Old age

13.97 'Old age' is not defined in HA 1996, Part 7. The Codes advise that applications concerning people aged over 60, should be 'considered carefully', and that local housing authorities should not assume that people over 60 will be automatically vulnerable nor, conversely, that people younger than 60 are ruled out of vulnerability on the basis of 'old age'. The Codes recommend that each case should be considered on its individual circumstances.[175] Such guidance is of little practical value and local housing authorities are left to determine for themselves whether a person aged 54 or 58 (or whatever age) can be said to be 'old' for these purposes.

13.98 Earlier editions of the Codes had suggested particular ages but this only produced unhelpful rigidity. For example, an early Code suggested that men reaching 65, should be accepted. 'Taken literally this would mean that a healthy man of 64 would not be vulnerable while the same man at 65 would be'.[176] Not surprisingly, therefore, there is no specific guidance offered by the current Codes, nor by any reported cases, as to what constitutes 'old age'.

Mental illness or (mental) handicap

13.99 The statutory term 'mental illness or handicap' plainly includes a wide range of disabilities. Mental illness and mental handicap are, however, two very different things. The reference to 'handicap' in this context embraces what, in somewhat dated language, has been described as 'subnormality or severe subnormality'[177] or, in more modern language, could be described as 'learning

173 *R v Waveney District Council ex p Bowers* [1983] QB 238, CA.
174 *Crossley v City of Westminster* [2006] EWCA Civ 140, [2006] HLR 26, CA.
175 English Code, para 10.15; Welsh Code, para 14.15.
176 *R v Waveney District Council ex p Bowers* [1983] QB 238, CA at 245, per Waller LJ.
177 *R v Bath City Council ex p Sangermano* (1984) 17 HLR 94, QBD at 101, per Hodgson J.

disability'.[178] In determining whether there is such illness or handicap contributing to current vulnerability, local housing authorities should have regard to any available medical opinion and to any advice available from an adult care or children's services authority or department. They should consider the nature and extent of the illness or handicap, and the relationship between the illness or handicap and the individual's ability to deal with the obvious difficulties associated with being homeless.

13.100 Those discharged from psychiatric hospitals or from hostels for people with mental health problems are likely to be vulnerable.[179] Although health authorities are supposed to make appropriate pre-discharge arrangements,[180] if the applicant is actually vulnerable, the fact that such arrangements should have been (or could have been) made is irrelevant.

13.101 Local housing authorities should clearly distinguish, in the decision notification dealing with this category of priority need, between any mental illness and any mental handicap.[181]

13.102 Where there is more than one mental condition, the local housing authority must consider the cumulative impact of the various conditions on the applicant, as well as any physical disability or other conditions that cumulatively might render the applicant vulnerable.[182]

13.103 A wide range of conditions has been explored in the case law as potentially or actually falling within the terms 'mental illness' and 'handicap'. These include:

(1)   accidental brain injury;[183]

(2)   subnormal intelligence (without any psychiatric disturbance or psychiatric history);[184]

(3)   depression;[185]

---

[178]   English Code, para 10.16; Welsh Code, para 14.16.

[179]   English Code, paras 10.16–10.17; Welsh Code, paras 14.16.

[180]   English Code, para 10.17; Welsh Code, para 14.17; Mental Health Act 1983, s 117. See **20.49–20.54**.

[181]   *R v Bath City Council ex p Sangermano* (1985) 17 HLR 94, QBD.

[182]   *Crossley v Westminster City Council* [2006] EWCA Civ 140, [2006] HLR 26, CA.

[183]   *R v Waveney District Council ex p Bowers* [1983] QB 238, CA; and *R v Lambeth London Borough Council ex p Carroll* (1988) 20 HLR 142, QBD.

[184]   *R v Bath City Council ex p Sangermano* (1985) 17 HLR 94, QBD.

[185]   *Griffin v City of Westminster Council* [2004] EWCA Civ 108, [2004] HLR 32 CA; *Chowdhoury v Newham London Borough Council* [2004] EWCA Civ 08, (2004) March *Legal Action*, p 25, CA; *Hall v Wandsworth London Borough Council* [2004] EWCA Civ 1740, [2005] HLR 23, CA; *Osmani v Camden London Borough Council* [2004] EWCA Civ 1706, [2005] HLR 22, CA; and *Shala v Birmingham City Council* [2007] EWCA Civ 624, [2008] HLR 8, CA.

(4)   epilepsy;[186]

(5)   persecutory delusion disorder and lack of insight;[187]

(6)   severe poly-drug dependence syndrome;[188] and

(7)   post-traumatic stress disorder.[189]

Physical disability

13.104 Physical disabilities that have an adverse impact on an applicant's ability to fend for him or herself when homeless may be readily discernible, but the Codes recommend that medical or adult care services advice should be sought wherever necessary.[190]

13.105 There is no requirement that any particular degree of disability is present, nor that it is of any particular duration. The phrase 'substantial disability' is not part of the statutory rubric.[191] Nor does HA 1996, Part 7 require a significant or permanent disability. The question is simply whether the relevant person is vulnerable wholly or partly by reason of his or her current physical disability.[192]

13.106 A local housing authority is not bound to treat someone as vulnerable as a result of a physical disability simply because the Department for Work and Pensions has awarded that person a benefit such as Disability Living Allowance.[193]

13.107 If there is any feature of the information available to the local housing authority that the applicant, or a member of his or her household, might be disabled, the local housing authority should make inquiries into whether or not

---

[186] *R v Wandsworth London Borough Council ex p Banbury* (1986) 19 HLR 76, QBD; and *R v Reigate and Banstead District Council ex p Di Domenico* (1988) 20 HLR 153, QBD.

[187] *R v Greenwich London Borough Council ex p Dukic* (1996) 29 HLR 87, QBD.

[188] *R v Camden London Borough Council ex p Pereira* (1999) 31 HLR 317, CA.

[189] *Shala v Birmingham City Council* [2007] EWCA Civ 624, [2008] HLR 8, CA; and *Sesay v Islington London Borough Council* (2009) September *Legal Action*, p 25, Clerkenwell & Shoreditch County Court.

[190] English Code, paras 10.16 and 10.18; Welsh Code, para 14.18.

[191] *R v Lambeth London Borough Council ex p Carroll* (1988) 20 HLR 142, QBD at 145, per Webster J.

[192] In *Wandsworth London Borough Council v Brown* [2005] EWCA Civ 907, the Court of Appeal refused permission to appeal against a first-instance judge's order varying the local housing authority's decision from one of no priority need to a decision that the applicant had a priority need. The applicant suffered from 'extreme sciatica, back pain, asthma, severe psoriasis and dermatitis and narcolepsy' and an 'extreme combination of a variety of very different ailments', which made the case unusual and one in which there could be only one conclusion – that he was vulnerable.

[193] *Mangion v Lewisham London Borough Council* [2008] EWCA Civ 1642, (2009) January *Legal Action*, p 26, CA; and *Simpson-Lowe v Croydon London Borough Council* [2012] EWCA Civ 131, (2012) April *Legal Action*, p 47, CA. See **10.50–10.64**.

that person is disabled. If he or she is disabled, that is a protected characteristic[194] and the local housing authority must take into account that the person has a protected characteristic under the Equality Act 2010.[195]

13.108 Where there is more than one physical disability, the local housing authority must consider the cumulative impact of the various conditions on the applicant, as well as any other conditions, such as mental illness or handicap, that cumulatively might render the applicant vulnerable.[196]

13.109 It is to be noted that HA 1996, Part 7 does not specifically deal with vulnerability arising through physical illness. Plainly a person suffering from, for example, influenza may be rendered 'vulnerable' in the relevant sense. But unless the local housing authority is prepared to accept the fact of physical illness as some 'other special reason',[197] vulnerability caused by it will not attract a finding of 'priority need'. On the other hand (as the Codes recognise), there will be circumstances in which acute long-term illness itself amounts to disability.[198]

Other special reason

13.110 If a person is vulnerable, but not by reason of any of the factors specified in HA 1996, Part 7, or the English Priority Need Order, the question is whether he or she is vulnerable by reason of some 'other special reason' or reasons.[199] This term is not defined in HA 1996, Part 7, or in the Codes. It is a free-standing category, and is not limited to physical or mental factors.

13.111 In *R v Kensington and Chelsea Royal London Borough Council ex p Kihara*,[200] the Court of Appeal held that 'special' means that the difficulties faced must be of an unusual degree of gravity. Asylum-seekers who were homeless, had no right to receive welfare benefits, had no income or capital, no family or friends, no opportunity to work and, in some cases, spoke no English were plainly in priority need for some 'other special reason'.[201]

13.112 There are no set or pre-determined groups of people who would fall within this category. Local housing authorities should keep an open mind, and consider the whole of an applicant's circumstances.[202]

---

[194] Equality Act 2010, ss 5–12.
[195] *Pieretti v Enfield London Borough Council* [2010] EWCA Civ 1104, [2011] HLR 3, CA.
[196] *Crossley v Westminster City Council* [2006] EWCA Civ 140, [2006] HLR 26, CA.
[197] See **13.110–13.119**.
[198] English Code, para 10.18; Welsh Code, para 14.16.
[199] HA 1996, s 189(1)(c).
[200] (1997) 29 HLR 147, CA.
[201] Since 3 April 2000, most asylum seekers who are destitute are not eligible for homelessness assistance and receive support and accommodation from the United Kingdom Border Agency (UKBA).
[202] English Code, paras 10.30–10.35; Welsh Code, paras 14.20–14.27.

13.113 Whilst reminding local housing authorities of the need to consider the relevant individual's circumstances, the Codes do give a number of examples of people whose circumstances might amount to their being vulnerable for an 'other special reason'. A number of cases have also come before the courts.

13.114 People who may be vulnerable due to an 'other special reason' can include those who are chronically sick, including people with HIV/AIDS-related illnesses. Local housing authorities should take into account not only physical symptoms, but also common social attitudes towards some of these illnesses.[203]

13.115 Young people who do not fall within any other category of priority need may also be vulnerable for some 'other special reason', and local housing authorities should consider the degree of support available to a young person, along with the cost and practicalities of finding and maintaining a home for the first time. Young people who were forced to leave the parental home, or who left it because of violence or sexual abuse, are particularly likely to be vulnerable.[204] In Wales, former care-leavers aged 21 or over who are vulnerable might fall within this category.[205] In England, former care-leavers who are vulnerable as a result of having been looked after, accommodated or fostered have a priority need under the Priority Need Order.[206]

13.116 People who flee their homes as a result of harassment that falls short of actual violence or threats of violence may be vulnerable for an 'other special reason'. Witnesses who may be at risk of intimidation could also fall within this category.[207]

13.117 Former asylum-seekers may fall within this category if they are vulnerable. Their experience of persecution in their country of origin and/or severe hardship in reaching the UK would be relevant, and local housing authorities should be sensitive to the fact that former asylum-seekers may be reluctant to discuss some of their experiences.[208]

---

[203] English Code, para 10.32; Welsh Code, para 14.22. See *Kata v Westminster City Council* [2011] EWCA Civ 1456, (2012) February *Legal Action*, p 13, CA, for a case where the local housing authority found that a person who was HIV positive was not vulnerable.

[204] English Code, para 10.33; Welsh Code, para 14.23. See also the Scottish cases of *Kelly v Monklands District Council 1985 SLT 165, OH*; and *Wilson v Nithsdale District Council 1992 SLT 1131, OH*.

[205] Welsh Code, para 14.23.

[206] SI 2002/2051, art 5(1). See **13.186–13.189**.

[207] English Code, para 10.34; Welsh Code, para 14.24. The Welsh Code also refers to people fleeing their homes as a result of violence that is not domestic violence; they would need to be vulnerable for an 'other special reason' in order to have a priority need.

[208] English Code, para 10.35; Welsh Code, para 14.26. See *Al-Oumian v Brent London Borough Council*(1999) June *Legal Action*, p 24, Willesden County Court; *Al-Kabi v Southwark London Borough Council* (2008) March *Legal Action*, p 21, Lambeth County Court; and *Sesay v Islington London Borough Council* (2008) September *Legal Action*, p 25, Clerkenwell & Shoreditch County Court. In *Shala v Birmingham City Council* [2007] EWCA Civ 624, [2008] HLR 8, CA the applicant suffered from depression and post-traumatic stress disorder as a result of her experiences as an Albanian Kosovan in the 1990s.

13.118 In Wales, local housing authorities are advised to consider whether rough sleepers may be vulnerable as a result of multiple needs, including mental health or substance misuse problems.[209]

13.119 Drug or alcohol addiction and the risk of relapsing could fall within this 'other special reason' category if the relevant person is vulnerable as a result of it.[210] In *R v Waveney District Council ex p Bowers*,[211] the Court of Appeal held that self-induced alcoholism would not normally result in a finding of 'vulnerability'. This was described as a 'grey area' in *Crossley v City of Westminster*.[212] Giving the judgment of the court, Sedley LJ said: 'drug addiction by itself, for all its personal and social consequences, cannot amount to a special reason for vulnerability which is capable of being addressed by housing'.[213] The local housing authority should, however, consider whether there are other factors, including the possibility of relapse into drug addiction if the applicant is on the streets, particular harm suffered as a result of the addiction, or the lack of family support available, which would render the applicant 'vulnerable' for an 'other special reason'. In *Crossley*, the applicant's combination of problems – he had spent his childhood from the age of three in care, he had developed his addiction to heroin at the age of 13, he had been sleeping rough from the age of 17, with short spells in hostels and in prison, he was chronically depressed and suffered from asthma and hepatitis C – were described as 'stark facts' pointing to a decision that he was vulnerable.[214]

Homeless 'as a result of an emergency'[215]

13.120 Any applicant (the only relevant person under this category) will have a priority need if currently homeless (or threatened with homelessness) as a 'result of an emergency such as a flood, fire or other disaster'.[216] There are therefore two questions for the local housing authority:

(1)   Is the applicant's present or threatened homelessness 'as a result of' an emergency?

(2)   If so, was the emergency one of a relevant type?

---

[209]   Welsh Code, para 14.25.
[210]   *R v Camden London Borough Council ex p Pereira* (1999) 31 HLR 317, CA; *R v Westminster City Council ex p Ortiz* (1993) 27 HLR 364, CA; *Hoolaghan v Motherwell District Council* 1997 CLY 6114, OH; *Tetteh v Kingston Royal London Borough Council* [2004] EWCA Civ 1775, [2005] HLR 21, CA; and *Ryde v Enfield London Borough Council* [2005] EWCA Civ 1281, (2005) January *Legal Action*, p 32, CA.
[211]   [1983] QB 238, CA.
[212]   [2006] EWCA Civ 140, [2006] HLR 26, CA.
[213]   [2006] EWCA Civ 140, [2006] HLR 26, CA at [30].
[214]   Another case involving multiple problems, including drug misuse, was *Payne v Kingston upon Thames Royal London Borough Council* (2008) March *Legal Action*, p 21, Central London Civil Justice Centre, where a decision that a single woman, who had been a victim of abuse and domestic violence, and had a history of mental health problems and of drug misuse, was not vulnerable was quashed.
[215]   HA 1996, s 189(1)(d).
[216]   English Code, para 10.42; Welsh Code, para 14.27.

Cause and effect

13.121 The 'emergency' must cause the actual or prospective loss of accommodation and therefore the current or threatened homelessness. The category is intended to deal with sudden emergencies rather than the loss of accommodation that has been anticipated for some time.[217] If the person is already 'homeless', in the technical sense used in HA 1996, Part 7,[218] before the emergency occurs, then the homelessness did not result from the emergency. For example, in one case, a caravan-dweller suddenly lost his caravan. But the caravan had been on a site where he had not had permission to station it or occupy it. So he had been homeless when the loss of the caravan occurred. Whilst the sudden loss of his home was 'an emergency', it did not cause his homelessness.[219] In another case, a local housing authority's decision that the applicant had become homeless as a result of the withdrawal of accommodation provided to him as an asylum-seeker, rather than as a result of his losing his home in Darfur, was not wrong in law. He was not therefore homeless as a result of an emergency.[220]

13.122 On the other hand, if a person loses his or her home as the result of an emergency, it is irrelevant (to the question of priority need) that he or she might have been made homeless anyway at a later date.[221] So, a person who is in no other sense in 'priority need' will be within this category if made homeless by an emergency (such as a fire) even if that occurs just before an imminent eviction from his or her accommodation for massive rent or mortgage arrears.

What type of emergency?

13.123 The words used at HA 1996, s 189(1)(d) are 'emergency such as a flood, fire or other disaster'. The courts have held that this wording means that the emergency must have some physical nature, such as a flood, fire or some similar event. But the flood or fire or other disaster need not have been naturally caused. The person made homeless by flooding from a burst communal water tank is as much in priority need as the person made homeless by reason of sea or river flooding. The person made homeless by an arsonist or by a fire caused by faulty electric wiring is as much in priority need as the victim made homeless by a forest fire or lightning strike. Homelessness caused by a sudden gas leak or explosion is likewise the result of an emergency. A person whose mobile home is stolen from its lawful pitch, site or mooring is also within this provision.[222]

---

[217] *R v Walsall Metropolitan Borough Council ex p Price* [1996] CLY 3068, QBD; and *R v Camden London Borough Council ex p Wait* (1986) 18 HLR 434, QBD.

[218] See **11.2–11.120.**

[219] *Higgs v Brighton and Hove City Council* [2003] EWCA Civ 895, [2004] HLR 2, CA.

[220] *Sadiq v Hackney London Borough Council* [2007] EWCA Civ 1507, (2008) April *Legal Action*, p 34, CA.

[221] *R v Camden London Borough Council ex p Wait* (1986) 18 HLR 434, QBD.

[222] *Higgs v Brighton and Hove City Council* [2003] EWCA Civ 895, [2004] HLR 2, CA.

13.124   On the other hand, homelessness resulting from the enforcement of a demolition order is not the result of an emergency.[223] Likewise, an unlawful eviction (where the locks were changed and the applicant's belongings placed outside) did not constitute some 'other disaster' falling within the term 'emergency'.[224]

13.125   The volcanic eruptions in Montserrat are an obvious example of an 'emergency' that falls within this subsection, and people fleeing from the eruption which caused the loss of their home will have a priority need.[225] Where a person resides in any building which has been made subject to an order of the magistrates court under the Greater London Council (General Powers) Act 1984, s 37[226] or s 38,[227] he or she is deemed to have a priority need by virtue of an emergency.[228]

ADDITIONAL CATEGORIES IN ENGLAND: THE PRIORITY NEED ORDER

13.126   The Homelessness (Priority Need for Accommodation) (England) Order 2002[229] came into force on 31 July 2002. Under the Order, there are six extra categories of people who have a priority need in addition to the four categories set out in HA 1996, Part 7 itself.[230] These additional categories only operate to confer priority need on the applicant personally.

A person aged 16 or 17[231]

13.127   A young person, who is aged 16 or 17, has a priority need simply by virtue of his or her age.[232] There is no additional requirement that he or she be 'vulnerable' or fall into any of the other priority need categories of HA 1996, Part 7, or the Order. There are only two exceptions specified in the Order:

(1)   'relevant' children; or

(2)   children who ought to be being accommodated by a children's services authority which owes them duties under the Children Act 1989, s 20.

---

[223]   *Noble v South Herefordshire District Council* (1985) 17 HLR 80, CA.
[224]   *R v Bristol City Council ex p Bradic* (1995) 27 HLR 584, CA.
[225]   *Telesford v Ealing London Borough Council* (2000) August *Legal Action*, p 26, Brentford County Court. English Code, para 10.42; Welsh Code, para 14.27.
[226]   Removal of occupants of dangerous buildings in outer London.
[227]   Removal of occupants of buildings in vicinity of dangerous structures, etc.
[228]   GLC (General Powers) Act 1984, s 39.
[229]   SI 2002/2051. See Appendix 2.
[230]   SI 2002/2051, arts 3–6.
[231]   SI 2002/2051, art 3.
[232]   English Code, paras 10.36–10.39 and Chapter 12.

13.128   In dealing with an application for homelessness assistance from such a young person, local housing authorities should consider whether the applicant:

(a)   is aged 16 or 17; and then

(b)   whether she or he:
    (i)   falls within the definition of 'a relevant child'; or
    (ii)   is owed a duty pursuant to the Children Act 1989, s 20.

13.129   A 16- or 17-year old applicant for homelessness assistance who falls within (or is likely to fall within) either of these exceptions may consider directing an application (or a further application) to a local housing authority in Wales.[233] As indicated,[234] there is no parallel to either of these exceptions to priority need status for a 16- or 17-year-old in the Welsh Order.[235] He or she will automatically be found to have a priority need by a local housing authority in Wales.

Age

13.130   In most cases, the child's age is unlikely to be in any doubt. If there is doubt, a local housing authority will have to make its own decision on the child's age, relying on the applicant's appearance, family and educational background and any ethnic or cultural considerations.[236]

13.131   The local housing authority must decide whether the child is 16 or 17 at the date of its initial decision or review decision, rather than at the date of application.

13.132   What should happen when a 17-year-old, approaching his or her eighteenth birthday, makes an application for homelessness assistance? The Local Government Ombudsman has found maladministration where local housing authorities have refused to help 17-year-olds who were attempting to make applications for homelessness assistance.[237]

---

[233]   If he or she prefers to be accommodated pursuant to a homelessness duty rather than a children's services duty.

[234]   See **13.214–13.218**.

[235]   SI 2001/607.

[236]   *R (B) v Merton London Borough Council* [2003] EWHC 1689 (Admin), [2003] 4 All ER 295. In the context of the provision of accommodation under Children Act 1989, s 20, the Supreme Court has held that if a child disagrees with a children's services' authority's assessment of his or her age, the child can bring judicial review proceedings and, unlike most claims in judicial review, ask the court to review the evidence available and make its own decision as to what age he or she is (*R (A) v Croydon London Borough Council, R (M) v Lambeth London Borough Council* [2009] UKSC 8, [2009] 1 WLR 2557, SC). It remains to be seen how this decision might fit into the review and appeal provisions of HA 1996, Part 7 (see Chapter 19).

[237]   See *Complaint against South Tyneside Metropolitan Borough Council*, 04/C/18995, 12 December 2005, where £2,000 compensation was recommended after the local housing authority failed to give a 17-year-old a homeless application form to complete or provide him with any interim accommodation. He returned after two months, by which time he had turned 18 and no longer had a priority need.

13.133 The Court of Appeal considered these circumstances in *Robinson v Hammersmith & Fulham London Borough Council*.[238] The guidance that it gave was in three parts.

13.134 First, the making of decisions on applications for homelessness assistance should not be postponed. The local housing authority's duty is to make its inquiries 'as quickly as possible'.[239] The issue of the applicant's priority need is a very straightforward question of fact, which would not normally take much time to determine. The Court of Appeal said:

> 'in the case of a 17-year-old child, it would not ... be lawful for a local authority to postpone the taking of a decision even for a short period on the basis that by postponing that decision the child will have reached the age of 18 before the decision is taken.'[240]

13.135 Second, a local housing authority cannot find that a young person approaching his or her eighteenth birthday does not have a priority need because he or she is 'so nearly 18 that the difference between 18 and 17, should be ignored'.[241] If, at the date of the decision, the young person is, as a matter of fact, 17 (even if the following day is his or her eighteenth birthday), he or she has a priority need.

13.136 Third, where the young person requests a review of any negative decision, but turns 18 before the review is concluded, it is not lawful for the local housing authority simply to state that, at the date of the review decision, the young person does not have a priority need:

> 'if the original decision was unlawful ... the review decision should have so held and made a decision that would have restored to the appellant the rights she would have had if the decision had been lawful.'[242]

13.137 It may be that the local housing authority has genuinely difficult inquiries to make into, for example: whether or not the young person is homeless from his or her parents' accommodation, or whether, in fact, the family home is still available to the young person and reasonable for him or her

---

[238] [2006] EWCA Civ 1122, [2007] HLR 7, CA.

[239] English Code, para 6.16.

[240] *Robinson v Hammersmith & Fulham London Borough Council* [2006] EWCA Civ 1122, [2007] HLR 7, CA at [38], per Waller LJ. See also *R (MM) v Lewisham London Borough Council* [2009] EWHC 416 (Admin), (2009) April *Legal Action*, p 23, Admin Ct, where the local housing authority simply failed to make a decision on an application from a 17-year-old for over four months. The Administrative Court judge said, 'I would urge the defendant to take action to ensure that ... steps are taken to ensure that the imminence of a child attaining 18 years is not taken as a basis for failing to take action and ... there is due and proper contact between its housing authority and its social services authority'.

[241] *Robinson v Hammersmith & Fulham London Borough Council* [2006] EWCA Civ 1122, [2007] HLR 7, CA at [29], per Waller LJ.

[242] *Robinson v Hammersmith & Fulham London Borough Council* [2006] EWCA Civ 1122, [2007] HLR 7, CA at [32], per Waller LJ.

to continue to occupy.[243] The English Code recommends that local housing authorities consider the possibility of collusion (in order to obtain homelessness assistance) between the parents and child,[244] and that they should also explore the possibility of mediation and/or reconciliation. Pursuing those avenues without any improper intent might delay the decision on an application until after the young person's eighteenth birthday. The Court of Appeal has held that a local housing authority is entitled:

'to have time to check the genuineness of the decision to exclude the child, and indeed the reasons given by the child for being excluded, for example where there may have been collusion.'[245]

13.138 However:

'if an authority are of the view that a child genuinely has no place to go unless a mediation can sort matters out, and a mediation cannot take place without depriving the child of a right it would otherwise have had, then in my view the authority has to take the view that its full duty must be performed, and use mediation in order to fulfil that duty.'[246]

13.139 As the last extract makes clear, if the local housing authority accepts that a main housing duty is owed to the 17-year-old, it can still use its mediation service to attempt to persuade the parent to welcome the child back, and, if successful, it will have performed the main housing duty by ensuring that the accommodation is provided at the parental home if that accommodation is suitable for the needs of the child.[247]

The exceptions

13.140 Both of the exceptions to this category are designed to ensure that young people to whom children's services have owed duties in the past, or do owe a present duty to accommodate by virtue of Children Act 1989, s 20, should be the responsibility of children's services. This is because young people in those circumstances are likely to have needs over and above the simple need for a roof over their heads, and those needs are best met by children's services.[248] As Baroness Hale put it in the House of Lords:

---

[243] See **11.2–11.120** and **11.75–11.120**.

[244] English Code, paras 8.12 and 12.10–12.11.

[245] *Robinson v Hammersmith & Fulham London Borough Council* [2006] EWCA Civ 1122, [2007] HLR 7, CA at [39], per Waller LJ.

[246] *Robinson v Hammersmith & Fulham London Borough Council* [2006] EWCA Civ 1122, [2007] HLR 7, CA at [41], per Waller LJ.

[247] HA 1996, s 206(1)(b) or (c); see **17.12** and see Chapter 18 on suitability.

[248] *R (M) v Hammersmith & Fulham London Borough Council* [2008] UKHL 14, [2008] 1 WLR 535, HL at [31] per Baroness Hale; *R (G) v Southwark London Borough Council* [2009] UKHL 26, [2009] 1 WLR 2399, HL; and *R (TG) v Lambeth London Borough Council* [2011] EWCA Civ 526, [2011] HLR 33, CA. See *Provision of Accommodation for 16 and 17 year old young people who may be homeless and/or require Accommodation* (April 2010, CLG and Children, Schools and Families) on CD-Rom.

'It is, perhaps, possible to envisage circumstances in which a 16 or 17 year old who is temporarily without accommodation is nevertheless not in need within the meaning of section 17(10): perhaps a child whose home has been temporarily damaged by fire or flood who can well afford hotel accommodation while it is repaired. . . . But it cannot seriously be suggested that a child excluded from home who is "sofa surfing" in this way, more often sleeping in cars, snatching showers and washing his clothes when he can, is not in need.'[249]

13.141 Following the two significant House of Lords' decisions on the housing needs of 16- and 17-year-olds,[250] the UK Government issued statutory guidance in April 2010: *Provision of Accommodation for 16 and 17 year old young people who may be homeless and/or require Accommodation.*[251] The guidance reinforces the decisions of the House of Lords: 'the 1989 [Children] Act takes precedence over the 1996 [Housing] Act',[252] and so primary responsibility for homeless teenagers will lie with children's services.

13.142 The case-law and government guidance have all emphasised joint working between local housing authorities and children's services. However, investigations by Shelter[253] and the magazine *Inside Housing*[254] have found that 'a substantial number of vulnerable children are still suffering from a failure of co-ordination between these two departments within a number of local authorities' in England.[255] The issue of joint working is explored further at **13.150–13.168**.

Relevant child

13.143 'A relevant child' is defined by the Children Act 1989, s 23A(2), as any child, aged 16 or 17, who was formerly being looked after by any local

---

[249] *R (G) v Southwark London Borough Council* [2009] UKHL 26, [2009] 1 WLR 2399, HL, per Baroness Hale at [28]. For an example of a young person who was accommodated by the local housing authority under HA 1996, s 193(2) main housing duty rather than by children's services, see *R (B) v Nottingham City Council* [2011] EWHC 2933 (Admin), (2011) December *Legal Action*, p 30, Admin Ct. The local housing authority was not wrong in law on the facts of that particular case when it decided that a pregnant 16-year-old was not a child in need.
[250] *R (M) v Hammersmith & Fulham London Borough Council* [2008] UKHL 14, [2008] 1 WLR 535, HL; and *R (G) v Southwark London Borough Council* [2009] UKHL 26, [2009] 1 WLR 2399, HL.
[251] April 2010, CLG and Children, Schools and Families at CD-Rom. HA 1996, s 182 requires that local housing authorities take the guidance in account when exercising their HA 1996 Part 7 functions. Local Authority Social Services Act 1970, s 7 requires children's services' departments to take the guidance into account when exercising children's services' functions. See **13.151–13.164**.
[252] Para 2.13 of *Provision of Accommodation for 16 and 17 year old young people who may be homeless and/or require Accommodation*.
[253] Referred to in *R (TG) v Lambeth London Borough Council* [2011] EWCA Civ 526, [2011] HLR 33, CA per Wilson LJ at [5].
[254] 'Who Cares?', *Inside Housing*, 7 January 2011.
[255] *R (TG) v Lambeth London Borough Council* [2011] EWCA Civ 526, [2011] HLR 33, CA per Wilson LJ at [5].

authority for a prescribed period of time while of a prescribed age, but who is no longer being looked after.[256] This exception, as described in the English Code,[257] is satisfied only if:

(1)   the child is 16 or 17; and

(2)   the child was 'looked after'[258] by a children's services authority:
      (a)   for at least 13 weeks,
      (b)   after the age of 14; and

(3)   has been looked after while he or she was 16 or 17; and

(4)   is no longer being looked after.

13.144   As the Code itself foreshadows,[259] each of these elements is subject to close technical definition in the Children Act 1989 (as amended) and in the Care Leavers (England) Regulations 2010.[260] If the terms of the exception appear to be satisfied, the local housing authority should obviously refer to the precise wording of the Children Act 1989 and the Regulations to confirm the actual position. Although the Code recommends that any uncertainty as to whether this exception applies should lead to children's services being contacted,[261] the decision as to whether the child meets the technical definition of 'relevant child' is for the local housing authority to make and not for children's services to decide.

A child owed duties under the Children Act 1989, s 20

13.145   A 16- or 17-year-old does not have automatic priority need if she or he is a person to whom a children's services authority 'owe a duty to provide accommodation' under the Children Act 1989, s 20.[262] Note that the exception only applies if the duty 'is' owed (that is currently owed). That the duty was owed in the past or might be owed in the future is irrelevant. A children's services authority is not obliged to notify a decision that it owes a young person the duty under Children Act 1989, s 20 in writing, so there is unlikely to be a convenient short-cut for inquiries by simply requesting sight of such a document.

13.146   Children owed duties under the Children Act 1989, s 20 are those children who appear to a children's services authority to require accommodation either:

---

[256]   Children Act 1989, Sch 2, para 19B; Care Leavers (England) Regulations 2010, SI 2010/2571, reg 3.
[257]   English Code, paras 10.37–10.39.
[258]   See **13.149**.
[259]   English Code, para 10.37.
[260]   SI 2010/2571, reg 3.
[261]   English Code, para 10.39.
[262]   SI 2001/2051, art 3(2).

(1)   because they are 16 or over and their welfare is otherwise likely to be seriously prejudiced; or

(2)   because they have no parents or other people who are able to provide accommodation for them.

13.147   Where a child has been provided with accommodation by children's services, there may be some doubt as to whether that accommodation was provided under the duty at Children Act 1989, s 20, or the power at Children Act 1989, s 17.[263] The courts have held that where accommodation has been provided as a result of a young person falling within the test at Children Act, s 20, the local authority cannot side-step its responsibility by recording or arguing that it was in fact acting under the Children Act 1989, s 17 power or some other legislation.[264] Equally, the children's services authority cannot side-step its responsibility by telling a child aged 16 or 17 who falls within the criteria at Children Act 1989, s 20 to make an application for homelessness assistance.[265]

Children's services' duties towards relevant children and 'looked after' children

13.148   The thrust of the amendments made to the Children Act 1989 by the Children (Leaving Care) Act 2000 is that children's services authorities should be responsible for meeting the accommodation and other needs of young people who have been in, but are no longer in, the care system (at least until they reach 18), or who have been 'looked after' under Children Act 1989, s 20. To accord such 16- and 17-year-olds priority need would shift the responsibility for accommodating young people on to local housing authorities when children's services should be arranging accommodation.[266] This policy aim is reinforced in the most recent UK government guidance: *Provision of Accommodation for 16 and 17 year old young people who may be homeless and/or require Accommodation.*[267]

---

[263]   See **20.55–20.73** for Children Act 1989, s 17; and **20.74–20.80** for Children Act 1989, s 20.
[264]   *Southwark London Borough Council v D* [2007] EWCA Civ 182, (2007) 10 CCLR 280, CA; *R (H) v Wandsworth London Borough Council, R (Barhanu) v Hackney London Borough Council, R (B) v Islington London Borough Council* [2007] EWHC 1082 (Admin), (2007) 10 CCLR 441, Admin Ct; and *R (L) v Nottinghamshire County Council* [2007] EWHC 2364 (Admin).
[265]   *R (G) v Southwark London Borough Council* [2009] UKHL 26, [2009] 1 WLR 2399, HL; *R (MM) v Lewisham London Borough Council* [2009] EWHC 416 (Admin), (2009) April *Legal Action*, p 23, Admin Ct *and R (TG) v Lambeth London Borough Council* [2011] EWCA Civ 526, [2011] HLR 33, CA. The Local Government Ombudsman recommended that a local authority pay a teenage woman £7,000 for its failure to provide her with services under Children Act 1989, s 20 and for being content for her to be dealt with solely by the housing department (*Complaint against Waltham Forest London Borough Council*, 08 016 986, 21 October 2009, (2010) February *Legal Action*, p 34).
[266]   *R (G) v Southwark London Borough Council* [2009] UKHL 26, [2009] 1 WLR 2399, HL.
[267]   April 2010, CLG and Children, Schools and Families, see CD-Rom.

13.149 Where a child is a relevant child, or is accommodated under Children Act 1989, s 20, he or she then becomes a 'looked after' child. The children's services authority is then responsible for safeguarding and promoting the child's welfare, including his or her educational achievement,[268] and for maintaining the child in other respects apart from providing accommodation. [269] In addition, if the 'looked after' 16- or 17-year-old has been looked after by the children's services authority for a total of 13 weeks or more at any time since the age of 14, he or she is entitled to services under the Children (Leaving Care) Act 2000. Those services include an assessment of the child's future needs, preparation of a detailed pathway plan for him or her, and a personal adviser.[270] The services continue until the child is 21, or has completed his or her education or training.[271] It is precisely because of these obligations of children's services towards 16- and 17-year-olds that the exceptions to this priority need category have been made.

Joint working between housing and children's services

13.150 In cases of uncertainty, the Code recommends that children's services be contacted to help ascertain whether the applicant is a relevant child or a child owed a Children Act 1989, s 20 duty.[272] The House of Lords has taken a stronger view and held that, when a 16- or 17-year-old presents himself or herself to the housing department as homeless, the housing department must make a referral to the children's services department as part of its ongoing inquiries into whether or not the young person has a priority need, or is a relevant child or is owed a Children Act 1989, s 20 duty. The children's services department should then carry out its own assessment in accordance with its responsibilities under the Children Act 1989.[273] It is precisely because 'relevant children' and children entitled to a Children Act 1989, s 20 duty have needs over and above the simple need for a roof over their heads that the Priority Need Order clearly contemplates that children's services should take the long term responsibility.[274]

13.151 The UK Government guidance emphasises the need for a joint approach, underpinned by a joint protocol, to prevent 16- and 17-year-olds in crisis from being passed between housing and children's services departments unnecessarily.[275] The statutory Guidance *Provision of Accommodation for 16*

---

[268] Children Act 1989, s 22(3) and (3A).
[269] Children Act 1989, s 23(1)(b), to be repealed and replaced by a new Children Act 1989, ss 22A–22F inserted by Children and Young Persons Act 2008, s 8 and not yet in force.
[270] Children Act 1989, s 23B.
[271] Children Act 1989, s 23C(7).
[272] English Code, para 10.39.
[273] *R (M) v Hammersmith & Fulham London Borough Council* [2008] UKHL 14, [2008] 1 WLR 535, HL at [29], per Baroness Hale. See **20.74–20.80** for children's services' responsibilities.
[274] *R (M) v Hammersmith & Fulham London Borough Council* [2008] UKHL 14, [2008] 1 WLR 535, HL at [31], per Baroness Hale. See also *R (G) v Southwark London Borough Council* [2009] UKHL 26, [2009] 1 WLR 2399, HL.
[275] *Provision of Accommodation for 16 and 17 year old young people who may be homeless and/or require Accommodation*, April 2010, CLG and Children, Schools and Families. See CD-Rom.

and 17 year old young people who may be homeless and/or require Accommodation[276] addresses various scenarios that housing and children's services departments may encounter when approached by a 16 or 17 year old who may be homeless.

13.152   The Guidance advises '[i]t is in the best interests of most young people aged 16 or 17 to live in the family home, or, where this is not safe or appropriate, with responsible adults in their wider family and friends network'.[277] In order to achieve this, children's services should consider providing services to prevent a young person from having to leave home at all. However, this preventative work should not delay an assessment of the young person's needs or the delivery of services, including accommodation, where the young person may be homeless or at risk of homelessness.

13.153   Where the young person first approaches the local housing authority, it has a duty to accept an application for homelessness assistance, to make inquiries into that application and to secure interim accommodation where there is reason to believe that the young person may be eligible for assistance, may be homeless and may be 16- or 17-years-old. The Guidance advises that bed and breakfast accommodation is unsuitable for 16- and 17-year-olds.[278]

13.154   If the young person may be homeless or may be likely to become homeless within 28 days, the local housing authority should immediately make a referral to children's services for an assessment.[279] This applies to all 16- and 17-year-old applicants. Local housing authorities are then advised to delay the making of the HA 1996, s 184 decision until children's services have completed their assessment of the young person's needs under the Children Act 1989.[280] That assessment should be undertaken and completed as soon as possible and in no more than ten days.[281]

---

[276]   April 2010, CLG and Children, Schools and Families.

[277]   Para 2.1 of the Guidance.

[278]   Paras 2.9–2.10 of the Guidance.

[279]   Surprisingly, there is nothing in HA 1996, Part 7, the English Code or the Guidance clarifying whether the child's consent should be sought for the referral to children's services and what steps should be taken if the child refuses to give consent. The starting-point will be that the child who has made an application for homelessness assistance is entitled to assume that the fact of the application and the details contained in it will remain confidential between the child and the local housing authority. It is for that reason that the child's consent to make the referral should be sought. However, a local housing authority falls within the organisations listed in Children Act 2004, s 11 which are under a duty to make arrangements to ensure their functions are discharged having regard to the need to promote and safeguard the welfare of children and it is this duty that may require a local housing authority to refer a child to children's services, even without the child's consent. See also *Working Together to Safeguard Children* (HM Government, March 2010).

[280]   The advice to delay sits rather uncomfortably with the general principle that inquiries into whether or not a duty is owed by a local housing authority should not normally be delayed: *Robinson v Hammersmith & Fulham London Borough Council* [2006] EWCA Civ 1122, [2007] HLR 7, CA. See **10.69–10.70**.

[281]   Para 2.11 of the Guidance.

13.155 The young person should continue to be accommodated by the local housing authority in interim accommodation until notification of the HA 1996, s 184 decision. Where children's services, having carried out their assessment of the young person's needs, have decided that he or she is a child in need of accommodation and that they have a duty under Children Act 1989, s 20 to provide accommodation, the local housing authority can complete its inquiries. The child will not have a priority need because he or she falls within the exception at art 3(2) of the Priority Need Order.[282]

13.156 Local housing authorities are reminded that they must consider all applications for homelessness assistance and comply with their duties to secure interim accommodation and notify a HA 1996, s 184 decision.

13.157 Where a 16- or 17-year-old first approaches children's services, either directly or through a referral by another agency, and he or she appears to be homeless or at risk of homelessness, children's services must assess whether the young person is a child in need and whether any duty is owed to him or her to provide accommodation under Children Act 1989.[283] If it appears that the young person has nowhere safe to stay that night, children's services must secure suitable emergency accommodation for him or her. Bed and breakfast accommodation is not considered suitable accommodation, even for emergencies. The immediate provision of accommodation means that he or she will have become a child to whom a local authority owes a duty to provide accommodation under Children Act 1989, s 20 and will not have a priority need under the Priority Need Order.[284]

13.158 The Guidance advises that there can be no doubt that where a young person requires accommodation as a result of one of the factors at Children Act 1989, s 20(1)(a)–(c) or (3), then that young person will be in need and must be provided with accommodation by children's services. That young person then becomes a 'looked after' child and will be entitled to all the duties owed to looked-after children.[285]

13.159 The local housing authority, having accepted an application for homelessness assistance, must still make inquiries into the application and notify the applicant of his or her decision.[286] The first question for the local housing authority will be whether or not the applicant is eligible and, if so, the next question will be whether he or she is homeless.[287] A child who is provided with accommodation under Children Act 1989, s 20 will no longer be homeless. A local housing authority can therefore determine the application for homelessness assistance and notify the applicant of its decision that he or she is not homeless and so no duty is owed.

---

[282] SI 2002/2051. See **13.145–13.147**.
[283] Para 2.15 of the Guidance.
[284] Para 2.16 of the Guidance. Art 3(2), SI 2002/2051.
[285] Para 2.23 of the Guidance. See **3.149**.
[286] HA 1996, s 184(1). See **Chapter 10**.
[287] HA 1996, s 184(1).

13.160 If the young person refuses accommodation offered under Children Act 1989, s 20, children's services must be clear that his or her decision has been reached after having been provided with all relevant information and that she or he is competent to make the decision.[288] Once accommodation has been lost because the child is refused it, and the child does not have any other accommodation, he or she will be homeless within the definition at HA 1996, ss 175–177.[289]

13.161 If Children Act accommodation is refused, or if the young person has been assessed by children's services as not having a need for accommodation, then the young person will no longer be the responsibility of children's services. If she or he is homeless, responsibility will lie with the local housing authority under HA 1996, Part 7. The local housing authority should then complete its inquiries and notify the young person of its decision. The child will have a priority need.[290] He or she should not be considered to have become homeless intentionally because of failing to take up an offer of accommodation from children's services.[291] Indeed, the Guidance advises that where a young person has had to leave accommodation because of his or her decision to refuse Children Act 1989, s 20 accommodation, he or she should not be considered to have become homeless intentionally.[292]

13.162 If, despite a children's services' assessment to the contrary, the local housing authority reaches a decision that the young person is owed a Children Act 1989, s 20 duty and that decision is disputed on review (or appeal) by the applicant, perhaps with children's services support, the case for the exercise of the discretionary power to accommodate pending review (or appeal) would seem compelling.[293]

13.163 Where the accommodation has been provided to the young person under one of the duties in HA 1996 Part 7, that is not necessarily the end of children's services' responsibilities. They should consider whether the child is still 'a child in need' and, if so, how provide other support and services, under Children Act 1989, s 17, in order to meet his or her needs.[294]

13.164 The bottom line is that both local housing authorities and children's services must work together and co-operate in order to meet the accommodation and other needs of children.[295] Children's services may ask local housing authorities to 'help in the exercise of any of their functions' under Children Act 1989 and local housing authorities are required to comply

---

[288] Paras 2.51–2.53 of the Guidance.
[289] See Chapter 9.
[290] Priority Need Order SI 2002/2051, art 3.
[291] Para 4.10 of the Guidance.
[292] Para 4.11 of the Guidance.
[293] HA 1996, s 188(3) and s 204(4). See **16.36–16.40** for accommodation pending review and **16.49–16.55** for accommodation pending appeal.
[294] Paras 4.1–4.12 of the Guidance.
[295] Chapter 5 of the Guidance.

with the request where possible.[296] Similarly local housing authorities can ask children's services authorities to assist them in discharging their functions under HA 1996, Part 7, and children's services authorities should co-operate by rendering such assistance as is reasonable in the circumstances.[297] The Guidance advises that local housing authorities and children's services agree written joint protocols which set out clear, practical arrangements for providing services to young people and their families and to 'prevent young people from being passed from pillar to post'.[298]

13.165 Unfortunately, there is no statutory mechanism available to resolve disagreements between different local authorities, or between different departments of a unitary authority, on these issues. If there is a dispute and neither the local housing authority nor the children's services authority is providing accommodation for the child under any statutory duty, the case for the exercise of the discretionary power to accommodate pending review (or appeal) would seem compelling.[299]

13.166 A 16- or 17-year old applicant who falls within (or is likely to fall within) either of the exceptions at art 3 of the Homelessness (Priority Need for Accommodation) (England) Order 2002[300] may consider directing an application (or a further application) to a local housing authority in Wales.[301] As indicated,[302] there is no parallel to either of these exceptions to priority need status for a 16- or 17-year-old in the Welsh Order.[303] He or she will automatically be found to have a priority need by a local housing authority in Wales.

13.167 Even if a homeless 16- or 17-year-old is the responsibility of children's services, the local housing authority's duty does not simply end as a result of the acceptance of the referral. If the local housing authority's inquiries have reached the stage of considering 'priority need', that process must be formally completed.[304] A local housing authority must therefore go on to consider

---

[296] Children Act 1989, s 27.
[297] HA 1996, s 213(1)(b).
[298] Para 5.2 of the Guidance. For a very stark example of a 16 year old who was passed from pillar to post, even though there was a joint protocol in place between the local housing authority and the children's services authority, see *Complaint against Kent County Council*, 09 017 510, and *Dover District Council*, 09 017 512, 31 July 2012 (2012) October *Legal Action*, p 38. In that case, the child had spent nine months, including over the winter period, sleeping in a tent and sometimes on sofas provided by friends, instead of being provided either by children's services or by the local hosing authority. The Ombudsman described these failures as 'inexcusable'.
[299] HA 1996, s 188(3) and 204(4) See **16.36–16.48** for accommodation pending review and **16.49–16.55** for accommodation pending appeal.
[300] SI 2002/2051. See **13.143–13.144** for the first exception and **13.145–13.147** for the second exception.
[301] If he or she prefers to be accommodated pursuant to a homelessness duty rather than a children's services duty.
[302] See **13.214–13.218**.
[303] SI 2001/607.
[304] HA 1996, s 184(3). Para 2.11 of the Guidance.

whether the applicant may have a priority need under one of the other categories of priority need (pregnancy, vulnerability, etc). The process must always conclude with a reasoned written decision. However, if children's services have provided accommodation under their powers or duties at Children Act 1989, s 17 or s 20, the more likely decision will normally be that the applicant is not homeless.

13.168 Local housing authorities are advised to work with children's services authorities in dealing with applications from 16- and 17-year-olds and to conduct joint assessments of children falling within this category.[305]

Housing responsibilities to 16- and 17-year-old applicants

13.169 The fact that most 16- and 17-year-olds now have priority need (without having to show any vulnerability) has led to concerns that local housing authorities will have an additional burden in accommodating such people when they are teenagers and then in the longer term. But, as the Code rightly indicates, there are at least three reasons why that burden should not be as great as feared.[306]

13.170 First, even if the young applicant is homeless and in priority need, she or he may have become homeless intentionally.[307] The Code reminds local housing authorities to be alive to the specific possibility of 'collusion' when dealing with young applicants aged 16 or 17 who may have been party to arrangements with their parents under which they were excluded from the parental home.[308]

13.171 Secondly, there is always the possibility of discharging any duty owed to the applicant by securing suitable accommodation provided by another 'person' instead of by the local housing authority itself.[309] That 'other person' might be a parent, relative or friend. The Code encourages local housing authorities specifically to consider reconciliation with those who have previously provided the teenager with accommodation and to draw on the help of children's services.[310] This should not be taken as a recommendation that a decision on the application might be deferred and the duty to provide interim accommodation[311] extended while these possibilities are explored. The local housing authority is really considering at this stage *how* its duty will be performed. It should have already notified the applicant of its decision on what

---

[305] English Code, para 10.39. Para 2.11 of the Guidance.
[306] English Code, paras 12.7–12.11.
[307] See *Denton v Southwark London Borough Council* [2007] EWCA Civ 623, [2008] HLR 11, CA, which concerned a homeless 21-year-old who had been excluded by his mother, and *White v Southwark London Borough Council* [2008] EWCA Civ 792, (2008) October *Legal Action*, p 37, CA, where the court held that children as young as 13 might be considered to have acted deliberately and thus made themselves intentionally homeless. See **14.64**.
[308] English Code, paras 12.10–12.11.
[309] HA 1996, s 206(1)(b). See **17.12**.
[310] English Code, paras 12.8–12.9.
[311] HA 1996, s 188(1). See **10.35–10.37** and **16.12–16.28**.

duty is owed, and should have replaced the interim accommodation with accommodation provided under the main housing duty (if applicable).[312]

13.172 Thirdly, many homeless 16- and 17-year-olds are likely to have needs over and above the simple need for a roof over their heads, and thus fall within the responsibility of children's services pursuant to s 20 of the Children Act 1989.[313]

13.173 Recognising the particular vulnerability of young people falling within this category, the Code advises that bed and breakfast is unlikely to be suitable for them.[314] More recent statutory UK government guidance[315] has gone further and advises:

> ' . . .accommodation must be suitable for a 16 and 17 year old and, in considering suitability, authorities should bear in mind that 16 and 17 year olds who are homeless and estranged from their family will be particularly vulnerable and in need of support. The Secretary of State considers that Bed and Breakfast accommodation is unsuitable for 16 and 17 year olds'.[316]

A broader view of the category

13.174 Although the provision in the English Priority Need Order only confers priority need on an applicant who is 16 or 17, the benefits are not restricted to single people. A young childless and homeless couple will find the main housing duty is owed if the application is made by one of them who is 16 or 17 years old (provided that the applicant is not found to have become homeless intentionally.)[317] So, for example, an 18-year-old living at home with his parents and wishing to establish a home with a 16-year-old partner who has been turned out by her parents can, on his partner's application as homeless, expect that they will be accommodated together.[318] Furthermore, a working teenager aged 16 or 17 living as part of a household made homeless can secure the benefits of the main housing duty for the whole family by making the

---

[312] See *Robinson v Hammersmith & Fulham London Borough Council* [2006] EWCA Civ 1122, [2007] HLR 7, CA.

[313] This should now routinely be the case following the House of Lords' decisions of *R (M) v Hammersmith & Fulham London Borough Council* [2008] UKHL 14, [2008] 1 WLR 535, HL and *R (G) v Southwark London Borough Council* [2009] *UKHL 26*, [2009] 1 WLR 2399, HL and the UK government statutory guidance: *Provision of Accommodation for 16 and 17 year old young people who may be homeless and/or require accommodation* (April 2010). See **13.151–13.164** and CD-Rom.

[314] English Code, para 12.14.

[315] *Provision of Accommodation for 16 and 17 year old young people who may be homeless* (CLG and Children, Schools and Families, April 2010), see CD-Rom.

[316] Para 2.10 of the Guidance.

[317] And assuming that they are not assessed as having a need for accommodation so that accommodation is provided by children's services under Children Act 1989, s 20.

[318] Had these provisions been in force, the wife in *Kaya v Haringey London Borough Council* [2001] EWCA Civ 677, [2002] HLR 1, CA, could have made a homeless application herself and would have been in priority need, thereby securing accommodation for herself and her husband.

application in his or her name.[319] The head of the household in the latter example could not achieve the same result, where the teenager is the only child at home, because the teenager is not 'dependent'.

A young person under 21[320]

13.175 Despite the apparent breadth of this category, the detail indicates that only a very small number of applicants have priority need by virtue of this provision.[321] Under it, an applicant now aged 18, 19 or 20 who was 'looked after, accommodated or fostered' at any time between the ages of 16 and 18 will have a priority need unless he or she is 'a relevant student'. In non-technical language, the criteria are likely to be fulfilled by recent care leavers who are not yet 21. If the applicant falls within this priority need category, he or she does not also need to be 'vulnerable' or fall into any other category.

13.176 The term 'looked after, accommodated or fostered'[322] takes its meaning from the Children Act 1989, s 24(2), which itself has been completely substituted by the Children (Leaving Care) Act 2000. The current definition is accurately set out in the English Code.[323] Case-law has provided some additional guidance on the 'looked after' element in that definition.[324]

13.177 As long as the applicant was 'looked after, accommodated or fostered' at some stage when he or she was 16, 17 or 18 years old, the criteria will be met. No minimum period of time during which he or she was 'looked after, accommodated or fostered' is prescribed.

13.178 Many of these former care leavers will be owed duties of support by children's services under Children Act 1989, ss 23C–24D including the duty to prepare and review a pathway plan, and to appoint a personal adviser.[325]

The exception to this category

13.179 The exception[326] applies where the applicant is a 'relevant student'.[327] That term is only met by a person:

---

[319] As happened in *R (Ogbeni) v Tower Hamlets London Borough Council* [2008] EWHC 2444 (Admin), (2008) *Legal Action* October, p 37, Admin Ct, where a 17-year-old applicant had a priority need and normally resided with his aunt, who was a member of his family. Accommodation had to be provided for both the applicant and his aunt.
[320] Homelessness (Priority Need for Accommodation) (England) Order 2002, SI 2002/2051, art 4.
[321] English Code, paras 10.40–10.41.
[322] SI 2002/2051, art 1(3).
[323] English Code, para 10.40.
[324] *R (Berhe) v Hillingdon London Borough Council and Secretary of State for Education and Skills* [2003] EWHC 2075 (Admin), [2003] All ER (D) 01 Sep, Admin Ct.
[325] Children Act 1989, ss 23C–24D.
[326] Disqualifying 18-, 19- or 20-year-olds who have been 'looked after, accommodated or fostered' from securing priority need by this route.
[327] SI 2002/2051, art 1(3). See English Code, para 10.40.

(1)   who is a care leaver; and

(2)   who is under 24[328] and to whom s 24B(3) of the Children Act 1989 applies; and

(3)   who is in full time higher or further education; and

(4)   whose term time accommodation is unavailable during vacation.

13.180 Children's services authorities continue to have duties to provide accommodation to those young people who meet these very specific conditions, and for that reason they are not accorded priority need under this provision.[329]

13.181 Applicants who fall within the very narrow exception of 'relevant student' cannot simply be turned away to the children's services authority which should be accommodating them. If the local housing authority's inquiries have reached the stage of considering 'priority need', that process must be formally completed. The local housing authority must therefore go on to consider whether the applicant may have a priority need under one of the other categories of priority need (pregnancy, vulnerability, etc). The process must always conclude with a reasoned written decision.[330] Of course, the hope would be that the children's services authority will have promptly met its duty to provide accommodation for an applicant within the exception, so that by the date of the decision on the application for homelessness assistance, the applicant will not be homeless.

Vulnerability: institutional backgrounds

13.182 People applying to local housing authorities in England and who are 'vulnerable' as a result of:

- having been 'looked after, accommodated or fostered'[331] (and who are aged 21 or over and not 'relevant students');[332] or

- having been a member of Her Majesty's regular naval, military or air forces; or

- having served a custodial sentence, been committed for contempt of court or other kindred offences, or having been remanded in custody,

---

[328] Children Act 1989, s 24B(3), to be amended to increase the age limit to 25 by Children and Young Persons Act 2008, s 23(2), not yet in force.
[329] Children Act 1989, s 24B(5); Children (Leaving Care) Act 2000; and Care Leavers (England) Regulations 2010, SI 2010/2571.
[330] HA 1996, s 184(3). See **10.66–10.74.**
[331] See **13.176.**
[332] See **13.175.**

all have a priority need.[333] Each sub-category is described in more detail in the following paragraphs.

13.183   To qualify, the applicant must be 'vulnerable' within the *Pereira* test.[334] So, simply having been in the military, in care, or in prison is not enough. The applicant must be vulnerable, and that vulnerability must be the result, in whole or in part, of having been in care, in custody or in the military.

13.184   The provisions do not require any immediate link between the end of military service, imprisonment or care and the application for homelessness assistance. They direct attention to the present vulnerability of the applicant. Although a person may be particularly vulnerable when first released, discharged, or at the point of leaving care, that may not be the only time at which he or she experiences relevant vulnerability. The provisions of the Order[335] will be met by any current vulnerability that is the result of the experience of a period in care, in the military or in prison, even if that period ended many months or years earlier.

13.185   Unlike the category of 'vulnerable' persons set out in HA 1996, Part 7,[336] this category of priority need can only be satisfied if the applicant personally is vulnerable for these reasons. A member of the applicant's household who is vulnerable as a result of one of these reasons does not confer priority need on the applicant. Obviously, in those circumstances, it would make sense for the vulnerable individual to apply in his or her own right for accommodation for his or her household.

A former care leaver aged 21 or over[337]

13.186   The local housing authority must address the following questions:

(1)   Is the person aged 21 or over?

(2)   Was he or she formerly looked after, accommodated or fostered?

(3)   Is he or she a relevant student?

(4)   Is he or she vulnerable?

(5)   Is that vulnerability *as a result of* having been looked after, accommodated or fostered?[338]

---

[333] SI 2002/2051, art 5.
[334] *R v Camden London Borough Council ex p Pereira* (1999) 31 HLR 317, CA, and see **13.75–13.119**.
[335] SI 2002/2051.
[336] HA 1996, s 189(1)(c).
[337] SI 2002/2051, art 5(1).
[338] English Code, paras 10.19–10.20.

13.187 The meanings of 'looked after, accommodated or fostered' and 'relevant student' are defined in the Priority Need Order.[339] If the applicant is a 'relevant student',[340] he or she cannot qualify under this category.

13.188 Unlike the category of care leavers aged 18, 19 and 20,[341] there is no requirement, for those aged 21 or over, that their period in care should have been at any particular age. The effects of a traumatic period in care (at any age) may only manifest themselves later in life.

13.189 The first three questions are therefore simple questions of fact for the local housing authority to determine. By contrast, determining:

(1)   whether the applicant is vulnerable; and

(2)   whether that vulnerability is *as a result of* having been 'looked after, accommodated or fostered'

require much more difficult judgments. The Code recommends that local housing authorities consider:

(1)   the length of time that the applicant was 'looked after, accommodated or fostered';

(2)   the reasons why the applicant was looked after, accommodated or fostered;

(3)   the length of time since that ended;

(4)   whether the applicant has been able to obtain or maintain accommodation since then; and

(5)   whether the applicant has existing support networks, particularly family, friends or a mentor.[342]

A person who is vulnerable as a result of having been a member of the armed forces[343]

13.190 The questions for the local housing authority are:

(1)   Was the applicant a member of the armed forces?

(2)   Is he or she vulnerable?

---

[339]   SI 2002/2051, art 1(3).
[340]   See **13.175**.
[341]   See **13.175–13.178**.
[342]   English Code, para 10.20.
[343]   SI 2002/2051, art 5(2).

(3) Is that vulnerability *as a result of* having been a member of the armed forces?[344]

13.191 The first question is a very straightforward question of fact, although military service is very broadly defined. The Order[345] refers to membership of 'Her Majesty's regular naval, military or air forces' without linking back to the much more technical definition previously used in HA 1996, Part 7.[346] The Code suggests that this definition includes a person who has been released following detention in a military correctional training centre.[347] It is difficult to see how the words could be met by a person who has been in anything other than the British armed services.

13.192 The next question is whether a person is 'vulnerable' according to the ordinary *Pereira* test.[348]

13.193 The final question is whether the applicant is vulnerable *as a result of* time spent in the armed forces. Local housing authorities are advised to consider:

(1) the length of time spent in the forces (they should not assume that vulnerability cannot occur after even a short period of service);

(2) the type of service that the applicant was engaged in (those on active service might find it more difficult to cope with civilian life);

(3) whether the applicant spent any time in a military hospital (possibly an indicator of a serious health problem or of post-traumatic stress);

(4) whether the Forces' medical and welfare advisers judged the individual to be particularly vulnerable and issued a Medical History Release Form;

(5) the length of time since discharge; and

(6) whether the applicant has any existing support networks, particularly family or friends.[349]

13.194 Some applicants (who have served for a long period or who have been medically discharged) ought to have been offered assistance with resettlement by the armed forces.[350] This does not mean that they are to be turned away by

---

[344] English Code, paras 10.21–10.23.
[345] SI 2002/2051.
[346] HA 1996, s 199(4) repealed by Housing and Regeneration Act 2008, ss 315((b), 321(1), Sch 16 from 1 December 2008 [England] and 30 March 2009 [Wales].
[347] English Code, para 10.21.
[348] *R v Camden London Borough Council ex p Pereira* (1999) 31 HLR 317, CA. See **13.75–13.119**.
[349] English Code, para 10.23.
[350] English Code, para 10.22.

the local housing authority or redirected to their former unit. In any event, such assistance from the armed forces is directed to the point of discharge, not to any later need for accommodation.

13.195 The Welsh Priority Need Order[351] does not contain the additional requirement of vulnerability.[352] Former members of the armed forces who may not be vulnerable might consider directing an application (or a further application) to a local housing authority in Wales.

A former prisoner who is vulnerable[353]

13.196 The questions for the local housing authority in dealing with an applicant who may fall within this category follow the same pattern as described for the previous two categories:

(1)   Is he or she vulnerable?

(2)   If so, is the vulnerability *as a result of* having served a custodial sentence, having been committed for contempt of court (or other kindred offences), or having been remanded in custody?[354]

13.197   The term 'custodial sentence' is defined to include:

- a sentence of imprisonment for those aged 21 or over;

- a sentence of detention for those aged under 18;

- a sentence of detention for public protection for those under 18 who commit serious offences;

- a sentence of detention for those under 18 who commit certain violent or sexual offences;

- a sentence of custody for life for persons under 21;

- a sentence of detention in a young offender institution for those aged between 18 and 21; and

- a detention and training order.[355]

---

[351]   SI 2001/607 (W 30).

[352]   SI 2001/607 (W 30), art 6. See **13.234–13.238**.

[353]   SI 2002/2051, art 5(3).

[354]   English Code, paras 10.24–10.27.

[355]   Powers of Criminal Courts (Sentencing) Act 2000, s 76; the references to sentence of custody for life and sentences of detention in a young offender institution are due to be repealed by the Criminal Justice and Court Services Act 2000, but no date for their repeal has yet been appointed (Criminal Justice and Court Services Act 2000, s 80(1)).

13.198 Being 'committed for contempt of court' refers to punishment under the inherent jurisdiction of the court to commit, and 'other kindred offences' refers to committals under the court's statutory powers.[356] Being 'remanded in custody' refers to being remanded by an order of the court, being remanded or committed to local authority accommodation, or being remanded, admitted or removed to hospital under the sentences available under the Mental Health Act 1983.[357]

13.199 The Code recommends that, in determining 'vulnerability', and whether it is the result of imprisonment or custody, local housing authorities should consider:

(1) the length of time served (it should not be assumed that vulnerability could not occur as a result of a short period of imprisonment);

(2) whether the applicant is receiving supervision from a criminal justice agency and any advice received from such an agency;

(3) the length of time since release;

(4) the extent to which the applicant has been able to obtain and maintain accommodation during that time; and

(5) whether the applicant has existing support networks, particularly family or friends, and how much of a positive influence those networks are likely to be.[358]

13.200 In one county court decision, the judge found that the local housing authority had been wrong to reject the opinion of a prison officer that the applicant was institutionalised, and had also been wrong to find that the applicant had a history of managing to secure housing when, in fact, his only accommodation in recent years had been insecure accommodation with a friend and he had previously been recalled to prison because he had not managed to secure housing.[359]

13.201 Former prisoners who have a priority need for this reason may still be found to have become homeless intentionally by the local housing authority if their homelessness arose as a result of their deliberate acts or omissions (which led them to prison and to lose their previous accommodation).[360] The Code

---

[356] Such as that at County Courts Act 1984, s 118.

[357] Referred to in the Order as being defined by the Powers of Criminal Courts (Sentencing) Act 2000, s 88. That section has been repealed and the definition is now found at Criminal Justice Act 2003, s 242(2). The references to the Mental Health Act 1983 are to the powers at ss 35, 36, 38 or 48, Mental Health Act 1983.

[358] English Code, para 10.25.

[359] *Kelly v City of Westminster Council* (2008) December *Legal Action*, p 27, Central London County Court.

[360] *R v Hounslow London Borough Council ex p R* (1997) 29 HLR 939, QBD; and *Stewart v Lambeth London Borough Council* [2002] EWCA Civ 753, [2002] HLR 40, CA.

reminds local housing authorities not to adopt a blanket policy of assuming that former prisoners who are homeless will have become homeless intentionally (or, indeed, always have become homeless unintentionally).[361] The Welsh Priority Need Order[362] does not contain the additional requirement of vulnerability.[363] Former prisoners who may not be vulnerable might consider directing an application (or a further application) to a local housing authority in Wales.

13.202 There is a considerable body of literature on some of the problems faced by ex-offenders in trying to find accommodation on their release from prison.[364]

A person who is vulnerable as a result of fleeing violence or threats of violence[365]

13.203 The questions for the local housing authority when dealing with an applicant who may fall within this category are:

(1) Did the person cease to occupy accommodation as a result of violence from another person or threats of violence from another person which were likely to be carried out?

(2) Is the person vulnerable?

(3) Is that vulnerability *as a result of* having ceased to occupy accommodation because of violence from another person or threats of violence from another person which were likely to be carried out?[366]

13.204 Although this category was intended primarily to benefit people without children who had been subject to domestic violence, its terms include people fleeing accommodation as a result of any type of violence (except self-inflicted harm). The Code refers to all forms of violence, including racially motivated violence.[367] A recent decision of the Supreme Court has held that where violence is 'domestic violence',[368] the definition of violence should be interpreted in the same sense as it is used in family proceedings: '"Domestic violence" includes physical violence, threatening or intimidating behaviour and

---

[361] English Code, para 10.27.
[362] SI 2001/607 (W 30).
[363] SI 2001/607 (W 30), art 7. See **13.239–13.245**.
[364] For example, *Locked Out* (Citizens' Advice Bureau, March 2007); *Homelessness Prevention and meeting housing need for ex-offenders: a Guide to Good Practice* (CLG, 2009); *Housing Ex-offenders* (House of Commons Library, SN/SP/2989, 7 March 2011); *Accommodation, Homelessness and re-offending of prisoners, results from the surveying prisoner crime reduction survey* (Ministry of Justice, 2012); and *Finding and Sustaining a Home in the Private Rented Sector – the essentials a guide for front-line staff working with homeless offenders* (Crisis, 2012).
[365] SI 2002/2051, art 6.
[366] English Code, paras 10.28–10.29.
[367] English Code, para 10.28.
[368] See **11.85**.

any other form of abuse which, directly or indirectly may give rise to the risk of harm.'[369] The Supreme Court declined to decide whether this extended definition of violence should also apply to people who might be fleeing from violence that was not domestic violence.[370]

13.205   The Code recommends that:

- the safety of the applicant and ensuring his or her confidentiality are of paramount concern;

- inquiries should not be made of the perpetrator; and

- the correct approach is to consider:

    '... the probability of violence, and not actions which the applicant could take (such as injunctions against the perpetrators).'[371]

13.206   This reflects the approach taken in relation to the question whether it would be reasonable for the applicant to continue to occupy accommodation in which violence is being experienced or threatened.[372]

13.207   In considering whether an applicant is vulnerable for this reason, local housing authorities are advised to take into account:

(1)   the nature of the violence or threats (whether a single but significant incident or a number of incidents over an extended period of time which have a cumulative effect);

(2)   the impact and likely effects of the violence or threats on the applicant's physical and mental health and well-being; and

(3)   whether the applicant has any existing support networks, particularly by way of family or friends.[373]

---

[369]   *Yemshaw v Hounslow London Borough Council* [2011] UKSC 3, [2011] 1 WLR 433, [2011] HLR 16, SC, Baroness Hale at [28] quoting the *Practice Direction (Residence and Contact Orders: Domestic Violence (No 2)* [2009] 1 WLR 251.
[370]   *Yemshaw v Hounslow London Borough Council* [2011] UKSC 3, [2011] 1 WLR 433, [2011] HLR 16, SC, Baroness Hale said: '[p]eople who are at risk of intimidating or harmful behaviour from their near neighbours are equally worthy of protection as are those who run the same risk from their relatives. But it may be less likely that they will suffer harm as a result of the abusive behaviour of their neighbours than it is in the domestic context. In practice, the threshold of seriousness may be higher' at [35]. For further discussion of the distinction to be drawn between 'domestic violence' and 'violence', see **11.83–11.92**.
[371]   English Code, para 10.28.
[372]   See **11.83–11.92**.
[373]   English Code, para 10.29.

13.208 Considering an applicant who claimed to have left his home because of threats of violence,[374] a county court judge held that the local housing authority should consider the following:

- Did the applicant leave his or her home due to threats?

- Were those threats likely to be carried out?

- Was he or she vulnerable?

13.209 In relation to the third question, the judge held that a person who is subject to threats of violence, and who is street homeless, is less likely to be able to protect himself or herself.[375]

13.210 To qualify under this category, the applicant must have actually left accommodation and have left it because of the violence or threatened violence. This need not be, but is very likely to have been, the accommodation which he or she had most recently occupied. Accordingly, the category will only apply infrequently to an applicant who is threatened with homelessness rather than actually homeless.

13.211 The Welsh Priority Need Order does not contain the additional requirement of vulnerability.[376] A person who has been subject to domestic violence, or is at risk of domestic violence if he or she returns home, who is not vulnerable and does not have a dependent child might consider directing an application for homelessness assistance (or a further application) to a local housing authority in Wales.

ADDITIONAL CATEGORIES IN WALES: THE WELSH PRIORITY NEED ORDER

13.212 The Homeless Persons (Priority Need) (Wales) Order 2001[377] came into force on 1 March 2001. It adds six additional categories of priority need to the four contained in HA 1996. Unlike the English Order, there is no reference in the Welsh Order to any new category which turns on an applicant being 'vulnerable'. If an applicant's circumstances mean that he or she falls within one of the categories, he or she will have a priority need.

13.213 The wording of the Order states that a person falling into one of the categories will have a priority need, suggesting that he or she must actually be the applicant. The Code, however, advises that local housing authorities should treat people as if they were in priority need if they reside with or might

---

[374] Not domestic violence.
[375] *Logan v Havering London Borough Council* (2007) May *Legal Action*, p 31, Romford County Court.
[376] SI 2001/607 (W 30), art 5.
[377] SI 2001/607 (W 30). See Appendix 3.

reasonably be expected to reside with people who qualify under the categories in the Order.[378] This probably goes further than the Order permits. To avoid any difficulty, it would be sensible for the application for homelessness assistance to be made by the individual who personally falls within the relevant category in the Order.

A person aged 16 or 17[379]

13.214   This category embraces all 16- and 17-year-olds. In contrast to the situation under the English Order,[380] there are no exceptions to this category.[381] There is certainly no requirement that the applicant be vulnerable or separated from his or her parents. It is simply being aged 16 or 17 that gives rise to the priority need.[382]

13.215   The Welsh Code correctly reflects the law as decided by the House of Lords, and guidance issued by the Welsh Assembly Government,[383] when it advises 'the duty within the Children Act 1989 under section 17 child in need and section 20 the duty to provide accommodation for a child in need takes precedence over the duties in the Housing Act 1996'.[384] It is also correctly emphasises joint working between housing and children's services departments.[385]

13.216   In 2010, the Welsh Assembly Government issued statutory guidance similar to that issued by the UK Government: *Provision of Accommodation for 16 and 17 year old young people who may be homeless*.[386] Like the English guidance,[387] it emphasises joint working between local housing authorities and children's services.[388] It also makes it clear that where a young person approaches a local housing authority for assistance with accommodation, and the local housing authority has reason to believe that the young person may be homeless, may be eligible for assistance and may be 16 or 17 years old, the local housing authority must perform its duties under HA 1996, Part 7, including securing interim accommodation.[389] If the young person may be homeless, or likely to become homeless within 28 days, the local housing authority should make an immediate referral to children's services for an assessment of the

---

[378]   Welsh Code, para 14.2.
[379]   SI 2001/607, art 4; Welsh Code, paras 14.38–14.41.
[380]   SI 2002/2051, art 3.
[381]   See **13.140–13.147** and Welsh Code, paras 14.38–14.41.
[382]   See **10.69–10.70** and **13.132–13.139** on the duties owed when a 17-year-old, approaching his or her eighteenth birthday, makes an application for homelessness assistance.
[383]   *Provision of Accommodation for 16 and 17 year old young people who may be homeless* (Welsh Assembly Government, September 2010) see CD-Rom.
[384]   Welsh Code, para 14.40.
[385]   Welsh Code, para 14.41.
[386]   Welsh Assembly Government, September 2010.
[387]   *Provision of Accommodation for 16 and 17 year old young people who may be homeless and/or require accommodation* (CLG and Children, Schools and Families, April 2010). See **13.151–13.164** and CD-Rom.
[388]   Chapter 5 of the Guidance.
[389]   Para 2.14 of the Guidance. See **16.12–16.28**.

child's needs.[390] That 'referral' should not involve turning the child away, but rather the local housing authority taking the application for homelessness assistance, providing interim accommodation where required, and then (if the applicant consents) notifying the children's services authority of the needs of the homeless child.[391]

13.217 Where children's services assess that a child is in need of accommodation and accommodation is to be provided under Children Act 1989, s 20, children's services must provide that accommodation.[392] If that is the case, the local housing authority will be likely to notify the child with its decision under HA 1996, s 184 that it does not have a duty to accommodate under HA 1996, Part 7, on the basis that the young person is no longer homeless.

13.218 The guidance advises that 'bed and breakfast accommodation for 16 and 17 year olds is not normally considered to be a suitable option'.[393] It also advises local housing authorities that 'where a 16 or 17 year old is required to leave accommodation as a result of his or her decision to refuse s 20 accommodation ... that decision should not be treated as deliberate action or inaction that contributed to intentional homelessness, subject to it being an informed and considered decision'.[394]

A person aged 18, 19 or 20[395]

13.219 Two specific groups within this age range are accorded priority need status by the Order: care leavers and those at risk of 'exploitation'. Both concepts are further refined.

13.220 If a person:

- is aged 18 or over, but under 21; and

- he or she was 'looked after, accommodated or fostered'; or

- is at particular risk of sexual or financial exploitation,

---

[390] Para 2.15 of the Guidance.
[391] What happens if the child does not consent? A local housing authority falls within the organisations listed in Children Act 2004, s 28 which are under a duty to make arrangements to ensure their functions are discharged having regard to the need to promote and safeguard the welfare of children and it is this duty that may require a local housing authority to refer a child to children's services, even without the child's consent. See also *Safeguarding Children: Working Together under the Children Act 2004* (Welsh Assembly Government, 2007).
[392] Chapter 3 of the Guidance, unless children's services can arrange for the child's needs to be met by providing other service such as support to return to the care of his or her family or other responsible adults (para 2.28 of the Guidance).
[393] Para 2.14 of the Guidance.
[394] Para 4.8 of the Guidance.
[395] SI 2001/607, art 3; Welsh Code, paras 14.29–14.37.

then he or she will have a priority need.

13.221 The definition of 'looked after, accommodated or fostered' is given in the Order[396] and is very broad. Although the shorthand commonly used for this rubric is 'care leaver', there is no requirement that the applicant has been in care. For example, the definition is met if the applicant has at some time in the past been 'privately fostered'.[397]

13.222 There is no minimum period of time during which the person must have been looked after, accommodated or fostered in order to qualify. Nor is there any specified age at which the applicant must have been looked after, accommodated or fostered.

13.223 Any young person (now aged 18, 19 or 20), who was 'looked after, accommodated or fostered' at any point in his or her life, for any period, will fall within this category.[398] The Welsh Code reminds local housing authorities of the guidance issued by the Welsh Assembly Government[399] and of importance of joint working with children's services departments.[400] The Welsh Code also advises that children who were, whilst they were being looked after, placed out of the area to which they were originally connected, and who wish to return to the area to which they were originally connected, should be accepted as having a local connection with that area, even where they were residing for a considerable time elsewhere.[401]

13.224 The second or alternative route to qualification under this provision is met by an 18-, 19- or 20-year-old who 'is at particular risk of sexual or financial exploitation'.[402]

13.225 The Welsh Code advises that certain young people may be at particular risk of sexual financial exploitation. Those young people include:

- a young person who is at risk of sexual abuse; or

- a young person who is at risk due to his or her sexual orientation; or

- a young person who is at risk of prostitution; or

- a young person who has learning disabilities; or

---

[396] SI 2001/607, art 3(2).

[397] SI 2001/607, art 3(2)(e).

[398] Welsh Code, para 14.30: 'anytime, *however short*, during their childhood in care' (emphasis in original).

[399] *Provision of Accommodation for 16 and 17 year old young people who may be homeless* (Welsh Assembly Government, 2010), see **13.216–13.218**, and CD-Rom.

[400] Welsh Code, para 14.32.

[401] Welsh Code, para 20.9. It also advises that the same provision should apply if any member of the applicant's household has a local connection in those circumstances. For 'member of the applicant's household', see **11.23–11.34**. For 'local connection', see **15.42–15.115**.

[402] Welsh Code, paras 14.35–14.37.

- a young person who is at risk of misuse of power or exercise of control by another person; or

- a young person who is at risk of financial extortion; or

- a young person who is on a low income (ie an income falling substantially below his or her needs), and is vulnerable due to a lack of alternative financial means (excluding students in further education.)[403]

13.226 The Code advises that local housing authorities should consider whether young persons would be at risk of further exploitation if they returned to live at their former homes, and that, where young people have histories of being sexually or financial exploited, they should normally be regarded as vulnerable unless there is strong evidence that they are no longer at risk. It is not good practice for local housing authorities always to expect evidence of sexual or financial exploitation.[404]

13.227 Note that the applicant must be at 'particular' risk for the terms of the Order to be satisfied, not merely subject to the general risk of sexual or financial exploitation that any young person may face. Presumably this additional criterion will be satisfied by some personal characteristic of the applicant (eg drug or alcohol dependency) or perhaps some special feature of his or her local area (eg prevalent street prostitution).

A person fleeing domestic violence or threatened domestic violence[405]

13.228 This category is satisfied if an applicant:

- has been subject to domestic violence; or

- is at risk of domestic violence; or

- is at risk of domestic violence if he or she returns home; and

- is without dependent children.[406]

13.229 Unlike the equivalent category in the English Order,[407] there is no need for the applicant to be vulnerable as a result of having fled accommodation in order to qualify in this category.

---

[403] Welsh Code, para 14.35.

[404] Welsh Code, paras 14.36–14.37. It is not clear why the word 'vulnerable' is used by the Code in this context. This category of priority need does not require any additional test that the applicant must be vulnerable. See the Scottish cases of *Kelly v Monklands District Council 1985 SLT 165, OH*; and *Wilson v Nithsdale District Council 1992 SLT 1131, OH*.

[405] SI 2001/607, art 5.

[406] Welsh Code, paras 14.42–14.46.

[407] SI 2002/2051, art 6. See **13.203–13.211**.

13.230 The other important distinction from the English Order is that only 'domestic' violence (presumably as defined in HA 1996, s 177(1))[408] rather than any other violence will result in a person falling into this category. A recent decision of the Supreme Court has held that the definition of domestic violence should be interpreted in the same sense as it is used in family proceedings: '"Domestic violence" includes physical violence, threatening or intimidating behaviour and any other form of abuse which, directly or indirectly may give rise to the risk of harm'.[409] The Welsh Code adopts the same definition.[410]

13.231 Although the description above this category (as given in the Order itself) refers to a person 'fleeing' domestic violence, that is not part of the words used in the relevant article in the order. It therefore embraces victims of actual or threatened domestic violence who have not yet left home. This enables an applicant to apply for accommodation and quickly be accepted as homeless, in priority need and unintentionally homeless, whilst still at home. She or he will therefore be able take the benefit of the main housing duty without first having to be provided with interim accommodation.

13.232 This category only applies to people without dependent children. Those who do have dependent children will have a priority need under the relevant category contained in HA 1996, Part 7.[411]

13.233 The Welsh Code advises that 'domestic violence' can occur in same-gender relationships as well as in mixed gender relationships.[412] Guidance on the sympathetic and careful nature of the inquiries to be carried out is given in the Welsh Code at paras 14.42–14.46.

A person homeless after leaving the armed forces of the Crown[413]

13.234 This category is met by any applicant who is a former member of the armed forces and:

(1) is homeless; and

(2) has been homeless since leaving the armed forces.[414]

---

[408] See **11.83–11.92**. It must be noted however that the Welsh Order itself does not define 'domestic violence', nor does it refer expressly to the definition in HA 1996 Part 7.

[409] *Yemshaw v Hounslow London Borough Council* [2011] UKSC 3, [2011] 1 WLR 433, [2011] HLR 16, SC, Baroness Hale at [28] quoting the *Practice Direction (Residence and Contact Orders: Domestic Violence (No 2)* [2009] 1 WLR 251. See **11.83–11.92**.

[410] Welsh Code, para 14.44.

[411] See **13.38–13.74**.

[412] Welsh Code, para 14.44. Violence from same-sex partners falls within the definition of 'domestic violence' at HA 1996, s 177(1), (1A) and s 178, as amended by the Civil Partnership Act 2004.

[413] SI 2001/607, art 6.

[414] Welsh Code, paras 14.47–14.51.

13.235 Unlike the English equivalent category,[415] there is no requirement that the applicant be 'vulnerable', whether by reason of service in the forces or otherwise.

13.236 Only service in the 'regular armed forces of the Crown' satisfies the condition for this category. The definition of 'armed forces' used is the technical one adopted in HA 1996.[416]

13.237 The emphasis is on a continuing chain of homelessness since discharge. The Code recommends that homelessness should be treated as lack of 'suitable permanent accommodation', ie not having had a tenancy or having been permanently settled with family or friends.[417]

13.238 The length of time since discharge is not in point; the issue is whether the applicant has remained homeless since he or she was discharged.[418]

A former prisoner who has been homeless since being released from custody[419]

13.239 To qualify under this category the applicant must:

(1) be a former prisoner; and

(2) be homeless; and

(3) have been homeless since leaving custody; and

(4) have a local connection with the local housing authority's area.[420]

13.240 Again, unlike the English equivalent,[421] there is no requirement that the former prisoner be 'vulnerable'.

13.241 A 'prisoner' is defined as 'any person for the time being detained in lawful custody as the result of a requirement imposed by a court that he or she be detained'.[422] That includes time spent on remand, in a young offender's institution or in prison, whether as a result of a conviction or not.[423] As with former members of the armed forces,[424] the emphasis is on a continuing chain of homelessness and local housing authorities are advised to consider whether

---

[415] SI 2002/2051, art 5(2). See **13.109–13.195**.
[416] HA 1996, s 199(4) repealed by Housing and Regeneration Act 2008 ss 315(b), 321(1), Sch 16; SI 2001/607, art 6(2).
[417] Welsh Code, para 14.50.
[418] Welsh Code, paras 14.50–14.51.
[419] SI 2001/607, art 7.
[420] Welsh Code, paras 14.52–14.61.
[421] SI 2002/2051, art 5(3). See **13.196–13.202**.
[422] SI 2001/607, art 7(2).
[423] Welsh Code, para 14.56.
[424] See **13.234–13.239**.

the applicant has 'failed to secure suitable accommodation and has therefore been unable to establish stable accommodation since leaving prison'.[425]

13.242 The inclusion of a 'local connection' requirement reflects a concern later expressed during the passage of the Homelessness Act 2002 through Parliament, when MPs representing constituencies containing sizeable prisons were anxious that their local housing authorities should not suddenly receive a host of applications from former prisoners. The solution in England was to restrict the extension of priority need to those former prisoners who were 'vulnerable' as a result of their imprisonment. The solution in Wales was to require that former prisoners must have a local connection with the local housing authority to which they apply in order to obtain the benefit of this priority need category.[426]

13.243 Local connection to an area cannot be acquired by residence as a result of lawful detention in that area.[427] A former prisoner would, therefore, not acquire a local connection in the area where his or her prison was situated, unless he or she had acquired a local connection with that area for a reason other than residence, eg by employment (either before or after the period of imprisonment).[428]

13.244 The wording leaves open the question of what happens if a prisoner has no local connection with any area, but otherwise falls within this category. Any local housing authority to which he or she chooses to apply must accept his or her application.[429] However, on a literal reading of this article,[430] a prisoner who has been homeless since release but has no local connection with any local housing authority will not be able to acquire a priority need under this category if he or she has directed his or her application for homelessness assistance to a local housing authority in Wales. The Welsh Code does not deal with that eventuality.

13.245 In contrast to the English Code, the Welsh Code specifically advises local housing authorities that the actions of former prisoners that led to their imprisonment should not also lead to their being considered intentionally homeless, unless the offence which resulted in the prison sentence was a direct breach of the tenancy agreement which led to repossession of the property.[431]

---

[425] Welsh Code, para 14.57.
[426] Welsh Code, paras 14.58–14.60.
[427] HA 1996, s 199(3)(b); Welsh Code, para 14.55 which notes that residence prior to imprisonment may give rise to a local connection. See **15.61**.
[428] Welsh Code, paras 14.55, 14.58–14.59. These paragraphs recognise that a former prisoner may wish to live in an area in which he or she has no local connection and suggests that this can be achieved through reciprocal arrangements between local housing authorities. See **15.234–15.239**.
[429] HA 1996, s 198(2). See **15.17–15.18**.
[430] SI 2001/607, art 7.
[431] Welsh Code, para 15.23.

Chapter 14

BECOMING HOMELESS INTENTIONALLY

INTRODUCTION

14.1 Once a local housing authority has determined that an applicant is homeless (or is threatened with homelessness), and that she or he is eligible for assistance, a duty under the Housing Act 1996 (HA 1996), Part 7 is owed to the applicant. In order to decide which precise duty is owed, the local housing authority must decide whether the applicant has a priority need[1] and whether she or he has become homeless (or has become threatened with homelessness) intentionally.

14.2 Because different duties arise depending upon the answers, the local housing authority must answer both of those two questions. Traditionally, if local housing authorities had decided that the applicant had no priority need, they felt it unnecessary to consider whether or not an applicant had become homeless intentionally (or had become threatened with homelessness intentionally). But now that there is a power available to the local housing authority to provide accommodation for people who do not have a priority need and who did not become homeless (or threatened with homelessness) intentionally, both questions must be asked and answered.[2]

14.3 For the first 20 years of statutory homelessness provision in the UK (1977–1997), the decision as to whether or not the homelessness of a priority need applicant had come about 'intentionally' was pivotal. Those who had not become homeless intentionally were treated as entitled to a permanent home. Those who had become homeless intentionally would merely be given temporary accommodation and then only for a very short period. Disputes about whether an applicant had become homeless 'intentionally' accordingly dominated the work of housing advisers and homelessness officers, and formed the bulk of the reported court cases on the statutory provisions. To have been found to have become 'homeless intentionally' was to be given what one judge described as the 'mark of Cain'.[3]

14.4 Much has changed since the early days of homelessness law. First, a decision of the House of Lords in 1996 exploded the myth that those applicants who had become homeless unintentionally were entitled to be provided with permanent homes under the statutory homelessness provisions.[4] Second, the new statutory framework of HA 1996 made it clear that the highest duty owed to any applicant would be met by the provision of temporary

---

[1] See Chapter 13.

[2] Housing Act 1996, s 192(3). In *Gaskin v Norwich City Council* [2007] EWCA Civ 1239, (2008) January *Legal Action*, p 38, CA, the local housing authority had reached a decision that the applicant did not have a priority need without considering the issue of whether she had become homeless intentionally. In subsequent proceedings, after it had found that she did have a priority need but had become homeless intentionally, that earlier approach was not criticised by the court.

[3] *Din v Wandsworth London Borough Council* (unreported) 23 June 1981, CA, per Ackner LJ, quoted in *Lambert v Ealing London Borough Council* [1982] 1 WLR 550, CA at 557, per Lord Denning MR.

[4] *R v Brent London Borough Council ex p Awua* [1996] AC 55, HL.

accommodation only.[5] Third, changes to the arrangements for allocation of social housing (most recently made by the Homelessness Act 2002) have required local housing authorities to give a preference to all homeless people, including those who have become homeless intentionally.[6] Fourth, a deepening crisis in the availability of decent affordable housing on the open market in many areas has made the search for alternative homes by those who become homeless intentionally all the more difficult.

14.5 For applicants whose applications for homelessness assistance are made to local housing authorities in England on or after 9 November 2012, local housing authorities will be permitted to bring the main housing duty[7] to an end by making them an offer of suitable private rented accommodation.[8] So even applicants who are not found to have become homeless intentionally are likely to have accommodation secured for them in the private rented sector.

14.6 In previous editions of this book, we stated that, as a result of the first four factors above, provision for ever longer periods of temporary accommodation must be made for applicants who have become homeless intentionally. The amendments inserted by the Localism Act 2011[9] mean that the period of occupation of accommodation provided under the main housing duty should also become correspondingly shorter. So the gap should have significantly narrowed between the duties owed to those in priority need who have become homeless intentionally, and those who did not become homeless intentionally, and that gap should continue to narrow. Statistics show, however, that the proportion of applicants for homelessness assistance found to have become homeless intentionally rose steadily rising after the implementation of HA 1996 in 1997 until 2006 and has since then remained at around 7% of all applicants for homelessness assistance.[10]

14.7 These changes have not rendered the question of 'becoming homeless intentionally' (or 'becoming threatened with homelessness intentionally') altogether academic. As any list of the different powers and duties in HA 1996,

---

[5]   HA 1996, s 193(2). See **17.23–17.168**.
[6]   HA 1996, s 167(2)(a) and (b). See **4.62–4.79**.
[7]   HA 1996, s 193(2), see**17.23–17.168**.
[8]   For 'private rented sector offers', see **17.109–17.131**.
[9]   Which apply to applicants for homelessness assistance whose applications were made on or after 9 November 2012 to a local housing authority in England; at the date of writing, the amendments to HA 1996 made by LA 2011, ss 148–149 had not been brought into effect in Wales.
[10] *Table 770: Decisions taken by local authorities under the Housing Act 1996 on applications by eligible households* (DCLG) shows that the number of decisions where the applicant had a priority need and had become homeless intentionally had been 3% of applicants for homelessness assistance each year from 1998 to 2002. From 2003, the proportion started rising to a high of 8% for 2008–2009 and since then has been at 7% (figures to second quarter 2012). No figures are shown for those applicants found not to have a priority need and to have become homeless intentionally. Applicants found to have a priority need and to have become homeless intentionally were around 4% of total applications for homelessness assistance made to local housing authorities in Wales for the first quarter of 2012 (*National Statistics on Homelessness*, Welsh Government, June 2012).

Part 7 indicates,[11] much still turns on whether actual (or threatened) homelessness was (or is) intentional. The English Code explains the policy reasoning behind the different duties owed to those applicants found to have become homeless intentionally and those found not to have become homeless intentionally:

> 'This recognises the general expectation that, wherever possible, people should take responsibility for their own accommodation needs and ensure that they do not behave in a way which might lead to the loss of their accommodation.'[12]

14.8 However, even an adverse finding that actual or threatened homelessness has been brought about 'intentionally' is simply the result of one local housing authority having applied a complex statutory test and its own judgment to the facts of the application. Two equally reasonable local housing authorities may quite lawfully reach different conclusions on the same statutory test and the same set of facts. This means that there are often prospects for an applicant, who has been found to have become homeless intentionally by one local housing authority, to apply to another local housing authority and find that a different conclusion will be reached.[13]

14.9 Likewise, it is important to appreciate that the adverse finding is one that is applicable only so long as the particular actual or threatened homelessness lasts. First, a person who is found to have become threatened with homelessness intentionally may apply again once actually homeless, in the hope that there may be a different finding about why he or she became homeless. Second, a person who is found to have become homeless intentionally may render that finding irrelevant to any future incidence of homelessness by obtaining settled accommodation. This limited life of a finding of becoming homeless (or threatened with becoming homeless) intentionally means that a fresh application can always be made to a local housing authority for assistance under HA 1996, Part 7, unless the facts are precisely the same on the new application as upon the occasion of the last application.[14] Obviously, to save repeating what may have been extensive recent investigations on a previous application, the local housing authority is entitled initially to rely on its original finding that the applicant had become homeless intentionally and to confine its inquiries to whether there has been any intervening settled accommodation or other factual change since the earlier finding.[15]

---

[11] See **17.9**.

[12] *Homelessness Code of Guidance for Local Authorities* (Communities and Local Government, Department for Education and Skills, Department of Health, July 2006) (the English Code), para 11.3, at Appendix 2 of this book; *Code of Guidance for Local Authorities Allocation of Accommodation and Homelessness 2012* (Welsh Government, August 2012) (the Welsh Code), para 15.1, see CD-Rom.

[13] See **9.46–9.52**.

[14] *R v Harrow London Borough Council ex p Fahia* (1996) 30 HLR 1124, HL; and *Begum v Tower Hamlets London Borough Council* [2005] EWCA Civ 340, [2005] HLR 34, CA. See **9.66–9.85**.

[15] See English Code, para 11.30; Welsh Code, paras 15.28–15.30.

14.10   There is no special provision dispensing with this question of whether an applicant has become homeless intentionally where he or she has made a fresh application for homelessness assistance to a local housing authority in England within two years of acceptance of a private rented sector offer.[16] Even though inquiry into priority need is dispensed with, the main housing duty, or the equivalent duty to those threatened with homelessness, will only apply where the local housing authority 'is not satisfied that the applicant became homeless intentionally'.[17] Local housing authorities will therefore be permitted to examine the reasons why the applicant has lost, or is facing the loss of, accommodation.

14.11   An applicant who is homeless but is *not found to have become homeless intentionally* and who does have a *priority need* is owed the highest duty under HA 1996, Part 7 (referred to as the 'main housing duty'). That duty requires the local housing authority 'to secure that accommodation is available for occupation by the applicant'.[18]

14.12   In contrast, an applicant who became homeless *intentionally* and who has a *priority need* will be owed lesser duties:

> '... to secure that accommodation is available for his occupation for such period as they consider will give him a reasonable opportunity of securing accommodation'[19]

and to

> '... provide him with (or secure that he is provided with) advice and assistance in any attempts he may make to secure that accommodation becomes available for his occupation.'[20]

14.13   There is also a duty to assess the applicant's housing needs.[21]

14.14   An applicant who does *not* have a *priority need* and who became homeless *intentionally* is owed a limited duty, which is that the local housing authority:

---

[16]   HA 1996, s 193(7AA) as amended by LA 2011, s 148(5) and made to applicants whose applications for homelessness assistance were made on or after 9 November 2012 to a local housing authority in England. See **17.109–17.131**. At the date of writing, the amendments to HA 1996 made by LA 2011, ss 148–149 had not been brought into effect in Wales.

[17]   HA 1996, s 195A(1) and (3) as inserted by LA 2011, s 149(4) for applicants whose applications for homelessness assistance were made on or after 9 November 2012 to a local housing authority in England. At the date of writing, the amendments to HA 1996 made by LA 2011, ss 148–149 had not been brought into effect in Wales. See **9.89–9.95**.

[18]   HA 1996, s 193(2). See **17.23–17.168**.

[19]   HA 1996, s 190(2)(a). English Code, para 11.4; Welsh Code, para 15.2. See **17.182–17.189**.

[20]   HA 1996, s 190(2)(b). English Code, para 11.4. See **17.201–17.214**.

[21]   HA 1996, s 190(4). English Code, para 11.4. See **17.201–17.214**.

'... shall provide him with (or secure that he is provided with) advice and assistance in any attempts he may make to secure that accommodation becomes available for his occupation.'[22]

14.15 There is also a duty to assess the applicant's housing needs.[23]

14.16 If an applicant is 'threatened with homelessness', there is a similar range of duties, depending upon whether or not he or she has a priority need and whether he or she has become threatened with homelessness intentionally.[24]

14.17 Further discussion as to the extent of these various duties, and the methods of performing them, is provided at Chapter 17.

14.18 In this Chapter, we consider the test used to determine whether or not someone has become homeless (or threatened with homelessness) intentionally, and then outline some of the common scenarios in which an applicant may or may not be found to have become homeless (or threatened with homelessness) intentionally. Because the circumstances of 'threatened with homelessness' and actual homelessness are treated differently in HA 1996, Part 7, the remainder of this Chapter deals separately with, first, 'becoming homeless intentionally'[25] and then with 'becoming threatened with homelessness intentionally'.[26]

MAKING INQUIRIES INTO 'BECOMING HOMELESS INTENTIONALLY'

14.19 A local housing authority must conduct such inquiries into an application as will enable it to determine what duty under HA 1996, Part 7 (if any) is owed.[27] Where the local housing authority is satisfied that an applicant is both eligible and homeless (or threatened with homelessness), it must then make such further enquires as will enable it to determine whether that particular applicant has become homeless or threatened with homelessness 'intentionally'.

14.20 Obviously, an individual and applicant-centred approach to the question is required. Local housing authorities should not adopt general policies which seek to predetermine that particular classes of applicant (eg tenants of the local housing authority who were evicted for arrears of rent or anti-social behaviour) will or will not be found to have become homeless intentionally.[28] Local housing authorities should make all necessary inquiries

---

[22] HA 1996, s 190(3). English Code, para 11.4; Welsh Code, para 15.2. See **17.201–17.214**.
[23] HA 1996, s 190(4). English Code, para 11.4. See **17. 201–17.214**.
[24] HA 1996, s 195(2) and (5). See **17.190–17.200**.
[25] See **14.25–14.162**.
[26] See **14.163–14.173**.
[27] HA 1996, s 184(1)(b).
[28] English Code, para 11.6; Welsh Code, para 15.3.

about each particular application and reach a decision in the light of those inquiries. If there is doubt about the matter at the conclusion of initial inquiries, then either inquiries should continue until the matter is free of doubt, or the benefit of the doubt should be given to the applicant and he or she should be found not to have become homeless (or threatened with homelessness) 'intentionally'.[29] If it is not possible for the local housing authority to satisfy itself that the applicant became homeless intentionally, because the events it is inquiring into occurred some years earlier and the facts are unclear, the applicant should be considered not to have become homeless intentionally.[30]

14.21 Any decision that an applicant has become homeless or threatened with homelessness intentionally should be accompanied by clear reasons for that finding, even though the formal decision being notified to the applicant is only the decision as to what precise HA 1996 Part 7 duty the applicant is owed.[31]

14.22 The burden of making the inquiries rests with the local housing authority. It is not for the applicant to prove his or her case, and satisfy the local housing authority that she or he did not become homeless intentionally. This was reinforced by the Court of Appeal in *O'Connor v Kensington and Chelsea Royal London Borough Council*,[32] where it was held that a local housing authority, when considering the question of whether the applicant had become homeless intentionally, should consider whether the applicant had been unaware of a relevant fact in good faith, regardless of whether this latter point had been raised by the applicant. A later Court of Appeal decision refined the point, adding that the decision-maker need not consider matters that were not raised by the applicant, unless those matters were within 'the circumstances of obviousness'.[33]

14.23 The Codes suggest that there is one exception to the general rule about the burden of proof: if an applicant is seeking to establish that he or she did not acquiesce in the deliberate actions of another member of his of her household (who has already been found to have caused the homelessness of the household), the burden is on the applicant to raise and demonstrate a lack of acquiescence in those actions.[34] This is probably putting the test too high: the

[29] *R v Thurrock Borough Council ex p Williams* (1981) 1 HLR 128, QBD, and see **10.19**.
[30] English Code, para 11.6; Welsh Code, para 15.4.
[31] English Code, paras 11.5–11.6; Welsh Code, paras 12.45–12.48; and *Southall v West Wiltshire District Council* (2002) October *Legal Action*, p 31, Swindon County Court.
[32] *O'Connor v Kensington and Chelsea Royal London Borough Council,* [2004] EWCA Civ 394, [2004] HLR 37, CA at [37], per Sedley LJ and at [54], per Waller LJ.
[33] *Aw-Aden v Birmingham City Council* [2005] EWCA Civ 1834, (2006) July *Legal Action*, p 29, CA, per Maurice Kay LJ at [12]. See *Bury Metropolitan Borough Council v Gibbons* [2010] EWCA Civ 327, [2010] HLR 33, CA, where one of the reasons why the review decision was held to be unlawful was that the decision-maker had failed to consider whether, on the facts, the applicant had been, in good faith, unaware of a relevant fact, namely the availability of housing benefit and his right to remain in possession until a possession order had been made.
[34] English Code, para 11.5; Welsh Code, para 15.4. See **10.15–10.19, 10.48–10.49** and **14.93–14.97**.

proper approach is that acquiescence may be assumed by the local housing authority 'in the absence of material which indicates to the contrary.'[35] Where there is any material that indicates that the applicant may not have acquiesced, the local housing authority must make inquiries in the usual way.[36]

14.24 If, during its inquiries, the local housing authority has reason to believe that an applicant whose household includes children under 18 might be found to have become homeless intentionally, it is under a duty to ask the applicant to give consent for his or her circumstances to be referred to the children's services authority, and then (if consent is given) to make that referral.[37] This will enable children's services to begin planning what assistance it might provide for the household if the local housing authority's final conclusion is that the applicant did become homeless intentionally. The local housing authority is obliged to follow up the referral by advising the children's services authority of the decision that it actually reaches on the application for homelessness assistance.[38]

THE STATUTORY MEANING

Overview

14.25 In the homelessness provisions of HA 1996, Part 7, the word 'intentionally' is not given its ordinary or dictionary meaning. It has a very tightly prescribed statutory meaning. Most obviously this is because, in the ordinary use of language, an applicant's homelessness is very often brought about, not by an intentional act of the applicant, but rather by the intentional act of another party (such as a landlord, parent or court bailiff) who has deliberately ejected the applicant. Moreover, it is something of a contradiction to suggest that an applicant has become homeless intentionally, since the whole point of the applicant making an application for homelessness assistance is to avoid or end his or her state of homelessness.

14.26 As Lord Denning MR observed, in one of the earliest homelessness cases:

'Many people would have thought that [the applicant's] conduct, however deplorable, was not 'deliberate' in the sense required by ... [the Act]. She did not deliberately do anything to get herself turned out.'[39]

14.27 Similarly, Lord Lowry said:

---

[35] *R v North Devon District Council ex parte Lewis* [1981] 1 WLR 328 at 333, per Woolf J.

[36] *R v West Dorset District Council ex parte Phillips* (1985) 17 HLR 336, QBD; and *N v Allerdale Borough Council* (2008) October *Legal Action*, p 38, Carlisle County Court.

[37] HA 1996, s 213A(1). English Code, para 11.29; Welsh Code, para 15.27. See **17.225–17.232**.

[38] HA 1996, s 213A(2) and (3).

[39] *R v Slough Borough Council ex p Ealing London Borough Council* [1981] 1 QB 801, CA at 809.

'No one really becomes homeless or threatened with homelessness intentionally; the word is a convenient label to describe the result of acting or failing to act as described in [the Act].'[40]

14.28 The statutory definition of 'becoming homeless intentionally' is that:

'... a person becomes homeless intentionally if he deliberately does or fails to do anything in consequence of which he ceases to occupy accommodation which is available for his occupation and which it would have been reasonable for him to continue to occupy.'[41]

14.29 This complex composite definition has been described as part of a statutory 'semantic nightmare'.[42]

14.30 Because each and every element of the composite must be in place before a local housing authority can be satisfied that an applicant 'became homeless intentionally', initial expectations (when the phrase was first enacted) were that it would only be satisfied infrequently. The first edition of the *Code of Guidance* in 1978 indicated that the number of applicants falling foul of it was 'expected to be small'.[43]

14.31 The statutory formulation is most practically approached by treating it as having five elements. To ensure that they are all in place, the local housing authority needs to address five questions in the course of its inquiries and decision-making. The necessary premise for the questions is that the applicant is currently homeless (ignoring, of course, any interim accommodation that the local housing authority may have provided), so that all the attention is directed to the past:

(1)   Was there a deliberate act or omission (which does not include an act or omission in good faith by a person unaware of a material fact)?[44]

(2)   Was that a deliberate act or omission by the applicant?[45]

(3)   Was it as a consequence of that deliberate act or omission that the applicant ceased to occupy accommodation?[46]

(4)   Was that accommodation available for the applicant's occupation and for occupation by members of the applicant's family who normally resided

---

[40]   *Din v Wandsworth London Borough Council* [1983] 1 AC 657, HL at 679, referring to Housing (Homeless Persons) Act 1977, s 17, containing the same definition of 'becoming homeless intentionally' as at HA 1996, s 191(1).

[41]   HA 1996, s 191(1).

[42]   *Roughead v Falkirk District Council* 1979 SCOLAG 188, per Sheriff Sinclair.

[43]   *Code of Guidance* (Department of Environment, 1978), para 2.19.

[44]   See **14.37–14.92**.

[45]   See **14.93–14.97**.

[46]   See **14.98–14.117**.

with the applicant and by persons with whom the applicant might reasonably have been expected to reside?[47]

(5) Would it have been reasonable for the applicant to have continued to occupy the accommodation?[48]

14.32 If the local housing authority's answer to *each* of these five questions is 'Yes', then the applicant will have 'become homeless intentionally'. If the answer to *any* of them is 'No', the applicant cannot have become homeless intentionally.

14.33 'Becoming threatened with homelessness intentionally' is also defined in HA 1996, Part 7, in similar but not identical terms.[49]

14.34 There is, in addition, a category of applicants who are deemed to have become homeless intentionally and to whom the five-question approach is not to be applied. An applicant is 'treated as' becoming homeless intentionally if:

(1) he or she has (in the past) entered into an arrangement to give up accommodation; and

(2) it was accommodation which it would have been reasonable to continue to occupy; and

(3) the purpose of the arrangement was to trigger entitlement to help under HA 1996, Part 7; and

(4) there is no other good reason why the applicant is homeless.[50]

14.35 This deeming provision is obviously designed to prevent collusive arrangements, but in practice is hardly ever used. Not only are the conditions tightly drawn, but they only deem the 'person' who 'enters into' the arrangement as having become homeless intentionally.[51] Its effect can therefore be avoided by a different member of the homeless household making the application for homelessness assistance.[52] There is a similar deeming provision in the definition of 'becoming threatened with homelessness intentionally'.[53]

14.36 The following paragraphs address, in turn, each of the five elements of the composite statutory definition of 'becoming homeless intentionally'.

---

[47] See **14.118–14.124**.
[48] See **14.125–14.143**.
[49] HA 1996, s 196(1) and (2); and discussed further at **14.163–14.173**.
[50] HA 1996, s 191(3). See also English Code, paras 11.8 and 11.28; Welsh Code, para 15.6. See **14.174–14.180**.
[51] HA 1996, s 191(3)(a).
[52] Discussed further at **14.180**.
[53] HA 1996, s 196(3). See **14.168**.

Was there a deliberate act or omission?

A deliberate act or omission

14.37 The first step in the statutory definition is that the applicant 'deliberately does or fails to do anything' which results in his or her loss of accommodation.[54] There is no definition of 'deliberate act' or 'deliberate omission' in HA 1996, Part 7.[55] Instead, HA 1996, Part 7, stipulates that some acts or omissions are not to be treated as deliberate, by providing that:

'... an act or omission in good faith on the part of a person who was unaware of any relevant fact shall not be treated as deliberate.'[56]

14.38 So the word 'deliberate' in this setting must connote a free election to act (or fail to act) in a particular way by a person in possession of all the relevant facts. As one English judge has put it:

'I am satisfied from a consideration of the whole of the section ... that "deliberately" is used in the ordinary sense of the word and is not to be narrowly construed. In particular the provisions of [the] subsection ... indicate that "deliberately" means "after a consideration of all the relevant facts".'[57]

14.39 The most obvious example of an act 'deliberately' done arises where an applicant has surrendered, or given notice on, his or her tenancy, or sold his or her house, and made no provision for future accommodation.[58] The most obvious example of a 'deliberate' omission would be failure to pay housing costs notwithstanding having the means and opportunity to pay them.

14.40 The English Code of Guidance introduces the notions of 'force' and 'fault':

'... an act or omission should not generally be treated as deliberate, even where deliberately carried out, if it was forced upon the applicant through no fault of their own.'[59]

14.41 Adopting the approach in this guidance and adding a non-statutory gloss to HA 1996, Part 7 itself, a non-deliberate act could therefore occur either when:

(1) someone was forced to do something; or

---

[54] HA 1996, s 191(1).
[55] The dictionary definition of 'deliberate' is 'intentional', which, in the context of HA 1996, s 191, seems to take one round in circles (*Shorter Oxford English Dictionary*, 1993).
[56] HA 1996, s 191(2).
[57] *Devenport v Salford City Council* (1983) 8 HLR 54, CA, per Waller LJ.
[58] See *Dyson v Kerrier District Council* [1980] 1 WLR 1205, CA (a case in which the applicant gave up long-term accommodation for a precarious winter let); and *F v Birmingham City Council* [2006] EWC Civ 1427, [2007] HLR 18, CA, where a tenant gave up her secure tenancy for unaffordable private rented accommodation.
[59] English Code, para 11.16; there is no equivalent in the Welsh Code.

(2) someone may have chosen to act in a particular way, but did so in ignorance of all the relevant facts.[60]

14.42 An example of the former would arise where the applicant had deliberately vacated accommodation, but did so because remaining there would lead to him or her experiencing further violence from a neighbour. Similarly, an applicant's choice to spend his or her last available money to buy food for hungry children rather than paying the rent is not, for the purposes of the legislation, 'deliberate'.[61] On the latter set of facts, a local housing authority argued:

> 'a person does or fails to do something "deliberately" if he makes a considered choice between two courses of action or inaction, either of which he is able to take. Thus, if he makes a considered decision to apply the only money he has in his pocket in maintaining his children instead of paying it to his landlord, he deliberately fails to pay the rent'.[62]

14.43 This submission was rejected. The Court of Appeal said:

> 'The purpose of … the … Act is to house the homeless. Admittedly it is no part of that purpose to house those whose homelessness has been brought upon them by their own fault. But equally it is no part of it to refuse housing to those whose homelessness has been brought upon them without fault on their part, for example by disability, sickness, poverty or even a simple inability to make ends meet.'[63]

Unaware of a relevant fact

14.44 The proviso dealing with ignorance of material facts can be difficult to operate in practice. First, the local housing authority must identify whether the fact of which the applicant was ignorant was 'relevant'. Second, assuming that there was ignorance of a relevant fact, it must ask whether the applicant acted 'in good faith'.[64]

14.45 As one judge has observed, the proviso is:

> '… not without its difficulties. It is to be noted that the test is not the reasonableness of the applicant's actions, but whether they were taken in

---

[60] The important question of an applicant's mental capacity at the time of the act or omission in this context is discussed at **14.63–14.69**.

[61] As happened in *R v Wandsworth London Borough Council ex p Hawthorne* (1995) 27 HLR 59, CA. See also *Adekunle v Islington London Borough Council* (2009) November *Legal Action*, p 25, Mayor's and City of London County Court, where the local housing authority had decided that the applicant's choice to sell her house in the face of serious financial difficulties was 'a conscious and deliberate decision' which fell within the definition of 'deliberate act'. The judge said that view was 'mistaken and wrong' in the circumstances where a person's conscious decision is taken 'in a situation where there is no realistic alternative'.

[62] *R v Wandsworth London Borough Council ex p Hawthorne* (1995) 27 HLR 59, CA at 63.

[63] *R v Wandsworth London Borough Council ex p Hawthorne* (1995) 27 HLR 59, CA at 63, per Nourse LJ.

[64] HA 1996, s 191(2).

ignorance. This may seem unjust. A person who takes the trouble to find out all the relevant facts, but makes a reasonable but mistaken judgment, cannot apparently claim the benefit of the section; a person who makes no enquiries at all and therefore acts in ignorance, may be able to do so. The omission of a test of reasonableness has been criticised in the courts (see for example *R v Tower Hamlets London Borough Council ex p Rouf*)[65] but the section remains unamended.'[66]

14.46 In using the words 'any relevant fact', Parliament has indicated that it intended a wide construction to be given to that phrase.[67] But 'relevant' to what? A person may have deliberately given up his or her existing home in the mistaken belief that there would be accommodation (or employment capable of funding accommodation) in a place to which he or she then moved. If that person was factually wrong about the availability of other accommodation (or employment) can that render the giving up of the original home not a 'deliberate' act?

14.47 In one case, a young woman gave up her home overseas to come to the UK in the mistaken belief that her family would accommodate her here. In another, a businessman gave up his home in the UK to move abroad in the mistaken belief that he would be pursuing a sound business venture overseas capable of financing alternative accommodation there. Both were ignorant of the true facts, but were these facts 'relevant' to the giving up of their homes? In both cases, the judges decided that they were 'relevant facts' that were capable of triggering the application of the proviso to what was otherwise manifestly the deliberate giving-up of their homes.[68]

14.48 Subsequently, the courts have drawn a distinction between 'matters of hope' and relevant facts.[69] In the case of a scientist who gave up accommodation in Belgium to come to the UK, the Court of Appeal described his prospects of finding suitable employment as resting on 'little more than a wing and a prayer'.[70] The question of good faith simply did not arise, because the scientist's over-optimism did not constitute a relevant fact.[71]

14.49 Note that what the individual has been ignorant of must have been a 'fact', and not the legal consequences of that fact. For example, an applicant

---

[65] *R v Tower Hamlets London Borough Council ex p Rouf* (1991) 23 HLR 460, CA.
[66] *R v Westminster City Council ex p Obeid* (1996) 29 HLR 389, QBD at 394, per Carnwath J.
[67] *R v Hammersmith and Fulham London Borough Council ex p Lusi* (1991) 23 HLR 260, QBD at 269, per Roch J.
[68] *R v Wandsworth London Borough Council ex p Rose* (1983) 11 HLR 105, QBD, and *R v Hammersmith and Fulham London Borough Council ex p Lusi* (1991) 23 HLR 260, QBD.
[69] See the analysis of relevant case law in *Aw-Aden v Birmingham City Council* [2005] EWCA Civ 1834, (2006) July *Legal Action*, p 29, CA.
[70] *Aw-Aden v Birmingham City Council* [2005] EWCA Civ 1834, (2006) July *Legal Action*, p 29, CA, per Maurice Kay LJ, at [11].
[71] Similarly, in *F v Birmingham City Council* [2006] EWCA Civ 1427, [2007] HLR 18, CA, where a young woman had 'closed her eyes to the obvious', in that case that housing benefit would not be available for the whole of the contractual rent, there was no relevant fact and thus the issue of whether she had acted in good faith did not arise for consideration.

who decides not to pay his or her housing costs, in the mistaken belief that this (and the consequent eviction) will not prejudice any subsequent application for homelessness assistance, has not acted in ignorance of any fact but rather in ignorance of the legal consequences of the deliberate omission to pay.[72] A secure tenant who leaves her home in fear of threats of violence cannot be said to have been unaware of the 'fact' that her security of tenure would be lost in her absence. That is not a fact but 'a legal result of the factual departure which she made'.[73] Likewise, it has been suggested that ignorance of legal rights is not ignorance of a 'fact'.[74] The Codes contain some confusing advice regarding the scenario of a former tenant who left his or her home in response to a valid notice from the landlord where the former tenant was genuinely unaware that he or she had a legal right to remain until a possession order (and even execution of the subsequent warrant). This scenario is described as 'a general example of an act made in good faith' even though the tenant had 'the belief that they had no legal right to continue to occupy the accommodation', which suggests an ignorance of the legal position.[75] More obviously, if, as a matter of fact, an applicant had to do something by a particular date to retain his or her home and did not understand that there was such a deadline, the applicant's failure to act will not have been deliberate, as it was in ignorance of a relevant 'fact'.[76]

14.50 Another scenario recently considered by the courts is where an applicant approaches a local housing authority for help with his or her housing situation and is either given the wrong advice, or not given any advice at all. In both *Ugiagbe v Southwark London Borough Council*[77] and *Bury Metropolitan Borough Council v Gibbons*,[78] assured shorthold tenants who had been given notices requiring possession by their landlords approached their local housing authorities. Neither of them were given advice that they were entitled to remain in their properties until a possession order had been made against them. They each left their accommodation upon the expiration of the notice. On their subsequent applications for homelessness assistance, they were found to have become homeless intentionally. The Court of Appeal found in each case that the local housing authorities' failure to give the correct advice had meant that they had not been acting deliberately when they left their tenancies.

---

[72] *R v Eastleigh Borough Council ex p Beattie (No 2)* (1984) 17 HLR 168, QBD.

[73] *R v Croydon London Borough Council ex p Toth* (1987) 20 HLR 576, CA at 582, per O'Connor LJ.

[74] *Brown v Hamilton District Council 1983 SLT 397*, per Lord Fraser and *R v Harrow London Borough Council ex p Weingold* (unreported) 24 August 1992, QBD.

[75] English Code, para 11.25; Welsh Code, para 15.20; see **14.50** for two other examples which appear at first sight to relate to ignorance of the law, but where the Codes advise that they might also be ignorance of a material fact.

[76] *R v Christchurch Borough Council ex p Conway* (1987) 19 HLR 238, QBD. In *Abdullahi v Brent London Borough Council* [2007] EWCA Civ 885, (2007) October *Legal Action*, p 26, CA, a woman's ignorance of her responsibility to pay the shortfall between her contractual rent and housing benefit was held to be a relevant fact and the issue of whether she had acted in good faith should have been considered by the local housing authority.

[77] [2009] EWCA Civ 31, [2009] HLR 35, CA.

[78] [2010] EWCA Civ 327, [2010] HLR 33, CA.

14.51 These two problem issues of 'relevant' and 'fact' come together in the situation in which an applicant leaves accommodation (A) to move to other accommodation (B) in the erroneous belief that he or she will be able to afford accommodation (B) or that the availability of benefits or employment will make property (B) affordable. If that all turns out to be wrong, can the applicant be said to have moved from (A) in ignorance of a relevant fact?[79] In *R v Westminster City Council ex p Obeid*, Carnwath J said:

> '... an applicant's appreciation of the prospects of future housing or future employment can be treated as "awareness of a relevant fact" for the purposes of the subsection, provided it is sufficiently specific (that is related to specific employment or specific housing opportunities) and provided it is based on some genuine investigation and not mere "aspiration". Although that interpretation may not accord with what one would normally understand by a reference in a statute to a "relevant fact", it is an interpretation by which I am bound. It is perhaps justified by the general intent of the Act, to ensure that those who find themselves under the extreme pressures of homelessness should not be penalised except for decisions made with their eyes fully open.'[80]

14.52 This formulation was approved by the Court of Appeal in *Aw-Aden v Birmingham City Council*[81] and in *Ugiagbe v Southwark London Borough Council*.[82]

Good faith

14.53 'Good faith' is a phrase introducing similar complexity.[83] HA 1996, Part 7 couples lack of awareness and 'good faith'. The test on lack of awareness is subjective: 'Was *the applicant* unaware of any relevant fact?' rather than 'would a reasonable person have been unaware of that fact?'[84] Then, if there was lack of awareness, the applicant must additionally have acted in 'good faith' for the act not to be considered 'deliberate' for the purposes of the definition of intentional homelessness.

---

[79]	This was precisely the scenario in *F v Birmingham City Council* [2006] EWCA Civ 1427, [2007] HLR 18, CA, where a tenant gave up her secure tenancy in the belief that housing benefit would be available for the whole of the contractual rent on a private rented tenancy. She had 'closed her eyes to the obvious' and so the issue of whether she had acted in good faith did not arise. There is a helpful synopsis of the issue of 'relevant fact' in the judgment of May LJ at [17].

[80]	*R v Westminster City Council ex p Obeid* (1996) 29 HLR 389, QBD, at 398.

[81]	[2005] EWCA Civ 1834, (2006) July *Legal* Action, p 29, CA, per Maurice Kay LJ, at [11].

[82]	[2009] EWCA Civ 31, [2009] HLR 35, CA, per Lloyd LJ, at [20].

[83]	HA 1996, s 191(2).

[84]	*O'Connor v Kensington and Chelsea Royal London Borough Council* [2004] EWCA Civ 394, [2004] HLR 37, CA at [30] and [34], per Sedley LJ.

14.54 A mistake of judgment may constitute an act in good faith, but not those instances based on 'wilful ignorance'[85] nor those based on 'mere aspiration'.[86] As the Court of Appeal put it in one case:

> '... the statutory dividing line ... comes not at the point where the applicant's ignorance of a relevant fact was due to his own unreasonable conduct, but at the point where, for example, by shutting his eyes to the obvious he can be said not to have acted in good faith.'[87]

14.55 If there is dishonesty, the act or omission cannot have been made in good faith.[88] Lloyd LJ has said in the Court of Appeal:

> 'the use of the phrase "good faith" carries a connotation of some kind of impropriety, or some element of misuse or abuse of the legislation. It is aimed at protecting local housing authorities from finding that they owe the full duty under Part 7 of the 1996 Act to a person who, despite some relevant ignorance, ought to be regarded as intentionally homeless ... Dishonesty is the most obvious kind of conduct which it would catch, and wilful blindness in the Nelsonian sense comes close to that.'[89]

14.56 'Foolish or imprudent' or unreasonable behaviour is not sufficient to put a person into the category of not acting in good faith.[90]

14.57 In *R v Westminster City Council ex p N-Dormadingar*,[91] the court set out the following principles to be considered by local housing authorities in relation to 'unaware of a relevant fact' and 'good faith':

(1) the applicant must show that he or she was unaware of some relevant fact existing at the date that the accommodation was given up;

(2) whether or not the applicant made any inquiries into the existence of that relevant fact is relevant to determining the applicant's awareness (or not) of its existence;

(3) a fact is relevant where, had the applicant been aware of it, he or she would have taken it into account in deciding whether to give up the accommodation;[92]

---

[85] *O'Connor v Kensington and Chelsea Royal London Borough Council* [2004] EWCA Civ 394, [2004] HLR 37, CA at [30] per Sedley LJ.

[86] *R v Westminster City Council ex p Obeid* (1996) 29 HLR 389, QBD at 397, per Carnwath J.

[87] *O'Connor v Kensington and Chelsea Royal London Borough Council* [2004] EWCA Civ 394, [2004] HLR 37, CA at [34], per Sedley LJ.

[88] English Code, para 11.26; *R v Barnet London Borough Council ex p Rughooputh* (1993) 25 HLR 607, CA.

[89] *Ugiagbe v Southwark London Borough Council* [2009] EWCA Civ 31, [2009] HLR, 35 CA at [27], per Lloyd LJ.

[90] *Ugiagbe v Southwark London Borough Council* [2009] EWCA Civ 31, [2009] HLR, 35 CA at [26], per Lloyd LJ.

[91] *R v Westminster City Council ex p N-Dormadingar* (1997) Times, 20 November, QBD.

[92] See **14.44–14.52**.

(4)   the fact must be sufficiently clear and definite for its existence to be objectively determined; and

(5)   an applicant's lack of foresight into the future, or a deficiency of the applicant's foresight into the future, is not unawareness of an existing fact.

14.58   Both Codes give examples of acts or omissions that could be made in good faith:[93]

(1)   a person accrues rent arrears, unaware that he or she may be entitled to housing benefit or other social security benefits;

(2)   an owner-occupier, faced with foreclosure or possession proceedings to which there is no defence, sells or surrenders the property before a possession order is obtained; and

(3)   a tenant faced with possession proceedings to which there is no defence surrenders the property to the landlord.

14.59   The latter two examples could be analysed as ignorance of the legal right to remain in the property. In relation to the last example, both Codes advise that the ignorance might be of 'the general pressure on the authority for housing' – a matter of fact rather than law.[94]

14.60   Note that the adverb 'deliberately' governs only the act or omission itself, not the outcome, or consequences, of the act or omission. The question is not: 'Has the applicant deliberately become homeless?' but rather: 'Has the applicant deliberately done something, or failed to do something, as a result of which he or she is now homeless?'[95]

14.61   Whilst each case must be considered on its own facts, the Codes and the courts have considered a number of different scenarios that provide some useful guidance.[96] Each is examined below.

Acts or omissions not generally considered deliberate

14.62   The Codes of Guidance suggest several circumstances in which acts or omissions of applicants 'should not' be considered to be 'deliberate'.[97]

(1) Incapacity

14.63   The Codes advise that where the local housing authority has reason to believe that an applicant was incapable of managing his or her affairs, for

---

[93]   English Code, para 11.27; Welsh Code, para 15.21.
[94]   English Code, para 11.27(iii); Welsh Code, para 15.21(iii).
[95]   *Devenport v Salford City Council* (1983) 8 HLR 54, CA.
[96]   English Code, paras 11.16–11.20; Welsh Code, paras 15.10–15.25.
[97]   English Code, para 11.17; Welsh Code, para 15.11.

example by reason of age, mental illness or disability, his or her act or failure to act at that time should not be considered to have been 'deliberate'.[98] The formulations in the Codes suggest that both the very old and the very young might be considered incapable as a result of their age.[99] Applying this approach, if the applicant was incapable at the date when the act or omission was committed, he or she will not have become homeless intentionally.

14.64 This guidance in the Codes should not be taken as meaning that young people and children cannot be found to have become homeless intentionally even when their deliberate acts were committed when they were children. In *Denton v Southwark London Borough Council*,[100] the Court of Appeal upheld a finding by the local housing authority that a young person had become homeless intentionally as a result of his deliberate actions when he was 21. In *White v Southwark London Borough Council*,[101] a Court of Appeal judge said that actions of children as young as 13 might be 'deliberate acts'.[102]

14.65 The English Code was published before the principles and structured approach to determining capacity in Mental Capacity Act 2005, ss 1–3 came into force.[103] The modern approach, set out in those sections, is that 'a person must be assumed to have capacity unless it is established that he lacks capacity'[104] When deciding whether or not a person has capacity to make a decision, the test is issue-specific, in other words whether the person has or had the capacity to make that particular decision, not whether he or she can make other (simpler or more complex) decisions.[105] An impairment or disturbance in the functioning of the mind or brain, which leads to the person being incapable of making a decision, may be permanent or temporary.[106] This very structured, careful approach should be applied by a local housing authority decision-maker considering whether or not an applicant for homelessness assistance had capacity at the date of commission of his or her deliberate act (or his or her omission to act).

14.66 The Welsh Code advises that local housing authorities might consider what advice and support was made available to someone who could be

---

[98] English Code, para 11.17(ii); Welsh Code, para 15.11(ii).
[99] Earlier editions of the Codes referred to 'old age' rather than 'age'.
[100] [2007] EWCA Civ 623, [2008] HLR 11, CA.
[101] [2008] EWCA Civ 792, (2008) October *Legal Action*, p 37, CA.
[102] Sir Peter Gibson, dismissing an application to bring a second appeal. Note that guidance from both the UK government (*Provision of Accommodation for 16 and 17 year old young people who may be homeless and/or require accommodation*, CLG and Department for Children, Schools and Families, April 2010) and the Welsh Government (*Provision of Accommodation for 16 and 17 year old young people who may be homeless*, Welsh Assembly Government, 2010) each advise that young people who have refused accommodation provided by children's services and who have lost such accommodation as a result should not be treated as having acted deliberately (English Guidance paras 4.10–4.11; Welsh Guidance paras 4.7–4.8).
[103] At the date of publication of the Welsh Code, the Mental Capacity Act 2005 had been in force for over five years. However, there is no reference to it in the Welsh Code.
[104] Mental Capacity Act 2005, s 1(2).
[105] MCA 2005, s 3.
[106] MCA 2005, s 2.

considered to be vulnerable[107] before he or she became homeless. If advice and support was offered, in order to prevent homelessness, but this was disregarded by the applicant, he or she might be considered to have become homeless intentionally. If the advice and support was not available to a vulnerable person, and he or she was not be able to manage his or her affairs without that advice and support, he or she could be considered not to have acted deliberately.[108]

14.67 Local housing authorities should also bear in mind their public sector equality duty at Equality Act 2010, s 149.[109] Local housing authorities should be making inquiries into the issue of capacity if there is any feature of the evidence presented to them that raises a real possibility that the applicant was disabled where that is relevant to the issue of whether he or she acted deliberately.[110]

14.68 Even if the applicant appears (at the date of his or her application) to be capable, he or she may have been temporarily incapable at the date that he or she committed the act or at the date when he or she omitted to act.

14.69 Although the phrasing in the Codes appears to reflect part of the priority need test for 'vulnerability',[111] it does not follow, just because an applicant has been found to be vulnerable (and thereby to have a priority need) at the date of the application for homelessness assistance, that he or she was incapable at the time when the accommodation was lost.[112]

(2) Limited capacity and/or frailty

14.70 Even if the applicant is generally capable of managing his or her own affairs and had a measure of capacity at the relevant time, both Codes advise local housing authorities to consider whether the particular act or omission leading to the loss of accommodation was 'the result of limited mental capacity; or a temporary aberration or aberrations caused by mental illness or frailty'.[113]

14.71 The English Code advises that a temporary aberration or aberrations may have been caused by an assessed substance abuse problem and that, in those circumstances, an act or omission should not be considered as deliberate.[114]

---

[107] See **13.75–13.119**.
[108] Welsh Code, para 15.15: the advice applies where the person's actions or omissions led to the loss of accommodation which he or she was occupying, not, of course, to any failure to accept advice designed to find alternative accommodation.
[109] See **4.196–4.209**.
[110] *Pieretti v Enfield London Borough Council* [2010] EWCA Civ 1104, [2011] HLR 3, CA.
[111] HA 1996, s 189(1)(c); see **13.75–13.119**.
[112] *R v Wirral Metropolitan Borough Council ex p Bell* (1995) 27 HLR 234, QBD.
[113] English Code, para 11.17(iii); Welsh Code, para 15.11(iii); *Hijazi v Kensington and Chelsea Royal London Borough Council* [2003] EWCA Civ 692, [2003] HLR 72, CA.
[114] See *Kendall v City of Westminster Council* (2009) November *Legal Action*, p 25, Central

(3) Lacking foresight or prudence

14.72 The act or omission may have been imprudent or have been a result of lack of foresight. If the applicant acted in good faith, it will not generally be considered that such act or omission was deliberate.[115]

(4) Financial difficulties beyond the applicant's control

14.73 The Codes give examples of a tenant not paying the rent as a result of housing benefit delays, or financial difficulties which were beyond the applicant's control.[116] Where the applicant was genuinely unable to keep up rent (or mortgage) payments, even after claiming benefits, and there was no further financial help available, giving up possession of the home would not generally be considered deliberate.[117] However, in those circumstances, the local housing authority is entitled to consider why the arrears accrued and the applicant's ability to meet the commitment to pay housing costs at the time that it was taken on.[118] That is because the 'act' of the applicant, which may have ultimately caused his or her homelessness, could have been the taking out of an impossible rent or mortgage commitment in the first place. The Welsh Code also advises that changes to the welfare benefit system may result in increased numbers of people struggling to meet their housing costs and that applicants should not be considered to have become homeless intentionally where their previously affordable accommodation became unaffordable as a result of changes in the local housing allowance or housing benefit.[119]

(5) Under duress

14.74 The English Code advises that an act or omission made when the applicant was under duress should not generally be considered deliberate.[120] There is no further explanation. An example would presumably be someone subjected to domestic violence who is required by his or her partner to give up any legal interest in the home.

(6) Fleeing violence

14.75 The Codes advise that where an applicant fled his or her home because of violence (or threats of violence likely to be carried out), but failed to pursue

---

London County Court. It is not clear what the English Code means by 'assessed' and whether there has to have been some formal process of assessment.

[115] English Code, para 11.17(v); Welsh Code, para 15.11(iv).
[116] English Code, para 11.17(i); Welsh Code, paras 15.11(i) and 15.12. See **14.182–14.191**.
[117] English Code, para 11.18; Welsh Code, paras 15.11(i) and 15.12. For a recent example, see *Adekunle v Islington London Borough Council* (2009) November *Legal Action*, p 25, Mayor's and City of London County Court.
[118] English Code, para 11.19; Welsh Code, para 15.13. See *William v Wandsworth London Borough Council* [2006] EWCA Civ 535, [2006] HLR 42, CA.
[119] Welsh Code, paras 15.31–15.33.
[120] English Code, para 11.17(iv).

all legal remedies against the perpetrator, neither the act of leaving nor the omission to use remedies should be considered 'deliberate'.[121]

14.76 However, the result may be different where the applicant's own misbehaviour had led to the violence or threats of violence.[122]

(7) Serving a prison sentence

14.77 The Welsh Code gives an example of a prisoner who has just served a sentence (and presumably lost his or her accommodation during the term of imprisonment) for offences which were not in themselves breaches of his or her tenancy agreement.[123] This reflects the Welsh Government's view that 'the actions that caused the person to be imprisoned ... should not be considered as grounds for regarding him or her as intentionally homeless', unless the offence which resulted in the sentence of imprisonment was a direct breach of the prisoner's tenancy agreement and led to the landlord obtaining possession of the property.[124]

14.78 In England, the tendency has been to treat the criminal act as having been 'deliberate', but then to focus on whether it was causative of the homelessness.[125]

Activities that may be regarded as 'deliberate'

14.79 The Codes of Guidance suggest a number of circumstances in which acts or omissions of applicants 'may be regarded as deliberate'.[126]

(1) Voluntary sale or voluntary non-payment of housing costs

14.80 If an applicant has chosen to sell his or her home where there was no risk of losing it, that action will generally be treated as having been 'deliberate'.[127] The question of whether any resultant homelessness was intentional will turn on other aspects of the statutory definition, eg whether it would have been reasonable to have continued in occupation of that home.[128]

14.81 Where a home has been lost for failure to meet liabilities for housing costs and where any rent or mortgage arrears accrued as a result of a 'wilful and persistent refusal to pay', the omission to pay will generally be treated as

---

[121] English Code, para 11.23; Welsh Code, para 15.22, which mentions the circumstances where legal remedies were not pursued because of 'fear of reprisal'. See **14.205–14.214**.

[122] English Code, para 11.20(vi); Welsh Code, para 15.23; and *R v Hammersmith and Fulham London Borough Council ex p P* (1990) 22 HLR 21, QBD. See **14.214** and **14.220**.

[123] Welsh Code, para 15.23. See **14.236–14.237**.

[124] Welsh Code, para 15.23.

[125] English Code, para 11.14. See **14.236**.

[126] English Code, para 11.20; Welsh Code, para 15.16.

[127] English Code, para 11.20(i); Welsh Code, para 15.16(i).

[128] See **14.125–14.143**.

having been 'deliberate'.[129] The Codes' emphasis on persistent and wilful default underscores the obvious point that non-payment caused by lack of funds will not be deliberate.[130] 'Wilful default' in making payment, however, is sufficient to establish a deliberate omission.[131]

(2) Neglecting affairs

14.82 An omission may be regarded as deliberate where 'someone could be said to have significantly neglected his or her affairs having disregarded sound advice from qualified persons'.[132] Into the scope of this example would fall an applicant who temporarily left accommodation without making arrangements for the rent to be paid in his or her absence.[133]

14.83 The courts have held that, where someone had been given inaccurate advice, or no advice at all, from a local housing authority and had therefore acted in ignorance of his or her legal rights, then the applicant's actions should not be construed as 'deliberate'.[134]

(3) Giving up a home

14.84 The Codes advise that 'voluntary surrender of adequate accommodation in this country or abroad which it would have been reasonable for the applicant to continue to occupy' may be regarded as a deliberate act.[135] Again, whether the applicant is likely to be found to have become homeless intentionally will turn on other parts of the statutory definition and, in particular, on whether it would have been reasonable to have continued occupying the accommodation given up.[136]

14.85 Where a father had permitted his three children to move from perfectly suitable accommodation with their mother to his one room accommodation, and, as a result of the presence of the children, he was then required to leave by his landlord, his conduct had been deliberate.[137]

---

[129] English Code, para 11.20(ii); Welsh Code, para 15.16(ii). For examples, see *William v Wandsworth London Borough Council* [2006] EWCA Civ 535, [2006] HLR 42, CA and *Watchman v Ipswich Borough Council* [2007] EWCA Civ 348, [2007] HLR 33, CA. See **14.182–14.191**.

[130] See **14.182–14.191**.

[131] *R v Wyre Borough Council ex p Joyce* (1983) 11 HLR 73, QBD, discussed at **14.49**.

[132] English Code, para 11.20(iii); Welsh Code, para 15.16(iii).

[133] *R v Wycombe District Council ex p Mahsood* (1988) 20 HLR 683, QBD.

[134] *Ugiagbe v Southwark London Borough Council* [2009] EWCA Civ 31, [2009] HLR 35, CA; *Bury Metropolitan Borough Council v Gibbons* [2010] EWCA Civ 327, [2010] HLR 33, CA. See **14.50**.

[135] English Code, para 11.20(iv); Welsh Code, para 15.16(iv). See **14.233**.

[136] For an unusual example involving joint owners see *Bellamy v Hounslow London Borough Council* [2006] EWCA Civ 535, [2006] HLR 42, CA. See **14.81** and **14.182–14.191**.

[137] *Oxford City Council v Bull* [2011] EWCA Civ 609, [2011] HLR 35, [2012] 1 WLR 203, CA. See **13.68**.

(4) Eviction for anti-social behaviour

14.86 The Codes suggest that 'where someone is evicted because of anti-social behaviour, nuisance to neighbours, harassment, etc', that behaviour may be treated as having been deliberate.[138] The nuisance or anti-social behaviour that brought about the eviction will often have been the deliberate 'act' of the applicant. In other cases, the applicant's deliberate 'omission' may have been his or her failure to control or remove the perpetrator of the nuisance, thus constituting his or her acquiescence in the perpetrator's nuisance behaviour.[139] In such cases a local housing authority is entitled to consider the behaviour of the family as a whole and to come to a decision that the applicant had either acquiesced in, or failed to prevent, the nuisance behaviour which had resulted in the family's eviction.[140] A tenant subject to a possession order on the grounds of waste to the property or deterioration of the furniture may also be considered to have committed a deliberate act (damage) or omission (failure to maintain).[141]

14.87 Local housing authorities need not restrict their application of this guidance to cases where tenants enjoying security of tenure have been subject to possession orders under one or more of the 'fault' grounds for possession.[142] If a private landlord refuses to renew an assured shorthold tenancy, and subsequently obtains a possession order following service of a notice given under the Housing Act 1988, s 21, the local housing authority is entitled to consider the reason for the landlord seeking possession. If it was due to the fault of the tenant, or members of the tenant's household, the loss of accommodation may be found to have been caused by the deliberate act of, or omission by, the tenant.[143]

(5) Inflicting violence

14.88 Perpetrators of 'violence or threats of violence', as defined by HA 1996, Part 7,[144] who are evicted because of their behaviour, may be considered to have committed a deliberate act.[145] Such an eviction may arise from the former landlord applying for possession on one or more of the grounds that specifically relate to nuisance, criminal convictions or domestic violence,[146] or as a result of the victim of domestic violence either:

---

[138] English Code, para 11.20(v); Welsh Code, para 15.16(v). See **14.199–14.204**.
[139] *Devenport v Salford City Council* (1983) 8 HLR 54, CA, and *R v Swansea City Council ex p John* (1982) 9 HLR 56, QBD. See **14.93–14.97**.
[140] *R v East Hertfordshire District Council ex p Bannon* (1986) 18 HLR 515, QBD.
[141] *R v Sevenoaks District Council ex p Reynolds* (1990) 22 HLR 250, CA.
[142] Housing Act 1988, Sch 2, Part 1 and Housing Act 1985, Sch 2.
[143] *R v Rochester upon Medway City Council ex p Williams* (1994) 26 HLR 588, QBD; *R v Nottingham City Council ex p Edwards* (1999) 31 HLR 33, QBD; and *Sheppard v Richmond upon Thames Royal London Borough* [2012] EWCA Civ 302, (2012) June *Legal Action*, p 36, CA.
[144] See HA 1996, s 177(1) and (1A). See **11.83–11.92**.
[145] English Code, para 11.20(vi)); the Welsh Code, para 15.16(vi). See **14.214** and **14.220**.
[146] Housing Act 1985, Sch 2, Grounds 2 and 2A; Housing Act 1988, Sch 2, Grounds 14 and 14A.

(1)   obtaining an occupation order in family court proceedings requiring the perpetrator to leave;[147] or

(2)   bringing the tenancy to an end by notice.

(6) Giving up tied accommodation

14.89   Where an applicant has been living in tied accommodation and leaves his or her job, thereby losing the accommodation, the local housing authority may well find that there has been a 'deliberate' act.[148] The Codes remind local housing authorities that they should go on to consider the other elements of the statutory definition, in particular whether it would have been reasonable for the employee to have continued in the employment and/or reasonable to have continued to occupy the accommodation. If the applicant has been dismissed, the local housing authority should make inquiries to ascertain whether the acts or omissions leading to the applicant's dismissal were the applicant's 'deliberate' acts or omissions. The English Code recommends that former members of the armed forces, who are required to vacate service quarters as a result of giving notice to leave the service, should not be considered to have become homeless intentionally.[149]

Summary of 'deliberate act or omission'

14.90   In summary, a deliberate act or omission is one that:

- is freely made;

- by a person (the applicant) in possession of all the relevant facts;

- who is not forced to act (or fail to act); and

- who is not unaware of a relevant fact.

14.91   If the applicant was unaware of a relevant fact, his or her act will not be considered deliberate if he or she acted in good faith, ie he or she was genuinely ignorant of that relevant fact and that ignorance was not based on an unrealistic degree of optimism, a shutting of the eyes to the obvious, or on dishonesty.

14.92   Even if the local housing authority finds that this limb of the test is satisfied, it cannot find that the applicant has become homeless intentionally unless the other four limbs are also made out.

---

[147]   Family Law Act 1996, s 33.
[148]   English Code, para 11.20(vii); Welsh Code, para 15.16(vii); and *R v Kyle and Carrick District Council ex p Speck* 1993 GWD 1566, OH.
[149]   English Code, para 11.15.

Was that deliberate act or omission *by the applicant?*

14.93 Each applicant is entitled to individual consideration of his or her application. This means that even where one member of a household has been found to have become homeless intentionally, an application from another member must still be individually considered. For this reason it is inappropriate to use the term 'intentionally homeless family'. An applicant can only be found to have become homeless intentionally if it was his or her deliberate act or omission that caused the homelessness.[150] Local housing authorities should therefore consider whether the particular applicant acted deliberately or deliberately failed to act and, if not, whether the applicant had acquiesced in the deliberate act or omission of another that led to the loss of accommodation. In this sense, acquiescence can be a deliberate failure to prevent another from acting or failing to act in a particular way.

14.94 Where an applicant's case is that he or she did not acquiesce in the deliberate act or omission of another member of the household (that has led to the loss of accommodation), the Codes suggest that the burden of proof rests on the applicant.[151] That slightly overstates the position and is not repeated in the specific part of the Codes dealing with the 'Whose conduct?' issue.[152] Perhaps a more accurate way of summarising the relevant law would be that there is a presumption (or a local housing authority is entitled to make an assumption or draw an inference), in the absence of any material indicating the contrary, that where one member of the household's conduct has been such that she or he would be regarded as having deliberately acted or failed to act in such a way as to cause the homelessness, the other household members were party to that conduct.[153] However, once there are positive assertions by an applicant (or some other evidence) that there was no acquiescence, such as one partner asserting that he or she had always protested at the other partner's failure to pay the rent or mortgage, the local housing authority must abandon any presumption, assumption or inference and inquire into the issue fully.[154]

14.95 The case law is replete with examples of everyday situations in which the question has arisen as to whether the applicant acquiesced in the conduct of another household member. This includes situations in which the other household member has:

---

[150] English Code, para 11.9; Welsh Code, para 15.7; *R v North Devon District Council ex p Lewis* [1981] 1 WLR 328, QBD, and *City of Gloucester v Miles* (1985) 17 HLR 292, CA.

[151] English Code, para 11.5; Welsh Code, para 15.4.

[152] English Code, para 11.9; Welsh Code, paras 15.7–15.9.

[153] *R v North Devon District Council ex p Lewis* [1981] 1 WLR 328, QBD.

[154] *R v West Dorset District Council ex p Phillips* (1985) 17 HLR 336, QBD; *R v Eastleigh Borough Council ex p Beattie (No 2)* (1984) 17 HLR 168, QBD; *R v East Northamptonshire Borough Council ex p Spruce* (1988) 20 HLR 508, QBD; *R v Thanet District Council ex p Groves* (1990) 22 HLR 223, QBD; *Quinton v East Hertfordshire District Council* (2003) April *Legal Action*, p 27, Luton County Court; and *N v Allerdale Borough Council* (2008) October *Legal Action*, p 38, Carlisle County Court.

- failed to pay the rent in circumstances where both partners were involved in managing the household's finances;[155] or

- terminated a joint tenancy;[156] or

- given up his or her job (to which tied accommodation was linked);[157] or

- changed jobs (from one to which future re-housing was linked to another with no promise of re-housing);[158] or

- misspent the money earmarked for housing costs (whether on drink, drugs or gambling);[159] or

- caused nuisance or annoyance to others;[160] or

- as head of the household, taken the family from secure to insecure accommodation;[161] or

- withheld the rent in the mistaken belief that there was an entitlement to do so on account of disrepair;[162] or

---

[155] *R v Barnet London Borough Council ex p O'Connor* (1990) 22 HLR 486, QBD; and *R v Nottingham City Council ex p Caine* (1996) 28 HLR 374, CA, where, in both cases, the local housing authority was entitled to find acquiescence.

[156] *R v Penwith District Council ex p Trevena* (1984) 17 HLR 526, QBD, where a decision that the former joint tenant remaining in occupation had acquiesced was held to be one that no reasonable local housing authority would have come to.

[157] *R v North Devon DC ex p Lewis* [1981] 1 WLR 328, QBD, where it was held that, on the evidence, the local housing authority was entitled to find acquiescence.

[158] *R v Mole Valley DC ex p Burton* (1989) 20 HLR 479, QBD, where the decision that the applicant had acquiesced in that behaviour was quashed. She had known of the behaviour but had also acted in good faith in believing his assurances that they would qualify for council housing.

[159] *R v West Dorset DC ex p Phillips* (1984) 17 HLR 336, QBD, where a decision that the wife had acquiesced (when she had informed the local housing authority that she did not know about the non-payment and had always said that the husband's drinking would lead to trouble) was quashed.

[160] *Smith v Bristol City Council* [1981] LAG Bull 287, CA; *Devenport v Salford City Council* (1983) 8 HLR 54, CA, where there was acquiescence; *R v Swansea City Council ex p John* (1982) 9 HLR 56, QBD, where a finding that the wife had acquiesced by failing to remove her husband who had caused nuisance was upheld; *R v East Hertfordshire District Council ex p Bannon* (1986) 18 HLR 515, QBD, where a finding that the conduct of the whole of the family was to blame and therefore the applicant had acquiesced was upheld; and *N v Allerdale Borough Council* (2008) October *Legal Action*, p 38, Carlisle County Court, where the local housing authority's inquiries into whether a mother had acquiesced in her son's anti-social behaviour were inadequate.

[161] *R v Tower Hamlets London Borough Council ex p Khatun (Asma)* (1993) 27 HLR 344, CA, where the wife was found to have acquiesced by having been content to leave the decisions to her husband.

[162] *R v Nottingham City Council ex p Caine* (1995) 28 HLR 374, CA, where the decision that the applicant had acquiesced was upheld, as she must have known of the non-payment.

- re-mortgaged the home to such an extent that the debt became unmanageable.[163]

14.96 In summary, the deliberate act or omission must have been by the applicant. In cases where the deliberate act or omission was by another member of the applicant's household, a local housing authority is entitled to presume that the applicant acquiesced in that conduct unless there is an assertion, or evidence, that the applicant did not acquiesce. Where there is an assertion, or evidence, that the applicant did not acquiesce, the local housing authority must then make full inquiries into the issue.[164]

14.97 Even if the local housing authority finds that this limb of the test is satisfied, it cannot find that the applicant has become homeless intentionally unless the other four limbs are also made out.

Was it as a consequence of that deliberate act or omission that the applicant ceased to occupy accommodation?

14.98 This requires consideration of two elements:

(1) Has there been any cessation of occupation at all?

(2) If so, did the deliberate act or omission cause the cessation of occupation?

14.99 Only if both are answered affirmatively will this limb of the statutory definition be made out.

Has there been any cessation of occupation at all?

14.100 The deliberate act or omission must have had the consequence that the applicant 'ceases to occupy' accommodation.[165] Accordingly, the applicant must have actually occupied the accommodation the loss of which was caused by his or her deliberate act or omission.[166] There need not have been continuous occupation at all times, but the accommodation must at least have been at the disposal of the applicant and available for his or her occupation at the time it was given up.[167]

---

[163] *R v Barnet London Borough Council ex p O'Connor* (1990) 22 HLR 486, QBD, where the decision that the wife had acquiesced was upheld – she had said that she left financial matters to her husband, but had signed two mortgage applications on which she had made false representations.

[164] In the unusual case of *Bellamy v Hounslow London Borough Council* [2006] EWCA Civ 535, [2006] HLR 42, CA, the applicant's account was that she was not aware that she, as a legal joint owner of her home with her mother, had a power to object to a sale. The local housing authority did not believe the applicant and the Court of Appeal held that the local housing authority had been entitled not to believe her.

[165] HA 1996, s 191(1).

[166] *R v Westminster City Council ex p Chambers* (1982) 6 HLR 24, QBD, and *Din v Wandsworth London Borough Council* [1983] 1 AC 657, HL.

[167] See the unusual facts of *R v Westminster City Council ex p Khan* (1991) 23 HLR 230, QBD,

14.101   The accommodation the applicant has ceased to occupy may have been anywhere in the world; local housing authorities are not restricted to considering accommodation the applicant has occupied in the UK.[168]

14.102   It follows that decisions by applicants:

(1)   to rid themselves of accommodation that they have not occupied; or

(2)   not to accept accommodation offered to them to occupy,

cannot result in findings that they have become homeless intentionally. In *R v Wandsworth London Borough Council ex p Oteng*,[169] the applicant left a home that she shared with her two sisters and, over two years later, she transferred her interest in the property to her mother. The local housing authority decided that she had become homeless intentionally as a result of voluntarily transferring her interest. The Court of Appeal rejected that approach. The transfer of interest had not caused the applicant to cease to occupy the accommodation – that had occurred two years earlier.[170]

14.103   Applying the correct approach, homeless applicants in temporary accommodation provided under HA 1996, Part 7 who refuse offers of accommodation cannot become homeless intentionally from the accommodation that they refuse, as they have never occupied it (although they may be found to have become homeless intentionally from temporary accommodation lost as a result of their refusal of other accommodation).[171] However, in such cases, local housing authorities should consider whether it was the refusal that caused the loss of the temporary accommodation, or whether there was some other reason for its loss.[172]

---

where the applicant had not actually occupied the accommodation, but it was held to have been at her disposal and available for her occupation; and see *Lee-Lawrence v Penwith District Council* [2006] EWCA Civ 1672, (2006) July *Legal Action*, p 29, CA, where holding the keys to a house provided on a tenancy and claiming housing benefit in order to pay the rent was held to be sufficient evidence to uphold a finding of occupation for the purposes of HA 1996, s 191(1).

[168]   English Code, para 11.10.

[169]   *R v Wandsworth London Borough Council ex p Oteng* (1994) 26 HLR 413, CA. See also *R v Westminster City Council ex p De Souza* (1997) 29 HLR 649, QBD.

[170]   In *Quaid v Westminster City Council* (2008) February *Legal Action*, p 41, Central London County Court, the applicant had committed offences while he was street homeless. He subsequently acquired a place at a Salvation Army hostel. He was convicted of those offences, sent to prison and lost the hostel place. The local housing authority found that he had become homeless intentionally as a result of the offences committed. The decision was varied to a decision that he had not become homeless intentionally. The commission of the offences had not caused the loss of the hostel place.

[171]   For example, *R v Brent London Borough Council ex p Awua* [1996] AC 55, HL.

[172]   *Sonde v Newham London Borough Council* (1999) June *Legal Action*, p 24, Bow County Court; and *R (Dragic) v Wandsworth London Borough Council* [2012] EWHC 1241 (Admin), (2012) July *Legal Action*, p 42, Admin Ct. See **14.238–14.240**.

Did that act or omission cause the cessation of occupation?

Identifying the operative causes of the loss of accommodation

14.104 In most situations, there will be a number of events that, taken together, caused the applicant to cease to occupy the accommodation. Some of those events may not be the direct causes of the loss of the accommodation, but may have started off the chain of events that led to the loss of accommodation.

14.105 HA 1996, Part 7 uses the word 'anything' to refer to what has been done (or failed to be done).[173] However, the subject of enquiry is not every act or omission in which the applicant engaged at the time she or he became homeless, or in the lead-up to that time. HA 1996, Part 7 is concerned only with the doing of (or failure to do) something 'in consequence of which' the applicant ceased to occupy his or her accommodation.

14.106 It is necessary, therefore, to identify the operative causes of the loss of accommodation, and then to consider whether any of those operative causes was the applicant's deliberate act or omission.[174] Such an operative cause can be doing (or failing to do) 'anything'.[175] If just one of the operative causes was the applicant's deliberate act or omission, that will be sufficient for the applicant to fall within this limb of the definition of having become homeless intentionally.[176]

14.107 Various judges have commented on the difficulties involved in establishing the cause or causes of the loss of accommodation. In *R v Hackney London Borough Council ex p Ajayi*,[177] Dyson J said:

> 'Questions of causation are notoriously difficult and, in my judgment, the Court should be slow to intervene to strike down the decisions of administrative bodies on such questions and should do so only in clear cases. I cannot accept that the effective cause should always be regarded in these cases as the chronologically immediate or proximate cause. In some cases, the cause closest in point of time will be regarded as the effective cause ... In others, the cause closest in time will be not so regarded.'[178]

14.108 In *O'Connor v Kensington and Chelsea Royal London Borough Council*[179] the applicant's father was terminally ill and the whole family

---

[173] HA 1996, s 191(1).

[174] See **14.37–14.97**.

[175] HA 1996, s 191(1).

[176] *O'Connor v Kensington and Chelsea Royal London Borough Council* [2004] EWCA Civ 394, [2004] HLR 37, CA.

[177] (1997) 30 HLR 473, QBD.

[178] *R v Hackney London Borough Council ex p Ajayi* (1997) 30 HLR 473, QBD at 479, per Dyson J, subsequently approved by the Court of Appeal in *William v Wandsworth London Borough Council* [2006] EWCA Civ 535, [2006] HLR 42, CA and in *Watchman v Ipswich Borough Council* [2007] EWCA Civ 348, [2007] HLR 33, CA.

[179] [2004] EWCA Civ 394, [2004] HLR 37, CA.

travelled to Ireland to his bedside, starting off a chain of events that eventually resulted in the loss of their accommodation in London. The father's illness was not an act or omission of the applicants and, although the decision to travel to Ireland was the applicants' act:

> '... nobody but a logician would say that it was in consequence of the family's going to Ireland to see a sick relative that they lost their accommodation.'[180]

The 'reasonable likelihood' test

14.109 A loss of accommodation must have occurred as a consequence of the applicant's deliberate act or omission. This does not mean that there needs to be any direct link between the nature of the act done (or the omission) and the occupation of accommodation. An applicant, who deliberately gambles at a casino and loses every resource he or she has, has done an act (the gambling) that is in itself entirely unrelated to the accommodation subsequently lost for failure to pay housing costs. A convicted international drug dealer who, while in prison, has his or her house confiscated and sold as a proceed of crime, has done an act (criminal drug dealing) wholly unrelated to the former home. The issue, however, is not whether the loss of the home was the intended consequence of the deliberate act or omission but whether it is *a* consequence.

14.110 This is not to say that acts or omissions wholly removed from any connection at all with the eventual loss of accommodation can always be counted if they, as a matter of fact, did 'cause' that loss. Without any sensible restraint on the plain words, absurd decisions might be made, eg that a father who chastised his son too harshly for the liking of the mother (who then excluded the father from her home) had lost his accommodation in consequence of the deliberate act of chastisement.[181] The courts have, accordingly, striven to identify a narrower basis on which the link between the act and its consequences must be made out rather than a simple test of strict causation. Through the case law a test of 'reasonable likelihood' has emerged.[182] The question to be posed is: 'Was the loss of the accommodation the reasonably likely result of what the applicant did?' Rather more straightforwardly, one judge has suggested that the correct approach is:

- to look at what the applicant did;

- find that the ultimate result was loss of accommodation; and

- then to ask 'if the fair-minded bystander could say to himself, "He asked for it".'[183]

---

[180] [2004] EWCA Civ 394, [2004] HLR 37, CA at [27] per Sedley LJ.

[181] *R v Westminster City Council ex p Reid* (1994) 26 HLR 690, QBD.

[182] *R v Hounslow London Borough Council ex p R* (1997) 29 HLR 939, QBD.

[183] *Robinson v Torbay District Council* [1982] 1 All ER 726, QBD at 731, per HHJ Goodall.

14.111 This approach of 'reasonable likelihood' has been approved by the Court of Appeal[184] and is to be preferred to a test of whether the act done was too 'remote' from the resultant loss of accommodation.[185]

14.112 The most recent formulation of the correct approach by the Court of Appeal is:

> 'What is called for, then, in a case where there are potentially multiple causes of an applicant's homelessness, is a careful judgment on the particular facts looking to see whether homelessness is shown to have been a likely consequence of the applicant's deliberate act, bearing in mind that it is the applicant's own responsibility for his homelessness that the statute is looking for. The precise question to be asked and answered of course relates to the time when the applicant in fact became homeless: that is the result of their Lordships' decision in *Din*.'[186]

14.113 Applying this approach, former prisoners, who are homeless on their release, face being found to have become homeless intentionally if the reasonably likely result of their deliberate acts in committing criminal offences, viewed objectively, was a sentence of imprisonment resulting in the loss of their accommodation.[187]

Intervening events

14.114 The causative link between the deliberate act or omission and the actual loss of accommodation must be in place throughout. An act or omission of a third party that actually causes the loss of accommodation will break that link. For example, an applicant may be on the brink of having his or her home repossessed for non-payment of rent or a mortgage, but if, on the eve of eviction, the house is burnt down by a third party, the homelessness cannot have been intentional, as it was not a consequence of the applicant's omission to pay. In *Gloucester City Council v Miles*,[188] the applicant left her home, but (because she did not give up her tenancy) she was not homeless. Finding her gone, her husband vandalised the home, rendering it uninhabitable; his act rendered her homeless. As Stephenson LJ put it:

---

[184] *Devenport v Salford City Council* (1983) 8 HLR 54, CA; *R v Westminster City Council ex p Reid* (1994) 26 HLR 691, CA; *Stewart v Lambeth London Borough Council* [2002] EWCA Civ 753, [2002] HLR 40, CA; and *Watchman v Ipswich Borough Council* [2007] EWCA Civ 348, [2007] HLR 33, CA.

[185] *R v Thanet District Council ex p Reeve* (1981) 6 HLR 31, QBD.

[186] *Watchman v Ipswich Borough Council* [2007] EWCA Civ 348, [2007] HLR 33, CA at [22], per Laws LJ referring to *Din v Wandsworth London Borough Council* [1983]1 AC 657, HL.

[187] *R v Hounslow London Borough Council ex p R* (1997) 29 HLR 939, QBD; *Minchin v Sheffield City Council* (2000) Times, 26 August, CA, and *Stewart v Lambeth London Borough Council* [2002] EWCA Civ 753, (2002) 34 HLR 40, CA. The Welsh Code, however, advises local housing authorities in Wales against finding intentional homelessness in such circumstances, unless the acts, which led to the applicant's imprisonment, were also breaches of his or her tenancy and led to the landlord obtaining possession of the property: Welsh Code, para 15.23. See **14.236–14.237**.

[188] *Gloucester City Council v Miles* (1985) 17 HLR 292, CA.

'The relevant questions – when, how and why did she become homeless – admit of only one answer: on vandalisation of her home.'[189]

14.115 Again, loss of accommodation by prisoners can provide classic examples of the operation of these provisions. Many prisoners will find difficulty in paying rent for their homes whilst they are in custody. Rent arrears and consequent loss of the tenancy may be inevitable. But if the landlord wrongfully repossesses without a court order, it will be that illegal eviction that actually causes the homelessness and the prisoner cannot have become homeless intentionally.[190] If the prisoner asks a third party to pay the rent and that third party fails to pay, that may, depending on the facts, result in a decision that the prisoner became homeless intentionally (because the prisoner has failed to make an effective arrangement),[191] or in a decision that the prisoner became homeless unintentionally (where a proper and genuine arrangement is frustrated by the third party stealing the prisoner's money rather than paying the rent).

14.116 In summary, the deliberate act or omission by the applicant must have caused him or her actually to cease to occupy accommodation. An applicant's decision to rid himself or herself of accommodation that he or she was not occupying, or to refuse an offer of accommodation, cannot fall within this limb of the test. In deciding whether the deliberate act or omission caused the cessation of occupation, the local housing authority must identify:

- the operative causes of the loss of accommodation; and

- whether any one of those operative causes was the deliberate act or omission by the applicant; and

- whether the cessation of accommodation was the reasonably likely result of the act or omission; and

- that there was no intervening event by a third party causing the loss of accommodation.

14.117 Even if the local housing authority finds that this limb of the test is satisfied, it cannot find that the applicant has become homeless intentionally unless the other four limbs are also made out.

---

[189] (1985) 17 HLR 292, CA, at 304. See also *Bolah v Croydon London Borough Council* (2008) February *Legal Action*, p 40, Central London County Court, where the applicant was homeless as a result of the expiry of her landlord's lease, not as a result of having withdrawn an application for homeless assistance made to another local housing authority. See also *Black v Wandsworth London Borough Council* (2008) February *Legal Action*, p 41, Lambeth County Court.

[190] *Wilkins v Barnet London Borough Council* (1998) December *Legal Action*, p 27, Watford County Court.

[191] *Stewart v Lambeth London Borough Council* [2002] EWCA Civ 753, [2002] HLR 40, CA.

Was the accommodation available for the applicant?

14.118 If the applicant deliberately did (or failed to do) something in consequence of which he or she ceased to occupy accommodation, the next question for consideration is whether the accommodation lost was accommodation that was available for his or her occupation.

14.119 In HA 1996, Part 7 the phrase 'available for his occupation' has a special meaning. The statutory definition relates both to the physical availability of the accommodation and to the nature and extent of the applicant's right to occupy it.[192] The same definition is used in determining whether an applicant is 'homeless'. The detail has already been explored in Chapter 11. The following paragraphs contain only a brief summary.

14.120 The accommodation must have been available for occupation by the applicant and by any person who normally resided with the applicant as a member of the applicant's family, and also available for occupation by any person who might reasonably have been expected to reside with the applicant at the date it was lost.[193]

14.121 The importance of this provision is to prevent a finding that the applicant has become homeless intentionally when what the applicant has lost was accommodation that could not actually accommodate his or her household. Frequently, it is applied to split or separated households that have no accommodation in which they can live together. For example:

- A head of household who left his or her home country and took up a hostel room for a single person in the UK will not become homeless intentionally when he or she is later asked to leave that hostel once the family arrives (because the single person's hostel was not accommodation 'available' to the family).[194]

- Two young people living in their respective parental homes may develop a relationship and have a child. If neither set of parents will accommodate their child's partner, neither of the two will become homeless intentionally when the parental home is lost (eg on ejection following a family dispute) because neither partner had accommodation 'available' to accommodate the other.[195]

14.122 However, a father who permitted his three children to leave perfectly satisfactory accommodation that they were occupying with their mother so as

[192] HA 1996, s 175(1) and s 176. See also English Code, paras 8.5–8.17; Welsh Code, paras 13.16–13.33. See further **11.17–11.167**.
[193] See HA 1996, s 176 for the definition of the applicant's household. See also *R v Wimborne Borough Council ex p Curtis* (1986) 18 HLR 79, QBD; *R v Hammersmith and Fulham London Borough Council ex p O'Sullivan* [1991] EGCS 110, QBD; and *R v Peterborough City Council ex p Carr* (1990) 22 HLR 206, QBD. See also **11.23–11.34**.
[194] *R v Westminster City Council ex p Ali* (1983) 11 HLR 83, QBD.
[195] *R v Peterborough City Council ex p Carr* (1990) 22 HLR 206, QBD.

to move into his one-room accommodation with him was held to have become homeless intentionally. His deliberate conduct in letting them move in subsequently led to his landlord requiring the family to leave the one room. The distinction between this case and the first example above is that, before the children moved in to live with their father, they did not reside with him and nor was it reasonable to expect that they would do so.[196]

14.123 In summary, the accommodation must have been actually available both for the applicant and any person who normally resided with him or her as a member of his or her family and for any person who might reasonably have been expected to reside with him or her at the date it was lost.

14.124 Even if the local housing authority finds that this limb of the test is satisfied, it cannot find that the applicant has become homeless intentionally unless the other four limbs are also made out.

Would it have been reasonable for the applicant to have continued to occupy the accommodation?

14.125 To reach this stage in the application of the 'becoming homeless intentionally' test, the local housing authority must have satisfied itself that it was by his or her own deliberate act (or failure to act) that the applicant ceased to occupy available accommodation. The last issue to be settled is whether it would (at the point at which the deliberate act was done) have been reasonable for the applicant to have remained in occupation. It cannot be over-emphasised that the question is not 'Was it reasonable for the applicant to leave?' but rather 'Was it reasonable for the applicant to have continued in occupation?'

14.126 This reasonableness aspect of the test is the parallel of the part of the definition of 'homelessness' which uses exactly the same rubric.[197] Cases decided on whether an applicant is homeless or not homeless, having regard to the reasonableness of continued occupation, are therefore equally relevant to decisions as to whether a person became homelessness intentionally.

14.127 The question of whether accommodation was 'reasonable to continue to occupy' involves consideration of all the circumstances at the time of the applicant's deliberate act or omission, and is not limited to the physical quality of the accommodation that the applicant has ceased to occupy.[198]

---

[196] *Oxford City Council v Bull* [2011] EWCA Civ 609, [2011] HLR 35, [2012] 1 WLR 203, CA.

[197] HA 1996, s 175(3). See also English Code, paras 8.18–8.32; Welsh Code, paras 13.16–13.33. See further **11.75–11.120**.

[198] *R v Broxbourne Borough Council ex p Willmoth* (1989) 22 HLR 118, CA. See *Moran v Manchester City Council, Richards v Ipswich Borough Council* [2008] EWCA Civ 378 at [49]–[50] per Wilson LJ. The case went to the House of Lords, which decided the discrete issue that women's refuges could not be accommodation that was reasonable for an applicant and her household to continue to occupy: *Ali & others v Birmingham City Council, Moran v Manchester City Council* [2009] UKHL 36, [2009] 1 WLR 1506, HL. However, their Lordships did not specifically overrule the list of general considerations set out by Wilson LJ at [49]. See **11.97**.

14.128 When considering whether accommodation was reasonable for the applicant to continue to occupy, a local housing authority is directed by HA 1996, Part 7 only to the reasonableness of *the applicant* remaining in occupation. But the local housing authority must also consider whether it was reasonable for other members of the applicant's household to continue to occupy as an element in determining whether accommodation was 'available' for occupation by the whole family unit.[199] If there is an issue as to whether the accommodation lost would not have been reasonable for other persons in the household to continue to occupy, the local housing authority must resolve that issue. In *R v Westminster City Council ex p Bishop* the local housing authority and the court were satisfied that it would have been reasonable for the applicant herself to have remained in occupation of the former home, but the issue of whether it would have been reasonable for her dependent daughter to have remained had not been properly considered by the local housing authority.[200] Rose LJ said:

'... accommodation can only be regarded as available for an applicant's occupation if both she and those members of her family who normally live with her can reasonably be expected to occupy it. Accordingly, although I accept that the question of reasonableness of continued occupation within [s 191(1)] has to be looked at in relation to the applicant herself, if, in the present case, it was reasonable for her daughter to leave, it could not, in my view, be said that it was reasonable for the applicant to have remained alone. The daughter's position was, therefore, as it seems to me, of great significance.'[201]

14.129 Accordingly, the English Code advises that, as part of determining whether it was reasonable to have continued to occupy, a local housing authority will find it 'necessary' to consider the circumstances of both the applicant 'and the household' in each case.[202]

14.130 There is an important distinction, prescribed by HA 1996, Part 7, between the test of 'reasonable to continue to occupy' to be applied where an applicant has ceased to occupy accommodation because of *violence* (or threats of violence that are likely to be carried out) and all other cases. As a matter of law, accommodation where, had the applicant continued to occupy it was probable that she or he (or a member of his or her household) would have been subject to violence or to threats of violence that were likely to be carried out, cannot be reasonable for the applicant to have continued to occupy.[203]

---

[199] See **11.21–11.34**.
[200] *R v Westminster City Council ex p Bishop* (1993) 25 HLR 459, CA.
[201] *R v Westminster City Council ex p Bishop* (1993) 25 HLR 459, CA at 465.
[202] English Code, para 11.22. See also *Sharif v Camden London Borough Council* [2011] EWCA Civ 463, [2011] HLR 32, CA and see also **11.22**. At the date of writing, Camden London Borough Council had been given permission to appeal to the Supreme Court but the appeal had not been heard.
[203] HA 1996, s 177(1). *Bond v Leicester City Council* [2001] EWCA Civ 1544, (2002) 34 HLR 6, CA. English Code, para 11.13; Welsh Code, paras 13.16–13.33 deal with 'reasonable to continue to occupy', and para 15.22 refers to fleeing domestic violence. See **11.81–11.92** and **14.205–14.214**. The Supreme Court has held that 'domestic violence' should be given a broad interpretation, including 'physical violence, threatening or intimidating behaviour and any

14.131 In all other cases, including cases of harassment that fall short of violence (or threats of violence that are likely to be carried out), the local housing authority should consider all the circumstances in determining whether it would have been reasonable for the applicant to have continued in occupation. Those circumstances could include:

- the availability or otherwise of alternative remedies to tackle the problem that drove the applicant to leave;

- the possibility of it being reasonable for the applicant to have continued to occupy the accommodation for at least the period it would have taken to arrange alternative accommodation; and

- any other relevant matters.

14.132 The local housing authority is specifically required by regulations to consider whether the accommodation that the applicant has ceased to occupy was *affordable* for him or her.[204] A local housing authority that fails to consider affordability when determining whether or not accommodation had been reasonable for the applicant to continue to occupy will find its decision quashed.[205] Obviously, whether or not accommodation was 'affordable' will be a critical factor where accommodation has been lost by reason of mortgage default or rent arrears.

14.133 In the specific case of women's refuges, the House of Lords has held that it would not be reasonable for a woman to continue to occupy a refuge indefinitely. Even if she is asked to leave the refuge because of her own deliberate act, therefore, she should not be found to have become homeless intentionally.[206]

14.134 On the face of it, the question whether it was reasonable for a particular applicant to have continued in occupation is directed to the specific circumstances of that applicant. However, HA 1996, Part 7 allows a local housing authority to inject a comparative element by comparing the situation that faced the applicant with the *general circumstances in relation to housing* in its area. A local housing authority, when determining whether it was reasonable for the applicant to have continued in occupation, is permitted (but not

---

other form of abuse which, directly or indirectly may give rise to the risk of harm' (*Yemshaw v Hounslow London Borough Council* [2011] UKSC 3, [2011] 1 WLR 433, [2011] HLR 16, SC, Baroness Hale at [28] quoting the *Practice Direction (Residence and Contact Orders: Domestic Violence (No 2)* [2009] 1 WLR 251). The same definition is used in the Welsh Code at para 13.20. See **11.85**.
[204] Homelessness (Suitability of Accommodation) Order 1996, SI 1996/3204. See Appendix 2. See **11.101** and **18.47–18.48**.
[205] *Odunsi v Brent London Borough Council* [1999] 6 CLD 348, Willesden County Court.
[206] *Ali & others v Birmingham City Council, Moran v Manchester City Council* [2009] UKHL 36, [2009] 1 WLR 1506, HL; the Welsh Code, para 13.23, says '[e]ach case should be considered on an individual basis . . . [but that] [a]pplicants are not required to remain in the refuge for a minimum period of time before an application for re-housing will be considered'.

required) to have regard to general housing circumstances in its area.[207] This element of comparison is also a feature of the definition of being 'homeless'.[208]

14.135 Where the accommodation that the applicant has lost was not within the local housing authority's district, and particularly if the accommodation was outside the UK, the question for the local housing authority is not 'was the accommodation reasonable to continue to occupy given general housing circumstances prevailing in the area where the accommodation was situated?' Instead, the question is 'was the accommodation reasonable to continue to occupy given the general housing circumstances prevailing in our own area?'

14.136 The reasonableness of continued occupation of accommodation that was given up (whether overseas or in the UK) has to be balanced against the general housing circumstances in the area of the local housing authority to which the applicant has applied.[209] That balancing exercise should include the prospects available to the applicant in the accommodation that he or she has ceased to occupy, including employment prospects, the availability of welfare benefits, the applicant's financial position, and the space and arrangement (and any overcrowding) of the accommodation lost.[210] Strict application of this test could mean that an applicant who gives up accommodation in an area of acute housing need would be best advised to direct an application for homelessness assistance to an area where the general circumstances in relation to housing were much better, in the hope of then being referred back to the first area once the main housing duty has been accepted.[211]

14.137 Where the local housing authority has elected to take general housing circumstances prevailing in its district into account, the courts will be loath to interfere with its assessment of those circumstances. It is the local housing authority that is in the best position to judge the seriousness of any housing crisis in its district and to determine whether the applicant's particular complaints about his or her previous accommodation took him or her out of the norm of difficult housing circumstances in the district.[212]

14.138 For their part, applicants must be careful not to jump the gun. The question for the local housing authority is: 'Was the accommodation reasonable for the applicant and members of his or her household to continue to occupy at the date of the applicant's deliberate act or omission?', not at some date in the future.[213] So an applicant who faces the prospect, perhaps in the

---

[207] HA 1996, s 177(2).

[208] See **11.93–11.119**.

[209] *R v Tower Hamlets London Borough Council ex p Monaf* (1988) 20 HLR 529, CA, and *De Falco v Crawley Borough Council* [1980] QB 460, CA.

[210] *R v Tower Hamlets London Borough Council ex p Ojo* (1991) 23 HLR 488, QBD, and *Osei v Southwark London Borough Council* [2007] EWCA Civ 787, [2008] HLR 15, CA.

[211] However, judicially developed control measures in relation to the law on referral of applications (see **15.162–15.165**) have made it somewhat more difficult for applicants to expect referral back to the first area by this route.

[212] *R v Brent London Borough Council ex p Bariise* (1999) 31 HLR 50, CA.

[213] *Din v Wandsworth London Borough Council* [1983] 1 AC 657, HL.

relatively near future, that the accommodation may become unreasonable to continue to occupy, would perhaps be best advised to wait until he or she is within 28 days of that situation crystallising and then make an application on the basis that he or she has become threatened with homelessness unintentionally.

14.139 Although the statutory formula appears to suggest that the relevant date, when considering whether it was 'reasonable for him to continue to occupy', is the date when the applicant ceases to be in occupation of the accommodation, the better view is that the test should be applied as at the date of any earlier act or omission (if any) that caused the accommodation to be lost. For example, as at the date of actual eviction, the defaulting mortgage borrower may have faced such a level of repayments as to make it impossible to say that it would be reasonable to have continued in occupation. Nevertheless, the applicant may have become homeless intentionally if it would have been reasonable to have continued in occupation at the date when the property was unwisely remortgaged or the borrowing was increased so that the level of instalments became unmanageable.[214]

14.140 The question whether it would have been reasonable for the applicant to continue in occupation of particular accommodation should be considered in light of all the facts that occurred *before* the applicant's deliberate act or omission which led to the loss of the accommodation. The local housing authority must ignore later deliberate acts or omissions when deciding whether it was reasonable for the applicant to continue in occupation.[215]

14.141 In summary, for an applicant to have become homeless intentionally, the accommodation that he or she was occupying, and lost, must have been reasonable for him or her to continue to occupy. The accommodation must also have been reasonable for anyone who normally resides with the applicant as a member of his or her family and for any other person who might reasonably be expected to reside with the applicant to continue to occupy. Accommodation cannot be reasonable for an applicant to continue to occupy if it was probable that continued occupation would have led to violence (or to threats of violence that were likely to be carried out) against the applicant or a member of his or her household. In all other cases, the local housing authority has to make a decision as to whether or not the accommodation was factually reasonable for the applicant and his or her household to continue to occupy, taking account, if it chooses, of the general housing circumstances prevailing in its area.

---

[214] In *Bellamy v Hounslow London Borough Council* [2006] EWCA Civ 535, CA, [2006] HLR 42, CA, the Court of Appeal held that it would have been reasonable for a joint legal owner to remain in the property whilst she contested any application for sale that her co-owner might make.

[215] *Denton v Southwark London Borough Council* [2007] EWCA Civ 623, [2008] HLR 11, CA.

14.142   The relevant date, when considering whether it was reasonable for the applicant to continue to occupy accommodation, should be the date of the deliberate act or omission that caused the loss of accommodation.[216]

14.143   Even if the local housing authority finds that this limb of the test is satisfied, it cannot find that the applicant has become homeless intentionally unless the other four limbs are also made out.

Breaking the chain of causation

14.144   The test for 'becoming homeless intentionally', as set out by HA 1996, Part 7, appears to be satisfied where a local housing authority has found that the applicant satisfies all five limbs:

(1)   there was a deliberate act or omission (which does not include an act or omission in good faith by a person unaware of a material fact);[217] and

(2)   that deliberate act or omission was that of the applicant;[218] and

(3)   the applicant ceased to occupy accommodation as a consequence of that deliberate act or omission;[219] and

(4)   that accommodation was available for the applicant's occupation and for occupation by members of the applicant's household;[220] and

(5)   it would have been reasonable for the applicant and for all members of his or her household to have continued to occupy the accommodation.[221]

14.145   However, the courts, in interpreting HA 1996, Part 7, have posed an additional question to be addressed before an applicant can be found to have become homeless intentionally.

Is the deliberate act (or omission), and the cessation of occupation it caused, an operative cause of the present homelessness?

14.146   As we have seen, the exercise of determining whether a person became homeless intentionally for the purpose of the statutory definition involves travelling back in time to consider the point at which (at the latest) that person ceased to occupy accommodation as a result of his or her own deliberate act or failure to act.[222] But this begs the question 'How far back?' Many applicants

---

[216]   See **14.37–14.92**.
[217]   See **14.37–14.92**.
[218]   See **14.93–14.97**.
[219]   See **14.98–14.117**.
[220]   See **14.118–14.124**. The applicant's household is defined at HA 1996, s 176. See **11.23–11.3**.
[221]   See **14.125–14.143**.
[222]   See **14.37–14.117**.

will at some point in their lives have given up accommodation it would have been reasonable to continue to occupy (not least on leaving a parental home on achieving adulthood). If local housing authorities were free to run backwards indefinitely when applying the statutory test, significant numbers of applicants could be found to have deliberately given up occupation of some accommodation during their lifetimes and investigations would be extensive and expensive.

Settled accommodation

14.147 The Codes advise that local housing authorities should consider only the current incidence of homelessness to examine whether it is the result of a past deliberate act or omission. They suggest, adopting an approach developed from the case law, that local housing authorities look back only to 'the last period of settled accommodation' and examine why the applicant left that.[223] In their earlier versions, the Codes had suggested that attention be focused on the 'most immediate cause' of present homelessness 'rather than events that may have taken place previously', but that approach was subsequently considered too narrow.

14.148 The current formulation correctly echoes the approach taken by the courts. They have decided that past intentional homelessness can be expunged by the subsequent acquisition of 'settled' accommodation. The phrase was first coined by Ackner LJ in *Din v Wandsworth London Borough Council*.[224] He said:

> 'To remove his self-imposed disqualification, he must therefore have achieved what can be loosely described as "a settled residence", as opposed to what from the outset is known … to be only temporary accommodation. What amounts to "a settled residence" is a question of fact and degree depending upon the circumstances of each individual case.'

14.149 Consequently, where housing was lost in circumstances meeting the statutory definition of becoming homeless intentionally, a local housing authority's inquiries can be limited to determining those circumstances and then to whether there has been any such settled accommodation since that loss of accommodation. The local housing authority is entitled to ignore the acquisition and loss of temporary or insecure accommodation (even if occupation of such accommodation brought the applicant's state of homelessness to an end for a time) and may track back to the loss of the last settled accommodation. That loss, looking at the whole history, may be the real reason for the present homelessness.[225]

---

[223] English Code, paras 11.11–11.12; Welsh Code, para 15.17 which advises that local housing authorities may wish to consider the original intention of the arrangement when the applicant took up occupation of that accommodation.

[224] *Din v Wandsworth London Borough Council* (unreported) 23 June 1981, CA, quoted by Lord Denning MR in *Lambert v Ealing London Borough Council* [1982] 1 WLR 550, CA at 557.

[225] In accordance with the principle that it is not for the applicant to prove his or her case (see **10.15–10.19** and **14.19–14.24**), the local housing authority must consider whether the facts as

14.150 Not surprisingly, a whole body of case law has developed as to the circumstances in which accommodation is to be treated as 'settled' for the purpose of applying this test. While the matter is one primarily for the local housing authority itself to determine on the facts of the particular application, it should take a careful and measured approach. In the words of a recently retired Justice of the Supreme Court:

> 'Given the grave difficulty of securing settled accommodation, and given too that the clear legislative objective underlying the concept of intentionality – to discourage people from needlessly leaving their accommodation and becoming homeless – is surely sufficiently achieved without too protracted a period of consequential disqualification from re-housing, it is much to be hoped that housing authorities will in general interpret benevolently the character of accommodation secured by applicants after a finding of intentionality, namely as to whether or not it is settled.'[226]

14.151 The case law has thrown up many helpful illustrations as to what some local housing authorities have respectively considered unsettled and settled accommodation for these purposes.

Not usually treated as 'settled' accommodation:

14.152

- Holiday lets.[227]

- Out of season (or winter) lettings.[228]

- Bed and breakfast or other short-term hostel style accommodation.[229]

- Tied accommodation linked to short fixed-term employment.[230]

- A temporary stay with relatives.[231]

- Decrepit caravans.[232]

---

disclosed by the applicant amount to there being intervening settled accommodation, whether or not the applicant has specifically raised the point (*Black v Wandsworth London Borough Council* (2008) February *Legal Action*, p 41, Lambeth County Court).
[226] *R v Merton London Borough Council ex p Ruffle* (1988) 21 HLR 361, QBD at 366–367, per Simon Brown J (as he then was).
[227] *Lambert v Ealing London Borough Council* [1982] 1 WLR 550, CA.
[228] *Dyson v Kerrier District Council* [1980] 1 WLR 1205, CA.
[229] *R v Harrow London Borough Council ex p Holland, R v Rushcliffe District Council ex p Summerson* (1992) 25 HLR 577, QBD.
[230] *R v Dacorum District Council ex p Wright* (unreported) 16 October 1991, QBD.
[231] *De Falco v Crawley Borough Council* [1980] QB 460, CA.
[232] *Davis v Kingston Royal London Borough Council* (1981) Times 28 March, CA.

- Lodging in a council house.[233]

- Accommodation in another country in breach of immigration laws.[234]

- Moving in temporarily with a cohabitant.[235]

- An insecure, statutorily overcrowded and unaffordable assured shorthold tenancy.[236]

- Precarious occupation, whether as a bare licensee or as an unlawful sub-tenant.[237]

- Occupation in a caravan on a site without permission.[238]

- A non-secure tenancy provided in performance of the main housing duty.[239]

Usually treated as settled accommodation:

14.153

- Freehold or leasehold ownership.

- A tenancy enjoying security of tenure.

- An indefinite licence or permission to occupy.

- Returning to long-term occupation of the parental home.[240]

- Indefinite stay with friends or relatives.[241]

- Tied accommodation as a long-term employee.

14.154 The most difficult application of the test of 'settled' accommodation arises where an applicant who had been found to have become homeless intentionally has subsequently obtained a tenancy with a private sector

---

[233] *R v Merton London Borough Council ex p Ruffle* (1988) 21 HLR 361, QBD, and *Mazzaccherini v Argyll and Bute District Council* (1987) SCLR 475.
[234] *R v Croydon London Borough Council ex p Easom* (1992) 25 HLR 262, QBD.
[235] *R v Purbeck District Council ex p Cadney* (1986) 17 HLR 534, QBD.
[236] *Mohamed v Westminster City Council* [2005] EWCA Civ 796, [2005] HLR 47, CA.
[237] *Gilby v Westminster City Council* [2007] EWCA Civ 604, [2008] HLR 7, CA.
[238] *Stewart v Kingston upon Thames RLBC* [2007] EWCA Civ 565, [2007] HLR 42, CA.
[239] *Ali v Haringey London Borough Council* [2008] EWCA Civ 132, (2008) April *Legal Action*, p 34, CA. For 'main housing duty' see **17.23–17.168**.
[240] *Robson v Kyle and Carrick District Council* (1994) SCLR 259.
[241] *Krishnan v Hillingdon London Borough Council* (1981) SCOLAG January 1981, p 137, and *Black v Wandsworth London Borough Council* (2008) February *Legal Action*, p 41, Lambeth County Court.

landlord. Since February 1997, any such letting will have been on an assured shorthold tenancy (AST) involving hardly any security of tenure. The Court of Appeal has rejected the proposition that because an AST is the normal or default tenancy in the private sector, it must always count as 'settled'.[242] The true question for the local housing authority is whether, having regard to the circumstances and terms of its creation, the AST can properly be treated as having provided 'settled' accommodation for the applicant.

14.155 The material consideration is (generally) the position at the commencement of the new accommodation, 'since if the causal link is broken at that point nothing that happens thereafter will mend it'.[243] Of course, the reverse is also true. An arrangement may not have been 'settled' at the outset, but may become so at a later stage (eg when an originally short-term tenancy is renewed for an extended term) and it is at that stage that the causal link from previously having become homeless intentionally may be severed.

14.156 Properly understood, the application of the 'settled' accommodation test is all about cause and effect. The search is for a causal link between past deliberate loss of accommodation and the present homelessness. The local housing authority is really asking itself whether the earlier intentional act is causative of the present homelessness. It will usually conclude that it is, unless there has been some intermediate 'settled' accommodation.

Other events breaking the causal link

14.157 However, there may potentially be other circumstances in which the causal chain between present unintentional homelessness and having become homelessness intentionally in the past may be broken. While it is well established that the obtaining of settled accommodation is sufficient to break the causal link between having become homeless intentionally in the past and the immediate homelessness in question, there has been some doubt whether that was the only way in which the causal link could be severed.[244]

14.158 Precisely when, and in what circumstances, such a situation might arise has been canvassed twice in the House of Lords.

14.159 In *R v Brent London Borough Council ex p Awua*,[245] Lord Hoffman reached no concluded view. He said the jurisprudence concerning 'settled' accommodation:

[242] *Knight v Vale Royal District Council* [2003] EWCA Civ 1258, [2004] HLR 9, CA.
[243] *R v Westminster City Council ex p Obeid* (1996) 29 HLR 389, QBD, at 400 per Carnwath J.
[244] In *R v Basingstoke and Deane District Council ex p Bassett* (1983) 10 HLR 125, QBD, the applicant and her husband gave up secure accommodation to go and stay with her husband's relations. The marriage then broke down, she left her in-laws' house and became homeless. She had not had any intervening settled accommodation and the local housing authority considered that she had therefore become homeless intentionally. Taylor J held that the final homelessness resulted from the breakdown of the marriage, not from the decision to give up the settled accommodation.
[245] *R v Brent London Borough Council ex p Awua* [1996] AC 55, HL.

'... is well-established (it was approved by this House in *Din*'s case) and nothing I have said is intended to cast any doubt upon it, although I would wish to reserve the question of whether the occupation of a settled residence is the sole and exclusive method by which the causal link can be broken.'[246]

14.160 In *R v Harrow London Borough Council ex p Fahia*,[247] both the first-instance judge and the Court of Appeal held that the chain of causation could be broken in ways other than by obtaining intervening settled accommodation. They held that the local housing authority had misdirected itself in looking only to the question whether Mrs Fahia had obtained settled accommodation. Harrow petitioned for leave to appeal to resolve this 'doubtful point of law', but later conceded that the chain of causation could be broken by means other than the obtaining of intervening settled accommodation. The Law Lords were invited, despite this concession, to decide the point, but considered:

' ... it would not be right to do so. The point may be one of some importance to local authorities generally and your Lordships should decline to express any view, one way or the other, on the point.'[248]

14.161 So this area of law remains in a state of flux. For the time being the position must be (in keeping with the Court of Appeal's decision in *Fahia*) that acquisition of settled accommodation is *not* necessarily the only way of breaking the causal chain between having previously become homeless intentionally and the present incident of homelessness.

14.162 Both aspects of the causation issue can arise where an applicant had given up accommodation in the UK in order to emigrate, and then later returns to the UK.[249] On the assumption that the statutory definition of 'becoming homeless intentionally' was met upon giving up the accommodation in the UK, the local housing authority must go on to ask whether that is the cause of the applicant's present homelessness. This will involve considering both whether the accommodation overseas was 'settled' and (if it was not) whether there was an intervening event, such as the applicant's marriage breaking up[250] or the overseas accommodation becoming otherwise unreasonable to continue to occupy, that caused the present homelessness.[251]

---

[246] *R v Brent London Borough Council ex p Awua* [1996] AC 55, per Lord Hoffmann referring to *Din v Wandsworth London Borough Council* [1983] 1 AC 657, HL.

[247] *R v Harrow London Borough Council ex p Fahia* [1998] 1 WLR 1396, HL.

[248] *R v Harrow London Borough Council ex p Fahia* [1998] 1 WLR 1396, HL at 1129, per Lord Browne-Wilkinson

[249] See **14.233–14.234**.

[250] The example cited by the English Code, para 11.12. See *Blackstock v Birmingham City Council* (2008) March *Legal Action*, p 22, Birmingham County Court.

[251] *R v Basingstoke and Deane Borough Council ex p Bassett* (1983) 10 HLR 125, QBD, and *R v Harrow London Borough Council ex p Louis* (1997) June *Legal Action*, p 23, QBD.

BECOMING THREATENED WITH HOMELESSNESS INTENTIONALLY

14.163 The wording in the statutory definition of 'becoming threatened with homelessness intentionally' is similar to, but not quite the same as, the definition of 'becoming intentionally homeless'.[252] After all, the applicant will still be in occupation of accommodation and much will turn on an early decision as to whether the applicant has become threatened with homelessness intentionally. If the decision is adverse to the applicant who is threatened with homelessness, she or he will receive only advice and assistance to avoid actual homelessness.[253] If the decision is that the applicant has not become threatened with homelessness intentionally, the local housing authority has the power (and, if the applicant has a priority need, will be obliged) to take steps to prevent actual homelessness.[254]

14.164 HA 1996, Part 7 provides that a person becomes threatened with homelessness intentionally if he or she has committed a deliberate act or omission the 'likely result of which' is that he or she will be forced to leave accommodation, but he or she has not yet had to leave.[255]

14.165 In order for the local housing authority to find that an applicant has become threatened with homelessness intentionally, it must also find that the accommodation is available for his or her occupation and that it would be reasonable for him or her to continue to occupy the accommodation. If the applicant has acted in good faith, but in ignorance of a relevant fact, he or she has not become threatened with homelessness intentionally, because the act or failure to act will not be treated as having been 'deliberate'.[256]

14.166 Several features of the main definition of 'becoming threatened with homelessness intentionally' are in precisely the same terms as those used to define 'becoming homeless intentionally'. The following components are discussed in detail above in relation to 'becoming homeless intentionally':

- 'deliberate' act or failure to act;[257]

- accommodation 'available for his occupation';[258] and

- 'reasonable for him to continue to occupy'.[259]

---

[252] HA 1996, s 196.
[253] HA 1996, s 195(5). See **17.201–17.214**.
[254] HA 1996, s 195(2), (9). See **17.190–17.200**.
[255] HA 1996, s 196(1).
[256] HA 1996, s 196(2).
[257] See **14.37–14.92**.
[258] See **14.118–14.124**.
[259] See **14.125–14.143**.

14.167 The missing element, loss of accommodation 'in consequence of' the act or failure to act, is replaced by a test of reasonable likelihood ('the likely result of which'), which in fact mirrors the approach taken by the courts in construing the term used in the definition of becoming homeless intentionally.[260]

14.168 As with 'becoming homeless intentionally', there is a separate provision dealing with collusive arrangements.[261] If the applicant has:

- entered into an arrangement under which he or she is required to cease to occupy accommodation; and

- the purpose of that arrangement is to enable him or her to receive homelessness assistance; and

- there is no other good reason why he or she is threatened with homelessness;

he or she has become threatened with homelessness intentionally.[262]

14.169 There is very little developed case law on becoming threatened with homelessness intentionally. This is perhaps because local housing authorities often find that they have insufficient time to conclude their inquiries before the applicant actually becomes homeless. The local housing authority can only reach a decision on the question within the relatively tight period of 28 days between the applicant first becoming 'threatened with homelessness' and the homelessness then crystallising.[263]

14.170 This shortage of cases has enabled the courts to avoid grappling with the problems of language and logic that arise where the applicant is facing homelessness from accommodation that would not constitute 'settled' accommodation and has previously been found to have become homeless intentionally. For example, an applicant who has previously been found to have become homeless intentionally may be within 28 days of actual homelessness as a result of his or her current landlord obtaining an order for possession to bring to an end an assured shorthold tenancy which both landlord and tenant understood would only last six months.

14.171 It is exceptionally difficult to bring that scenario within the strict definition of 'becoming threatened with homelessness intentionally'. To do so would require a decision that the previous act that caused the applicant to become homeless intentionally was the act 'the likely result' of which was that

---

[260] See **14.109–14.112**.
[261] See **14.174–14.180**.
[262] HA 1996, s 196(3).
[263] HA 1996, s 175(4). See **11.129–11.133**.

the current accommodation would be lost. The attempt by Brightman LJ to square this particular circle[264] has been described as 'distinctly odd'[265] and has attracted adverse judicial comment.[266]

14.172 The better view is perhaps that the causal connection approach cannot properly work to link past intentional homelessness to present intentional threatened homelessness. If that is right, an applicant, who would be likely, if homeless, to be found to have become homeless intentionally because she or he has not acquired settled accommodation since previous intentional homelessness, would do well to apply as soon as she or he is threatened with homelessness from current unsettled accommodation and to press for an early decision.

14.173 A local housing authority cannot find that an applicant has become homeless intentionally unless he or she has actually become homeless and, likewise, cannot find an applicant to have become threatened with homelessness intentionally until he or she is actually threatened with homelessness, ie is within 28 days of becoming homeless.[267]

ENTERING INTO AN ARRANGEMENT TO CEASE TO OCCUPY ACCOMMODATION

14.174 Until 1997, an applicant could only be considered to have become homeless intentionally by falling foul of the five-part statutory definition considered above. However, HA 1996, Part 7 introduced a wholly new and separate class of intentional homelessness. If the statutory requirements of that category are met, then the applicant is deemed to have become homeless intentionally without consideration of the longstanding five-part definition.

14.175 Under these provisions, if a local housing authority decides that an applicant has entered into an arrangement by which he or she was required to leave accommodation, and that the purpose of that arrangement was to enable the applicant to receive homelessness assistance, he or she will have become homeless intentionally.[268]

14.176 The essential elements are that:

(1) the applicant is homeless; and

(2) he or she had previously entered into an arrangement under which she or he would be required to leave accommodation; and

---

[264] *Dyson v Kerrier District Council* [1980] 1 WLR 1205, CA.
[265] D Hoath *Homelessness* (Sweet & Maxwell, 1983), p 114.
[266] *Din v Wandsworth London Borough Council* [1983] 1 AC 657, HL at 678–679, per Lord Lowry.
[267] *R v Rugby Borough Council ex p Hunt* (1992) 26 HLR 1, QBD.
[268] HA 1996, s 191(3).

(3)   the accommodation to which that arrangement applied would have been reasonable to continue to occupy; and

(4)   the purpose of the arrangement was to enable the applicant to become entitled to HA 1996, Part 7 assistance; and

(5)   there is no other good reason for the applicant's present homelessness.[269]

14.177   The English Code advises that particular care should be taken when local housing authorities assess applications from 16- or 17-year-olds in respect of this new definition.[270] The Welsh Code refers to collusion 'with friends or relatives' and 'between landlords and tenants'.[271]

14.178   The statutory provision is obviously directed to preventing collusion to bring about homelessness that would result in HA 1996, Part 7 duties. Collusion could occur in informal arrangements, between friends or relations, or in the more formal relationship between landlord and tenant. Even if there has been collusion, the applicant will not have become homeless intentionally if the accommodation given up was not reasonable for the applicant to continue to occupy.[272] If the applicant was staying with friends or relatives, the relationship may have broken down to such an extent that the accommodation has become unreasonable to continue to occupy.

14.179   The Codes advise that an 'other good reason' why an applicant may be homeless might include overcrowding, or an obvious breakdown in relations between the applicant and his or her host.[273] In those circumstances, an applicant will not be caught by this test.

14.180   Local housing authorities must be satisfied that collusion exists and should not rely on hearsay or unfounded suspicions if they are to find that the applicant became homeless intentionally under this provision. As already noted,[274] the provision is hardly ever used in practice by local housing authorities to sustain a decision that the applicant became homeless intentionally, and it can be avoided altogether by ensuring that the application for homelessness assistance is made by someone other than the person who entered into the arrangement. As already indicated, there is an equivalent provision to prevent collusion by those who are threatened with homelessness.[275]

---

[269]   HA 1996, s 191(3).
[270]   English Code, para 11.28; See **13.127–13.174**.
[271]   Welsh Code, para 15.26. See **13.214–13.218**.
[272]   See **14.125–14.143**.
[273]   English Code, para 11.28; Welsh Code, para 15.24.
[274]   See **14.34–14.35**.
[275]   See **14.168**.

COMMON SCENARIOS

14.181 The remainder of this Chapter seeks to apply the above analysis of the statutory definitions of 'becoming homeless intentionally' and 'becoming threatened with homelessness intentionally' to common factual circumstances in which local housing authorities may be called upon to apply those tests.

Rent or mortgage arrears

14.182 The local housing authority will need to consider why it was that the applicant accrued the rent or mortgage arrears that caused the loss of accommodation.[276] If the applicant had simply refused to pay the rent or mortgage payments and had spent the money elsewhere, that would constitute a deliberate act (spending it) or omission (to pay it towards housing costs) necessary to satisfy the first part of the definition of becoming homeless intentionally.[277]

14.183 But the enquiry cannot stop there, because, if the accommodation was unaffordable for the applicant, in that he or she could not afford the housing costs as well as meet the ordinary necessities of life, the property would not be reasonable for the applicant and the members of his or her household to continue to occupy.[278] What constitute 'the ordinary necessities of life' may vary according to the individual circumstances of each applicant and is a question of fact for the local housing authority to decide, having regard to the matters set out in a statutory order.[279]

14.184 Of course, the two elements of (1) a deliberate act and (2) the reasonableness of continued occupation may overlap. That is particularly likely where the deliberate act of the applicant has itself arguably rendered the accommodation unaffordable. The local housing authority is entitled to consider the applicant's financial position both when he or she first obtained the accommodation, and throughout the occupation of that property. So, for example, if the applicant had been able to afford the mortgage for the accommodation when it was first acquired, but had later taken on an additional loan that became unaffordable, that decision to extend the lending

---

[276] Or, in the case of an applicant threatened with homelessness, why the applicant might have accrued the arrears which are threatening to cause the loss of accommodation.

[277] See *William v Wandsworth London Borough Council* [2006] EWCA Civ 535, [2006] HLR 42, CA; and *Bury Metropolitan Borough Council v Gibbons* [2010] EWCA Civ 327, [2010] HLR 33, CA.

[278] Homelessness (Suitability of Accommodation) Order, SI 1996/3204. English Code, paras 8.29 and 11.17–11.19; Welsh Code, paras 13.29–13.30. See also *R v Hillingdon London Borough Council ex p Tinn* (1988) 20 HLR 305, QBD; *R v Wandsworth London Borough Council ex p Hawthorne* [1994] 1 WLR 1442, CA; *R v Brent London Borough Council ex p Baruwa* (1997) 29 HLR 915, CA; *Saunders v Hammersmith and Fulham London Borough Council* [1999] 6 CLD 347, West London County Court; and *Bernard v Enfield London Borough Council* [2001] EWCA Civ 1831, (2002) 34 HLR 46, CA and **11.101**. For affordability in relation to suitability, see **18.47–18.48**.

[279] Homelessness (Suitability of Accommodation) Order, SI 1996/3204.

or remortgage the property could properly be described as a deliberate act which, eventually, led to the loss of accommodation.[280] Equally, if the applicant's financial difficulties occurred as a result of his or her raising a secured loan to finance an unsuccessful business venture (which led to inability to meet repayments), the local housing authority would be entitled to consider the prospects of that venture as they appeared at the time that the mortgage was taken out.[281] If the applicant genuinely believed that the business venture would be sound, he or she will have acted in good faith in taking out a mortgage to finance it. However, if that judgment involved an unrealistic degree of optimism or any dishonesty, he or she will not have acted in good faith.[282] Two Court of Appeal decisions have upheld local housing authorities' decisions that the taking out of a mortgage that was unaffordable was a deliberate act which subsequently rendered the applicants homeless and therefore they had become homeless intentionally.[283]

14.185 If an applicant was receiving welfare benefits to help with the accommodation costs, the local housing authority should not simply assume that the housing costs were therefore affordable, but should still look at all the circumstances. Even if the applicant failed to use his or her available welfare benefits to pay his or her rent or mortgage, the property might still be unaffordable in any event due to the shortfall between the benefit received and the contractual rent or mortgage payments.[284]

14.186 If the applicant failed to apply for benefit to which he or she would have been entitled, that would generally be considered to have been a deliberate omission. However, if he or she was genuinely unaware of his or her entitlement to benefit, he or she may not have been guilty of deliberate omission if she or he acted in good faith.[285]

---

[280] *R v Barnet London Borough Council ex p Rughooputh* (1993) 25 HLR 607, CA; and *R v Wandsworth London Borough Council ex p Onwudiwe* (1993) 26 HLR 302, CA.

[281] *R v Exeter City Council ex p Tranckle* (1994) 26 HLR 244, CA; and *R v Warrington Borough Council ex p Bryant* (2000) October *Legal Action*, p 24, QBD.

[282] English Code, para 11.26. See also *R v Hammersmith and Fulham London Borough Council ex p Lusi* (1991) 23 HLR 260, QBD.

[283] *William v Wandsworth London Borough Council* [2006] EWCA Civ 535, [2006] HLR 42, CA; and *Watchman v Ipswich Borough Council* [2007] EWCA Civ 348, [2007] HLR 33, CA.

[284] *R v Shrewsbury and Atcham Borough Council ex p Griffiths* (1993) 25 HLR 613, QBD; *R v Brent London Borough Council ex p Grossett* (1996) 28 HLR 9, CA; *Ahmed v Westminster City Council* (1999) June *Legal Action*, p 24, Central London County Court; and *Odunsi v Brent London Borough Council* [1999] CLY 3063, Willesden County Court.

[285] *R v Tower Hamlets London Borough Council ex p Saber* (1992) 24 HLR 611, QBD; and *R v Westminster City Council ex p Moozary-Oraky* (1993) 26 HLR 213, QBD; *Bury Metropolitan Borough Council v Gibbons* [2010] EWCA Civ 327, [2010] HLR 33, CA; and *Essex v Birmingham City Council* (2012) August *Legal Action*, p 28, Birmingham County Court. Note that in *F v Birmingham City Council* [2006] EWCA Civ 1427, [2007] HLR 18, CA, a tenant had 'closed her eyes to the obvious' when she gave up a secure tenancy for a private rented tenancy in ignorance of the fact that housing benefit would not cover the whole of the contractual rent and therefore the issue of good faith did not arise. In different circumstances, in *Abdullahi v Brent London Borough Council* [2007] EWCA Civ 885, (2007) October *Legal Action*, p 26, CA, an assured tenant's ignorance of the shortfall between contractual rent and housing benefit

14.187 The Codes advise that non-payment of rent due to housing benefit delays which were beyond the applicant's control should not generally be considered deliberate.[286] This guidance must refer to situations where a landlord is entitled to a mandatory order of possession, either based on rent arrears[287] or as a result of a notice requiring possession,[288] and the court had no discretion to adjourn or refuse a possession order, even though the arrears might be due to be paid by a late determination of housing benefit entitlement.[289] The Welsh Code advises that 'applicants should not be considered to have become homeless intentionally in circumstances where the accommodation which was previously affordable, became unaffordable as a result of changes in the rate of their local housing allowance/housing benefit'.[290]

14.188 Occupiers in financial difficulties would do well to approach the local housing authority for help at an early stage. They certainly cannot assume that, if they leave the accommodation because of financial difficulties, they will not be found to have become homeless intentionally. If they have left, the local housing authority will consider whether leaving the accommodation was the only option available to them, ie whether or not it would have been reasonable to have continued in occupation at the date when they left. If the applicant is still in the accommodation, the local housing authority can at least decide the issue of whether he or she has become threatened with homelessness intentionally while the family is in occupation.[291] In *R v Leeds City Council ex p Adamiec*,[292] the applicant considered that he could no longer afford his mortgage and contracted to sell his home. The local housing authority decided that he had become threatened with homelessness intentionally. His finances at the date he contracted to sell were not such that his accommodation was unaffordable. The decision was upheld, but the judge noted that:

---

was a relevant fact which required consideration of whether she had acted in good faith. For 'relevant fact', see **14.44–14.52**. For 'good faith', see **14.53–14.61**.

[286] English Code, para 11.17(i); Welsh Code, para 15.11(i).

[287] Housing Act 1988, Sch 2, Ground 8.

[288] Housing Act 1988, s 21.

[289] In *Houghton v Sheffield City Council* [2006] EWCA Civ 1799, (2007) March *Legal Action*, p 18, CA, the applicant was found to have become homeless intentionally even though, at the date the possession order had been made against him, he had reduced his rent arrears from £1,000 to £7. A first-instance judge found that the local housing authority's decision was perverse, and that he had not become homeless intentionally, and the Court of Appeal refused the local housing authority permission to bring a second appeal. For applicants who are homeless as a result of possession orders, see **14.19–14.204**.

[290] Welsh Code, paras 15.31–15.33.

[291] Indeed if the local housing authority fails to recognise that an approach for assistance with accommodation may be an application for homelessness assistance (HA 1996, s 183, see **9.8–9.63**) and fails to make a decision and provide the applicant with advice and assistance (if he or she is threatened with homelessness, HA 1996 s 195(2)), that very failure by the local housing authority could result in the applicant not having acted deliberately when he or she subsequently leaves the accommodation: *Bury Metropolitan Borough Council v Gibbons* [2010] EWCA Civ 327, [2010] HLR 33, CA.

[292] (1992) 24 HLR 138, QBD.

'... [W]ere he not to get work in a month or two, and if he were to be threatened with repossession, it would almost certainly at that stage have been unreasonable to expect him not to sell his home. But that stage had not yet been reached.'[293]

14.189   The local housing authority is, accordingly, entitled to consider how desperate the applicant's financial position was and whether, for example, his or her creditors were actually threatening to recover loans or obtain possession of the accommodation or not.[294] The correct approach has been crisply stated in this way:

'As a matter of common sense, it seems to me that it cannot be reasonable for a person to continue to occupy accommodation when they can no longer discharge their fiscal obligations in relation to that accommodation, that is to say, pay the rent and make the mortgage repayments, without so straining their resources as to deprive themselves of the ordinary necessities of life, such as food, clothing, heat, transport and so forth.'[295]

14.190   A local housing authority is entitled to presume that, where one partner in a household accrued rent or mortgage arrears, the other partner acquiesced in that behaviour.[296] If, however, the applicant asserts that he or she did not acquiesce and puts forward some relevant material, the local housing authority must make inquiries into that assertion.[297] Where the applicant has been actively involved in the family finances, the local housing authority may be entitled to find that he or she acquiesced in a decision not to pay the rent or mortgage arrears, or to over-extend the family budget.[298]

14.191   Decisions as to whether or not the applicant could have afforded to pay both the housing costs and the ordinary necessities of life apply equally to accommodation that has been lost outside the UK. If an applicant gives up accommodation overseas in order to migrate to the UK for economic reasons, the question for the local housing authority is whether or not the applicant could have afforded to pay his or her housing costs and the ordinary necessities of life in the overseas accommodation. If not, the accommodation will not have been reasonable for the applicant and members of his or her household to have continued to occupy.[299]

---

[293]   (1992) 24 HLR 138, QBD at 153, per Webster J.
[294]   *R v Tower Hamlets London Borough Council ex p Ullah* (1992) 24 HLR 680, QBD; and *R v Westminster City Council ex p Ali* (1997) 29 HLR 580, QBD.
[295]   *R v Hillingdon London Borough Council ex p Tinn* (1988) 20 HLR 305, QBD at 308, per Kennedy J. See, more recently, *Adekunle v Islington London Borough Council* (2009) November *Legal Action*, p 25, Mayor's and City of London County Court.
[296]   See the discussion on acquiescence at **14.93–14.97**.
[297]   *R v Wyre Borough Council ex p Joyce* (1983) 11 HLR 73, QBD; *R v West Dorset District Council ex p Phillips* (1985) 17 HLR 336, QBD; *R v Eastleigh Borough Council ex p Beattie (No 2)* (1985) 17 HLR 168 QBD; *R v East Northamptonshire Borough Council* (1988) 20 HLR 508, QBD; *R v Thanet District Council ex p Groves* (1990) 22 HLR 223, QBD; and *Quinton v East Hertfordshire District Council* (2003) April *Legal Action*, p 27, Luton County Court.
[298]   *R v Barnet London Borough Council ex p O'Connor* (1990) 22 HLR 486, QBD; and *R v Nottingham City Council ex p Caine* (1996) 28 HLR 374, CA.
[299]   *R v Islington London Borough Council ex p Bibi* (1996) 29 HLR 498, QBD.

Tenants facing possession proceedings

14.192 Most landlords cannot lawfully obtain possession of tenanted premises without obtaining an order for possession.[300] The legal proceedings may not be the tenant's fault, there may be no defence and the tenant may be anxious to leave before a court hearing, not least to avoid liability for court costs. If the tenant chooses to leave, that may be a perfectly reasonable thing to do, but there may still be a finding that he or she became homeless intentionally if it would have been reasonable to have remained in occupation.[301]

14.193 If the application for homelessness assistance is made while the tenant is still in occupation, it is for the local housing authority to decide whether or not it would be reasonable for the tenant in those circumstances to continue to occupy the accommodation until a possession order is obtained and/or executed. The Codes advise that the local housing authority should take into account:

- the general cost to the local housing authority of accepting a duty;

- the positions of the tenant and the landlord;

- the likelihood that the landlord will actually proceed;

- the burden on the courts of unnecessary proceedings where there is no defence to a possession claim; and

- general housing circumstances (if they wish to do so).[302]

14.194 Both Codes advise that:

- where an assured shorthold tenant has received a proper Housing Act 1988, s 21 notice;[303] and

- the local housing authority is satisfied that the landlord intends to seek possession; and

---

[300] Protection from Eviction Act 1977, ss 1–3.

[301] In *Ugiagbe v Southwark London Borough Council* [2009] EWCA Civ 31, [2009] HLR 35, CA, an assured shorthold tenant left the premises before the landlord served a Housing Act 1988, s 21 notice or started possession proceedings. Having been told by the landlord to leave, she sought advice from a local housing authority advice centre which told her to go to the Homeless Persons Unit who would put her into temporary accommodation. The advice centre did not tell her that she had the right to remain in the property until the landlord obtained a possession order. Had she gone to the Homeless Persons Unit, she would have been advised accordingly. The Court of Appeal found that she was ignorant of a relevant fact (her security of tenure) and that her failure to obtain that advice had been in good faith. See also *Bury Metropolitan Borough Council v Gibbons* [2010] EWCA Civ 327, [2010] HLR 33, CA.

[302] English Code, para 8.31; Welsh Code, para 13.32.

[303] Housing Act 1988, s 21.

- it is satisfied that there would be no defence to a claim for a possession order,

it is unlikely to be reasonable for the applicant to continue to occupy the accommodation beyond the date given in the s 21 notice.[304]

14.195 Local housing authorities should consider any other application from a tenant facing possession proceedings on its own facts.

14.196 It follows from the guidance regarding assured shorthold tenants that other tenants who have been served with notices terminating their tenancies or requiring them to give possession, who would face possession proceedings to which they would have no defence, are also unlikely to be considered to be occupying accommodation that is reasonable to continue to occupy. The crucial issue is, of course, the intention of the landlord to bring possession proceedings once the notice has expired.

14.197 The local housing authority is entitled to take into account the general housing conditions prevailing in its district when considering whether or not it would be reasonable for the tenant to remain in occupation pending any inevitable possession proceedings.[305] However, a tenant who surrenders accommodation rather than waiting for inevitable possession proceedings may be acting in ignorance of a material fact (i e the general housing circumstances prevailing in the district), and such an act could not have been done 'deliberately' if done in good faith.[306]

14.198 Of course, the local housing authority is also entitled to take into account the landlord's reasons for requiring possession.[307]

---

[304] English Code, para 8.32; Welsh Code, paras 13.32 and 15.21(iii). The latter sub-paragraph of the Welsh Code advises 'the authority may consider that it would have been reasonable for the tenant to continue to occupy the accommodation, the tenant would not have become homeless deliberately if they [sic] had taken a contrary view in ignorance of material facts e g the general pressure on the authority for housing assistance'. See also *R v Newham London Borough Council ex p Ugbo* (1993) 26 HLR 263, QBD; and *Mondeh v Southwark London Borough Council* (2010) November *Legal Action*, p 19, Lambeth County Court. Where an applicant's application for homelessness assistance is made to a local housing authority in England on or after 9 November 2012 and within two years of having accepted a private rented sector offer (HA 1996, s 193(7AA) amended by LA 2011, s 148(5), see **17.109–17.131**), he or she will be deemed to be threatened with homelessness on the date that a valid HA 1988, s 21 notice is served and deemed to be homeless on the date of expiration of that notice (HA 1996 s 195A(2) and (4) inserted by LA 2011, s 149(4)). See **11.121–11.128**. At the date of writing, the amendments to HA 1996 made by LA 2011, ss 148–149 had not been brought into effect in Wales.

[305] HA 1996, s 177(2).

[306] English Code, paras 11.25 and 11.27(iii); Welsh Code, para 15.21(iii).

[307] See **14.199–14.204**. This applies even where an applicant to a local housing authority in England whose application is made on or after 9 November 2012 is deemed to be homeless or threatened with homelessness as a result of a valid HA 1988 s 21 notice having been served by the landlord (HA 1996 s 195A(2) and (4), inserted by LA 2011, s 149(4)). See **11.121–11.128**. At the date of writing, the amendments to HA 1996 made by LA 2011, ss 148–149 had not been brought into effect in Wales.

Loss of accommodation as a result of a possession order

14.199 As already referred to,[308] most owner-occupiers and tenants of rented accommodation are entitled not to be evicted unless a possession order has been made against them. In one sense, occupiers who leave or are evicted from property as a result of a possession order cannot be said to have become homeless intentionally. They have been required to leave by a Court against their wishes.

14.200 However, applying the 'operative cause'[309] and 'reasonable likelihood'[310] tests described above, local housing authorities are entitled to consider the reasons for the bringing of possession proceedings.[311] Possession proceedings themselves fall into three categories:

- claims for possession where the reason is said to be some fault by the tenant;

- claims for possession where there is no obligation on the landlord to show fault; and

- claims for possession brought by lenders.

14.201 The Court of Appeal has declined an invitation to hold that a local housing authority is always obliged to accept what is said on the face of a possession order (such as the correct figures for the arrears).[312] However, it would be unusual for a local housing authority to come to a different decision from the facts as determined by the judge and recorded on the face of the order. There may, however, be a number of matters that were not raised before or considered by a judge hearing the possession claim that could be relevant to the question of whether the occupier has become homeless intentionally.

14.202 Where the claim for possession is brought by a landlord who alleges fault on the part of a secure or assured tenant,[313] the court hearing the claim for possession will determine whether there has been fault, so as to entitle the landlord to possession, and will normally consider whether it is reasonable to make an order for possession and whether the order should be postponed on terms.[314] A tenant evicted as a result of one of these 'fault-based' grounds for possession is likely to find that the local housing authority decides that he or

---

[308] See **11.58–11.77**.

[309] See **14.104–14.108**.

[310] See **14.109–14.113**.

[311] *Devenport v Salford City Council* (1988) 8 HLR 54, CA; and *Bratton v Croydon London Borough Council* [2002] EWCA Civ 1494, (2002) December *Legal Action*, p 22, CA.

[312] *Green v Croydon London Borough Council* [2007] EWCA Civ 1367, (2008) *Legal Action*, p 41, CA.

[313] Under Housing Act 1985, Sch 2, Part 1 (secure tenants) or Housing Act 1988, Sch 2, Grounds 8, 10, 11, 12, 13, 14, 15, or 17 (assured tenants).

[314] The exception is Housing Act 1988, Sch 2, Ground 8, where the landlord is entitled to possession if the ground is made out.

she has become homeless intentionally for the same reason that the court decided to make a possession order. Common scenarios include where the tenant has accrued rent arrears or has been found responsible for nuisance behaviour.[315] Normally, in these fault-based claims for possession, the tenant will have had the opportunity to put everything that is relevant to a decision as to whether he or she had become homeless intentionally to the judge hearing the possession claim, and so it would be unusual for there to be additional relevant facts to be put before the local housing authority.

14.203 Where the possession claim has been brought without any need for the landlord to show that the tenant is at fault, such as possession proceedings brought under Housing Act 1988, s 21 against assured shorthold tenants, or proceedings by local housing authorities against introductory, demoted or non-secure tenants, then very little information will have been put before the judge. The local housing authority is entitled to consider the reasons for the landlord's decision to bring (and continue) possession proceedings and, of course, must hear the tenant's side of the story. If those reasons are because of the fault of the tenant, he or she may have become homeless intentionally, even though the possession claim was not brought on any of the fault-based grounds.[316]

14.204 Where the occupier is evicted as a result of mortgage foreclosure proceedings, the reason for the bringing of the proceedings will have been the occupier having accrued arrears under the mortgage, and the local housing authority will be entitled to consider the reasons for those arrears and for the decision to take out the mortgage in the first place.[317]

---

[315] For cases concerning rent arrears, see: *R v Wandsworth London Borough Council ex p Hawthorne* [1994] 1 WLR 1442, CA; *R v Brent London Borough Council ex p Baruwa* (1997) 29 HLR 915, CA; and *R v Newham London Borough Council ex p Campbell* (1994) 26 HLR 183, QBD (where the real cause of homelessness was not the reason for the making of the possession order). For cases concerning nuisance behaviour, see: *Devenport v Salford City Council* (1983) 8 HLR 54, CA; *R v Swansea City Council ex p John* (1983) 9 HLR 56, QBD (where the tenant had acquiesced in her partner's nuisance behaviour and so had become homeless intentionally); *Griffiths v St Helens Metropolitan Borough Council* [2004] 142 Housing Aid Update, St Helens County Court, noted at Madge & Sephton *Housing Law Casebook* (LAG, 5th edn, 2012), T23.5 (where the tenant had tried to stop her children's misconduct and had not become homeless intentionally); and *Walcot v Lambeth London Borough Council* [2006] EWCA Civ 809, (2006) September *Legal Action*, p 14, CA. In *Sheppard v Richmond-upon-Thames Royal London Borough Council* [2012] EWCA Civ 302 (2012) June *Legal Action*, p 36, CA, the possession order had been made because of the tenant's breach of her tenancy agreement by refusing to allow gas safety checks.

[316] *Bratton v Croydon London Borough Council* [2002] EWCA Civ 1494, (2002) December *Legal Action*, p 22, CA. See *Houghton v Sheffield City Council* [2006] EWCA Civ 1799, (2007) March *Legal Action*, p 18, where a local housing authority was wrong to find that a tenant who had reduced arrears from £1,000 to £7, but was still subject to a possession order, had become homeless intentionally.

[317] See **14.182–14.191**.

Leaving accommodation because of violence or threats of violence or harassment

Violence or threats of violence

14.205 As a matter of law, if the local housing authority finds that it is probable that, if the applicant continues to occupy his or her accommodation, he or she or a member of his or her household will be subject to violence or threats of violence that are likely to be carried out, the accommodation cannot be reasonable for the applicant and members of his or her household to continue to occupy.[318] The applicant is already 'homeless' and may therefore leave without a finding that he or she has become homeless intentionally.

14.206 For these purposes, 'violence' and 'threats of violence' can include sexual or physical abuse from another member of the family[319] or any other form of actual or threatened violence. Where that 'violence' is 'domestic violence',[320] the Supreme Court has held that violence should be given a broad interpretation including 'physical violence, threatening or intimidating behaviour and any other form of abuse which, directly or indirectly may give rise to the risk of harm'.[321] The Supreme Court declined to decide whether that broad interpretation should also be applied in cases of non-domestic violence.

14.207 A failure to pursue legal remedies against the perpetrator because of fears of reprisal, or because the applicant was unaware of the remedies available, should not generally be considered a deliberate omission if the applicant was acting in good faith.[322]

14.208 Where a woman leaves her accommodation because of domestic violence, and goes to a women's refuge, the refuge will not be reasonable to continue to occupy indefinitely.[323] Consequently, the local housing authority should look back to the reasons why the woman left her accommodation, and whether it was due to violence, or threats of violence that were likely to have been carried out if she continued in occupation, as defined at HA 1996, s 177(1).

---

[318] HA 1996, s 177(1). See also English Code, paras 8.19–8.25, 11.13, 11.23; Welsh Code, paras 13.18–13.26 and 15.22). *Bond v Leicester City Council* [2001] EWCA Civ 1544, (2002) 34 HLR 6, CA. See **11.83–11.92**.

[319] *R v Northampton Borough Council ex p Clarkson* (1992) 24 HLR 529, QBD.

[320] Defined by reference to the relationship between the perpetrator and the victim (HA 1996, s 177(1A) and s 178), see **11.86**.

[321] *Yemshaw v Hounslow London Borough Council* [2011] UKSC 3, [2011] 1 WLR 433, [2011] HLR 16, SC, Baroness Hale at [28] quoting the *Practice Direction (Residence and Contact Orders: Domestic Violence (No 2)* [2009] 1 WLR 251). The Welsh Code contains the same definition at para 13.20. See **11.8**.

[322] English Code, para 11.23; Welsh Code, para 15.22.

[323] *Ali & others v Birmingham City Council, Moran v Manchester City Council* [2009] UKHL 36, [2009] 1 WLR 1506, HL.

Harassment not amounting to violence or threats of violence

14.209 If the applicant says that he or she left accommodation due to harassment, on a scale that does not amount to violence or threats of violence that are likely to be carried out, the local housing authority should determine whether, in all the circumstances, including (if it chooses) taking into account general housing conditions in its district, the accommodation was reasonable for the applicant to continue to occupy.[324] Many of the cases that considered this point were decided before the enactment of the current statutory formula, 'reasonable for him to continue to occupy' in respect of violence or threats of violence that were likely to be carried out.[325] Those cases now only apply to a lower level of harassment: one that does not amount to violence or threats of violence that are likely to be carried out.

14.210 When considering non-violent harassment cases, local housing authorities are entitled to make inquiries into whether or not the applicant could have arranged to move away (eg by arranging a sale or through a transfer), and the extent to which it might be reasonable for the applicant to have continued to occupy the accommodation whilst that move was arranged.[326] Similarly, local housing authorities are entitled to consider whether it would have been reasonable for the applicant to have continued to occupy the accommodation with police protection rather than to have simply left.[327]

14.211 Once an applicant has raised the issues of violence, threats of violence and/or lower-level harassment, the local housing authority has a duty to make all necessary inquiries of all agencies that have been involved.[328] The burden rests on the local housing authority and not on the applicant.[329] The local housing authority must make a finding of fact as to whether or not it accepts the applicant's account of events.[330] If significant matters are to be held against the applicant, they should first be put to him or her for comment.[331] Having made that finding of fact, the local housing authority should then consider whether it is probable that continued occupation of the accommodation would have led to violence or threats of violence against the applicant. If it was probable, the accommodation was not reasonable to continue to occupy and the applicant cannot have become homeless intentionally. If violence or threats

---

324 English Code, para 8.34; Welsh Code, para 13.26.

325 HA 1996, ss 175(3), 177(1). See **11.83–11.92**.

326 *R v Hillingdon London Borough Council ex p H* (1988) 20 HLR 554, QBD, and *R v Newham London Borough Council ex p McIlroy* (1991) 23 HLR 570, QBD.

327 *R v Croydon London Borough Council ex p Toth* (1988) 20 HLR 576, CA.

328 *Hawa Abdilah Ali v Newham London Borough Council* (2000) November *Legal Action*, p 23, Bow County Court.

329 *R v Barnet London Borough Council ex p Babalola* (1995) 28 HLR 196, QBD.

330 *R v Newham London Borough Council ex p Bones* (1993) 25 HLR 357, QBD. See *Eren v Haringey London Borough Council* [2007] EWCA Civ 1796, (2007) June *Legal Action*, p 38, CA, and *Rodrigues v Barking & Dagenham London Borough Council* [2008] EWCA Civ 271, (2008) June *Legal Action*, p 33, CA, for examples of cases where the local housing authority did not believe the applicant.

331 *R v Brent London Borough Council ex p McManus* (1995) 25 HLR 643, QBD.

of violence were not probable, the local housing authority should consider whether, in all the circumstances, it was reasonable for the applicant to continue to occupy the accommodation. If the applicant's account is accepted, the local housing authority should give proper, adequate and intelligible reasons if it concludes that the accommodation was, in any event, reasonable for the applicant to continue to occupy.[332]

14.212 The question for the local housing authority is whether it was reasonable for the applicant *and* all other members of his or her household to continue to occupy the accommodation.[333] If the violence, threat of violence or harassment was directed against a member of the household, rather than the applicant, the accommodation will still not be reasonable for the applicant to continue to occupy.[334]

14.213 Where the applicant has actually been responsible for violence, threats of violence, harassment or nuisance behaviour and has lost his or her home as a result, he or she will generally be considered to have committed a deliberate act leading to the loss of accommodation.[335] An applicant who has not directly participated in nuisance behaviour carried out by another household member may have acquiesced if he or she failed to take any steps to prevent the behaviour.[336]

14.214 However, if the accommodation has been lost for any other reason, not related to the applicant's deliberate act, even though the applicant has also been guilty of violent behaviour, he or she will not have become homeless intentionally.[337] If the applicant's own behaviour has led to the harassment, that behaviour can constitute a deliberate act, and he or she could be found to have become homeless intentionally.[338]

Exclusion by friends or relatives

14.215 Where people are living with friends or relatives, but are not themselves the tenant or owner of the accommodation, they are usually bare licensees or tenants with no statutory protection.[339] Their host will be entitled to require them to leave, provided that the licence or tenancy is terminated upon reasonable notice, which might be as little as 24 hours.

---

[332] *R v Westminster City Council ex p Ermakov* [1996] 2 All ER 302, CA.

[333] See **11.21–11.34** and **11.75–11.128**.

[334] *R v Westminster City Council ex p Bishop* (1993) 25 HLR 459, CA.

[335] English Code, para 11.20(vi); Welsh Code, para 15.16(vi). See also *Devenport v Salford City Council* (1983) 8 HLR 54, CA, and *R v Swansea City Council ex p John* (1983) 9 HLR 56, QBD.

[336] See **14.93–14.97**.

[337] *R v Westminster City Council ex p Reid* (1994) 26 HLR 690, QBD; *R v Leeds City Council ex p Collier* (1998) June *Legal Action*, p 14, QBD; and *Demirtas v Islington London Borough Council* (2003) April *Legal Action*, p 27, Mayor's and City of London County Court.

[338] *R v Hammersmith and Fulham London Borough Council ex p P* (1990) 22 HLR 21, QBD.

[339] Such as that protection provided by Protection from Eviction Act 1977, s 3.

14.216 The local housing authority is entitled in these cases to consider the reasons for the host's decision to exclude. It is not unusual for guests in these circumstances to have been staying with their hosts in overcrowded accommodation and for the accommodation therefore not to have been reasonable for the guests to continue to occupy.[340]

14.217 It might, however, have been the applicant's own conduct that led to the decision to exclude him or her from accommodation that would otherwise have been reasonable for him or her to continue to occupy. In *Denton v Southwark London Borough Council*,[341] the Court of Appeal held that a 21-year-old had become homeless intentionally after his mother had excluded him because of his unreasonable conduct. Arden LJ said:

> 'it is essential when people live together, that they show appropriate respect for each other's needs and follow any requests that one reasonably makes to the other. This is not a case where the mother was laying down inappropriate rules.'[342]

14.218 The situation would be different if the mother's rules had been unreasonable.[343]

14.219 If accommodation has become unreasonable to continue to occupy as a result of the applicant's deliberate act or omission, the fact that it was unreasonable when the applicant lost the accommodation should be disregarded.[344]

14.220 Perpetrators of domestic violence who are excluded from, or lose, their family home as a result of that violence could be found to have become homeless intentionally.[345]

Unsatisfactory accommodation

14.221 When considering the accommodation from which the applicant became (or is about to become) homeless, a local housing authority should consider the property's physical conditions and any overcrowding when deciding whether the accommodation was reasonable for the applicant (and members of his or her household) to have continued to occupy.[346]

---

[340] See **14.125–14.143** for 'reasonable to continue to occupy' and **14.221–14.226** for unsatisfactory accommodation.

[341] [2007] EWCA Civ 623, [2008] HLR 11, CA.

[342] *Denton v Southwark London Borough Council* [2007] EWCA Civ 623, [2008] HLR 11, CA at [21], per Arden LJ.

[343] In *White v Southwark London Borough Council* [2008] EWCA Civ 792, (2008) October *Legal Action*, p 37, CA, the Court of Appeal said that actions of children as young as 13 might be 'deliberate acts' and could be considered, even if the applicant was currently an independent young person. See also *Hassan v Brent London Borough Council* [2008] EWCA Civ 1385, (2009) February *Legal Action*, p 32, CA.

[344] *Denton v Southwark London Borough Council* [2007] EWCA Civ 623, [2008] HLR 11, CA.

[345] English Code, para 11.20(v); Welsh Code, para 15.16(vi).

[346] English Code, para 8.34; Welsh Code, paras 13.27.

14.222 Local housing authorities are entitled to take into account (if they choose) the general housing conditions prevailing in their district when considering the question of reasonableness of continued occupation.[347] This is the case whether the relevant accommodation is in the local housing authority's own district, elsewhere in the UK, or outside the UK.[348] The local housing authority should not rely on assertions as to the general level of overcrowding or unfitness in its district, but should address itself to the particular degree of overcrowding or unfitness experienced by the applicant.[349]

14.223 Overcrowding which may render accommodation unreasonable for continued occupation is not restricted to statutory overcrowding.[350] If there are any medical needs arising as a result of the overcrowding or the physical condition of the property, they are relevant to the question of whether it would have been reasonable to continue to occupy.

14.224 Even when taking into account general housing conditions in its district, a local housing authority would normally be wrong to conclude that it would have been reasonable for a husband, wife and four children to have continued to occupy one room.[351] However, a local housing authority's decision that it would be reasonable, taking into account the shortage of accommodation in its district, for a separated husband to continue to occupy the same accommodation as his wife and her new boyfriend was not wrong in law.[352] In addition, where three children had satisfactory accommodation with their mother, and their father permitted them to leave that accommodation and live with him in his one-room accommodation (so that the landlord required them to leave), the father's actions in permitting his children to leave satisfactory accommodation so as to reside with him were held to be deliberate and he had become homeless intentionally.[353]

14.225 It is not appropriate for a local housing authority to conclude that the applicant has become homeless intentionally where the accommodation had

---

[347] HA 1996, s 177(2); *R v Brent London Borough Council ex p Bariise* (1999) 31 HLR 50, CA.

[348] *R v Tower Hamlets London Borough Council ex p Monaf* (1988) 20 HLR 529, CA; *R v Tower Hamlets London Borough Council ex p Ojo* (1991) 23 HLR 488, QBD; *R v Tower Hamlets London Borough Council ex p Bibi* (1991) 23 HLR 500, QBD; and *Osei v Southwark London Borough Council* [2007] EWCA Civ 787, [2008] HLR 15, CA.

[349] *Mohamoud v Greenwich London Borough Council* (2003) January *Legal Action*, p 23, Woolwich County Court.

[350] *R v Westminster City Council ex p Alouat* (1989) 21 HLR 477, QBD.

[351] *R v Hillingdon London Borough Council ex p Islam* [1983] 1 AC 688, HL, although the opposite conclusion was not wrong in law in *R v Tower Hamlets London Borough Council ex p Uddin* (1993) June *Legal Action*, p 15, QBD. See also *R v Harrow London Borough Council ex p Louis* (1997) June *Legal Action*, p 23, QBD; and *R v Kensington and Chelsea Royal London Borough Council ex p Silchenstedt* (1997) 29 HLR 728, QBD.

[352] *R v Kensington and Chelsea Royal London Borough Council ex p Moncada* (1996) 29 HLR 289, QBD.

[353] *Oxford City Council v Bull* [2011] EWCA Civ 609, [2011] HLR 35, [2012] 1 WLR 203, CA.

become overcrowded (and is no longer reasonable to continue to occupy) as a result of the applicant's deliberate acts in having more children, or otherwise expanding his or her family.[354]

14.226 Other issues arising on the question of whether accommodation might not have been reasonable to have continued to occupy include the adequacy of fire prevention and escape facilities to the property and/or whether the accommodation was fit for human habitation.[355]

Medical needs

14.227 An applicant's medical needs can render the accommodation the applicant has left unreasonable to have continued to occupy.

14.228 Where medical issues are raised in relation to whether or not accommodation was reasonable to continue to occupy, the local housing authority is under a duty to inquire into them.[356] The local housing authority must consider the medical needs of the applicant and of all members of his or her household, together with any other factors which may, cumulatively, have resulted in the accommodation having been unreasonable to continue to occupy.[357]

14.229 If the applicant leaves accommodation that he or she anticipates will in the future become unreasonable to continue to occupy (such as where a pregnant applicant has been told that the property will not be suitable for her baby), he or she may still have become homeless intentionally if, at the particular time when the applicant left, the property was then reasonable to continue to occupy at least for some further period.[358]

14.230 The location of the accommodation and its effect on the applicant's state of health, or the health of members of his or her household, can be relevant and can render accommodation not reasonable for continued occupation, although in making its assessment the local housing authority would be entitled to take into account general housing conditions in its own area.[359]

---

[354] *R v Eastleigh Borough Council ex p Beattie (No 1)* (1984) 10 HLR 134, QBD; and *R v Tower Hamlets London Borough Council ex p Hoque* (1993) Times 20 July, QBD.

[355] *R v Kensington and Chelsea Royal London Borough Council ex p Ben-El-Mabrouk* (1995) 27 HLR 564, CA; and *R v Haringey London Borough Council ex p Flynn* (1995) June *Legal Action*, p 21, QBD.

[356] *R v Wycombe District Council ex p Homes* (1990) 22 HLR 150, QBD. The Welsh Code advises that local housing authorities should also consider a person's vulnerability: paras 15.14–15.15.

[357] *R v Westminster City Council ex p Bishop* (1993) 25 HLR 459, CA.

[358] *R v Brent London Borough Council ex p Yusuf* (1997) 29 HLR 48, QBD; but see also *R v Medina District Council ex p Dee* (1992) 24 HLR 562, QBD.

[359] *R v Waltham Forest London Borough Council ex p Green* (1997) December *Legal Action*, p 15, QBD.

14.231 The question for the local housing authority is not whether an applicant's medical needs, or those of his or her family members, would be better served elsewhere, but whether their medical needs rendered the accommodation unreasonable to continue to occupy at the date when the applicant left it.[360]

Employment and other social or economic prospects

14.232 The opportunities for employment (and any other financial prospects) that were available to the applicant at the accommodation may need to be taken into account in determining whether it would have been reasonable for him or her to have continued to occupy it.[361] Relevant matters may include employment prospects, any available capital or savings, debts, the availability of social security benefits and any other means of support, as well as the extent to which the applicant was socially isolated and any affect on his or her health as a result.[362]

14.233 Frequently, cases on this point will relate either to applicants migrating to the UK from elsewhere in the world for economic reasons, or to UK residents deciding to emigrate and then returning to the UK, again for economic reasons. The question for the local housing authority is not whether it was reasonable for the applicant to seek to live in (or return to) the UK, but rather whether it would have been reasonable to have continued to occupy the accommodation overseas. Local housing authorities should avoid decisions containing such phrases as 'you brought your family to the UK without making reasonable provision for their accommodation', as they suggest that the wrong issue is being addressed. The true focus of inquiry is whether it would have been reasonable for the applicant and his or her household to have remained in their accommodation overseas. The issue for the local housing authority is not why the applicant has left a particular country to come to the UK, but why he or she has left the particular accommodation in that country.[363]

14.234 Where the applicant raises the issue of the lack of employment prospects if he or she had continued to occupy his or her previous

[360] *R v Wandsworth London Borough Council ex p Nimako-Boateng* (1984) 11 HLR 95, QBD.
[361] *R v Kensington and Chelsea Royal London Borough Council ex p Bayani* (1990) 22 HLR 406, CA.
[362] *R v Hammersmith and Fulham London Borough Council ex p Duro-Rama* (1983) 9 HLR 71, QBD; *R v Kensington and Chelsea Royal London Borough Council ex p Cunha* (1989) 21 HLR 16, QBD; *R v Camden London Borough Council ex p Aranda* (1997) 30 HLR 76, CA; *R v Camden London Borough Council ex p Cosmo* (1997) 30 HLR 817, QBD; *R v Wandsworth London Borough Council ex p Dodia* (1998) 30 HLR 562, QBD; *Kacar v Enfield London Borough Council* (2001) 33 HLR 5, CA; *Mohammed v Waltham Forest London Borough Council* (2002) October *Legal Action*, p 30, Bow County Court (permission to appeal refused by CA at [2002] EWCA Civ 1241, (2002) December *Legal Action*, p 22); and *Aw-Aden v Birmingham City Council* [2005] EWCA 1834, (2006) July *Legal Action*, p 29, CA.
[363] *R v Westminster City Council ex p Guilarte* (1994) June *Legal Action*, p 13, QBD.

accommodation, the local housing authority is bound to make inquiries into that issue to see whether it would in fact have been reasonable for the applicant to have remained in occupation.[364]

14.235 If the applicant has lost tied accommodation as a result of his or her employment having come to an end, the local housing authority is entitled to consider whether his or her deliberate act or omission (in resigning or on being dismissed for misconduct) led to the loss of employment and hence the loss of accommodation.[365] Even if it finds such a deliberate act or omission, it must of course go on to consider whether the accommodation was available to the applicant and reasonable for him or her to have continued to occupy.

Ex-prisoners

14.236 The courts have held that the commission of a criminal offence, where the reasonably likely result is that the applicant will be sent to prison, can constitute a deliberate act as a consequence of which the applicant's accommodation may be lost. As a result, local housing authorities are entitled to find that a prisoner who loses his or her accommodation during the period of imprisonment because of inability to keep up payments for an unoccupied home has become homeless intentionally.[366] This conclusion was held not be wrong in law even in the case of a prisoner who made arrangements with his sister that she would pay the rent and a contribution to the arrears (required under a suspended possession order) during his sentence, when she then failed to honour the agreement.[367]

14.237 The Welsh Code advises that applicants who have just served a prison sentence and who find themselves homeless on release should not be considered to have become homeless intentionally unless the offences were themselves breaches of their previous tenancy agreements and led to the loss of the accommodation.[368]

---

[364] *Bowen v Lambeth London Borough Council* (1999) December *Legal Action*, p 22, Lambeth County Court; and *R v Westminster City Council ex p Augustin* (1993) 25 HLR 281, CA.

[365] English Code, para 11.20(vii); Welsh Code, para 15.16(vii). See also *R v Kyle and Carrick District Council ex p Speck* 1993 GWD 1566, OH.

[366] *R v Hounslow London Borough Council ex p R* (1997) 29 HLR 939, QBD; and *Minchin v Sheffield City Council* (2000) Times, 26 April, CA. In *Minchin v Sheffield City Council*, the fact that the applicant had moved house after the commission of offences was irrelevant to her subsequently being found to have become homeless intentionally. In *Quaid v Westminster City Council* (2008) February *Legal Action*, p 41, Central London County Court, the applicant had not become homeless intentionally because he had committed offences when street homeless. It was not reasonably likely at the time that he had committed the offences that he would lose accommodation acquired after the offences had been committed. See also English Code, para 11.14.

[367] *Stewart v Lambeth London Borough Council* [2002] EWCA Civ 753, [2002] 34 HLR 40, CA.

[368] Welsh Code, para 15.23.

Accommodation withdrawn by a local housing authority on completion of its homeless duty

14.238 Accommodation provided by the local housing authority while it is making inquiries,[369] or under the various short-term accommodation duties[370] or powers,[371] is unlikely to be settled accommodation and so unlikely to be relevant to any question of having become homeless intentionally.

14.239 However, where an applicant loses accommodation provided under the main housing duty,[372] the question arises whether that accommodation was lost as a result of the deliberate act or omission of the applicant.[373]

14.240 In the landmark case of *R v Brent London Borough Council ex p Awua*,[374] the House of Lords held that there was no requirement that the accommodation lost by a person who had become homeless intentionally should have been settled accommodation. As a result, Ms Awua had become homeless intentionally because she had lost her accommodation temporarily provided to her under the main housing duty as a result of her having refused an offer of accommodation.[375]

---

[369] HA 1996, s 188(1). See **16.12–16.28**.

[370] HA 1996, s 190(2)(a) (see **17.182–17.189**) and s 200(1) (see **15.157–15.160**).

[371] HA 1996, s 188(3) (see **16.36–16.48**), s 190(3) (see **17.215–17.222**), s 200(5) (see **16.56–16.63**) and s 204(4) (see **16.49–16.55**).

[372] HA 1996, s 193. See **17.23–17.168** for the main housing duty and **17.42–17.168** for the ending of that duty.

[373] HA 1996, s 193(9) permits the applicant to make a fresh application to the local housing authority. For circumstances in which that application will be accepted, see **9.66–9.85** and **17.169–17.170**. Acceptance of the application, however, does not prevent a local housing authority from determining that the applicant has become homeless intentionally. For such a scenario, see *R (Dragic) v Wandsworth London Borough Council* [2012] EWHC 1241 (Admin), (2012) July *Legal Action*, p 42, Admin Ct.

[374] [1996] AC 55, (1995) 27 HLR 453, HL.

[375] See *Amanuel v Southwark London Borough Council* [2007] EWCA Civ 854, (2007) September *Legal Action*, p 18, CA; and *Ali v Haringey London Borough Council* [2008] EWCA Civ 132, (2008) April *Legal Action*, p 34, CA. Care must be taken to identify the reason for the loss of the accommodation: see *Bolah v Croydon London Borough Council* (2008) February *Legal Action*, p 40, Lambeth County Court. In *Keita v Southwark London Borough Council* [2008] EWCA Civ 963, (2008) October *Legal Action*, p 38, CA, the accommodation lost had not been provided under homelessness duties, but was terminated by the landlord charity after the applicant had refused an offer of accommodation. Where young people aged 16 or 17 years old refuse offers of accommodation provided under Children Act 1989, s 20 duties, statutory government guidance advises that they should not be considered to have become homeless intentionally when accommodation is subsequently withdrawn as a result of that refusal: (*Provision of Accommodation for 16 and 17 year old young people who may be homeless and/or require accommodation*, CLG and Department for Children, Schools and Families, April 2010), paras 4.10–4.11; *Provision of Accommodation for 16 and 17 year old young people who may be homeless*, Welsh Assembly Government Circular 025/2010, September 2010, paras 4.7–4.8).

Chapter 15

REFERRAL BETWEEN LOCAL HOUSING AUTHORITIES

INTRODUCTION

15.1 The referral provisions in the Housing Act 1996 (HA 1996), Part 7 ensure that responsibility for accommodating those who are homeless is spread fairly between local housing authorities. Without a coherent set of rules governing which local housing authority owes a housing duty, homeless applicants would end up in the same position as their predecessors under the Poor Laws, when:

> '... each parish was responsible for the relief of those who were poor and unable to work. When a poor man moved from one parish to another, the question arose: which parish was responsible? The disputes, Blackstone tells us, "created an infinity of expensive lawsuits between contending neighbourhoods, concerning those settlements and removals".'[1]

15.2 In order to avoid intractable disputes (including 'expensive lawsuits'), HA 1996, Part 7 lays out the conditions under which local housing authorities can transfer responsibility for applicants by referring them to other local housing authorities. The conditions *only* apply to those applicants whom the first-approached local housing authority has already decided are homeless, are eligible for assistance, have a priority need and have not become homeless intentionally. Unless those applicants were referred, the main HA 1996, s 193(2) duty would be owed to them.[2] The referral provisions do not apply to applicants who have been found to be threatened with homelessness, or not to have a priority need, or to have become homeless intentionally.

15.3 In very broad terms, there are three sets of circumstances in which a local housing authority can refer a homeless applicant to another local housing authority.[3] These are:

(1)   where the applicant and his or her household have no connection with the area to which application for homelessness assistance has been made but do have a connection with another area to which they can safely be returned;[4] or

(2)   where an applicant whose application for homelessness assistance was made to a local housing authority in England[5] on or after 9 November

---

[1]   *R v Slough Borough Council ex p Ealing London Borough Council* [1981] QB 801, CA at 808, per Lord Denning.

[2]   HA 1996, s 198(1).

[3]   There are special additional rules permitting local housing authorities to refer certain asylum-seekers to another local housing authority has agreed to accept the referral. These rules only apply to applicants whose applications for homelessness assistance were made on or before 3 April 2000. For a discussion of those rules see the first or second editions of this book (Jan Luba QC and Liz Davies, 1st edn, 2006; 2nd edn, 2010).

[4]   HA 1996, s 198(2) and (2A). See **15.42–15.115**.

[5]   At the date of writing, the amendments to HA 1996 made by the Localism Act 2011, ss 148–149 had not been brought into effect in Wales.

2012 had accepted a private rented sector offer[6] from that local housing authority which was located in the district of another local housing authority, and the applicant has made another application for homelessness assistance to the other local housing authority in England within two years of the date of acceptance;[7] or

(3)	where the applicant has been recently placed in the local housing authority's area by another local housing authority under its homelessness functions, but has become homeless again.[8]

15.4	The second condition only applies to referrals between local housing authorities in England, because the amendments to HA 1996 made by Localism Act 2011, ss 148–149 had not, at the date of writing, been brought into effect in Wales.[9] It is the authors' view that the third condition now only applies to referral between local housing authorities in England and, possibly, from local housing authorities in England to local housing authorities in Wales.[10] However, it should be noted that the Welsh Code of Guidance[11] does contain guidance that the third condition applies to referrals between local housing authorities in Wales, and between local housing authorities in both England and in Wales.[12]

---

[6]	HA 1996, s 193(7AA)–(7AC) as amended by LA 2011, s 148(5)–(7). Private rented sector offers can be made to applicants whose applications for homelessness assistance were made to a local housing authority in England on or after 9 November 2012. See **17.109–17.131**. At the date of writing, the amendments to HA 1996 made by LA 2011, ss 148–149 had not been brought into effect in Wales.

[7]	HA 1996, s 198(2ZA) and (2A), amended by LA 149(6)–(8), and applicable to applicants whose applications for homelessness assistance were made to a local housing authority in England on or after 9 November 2012. At the date of writing, the amendments to HA 1996 made by LA 2011, ss 148–149 had not been brought into effect in Wales. See **15.116–15.131**.

[8]	HA 1996, s 198(4). See **15.132–15.145**.

[9]	The second condition will apply to referrals between local housing authorities in England, and between local housing authorities in England or in Wales, when the amendments to HA 1996 made by LA 2011, ss 148–149 are brought into effect in Wales.

[10]	This is because the third condition only applies where the applicant was placed by one local housing authority in the district of the second local housing authority within a 'prescribed period'. The 'prescribed period' was first contained in the Homelessness (England) Regulations 2000, SI 2000/701, reg 6, which was applied to Wales by the Homelessness (Wales) Regulations 2000, SI 2000/1079, reg 2. The Homelessness (Wales) Regulations 2000, SI 2000/1079, were revoked in their entirety from 9 October 2006 by the Homelessness (Wales) Regulations 2006, SI 2006/2646 (W 227), reg 6. The Homelessness (Wales) Regulations 2006, SI 2006/2646 (W 227) do not contain a prescribed period. In the absence of any prescribed period, local housing authorities in Wales cannot operate HA 1996, s 198(4), except for applications for homelessness assistance made before 9 October 2006. The prescribed period to be operated by local housing authorities in England is at reg 3 of the Allocation of Housing and Homelessness (Miscellaneous Provisions) (England) Regulations 2006 (SI 2006/2527), at Appendix 2 of this book. See **15.133**.

[11]	*Code of Guidance for Local Authorities: Allocation of Accommodation and Homelessness 2012* (Welsh Government, August 2012) (the Welsh Code): see CD-Rom.

[12]	Welsh Code, paras 20.3–20.5, relying on the prescribed period at Homelessness (Wales) Regulations 2000, SI 2000/1079, reg 2, even though that regulation has been revoked.

15.5 If the statutory conditions are satisfied, responsibility for a homeless applicant can be transferred from one local housing authority to another.

15.6 Several judges have remarked on the parallels with the Poor Laws:

'... it is all very reminiscent of the operation of the Poor Law of the nineteenth century and before, all dressed up in modern language.'[13]

'Given the pressures on many housing authorities, the natural tendency would be to try to export the homeless whenever possible. Moving the needy beyond the parish boundary has a long history.'[14]

15.7 Local housing authorities are not required to use these provisions. They are free to accept all those who apply to them. So, although they have power to make inquiries into an applicant's connection with another district if they wish, there is no obligation upon them to do so.[15]

15.8 However, if local housing authorities do choose to make those inquiries, the tests that they must apply to determine whether a referral can be made are strictly defined at HA 1996, s 198(2), or (2ZA), and (2A), or (4). If the conditions are not met, no referral to another local housing authority can be made and the first-approached local housing authority must perform its HA 1996, s 193(2) duty towards the applicant. If the local housing authority decides that the conditions are met, it retains a discretion, even at that stage, as to whether or not to make a referral. There is no obligation to do so.

15.9 Accordingly, there are potentially three decisions for a local housing authority to make in relation to each applicant:

(1)   whether or not to make inquiries into the question of any local connection at all; if so,

(2)   whether the conditions for referral as defined at either HA 1996, s 198(2), or (2ZA), and (2A), or (4) are met; and, if so,

(3)   whether or not to notify another local housing authority of its opinion that the conditions are met.

15.10 Given that the conditions for referral only apply to those applicants who would otherwise be owed a main housing duty[16] by the local housing authority making the referral, the applicants affected have a right to be

---

[13]   *R v Hammersmith and Fulham London Borough Council ex p O'Brien* (1985) 17 HLR 471, QBD at 474, per Glidewell J.

[14]   *R v Slough Borough Council ex p Khan* (1996) 27 HLR 492, QBD at 496, per Toulson J (then Mr Roger Toulson QC).

[15]   HA 1996, s 184(2). *Homelessness Code of Guidance for Local Authorities* (Communities and Local Government, Department for Education and Skills, Department of Health, July 2006) (the English Code), paras 18.2–18.5, at Appendix 2 of this book. Welsh Code, para 20.1.

[16]   HA 1996, s 193(2). See **17.23–17.168**.

accommodated throughout the decision-making process. The duty to accommodate falls first on the first-approached local housing authority, and then on the local housing authority to which the referral is made.[17]

15.11 Applicants are most likely to seek assistance from the local housing authority for the district in which they want to live and so would be expected to dispute a decision to refer them to another local housing authority. It is therefore no surprise that applicants are entitled to request reviews of several of the decisions involved in the referral process. They may request reviews of any decision that they should be referred to another local housing authority, any decision that the conditions for referral are made out, and any decision as to the duties owed to them as a result.[18] Obviously, if any of those review decisions contain an error of law, the applicants may appeal to the county court.[19]

15.12 In order to avoid homeless applicants being caught in 'a game of battledore and shuttlecock – with the homeless the shuttlecock and the housing authorities wielding the battledore',[20] local housing authorities are obliged to accept a referral if the conditions for referral are met. If the local housing authority, which has been asked to accept a referral, disputes whether the conditions are met, a referee can be appointed. Those arrangements are described in detail in the English Code, Annex 18.[21] The local housing authorities involved are then bound by the referee's decision. However, the applicant still has the right to request a review of the referee's decision (and subsequently to appeal to the county court on a point of law).[22]

15.13 There are special additional rules permitting local housing authorities to refer certain asylum-seekers (those who are eligible for homelessness assistance and to whom a HA 1996, s 193(2) main housing duty would otherwise be owed) to another local housing authority that has agreed to accept the referral.[23] These rules only apply to applicants whose applications for homelessness assistance were made on or before 3 April 2000. There is a discussion of those rules in previous editions of this book.[24]

15.14 There are also additional rules concerning former asylum-seekers who occupied accommodation provided by the United Kingdom Border Agency (UKBA, formerly National Asylum Support Service or NASS) in Scotland and subsequently made applications for homelessness assistance to local housing authorities in England or in Wales. In those cases, local housing authorities in

---

[17] HA 1996, s 200. See **15.157–15.160**.
[18] HA 1996, s 202(1)(c), (d) and (e). See **19.16–19.26**.
[19] HA 1996, s 204(1).
[20] *R v Slough Borough Council ex p Ealing London Borough Council* [1981] QB 801, CA at 808, per Lord Denning.
[21] The Local Authorities' Agreement is not reproduced in the Welsh Code, but reference is made to it at para 20.8 of the Welsh Code.
[22] HA 1996, s 202(1)(d). See **15.174–15.191** and **19.23–19.25**.
[23] HA 1996, s 198(4A) and (4B).
[24] Jan Luba QC and Liz Davies, 1st edn, 2006; 2nd edn, 2010.

England or in Wales are not subject to the main housing duty,[25] but instead may provide accommodation for a limited period and provide advice and assistance to help the applicant apply to a local authority in Scotland, or make other arrangements for accommodation.[26] These rules are discussed towards the end of this Chapter.[27]

15.15 Throughout this Chapter, we use the statutory terms of 'notifying local housing authority' and 'notified local housing authority' to indicate respectively the local housing authority first receiving the application for homelessness assistance and subsequently making the referral (the 'notifying local housing authority'), and the local housing authority receiving the referral (the 'notified local housing authority').

15.16 The Chapter concludes with a review of the circumstances in which applicants may be accommodated outside the district in which they sought to be housed but without the local housing authority invoking any referral procedure.

THE RIGHT TO MAKE AN APPLICATION FOR HOMELESSNESS ASSISTANCE TO ANY LOCAL HOUSING AUTHORITY

15.17 A homeless person is free to apply to any local housing authority in England, Wales or Scotland (or to the Housing Executive in Northern Ireland) for assistance with accommodation. There is no prior condition that the applicant must apply to the local housing authority for any particular district. There is no filter that prevents an applicant who has no connection with a particular local housing authority from applying to that local housing authority. Once the application for homelessness assistance has been made, and there is reason to believe that the applicant may be homeless or threatened with homelessness, the local housing authority must conduct inquiries and make its decision as to whether or not the applicant is eligible and, if so, whether a duty and (if so) what duty, is owed to the applicant under HA 1996, Part 7.[28] Any local housing authority that tells an applicant that he or she has applied to the wrong local housing authority, that he or she cannot apply to that particular local housing authority, or that no inquiries will be made because he or she does not appear to have a connection with its district, is acting unlawfully.[29]

---

[25] HA 1996, s 193(2). See Chapter 17, at **17.23–17.168**.
[26] Asylum and Immigration (Treatment of Claimants etc) Act 2004, s 11(2) and (3) in force from 4 January 2005. See **15.192–15.201**.
[27] See **15.192–15.201**.
[28] HA 1996, s 184(1) and (3).
[29] *R v Slough Borough Council ex p Ealing London Borough Council* [1981] QB 801, CA; and *R v Tower Hamlets London Borough Council ex p Camden London Borough Council* (1988) 21 HLR 197, QBD.

15.18 Because well-informed applicants may shop around between different local housing authorities,[30] it must be emphasised that the conditions for referral under the referral provisions only apply to applicants to whom the notifying local housing authority would otherwise owe a main housing duty[31] (ie those who are homeless, eligible for assistance, have a priority need, and did not become homeless intentionally). No other applicants can be referred. Applicants who:

- are threatened with homelessness; or

- do not have a priority need; or

- have become homeless intentionally,

remain the responsibility of the local housing authority to which they have applied, and the limited duties owed to those applicants must be performed by that local housing authority. Put another way, the duties to provide:

- interim accommodation pending inquiries,[32]

- help for those who became homeless intentionally,[33]

- assistance to those threatened with homelessness,[34]

- protection for an applicant's property,[35] and

- any other assistance under HA 1996, Part 7 (except the main housing duty),

cannot be transferred using the referral provisions.[36]

DISCRETIONARY POWER TO MAKE INQUIRIES INTO THE CONDITIONS FOR REFERRAL

Introduction

15.19 As soon as a local housing authority has 'reason to believe' that an applicant for assistance under HA 1996, Part 7 may be homeless or threatened with homelessness, it must make inquiries to satisfy itself whether the applicant

---

[30] Where an applicant for homelessness assistance has made an earlier, or a simultaneous, application to a different local housing authority, see **9.46–9.52**.
[31] HA 1996, s 193(2), see**17.23–17.168**.
[32] HA 1996, s 188(1). See **16.12–16.28**.
[33] HA 1996, s 190. See **17.182–17.189** and **17.201–17.214**.
[34] HA 1996, s 195. See **17.190–17.200** and **17.201–17.214**.
[35] HA 1996, s 211. See **17.233–17.254**.
[36] English Code, para 18.3; Welsh Code, para 20.1.

is eligible and whether any duty, and if so what duty, is owed to the applicant.[37] It *may* also make inquiries into whether the applicant has a 'local connection' with the district of any other local housing authority in England, Wales or Scotland (which is one of the requirements enabling a referral to be made).[38] However, there is no obligation to make those latter inquiries. Even if the applicant self-evidently has no connection with the local housing authority to which he or she has applied, and has an obvious connection with another local housing authority, the first local housing authority can choose not to make inquiries into that connection.

15.20 Applicants cannot insist that the local housing authority to which they apply makes inquiries into their local connection. If the local housing authority decides not to make those inquiries, the applicant has no right to request a review of that decision, as it is not a decision that falls within one of the categories of decisions capable of review.[39] Any legal challenge could only be brought by judicial review.[40] Although many local housing authorities, anxious to reduce pressure on their resources, will want to consider the possibility of referring an applicant to another local housing authority, local housing authorities are also entitled to assume that an applicant has applied to the local housing authority in whose district he or she would want to be housed.[41]

15.21 If an applicant does find that he or she has made an application for homelessness assistance to the wrong local housing authority, and is then disappointed that it decides not to make inquiries into his or her local connection elsewhere, there are three alternative courses of action available.

15.22 First, he or she could withdraw the first application and apply afresh to the local housing authority in whose district he or she wants to live.[42] That would only be possible before the first local housing authority had notified the applicant of its decision on the first application.[43]

15.23 Second, the applicant could seek to persuade the first local housing authority that he or she should be provided with accommodation in the district of the local housing authority where he or she wishes to live. The first local housing authority could facilitate that by arranging for a private rented sector

[37] HA 1996, s 184(1). See **9.57–9.65, 10.35–10.37** and **10.66–10.74**.
[38] HA 1996, s 184(2). See **10.2** and **10.13**.
[39] HA 1996, s 202(1); see *Hackney London Borough Council v Sareen* [2003] EWCA Civ 351, [2003] HLR 54, CA.
[40] See **19.224–19.250**.
[41] *Hackney London Borough Council v Sareen* [2003] EWCA Civ 351, [2003] HLR 54, CA at [42], per Auld LJ.
[42] English Code, para 6.26; Welsh Code, para 12.50. See **9.14–9.22**.
[43] Otherwise the applicant runs the risk of refusing, or becoming homeless intentionally following an offer of suitable HA 1996, s 193 accommodation, or, in the case of an applicant whose application for homelessness assistance was made to a local housing authority in England on or after 9 November 2012, of a suitable private rented sector offer (HA 1996, s 193(7AA) as amended by LA 2011, s 148(5)), and a subsequent finding that the duty towards him or her has ended. See **17.55–17.66** and **17.119–17.131** [England] and **17.136–17.137** [Wales].

offer in that district;[44] by nominating the applicant to the second local housing authority under its housing allocation scheme;[45] or by nomination to a private registered provider of social housing in England or registered social landlord in Wales operating in that district.[46]

15.24 Third, the applicant could (if still homeless or threatened with homelessness) promptly apply direct to the local housing authority in whose district he or she wishes to live, while leaving the first application pending.

What inquiries can the local housing authority make?

15.25 If the local housing authority does choose to make inquiries into the applicant's local connection, the results of those inquiries will only become relevant once the local housing authority has determined what duty, if any, it owes the applicant and, even then, only if the decision it has made is that it would otherwise owe the main housing duty under HA 1996, s 193(2).

15.26 Given that the conditions for referral only apply to those applicants to whom the local housing authority would owe a main housing duty, it may make practical sense for a local housing authority not to make inquiries into any local connection until it has completed the remainder of its inquiries and made decisions upon them. If an applicant appears to have become homeless intentionally or not to have a priority need, there is no point devoting additional resources to making wasteful inquiries into the question of local connection.[47]

15.27 The local housing authority may only make inquiries into whether the applicant has a local connection with the district of any other local housing authority in England, Wales or Scotland.[48] A local connection with a local

[44] 'Private rented sector offer', as defined at HA 1996, s 193(7AA) as amended by LA 2011, s 148(5), can only be made to an applicant whose application for homelessness assistance was made to a local housing authority in England on or after 9 November 2012, see **17.109–17.131**. At the date of writing, the amendments to HA 1996 made by LA 2011, ss 148–149 had not been brought into effect in Wales. A local housing authority in Wales could, nevertheless, arrange for a private landlord to offer the applicant an assured shorthold tenancy in another local housing authority's district under HA 1996 s 193(2) (see **17.136–17.137**) or under s 193(7B) ('qualifying offer of an assured shorthold tenancy') which an applicant is free to accept or refuse, see **17.147–17.154**.

[45] HA 1996, s 159(2)(b). See *R (W) v Sheffield City Council* [2005] EWHC 720 (Admin), where Mr W, who had been referred by Westminster to Sheffield, sought to persuade Sheffield that its duty to provide suitable accommodation for him could only be performed by arranging for accommodation in Westminster. See also para 6.4 of the Local Authorities' Agreement at Annex 18 of the English Code, which recommends that local housing authorities should consider their ability to nominate in order to avoid 'causing undue disruption'. See also **15.234–15.239**.

[46] HA 1996, s 159(2)(c); See Chapter 6 of this book.

[47] English Code, paras 6.14 and 18.4; Welsh Code, paras 12.11 and 20.1.

[48] HA 1996, s 184(2).

housing authority elsewhere is not relevant.[49] In particular, a connection with other parts of the UK (eg Northern Ireland)[50] would not trigger the referral provisions in HA 1996, s 198.

15.28 Curiously, HA 1996, Part 7 limits the subject matter of the discretionary inquiries to whether the applicant himself or herself has a connection elsewhere.[51] A local housing authority which confined its inquiries only to that question would find it impossible to determine whether the conditions for referral to another local housing authority were in fact satisfied or not. As the remainder of this Chapter indicates, the referral conditions are detailed and complex and go well beyond the question of whether the applicant personally has a local connection with the district of another local housing authority. The local housing authority which receives an application for homelessness assistance, and wishes to pursue the possibility of referring the main housing duty, will want to start by inquiring into whether the applicant has a real connection with its district or with the district of any local housing authority.[52] It will also need to know whether:

(1)   the applicant or any member of his or her household has a local connection with its own area;[53] and whether

(2)   any other member of the applicant's household has a local connection with another local housing authority's area;[54] and whether

(3)   in the case of an application for homelessness assistance made to a local housing authority in England on or after 9 November 2012,[55] the applicant had been placed in its area as a result of having accepted a private rented sector offer[56] from another local housing authority and subsequently made his or her application for homelessness assistance within two years of the date of acceptance;[57] and whether

---

[49]   *R v Westminster City Council ex p Esmail* (1989) June *Legal Action*, p 25, QBD.
[50]   See Box 1 at **12.66**. See also **15.213–15.222**.
[51]   HA 1996, s 184(2).
[52]   *X v Ealing London Borough Council* (2010) November *Legal Action*, p 19, Brentford County Court. See *R v Eastleigh Borough Council ex p Betts* [1983] 2 AC 613, HL, and 15.51 for 'real connection'.
[53]   HA 1996, s 198(2)(a).
[54]   HA 1996, s 198(2)(b).
[55]   At the date of writing, the amendments to HA 1996 made by LA 2011, ss 148–149 had not been brought into effect in Wales.
[56]   HA 1996, s 193(7AA) as amended by LA 2011, s 148(5), and made to applicants whose applications for homelessness assistance were made to a local housing authority in England on or after 9 November 2012, see **17.109–17.131**. At the date of writing, the amendments to HA 1996 made by LA 2011, ss 148–149 had not been brought into effect in Wales.
[57]   HA 1998, s 198(2ZA) inserted by LA 2011, s 149(6). See **15.121–15.131**. At the date of writing, the amendment to HA 1996 made by LA 2011, ss 148–149 had not been brought into effect in Wales.

(4)   the applicant (or any member of his or her household) would be at risk of actual or threatened violence if returned to another area;[58] and whether

(5)   (in the case of an application for homelessness assistance made to a local housing authority in England) the applicant had been placed in its area by another local housing authority acting under the homelessness provisions of HA 1996, Part 7.[59]

15.29   Self-evidently, inquiries into those matters would go well beyond the scope of those expressly mentioned in HA 1996, s 184(2), and so the local housing authority will rely entirely upon the applicant and others voluntarily responding to its inquiries.

15.30   Accordingly, where the local housing authority has received an application for homelessness assistance, has opted to make inquiries into the matter and has discovered that the applicant has a local connection elsewhere, it cannot simply assume that all the other ingredients of the conditions for a referral are made out. It must go on to explore whether the other conditions for referral are satisfied.[60]

THE CONDITIONS FOR REFERRAL

Introduction

15.31   The preliminary condition for *any* referral is that the local housing authority in receipt of the application for homelessness assistance is satisfied that it would itself owe the applicant the main housing duty.[61]

15.32   Beyond that, the detailed conditions for referral are set out in HA 1996, s 198. There are three separate and alternative tranches of conditions for referral contained in the statute. The second and third sets of conditions for referral apply only to referrals between local housing authorities in England.[62] The third set of conditions may possibly, apply to referrals by local housing authorities in England to local housing authorities in Wales.

---

[58]   HA 1996, s 198(2)(c).

[59]   HA 1996, s 198(4). It is the authors' view that this last condition does not apply to applications for homelessness assistance made to local housing authorities in Wales, but the Welsh Code, paras 20.3–20.5 takes a different view and advises that it does apply. See fn 10 and **15.132–15.145**.

[60]   *R v Slough Borough Council ex p Khan* (1995) 27 HLR 492, QBD; and *R v Greenwich London Borough Council ex p Patterson* (1994) 26 HLR 159, CA.

[61]   HA 1996, ss 193(1) and 198(1).

[62]   The second set of conditions is inserted into HA 1996 by LA 2011, s 149. At the date of writing, the amendments to HA 1996 made by LA 2011, ss 148–149 had not been brought into effect in Wales. It is the authors' view that the third set of conditions does not apply to applications for homelessness assistance made to local housing authorities in Wales (see fn 10 and 15.132–15.145). However, the Welsh Code, paras 20.3–20.5, advises that this set of conditions does apply.

15.33 The *first* set of 'conditions for referral' is found in HA 1996, s 198(2) and (2A). These are that:

(1) neither the applicant nor any person who might reasonably be expected to reside with the applicant has a local connection with the district of the local housing authority to which the application for homelessness assistance was made; and

(2) either the applicant or a person who might reasonably be expected to reside with the applicant has a local connection with the district of another local housing authority in England, Wales or Scotland; and

(3) neither the applicant nor any person who might reasonably be expected to reside with the applicant will run the risk of domestic violence in that other district; and

(4) neither the applicant nor any person who might reasonably be expected to reside with the applicant has suffered violence in the district of that other local housing authority; or,

(5) if violence has been suffered, it is not probable that a return to that district will lead to further violence of a similar kind against that person.[63]

15.34 This set of conditions requires additional consideration of the concept of 'local connection'.[64]

15.35 The *second* set of 'conditions for referral' is to be found in HA 1996, s 198(2ZA)[65] and (2A).[66] The conditions apply to applicants who made applications for homelessness assistance to a local housing authority in England on or after 9 November 2012, who had accepted a private rented sector offer[67] from that local housing authority located in the district of another local housing authority in England and who subsequently make a new application for homelessness assistance to the other local housing authority within two years of the date of acceptance[68] of the private rented sector offer. The conditions are that:

---

63 HA 1996, s 198(2A).
64 See **15.42–15.115**.
65 Inserted by LA 2011, s 149(6) and applicable to applicants whose applications for homelessness assistance were made on or after 9 November 2012 to a local housing authority in England. At the date of writing, the amendments to HA 1996 made by LA 2011, ss 148–149 had not been brought into effect in Wales. See **15.116–15.131**.
66 Amended by LA 2011, s 149(7) and applicable to applicants whose applications for homelessness assistance were made on or after 9 November 2012 to a local housing authority in England. At the date of writing, the amendments to HA 1996 made by LA 2011, ss 148–149 had not been brought into effect in Wales. See **15.116–15.131**.
67 HA 1996, s 193(7AA)–(7AC) as amended by LA 2011, s 148(5)–(7) and applicable to applicants whose applications for homelessness assistance were made on or after 9 November

(1)   the applicant accepted a private rented sector offer made by one local housing authority (authority B) in the district of another local housing authority (authority A); and

(2)   within two years of the date of acceptance, the applicant makes an application for homelessness assistance to authority A; and

(3)   neither the applicant nor any person who might reasonably be expected to reside with the applicant will run the risk of domestic violence in the district of authority B; and

(4)   neither the applicant nor any person who might reasonably be expected to reside with him or her has suffered violence in the district of authority B; or

(5)   if violence has been suffered, it is not probable that a return to the district of authority B will lead to further violence of a similar kind against that person.[69]

15.36   Each of these sets of conditions requires additional consideration of the concepts of 'violence'[70] and 'domestic violence'.[71] There must also be a determination by the local housing authority as to those persons with whom the applicant 'might reasonably be expected to reside' – a phrase that is not confined to those with whom the applicant is, or has been, living immediately prior to the application for homelessness assistance.[72]

15.37   The *third* set of 'conditions for referral' is to be found in HA 1996, s 198(4). It now applies only to local housing authorities in England.[73]

[   ] 2012 to a local housing authority in England. At the date of writing, the amendments to HA 1996 made by LA 2011, ss 148–149 had not been brought into effect in Wales. See **17.109–17.118**.

[68]   The new application for homelessness assistance will fall within the special provisions at HA 1996 s 195A inserted by LA 2011, s 149(4) and applicable to applicable to applicants whose applications for homelessness assistance were made on or after 9 November 2012 to a local housing authority in England. At the date of writing, the amendments to HA 1996 made by LA 2011, ss 148–149 had not been brought into effect in Wales. See **9.89–9.95**.

[69]   HA 1996, s 198(2ZA) and (2A) as amended by LA 2011, s 149(6) and (7) and applicable to applicants whose applications for homelessness assistance were made on or after 9 November 2012 to a local housing authority in England. At the date of writing, the amendments to HA 1996 made by LA 2011, ss 148–149 had not been brought into effect in Wales. See **15.116–15.131**.

[70]   Defined at HA 1996, s 198(3). See **15.98–15.111**.

[71]   Defined at HA 1996, s 198(3). See **15.102–15.104**.

[72]   See HA 1996, s 176 and see **11.23–11.34**.

[73]   Although the Welsh Code advises that it also applies to referrals between local housing authorities in Wales, and between local housing authorities in England or Wales, paras 20.3–20.5. See fn 10 for the authors' view as to why it does not apply to applications made to local housing authorities in Wales.

15.38 The conditions are that:

(1) the applicant was placed in accommodation in the district of the local housing authority to which he or she has applied (authority A) by another local housing authority (authority B); and

(2) that placement was made in pursuance of authority B's functions under HA 1996, Part 7; and

(3) the application for homelessness assistance to authority A is made within a prescribed period.

15.39 For local housing authorities in England, the prescribed period is the total of five years plus the period between the date of the applicant's application for homelessness assistance to authority A and the date when the applicant was placed in authority B.[74]

15.40 If this third set of conditions is met, the applicant can be referred by authority A to authority B. There is no additional requirement on authority A to consider whether the applicant ever had a local connection with authority B or has, more recently, acquired a local connection with its district. Nor is there any requirement to consider whether the applicant or any member of his or her household would be subject to domestic or other violence in the district of authority B.

15.41 Each set of conditions for referral is now separately considered.

The first set of conditions for referral – 'local connection'

Overview

15.42 The lynchpin of the first set of referral conditions is the concept of 'local connection'. That phrase is not itself defined by HA 1996, Part 7. The legislation simply limits the relevant methods by which a local connection can be acquired to one or more of the circumstances specified in HA 1996, s 199. The circumstances are that:

(1) the person is, or was in the past, normally resident in a district and his or her residence there is, or was, of his or her own choice;[75] or

(2) the person is employed in the district;[76] or

---

[74] Allocation of Housing and Homelessness (Miscellaneous Provisions) (England) Regulations 2006, SI 2006/2527, reg 3, for applications to local housing authorities made on or after 9 October 2006. See Appendix 2. The prescribed period was the same for applications made up to and including 31 May 2006 (Homelessness (England) Regulations 2000, SI 2007/701, reg 6). For applications made between 1 June 2006 and 8 October 2006, the position is unclear, since there was no prescribed period.

[75] HA 1996, s 199(1)(a). See **15.54–15.65**.

[76] HA 1996, s 199(1)(b). See **15.66–15.71**.

(3)　the person has a connection with the district through family associations;[77] or

(4)　the person has a connection with the district through special circumstances;[78] or

(5)　the person was provided with accommodation in the district (in England or Wales) under s 95 of the Immigration and Asylum Act 1999 (dispersal of asylum-seekers).[79]

15.43　Each of the above circumstances will be examined in turn in this Chapter.

15.44　When considering whether the circumstances sufficient to establish a 'local connection' are made out, a local housing authority must have regard to both HA 1996, Part 7 and the relevant Code of Guidance. In addition, local housing authorities have also agreed and adopted additional guidance as to the interpretation of some of these statutory provisions.[80] The House of Lords has confirmed that local housing authorities are entitled to consider that additional guidance when making their decisions.[81] As Chadwick LJ put it in a later case:

> 'It is desirable that the notified authority – who is being asked to assume the burden of providing accommodation for the applicant in the place of the notifying authority – should be able to accept the view of the notifying authority both that the applicant has no local connection with the district of the notifying authority and that the applicant does have a local connection with their own district. Ready agreement is unlikely to be achieved on those two points unless both the notifying authority and the notified authority are able to approach the question from a common basis. It is the need for that common basis which, as it seems to me, provides the imperative for all authorities to apply the guidelines "generally to all applications which come before them".'[82]

15.45　If they do take the guidance into account, local housing authorities must still ensure that they consider the applicant's individual circumstances, particularly any exceptional circumstances, before reaching a decision.[83]

---

[77]　HA 1996, s 199(1)(c). See **15.72–15.81**.

[78]　HA 1996, s l99(1)(d). See **15.82–15.87**.

[79]　HA 1996, s 199(6), added by Asylum and Immigration (Treatment of Claimants, etc) Act 2004, s 11(1) and in force from 4 January 2005. The Welsh Code does not mention this fifth circumstance at all (Welsh Code, para 20.7). See **15.88–15.94**.

[80]　Guidelines for Local Authorities and Referees agreed by Association of London Government (ALG), Convention of Scottish Local Authorities (CoSLA), Local Government Association (LGA), Welsh Local Government Association (WLGA), reproduced at English Code, Annex 18. It applies to local housing authorities in both England and Wales. The Welsh Code does not contain a copy of the Agreement although it refers to it at paras 20.21–20.25.

[81]　*R v Eastleigh Borough Council ex p Betts* [1983] 2 AC 613, HL at 627, per Lord Brightman.

[82]　*Ozbek v Ipswich Borough Council* [2006] EWCA Civ 534, [2006] HLR 41, CA at [39] per Chadwick LJ.

[83]　*R v Harrow London Borough Council ex p Carter* (1992) 26 HLR 32, QBD.

15.46 If they embark on inquiries into local connection at all, local housing authorities should consider each of the five circumstances in which an applicant, or a member of his or her household, may acquire a local connection.[84] It is not sufficient merely to establish that a local connection has been acquired by the applicant with the district of another local housing authority through one of the specified categories. The local housing authority must go on to consider what other local connections the applicant or his or her household members may have. Consideration of all the categories might reveal that the applicant, or a member of his or her household, has a local connection with the very local housing authority to which he or she applied.[85] If that is the case, the conditions for referral will not be met. Alternatively, it might be the case that the applicant or a member of his or her household has a local connection with more than one local housing authority (other than that to which he or she applied), in which case the conditions for referral are met, but the relative strengths of the connections[86] and the applicant's preference[87] are relevant when deciding which local housing authority should be notified by the local housing authority to whom the applicant has applied.[88]

15.47 The House of Lords held in *Mohammed v Hammersmith and Fulham London Borough Council*[89] that the relevant date for determining whether an applicant has a local connection, and with which local housing authority, is the date of the decision that the local housing authority (or local housing authorities jointly, or a referee) makes on the question or (if a review is requested) the date of the review decision. Although in that case, the House of Lords was concerned with the definition of 'normally resident', the principle must apply to any of the other statutory circumstances that fall to be considered. So, if an applicant acquires a family association or becomes employed in a local housing authority's district after his or her application for homelessness assistance but before the date of decision, or even the review decision, the question of local connection must be considered on the facts at that later date, not as at the date of application. More commonly, of course, the applicant might have been 'resident' in the local housing authority's district for long enough since applying to have established a local connection[90] by the time of the initial decision or review, even though the period of residence in the

---

84   *R v Slough Borough Council ex p Khan* (1995) 27 HLR 492, QBD.
85   English Code, para 18.13; Welsh Code, para 20.10. See *X v Ealing London Borough Council* (2010) November *Legal Action*, p 19 Brentford County Court where a county court judge decided that the correct approach was to ask first whether or not an application had a real connection (as described by the House of Lords in *R v Eastleigh Borough Council ex p Betts* [1983] 2 AC 613, HL, see **15.51**) with a local housing authority's district and then whether or not that connection arose by reason of any of the factors specified at HA 1996, s 199(1).
86   See **15.52** and **15.114**.
87   English Code, para 18.14; Welsh Code, para 20.11.
88   English Code, Annex 18, para 4.11.
89   [2001] UKHL 57, [2002] 1 AC 547, HL.
90   Under HA 1996, s 199(1)(a).

district prior to the application for homelessness assistance had not been long enough to establish such a local connection.[91]

15.48 It is possible for a person not to have a local connection with any local housing authority in England, Wales or Scotland. The example given in the Welsh Code is where a person has 'had an unsettled way of life for many years'.[92] Former prisoners, former long-term hospital residents, former servicemen or servicewomen, etc, may likewise not have a local connection with any district at all. Neither would someone newly arrived in the UK, with no prior period of residence in England, Wales or Scotland, who was not employed and who had no family associations here. If there is no local connection anywhere, the conditions for referral are not met and the applicant remains the responsibility of the local housing authority to which he or she applied.[93]

15.49 Three additional points about local connection must be made before the individual ingredients are considered further.

15.50 First, HA 1996, Part 7 does not exhaustively define 'local connection'. Most obviously, a person may have a local connection with an area but it may arise from circumstances falling outside the prescribed list of circumstances. If that is the case, that connection would not fall within the definition of 'local connection' for the purposes of HA 1996, Part 7. For example, the connection a person has with an area because it was the place of his or her birth would be immaterial: 'A local connection not founded upon any of the four stated factors is irrelevant'.[94]

15.51 There is another sense in which the subsection does not exhaustively define 'local connection'. A 'local connection' with a district is something more than simply *a* connection by residence, employment, etc. While one of the five prescribed circumstances is a necessary pre-condition for a local connection, it is not sufficient alone to establish a local connection. For example, a person may have employment in an area, but it may be of only a transient or very part-time nature. A person may have 'family associations' with an area because his or her parents live there, but might be estranged from their parents and not have seen or spoken to them for years. What is required is that the connection by a person (by having been 'normally resident', 'employed', or having 'family associations' in an area) is of sufficient quality to amount to a present 'local connection'. As the House of Lords has put it, a local connection is a connection which has been built up or established so as to have become 'a connection in real terms'.[95]

---

[91] See, for example, *Fetaj v Lambeth London Borough Council* (2002) September *Legal Action*, p 31, Lambeth County Court.
[92] Welsh Code, para 20.14.
[93] English Code, para 18.22; Welsh Code, para 20.14.
[94] *R v Eastleigh Borough Council ex p Betts* [1983] 2 AC 613, HL per Lord Brightman. There are now five stated factors, see **15.42**.
[95] *R v Eastleigh Borough Council ex p Betts* [1983] 2 AC 613, HL per Lord Brightman. See *X v*

15.52 Second, different local connections may be of different comparative strengths. For example, a person might be said to have a stronger local connection with the place in which she or he lives than with the place where she or he works. If the applicant (or anyone who might reasonably be expected to live with him or her) has *any* local connection (based on one or more of the five statutory circumstances) with the local housing authority to which an application for homelessness assistance has been made, the strength of that local connection is irrelevant. The conditions for referral will not be made out and the referral provisions cannot be used, even if the applicant has a much stronger local connection with another local housing authority.[96] But where there is no local connection with the district of the local housing authority applied to, but local connections with two or more other districts, the respective strengths of the local connections elsewhere, along with the applicant's preference, will be a factor for the first local housing authority in determining to which other local housing authority it should direct the referral.[97]

15.53 Third, the relevant local connection is with the 'district' of a local housing authority. That must mean with any part of the geographical area of that authority. So, a person who lives (and has always lived) just inside the boundaries of Borough A will have a local connection with that borough even if, in practice, most of his or her time is spent in neighbouring Borough B (for shopping, education, recreation or leisure purposes). None of the interesting questions which might arise in relation to local connection when district boundaries are moved (eg by implementation of recommendations of the Boundary Commission) have yet been considered by the courts.

The relevant statutory circumstances

(1) Normal residence of his or her own choice[98]

15.54 A person must have been 'normally resident' in a district in order to acquire a local connection with that district by having lived there. 'Normal residence' is to be understood as meaning 'the place where at the relevant time the person in fact resides'.[99] There is no need for the place to be a permanent home, or even to be the place where a person most wants to be living.

> 'So long as that place where he eats and sleeps is voluntarily accepted by him, the reason why he is there rather than somewhere else does not prevent that place from being his normal residence. He may not like it, he may prefer some other place, but that place is for the relevant time the place where he normally resides. If a person, having no other accommodation, takes his few belongings and moves into a barn

---

Ealing London Borough Council (2010) November *Legal Action*, p 19 Brentford County Court for an example of a connection based on special circumstances amounting to a connection in real terms, see **15.85**.

96 English Code, para 18.13; Welsh Code, para 20.10.
97 English Code, para 18.14 and Annex 18 para 4.11; Welsh Code, para 20.11.
98 HA 1996, s 199(1)(a).
99 *Mohamed v Hammersmith and Fulham London Borough Council* [2001] UKHL 57, [2002] 1 AC 547, HL at [17], per Lord Slynn.

for a period to work on a farm that is where during that period he is normally resident, however much he might prefer some more permanent or better accommodation. In a sense it is "shelter" but it is also where he resides.'[100]

15.55 Applying this approach, even occupation of interim accommodation, provided under a local housing authority's homelessness duties, constitutes 'normal residence'. Likewise, occupation of accommodation provided under community care or other duties will be accommodation in which the applicant normally resides.

15.56 The assessment that has to be made in a 'residence' case:

'... is not whether the homeless person is now or was in the past normally resident in the area of the notifying authority, but whether the applicant has now a local connection with either area based upon the fact that he is now or was in the past normally resident in that area.'[101]

15.57 The Local Authorities' Agreement[102] suggests that a working definition of normal residence sufficient to establish a 'local connection' should be residence for at least six months in an area during the previous 12 months, or for not less than three years during the previous five-year period.[103] Local housing authorities may apply that working definition, although each case must be considered on its own particular facts.[104]

15.58 The concept of normal residence being 'of his own choice' was considered by the House of Lords in *Al-Ameri v Kensington and Chelsea Royal London Borough Council*.[105] It decided that 'choice' in this context refers to a person's choice to go and live in a particular district. The district must have been selected by the individual, rather than by some other person (for example, by an official or a Secretary of State). The particular situation in *Al-Ameri* (asylum-seekers occupying accommodation provided under the then National Asylum Support Service (NASS) scheme) has since been specifically addressed by legislation.[106] However, the general definition of 'his own choice' remains. The House of Lords decision confirmed, for example, that children moved from one district to another by their parents would not have been resident in the new district 'of their own choice'.[107]

15.59 This freedom of choice aspect cannot be extrapolated too far. A person who moves from one area to another as a consequence of his or her employer

[100] *Mohamed v Hammersmith and Fulham London Borough Council* [2001] UKHL 57, [2002] 1 AC 547, HL at [17], per Lord Slynn.
[101] *R v Eastleigh Borough Council ex p Betts* [1983] 2 AC 613, HL, per Lord Brightman.
[102] See **15.167–15.173**.
[103] English Code, Annex 18, para 4.1(i).
[104] *R v Eastleigh Borough Council ex p Betts* [1983] 2 AC 613, HL.
[105] *Al-Ameri v Kensington and Chelsea Royal London Borough Council* [2004] UKHL 4, [2004] 2 AC 159, HL.
[106] HA 1996, s 199(6) and (7) as amended. See **15.88–15.94**.
[107] See also English Code, Annex 18, para 4.1(iii).

relocating might be said to be simply falling in line with a choice made by another, and the point could be made with even more force about the employee's partner. However, in reality, the employee has chosen to move rather than to resign and the employee's partner has chosen to follow. Their residence is, accordingly, of their 'own choice'. Much more acute difficulties arise with the 'own choice' concept when an applicant to the local housing authority for District A has become resident in District A as a result of having been placed there by District B in pursuance of its statutory duties to accommodate the applicant. Those statutory obligations might include the making of a private rented sector offer to the applicant by a local housing authority in England.[108] In one sense this was not residence of the applicant's 'own choice'. On the other hand, the applicant was not obliged to accept the accommodation in District A as offered by District B.[109]

Exceptions to normal residence of his or her own choice

Military service

15.60 Prior to 1 December 2008, people who were serving in the armed forces of the Crown, and people who might reasonably be expected to reside with them, were not considered as normally resident in a district of their own choice (HA 1996, s 199(3)(a)). This exception was repealed by s 315 of the Housing and Regeneration Act 2008 and does not apply to applications for homelessness assistance made to local housing authorities in England on or after 1 December 2008,[110] nor to applications for homelessness assistance made to local housing authorities in Wales on or after 30 March 2009.[111]

Detention

15.61 Residence in a district is not 'of his own choice' if it occurs because a person is detained under the authority of an Act of Parliament.[112] This refers to any form of detention authorised by statute and therefore embraces detentions, for example, as a result of having been remanded in custody,[113]

---

[108] HA 1996, s 193(7AA)–(7AC) amended by LA 2011, s 148(5)–(7) and applicable to applicants whose applications for homelessness assistance were made on or after 9 November 2012 to a local housing authority in England. At the date of writing, the amendments to HA 1996 made by LA 2011, ss 148–149 had not been brought into effect in Wales. See **17.109–17.131**. In those circumstances the second set of referral conditions at HA 1996, s 198(2ZA) and (2A) amended by LA 2011, s 149(6)–(7) may arise. See **15.116–15.131**.

[109] This problem is side-stepped for local housing authorities in England by the second and third set of referral conditions available to District A when this scenario arises (HA 1996, s 198(4)). See also **15.116–15.131** and **15.132–15.145**. See **fn 10** for the authors' view as to why the third set of referral conditions does not apply to local housing authorities in Wales.

[110] Housing and Regeneration Act 2008 (Commencement No 2 and Transitional, Saving and Transitory Provisions) Order 2008, SI 3068/2008, art 4(10).

[111] Housing and Regeneration Act 2008 (Commencement No 1) (Wales) Order 2009, SI 773/2009 (W 65) (C 48).

[112] HA 1996, s 199(3)(b).

[113] Criminal Justice Act 2003, s 242(2).

having been given a custodial sentence,[114] or having been detained under the Mental Health Act 1983.[115] Periods of residence in a district prior to detention are not excluded and can count towards normal residence for the purposes of HA 1996, Part 7.[116] This exception encompasses spouses or other family members of detainees, who come to reside in the district in order to be close to their detained relative. Therefore, the person who moves from District A to District B to be near her partner, who is detained in District B, cannot acquire a local connection with District B unless either:

(1)   a connection other than through normal residence is available (eg she becomes employed in District B); or

(2)   there is a period of fresh residence (eg if she remained in District B after her partner was released, or after she had ended the relationship but chose to remain in the district).

Other exceptions

15.62   The Secretary of State and the Welsh Ministers have the power to specify circumstances in which residence in a district is not to be treated as being of a person's own choice.[117] To date, neither the Secretary of State nor the Welsh Ministers have exercised that power.

15.63   Previous editions of the Local Authorities' Agreement, recommended that local housing authorities also treat time spent in hospital or time spent in an institution in which households are accepted only for a limited period (eg mother and baby homes, refuges, rehabilitation centres) as exceptions for the purposes of determining local connection. These examples, not repeated in the current edition,[118] illustrate the point that having normal residence of one's own choice in an area is not sufficient. Such residence must have the character, additionally, of establishing a 'local connection' with a local housing authority's district. The examples given were of normal residence of choice which *may* be thought, as a general rule, not to be of sufficient character to establish a local connection.

Former asylum-seekers

15.64   Former asylum-seekers who previously lived in accommodation provided by the UKBA under s 95 of the Immigration and Asylum Act 1999 (formerly known as 'NASS accommodation') do not reside in that district of their own choice.[119] However, asylum-seekers who occupied accommodation provided under IAA 1999, s 95 (the main duty to provide accommodation and

---

114   Powers of Criminal Courts (Sentencing) Act 2000, s 76.
115   Mental Health Act 1983, ss 2–3.
116   English Code, para 18.16; Welsh Code, para 20.13.
117   HA 1996, s 199(5)(b).
118   At English Code, Annex 18.
119   *Al-Ameri v Kensington and Chelsea Royal London Borough Council* [2004] UKHL 4, [2004] 2 AC 159, HL.

support) are deemed to have a local connection with the local housing authority in whose district that accommodation is situated.[120] This deeming provision does not apply to asylum-seekers who only occupied accommodation provided under IAA 1999, s 98 (temporary support) or s 4 (hard cases support), nor to asylum-seekers who were provided with accommodation by local authorities under the Asylum Seekers (Interim Provisions) Regulations 1999.[121]

15.65 Scottish law provides that residence in accommodation provided under the IAA 1999, s 95 cannot constitute residence 'of his own choice', and so asylum seekers dispersed to Scotland by the UKBA do not, as a matter of law, acquire a local connection with a local authority in Scotland under this provision.[122]

(2) Employment[123]

15.66 An applicant, or a member of his or her household, who is employed in a district may acquire a local connection with that district by virtue of that employment. The Codes suggest that the person must actually work in the district, in the sense of being physically present, for the employment to establish a local connection, and so it would not be sufficient, as in the case of a peripatetic employee, for the employer's head office to be located there.[124]

15.67 Both HA 1996, Part 7 and the Codes use the present tense ('is employed').[125] The question is therefore whether the applicant, or a member of his or her household, is employed in the relevant district at the date of the initial decision or review decision.[126] However, the simple fact of such current employment will not necessarily establish a local connection in itself. To build up and establish a local connection there will usually need to have been 'a period of employment',[127] although neither HA 1996, Part 7 nor the Codes

---

[120] By HA 1996, s 199(6). English Code, paras 18.17–18.19. Surprisingly, there is no mention of this fifth local connection in the Welsh Code, see para 20.7. See **15.88–15.94**.

[121] SI 1999/3056; in the latter case, reg 6(2) is identical to Immigration and Asylum Act 1999, s 95, so that an asylum-seeker's preference as to the location of accommodation is not to be taken into account by local housing authorities; see *Ciftci v Haringey London Borough Council* (2004) January *Legal Action*, p 32, Central London County Court.

[122] Housing (Scotland) Act 1987, s 27 as amended by Homelessness etc (Scotland) Act 2003, s 7. As a result, there are lesser duties imposed on local housing authorities in England and in Wales who receive applications for homelessness assistance from asylum seekers previously dispersed to Scotland (see **15.192–15.201**). The Scottish Ministers have the power to suspend Housing (Scotland) Act 1987, s 27, so as to end referral between local housing authorities (Homelessness etc (Scotland) Act 2003, s 8). They have not as yet exercised this power, see **15.220**. English Code, paras 18.20–18.21.

[123] HA 1996, s 199(1)(b).

[124] English Code, para 18.10; Welsh Code, para 20.7(ii), although this is a difficult approach to apply to employment that is mobile, such as a mobile tradesperson working in a number of local housing authority districts in a metropolitan area, or a pilot spending more time in the air than in the airport where he or she is based.

[125] HA 1996, s 199(1)(b).

[126] *R v Ealing London Borough Council ex p Fox* (1998) *The Times*, 9 March, QBD.

[127] *Betts v Eastleigh Borough Council* [1983] 2 AC 613, HL at 627, per Lord Brightman.

suggest any particular period of employment. If the person's connection with an area is through past employment that will count, if at all, only if it amounts to 'special circumstances'.[128]

15.68   Further, the Local Authorities' Agreement suggests that, if it is to found a local connection, employment should not be of a casual nature. It then suggests that employers be asked for confirmation of both the fact of employment and its non-casual nature.[129] This inquiry is obviously unnecessary if the applicant can produce a written statement of the terms and conditions of employment or a fixed-term contract.

15.69   Employment can be full-time or part-time and include both paid and unpaid employment.[130] For example, an unpaid pastor in a church has been held to have a local connection with a district by virtue of that employment.[131]

15.70   Prior to 1 December 2008, people who were serving in the armed forces of the Crown were not considered as employed in a district (HA 1996, s 199(2)). This exception has been repealed by s 315 of the Housing and Regeneration Act 2008 and does not apply to applications for homelessness assistance made to local housing authorities in England on or after 1 December 2008,[132] nor to applications for homelessness assistance made to local housing authorities in Wales on or after 30 March 2009.[133]

15.71   There is provision for the Secretary of State or the Welsh Ministers to specify other circumstances in which a person is not to be treated as employed in a district, but this power has not been exercised in either jurisdiction.[134]

(3) Family associations[135]

15.72   An applicant, or a member of his or her household, may have a local connection with a district if he or she has family associations with that district. 'Family associations' are not defined in HA 1996, Part 7. The Local Authorities' Agreement suggests that the phrase should 'normally' be understood to refer to 'parents, adult children or brothers and sisters' and that only in 'exceptional circumstances' should the place of residence of other relatives be taken into account.[136] In the past, this approach received a measure of judicial support:

---

[128]   HA 1996, s 199(1)(d). See also **15.82–15.87**.
[129]   English Code, Annex 18, para 4.1(ii).
[130]   *R v Ealing London Borough Council ex p Fox* (1998) Times, 9 March, QBD.
[131]   *Sarac v Camden London Borough Council* (2002) June *Legal Action*, p 28, Central London County Court.
[132]   Housing and Regeneration Act 2008 (Commencement No 2 and Transitional, Saving and Transitory Provisions) Order 2008, SI 3068/2008, art 4(10).
[133]   Housing and Regeneration Act 2008 (Commencement No 1) (Wales) Order 2009, SI 773/2009 (W 65) (C 48). See Welsh Code, para 20.12.
[134]   HA 1996, s 199(5)(a).
[135]   HA 1996, s 199(1)(c).
[136]   English Code, Annex 18, para 4.1(iii).

'In my opinion family associations do not extend beyond parents, adult children or brothers and sisters. First cousins once removed (or cousins of any description) cannot provide the necessary connection.'[137]

15.73 In *R v Hammersmith and Fulham London Borough Council ex p Avdic*, it had been conceded that a first cousin once removed did not amount to a 'family association'. In a later case, *R v Ealing London Borough Council ex p Fox*, that expression of judicial opinion was directly followed and a local housing authority's decision that an uncle did not constitute a sufficiently close relative to establish a 'family association' was held not to be wrong in law.[138]

15.74 However, the better and more recent view, which has also received some support from the Court of Appeal, is that the question falls to be decided having regard to the fact-specific characteristics of the individual case:

'... the starting point is the position of the applicant and his household and, in having regard to both "family association" and "special circumstances", while we do not discourage general rules such as are to be found in the Local Authority Agreement, we note that Parliament left those broad phrases undefined and to be judged as a matter of fact and degree in every case. For instance, the actual closeness of the family association may count for more than the precise degree of consanguinity.'[139]

15.75 In *Ozbek v Ipswich Borough Council*,[140] the Court of Appeal specifically rejected a submission that that only near relatives could found the basis for a local connection because of 'family associations'. Considering the judicial observations in *R v Hammersmith & Fulham London Borough Council ex p Avdic*,[141] Chadwick LJ said that those observations were not authority for the proposition that only near relatives (parents, siblings, children) could provide a 'family association' and said that the relevant question is:

'whether, in the particular circumstances of the individual case, the bond between the applicant and one or more members of the extended family was of such a nature that it would be appropriate to regard those members of the extended family as "near relatives" in the sense in which that concept is recognised in the Referral Guidelines.'[142]

---

[137] *R v Hammersmith and Fulham London Borough Council ex p Avdic* (1996) 28 HLR 897, QBD at 899, per Tucker J, confirmed on appeal at (1998) 30 HLR 1, CA.
[138] (1998) Times, 9 March, QBD.
[139] *Surdonja v Ealing London Borough Council* (2000) 32 HLR 481, CA at 489, per Henry LJ. Recent cases have stressed the importance of the local housing authority's role in fact-finding, see, for example, *Bellis v Woking Borough Council* [2005] EWCA Civ 1671, (2006) February Legal Action, p 31, CA, where there was no error of law in the local housing authority's rejection of contact with a separated father as 'family association'.
[140] [2006] EWCA Civ 534, [2006] HLR 41, CA.
[141] (1996) 28 HLR 897, QBD; see **15.71**.
[142] *Ozbek v Ipswich Borough Council* [2006] EWCA Civ 534, [2006] HLR 41, CA at [43]–[44] and [49], per Chadwick LJ.

15.76 Sedley LJ said that, if the judge in *Avdic* had meant to confine 'family association' to near relatives, he was wrong and his judgment should not be followed in that regard. He gave examples of relatives whose presence might found a 'family association' as 'grandparents or uncles and aunts by whom the applicant had been brought up' and emphasised that 'the character of the family association must be at least as relevant – probably more relevant – than the degree of consanguinity'.[143]

15.77 Accordingly, the family relationship does not have to be one of blood or marriage. For example, an unmarried step-parent has been held to be a sufficiently close relative to provide a family association.[144]

15.78 The current edition of the English Code shows that the Secretary of State takes a similar view:

> 'the Secretary of State considers that [family associations] may extend beyond parents, adult children, or siblings. They may include association with other family members such as step-parents, grandparents, grandchildren, aunts or uncles provided that there are sufficiently close links in the form of frequent contact, commitment or dependency. Family associations may also extend to unmarried couples, provided that the relationship is sufficiently enduring, and to same sex couples.'[145]

15.79 Local housing authorities, certainly in England, are therefore advised against applying the guidelines in the Local Authorities' Agreement rigidly.[146]

15.80 The Local Authorities' Agreement recommends that, in order to give rise to a local connection, the family members relied upon as 'family associations' should have been resident in the district for a period of at least five years at the date of application for homelessness assistance.[147] But no rule to this effect is contained in HA 1996 Part 7, and the individual circumstances of a particular case might indicate that a shorter period of residence by a relation is sufficient. Local housing authorities need to guard against the temptation simply to apply the five-year yardstick to every case.[148] This is

---

[143] *Ozbek v Ipswich Borough Council* [2006] EWCA Civ 534, [2006] HLR 41, CA at [64], per Sedley LJ.

[144] *Munting v Hammersmith and Fulham London Borough Council* (1998) March *Legal Action*, p 15, West London County Court.

[145] English Code, para 18.10. There is no specific guidance in the Welsh Code.

[146] Local housing authorities in Wales, even though not subject to the same guidance, should certainly ensure that they apply the Court of Appeal's approach in *Ozbek v Ipswich Borough Council* [2006] EWCA Civ 534, [2006] HLR 41, CA.

[147] English Code, Annex 18, para 4.1(iii).

[148] See *R v Harrow London Borough Council ex p Carter* (1992) 26 HLR 32, QBD at 37, where the applicant's sister had lived in the Harrow area for only four years. Roger Henderson QC, sitting as a deputy High Court judge, said: 'It will be seen that that clause of the agreement, if applied rigidly, would mean that a family association would not normally arise if a homeless person's sister had been resident in Harrow for less than five years, but the agreement would not preclude this abnormally. Thus, to say without more ado that Mrs Carter had no local connection with Harrow because her sister had lived in Harrow for between four and five years

particularly so in the cases of refugees or other recent arrivals to the UK, where local housing authorities should bear in mind that the relatives may not have had five years in which to build up a residence period in any district in the UK.[149]

15.81 The 'family associations' variant of local connection is an acknowledgment of 'the continuity of support that family associations can give'.[150] Accordingly, a local housing authority should not be relying on it in order to identify a connection with an area other than one where the applicant positively wants to live. The applicant must indicate a wish to be near those members of his or her family for a local connection to be acquired through 'family associations'. As the Local Authorities' Agreement sensibly acknowledges, a referral should not be made under 'family associations' if the applicant objects to being referred to a district in which other members of his or her family live.[151]

(4) Special circumstances[152]

15.82 A person may have a local connection with a particular district if his or her connection with it arises because of 'special circumstances'.[153] Unsurprisingly, these are not defined in HA 1996, Part 7. The deliberately wide term embraces 'all special circumstances which can contribute to such a socially beneficial "local connection"' with an area.[154]

15.83 The Codes give as an example 'the need to be near special medical or support services which are available only in a particular district'.[155]

15.84 The Local Authorities' Agreement suggests that this category 'may be particularly relevant in dealing with people who have been in prison or in hospital' and gives an example of a person seeking to return to an area where he or she was brought up or lived for a considerable length of time.[156]

15.85 Absent a statutory definition, and with only limited guidance given by the Codes and the Local Authorities' Agreement, it is no surprise to find that a wide range of circumstances have been advanced (often unsuccessfully) as being sufficiently 'special' for these purposes. These include:

---

would have been erroneous (a) because the agreement is no more than a guideline, (b) because the agreement did not so provide and (c) because, in Mrs Carter's predicament with four small children, any form of sisterly support might well make a significant difference in coping with her parental responsibilities.'

[149] *Ozbek v Ipswich Borough Council* [2006] EWCA Civ 534 [2006] HLR 41, (2006) June *Legal Action*, p 36, CA, at [46], per Chadwick LJ and at [65], per Sedley LJ.

[150] *Surdonja v Ealing London Borough Council* (2000) 32 HLR 481, CA at 485, per Henry LJ.

[151] English Code Annex 18, para 4.1(iii).

[152] HA 1996, s 199(1)(d).

[153] HA 1996, s 199(1)(d).

[154] *Surdonja v Ealing London Borough Council* (2000) 32 HLR 481, CA at 485, per Henry LJ.

[155] English Code, para 18.10; Welsh Code, para 20.7(iv).

[156] English Code, Annex 18, para 4.1(iv).

- the need to visit a particular mosque and attend a particular school;[157]

- medical advice that an applicant needed to live in a warmer area;[158]

- residence (not for a sufficient period to constitute normal residence under HA 1996, s 199(1)(a)), first with the man with whom the applicant believed that she was going to live and, secondly, in a woman's refuge;[159]

- the need to remain in the London area to receive medical treatment (the local housing authority was entitled to take the view that the medical treatment required was also available in the notified local housing authority's district);[160]

- the applicant's need for care and assistance would not be met in the notified local housing authority's district;[161]

- the applicant's traumatic experiences before fleeing as a refugee, the existence of an ethnic minority community of same-language speakers in the local housing authority's district, and enrolment at a local college;[162]

- the fact that the applicant's children had special educational needs and were making rapid progress at a particular local school;[163]

- a fear of leaving the area by reason of the risk of violence that might be experienced elsewhere;[164]

- membership of a church community around which the applicant's social life revolved;[165]

---

[157] *R v Westminster City Council ex p Benniche* (1996) 29 HLR 230, CA, where the local housing authority's decision of 'no special circumstances' on the facts was not wrong in law.

[158] *R v East Devon District Council ex p Robb* (1997) 30 HLR 922, QBD, where the local housing authority was wrong in law not to have considered this as a potentially special circumstance.

[159] *R v Southwark London Borough Council ex p Hughes* (1998) 30 HLR 1082, QBD, where the local housing authority was wrong in law not to have considered this as a potentially special circumstance.

[160] *R v Hammersmith and Fulham London Borough Council ex p Avdic* (1998) 30 HLR 1, CA, where the local housing authority's decision of no special circumstances on the facts was not wrong in law.

[161] *Connor v Brighton and Hove Council* [1998] EWCA Civ 1396, (1999) August *Legal Action*, p 29, CA, where the local housing authority's decision of no special circumstances on the facts was not wrong in law.

[162] *R v Kensington and Chelsea Royal London Borough Council ex p Bishop* (unreported) 11 February 1983, QBD.

[163] *R v Harrow London Borough Council ex p Carter* (1992) 26 HLR 32, QBD, where the local housing authority should have considered those circumstances.

[164] *R v Islington London Borough Council ex p Adigun* (1986) 20 HLR 600, QBD, where the local housing authority's decision of no special circumstances on the facts was not wrong in law.

[165] *R v White Horse District Council ex p Smith and Hay* (1984) 17 HLR 160, QBD, where the local housing authority's decision of no special circumstances on the facts was not wrong in law. See also *R (Gebremarium) v Westminster City Council* [2009] EWHC 2254 (Admin), (2009) November *Legal Action*, p 26, Admin Ct.

- 14 years' previous residence in the area in which the applicants' children had attended school and in which the family still had friends;[166] and

- a former asylum-seeker's decision to seek accommodation in an area because her daughter had secured a bursary to study at a private school in that area, and where the daughter had been in that school for three months.[167]

15.86 The generally strict line taken by the courts (rejecting most of the above cases) reflects the fact that Parliament has left it to local housing authorities to determine whether there are sufficiently 'special' circumstances to amount to a local connection. However, a local housing authority must not gloss the statutory language by seeking some extra-special or particularly pressing 'special circumstances'. For example, a local housing authority considering an application based on a 'special circumstances' connection was held to have misdirected itself by looking for 'an essential compassionate, social or support need' to be in a particular area.[168]

15.87 Local housing authorities are advised in the Local Authorities' Agreement that, if they are referring on the basis that an applicant has no local connection with their area, but does have a local connection with another area under this category, they should only do so with the prior consent of the notified local housing authority.[169]

(5) Deemed 'local connection' for some former asylum-seekers[170]

15.88 By virtue of amendments made to HA 1996, Part 7 in 2005, a 'local connection' is deemed to have been acquired by a person with the district of any local housing authority in England or Wales in which he or she, while an asylum-seeker, was provided with accommodation under s 95 of the Immigration and Asylum Act 1999. The accommodation could have been provided 'at any time', ie before or after this provision for deemed local connection was enacted.[171]

---

[166] *R v Waltham Forest London Borough Council ex p Koutsoudis* (unreported) 1 September 1986, QBD.

[167] *X v Ealing London Borough Council* (2010) November *Legal Action*, p 19, Brentford County Court where the local housing authority's decision that there were no special circumstances was wrong in law, and no reasonable local housing authority could have decided other than that the applicant had a local connection.

[168] *Surdonja v Ealing London Borough Council* (2000) 32 HLR 481, CA at 494, per Henry LJ.

[169] English Code, Annex 18, para 4.2.

[170] HA 1996, s 199(6) as so added and in force from 4 January 2005. See English Code, paras 18.17–18.19. This deemed local connection applies to local housing authorities in Wales. Surprisingly, there is no mention of it in the Welsh Code (see para 20.7).

[171] HA 1996, s 199(6), as amended and in force from 4 January 2005.

15.89   The effect of this deeming provision is that former asylum-seekers, who previously occupied accommodation provided by the UKBA, will acquire a local connection with the local housing authority in whose district the UKBA accommodation was situated.[172]

15.90   Since HA 1996, s 199(6) specifies 'at any time', a former asylum-seeker will retain a local connection with that district for ever. Even if the UKBA accommodation came to an end some considerable time before the applicant's subsequent application for homelessness assistance, and even if the applicant had since then moved around the country and acquired a local connection with other local housing authorities, he or she will retain a local connection with that original district. It appears that the local connection cannot be lost, although it becomes of less importance if the former asylum-seeker is able to establish a local connection with another local housing authority (for example, by employment) and makes the application for homelessness assistance there.[173]

15.91   The lifetime acquisition of deemed local connection applies not just to the asylum-seeker, but also, it would seem, to every member of his or her household who had been 'provided with' UKBA accommodation in that area. Applying that deemed local connection to a homeless applicant's household means that any member of the applicant's household who had, in the past, been provided with UKBA accommodation, whether in his or her own right or as part of the household of an asylum-seeker, therefore acquires a local connection.[174] Nor does there appear to be any minimum period during which the asylum-seeker must occupy the UKBA accommodation for it to trigger a deemed local connection.[175]

---

[172] As was the case in *Ozbek v Ipswich Borough Council* [2006] EWCA Civ 534, [2006] HLR 41, CA, where the applicant had a local connection with Portsmouth, having lived in NASS accommodation there for just under three months. In *Danesh v Kensington & Chelsea Royal London Borough Council* [2006] EWCA Civ 1404, [2007] HLR 17, CA, the applicant had spent 14 months in Home Office accommodation. See also *R (Gebremarium) v Westminster City Council* [2009] EWHC 2254 (Admin), (2009) November *Legal Action*, p 26, Admin Ct.

[173] English Code, para 18.19. For an example of a former asylum-seeker who had both a local connection because of special circumstances with the district of the local housing authority to which she had applied, and a deemed local connection with another local housing authority because of occupying accommodation there which had been provided under Immigration and Asylum Act 1999, s 95, see *X v Ealing London Borough Council* (2010) November *Legal Action*, p 19, Brentford County Court.

[174] Thus, for example, a former asylum-seeker, or the child of a former asylum-seeker, who marries a British citizen and moves into that British citizen's household has a deemed local connection with the district in which the UKBA accommodation was provided. If there is no other local connection held by the applicant or any members of his or her household with the district of a different local housing authority, the conditions for referral will be met (HA 1996, s 198(2)).

[175] So, if a person moves into UKBA accommodation in District A on a Monday (having lived in District B for the previous nine months), is accorded refugee status on the Tuesday, and that accommodation burns down on the Wednesday, he or she will have a local connection with District A, and his or her application for homelessness assistance made on Thursday to District A could not be referred to District B or anywhere else.

15.92 There are two statutory qualifications to the deemed local connection triggered by occupation of UKBA accommodation. First, the deemed local connection is only acquired with the district in which the *last* accommodation provided by the UKBA was situated. If the asylum-seeker was moved around by the UKBA, it is only the last accommodation that can be considered as giving rise to the deemed local connection.[176] Second, accommodation provided by the UKBA in an accommodation centre[177] cannot constitute accommodation by which an applicant acquires a deemed local connection.[178]

15.93 The deemed local connection category specifically refers to accommodation which was provided under s 95 of the Immigration and Asylum Act 1999. That is the main statutory power available to the Secretary of State to provide accommodation to asylum-seekers. It does not refer to other temporary accommodation, including accommodation provided under IAA 1999, s 98,[179] or to hard cases support,[180] or to accommodation provided by local authorities.[181] Former asylum-seekers who were accommodated only under one of these latter provisions, therefore, will not have acquired a deemed local connection.

15.94 The deemed local connection provisions are only part of homelessness legislation for *England and Wales* – there is no such deeming provision in Scotland. Instead, UKBA accommodation provided under s 95 of the Immigration and Asylum Act 1999 in Scotland is specifically not capable of giving rise to a local connection by virtue of normal residence because it is not 'residence of his own choice'.[182] Asylum-seekers who occupied UKBA accommodation in Scotland do not, therefore, acquire a local connection with the local authority in Scotland for the area in which that accommodation is situated, by virtue of such residence alone. Instead, the main housing duty under HA 1996, s 193(2) to provide accommodation (if owed by a local housing authority in England to a former resident of UKBA accommodation in Scotland) is modified by s 11(2) and (3) of the Asylum and Immigration (Treatment of Claimants etc) Act 2004, so that former asylum-seekers are provided with accommodation for a period, giving him or her a reasonable opportunity of securing accommodation, and are given advice and assistance either to apply to a local authority in Scotland as homeless or to find his or her own accommodation.[183] These rules are discussed later in this Chapter.[184]

---

[176] HA 1996, s 199(7)(a) as amended; English Code, para 18.18(a).

[177] Nationality, Immigration and Asylum Act 2002, s 22; English Code, para 18.18(b). Plans to build accommodation centres were abandoned by the government.

[178] HA 1996, s 199(7)(b), as amended.

[179] Immigration and Asylum Act 1999, s 98. See *Berhane v Lambeth London Borough Council* [2007] EWHC 2702, (2008) March *Legal Action*, p 21, QBD.

[180] Immigration and Asylum Act 1999, s 4.

[181] SI 1999/3056.

[182] Housing (Scotland) Act 1987, s 27, as amended.

[183] Asylum and Immigration (Treatment of Claimants etc) Act 2004, s 11(2) and (3), in force from 4 January 2005; English Code, paras 18.20–18.21.

[184] See **15.192–15.201**.

Who acquires a local connection?

15.95 A relevant local connection may have been acquired (or deemed to have been acquired) by the applicant or by any person who might reasonably be expected to reside with the applicant.[185]

15.96 Any local housing authority choosing to investigate the question of local connection must obviously, therefore, make inquiries into any potential local connection that any of the people who might reasonably be expected to reside with the applicant might have, either with its own district or any other district in England, Wales or Scotland.

15.97 The extent of any local connection enjoyed by any other member of the household (if that local connection is different from any enjoyed by the applicant) could be relevant in various scenarios. For example:

(1)   The applicant has no local connection with the local housing authority to which she or he has applied and does have a local connection with another local housing authority, but a member of his or her household has a local connection with the local housing authority to which the application has been made: the conditions for referral are not met and the applicant cannot be referred.

(2)   Neither the applicant nor any member of his or her household has a local connection with the local housing authority to which she or has applied, the applicant has a local connection with another local housing authority and a member of the applicant's household has a local connection with a different local housing authority: the conditions for referral are met, but the local housing authority dealing with the application has a discretion as to which local housing authority it will refer the applicant to (if it decides to make any referral).[186]

(3)   The applicant has a connection with the local housing authority applied to, but a member of the household has a stronger connection with the district of another local housing authority: if the applicant has a local connection with the district to which application has been made, there can be no referral – the connection of the other household member(s) is irrelevant.

---

[185] HA 1996, s 198(2). See also English Code, para 18.7, and Annex 18, para 4.1; Welsh Code, para 20.2. The question of whether it is reasonable to expect a person to reside with the applicant arises both in relation to homelessness and priority need and is discussed at **11.30–11.32, 13.57–13.59** and **13.70–13.74**.

[186] See **15.146–15.150**.

Risk of domestic or other violence[187]

15.98 Even if the applicant is owed the main housing duty[188] and he or she, or a member of his or her household:

(1) does not have a local connection with the district of the local housing authority to which the application is made; and

(2) does have a local connection with the district of another local housing authority in England, Scotland or Wales,

the local housing authority in receipt of the application, and which has opted to consider local connection questions, must then inquire into whether or not:

(1) the applicant, or any member of his or her household, would run the risk of domestic violence in that other local housing authority's district; and

(2) the applicant, or any member of his or her household, had suffered violence in the district of that other local housing authority and it is probable that there would be further violence of a similar kind if he or she returned to that district.

15.99 The local housing authority is obliged to make inquiries itself into the risk of violence or domestic violence; it is not sufficient for it to wait for the applicant to volunteer any relevant information.[189]

15.100 The wording of the statutory provisions puts victims of domestic violence in a slightly different position from victims of other violence.

15.101 'Violence' is defined in HA 1996 as 'violence from another person or threats of violence from another person which are likely to be carried out'.[190] The Codes contain very broad definitions of 'violence', including 'domestic violence' and local housing authorities are advised not to apply the test restrictively.[191] Where the violence is 'domestic violence', a broad interpretation should be applied that encompasses not just physical violence but also 'threatening or intimidating behaviour and any other form of abuse which, directly or indirectly may give rise to the risk of harm'.[192]

---

[187] HA 1996, s 198(2)(c), (2A) and (3).
[188] At HA 1996, s 193(2). See**17.23–17.168**.
[189] *R v Greenwich London Borough Council ex p Patterson* (1994) 26 HLR 159, CA.
[190] HA 1996, s 198(3). The definition is the same as that applying to the definition of homelessness at HA 1996, s 177(1). See **11.81–11.93**.
[191] English Code, paras 8.21 and 18.23–18.25; Welsh Code, paras 13.20 and 20.15. See **11.85** and **15.106**.
[192] *Yemshaw v Hounslow London Borough Council* [2011] UKSC 3, [2011] 1 WLR 433, [2011] HLR 16, SC, Baroness Hale at [28] quoting the *Practice Direction (Residence and Contact Orders: Domestic Violence (No 2)* [2009] 1 WLR 251). See **11.85** for a discussion as to whether or not this broad interpretation should be applied to violence that is not domestic violence.

Domestic violence

15.102 Violence is 'domestic violence' if it is from a person who is associated with the victim.[193] The phrase 'a person who is associated with the victim' is defined at HA 1996, s 178 and includes:

- spouses and former spouses;

- civil partners and former civil partners;

- cohabitants and former cohabitants (heterosexual or same-sex);

- people who live or used to live in the same household;

- relatives;

- people who have agreed to marry each other or to enter into a civil partnership; and

- people who share the parentage of, or parental responsibility for, a child (including the relationship between natural and adoptive parents).[194]

15.103 The definition also includes adoptive and natural parents of a child, step-relatives, grandparents and grandchildren, siblings, uncles, aunts, nieces and nephews, and in-laws or former in-laws (including relatives of a civil partner or former civil partner).[195]

15.104 If the issue of domestic violence is the subject of inquiries, the test is whether the applicant, or a member of the applicant's household, will run the risk of domestic violence in the district of the local housing authority intended to be notified.[196] It follows, therefore, that that person need not actually have been subject in the past to actual or threatened domestic violence there. Obviously, if there has been domestic violence, the relevant question to ask is whether it will recur. However, even where there has been no domestic violence in the past, if there is information that leads to the conclusion that the person would be at risk of violence, or threats of violence which are likely to be carried out, from an associated person, the conditions for referral are not made out.[197]

---

[193] HA 1996, s 198(3).

[194] Civil Partnership Act 2004, s 81 and Sch 8, para 61 amend s 178 to include references to civil partnerships and same-sex couples living together as though they were civil partners, in force from 5 December 2005.

[195] HA 1996, s 178(1), (2), (3). See also **11.86**.

[196] HA 1996, s 198(2)(c).

[197] For example, the applicant may have fled the family home in District A as a result of domestic violence experienced there. One of the perpetrators of the violence may have moved to District B, while the other remained in District A. On an application to District C, the applicant cannot be referred to either District A or District B if as a matter of fact he or she would now run the risk of domestic violence in either district.

Other violence

15.105 If there is no *domestic* violence, the test is slightly different (although the Codes of Guidance do not draw attention to, or give guidance upon, the difference.)[198] There must have been 'violence', as defined by HA 1996,[199] suffered in the district of the local housing authority likely to be notified, and it must be probable that the return to that district will lead to further violence of a similar kind.[200] The past violence may have been carried out by any person, not being a person associated with the victim.[201]

15.106 In *Danesh v Kensington & Chelsea Royal London Borough Council,*[202] the Court of Appeal held that 'violence' in HA 1996, s 198(3) means 'physical violence' and the word 'violence' on its own 'does not include threats of violence or acts or gestures, which lead someone to fear physical violence'.[203] In *Yemshaw v Hounslow London Borough Council,*[204] the Supreme Court declined to decide whether the broader definition of violence in the context of domestic violence,[205] also applied to violence outside the domestic context.

15.107 It follows that there are two questions for the local housing authority:

(1) Has there been physical 'violence'?

(2) Is it 'probable' that the victim's return to the notified local housing authority's district will lead to 'further violence of a similar kind' against the same victim?

15.108 The local housing authority may also want to ask itself whether there has been conduct which directly or indirectly gives rise to the risk of harm and which amounts to violence, or whether there have been threats of such conduct and the threats are likely to be carried out. If so, it is possible that the applicant or a member of his or her household has been subject to violence and the next question would be whether the victim's return to the notified local housing authority's district will lead to 'further violence of a similar kind' against the same victim. Probable' means 'more likely than not'.[206]

---

[198] English Code, paras 18.23–18.25; Welsh Code, paras 20.15–20.16.

[199] HA 1996, s 198(3). See **11.81–11.93** and **15.101**.

[200] HA 1996, s 198(2A).

[201] The Welsh Code advises that 'violence of a similar kind' should be taken 'to mean any violence forming a pattern of conduct against them, even where the individual perpetrators may vary' (Welsh Code, para 20.15), thus including violence from different gang members or other groups of individuals.

[202] [2006] EWCA Civ 1404, [2007] HLR 17, CA.

[203] *Danesh v Kensington & Chelsea RLBC* [2006] EWCA Civ 1404, [2007] HLR 17, CA at [14], per Neuberger LJ.

[204] [2011] UKSC 3, [2011] 1 WLR 433, [2011] HLR 16, SC per Baroness Hale at [35]

[205] Per Baroness Hale at [35]. See **11.85**.

[206] *Bond v Leicester City Council* [2001] EWCA Civ 1544, [2002] HLR 6, CA.

15.109 The local housing authority is entitled to take the applicant's perceptions, fears or concerns into account, but it is for the local housing authority to decide the facts, in order to answer these two questions objectively.[207]

15.110 It follows that if there is a probability of violence, other than domestic violence, which is of a different kind to that previously experienced, the test will not be made out. Similarly, if any violence in the future were to be directed against another member of the household, the test will not be made out. Although there would be no statutory bar on a local housing authority referring a victim back to an area in which a different kind of non-domestic violence was likely to be suffered by another member of the household, it might be expected that a local housing authority would exercise its discretion *not* to refer in those circumstances.

15.111   The factual decisions as to:

(1)   whether there is a risk of domestic violence; or

(2)   whether other violence occurred in the past; and

(3)   whether it is probable that there will be further violence of a similar kind in future,

are for the local housing authority to make, and its decisions will be upheld by the courts, provided that it lawfully applies the correct statutory tests.[208]

Conditions for referral by reason of local connection – a summary

15.112   Only if:

- the applicant is eligible, did not become homeless intentionally and has a priority need; and

- neither the applicant, nor any member of his or her household, has a local connection with the district of the local housing authority to which he or she has applied; and

- either the applicant, or a member of his or her household, has a local connection with the district of another local housing authority in England, Wales or Scotland; and

---

[207]   *Danesh v Kensington & Chelsea Royal London Borough Council* [2006] EWCA Civ 1404, [2007] HLR 17, CA at [26], per Neuberger LJ.

[208]   *R v Islington London Borough Council ex p Adigun* (1988) 20 HLR 600, QBD; *Danesh v Kensington & Chelsea Royal London Borough Council* [2006] EWCA Civ 1404, [2007] HLR 17, CA.

- there is no risk of domestic violence to the applicant or any member of his or her household in the district of the other local housing authority; and

- neither the applicant, nor any member of his or her household, had suffered violence in the other local housing authority's district; and

- if either the applicant, or a member of his or her household, had suffered violence in the other local housing authority's district, it is not probable that there will be further violence of a similar kind against that person,

are the conditions for referral under the local connection route made out.

15.113 It follows that there can be no referral if:

- the applicant or a member of his or her household has a local connection with the local housing authority to which the application was made – the conditions for referral are not met; or

- there is no local connection with any local housing authority in England, Wales or Scotland – the conditions for referral are not met and the applicant remains the responsibility of the original local housing authority; or

- the applicant is ineligible, or only threatened with homelessness, or does not have a priority need, or became homeless intentionally.

15.114 Where the conditions for referral are met, and there is a local connection with *two or more* different local housing authorities (not including the local housing authority which received the application), the original local housing authority has a discretion as to which of the other local housing authorities it should refer the applicant (if any). When considering that discretion, it should take into account the applicant's own preference, as well as the relative strengths of the different local connections.[209]

15.115 Even if all the conditions for a referral are made out, the local housing authority is under no obligation to refer and has an unqualified discretion as to whether or not to refer.[210]

---

[209] English Code, para 18.14, and Annex 18, para 4.12; Welsh Code, para 20.11.
[210] See **15.146–15.150**.

The second set of conditions for referral – acceptance of a private rented sector offer made by a local housing authority in England in the area of a different local housing authority in England[211]

Introduction

15.116 The second circumstances in which the conditions for referral are met is much more self-contained and has nothing to do with the statutory definition of 'local connection'.[212] It arises where:

(1) an applicant had made an application for homelessness assistance on or after 9 November 2012 to a local housing authority in England; and

(2) the applicant had accepted a private rented sector offer[213] from that local housing authority of accommodation located in the district of another local housing authority in England; and

(3) the applicant subsequently made a further application for homelessness assistance to the second local housing authority in England within two years of the date of acceptance of that offer.[214]

15.117 Its purpose is to ensure that the applicants in those circumstances – who benefit from special provisions whereby the main housing duty or equivalent duty to those threatened with homelessness will be owed to most applicants whether or not they have a priority need[215] – remain the responsibility of the local housing authority which made the private rented sector offer. In particular, the availability of private rented sector offers and the restrictions on housing benefit make it likely that local housing authorities operating in areas of high private sector rents will make private rented sector offers in districts where rents are less expensive. If the assured shorthold tenancies secured under these arrangements end within two years of the date of

---

[211] HA 1996, s 198(2ZA) and (2) amended by LA 2011, s 149(5)–(7) and applicable to applicants whose applications for homelessness assistance were made on or after 9 November 2012 to a local housing authority in England. At the date of writing, the amendments to HA 1996 made by LA 2011, ss 148–149 had not been brought into effect in Wales.

[212] See **15.42–15.115**.

[213] HA 1996, s 193(7AA)–(7AC) amended by LA 2011, s 148(5)–(7) and applicable to applicants whose applications for homelessness assistance were made on or after 9 November 2012 to a local housing authority in England. At the date of writing, the amendments to HA 1996 made by LA 2011, ss 148–149 had not been brought into effect in Wales. See **17.109–17.118**.

[214] HA 1996 198(2ZA) and (2) amended by LA 2011, s 149(6) and (7) and applicable to applicants whose applications for homelessness assistance were made on or after 9 November 2012 to a local housing authority in England. At the date of writing, the amendments to HA 1996 made by LA 2011, ss 148–149 had not been brought into effect in Wales.

[215] HA 1996, s 195A(1) and (3) inserted by LA 2011, s 149(4) and applicable to applicants whose applications for homelessness assistance were made on or after 9 November 2012 to a local housing authority in England. At the date of writing, the amendments to HA 1996 made by LA 2011, ss 148–149 had not been brought into effect in Wales. See **9.89–9.95**.

acceptance, it is the local housing authority which made the private rented sector offer which will subsequently owe a main housing duty to the applicant.[216]

15.118 This set of conditions for referral apply where both the first application and the subsequent application for homelessness assistance were made to local housing authorities in England.[217] The first application for homelessness assistance will have been made on or after 9 November 2012.[218]

15.119 This second set of conditions for referral does not apply in Scotland and cannot be used by a local housing authority in England to refer an applicant to a local authority in Scotland.[219]

15.120 At the time of writing, no specific guidance had been issued. The provisions of the Local Authorities' Agreement will apply, where relevant, to any disputes between local housing authorities as to whether or not this set of conditions for referral is met.[220]

The second set of conditions

15.121 The second set of conditions for a referral will be met where:

(1) the applicant makes an application for homelessness assistance to a local housing authority in England (authority A) on or after 9 November 2012;[221] and

(2) the applicant had previously applied to a local housing authority in England (authority B) on or after 9 November 2012;[222] and

---

[216] HA 1996, s 195A inserted by LA 2011, s 149(4) and applicable to applicants whose applications for homelessness assistance were made on or after 9 November 2012 to a local housing authority in England. At the date of writing, the amendments to HA 1996 made by LA 2011, ss 148–149 had not been brought into effect in Wales. See **9.89–9.95**.

[217] At the date of writing, the amendments to HA 1996 made by LA 2011, ss 148–149 had not been brought into effect in Wales.

[218] Localism Act 2011 (Commencement No 2 and Transitional Provisions) (England) Order 2012, SI 2012/2599 (c 104). See Appendix 2.

[219] Because HA 1996, s 198(2ZA) as inserted by LA 2011, s 149(5) and (6) only applies to local housing authorities in England where the application for homelessness assistance was made on or after 9 November 2012. Housing (Scotland) Act 1987, s 33 (the Scottish equivalent to HA 1996, s 198) does not contain an equivalent provision to HA 1996, s 198(2ZA) as amended by LA 2011, s 149(5) and (6). See Local Authorities' Agreement, English Code, Annex 18, para 3.3.

[220] English Code, Annex 18.

[221] HA 1996, s 198(2ZA) as amended by LA 2011, s 149(5) and (6) and applicable to applicants whose applications for homelessness assistance were made on or after 9 November 2012 to a local housing authority in England. At the date of writing, the amendments to HA 1996 made by LA 2011, ss 148–149 had not been brought into effect in Wales.

[222] The date when the amendments to HA 1996 made by LA 2011, ss 148–149 came into force (see Localism Act 2011 (Commencement No 2 and Transitional Provisions) (England) Order 2012, SI 2012/2599 (c 104)). At the date of writing, the amendments to HA 1996 made by LA 2011, ss 148–149 had not been brought into effect in Wales.

(3)   authority B had made the applicant a private rented sector offer[223] in order to bring the main housing duty to an end,[224] of accommodation in the district of authority A;[225] and

(4)   the applicant had accepted the private rented sector offer;[226] and the applicant has made an application for homelessness assistance to authority A within two years of the date of his or her acceptance of the offer;[227] and

(5)   neither the applicant nor any member of the applicant's household will run the risk of domestic violence in the district of authority B;[228] and

(6)   neither the applicant, nor any member of his or her household, had suffered violence or threats of violence that were likely to be carried out in the district of authority B;[229] and

(7)   if either the applicant, or a member of his or her household, had suffered violence in the district, of authority B, it is not probable that there will be further violence of a similar kind against that person.[230]

---

[223]   HA 1996, s 193(7AA) as amended by LA 2011, s 148(5) and applicable to applicants whose applications for homelessness assistance were made on or after 9 November 2012 to a local housing authority in England. At the date of writing, the amendments to HA 1996 made by LA 2011, ss 148–149 had not been brought into effect in Wales. See **17.109–17.131**.

[224]   HA 1996, ss 193(7AA)–(7AC) as amended by LA 2011, s 148(5)–(7) and applicable to applicants whose applications for homelessness assistance were made on or after 9 November 2012 to a local housing authority in England. At the date of writing, the amendments to HA 1996 made by LA 2011, ss 148–149 had not been brought into effect in Wales. See **17.23–17.168**.

[225]   HA 1996, s 198(2ZA)(a) amended by LA 2011, s 149(6) and applicable to applicants whose applications for homelessness assistance were made on or after 9 November 2012 to a local housing authority in England. At the date of writing, the amendments to HA 1996 made by LA 2011, ss 148–149 had not been brought into effect in Wales.

[226]   HA 1996, s 193(7AA)(a) amended by LA 2011, s 148(6) applicable to applicants whose applications for homelessness assistance were made on or after 9 November 2012 to a local housing authority in England. At the date of writing, the amendments to HA 1996 made by LA 2011, ss 148–149 had not been brought into effect in Wales. See **17.109–17.118**.

[227]   HA 1996, s 198(2ZA)(a) amended by LA 2011, s 149(6) and applicable to applicants whose applications for homelessness assistance were made on or after 9 November 2012 to a local housing authority in England. At the date of writing, the amendments to HA 1996 made by LA 2011, ss 148–149 had not been brought into effect in Wales. See **9.89–9.95**.

[228]   HA 1996, s 198(2ZA)(b) amended by LA 2011, s 149(6) and applicable to applicants whose applications for homelessness assistance were made on or after 9 November 2012 to a local housing authority in England. At the date of writing, the amendments to HA 1996 made by LA 2011, ss 148–149 had not been brought into effect in Wales. See **15.98–15.104**.

[229]   HA 1996, s 198(2A) amended by LA 2011, s 149(7) and applicable to applicants whose applications for homelessness assistance were made on or after 9 November 2012 to a local housing authority in England. At the date of writing, the amendments to HA 1996 made by LA 2011, ss 148–149 had not been brought into effect in Wales. See **15.98–15.101** and **15.105–15.111**.

[230]   HA 1996, s 198(2A) amended by LA 2011, s 149(7) and applicable to applicants whose applications for homelessness assistance were made on or after 9 November 2012 to a local housing authority in England. At the date of writing, the amendments to HA 1996 made by LA 2011, ss 148–149 had not been brought into effect in Wales. See **15.107–15.110**.

15.122   It should be noted that the relevant two-year period is that between the date of the applicant's acceptance of the private rented sector offer from authority B and the date of his or her application for homelessness assistance to authority A. It is not from the date of the commencement of the tenancy.

15.123   The applicant will also be entitled to the benefit of the special provisions in HA 1996, s 195A.[231] For most applicants, they will not have to have a priority need in order to be entitled to the main housing duty or the equivalent duty owed to those threatened with homelessness.[232] They will also be deemed to be threatened with homelessness on the date on which they are given a valid HA 1988, s 21 notice and deemed to be homeless on the date on which the notice expires.[233] These special provisions only apply on the first occasion when an applicant makes an application within two years of acceptance of a private rented sector offer.[234] If the applicant subsequently accepts a second private rented sector offer, there are no special provisions if the applicant later makes a fresh application for homelessness assistance.

15.124   Unlike the special provisions in HA 1996, s 195A,[235] this set of conditions for referral applies to all applicants who have accepted a private rented sector offer from one local housing authority in the district of another local housing authority and then make an application for homelessness assistance within two years of acceptance. It does not matter whether the application being considered follows a first acceptance of a private rented sector offer, or a second, third or fourth acceptance. If the application for homelessness assistance is made within two years of any acceptance of a private rented sector offer, this set of conditions for referral will apply.

---

[231]   Inserted by LA 2011, s 149(4) and in force from 9 November 2012. See **9.89–9.95**. The exception is where the applicant is only owed the main housing duty because of the presence in his or her household of a 'restricted person' (defined at HA 1996, s 184(7), see **12.32–12.47**). If that is the case, the applicant must still have a priority need in order to be entitled to the main housing duty or the equivalent duty to those threatened with homelessness (HA 1996 s 195A(5) inserted by LA 2011, s 149(4) and in force from 9 November 2012), see **17.155–17.162**.

[232]   HA 1996, s 195A(1) and (3) inserted by LA 2011, s 149(4) and applicable to applicants whose applications for homelessness assistance were made on or after 9 November 2012 to a local housing authority in England. At the date of writing, the amendments to HA 1996 made by LA 2011, ss 148–149 had not been brought into effect in Wales. See **9.89–9.95**.

[233]   HA 1996, s 195A(2) and (4) inserted by LA 2011, s 149(4) and applicable to applicants whose applications for homelessness assistance were made on or after 9 November 2012 to a local housing authority in England. At the date of writing, the amendments to HA 1996 made by LA 2011, ss 148–149 had not been brought into effect in Wales. See **9.89–9.95**. For priority need, see Chapter 13.

[234]   HA 1996, s 195A(6) inserted by LA 2011, s 149(4) and applicable to applicants whose applications for homelessness assistance were made on or after 9 November 2012 to a local housing authority in England. At the date of writing, the amendments to HA 1996 made by LA 2011, ss 148–149 had not been brought into effect in Wales. See **9.89–9.95** and **11.121–11.128**.

[235]   Inserted by LA 2011, s 149(4) and applicable to applicants whose applications for homelessness assistance were made on or after 9 November 2012 to a local housing authority in England. At the date of writing, the amendments to HA 1996 made by LA 2011, ss 148–149 had not been brought into effect in Wales. See **9.89–9.95**.

15.125 This set of conditions does not require the applicant to be currently living in the private rented sector accommodation, which he or she had accepted. It may be that the tenancy has ended and the applicant has managed to find his or her own accommodation, whether another assured shorthold tenancy or some much more insecure arrangement. If the application for homelessness assistance is made within two years of the date of acceptance of the private rented sector offer, this set of conditions for referral will apply.

15.126 This set of conditions for referral should take precedence over the first set of conditions for referral, based on 'local connection',[236] because HA 1996, s 198(2ZA)[237] is clear that the set of conditions for referral is made out if the tests at HA 1996, s 198(2ZA) and (2) are satisfied. Accordingly, it should be irrelevant that the applicant, or a member of his or her household, has acquired any local connection with the district of authority B.

15.127 The second set of conditions for referral is not satisfied if the application for homelessness assistance is made to authority A more than two years after the date of acceptance of the private rented sector offer. If the application is made on the two-year anniversary itself, or any time after that, this set of conditions for referral will not apply and the only relevant set of conditions would be those relating to 'local connection'.[238] Indeed an applicant would probably have acquired a local connection to authority A as a result of having resided in authority B's district by choice for a period of two years or more.[239]

15.128 The second set of conditions is also not satisfied if the applicant is someone other than the person who accepted the private rented sector offer.[240] However, the special provisions at HA 1996, s 195A[241] only apply to re-applications made by the same person who had accepted the private rented sector offer.[242] So if the household would need to take advantage of those special provisions (perhaps because there is no longer any member of a

---

[236] HA 1996, s 198(2) and (2A) as amended by LA 2011, s 149(5). See **15.42–15.115**.

[237] As amended by LA 2011, s 149(5)–(6) and applicable to applicants whose applications for homelessness assistance were made on or after 9 November 2012 to a local housing authority in England. At the date of writing, the amendments to HA 1996 made by LA 2011, ss 148–149 had not been brought into effect in Wales.

[238] HA 1996, s 198(2) and (2A), see **15.42–15.115**.

[239] HA 1996, s 199(1)(a). See **15.54–15.65**.

[240] HA 1996, s 198(2ZA) amended by LA 2011, s 149(6) and applicable to applicants whose applications for homelessness assistance were made on or after 9 November 2012 to a local housing authority in England. At the date of writing, the amendments to HA 1996 made by LA 2011, ss 148–149 had not been brought into effect in Wales.

[241] Inserted by LA 2011, s 149(4) and applicable to applicants whose applications for homelessness assistance were made on or after 9 November 2012 to a local housing authority in England. At the date of writing, the amendments to HA 1996 made by LA 2011, ss 148–149 had not been brought into effect in Wales. See **9.89–9.95**.

[242] HA 1996 s 195A as inserted by LA 2011, s 149(4) and applicable to applicants whose applications for homelessness assistance were made on or after 9 November 2012 to a local housing authority in England. At the date of writing, the amendments to HA 1996 made by LA 2011, ss 148–149 had not been brought into effect in Wales. See **9.89–9.95**.

household who has a priority need),[243] the application should be made by the person who had accepted the private rented sector offer. On the other hand, if there is no benefit to the household in the special provisions at HA 1996, s 195A (because any member of the household would have a priority need[244]), and the household would wish to avoid a referral back to authority B, the applicant could be a different member of the household from the one who had accepted the private rented sector offer.

15.129 It must be emphasised that the conditions stipulated are conditions for formal referral. Authority A cannot merely turn the applicant away to apply for himself or herself at authority B. The referral can only be made after authority A has satisfied itself, on completion of inquiries into whether the applicant is homeless,[245] whether he or she is eligible for assistance,[246] whether he or she has a priority need,[247] and whether he or she became homeless intentionally,[248] that it would otherwise owe the applicant a main housing duty (at HA 1996, s 193(2)[249]). The duty to provide interim accommodation pending the outcome of those inquiries,[250] to provide accommodation to those found to have become homeless intentionally,[251] or to provide advice and assistance[252] remains on authority A.

15.130 Authority A must make inquiries into all five limbs of the test in HA 1996, s 198(2ZA) and (2A).[253] The conditions for referral will not be satisfied merely by authority A establishing that the applicant had accepted a private rented sector offer[254] from authority B and that the application for

---

[243] See Chapter 13.
[244] See Chapter 13 for 'priority need' and see **17.171–17.181** for the duties owed under HA 1996 s 195A.
[245] HA 1996 ss 175–177, see Chapter 9.
[246] HA 1996, s 185, see Chapter 12.
[247] See Chapter 13. Unless the applicant is making a fresh application for homelessness assistance to a local housing authority in England within two years of accepting a private rented sector offer (HA 1996 s 193(7AA) as amended by LA 2011, s 148 (5)). If that is the case, he or she will normally benefit from the special provision at HA 1996 s 195A (inserted by LA 2011, s 149(4)) and applicable to applicants whose applications for homelessness assistance were made on or after 9 November 2012 to a local housing authority in England. At the date of writing, the amendments to HA 1996 made by LA 2011, ss 148–149 had not been brought into effect in Wales. If the applicant is benefiting from those special provisions, he or she will not need to have a priority need in order to be entitled to the main housing duty at HA 1996 s 193(2). See **9.89–9.95** and **17.171–17.181**.
[248] HA 1996, s 191. See Chapter 14.
[249] See **17.23–17.168**.
[250] HA 1996, s 188(1). See **16.12–16.28**.
[251] HA 1996, s 190(2)(a). See **17.182–17.189**.
[252] HA 1996, s 190(3) and 192(2). See **17.201–17.214**.
[253] As amended by LA 2011, s 148(5) and (7) and applicable to applicants whose applications for homelessness assistance were made on or after 9 November 2012 to a local housing authority in England. At the date of writing, the amendments to HA 1996 made by LA 2011, ss 148–149 had not been brought into effect in Wales. See **15.121**.
[254] HA 1996 s 193(7AA) as amended by LA 2011, s 148(5) and applicable to applicants whose applications for homelessness assistance were made on or after 9 November 2012 to a local housing authority in England. At the date of writing, the amendments to HA 1996 made by LA 2011, ss 148–149 had not been brought into effect in Wales. See **17.109–17.118**.

homelessness assistance was made within two years of the date of the acceptance. Authority A must also inquire into whether the applicant or any member of his or her household will run the risk of domestic violence in the district of authority B,[255] whether the applicant, or any member of his or her household, had suffered violence or threats of violence that were likely to be carried out in the district of authority B;[256] and (if either the applicant, or a member of his or her household, had suffered violence in the district of authority B) whether is probable that there will be further violence of a similar kind against that person.[257]

15.131 It should also be remembered that authority A retains a discretion whether or not to refer the applicant to authority B.[258] It may be that, even if this set of conditions for referral are made out, if the applicant also has a local connection with authority A, it would be reasonable on the facts of a particular case for authority A to decide not to refer him or her to authority B.

The third set of conditions for referral – out of district placements

Introduction

15.132 The third circumstance in which the conditions for referral are met is also more self-contained.[259] It arises where an applicant has previously been placed by another local housing authority in the district of the local housing authority to which a new application for homelessness assistance is being made. It is different from the second set of conditions for referral in that it applies where an applicant was occupying accommodation secured in performance of HA 1996, Part 7 duties[260] rather than having accepted a private rented sector offer which brought those HA 1996, Part 7, duties to an end.[261]

---

[255] HA 1998, s 198(2ZA)(b) amended by LA 2011, s 149(6) and applicable to applicants whose applications for homelessness assistance were made on or after 9 November 2012 to a local housing authority in England. At the date of writing, the amendments to HA 1996 made by LA 2011, ss 148–149 had not been brought into effect in Wales. See **15.98–15.104**.
[256] HA 1996, s 198(2A) amended by LA 2011, s 149(7) and in force from applicable to applicants whose applications for homelessness assistance were made on or after 9 November 2012 to a local housing authority in England. At the date of writing, the amendments to HA 1996 made by LA 2011, ss 148–149 had not been brought into effect in Wales. See **15.98–101** and **15.105–15.111**.
[257] HA 1996, s 198(2A) amended by LA 2011, s 149(7) applicable to applicants whose applications for homelessness assistance were made on or after 9 November 2012 to a local housing authority in England. At the date of writing, the amendments to HA 1996 made by LA 2011, ss 148–149 had not been brought into effect in Wales. See **15.107–15.110**.
[258] HA 1998, s 198(1). See **15.146–15.150**.
[259] See **15.35–15.45**.
[260] Under HA 1996, ss 188, 190(2)(a), 192(3) or 200.
[261] HA 1996 ss 193(7AA – (7AC) amended by LA 2011, s 148(5)–(7) and applicable to applicants whose applications for homelessness assistance were made on or after 9 November 2012 to a local housing authority in England. At the date of writing, the amendments to HA 1996 made by LA 2011, ss 148–149 had not been brought into effect in Wales. See 17.109–17.118 for the provisions by which acceptance of a private rented sector offer brings the main housing duty to an end. See 15.116–15.131 for the second set of conditions for referral.

15.133 Its purpose is to underscore the statutory presumption that homeless households should be accommodated in the district to which they first apply by ensuring that a local housing authority cannot relieve itself of some future responsibility by placing the applicant outside its own district.[262] It was enacted in 1996 to meet the phenomenon of increasing numbers of local housing authorities placing their homeless households in other local housing authorities' districts. These conditions for referral no longer apply to local housing authorities in Wales considering any applications for homelessness assistance made on or after 9 October 2006. This is because the conditions for referral depend upon the operation of a 'prescribed' period and no such period has been prescribed in Wales.[263]

15.134 The Local Authorities' Agreement refers to the third set of conditions for referral as 'for Welsh authorities only'.[264] This is out of date and should be read as 'for authorities in England only'.

15.135 The Codes and the Agreement are silent on what should happen if a local housing authority in England wishes to refer under these conditions to a local housing authority in Wales, or indeed vice versa.[265]

15.136 This third set of conditions for referral does not apply in Scotland and cannot be used by a local housing authority in England or in Wales to refer an applicant to a local authority in Scotland.[266]

The third set of conditions

15.137 The conditions for a referral will be met where:

(1) the applicant had been placed in the district of the local housing authority to which he or she has now applied (authority A) by another local housing authority (authority B) in performance of any of authority B's homelessness functions; and

---

[262] HA 1996, s 208(1); see **15.226–15.233** and **18.58–18.68**.

[263] HA 1996, s 198(4). The prescribed period for local housing authorities in Wales was the same as that prescribed for local housing authorities in England. It was to be found in the Homelessness (England) Regulations 2000, SI 2000/701, reg 6, applied to Wales by the Homelessness (Wales) Regulations 2000, SI 2000/1079 (W 72), reg 2. The Homelessness (Wales) Regulations 2006, SI 2006/2646 (W 227), reg 6, revoked the Homelessness (Wales) Regulations 2000 and therefore the application of the prescribed period. There is no prescribed period in the Homelessness (Wales) Regulations 2006, SI 2006/2646 (W 227). However, the Welsh Code advises that this third set of conditions does apply to local housing authorities in Wales and refers to Homelessness (Wales) Regulations 2000, SI 2000/1079 (W 72), reg 2 (Welsh Code, paras 20.3–20.5). See **15.4**.

[264] English Code, Annex 18, paras 3.2(d) and 4.4.

[265] See **15.206–15.208**.

[266] Because HA 1996, s 198(4) only applies to local housing authorities in England and Wales and Housing (Scotland) Act 1987, s 33 (the Scottish equivalent to HA 1996, s 198) does not contain an equivalent provision to HA 1996, s 198(4). See Local Authorities' Agreement, English Code, Annex 18, para 3.3 and **15.213–15.216**.

(2) the current application is made within a prescribed period running from the date of the application for homelessness assistance to authority B; and

(3) the duty owed by authority A would be the main homelessness duty owed to an eligible, homeless person who has a priority need and did not become homeless intentionally.[267]

15.138 The currently prescribed period is five years *plus* any period between the date of the applicant's original application to authority B and the date of being placed in the accommodation in authority A's district.[268] This aggregate period is then applied running backwards from the date of the application to authority A (not from the date of authority A's decision on that application).[269] The advice on the duration of the prescribed period in the Codes of Guidance and the Local Authorities' Agreement is slightly imprecise.[270] The better approach is to use the precise formula as given in the regulation.[271]

15.139 This set of conditions for referral applies regardless of which of authority B's statutory homelessness functions it was carrying out when it provided the accommodation. Throughout the whole of the prescribed period, authority B retains responsibility for that applicant. A local housing authority which moves a homeless household over a series of districts (eg interim accommodation in District A, followed by short-term temporary accommodation in District C, and then longer term temporary accommodation in District D) will find that it is triggering a new prescribed period of responsibility on each move.

15.140 This third set of conditions for referral may be satisfied whether the applicant has become homeless from the accommodation actually provided by authority B or from some other accommodation in authority A's district. An applicant provided with accommodation in authority A's district by authority B may have found his or her own accommodation in authority A's district. However, if he or she becomes homeless again and applies to authority A within the prescribed period, the conditions for referral will be met and authority A may refer him or her back to authority B.

15.141 It has already been noted that the statutory scope of initial inquiries that a local housing authority undertakes on an application for homelessness assistance has not been expressly expanded to include the information required

---

[267] HA 1996, s 198(4).

[268] Allocation of Housing and Homelessness (Miscellaneous Provisions) Regulations 2006, SI 2006//2527, reg 3. English Code, Annex 18, para 3.2(d).

[269] So, if the applicant applied to local housing authority B on 3 June 2006 and was placed in the district of local housing authority A on 3 January 2007 (six months later) the prescribed period would not have expired until 3 January 2012 (five years and six months in all). If he or she applied to authority A on 30 August 2011, the conditions for referral to authority B will be met, even if authority A's decision is taken several weeks or months later. If he or she applied to authority A on 1 September 2012, the conditions for referral will not be met.

[270] English Code, Annex 18, para 3.2(d).

[271] SI 2006/2527, reg 3.

to make out this third set of conditions for referral.²⁷² Certainly there is no obligation on an applicant to volunteer (without being asked) the fact that he or she came into the local housing authority's district on placement by another local housing authority.

15.142 As with the second set of conditions for referral,²⁷³ it must be emphasised that these are conditions for formal referral. Authority A cannot merely turn the applicant away to apply for himself or herself at authority B. The referral can only be made after authority A has satisfied itself, on completion of inquiries into eligibility, homelessness, priority need and whether or not the applicant has become homeless intentionally, that it would otherwise owe the applicant a main housing duty.²⁷⁴ The duty to provide interim accommodation pending those inquiries,²⁷⁵ to provide accommodation to those found to have become homeless intentionally,²⁷⁶ or to provide advice and assistance²⁷⁷ remains on authority A.

15.143 Since this third set of conditions for referral is separate from the conditions governing a local connection referral under the first set of conditions, it must follow that there is no strict need for authority A to consider whether the applicant might be at risk of domestic or other violence if he or she is referred back to authority B. However, authority A retains a discretion whether or not to refer,²⁷⁸ once it has decided that the conditions are met, and any risk of violence would be relevant to the exercise of that discretion.

15.144 It must also follow that, even if the applicant has acquired a local connection with the district of authority A, by residence, employment, family association or special circumstances, the third set of conditions for referral is still met. Although, if the applicant has a local connection with authority A, particularly if he or she is employed in that district or has family associations, this should be a relevant consideration when authority A is deciding whether or not to exercise its discretion to refer.

15.145 The third set of conditions for referral is only met if the applicant to authority A was also the applicant to authority B. They do not apply to people with whom the applicant resides or might reasonably be expected to reside. This suggests that, if the placement in the district of authority A was as a result of

---

²⁷² See **15.17**.
²⁷³ HA 1996, s 198(2ZA) and (2A) as amended by LA 2011, s 149(5) and (7) and applicable to applicants whose applications for homelessness assistance were made on or after 9 November 2012 to a local housing authority in England. At the date of writing, the amendments to HA 1996 made by LA 2011, ss 148–149 had not been brought into effect in Wales. See **15.116–15.131**.
²⁷⁴ HA 1996, s 193(2). See **17.23–17.168**.
²⁷⁵ HA 1996, s 188(1). See **16.12–16.28**.
²⁷⁶ HA 1996, s 190(2)(a). See **17.182–17.189**.
²⁷⁷ HA 1996, s 190(3) and 192(2). See **17.201–17.214**.
²⁷⁸ See **15.146–15.150**.

authority B's duty owed to one member of the household, another member of the household could apply to authority A and the third set of conditions for referral would not be made out.

THE DECISION WHETHER OR NOT TO REFER

15.146 Once a local housing authority has decided that one of the three sets of conditions for referral are met, it must then decide whether or not to notify the other local housing authority of its opinion.[279] A local housing authority that failed properly to consider its discretion whether to refer, having determined that the conditions for referral were met, would have erred in law.[280] However, given the shortfall between housing supply and demand in many areas, there is nothing to prevent a local housing authority from adopting a general policy that it will normally refer an applicant in respect of whom the conditions are fulfilled, provided that it ensures that it considers any particular circumstances of an individual case that would suggest that a departure from the general policy should be made.[281]

15.147 Obviously, the applicant's personal circumstances (including any risk of violence that does not fall within any of the statutory criteria prohibiting referral) are relevant to the local housing authority's decision whether or not to notify.[282] There will be other cases in which the conditions for a referral are only tenuously met and where, for that reason and perhaps others, it would not be right to use the power to refer. In those and other cases the local housing authority will want to consider 'whether it is in the public interest' to accept the main housing duty or make a referral, taking into account the public expenditure involved, whether a referral involves disruption to an applicant's employment or education, etc.[283] In a case involving former asylum-seekers, who had a local connection by reason of having occupied accommodation provided by the UKBA, the notifying local housing authority was entitled to take into account the burden on its own resources and the giving of effect to Parliament's policy of dispersal of asylum-seekers. Absence of family or friends in the district of the notified local housing authority was not a sufficient reason for the notifying local housing authority to decide against making a referral.[284]

15.148 In addition, when considering a referral, local housing authorities may take into account, where it is relevant, the general housing circumstances prevailing in the district of the local housing authority potentially to be notified, particularly in cases where the applicant had made a previous application to that local housing authority and the two local housing

---

[279] HA 1996, s 198(1).
[280] *R v East Devon District Council ex p Robb* (1997) 30 HLR 922, QBD.
[281] English Code, para 18.5; Welsh Code, para 20.1.
[282] *R v Harrow London Borough Council ex p Carter* (1994) 26 HLR 32, QBD.
[283] Local Authorities' Agreement, English Code, Annex 18, para 3.4.
[284] *Ozbek v Ipswich Borough Council* [2006] EWCA Civ 534, [2006] HLR 41, CA at [61], per Chadwick LJ; see **15.72–15.81**.

authorities had come to different conclusions as to the nature of the homelessness duty owed to the applicant.[285]

15.149 Where the applicant or a member of his or her household has a local connection with more than one local housing authority (other than the local housing authority to which the application has been made), the notifying local housing authority is advised by the Local Authorities' Agreement to weigh up all the relevant factors in deciding which local housing authority to notify. The relevant factors include the applicant's own preference, and the relative strength of any residential local connection in relation to connections established by employment, family associations or special circumstances.[286]

15.150 There is no requirement on any local housing authority to notify another local housing authority of an application for homelessness assistance, even where it has decided that the conditions for referral are met. Local housing authorities are free to accept all those to whom they owe the main housing duty under HA 1996, s 193(2) duty, regardless of whether either set of the conditions for referral is met.[287]

NOTIFICATION DUTIES

Notification to the applicant[288]

15.151 Where any question of referring to another local housing authority arises, the local housing authority which received the application must notify the applicant of its decision-making on two occasions:[289]

(1) 'the first notification': when it has decided that the conditions for referral are met, and that it intends to notify another local housing authority of that opinion;[290] and

(2) 'the second notification': when it has later been decided (by the two local housing authorities agreeing, or by a referee) that the conditions for referral are or are not met.[291]

15.152 Each notification to the applicant must inform him or her that he or she has a right to request a review of the decision and of the 21-day period in which a review must be requested.[292] At all times, there is a duty on one of the

---

[285] Local Authorities' Agreement, English Code, Annex 18, para 3.4. *R v Newham London Borough Council ex p Tower Hamlets London Borough Council* [1991] 1 WLR 1032, CA.

[286] English Code, para 18.14 and Annex 18, para 4.11.

[287] English Code, para 18.4; Welsh Code, para 20.1.

[288] See also **10.66–10.81**.

[289] See English Code, paras 18.26–18.30; Welsh Code, paras 20.17–20.20.

[290] HA 1996, s 200(1).

[291] HA 1996, s 200(2).

[292] HA 1996, ss 184(4) and 200.

local housing authorities to accommodate the applicant, but which local housing authority is subject to that duty varies according to the progress of the notification.[293]

15.153 The *first* notification duty enables a local housing authority, in effect, to give the applicant a 'minded to refer' notification so that all the issues can be explored with the applicant before another local housing authority is troubled with what might transpire to be an inappropriate or impermissible referral. Alternatively, if the question of referral appears straightforward, it permits one local housing authority to give notice of referral to another straight away, whilst simultaneously also notifying the applicant that this has been done.

15.154 Once the *second* notification has been given to the applicant, the notifying local housing authority is no longer under a duty to provide accommodation for the applicant.[294] The notified authority becomes subject to the HA 1996, s 193(2) main housing duty.[295] The notifying local housing authority may continue to accommodate pending any review or appeal.[296]

Notification procedures between local housing authorities

15.155 Once the notifying local housing authority has formed the opinion that the conditions for referral are met and decided that a referral should be made, it is advised first to contact the local housing authority which it intends to notify by telephone and then confirm the notification in writing.[297] A pro-forma written notification is provided in the Local Authorities' Agreement.[298] Each local housing authority is expected to have a nominated officer to deal with such notifications as are received. Unless there is likely to be a dispute between the local housing authorities, the notified local housing authority should immediately start to make appropriate arrangements to provide accommodation and not wait for the written confirmation to arrive.[299] If it does accept responsibility (or is found by a referee to be responsible), the notified local housing authority should reimburse the notifying local housing authority for the cost of the accommodation it has provided to the applicant, unless there has been undue delay in making the referral.[300]

---

[293] See also **15.157–15.160**.

[294] HA 1996, s 200(1) and (5); English Code, para 18.27; Welsh Code, para 20.18.

[295] HA 1996, s 200(4).

[296] HA 1996, s 200(5); English Code, para 18.29; Welsh Code, para 20.19. See *R (Gebremarium) v Westminster City Council* [2009] EWHC 2254 (Admin), (2009) November *Legal Action*, p 26, Admin Ct, where the Administrative Court refused permission to seek a judicial review against Westminster's decision not to provide accommodation under HA 1996, s 200(5) pending a s 202 review of its decision to refer the claimant to Cardiff. See also **16.56–16.63**.

[297] English Code, Annex 18, para 6.1.

[298] English Code, Annex 18.

[299] English Code, Annex 18, para 6.1.

[300] English Code, Annex 18, para 7.3.

15.156 The notified local housing authority should reply to the notifying local housing authority (confirming whether or not it accepts responsibility) within 10 days of receiving the written confirmation of notification.[301]

DUTIES TO PROVIDE ACCOMMODATION

15.157 Once the first notification[302] has been given to the applicant, the notifying local housing authority's duty to provide interim accommodation for the applicant comes to an end.[303] In its place, a duty to provide accommodation under HA 1996, s 200(1) arises on the notifying local housing authority and runs until the second notification has been given.[304]

15.158 Once the second notification[305] has been given to the applicant, the duty to provide accommodation passes to the notified local housing authority.[306] If the applicant requests a review of that notification,[307] the notifying local housing authority has a power, but not a duty, to provide accommodation pending the determination of the review (and a similar power to provide accommodation pending the determination of any appeal against that review decision). The notified local housing authority, meanwhile, owes the HA 1996, s 193(2) main housing duty to provide accommodation for the applicant.[308]

15.159 The Local Authorities' Agreement recommends that local housing authorities 'should try to avoid causing undue disruption to the applicant' and consider reciprocal arrangements so as to avoid having to move a household.[309]

15.160 If, after the first notification, it is decided that the conditions for referral are *not* met, the notifying local housing authority's duty to the applicant becomes the main housing duty owed under HA 1996, s 193(2).[310]

---

[301] English Code, Annex 18, para 6.5.
[302] See also **15.151** and **15.153**.
[303] HA 1996, s 188(1) and (3).
[304] See **16.56–16.63** for further details on the nature and extent of this duty.
[305] See **15.151** and **15.154**.
[306] HA 1996, s 200(4).
[307] See also **19.23–19.25**.
[308] See also **17.23–17.168**.
[309] English Code, Annex 18, para 6.4; see **15.234–15.239**.
[310] HA 1996, s 200(3).

DISPUTES BETWEEN LOCAL HOUSING AUTHORITIES

15.161   Where the notified local housing authority disagrees with the opinion of the notifying local housing authority, as to whether the conditions for a referral are made out, there is a special procedure for resolution of the dispute.[311]

15.162   However, the notified local housing authority may have a more fundamental disagreement with the referral. It may disagree with one or more of the notifying local housing authority's earlier decisions: that the applicant is homeless, eligible for assistance, has a priority need and did not become homeless intentionally. In other words, it may dispute the proposition that the applicant is owed the HA 1996, s 193(2) main housing duty at all. The sense of grievance may be particularly strong when the notified local housing authority had previously accepted an application by the very same applicant, but had decided that the main housing duty was not owed (perhaps because the notified local housing authority had decided that the applicant had become homeless intentionally). The prospect of the applicant then applying to a different local housing authority, with which he or she has no local connection, and that local housing authority inquiring into the same facts, but coming to a different conclusion and then referring the performance of the main housing duty back to the original local housing authority is not one that the original local housing authority would find attractive. Although this may seem harsh to the notified local housing authority, an essential premise is that the notifying local housing authority has investigated all the circumstances 'with the same degree of care and thoroughness ... as it would for any other case'.[312]

15.163   The courts have made it very clear that, once a local housing authority has determined that the main housing duty is owed, and has notified another local housing authority that the conditions for referral are met, the notified local housing authority cannot re-open or go behind the inquiries and decisions made by the notifying authority as to the existence of the main housing duty.[313]

15.164   If it remains dissatisfied, the notified local housing authority can challenge, through judicial review, the lawfulness of the inquiries made by the notifying local housing authority before it came to its decision that the main housing duty was owed, or the legality of the decision itself. In *R v Tower Hamlets London Borough Council ex p Camden London Borough Council*,[314] the notifying local housing authority (Camden) should have made inquiries of the notified local housing authority (Tower Hamlets) and considered Tower Hamlets' reasons for finding that the applicant had become homeless intentionally, before making its own decision that a main housing duty was owed. In *R v Newham London Borough Council ex p Tower Hamlets London*

---

[311]   See **15.155–15.156**.
[312]   Local Authorities' Agreement, English Code, Annex 18, para 6.3.
[313]   *R v Slough Borough Council ex p Ealing London Borough Council* [1981] QB 801, CA.
[314]   (1989) 21 HLR 197, QBD.

Borough Council,[315] Newham notified Tower Hamlets of its intention to refer an applicant whom Tower Hamlets had previously found to have become homeless intentionally. Tower Hamlets successfully challenged the lawfulness of Newham's inquiries into the question of whether the applicant had become homeless intentionally.

15.165 Similarly, if the applicant applied to the notifying local housing authority after refusing an offer of accommodation from the notified local housing authority (and the notified local housing authority had decided that its duty to the applicant had come to an end), the notifying local housing authority could be challenged for failing to conclude that there had been no fresh incidence of homelessness.[316] If the notified local housing authority disputes, but does not challenge in the courts, the lawfulness of the notifying local housing authority's decision that a main housing duty would be owed, it cannot simply refuse to accept the referral. Nor can it seek to raise the matter as part of the procedures for resolving disputes over whether the conditions for referral are satisfied. It is bound by the notifying local housing authority's decision unless that decision is withdrawn or is successfully challenged, and quashed, in judicial review proceedings.[317] An applicant should never be required to bring his or her own legal proceedings to compel a local housing authority to act on a referral.

15.166 The notified local housing authority can, however, perfectly properly dispute the notifying local housing authority's opinion that the conditions for referral are met. The following paragraphs explain the procedure involved.

Determining disputes about whether the conditions for referral are met

15.167 The arrangements for resolving disputes between local housing authorities as to whether any of the three sets of conditions for referral is met have been negotiated and agreed between the organisations representing local authorities in England, Wales and in Scotland and have been approved by the Secretary of State.[318]

15.168 If the notified local housing authority wishes to challenge the referral, in the sense of contending that the conditions for referral are not made out, it must state its written reasons in full within 10 days of receiving the referral

---

[315] [1991] 1 WLR 1032, CA.

[316] *R v Hammersmith and Fulham London Borough Council ex p O'Brien* (1985) 17 HLR 471, QBD.

[317] *R (Bantamagbari) v Westminster City Council* [2003] EWHC 1350 (Admin), (2003) July *Legal Action*, p 27, Admin Ct; and *R (Enfield London Borough Council) v Broxbourne Borough Council* [2004] EWHC 1053 (Admin), (2004) May *Legal Action*, p 26, Admin Ct.

[318] Homelessness (Decisions on Referrals) Order 1998, SI 1998/1578, made under the Secretary of State's powers at HA 1996, s 198(5) and approving the Guidelines for Local Authorities and Referees Agreement at English Code, Annex 18. The Agreement is not reproduced in the Welsh Code which refers to the Agreement at paras 20.8 and 20.21–20.24.

notification.[319] On receipt of that response, the notifying local housing authority may accept the notified local housing authority's position and withdraw the referral.

15.169 However, if there is no agreement between the two local housing authorities, the question of whether the conditions for referral are met should be decided by a referee. The referee should be appointed within 21 days of notification to the notified local housing authority of the referral.[320] The local housing authorities agree to be bound by the referee's decision. The two local housing authorities may themselves find and appoint an agreed referee, but if they cannot agree on the identity of the referee, one will be appointed by the chairperson of their appropriate local government organisation.[321] The request for a referee to be appointed should be jointly made, or can be made by the notifying local housing authority alone if the notified local housing authority has failed to agree to accept the referral within six weeks of the referral having been made.[322]

15.170 The referee, once appointed, invites both local housing authorities to submit representations within 14 working days. Each local housing authority will have the opportunity to consider the other's representations, and to comment in writing on those representations within a further 10 working days. If the representations are insufficient, the referee can invite further representations on any issue that he or she considers necessary. Although the applicant is not a party to this particular aspect of the dispute, he or she should be sent the local housing authorities' representations. It is up to the referee whether the applicant should be invited to comment, or to make written representations. The referee may choose to hold an oral hearing and the Local Authorities' Agreement advises that an oral hearing might be necessary or more convenient where the applicant is illiterate, where English is not his or her first language, or where further information is necessary for the issues to be resolved.[323]

15.171 The referee's decision must be given in writing. The Local Authorities' Agreement recommends that the decision should be reached 'as quickly as possible' and normally within one month from receipt of both the local housing authorities' written representations.[324] The decision should record the issues, the referee's findings of fact, the decision and the reasons for the decision. Copies should be sent to both local housing authorities and the

---

[319] English Code, Annex 18, para 10.2.
[320] English Code, Annex 18, para 10.3.
[321] There is a small panel of referees established by the local authority organisations to perform this function. The list of panel members is maintained by the Local Government Association.
[322] English Code, Annex 18, paras 10.6–10.7.
[323] English Code, Annex 18, paras 13.1–14.3.
[324] English Code, Annex 18, para 13.5.

appropriate local government organisation. The notifying local housing authority should inform the applicant of the decision.[325] One judge described the aims of the procedure:

> 'the legislature intended that these matters should be disposed of within a particular specified time frame and "as quickly as possible" and "promptly". It is also obvious from the terms of that guidance that it is, as one would expect, contemplated by the legislature that the relevant applicant should be kept informed of what is going on, to a reasonable extent.'[326]

15.172 The applicant may then request a review of the referee's decision, in which case a reviewer will have to be appointed by agreement between the two local housing authorities; this would commonly be another referee from the panel maintained by the local authority associations.[327]

15.173 The written decisions of the referees are collected by the local government associations and distributed among other members of the panel of referees (no doubt to encourage consistency of decision-making). They are not officially published. By the end of 2004 only some 120 decisions had been made by referees since the inception of the scheme in 1977. The great bulk had been made in the early years and over the past decade no more than a handful of disputes has been resolved by referees each year.[328]

CHALLENGES BY THE APPLICANT

15.174 The applicant has the right to request the review of a number of the decisions that a local housing authority may make in connection with referral procedures, including:

(1) any decision made by the local housing authority to which the applicant applied, to notify another local housing authority;[329]

(2) any decision reached, by agreement between the two local housing authorities or by a referee's decision, that the conditions for referral are met;[330] and

---

[325] English Code, Annex 18, paras 15.1 and 17.1–17.2.
[326] *Berhane v Lambeth London Borough Council* [2007] EWHC 2702, (2008) March *Legal Action*, p 21, QBD, at [36] per Eady J.
[327] Allocation of Housing and Homelessness (Review Procedures) Regulations 1999, SI 1999/71, reg 7. See also **19.80–19.81**.
[328] In November 1980 the then London Boroughs Association produced an indexed Digest covering decisions 1–25. A supplement in May 1982 added decisions 26–43. A second update in December 1986 added and indexed decisions up to No 60. However, production of the Digest ceased with the issue of a final supplement in 1993 (which added decisions up to and including No 89 to the text).
[329] HA 1996, s 202(1)(c). See **19.16–19.22**.
[330] HA 1996, s 202(1)(d). See **19.23–19.25**.

(3)   any decision[331] by either of the two local housing authorities as to which of them is subject to the main housing duty.[332]

15.175   Those rights, read together with the requirements of notification to the applicant,[333] have the effect that, during the referral process, the applicant could substantively challenge decisions to make a referral on two occasions and on a number of issues. The applicant will receive two decisions:

(1)   a decision made by the local housing authority to which he or she applied to notify another local housing authority;[334] and then

(2)   a decision reached by agreement between the two local housing authorities or by a referee that the conditions for referral are met.[335]

15.176   Both of those decisions can be challenged by the applicant making a request for a review if the applicant wishes to do so.

15.177   The applicant has, in effect, the right to request a review in relation to a local connection referral, *of the notifying local housing authority's decision* that:

(1)   the applicant, or a member of his or her household, has no local connection with it; or

(2)   the applicant, or a member of his or her household, has a local connection with the district of another local housing authority; or

(3)   the applicant, or a member of his or her household, will not run the risk of domestic violence in the district of the other local housing authority; or

(4)   the applicant, or a member of his or her household, has not suffered violence in the district of the other local housing authority; or

(5)   the applicant, or a member of his or her household, has suffered violence, but it is not probable that any return to the other local housing authority's district will lead to further violence of a similar kind against the victim; or

(6)   the other local housing authority should be notified of the local housing authority's decision that the conditions for referral are met.

---

[331]   Under HA 1996, s 200(3) or (4).
[332]   HA 1996, s 202(1)(e). Now redundant: see **19.26**.
[333]   See **15.151–15.154**.
[334]   HA 1996, s 184(4) and (5). See **10.66–10.81** and **15.151–15.153**.
[335]   HA 1996, s 200(2).

15.178 In addition, the applicant has the right to request a review, following a referral, *of both local housing authorities' decisions*, or *of a referee's decision*, that:

(1) the applicant, or a member of his or her household, has no local connection with the local housing authority to which he or she applied; or

(2) the applicant, or a member of his or her household, has a local connection with the district of another local housing authority; or

(3) the applicant, or a member of his or her household, will not run the risk of domestic violence in the district of the other local housing authority; or

(4) the applicant or a member of his or her household, has not suffered violence in the other local housing authority's district; or

(5) the applicant, or a member of his or her household, has suffered violence, but it is not probable that any return to the other local housing authority's district will lead to further violence of a similar kind against the victim.

15.179 In relation to the second set of conditions for referral between local housing authorities in England,[336] the applicant has the right to request a review *of the notifying local housing authority's decision* that:

(1) he or she accepted a private rented sector offer[337] from another local housing authority and has made his or her application for homelessness assistance within two years of the date of acceptance;[338] or

(2) he or she, or a member of his or her household, will not run the risk of domestic violence in the district of the other local housing authority;[339] or

---

[336] HA 1996 s 198(2ZA) and (2A) amended by LA 2011, s 149 (5)–(7) and applicable to applicants whose applications for homelessness assistance were made on or after 9 November 2012 to a local housing authority in England. At the date of writing, the amendments to HA 1996 made by LA 2011, ss 148–149 had not been brought into effect in Wales. See **15.116–15.131**.

[337] HA 1996, s 193(7AA) amended by LA 2011, s 148 (5) and applicable to applicants whose applications for homelessness assistance were made on or after 9 November 2012 to a local housing authority in England. At the date of writing, the amendments to HA 1996 made by LA 2011, ss 148–149 had not been brought into effect in Wales. See **17.109–17.118**.

[338] HA 1996, s 198(2ZA)(a) applicable to applicants whose applications for homelessness assistance were made on or after 9 November 2012 to a local housing authority in England. At the date of writing, the amendments to HA 1996 made by LA 2011, ss 148–149 had not been brought into effect in Wales. See **9.89–9.95** and **15.116–15.131**.

[339] HA 1996, s 198(2ZA) (b) amended by LA 2011, s 149(5) and (6) and applicable to applicants whose applications for homelessness assistance were made on or after 9 November 2012 to a local housing authority in England. At the date of writing, the amendments to HA 1996 made by LA 2011, ss 148–149 had not been brought into effect in Wales. See **15.98–15.104** and **15.121–15.131**.

(3)   he or she, or a member of his or her household, has not suffered violence in the district of the other local housing authority;[340] or

(4)   he or she, or a member of his or her household, has suffered violence, but it is not probable that any return to the other local housing authority's district will lead to further violence of a similar kind against the victim;[341] or

(5)   the other local housing authority should be notified of the local housing authority's decision that the conditions for referral are met.[342]

15.180   In addition, the applicant has the right to request a review, following a referral, *of both local housing authorities' decisions,* or *of a referee's decision,* that:

(1)   he or she accepted a private rented sector offer[343] from another local housing authority and has made his or her application for homelessness assistance within two years of the date of acceptance;[344] or

(2)   he or she, or a member of his or her household, will not run the risk of domestic violence in the district of the other local housing authority;[345] or

(3)   he or she, or a member of his or her household, has not suffered violence in the district of the other local housing authority;[346] or

---

[340]   HA 1996, s 198(2A) amended by LA 2011 (5) and (7) applicable to applicants whose applications for homelessness assistance were made on or after 9 November 2012 to a local housing authority in England. At the date of writing, the amendments to HA 1996 made by LA 2011, ss 148–149 had not been brought into effect in Wales. See **15.98–15.101** and **15.105–15.108**.

[341]   HA 1996, s 198(2A) amended by LA 2011 (5) and (7) applicable to applicants whose applications for homelessness assistance were made on or after 9 November 2012 to a local housing authority in England. At the date of writing, the amendments to HA 1996 made by LA 2011, ss 148–149 had not been brought into effect in Wales. See **15.98–15.101**, **15.105–15.111** and **15.121–15.131**.

[342]   HA 1996, s 198(1). See **15.146–15.150**.

[343]   HA 1996, s 193(7AA) as amended by LA 2011 (5) and applicable to applicants whose applications for homelessness assistance were made on or after 9 November 2012 to a local housing authority in England. At the date of writing, the amendments to HA 1996 made by LA 2011, ss 148–149 had not been brought into effect in Wales. See **17.109–17.118**.

[344]   HA 1996, s 198(2ZA)(a) amended by LA 2011 (5) and (7) applicable to applicants whose applications for homelessness assistance were made on or after 9 November 2012 to a local housing authority in England. At the date of writing, the amendments to HA 1996 made by LA 2011, ss 148–149 had not been brought into effect in Wales. See **9.89–9.95** and **15.121–15.131**.

[345]   HA 1996 s 198(2ZA)(b) amended by LA 2011 (5) and (7) applicable to applicants whose applications for homelessness assistance were made on or after 9 November 2012 to a local housing authority in England. At the date of writing, the amendments to HA 1996 made by LA 2011, ss 148–149 had not been brought into effect in Wales. See **15.98–15.104**.

[346]   HA 1996 s 198(2A) amended by LA 2011 (5) and (7) applicable to applicants whose applications for homelessness assistance were made on or after 9 November 2012 to a local

(4) he or she, or a member of his or her household, has suffered violence, but it is not probable that any return to the other local housing authority's district will lead to further violence of a similar kind against the victim.[347]

15.181 For applicants to local housing authorities in England,[348] in relation to the third set of conditions for referral,[349] the applicant has the right to request a review of any decision *by the notifying local housing authority* (authority A) that:

(1) the applicant was, on a previous application to authority B, placed in the district of authority A in performance of authority B's homelessness functions; or

(2) that the previous application to authority B was made within the prescribed period of the application to authority A; or

(3) that authority A should notify authority B of its decision that these conditions for referral are met.

15.182 In addition, the applicant has the right to request a review, following a referral, of *both local housing authorities' decisions*, or *of a referee's decision*, that:

(1) the applicant was on a previous application to authority B placed in the district of authority A in performance of authority B's homelessness functions; or

(2) the previous application was within the prescribed period.

15.183 However, there is *no* statutory right to request a review of any of the other decisions involved in the process, including:

(1) a decision, by the local housing authority to which he or she has applied, to make or not to make inquiries into local connection or the other conditions of referral;[350]

---

housing authority in England. At the date of writing, the amendments to HA 1996 made by LA 2011, ss 148–149 had not been brought into effect in Wales. See **15.98–15.101** and **15.104–15.111**.

[347] HA 1996, s 198(2A) amended by LA 2011 (5) and (7) applicable to applicants whose applications for homelessness assistance were made on or after 9 November 2012 to a local housing authority in England. At the date of writing, the amendments to HA 1996 made by LA 2011, ss 148–149 had not been brought into effect in Wales. See **15.98–15.101** and **15.104–15.111**.

[348] It is the authors' view that this third set of conditions for referral does not apply to local housing authorities in Wales, but the Welsh Code, paras 20.3–20.5, advises that it does. See **15.133**.

[349] HA 1996, s 198(4). See **15.132–15.145**.

[350] HA 1996, s 184(2); *Hackney London Borough Council v Sareen* [2003] EWCA Civ 351, [2003] HLR 54, CA. See **15.19–15.24**.

(2)   a decision by the local housing authority that the conditions of referral are met, but that another local housing authority should not be notified of the application;[351] and

(3)   a decision by the notifying local housing authority not to exercise its power to provide accommodation pending determination of a request for a review of the decision made by the two local housing authorities jointly or by the referee.[352]

15.184   Challenges to those decisions can only be brought by judicial review.[353]

15.185   The procedure for requesting a review of any decision by the notifying local housing authority is the same as for any other request for a review, and the reviewer will be appointed by the notifying local housing authority in the usual way.[354] The trigger for a request for a review is notification to the applicant of one of the decisions .[355]

15.186   If the request is to review a decision made as to whether the conditions for referral are met, the decision will have been made either by agreement between the notifying and notified local housing authorities, or by a referee. In either case, the request should be made to the notifying local housing authority.[356]

15.187   If the decision was one made by agreement between the two local housing authorities, then the review must be undertaken by them jointly.[357] Presumably this will mean an arrangement for a joint committee or a joint panel of officers.

15.188   If a referee made the decision, then the reviewer should be a person jointly appointed by the local housing authorities within five working days from the day on which the review request was received by the notifying local housing authority.[358] This appointee could be anyone to whom both local housing authorities are prepared to entrust the review process.[359] If an appointment is not agreed within that time frame, the notifying local housing authority (which has received the review request) has a further five working

[351]   HA 1996, s 198(1). See **15.146–15.150**.
[352]   HA 1996, s 200(5). See *R (Gebremarium) v Westminster City Council* [2009] EWHC 2254 (Admin), (2009) November *Legal Action*, p 26, Admin Ct for an example of an unsuccessful challenge in judicial review to Westminster's decision not to exercise its HA 1996, s 200(5) power pending a review of its decision to refer her to Cardiff. See also **15.158** and **16.62–16.63**.
[353]   See **19.224–19.250**.
[354]   See **19.52–19.64** and **19.76–19.79**.
[355]   *Berhane v Lambeth London Borough Council* [2007] EWHC 2702, (2008) March *Legal Action*, p 21, QBD. Those decisions are described at **15.177, 15.179** and **15.181**.
[356]   Allocation of Housing and Homelessness (Review Procedures) Regulations 1999, SI 1999/71, reg 6(1)(b). Those decisions are described at **15.178, 15.180** and **15.182**.
[357]   SI 1999/71, reg 1(2)(b)(i).
[358]   SI 1999/71, reg 7(1).
[359]   English Code, Annex 18, para 20.2; Welsh Code, paras 20.23 and 21.12–21.13.

days to ask the chair of the Local Government Association (LGA)[360] to appoint another referee.[361] The chair of the LGA must then appoint a referee within a further seven days[362] from among the membership of a panel appointed by the LGA.[363] That person then undertakes the review. Although this may appear to be a very tight time frame,[364] the membership of the panel comprises only a handful of referees, one of whom is already eliminated because he or she took the decision.[365] Whether appointed by the local housing authorities or by the LGA, the reviewer will in this Chapter be referred to as to the 'appointed' reviewer.[366]

15.189 Once the appointed reviewer has been appointed, the local housing authorities should supply the reasons for the decision under review, together with information and evidence in support. The appointed reviewer will inform the applicant of the procedure to be followed during the review process and that he or she may make written representations. The request for a review and representations made by the applicant should be sent to the local housing authorities and they should be invited to respond. If there is thought to be a deficiency or irregularity in the original decision, further written or oral representations should be invited.[367]

15.190 If the appointed reviewer is a person appointed by agreement between the two local housing authorities, the review decision must be notified to the applicant within 10 weeks from the date of the request for the review.[368] If the appointed reviewer was appointed from a panel, the period is 12 weeks for notification to the applicant, and the review decision will be notified to the local housing authorities one week prior to notification to the applicant, in order to give the local housing authorities concerned time to notify a review decision within the 12-week period.[369]

15.191 Once the review has been determined, and the decision on review notified to the applicant, the applicant may appeal to the county court against

[360] Or Convention of Scottish Local Authorities, if the notified authority is in Scotland.
[361] Allocation of Housing and Homelessness (Review Procedures) Regulations 1999, SI 1999/71, reg 7(2); English Code, Annex 18, para 20.2.
[362] English Code, Annex 18, para 20.2; Welsh Code, para 21.12; it is unclear from the Regulations whether the LGA has seven working days or seven non-working days. The English Code refers to the five-day period as 'working days' and to the seven-day period simply as 'seven days', which suggests that the Regulations mean seven working days, including non-working days. The Welsh Code refers to each period as 'working days', paras 21.12.
[363] Allocation of Housing and Homelessness (Review Procedures) Regulations 1999, SI 1999/71, reg 7(2)(b) and (3).
[364] SI 1999/71, reg 7(7) defines 'working day'.
[365] SI 1999/71, reg 7(6).
[366] SI 1999/71, reg 7 refers to the reviewer appointed in these circumstances as 'the appointed person'.
[367] SI 1999/71, regs 6(3), 7(4), (5), 8(1) and (2); and see **19.87–19.101**.
[368] SI 1999/71, reg 9(1)(b).
[369] SI 1999/71, reg 9(1)(c) and (3). The Local Authorities' Agreement does not refer to the 12-week period for disputes between local housing authorities in England (English Code, Annex 18, paras 9.1–9.6), but the Regulation is still in force.

the review decision. The exercise of this right is entirely separate from any dispute that may be going on between the two local housing authorities. In one case, the county court judge's decision to adjourn the appeal whilst the notifying and notified local housing authorities sought to resolve their dispute was criticised by an appeal judge because it 'denies the appellant effective access to the court, where there is, or is likely to be, undue delay on the part of the relevant respondent.'[370]

SPECIAL RULES FOR FORMER ASYLUM-SEEKERS

15.192   The special rules are intended to mirror the dispersal provisions for asylum-seekers contained in Immigration and Asylum Act 1999 and implemented by the UKBA. They will be repealed whenever HA 1996, s 186 is repealed.[371] There is provision to repeal HA 1996, s 186 by statutory instrument; that power has not yet been exercised but, no doubt, will be when there are no longer any eligible asylum-seekers receiving homelessness assistance.[372] Since the only applicants who can be affected by these special rules are those who made their applications for homelessness assistance before 3 April 2000, this edition of this book does not set out the special rules. Reference can be made to the first or second editions of this book.[373]

The power to assist former asylum-seekers who occupied UKBA accommodation in Scotland

15.193   Former asylum-seekers who leave accommodation in Scotland provided by the UKBA under Immigration and Asylum Act 1999, s 95 and then apply as homeless to local housing authorities in England or Wales will not normally have a local connection with the district of the local authority in Scotland (unless by reason of employment, family associations, or some other special circumstance).

15.194   If such former asylum-seekers do not have a local connection with any other local housing authority in England or Wales, they would ordinarily be owed the HA 1996, s 193(2) main housing duty by the local housing authority in England or in Wales to which they applied. However, legislation passed in 2004 provides that where local housing authorities in England or Wales would otherwise have a main housing duty[374] towards those former asylum-seekers, the duty does not apply.[375]

---

[370] *Berhane v Lambeth London Borough Council* [2007] EWHC 2702, (2008) March *Legal Action*, p 21, QBD, at [43] per Eady J.
[371] SI 1999/3126, reg 7.
[372] Immigration and Asylum Act 1999, ss 117(5), 169(3) and Sch 16.
[373] Luba and Davies *Housing Allocation and Homelessness* (1st edn, 2006; 2nd edn, 2010).
[374] HA 1996, s 193(2). See **17.23–17.168**.
[375] Asylum and Immigration (Treatment of Claimants etc) Act 2004, s 11(2) and (3), in force from 4 January 2005.

15.195 Instead, the local housing authority in England or in Wales has a power (but no duty):

- to provide accommodation for the former asylum-seeker for a period that would give him or her a reasonable opportunity of obtaining accommodation; and

- to provide advice and assistance with any attempts he or she may make to obtain his or her own accommodation.[376]

15.196 The idea is that the former asylum-seeker will either obtain his or her own accommodation in England or Wales, with assistance from the local housing authority (if the local housing authority chooses to provide it), or will return to Scotland and make an application for homelessness assistance to a local authority in Scotland.[377] Indeed, the English Code specifically suggests that the local housing authority consider:

> 'providing such advice and assistance as would enable the applicant to make an application for housing to the Scottish authority in the district where the section 95 accommodation was last provided, or to another Scottish authority of the applicant's choice.'[378]

15.197 Since, under Scottish law, the former asylum-seeker will most likely have no local connection with any local housing authority in England, Wales or Scotland, a local authority in Scotland will be subject to the main housing duty. There is no need for the former asylum-seeker to apply to the Scottish local authority in Scotland in whose district he or she had been accommodated by the UKBA.[379] He or she could apply to any Scottish local authority.

15.198 The extraordinary effect of this provision is to put a former asylum-seeker who was dispersed to Scotland by the UKBA but has become homeless unintentionally from UKBA accommodation and wishes to apply for accommodation to a local housing authority in England or in Wales in a worse position than a person who has become homeless intentionally. At least an applicant who has become homeless intentionally (who also had a priority need) would be owed a temporary accommodation *duty* by the local housing authority to which he or she had applied.[380] Moreover, the local housing

---

[376] Asylum and Immigration (Treatment of Claimants etc) Act 2004, s 11(3)(b), in force from 4 January 2005.

[377] Since an application for homelessness assistance can be made in any manner and should not require completion of the local housing authority's standard form, the former asylum-seeker could be assisted to make an application to any local authority in Scotland by writing, by fax, or even by email. There should be no need to leave any accommodation provided by the local housing authority in England or in Wales until the local authority in Scotland has notified the applicant that the application for homelessness assistance has been received and that suitable accommodation will be provided.

[378] English Code, para 18.21. Surprisingly, there is no reference in the Welsh Code to this power.

[379] English Code, para 18.21.

[380] HA 1996, s 190(2)(a). See **17.182–17.189**.

authority in England or in Wales is permitted no discretion. If the conditions are made out, no duty is owed to the former asylum-seeker.

15.199 Any decision by the local housing authority that such an applicant is caught by these provisions and not owed the main housing duty[381] would be a decision as to 'what duty (if any) is owed'. The applicant would have a right to request a review of that decision under HA 1996, s 202(1)(b).

15.200 The powers given to local housing authorities in England or in Wales under the Asylum and Immigration (Treatment of Claimants etc) Act 2004 (whether or not to provide accommodation and/or whether or not to provide advice and assistance) are discretionary powers and carry no statutory right to request a review. If a local housing authority decided not to exercise these powers, any challenge could only be brought on a point of law in judicial review proceedings.[382]

15.201 An applicant who had been provided with accommodation under the interim duty owed by the local housing authority in England or in Wales would be entitled to reasonable notice of the termination of that accommodation.[383]

CROSS-BORDER REFERRALS

15.202 All the countries of the UK[384] operate statutory homelessness schemes. This book is concerned only with the detailed scheme for England and Wales found in HA 1996, Part 7. But cross-border referrals may arise between local housing authorities in England or in Wales and when local housing authorities in England or in Wales make referrals to, or are asked to receive referrals from, other countries in the UK.

Referrals within England and Wales

15.203 The referral arrangements in HA 1996, Part 7 govern all formal referrals between local housing authorities in England or Wales. They apply to referrals between:

* a local housing authority in Wales and one or more other local housing authorities in Wales;

* a local housing authority in England and one or more other local housing authorities in England;

---

[381] HA 1996, s 193(2). See **17.23–17.168**.
[382] See **19.224–19.250** for judicial review.
[383] HA 1996, s 188(1); *R v Newham London Borough Council ex p Ojuri (No 3)* (1999) 31 HLR 631, QBD.
[384] England, Wales, Scotland and Northern Ireland. See Interpretation Act 1978, s 5 and Sch 1; and see Box 1 at **12.66**.

- a local housing authority in England and one or more local housing authorities in Wales; and

- a local housing authority in Wales and one or more local housing authorities in England.

15.204 Since devolution, the Welsh Ministers has had their own powers to make secondary legislation[385] and to issue their own homelessness guidance.[386] They have exercised these powers in relation to the homelessness provisions. There is a separate Code of Guidance in Wales and the regulations made by the Welsh Ministers do not mirror precisely those made by English ministers. The net result is a potential for disparity between the treatment of an application for homelessness assistance by a local housing authority in Wales as compared to that by a local housing authority in England. An applicant to a local housing authority in Wales might well be accepted as having priority need in circumstances in which no priority need would be found by a local housing authority in England (because of the different wording of the two Priority Need Orders).[387] The result may be that an applicant is found to be owed the main housing duty by a local housing authority in Wales when no such duty would be found by a local housing authority in England (and indeed may have been positively rejected on a previous application to a local housing authority in England).[388]

15.205 These nuances cannot, however, make any difference to the application of the first set of referral conditions discussed in this Chapter.[389] For example, if a local housing authority in Wales finds that it owes the main duty to an applicant who has no local connection with its district but who does have a local connection with a local housing authority in England(and would run no risk of violence by returning there), it may make a referral. No doubt, in considering the exercise of its discretion whether to refer,[390] it might wish to take into account that, on the same facts, the notified local housing authority might not have owed the main housing duty at all.

15.206 However, as this Chapter has described, an applicant to a local housing authority in England who was placed in that local housing authority's district by another local housing authority as a result of the acceptance by the

---

[385] Orders and Regulations. The power was originally exercisable by the National Assembly for Wales and transferred to the Welsh Assembly Government effective from 25 May 2007. The Welsh Assembly Government is now known as the Welsh Government.

[386] Government of Wales Act 1998 and Government of Wales Act 2006, s 161 and Sch 11, para 30.

[387] See **13.126–13.211** (English Priority Need Order), and **13.212–13.245** (Welsh Priority Need Order). The Welsh Code refers to these differences, see para 20.8.

[388] There are also different legislative provisions in England and Wales governing eligibility (see Chapter 12 of this book) and different guidance on decisions about whether or not an applicant has become homeless intentionally (see Chapter 14 of this book).

[389] See **15.42–15.115**.

[390] See **15.146–15.150**.

applicant of a private rented sector offer[391] or in performance of the local housing authority's homelessness functions could be referred back to the first local housing authority under the second[392] or third[393] set of conditions for referral.[394] This is not the case for applications to local housing authorities in Wales.[395]

15.207 Where the two local housing authorities involved are both local housing authorities in England, then the conditions for referral can be operated without difficulty. However, what happens in the following circumstances:

(1) Where an applicant to a local housing authority in Wales had previously accepted a private rented sector offer made by a local housing authority in England in the district of the local housing authority in Wales and the applicant makes a fresh application for homelessness assistance to the local housing authority in Wales within two years of the date of acceptance of the offer?

(2) Where an applicant to a local housing authority in Wales has previously been placed in that local housing authority's district, within the prescribed period by a local housing authority in England, in pursuance of its homelessness functions?

(3) Where an applicant applies to a local housing authority in England, having previously been placed in its district by a local housing authority in Wales?

15.208 There is nothing in HA 1996, Part 7, the Regulations, either of the Codes or the Local Authorities' Agreement that sheds any light on these cross-border problems. The authors' view is that it would certainly be difficult for local housing authority in Wales, in the first and second scenarios, to attempt to apply the conditions for referral at HA 1996, s 198(2ZA) and (2), and (4). It remains to be seen whether a local housing authority in England in the third scenario could attempt to apply those conditions to refer to a local housing authority in Wales under HA 1996, s 198(4).

---

[391] HA 1996, s 193(7AA) as amended by LA 2011, s 148(5) applicable to applicants whose applications for homelessness assistance were made on or after 9 November 2012 to a local housing authority in England. At the date of writing, the amendments to HA 1996 made by LA 2011, ss 148–149 had not been brought into effect in Wales. See **17.109–17.118**.

[392] HA 1996, s 198(2ZA) and (2A) as amended by LA 2011, s 149(5) and (7), applicable to applicants whose applications for homelessness assistance were made on or after 9 November 2012 to a local housing authority in England. At the date of writing, the amendments to HA 1996 made by LA 2011, ss 148–149 had not been brought into effect in Wales. See **15.116–15.131**.

[393] HA 1996, s 198(4). See **15.132–15.145**.

[394] See **15.116-15.145**.

[395] See **15.133** for the authors' view as to why the third set of conditions does not apply to local housing authorities in Wales. However, the Welsh Code, paras 20.3–20.5, advises that this set of conditions for referral does apply to local housing authorities in Wales.

Referrals to the Isles of Scilly

15.209   The Isles of Scilly are administratively part of England,[396] but special measures have been taken to protect the very limited stock of social housing on those islands. HA 1996[397] enables the Secretary of State to make an order adapting HA 1996, Part 7 in its application to the Isles of Scilly, and that power has been used.[398] So, for example, there are special provisions governing eligibility for applicants applying there.[399]

15.210   To prevent these eligibility rules being circumvented by an application directed initially to a local housing authority elsewhere, modifications have been made by Order to arrangements for referral by other local housing authorities to the Isles of Scilly Council.

15.211   If a homeless applicant applies to a local housing authority elsewhere in England or in Wales and the conditions for a local connection referral to the Council of the Isles of Scilly would otherwise be met, they are displaced by other rules. The intended effect of the Order[400] is that the applicant will only have a local connection with the Isles of Scilly if she or he has resided in the district of the Isles of Scilly Council for two years and six months during the three years prior to the date that the latest application for homelessness assistance is made. If that period of residence is established, there is deemed local connection in place of the normal local connection provisions.[401]

15.212   It is recognised that the Isles of Scilly may need to accommodate some of its homeless applicants on the mainland. As a result, local housing authorities in England can refer back to the islands if the second or third sets of conditions for a referral is made out.[402] This is because the power to modify HA 1996[403] has not been used in relation to this set of conditions.

Referrals to Scotland

15.213   The provisions of HA 1996, Part 7 enable local housing authorities in either England or in Wales to make referrals to local authorities in Scotland in just the same way as they might make a referral to another local housing authority in England or Wales. The Local Authorities' Agreement[404] was drawn up in co-operation with the Confederation of Scottish Local Authorities

---

[396]   Interpretation Act 1978, s 5 and Sch 1.

[397]   HA 1996, s 225(1).

[398]   Homelessness (Isles of Scilly) Order 1997, SI 1997/797.

[399]   Discussed at **12.241–12.242**.

[400]   Which is not well drafted.

[401]   HA 1996, s 199(1).

[402]   See **15.116–15.145**. However, for either of the second or third conditions for referral to apply, the Isles of Scilly would have had to have made private rented sector offers of accommodation or to have secured accommodation for an applicant in the district of a local housing authority in England, which seems unlikely.

[403]   HA 1996, s 225(2).

[404]   See **15.167–15.173**.

(CoSLA) and applies in the same way to referrals to local authorities in Scotland as it would to any other referral.

15.214 The Local Authorities' Agreement provides that, where there is a cross-border dispute, the relevant law to be applied is that relevant to the location of the notified local housing authority.[405] This only applies to the issue of whether or not the conditions for referral are or are not made out, and not to any other disagreements that the notified local housing authority may have with the decision of the notifying local housing authority.[406]

15.215 The only procedural difference is that if the notified local authority (in Scotland) does not accept that the conditions for referral are made out and is unable to agree with the notifying local housing authority (in England or in Wales) on the identity of a referee to resolve the dispute, then it is CoSLA which appoints a referee in default of such agreement.[407] The adjudication will then be governed by the procedural rules in the Homelessness (Decisions on Referrals) (Scotland) Order 1998.[408]

15.216 If the conditions for a referral are not made out, a local housing authority in England or in Wales may nevertheless invite a local authority in Scotland to assist in the discharge of HA 1996, Part 7 functions. The local authority in Scotland would be bound to co-operate with that request to such extent as was reasonable in the particular circumstances.[409]

Referrals from Scotland

15.217 The capacity of a local authority in Scotland to refer an application for homelessness assistance to a local housing authority in England or Wales will primarily be regulated by the law of Scotland (which is beyond the scope of this book). It must be noted, however, that there are several differences in the operation of homelessness provisions, including those relating to referrals, as between Scotland and England and Wales. For example:

- applicants in Scotland have no statutory right to seek a review of a decision to refer them to a local housing authority in England or Wales;

---

[405] Local Authorities' Agreement, English Code, Annex 18, para 11.4.
[406] See **15.161–15.165**.
[407] Local Authorities' Agreement, English Code, Annex 18, para 10.6.
[408] Homelessness (Decisions on Referrals) (Scotland) Order 1998, SI 1998/1603.
[409] HA 1996, s 213(1).

- the second and third sets of conditions for a statutory referral (reference back to a local housing authority which made a private rented sector offer or placed the applicant in the present local housing authority's area)[410] do not extend to Scotland;[411] and

- the deemed local connection for residents of UKBA accommodation[412] is not part of the law of Scotland.

15.218 However, if a local authority in Scotland (applying the law of Scotland) forms the opinion that the conditions for a referral to a local housing authority in England or Wales are met, it may notify the local housing authority in England or in Wales to that effect. If the notified local housing authority accepts that the conditions for a referral are satisfied, then the application is referred in the normal way. If the local housing authority in England or in Wales does not accept that the necessary conditions are satisfied, a referee will be appointed by agreement or in default by the Local Government Association.[413] The adjudication will then be governed by the procedural rules in the Homelessness (Decisions on Referrals) Order.[414]

15.219 If the conditions for a referral are not made out, a local authority in Scotland may nevertheless invite a local housing authority in England or Wales to assist in the discharge of its homelessness duties. The local housing authority in England or in Wales would be bound to co-operate with that request to such extent as was reasonable in the particular circumstances.[415]

15.220 The Homelessness etc (Scotland) Act 2003 contains powers under which ministers of the Scottish Executive may effectively abolish the referral powers of local authorities in Scotland so that responsibility for a homeless person in Scotland will remain with the local authority to which an applicant first applies.[416] The powers have yet to be used.

---

[410] Second set of conditions at HA 1996, s 198(2ZA) and (2A)(4) as amended by LA 2011, s 149(5) and (7) applicable to applicants whose applications for homelessness assistance were made on or after 9 November 2012?? to a local housing authority in England. At the date of writing, the amendments to HA 1996 made by LA 2011, ss 148–149 had not been brought into effect in Wales. See**15.116–15.131**. Third set of conditions at HA 1996, s 198(4), see paras **15.132–15.145**.

[411] Because LA 2011 does not apply to Scotland and because there is no mechanism for prescribing the relevant period.

[412] HA 1996, s 199(6) and (7), added by Asylum and Immigration (Treatment of Claimants etc) Act 2004, s 11(1), in force from 4 January 2005.

[413] Local Authorities' Agreement, English Code, Annex 18, para 10.3; Welsh Code, paras 20.21–20.24.

[414] SI 1998/1603. See Local Authorities' Agreement, English Code, Annex 18, para 11.4.

[415] HA 1996, s 213.

[416] Homelessness (Scotland) Act 2003, s 8.

Northern Ireland

15.221   Northern Ireland has its own self-contained legislative scheme for homelessness.[417] No doubt because there is a single authority dealing with applications for homelessness assistance in Northern Ireland (the Housing Executive), there are no 'local connection' or other referral provisions in the scheme. There is no power for the Executive to refer an application to a local housing authority in England, Scotland or Wales. Likewise, there is no power to make a referral in the other direction. Any referral could therefore only be through informal, co-operative arrangements.[418]

The Isle of Man

15.222   The Isle of Man has its own separate jurisdiction and, indeed, a self-contained legislative scheme defining the right of residence.[419] There are no legislative powers permitting referrals from the Isle of Man to local housing authorities in England or in Wales, or vice versa. Any referral could only, therefore, be informal through co-operative mechanisms, and the Isle of Man would be unlikely to co-operate unless the applicant had the right to reside under its statutes.

INFORMAL REFERRALS

15.223   This Chapter has been primarily concerned with the formal mechanisms by which a local housing authority can refer a successful homelessness applicant to another local housing authority to be accommodated in another local housing authority's district. Where those provisions do not apply, the normal rule is that the local housing authority that has accepted the application must accommodate the applicant in its own area.[420]

15.224   But there is a wide range of circumstances beyond those covered by the formal referral arrangements when the provision of accommodation in the area of another local housing authority may be appropriate. For example:

- the applicant may not be safe (in that there is a risk of domestic or other violence) in the district of the local housing authority which has accepted his or her application and with which she or he may enjoy a local connection;[421] or

---

[417]   Housing (Northern Ireland) Order 1988, SI 1988/1990, as amended.
[418]   See **15.234–15.239**.
[419]   Residence Act 2001, s 9 (not yet brought into effect).
[420]   HA 1996, s 208(1).
[421]   English Code, para 16.7; Welsh Code, paras 20.15–20.16.

- the applicant may have other compelling reasons (eg relating to health or education or the need to be near a carer) for asking that local housing authority to provide accommodation in another local housing authority's district; or

- the local housing authority may simply be unable to provide any accommodation which is suitable for the applicant in its own district; or

- the local housing authority may have sought to make a referral under the formal provisions, and then been satisfied by the notified local housing authority's response that the conditions for referral were not made out, yet the applicant may still wish to be accommodated in the other local housing authority's area.

15.225 The following paragraphs explore the extent to which there is scope under HA 1996, Part 7 for a local housing authority to provide accommodation in another local housing authority's district outside the tailor-made referral provisions.

Unilateral placements in another district

15.226 Strictly, a local housing authority which has accepted a responsibility to accommodate an applicant, but finds that it is not 'reasonably practicable' to accommodate that applicant in its own district, can provide accommodation in the district of another local housing authority (provided that it is suitable), and may do so without any prior reference to that other local housing authority at all.[422]

15.227 A local housing authority might be tempted to do precisely that when it comes to its most needy and vulnerable applicants, so that the burden of meeting their special needs (for example, in relation to education or adult care or children's services) falls on another district.[423] So as to meet this point directly, the Codes advise that these households should be given priority for placement *within* the district of the local housing authority to which they have applied rather than being placed in another district.[424]

15.228 Where an 'out of district'[425] placement is made, HA 1996, Part 7 requires the placing local housing authority to give notice of any such placement to the other local housing authority.[426] Notice is not required in

---

[422] HA 1996, s 208(1). When considering whether it is 'reasonably practicable' to provide accommodation in its own district, a local housing authority is entitled to have regard to any financial savings that might be achieved by out of borough placements, and to any differences in the quality of accommodation available within its district or out of borough (*R (Calgin) v Enfield London Borough Council* [2005] EWHC 1716 (Admin), [2006] HLR 4, Admin Ct).

[423] See the comments of Latham LJ in *R v Newham London Borough Council ex p Sacupima* (2001) 33 HLR 2, CA at [31].

[424] English Code, para 16.7; Welsh Code, para 18.9–18.10.

[425] English Code, paras 16.8–16.9; Welsh Code, paras 18.9–18.10.

[426] HA 1996, s 208(2). See also English Code, para 16.8; Welsh Code, para 18.10.

advance but must be given within 14 days of the provision of accommodation in the notified local housing authority's district.[427]

15.229 HA 1996, Part 7, sets out the formal requirements of the notice (name of applicant, address of the accommodation, etc) including the provision of the date on which accommodation was provided to the applicant.[428]

15.230 The duty to notify an 'out of district' placement applies whenever a local housing authority is discharging any accommodation duty owed under HA 1996, Part 7 by securing accommodation in another district, whether the accommodation being provided is provided by a social or private sector landlord or anyone else. Thus, it is not confined to placement of those owed the main housing duty under HA 1996, s 193(2). It applies whenever accommodation is being provided, whether it is on an interim basis pending a decision on an application,[429] as part of the assistance required to be given to a priority need homeless household where the applicant has become homeless intentionally,[430] in performance of the main housing duty[431] or of any other HA 1996, Part 7 accommodation duty. Experience suggests that, particularly in relation to the first category where there can be a reasonably rapid turnover of households, the notification duty is honoured in the breach.

15.231 The duty to notify does not apply where a local housing authority owes the main housing to an applicant and makes him or her a private rented sector offer in the district of another local housing authority.[432] This is surprising as the second local housing authority will become responsible for education, adult care or children's services and any other needs that the applicant and his or her household has. In addition, if the applicant makes a further application for homelessness assistance to the second local housing authority more than two years after he or she had accepted the private rented sector offer, any duty to accommodate under HA 1996, Part 7 will fall on the second local housing authority.[433]

15.232 The simple dispatch of a notice is not sufficient to relieve the placing local housing authority of any responsibility for the homeless household. The Codes remind placing local housing authorities to consider the particular needs

---

[427] HA 1996, s 208(4).
[428] HA 1996, s 208(3).
[429] HA 1996, s 188(1). See **16.12–16.28**.
[430] HA 1996, s 190(2)(a). See **17.18–17.189**.
[431] HA 1996, s 193(2). See **17.23–17.168**.
[432] HA 1996, s 193(7AA)–(7AC) as amended by LA 2011, s 148(5)–(7) and applicable to applicants whose applications for homelessness assistance were made to a local housing in England on or after 9 November 2012. At the date of writing, the amendments to HA 1996 made by LA 2011, ss 148–149 had not been brought into effect in Wales. See **17.109–17.131**.
[433] Because the second set of conditions for referral at HA 1996 s 198(2ZA) and (2), applicable to applicants whose applications for homelessness assistance were made to a local housing in England on or after 9 November 2012, will not apply. At the date of writing, the amendments to HA 1996 made by LA 2011, ss 148–149 had not been brought into effect in Wales. See **15.116–15.131**.

of a household being accommodated out of the area and advise that households who need adult care or children's services support or need to maintain links with specialist medical services, special schools or other essential services within the authority's district should be given priority for accommodation within that district.[434]

15.233 Where a household is placed in a different district from the district of the local housing authority to which it applied, it might be prudent for that household to apply for long-term social housing under *both* local housing authorities' allocation schemes.

Placements by co-operation between local housing authorities

15.234 HA 1996, Part 7, the Codes and the Local Authorities' Agreement are all replete with references to the need for local housing authorities to co-operate with one another in their dealings with homeless applicants. Obviously, it is particularly important for local housing authorities to co-operate where a homeless household is being re-located from the district of the local housing authority to which it applied to another local housing authority's district.

15.235 The legislation facilitates that necessary co-operation in two ways. First, HA 1996, Part 7 requires any local housing authority receiving a request for assistance in discharging HA 1996, Part 7 functions from another local housing authority, to give such assistance as is reasonable in the circumstances.[435] Second, HA 1996, Part 7 enables a local housing authority to perform its housing functions by securing accommodation for the applicant from 'some other person' than the local housing authority itself.[436] That 'other person' might be a different local housing authority.

15.236 The most frequent instance of local housing authorities co-operating occurs when authorities with surplus accommodation make that stock available to other local housing authorities. These arrangements are particularly encouraged by the Codes.[437] Increasingly sophisticated schemes have been developed to match homeless applicants who apply to high demand areas with accommodation in lower demand areas (even though they may have previously had no connection with those areas). Most of those schemes work on the premise that the applicant is willing to take up the opportunity of a home elsewhere.

15.237 The power given to local housing authorities in England to make private rented sector offers,[438] coupled with the restrictions on the levels of

---

[434] English Code, para 16.9; Welsh Code, para 18.9.
[435] HA 1996, s 213(1). See also English Code, para 16.29; Welsh Code, para 18.33.
[436] HA 1996, s 206(1)(b).
[437] English Code, paras 5.1–5.11 and 16.29; Welsh Code, para 18.38.
[438] HA 1996, s 193(7AA) as amended by LA 2011, s 148(5) and applicable to applicants whose applications for homelessness assistance were made to a local housing in England on or after 9

housing benefit paid to claimants, make it more likely that local housing authorities in districts where private rents are high will make private rented sector offers in districts where the rents are comparatively cheaper. The effects of such placements have yet to be seen.

15.238 It is not permissible is for the local housing authority (to which an applicant has applied) to use the mere existence or activation of these co-operative arrangements as a purported performance of its own duties.[439] However, where a local housing authority has satisfied itself that another local housing authority is prepared to accommodate the applicant and that the accommodation to be provided for the applicant will be suitable, the main housing duty owed to an applicant can be performed upon the other local housing authority accepting that it would accommodate him or her.[440]

15.239 The second common form of co-operative out-of-district placements is a reciprocal arrangement, whereby one local housing authority agrees to accommodate an applicant who has applied as homeless elsewhere, and, in response, can place one of its homeless applicants in the transferring local housing authority's district. The Codes advise local housing authorities that this form of co-operation is particularly appropriate where an applicant has 'special housing needs' which can better be met in one area than another, or where the applicant needs be placed elsewhere to avoid the risk of violence in the area of the local housing authority to which he or she applied.[441] The Local Authorities' Agreement also promotes such reciprocal arrangements where, for one reason or another, a strict application of the formal referral rules would not result in a successful referral.[442]

November 2012. At the date of writing, the amendments to HA 1996 made by LA 2011, ss 148–149 had not been brought into effect in Wales. See **17.109–17.131**.

[439] See *R v Bromley London Borough Council ex p Cafun* (2001) January *Legal Action*, p 27, Admin Ct, where Bromley had told the applicant that Greenwich, its neighbouring borough, would accommodate her. The court held that simple activation of the co-operative arrangements between the two boroughs was not enough. Bromley had to ensure that accommodation suitable for that particular applicant was actually going to be provided by Greenwich before its duty could be said to have been performed. Had *Bromley* satisfied itself that was the case, placing her in Greenwich would potentially have been lawful and its duty would have been discharged.

[440] *R v Bristol City Council ex p Browne* [1979] 1 WLR 1437, QBD.

[441] English Code, para 16.29. Welsh Code, para 8.9 advises that a reason to place out of borough might include where the applicant or a member of his or her household has been at risk of hate crime, or where ex-offenders or drug/alcohol users would benefit from being accommodated outside the district to help break links with previous contacts who could exert a negative influence. See also Welsh Code, para 18.38.

[442] For example, where the only ground for a local connection with the notified local housing authority would be 'special circumstances' or where a local connection is made out with the notifying local housing authority but the applicant does not wish to live in that local housing authority's area: English Code, Annex 18, paras 4.2 and 6.4.

Chapter 16

INTERIM ACCOMMODATION – DUTIES AND POWERS

INTRODUCTION

16.1 In the course of the consideration of any Housing Act 1996 (HA 1996) Part 7 application for accommodation (made by a person who has given reason to believe that he or she may be homeless or threatened with homelessness) there will be periods of time when it is not clear what duty (if any) will ultimately be owed to the applicant. That is most obviously the case between the date of the application and the date when the first decision on it is made. But it may also be true at later stages, eg pending a review or appeal, or where a referral to another local housing authority is under way. HA 1996, Part 7 requires that in some circumstances the local housing authority *must* secure accommodation during those 'interim' periods. In other circumstances, local housing authorities are given *powers* to secure accommodation during those periods. This Chapter examines those duties and powers; it refers throughout to 'interim accommodation' to describe the accommodation secured during any of those periods.

THE DUTIES AND POWERS IN OUTLINE

16.2 If a local housing authority has reason to believe that an applicant may be homeless, eligible for assistance and have a priority need, it is under an absolute duty to secure accommodation for the applicant, and members of his or her household, pending its decision as to whether it owes any other duty to the applicant under HA 1996, Part 7.[1]

16.3 Even if the local housing authority has reason to believe that it may eventually refer the applicant to another local housing authority under the provisions described in Chapter 15, it must secure accommodation pending notification of that decision.[2] The initial 'interim' duty is therefore owed to those who have no connection at all with the area of the local housing authority to which they have applied, as well as to those who do have such a local connection.

16.4 The duty ends automatically when the local housing authority's decision is notified to the applicant.[3] If the applicant later requests a statutory review of one of the local housing authority's decisions (if the decision is capable of review),[4] the local housing authority has a power, but not a duty, to secure accommodation pending the outcome of the review.[5]

16.5 There is a similar power, but no duty, to secure accommodation pending the determination of an appeal to the county court.[6]

---

[1]   Housing Act 1996, s 188(1). See **16.12–16.28**.
[2]   HA 1996, s 188(2). See **15.17–15.18** and **16.17–16.18** and **16.56**.
[3]   HA 1996, s 188(3). See also **16.23–16.27**.
[4]   See **19.12–19.37**.
[5]   HA 1996, s 188(3). See also **16.36–16.48**.
[6]   HA 1996, s 204(4). See also **16.49–16.55**.

16.6 Where an applicant makes an application for homelessness assistance to a local housing authority in England[7] within two years of the date of his or her acceptance of a private rented sector offer,[8] and the local housing authority has reason to believe that the main housing duty may apply,[9] the local housing authority must secure interim accommodation for the applicant and his or her household until notification of the decision on the application. This duty applies regardless of whether the applicant has a priority need.[10]

16.7 Powers and duties to secure interim accommodation may also be triggered by a decision to refer an application, made by someone who would otherwise be owed the main housing duty, to a different local housing authority. If, following a decision to refer the applicant to another local housing authority under any of the three conditions for referrals,[11] the applicant requests a review (and/or subsequently brings an appeal against that review decision), the notifying local housing authority has a power, but no duty, to continue to secure accommodation pending the review (and/or the appeal).[12] Even if the decision to refer to another local housing authority is not challenged by the applicant, the notifying local housing authority is under a duty to secure accommodation until the applicant has been notified that the notified local housing authority accepts that the conditions for referral are fulfilled or any dispute between the local housing authorities is finally resolved.[13]

16.8 The Codes provide guidance on the interim duties to accommodate,[14] and on how and when local housing authorities should exercise their powers to secure interim accommodation.[15]

---

[7] At the date of writing, the amendments to HA 1996 made by LA 2011, ss 148–149 had not been brought into effect in Wales.

[8] HA 1996, s 193(7AA)–(7AC) amended by Localism Act 2011, s 148(5)–(7) applicable to applicants whose applications for homelessness assistance were made to a local housing in England on or after 9 November 2012. At the date of writing, the amendments to HA 1996 made by LA 2011, ss 148–149 had not been brought into effect in Wales. See **17.109–17.118**.

[9] The main housing duty will apply where the local housing authority is satisfied that the applicant is homeless, eligible for assistance and is not satisfied that he or she became homeless intentionally: HA 1996, s 195A(1) inserted by LA 2011, s 149(4) and applicable to applicants whose applications for homelessness assistance were made to a local housing in England on or after 9 November 2012. If the local housing authority would only be satisfied that the main housing duty would apply because of the presence in the applicant's household of a restricted person, the special provisions at HA 1996 s 195A inserted by LA 2011, s 149(4) will not apply. At the date of writing, the amendments to HA 1996 made by LA 2011, ss 148–149 had not been brought into effect in Wales. See **9.89–9.95**.

[10] HA 1996, s 188(1A) inserted by LA 2011, s 149(2) and applicable to applicants whose applications for homelessness assistance were made to a local housing in England on or after 9 November 2012. At the date of writing, the amendments to HA 1996 made by LA 2011, ss 148–149 had not been brought into effect in Wales. See **16.291 6.35**.

[11] As described in Chapter 15.

[12] HA 1996, ss 200(5) and 204(4). See **16.62–16.63**.

[13] HA 1996, s 200(1)–(4). See **15.157–15.160** and **16.57–16.61**.

[14] *Homelessness Code of Guidance for Local Authorities* (Communities and Local Government, Department for Education and Skills, Department of Health, July 2006) (the English Code),

16.9 Where a local housing authority owes a duty to secure interim accommodation (or exercises a power to secure it), powers and duties to safeguard the applicant's furniture and other possessions may be triggered. Property protection is dealt with separately in Chapter 17.[16]

16.10 An applicant who is occupying interim accommodation is still 'homeless' within the statutory definition at HA 1996, ss 175–177.[17] He or she is therefore entitled to a reasonable preference within a local housing authority's allocation scheme under HA 1996, s 167(2)(a).[18]

16.11 Each of the duties and powers to secure interim accommodation is now considered in turn, followed by a review of common issues which apply to all forms of provision (as to the quality, size, location, cost, etc) of interim accommodation. The Chapter concludes with guidance on:

- the enforcement of duties;[19]

- challenges to refusals to exercise powers;[20] and

- the limited availability of compensation.[21]

THE DUTIES AND POWERS IN DETAIL

The initial duty to secure interim accommodation

16.12 The initial duty to secure interim accommodation[22] is triggered when the local housing authority has 'reason to believe' that an applicant may be 'homeless',[23] may be 'eligible for assistance',[24] and may have a 'priority need'.[25] This is a very low threshold.[26] The governing word is 'may', which must be

---

Chapter 7. *Code of Guidance for Local Authorities Allocation of Accommodation and Homelessness 2012* (Welsh Government, August 2012) (the Welsh Code), paras 12.14–12.19.
[15] English Code, Chapter 15; Welsh Code, paras 21.15–21.18 and 21.21–21.26.
[16] See **17.233–17.254**.
[17] *R (Alam) v Tower Hamlets London Borough Council* [2009] EWHC 44 (Admin), (2009) March *Legal Action*, p 24, Admin Ct. See Chapter 11 for statutory definition of 'homeless'.
[18] See **4.62–4.70**.
[19] See **16.981–6.102**.
[20] See **16.103–16.127**.
[21] See **16.128–16.132**.
[22] HA 1996, s 188(1).
[23] See Chapter 11.
[24] See Chapter 12.
[25] See Chapter 13.
[26] See *R (Kelly & Mehari) v Birmingham City Council* [2009] EWHC 3240 (Admin), (2010) January *Legal Action*, p 35, Admin Ct; English Code, para 7.3; and Welsh Code, para 12.14. See **16.191–6.21**. See also the following Local Government Ombudsman's decisions: *Complaint against Haringey London Borough Council*, 06/A/12508, 30 June 2008, (2008) August *Legal Action*, p 42; *Complaint against Hounslow London Borough Council*, 07/A/14216, 14 April 2009, (2009) June *Legal Action*, p 34; *Complaint against Hammersmith & Fulham London Borough Council*, 09 001 262, 21 January 2010, (2010) March *Legal Action,* p 31; *Complaint against*

understood to apply to all the elements of the statutory formula. So the threshold is met when a local housing authority has reason to believe that an applicant:

- 'may' be homeless; and also

- 'may' be eligible; and also

- 'may' have a priority need.

16.13 These are some of the issues that the local housing authority will be making inquiries into, in due course, in order to determine what duty (if any) is ultimately owed to the applicant under HA 1996, Part 7.

16.14 Four additional points should be noted.

16.15 First, no interim accommodation duty is owed to an applicant who may be simply 'threatened with' homelessness. There is not even a power to secure interim accommodation for such an applicant.

16.16 Second, the question whether the initial duty is owed may arise not only when the initial application is made but also at any stage before the local housing authority's decision on the application has been notified to the applicant. For example, where a local housing authority is making its inquiries into an application made by an applicant who appears to be threatened with homelessness, it is not under a duty to secure interim accommodation.[27] However, if, before the local housing authority has concluded its inquiries and notified the applicant of its decision, the situation changes and the local housing authority has reason to believe that the applicant may actually be homeless (and there is also reason to believe that the applicant may be eligible and may have a priority need), the duty to secure interim accommodation is immediately triggered. Similarly, if an applicant who appears to be homeless but has not previously been considered potentially to have a priority need suddenly acquires what appears to be a priority need,[28] the duty would be triggered.

16.17 Third, the initial duty arises irrespective of any local connection the applicant may have with any other local housing authority.[29]

Birmingham City Council, 10 010 323, 20 December 2010 (2011) March *Legal Action*, p 27; *Complaint against Hounslow London Borough Council*, 10 019 388, 5 October 2011, (2011) December *Legal Action*, p 29; *Complaint against Newham London Borough Council*, 11 000 383, 8 March 2012, (2012) March *Legal Action*, p 34; and *Complaints against Kent County Council and Dover District Council*, 09 017 510 and 09 017 512, 31 July 2012, (2012) October *Legal Action*, p 38. See **16.132**.

[27] HA 1996, ss 184(1) and 188(1).

[28] For example, the discovery of a pregnancy.

[29] HA 1996, s 188(2).

16.18 Fourth, the initial duty to secure interim accommodation is not a duty capable of being referred to another local housing authority under the conditions for referral described in Chapter 15.

16.19 If the local housing authority does have reason to believe that the applicant may be homeless, may be eligible and may have a priority need, the duty to secure initial interim accommodation is an absolute one. The local housing authority must secure that accommodation is available; it cannot postpone that duty, which is triggered as soon as the requisite 'reason to believe' is present. One local housing authority's application form contained the following instruction to its officers: 'unless the applicant and family are at risk of harm, they should be advised to return to the homeless address whereby a visiting officer will attend the property'. As a result of that instruction, the local housing authority failed to engage with the criteria at HA 1996, s 188(1) and failed to provide accommodation to applicants for homelessness assistance whom it had reason to believe may be homeless, may be eligible and may have a priority need. A Judge said:

> 'The approach of the Council to their obligations under Section 188 at the very least lacks legal coherence and a proper consideration of the relevant Section 188 criteria. So far as the Council are concerned that failure had and, insofar as that practice continues, continues to have, the effect of avoiding their obligations under Section 188.'[30]

16.20 The same local housing authority was later alleged to be operating a variety of systems in order to avoid the duty to secure interim accommodation. In a subsequent case, it agreed that apparent instructions that 'all single homeless . . . must be referred to the appropriate funded support service. We should not be completing a homeless application' were unlawful.[31]

16.21 There was also a suggestion that the same local housing authority was encouraging its officers to make a decision on an application for homelessness assistance on the same day as the application was received, so that the duty to secure interim accommodation at HA 1996, s 188(1) would not arise. The judge said:

> '[t]here is no doubt that a blanket 'same day' policy, which requires a decision on the homeless application and, in consequence, the interim accommodation all in one day would be unlawful ... it would only be "in the most straightforward of cases that a decision can be reached on the same day as the application itself".'[32]

---

[30] *R (Kelly & Mehari) v Birmingham City Council* [2009] EWHC 3240 (Admin), (2010) January *Legal Action*, p 35, Admin Ct, at [40], per Hickinbottom J.

[31] *R (Khazai) v Birmingham City Council* [2010] EWHC 2576 (Admin), (2010)) December *Legal Action*, p 37, Admin Ct.

[32] *R (Khazai) v Birmingham City Council* [2010] EWHC 2576 (Admin), (2010) December *Legal Action*, p 37, Admin Ct per Foskett J at [47] quoting from the instruction to local housing authority staff that was under scrutiny. See also Welsh Code, para 12.9.

16.22 If the local housing authority refuses to secure initial interim accommodation when the statutory conditions are fulfilled or, before the duty ends, withdraws any accommodation secured, it is in breach of its statutory duty. The applicant is entitled to bring judicial review proceedings for a mandatory order that accommodation be secured immediately.[33]

16.23 The duty to secure accommodation under the initial interim duty ends when the local housing authority's decision on the applicant's application (whether the applicant is 'eligible' and, if so, what duty if any is owed to him or her) is notified to the applicant.[34] The initial interim duty does not end when the decision is taken. It ends only when that decision is 'notified to' the applicant in writing.[35] The decision may acknowledge that a further duty is owed to the applicant, or that no duty is owed. The initial accommodation duty ends whatever the content of the decision.

16.24 Where the local housing authority decides that it owes the applicant a duty to secure accommodation, the notification letter ought sensibly to spell out how that accommodation duty is going to be met from the moment of notification, because the interim duty to accommodate has ceased from the moment that the applicant receives the letter. Much confusion is caused by notifications which accept the main housing duty (under HA 1996, s 193(2)) but do not spell out how it is going to be performed from that day forward.

16.25 If the decision is adverse (in the sense that it notifies a decision that the main housing duty is not owed to the applicant), the applicant might exercise his or her right to a review. This cannot keep the initial interim accommodation duty running. Any further accommodation secured by the local housing authority will either be the result of any limited accommodation duty owed to the applicant as notified in the decision letter,[36] or will be the result of the local housing authority exercising its power to secure accommodation pending review.[37]

16.26 The fact that the initial interim accommodation duty is brought to an end by notification of the decision does not mean that the accommodation that has been secured will be instantly withdrawn. The local housing authority may secure the same accommodation for the applicant in performance of any other accommodation duty it owes.

---

[33] See **16.98–6.102**.

[34] HA 1996, s 188(3). In *O'Callaghan v Southwark London Borough Council* (2010) May *Legal Action*, p 23, Lambeth County Court, the applicant had been provided with interim accommodation under the initial duty at HA 1996, s 188(1). No decision on her application for homelessness assistance was ever notified to her. As a consequence, when she was required to leave that accommodation and made a fresh application for homelessness assistance, she could not be found to have become homeless intentionally from that accommodation because her earlier period of homelessness had never ended. See **8.72**, and **9.64–9.65** and **11.13**.

[35] For 'notification of s 184 decision', see **10.66–10.81**.

[36] For example, the duty to secure accommodation owed to a person found to have become homeless intentionally under HA 1996, s 190(2)(a). See **17.182–17.189**.

[37] HA 1996, s 188(3). See **16.36–16.48**.

16.27 If there is no further accommodation duty owed, and the local housing authority is not willing to exercise its power to continue to secure accommodation pending review (or is not asked to exercise this power), the actual termination of the accommodation arrangement is discussed later in this Chapter under 'Termination of the Accommodation'.[38]

16.28 Any failure by the local housing authority to comply with its statutory duty will be an error of law. The applicant is entitled to bring judicial review proceedings for a mandatory order that accommodation be secured immediately.[39]

The duty to secure interim accommodation where there is a re-application for homelessness assistance to a local housing authority in England within two years of acceptance of a private rented sector offer[40]

16.29 Special provisions apply where an applicant, having accepted a private rented sector offer made by a local housing authority in response to an earlier application for homelessness assistance,[41] makes a fresh application for homelessness assistance to a local housing authority in England within two years of the date of his or her acceptance of the offer.

16.30 If the local housing authority has reason to believe that the main housing duty[42] may apply in these circumstances, it is under a duty to secure interim accommodation for the applicant and his or her household.[43] This duty applies whether or not there is any reason to believe that the applicant has a priority need. This is because most applicants in these circumstances will be entitled to the main housing duty whether or not they have a priority need.[44]

---

[38] See **16.93–16.97**. Issues relating to the cost, quality, location or terms of the occupation of the accommodation secured under the initial interim duty are discussed at **16.64–16.88**.

[39] See **16.102** and **19.224–19.250**.

[40] HA 1996, s 188(1A) inserted by LA 2011, s 149(2) and applicable to applicants whose applications for homelessness assistance were made on or after 9 November 2012 to a local housing authority in England. At the date of writing, the amendments to HA 1996 made by LA 2011, ss 148–149 had not been brought into effect in Wales.

[41] HA 1996, s 193(7AA)–(7AC) amended by LA 2011, s 148(5)–(7) and applicable to applicants whose applications for homelessness assistance were made on or after 9 November 2012 to a local housing authority in England. At the date of writing, the amendments to HA 1996 made by LA 2011, ss 148–149 had not been brought into effect in Wales. See **17.109–17.118**.

[42] HA 1996, s 193(2). See **17.23–17.168**.

[43] HA 1996, s 188(1A) inserted by LA 2011, s 149(2) applicable to applicants whose applications for homelessness assistance were made on or after 9 November 2012 to a local housing authority in England. At the date of writing, the amendments to HA 1996 made by LA 2011, ss 148–149 had not been brought into effect in Wales.

[44] HA 1996, s 195A(1) inserted by LA 20111, s 149(4) applicable to applicants whose applications for homelessness assistance were made on or after 9 November 2012 to a local housing authority in England. At the date of writing, the amendments to HA 1996 made by LA 2011, ss 148–149 had not been brought into effect in Wales. See **9.89–9.95**. The exception is where the local housing authority would not be satisfied that the main housing duty, or equivalent duty to those threatened with homelessness, is owed without having regard to a restricted person

16.31 In order for the main housing duty to apply, the local housing authority will only have to be satisfied that the applicant:

- is homeless; and

- is eligible for assistance; and

- did not become homeless intentionally.[45]

16.32 Obviously for the duty to secure *interim* accommodation to apply, the local housing authority need not be satisfied of any of these tests. It just has to have 'reason to believe' that the applicant may pass each of those conditions. The threshold is a low one.[46]

16.33 There is no duty to secure interim accommodation if the local housing authority only has reason to believe that an applicant may be threatened with homelessness, and may be entitled to the main duty owed to those threatened with homelessness.[47]

16.34 The duty to secure interim accommodation in these circumstances ends upon the notification to the applicant of the decision on the most recent application for homelessness assistance.[48]

16.35 Given that an applicant to whom these special provisions apply is deemed to be threatened with homelessness at the date of service of a valid HA 1988, s 21 notice, and is deemed to be homeless upon the expiration of the notice, many applicants will make fresh applications for homelessness assistance while they are still occupying their private rented accommodation.[49] The interim accommodation duty will apply once the date stipulated in the notice for giving up possession has been reached.[50] In those circumstances, it may be possible for the local housing authority to perform that duty by arranging with the landlord for the applicant and his or her household to

---

(HA 1996, s 195A inserted by LA 2011, s 149(4)). In those cases, there would have to be reason to believe that the applicant might have a priority need.

[45] HA 1996, s 195A(1) inserted by LA 2011, s 149(4) applicable to applicants whose applications for homelessness assistance were made on or after 9 November 2012 to a local housing authority in England. At the date of writing, the amendments to HA 1996 made by LA 2011, ss 148–149 had not been brought into effect in Wales. See **9.89–9.95**.

[46] See **16.12, 16.19–16.21**.

[47] HA 1996, s 195(2), see **17.190–17.200** for duties owed to those threatened with homelessness.

[48] HA 1996, s 188(3). See **16.23–16.26** and **16.93–16.97**.

[49] HA 1996, s 195A(2) and (4) inserted by LA 2011, s 149(4) applicable to applicants whose applications for homelessness assistance were made on or after 9 November 2012 to a local housing authority in England. At the date of writing, the amendments to HA 1996 made by LA 2011, ss 148–149 had not been brought into effect in Wales. See **9.89–9.95** and **11.121–11.128**.

[50] HA 1996, s 195A(2) inserted by LA 2011, s 149(4) and applicable to applicants whose applications for homelessness assistance were made on or after 9 November 2012 to a local housing authority in England. At the date of writing, the amendments to HA 1996 made by LA 2011, ss 148–149 had not been brought into effect in Wales.

remain in the private rented accommodation. However, if the applicant is required to leave that accommodation, the local housing authority will have to secure interim accommodation for him or her.

Power to secure interim accommodation pending a statutory review[51]

16.36 Some of the decisions made by a local housing authority on an application for homelessness assistance under HA 1996 Part 7 carry a right to a statutory review.[52] If the applicant requests a review of such a decision, the local housing authority has a power, but not a duty, to secure accommodation until the review has been concluded.[53]

16.37 That power can be exercised irrespective of the nature of the decision which is being reviewed (provided it is a decision which may be subject to statutory review) and regardless of whether the applicant has previously had any accommodation (interim or otherwise) secured for him or her by the local housing authority.

16.38 The local housing authority is not required automatically to consider the exercise of the power every time it receives a request for review. An applicant who wants interim accommodation, pending a decision on the review, should ask for it. There is no need for the request to be made in writing or on any particular form.

16.39 Once a request has been made, a local housing authority that refuses even to consider, or simply fails to consider, the exercise of its power would be acting unlawfully and may be vulnerable to a judicial review challenge.[54] Likewise, a local housing authority which decided *never* to exercise the discretionary power to accommodate pending review would be unlawfully fettering that discretion.

16.40 Busy local housing authorities, receiving large numbers of requests for reviews, may receive almost as many requests for accommodation pending decisions on those reviews. Although each such application must be given individual consideration, local housing authorities may draw up and apply policies governing the circumstances when they will exercise their powers to secure such accommodation. Local housing authorities that adopt policies restricting the provision of discretionary interim accommodation pending review to 'exceptional circumstances' are not necessarily acting unlawfully. But any such policy must be flexible enough to ensure that individual consideration is given to the circumstances of each applicant requesting interim accommodation pending review.[55]

---

[51] HA 1996, s 188(3).
[52] HA 1996, ss 202(1) and (1A) provide an exhaustive list. See also **19.12–19.37**.
[53] HA 1996, ss 188(3) and 195(8).
[54] For challenges to a refusal to exercise the power, see **16.103–16.127**.
[55] English Code, paras 15.12–15.20; Welsh Code, paras 21.15–21.18.

16.41   It is not unlawful for the decision-maker who made the original decision that is the subject of the review also to make the decision as to whether or not accommodation will be secured pending a statutory review.[56]

16.42   When a local housing authority considers the individual circumstances of each applicant, it must take into account:

- the strength of the applicant's case on review;

- whether any new material, information or argument has been raised since the decision which is the subject of the review was made;

- the personal circumstances of the applicant;

- the consequences for the applicant if accommodation is not secured; and

- any other relevant considerations.[57]

16.43   The task of taking into account these various factors is often referred to as the '*Mohammed* balancing exercise' (after the name of the case in which the factors were set out).[58]

16.44   Where a local housing authority has been provided with new information (in the sense that it was not available when the decision which is the subject of the review was made), the officer deciding on the request for interim accommodation pending review should consider the extent to which that material affects the strength of the applicant's case on review.[59] In deciding whether to exercise its power to secure interim accommodation pending review, a local housing authority is also entitled to take into account the demands on its resources involved in securing interim accommodation, the scarcity of accommodation and the demand for accommodation from other homeless applicants (provided that it does also consider the applicant's individual circumstances).[60]

16.45   In *R (Paul-Coker) v Southwark London Borough Council*,[61] the local housing authority had decided that the applicant was not eligible because she

---

[56]   *R (Abdi) v Lambeth London Borough Council* [2007] EWHC 1681 (Admin), [2008] HLR 5, Admin Ct.

[57]   *R v Camden London Borough Council ex p Mohammed* (1998) 30 HLR 315, QBD; and *R v Newham London Borough Council ex p Lumley* (2001) 33 HLR 11, QBD.

[58]   *R v Camden London Borough Council ex p Mohammed* (1998) 30 HLR 315, QBD.

[59]   *R v Newham London Borough Council ex p Lumley* (2001) 33 HLR 11, QBD.

[60]   *R (Cole) v Enfield London Borough Council* [2003] EWHC 1454 (Admin), (2003) August *Legal Action*, p 32, Admin Ct. For examples of local housing authorities correctly applying the '*Mohammed* factors', see *R (Lusamba) v Islington London Borough Council* [2008] EWHC 1149 (Admin), (2008) July *Legal Action*, p 22, Admin Ct; and *R (Sadek) v Westminster City Council* [2012] EWCA Civ 803, (2012) August *Legal Action*, p 28, Admin Ct.

[61]   [2006] EWHC 497 (Admin), [2006] HLR 32, Admin Ct.

was not habitually resident in the UK.[62] She requested interim accommodation pending a review and her solicitors made a number of representations, both in relation to her personal circumstances and by providing new information that could have an effect on the review decision. The Administrative Court held that 'there was a complete absence of any explanation or reasoning in the decision letter dealing with these various important aspects of the case' and that the local housing authority, whilst referring to the *Mohammed* balancing exercise, had actually only paid 'lip-service' to it.[63]

16.46   This decision reminds local housing authorities that 'lip-service' is not good enough. They must actually consider the representations made in support of the request for interim accommodation pending review and consider them in relation to the *Mohammed* factors.

16.47   The benefit of the power to secure interim accommodation pending a statutory review, and pending an appeal to the county court,[64] is not available to:

- nationals of other European Economic Area (EEA) states; and

- refugees given refugee status by other states (including EEA states); and

- former asylum-seekers who have failed to co-operate with removal directions; and

- people who are unlawfully present in the UK; and

- failed asylum-seekers with dependent children,

unless the local housing authority decides that securing accommodation is necessary in order to prevent a breach of the applicant's rights under the European Convention on Human Rights or under European Union law.[65] If interim accommodation is requested for former asylum-seekers who have failed to co-operate with removal directions, those who are unlawfully present in the

[62]   See **12.164–12.179**.
[63]   *R (Paul-Coker) v Southwark London Borough Council* [2006] EWHC 497 (Admin), [2006] HLR 32, Admin Ct, at [49], per Forbes J.
[64]   HA s 204(4). See **16.49–16.55**.
[65]   Nationality Immigration and Asylum Act 2002, Sch 3, para 3; see **16.54**, **20.46–20.48** and **20.65–20.73**, and English Code, para 15.3. Although this statutory restriction on he power to secure interim accommodation applies to local housing authorities in both England and Wales, there is no reference to it in the Welsh Code. See also *R (Mohammed) v Harrow London Borough Council* [2005] EWHC 3194 (Admin), [2006] HLR 18, Admin Ct, where the local housing authority's decision that accommodation was not 'necessary' to avoid a breach of European Union rights, as the claimant was not a worker or work-seeker and therefore not exercising those rights, contained no error of law.

UK, or for certain failed asylum-seekers with dependent children, local housing authorities are required to inform the United Kingdom Border Agency.[66]

16.48 Any refusal to secure accommodation under this power can only be challenged if there is an error of law. Challenges are brought by judicial review proceedings.[67]

Power to secure interim accommodation pending an appeal to the county court[68]

16.49 Review decisions (and original decisions which can be subject to a statutory review) can be appealed to the county court.[69] The fact that an applicant might lodge or has lodged an appeal does not impose a duty on the local housing authority to accommodate the applicant pending the hearing of that appeal. Sadly, in many areas appeals cannot be heard for some weeks or months after they are lodged.

16.50 However, there is a discretionary power available for the local housing authority to secure interim accommodation at two stages:

(1) during the 21-day period between notification of the review decision and the normal deadline for issue of a county court appeal;[70] and/or

(2) pending the determination of the appeal itself, once made.[71]

16.51 The power can *only* be used where the local housing authority has already either:[72]

(a) owed one of the following duties to the applicant:
   (i)   the duty to secure initial interim accommodation;[73] or
   (ii) the duty to secure accommodation for a reasonable period owed to an applicant found to have become homeless intentionally;[74] or
   (iii) the duty to secure accommodation pending referral under the 'conditions for referral' provisions;[75] or

66   Nationality Immigration Asylum Act 2002, Sch 3, para 14; English Code, para 9.24. It is unlikely that any of those classes of people would be eligible for assistance. See Chapter 12.
67   See **16.103–16.112** and **19.224–19.250**.
68   HA 1996, s 204(4).
69   HA 1996, s 204(1). See **19.146–19.201**.
70   HA 1996, s 204(4)(a).
71   HA 1996, s 204(4)(b).
72   HA 1996, s 204(4).
73   HA 1996, s 188(1). See **16.12–16.28**.
74   HA 1996, s 190(2). See **17.182–17.189**.
75   HA 1996, s 200. See **15.157–15.160** and **16.56–16.61**.

(b) had the power (whether it exercised it or not) to accommodate the applicant pending a review of a decision that, although in priority need, the applicant had become threatened with homelessness intentionally.[76]

16.52 The common thread running through the above list is that the applicant either has, or the local housing authority initially had reason to believe that he or she might have, a priority need. Where the local housing authority has not been subject to any of those duties or that power, there is no power under HA 1996, Part 7 for a local housing authority to secure interim accommodation pending appeal. Where the power is available, an applicant may invite the local housing authority to exercise it while an appeal is being considered, prepared, or later, once the appeal has been lodged.

16.53 When considering whether or not to exercise a power to accommodate, pending appeal to the county court, a local housing authority should carry out the same balancing exercise as it is required to undertake when considering a request for interim accommodation pending review.[77] It should consider all the relevant circumstances, and any new information, material or argument. It is required to consider the applicant's grounds of appeal, as part of its consideration of the merits of the case, but would not normally be expected to refer to any of the grounds of appeal in its decision letter, unless there is some important and striking ground which requires specific comment.[78] In addition, it will need to consider the applicant's personal and household circumstances, along with the terms of any general policy it has adopted governing its discretion (if any), and the resources available.[79]

16.54 This power to secure interim accommodation pending appeal to the county court is not available to:

• nationals of other EEA states; and

• refugees given refugee status by other EEA states; and

• former asylum-seekers who have failed to co-operate with removal directions; and

• people who are unlawfully present in the UK; and

• failed asylum-seekers with dependent children,

---

[76] HA 1996, s 195(8).
[77] See **16.42–16.46**.
[78] *Lewis v Havering London Borough Council* [2006] EWCA Civ 1793, [2007] HLR 20, CA.
[79] English Code, paras 15.21–15.24; Welsh Code, paras 21.21–21.26. For the possibility of challenging a refusal to accommodate pending appeal, see **16.113–16.127** and **19.202–19.212**.

unless the local housing authority considers it necessary in order to prevent a breach of rights under the European Convention on Human Rights or European Union law.[80]

16.55 Challenges to a local housing authority's refusal to secure accommodation pending the determination of the county court appeal are brought by a separate appeal, also on a point of law, to the county court under HA 1996, s 204A.[81]

Powers and duties to secure interim accommodation for applicants referred under the conditions for referral provisions

16.56 Whichever local housing authority an applicant applies to, if that local housing authority has reason to believe that the applicant may be homeless, eligible for assistance, and have a priority need, the duty to secure initial interim accommodation is triggered.[82] Interim accommodation must be secured, irrespective of whether or not the applicant appears to have a local connection with the local housing authority.[83] That duty continues while it carries out its inquiries.

16.57 If the local housing authority's conclusion upon those inquiries is that the applicant:

(1) is homeless; and

(2) is eligible; and

(3) has a priority need; and

(4) did not become homeless intentionally,

---

[80] Nationality Immigration and Asylum Act 2002, s 54 and Sch 3, paras 1 and 3, in force from 8 January 2003; see **16.47**, **20.46–20.48** and **20.65–20.73**, and English Code, para 15.3. Although this statutory restriction on the power to secure interim accommodation applies to local housing authorities in both England and Wales, there is no reference to it in the Welsh Code. If accommodation is requested by a former asylum-seeker who has failed to co-operate with removal directions, anyone unlawfully present in the UK or a failed asylum-seeker with dependent children, the local housing authority is under an obligation to inform the UKBA (Nationality, Immigration and Asylum Act 2002, Sch 3, para 14; English Code, para 9.24). In practice, there are very few people who might be eligible who would also fall within one of those three categories (see Chapter 12).

[81] See **16.113–16.127** and **19.202–19.212**.

[82] See **16.12–16.28**. In the case of an application for homelessness assistance made to a local housing authority in England within two years of acceptance of a private rented sector offer, the duty to secure interim accommodation applies whether or not there is reason to believe that the applicant may have a priority need (HA 1996, s 188(1A) inserted by LA 2011, s 149(2) and applicable to applicants whose applications for homelessness assistance were made on or after 9 November 2012 to a local housing authority in England). At the date of writing, the amendments to HA 1996 made by LA 2011, ss 148–149 had not been brought into effect in Wales. See **16.29–16.35**.

[83] HA 1996, s 188(2).

it would normally be subject to the main housing duty.[84] But if it considers that the conditions for referral of that duty to another local housing authority are made out, it may notify the other local housing authority that it holds that opinion.[85] The notifying local housing authority ('the first local housing authority') must notify the applicant that it has notified, or intends to notify, another local housing authority ('the second local housing authority') of its opinion.[86]

16.58   The effect of these two notices is:

(a)   to bring to an end the initial interim duty to accommodate;[87] and

(b)   to defer the triggering of the main housing duty[88] until the conditions for referral issue is resolved.[89]

16.59   HA 1996, Part 7, therefore, creates a further interim duty on the first local housing authority so that it is required to continue to accommodate the applicant.[90] That further interim duty, which has been triggered by a notice given to the applicant by the first local housing authority, ends only when the applicant receives a further notice from the first local housing authority. That further notice will contain the final decision (reached by agreement between the notified and notifying authorities) that the conditions of referral are, or are not, met. If there is a dispute between the two local housing authorities, the first local housing authority remains under the duty to secure interim accommodation until the dispute is resolved.

16.60   If the applicant is notified of a decision that the conditions for referral are *not* met, then the interim duty falls away and is replaced by the main housing duty owed by the first local housing authority.[91]

16.61   If, however, the applicant is notified that both local housing authorities agree (or it has been determined by arbitration) that the conditions for referral *are* met, then the interim duty to accommodate on the first local housing

---

[84]   HA 1996, s 193(2). Where the applicant is making an application for homelessness assistance to a local housing authority in England within two years of the acceptance by him or her of a private rented sector offer, the main housing duty will apply whether or not the applicant has a priority need (HA 1996, s 195A(1) inserted by LA 2011, s 149(4) and applicable to applicants whose applications for homelessness assistance were made on or after 9 November 2012 to a local housing authority in England). At the date of writing, the amendments to HA 1996 made by LA 2011, ss 148–149 had not been brought into effect in Wales. See **17.23–17.168** for 'main housing duty' and **17.171–17.181** for the special rules for applicants re-applying within two years of acceptance of a private rented sector offer.

[85]   HA 1996, s 198(1). See **15.155–15.156**.

[86]   HA 1996, s 184(4). See **15.151–15.154**.

[87]   By the notification to the applicant under HA 1996, ss 184(4) and 200(1).

[88]   HA 1996, s 193(2). See **17.23–17.168**.

[89]   HA 1996, s 200(1).

[90]   HA 1996, s 200(1). See English Code, paras 18.26–18.30; Welsh Code, paras 20.17–20.18.

[91]   HA 1996, s 200(3).

authority comes to an end. The second local housing authority is then subject to a duty to secure accommodation for the applicant under the main housing duty.[92]

16.62 If the applicant requests a review of the decision to refer, and asks to remain in accommodation secured by the first local housing authority while the review is considered, the first local housing authority has no further duty but does have a discretionary power to continue to secure interim accommodation pending review and, later, pending any appeal to the county court.[93] The refusal to exercise that power cannot be subject to a statutory review or an appeal to the courts. Any challenge would have to be by way of judicial review.[94]

16.63 Obviously, when the first local housing authority considers whether or not to exercise its discretion to secure interim accommodation in these circumstances, one of the factors that it will take into account is the fact that there is an existing duty on the second local housing authority to secure accommodation and that therefore, if the applicant is willing to take it up, he or she will no longer be homeless.

GENERAL ISSUES ABOUT INTERIM ACCOMMODATION

Interim accommodation for whom?

16.64 Where a local housing authority owes an interim accommodation duty, or exercises a power to secure interim accommodation, the accommodation secured must be 'available' for the applicant's occupation. This means not only 'available' in the practical sense (that the applicant must be able to get to it), but also in the technical sense of 'available' as accommodation both for the applicant and for members of his or her household.[95] In short, the accommodation secured must be capable of providing for:

(1)   the applicant; and

(2)   those who normally live with the applicant as members of his or her family; and

(3)   any others with whom it is reasonable to expect him or her to reside.[96]

---

[92]   HA 1996, s 200(4).

[93]   HA 1996, ss 200(5) and 204(4).

[94]   Examples of unsuccessful applications for permission to bring judicial review proceedings to challenge a local housing authority's decision not to secure accommodation pending review of a decision that the applicant should be referred to another local housing authority can be found at *R (Gebremarium) v Westminster City Council* [2009] EWHC 2254 (Admin), (2009) November *Legal Action*, p 26, Admin Ct and *R (Fadol) v Westminster City Council* [2012] EWHC 1399 (Admin), (2012) July *Legal Action*, p 42, Admin Ct.

[95]   HA 1996, s 176. This technical meaning of 'available' is fully discussed at **11.21–11.34**.

[96]   HA 1996, s 176. See **11.21–11.34**.

16.65 Therefore, the interim accommodation duty (or exercise of power) cannot be performed by securing separate units of interim accommodation in different buildings (eg rooms in two hotels some distance apart) for the same household. It could possibly be performed by securing adjoining or adjacent units of accommodation (such as separate rooms in the same building or two neighbouring houses).[97]

Suitable interim accommodation

16.66 Where the local housing authority falls under a duty to secure interim accommodation, or exercises a power to secure such accommodation, the accommodation actually secured must be 'suitable' for the applicant (a requirement additional to its being 'available' for his and her household).[98]

16.67 Whether or not the accommodation is 'suitable' is primarily a matter for the local housing authority, but consideration of suitability must focus on whether the accommodation is suitable for the particular applicant.[99] Factors relevant to that decision include:

(1)   the space and arrangement of the accommodation;

(2)   health and safety considerations;

(3)   the affordability of the accommodation;[100]

(4)   the location of it;[101]

(5)   the applicant's medical and physical needs and those of his or her household;

(6)   other social considerations;

(7)   any risk of violence or racial harassment;

(8)   the need for security and a secret location for those fleeing domestic violence, including single-sex accommodation where necessary; and

(9)   any other circumstances that may be relevant in a particular case.[102]

---

[97]   *R v Ealing London Borough Council ex p Surdonja* (1998) 31 HLR 686, QBD and see *Sharif v Camden London Borough Council* [2011] EWCA Civ 463, [2011] HLR 32, CA (at the date of writing, Camden London Borough had been granted permission to appeal to the Supreme Court and the appeal had not yet been heard).

[98]   HA 1996, ss 206 and 210. See also English Code, para 7.5; Welsh Code, paras 12.14 and 12.18–12.19.

[99]   The wording is 'suitable for a person': HA 1996, s 210(1).

[100]   Homelessness (Suitability of Accommodation) Order 1996, SI 1996/3204. See Appendix 2.

[101]   See **16.70–16.73**.

[102]   English Code, paras 17.1–17.8; Welsh Code, Chapter 19.

16.68 The fact that accommodation is being secured for an 'interim' period only is relevant to the local housing authority's decision as to whether or not it is suitable. Accommodation that would not be suitable in the long term may be suitable in the short term.[103] Obviously, the urgency of securing the accommodation is a relevant consideration. Whilst local housing authorities are entitled to maintain policies as to the way in which they will secure the provision of interim accommodation, they are still required to consider, in each and every case, whether the accommodation is in fact suitable for the individual needs of the applicant. There is a minimum standard of suitability below which the accommodation must not fall, regardless of the urgency of the situation and any shortage of resources experienced by the local housing authority.[104]

16.69 If the accommodation is unsuitable, the local housing authority is in breach of its duty. The duty to secure suitable interim accommodation is enforceable by taking judicial review proceedings. The applicant could apply for a mandatory order requiring the local housing authority to secure suitable accommodation forthwith. The local housing authority cannot rely on shortage of available accommodation or lack of resources as a defence to its failure to secure suitable accommodation. However, the courts have stressed that judicial review is a discretionary remedy, even where a local housing authority is in breach of its statutory duty. Applicants and their advisers should not be too quick to rush to court where a local housing authority is doing all that it reasonably can to meet its duty and the applicant is not without at least some shelter.[105]

Location of interim accommodation

16.70 The location of interim accommodation is obviously relevant to the question of whether or not it is suitable. Applicants may need accommodation to be in a particular area or district in order to be able to take their children to school, to get to work or to college, to ensure that their children have contact with any non-resident parent, or just to keep in touch with family and friends.[106] Likewise, there may be a need to be near a particular medical facility. Clearly, the length of time that the applicant may expect to be in interim accommodation is also relevant to the question of whether the location of the accommodation renders it unsuitable.

16.71 Local housing authorities are required by HA 1996, Part 7 to secure interim accommodation in their own districts, so far as that is reasonably

---

[103] English Code, para 17.7.

[104] *R v Newham London Borough Council ex p Ojuri (No 2)* (1998) 31 HLR 452, QBD; and *R v Newham London Borough Council ex p Sacupima* [2001] 1 WLR 563, (2001) 33 HLR 2, CA.

[105] *R v Newham London Borough Council ex p Sacupima* [2001] 1 WLR 563, (2001) 33 HLR 2, CA; and *Ali v Birmingham City Council, Moran v Manchester City Council* [2009] UKHL 36, [2009] 1 WLR 1506, per Lord Hope at [4]. See English Code, para 7.5.

[106] See *R v Newham London Borough Council ex p Ojuri (No 2)* (1998) 31 HLR 452, QBD; *R v Newham London Borough Council ex p Sacupima* (2001) 33 HLR 2, CA; and *R (Yumsak) v Enfield London Borough Council* [2002] EWHC 280 (Admin), (2003) 35 HLR 1, Admin Ct, for examples of all these difficulties.

practicable.[107] If a local housing authority does accommodate homeless applicants outside its own district (because there is no reasonably practicable way of accommodating them in its own district), it is required formally to notify the local housing authority for the district in which the applicant has been placed.[108] This duty to notify applies even to the most minimal period of interim accommodation. The notification must be in writing and contain certain information prescribed by HA 1996, s 208(3). It must be given within 14 days from the accommodation being made available to the applicant. It is therefore an additional administrative deterrent to making placements out-of-district.

16.72 The Codes recommend that households who need adult care or children's services support or have links with other essential services such as specialist medical services or special schools should be given priority for accommodation within the local housing authority's own district.[109]

16.73 Even when the conditions for placement outside local housing authorities' own districts are legitimately fulfilled, local housing authorities are not relieved of their continuing duties under HA 1996, Part 7, simply by placing applicants outside their own districts. The applicants continue to be the responsibility of the local housing authority to which they applied. However, if a local housing authority decides that it no longer owes a duty to secure interim accommodation for the applicant, and the applicant then needs help from adult care or children's services, that help will be available from the adult care or children's services departments of the local housing authority for the district where he or she was actually residing in the interim accommodation.[110]

Type of interim accommodation

16.74 A local housing authority which is subject to a duty to secure interim accommodation (or is using its powers to secure such accommodation) is not obliged to provide the applicant with local housing authority housing.[111] It may secure accommodation in any of the three ways open to it in performing any

---

[107] HA 1996, s 208(1): this provision was not in the Housing (Homeless Persons) Act 1977 or the Housing Act 1985, but was introduced in HA 1996, Part 7 to bring an end to the phenomenon of local housing authorities routinely placing applicants in other local housing authorities' districts, either because there was no accommodation available within a local housing authority's own district or, more commonly, simply because accommodation in other districts could be secured more cheaply. In *R (Calgin) v Enfield London Borough Council* [2005] EWHC 1716 (Admin), [2006] HLR 4, Admin Ct, the Administrative Court held that, when considering whether it is 'reasonably practicable' to secure accommodation in its own district, a local housing authority is entitled to have regard to any financial savings that might be achieved by out-of-borough placements.

[108] See **15.226–15.233, 18.58–18.68**; HA 1996, s 208(2)–(4); English Code, paras 16.7–16.9; Welsh Code, paras 18.9–18.10.

[109] English Code, para 16.9; Welsh Code, para 18.9, refers to 'health, social and personal needs'.

[110] *R (Stewart) v Hammersmith and Fulham London Borough Council, Wandsworth London Borough Council and Lambeth London Borough Council* [2001] EWHC 709 (Admin), (2001) 4 CCLR 466, Admin Ct.

[111] Indeed, the English Code contains guidance that it would not generally be appropriate for

housing function under HA 1996, Part 7.[112] The three ways are explored in more detail in Chapter 18[113] but are, in summary:

(1)   by providing accommodation itself;

(2)   by arranging for someone else to secure accommodation; or

(3)   by giving the applicant such advice and assistance as secures that accommodation is made available by someone else.

16.75   If the local housing authority is securing interim accommodation itself (option (1)), such accommodation would most likely be a place in a council-run hostel, a tenancy of a short-life local housing authority property, or some other non-secure local housing authority housing.[114]

16.76   If interim accommodation is being secured under options (2) or (3), it will often be in a hotel or hostel run privately or by a voluntary organisation, or a letting on a short-term tenancy from a private landlord or housing association. In the latter case, applicants are often offered what purport to be assured shorthold tenancies, although, as a matter of law, they cannot be any form of assured tenancy at all, not even an assured shorthold tenancy, unless the landlord notifies the applicant that the tenancy is to be regarded as an assured or assured shorthold tenancy.[115]

16.77   Generally, these arrangements for interim accommodation are unlikely to be subject to the Protection from Eviction Act 1977 and so can be terminated by the landlord upon reasonable notice.[116]

16.78   The various different ways in which the accommodation functions can be met are explored in more detail in Chapter 18, but there are two arrangements which are particularly common ways of securing interim accommodation. They are the arrangements commonly referred to as 'homeless at home' and 'bed and breakfast'.

'Homeless at home'

16.79   Many applications under HA 1996, Part 7 are made by individuals who have been asked to leave the homes of friends or relatives with whom they have been staying. An applicant who indicates that he or she has been asked to leave such accommodation plainly gives a local housing authority 'reason to believe'

---

social housing to be used as temporary accommodation (English Code, paras 16.6 and 16.12); see also Welsh Code, paras 18.15–18.18, which are not so specific.

[112]   HA 1996, s 206(1).

[113]   See **18.1** and **18.8–18.10**.

[114]   Under Housing Act 1985, Sch 1, para 4, none of those would amount to the grant of a secure tenancy or licence. See English Code, paras 16.11–16.14; Welsh Code, paras 18.15–18.19.

[115]   HA 1996, s 209(2). English Code, paras 16.15–16.16; Welsh Code, paras 18.20–18.34.

[116]   *Desnousse v Newham London Borough Council* [2006] EWCA Civ 547, [2006] HLR 38, CA; English Code, para 7.11; Welsh Code, paras 12.51–12.54.

that he or she 'may' be homeless. If there is reason to believe that he or she may also be eligible and may have a priority need, then the duty to secure interim accommodation is triggered.[117]

16.80 In that situation the local housing authority may consider performing its interim duty by arranging[118] for the friend or relative to provide further accommodation, at least until it concludes its inquiries and notifies its decision to the applicant. Often friends or relatives are prepared to do this, on the assumption (which is not always correct) that this will only be for a matter of days. From the applicant's perspective, remaining where he or she is may be more attractive than other forms of interim accommodation that the local housing authority might provide. For obvious reasons, this common form of performance of the interim accommodation duty is called 'homeless at home'.

16.81 The arrangement is not altogether easy to square with the scheme of HA 1996, Part 7, not least because the readiness of the friend/relative to accommodate may suggest that there was no homelessness or threat of homelessness in the first place (or that the original request to leave was part of an arrangement to take advantage of HA 1996, Part 7).[119]

16.82 However, in practice these issues are overlooked. 'Homeless at home' has been a feature of the provision of interim accommodation for homeless applicants for over 20 years.[120] Furthermore, even though local housing authorities make substantial savings by performing their duty in this way, rather than by paying for alternative forms of accommodation, it is very rare for a local housing authority to offer or pay anything to friends or relatives for providing this service. Many friends and relatives fail to make payment a term for their co-operation.

16.83 It is important that the 'homeless at home' arrangement is made in the correct way. The accommodation must be 'secured' by the local housing authority.[121] It is not sufficient for an applicant to be told 'go back and see if they will let you stay until we make our decision'. It is for the local housing authority to ensure that accommodation is available, not for the applicant to take a chance that it might be.

16.84 Plainly, the local housing authority must also make sufficient investigations to satisfy itself that the 'homeless at home' arrangement can secure 'suitable' accommodation for the applicant.[122]

---

[117] HA 1996, s 188(1). See also **16.12–16.28**.

[118] Under options (2) or (3) at **16.74**.

[119] See **11.2–11.17** and **14.174–14.180**.

[120] Indeed the DCLG's quarterly statistics on homelessness exclude 'homeless at home' from the statistics on applicants occupying temporary accommodation (Table 783: Statutory Homelessness, households in temporary accommodation by type of accommodation and region, DCLG).

[121] HA 1996, ss 188(1) and 206(1).

[122] See Chapter 18.

16.85 A driving force behind the popularity of 'homeless at home' has been the applicant's fear that the only alternative interim arrangement will be bed and breakfast accommodation. With that form of provision effectively outlawed for applicants with family commitments, the future of 'homeless at home' may be thought uncertain.[123]

16.86 Where an applicant has made his or her application for homelessness assistance on the basis that he or she has accommodation available, but that accommodation is not reasonable for him or her to continue to occupy,[124] it may still be suitable for the purposes of interim accommodation. That is because the local housing authority is required to consider whether the accommodation is not reasonable to continue to occupy over time, even though the applicant could remain there in the short term.[125] However, if the accommodation is not reasonable for the applicant to continue to occupy for one more night, then it will not be suitable accommodation and the local housing authority should secure an alternative form of accommodation in performance of its interim duty.

'Bed and breakfast' and other 'shared accommodation'

16.87 Local housing authorities are advised against using bed and breakfast accommodation for the provision of interim accommodation to any homeless applicant, except on the rare occasions when it may be the most appropriate option for that particular applicant.[126]

16.88 In both England and Wales, there are now statutory instruments that deem bed and breakfast accommodation and, in the case of Wales, other shared accommodation, not to be suitable accommodation for certain applicants and with certain exceptions.[127] Suitability of bed and breakfast accommodation is discussed in Chapter 18.[128]

---

[123] Homelessness (Suitability of Accommodation) (England) Order 2003, SI 2003/3326 (see **18.114–18.119**) and Homelessness (Suitability of Accommodation) (Wales) Order 2006, SI 2006/650 (W 71) (see **18.120–18.128**).

[124] HA 1996, ss 175 and 176; see **11.75–11.120**.

[125] *Ali & others v Birmingham City Council, Moran v Manchester City Council* [2009] UKHL 36, [2009] 1 WLR 1506, HL.

[126] English Code, paras 7.6, 16.28 and 17.24–17.38; Welsh Code, paras 18.35–18.37 and 19.10–19.29.

[127] The UK Government and the Welsh Assembly Government both advise in statutory guidance that bed and breakfast accommodation will not be suitable for 16- and 17-year-old applicants (*Provision of Accommodation for 16 and 17 year old young people who may be homeless and/or require Accommodation*, April 2010, CLG and Children, Schools and Families, paras 2.9–2.10; *Provision of Accommodation for 16 and 17 year old young people who may be homeless*, Welsh Assembly Government, September 2010, para 2.14). See **18.113** for the advice in the statutory guidance, **18.1141–8.119** for the English Order and **18.120–18.128** for the Welsh Order.

[128] See **18.107–18.128**.

Rejection of the accommodation (explicit or implied)

16.89   Where interim accommodation is secured for an applicant (whether under a power or a duty) the applicant is, of course, under no obligation to accept it. In particular, an applicant offered initial interim accommodation may (on receiving the details of it) prefer to make other arrangements pending the local housing authority's decision on his or her application. That will bring the local housing authority's initial interim accommodation duty to an end (unless it is revived by any change of circumstances), because it is not obliged to hold open accommodation that the applicant has rejected. Importantly, however, the duty to inquire into the application is *not* brought to an end by the rejection of interim accommodation. Indeed, the outcome of those inquiries might well be affected by the results of the applicant's own attempts to meet interim accommodation needs. If he or she finds anything other than crisis accommodation,[129] then he or she will not be 'homeless' at the date of decision. On the other hand, detriment to the applicant resulting from a failure to secure anything other than crisis accommodation may help demonstrate that an applicant is 'vulnerable' and for that reason has a priority need.[130]

16.90   Local housing authorities must ensure that the applicant has actually rejected the accommodation before deciding that their initial interim accommodation duty has come to an end. One local housing authority was subject to judicial review proceedings when it refused to secure further interim accommodation, insisting that the applicant had rejected the accommodation, after the applicant had arrived at the accommodation a day late.[131]

16.91   Having taken up occupation of the interim accommodation, the applicant may, of course, subsequently reject it. Again, that will release the local housing authority from the accommodation duty. Rejection may be express or implied. For example, the applicant could simply walk out (and not return). Or the applicant's conduct might manifest a rejection of the accommodation: for example, if the applicant flouts the terms on which the accommodation is available or, in extreme cases, damages or destroys the accommodation. Where the local housing authority is minded to treat the applicant's behaviour as an implied rejection, it should normally give the applicant a warning and an opportunity to provide an explanation for his or her conduct.[132] Particular sensitivity is needed when the applicant is in poor mental health (a phenomenon that is not infrequent, given the stressful nature of homelessness).

---

[129]   See **11.11–11.14**.
[130]   See **13.75–13.119**.
[131]   *R (Carstens) v Basildon District Council* (2006) CO/923/2006, (2007) September *Legal Action*, p 18, Admin Ct.
[132]   *R v Kensington and Chelsea Royal London Borough Council ex p Kujtim* [1999] 4 All ER 161, (2000) 32 HLR 579, CA.

16.92 An applicant who rejects initial interim accommodation before having taken up occupation of it will not, for that reason, have become homeless intentionally.[133]

Termination of the accommodation

16.93 Once a duty to secure interim accommodation has ended, or a local housing authority decides that it will no longer exercise a power to secure interim accommodation, the applicant's legal right to occupation of the accommodation may need to be brought to an end.

16.94 The length of any notice period that the applicant is entitled to be given if he or she is required to leave the interim accommodation depends first on the terms of the licence or tenancy under which she or he has been occupying it. She or he cannot be excluded on shorter notice than is provided for in that tenancy or licence agreement.

16.95 However, almost by definition, any agreement for occupation of 'interim' accommodation will provide for quite short notice. Ordinarily, whatever the agreement itself says, those tenancies and licences that fall within the scope of the Protection from Eviction Act 1977 can only be terminated by the landlord on at least four weeks' written notice and the landlord will require a possession order from the court before he or she is entitled to obtain possession. But much of the accommodation secured as interim accommodation is provided under licences excluded from that protection.[134] In particular, a licence to occupy a local authority hostel is excluded from protection,[135] and so all that the local housing authority or the hostel manager need do is give the applicant reasonable notice to leave.[136]

16.96 Even in respect of the types of accommodation which might otherwise ordinarily fall within the scope of the Protection from Eviction Act 1977 (such as self-contained accommodation), the courts have not been inclined to apply the provisions of the Protection from Eviction Act 1977 to interim accommodation which is occupied under a licence. The approach taken has been that it is incompatible with a scheme for interim accommodation that the occupier should be entitled to four weeks' notice and then to the benefit of the further inevitable delay while possession is obtained through the courts.[137] However, the courts have so far left unanswered the question of whether interim accommodation occupied under *a tenancy* should be subject to the

---

[133] See **14.100–14.103**.
[134] Protection from Eviction Act 1977, s 3A lists the exclusions.
[135] Protection from Eviction Act 1977, s 3A(8).
[136] *Minister of Health v Bellotti* [1944] 1 KB 298, CA.
[137] *Mohammed v Manek and Kensington and Chelsea Royal London Borough Council* (1995) 27 HLR 439, CA; *Gibson v Paddington Churches Housing Association* (2003) November *Legal Action*, p 16, Central London County Court; and *Desnousse v Newham London Borough Council* [2006] EWCA Civ 547, [2006] HLR 38, CA.

Protection from Eviction Act 1977.[138] After all, if Parliament had intended to exclude interim accommodation from the benefit of the Protection from Eviction Act 1977, it could easily have done so by amending that Act when it introduced HA 1996, Part 7.

16.97   Even if there is no minimum notice required and no need to obtain a possession order, this does not mean that the local housing authority can simply eject applicants accommodated on an interim basis. Local housing authorities must act reasonably, as any public authority would. The obligation to behave reasonably requires that the applicant be given at least some opportunity to find some other accommodation before the interim accommodation is withdrawn.[139] Reasonable notice in those circumstances should obviously be more than 24 hours[140] and periods of six or seven days have also been held to be too short to constitute reasonable notice.[141] In a case in which the right to occupy interim accommodation was ended by new legislation, a judge suggested that the reasonable notice ought to be at least the period the local housing authority would have given to a person found to have become homeless intentionally.[142]

ENFORCEMENT OF DUTIES (AND CHALLENGES TO REFUSALS TO EXERCISE POWERS) TO SECURE INTERIM ACCOMMODATION

16.98   None of the decisions that a local housing authority might make in relation to its powers or duties to secure 'interim' accommodation can be subject to the statutory review procedure. None of the following decisions about the provision of interim accommodation, which may be among the most critical to be made concerning an applicant, are covered by the statutory review procedure:

(1)   a decision that no duty to secure interim accommodation is owed;

(2)   a decision that a power to secure interim accommodation will not be exercised;

---

[138]   *Desnousse v Newham London Borough Council* [2006] EWCA Civ 547, [2006] HLR 38, CA, at [69], per Lloyd LJ.

[139]   English Code, paras 7.10–7.12; Welsh Code, paras 12.51–12.54; and *R v Secretary of State for the Environment ex p Shelter* [1997] COD 49, QBD, applied in *R v Newham London Borough Council ex p Ojuri (No 3)* (1999) 31 HLR 631, QBD.

[140]   *R v Newham London Borough Council ex p Ojuri (No 3)* (1999) 31 HLR 631, QBD.

[141]   *R v Newham London Borough Council ex p Pembele* (1999) January *Legal Action*, p 27, QBD; *R v Westminster City Council ex p Abdulkadir* (1999) August *Legal Action*, p 29, QBD, although in *R v Newham London Borough Council ex p Lumley* (2001) 33 HLR 11, QBD, it was said *obiter* that six clear days' notice would not be unreasonable for a young single man.

[142]   *R v Secretary of State for the Environment ex p Shelter* [1997] COD 49, QBD, per Carnwath J.

(3) a decision as to how a duty to secure interim accommodation will be performed or a power exercised;

(4) a decision as to which members of the applicant's household will be accommodated under the duty or the exercise of the power to secure interim accommodation ; and

(5) a decision as to whether the interim accommodation is suitable.

16.99 There is no statutory obligation to notify the applicant of these decisions (in writing or otherwise), nor is there a statutory obligation to give reasons for those decisions.[143]

16.100 Although these decisions, if disputed, could be the subject of a formal complaint to the local housing authority under its complaints procedure and (ultimately) to the Local Government Ombudsmen,[144] the applicant will usually need the urgent provision of accommodation, and this can only be obtained (if at all) by a legal challenge to the decision.

16.101 Any challenge to the suitability of accommodation secured under any of these duties or powers to secure interim accommodation can only be brought by judicial review.[145] There is no right to request a statutory review of the suitability of interim accommodation and no appeal to the county court on such an issue.

Refusal to comply with a statutory duty

16.102 When the local housing authority is failing to comply with its acknowledged statutory duty, the position is relatively straightforward. Although the applicant cannot sue in the ordinary way for damages and for an injunction to compel the local housing authority to perform its duty,[146] he or she is not left without recourse to the courts. If the local housing authority fails to secure interim accommodation when it is under a duty to do so, the appropriate procedure is to bring a claim for judicial review,[147] including an application for both an interim and final mandatory order requiring the local housing authority to comply with its statutory duty.

---

[143] It is obviously good administrative practice for decisions to be recorded in writing and, where appropriate, to be explained by written reasons.

[144] Or to the Public Services Ombudsman for Wales. See **19.238–19.245**.

[145] See **19.251–19.258**.

[146] *O'Rourke v Camden London Borough Council* [1998] AC 188, HL.

[147] The procedure is explained at **19.224–19.250**.

Refusal to exercise power to secure interim accommodation pending review

16.103   Where a local housing authority has:

- failed to consider a request for interim accommodation pending review; or

- refused to secure interim accommodation pending a review; or

- decided to secure interim accommodation for a limited period only; or

- decided to withdraw interim accommodation that had been secured pending the review, before the notification of the review decision,

the appropriate avenue for the applicant to challenge any of these decisions is to bring a claim by way of judicial review. In order to succeed, the applicant must show that the local housing authority's decision (or failure to make one) was wrong in law.

16.104   Challenges to local housing authorities' decisions not to exercise a discretionary power are generally much more difficult for the applicant than challenges for breach of statutory duty. The courts can be particularly reluctant to intervene where Parliament has left local housing authorities free of duties and enjoying a discretion to exercise (or not exercise) powers.

16.105   The principles that a local housing authority must consider when deciding whether or not to secure interim accommodation pending review are set out in *R v Camden London Borough Council ex p Mohammed*.[148]

16.106   On applying for permission to bring a claim by way of judicial review, the applicant can also apply for an interim injunction requiring the local housing authority to secure accommodation pending the determination of the judicial review proceedings. The test that the Administrative Court will apply in considering whether or not to make an interim injunction is two-fold:

- whether the claim raises a serious issue to be tried;[149] and

- the balance of convenience including the wider public interest.[150]

---

[148]   *R v Camden London Borough Council ex p Mohammed* (1998) 30 HLR 315, QBD. See also **16.421–6.46**, and English Code, paras 15.12–15.20; Welsh Code, paras 21.15–21.18.

[149]   This test includes considering whether the claimant can demonstrate a real prospect of succeeding at trial (*R (Medical Justice) v SSHD* [2010] EWHC 1425 (Admin), Admin Ct.

[150]   *American Cyanamid Co v Ethicon Ltd* [1975] AC 396, HL; and *R v Kensington and Chelsea Royal London Borough Council ex parte Hammell* [1989] 1 QB 518, CA.

16.107 The onus is on the applicant to show that the claim raises a serious issue to be tried, where he or she is applying for an interim injunction.[151]

16.108 In cases of emergency, where the applicant is or is about to be street homeless, an application for an interim injunction can be made out of hours and over the telephone to a duty Administrative Court judge. In *R (Lawer) v Restormel Borough Council*,[152] the applicant's legal representatives were reminded that applications in these circumstances are exceptional and of the importance of their duties:

- to make full and frank disclosure of all the relevant documents to the judge; and

- to ensure that there has been compliance with the pre-action protocol in judicial review claims and service on the local housing authority's legal department.[153]

16.109 In practice, if the Administrative Court judge considers that the claim for judicial review has merit, the balance of convenience is likely to be in favour of making an interim injunction, since otherwise the applicant would be homeless.

16.110 Many judicial review claims against refusals to secure interim accommodation are disposed of at the time of, or shortly after, consideration of whether or not permission should be granted to bring the claim. If permission is refused, unless there is to be an appeal, that is the end of the matter for the applicant. If permission is granted, and an interim injunction made requiring the local housing authority to accommodate the applicant until the judicial review claim has been determined,[154] many local housing authorities will then agree to accommodate pending review. Even if there is no agreement, it is not unusual for the review decision to be notified to the applicant before the judicial review claim has been finally heard, and so the claim for judicial review becomes academic.

16.111 If the judicial review claim does proceed to a full hearing, the claim might be dismissed (if there is no error of law). If the claim succeeds, and the Administrative Court decides that the local housing authority did make an error of law in one or more of its decisions, it can set the decision aside (a 'quashing order'). The local housing authority will either have to reconsider its

---

[151] *R (Omatoyo) v City of Westminster Council* [2006] EWHC 2572 (Admin), (2006) December *Legal Action*, p 21, Admin Ct.

[152] [2007] EWHC 2299 (Admin), [2008] HLR 20, Admin Ct.

[153] See **19.226–19.232**. And see also *R (Sadek) v Westminster City Council* [2012] EWCA Civ 803, (2012) August *Legal Action*, p 28, Admin Ct.

[154] Permission is granted where there is a reasonably arguable case. An interim mandatory injunction requires a serious issue to be tried. The fact that permission has been granted, whilst not determinative, is certainly a relevant factor when the court considers whether an interim injunction should continue (*R (Omatoyo) v City of Westminster Council* [2006] EWHC 2572 (Admin), (2006) December *Legal Action*, p 21, Admin Ct).

decision or the Administrative Court may make a mandatory order requiring the local housing authority to secure accommodation until the review decision has been notified to the applicant.

16.112 The *R (Paul-Coker) v Southwark London Borough Council*[155] case is an example of the Administrative Court deciding that a local housing authority, when it referred to the criteria involved in the *Mohammed* balancing-exercise, was in fact paying 'lip-service' to them. The refusal to exercise the power to secure accommodation in that case was unlawful.

Refusal to exercise a power to secure interim accommodation pending appeal

16.113 If the local housing authority refuses to secure interim accommodation pending appeal (or if it decides to secure interim accommodation for a limited period only), there is no right to a statutory review of that decision. Instead, the applicant has the right to appeal against that refusal. The appeal lies to the county court on a point of law.[156] To distinguish this appeal from the main or substantive appeal (usually brought against the review decision of the local housing authority) it is described in the paragraphs that follow as the 'accommodation appeal'.

16.114 The principles that a local housing authority must consider when deciding whether or not to secure interim accommodation pending appeal are set out in *R v Camden London Borough Council ex p Mohammed*.[157]

16.115 The accommodation appeal may be against:

(1)   the refusal to accommodate at all pending appeal; or

(2)   a decision to exercise the power to accommodate only for a limited period; or

(3)   a decision to withdraw interim accommodation that had been secured pending appeal.[158]

16.116 There is no appeal on the facts. The applicant must show that the local housing authority's refusal, decision or withdrawal was wrong in law. The court will adopt the principles applied generally in judicial review claims when it considers the lawfulness of the local housing authority's decision-making.[159]

---

[155]   *R (Paul-Coker) v Southwark London Borough Council* [2006] EWHC 497 (Admin), [2006] HLR 32, Admin Ct; and see **16.42–16.46**.
[156]   HA 1996, s 204A(2). See **19.202–19.212**.
[157]   *R v Camden London Borough Council ex p Mohammed* (1998) 30 HLR 315, QBD. See also **16.421–6.46**, and English Code, paras 15.21–15.24; Welsh Code, paras 21.21–21.26.
[158]   HA 1996, s 204A(2).
[159]   HA 1996, s 204A(4)(b). See **19.157–19.166**.

16.117 Prior to 30 September 2002, challenges to refusals to secure accommodation pending appeal were brought by way of judicial review.[160] The Court of Appeal had held that if the guidance given in *R v Camden London Borough Council ex p Mohammed*[161] had been followed by a local housing authority, when considering whether or not to secure interim accommodation pending appeal, challenges to the exercise of that discretion were likely to be futile, and applications for judicial review should only be brought in exceptional cases. The appropriate step for an applicant without accommodation was to seek to expedite the hearing of his or her substantive appeal, rather than challenge the refusal to accommodate pending appeal.[162]

16.118 The Court of Appeal has taken the same approach now that challenges to refusals are brought by way of a county court appeal rather than by way of judicial review.[163] If the local housing authority has properly directed itself in accordance with the *Mohammed* principles,[164] the court will not intervene. The county court hearing an accommodation appeal should not embark on a consideration of the merits of the main or main or substantive appeal.

16.119 If the local housing authority has not properly directed itself, then the court will quash the decision and will consider whether it should exercise its power to order the local housing authority to secure interim accommodation pending appeal.[165]

16.120 This decision in *Francis v Kensington and Chelsea Royal London Borough Council*,[166] begs the question as to what 'properly directed itself' means. Certainly, where a local housing authority fails to consider, at all, a request for accommodation pending appeal, it cannot be said to have properly considered the right factors, and must therefore have erred in law. Conversely, where a local housing authority has set out the *Mohammed* factors and carefully considered each of those, along with any other points raised by the applicant, then the decision is unlikely to be wrong in law.

16.121 In practice, the decision in *Francis* means that accommodation appeals may now be rarely brought, but in the rare cares in which they may justifiably be brought they may well succeed.[167]

---

[160] *Ali v Westminster City Council* [1999] 1 WLR 384, (1999) 31 HLR 349, CA.

[161] *R v Camden London Borough Council ex p Mohammed* (1998) 30 HLR 315, QBD. See also **16.42–16.46**.

[162] *R v Brighton and Hove Borough Council ex p Nacion* (1999) 31 HLR 1095, CA.

[163] *Francis v Kensington and Chelsea Royal London Borough Council* [2003] EWCA Civ 443, [2003] 35 HLR 50, CA; and *Brookes v Croydon London Borough Council* [2004] EWCA Civ 439, (2004) June *Legal Action*, p 31, CA.

[164] *R v Camden London Borough Council ex p Mohammed* (1998) 30 HLR 315, QBD. See also **16.42–16.46**.

[165] See also **16.122–16.127**.

[166] [2003] EWCA Civ 443, [2003] 35 HLR 50, CA.

[167] As did the applicants in *Onyaebor v Newham London Borough Council* (2004) May *Legal Action*, p 27, Bow County Court; and *Quadir v Tower Hamlets London Borough Council* (2011),

16.122 If the accommodation appeal succeeds, the court may quash the decision appealed against. At that point, the court may either refer the matter back to the local housing authority for re-consideration of the request for accommodation pending appeal, or it may make an order requiring the local housing authority to secure interim accommodation. It can only make the latter order if it is satisfied that:

> '... failure to exercise the section 204(4) power in accordance with the order would substantially prejudice the applicant's ability to pursue the main appeal.'[168]

16.123 This is a strikingly different test from that governing the local housing authority's own exercise of discretion. The determinative factor for the court can only be the ability of the applicant to pursue his or her main or substantive appeal with or without the provision of accommodation. Whilst an applicant's other personal circumstances may be relevant, they cannot be determinative.[169]

16.124 An order to accommodate made by the court cannot extend beyond the conclusion of the main appeal. In other words, the county court has no jurisdiction to order the provision of accommodation pending any further appeal beyond the county court.

16.125 Accommodation appeals, like main or substantive appeals, can only be heard by a circuit judge or recorder, not by a district judge.[170]

16.126 Applications for interim orders, requiring the provision of accommodation pending determination of the accommodation appeal, can be made before the full accommodation appeal is heard. A judge hearing an interlocutory application will have to decide:

(1) whether there is an arguable error of law in the decision being appealed against; and, if so,

(2) whether, arguably, the ability of the applicant to pursue his or her main appeal would be substantially prejudiced if accommodation were not secured.

(2012) April *Legal Action*, p 47, Central London Civil Justice Centre. For an example of an appeal which did not succeed, see *Hafiz & Haque v Westminster City Council* [2012] EWHC 1392 (QB), (2012) July *Legal Action*, p 42, QBD.

[168] HA 1996, s 204A(6).

[169] For example, in *Quadir v Tower Hamlets London Borough Council* (2011), (2012) April *Legal Action*, p 47, Central London Civil Justice Centre, the appeal against the refusal to secure accommodation pending appeal was successful, and the local housing authority's refusal was quashed by the judge. However, the judge did not consider that the strict test at HA 1996, s 204A(6) was satisfied and did not make an order requiring the local housing authority to secure interim accommodation.

[170] CPR 1998, Pt 2, PD2B, para 9.

16.127 An interim order can only be made if the judge takes the view that both of those points are arguable by the applicant, and that the balance of convenience favours the making of an interim order.[171]

Compensation claims

16.128 Where a local housing authority wrongly fails to secure interim accommodation, in breach of its statutory duty so to do, the applicant cannot sue for compensation for loss, in the normal way, in respect of that breach of statutory duty[172] nor can he or she recover damages for that breach as an ancillary remedy in a claim by way of judicial review.[173] Nor can the applicant recover damages for any breach of the right to respect for his or her home[174] because, by definition, she or he has, at this point, no home to 'respect'. The right to 'respect for his home' does not encompass a right to a home.[175] There may be a legal right to compensation[176] if the breach of duty reduces the applicant to circumstances amounting to inhuman or degrading treatment,[177] or infringes his or her right to respect for private or family life.[178]

16.129 The absence of a general right to compensation in these circumstances makes it even more important that the applicant promptly obtains a mandatory order in judicial review proceedings requiring the local housing authority to perform its duty. Normally, any financial or other loss caused in the period before an order is obtained could only be recovered through a complaint under

---

[171] HA 1996, s 204(4)(a) and see *Hafiz & Haque v Westminster City Council* [2012] EWHC 1392 (QB), (2012) July *Legal Action*, p 42, QBD.

[172] *O'Rourke v Camden London Borough Council* [1998] AC 188, HL.

[173] *R v Ealing London Borough Council ex p Parkinson* (1997) 29 HLR 179, QBD, per Laws J. In some circumstances, it might be possible to claim damages for the tort of misfeasance in public office. In the only attempt known to the authors of a claim for damages for this tort being brought in connection with homelessness duties, the Judge said: '[w]hilst . . . I would be reluctant to conclude that a claim for misfeasance in a public office could *never* be brought in a situation that reflects a breach of Part 7, the circumstances in which such a claim could successfully be brought would . . . be extremely limited' (*R (Kharzai & others) v Birmingham City Council* [2010] EWHC 2576 (Admin), (2010) December *Legal Action*, p 37, Admin Ct per Foskett J at [44]).

[174] Protected by Art 8 of the European Convention on Human Rights: Human Rights Act 1998, Sch 1.

[175] *O'Rourke v UK (Application 39022/97)* (unreported) 26 June 2001, ECtHR.

[176] Human Rights Act 1998, s 8(2).

[177] Under Art 3 of the European Convention on Human Rights: Human Rights Act 1998, Sch 1; see **19.246–19.250** and **20.90–20.98**; *O'Rourke v UK (Application 39022/97)* (unreported) 26 June 2001, ECtHR.

[178] Under Art 8 of the European Convention on Human Rights. See *R (B) v Southwark London Borough Council (No 2)* (2004) January *Legal Action*, p 32, in which the local housing authority settled a claim for compensation for £3,000 where the failure to secure interim accommodation caused the applicant to stay in prison unnecessarily for an additional weekend. See **20.99–20.102**.

the local housing authority's own complaints procedure (or thereafter by further complaint to the Local Government Ombudsmen).[179]

16.130 Even where an applicant has been provided with interim accommodation, the local housing authority will be in breach of its statutory duties if the accommodation is not 'suitable'. Again, the normal rule is that the applicant cannot sue for recompense.[180] However, where the standard of accommodation is so unsuitable that it infringes an applicant's right to respect for his or her home, family or private life, damages could be awarded for breach of the Human Rights Act 1998, Sch 1, Art 8(1).[181] Where the evidence shows that the conditions of the accommodation do infringe an applicant's rights under Art 8(1), the burden rests on the local housing authority to show that the interference with those rights was justified and proportionate under Art 8(2).[182]

16.131 Precisely because Art 8(1) does not provide a right to a home,[183] merely the right to respect for the applicant's existing home, any claims brought under it are likely to relate to the interference, as a result of the condition of the accommodation, with the applicant's right to respect for his or her family or private life.[184] For example, placing a London family in interim accommodation in Birmingham, when the child needed to retain contact with her father in London, was found to be contrary to the family's right to respect for their family life.[185] On the other hand, a claim for damages for 29 weeks spent in grossly overcrowded and unsuitable accommodation did not succeed as the applicant was not deprived of her home, she was not separated from her children and the health problems caused by the unsuitable accommodation were not so grave as to constitute an interference with her private life.[186] Damages were awarded for breach of the applicant's right to respect for her family and private life where a wheelchair-bound woman was restricted to a single room in unsuitable temporary accommodation for over two years.[187] However, where an elderly woman had been effectively confined to her bedroom as a result of the steepness of the stairs in the family's temporary accommodation, and had missed the family interaction that took place principally in the kitchen, the local housing authority was held not to have

---

[179] Or the Public Services Ombudsman for Wales. See **19.251–19.258**. For an example, see *Complaint against Newham London Borough Council*, 11 000 383, 8 March 2012, (2012) May *Legal Action*, p 34.

[180] *R v Ealing London Borough Council ex p Parkinson* (1997) 29 HLR 179, QBD.

[181] Human Rights Act 1998, s 8, Sch 1; *R (Bernard) v Enfield London Borough Council* [2002] EWHC 2282 (Admin), (2003) 35 HLR 27, Admin Ct.

[182] *R (Yumsak) v Enfield London Borough Council* [2002] EWHC 280 (Admin), [2003] HLR 1, Admin Ct.

[183] See **19.246–19.250** and **20.99–20.102**.

[184] *R (Morris) v Newham London Borough Council* [2002] EWHC 1262 (Admin), (2002) July *Legal Action*, p 27, Admin Ct.

[185] *R (Yumsak) v Enfield London Borough Council* [2002] EWHC 280 (Admin), [2003] HLR 1, Admin Ct.

[186] *R (Morris) v Newham London Borough Council* [2002] EWHC 1262 (Admin), (2002) July *Legal Action*, p 27, Admin Ct.

[187] *R (Bernard) v Enfield London Borough Council* [2002] EWHC 2282 (Admin), (2003) 35 HLR 27, Admin Ct.

interfered with her right to respect for her family life. It had secured accommodation, made offers of alternative accommodation that had been rejected, and had provided practical help. The obligations under Human Rights Act 1998, Sch 1, imposed on the local housing authority did not extend to creating a set of circumstances in which all major impediments to the full enjoyment of family life were removed.[188]

16.132 Alternatively, complaint could be made to the Local Government Ombudsmen or Public Services Ombudsman for Wales that the local housing authority has been guilty of maladministration. Indeed, any awards of compensation for interference with an applicant's rights under Art 8(1) of the Human Rights Act 1998, Sch 1, are likely to be assessed by reference to the sums recommended as compensation for maladministration by the Local Government Ombudsmen in other cases.[189]

---

[188] *Anufrijeva v Southwark London Borough Council* [2003] EWCA Civ 1406, CA, [2004] 1 All ER 833, CA.
[189] *R (Bernard) v Enfield London Borough Council* [2002] EWHC 2282 (Admin), (2003) 35 HLR 27, Admin Ct. See **19.246–19.250**.

Chapter 17

DUTIES AND POWERS TO ASSIST
THE HOMELESS

INTRODUCTION

17.1 The Housing Act 1996 (HA 1996) Part 7 ('Homelessness') places a wide range of duties on a local housing authority when it receives an application for homelessness assistance; it also supplies the local housing authority with a range of powers. The full portfolio of *duties* extends from a simple duty to notify a decision at one end of the spectrum to an obligation to accommodate the applicant (until he or she can find a home of his or her own) at the other. The range of discretionary *powers* extends from care of personal possessions to provision of a temporary home.

17.2 Other Chapters in this book have already examined the powers and duties relating to:

- homelessness reviews and strategies (Chapter 7);

- decisions and notifications (Chapter 10); and

- provision of interim accommodation (Chapter 16).

17.3 This Chapter explores the remaining powers and duties, focusing on the most important of all the duties – the 'main housing duty' to accommodate the applicant.[1]

Notification to the applicant

17.4 The applicant will know which *duty* is owed to him or her from the notification letter issued once the local housing authority has completed its inquiries and decided 'whether any duty, and if so what duty, is owed to' the applicant under HA 1996, Part 7.[2]

17.5 Although there is no express requirement to consider whether to exercise a *power*, nor an obligation to notify any decision on the exercise of that power, it might be expected that local housing authorities would consider the relevant powers in HA 1996, Part 7 and, at least if requested, explain their decisions on whether or not to exercise them.

17.6 If the applicant is a 'restricted case',[3] or 'restricted threatened homelessness case',[4] because of the presence in his or her household of a 'restricted person',[5] the local housing authority has special notification duties.[6]

---

1   Housing Act 1996, s 193(2). See **17.23–17.168**.
2   HA 1996, s 184(1). See **10.66–10.81**.
3   HA 1996, s 193(3D), inserted by Housing and Regeneration Act 2008, Sch 15, para 5, in force for applications made on or after 2 March 2009. See **12.32, 12.47** and **17.155–17.168**.
4   HA 1996, s 195(4B), inserted by Housing and Regeneration Act 2008, Sch 15, para 6, in force for applications made on or after 2 March 2009. See **17.196–17.200**.
5   HA 1996, s 184(7), inserted by Housing and Regeneration Act 2008, Sch 15, para 3, in force for applications made on or after 2 March 2009. See **10.38–10.40,** and **12.32–12.47**.

Overview of duties and powers

17.7   Every applicant is owed at least one duty: the duty that the local housing authority must notify a decision on his or her application.[7]

17.8   Beyond notification of the decision, no further duty under HA 1996, Part 7 is owed to an applicant who is ineligible for assistance,[8] or to one who is neither homeless nor threatened with homelessness.[9] There is no duty to give advice and assistance to those applicants, but they may receive advice from the local housing authority's homelessness advice service.[10] They may also benefit from the power to take care of their possessions.[11]

17.9   The duties owed to the other classes of applicant (generally the vast bulk of applicants) depend on whether they became homeless intentionally or unintentionally (or became threatened with homelessness intentionally or unintentionally),[12] and on whether or not they have a priority need.[13] For ease of reference the main duties and powers listed below have been divided up by reference to the key findings on the questions of intentionality and priority need:

Applicants who have not become homeless intentionally

- In priority need:
    - the 'main housing *duty*' to secure accommodation;[14] or
    - for applicants to a local housing authority in Wales,[15] the 'main housing *duty*' to secure accommodation and a *duty* to be given a copy of the statement in the authority's allocation statement on offering choice to people allocated housing accommodation;[16] or
    - if referred to another local housing authority:[17]
        - a *duty* to notify the applicant that the local housing authority intends to refer him or her and to inform the applicant of the reasons for it;[18] and

---

[6]   HA 1996, s 184(3A), inserted by Housing and Regeneration Act 2008, Sch 15, para 3, in force for applications made on or after 2 March 2009. See **10.82–10.85**.

[7]   HA 1996, s 184(1) and (3). See **10.1** and **10.66–10.81**.

[8]   See Chapter 12.

[9]   See Chapter 11.

[10]   HA 1996, s 179. See **9.4–9.7**.

[11]   HA 1996, s 211(3). See **17.233–17.254**.

[12]   See Chapter 14.

[13]   See Chapter 13.

[14]   HA 1996, s 193(2). See **17.23–17.168**.

[15]   And for applicants whose applications for homelessness assistance were made before 9 November 2012 to a local housing authority in England.

[16]   HA 1996, s 193(3A) repealed by Localism Act 2011, s 148(2) for applicants whose applications for homelessness assistance were made on or after 9 November 2012 to a local housing authority in England. At the date of writing, the amendments to HA 1996, Part 7, made by LA 2011, ss 148–149 had not been brought into effect in Wales. See **17.132–17.158**.

[17]   See Chapter 15.

[18]   HA 1996, s 184(4). See **15.151–15.154**.

- an *interim duty* to secure accommodation until the applicant is notified that the conditions for referral have been met;[19] and
- a *duty* to secure accommodation if conditions for referral are not met;[20] or
- a *power* to secure accommodation if the conditions for referral are met and the applicant requests a review,[21] or
  - if the applicant is a 'restricted case', modifications to the main housing *duty*.[22]

- Not in priority need:
  - a duty to provide advice and assistance;[23] and
  - a *power* to secure accommodation;[24] and
  - for applications made on or after 9 November 2012 to a local housing authority in England,[25] and also made within two years of acceptance of a private rented sector offer,[26] the main housing *duty*.[27]

Applicants who have become homeless intentionally

- In priority need:
  - a *duty* to provide advice and assistance;[28] and
  - a *duty* to secure accommodation for such period as will give the applicant a reasonable period to obtain accommodation for him or herself.[29]

- Not in priority need:

---

[19] HA 1996, s 200(1) and see **15.157–15.160** and **16.56–16.63**.

[20] HA 1996, s 200(3) and s 193(2).

[21] HA 1996, s 200(5), and see **15.154** and **16.62**.

[22] HA 1996, s 193(7AA)–(7AD) amended by LA 2011, s 148(5)–(7), for applicants whose applications for homelessness assistance were made on or after 9 November 2012 to a local housing authority in England. For the modifications in those cases, see **17.159–17.162**. At the date of writing, the amendments to HA 1996 made by LA 2011, ss 148–149 had not been brought into effect in Wales, see **17.163–17.168**.

[23] HA 1996, s 192(2); see **17.201–17.214**.

[24] HA 1996, s 192(3); see **17.215–17.222**.

[25] At the date of writing, the amendments to HA 1996 made by LA 2011, ss 148–149 had not been brought into effect in Wales.

[26] 'Private rented sector offer' is defined at HA 1996, s 193(7AA) as amended by LA 2011, s 148(5) and made to applicants whose applications for homelessness assistance were made on or after 9 November 2012 to a local housing authority in England. See **9.89–9.95** and **17.109–17.131**. At the date of writing, the amendments to HA 1996 made by LA 2011, ss 148–149 had not been brought into effect in Wales.

[27] HA 1996, s 195A(1) inserted by LA 2011, s 149(4), for applicants whose applications for homelessness assistance were made on or after 9 November 2012 to a local housing authority in England. See **17.171–17.181**. There is an exception where the local housing authority would not be satisfied that the main housing duty is owed to the applicant without the presence of a 'restricted person' (HA 1996, s 184(7), see **17.173**), in which case the applicant must still have a priority need in order to be owed the main housing duty (HA 1996, s 195A(5) inserted by LA 2011, s 149(4))..

[28] HA 1996, s 190(2)(b); see **17.201–17.214**.

[29] HA 1996, s 190(2)(a); see **17.182–17.189**.

-       a *duty* to provide advice and assistance.[30]

Applicants who have *not* become threatened with homelessness intentionally

*   In priority need:
    -       a *duty* to take reasonable steps to ensure that accommodation does not cease to be available;[31] and
    -       a *duty* to secure accommodation if the previous accommodation ceases to be available;[32] or
    -       if the applicant is a 'restricted threatened homelessness case', modifications to the *duty* to secure accommodation if the previous accommodation ceases to be available.[33]

*   Not in priority need:
    -       a *duty* to provide advice and assistance;[34] and
    -       a *power* to take reasonable steps to ensure that accommodation does not cease to be available;[35] or
    -       if the applicant whose application for homelessness assistance is made to a local housing authority in England on or after 9 November 2012[36] and is re-applying within two years of acceptance of a private rented sector offer,[37] a *duty* to take reasonable steps to ensure that accommodation does not cease to be available; and a *duty* to secure accommodation if the previous accommodation ceases to be available.[38]

Applicants who have become threatened with homelessness intentionally

*   In priority need:

---

[30]   HA 1996, s 190(3); see **17.201–17.214**.

[31]   HA 1996, s 195(2); see **17.190–17.200**.

[32]   HA 1996, s 193(2); see **17.123–17.168**.

[33]   HA 1996, s 195(4A)–(4B) inclusive as amended by LA 2011, s 148(3), for applicants whose applications for homelessness assistance were made on or after 9 November 2012 to a local housing authority in England, see **17.196–17.199**. At the date of writing, the amendments to HA 1996 made by LA 2011, ss 148–149 had not been brought into effect in Wales, see **17.196–17.198** and **17.200**.

[34]   HA 1996, s 195(5); see **17.201–17.214**.

[35]   HA 1996, s 195(9); see **17.215–17.222**.

[36]   At the date of writing, the amendments to HA 1996 made by LA 2011, ss 148–149 had not been brought into effect in Wales.

[37]   HA 1996, s 193(7AA) as amended by LA 2011, s 148(5), for applicants whose applications for homelessness assistance were made on or after 9 November 2012 to a local housing authority in England. See **9.89–9.95** and **17.109–17.131**. At the date of writing, the amendments to HA 1996 made by LA 2011, ss 148–149 had not been brought into effect in Wales.

[38]   HA 1996, s 195A(3) inserted by LA 2011, s 149(4), for applicants whose applications for homelessness assistance were made on or after 9 November 2012 to a local housing authority in England. See **9.89–9.95** and **17.171–17.181**. There is an exception where the local housing authority would not be satisfied that the main duty is owed to the applicant without the presence of a 'restricted person' (HA 1996, s 184(7), see **10.38–10.40** and **12.32–12.47**), in which case the applicant must still have a priority need in order to be owed the main duty (HA 1996, s 195A(5) inserted by LA 2011, s 149(4)). See **17.173**.

- a *duty* to provide advice and assistance.[39]

• Not in priority need:
  - a *duty* to provide advice and assistance.[40]

17.10 These duties and powers are summarised in both the English and Welsh Codes and those summaries are accompanied by considerable statutory guidance.[41]

Duties and powers to secure accommodation

17.11 A number of duties (and powers) by which local housing authorities are obliged to (or may) 'secure' accommodation for an applicant are set out in HA 1996, Part 7. The duties and powers to secure accommodation of an 'interim' nature are described in Chapter 16. In this Chapter, the focus is on those accommodation duties and powers triggered by the local housing authority's decision on an application for homelessness assistance.

17.12 To save endless repetition, each time HA 1996, Part 7 deals with a different accommodation duty or power, it describes the performance of those duties or powers as being the performance of a 'housing function'.[42] It then sets out some common characteristics which apply to each housing function. These are:

(1) a requirement that accommodation secured for the applicant must be 'suitable';[43]

(2) a requirement that such accommodation be 'available' not only for the applicant but also for others in his or her household;[44]

(3) three different methods by which the duty or power can be performed:
   (a) provision of the local housing authority's own housing;[45] or
   (b) housing from some other person;[46] or
   (c) advice and assistance that secures housing;[47]

(4) a power to impose reasonable charges for accommodation;[48]

---

[39] HA 1996, s 195(5); see **17.201–17.214**.
[40] HA 1996, s 195(5); see **17.201–17.214**.
[41] *Homelessness Code of Guidance for Local Authorities* (Communities and Local Government, Department for Education and Skills, Department of Health, July 2006), (the English Code), Chapter 14. *Code of Guidance for Local Authorities Allocation of Accommodation and Homelessness 2012* (Welsh Government, August 2012) (the Welsh Code), Chapter 18.
[42] HA 1996, s 205.
[43] HA 1996, ss 206(1) and 210. See Chapter 18.
[44] HA 1996, s 176, and see the discussion at **11.23–11.34**.
[45] HA 1996, s 206(1)(a).
[46] HA 1996, s 206(1)(b).
[47] HA 1996, s 206(1)(c).
[48] HA 1996, s 206(2). See **17.16–17.20**.

(5) a presumption that accommodation will be secured in the local housing authority's own district;[49] and

(6) modifications to security of tenure provisions, which might otherwise apply to such accommodation.[50]

17.13 In 'restricted cases',[51] there are additional modifications to some duties.

17.14 Where the applicant who is owed the main housing duty made his or her application for homelessness assistance to a local housing authority in England[52] on or after 9 November 2012, the local housing authority is no longer obliged to give a statement of its policy on 'choice' in its allocation scheme.[53] This is because the expectation is that the main housing duty will be brought to an end by the making of a private rented sector offer.[54] Applicants who also wish to apply to the local housing authority's allocation scheme can make their own inquiries as to whether or not the scheme offers 'choice'.[55]

17.15 Local housing authorities in Wales[56] remain under an obligation to give most applicants owed the main housing duty a copy of the statement on 'choice' in their allocation schemes.[57]

Charging for accommodation

17.16 The local housing authority can secure accommodation for applicants free of charge. More usually it will require the applicant to pay whatever amount the local housing authority considers he or she can reasonably afford. The local housing authority has power to require the applicant to pay 'such reasonable charges as they may determine' in respect of the accommodation secured, by itself or by another person.[58] Where the local housing authority is

---

[49] HA 1996, s 208(1); see **15.226–15.233, 16.70–16.73** and **18.58–18.68**.
[50] HA 1996, s 209; and see also Housing Act 1985, Sch 1, para 4.
[51] HA 1996, s 193(3B), see **10.38–10.40, 10.82–10.85** and **12.32–12.47**. For the modifications to the main housing duty owed to a restricted case where the applicant made his or her application for homelessness assistance to a local housing authority in England on or after 9 November 2012, see **17.155–17.162**. For the modifications where the applicant made his or her application for homelessness assistance to a local housing authority in Wales, see **17.163–17.168**.
[52] At the date of writing, the amendments to HA 1996 made by LA 2011, ss 148–149 had not been brought into effect in Wales.
[53] HA 1996, s 193(3A) repealed by LA 2011, s 148(3).
[54] HA 1996, s 193(7AA)–(7AD) amended by LA 2011, s 148(5)–(7) and made to applicants whose applications for homelessness assistance were made on or after 9 November 2012 to local housing authorities in England. See **17.109–17.131**. At the date of writing, the amendments to HA 1996 made by LA 2011, ss 148–149 had not been brought into effect in Wales.
[55] HA 1996 Part 6, see **5.1–5.60**.
[56] And local housing authorities in England where the application for homelessness assistance was made before 9 November 2012.
[57] HA 1996, s 193(3A). The exception is for 'restricted cases' (see HA 1996, s 193(3B)). For 'restricted case', see **10.38–10.40, 10.82–10.85** and **12.32–12.47**.
[58] HA 1996, s 206(2)(a).

itself paying for the accommodation,[59] it can require the applicant to pay 'such reasonable amount' towards the cost as it may determine.[60]

17.17 The local housing authority's performance of its duty to secure accommodation is not contingent upon the applicant paying any charges imposed.[61] Obviously, if an unpaid charge leads to loss of the accommodation, this may give rise to a further incidence of homelessness.

17.18 What is a 'reasonable' charge or amount will vary according to the type, nature and extent of the accommodation and the personal circumstances of the applicant.[62] Indeed, local housing authorities are required to consider 'affordability' as a function of 'suitability' whenever they secure accommodation.[63] Plainly, it would not be reasonable to impose a level of charges that pushed the applicant below subsistence levels of income.[64] Somewhat surprisingly, beyond a reminder to local housing authorities that they should not place applicants in accommodation where the costs are such that they cannot afford the basic essentials, or would have to resort to welfare benefits, the Codes fail to provide any further guidance.[65]

17.19 There is no right to a statutory review of the amount charged by the local housing authority unless:

(1) it could be said that the level of charging rendered the accommodation 'unsuitable'; and

(2) the accommodation is being secured under one of the duties which carry a right to a review of its suitability.[66]

---

[59] For example, where it is paying rent for accommodation that it is leasing from a private owner.

[60] HA 1996, s 206(2)(b).

[61] *R v Tower Hamlets London Borough Council ex p Khalique* (1994) 26 HLR 517, QBD, at 523.

[62] In *R (Best) v Oxford City Council* [2009] EWHC 608 (Admin), (2009) May *Legal Action*, p 27, Admin Ct, it appears that the applicant argued that she could not afford to pay the charges because she was not entitled to housing benefit, but that the local housing authority did not agree and had decided that she had the resources to pay.

[63] Homelessness (Suitability of Accommodation) Order 1996, SI 1996/3204. See **18.47–18.48** and Appendix 2.

[64] *R v Argyll and Bute District Council* (1986) SCOLAG 100, Sh Ct.

[65] English Code, paras 17.39–17.40; Welsh Code, paras 19.3–9.31. See *Eryurekler v Hackney London Borough Council* (2010) May *Legal Action*, p 24, Clerkenwell & Shoreditch County Court where the Judge held that the local housing authority had failed to consider the contents of the relevant paragraph of the Code and to apply the guidance at English Code, para 17.42 to an applicant who was receiving child tax credits. See also **11.101**.

[66] HA 1996, s 202(1)(f) gives a right to request a review of the suitability of accommodation secured under HA 1996, ss 190(2), 193(2) and 195, or any offer of HA 1996, Part 6 accommodation (see **19.27–19.32**). The right to request a review of the suitability of private rented sector offers, for applicants whose applications for homelessness assistance were made to a local housing authority in England on or after 9 November 2012, is at HA 1996, s 202(1)(g) as amended by LA 2011, s 149(9), see **19.33–19.34**. At the date of writing, the amendments to HA 1996 made by LA 2011, ss 148–149 had not been brought into effect in Wales. For applicants who are 'restricted cases' (HA 1996, s 193(3B)) and whose applications for homelessness assistance are made to a local housing authority in England before

17.20   Otherwise, the amount of the charge can be disputed through the local housing authority's complaints procedure, and thereafter with a complaint to the Ombudsmen, or (where an error of law is alleged) by a challenge by way of judicial review.[67]

Terms on which accommodation is secured

17.21   Beyond the requirement of suitability and the power to impose charges, HA 1996, Part 7 does not prescribe the terms on which the accommodation must be secured. These will be a matter of agreement (at least notionally) between the accommodation provider, which may be the local housing authority itself, and the applicant. If the terms offered are standard terms, then the provisions of the Unfair Terms in Consumer Contracts Regulations[68] are likely to apply.[69]

17.22   Because the local housing authority securing the accommodation is a public authority, it must fix any terms of occupation bearing in mind the applicant's rights to respect for his or her private and family life.[70]

THE 'MAIN HOUSING DUTY': TO SECURE ACCOMMODATION

The main housing duty in outline

17.23   The highest duty to secure accommodation that can be owed under HA 1996, Part 7[71] is often colloquially called the 'full housing duty', but HA 1996, Part 7 refers to it as the 'main housing duty'.[72] We use the statutory language to refer to the duty throughout this Chapter and this book.

Historical overview of the main housing duty

17.24   When the statutory homelessness provisions were first introduced, the Codes and the courts treated this main housing duty as requiring the provision of what was then called 'permanent accommodation', which was understood to mean a periodic tenancy of local housing authority property.

---

9 November 2012 or to a local housing authority in Wales, the right to request a review of a suitability of a private accommodation offer (HA 1996, s 193(7AD) unamended) is at HA 1996, s 202(1)(g) in its original enacted form. See **19.35–19.37**.

[67]   For complaints see **19.251–19.258** and for judicial review, see **19.224–19.250**.

[68]   Unfair Terms in Consumer Contracts Regulations 1999, SI 1999/2083. For an example of a review by the Office of Fair Trading (OFT) of the fairness (or otherwise) of the standard terms of a non-secure tenancy supplied to a homeless family, see OFT Press Release 163/05 (30 August 2005).

[69]   *R (Khatun) v Newham London Borough Council* [2004] EWCA Civ 55, [2004] HLR 29, CA.

[70]   Human Rights Act 1998, Sch 1, art 8; *Orejudos v Kensington and Chelsea Royal London Borough Council* [2003] EWCA Civ 1967, [2004] HLR 23, CA.

[71]   HA 1996, s 193(2).

[72]   Used in this sense in HA 1996, s 200(3).

17.25 In 1996 the House of Lords decided that the wrong approach had been taken over the course of the previous two decades, and that the duty could be discharged by the simple provision of accommodation for such period as the local housing authority considered was suitable.[73] HA 1996, Part 7, as originally enacted, brought a new approach, under which the main housing duty became a duty to accommodate temporarily for a minimum of two years, with a statutory discretion to extend that period. That remained the law for over five years.

17.26 From 2003, the main housing duty is a duty to accommodate indefinitely.[74] The duty can only come to an end by the happening of events specifically prescribed by HA 1996, s 193(5)–(7F) inclusive.[75] However, for applicants whose applications for homelessness assistance are made on or after 9 November 2012 to a local housing authority in England, amendments to HA 1996, Part 7, introduced by the Localism Act 2011, envisage that most applicants will be made private rented sector offers in order to bring the main housing duty to an end.[76] While the duty is therefore indefinite, the period of time during which applicants might expect to occupy accommodation under the main housing duty is likely to be considerably shorter than in the past. At the date of writing, the amendments to HA 1996 made by LA 2011, ss 148–149 have not been brought into effect in Wales.

The current position

17.27 The 'main housing duty' is owed to applicants who are homeless,[77] eligible for assistance,[78] have a priority need,[79] did not become homeless intentionally,[80] and whom the local housing authority does not intend to refer to another local housing authority under the conditions for referral.[81]

---

[73] *R v Brent London Borough Council ex p Awua* [1996] 1 AC 55, HL.
[74] HA 1996, Part 7, as amended by Homelessness Act 2002.
[75] See **17.42–17.168**.
[76] HA 1996, s 193(7AA)–(7AC) amended by LA 2011, s 148(5)–(7) and made to applicants whose applications for homelessness assistance were made on or after 9 November 2012 to local housing authorities in England. See **17.109–17.131**. At the date of writing, the amendments to HA 1996 made by LA 2011, ss 148–149 had not been brought into effect in Wales..
[77] See Chapter 11.
[78] See Chapter 12.
[79] See Chapter 13. There is an exception from the requirement that an applicant must have a priority need in order to be owed the main housing duty where the applicant is making a fresh application for homelessness assistance to a local housing authority in England on or after 9 November 2012, within two years of the date of acceptance by the applicant of a private rented sector offer (HA 1996, s 195A inserted by LA 2011, s 149(4)). At the date of writing the amendments to HA 1996 made by LA 2011, ss 148–149 had not been brought into effect in Wales. For HA 1996, s 195A, see **9.89–9.95** and **17.171–17.181**. It should be noted that where the main housing duty or equivalent duty owed to those threatened with homelessness would only be owed to the applicant because of the presence of a restricted person, the applicant must still have a priority need in order to be owed the main housing duty (HA 1996, s 195A(5) inserted by LA 2011, s 149(4)), see **17.173**.
[80] See Chapter 14.
[81] See Chapter 15.

17.28   The duty is 'to secure that accommodation is available for occupation by the applicant' and by his or her household (ie by all other persons who normally reside with the applicant as a member of his or her family, or who might reasonably be expected to reside with the applicant).[82]

17.29   Although the duty is not limited to any particular minimum or maximum period, and in that sense can be owed indefinitely, it is important to emphasise that the duty owed is simply to secure 'accommodation' for the time being. It is not a duty to provide a lasting home. HA 1996, Part 7 is a safety net statutory scheme designed to resolve or prevent homelessness. The 'main housing duty' is the highest form of that safety net. Under that duty, accommodation is secured until the applicant is able, with any appropriate assistance, to resolve his or her longer term housing needs. That longer term need might be met by the provision of a tenancy of social housing,[83] in which case the applicant will need the assistance of HA 1996, Part 6 (Allocation of Housing Accommodation) described in Chapters 1–6 of this book.

17.30   Alternatively, for applications for homelessness assistance made to a local housing authority in England on or after 9 November 2012,[84] the applicant might be made a private rented sector offer, designed to bring the main housing duty to an end whether the applicant accepts or rejects it.[85] If the applicant does accept the private rented sector offer and subsequently makes an application for homelessness assistance within two years of the date of acceptance, he or she will not normally need to have a priority need in order to be entitled to the main housing duty again.[86]

---

[82]   HA 1996, s 176. This extension of the duty to the other household members is considered at **11.23–11.34**. See *R (Ogbeni) v Tower Hamlets London Borough Council* [2008] EWHC 2444 (Admin), (2008) October *Legal Action*, p 37, Admin Ct, where the local housing authority was wrong to refuse to secure accommodation to a 17-year-old applicant and to his aunt, who normally resided with him as a member of his family.

[83]   HA 1996, s 193(6)(c) or (7) as amended by LA 2011, s 148(4), for applicants whose applications for homelessness assistance were made on or after 9 November 2012 to local housing authorities in England. See **17.79–17.108**. At the date of writing, the amendments to HA 1996 made by LA 2011, ss 148–149 had not been brought into effect in Wales. See **17.136–17.146**.

[84]   At the date of writing, the amendments to HA 1996 made by LA 2011, ss 148–149 had not been brought into effect in Wales.

[85]   HA 1996, s 193(7AA)–(7AC) as amended by LA 2011, s 148(5)–(7), for applicants whose applications for homelessness assistance were made on or after 9 November 2012 to local housing authorities in England. See **17.109–17.131**. At the date of writing, the amendments to HA 1996 made by LA 2011, ss 148–149 had not been brought into effect in Wales.

[86]   HA 1996, s 195A(1) and (3) inserted by LA 2011, s 149(4), for applicants whose applications for homelessness assistance were made on or after 9 November 2012 to local housing authorities in England. See **9.89–9.95** and **17.171–17.181**. At the date of writing, the amendments to HA 1996 made by LA 2011, ss 148–149 had not been brought into effect in Wales. The exception is where the applicant would not be owed the main housing duty if it were not for the presence of a restricted person in his or her household, in which case he or she will still have to have a priority need in order to be owed any accommodation duties (HA 1996, s 195A(5) inserted by LA 2011, s 149(4)) see **17.173**.

17.31 At the date of writing, the amendments to HA 1996 made by LA 2011, ss 148–149 had not been brought into effect in Wales. However, the Welsh Government advises in the Welsh Code that '[h]omelessness applications should not be the main route into social housing, and applicants should be encouraged to consider other options where practicable'.[87] Those other options would include the making of a qualifying offer of a suitable assured shorthold tenancy which an applicant would be free to accept or refuse without the main housing duty coming to an end.[88]

What sort of accommodation?

17.32 Like all other accommodation secured under HA 1996, Part 7, what is secured under the 'main housing duty' must meet prescribed statutory requirements.[89] The accommodation secured must be 'suitable'[90] for the needs of the applicant and of his or her household.[91] So far as is reasonably practicable, it should be secured within the local housing authority's own district.[92] The local housing authority may provide its own accommodation, provide suitable accommodation from some other person, or give advice and assistance so as to obtain suitable accommodation for the applicant from some other person.[93]

17.33 No particular security of tenure is required or conferred. If the accommodation has been secured from a private landlord, private registered provider of social housing in England or registered social landlord in Wales, it will usually be offered by that landlord on an assured shorthold tenancy. Accommodation secured from the local housing authority's own stock will be let on non-secure, non-introductory tenancies, unless the local housing authority notifies an applicant that the tenancy is to be a secure or introductory tenancy.[94]

17.34 An offer of accommodation which was not suitable for the applicant at the date it fell to be accepted could operate as an offer of suitable

---

[87] Welsh Code, para 18.16.

[88] HA 1996, s 193(7B)–(7D) prospectively repealed by LA 2011, s 148(8). At the date of writing, the amendments to HA 1996 made by LA 2011, ss 148–149 had not been brought into effect in Wales. For 'qualifying offer', see **17.147–17.154**.

[89] See **17.12**.

[90] See Chapter 18.

[91] HA 1996, ss 206 and 210.

[92] HA 1996, s 208(1); see **15.226–15.233, 16.70–16.73** and **18.58–18.68**.

[93] HA 1996, s 206(1).

[94] Housing Act 1985, Sch 1, para 4. See English Code, para 16.13; Welsh Code, para 18.17. In *Westminster City Council v Boraliu* [2007] EWCA Civ 1339, (2008) March *Legal Action*, p 18, *CA* the Court of Appeal held that HA 1985, Sch 1, para 4 applied to all tenancies granted by local housing authorities in performance of their housing functions under HA 1996, Part 7, whether the property occupied was local housing authority stock, or had been leased from another landlord by the local housing authority.

accommodation if it was accompanied with certain, binding and enforceable assurances about the works to be carried out to render it suitable before it is occupied.[95]

17.35 The concept of 'suitability' and its application to such matters as the location, affordability and size of accommodation secured under the main duty, is discussed in Chapter 18. Regulations have prescribed that private rented sector offers[96] will only be suitable if there has been compliance with the tests set out in Homelessness (Suitability of Accommodation) (England) Order 2012.[97] Those tests are discussed at **18.51–18.54**.

When does the duty start?

17.36 The main housing duty is triggered as soon as the local housing authority is satisfied that all four components required to activate the duty (eligibility, homelessness, priority need and a decision that the local housing authority is not satisfied that the applicant has become homeless intentionally) are in place.[98]

17.37 The commencement of the duty is not dependent on notification being given to the applicant, but it is owed as soon as the local housing authority is 'satisfied' that the components are in place. That may be some hours or days before the formal written notification is delivered. The only circumstance in which such satisfaction does not trigger the main housing duty is if the local housing authority refers the homeless person's application to another local housing authority under the conditions for referral.[99]

17.38 The duty is an unqualified one and, once the components are in place, its performance cannot be deferred. A local housing authority must secure accommodation, and it must be suitable, from the date the duty is first owed. The local housing authority cannot avoid the immediate performance of the

---

[95] *Boreh v Ealing London Borough Council* [2008] EWCA Civ 1176, [2009] HLR 22, CA. See also *Norris v Milton Keynes Council* [2010] EWCA Civ 77, April *Legal Action,* p 26, CA.

[96] For 'private rented sector offer', see HA 1996, s 193(7AC) as amended by LA 2011, s 148(7). This applies to applicants whose applications for homelessness assistance were made on or after 9 November 2012 to a local housing authority in England. At the date of writing, the amendments to HA 1996 made by LA 2011, ss 148–149 had not been brought into effect in Wales. See **17.109–17.131** and **18.51–18.54**.

[97] Homelessness (Suitability of Accommodation) (England) Order 2012, SI 2012/2601, see Appendix 2.

[98] Where an applicant is making an application for homelessness assistance to a local housing authority in England on or after 9 November 2012, and within two years of his or her acceptance of a 'private rented sector offer' (HA 1996, s 193 (7AA) as amended by LA 2011, s 148(5), see **17.109–17.118**), he or she will not need to have a priority need in order to be entitled to the main housing duty (HA 1996, s 195A(1) as inserted by LA 2011, s 149(4)). See **9.89–9.95** and **17.171–17.181**. At the date of writing, the amendments to HA 1996 made by LA 2011, ss 148–149 had not been brought into effect in Wales.

[99] That action would cause a different accommodation duty to trigger under HA 1996, s 200(1). See **15.157–15.160** and **16.56–16.63**.

duty by reference to the other demands on its housing services or its available stock.[100] The whole point of the safety net duty is that it kicks in immediately once its components are met.

17.39 If the local housing authority fails to secure suitable accommodation, the applicant can apply for a mandatory order in judicial review proceedings requiring the local housing authority to comply with its duty.[101]

17.40 If the breach of duty is technical or minor, and the local housing authority can demonstrate it has done its best to comply with the duty, permission to bring a judicial review claim may be refused.[102]

17.41 Local housing authorities in Wales, and local housing authorities in England in respect of applicants whose applications for homelessness assistance were made before 9 November 2012,[103] must also give the applicant a copy of their statement on their policy within their allocation scheme on offering applicants a choice of accommodation and on the opportunity to express preferences about the accommodation to be allocated.[104]

How can the duty come to an end?

17.42 Once the local housing authority is under a main housing duty to secure accommodation for the applicant, that duty can only end if one of the events set out in HA 1996, s 193(5)–(7F) occurs.[105] The list of those events is exhaustive, so if there is a change of circumstances not featuring among the events specified, the duty is not brought to an end.[106] For example, where an applicant who had a priority need and was entitled to the main housing duty had a change of circumstances such that he no longer had a priority need, the local housing authority still had a duty towards him, because such a change is not among the listed events.[107]

---

[100] *Codona v Mid-Bedfordshire District Council* [2004] EWCA Civ 925, [2005] HLR 1, CA, at [36], per Auld LJ.

[101] See **19.222–19.250**.

[102] *R v Newham London Borough Council ex p Sacupima* (2000) 33 HLR 2, CA, at [17].

[103] Localism Act 2011 (Commencement No 2 and Transitional Provisions) (England) Order, SI 2012/2599 (c.109), see Appendix 2. At the date of writing, the amendments to HA 1996 made by LA 2011, ss 148–149 had not been brought into effect in Wales.

[104] HA 1996, s 193(3A) repealed by LA 2011, s 148(3) in respect of applications for homelessness assistance made on or after 9 November 2012 to a local housing authority in England. At the date of writing, the amendments to HA 1996 made by LA 2011, ss 148–149 had not been brought into effect in Wales. The duty is not owed to 'restricted cases' or to 'restricted threatened homelessness cases', see **17.164**.

[105] HA 1996, s 193(5)–(7F) as amended by LA 2011, s 148 in respect of applicants whose applications for homelessness assistance were made on or after 9 November 2012 to local housing authorities in England. See **17.54–17.131**. At the date of writing, the amendments to HA 1996 made by LA 2011, ss 148–149 had not been brought into effect in Wales. See **17.132–17.154**.

[106] *R v Hackney London Borough Council ex p K* (1997) 30 HLR 760, CA.

[107] *R v Brent London Borough Council ex p Sadiq* (2001) 33 HLR 525, QBD.

17.43 Of course, if the local housing authority discovers that its decision that the main housing duty is owed was obtained as a result of fraud, or made under a fundamental mistake of fact, it may re-open that decision and, on further inquiries, may decide that it does not owe the main housing duty after all.[108]

17.44 The events that can cause the duty to end are:

(1) the refusal by an applicant of suitable accommodation secured in performance of the main housing duty;[109]

(2) the applicant ceasing to be eligible for assistance;[110]

(3) the applicant becoming homeless intentionally from his or her main housing duty accommodation;[111]

(4) the applicant accepting an offer of a tenancy made under HA 1996, Part 6;[112]

(5) the applicant accepting an offer of an assured, but not an assured shorthold, tenancy from a private landlord, including a private registered provider in England or registered social landlord in Wales;[113]

(6) the applicant voluntarily ceasing to occupy his or her main housing duty accommodation as his or her only or principal home;[114]

(7) the applicant refusing a final offer of suitable accommodation made under HA 1996, Part 6;[115]

(8) for applicants whose applications were made on or after 9 November 2012 to a local housing authority in England, the applicant accepting a private rented sector offer;[116]

---

[108] *Porteous v West Dorset District Council* [2004] EWCA Civ 244, [2004] HLR 30, CA.

[109] HA 1996, s 193(5) as amended by LA 2011, s 148(3) for applicants whose applications for homelessness assistance were made on or after 9 November 2012 to local housing authorities in England. See **17.55–17.66**. At the date of writing, the amendments to HA 1996 made by LA 2011, ss 148–149 had not been brought into effect in Wales. See **17.136–17.137**.

[110] HA 1996, s 193(6)(a). See **17.67–17.69**.

[111] HA 1996, s 193(6)(b). See **17.70–17.74**.

[112] HA 1996, s 193(6)(c). See **17.79–17.87**.

[113] HA 1996, s 193(6)(cc). See **17.88–17.91**.

[114] HA 1996, s 193(6)(d). See **17.75–17.78**.

[115] HA 1996, s 193(7)–(7A) as amended by LA 2011, s 148(4) and (5) for applicants whose applications for homelessness assistance were made on or after 9 November 2012 to local housing authorities in England. See **17.92–17.108**. At the date of writing, the amendments to HA 1996 made by LA 2011, ss 148–149 had not been brought into effect in Wales. See **17.138–17.146**.

[116] HA 1996, s 193(7AA)(a) amended by LA 2011, s 148(5). At the date of writing, the amendments to HA 1996 made by LA 2011, ss 148–149 had not been brought into effect in Wales. See **17.109–17.118**.

(9) for applicants whose applications were made on or after 9 November 2012 to a local housing authority in England, the applicant refusing a private rented sector offer;[117] or

(10) for applicants to local housing authorities in Wales,[118] the applicant accepting a qualifying offer of an assured shorthold tenancy from a private landlord, including from a private registered provider [England] or registered social landlord [Wales].[119]

17.45 From this list it is clear that the duty may end when the applicant *refuses* three types of offer of suitable accommodation:

- an offer of accommodation made in performance of the main housing duty itself;[120] or

- a final offer made under HA 1996, Part 6;[121] or

- a private rented sector offer[122] made to an applicant whose application for homelessness assistance has been made to a local housing authority in England[123] on or after 9 November 2012.

17.46 If, unusually, an offer of accommodation is made outside of these provisions, an applicant would be free to refuse it without fear that the main housing duty would end.

---

[117] HA 1996, s 193(7AA)(b)–(7AC) amended by LA 2011, s 148 (5)–(7). At the date of writing, the amendments to HA 1996 made by LA 2011, ss 148–149 had not been brought into effect in Wales. See **17.119–17.131**.

[118] And for applicants whose applications for homelessness assistance were made before 9 November 2012 to local housing authorities in England. HA 1996, s 193(7B)–(7E) repealed by LA 2011, s 148(8) for applicants whose applications for homelessness assistance were made on or after 9 November 2012 to a local housing authority in England At the date of writing, the amendments to HA 1996, Part 7, made by LA 2011, ss 148–149 had not been brought into effect in Wales.

[119] HA 1996, s 193(7AA)–(7AC) prospectively amended by LA 2011, s 148(5)–(7). At the date of writing, the amendments to HA 1996, Part 7, made by LA 2011, ss 148–149 had not been brought into effect in Wales. See **17.147–17.154**.

[120] HA 1996, s 193(5) as substituted by LA 2011, s 148(3), for applicants whose applications were made on or after 9 November 2012 to a local housing authority in England. At the date of writing, the amendments to HA 1996 made by LA 2011, ss 148–149 had not been brought into effect in Wales and reference should be made to HA 1996, s 193(5) as originally enacted. See **17.55–17.66** (England) and **17.136–17.137** (Wales).

[121] HA 1996, s 193(7) and (7A) as amended by LA 2011, s 148(4), for applicants whose applications were made on or after 9 November 2012 to a local housing authority in England. At the date of writing, the amendments to HA 1996 made by LA 2011, ss 148–149 had not been brought into effect in Wales and reference should be made to HA 1996, s 193(7) and (7A) as originally enacted. See **17.92–17.108** (England) and **17.138–17.146** (Wales).

[122] HA 1996, s 193(7AA)–(7AC) as amended by LA 2011, s 148(5)–(7). At the date of writing the amendments to HA 1996 made by LA 2011, ss 148–149 had not been brought into effect in Wales. See **17.118–17.131**.

[123] At the date of writing, the amendments to HA 1996 made by LA 2011, ss 148–149 had not been brought into effect in Wales.

17.47 Because the consequence of refusal of any of these offers can be to bring the main housing duty to an end, applicants contemplating refusing an offer, and their advisers, should first ensure that they are very clear whether the offer is made under any of these three provisions or not.

Decisions and challenges about the ending of the main housing duty

17.48 There is a common misconception that it is for the local housing authority to decide whether or not the main housing duty has ended. In fact, HA 1996, Part 7, simply prescribes that, on the happening of one of the events listed above, the local housing authority 'shall cease to be subject to the duty'.[124] In other words, the main housing duty ends automatically and without any need for a freestanding decision to that effect by the local housing authority. In consequence, there is no obligation on a local housing authority to 'notify' any such decision to the applicant (subject to an exception at HA 1996, s 193(5)).[125]

17.49 However, many of the events which terminate the main housing duty are dependent upon the local housing authority being 'satisfied' that a particular situation has come about (eg that accommodation refused by the applicant was suitable).[126] Most local housing authorities will notify the applicant of their conclusions and indicate that, as a result, they consider that the main housing duty has ended. These are colloquially called 'discharge of duty' letters.

17.50 A decision made by a local housing authority that events have occurred that bring to an end its main housing duty owed to the applicant has been held to constitute a decision as to 'what duty (if any) is owed to him'. The applicant therefore has a right to request a review of the decision to treat the main housing duty as at an end.[127]

17.51 Quite apart from this general right to a statutory review of any decision that events have occurred which bring the main housing duty to an end, the applicant also has a separate freestanding right to request a review of any decision that accommodation offered in performance of the main housing duty, as a final offer under HA 1996, Part 6 or as a private rented offer[128] is

---

[124] HA 1996, s 193(5), (6), (7) and (7AA) as amended by LA 2011, s 148(3)–(5), for applicants whose applications for homelessness assistance were made to a local housing authority in England on or after 9 November 2012. At the date of writing, the amendments to HA 1996 made by LA 2011, ss 148–149 had not been brought into effect in Wales.

[125] See **17.49–17.50**.

[126] HA 1996, s 193(5) and (7) as amended by LA 2011, s 148(3)–(4), for applicants whose applications for homelessness assistance were made to a local housing authority in England on or after 9 November 2012. At the date of writing, the amendments to HA 1996 made by LA 2011, ss 148–149 had not been brought into effect in Wales.

[127] HA 1996, s 202(1)(b). *Warsame v Hounslow London Borough Council* (2000) 32 HLR 335, CA.

[128] HA 1996, s 193(7AA)–(7AC) as amended by LA 2011, s 148(5)–(7), for applicants whose applications for homelessness assistance were made to a local housing authority in England on

suitable.[129] If an applicant receives an offer of accommodation under any of the three provisions,[130] and he or she believes that the accommodation is not suitable, there is the right both to request a review of the decision that the property is suitable, and to accept the property in any event.[131] This must always be the sensible course of action for an applicant to take. Otherwise, she or he may lose the suitability review and find that the offer has meanwhile been withdrawn.[132]

17.52 Where the local housing authority has decided to end its duty because the applicant has refused an offer of suitable accommodation,[133] and the applicant then requests a review of that decision (as he or she is entitled to do), the scope of the review will be different from the scope of reviews of other decisions. The normal rule for reviews is that the reviewing officer should consider all the facts, law and circumstances at the date of the review decision.[134] The Court of Appeal has considered whether the normal rule should apply to cases involving refusals of offers. In *Osseily v Westminster City Council*,[135] it held that there was no obligation on the local housing authority to keep open the offer of accommodation until the review had been determined. In *Omar v Westminster City Council*,[136] the Court of Appeal considered the position where, at the date of refusal, the accommodation was unsuitable, but subsequent events had rendered it suitable by the date of the review decision. The Court of Appeal held that:

> 'the correct question for the reviewer is whether the council were right, as at the date of that original decision; and for that purpose what they should be examining is the facts that existed as of that date, albeit they may discover what facts existed as at that date, between the date of that original decision and the date of review.'[137]

---

or after 9 November 2012. At the date of writing, the amendments to HA 1996, Part 7, made by LA 2011, ss 148–149 had not been brought into effect in Wales. See **17.109–17.131**.

[129] HA 1996, s 202(1)(f) and (g) as amended by LA 2011, s 149(9). See **19.27–19.32**.

[130] See Chapter 18.

[131] HA 1996, s 202(1A).

[132] The Court of Appeal has made it clear that, once an offer of accommodation has been refused and the local housing authority has decided that its duty has come to an end, there is no obligation on the local housing authority to keep the accommodation available for the applicant while a review is being carried out (*Osseily v Westminster City Council* [2007] EWCA Civ 1108, [2008] HLR 18, CA).

[133] For a refusal of main housing duty accommodation (HA 1996, s 193(5) as amended by LA 2011, s 148(3)), see **17.55–17.66** (England) and **17.136–17.137** (Wales). For a refusal of a final offer of Part 6 accommodation (HA 1996, s 193(7) and (7A) as amended by LA s 148 (3) and (4)), see **17.92–17.108** (England) and **17.138–17.146** (Wales). For a refusal of private rented sector offered accommodation (HA 1996, s 193(7AA)–(7AC) as amended by LA 2011, s 148(5)–(7)), see **17.119–17.131**. At the date of writing, the amendments to HA 1996 made by LA 2011, ss 148–149 had not been brought into effect in Wales.

[134] *Mohammed v Hammersmith & Fulham London Borough Council* [2001] UKHL 57, [2002] 1 AC 547, HL; and *Crawley Borough Council v B* (2000) 32 HLR 636, CA. See **19.107–19.114**.

[135] [2007] EWCA Civ 1108, [2008] HLR 18, CA.

[136] [2008] EWCA Civ 421, [2008] HLR 36, CA.

[137] *Omar v Westminster City Council* [2008] EWCA Civ 421, [2008] HLR 36, CA, at [32], per Waller LJ.

17.53 A third decision of the Court of Appeal concerned accommodation which, at the date when the applicant was required to accept it, was not suitable but there were works proposed that would render it suitable. In *Boreh v Ealing London Borough Council*,[138] the Court of Appeal held that there would only be an offer of suitable accommodation in those circumstances if the offer were accompanied with certain, binding and enforceable assurances about what work would be carried out after acceptance and before occupation.[139] A reviewing officer should not take into account the works subsequently carried out if they had not been contained in such assurances.

The events that may cause the main housing duty to end

17.54 HA 1996, s 193(7)–(7AC)[140] contains a list of nine events which may cause the main housing duty to come to an end. Each of those events could apply to any applicant for homelessness assistance whose application was made on or after 9 November 2012 to a local housing authority in England. For applicants whose applications were made before 9 November 2012, or for applicants to local housing authorities in Wales, there are only eight events.[141] The principal difference between the main housing duty owed by local housing authorities in England and that owed by local housing authorities in Wales[142] is that a local housing authority in England can bring the duty to an end by making the applicant a private rented sector offer.[143] The duty will come to an end if the applicant accepts or refuses it.[144] Local housing authorities in Wales can make an applicant a qualifying offer of an assured shorthold tenancy.[145] If the applicant accepts it, the main housing duty will come to an end. However, if the applicant refuses a qualifying offer of an assured shorthold tenancy made by a local housing authority in Wales,[146] the main housing duty will not end.[147]

---

[138] [2008] EWCA Civ 1176, [2009] HLR 22, CA.

[139] The Court of Appeal in *Boreh v Ealing London Borough Council* [2008] EWCA Civ 1176, [2009] HLR 22, CA, did not specify that the assurances must be to the effect that the works would be carried out before the accommodation is to be occupied. However, it follows that if the accommodation before works were carried out was not suitable for occupation by the applicant, then the works should be carried out before occupation commences. See also *Norris v Milton Keynes Council* [2010] EWCA Civ 77, (2010) April *Legal Action*, p 26, CA.

[140] As amended by LA 2011, s 148(3)–(7), for applicants whose applications for homelessness assistance were made to a local housing authority in England on or after 9 November 2012. At the date of writing, the amendments to HA 1996 made by LA 2011, ss 148–149 had not been brought into effect in Wales.

[141] See **17.134**.

[142] And by local housing authorities in England to applicants whose applications for homelessness assistance were made before 9 November 2012.

[143] HA 1996, s 193(7AC) as amended by LA 2011, s 148(7). See **17.109–17.131**.

[144] HA 1996, s 193(7AA)–(7AC) as amended by LA 2011, s 148(5)–(7). See **17.109–17.118** for when the applicant accepts the private rented sector offer. See **17.119–17.131** for when the applicant refuses the private rented sector offer.

[145] HA 1996, s 193(7B). See **17.147–17.154**.

[146] Or by a local housing authority in England to an applicant whose application for homelessness assistance was made before 9 November 2012.

[147] HA 1996, s 193(7B)–(7C), see **17.149**.

England

(1) Refusal of main housing duty accommodation[148]

17.55 For the main housing duty to end for this reason, HA 1996, s 193(5)[149] prescribes a number of fairly strict conditions which must all be fulfilled. These conditions are that:

(1) the accommodation has been offered in performance of the main housing duty;[150] and

(2) the local housing authority is satisfied that it is 'suitable' accommodation; and

(3) the applicant has been informed of the consequences of refusal or acceptance of the offer;[151] and

(4) the applicant has been informed of the right to seek a review of the suitability of the offered accommodation; and

(5) the applicant refuses the offer; and

(6) the local housing authority notifies the applicant that it regards the main housing duty as having ended as a result of the refusal.[152]

17.56 Where a fixed-term assured shorthold tenancy is being offered in performance of the main housing duty, the Court of Appeal has held that the local housing authority should explain in the offer letter that:

---

[148] HA 1996, s 193(5) as amended by LA 2011, s 148(3), for applicants whose applications for homelessness assistance were made to a local housing authority in England on or after 9 November 2012. The amended HA 1996, s 193(5) means that the applicant is informed of the consequences of accepting the offer, in other words, that the applicant knows that the main housing duty continues and that the offer is not either a final offer of HA 1996, Part 6, accommodation or a private rented sector offer. At the date of writing, the amendments to HA 1996 made by LA 2011, ss 148–149 had not been brought into effect in Wales. English Code, para 14.7(v).

[149] HA 1996, s 193(5) as amended by LA 2011, s 148(3), for applicants whose applications for homelessness assistance were made to a local housing authority in England on or after 9 November 2012.

[150] The exact text is 'not an offer of accommodation under Part 6 or a private rented sector offer' (HA 1996, s 193(5) as substituted by LA 2011, s 148(3)).

[151] HA 1996, s 193(5), the words 'or acceptance' were inserted by LA 2011, s 148(3), for applicants whose applications for homelessness assistance were made to a local housing authority in England on or after 9 November 2012. At the date of writing, the amendments to HA 1996 made by LA 2011, ss 148–149 had not been brought into effect in Wales.

[152] HA 1996, s 193(5) as amended by LA 2011, s 148(3) for applicants whose applications for homelessness assistance were made to a local housing authority in England on or after 9 November 2012. At the date of writing, the amendments to HA 1996 made by LA 2011, ss 148–149 had not been brought into effect in Wales. See English Code, para 14.17(v).

'the authority acknowledges the accommodation would be temporary if the private landlord lawfully exercises his right to recover possession after the end of the fixed term and that, if that happens and assuming that the applicant's circumstances have not materially changed, the authority accepts that it would again become obliged to perform its duty under the section to secure that accommodation is available for occupation by the applicant.'[153]

17.57 The conditions refer to two sets of rights to request a review:

(a) a review of the decision as to suitability;[154] and

(b) a review of the decision that the duty is regarded as ended.[155]

17.58 This reflects the fact that the applicant will have received two letters. The first letter offered the accommodation on the basis that it was suitable, outlined the right to seek a review of suitability, and warned of the consequences of refusal. The second, following a refusal, notified the applicant of the fact that the local housing authority considered that the main housing duty had ended. Because an applicant can request a review whilst simultaneously accepting the accommodation (and thus preserve his or her position), it should become less common for the second letter to be sent.[156] Indeed, the Codes go further than HA 1996, s 193(5) and advise that the applicant should be specifically told that he or she will be able both to accept and to seek a review in an even earlier letter – the letter notifying the applicant of the local housing authority's decision under HA 1996, s 184.[157] In *Ali v Birmingham City Council*,[158] the Court of Appeal held that '"inform" in [HA 1996, Part 7] is … to be construed as requiring information to be conveyed in understandable English' and that 'notify' requires the giving of a notice which imports a degree of formality.[159]

17.59 There is no obligation for the information to be given to the applicant in the same letter as the offer. It may have been provided in an earlier communication. The Court of Appeal has held that it is 'essentially a matter of fact and degree' whether or not any period between the notification and the offer itself means that the applicant has or has not been informed of his or her statutory rights. In the case, considered by the Court of Appeal,[160] there had been a month between the information being conveyed to the applicant and the offer being made, with no other relevant events occurring during that month. If

---

[153] *Griffiths v St Helens Council* [2006] EWCA Civ 160, [2006] HLR 29, CA, at [42], per May LJ.
[154] HA 1996, s 202(1)(f). See **19.27–19.32**.
[155] HA 1996, s 202(1)(b). See **19.14–19.15**. For the specific considerations where an offer has been refused, see **17.52–17.53** and **19.114**.
[156] HA 1996, s 202(1A), added by Homelessness Act 2002, s 8 (in force from 26 February 2002) and overturning the effect of *Alghile v Westminster City Council* [2001] EWCA Civ 363, (2001) 33 HLR 627, CA.
[157] English Code, para 19.3.
[158] [2009] EWCA Civ 1279, [2011] HLR 17, CA.
[159] *Ali v Birmingham City Council* [2009] EWCA Civ 1279, [2011] HLR 17, CA at [39], per Sir Anthony May.
[160] *Vilvarasa v Harrow London Borough Council* [2010] EWCA Civ 1278, [2011] HLR 12, CA.

there was a longer period between the information being conveyed and the offer being made, and especially if there had been other correspondence during that period between the local housing authority and the applicant, it might be the length of that period meant that the applicant had been not been informed of the consequences before refusing the offer of accommodation.[161]

17.60 A decision by the local housing authority that its main housing duty has come to an end as a result of this provision could arise at any time during the performance of the HA 1996, s 193(2) main housing duty. So, where an applicant is offered a move from his or her current accommodation secured under the main housing duty to suitable accommodation and refuses to move, he or she may find that the main housing duty has come to an end.[162] If the applicant is notified that the main housing duty has come to an end as a result of his or her refusal of main housing duty accommodation, local housing authorities should be alert to the possibility that an applicant's request for a review might either be made in respect solely of the suitability of the offer[163] or have been made in respect of an actual or anticipated decision that the duty has come to an end. So the applicant might request a review because he or she believes that he or she did not refuse the offer, or had not been informed of the consequences of refusal or acceptance of the offer. The local housing authority must ensure that it deals with all the issues that arise on a HA 1996, s 193(5)[164] decision that the duty has ended and not confine the review only to the issue of suitability of the accommodation.[165]

17.61 The key issue for the applicant is likely to be the suitability or otherwise of the accommodation offered.[166] It may be that accommodation offered was not suitable at the date when it fell to be accepted, eg if it was not wheelchair-accessible. If accompanied by certain, binding and enforceable assurances about the work to be carried out after acceptance but before occupation, the accommodation may be suitable and a refusal of the offer may result in the ending of the main housing duty under this provision.[167] However, where no such assurance had been given by the date for acceptance, it will not have been an offer of suitable accommodation.

---

[161] *Vilvarasa v Harrow London Borough Council* [2010] EWCA Civ 1278, [2011] HLR 12, CA per Munby LJ at [23].

[162] *Muse v Brent London Borough Council* [2008] EWCA Civ 1447, (2009) February *Legal Action*, p 32, CA; *Vilvarasa v Harrow London Borough Council* [2010] EWCA Civ 1278, [2011] HLR 12, CA; and *Nzamy v Brent London Borough Council* [2011] EWCA Civ 283, [2011] HLR 20, CA.

[163] Under HA 1996, s 202(1)(f). See **19.27–19.32**.

[164] As amended by LA 2011, s 148(3) and for applicants whose applications for homelessness assistance were made to a local housing authority in England on or after 9 November 2012. At the date of writing, the amendments to HA 1996 made by LA 2011, ss 148–149 had not been brought into effect in Wales.

[165] *Nzamy v Brent London Borough Council* [2011] EWCA Civ 283, [2011] HLR 20, CA.

[166] See Chapter 18.

[167] *Boreh v Ealing London Borough Council* [2008] EWCA Civ 1176, [2009] HLR 22, CA; and *Norris v Milton Keynes Council* [2010] EWCA Civ 77, (2010) April *Legal Action*, p 26, CA.

17.62 The expectation is that, following receipt of the offer of main housing duty accommodation, the applicant should have a reasonable opportunity to consider the offer and inspect the accommodation. This reflects best practice as set out in the Codes of Guidance.[168] Circumstances might compel the local housing authority to require an immediate acceptance or rejection of the offer, even if the applicant has not had the opportunity to see it or consider it. The safeguards, if the local housing authority insists on an immediate acceptance or rejection, are that:

(1) the local housing authority must have satisfied itself that the accommodation is suitable;[169] and

(2) it must have notified the applicant of the right to a review;[170] and

(3) the applicant can both accept and seek a review.[171]

17.63 The Court of Appeal has held that these safeguards are sufficiently compliant with the statutory scheme, and that there is no separate right for applicants to view, and comment on, the accommodation before being required to accept or reject it.[172]

17.64 The English Code of Guidance, published after the Court of Appeal's decision, contains a recommendation from the Secretary of State that applicants should be:

> 'given the chance to view accommodation before being required to decide whether they accept or refuse an offer, and before being required to sign any written agreement relating to the accommodation.'[173]

17.65 This suggests that local housing authorities should normally give the applicant an opportunity to view the accommodation, even though they are not strictly required to under HA 1996, s 193(5).[174]

---

[168] English Code, para 14.22; Welsh Code, para 16.30.

[169] HA 1996, s 193(5) as amended by LA 2011, s 148(3), for applicants whose applications for homelessness assistance were made to a local housing authority in England on or after 9 November 2012. At the date of writing, the amendments to HA 1996 made by LA 2011, ss 148–149 had not been brought into effect in Wales.

[170] HA 1996, s 193(5) as amended by LA 2011, s 148(3), for applicants whose applications for homelessness assistance were made to a local housing authority in England on or after 9 November 2012. At the date of writing, the amendments to HA 1996 made by LA 2011, ss 148–149 had not been brought into effect in Wales.

[171] HA 1996, s 202(1)(f) and (1A). See **19.27–19.32** and **19.41–19.49**.

[172] *R (Khatun) v Newham London Borough Council* [2004] EWCA 55, [2004] HLR 29, CA. In *Abed v Westminster City Council* [2011] EWCA Civ 1406, (2012) January *Legal Action*, p 21, CA, the Court of Appeal held that any deficiency leading up to the offer of accommodation to the applicant, such as a failure to assess the suitability of accommodation, could be overcome by the review process.

[173] English Code, para 14.18. See also Welsh Code, para 16.30.

[174] As amended by LA 2011, s 148(3) and for applicants whose applications for homelessness

17.66 The key ingredient to the ending of the duty under this first route is that the applicant has *refused* the accommodation offered. The statutory wording is that the applicant 'refuses' an offer – not simply fails to accept it. This must mean something more than that the applicant has not replied to the making of an offer. The local housing authority must be able to identify something that amounts to unequivocal rejection following receipt of the offer.[175]

(2) Because the applicant ceases to be eligible[176]

17.67 When an applicant ceases to be eligible for homelessness assistance, the main housing duty ends. Eligibility is primarily determined by immigration status,[177] so the trigger to the ending of the main housing duty in these circumstances will normally be a change in that status.[178]

17.68 HA 1996, s 193(6)(a) makes it clear that the issue is whether *the applicant* has ceased to be eligible. The main housing duty does not end if it is some other member of the applicant's household who ceases to be eligible for assistance, even if it is the very household member whose presence conferred priority need on the applicant in the first place. In those circumstances, the main housing duty will continue.

17.69 There is some debate as to whether or not a local housing authority needs to make a decision that the main housing duty has ended because the applicant is no longer eligible, since the issue is not a matter of discretion.[179] It is recognised, however, that the question of whether the applicant has ceased to be eligible may be disputed, and in those circumstances it would seem right for there to be a decision by the local housing authority, which can then be the subject of a request for a statutory review.[180]

(3) Because the applicant becomes homeless intentionally from the main housing duty accommodation[181]

17.70 When the local housing authority is deciding whether the main housing duty has ended for this reason, it should apply the definition of intentional

---

assistance were made to a local housing authority in England on or after 9 November 2012. At the date of writing, the amendments to HA 1996 made by LA 2011, ss 148–149 had not been brought into effect in Wales.
[175] *R v Haringey London Borough Council ex p Muslu* (2001) February *Legal Action*, p 29, QBD.
[176] HA 1996, s 193(6)(a). English Code, para 14.17(vi).
[177] See Chapter 12.
[178] As happened in *Tower Hamlets London Borough Council v Deugi* [2006] EWCA Civ 159, [2006] HLR 28, CA, where the applicant had originally been eligible as a result of being the primary carer of a dependent child who was in full-time education (see **12.154–12.155**). She ceased to be eligible when the child left full-time education.
[179] See the comments by May LJ in *Tower Hamlets London Borough Council v Deugi* [2006] EWCA Civ 159, [2006] HLR 28, CA, at [33].
[180] HA 1996, s 202(1)(b). See **19.14–19.15**.
[181] HA 1996, s 193(6)(b); English Code, para 14.17(vii); Welsh Code, para 16.29(vii).

homelessness contained in HA 1996, Part 7[182] . In *Orejudos v Kensington and Chelsea Royal London Borough Council*[183] the applicant was absent, despite warnings, on ten different occasions (over a period of more than a year) from hostel accommodation provided in performance of the main housing duty. In breach of the conditions of his occupancy, he had failed to give reasons for his absences in advance.[184] The local housing authority terminated his booking, decided that he had become homeless intentionally and concluded that its duty toward him had ended. That decision was upheld on review, on appeal to the county court and on a further appeal to the Court of Appeal. Similarly, where an applicant lost her main housing duty accommodation because she did not pay the rent, and the local housing authority rejected her argument that she did not have the resources to pay for the accommodation, she had become homeless intentionally from the main housing duty accommodation.[185] It is, of course, a necessary pre-requisite that the applicant has actually been rendered homeless by termination of any rights to occupy the main housing duty accommodation. The duty does not end simply because the applicant has become threatened with homelessness intentionally.

17.71   The applicant has a right to request that the local housing authority reviews its decision that the main housing duty has ended for this reason.[186]

17.72   The applicant has the right to make a further application for homelessness assistance.[187] It might be that the decision notified to the applicant on the new application for homelessness assistance is that he or she has become homeless intentionally as a result of the accommodation provided under main housing duty having come to an end. However, the local housing authority will still have to make inquiries into all of the elements of the test at HA 1996, s 191(1) and (2).[188] Unless it is able to complete its inquiries and to notify the applicant of its decision on his or her further application for homelessness assistance on the same day that the application is made, the local housing authority will have to secure interim accommodation for the applicant and his or her household.[189]

17.73   If the decision notified to the applicant is that he or she has a priority need and that the local housing authority is satisfied that he or she became

---

[182]   HA 1996, s 191. See English Code, para 14.17(vii) and, for the appropriate application of that definition. see Chapter 14 of this book.

[183]   [2003] EWCA Civ 1967, [2004] HLR 23, CA.

[184]   *Orejudos v Kensington and Chelsea Royal London Borough Council* [2003] EWCA Civ 1967, [2004] HLR 23, CA.

[185]   *R (Best) v Oxford City Council* [2009] EWHC 608 (Admin), (2009) May *Legal Action*, p 27, Admin Ct.

[186]   HA 1996, s 202(1)(b). See **19.14–19.15**.

[187]   HA 1996, s 193(9). The local housing authority is not permitted to refuse to accept the fresh application for homelessness assistance since the factual circumstances leading to the applicant being homeless will be different to those in existence at the date of his or her first application for homelessness assistance. See **9.66–9.85** and **17.169–17.170**.

[188]   See Chapter 14.

[189]   If the local housing authority has reason to believe that the applicant may be homeless, may be eligible for assistance and may have a priority need: HA 1996, s 188(1). See **16.12–16.28**.

homeless intentionally, the local housing authority must provide accommodation for the applicant and his or her household for such period as it decides would give him or her a reasonable opportunity to secure his or her own accommodation.[190] In addition, the applicant will have the right to request a review of a decision that he or she had become homeless intentionally.[191]

17.74 In one case, an applicant argued that once his main housing duty accommodation ended under this provision, the local housing authority should provide him with accommodation for such period as would give him a reasonable opportunity to secure his own accommodation.[192] By the time the appeal was heard, the applicant had been accommodated by friends and relatives for six months and the appeal was dismissed by the county court judge on the basis that it had become academic and futile. The Court of Appeal refused permission to appeal on the grounds that the decision had been justified on the facts, but reserved for another occasion whether a different result might be required in 'a starker case'.[193]

(4) Because the applicant voluntarily ceases to occupy the main housing duty accommodation[194]

17.75 The main housing duty will come to an end where the applicant voluntarily ceases to occupy, as his or her only or principal home, the accommodation made available under the main housing duty. The test to be applied in relation to the cessation of occupation is the same test as that used for determining whether a tenant of social housing has lost security of tenure because he or she no longer occupies accommodation as his or her only or principal home.[195] The test is not met, and the main housing duty will not have ended, merely because the applicant has been staying somewhere else temporarily.[196] Additionally, if the applicant has ceased to occupy, he or she must have done so 'voluntarily'. This requirement is especially important where the applicant has been accommodated because she or he is vulnerable as a result of mental illness.[197] Its presence corresponds to the requirement in the definition of 'becoming homeless intentionally' that the applicant's actions must have been 'deliberate'.[198]

---

[190] HA 1996, s 190(2)(a). See **17.182–17.189**.

[191] HA s 202(1)(b). See **19.14–19.15**.

[192] HA 1996, s 190(2)(a), see **17.182–17.189**.

[193] *Newman v Croydon London Borough Council* [2008] EWCA Civ 1591, (2009) *Legal Action*, p 22, CA. See also *R (Dragic) v Wandsworth London Borough Council* [2012] EWHC 1241 (Admin) (2012) July *Legal Action*, p 42, Admin Ct, where the applicants took the route of re-applying after the main housing duty had come to an end.

[194] HA 1996, s 193(6)(d). See English Code, para 14.17(viii).

[195] Housing Act 1985, s 81 (secure tenants) and Housing Act 1988, s 1 (assured tenants). See *Islington London Borough Council v Boyle* [2011] EWCA Civ 1450, [2012] HLR 18, CA.

[196] *Crawley Borough Council v Sawyer* (1987) 20 HLR 98, CA.

[197] As was the case in *R v Kensington and Chelsea Royal London Borough Council ex p Kujtim* (1999) 32 HLR 579, CA.

[198] HA 1996, s 191(1). See **14.37–14.92**.

17.76 The applicant has a right to request that the local housing authority reviews its decision that the main housing duty has ended for this reason.[199]

17.77 Alternatively, the applicant has the right to make a further application for homelessness assistance.[200] The local housing authority may have to secure interim accommodation for him or her and his or her household.

17.78 A decision, again subject to a right to seek a review, may be taken on the new application and the question as to whether he or she had voluntarily ceased to occupy the main housing duty accommodation can be determined through that process. If that decision is that the applicant had become homeless intentionally as a result of the loss of main housing duty accommodation and also has a priority need, the local housing authority will be under a duty to provide accommodation for the applicant for such period as will give him or her a reasonable opportunity to secure his or her own accommodation.[201] The applicant will also have the right request a review of a decision that he or she had become homeless intentionally.[202]

(5) By acceptance of a HA 1996, Part 6 offer[203]

17.79 An applicant owed the main housing duty will normally have applied to the same local housing authority for an allocation of a social housing tenancy under the provisions of HA 1996, Part 6 ('Allocation of housing accommodation').

17.80 Because all homeless persons (including those owed the main housing duty) are entitled to a reasonable preference in an allocation scheme,[204] an offer under HA 1996, Part 6 could be made quite quickly. In some circumstances, a HA 1996, Part 6 offer could be made immediately upon the main housing duty being triggered.[205] If that offer is accepted, then it may not be necessary to secure any accommodation under the main housing duty at all.

17.81 Where the applicant has been provided with accommodation from a local housing authority or from a private registered provider under the main housing duty, the subsequent offer under HA 1996, Part 6 might be of a

---

[199] HA 1996, s 202(1)(b). See **19.14–19.15**.
[200] HA 1996, s 193(9). The local housing authority is not permitted to refuse to accept the fresh application for homelessness assistance since the factual circumstances leading to the applicant being homeless will be different to those in existence at the date of his or her first application for homelessness assistance. See **9.66–9.85** and **17.169–17.170**.
[201] See **9.80** and **14.238–14.240** for a more detailed discussion of the issues arising on a further application for homelessness assistance in these circumstances.
[202] HA 1996, s 202(1)(b). See **19.14–19.15**.
[203] HA 1996, s 193(6)(c). See English Code, para 14.17(i).
[204] See **4.62–4.79**.
[205] English Code, paras 3.22 and 14.15.

tenancy of the very same property. If that offer is accepted, the local housing authority, or private registered provider will notify the applicant of his or her new tenancy status.[206]

17.82 Prior to the changes made by the Homelessness Act 2002, most local housing authorities made only a single offer of HA 1996, Part 6 accommodation to applicants owed the main housing duty. The expectation under choice-based lettings schemes,[207] is that the applicant should be free to bid for properties, without any penalties or risks to his or her temporary accommodation. The current statutory framework was specifically introduced so that those owed the main housing duty would have:

> '... a reasonable period in which they can exercise the same degree of customer choice of settled accommodation as is available to other people with urgent housing needs waiting on the housing register'.[208]

17.83 Precisely for this reason, there is no requirement in HA 1996, Part 7 that *all* the HA 1996, Part 6 offers made to an applicant should be of 'suitable' accommodation or that any reasons are required to be given by the applicant for refusal of those offers. There is no right to a statutory review of the suitability of offers that are *not* expressed to be 'final' offers.

17.84 An applicant who accepts an offer, only to find subsequently that it is unsuitable, will simply apply for a transfer to alternative accommodation in the ordinary way.[209]

17.85 However, when a 'final' offer is made under HA 1996, Part 6, there is not the same flexibility. If a local housing authority's policy is to make one offer only to its HA 1996, Part 6 applicants, then the only offer made to someone owed the main HA 1996, Part 7 housing duty will be 'a final offer', and there may be consequences if the applicant refuses it.[210]

17.86 The local housing authority cannot make a 'final' offer of HA 1996, Part 6 accommodation without first being satisfied that the accommodation is suitable for the applicant and his or her household.[211]

---

[206] English Code, paras 16.12–16.13. For applicants to local housing authorities in Wales, the accommodation might have been secured from the local housing authority or from a registered social landlord.

[207] HA 1996, Part 6, see Chapter 5.

[208] 'Quality and Choice: A Decent Home for All' (DETR Green Paper, April 2000), para 9.43.

[209] See **2.57–2.68**.

[210] HA 1996, s 193(7) and (7A) as amended by LA 2011, s 148(4), for applicants whose applications for homelessness assistance were made on or after 9 November 2012 to a local housing authority in England. At the date of writing, the amendments to HA 1996 made by LA 2011, ss 148–149 had not been brought into effect in Wales. See **17.92–17.108** (England) and **17.138–17.146** (Wales).

[211] HA 1996, s 193(7F) as amended by LA 2011, s 148(9), for applicants whose applications for homelessness assistance were made on or after 9 November 2012 to a local housing authority in England. At the date of writing, the amendments to HA 1996 made by LA 2011, ss 148–149 had not been brought into effect in Wales. Applicants whose applications for homelessness

17.87　The applicant has a right to request that the local housing authority reviews its decision that the duty has ended for this reason.[212] However, since the main housing duty only ends as a result of the voluntary acceptance by the applicant of accommodation, it would seem unlikely that the applicant would want to challenge such a decision.

(6) By acceptance of an offer of an assured tenancy[213]

17.88　The main housing duty will end if the applicant accepts an assured tenancy offered by a private landlord (including by a private registered provider[214]). In this context, assured tenancy does not include an assured shorthold tenancy.[215] It follows that it would also not be a private rented sector offer.[216]

17.89　The offer will have been made other than as a result of a nomination under the local housing authority's allocation scheme (HA 1996, Part 6).[217] Such an offer may have been elicited from a private sector landlord by a local housing authority seeking homes for its homeless households. Or it may have come from a private registered provider to which the applicant had applied directly for a tenancy.[218]

17.90　An offer of an assured tenancy, made separately from the HA 1996, Part 6 process, may be refused by the applicant with no adverse consequences upon the main housing duty, unless the accommodation is subsequently re-offered to him or her as a final HA 1996, Part 6 offer.[219] The local housing authority cannot make a 'final' offer of HA 1996, Part 6 accommodation without first being satisfied that the accommodation is suitable for the applicant and his or her household.[220]

---

assistance were made before 9 November 2012, or were made to a local housing authority in Wales, are also entitled to have the local housing authority consider whether it had been reasonable for them to accept the final offer (HA 1996, s 193(7F)). See**17.99** and **17.140–17.144**. See English Code, paras 14.21–14.22.

[212]　HA 1996, s 202(1)(b). See **19.14–19.15**.

[213]　HA 1996, s 193(6)(cc). See English Code, para 14.17(ii).

[214]　Or, for applicants to local housing authorities in Wales, by a registered social landlord.

[215]　HA 1996, s 193(6)(cc).

[216]　Because a 'private rented sector offer' can only be an offer of an assured shorthold tenancy: HA 1996, s 193(7AA)–(7AC) as amended by LA 2011, s 148(5)–(7), for applicants whose applications for homelessness assistance were made on or after 9 November 2012 to a local housing authority in England. At the date of writing, the amendments to HA 1996 made by LA 2011, ss 148–149 had not been brought into effect in Wales. See **17.110**.

[217]　Because the acceptance of HA 1996, Part 6 offers is dealt with separately in HA 1996, s 193(6)(c).

[218]　English Code, Annex 5, paras 8–12. See Chapter 6 of this book. For applicants to local housing authorities in Wales, the accommodation may have come from a registered social landlord.

[219]　See **17.92–17.108**.

[220]　HA 1996, s 193(7F) as amended by LA 2011, s 148(9), for applicants whose applications for homelessness assistance were made on or after 9 November 2012 to a local housing authority in England. At the date of writing, the amendments to HA 1996 made by LA 2011, ss 148–149 had not been brought into effect in Wales. Applicants whose applications for homelessness

17.91 The applicant has a right to request that the local housing authority reviews its decision that the duty has ended for this reason.[221] However, since the main housing duty only ends as a result of the voluntary acceptance by the applicant of accommodation, it would seem unlikely that the applicant would want to challenge such a decision.

(7) By refusal of a final offer made under HA 1996, Part 6[222]

17.92 Where the applicant refuses an offer of accommodation made under HA 1996, Part 6, the main housing duty will end if the following requirements are all fulfilled:

(1) the applicant was offered accommodation under HA 1996, Part 6;[223] and

(2) the offer was made in writing;[224] and

(3) the offer stated that it was a 'final offer for the purposes of section 193(7)';[225] and

(4) the local housing authority had satisfied itself that the accommodation was 'suitable' for the applicant;[226] and

(5) the applicant is not under contractual or other obligations in respect of his or her existing accommodation which he or she cannot bring to an end before being required to take up the offer;[227] and

---

assistance were made before 9 November 2012 to a local housing in England, or were made to a local housing authority in Wales, are also entitled to have the local housing authority consider whether it had been reasonable for them to accept the final offer (HA 1996, s 193(7F)). See **17.99** and **17.140–17.144**. See English Code, paras 14.21–14.22.

[221] HA 1996, s 202(1)(b). See **19.14–19.15**.

[222] HA 1996, s 193(7) and (7A) as amended by LA s 148(4), for applicants whose applications for homelessness assistance were made on or after 9 November 2012 to a local housing authority in England. At the date of writing, the amendments to HA 1996 made by LA 2011, ss 148–149 had not been brought into effect in Wales. See English Code, para 14.17(iv).

[223] HA 1996, s 193(7) as amended by LA 2011, s 148(4), for applicants whose applications for homelessness assistance were made on or after 9 November 2012 to a local housing authority in England. At the date of writing, the amendments to HA 1996 made by LA 2011, ss 148–149 had not been brought into effect in Wales.

[224] HA 1996, s 193(7A).

[225] HA 1996, s 193(7A).

[226] HA 1996, s 193(7F)(a) as amended by LA 2011, s 148(9), for applicants whose applications for homelessness assistance were made on or after 9 November 2012 to a local housing authority in England. At the date of writing, the amendments to HA 1996 made by LA 2011, ss 148–149 had not been brought into effect in Wales.

[227] HA 1996, s 193(7F) and (8) as amended by LA 2011, s 148(9)–(10), for applicants whose applications for homelessness assistance were made on or after 9 November 2012 to a local housing authority in England. At the date of writing, the amendments to HA 1996 made by LA 2011, ss 148–149 had not been brought into effect in Wales. HA 1996, s 193(7F) as originally enacted contained a requirement that the local housing authority must also be satisfied that it would have been reasonable for the applicant to have accepted the accommodation. See **17.140–17.144**.

(6) the applicant had been informed of the possible consequences of refusal or acceptance of the offer;[228] and

(7) the applicant had been told of the right to request a review of the suitability of the accommodation;[229] and

(8) the offer was refused.[230]

17.93 This possible avenue to the ending of the main housing duty only applies to a 'final offer' of HA 1996, Part 6 accommodation.

Notification of final offer

17.94 The applicant will know whether or not the offer is a 'final offer' because the written notification must not only state that it is, but must also state that it is being treated as such for the purposes of the specific subsection in HA 1996, Part 7.[231] Meeting all of these different requirements, which enable the local housing authority to bring the main housing duty to an end under this route, requires careful organisation by the allocation staff and the homelessness staff.[232]

17.95 The formula for the ending of the main housing duty by refusal of a final offer of accommodation offered under HA 1996, Part 6 potentially triggers two sets of rights to request a review:

(1) a right to request a review of the decision as to suitability;[233] and

(2) a right to request a review of the decision that the duty is regarded as ended.[234]

---

[228] HA 1996, s 193(7) as amended by LA 2011, s 148(4), for applicants whose applications for homelessness assistance were made on or after 9 November 2012 to a local housing authority in England. At the date of writing, the amendments to HA 1996 made by LA 2011, ss 148–149 had not been brought into effect in Wales.

[229] HA 1996, s 193(7) as amended by LA 2011, s 148(4), for applicants whose applications for homelessness assistance were made on or after 9 November 2012 to a local housing authority in England. At the date of writing, the amendments to HA 1996 made by LA 2011, ss 148–149 had not been brought into effect in Wales.

[230] HA 1996, s 193(7) as amended by LA 2011, s 148(4), for applicants whose applications for homelessness assistance were made on or after 9 November 2012 to a local housing authority in England. At the date of writing, the amendments to HA 1996 made by LA 2011, ss 148–149 had not been brought into effect in Wales.

[231] The letter need not contain the exact words in HA 1996, s 193(7) (as amended by LA 2011, s 148(4)), provided that it conveys every matter of substance required by s 193(7): *Omar v Birmingham City Council* [2007] EWCA Civ 610, [2007] HLR 43, CA.

[232] Particularly so where these functions are separately managed within the particular local housing authority.

[233] HA 1996, s 202(1)(f). See **19.27–19.32**.

[234] HA 1996, s 202(1)(b). See **19.14–19.15**. For the specific considerations where an offer has been refused, see **17.52–17.53** and **19.114**.

17.96 This reflects the fact that the applicant will have received two letters. The first will have offered the accommodation on the basis that it was a final offer, outlined the right to seek a review of suitability, and warned of the consequences of refusal. The second, following a refusal, will have notified the applicant that the local housing authority considers the main housing duty to come to an end. The Court of Appeal has held that it is desirable for all the issues arising on refusal to be reviewed at the same time. It should be made clear to the applicant that he or she has a right to a review of the suitability of the accommodation alone and/or of all the other elements of HA 1996, s 193(7) as amended.[235]

17.97 Because an applicant can both request a review and also simultaneously accept the accommodation (and thus preserve his or her position), it should become less common for the stage to be reached at which the second letter comes to be sent.[236]

17.98 Indeed, the Code goes further than HA 1996, Part 7 in requiring that the applicant should be specifically told that he or she can both accept and seek a review in the letter in which the applicant is notified of the local housing authority's decision on his or her application.[237] This should ensure that offers are almost always accepted, even if a review is to be pursued.

Suitable accommodation

17.99 Before the offer is put to the applicant, the local housing authority must only satisfy itself that the accommodation offered is suitable. The question of suitability of accommodation is considered in Chapter 18.

Contractual or other obligations

17.100 Prior to the amendments made to HA 1996, Part 7, by LA 201, s 148, the local housing authority was also obliged to consider whether it would be reasonable for the applicant to accept the offer of accommodation.[238]

---

[235] *Ravichandran v Lewisham London Borough Council* [2010] EWCA Civ 755, [2010] HLR 42, CA. While the specific point that the Court of Appeal was considering (whether it had been reasonable for the applicants to accept the offer) no longer arises following the amendments to HA 1996, s 193(7F) by LA 2011, s 148(9), the general point that applicants should not be deprived of a review decision that considers all the separate elements of a HA 1996, s 193(7) (as amended by LA 2011, s 148(4)) decision still applies.

[236] HA 1996, s 202(1A). See **19.41–19.49**.

[237] English Code, para 19.3.

[238] HA 1996, s 193(7F) as originally enacted and still relevant to applicants whose applications for homelessness assistance were made before 9 November 2012 to a local housing authority in England and to applicants to local housing authorities in Wales. At the date of writing, the amendments to HA 1996 made by LA 2011, ss 148–149 had not been brought into effect in Wales. See **17.140–17.144**.

17.101 Since the coming into force of the amendments to HA 1996, s 193(7F), by LA 2011, s 148(9), on 9 November 2012, this requirement has been repealed. However, the elements of HA 1996, s 193(7)[239] will not be made out where the applicant is:

- under contractual or other obligations in respect of his or her existing accommodation; and

- not able to bring those obligations to an end before being required to take up the offer.[240]

17.102 This means that if an applicant cannot end the term of his or her tenancy or licence in order to take up the offer of HA 1996, Part 6 accommodation, even though that accommodation is suitable and all the other elements of HA 1996, s 193(7)[241] are made out, the local housing authority cannot decide that its main housing duty has come to an end as a result of the applicant's refusal of the offer.

17.103 In practice, this is likely to apply to applicants who are occupying main housing duty accommodation on a fixed-term tenancy, with no break clause. For applicants whose applications for homelessness assistance were made to a local housing authority in England before 9 November 2012, or applicants whose applications for homelessness assistance are made to a local housing authority in Wales, the requirement that the local housing authority consider whether it would be reasonable for the applicant to accept the offer of accommodation is still in force. That requirement is discussed at **17.140–17.144**.

Opportunity to consider the offer

17.104 While the requirement for it to be reasonable for the applicant to accept the offer of accommodation has been repealed,[242] local housing

---

[239] As amended by LA 2011, s 148(4) for applicants whose applications for homelessness assistance were made on or after 9 November 2012 to a local housing authority in England. At the date of writing, the amendments to HA 1996 made by LA 2011, ss 148–149 had not been brought into effect in Wales.

[240] HA 1996, s 193(7F) and (8) as amended by LA 2011, s 148(9) and (10) for applicants whose applications for homelessness assistance were made on or after 9 November 2012 to a local housing authority in England. At the date of writing, the amendments to HA 1996 made by LA 2011, ss 148–149 had not been brought into effect in Wales.

[241] As amended by LA 2011, s 148(4), for applicants whose applications for homelessness assistance were made on or after 9 November 2012 to a local housing authority in England. At the date of writing, the amendments to HA 1996 made by LA 2011, ss 148–149 had not been brought into effect in Wales.

[242] HA 1996, s 193(7F) amended by LA 2011, s 148(9) for applicants whose applications for homelessness assistance were made on or after 9 November 2012 to a local housing authority in England. At the date of writing, the amendments to HA 1996 made by LA 2011, ss 14–49 had not been brought into effect in Wales.

authorities should still act fairly and take into account the advice in the English Code in giving applicants a reasonable opportunity to consider final offers of HA 1996, Part 6 accommodation.[243]

17.105 There is no set reasonable period. The appropriate length of time depends on the applicant's circumstances. Local housing authorities should take into account that:

- applicants should have a longer period in which to consider offers made under HA 1996, Part 6 than the period they have in which to consider offers of temporary accommodation;

- applicants may wish to seek advice; and

- applicants may not be familiar with the property offered.

17.106 If the applicant is in hospital or temporarily absent, the local housing authority should take that into account.[244]

17.107 The Secretary of State recommends that applicants should be given the opportunity to view the accommodation before deciding whether to accept or reject it.[245]

Refusal of offer

17.108 The key ingredient for ending the duty in these circumstances is that the applicant has *refused* the HA 1996, Part 6 accommodation offered. The wording in HA 1996, s 193(7) is that the applicant 'refuses' a final offer. It is not sufficient that there has been a simple failure to accept it. This must mean something more than that the applicant has failed to respond to an offer made to him or her. The local housing authority must be able to identify something that amounts to unequivocal rejection following receipt of the offer.[246]

(8) By acceptance of a private rented sector offer[247]

17.109 Since the coming into force of the amendments to HA 1996, s 193, by LA 2011, s 148[248] on 9 November 2012, local housing authorities in England

---

[243] English Code, paras 14.2–4.22. For the advice in the Welsh Code, see **17.145**.

[244] English Code, para 14.22.

[245] English Code, para 14.18.

[246] *R v Haringey London Borough Council ex p Muslu* (2001) February *Legal Action*, p 29, QBD.

[247] HA 1996, s 193(7AA)–(7AC) as amended by LA 2011, s 148(5)–(7) for applicants whose applications for homelessness assistance were made on or after 9 November 2012 to a local housing authority in England. At the date of writing, the amendments to HA 1996 made by LA 2011, ss 148–149 had not been brought into effect in Wales.

[248] For applicants whose applications for homelessness assistance were made on or after 9 November 2012 to a local housing authority in England. At the date of writing, the amendments to HA 1996 made by LA 2011, ss 148–149 had not been brought into effect in Wales.

have been able to make private rented sector offers to applicants owed the main housing duty whose applications for homelessness assistance were made on or after 9 November 2012.

17.110 A 'private rented sector offer' is defined at HA 1996, s 193(7AC)[249] as being:

(a) an offer of an assured shorthold tenancy made by a private landlord to the applicant in relation to any accommodation which is, or may become, available for the applicant's occupation; and

(b) is made, with the approval of the local housing authority, in pursuance of arrangements made by the authority with the landlord with a view to bringing the local housing authority's main housing duty to an end; and

(c) the tenancy being offered is a fixed-term tenancy (within the meaning of Housing Act 1988 Part 1) for a period of at least 12 months.

17.111 Power is given to the Secretary of State to provide by regulations that the minimum term may be increased from 12 months.[250] That power has not been exercised. However, local housing authorities can choose to make private rented sector offers of tenancies with terms longer than the minimum of 12 months.

17.112 Local housing authorities may choose to make private rented sector offers to applicants who are owed the main housing duty under HA 1996, s 193(2). However, where the applicant is a restricted case,[251] HA 1996, s 193(7AD) requires local housing authorities to bring any main housing duty to an end by making a private rented sector offer 'so far as reasonably practicable'.

17.113 The accommodation offered by way of a private rented sector offer must be suitable for the needs of the applicant and the members of his or her household.[252] In addition to all the general considerations provided by HA 1996, Part 7, and by case law, the Secretary of State has made the Homelessness

[249] As amended by LA 2011, s 148 (7) and applicable to applicants whose applications for homelessness assistance were made on or after 9 November 2012 to a local housing authority in England. At the date of writing, the amendments to HA 1996 made by LA 2011, ss 148–149 had not been brought into effect in Wales.

[250] HA 1996, s 193(10)–(12) as inserted by LA 2011, s 148(11) for applicants whose applications for homelessness assistance were made on or after 9 November 2012 to a local housing authority in England. At the date of writing, the amendments to HA 1996 made by LA 2011, ss 148–149 had not been brought into effect in Wales.

[251] HA 1996, s 193(3B), see **10.38–10.40, 10.82–10.85, 12.32–12.47** and **17.155–17.168**.

[252] HA 1996, s 193(7F) as amended by LA 2011, s 148(9) and s 206, for applicants whose applications for homelessness assistance were made on or after 9 November 2012 to a local housing authority in England. At the date of writing, the amendments to HA 1996 made by LA 2011, ss 148–149 had not been brought into effect in Wales. See Chapter 18 for general considerations regarding suitability.

(Suitability of Accommodation) (England) Order 2012[253] which contains specific prescriptions regarding the physical characteristics and the management of a property offered by way of a private rented sector offer.[254]

17.114 The applicant will know that this is an offer designed to bring the main housing duty to an end, rather than an offer of main housing duty accommodation, because of the special notification requirements.

17.115 Before or, at the latest, at the same time as the private rented sector offer is made, the local housing authority must:

(1) inform the applicant in writing[255] of the possible consequences of refusal or acceptance of the offer;[256] and

(2) inform the applicant in writing of his or her right to request a review of the suitability of the private rented sector offer;[257] and

(3) unless the applicant is a 'restricted case',[258] inform him or her in writing of the effect of the special provisions at HA 1996, s 195A of a further application for homelessness assistance to a local housing authority in England within two years of the date of acceptance of the offer;[259]

(4) be satisfied that the offer is 'suitable' for the applicant and his or her household;[260] and

---

[253] SI 2012/2601. In force from 9 November 2012.
[254] See Chapter 18 for general considerations on suitability and **18.51–18.54** for the specific requirements in relation to a private rented sector offer. See stop-press for statutory guidance issued by DCLG.
[255] The letter need not contain the exact words in HA 1996, s 193(7AB) (as amended by LA 2011, s 148(6)), provided that it conveys every matter of substance required by s 193(7) (*Omar v Birmingham City Council* [2007] EWCA Civ 610, [2007] HLR 43, CA).
[256] HA 1996, s 193(7AA)–(7AB) amended by LA 2011, s 148(5) and (6).
[257] HA 1996, s 193(7AA)–(7AB) amended by LA 2011, s 148(5) and (6).
[258] HA 1996, s 193(3B). See **10.38–10.40, 10.82–10.85** and **12.32–12.47**.
[259] HA 1996, s 193(7AA)–(7AB) amended by LA 2011, s 148(5) and (6), for applicants whose applications for homelessness assistance were made on or after 9 November 2012 to a local housing authority in England. At the date of writing, the amendments to HA 1996 made by LA 2011, ss 148–149 had not been brought into effect in Wales. For the special provisions governing a re-application for homelessness assistance within two years of acceptance of a private rented sector offer, see HA 1996, s 195A inserted by LA 2011, s 149(4), for applicants whose applications for homelessness assistance were made on or after 9 November 2012 to a local housing authority in England. At the date of writing, the amendments to HA 1996 made by LA 2011, ss 148–149 had not been brought into effect in Wales. See **9.89–9.95** and **17.171–17.181**.
[260] HA 1996, s 193(7AA) amended by LA 2011, s 148(5) For 'suitability' in general, see Chapter 18. For the specific requirements governing the suitability of a private rented sector offer, see **18.51–18.54**.

(5) be satisfied that the applicant is not under contractual or other obligations in respect of his or her existing accommodation, or, that if he or she is, he or she is able to bring those obligations to an end before being required to take up the offer.[261]

17.116 The applicant will know that this is an offer designed to bring the main housing duty to an end, rather than an offer of main housing duty accommodation, because of the special notification requirements.[262]

17.117 If the applicant accepts the offer, the local housing authority has to do is to notify the applicant that the main housing duty has come to an end as a result of his or her acceptance.

17.118 The applicant might wish to request a review of the suitability of the accommodation offered.[263] As with other offers, he or she should usually be advised both to accept the offer and to request a review simultaneously.[264] The question arises as to what happens if the applicant, having accepted the fixed-term tenancy, is then informed by the local housing authority that his or her request for a review has been successful and the local housing authority agrees that the accommodation was not suitable? The applicant at that point may wish to terminate the tenancy but will not be able to do so unless the terms of the tenancy contain a break clause. Alternatively, it may be that the accommodation is not suitable for a private rented sector offer, but might be considered suitable accommodation for main housing duty accommodation.[265] A third possibility might be that the local housing authority intervenes and pays the landlord any rent for the remaining period of the term of the tenancy, so that the applicant can move out of the accommodation without incurring debt.

---

[261] HA 1996, s 193(7F) and (8) as amended by LA 2011, s 148(9) and (10), for applicants whose applications for homelessness assistance were made on or after 9 November 2012 to a local housing authority in England. At the date of writing, the amendments to HA 1996 made by LA 2011, ss 148–149 had not been brought into effect in Wales.

[262] HA 1996, s 193(7AA)–(7AC) amended by LA 2011, s 148(5) and (6), for applicants whose applications for homelessness assistance were made on or after 9 November 2012 to a local housing authority in England. At the date of writing, the amendments to HA 1996 made by LA 2011, ss 148–149 had not been brought into effect in Wales. See **17.115**.

[263] HA 1996, s 202(1)(g) as amended by LA 2011, s 149(9), for applicants whose applications for homelessness assistance were made on or after 9 November 2012 to a local housing authority in England. At the date of writing, the amendments to HA 1996 made by LA 2011, ss 148–149 had not been brought into effect in Wales.

[264] HA 1996, s 202(1A).

[265] On the basis that expected duration of occupation is relevant to whether or not accommodation is suitable (*Ali v Birmingham City Council, Moran v Manchester City Council* [2009] UKHL 36, [2009] 1 WLR 1506, [2009] HLR 41, HL) and so accommodation that was not suitable for the term of the private rented sector offer could be suitable as performance of the main housing duty at HA 1996, s 193(2). See **18.69–18.70**.

(9) By refusal of a private rented sector offer[266]

17.119 Since the coming into force of the amendments to HA 1996, s 193, by LA 2011, s 148[267] on 9 November 2012, local housing authorities in England have been able to make private rented sector offers to applicants owed the main housing duty whose applications for homelessness assistance were made on or after 9 November 2012.

17.120 The main housing duty will end where an applicant refuses a private rented sector offer.

17.121 There are a complex series of notifications to be made by the local housing authority to the applicant, so as to ensure that the applicant is fully informed of the consequences if he or she decides to refuse the offer.[268]

17.122 The first notification to the applicant will have been on, or before, the private rented sector offer was made to the applicant. By the time of the offer, the applicant must have been informed in writing[269] of:

(1)   the possible consequences of refusal or acceptance of the offer;[270] and

(2)   his or her right to request a review of the suitability of the offer;[271] and

(3)   unless the applicant is a restricted case,[272] of the special provisions at HA 1996, s 195A[273] which will be triggered if he or she makes a further

---

[266]   HA 1996, s 193(7AA)–(7AC) as amended by LA 2011, s 148(5)–(7) for applicants whose applications for homelessness assistance were made on or after 9 November 2012 to a local housing authority in England. At the date of writing, the amendments to HA 1996 made by LA 2011, ss 148–149 had not been brought into effect in Wales.

[267]   For applicants whose applications for homelessness assistance were made on or after 9 November 2012 to a local housing authority in England. At the date of writing, the amendments to HA 1996 made by LA 2011, ss 148–149 had not been brought into effect in Wales.

[268]   HA 1996, s 193(7AA)–(7AC) as amended by LA 2011, s 148(5)–(7) for applicants whose applications for homelessness assistance were made on or after 9 November 2012 to a local housing authority in England. At the date of writing, the amendments to HA 1996 made by LA 2011, ss 148–149 had not been brought into effect in Wales.

[269]   The letter need not contain the exact words in HA 1996, s 193(7AB) (as amended by LA 2011, s 148(6)), provided that it conveys every matter of substance required by s 193(7): *Omar v Birmingham City Council* [2007] EWCA Civ 610, [2007] HLR 43, CA.

[270]   HA 1996, s 193(7AB) amended by LA 2011, s 148(6) for applicants whose applications for homelessness assistance were made on or after 9 November 2012 to a local housing authority in England. At the date of writing, the amendments to HA 1996 made by LA 2011, ss 148–149 had not been brought into effect in Wales.

[271]   HA 1996, s 193(7AB)(b) amended by LA 2011, s 148(6) for applicants whose applications for homelessness assistance were made on or after 9 November 2012 to a local housing authority in England. At the date of writing, the amendments to HA 1996 made by LA 2011, ss 148–149 had not been brought into effect in Wales.

[272]   HA 1996, s 193(3B). See **10.38–10.40, 10.82–10.85** and **12.32–12.47** for 'restricted cases' and see **17.155–17.168** for the special duties to restricted cases.

[273]   As inserted by LA 2011, s 149(4) for applicants whose applications for homelessness assistance

application for homelessness assistance to a local housing authority in England within two years of the date of acceptance of the offer.[274]

17.123 For 'private rented sector offer' see **17.110**. The offer must be suitable for the needs of the applicant and of his or her household. In addition to all the general considerations provided by HA 1996 and by case law, the Secretary of State has made the Homelessness (Suitability of Accommodation) (England) Order 2012[275] which contains specific prescriptions regarding the physical characteristics and the management of a property offered by way of a private rented sector offer.[276]

17.124 If an applicant, having received this information, refuses the private rented sector offer, and the local housing authority is not willing to make him or her another offer, or to continue to secure accommodation under the main housing duty, it will notify him or her accordingly. That second notification will contain the local housing authority's decision that the main housing duty has ended as a result of the applicant's refusal and its reasons for that decision. The issues to be addressed by the local housing authority in deciding whether the duty has ended are:

(1)   whether the applicant was informed in writing of the possible consequences of refusal or acceptance of the private rented sector offer, of his or her right to request a review of the suitability of the accommodation and (in most cases) of the effect under HA 1996, s 195A[277] of a further application to a local housing within two years of acceptance of the offer;[278] and

(2)   whether the accommodation offered was a private rented sector offer;[279] and

(3)   whether the applicant refused the offer;[280] and

(4)   whether the offer was suitable for the needs of the applicant and of his or her household;[281] and

---

were made on or after 9 November 2012 to a local housing authority in England. At the date of writing, the amendments to HA 1996 made by LA 2011, ss 148–149 had not been brought into effect in Wales. See **9.89–9.95** and **17.171–17.181**.

[274]   HA 1996, s 193(7AB)(c) as amended by LA 2011, s 148 (6) for applicants whose applications for homelessness assistance were made on or after 9 November 2012 to a local housing authority in England. At the date of writing, the amendments to HA 1996 made by LA 2011, ss 148–149 had not been brought into effect in Wales.

[275]   SI 2012/2601. In force from 9 November 2012.

[276]   See Chapter 18 for general considerations on suitability and **18.51–18.54** for the specific requirements in relation to a private rented sector offer.

[277]   As inserted by LA 2011, s 149(4). See **9.89–9.95** and **17.171–17.181**.

[278]   HA 1996, s 193(7AB) as amended by LA 2011, s 148(6).

[279]   HA 1996, s 193(7AC) as amended by LA 2011, s 148(6). See **17.110**.

[280]   HA 1996, s 193(7AA)(b) amended by LA 2011, s 148(5).

[281]   HA 1996, s 193(7F) as amended by LA 2011, s 148(9). For 'suitability', see Chapter 18. For the specific issues relating to suitability of private rented sector offers, see **18.51–18.54**.

(5)   whether the applicant was under contractual or other obligations in relation to his or her existing accommodation;[282] and

(6)   if the applicant was under such contractual or other obligations, whether he or she was able to bring those obligations to an end before being required to take up the tenancy.[283]

17.125   The local housing authority will also inform the applicant of his or her right to request a review of the decision that the main housing duty has come to an end[284] and of the time within the request for the review should be made.

17.126   Whilst a key issue for most applicants who refuse private rented sector offers is likely to have been the suitability of that offer, it may be that the applicant is challenging another part of the local housing authority's decision, for example disputing whether the accommodation offered was a private rented sector offer, or whether he or she could have brought his or her contractual obligations to an end.

17.127   During the passage through Parliament of the Localism Act 2011, concern was raised about the possible cost, quality and location of accommodation offered by way of private rented sector offers. The new Homelessness (Suitability of Accommodation) (England) Order 2012[285] contains a list of 10 factors relating to the physical condition of the property and the character of the landlord. Each of those factors must be complied with before a local housing authority can be satisfied that the accommodation offered is suitable.[286]

17.128   The Order[287] also contains a non-exhaustive list of factors relating to the location of the accommodation offered by way of a private rented sector offer. The local housing authority must take into account:

- where the accommodation is situated outside of its district, the distance of the accommodation from its district;

- the significance of any disruption which would be caused by the location of the accommodation to the employment, caring responsibilities or education of the applicant or of members of the applicant's household;

- the proximity and accessibility of the accommodation to medical facilities and other support are currently used by or provided to the applicant, or

---

282   HA 1996, s 193(7F) and (8) as amended by LA 2011, s 148(9) and (10). See **17.101–17.103**.
283   HA 1996, s 193(8) amended by LA 2011, s 148(10).
284   HA 1996, s 202(1)(b)
285   SI 2012/2601.
286   See Chapter 18, at **18.51**.
287   SI 2012/2601.

used by or provided to members of the applicant's household, and which are essential to the applicant's well-being or to the well-being of members of the applicant's household; and

• the proximity and accessibility of the accommodation to local services, amenities and transport.[288]

17.129　There has been no new guidance published specifically on the cost and affordability of accommodation offered as a private rented sector offer. Local housing authorities are directed by specific statutory instrument[289] to consider the applicant's financial resources (including any welfare benefits) and the total costs of the accommodation. If the accommodation is not affordable, it will not be suitable.[290] The English Code also contains guidance on the cost of accommodation.[291]

17.130　An applicant may raise any other issue, relating to the accommodation offered and/or to his or her personal circumstances or those of any member of his or her household, as a reason why the accommodation offered is not suitable for him or her and his or her household.[292]

17.131　The key ingredient for ending the duty in these circumstances is that the applicant has *refused* the private rented sector offer. The wording in HA 1996, s 193(7AA)(b)[293] is that the applicant 'refuses' a private rented sector offer. It is not sufficient that there has been a simple failure to accept it. This must mean something more than that the applicant has failed to respond to an offer made to him or her. The local housing authority must be able to identify something that amounts to unequivocal rejection following receipt of the offer.[294]

Wales[295]

17.132　At the date of writing, the Welsh Government had not announced when, or indeed, whether the amendments to HA 1996 made by LA 2011, ss 148–149, especially those enabling private rented sector offers to be made, would be brought into effect.

---

[288]　SI 2012/2601, Art 2. See **18.52**.
[289]　Homelessness (Suitability of Accommodation) Order 1996, SI 1996/3204, at Appendix 2.
[290]　SI 1996/3204, Art 2.
[291]　English Code, paras 17.3–7.40. For more on 'affordability', see **18.47–18.48**.
[292]　English Code, Chapter 17 contains guidance on suitability. See Chapter 18 of this book.
[293]　As amended by LA 2011, s 148(5) for applicants whose applications for homelessness assistance were made on or after 9 November 2012 to a local housing authority in England. At the date of writing, the amendments to HA 1996, Part 7, made by LA 2011, ss 148–149 had not been brought into effect in Wales.
[294]　*R v Haringey London Borough Council ex p Muslu* (2001) February *Legal Action*, p 29, QBD.
[295]　This section also applies to local housing authorities in England where they are dealing with applicants whose applications for homelessness assistance were made on or after 9 November 2012.

17.133 Until the amendments to HA 1996 made by LA 2011, ss 148–149 are brought into effect, local housing authorities in Wales are not able to make 'private rented sector offers',[296] so that the main housing duty will come to an end if the applicant refuses the offer.[297] The list of events that can bring the main housing duty to an end for applicants to local housing authorities in Wales will also apply to a local housing authorities in England who owe a duty to applicants whose applications for homelessness assistance were made before 9 November 2012.[298]

17.134 Those events are:

(1) the applicant refuses suitable main housing duty accommodation;[299] or

(2) the applicant ceases to be eligible for assistance;[300] or

(3) the applicant becomes homeless intentionally from the accommodation made available for his or her occupation;[301] or

(4) the applicant accepts an offer of accommodation under Part 6 HA 1996;[302] or

(5) the applicant accepts an offer of an assured tenancy (other than an assured shorthold tenancy) from a private landlord;[303] or

(6) the applicant voluntarily ceases to occupy as his or her only or principal home the main housing duty accommodation;[304] or

(7) the applicant refuses a final offer of Part 6 accommodation;[305] or

(8) the applicant accepts a qualifying offer of an assured shorthold tenancy.[306]

17.135 HA 1996, s 193(6) – which contains the events listed at (2)–(6) in this list – was not amended by LA 2011 and so reference can be made to the descriptions of those events for applications to local housing authorities in

---

[296] HA 1996, s 193(7AC) amended by LA 2011, s 148 (7). See **17.109–17.131**.
[297] HA 1996, s 193(7AA) (b) amended by LA 2011, s 148(5). See **17.119–17.131**.
[298] The date of commencement of the amendments to HA 1996 Part 7 made by LA 2011, ss 148–149 in England. Localism Act 2011 (Commencement No 2 and Transitional Provisions) (England) Order, SI 2012/2599 (c.109), see Appendix 2.
[299] HA 1996, s 193(5), and Welsh Code, para 16.29(v), see **17.136–17.139**.
[300] HA 1996, s 193(6)(a), and Welsh Code, para 16.29(vi), see **17.67–17.69**.
[301] HA 1996, s 193(6)(b), and Welsh Code, para 16.29(vii), see **17.70–17.74**.
[302] HA 1996, s 193(6)(c), and Welsh Code, para 16.29(i), see **17.79–17.87**.
[303] HA 1996, s 193(6)(cc), Welsh Code para 16.29(ii) and see **17.88–17.91**.
[304] HA 1996, s 193(6)(d), and Welsh Code see para 16.29(viii), see **17.75–17.78**.
[305] HA 1996, s 193(7) and (7A), and Welsh Code, para 16.29(iv), see **17.138–17.146**.
[306] HA 1996, s 193(7B), and Welsh Code, para 16.31. See **17.147–17.154**.

England.[307] We deal in the following sections with the first, seventh and eighth events on the list as they operate in Wales.[308] Reference can also be made to the descriptions of the first and seventh events in England.[309]

Refusal of main housing duty accommodation[310]

17.136　HA 1996, s 193(5) prior to amendment by LA 201, s 148(3) is almost identical to its amended text and so reference should be made to **17.55–17.66**. However, there is no requirement on the local housing authority to have specified that the accommodation offered was not an offer of accommodation under HA 1996, Part 6, or a private rented sector offer. The local housing authority simply has to inform the applicant of:

(1)　the possible consequence of refusal of the accommodation; and

(2)　his or her right to request a review of the suitability of the accommodation.

17.137　The Welsh Code advises that applicants should be given the chance to view accommodation provided in performance of the main housing duty before being required to decide whether they accept or refuse it and before being required to sign any written agreement, such as a tenancy, relating to the accommodation.[311]

Refusal of a final offer of Part 6 accommodation[312]

17.138　HA 1996, s 193(7) and (7A), prior to amendment by LA 201, s 148(4), are also almost identical to their amended texts. Reference should be made to **17.92–17.108**.

17.139　There are two differences:

(1)　a local housing authority in Wales is only required to inform the applicant of the consequences of refusal of the offer, not of the consequences of acceptance;[313] and

---

[307]　HA 1996, s 193(6)(a), see **17.67–17.69**. HA 1996, s 193(6)(b), see **17.70–17.74**. HA 1996, s 193(6)(c), see **17.79–17.87**. HA 1996, s 193(6)(cc), see **17.88–17.91**. HA 1996, s 193(6)(d), see **17.75–17.78**.

[308]　For 'refusal of main housing duty accommodation', see **17.136–17.137**. For 'refusal of a final offer of Part 6 accommodation', see **17.138–17.146**. For 'acceptance of a qualifying offer of an assured shorthold tenancy', see **17.147–17.154**.

[309]　For 'refusal of main housing duty accommodation' in England, see **17.55–17.66**. For 'refusal of a final offer of Part 6 accommodation' in England, see **17.92–17.108**.

[310]　HA 1996, s 193(5) prior to amendment by LA 2011, s 148, Welsh Code, para 16.29(v).

[311]　Welsh Code, para 16.30.

[312]　HA 1996, s 193(7)–(7A) prior to amendment by LA 2011, s 148, Welsh Code, para 16.29(iv).

[313]　HA 1996, s 193(7) prior to amendment by LA 2011, s 148.

(2) a local housing authority in Wales must be satisfied that it was reasonable for the applicant to accept the offer of accommodation.[314]

17.140 This last point requires the local housing authority to think ahead and consider what the circumstances are likely to be when the applicant receives the offer. For example, the local housing authority must consider the contractual or other obligations (such as to notice) that the applicant may owe in respect of his or her existing accommodation. The local housing authority should consider whether the applicant will be able to bring those obligations to an end before he or she is required to take up the offered accommodation.[315]

17.141 There may be a host of other reasons why it may not be reasonable to expect an applicant to take up even a final offer of suitable accommodation made under HA 1996, Part 6. HA 1996, Part 7:

'… makes it clear that the question whether it was reasonable for an applicant to accept accommodation is distinct from the question whether the accommodation was suitable. There may be circumstances in which it is reasonable to refuse to accept accommodation which is suitable.'[316]

17.142 The Court of Appeal held in *Slater v Lewisham London Borough Council*[317] that there are two separate elements: (1) the suitability of the accommodation and (2) whether or not it would have been reasonable to accept the offer, and the local housing authority must consider and be satisfied in respect of each of those elements. In considering how the local housing authority should test the question of whether or not it would have been reasonable to accept the offer, the Court of Appeal held that an approach centred on the specific attributes of the applicant was required:

'the decision-maker must have regard to all the personal characteristics of the applicant, her needs, her hopes and her fears and then taking account of those individual aspects, the subjective factors, ask whether it is reasonable, an objective test, for the applicant to accept. The test is whether a right-thinking local housing authority would conclude that it was reasonable that *this applicant* should have accepted the offer of *this* accommodation.'[318]

17.143 Given the potential consequences of refusal, applicants must be allowed a reasonable period in which to consider final offers of HA 1996, Part 6 accommodation. There is no set reasonable period. The appropriate

---

[314] HA 1996, s 193(7F) prior to amendment by LA 2011, s 148.
[315] HA 1996, s 193(8).
[316] *Warsame v Hounslow London Borough Council* (2000) 32 HLR 335, CA, at 339, per Chadwick LJ.
[317] [2006] EWCA Civ 394, [2006] HLR 37, CA.
[318] *Slater v Lewisham London Borough Council* [2006] EWCA Civ 394, [2006] HLR 37, CA, at [34], per Ward LJ. This approach was followed and applied by the Court of Appeal in *Ahmed v Leicester City Council* [2007] EWCA Civ 843, [2008] HLR 6, CA. See also *Ahad v Tower Hamlets London Borough Council* [2008] EWCA Civ 606, (2008) July *Legal Action*, p 22, CA.

length of time depends on the applicant's circumstances. Local housing authorities should take into account that:

- applicants should have a longer period in which to consider offers made under HA 1996, Part 6 than the period they have in which to consider offers of temporary accommodation;

- applicants may wish to seek advice; and

- applicants may not be familiar with the property offered.

17.144 If the applicant is in hospital or temporarily absent, the local housing authority should take that into account.[319]

17.145 The Welsh Code advises that applicants should be given the opportunity to view the accommodation before deciding whether to accept or reject it and before being asked required to sign any written tenancy agreement.[320]

17.146 As already discussed,[321] when a local housing authority is deciding whether or not its duty has come to an end as a result of the refusal of a Part 6 offer, it must consider both the suitability of the accommodation and, as a separate issue, whether or not it was reasonable for the applicant to accept the offer. Those two issues could each be considered in a single review decision relating to the suitability of the offer, or in a review of the decision that the duty has come to an end. However, where a local housing authority failed to consider in either of those review decisions whether or not it had been reasonable for an applicant to accept an offer, the review decision was held to be unlawful.[322]

Acceptance of a qualifying offer of an assured shorthold tenancy[323]

17.147 The main housing duty ends if an applicant accepts a qualifying offer of an assured shorthold tenancy from a private landlord, including from a registered social landlord,[324] of suitable accommodation which is available or will be made available to him or her to occupy.[325]

17.148 The offer must be of accommodation that the local housing authority has already satisfied itself is suitable for the needs of the applicant and his or

---

[319] Welsh Code, para 16.34.
[320] Welsh Code, para 16.30.
[321] See **17.140–17.144**.
[322] *Ravichandran v Lewisham London Borough Council* [2010] EWCA Civ 755, [2010] HLR 42, CA.
[323] HA 1996, s 193(7B)–(7F) prior to amendment by LA 2011, s 148; Welsh Code, para 16.31.
[324] Or, in England, a private registered provider.
[325] HA 1996, s 193(7B).

her household. The local housing authority must also be satisfied, before the offer is made, that it is reasonable for the applicant to accept the offer.[326]

17.149 However, even though the accommodation must be suitable and reasonable to accept, the applicant is free to *refuse* a qualifying offer of an assured shorthold tenancy made under these provisions without fear of any consequences.[327]

17.150 The Welsh Code advises that local housing authorities should work with private landlords to make qualifying offers of assured shorthold tenancies and that this should be 'considered as a mainstream element' of securing housing for the homeless.[328] In other words, while the Welsh Government has not, at the date of writing, permitted local housing authorities to make private rented sector offers,[329] it is encouraging local housing authorities to make use of the private rented sector. The difference is that an applicant will not face the loss of the main housing duty if he or she refuses a suitable qualifying offer of an assured shorthold tenancy.

17.151 A 'qualifying offer' is defined as:

(1) an offer made with the approval of the local housing authority, in pursuance of arrangements made between the local housing authority and the landlord, with a view to ending the local housing authority's main housing duty;

(2) of a fixed term tenancy (although there is no minimum period); and

(3) accompanied by a written statement informing the applicant of the length of the fixed term and explaining in ordinary language that there is no obligation to accept, but that the main housing duty will end if the offer is accepted.[330]

17.152 The applicant must sign an acknowledgment that he or she has understood that statement.[331]

17.153 These procedures, described as 'elaborate' by one Court of Appeal judge:

---

[326] HA 1996, s 193(7F)(b).
[327] HA 1996, s 193(7C). If the offer of an assured shorthold tenancy is being made in performance of the main housing duty, instead of being a qualifying offer designed to end the main housing duty, and is suitable, refusal of the offer will bring the duty to an end under HA 1996, s 193(5). See **17.136–17.137**.
[328] Welsh Code, para 18.27.
[329] HA 1996, s 193(7AC) as amended by LA 2011, s 148(6) for applicants whose applications were made to a local housing authority in England on or after 9 November 2012. At the date of writing, the amendments to HA 1996 made by LA 2011, ss 148–149 had not been brought into effect in Wales. See **17.110** for 'private rented sector offer'.
[330] HA 1996, s 193(7D).
[331] HA 1996, s 193(7E).

'are there to recognise that, on the one hand, assured shorthold tenancies from private landlords have their disadvantages ... but that, on the other hand, some homeless applicants may reasonably prefer to accept the offer of such a tenancy, rather than remain in temporary accommodation for a long time until they may be offered secure accommodation under Part 6.'[332]

17.154 The applicant has a right to request that the local housing authority reviews its decision that the main housing duty has ended for this reason.[333] However, since the main housing duty only ends as a result of the voluntary acceptance by the applicant of accommodation, it would seem unlikely that the applicant would want to challenge such a decision.[334]

The special rules for 'restricted cases'[335]

The definition of 'restricted case'

17.155 An applicant is a 'restricted case' where:

- the applicant is eligible;[336] and

- the applicant's household contains a 'restricted person';[337] and

- it is the presence in the household of the restricted person that has led to the main housing duty having been accepted.[338]

17.156 A 'restricted person'[339] is defined as a person:

- who is not eligible for assistance under HA 1996, Part 7;[340] and

- who is subject to immigration control within the meaning of the Asylum and Immigration Act 1996;[341] and

- who either does not have leave to enter or remain in the UK; or

---

[332] May LJ in *Griffiths v St Helens Council* [2006] EWCA Civ 160, [2006] HLR 29, CA, at [36].
[333] HA 1996, s 202(1)(b). See **19.14–19.15**.
[334] If the applicant did request a review and the decision on review was that it had not been reasonable for the applicant to accept the offer, the applicant will be homeless and the main housing duty will continue.
[335] HA 1996, s 193(3B), inserted by Housing and Regeneration Act 2008, Sch 15, para 5, in force for applications made on or after 2 March 2009.
[336] See Chapter 12.
[337] HA 1996, s 184(7), inserted by Housing and Regeneration Act 2008, Sch 15, para 3, in force for applications made on or after 2 March 2009.
[338] HA 1996, s 193(3B), inserted by Housing and Regeneration Act 2008, Sch 15, para 5, in force for applications made on or after 2 March 2009.
[339] HA 1996, s 184(7), inserted by Housing and Regeneration Act 2008, Sch 15, para 3, in force for applications made on or after 2 March 2009.
[340] See Chapter 12.
[341] See **12.64–12.70**.

- whose leave to enter or remain in the UK is subject to a condition to maintain and accommodate himself, and any dependents, without recourse to public funds.

17.157 Importantly, a restricted case only arises where the applicant's entitlement to the main housing duty is *solely* because of the presence in the applicant's household of a restricted person. For example, if it was only the presence of the restricted person that resulted in the applicant becoming homeless, or having a priority need, the applicant's case would be a restricted case. However, if the applicant would be entitled to the main housing duty regardless of the presence of the restricted person (if, for example, the applicant himself or herself had a priority need, or there were other members of the applicant's household whose presence entitled the applicant to a priority need), the applicant's case would not be a restricted case.

17.158 The applicant will know whether his or her case is a 'restricted case', because the local housing authority is required to notify him or her that the main housing duty is owed because of the presence in his or her household of a restricted person.[342] The applicant will have the right to request a review of any decision that he or she is a 'restricted case'.[343]

The modifications to the main housing duty

England

17.159 Following the amendments to HA 1996, Part 7, by LA 2011, ss 148 and 149,[344] the distinction between applicants who are restricted cases and those who are not has become less significant in England.

17.160 For restricted cases, the main housing duty is modified in two ways:

(1) the local housing authority is required, so far as reasonably practicable, to bring its main housing duty to an end by making the applicant a private rented sector offer;[345] and

(2) where an applicant is offered a private rented sector offer, he or she need not be informed in writing of the effect under HA 1996, s 195A of a further application to a local housing authority within two years of acceptance of the offer.[346]

---

[342] HA 1996, s 184(3A), inserted by Housing and Regeneration Act 2008, Sch 15, para 2, in force for applications made on or after 2 March 2009. See **10.82–10.85**.

[343] Such a decision would be a decision as to 'what duty (if any)' is owed to the applicant and therefore carries a right to request a review at HA 1996, s 202(1)(b). See **19.14–19.15**.

[344] For applicants whose applications were made on or after 9 November 2012 to a local housing authority in England. At the date of writing, the amendments to HA 1996 made by LA 2011, ss 148–149 had not been brought into effect in Wales.

[345] HA 1996, s 193(7AD).

[346] HA 1996, s 193(7AB)(c) amended by LA 2011, s 148(6), for applicants whose applications were made on or after 9 November 2012 to a local housing authority in England. At the date of

17.161 The reason for this second modification is because part of the special provisions at HA 1996, s 195A[347] do not apply to an applicant to whom the main housing duty, or equivalent duty to those threatened with homeless, is only owed because of the presence in his or her household of a restricted person.[348] For applicants who are not restricted cases, the special provisions at HA 1996, s 195A enable an applicant to be owed the main housing duty, or the equivalent duty to those threatened with homelessness, regardless of whether the applicant has a priority need. However, applicants for whom the main housing duty, or equivalent duty to those threatened with homeless, is only owed because of the presence in his or her household of a restricted person, will still have to have a priority need in order to be owed either of those duties.

17.162 An applicant who has a restricted person in his or her household will still be entitled, however, to the benefit of the other special provisions at HA 1996, s 195A – deeming an applicant to be threatened with homelessness and homeless when a valid Housing Act 198, s 21 notice is served.[349]

Wales

17.163 The following modifications apply to restricted cases, where the application for homelessness assistance was made to a local housing authority in Wales (or to a local housing authority in England prior to 9 November 2012).[350]

Statement on choice in allocation scheme

17.164 HA 1996, s 193(3A) is modified so that applicants who are 'restricted cases' need not be given a copy of the local housing authority's statement on 'choice' in its allocation scheme.[351] This is presumably because the applicant who is a restricted case is not entitled to reasonable preference as a result of being owed the main housing duty.[352] It should be remembered, however, that

---

writing, the amendments to HA 1996 made by LA 2011, ss 148–149 had not been brought into effect in Wales. For HA 1996, s 195A, see **9.89–9.95** and **17.171–17.181**.

[347] See **9.89–9.95** and **17.171–17.181**.
[348] HA 1996, s 195A(5) inserted by LA 2011, s 149(4), for applicants whose applications were made on or after 9 November 2012 to a local housing authority in England. At the date of writing, the amendments to HA 1996 made by LA 2011, ss 148–149 had not been brought into effect in Wales. See **9.89–9.95** and **17.171–17.181**.
[349] HA 1996, s 195A (2) and (4) inserted by LA 2011, s 149(4), for applicants whose applications were made on or after 9 November 2012 to a local housing authority in England. At the date of writing, the amendments to HA 1996 made by LA 2011, ss 148–149 had not been brought into effect in Wales. See **9.94** and **11.121–11.128**.
[350] At the date of writing, the amendments to HA 1996 made by LA 2011, ss 148–149 had not been brought into effect in Wales. The amendments were brought into effect for applicants to local housing authorities in England who made their applications on or after 9 November 2012 (SI 2012/2599, see Appendix 2). There is no guidance in the Welsh Code.
[351] HA 1996, s 193(3B).
[352] See **4.79**.

the applicant may still be within another reasonable preference category other than those arising as a result of the applicant being homeless or being owed the main housing duty.[353]

An offer of 'private accommodation'

17.165   The main housing duty is modified so that the duty comes to an end for an applicant who is a restricted case if he or she accepts or refuses an offer of 'private accommodation'.[354]

17.166   An offer is an offer of 'private accommodation' if:

- it is an offer of an assured shorthold tenancy made by a private landlord; and

- it is made with the approval of the local housing authority in pursuance of arrangements made by the local housing authority with the landlord with a view to bringing the main housing duty to an end; and

- it is a fixed term tenancy for a period of at least 12 months.[355]

17.167   For the duty to come to an end, the applicant must have been informed of:

- the possible consequences of refusal of the offer; and

- that he or she has the right to request a review of the suitability of the accommodation.[356]

17.168   The private accommodation offer should not be approved by the local housing authority unless it is satisfied:

- that the accommodation is suitable for the needs of the applicant and his or her household; and

- that it is reasonable for the applicant to accept the offer.[357]

Re-applying after the main housing duty ends

17.169   An applicant in respect of whom the main housing duty has ended is free to make a new application for homelessness assistance to the same local housing authority, or any other authority, at any time.[358]

---

[353]   HA 1996, s 167(2)(c), (d) or (e) as amended by LA 2011, s 147(5). See **4.80–4.114**.
[354]   HA 1996, s 193(7AA)–(7AC) prior to amendment by LA 2011, s 148.
[355]   HA 1996, s 193(7AC) prior to amendment by LA 2011, s 148.
[356]   HA 1996, s 193(7AB) prior to amendment by LA 2011, s 148.
[357]   HA 1996, s 193(7F) prior to amendment by LA 2011, s 148.
[358]   HA 1996, s 193(9).

17.170   However, if the application is made to the same local housing authority, it will be entitled to rely on the termination of the earlier duty towards the applicant, and will not come under a new duty to secure accommodation or provide other assistance unless there are new facts put forward on the new application.[359]

The special rules for applicants re-applying within two years of acceptance of a private rented sector offer – England[360]

17.171   The introduction of the facility for local housing authorities to end the main housing duty[361] by making private rented sector offers,[362] of tenancies of as minimum duration of only 12 months,[363] raised the spectre of an applicants for homelessness assistance constantly re-applying for homelessness assistance. As each private let came to an end, the applicant would once again apply for homeless assistance and would need to pass, once again, through the obstacle course of HA 1996, Part 7 before being owed another main housing duty and made just another short-term private rented sector offer.

17.172   To meet this possibility, at least in part, the UK government brought forward the arrangements contained in what is now HA 1996, 195A. In short, it provides that the main housing 'duty remains with the placing local authority for a two-year period'.[364] This is achieved by providing that if an applicant becomes homeless within two years of the acceptance of a suitable private rented sector offer, and applies again for homelessness assistance, he or she will be fast-tracked through HA 1996, Part 7 to the main housing duty again with the benefit of special provisions and, most particularly:

(1)   irrespective of whether he or she still has a priority need for accommodation; and

(2)   without needing to face possession proceedings brought by the private sector landlord.

---

[359]   *R v Harrow London Borough Council ex p Fahia* [1998] 1 WLR 1396, HL; and *Begum v Tower Hamlets London Borough Council* [2005] EWCA Civ 340, [2005] HLR 34, CA. See also **9.66–9.84** and **14.238–14.240**.

[360]   HA 1996, s 195A inserted by LA 2011, s 149(4) for applicants whose applications for homelessness assistance were made on or after 9 November 2012 to a local housing authority in England. At the date of writing, the amendments to HA 1996 made by LA 2011, ss 148–149 had not been brought into effect in Wales. See **9.89–9.95**.

[361]   HA 1996, s 193(2), see **17.23–17.168**.

[362]   HA 1996, s 193(7AA)–(7AC) as amended by LA 2011, s 148(5)–(7) for applicants whose applications for homelessness assistance were made on or after 9 November 2012 to a local housing authority in England. At the date of writing, the amendments to HA 1996 made by LA 2011, ss 148–149 had not been brought into effect in Wales. See **17.109–17.131**.

[363]   HA 1996, s 193(7AC)(c) as amended by LA 2011, s 148(7) for applicants whose applications for homelessness assistance were made on or after 9 November 2012 to a local housing authority in England. At the date of writing, the amendments to HA 1996 made by LA 2011, ss 148–149 had not been brought into effect in Wales. See **17.110–17.111**.

[364]   Parliamentary Under-Secretary of State for Communities and Local Government (Andrew Stunell MP), *Hansard*, Public Bill Committee on the Localism Bill, 3 March 2011, col 787.

17.173 The first special provision is that he or she will not normally need a priority need in order to be owed the main housing duty or equivalent duty to those threatened with homelessness.[365] The exception is where the applicant would only be owed either of those duties because of the presence in his or her household of a restricted person.[366] Even if this is the case, the presence of the restricted person might give the applicant a priority need and so he or she would be then owed the main housing duty or equivalent duty to those threatened with homelessness.

17.174 The second special provision is that applicants are deemed to be threatened with homelessness from the date that a valid HA 1988, s 21 notice is given to them and are deemed to be homelessness on the day on which the notice expires.[367]

17.175 An applicant should therefore make his or her application for homelessness assistance as soon as he or she is given a valid HA 1988, s 21 notice by the private sector landlord. If the notice is valid, the local housing authority must accept that he or she is threatened with homelessness.[368] There may be some further inquiries to be carried out into the issues of the applicant is eligible for assistance[369] and whether or not he or she became threatened with homelessness intentionally.[370] However, if the local housing authority is able to make its decision on the application during the two months of the HA 1988, s 21 notice, and is not satisfied that the applicant become threatened with homelessness intentionally, it will be subject to the duty at HA 1996, s 195(2) to take reasonable steps to secure that the accommodation does not cease to be available for the applicant's occupation.[371] If those reasonable steps do not succeed in retaining the accommodation for the applicant when the notice expires, the main housing duty will be owed to the applicant.[372]

17.176 Many landlords serve a Housing Act 1988, s 21, notice at the beginning of the tenancy, so that the date on which possession is required is the last day of the fixed-term tenancy which can be no sooner than 12 months. The deeming provisions at HA 1996, s 195A (4) states clearly that the applicant will be threatened with homelessness from the date on which the notice is given so that, even if the notice is not due to expire for 12 months, the applicant is threatened with homelessness. The implication is that the applicant will be threatened with homelessness throughout the whole term of the tenancy.

---

[365] HA 1996, s 195A(1) and (3) inserted by LA 2011, s 149(4).
[366] HA 1996, s 195A(5) inserted by LA 2011, s 149(4). For 'restricted person', see **12.32–12.47**.
[367] HA 1996, s 195A(2) and (4) inserted by LA 2011, s 149(4).
[368] HA 1996, s 175(4), see **11.129–11.123**.
[369] HA 1996, s 185, see Chapter 12.
[370] HA 1996, s 191. See Chapter 14.
[371] HA 1996, s 195A(3) inserted by LA 2011, s 149(4). For HA 1996, s 195(2) duty, see **17.190–17.200**.
[372] HA 1996, s 193(2) and 195(4), for 'main housing duty', see **17.190–17.200** and **17.23–17.168**.

17.177   If the decision on the application is taken on or after the date on which the notice expires, the applicant will be deemed to be homeless.[373] If the decision is that he or she is eligible for assistance and did not become homeless intentionally, the main housing duty will be owed.[374] The local housing authority may be able to persuade the landlord to permit the applicant to remain in the accommodation. If it succeeds in doing so, the applicant might be made a further private rented sector offer[375] (of that same accommodation) or simply remain in the accommodation in performance of the main housing duty under a periodic tenancy or licence whilst the local housing authority makes him or her another offer of accommodation.[376]

17.178   Obviously if the landlord does not agree to the applicant remaining after the expiry of the notice, the main housing duty will have to be performed by securing accommodation elsewhere for the applicant and his or her household.

17.179   If the private rented sector offer was in the district of authority A, but had been offered to the applicant by authority B, and the applicant makes his or her further application for homelessness assistance to authority A, authority A can refer the performance of the main housing duty back to authority B provided that neither the applicant nor any member of his or her household will run the risk of domestic violence in the district of authority B.[377]

17.180   As already noted, the special rules do not exclude consideration of whether the applicant is eligible for assistance, and of whether he or she become homeless (or threatened with homelessness) intentionally. If the applicant is not eligible for assistance, then no duty will be owed.[378] If the applicant is found to have become homeless intentionally from the private rented accommodation, eg because it was his or her actions that led the landlord to serve a HA 1988, s 21 notice, then the applicant will be entitled to advice and assistance in any attempts he or she may make to secure his or her own accommodation[379] and, if the applicant also has a priority need, to short-term accommodation under HA 1996, s 190(2)(a).[380] It may be that the local housing authority can arrange with the private landlord that the

---

[373] HA 1996, s 195A(2) inserted by LA 2011, s 149(4) and for applicants whose applications for homelessness assistance were made on or after 9 November 2012 to a local housing authority in England. At the date of writing, the amendments to HA 1996 made by LA 2011, ss 148–149 had not been brought into effect in Wales.

[374] HA 1996, s 193(2), see **17.23–17.168**.

[375] HA 1996, s 193(7AC) as amended by LA 2011, s 148(7).

[376] The accommodation then being secured by the local housing authority under the main housing duty at HA 1996, s 193(2). See **17.32–17.35**.

[377] HA 1996, s 198(2ZA) and (2A) inserted and amended by LA 2011, s 149(6)–(8) and in force from 9 November 2012. See **15.116–15.131**.

[378] HA 1996, s 183(2).

[379] HA 1996, s 190(3), see **17.201–17.214**.

[380] See **17.182–17.189**. The special provisions at HA 1996, s 195A(1) and (3) only exclude priority need from consideration if the applicant is entitled to the main housing duty or equivalent duty to those threatened with homelessness. They do not apply where the local housing authority is satisfied that the applicant has become homeless intentionally and so the issue of

accommodation previously occupied as a result of the private rented sector offer can now be offered to the applicant again, perhaps if the local housing authority's assistance were to include help with a rent deposit or a rent guarantee.

17.181 These special provisions only apply once.[381] If, on a re-application within two years of acceptance of a private rented sector offer, the applicant accepts another private rented sector offer (which might be of the same or different accommodation), and that subsequently comes to an end, he or she will have to apply in the usual way and will need to have a priority need in order to be owed any of the accommodation duties.

DUTY TO SECURE ACCOMMODATION FOR A PERIOD THAT WILL GIVE THE APPLICANT A REASONABLE OPPORTUNITY OF SECURING HIS OR HER OWN ACCOMMODATION[382]

17.182 This duty is owed to an applicant whom the local housing authority is satisfied is eligible, is homeless and has a priority need but whom it is also satisfied became homeless intentionally. The duty is triggered as soon as those conditions are fulfilled, although the local housing authority will provide written notification to the applicant indicating that this is the duty that it owes to him or her.[383] The duty owed by the local housing authority is to secure accommodation 'for such period as they consider will give him a reasonable opportunity of securing accommodation for his occupation'.[384] The accommodation secured for this period must meet all the usual requirements.[385] The local housing authority also has a duty to provide advice and assistance in the applicant's search for his or her own accommodation.[386]

17.183 The applicant owed these duties is likely to have been provided with interim accommodation pending the decision on his or her application. In that situation, the usual course will be for the local housing authority to continue

---

priority need will be relevant to whether or not the local housing authority owes a short-term duty to accommodate under HA 1996, s 190(2)(a).

[381] HA 1996, s 195A(6) inserted by LA 2011, s 149(4).

[382] HA 1996, s 190(2)(a). See English Code, paras 14.27–14.29; Welsh Code, paras 16.20–16.22.

[383] HA 1996, s 184(3). See **10.66–10.81**. Where a local housing authority had rejected the contention that it owed this duty to accommodate an applicant whom it had found to have become homeless intentionally, it was ordered to pay the costs of the applicant's judicial review claim. The prospect of the local housing authority losing the judicial review was 'towards the obvious end of the spectrum': per Walker J in *R (Dumbaya) v Lewisham London Borough Council* [2008] EWHC 1852 (Admin), (2008) September *Legal Action*, p 25, Admin Ct.

[384] HA 1996, s 190(2)(a).

[385] Described at **17.12**.

[386] See English Code, paras 14.27–14.29; Welsh Code, paras 16.6–16.10 and 16.22; and see **17.132–17.145**.

the provision of that same accommodation for whatever further period it has decided will satisfy its duty. If it has not previously secured accommodation, it must do so for that same period.

17.184 Local housing authorities, having strategic responsibility for housing in their districts, are uniquely well placed to determine what sort of period an applicant will require in order to have a 'reasonable opportunity' of finding housing locally. The duty is not to secure accommodation for as long as it actually takes the applicant to find his or her own housing. It is instead to secure accommodation for the period that the local housing authority considers will give the applicant a 'reasonable opportunity' to find and secure accommodation for himself or herself.

17.185 Plainly the period required will be longer in areas of housing shortage. Some examples considered by the courts are:

- where a period of four days for an applicant with a family was unlawfully short and a period of months might be expected;[387]

- an initial decision to give a single parent of three children six or seven days' accommodation could not be considered reasonable, but there was no error of law in the local housing authority's subsequent decision not to extend the period beyond 28 days;[388]

- where a judge decided that accommodation secured under HA 1996, s 190(2)(a) would have been for a maximum period of three months;[389]

- where a judge decided that he should grant an interim injunction requiring the local housing authority to continue to secure accommodation to the applicant, where the evidence was that within a week the claimant would be able to clear previous arrears, secure housing benefit and with the help of a bond scheme, secure a private sector tenancy;[390] and

- where a judge held that it was not wrong in law for a local housing authority to decide that a 28-day period was a 'reasonable period' for a single mother with a four-year-old son.[391]

---

[387] *De Falco v Crawley Borough Council* [1980] QB 460, HL.

[388] *R (Nipyo) v Croydon London Borough Council* [2008] EWHC 847 (Admin), [2008] HLR 37, Admin Ct. In an application for permission to bring a judicial review claim.

[389] *Newman v Croydon London Borough Council* [2008] EWCA Civ 1176, (2009) April *Legal Action*, p 22, CA.

[390] *R (Anwar) v Manchester City Council* [2009] EWHC 2876 (Admin), (2010) January *Legal Action*, p 36, Admin Ct.

[391] *R (Savage) v Hillingdon London Borough Council* [2010] EWHC 88 (Admin), March *Legal Action*, p 31, Admin Ct.

17.186 The Codes advise that the appropriate period for each case should be considered on its merits.[392] The Codes encourage local housing authorities, when fixing the period, to take into account local housing circumstances and the supply of accommodation in the district, as well as the applicant's resources, his or her ability to fund rent in advance and pay a deposit for a private sector tenancy, and any other relevant circumstances. Perhaps the most relevant material that might help to assess the period that the applicant will require will come from the personal assessment of his or her housing needs conducted by the local housing authority itself.[393] Indeed, it is difficult to see how, save in the most straightforward case, the local housing authority could fix the period (except perhaps on a provisional basis) until the assessment had been completed.

17.187 The Court of Appeal has held that, when considering what period would give the applicant a 'reasonable opportunity', the local housing authority should consider what is reasonable from an applicant's standpoint, having regard to his or her circumstances and in the context of accommodation potentially available. Considerations peculiar to the local housing authority, such as the extent of its resources and the other demands on its resources, are not to be taken into account when determining the length of the period.[394]

17.188 If the applicant wants to challenge the local housing authority's decision as to the length of the period that it considers will give him or her 'a reasonable opportunity' of securing his or her own accommodation, he or she must bring a claim for judicial review. This is because it is a dispute over the way in which the local housing authority is performing its duty, not over what duty, if any, is owed to the applicant, and so the statutory right to request a review is not available.[395]

17.189 Accommodation secured under this statutory duty is unlikely to be protected by the Protection from Eviction Act 1977 because it is usually provided under a licence and for a short period of time.[396] It can therefore be terminated on reasonable notice, but with no obligation on the landlord to obtain a possession order.[397]

---

[392] English Code, para 14.28; Welsh Code, para 16.21.

[393] HA 1996, s 190(4). See **17.201–17.214**.

[394] *R (Conville) v Richmond upon Thames London Borough Council* [2006] EWCA Civ 718, [2006] HLR 45, CA.

[395] *R (Conville) v Richmond upon Thames London Borough Council* [2006] EWCA Civ 718, [2006] HLR 45, CA. For judicial review, see **19.224–19.250**.

[396] For more on tenure and statutory protection from eviction, see **18.83–18.97**.

[397] Protection from Eviction Act 1977, s 3. See **16.74–16.88**. *Desnousse v Newham London Borough Council* [2006] EWCA Civ 547, [2006] HLR 38, CA, but note that this case was concerned with accommodation occupied under a licence, not a tenancy, and left open the question of whether the position might be different if the accommodation is let under a tenancy (per Lloyd LJ at [69]).

DUTY TO TAKE REASONABLE STEPS TO SECURE THAT ACCOMMODATION DOES NOT CEASE TO BE AVAILABLE[398]

17.190　If a local housing authority is satisfied that an applicant is eligible, is threatened with homelessness unintentionally, and also has a priority need, its duty is to take reasonable steps to secure that accommodation does not cease to be available for the occupation of the applicant and his or her household.[399] The applicant will be informed that this is the duty that he or she is owed in the notification of the decision on his or her application.[400]

17.191　In performing its duty under HA 1996, Part 7, the local housing authority will usually first consider what can be done to keep the applicant in the accommodation in which he or she is threatened with homelessness. In *Bury Metropolitan Borough Council v Gibbons*,[401] a local housing authority failed to recognise that an applicant was making an application for homelessness assistance, and that he was threatened with homelessness, and therefore failed to take reasonable steps to secure that the accommodation did not cease to be available for his occupation. After he left the accommodation and made a further application for homelessness assistance, he was found to have become homeless intentionally. That decision was overturned as being wrong in law. The accommodation had not been lost by any deliberate act of the applicant but by the failure of the local housing authority to recognise and perform its duties to him.

17.192　The Codes suggest that in deciding how to perform its duty, the local housing authority should consider:

- the possibility of constructive negotiations with the applicant's landlord (if the applicant is living in the private rented sector and facing repossession);

- the scope for mediation (if the applicant has been asked to leave accommodation provided by family or friends);

- providing support to the household so as to ease any pressures that may have led to a request that the applicant should leave the accommodation; and

- providing assistance with any specific problems that can be addressed, such as housing benefit delays.[402]

---

[398]　HA 1996, s 195(2).
[399]　HA 1996, s 195(2). See English Code, paras 14.6–14.9; Welsh Code, paras 16.12–16.15 for guidance.
[400]　HA 1996, s 184(3). See **10.66–10.81**.
[401]　[2010] EWCA Civ 327, [2010] HLR 33, CA.
[402]　English Code, para 14.7; Welsh Code, para 16.13.

17.193 The local housing authority's homelessness review and strategy should be consulted for the specific help that should be available in the district for those facing the prospect of homelessness and who are trying to retain their homes.[403]

17.194 If the local housing authority is unable to ensure the retention of the accommodation in which the applicant is threatened with homelessness, the local housing authority will then itself be under a duty to secure accommodation for the applicant and the members of his or her household.[404] That duty must be performed in accordance with the requirements that attach to all of the housing functions under HA 1996, Part 7.[405]

17.195 The duty is not time limited and so could be owed indefinitely. It is brought to an end only in circumstances which would (as necessarily modified) bring the main housing duty to an end.[406]

The special rules for 'restricted threatened homelessness cases'[407]

17.196 A 'restricted threatened homelessness case' is defined as a case in which the duty would not have arisen without the presence in the applicant's household of a restricted person.[408]

17.197 A restricted threatened homelessness case only arises where the applicant's entitlement to the duty is *solely* because of the presence in the applicant's household of a restricted person. For example, if it was the presence of the restricted person that resulted in the applicant becoming threatened with homeless, or having a priority need, the applicant's case would be a restricted case. However, if the applicant would be entitled to the duty regardless of the presence of the restricted person (if, for example, the applicant himself or herself had a priority need, or there were other members of the applicant's household whose presence entitled the applicant to a priority need), the applicant's case would not be a restricted threatened homelessness case.

17.198 The applicant will know whether or not his or her case is a 'restricted threatened homelessness case', because the local housing authority is required to notify him or her that the duty is owed because of the presence in his or her

---

[403] See Chapter 8.
[404] HA 1996, s 195(4).
[405] See **17.12**.
[406] HA 1996, s 195(4). Those circumstances are reviewed at **17.42–17.168**.
[407] HA 1996, s 195(4B), inserted by Housing and Regeneration Act 2008, Sch 15, para 6, in force for applications made on or after 2 March 2009.
[408] HA 1996, s 195(4B), inserted by Housing and Regeneration Act 2008, Sch 15, para 6, in force for applications made on or after 2 March 2009. 'Restricted person' is defined at HA 1996, s 184(7); and see **10.38–10.40** and **12.32–12.47**.

household of a restricted person.[409] The applicant will have the right to request a review of any decision that he or she is a 'restricted threatened homelessness case'.[410]

The modifications to the duty

England

17.199   For applications made to local housing authorities in England on or after 9 November 2012,[411] the distinction between applicants who are restricted threatened homelessness cases and those who are not becomes less important. If the accommodation from which the applicant is threatened with homelessness cannot be secured for his or her occupation, the main housing duty at HA 1996, s 193(2) will apply.[412] The applicant will accordingly become a 'restricted case'.[413] The main housing duty is modified in two ways for restricted cases:

- the local housing authority is required to end the main housing duty by making the applicant a private rented sector offer,[414] so far as that is reasonably practicable;[415] and

- when the local housing authority makes a private rented sector offer to the applicant, it is not required to inform the applicant in writing of the effect of the special provisions of HA 1996, s 195A.[416]

Wales

17.200   For local housing authorities in Wales, and for local housing authorities in England dealing with applicants whose applications for

---

[409]   HA 1996, s 184(3A), inserted by Housing and Regeneration Act 2008, Sch 15, para 2, in force for applications made on or after 2 March 2009. See **10.82–10.85**.

[410]   Such a decision would be a decision as to 'what duty (if any)' is owed to the applicant and therefore carries a right to request a review at HA 1996, s 202(1)(b). See **19.14–19.15**.

[411]   The date of commencement of the amendments to HA 1996 made by LA 2011, ss 148–149 (see SI 2012/2061). At the date of writing, the amendments to HA 1996 made by LA 2011, ss 148–149 had not been brought into effect in Wales.

[412]   For 'main housing duty' see **17.23–17.168**.

[413]   HA 1996, s 193(3B), see **17.155**.

[414]   HA 1996, s 193(7AC) as amended by LA 2011, s 148(7) for applicants whose applications for homelessness assistance was made on or after 9 November 2012 to a local housing authority in England. At the date of writing, the amendments to HA 1996 made by LA 2011, ss 148–149 had not been brought into effect in Wales. See **17.110**.

[415]   HA 1996, s 193(7AD), see **17.109–17.131**.

[416]   IHA 1996, s 193(AB)(c) as amended by LA 2011, s 148(6). HA 1996, s 195A inserted by LA 2011, s 149(4) for applicants whose applications for homelessness assistance was made on or after 9 November 2012 to a local housing authority in England. At the date of writing, the amendments to HA 1996 made by LA 2011, ss 148–149 had not been brought into effect in Wales. See **9.89–9.95** and **17.171–17.181** for the effect of HA 1996, s 195A.

homelessness assistance were made before 9 November 2012,[417] the normal duty at HA 1996, s 195 owed to restricted threatened homelessness cases is modified in two ways:

- by removing the requirement to give the applicant a copy of the local housing authority's statement on 'choice' in its allocation scheme,[418] and

- if the applicant becomes homeless from the accommodation from which he or she was threatened with homelessness, so that the main housing duty at HA 1996, s 193(2)[419] is owed,[420] by requiring the local housing authority to bring the duty to an end by an offer of 'private accommodation' so far as is reasonably practicable.[421]

DUTY TO PROVIDE ADVICE AND ASSISTANCE

17.201 For more than two decades the duty to provide advice and assistance was a much-neglected aspect of the regime of powers and duties now to be found in HA 1996, Part 7. However, it has been transformed by the Homelessness Act 2002 and, most particularly, by the innovative requirement that 'the applicant's housing needs' should be assessed in every case in which the duty is owed, leading to person-specific advice and assistance, tailor-made for the individual applicant.

17.202 Duties to provide advice and assistance are owed to applicants who:

(1) became homeless unintentionally and do not have a priority need;[422] or

(2) became homeless intentionally, whether they have a priority need or not;[423] or

(3) became threatened with homelessness unintentionally and do not have a priority need;[424] or

---

[417] The date of commencement of the amendments to HA 1996 made by LA 2011, ss 148–149 (see SI 2012/2061). At the date of writing, the amendments to HA 1996 made by LA 2011, ss 148–149 had not been brought into effect in Wales.

[418] HA 1996, s 195(3A) prior to repeal by LA 2011, s 149(3). This is presumably because the applicant is not entitled to reasonable preference as a result of being owed the duty. It should be remembered, however, that the applicant may still be entitled to any reasonable preference other than those arising as a result of the applicant being homeless or being owed this duty or the main housing duty. See **4.79**.

[419] See **17.23–17.168**.

[420] HA 1996, s 195(4A). See **17.194**.

[421] HA 1996, s 193(7AD), see**17.165–17.168**.

[422] HA 1996, s 192(2).

[423] HA 1996, s 190(2)(b) and (3).

[424] HA 1996, s 195(5)(a).

(4)   became threatened with homelessness intentionally, whether they have a priority need or not.[425]

17.203   The duty owed to an applicant in either of the first two categories is to provide:

'... advice and assistance in any attempts he may make to secure that accommodation becomes available for his occupation.'[426]

17.204   The duty in respect of the second two categories of applicant is to provide advice and assistance with:

'... any attempts he may make to secure that accommodation does not cease to be available for his occupation.'[427]

17.205   Before the advice and assistance is provided under these duties, the particular applicant's housing needs must be assessed so that the advice and assistance can be tailored to meet the applicant's individual needs.[428] The quality and extent of the assessment will therefore be crucial in order to formulate properly the advice and assistance necessary to help the applicant best. The assessment should be undertaken after the decision on the application has been notified and before the advice and assistance is actually provided.[429]

17.206   The scope of the assessment of the applicant's housing needs (for the future) is wider than the scope of the inquiries the local housing authority will have already made under HA 1996, Part 7 (which essentially look to the past and present).[430] Local housing authorities should identify any factors making it difficult for the applicant to obtain accommodation, such as poverty, outstanding debts, health problems, disabilities, whether or not English (or Welsh) is the applicant's first language, and so on. They should take account of the factors that originally led to the applicant's homelessness (or threatened homelessness) and consider his or her ability to obtain and maintain

[425] HA 1996, s 195(5)(b).
[426] HA 1996, ss 190(2) and 192(2)(b).
[427] HA 1996, s 195(5).
[428] HA 1996, ss 190(4), 192(4) and 195(6). See English Code, paras 14.4 and 14.29; Welsh Code, paras 16.4–16.10 for guidance. Surprisingly the current edition of the English Code contains *less* guidance on the duty to provide advice and assistance than previous editions did. It cross-refers to the advice provided on the local housing authority's duty to ensure that a free advice and information service is provided under HA 1996, s 179. The latter service is, of course, provided under a different statutory duty available to anyone, not just applicants for homelessness assistance, and, crucially, does not contain the important requirement to assess an applicant's housing needs before providing the advice and assistance. See **9.4–9.7**.
[429] *R (Savage) v Hillingdon London Borough Council* [2010] EWHC 88 (Admin), (2010) March *Legal Action*, p 10, Admin Ct.
[430] Although in one particular case a Judge decided that the local housing authority did not need to find out any more information than it had already ascertained as a result of its statutory inquiries for it to make a lawful assessment of the applicant's housing needs as those inquiries had already generated sufficient material about housing needs to enable an assessment to be made: *R (Savage) v Hillingdon London Borough Council* [2010] EWHC 88 (Admin), (2010) March *Legal Action*, p 10, Admin Ct.

accommodation and also consider the type of accommodation (including size, location, affordability and any special needs) that would be appropriate for the applicant.[431]

17.207 The advice and assistance actually provided must include information about the likely availability of the type of accommodation appropriate to the applicant's housing needs in the local housing authority's district, including in particular the location and sources of that type of accommodation.[432] Gone are the days when all that applicants would receive under this duty was a general list of local estate or letting agents or hostels. If applicants are referred to local landlords or letting agencies under this duty nowadays, the local housing authority must have satisfied itself that those landlords or agencies will be in a position to supply the sort of accommodation required by the applicant.

17.208 If the applicant cannot afford to provide a deposit, or to pay rent in advance, in order to obtain private rented accommodation, the local housing authority should consider offering a rent guarantee. Local housing authorities may provide deposits and/or guarantees themselves.[433] Local housing authorities' powers to pay deposits are derived from Local Government Act 1988, s 24 and require consent from the Secretary of State or Welsh Government.[434] Consent C permits local housing authorities to provide financial assistance for the purposes of acquiring or improving a property that is to be privately let as housing accommodation. Local housing authorities might also consider paying the costs of drawing up tenancy agreements, making small one-off grants to landlords to encourage them to let to households owed homelessness duties, paying indemnities to guarantee tenancy obligations, and making discretionary housing payments to meet any shortfall between the rent and the amount of housing benefit payable. When deciding whether or not to provide such financial assistance, local housing authorities must act reasonably and in accordance with their duties towards all their tax and rent payers.[435]

17.209 Often local housing authorities will have policies governing to whom they will pay rent deposits or guarantees. They are not permitted to fetter their discretion and so must consider each individual who may need a rent deposit or guarantee individually.[436]

17.210 The advice and assistance provided to an applicant who needs to acquire his or her own accommodation should include:

---

[431] English Code, para 14.4; Welsh Code, para 16.5.
[432] HA 1996, ss 190(5), 192(5) and 195(7).
[433] English Code, paras 14.29 and 16.20; Welsh Code, paras 16.6–16.10. The statutory power is in Local Government Act 1988, ss 24–25.
[434] The General Consents under Local Government Act 1988, s 25 (local authority assistance for privately let housing).
[435] English Code, para 16.20; Welsh Code, paras 16.9–16.10.
[436] *R (Conville) v Richmond upon Thames Royal London Borough Council* [2006] EWCA Civ 718, [2006] HLR 45, CA; and *R (Savage) v Hillingdon London Borough Council* [2010] EWHC 88 (Admin), (2010) March *Legal Action*, p 31, Admin Ct.

- details of how to apply for accommodation from local private registered providers or registered social landlords;

- details of the local housing authority's allocation scheme under HA 1996, Part 6, and of the right to apply for an allocation; and

- details of assistance available for those who would have difficulty in making an application to the allocation scheme without assistance.[437]

17.211 The local housing authority can arrange for the required advice and assistance to be provided by someone else (for example, by an independent housing advice agency) but first it must have carried out the assessment of the applicant's housing need itself, unless that function has been contracted out.[438] Only on completion of the assessment will it know which agency can provide the assistance appropriate to meet the applicant's particular housing needs.

17.212 There is *no* right to request a review of:

- any failure by the local housing authority to assess the applicant's needs;

- the conduct or results of the assessment;

- the content of the advice provided;

- the scope or quality of the assistance provided; or

- any other aspect of the local housing authority's performance of this duty.

17.213 If there is a claim by the applicant that:

- the local housing authority has failed to comply with its statutory duty to provide advice and assistance, or

- that it has failed to carry out an assessment,

the appropriate procedure is to bring judicial review proceedings seeking a mandatory order requiring the local housing authority to perform its duty.[439]

17.214 If the applicant seeks to challenge the local housing authority's assessment of his or her housing needs, or the decision as to the type of advice and assistance that will be provided, the appropriate procedure is to seek a quashing order in proceedings for judicial review.

---

[437] English Code, paras 2.9–2.15, 14.4 and 14.29; Welsh Code, para 16.6.
[438] See **21.21–21.25**.
[439] See **19.224–19.250**.

POWERS TO SECURE ACCOMMODATION[440]

17.215 Since 2003, local housing authorities have had a power to secure accommodation for the applicant's occupation if the applicant did not become homeless intentionally and does not have a priority need.[441] The power is therefore targeted at the single non-priority homeless and at childless couples (not otherwise falling into the priority need categories). There is no maximum or minimum limit on the period for which such accommodation can be secured. If the power is exercised, then the normal requirements for the performance of any housing function apply.[442] There is a parallel power to take reasonable steps to secure that accommodation does not cease to be available for applicants who are unintentionally threatened with homelessness and do not have a priority need.[443]

17.216 An applicant who is the beneficiary of one of these powers will also have had the benefit of an assessment of housing need and the provision of advice and assistance.[444] Indeed, if accommodation is secured under these powers, the duty to provide advice and assistance (in any attempt that the applicant may make to obtain accommodation for him or herself) remains. So, if the accommodation is only secured for a temporary period,[445] advice and assistance must be directed to meeting the applicant's housing needs once the accommodation is withdrawn.

17.217 If local housing authorities use their own stock in order to secure the accommodation, any tenancies granted under those powers cannot be secure or introductory tenancies.[446]

17.218 When considering whether or not to use these powers, a local housing authority must take into account other demands on its housing stock (in particular the legitimate expectation of applicants to the allocation scheme that its own stock will be allocated according to the provisions of that scheme), together with the need to secure accommodation to other homeless persons as a result of its duties under HA 1996, Part 7. The powers are, as a result, most likely to be exercised where the supply of the appropriate type of accommodation matches or exceeds local demand.

---

[440] HA 1996, s 192(3), added by Homelessness Act 2002, s 5 (in force from 31 July 2002 [England] or 30 September 2002 [Wales]). See also English Code, paras 15.5–15.11; Welsh Code, paras 18.49–18.51 for guidance.

[441] HA 1996, s 192(3), as added.

[442] See **17.12**.

[443] HA 1996, s 195(9).

[444] HA 1996, s 192(2) and (4).

[445] The Codes recommend that this power should be exercised to secure accommodation 'for a limited period only ... as part of a managed programme of accommodation': English Code, para 15.10; Welsh Code, para 18.51.

[446] Secure and introductory tenancies can only be allocated in accordance with the provisions of HA 1996, Part 6; see Chapter 1. English Code, para 15.6; Welsh Code, para 18.50.

17.219　The English Code suggests that accommodation might be secured under the powers for homeless key workers who do not have a priority need, particularly where it would be in the interests of the local community for accommodation to be provided for key workers to live in the local housing authority's district.[447] Recruiting workers to perform key public sector services (e g in hospitals, schools, fire services, or the police) is obviously an easier task if accommodation close by can be provided. The power can be used to secure short-term accommodation in the local housing authority's district for key workers to occupy as part of a managed programme to allow the applicants to obtain more settled accommodation in due course.

17.220　The English Code also suggests that local housing authorities should consider exercising their powers so as to comply with the European Convention on Human Rights and in circumstances where, if an available power was not exercised, they might be acting in a way incompatible with an applicant's Convention rights.[448] The expectation is therefore that the power may be used to secure accommodation where the applicant would normally have a priority need except that the member of his or her household who would confer the priority need is not eligible for assistance,[449] or where the applicant would be at risk of suffering inhuman or degrading treatment if accommodation was not secured.[450]

17.221　If accommodation is secured under these powers, it should be explained to the applicant that the accommodation is not secured for the long term and that the local housing authority and the applicant are expected to work together to obtain more settled long-term accommodation. If the accommodation is subsequently withdrawn from the applicant, reasonable notice of termination should be given.

17.222　There is no right to request a review of any refusal to exercise these powers in the applicant's favour, or of the local housing authority's decision as to the period for which the power will be exercised. A challenge to any of those decisions can only be brought by way of judicial review.

WHEN THE DUTIES AND POWERS EXPIRE

17.223　Nothing in HA 1996, Part 7 addresses the factual situation that arises when the period for which accommodation has been secured, whether under a

---

[447]　English Code, para 15.9.

[448]　English Code, para 15.8.

[449]　HA 1996, s 185(4) as amended; *R (Morris) v Westminster City Council* [2005] EWCA 1184, [2006] HLR 8, CA. A refusal to exercise the power in favour of an applicant who had an ineligible young dependent child was not considered unlawful in *R (Bangura) v Southwark London Borough Council* [2007] EWHC 1681 (Admin), (2007) September *Legal Action*, p 18, Admin Ct. See **12.28–12.31**.

[450]　See *R (Limbuela) v Secretary of State for the Home Department* [2005] UKHL 66, [2006] 1 AC 396, HL, and **20.90–20.98**.

power or duty, comes to an end. Normally there is no further statutory duty to accommodate under HA 1996, Part 7 when those duties end.[451] If a review or appeal is being pursued, the local housing authority may have a discretion to accommodate,[452] but otherwise there will be no continuing statutory obligation.

17.224 However, even when a duty or power has expired, it does not follow that the applicant will be instantly on the streets. A local housing authority, like any other public body, must behave reasonably and so ensure that the applicant has had sufficient warning of the termination of accommodation to make alternative arrangements.[453] It must, of course, give whatever notice is required to bring the existing tenancy or licence to an end, and in some circumstances will need to apply for an order for possession.[454] An applicant who has been given a non-secure tenancy of accommodation owned by the local housing authority may be able to argue in the possession proceedings that his or her circumstances are sufficiently exceptional that it would not be proportionate to make a possession order against him or her.[455]

ADDITIONAL DUTIES AND POWERS

Duties to applicants whose household includes a person under 18

17.225 Special provision is made in HA 1996, Part 7 for situations in which it appears to a local housing authority that it will be unlikely to owe the main housing duty to a family with dependent children. The objective is to ensure that in those cases, where HA 1996, Part 7 will not provide the necessary safety net of the main housing duty, the alternative safety net of provision of accommodation for children (under the Children Act 1989) is ready to be used by the time the local housing authority reaches its negative decision.

---

[451] Although it may be that the ending of main housing duty accommodation should be followed by a more limited duty, for example if the applicant is found to have become homeless intentionally but also to have a priority need. See *Newman v Croydon London Borough Council* [2008] EWCA Civ 1591, (2009) April *Legal Action*, p 22, CA, where the Court of Appeal refused permission to appeal on the grounds that the decision had been justified on the facts, but reserved for another occasion whether a different result might be required in 'a starker case'.

[452] See **16.36–16.55**.

[453] *R v Secretary of State for the Environment ex p Shelter and the Refugee Council* [1997] COD 49, QBD, and *R v Newham London Borough Council ex p Ojuri (No 5)* (1999) 31 HLR 631, QBD.

[454] These issues (and in particular the question of what reasonable notice must be given) are explored further at **18.83–16.97**.

[455] Article 8, Sch 1, Human Rights Act 1998. The issue of Article 8 and proportionality as a defence to possession proceedings is complex and beyond the scope of this book. See Luba, McConnell, Gallagher and Madge *Defending Possession Proceedings* (7th edn, 2010; and the online update, March 2011).

17.226 Where the applicant's household[456] includes a person under the age of 18, and the local housing authority has reason to believe that the applicant:

(1)   may not be eligible for assistance; or

(2)   may have become homeless intentionally; or

(3)   may have become threatened with homelessness intentionally,

the local housing authority must ask the applicant to consent to the referral of the essential facts of his or her case to the local children's services department or authority.[457] The local housing authority should not wait until its actual decision is made on the application under HA 1996, Part 7, but must obtain consent when the threshold conditions are met, which will usually be almost immediately after the application for homelessness assistance has been made.

17.227 This obligation is not triggered where the application is received from a lone applicant who is under 18, because such cases are covered by different liaison arrangements.[458]

17.228 Once the consent has been given, the essential facts and details of the application and of the subsequent HA 1996, Part 7 decision must be communicated to the children's services authority.[459] This early notification obligation applies to unitary authorities (thus requiring notification between departments) as well as to separate local housing authorities and children's services authorities.[460] Children's services should be alerted as quickly as possible, so as to have an opportunity to consider the case and plan their response well before the local housing authority has concluded its inquiries and reached any negative HA 1996, Part 7 decision.

17.229 If the applicant does not give his or her consent, the local housing authority may still disclose information about an application to the children's services department if it has reason to believe that a child is, or may be, at risk of significant harm.[461]

---

[456] In this context, the word 'household' is used to mean those persons who normally reside with the applicant as a member of his or her family, and any other persons who might reasonably be expected to reside with the applicant; see HA 1996, s 176 and **11.23–11.34**.

[457] HA 1996, s 213A(2).

[458] See **13.127–13.174** (England) and **13.214–13.218** (Wales). See also *R (M) v Hammersmith & Fulham London Borough Council* [2008] UKHL 14, [2008] 1 WLR 535, HL; *R (G) v Southwark London Borough Council* [2009] UKHL 26, [2009] 1 WLR, 2399, HL; *Provision of Accommodation for 16 and 17 year old young people who may be homeless and/or require Accommodation*, (April 2010, CLG and Children, Schools and Families) and *Provision of Accommodation for 16 and 17 year old young people who may be homeless* (Welsh Assembly Government, September 2010).

[459] HA 1996, s 213A(1) and (2). See also English Code, Chapter 13; Welsh Code, Chapter 17 for guidance.

[460] HA 1996, s 213A(3).

[461] HA 1996, s 213A(4). See also English Code, para 13.7; Welsh Code, para 17.4.

17.230 HA 1996, Part 7 contains a provision designed to ensure that the local housing authority cannot simply wash its hands of the applicant and pass responsibility to children's services. In the case of an applicant whose household includes a person under 18 and whom the local housing authority has decided:

- is ineligible for assistance; or

- has become homeless intentionally; or

- has become threatened with homelessness intentionally,

the children's services authority can call upon the local housing authority to provide such advice and assistance as is reasonable in the circumstances to help with the exercise of any children's services functions under Part 3 of the Children Act 1989.[462] In this way it is intended that there should be a seamless scheme of social welfare provision for the most vulnerable families. In a Parliamentary debate initiated by a former housing minister, the previous government spelt out its understanding that the scheme should work in this way.[463]

17.231 Any disagreement between the local housing authority and the children's services authority should be resolved by discussion and negotiation and not by litigation.[464]

17.232 The assistance that the applicant, or, more particularly, the applicant's children, can expect to receive from children's services under the Children Act 1989 is outlined in Chapter 20.[465]

Duties and powers to protect the applicant's property

Introduction

17.233 The provisions of HA 1996, Part 7 recognise that a safety net scheme of assistance for the homeless will not be comprehensive if all it achieves is shelter for the people involved. Most applicants who are actually homeless or threatened with homelessness will also have at least a few personal possessions that need safeguarding, ranging from a single bag containing a change of clothes at one extreme to a full house of furniture, personal possessions and pets at the other. HA 1996, Part 7 imposes duties, and provides powers, for the safeguarding of these possessions.[466]

---

[462] HA 1996, s 213A(5) and (6).
[463] *Hansard*, HC Deb, vol 417, cols 1092–1098 (6 February 2004).
[464] *R v Northavon District Council ex p Smith* [1994] 2 AC 402, HL, at 410 per Lord Templeman.
[465] See **20.55–20.73**.
[466] HA 1996, ss 211–212.

When duties are owed

17.234 A duty is owed to certain applicants[467] where the local housing authority has reason to believe that:

(1) there is a danger of loss of, or damage to, any of the applicant's personal property; and

(2) the danger arises because the applicant is unable to protect or deal with that property; and

(3) no other suitable arrangements have been or are being made.[468]

17.235 'Danger' in this context means a genuine or real danger. That is, something more than a possible danger, a slight risk or remote possibility of injury. It denotes a 'likelihood of harm'.[469] The duty will not therefore be triggered simply because property was left behind in a secure locked flat which was regularly visited by the applicant or by others on his or her behalf, giving rise to no greater risk of burglary than that experienced by a householder who is temporarily away from home.[470] Of course, the situation would be entirely different if the flat were insecure with 'a front door opened and banging in the wind', or the property was 'left in the gutter' after an eviction.[471]

17.236 If the local housing authority is or has been subject to:

(1) an interim duty to accommodate; or

(2) any of the accommodation duties towards people found to be homeless or threatened with homelessness; or

(3) any of the accommodation duties towards applicants whose cases are being considered for referral,

it owes an applicant the duty to take reasonable steps to prevent the loss of property or prevent or mitigate any damage to it.[472]

17.237 Even if no such duty is or was owed to an applicant,[473] the local housing authority has a power to take any steps it considers reasonable in order to protect personal property.[474]

---

[467] Identified at HA 1996, s 211(2). See **17.236**.
[468] HA 1996, s 211(1). See English Code, Chapter 20; Welsh Code, paras 16.40–16.45 for guidance.
[469] *Deadman v Southwark London Borough Council* (2001) 33 HLR 75, CA, at [20], per Ward LJ. See English Code, para 20.6.
[470] *Deadman v Southwark London Borough Council* (2001) 33 HLR 75, CA at [21], per Ward LJ.
[471] *Deadman v Southwark London Borough Council* (2001) 33 HLR 75, CA, at [25], per Ward LJ.
[472] HA 1996, s 211(2).
[473] Because he or she has been found not to be homeless or threatened with homelessness, or not to be eligible for assistance, and was never secured with interim accommodation.
[474] HA 1996, s 211(3).

17.238 The local housing authority should therefore start by asking and answering the following questions:

(1)　Is there a danger of loss or damage?

(2)　Is that because the applicant is unable to protect or deal with his or her possessions?

(3)　Is that because no other suitable arrangements have been made or are being made?

17.239 The local housing authority is only under the duty imposed by HA 1996, Part 7, if all of the questions are answered positively.

17.240 If the applicant seeks to challenge a local housing authority's decision that all or any of the questions are to be answered 'No', the only challenge would lie in a claim by judicial review on the basis that the local housing authority's decision was wrong in law.[475]

17.241 If the answer to all three questions is 'Yes', then the next question for the local housing authority is whether it owes or has owed the applicant any of the duties identified at **17.236**. If it has done, even if that duty has since ended, it remains under a duty to take reasonable steps to prevent any loss of, or damage to, the property. If the local housing authority never owed the applicant any of those duties, it may still choose to take reasonable steps to prevent loss or damage.

The extent of the duty to prevent loss or damage

17.242 The local housing authority can deal with the personal property in any way that is reasonably necessary in order to prevent or mitigate loss or damage to it. This includes storing the property itself, or arranging for it to be stored by some other person.[476] If the applicant's previous home is still available, the local housing authority may be able to arrange for the personal property to remain there if it can be adequately protected.[477]

17.243 The local housing authority has the right to impose conditions before it will take any steps to deal with personal property. These conditions can include levying reasonable charges and specifying in what circumstances the local housing authority may dispose of the property (usually upon reasonable notice to the applicant or if the applicant loses touch with the local housing authority and cannot be traced).[478]

---

[475]　*Deadman v Southwark London Borough Council* (2001) 33 HLR 75, CA. There is no right to request a statutory review in respect of any of the functions of the local housing authority that relate to the protection of possessions.

[476]　HA 1996, s 212(1).

[477]　English Code, para 20.7.

[478]　HA 1996, s 211(4). English Code, para 20.10; Welsh Code, para 16.43.

17.244 In order to perform the duty and protect the property, the local housing authority is entitled to enter the applicant's usual or last place of residence at all reasonable times.[479]

Which possessions must be protected?

17.245 The powers and duties are concerned with the 'personal property' of the applicant. This is enlarged by HA 1996, Part 7 to embrace the 'personal property of any person who might reasonably be expected to reside with him'.[480] That terminology echoes wording used elsewhere in HA 1996, Part 7.[481] It is wide enough to include those with whom an applicant resides and others with whom an applicant proposes to reside.

17.246 The term 'personal property' is not defined in HA 1996, Part 7. Given the wide variety of ways in which individuals accumulate possessions, the range will be enormous. In *R v Chiltern District Council ex p Roberts*,[482] the applicants were travelling showmen and the question arose as to whether their fairground equipment constituted their 'personal property'. Although, in the event, the case did not turn on the point, the judge said of 'personal property':

> 'I am inclined to the view that it would not extend to equipment used by an applicant in his business, at any rate where the business is conducted other than at the relevant accommodation ... The adjective "personal" is used to distinguish not only from real property, but from property used for commercial purposes, particularly if used elsewhere.'[483]

17.247 Nowadays, local housing authorities will want to avoid too restrictive a definition of personal property. Otherwise, they may run the risk of breaching the obligation on public authorities to take positive measures to prevent individuals losing their possessions contrary to the European Convention on Human Rights, Art 1, First Protocol.[484]

17.248 The most controversial issues in day-to-day practice arise where the personal possessions include pets. No local housing authority would deny that a goldfish bowl was 'personal property' – so, no less, the goldfish inside it. The safeguard for a local housing authority faced with a menagerie of cats, dogs and other pets is the power to impose, in advance, a condition that the applicant pays a reasonable charge for the action it takes.[485] Obviously, for applicants on a low income, the amount that is 'a reasonable charge' for them to pay may not meet the full cost to the local housing authority. But even the poorest applicant will have been paying something to feed the pets and so could be expected to pay a weekly charge equivalent to that amount so as to

---

[479]   HA 1996, s 212(1)(a).
[480]   HA 1996, s 211(5).
[481]   See **11.23–11.34**.
[482]   (1990) 23 HLR 387, QBD.
[483]   *R v Chiltern District Council ex p Roberts* (1990) 23 HLR 387, QBD, at 396, per Pill J.
[484]   Human Rights Act 1998, Sch 1.
[485]   HA 1996, s 211(4)(a).

contribute to kennelling or other fees. Local housing authorities troubled by the need to arrange kennelling for a few dogs should sympathise with Harlow District Council, which faced the prospect of dealing with a homeless applicant with 56 cats.[486]

The ending of the duty

17.249 In most cases, the duty to protect possessions will end at the same time as the most common form of the termination of the main housing duty, ie with the applicant's move to a longer-term home. But this is not necessarily so. In one case the main housing duty ended by the applicant becoming homeless intentionally from his accommodation secured under HA 1996, Part 7. The duty to protect his possessions did not cease, and the local housing authority which had wrongly disposed of his personal possessions later agreed to pay £6,000 compensation and waive its storage charges.[487]

17.250 If the applicant requests that his or her property is moved to a particular address (whether it is the applicant's new long-term home or anywhere else), and the local housing authority agrees, the duty will have ended once the property has been moved. The authority must inform the applicant that this will be the case before it agrees to move the property.[488]

17.251 Otherwise, the duty ceases if the local housing authority no longer has reason to believe that there is a threat of loss of, or damage to, the applicant's property. For example, there may have been a change of circumstances in that the applicant has found accommodation or has become able to afford to pay private storage charges.

17.252 Once the duty has ended, the local housing authority retains a power to continue to store any property previously in storage, upon the same or modified conditions.[489]

17.253 If the local housing authority is no longer under the duty, and no longer intends to exercise the power, to store the property, it must notify the applicant of that fact. The notification must include the reasons for the decision that the duty no longer applies.[490]

17.254 Once the local housing authority has accepted a duty, then it is under a private law obligation to the applicant as bailee of his or her goods until the duty is discharged and the goods are collected.[491] If property is damaged or destroyed, the applicant would be entitled to bring a private law action for

---

[486] *Harlow District Council v Sewell* [2000] JHL D29.
[487] *Complaint against Sutton London Borough Council*, 03/B/6452, 9 December 2004, (2005) April *Legal Action*, p 30.
[488] HA 1996, s 212(2); English Code, para 20.12; Welsh Code, para 16.42.
[489] HA 1996, s 212(3).
[490] HA 1996, s 212(4).
[491] *Mitchell v Ealing London Borough Council* [1979] QB 1, QBD.

damages for breach of that duty, conversion and/or trespass to goods. The local housing authority may have a defence available if it can show that it took all reasonable steps to prevent the loss or damage, or if the loss or damage was not reasonably foreseeable.

FAILURE TO COMPLY WITH ANY STATUTORY DUTY

17.255 If the local housing authority fails to comply with any of the duties owed to the applicant discussed in this Chapter, the appropriate remedy is a claim for a mandatory order in judicial review proceedings, requiring it to comply with its duty. Each of the different duties is absolute and cannot be deferred (unless specifically qualified in HA 1996, Part 7) once the statutory components or trigger factors are in place. However, as already indicated, no court will make a mandatory order where a local housing authority has not been acting unreasonably in its attempts to perform its duties as quickly as possible.[492]

17.256   There is no common law or statutory provision that gives the applicant a right to financial compensation (damages) if the local housing authority fails to comply with any of these duties,[493] unless the failure constitutes breach of the applicant's rights under the European Convention on Human Rights.[494] If that is the case, damages under the Human Rights Act 1998, s 8 may be awarded.[495]

17.257   The applicant may prefer to seek recompense through the complaints scheme of the local housing authority and thereafter by further complaint to the Local Government Ombudsmen or the Public Services Ombudsman for Wales.[496]

17.258   An applicant might have a legitimate expectation that the duty owed to him or her will be performed in a particular way, such as where the local housing authority had stated to the applicant that the duty would be performed by the provision of a certain type of accommodation (eg a 'permanent home' or 'a council tenancy'). Where an applicant has a legitimate expectation that the duty towards him or her will be performed in a certain way, the Administrative Court in judicial review proceedings may intervene to uphold that legitimate expectation.[497] It will be for the local housing authority (subject to the supervision of the court) to decide how that expectation should be

---

[492]   *R v Newham London Borough Council ex p Mashuda Begum* (2000) 32 HLR 808, QBD.
[493]   *R v Ealing London Borough Council ex p Parkinson* (1995) 29 HLR 179, QBD, unless the local housing authority fails to prevent loss or damage to property, having accepted a duty under HA 1996, s 211.
[494]   HRA 1998, Sch 1, right to respect for the applicant's home, family and private life and correspondence.
[495]   See **19.246–19.250** and **20.99–20.102**.
[496]   See **19.251–19.258**.
[497]   For judicial review, see **19.224–19.250**.

honoured. For example, the local housing authority may agree, or the court may order, that the applicant's points within the allocation scheme should include a number of points for legitimate expectation.[498]

---

[498] *R (Bibi and Al-Nashed) v Newham London Borough Council* [2001] EWCA Civ 607, (2001) 33 HLR 955, CA; *R (Ibrahim) v Redbridge London Borough Council* [2002] EWHC 2756 (Admin), (2003) February *Legal Action*, p 35, Admin Ct; and *R (Bibi) v Newham London Borough Council* [2003] EWHC 1860 (Admin), (2003) September *Legal Action*, p 28, Admin Ct.

Chapter 18

SUITABILITY OF ACCOMMODATION

INTRODUCTION

18.1 There are three distinct stages at which, in applying the homelessness provisions of the Housing Act 1996 (HA 1996), Part 7, the question of the 'suitability' of accommodation may arise:

(1) in the provision of interim accommodation (pending an initial decision, a review decision, an appeal decision, or the outcome of a local connection referral);[1]

(2) in the provision of accommodation in performance of a housing duty owed under HA 1996, Part 7, or pursuant to a power to accommodate given by it;[2] or

(3) in the making of offers of accommodation where those offers are relied upon to release the local housing authority from duties owed under HA 1996, Part 7.[3]

18.2 Guidance as to 'suitability' is also given in each of the two Codes of Guidance.[4] At the date of writing, it was expected that there would be additional statutory guidance for local housing authorities in England to take into account when considering the suitability of a private rented sector offer.[5]

'Suitable' accommodation for whom?

18.3 Any accommodation secured by a local housing authority in performance of its duties or the exercise of its powers under HA 1996, Part 7, or offered with a view to achieving a release from its duties, must be 'suitable'. But suitable for whom?

18.4 The focus throughout HA 1996, Part 7 is on the 'applicant'.[6] Accommodation secured for the applicant must be 'available' for him or her. 'Available' is given a special meaning, ensuring that accommodation is 'available' not only for the applicant, but also for all those people who might

---

[1] For 'suitability' in this context see **16.66–16.69**.
[2] See Chapter 17.
[3] See **17.23–17.53, 17.55–17.66, 17.92–17.131, 17.136–17.154, 17.182–17.189, 17.190–17.195** and **17.215–17.222**.
[4] See for general guidance *Homelessness Code of Guidance for Local Authorities* (Department for Communities and Local Government, Department for Education and Skills, Department of Health, July 2006) (the English Code), Chapters 16–17. *Code of Guidance for Local Authorities Allocation of Accommodation and Homelessness* (Welsh Government, August 2012) (the Welsh Code), Chapters 18–19.
[5] See Stop Press and Appendix 4.
[6] See HA 1996, s 193(2) for one example.

loosely be included in his or her household.[7] There is no precise mirroring of this expanded approach, beyond the needs of the individual applicant, in the treatment of 'suitability'.

18.5   When dealing with 'suitability', HA 1996, Part 7 refers to suitability for 'a person' rather than for 'the applicant'.[8] From this, one can infer that the determination of suitability requires regard not only for the individual needs of the applicant, but also for the needs of all those other persons who are members of the applicant's family who normally reside with him or her and of anyone else who might reasonably be expected to reside with him or her.[9] This is certainly the approach taken in the Codes of Guidance, which, when dealing with suitability, specifically direct attention not only to the applicant but also to others in his or her family or household.[10]

18.6   In one of the leading modern cases on 'suitability', the Court of Appeal proceeded on the uncontested assumption that the accommodation:

> '... has to be suitable for the particular homeless person *and his or her family*. There is no doubt that the question of whether or not the accommodation is suitable requires an assessment of all the qualities of the accommodation in the light of the needs and requirements of the homeless person *and his or her family*.'[11]

18.7   'Family' was there used by the court in the sense of the household for whom accommodation must be made available.[12]

'Suitable' accommodation from whom?

18.8   When performing a duty (or exercising a power) to secure accommodation, a local housing authority need not provide the particular

---

[7]   As defined at HA 1996, s 176. See **11.23–11.34**. See *R (Ogbeni) v Tower Hamlets London Borough Council* [2008] EWHC 2444 (Admin), (2008) October *Legal Action*, p 37, Admin Ct.

[8]   HA 1996, s 210(1).

[9]   HA 1996, ss 176, 206 and 210.

[10]   English Code, para 16.3; Welsh Code, paras 19.3 and 19.7 (all referring to 'household'). In *R (McCammon-Mckenzie) v Southwark London Borough Council* [2004] EWHC 612 (Admin), [2004] All ER (D) 174 (Mar), Admin Ct, accommodation was not suitable for the applicant because her 16-year-old son could not occupy it with her (and had been taken into care as a result). Two separate self-contained units of accommodation were not suitable for a family which would have needed to split up in order to occupy the units: *Sharif v Camden London Borough Council* [2011] EWCA Civ 463, [2011] HLR 32, CA (at the date of writing, Camden London Borough Council had been granted permission to appeal to the Supreme Court and the appeal had not been heard).

[11]   *R v Newham London Borough Council ex p Sacupima* (2001) 33 HLR 2, CA, at [28], per Latham LJ (emphasis added). More recently, the Court of Appeal referred to 'suitability': 'having regard to the circumstances of the occupant and his or her resident family' (*Codona v Mid-Bedfordshire District Council* [2004] EWCA Civ 925, [2005] HLR 1, CA, at [46], per Auld LJ). The House of Lords in *Ali & others v Birmingham City Council, Moran v Manchester City Council* [2009] UKHL 36, [2009] 1 WLR 1506, HL also referred to 'homeless families' rather than to 'applicants'.

[12]   *R v Newham London Borough Council ex p Sacupima* (2001) 33 HLR 2, CA, at [32].

accommodation itself. HA 1996, Part 7 enables the securing of accommodation to be achieved in any one of three ways. These are:[13]

(1) by the local housing authority itself providing the accommodation.[14] This might be, for example, by providing council-owned housing, a place in a council-run hostel or supported housing scheme, or accommodation that the local housing authority has itself rented from a private owner;[15] or

(2) by obtaining accommodation for the applicant from some other person.[16] The other person may be a private landlord, a private registered provider in England or registered social landlord in Wales, another local housing authority, an adult care and children's services authority, a voluntary organisation or anyone else;[17] or

(3) by giving the applicant such advice and assistance that she or he is able to obtain accommodation from another person.[18] This would include helping an applicant to purchase accommodation from another person using her or his own funds.[19]

18.9 It is the local housing authority, and not the applicant, that chooses which of the three options will be used. For some local housing authorities (those which have transferred all their housing stock and other accommodation to new owners), only the latter two options will be available.

18.10 Where the local housing authority is relying on an offer of 'suitable' accommodation to release it from the duty under HA 1996, Part 7 that it already owes, that offer may be of local housing authority accommodation (its own or obtained from another local housing authority) or of private registered provider or registered social landlord property, or of an assured shorthold tenancy from a private landlord.[20] An assured shorthold tenancy might be offered in performance of the main housing duty at HA 1996, s 193(2.)[21] For applicants whose applications for homelessness assistance were made on or after 9 November 2012 to a local housing authority in England, an assured shorthold tenancy might be offered in order to end the main housing duty by way of a 'private rented sector offer'. For applicants whose applications for

---

[13] HA 1996, s 206(1).
[14] HA 1996, s 206(1)(a).
[15] English Code, paras 16.11–16.16; Welsh Code, paras 18.15–18.22.
[16] HA 1996, s 206(1)(b).
[17] English Code, paras 16.17–16.31; Welsh Code, paras 18.23–18.34 and 18.38.
[18] HA 1996, s 206(1)(c).
[19] English Code, paras 16.32–16.36; Welsh Code, paras 18.41–18.44.
[20] The private landlord option is available for applicants whose applications for homelessness assistance were made on or after 9 November 2012 to a local housing authority in England (HA 1996, S 193(7) as amended by Localism Act 2011, s 148(4)). See **17.109–17.131**.At the date of writing, the amendments to HA 1996 made by LA 2011, ss 148–149 had not been brought into effect in Wales. Local housing authorities in Wales can make qualifying offers, which an applicant is free to accept or refuse, see **17.147–17.154**.
[21] See **17.32–17.35**, **17.55–17.68** and **17.136–17.137**.

homelessness assistance are made to a local housing authority in Wales,[22] an assured shorthold tenancy might be offered as a 'qualifying offer',[23] which the applicant is free to accept or to refuse, or as a 'private accommodation offer'[24]to an applicant who is a restricted case.[25]

Suitability in general

18.11 In determining whether accommodation is 'suitable', local housing authorities must consider the applicant and his or her household's particular individual needs. A general assessment of what accommodation may be suitable could be made in advance (for example, that a unit of accommodation of a particular size or type is likely to be required). However, the question posed by HA 1996, Part 7 is whether the specific property secured for, or offered to, the applicant is 'suitable'.[26] Accordingly, local housing authorities cannot adopt blanket policies prescribing that certain types of accommodation will be suitable in certain circumstances.[27] If the applicant raises a reason why the accommodation that has been secured or offered is not suitable, the local housing authority must consider that particular reason. It cannot restrict itself to general considerations of whether the accommodation would be suitable for the average or ordinary applicant.[28]

18.12 The duty to secure suitable accommodation is a continuing one. If an applicant's circumstances change, so that the accommodation secured in performance of a power or duty ceases to be suitable, the local housing authority has a duty to secure other, suitable accommodation.[29]

---

22   And applicants to local housing authorities in England whose applications for homelessness assistance were made before 9 November 2012.

23   HA 1996, s 193(7B)–(7F), see **17.147–17.154**.

24   HA 1996, s 193(7AC), see **17.165–17.168**.

25   For 'restricted cases', see **12.32–12.47** and **17.155–17.168** and **17.196–17.200**.

26   *R v Lambeth London Borough Council ex p Touhey* (1999) 32 HLR 707, QBD, at 716, 723 and 727, per Richards J.

27   English Code, para 17.4; Welsh Code, para 19.7.

28   *R v Brent London Borough Council ex p Omar* (1991) 23 HLR 446, QBD.

29   *R (Zaher) v Westminster City Council* [2003] EWHC 101 Admin, [2003] All ER (D) 253 (Jan), Admin Ct; and *R v Newham London Borough Council ex p Mashuda Begum* (1999) 32 HLR 808, QBD; English Code, para 17.8; and Welsh Code, para 18.1. An applicant in this situation, faced with a move from unsuitable accommodation to accommodation that the local housing authority has secured for him or her and has decided is suitable, will be at risk of the local housing authority deciding that its main housing duty has come to an end under HA 1996, s 193(5) if he or she refuses the offer of suitable accommodation (*Muse v Brent London Borough Council* [2008] EWCA Civ 1447, (2009) February *Legal Action*, p 32, CA; *Vilvarasa v Harrow London Borough Council* [2010] EWCA Civ 1278, [2011] HLR 12, CA and *Nzamy v Brent London Borough Council* [2011] EWCA Civ 283, [2011] HLR 20, CA). For the ending of the main housing duty under HA 1996, s 193(5) see **17.55–17.66** (England) and **17.136–17.137** (Wales).

The bottom line

18.13 Where accommodation is being secured under HA 1996, Part 7, it must be 'suitable'. That represents a statutory bottom line. As later parts of this Chapter demonstrate, 'suitability' is a flexible concept – what may be suitable for a few nights may not be suitable for a longer period.[30] But there is always an irreducible minimum standard below which accommodation must not fall:

> 'Although financial constraints and limited housing stock are matters that can be taken into account in determining suitability, there is a minimum and one must look at the needs and circumstances of the particular family and decide what is suitable for them, and there will be a line to be drawn below which the standard of accommodation cannot fall. If the accommodation falls below that line, and is accommodation which no reasonable local authority could consider to be suitable to the needs of the applicant, then the decision will be struck down, and an appeal to the resources argument will be of no avail.'[31]

18.14 The courts recognise that, from time to time, local housing authorities may find it simply impossible to secure 'suitable' accommodation. Strictly, the local housing authority concerned will be immediately in breach of an acknowledged statutory duty. On any legal challenge it will need compelling evidence in order to avoid the making of a mandatory order.[32] After all, if there is no accommodation reasonable for the applicant to occupy, he or she will still be 'homeless'.[33]

18.15 In *Codona v Mid-Bedfordshire District Council*,[34] Auld LJ, giving the leading judgment, surveyed the case law and held that there are three aspects of the issue of whether or not accommodation is 'suitable':

> '(1) suitability to a *Wednesbury* minimum level of suitability in the nature, location and standard of condition of the accommodation having regard to the circumstances of the applicant and his or her resident family, including the duration of their likely occupation of it;
>
> (2) the absolute nature of the duty which, though coupled with an elastic concept of suitability taking account of financial constraints and limited availability of accommodation, is not so elastic as to permit an offer below the *Wednesbury* minimum standard (or … outside the margin of appreciation); and
>
> (3) special consideration, in the regulatory provision for and in decision-making in individual cases, for the housing needs of particularly vulnerable applicants such

---

30 English Code, para 17.7.
31 *R v Newham London Borough Council ex p Sacupima* (2001) 33 HLR 2, CA, approving the first-instance decision of Dyson J, who had quoted Collins J in *R v Newham London Borough Council ex p Ojuri (No 3)* (1998) 31 HLR 452, QBD.
32 See *R v Lambeth London Borough Council ex p Touhey* (2000) 32 HLR 707, QBD.
33 HA 1996, s 175(3). See **11.75–11.120**.
34 [2004] EWCA Civ 925, [2005] HLR 1, CA.

as traditional gypsies with a view, so far as practicable and when considered with all the other circumstances, to facilitating their traditional way of life.'[35]

18.16 Where the applicant for homelessness assistance is applying on the basis that, although he or she has accommodation that is available for him or her, the accommodation is not reasonable to continue to occupy,[36] the accommodation might still be suitable for the applicant to occupy.[37] This is because the local housing authority will have to ask, and answer, two separate questions:

(1) Is the accommodation reasonable for the applicant to continue to occupy for as long as he or she would have to do unless the local housing authority takes action? If the answer is 'No', the applicant will be homeless.

(2) If the applicant is entitled to the main housing duty, is the accommodation suitable for him or her to occupy for the period during which the applicant can expect to live there until he or she receives an HA 1996, Part 6 offer or other accommodation?[38]

18.17 If the accommodation is not reasonable for the applicant to continue to occupy for one more night, then it will also not be suitable accommodation.[39]

Disputes over 'suitability'

Avenues for challenge

18.18 Although all accommodation secured under HA 1996, Part 7 must be 'suitable', not every decision about suitability is amenable to the statutory review procedure.[40]

18.19 The applicant has the right to request a review of a decision by the local housing authority that accommodation offered to him or her is suitable if:

(1) the accommodation has been secured in 'discharge of their duty'; and

(2) that duty is one of the duties owed under HA 1996, ss 190–193 or s 195;[41] or

---

[35] At [46].
[36] HA 1996, ss 175 and 176; see **11.8–11.174** for available accommodation and **11.175–11.120** for reasonable to continue to occupy.
[37] *Ali & others v Birmingham City Council, Moran v Manchester City Council* [2009] UKHL 36, [2009] 1 WLR 1506, HL.
[38] *Ali & others v Birmingham City Council, Moran v Manchester City Council* [2009] UKHL 36, [2009] 1 WLR 1506, HL, at [46]–[48], per Baroness Hale.
[39] *Ali & others v Birmingham City Council, Moran v Manchester City Council* [2009] UKHL 36, [2009] 1 WLR 1506, HL, at [47], per Baroness Hale.
[40] HA 1996, s 202(1). See **18.180–18.186** and **19.8–19.141** for a full description of that procedure.
[41] HA 1996, s 202(1)(b) includes reference to HA 1996, s 196 as one of the sections providing for a duty under HA 1996, Part 7, but this section contains a definition and not a duty.

(3)   the offer relied upon is made under a local housing authority's allocation scheme adopted under HA 1996, Part 6 and is intended to bring to an end the main housing duty in HA 1996, Part 7;[42] or

(4)   for applicants whose applications for homelessness assistance were made to local housing authorities in England on or after 9 November 2012,[43] a private rented sector offer intended to bring the duty to an end;[44] or

(5)   for applicants whose applications for homelessness assistance were made to local housing authorities in Wales,[45] and who are restricted cases,[46] a private accommodation offer intended to bring the duty to an end.[47]

18.20   It is plain, therefore, that there is no right to a statutory review of the suitability of accommodation offered in the exercise of a power.[48] Presumably, this is a statutory representation of the maxim 'beggars can't be choosers'.

18.21   Even if the offer is made under a duty to accommodate, it must be under one of the specifically prescribed duties for there to be a right to a statutory review.

18.22   In order to attract the right to request a review, the offer must be made in order to release the local housing authority from the main housing duty, and the offer must either be the 'final' offer of accommodation offered under HA 1996, Part 6[49] or, for applicants whose applications for homelessness assistance were made on or after 9 November 2012 to local housing authorities in England,[50] a private rented sector offer.[51] Any other offer made under HA 1996, Part 7, such as an offer of HA 1996, Part 6 which was not made as a final

---

[42]   HA 1996, s 202(1)(f). See **19.27–19.32**.
[43]   At the date of writing, the amendments to HA 1996 made by LA 2011, ss 148–149 had not been brought into effect in Wales.
[44]   As defined at HA 1996, s 193(7AA)–(7AC) as amended by LA 2011, s 148 (5)–(7) for applicants whose applications for homelessness assistance were made on or after 9 November 2012 to a local housing authority in England. At the date of writing, the amendments to HA 1996 made by LA 2011, ss 148–149 had not been brought into effect in Wales. The right to request a review is at HA 1996, s 202(1)(g) as amended by LA 2011, s 149(9).
[45]   And applicants to local housing authorities in England whose applications for homelessness assistance were made before 9 November 2012.
[46]   HA 1996, s 193(3B), see **12.32–12.47** and **17.155–17.158**.
[47]   HA 1996, s 193(7AA)–(7AC) prior to amendment by LA 2011, s 148. See **17.165–17.168**. The right to request a review is at HA 1996, s 202(1)(f) prior to amendment by LA 2011, s 149(9).
[48]   For example, under HA 1996, s 192(3) or s 195(9). Any challenge would have to be brought by way of judicial review.
[49]   HA 1996, s 193(7)–(7A) as amended by LA 2011, s 148(4), for applicants whose applications for homelessness assistance are made to a local housing authority in England on or after 9 November 2012. See **17.109–17.131**.
[50]   At the date of writing, the amendments to HA 1996 made by LA 2011, ss 148–149 had not been brought into effect in Wales.
[51]   HA 1996, s 193(7AA)–(7AC) as amended by LA 2011, s 148(5)–(7). See **17.109–17.131**.

offer, or an offer of an assured tenancy made outside HA 1996, Part 6 and not made as a private rented sector offer, would not attract the right to request a review.[52]

18.23 If a review on suitability is available and has been requested by the applicant, but is either unsuccessful or has not been determined by the local housing authority, the applicant can appeal to the county court on a point of law.[53]

18.24 'Suitability' decisions that do not fall within the scope of the statutory review scheme will need to be challenged by way of judicial review proceedings or under the local housing authority's complaints procedure.[54]

18.25 If the local housing authority and the applicant are agreed that accommodation which has been offered or secured is *not* suitable, the appropriate procedure in order to obtain suitable accommodation is for the applicant to bring judicial review proceedings for a mandatory order requiring the local housing authority to secure such suitable accommodation. That remedy is discretionary. The Administrative Court could refuse permission to seek judicial review if the breach of statutory duty was not particularly significant and of short duration,[55] or could refuse to make a mandatory order if the local housing authority demonstrated that it was doing all that it could to secure suitable accommodation.[56] But if there is plain and continuing failure and no clear evidence that everything possible is being done, the Administrative Court should grant a mandatory order.[57]

Grounds for challenge

18.26 The question of whether or not accommodation is 'suitable' is a factual one for the local housing authority to answer. It is not for the applicant, the applicant's adviser, or for a judge to determine.

18.27 Any applicant wishing to challenge the decision in the courts, and to argue that no reasonable local housing authority would have found that the accommodation was suitable for his or her needs, has a high hurdle to overcome.[58]

---

[52] A right to request a review is also available to an applicant who is a restricted case and who has been made a private accommodation offer, see **17.165–17.168**.
[53] HA 1996, s 204(1). See **19.146–19.201**.
[54] See 18.19 and **19.224–19.250**.
[55] *R v Newham London Borough Council ex p Sacupima* (2001) 33 HLR 2, CA, at [17].
[56] *R v Lambeth London Borough Council ex p Touhey* (2000) 32 HLR 707, QBD.
[57] *R v Newham London Borough Council ex p Mashuda Begum* (2000) 32 HLR 808, QBD; and *R (McCammon-Mckenzie) v Southwark London Borough Council* [2004] EWHC 612 (Admin), [2004] All ER (D) 174 (Mar), Admin Ct.
[58] *R v Haringey London Borough Council ex p Karaman* (1996) 29 HLR 366, QBD. See also *Watson v Wandsworth London Borough Council* [2010] EWCA Civ 1558, [2011] HLR 9, CA where a first-instance judge's conclusion that a review decision that accommodation was suitable had been perverse was overturned by the Court of Appeal.

18.28 A challenge may have a better prospect of success if it attacks the local housing authority's procedure in reaching its decision, or alleges a failure to consider a specific point raised, or a failure to have regard to a matter which ought to have been taken into account.

FACTORS THAT THE LOCAL HOUSING AUTHORITY MUST TAKE INTO ACCOUNT

18.29 As a matter of law, when it is determining whether particular accommodation is 'suitable', local housing authorities in both England and Wales are required to consider six matters:

(1) the provisions of the Housing Act 1985 relating to slum clearance and overcrowding;[59] and

(2) the provisions of Parts 1–4 of the Housing Act 2004 relating to housing conditions, houses in multiple occupation and licensing of accommodation;[60] and

(3) the affordability of the accommodation;[61] and

(4) the public sector equality duty at Equality Act 2010, s 149.[62] and

(5) the guidance given in the Codes of Guidance;[63] and

(6) the relevant content (if any) of their own homelessness strategies.[64]

18.30 Local housing authorities in England should also be aware that bed and breakfast accommodation made available under their duties to secure accommodation is deemed not to be suitable for applicants with family commitments, unless no other accommodation is available (and even then for at most only a 6-week period).[65] From 9 November 2012, they must also take into account the location of the accommodation offered, including four factors specified and any other issues relevant to the location.[66]

---

[59] HA 1996, s 210(1); Housing Act 1985, Parts 9 and 10. See **18.37–18.39**.

[60] HA 1985, s 210(1); Housing Act 2004 Parts 1–4. See **18.40–18.46**.

[61] HA 1996, s 210(2); Homelessness (Suitability of Accommodation) Order 1996, SI 1996/3204. See **18.47–18.48** and Appendix 2.

[62] *Pieretti v Enfield London Borough Council* [2010] EWCA Civ 1104, [2011] HLR 3, CA, see **18.49–18.50**.

[63] HA 1996, s 182(2). Guidance on suitability is at English Code, Chapter 17; Welsh Code, Chapter 19.

[64] Homelessness Act 2002, s 1(5). See **7.94–7.95**.

[65] Homelessness (Suitability of Accommodation) (England) Order 2003, SI 2003/3326. See **18.114–18.119** and Appendix 2.

[66] Homelessness (Suitability of Accommodation) (England) Order 2012, SI 2012/2601, in force 9 November 2012. See Appendix 2 and **18.52** and **18.62**.

18.31 Local housing authorities in England considering the making of a private rented sector offer[67] must also take into account 10 factors relating to physical condition and management of the property set out at arts 2 and 3 of Homelessness (Suitability of Accommodation) (England) Order 2012).[68]

18.32 Local housing authorities in Wales are required to take into account four other matters when deciding whether accommodation is suitable for a person in priority need[69] where the accommodation is secured under a statutory duty. Those are:

(a)   the specific health needs of the person;

(b)   the proximity and accessibility of adult care and children's services;

(c)   the proximity and accessibility of the support of the family or other support services; and

(d)   any disability of the person.[70]

18.33 Local housing authorities in Wales are prohibited from using bed and breakfast accommodation and other shared accommodation for all applicants who have a priority need except for very tightly defined periods of no more than two or six weeks (depending on the standard of the accommodation).[71]

18.34 The local housing authority's file notes, if not the terms of any letter written to the applicant, should demonstrate that these mandatory factors have been considered in respect of each unit of accommodation offered or secured. The presence of these factors in the statutory scheme ensures that a local housing authority cannot rely on accommodation offered unless it has informed itself, at least, of the physical attributes of the specific accommodation and its cost.

---

[67]   HA 1996, s 193(7AA)–(7AC) as amended by LA 2011, s 148 (5)–(7) made to applicants whose applications for homelessness assistance were made on or after 9 November 2012 to a local housing authority in England. At the date of writing, the amendments to HA 1996 made by LA 2011, ss 148–149 had not been brought into effect in Wales. See **17.109–17.131**.

[68]   SI 2012/2601. See Appendix 2. See **18.51–18.54**.

[69]   All applicants who are beneficiaries of any of the statutory duties to secure accommodation will have, or the local housing authority will have reason to believe that they may have, a priority need.

[70]   Homelessness (Suitability of Accommodation) (Wales) Order 2006, SI 2006/650 (W 71), art 3, in force from 3 April 2006. See also Welsh Code, para 19.12 and see **18.55–18.57** and Appendix 3.

[71]   Homelessness (Suitability of Accommodation) (Wales) Order 2006, SI 2006/650 (W 71); Welsh Code, para 19.13–19.29. See **18.120–18.128**.

18.35 Beyond the mandatory matters, however, numerous judicial decisions – most recently reviewed and applied by the Court of Appeal in *Codona v Mid-Bedfordshire District Council*[72] – have confirmed that 'suitability' has 'a broad meaning'.

> 'It must, as a matter of common-sense encompass considerations of the range, nature and location of accommodation as well as of its standard of condition and the likely duration of the applicant's occupancy of it. Standards of the condition of property are clearly important.'[73]

18.36 In the rest of this Chapter, we consider first the mandatory matters set out at **18.29**(1)–(4) above;[74] second, the additional statutory factors for local housing authorities in England,[75] third the additional statutory factors for local housing authorities in Wales;[76] and then the broader range of matters relevant to 'suitability'.[77]

Slum clearance and overcrowding

18.37 The provisions of the Housing Act 1985 direct local housing authorities to take action where dwelling houses in their districts are in such condition as to require demolition or clearance or are statutorily overcrowded.[78]

18.38 These strategic responsibilities would be wholly undermined if homeless households were to be placed in such poor or overcrowded premises at the initiative of the very same local housing authority. For that reason, the local housing authority is required by HA 1996, Part 7 to 'have regard to' those statutory provisions addressing such housing conditions when considering what would be 'suitable' accommodation.[79]

18.39 HA 1996, Part 7 does not expressly say that accommodation which fails to meet statutory minimum standards or would be statutorily overcrowded is never suitable. It follows, therefore, that a local housing authority could determine that the state of the accommodation contravenes the statutory standards, but that it is still suitable, although it would seem that the local housing authority would need some compelling reasons for such a determination.

---

[72] [2004] EWCA Civ 925, [2005] HLR 1, CA.
[73] Auld LJ at [34].
[74] **18.37–18.50**.
[75] Homelessness (Suitability of Accommodation) (England) Order 2012, SI 2012/2601, see **18.51–18.54** and Appendix 2.
[76] Homeless (Suitability of Accommodation) (Wales) Order 2006, SI 2006/650 (W 71), see **18.55–18.57** and Appendix 3.
[77] **18.58–18.104**.
[78] Housing Act 1985, Parts 9 and 10. See English Code, Annex 16 for the definition of statutory overcrowding.
[79] HA 1996, s 210(1).

Housing conditions, houses in multiple occupation and licensing of accommodation

18.40	The Housing Act 2004 amended the statutory rubric of the mandatory considerations on the question of 'suitability' with effect from 6 April 2006 in England (16 June 2006 in Wales). From that date, local housing authorities should have regard to 'slum clearance and overcrowding and Parts 1 to 4 of the Housing Act'.[80] The following paragraphs provide only a summary outline of the scope of Parts 1–4 of the Housing Act 2004 to which the amended text now draws attention.[81]

18.41	Part 1 of the Housing Act 2004[82] contains duties and powers enabling local housing authorities to inspect the condition of residential premises in their areas and to assess them for hazards. A 'hazard' is a risk of harm to the health of an actual or potential occupier deriving from a deficiency in the dwelling or neighbouring land. Where there are hazards identified as 'Category One' hazards, the local housing authority will be under a duty to take enforcement action. Where there are 'Category Two' hazards, the local housing authority has a power, not a duty, to require remedial action. The hazards relate to physiological requirements (damp and mould growth, excess cold or heat, pollutants), psychological requirements (relating to space, security, light and noise), protection against infection and protection against accident. The assessment of hazards is a complex process, including an assessment of the likelihood of an occurrence, the risk to health and safety of an actual or potential occupant, and the spread of possible harms.[83]

18.42	Neither the Housing Act 2004, nor the amended HA 1996, s 210, provide that accommodation will be, as a matter of law, unsuitable if it constitutes a Category One or Category Two hazard. However, the English Code contains a recommendation from the Secretary of State that, as a minimum, local housing authorities should ensure that accommodation secured under HA 1996, Part 7 duties is free of Category One hazards.[84] This should not be read as guidance that 'suitable accommodation' can contain Category Two hazards. The local housing authority should still explicitly consider the condition of the building and the risk to health and safety when deciding whether it is suitable.

---

[80]	HA 1996, s 210(1), amended by Housing Act 2004, s 265 and Sch 15, para 43 with effect from 6 April 2006 [England] and 16 June 2006 [Wales]: Housing Act 2004 (Commencement No 5 and Transitional Provisions and Savings) (England) Order 2006, SI 2006/1060, arts 1(1), (3)(c) and 2(1)(d); and Housing Act 2004 (Commencement No 3 and Transitional Provisions and Savings) (Wales) Order 2006, SI 2006/1535, arts 1(2)(c) and 2(b).

[81]	Useful summaries are given at paras 17.10–17.23 of the English Code; and at paras 19.3–19.6 of the Welsh Code.

[82]	Housing Act 2004, ss 1–54.

[83]	English Code, paras 17.10–17.15; Welsh Code, paras 19.3–19.4.

[84]	English Code, para 17.15; Welsh Code is more circumspect at para 19.3.

18.43 Part 2[85] of the Housing Act 2004 requires that houses in multiple occupation (HMOs), which include privately owned bed and breakfast and hostel accommodation, should be licensed by local housing authorities. For a licence to be granted, the local housing authority must be satisfied that the house is reasonably suitable for occupation by a specified number of persons or households, that the proposed licence holder and manager are both fit and proper persons and that the proposed management arrangements are satisfactory.[86]

18.44 Local housing authorities also have a discretionary power, in Part 3[87] of the Housing Act 2004, to designate areas in their districts as areas where there will be a requirement for the licensing of all privately rented housing.[88]

18.45 Where a local housing authority decides that there is no reasonable prospect of being able to grant a licence for a property under Parts 2 or 3 of the Housing Act 2004, Part 4[89] of Housing Act 2004 obliges the local housing authority to make a management order, taking over the management of the property. The local housing authority may also make management orders in respect of HMOs which do not fall within Parts 2 or 3 of the Housing Act 2004 and so do not require licences. Management orders may also be made where the local housing authority believes that they are necessary for the health and safety of the occupiers of the property, or of others in the vicinity. Local housing authorities can make interim management orders (for a maximum period of 12 months) and final management orders (maximum period five years).

18.46 There is nothing in the statutory scheme (HA 1996 and Housing Act 2004, Parts 2–4) explicitly providing that a house in multiple occupation which does not comply with these provisions is not 'suitable' accommodation. It would be difficult to describe a dwelling for which the owner does not have the requisite licence, or where he or she is in breach of the licence conditions, as 'suitable'. The English Code of Guidance directs local housing authorities to consider these provisions in particular when considering the suitability of bed and breakfast accommodation.[90]

Affordability

18.47 The local housing authority is directed, by specific statutory order, to consider the applicant's financial resources (including any available social

---

[85] Housing Act 2004, ss 55–78.
[86] English Code, paras 17.18–17.22; Welsh Code, paras 19 5–19.6. There are different regulations governing standards of management in England and in Wales.
[87] Housing Act 2004, ss 79–100.
[88] English Code, para 17.23; Welsh Code, para 19.5.
[89] Housing Act 2004, ss 101–147.
[90] English Code, para 17.38; see **18.107–18.113**.

security benefits), and the total costs of the accommodation, in determining whether particular accommodation would be 'suitable'.[91]

18.48   The Codes suggest that accommodation will not be suitable if the applicant's net income, after payment of housing costs, would be significantly less than Income Support or Jobseekers Allowance levels.[92] Nor will it be suitable if the applicant would not be able to afford basic essentials such as food, clothing, heating, or transport as well as the costs of the accommodation. Applicants who are in low-paid employment should not be placed in accommodation where they could only meet the housing costs by resorting to claiming benefit. If there is likely to be a substantial shortfall between housing benefit and the contractual rent, which the applicant would have to find from his or her own resources, accommodation will not be suitable.[93]

Public sector equality duty

18.49   The Equality Act 2010, s 149[94] requires all public authorities, including local housing authorities, to have

'due regard to the need to—

(a)   eliminate discrimination, harassment, victimisation and any other conduct that is prohibited by or under this Act;

(b)   advance equality of opportunity between persons who share a relevant protected characteristic and persons who do not share it;

(c)   foster good relations between persons who share a relevant protected characteristic and persons who do not share it'.[95]

18.50   They must have such 'due regard' when exercising any of their functions under HA 1996, Part 7. So the duty to have 'due regard' to these equality issues applies not only when a local housing authority is deciding policy questions but also to any decisions taken in respect of individual applications.[96]

---

[91]   Homelessness (Suitability of Accommodation) Order 1996, SI 1996/3204, at Appendix 2.
[92]   English Code, paras 17.39–17.40; Welsh Code, paras 19.30–19.31.
[93]   See *Eryurekler v Hackney London Borough Council* (2010) May *Legal Action*, p 24, Clerkenwell & Shoreditch County Court.
[94]   In force from 5 April 2011.
[95]   Equality Act 2010, s 149(1).
[96]   *Pieretti v Enfield London Borough Council* [2010] EWCA Civ 1104, [2011] HLR 3, CA.

Additional statutory factors for local housing authorities in England[97]

Private rented sector offers[98]

18.51 A 'private rented sector offer'[99] will only be of suitable accommodation if the local housing authority is satisfied of all of the following:

(a) that the accommodation is in a reasonable physical condition; and

(b) that the electrical equipment supplied with the accommodation meets the requirements of regs 5 and 7 of the Electrical Equipment (Safety) Regulations 1994;[100] and

(c) that the landlord has taken reasonable fire safety precautions with the accommodation and any furnishings supplied with it; and

(d) that the landlord has taken reasonable precautions to prevent the possibility of carbon monoxide poisoning in the accommodation; and

(e) that the landlord is a fit and proper person to act in the capacity of landlord, following consideration of whether he or she has:
  (i) committed any offence involving fraud or other dishonesty, or violence or drugs, or any offence listed in Sch3 to the Sexual Offences Act 2003;[101]
  (ii) practised unlawful discrimination on grounds of sex, race, age, disability, marriage or civil partnership, pregnancy or maternity, religion or belief, sexual orientation, gender identity or gender reassignment in, or in connection with, the carrying out of any business; and
  (iii) contravened any provision of the law relating to housing or of landlord or tenant law; and
  (iv) acted otherwise than in accordance with any applicable code of practice for the management of a house in multiple occupation, approved under Housing Act 2004, s 233;

---

[97] Homelessness (Suitability of Accommodation) Order 2012, SI 2012/2601, see Appendix 2, in force 9 November 2012.

[98] At the date of writing, the amendments to HA 1996 made by LA 2011, ss 148–149 had not been brought into effect in Wales.

[99] HA 1996, s 193(7AC) as amended by LA 2011, s 148(7) made to applicants whose applications for homelessness assistance were made on or after 9 November 2012 to a local housing authority in England. At the date of writing, the amendments to HA 1996 made by LA 2011, ss 148–149 had not been brought into effect in Wales. See **17.109–17.131**.

[100] SI 1994/3260. The Regulations require electrical equipment to be safe and in conformity either with EU harmonised standards or UK domestic standards.

[101] The Schedule as amended specifies 175 offences which are to be notified as sexual offences under Sexual Offences Act 2003, Part 2.

(f)   that where it is a house in multiple occupation subject to licensing under Housing Act 2004, s 55, it is licensed; and

(g)   that where it is a house in multiple occupation subject to additional licensing under Housing Act 2004, s 54, it has that additional licence; and

(h)   that the property has a valid Energy Performance Certificate; and

(I)   that the property has a current gas safety record in accordance with Gas Safety (Installation and Use) Regulations 1998;[102] and

(j)   that the landlord has provided a written tenancy agreement which he or she proposes to use for the purposes of a private rented sector offer and the local housing authority considers the agreement to be adequate.[103]

Any accommodation offered

18.52   The Order[104] also contains a non-exhaustive list of factors relating to the location of any accommodation. The local housing authority must take into account:

- where the accommodation is situated outside of its district, the distance of the accommodation from its district;

- the significance of any disruption which would be caused by the location of the accommodation to the employment, caring responsibilities or education of the applicant or of members of the applicant's household;

- the proximity and accessibility of the accommodation to medical facilities and other support which are currently used by or provided to the applicant, or used by or provided to members of the applicant's household, and which are essential to the applicant's well-being or to the well-being of members of the applicant's household; and

- the proximity and accessibility of the accommodation to local services, amenities and transport.[105]

18.53   These four factors must be considered by the local housing authority. The local housing authority must also, of course, consider any other factors regarding the location of the accommodation that might be relevant to its suitability, whether those other factors are already known to the local housing authority or are raised by the applicant.[106]

---

[102]   SI 1998/2451.
[103]   SI 2012/2601, art 3. See Appendix 2.
[104]   SI 2012/2601.
[105]   SI 2012/2601, art 2. See **18.58–18.186.**
[106]   For examples, the issues raised at English Code, para 17.41. See **18.58–18.104.**

18.54 At the date of writing, guidance on the Order was due to be published by DCLG.[107]

Additional statutory factors for local housing authorities in Wales[108]

18.55 Local housing authorities in Wales are additionally directed to consider:

(a) the specific health needs of the person;

(b) the proximity and accessibility of adult care and children's services;

(c) the proximity and accessibility of the support of the family or other support services; and

(d) any disability of the person,[109]

when determining whether or not accommodation is suitable for the needs of any person who has a priority need. In practice, this will mean all applicants for homelessness assistance for whom a duty to secure accommodation has been accepted.

18.56 These additional matters clearly reflect a concern that applicants who need specific support should be secured with accommodation that enables their support to be maintained. The suggestion is that accommodation should be located within a reasonable travelling distance of such services or networks as:

• hospitals, if the applicant or members of his or her household regularly attend hospitals;

• adult care and children's services, if support for health needs or children is being provided;

• family, friends or carers; or

• other facilities used by people with disabilities such as day centres etc.

18.57 These additional considerations apply to accommodation secured under any of the HA 1996, Part 7 *duties*, but not to accommodation secured under HA 1996, Part 7 *powers*.[110]

---

[107] See Stop Press and Appendix 4.
[108] Homelessness (Suitability of Accommodation) Wales Order 2006, SI 2006/650 (W 71), see Appendix 3. Welsh Code paras 18.11–18.14 and 19.10–19.29
[109] Homelessness (Suitability of Accommodation) (Wales) Order 2006, SI 2006/650 (W 71), art 3, in force from 3 April 2006.
[110] Homelessness (Suitability of Accommodation) (Wales) Order 2006, SI 2006/650 (W 71), art 1(5).

PARTICULAR ASPECTS OF 'SUITABILITY'

Location

18.58 The location of the accommodation secured or offered is always relevant to the decision as to whether or not it is suitable.[111]

18.59 Local housing authorities are under a duty to secure accommodation for applicants in their own districts, so far as is reasonably practicable.[112] It will not be 'reasonably practicable' for accommodation to be secured locally where the applicant or a member of his or her household would be at risk of violence if housed in the local housing authority's own district.[113]

18.60 If, exceptionally, suitable accommodation is secured by a local housing authority outside its own district, it must give written notice to the local housing authority for the district where the accommodation is situated, because it is that local housing authority that will have to provide other, non-housing services such as adult care and children's services, education, health care, etc.[114]

18.61 Normally, accommodation will be secured in the local housing authority's own area and the issue of location will focus on location within the local housing authority's boundaries. The Codes recommend that local housing authorities should avoid placing people in isolated accommodation, and that, wherever possible, they should be placed in accommodation as close as possible to where they were previously living. The need to travel to places of employment and/or education is also relevant. Care should be taken to minimise disruption to any young person's education.[115]

18.62 Local housing authorities in England considering the suitability of accommodation are required to take into account the following four non-exhaustive factors relating to the location of the accommodation:

- where the accommodation is situated outside of the local housing authority's district, the distance of the accommodation from its district;

---

[111] English Code, paras 17.4 and 17.41; Welsh Code, para 19.8. See also *R v Newham London Borough Council ex p Sacupima* (2001) 33 HLR 2, CA; *Codona v Mid-Bedfordshire District Council* [2004] EWCA Civ 925, [2005] HLR 1, CA.

[112] HA 1996, s 208(1). They are entitled to conclude that cheaper accommodation outside of their district would render the provision of more expensive accommodation within their district not 'reasonably practical': *R (Calgin) v Enfield London Borough Council* [2005] EWHC 1716 (Admin), [2006] HLR 4, Admin Ct. In deciding whether out of borough accommodation should be offered, the local housing authority should consider whether there is suitable accommodation available within the borough: *Sevine v Enfield London Borough Council* (2009) January *Legal Action*, p 27, Central London County Court.

[113] English Code, paras 16.7 and 17.6; Welsh Code, paras 18.9–18.10 which advises that 'violence' may include 'hate crime' and that ex-offenders or drug or alcohol users might benefit from being outside the district to help break links with previous contacts who could exert a negative influence.

[114] HA 1996, s 208(2)–(4). See **15.226–15.233**.

[115] English Code, para 17.41; Welsh Code, paras 18.11–18.14.

- the significance of any disruption which would be caused by the location of the accommodation to the employment, caring responsibilities or education of the applicant or of members of the applicant's household;

- the proximity and accessibility of the accommodation to medical facilities and other support which are currently used by or provided to the applicant, or used by or provided to members of the applicant's household, and which are essential to the applicant's well-being or to the well-being of members of the applicant's household; and

- the proximity and accessibility of the accommodation to local services, amenities and transport.[116]

18.63 The additional statutory matters to be considered by local housing authorities in Wales specifically refer to the proximity and accessibility of various support services and, therefore, by implication to the location of the accommodation.[117]

18.64 The applicant's need for family or other support in a particular area is relevant to the question of suitability,[118] as are any particular cultural considerations such as the need to be near particular shops or community centres. When considering the applicant's needs to be located in a particular area, however, the local housing authority can also take into account the length of time that accommodation is to be secured for. The shorter the period of time, the more the applicant could be expected to endure a certain degree of disruption to normal arrangements.[119]

18.65 The risk of the applicant suffering harassment or violence, and any particular vulnerability of the applicant and his or her household, in certain geographic areas is also relevant to the question of whether the location of the accommodation is suitable.[120] Where accommodation situated on an estate renowned for racist attacks was offered to an Asian family, the local housing authority had to have regard to the incidence of racist attacks and racial

---

[116] SI 2012/2601, art 2. At the date of writing, guidance is due to be published by the UK government. See Stop Press for details.

[117] Homelessness (Suitability of Accommodation) (Wales) Order 2006, SI 2006/650 (W 71), art 3; Welsh Code, paras 18.11–18.14. See **18.55–18.57**.

[118] *Mohamud v Haringey London Borough Council* (2000) November *Legal Action*, p 23, Edmonton County Court; and see Homelessness (Suitability of Accommodation) (Wales) Order, SI 2006/650 (W 71), art 3(c) directing local housing authorities in Wales specifically to consider the proximity and accessibility of the support of family or other support services; see **18.55–18.57**. In *Abdullah v Westminster City Council* [2007] EWCA Civ 1566, (2007) November *Legal Action*, p 38, CA, the reviewing officer found that the applicant 'would not be unable to cope' in accommodation outside the local housing authority's district and away from her social support network. The reviewing officer's decision was not wrong in law.

[119] *R v Westminster City Council ex p Abo-Ragheed* CO/4020/2000 (unreported) 27 November 2000, QBD.

[120] *R v Islington London Borough Council ex p Okocha* (1997) 30 HLR 191, QBD.

harassment, as well to evidence showing a general under-reporting of racist attacks in making its assessment of 'suitability'.[121]

18.66 Where the applicant alleges risk of violence, the local housing authority should consider the actual degree of risk to the applicant, the frequency of visits made by the perpetrator to the area, and any risk from friends or relatives of the perpetrator.[122]

18.67 The risk of violence in a particular location to an applicant who had given or was to give evidence in a murder trial has been held to be a relevant consideration on the question of 'suitability'.[123]

18.68 The English Code recommends that applicants who have suffered domestic violence may need to have 'gender-specific' accommodation, whose location is kept a secret and which has security measures and appropriate staffing.[124]

Duration of likely occupation

18.69 If the accommodation offered is a final offer of accommodation under HA 1996, Part 6 (relied upon to release the local housing authority from the main housing duty),[125] it would not necessarily be unreasonable for the local housing authority, when considering 'suitability', to expect the applicant to change schools, doctors, etc, although each case has to be considered on its individual facts.[126] However, it could be far more disruptive for an applicant offered accommodation under HA 1996, Part 7 to have to make those changes, as he or she would only be occupying the accommodation until the duty under HA 1996, Part 7 ended. It might also be disruptive for an applicant given a private rented sector offer[127] to have to make those changes, since the applicant may not have any legal right to occupy the accommodation offered for more

---

[121] *R v Tower Hamlets London Borough Council ex p Subhan* (1992) 24 HLR 541, QBD; see also *Villaruel v Richmond upon Thames* (2003) March *Legal Action*, p 31, Brentford County Court.

[122] *R v Southwark London Borough Council ex p Solomon* (1994) 26 HLR 693, QBD; *R v Hackney London Borough Council ex p Decordova* (1995) 27 HLR 108, QBD; *R v Haringey London Borough Council ex p Karaman* (1997) 29 HLR 366, QBD; and *Watson v Wandsworth London Borough Council* [2010] EWCA Civ 1558, [2011] HLR 9, CA.

[123] *R v Lambeth London Borough Council ex p Woodburne* (1997) 29 HLR 836, QBD; and see *R v Islington London Borough Council ex p B* (1997) 30 HLR 706, QBD.

[124] English Code, para 17.6.

[125] HA 1996, s 193(7) and (7A) as amended by LA 2011, s 148(4) for applicants whose applications for homelessness assistance were made on or after 9 November 2012 to a local housing authority in England. At the date of writing, the amendments to HA 1996 made by LA 2011, ss 148–149 had not been brought into effect in Wales. See **17.92–17.108** (England) and **17.138–17.146** (Wales).

[126] *R v South Holland District Council ex p Baxter* (1998) 30 HLR 1069, QBD; and *Williams v Birmingham City Council* [2007] EWCA Civ 691, [2008] HLR 4, CA.

[127] HA 1996, s 193(7AC) as amended by LA 2011, s 148(7) and made to applicants whose applications for homelessness assistance were made on or after 9 November 2012 to a local housing authority in England. At the date of writing, the amendments to HA 1996 made by LA 2011, ss 148–149 had not been brought into effect in Wales. See **17.109–17.131**.

than 12 months. It is for that reason that the Homelessness (Suitability of Accommodation) (England) Order 2012[128] specifically requires local housing authorities to consider the issue of the significance of any disruption to employment, caring responsibilities or education for the applicant and any member of his or her household, when considering the suitability of a private rented sector offer.[129]

18.70 The duration of expected occupation is relevant to whether or not accommodation is suitable:

> 'What is suitable for occupation in the short term may not be suitable for occupation in the medium term, and what is suitable for occupation in the medium term may not be suitable for occupation in the longer term.'[130]

Space and arrangement

18.71 The English Code provides that space and arrangement of the accommodation are 'key factors' in determining its suitability.[131] But that, like the judicial pronouncement from which it is drawn,[132] is not intended to suggest to the local housing authority that it must do anything other than consider *all* relevant matters.

18.72 Particular issues in relation to space and arrangement of accommodation can arise where there are children in the household, or elderly or disabled persons.[133] Accommodation which is not suitable and requires adaptations could be an offer of suitable accommodation (for the purpose of determining whether a refusal would bring the main housing duty to an end under HA 1996, s 193(5)[134] or (7)[135] or as a private rented sector offer[136]) if the offer is

---

[128]   SI 2012/2601, see Appendix 2.
[129]   SI 2012/2601, Art 2. See **17.110** for 'private rented sector offer'.
[130]   *Ali & others v Birmingham City Council, Moran v Manchester City Council* [2009] UKHL 36, [2009] 1 WLR 1506, HL, at [47] per Baroness Hale.
[131]   English Code, para 17.4; not in the Welsh Code.
[132]   *R v Brent London Borough Council ex p Awua* [1996] AC 55, HL, at 72, per Lord Hoffmann.
[133]   English Code, para 17.5.
[134]   Amended by LA 2011, s 148(3) for applicants whose applications for homelessness assistance were made on or after 9 November 2012 to a local housing authority in England. At the date of writing, the amendments to HA 1996 made by LA 2011, ss 148–149 had not been brought into effect in Wales. See **17.55–17.66** (England) and **17.136–17.137** (Wales).
[135]   HA 1996, s 193(7)–(7A) as amended by LA 2011, s 148(4) for applicants whose applications for homelessness assistance were made on or after 9 November 2012 to a local housing authority in England. At the date of writing, the amendments to HA 1996 made by LA 2011, ss 148–149 had not been brought into effect in Wales. See **17.92–17.108** (England) and **17.138–17.146** (Wales).
[136]   HA 1996, s 193(7AC) as amended by LA 2011, s 148(7) for applicants whose applications for homelessness assistance were made on or after 9 November 2012 to a local housing authority in England. At the date of writing, the amendments to HA 1996 made by LA 2011, ss 148–149 had not been brought into effect in Wales. See **17.109–17.131**.

accompanied with certain, binding and enforceable assurances as to the adaptations to be carried out before it is to be occupied in order to render the accommodation suitable.[137]

18.73 Where there are children, issues such as insecure door and window locks, access to a dangerous balcony, and inoperative fire doors will be relevant. They could produce a genuine risk to the health or safety of a child, and the local housing authority would be under a duty to consider those matters.[138]

18.74 Where the applicant, or any member of his or her household, is disabled, then the accessibility of the accommodation itself is relevant, as is the internal layout in terms of the provision of accessible bathroom and toilet facilities.[139]

18.75 In one case a local housing authority offered a five-bedroom house with one combined bathroom and toilet to an applicant to occupy with her husband, her ten children and two other family members. The applicant said that this accommodation could not be suitable as it would involve 14 people sharing one toilet. Rejecting that claim, the judge said that, when determining what is suitable accommodation, the local housing authority is entitled to take account of any general shortage of accommodation available to it in its district and the nature of the accommodation actually available to it.[140]

Standard of accommodation

18.76 Although the courts have recognised a minimum standard of suitability below which accommodation must not fall,[141] once that threshold is met it is for the local housing authority to determine the standard of the accommodation offered or secured. It must be remembered that even the 'main housing duty' under HA 1996, s 193(2) is only a safety net provision of temporary accommodation until the applicant's longer term housing needs are resolved. It would be wrong to raise expectations that this short-term accommodation will be of a high standard.

18.77 A local housing authority is entitled to have regard to the 'realities' in terms of the accommodation it can offer in areas of high demand where, therefore, 'a high standard of suitability cannot be obtained'.[142] The statutory

---

[137] *Boreh v Ealing London Borough Council* [2008] EWCA Civ 1176, [2009] HLR 22, CA.

[138] *R v Newham London Borough Council ex p Gentle* (1993) 26 HLR 466, QBD.

[139] *R (Amirun Begum) v Tower Hamlets London Borough Council* [2002] EWHC 633 (Admin), (2003) 35 HLR 8, Admin Ct; and *Boreh v Ealing London Borough Council* [2008] EWCA Civ 1176, [2009] HLR 22, CA. See also the somewhat surprising decision in *McDermott v Croydon London Borough Council* [2011] EWCA Civ 1696 (2012) April *Legal Action*, p 47, CA, that there was no error of law where a local housing authority had decided that accommodation was suitable even where a disabled man could not access the kitchen, since his disability prevented him from using the kitchen facilities even if he could get access.

[140] *R v Camden London Borough Council ex p Jibril* (1997) 29 HLR 785, QBD.

[141] See **18.13–18.17**.

[142] *R v Brent London Borough Council ex p Omar* (1991) 23 HLR 446, QBD, at 459 per Henry J.

references to 'slum clearance' and 'overcrowding' as mandatory considerations[143] indicate 'a relatively modest minimum standard that is relevant to the determination of suitability'.[144]

18.78 Obviously, once the applicant has taken up occupation of the accommodation, he or she can rely on the express or implied provisions of the tenancy agreement to secure any necessary repairs. Disrepair, and any other problems with the standard of the property (eg lack of soundproofing), can also be addressed by inviting the local Environmental Health Officer to inspect the accommodation.

18.79 Where the accommodation is offered under the allocation arrangements adopted under HA 1996, Part 6 (normally of long-term housing accommodation), a higher standard might be expected before the offer was to be considered 'suitable'.

Medical needs

18.80 The medical needs of the applicant and his or her household are clearly relevant to the question of suitability. When considering the suitability of accommodation offered to an applicant who has raised both medical and non-medical reasons as to why it might not be suitable, the local housing authority must take an overall or composite view of the applicant's needs.[145]

18.81 Where an applicant suffering from post-traumatic stress disorder rejected an offer of accommodation situated on the twenty-seventh floor, the local housing authority was under a duty to consider the medical evidence properly.[146] Where an applicant produced evidence that she had suffered a violent sexual assault on a housing estate, the local housing authority was under a duty to consider that evidence when deciding whether the offer of accommodation on an estate was suitable.[147] A local housing authority's decision that a property on the third or fourth floor, with no access by lift, was suitable for a single parent who suffered from back problems and who had two young children was quashed because it had failed to have proper or adequate regard to the medical evidence.[148] It was not wrong in law for a local housing

---

[143] See **18.37–18.39**. The Local Government Ombudsman found maladministration when an applicant was told to accept accommodation that was 'filthy' and in such a state as to be 'stomach turning'. The local housing authority paid the applicant £2,450 on the Ombudsman's recommendation in recognition of the distress caused (*Complaint against Nottingham City Council*, 05/C/02965, 19 April 2007).

[144] *R v Camden London Borough Council ex p Jibril* (1997) 29 HLR 785, QBD, at 792 per Stephen Richards sitting as a deputy High Court judge.

[145] *R v Lewisham London Borough Council ex p Dolan* (1993) 25 HLR 68, QBD.

[146] *R v Kensington and Chelsea Royal London Borough Council ex p Campbell* (1996) 28 HLR 160, QBD.

[147] *R v Islington London Borough Council ex p Thomas* (1997) 30 HLR 111, QBD, although, once the local housing authority had considered the medical evidence and decided that the offer was suitable, its decision was upheld.

[148] *R v Haringey London Borough Council ex p Sampaio* (1999) 31 HLR 1, QBD.

authority to have offered a maisonette with 13 internal steps to an applicant who suffered chronic back pain, even though there was medical evidence that climbing stairs would aggravate her back pain.[149] A local housing authority was wrong in law not to have obtained any information as to the risk to an applicant who suffered from epilepsy of occupying a small studio-bedsit property, where she said that she was at greater risk of injury during a fit than she would have been had she had larger accommodation.[150]

18.82   Local housing authorities in Wales are specifically directed to consider the health needs of the applicant, and any disability, along with proximity and accessibility of support services, when making a decision on the suitability of accommodation.[151]

Terms and tenure

18.83   The provisions of HA 1996, Part 7 do not require accommodation to be secured or offered on any particular terms, for any particular period, or with any security of tenure, in order for it to be 'suitable'.[152] However, if the accommodation is being offered on 'standard terms' set by the accommodation provider, those terms must be 'fair'.[153] A 'private rented sector offer'[154] must have a minimum fixed term for 12 months[155] and must be an assured shorthold tenancy.[156]

18.84   If the accommodation is self-contained premises, occupation is likely to be under a tenancy rather than on a licence. But even then the fairly minimal

---

[149]   *Abdi v Wandsworth London Borough Council* [2006] EWCA Civ 1099, (2006) October *Legal Action*, p 26, CA.
[150]   *Nazokkar v Barnet London Borough Council* (2011), February *Legal Action*, p 45, Central London Civil Trial Centre.
[151]   Homelessness (Suitability of Accommodation) (Wales) Order 2006, SI 2006/650 (W 71), art 3. See **18.55–18.57**.
[152]   Save that it must be affordable; see **18.47–18.48**.
[153]   In that they must not contravene the Unfair Terms in Consumer Contracts Regulations 1999, SI 1999/2083: *R (Khatun) v Newham London Borough Council* [2004] EWCA Civ 55, [2004] HLR 29, CA.
[154]   HA 1996, s 193(7AC) as amended by LA 2011, s 148(7) made to applicants whose applications for homelessness assistance were made on or after 9 November 2012 to a local housing authority in England. At the date of writing, the amendments to HA 1996, ss 148–149 had not been brought into effect in Wales. See Chapter **17.110** for private rented sector offers and **18.51–18.54** for the specific factors relating to suitability of private rented sector offers.
[155]   HA 1996, s 193(7AC)(c) as amended by LA 2011, s 148(7), see **17.110**. For applicants to local housing authorities in Wales, or to local housing authorities in England where their applications were made before 9 November 2012, a 'qualifying offer' (HA 1996, s 193(7D)(d)) must be for a fixed-term but no minimum period is specified. See **17.147–17.154**. For applicants to local housing authorities in Wales, or to local housing authorities in England where their applications for homelessness assistance were made before 9 November 2012, and who are 'restricted cases' (HA 1996, s 193(3B) see **12.32–12.47**), a 'private accommodation offer' must have a minimum fixed-term of 12 months (HA 1996, s 193(7AC)(c) prior to amendment by LA 2011), see **17.165–17.168**. Both 'qualifying offers' and 'private accommodation offers' must be of assured shorthold tenancies.
[156]   HA 1996, s 193(7AC)(a) as amended by LA 2011, s 148(7).

protection of the Protection from Eviction Act 1977 may not be available in respect of accommodation secured under HA 1996, Part 7.[157]

18.85 Although local housing authority accommodation can be secured under HA 1996, Part 7, it cannot be made available on a secure or introductory tenancy.[158] Likewise, accommodation rented by the local housing authority from a private owner and sub-let to the occupier will not be offered under a secure or introductory tenancy.[159] The occupier will simply be a bare contractual tenant.

18.86 Accommodation obtained from a private landlord or a private registered provider or registered social landlord to fulfil any interim duties will not be offered on an assured tenancy. So applicants will normally occupy their accommodation under, at best, assured shorthold tenancies.[160] An assured shorthold tenancy offered in performance of the main housing duty at HA 1996, s 193(2) was held by the Court of Appeal in principle to constitute an offer of suitable accommodation.[161]

18.87 The absence of any particular requirement for a minimum term, or for any security or stability, might enable a local housing authority to perform its duties under HA 1996, Part 7 by moving an applicant through a succession of very short-term placements. However, each unit of accommodation must itself be suitable. Furthermore, the very fact that the accommodation offered is yet another short-term placement, with minimum stability for the applicant, could, depending on the particular circumstances, render the accommodation 'not suitable'. The Welsh Code takes a different approach, advising that local housing authorities should test new approaches so as to reduce uncertainty and lack of security for applicants, such as converting accommodation used as 'temporary accommodation' into more settled housing, generally by making a qualifying offer[162] of an assured shorthold tenancy.[163]

18.88 In a landmark case decided under the homelessness provisions of Part 3 of the Housing Act 1985,[164] the House of Lords held that a local housing

---

[157] See the discussion at **16.93–16.97** and **17.224**.
[158] Housing Act 1985, Sch 1, para 4. English Code, para 16.13; Welsh Code, para 18.17. See *Westminster City Council v Boraliu* [2007] EWCA Civ 1339, [2008] HLR 42, CA.
[159] Housing Act 1985, Sch 1, para 6. English Code, paras 16.15–16.16; Welsh Code, paras 18.20–18.22.
[160] HA 1996, s 209. English Code, paras 16.21–16.22; Welsh Code, paras 18.24–18.29.
[161] *Griffiths v St Helens Council* [2006] EWCA Civ 160, [2006] HLR 29, CA.
[162] HA 1996, s 193(7B) for applicants to local housing authorities in Wales and applicants whose application for homelessness assistance were made before 9 November 2012 to local housing authorities in England. See **17.147–17.154** for qualifying offers.
[163] Welsh Code, paras 18.52–18.54.
[164] *R v Brent London Borough Council ex p Awua* [1996] AC 55, HL. Prior to this decision, it had been widely assumed that the duty at s 65(2) of the Housing Act 1985 to secure suitable accommodation for applicants required local housing authorities to grant secure tenancies from their own stock.

authority was not required to provide permanent accommodation in performing its duty to applicants for homelessness assistance. Lord Hoffmann said:

> '[T]here is no reason why temporary accommodation should ipso facto be unsuitable. If the tenure is so precarious that the person is likely to have to leave within 28 days without any alternative accommodation being available, then he remains threatened with homelessness and the council has not discharged its duty. Otherwise, it seems to me that the term for which the accommodation is provided is a matter for the council to decide. Provided that the decision is not *Wednesbury* unreasonable ... I do not think that the courts should lay down requirements as to security of tenure.'[165]

18.89 Following on from that decision, the Court of Appeal held that a local housing authority could perform its duty to secure 'suitable' accommodation by arranging for assured shorthold tenancies for applicants.[166] Evans LJ considered that the tenure of the accommodation secured could be relevant to the local housing authority's decision as to whether or not the accommodation was 'suitable' and held:

> '[T]he House of Lords' ruling that there is no requirement of permanence does not lead to the conclusion that there is no temporal requirement whatever. In my judgment the question of tenure is not left to the unfettered discretion of the [local housing] authority: its decision must be proportionate to the relevant circumstances of the particular case. These include, in my judgment, both the needs of the applicant and the situation in the local housing market.'[167]

18.90 These cases were considering the duty to secure suitable accommodation under s 65(2) of the Housing Act 1985 which was the statutory predecessor to HA 1996, Part 7.

18.91 Between 1997 and 2012, accommodation offered under HA 1996, Part 6 with a view to releasing the local housing authority from the main housing duty was usually offered as an assured, introductory or secure tenancy.[168] At the date of writing, that remains the case for applicants whose applications for homelessness assistance are made to local housing authorities in Wales or were made before 9 November 2012 to local housing authorities in England.[169] From 9 November 2012, local housing authorities in England will also be released

---

[165] *R v Brent London Borough Council ex p Awua* [1996] AC 55, HL, at 72, per Lord Hoffmann.
[166] *R v Wandsworth London Borough Council ex p Mansoor & Wingrove* (1996) 29 HLR 801, CA.
[167] *R v Wandsworth London Borough Council ex p Mansoor & Wingrove* (1996) 29 HLR 801, CA, at 811, per Evans LJ, followed and quoted with approval by Laws J (as he then was) when considering the duty under Housing Act 1985, s 65(2) in *R v Lambeth London Borough Council ex p Ekpo-Wedderman* (1998) 31 HLR 498, QBD; and by Richards J in *R v Lambeth London Borough Council ex p Touhey* (1999) 32 HLR 707, QBD.
[168] HA 1996, s 193(7). See **17.79–17.108** (England) and **17.79–17.91** and **17.138–17.146** (Wales).
[169] SI 2012/2599. At the date of writing, the amendments to HA 1996 made by LA 2011, ss 148–149 had not been brought into effect in Wales.

from the main housing duty by the making of a private rented sector offer as well as by making final offers under HA 1996, Part 6, if they choose to do so.[170]

18.92 In 2006, the Court of Appeal considered the distinction between local housing authorities offering assured shorthold tenancies under what were then known as 'qualifying offers'[171] (so bringing the main housing duty to an end if accepted by the applicant)[172] and offering them in performance of the main housing duty at HA 1996, s 193(2).[173] Considering 'qualifying offers',[174] May LJ said:

> 'The elaborate provisions for a qualifying offer of an assured shorthold tenancy from a private landlord in sub-section (7B) are there to recognise that, on the one hand, assured shorthold tenancies from private landlords have their disadvantages – the rent is not controlled and the tenure is technically insecure – but, on the other hand, some homeless applicants may reasonably prefer to accept the offer of such a tenancy rather than remain in temporary accommodation for a long time until they may be offered secure accommodation under Part 6. Some homeless applicants may therefore be prepared to accept an offer of an assured shorthold tenancy from a private landlord as the permanent accommodation which in practice it is often capable of being. But they must only do so with their eyes fully open, and the local housing authority must be satisfied that it is reasonable for the applicant to accept the offer. Applicants are entitled to reject the offer. But if they do accept it, the local housing authority's duty ceases.'[175]

18.93 When an assured shorthold tenancy is offered in performance of the main housing duty, it:

> 'may be technically insecure, but may in practice extend for a number of years. If the applicant accepts the offer and the accommodation subsequently ceases to be available, the authority's duty will have to be performed again, assuming that the applicant's circumstances have not otherwise relevantly changed.'[176]

18.94 For local housing authorities in England considering making private rented sector offers[177] to applicants whose applications for homelessness

---

[170] HA 1996, s 193(7AA)–(7AC) amended by LA 2011, s 148(5)–(7), see **17.109–17.131**.

[171] HA 1996, s 193(7B). At the date of writing, qualifying offers can be made to applicants whose applications for homelessness assistance are made to local housing authorities in Wales or were made before 9 November 2012 to local housing authorities in England.

[172] HA 1996, s 193(7B)–(7D) for applicants whose applications for homelessness assistance are made to local housing authorities in Wales or were made before 9 November 2012 to local housing authorities in England. See **17.147–17.154**.

[173] *Griffiths v St Helens Council* [2006] EWCA Civ 160, [2006] HLR 29, CA.

[174] HA 1996, s 193(7B). At the date of writing qualifying offers can be made to applicants whose applications for homelessness assistance are made to local housing authorities in Wales or were made before 9 November 2012 to local housing authorities in England.

[175] *Griffiths v St Helens Council* [2006] EWCA Civ 160, [2006] HLR 29, CA at [36]

[176] *Griffiths v St Helens Council* [2006] EWCA Civ 160, [2006] HLR 29, CA at [38].

[177] HA 1996, s 193(7AC) as amended by LA 2011, s 148(7) for applicants whose applications for homelessness assistance are made to local housing authorities in England on or after 9 November 2012. At the date of writing, the amendments to HA 1996 made by LA 2011, ss 148–149 had not been brought into effect in Wales. See **17.110**.

assistance were made on or after 9 November 2012,[178] this point will apply to those private sector rented offers. Local housing authorities in England should be careful to inform applicants whether an assured shorthold tenancy is being offered to them as a performance of the main housing duty[179] or in order to bring that duty to an end ie as a private sector rented offer.[180]

18.95　The applicant should know if the offer is made in performance of the main housing duty because the local housing authority must inform him or her that the offer of accommodation is not an offer of accommodation made under HA 1996, Part 6, nor is it a private rented sector offer.[181]

18.96　Similarly, an applicant will know that an offer is a private rented sector offer[182] because the local housing authority must have informed him or her:

- of the possible consequences of refusal or acceptance of the offer; and

- that he or she has the right to request a review of the suitability of the accommodation; and

- of the special provisions if he or she subsequently makes an application for homelessness assistance within two years of the date of his or her acceptance of the offer.[183]

18.97　Where an applicant has been given an assurance that she or he would be given a secure tenancy, that assurance can constitute a legitimate expectation.[184] The local housing authority is then under a duty, when considering what accommodation is suitable for the needs of the applicant and his or her household, to take into account the applicant's legitimate expectation to be given a secure tenancy. That does not amount to a duty to give the applicant automatic priority above other applicants on the local housing

---

[178] Localism Act 2011 (Commencement No 2 and Transitional Provisions) (England) Order 2012, SI 2012/2599.

[179] HA 1996, s 193(2) and (5). See **17.55–17.66**.

[180] See **17.109–17.131**.

[181] HA 1996, s 193(5) as amended by LA 2011, s 148(3) for applicants whose applications for homelessness assistance are made to local housing authorities in England on or after 9 November 2012. At the date of writing, the amendments to HA 1996 made by LA 2011, ss 148–149 had not been brought into effect in Wales. See **17.55–17.66**.

[182] HA 1996, s 193(7AC) as amended by LA 2011, s 148(7) for applicants whose applications for homelessness assistance are made to local housing authorities in England on or after 9 November 2012. At the date of writing, the amendments to HA 1996 made by LA 2011, ss 148–149 had not been brought into effect in Wales. See **17.110**.

[183] HA 1996, s 193(7AB) as amended by LA 2011, s 148(6) applicants whose applications for homelessness assistance are made to local housing authorities in England on or after 9 November 2012. At the date of writing, the amendments to HA 1996 made by LA 2011, ss 148–149 had not been brought into effect in Wales. See **17.105** and **17.122**. For the special provisions at HA 1996, s 195A inserted by LA 2011, s 149(4), see **9.89–9.95**. There is no obligation to notify the third point to restricted cases: HA 1996, s 193(7AB)(c) amended by LA 2011, s 148(6).

[184] Where such assurances have been given, they were usually given to applicants under Housing Act 1985, Part III: the previous homelessness provisions. See **4.53–4.54**.

authority's allocation scheme, but it does require it to adopt some method, such as the provision of additional points, to reflect that legitimate expectation.[185]

The applicant's views

18.98 The decision on suitability is for the local housing authority to make. HA 1996, Part 7 does not prescribe any specific inquiries to be undertaken before a local housing authority can determine whether particular accommodation will be suitable for a specific applicant. It need only ensure that it has had regard to the six prescribed matters it is required to consider in every case,[186] and to any other matters relevant to the circumstances of a particular case.

18.99 It may, if it wishes, invite the applicant's views on any general issues affecting the suitability of accommodation for him or her, or on a specific proposed offer or provision of accommodation. Indeed, the Codes contain advice that applicants should be given a chance to view the accommodation before being required to accept or refuse it.[187] This advice was published after the Court of Appeal's decision in *R (Khatun) v Newham London Borough Council*,[188] which held that there was no such obligation, and can therefore be taken as suggesting that viewing the accommodation is, at the very least, good practice.

18.100 However, a local housing authority may decide that the applicant's views as to suitability can be sufficiently aired at the review stage.[189]

Other considerations

18.101 Where a basement property on a large housing estate reminded the applicant, who was a refugee, of the prison in which she had been confined and tortured, the court quashed the local housing authority's decision that the accommodation was suitable, holding that this was an exceptional case.[190]

18.102 Where accommodation that was originally suitable was occupied by squatters before the applicant had been able to move in, it was held to be no longer suitable.[191] A local housing authority's decision, however, that squatted

---

[185] *R (Bibi and Al-Nashed) v Newham London Borough Council* [2001] EWCA Civ 607, (2001) 33 HLR 955, CA; *R (Ibrahim) v Redbridge London Borough Council* [2002] EWHC 2756 (Admin), (2003) February *Legal Action*, p 35, Admin Ct; and *R (Bibi) v Newham London Borough Council* [2003] EWHC 1860 (Admin), (2003) September *Legal Action*, p 28, Admin Ct. See **4.53–4.54**.

[186] See **18.29–18.57**.

[187] English Code, para 14.18; Welsh Code, para 16.30.

[188] [2004] EWCA Civ 55, [2005] HLR 29, CA.

[189] *R (Khatun) v Newham London Borough Council* [2004] EWCA Civ 55, [2005] HLR 29, CA. See also *Abed v Westminster City Council* [2011] EWCA Civ 1406, (2012) January *Legal Action*, p 21, CA.

[190] *R v Brent London Borough Council ex p Omar* (1991) 23 HLR 446, QBD.

[191] *R v Lambeth London Borough Council ex p Campbell* (1994) 26 HLR 618, QBD.

accommodation would be suitable once it had been repossessed and refurbished was held not to contain errors of law.[192]

18.103 Where an applicant had a cultural aversion to conventional bricks and mortar accommodation (having lived as a traveller all her life), an offer of conventional housing was held to be unsuitable for her needs. The local housing authority had failed to accord sufficient respect to her rights under the European Convention on Human Rights, Art 8(1).[193] However, if no sites or pitches are available, the local housing authority is not in breach of its statutory duty, nor of the applicant's rights under the Convention by making an offer of conventional accommodation unless that accommodation falls below the *Wednesbury* minimum standards of suitability.[194]

18.104 The English Code recommends that local housing authorities should be 'sensitive' to the importance of pets to some applicants, particularly elderly people and/or rough sleepers, when considering the suitability of accommodation offered.[195] If pets cannot be accommodated with the applicant, separate provision to kennel or otherwise look after them would fall under a local housing authority's duty to protect the applicant's property.[196]

TYPES OF ACCOMMODATION THAT MAY BE 'SUITABLE'

18.105 The Codes offer considerable guidance as to the types of accommodation that might be used by a local housing authority seeking to perform duties owed under HA 1996, Part 7 to secure 'suitable' accommodation.

18.106 The following review deals first with the forms of accommodation least likely to be suitable and progresses to accommodation more likely to be suitable.

Bed and breakfast accommodation

Generally

18.107 In general, bed and breakfast accommodation should only be regarded as suitable accommodation for any applicant when emergency accommodation

---

[192] *R v Ealing London Borough Council ex p Denny* (1995) 27 HLR 424, QBD.
[193] *R (Price) v Carmarthenshire County Council* [2003] EWHC 42 (Admin), (2003) March *Legal Action*, p 30, Admin Ct.
[194] English Code, para 16.38; Welsh Code, paras 18.46; and *Codona v Mid-Bedfordshire District Council* [2004] EWCA Civ 925, [2005] HLR 1, CA. See also *Thompson v Mendip District Council* (2010) April 2011 *Legal Action*, p 31, Taunton County Court; and *Sheridan v Basildon Borough Council* [2012] EWCA Civ 335, [2012] HLR 19, CA. See **18.13–18.17**.
[195] English Code, para 17.42.
[196] HA 1996, ss 211–212. See **17.233–17.254**.

is required at very short notice, and there is simply no better accommodation available. It should only be used as a last resort and for the shortest period possible.[197]

18.108 Bed and breakfast accommodation allocated to a family with six children, in a hostel where the other residents were single men with histories of drug abuse, psychiatric illness and violent behaviour, was held not to be suitable for the family's needs.[198] In a case where the applicant had occupied bed and breakfast accommodation for over 18 months, in circumstances where her 16-year old son could not live there and had been taken into care, the Administrative Court held that 'the time has now come when the claimant cannot expect to return to hostel accommodation'.[199]

18.109 Relevant considerations on whether or not bed and breakfast accommodation may be suitable include:

(1) the length of time that the applicant and his or her household are expected to occupy it;

(2) the efforts made by the local housing authority to find other suitable accommodation;

(3) the degree of likelihood of suitable accommodation becoming available in the near future; and

(4) any other factors affecting the individual applicant.

18.110 However, lack of resources available to the local housing authority is not a relevant consideration.[200]

18.111 Where bed and breakfast accommodation has been secured, local housing authorities should ensure that the accommodation is of a good standard. Bed and breakfast accommodation will normally be provided in a building which falls within the definition of a house in multiple occupation. Minimum standards are set out in the Codes of Guidance.[201]

18.112 If bed and breakfast accommodation has been secured under the local housing authority's duty to secure suitable interim accommodation,[202] and the local housing authority subsequently accepts a main housing duty,[203] it must

---

[197] English Code, paras 17.24–17.35; Welsh Code, paras 18.35–18.37 and 19.12–19.29.
[198] *Driver v Purbeck District Council* (1999) 10 CLD 407, Bournemouth County Court.
[199] *R (McCammon-Mckenzie) v Southwark London Borough Council* [2004] EWHC 612 (Admin), [2004] All ER (D) 174 (Mar), Admin Ct, at [15], per Keith J.
[200] *R (Khan) v Newham London Borough Council* [2001] EWHC (Admin) 589, (2001) October *Legal Action*, p 16, Admin Ct.
[201] English Code, paras 17.35–17.38 and Annex 17; Welsh Code, paras 19.12–19.29. See **18.40–18.46**.
[202] HA 1996, s 188(1). See **16.12–16.28**.
[203] HA 1996, s 193(2). See **17.23–17.168**.

consider anew whether or not the bed and breakfast accommodation is suitable for the needs of the applicant and his or her household with reference to that new duty.[204]

18.113 The Secretary of State and the Welsh Assembly Government have each advised, in statutory guidance, that bed and breakfast accommodation is not considered to be suitable accommodation for the needs of homeless 16- and 17-year-olds.[205]

The special rules in England

18.114 For local housing authorities in England, from 1 April 2004, bed and breakfast accommodation has been deemed to be unsuitable for applicants with family commitments.[206] It can only be used at all where 'no accommodation other than bed and breakfast is available[207] and for no longer than a total period of six weeks.[208] The six-week period does not include any periods of occupation before the rules came into force on 1 April 2004. Where an applicant has been referred from one local housing authority to another under the conditions of referral,[209] any period spent in accommodation secured by the notifying local housing authority will be disregarded when calculating the total period of occupation. The Code of Guidance advises that, even if these two conditions are satisfied, bed and breakfast accommodation should only be used 'as a last resort'.[210]

18.115 It follows that a local housing authority is required to satisfy itself that no other accommodation is available. The Code of Guidance is unclear how a local housing authority in England can demonstrate that 'no other accommodation' can be secured for the applicant in order to be able to justify its use of bed and breakfast. It simply advises that, in making the determination that no other accommodation can be secured, local housing authorities should take account of the cost to the local housing authority in securing accommodation, its affordability and location. A local housing authority is not under an obligation to include accommodation which is to be allocated under its allocation scheme when considering whether there is any alternative accommodation.[211] This suggests that a local housing authority

[204] *R (Chowdhury) v Newham London Borough Council* (2002) November *Legal Action*, p 24, Admin Ct (permission hearing); and *R (Cano) v Kensington and Chelsea Royal London Borough Council* [2002] EWHC 436 (Admin), (2002) December *Legal Action*, p 22, Admin Ct.
[205] *Provision of Accommodation for 16 and 17 year old young people who may be homeless and/or require Accommodation*, (April 2010, CLG and Children, Schools and Families); and *Provision of Accommodation for 16 and 17 year old young people who may be homeless* (Welsh Assembly Government, September 2010) and Welsh Code, para 19.14. See also **13.127–13.174** (England) and **13.214–13.218** (Wales).
[206] Homelessness (Suitability of Accommodation) (England) Order 2003, SI 2003/3326.
[207] SI 2003/3326, art 4(1)(a). English Code, paras 17.25–17.29.
[208] SI 2006/3326, art 4(1)(b).
[209] See Chapter 15.
[210] English Code, para 17.26.
[211] English Code, para 17.30.

could decide to secure bed and breakfast accommodation even though an empty council home or a stay at a five-star hotel might be technically 'available'. The authors, with respect, doubt the correctness of this particular guidance. We suggest that, for a local housing authority to demonstrate that no other accommodation was available, it must show that it has done more than merely check with its usual providers of short-term accommodation. It should have considered all possible means of providing accommodation other than bed and breakfast, including considering whether it has any empty properties that could be made available, making inquiries of all potential providers, both in its own district and any other districts where it would be suitable for the applicant and his or her household to be located for the expected duration.

18.116 It should also be noted that the obligation is a continuing one throughout the six-week period. It may be that no accommodation other than bed and breakfast is available for the first night after the local housing authority has come under a duty to secure accommodation, and so bed and breakfast accommodation will not be deemed to be unsuitable. That does not mean, however, that the local housing authority is then relieved of its obligation to consider whether any other accommodation is available after the first night. It cannot simply leave the applicant and his or her household in the bed and breakfast accommodation for a total period of six weeks.[212]

18.117 'Applicants with family commitments' are defined as applicants who are pregnant, or with whom a pregnant woman resides or might reasonably be expected to reside, or applicants with whom dependent children reside or might reasonably be expected to reside.[213]

18.118 'Bed and breakfast accommodation' is defined as accommodation which is not separate, self-contained premises and where a toilet, personal washing facilities or cooking facilities are shared between more than one household.[214] It does not include accommodation owned or managed by a local housing authority, a PRP or a voluntary organisation, and so use of bed and breakfast establishments owned by any of those organisations is not, as a matter of law, deemed unsuitable (although it may still be unsuitable for the particular needs of a specific applicant).[215]

18.119 This prohibition on the use of bed and breakfast by local housing authorities in England does not apply where accommodation is being secured in the exercise of a power, eg the power to accommodate pending a review or appeal.[216]

---

[212] The six-week period 'does not allow the temporarily accommodating council to sit back – it must make all efforts to find suitable accommodation' said Collins J in *R (Nagaye) v Bristol City Council* (2005) CO/3477/2005, (2005) August *Legal Action*, p 19, Admin Ct (consideration of permission).

[213] SI 2003/3326, art 2. English Code, para 17.26.

[214] SI 2003/3326, art 2. English Code, para 17.27.

[215] SI 2003/3326, art 2.

[216] SI 2003/3326, art 1(2). See **16.36–16.48, 16.49–16.55** and **17.215–17.222**.

The special rules in Wales

18.120 The special rules applying to the determination of 'suitable' by local housing authorities in Wales came into force in stages, concluding on 2 April 2008.[217] The Welsh legislation deals with use of bed and breakfast accommodation and, separately, other 'shared accommodation'.

18.121 'Bed and breakfast accommodation' has the same statutory definition in Wales as it does in England.[218] The Welsh Order requires that 'bed and breakfast accommodation' must meet one of two standards – the 'basic' and the 'higher' standard – in order to be 'suitable'.[219]

18.122 'Basic standard' is defined as accommodation that meets all the prescribed statutory requirements and has a manager who has been deemed by the local housing authority to be a fit and proper person with the ability to manage bed and breakfast accommodation.[220] 'Higher standard' is basic standard accommodation which also complies with various additional standards relating to minimum amounts of space, adequate heating, facilities for storing and cooking food, exclusive washing and toilet facilities, lockable entrance doors and a common room.[221]

18.123 There is also an additional category of 'small Bed and Breakfast accommodation', defined as bed and breakfast accommodation where the manager resides on the premises and there are fewer than seven bedrooms available for letting.[222]

18.124 As in England, the legislation applies only to accommodation secured under HA 1996 *duties*, not powers.[223] Periods of occupation before the relevant provisions of the legislation came into force are to be disregarded when calculating the total period of occupation.[224] If an applicant is referred from one local housing authority to another under the conditions of referral,[225] the period spent in accommodation secured by the notifying local housing authority will be disregarded when calculating the total period of occupation.[226]

---

[217] Homelessness (Suitability of Accommodation) (Wales) Order 2006, SI 2006/650 (W 71), art 1; Welsh Code, paras 19.10–19.29.

[218] SI 2006/650, art 2; Welsh Code, para 19.13; and see **18.118**.

[219] Detailed guidance is given in the Welsh Code at paras 19.21–19.290.

[220] SI 2006/650, art 2; Welsh Code, para 19.23.

[221] SI 2006/650, art 2 and Schedule; Welsh Code, para 19.24.

[222] SI 2006/650, art 2; Welsh Code, para 19.18.

[223] See **18.119**.

[224] Homelessness (Suitability of Accommodation) (Wales) Order 2006, SI 2006/650 (W 71), arts 6(4)(a) and 9(4)(a).

[225] See Chapter 15.

[226] Homelessness (Suitability of Accommodation) (Wales) Order 2006 SI 2006/650 (W 71), arts 6(4)(b) and 9(4)(b).

The rules since 7 April 2008

18.125 Since 7 April 2008, bed and breakfast accommodation has not been regarded as suitable for any applicant who has a priority need unless it is occupied for no more than 2 weeks (basic standard) or 6 weeks (higher standard).[227] If an offer of suitable alternative accommodation has been made during those periods and the person has chosen to remain in his or her bed and breakfast accommodation, higher standard small bed and breakfast accommodation can be considered suitable for an indefinite period.[228] In the case of basic standard small bed and breakfast accommodation, two offers of suitable alternative accommodation must be made and refused for it to be considered suitable indefinitely.[229]

18.126 The Welsh Order also effectively outlaws use of 'shared accommodation', which it defines as accommodation which is not separate, self-contained premises and where a toilet, personal washing facilities or cooking facilities are shared between more than one household, provided that it is not an institution registered under the Care Standards Act 2000.[230] Unlike 'bed and breakfast accommodation', 'shared accommodation' can be owned or managed by local housing authorities, registered social landlords or voluntary organisations.

18.127 Since 7 April 2008, 'shared accommodation' has not been regarded as suitable for an applicant who has a priority need unless it meets the higher standard.[231] Basic standard shared accommodation may be regarded as suitable for a period of no more than two weeks, or for a six-week period if during the initial two-week period an offer of suitable alternative accommodation has been made but the person has chosen to remain in the basic standard shared accommodation.[232]

18.128 If the 'shared accommodation' was owned or managed by a local authority or by a registered social landlord and was being used on 7 April 2008 for accommodation under HA 1996, Part 7, this provision did not apply until 4 April 2011.[233]

Hostels

18.129 The Codes recommend that hostels may secure suitable accommodation for applicants who would benefit from a supported environment. However, they warn against an automatic assumption that hostels will be the most appropriate form of accommodation for all vulnerable people. Those for whom it is more likely to be suitable are those experiencing a temporary crisis, so that

---

[227] SI 2006/650, arts 7 and 9; Welsh Code, paras 19.17–19.20.
[228] SI 2006/650, art 9(d) and (e); Welsh Code, para 19.18.
[229] SI 2006/650, art 9(c) and (d); Welsh Code, para 19.18.
[230] SI 2006/650, art 2; Welsh Code, para 19.20.
[231] SI 2006/650, art 8, Welsh Code, para 19.20.
[232] SI 2006/650, art 9(f) and (g); Welsh Code, para 19.20.
[233] SI 2006/650, art 10.

hostel accommodation provides an opportunity for them to take stock and then move on to live independently, or those whose need for a supported environment has been identified by a adult care services authority or department in a community care assessment.[234]

18.130 The hostels referred to in the Code are not the night shelter variety that simply secure accommodation overnight, leaving the applicant homeless again the next day.[235]

18.131 Some hostels, if privately run, will fall within the English or Welsh definitions of 'bed and breakfast' accommodation.[236] Since 7 April 2008, privately run hostels in Wales have been likely to fall within the definition of 'shared accommodation'.[237]

18.132 Hostels are also likely to fall within the definition of houses in multiple occupation and be subject to Parts 1–4 of the Housing Act 2004.[238]

Lodgings

18.133 Some young applicants, particularly those who are vulnerable, may benefit from lodgings rather than hostel or self-contained accommodation. Generally, such lodgings would be offered by landlords who provide a service for young people with support needs.[239]

Women's refuges

18.134 Women's refuges should generally be considered as emergency accommodation only and not be used to perform accommodation duties under HA 1996, Part 7.[240] Whether or not a particular refuge is suitable for a particular woman and her household will depend on the particular characteristics of the refuge and the applicant. The Codes of Guidance remind local housing authorities that using women's refuges to secure accommodation for female homeless applicants (and their children, if any) takes up bed space that would otherwise be available for the emergency occupation of women

---

[234] English Code, paras 16.25–16.26; Welsh Code, paras 18.31–18.32.
[235] *R v Waveney District Council ex p Bowers* [1983] QB 238, CA.
[236] For bed and breakfast accommodation generally, see **18.107–18.113**. For the English rules, see **18.114–18.119**. For the Welsh rules, see **18.120–18.128**.
[237] See **18.125–18.128**.
[238] See **18.40–18.46**.
[239] English Code, para 16.24; Welsh Code, para 18.30.
[240] See **11.12** and **11.113**. See also Baroness Hale in *Ali & others v Birmingham City Council, Moran v Manchester City Council* [2009] UKHL 36, [2009] 1 WLR 1506, HL, when she said, referring to submissions made by the Women's Aid Federation of England and Wales: 'They point out that a refuge is not simply crisis intervention for a few nights. It is a safe haven in which to find peace and support. But it is not a place to live. There are rules which are necessary for the protection of residents but make it impossible to live a normal family life. It is a place to gather one's strength and one's thoughts and to decide what to do with one's life.' per Baroness Hale at [43].

fleeing domestic violence. Where local housing authorities are able to persuade refuge organisers to make places available for applicants to whom HA 1996, Part 7 duties are owed, those places should be used for the minimum period possible.[241]

Mobile homes

18.135 Mobile homes are unlikely to be suitable for families with children, for the elderly, or for disabled applicants. Generally, if used at all, they should be used for emergency accommodation, when the local housing authority has not had an opportunity to arrange anything else. Holiday caravans should not be regarded as suitable at all.[242]

18.136 If the applicant normally occupies moveable accommodation and is homeless because she or he has no place at which to place the moveable home and reside in it,[243] the local housing authority is not required to provide a site or berth itself, but should consider whether sites, berths or pitches are reasonably available.[244] These may be its own sites, sites provided by other local housing authorities (in which case provision can be made by arrangement with the appropriate local housing authority), or private sites on which the local housing authority has been able to persuade the owner to receive the applicant and his or her home.[245]

18.137 Where an applicant has a strong cultural aversion to living in bricks-and-mortar accommodation, the only accommodation that would be suitable for his or her needs would be the provision of mobile or caravan accommodation, or a site on which to put the caravan or other mobile accommodation.[246]

Accommodation leased from a private landlord

18.138 Local housing authorities are able to lease accommodation from private owners, and then let it themselves to applicants who are owed a housing duty. This option, known as 'private sector leasing', is recommended in the Codes as a far preferable alternative to bed and breakfast accommodation.[247]

---

[241] English Code, para 16.27; Welsh Code, para 18.34.
[242] English Code, para 16.30; Welsh Code, para 18.39.
[243] HA 1996, s 175(2)(b). See **11.70–11.73**.
[244] English Code, para 16.37; Welsh Code, para 18.45.
[245] HA 1996, s 206(1)(a)–(c).
[246] *R (Price) v Carmarthenshire County Council* [2003] EWHC 42 (Admin), (2003) March *Legal Action*, p 31, Admin Ct; *Codona v Mid-Bedfordshire District Council* [2004] EWCA Civ 925, [2005] HLR 1, CA; Thompson v Mendip District Council (2010) April 2011 *Legal Action*, p 31, *Taunton County Court;* and *Sheridan v Basildon Borough Council* [2012] EWCA Civ 335, [2012] HLR 19, CA. However, note that 'if there is no prospect of a suitable site for the time being, there may be no alternative solution' (English Code, para 16.38; Welsh Code, para 18.46). See **18.162–18.172**.
[247] English Code, paras 16.15–16.16; Welsh Code, 18.20–18.22.

Although the applicant becomes a tenant of the local housing authority, this is not an introductory or secure tenancy.[248]

18.139 In accordance with the UK government's target of reducing the use of temporary accommodation,[249] the English Code encourages local housing authorities to plan ahead to when their leases of private rented accommodation are likely to expire, and then consider negotiating with the private owner to see if he or she would be willing to make an offer of the same accommodation directly to the applicant occupying it.[250] For local housing authorities in England dealing with applicants whose applications for homelessness assistance were made on or after 9 November 2012,[251] that offer would probably be a private sector rented offer[252] designed to bring the main housing duty to an end.[253] For applicants whose applications for homelessness assistance are made to local housing authorities in Wales,[254] the offer could be a 'qualifying offer'.[255] The Welsh Code advises that local housing authorities should explore making qualifying offers of accommodation being occupied by applicants under the main housing duty at HA 1996, s 193(2)[256] so as to turn accommodation from 'temporary to settled'.[257]

Local housing authority properties

18.140 Local housing authorities can use their own stock to secure accommodation under their HA 1996, Part 7 duty.[258] Tenancies granted by local housing authorities in performance of their own homelessness duties will not be secure or introductory tenancies.[259] The English Code advises against the use of social housing for temporary accommodation, except for short periods.[260]

---

[248] Housing Act 1985, Sch 1, para 6. *Westminster City Council v Boraliu* [2007] EWCA Civ 1339, [2008] HLR 42, CA. See **18.140**.

[249] See **8.12**.

[250] English Code, paras 16.39–16.43.

[251] SI 2012/2599 (c 104). At the date of writing, the amendments to HA 1996 made by LA 2011, ss 148–149 had not been brought into effect in Wales.

[252] HA 1996, s 193(7AC) as amended by LA 2011, s 148(7) for applicants whose applications for homelessness assistance are made to local housing authorities in England on or after 9 November 2012. At the date of writing, the amendments to HA 1996 made by LA 2011, ss 148–149 had not been brought into effect in Wales. See **17.110**.

[253] HA 1996, s 193(7AA)–(7AC) amended by LA 2011, s 148(5)–(7) for applicants whose applications for homelessness assistance are made to local housing authorities in England on or after 9 November 2012. At the date of writing, the amendments to HA 1996 made by LA 2011, ss 148–149 had not been brought into effect in Wales. See **17.109–17.131**.

[254] Or applicants whose applications for homelessness assistance are made before 9 November 2012 to a local housing authority in England.

[255] HA 1996, s 193(7B), see **17.147–17.154**.

[256] See **17.23–17.41**.

[257] Welsh Code, paras 18.27 and 18.52–18.54.

[258] HA 1996, s 206(1)(a). See also English Code, paras 16.12–16.13; Welsh Code, paras 18.15–18.18.

[259] Housing Act 1985, Sch 1, para 4. See English Code, para 16.13.

[260] English Code, para 16.12; Welsh Code, para 18.16, which suggests applicants should be encouraged to consider 'other options where practicable'.

Accommodation provided by other local housing authorities or social landlords

18.141 Local housing authorities may request other local housing authorities and other social landlords to assist them in the performance of their duties by providing accommodation for applicants who are owed housing duties. If requested, those bodies must co-operate and render assistance so far as is reasonable in the circumstances.[261] Other local housing authorities and social landlords could therefore assist either by providing temporary accommodation to meet a duty owed under HA 1996, Part 7, or by agreeing to accept a nomination made under the local housing authority's allocation scheme, thus enabling the local housing authority which owes the HA 1996, Part 7 duty to make the applicant an offer of HA 1996, Part 6 accommodation, so as to release it from its HA 1996, Part 7 duties.

18.142 A local housing authority cannot normally discharge its responsibility to secure 'suitable' accommodation by leaving the identification of the actual unit of accommodation to another local housing authority or social housing landlord. The decision about 'suitability' remains with the local housing authority which owes the HA 1996, Part 7 duty, so it must be able to assess the suitability of a specific property.[262]

18.143 If temporary accommodation is obtained from another local housing authority, the housing duty owed towards the applicant remains with the first local housing authority to which the applicant applied.

18.144 These voluntary arrangements are different from the arrangements for the referral of an applicant under the conditions for referral.[263] The Codes advise that accommodation secured under such voluntary, and often reciprocal, arrangements is particularly appropriate for the needs of applicants who might be at risk of violence or serious harassment in the area of the local housing authority to which they applied.[264]

Accommodation provided by private registered providers or by registered social landlords

18.145 As already noted,[265] local housing authorities can discharge their duty to secure accommodation by ensuring that suitable accommodation is obtained from another person.[266] That might be a private landlord or a private registered provider or registered social landlord.

---

[261] HA 1996, s 213. See also English Code, paras 16.23 and 16.29; Welsh Code, 18.38.
[262] *R (Cafun) v Bromley London Borough Council* [2000] All ER (D) 1425, Admin Ct.
[263] See **15.31–15.150**.
[264] English Code, para 16.29; Welsh Code, para 18.38.
[265] See **18.8–18.10**.
[266] HA 1996, s 206(1)(b).

18.146 Private registered providers and registered social landlords are required by HA 1996, s 213(1)(a) and by regulatory guidance to provide assistance to local housing authorities in the carrying out of those local housing authorities' homelessness duties.[267]

18.147 Where nomination arrangements have been set up, an offer of an assured, or an assured shorthold, tenancy from a private registered provider or registered social landlord could be made under the local housing authority's allocation scheme, and would therefore be capable of amounting to a final offer of accommodation made under HA 1996, Part 6, sufficient to release the local housing authority from the main housing duty.[268]

Accommodation provided by private landlords

18.148 Private landlords can also make accommodation available to help the local housing authority meet duties owed under HA 1996, Part 7. The Court of Appeal has held that assured shorthold tenancies can be secured under the local housing authority's main housing duty,[269] provided that, if the accommodation subsequently ceases to be available and the applicant's circumstances have not changed, the local housing authority acknowledges that its main housing duty will have to be performed again.[270]

18.149 It is not unusual for there to be confusion as to the identity of the landlord in these circumstances. Accommodation is often secured under tripartite arrangements between a property owner, a local housing authority and an applicant.[271] That accommodation could either have been leased by the local housing authority from the private landlord,[272] or the local housing authority may have arranged for the applicant to be granted a tenancy by the property owner. The identity of the landlord is therefore a question of fact.[273]

18.150 Since 9 November 2012, local housing authorities in England, dealing with applicants whose applications for homelessness assistance were made on

---

[267] HA 1996, s 213. See also English Code, paras 16.18–16.22 and Annex 5; Welsh Code, para 18.38. *The Regulatory Framework for Social Housing in England from April 2012* (2012, Homes and Communities Agency) and *Regulatory Framework for Housing Associations Registered in Wales* (2011, Welsh Government).

[268] HA 1996, s 193(6)(c), (cc) and (7)–(7A), see **17.79–17.108** (England) and **17.79–17.87** and **17.138–17.146** (Wales).

[269] HA 1996, s 193(2). See **17.23–17.41**.

[270] *Griffiths v St Helens Council* [2006] EWCA Civ 160, [2006] HLR 29, CA.

[271] *Apczynski v Hounslow London Borough Council* [2006] EWCA Civ 1833, (2007) April *Legal Action*, p 21, CA, at [6] per Neuberger LJ. In that case, the applicant occupied a room in a hotel owned by a private company, having been booked into the hotel by the local housing authority in performance of its housing duty owed to the applicant. He brought a claim against the local housing authority for damages for disrepair to the room. His claim was dismissed because the local housing authority was not his landlord.

[272] See **18.138–18.139**.

[273] *Apczynski v Hounslow London Borough Council* [2006] EWCA Civ 1833, (2007) April *Legal Action*, p 21, CA.

or after 9 November 2012,[274] have been able to bring their main housing duty to an end if an applicant accepts or refuses a private rented sector offer.[275] A private rented sector offer is:

- an offer of an assured shorthold tenancy made by a private landlord to the applicant in relation to any accommodation which is, or may become, available for the applicant's occupation; and

- made, with the approval of the local housing authority, in pursuance of arrangements made by the local housing authority with the landlord with a view to bringing the local housing authority's main housing duty to an end; and

- a fixed-term tenancy for a period of at least 12 months.[276]

18.151 There is provision for the Secretary of State in England to make regulations increasing the minimum length of the fixed term.[277] This power has not been exercised by the Secretary of State. However, the Secretary of State has made the Homelessness (Suitability of Accommodation) (England) Order 2012[278] containing a non-exhaustive list of four factors to be considered regarding the location of the accommodation and ten specific tests on the physical condition of the property and the standard of management of it before a private rented sector offer can be considered to be suitable.[279]

18.152 An applicant will know whether an assured shorthold tenancy is being offered to him or her in performance of the main housing duty[280] or as a private rented sector offer because there are specific notification requirements. If the accommodation is being offered under the main housing duty, the local housing authority must inform the applicant that the offer is not an offer of accommodation under HA 1996, Part 6 or a private rented sector.[281] Where a

---

[274] SI 2012/2601 (c 104). At the date of writing, the amendments to HA 1996 made by LA 2011, ss 148–149 had not been brought into effect.

[275] HA 1996, s 193(7AA)–(7AC) amended by LA 2011, s 148(5)–(7) for applicants whose applications for homelessness assistance are made on or after 9 November 2012 to a local housing authority in England. At the date of writing, the amendments to HA 1996 made by LA 2011, ss 148–149 had not been brought into effect in Wales. See **17.109–17.131**.

[276] HA 1996, s 193(7AC) amended by LA 2011, s 148(7) for applicants whose applications for homelessness assistance are made on or after 9 November 2012 to a local housing authority in England. At the date of writing, the amendments to HA 1996 made by LA 2011, ss 148–149 had not been brought into effect in Wales. See **17.110**.

[277] HA 1996, s 193(10)–(12) inserted by LA 2011, s 148(9) for applicants whose applications for homelessness assistance are made on or after 9 November 2012 to a local housing authority in England. At the date of writing, the amendments to HA 1996 made by LA 2011, ss 148–149 had not been brought into effect in Wales..

[278] SI 2012/2601. At the date of writing, statutory guidance was due to be published. See Stop press.

[279] See **18.51–18.54**.

[280] HA 1996, s 193(2) and (5). See **17.23–17.40** and **17.55–17.66** (England) **17.136–17.137** (Wales).

[281] HA 1996, s 193(5)(b) as amended by LA 2011, s 148(3) and for applicants whose applications for homelessness assistance are made on or after 9 November 2012 to a local housing authority

private rented sector offer is being made, and so the main housing duty will be brought to an end if the applicant accepts or refuses the offer, the applicant must be informed in writing of:

- the possible consequence of refusal or acceptance of the offer; and

- that he or she has the right to request a review of the suitability of the accommodation; and

- of the special provisions if he or she makes an application for homelessness assistance within two years of the date of the acceptance of the offer.[282]

18.153 Precisely because the applicant has the right to request a review of the suitability of accommodation, the fixed-term tenancy must contain a break clause in order to be suitable. Otherwise what happens if the applicant accepts the offer and requests a review of the suitability of accommodation and the review is successful? Without a break clause, the applicant remains contractually committed to pay rent for the remainder of the term (which must be 12 months or may be longer.)[283]

PARTICULAR APPLICANTS AND THEIR NEEDS

18.154 Precisely because the question of 'suitability' requires a person-centred approach, considerable statutory guidance is offered for those cases in which the provision of accommodation will need to be handled with particular sensitivity.

18.155 The Codes identify that some applicants may need support from adult care or children's services to assist them to maintain the accommodation which is to be secured. Local housing authorities should therefore consider whether an applicant has support needs and, if so, make arrangements for effective links with other agencies (eg the Supporting People team, adult care or children's services, and the health authority) so that a joint assessment of the applicant's housing needs can be carried out. The assessment should include consideration of what settled accommodation would be suitable for the needs of the applicant.[284]

---

in England. At the date of writing, the amendments to HA 1996 made by LA 2011, ss 148–149 had not been brought into effect in Wales. See **17.55–17.66**.

[282] HA 1996, s 193(7AB) as amended by LA 2011, s 148(6) and for applicants whose applications for homelessness assistance are made on or after 9 November 2012 to a local housing authority in England. For the special provisions for new applications see HA 1996, s 195A inserted by LA 2011, s 149(4) and in force from 9 November 2012 and see **9.89–9.95** and **17.171–17.181**. There is no obligation to notify the third point to restricted cases, see **17.159–17.162**. At the date of writing, the amendments to HA 1996 made by LA 2011, ss 148–149 had not been brought into effect in Wales.

[283] See **17.110**.

[284] English Code, Chapter 4, particularly paras 4.16–4.18, and para 16.4; Welsh Code,

18.156 There are special provisions governing the suitability of accommodation that is secured for eligible asylum-seekers. Since the duty to accommodate eligible asylum-seekers only applies to applicants whose applications for homelessness assistance were made prior to 3 April 2000, and who are still owed a main housing duty under HA 1996, s 193(2), we do not deal with these special provisions.[285]

Young people

18.157 Providing 'suitable' accommodation for young people can superficially seem difficult because of the rule that minors (persons aged under 18) cannot be the legal owners of an interest in land, which includes a tenancy. But they can be beneficial owners under a trust, and a tenancy granted to a young person takes effect as the grant of that tenancy on trust for the young person. The Codes recommend that children's services departments are asked to underwrite the tenancy and thus guarantee the rent in order to avoid a landlord's concern that he or she may not be able to recover rent from a minor.[286] This advice was described as 'not particularly informative' by the Court of Appeal in a case which discussed the legal framework surrounding the attempt to grant a tenancy to a minor.[287] The Court of Appeal held that, where a local housing authority purports to grant a tenancy to a minor, and the terms and conditions of that tenancy contain no reference to the tenant being a minor, the local housing authority holds the land in trust for the minor. As a result, it was a breach of that trust for the local housing authority to purport to serve a notice to quit on the minor, and the notice to quit was not effective to terminate the tenancy. To overcome these difficulties, the Court of Appeal suggested that licences to occupy accommodation where the minor does not have exclusive possession of that accommodation should normally be granted. Alternatively, the authors suggest, a tenancy could contain a declaration of trust appointing another person as the legal owner and trustee of the land.

18.158 Some homeless young people may need help with managing tenancies or with household budgeting. Close liaison with children's services and the local Supporting People team is recommended as essential. Other young people may benefit from supported accommodation before they are sufficiently

---

paras 18.4–18.5. The Local Government Ombudsman found maladministration where a vulnerable applicant who was being moved from one unit of temporary accommodation to another ended up with overlapping liabilities to pay rent. The Ombudsman said '[a]lthough the council says it offered and provided a degree of support, there apparently is not evidence to support substantial support and other advice' (*Complaint against Birmingham City Council*, 10 000 145, 20 December 2010, (2011) March *Legal Action*, p 28).

[285] Reference can be made to the first and second editions of this book (Jan Luba QC and Liz Davies, 1st edn, 2006; 2nd edn 2010).

[286] English Code, para 16.31; Welsh Code, para 18.40. See also *Complaint against Dover District Council*, 09 017 510, 31 July 2012 (2012) October *Legal Action*, p 38 where maladministration was found when the local housing authority failed to consider the advice in the Code and the other statutory guidance.

[287] *Alexander-David v Hammersmith & Fulham London Borough Council* [2009] EWCA Civ 259, [2009] HLR 39, CA, per Sullivan LJ at [13].

independent to manage a tenancy, although local housing authorities are reminded that they must consider each applicant's individual circumstances and not just assume that supported accommodation will be suitable for all young people. Generally, if the minor is also a parent, semi-independent accommodation with support is recommended. If the young parent is aged less than 16, she or he should always be referred to children's services for an assessment of his or her care needs.[288]

18.159 In *R (M) v Hammersmith & Fulham London Borough Council*,[289] the House of Lords held that local housing authorities should always refer children, aged less than 18 years, for an assessment by children's services. The expectation is that, unless the child's need for accommodation is relatively short-term, the responsibility for providing accommodation should be met by children's services under Children Act 1989, s 20, and so the child will receive not just accommodation but also the additional assistance to help and support him or her in the transition to independent adult living. The House of Lords stressed joint working between local housing authorities and children's services.

18.160 The referral to children's services does not avoid the local housing authority's duty to secure accommodation to the child while children's services carry out an assessment and consider whether he or she is a child in need pursuant to Children Act 1989, s 20.[290] This emphasis on joint working between local housing authorities and children's services' authorities was reiterated by the House of Lords in *R (G) v Southwark London Borough Council*,[291] where the children's services' department was criticised for referring a homeless 17-year-old to the housing department, to make an application for homelessness assistance, rather than assessing the child's needs under the Children Act 1989. Both the UK government and the Welsh Government subsequently published statutory guidance to local housing authorities and children's services. Each set of guidance emphasises that homeless children are likely to be children 'in need' and services should primarily be provided under Children Act 1989.[292] If the child is being accommodated under HA 1996, Part 7 duties, each set of guidance advises that bed and breakfast accommodation would not be suitable.

Families with children

18.161 When offering or securing accommodation for families with children, local housing authorities are advised to ensure that all babies and young

---

[288] English Code, paras 12.15–12.17.
[289] [2008] UKHL 17, [2008] 1 WLR 535, HL, see **13.273**.
[290] See **13.145–13.168** (England) and **13.214–13.218** (Wales) and **20.74–20.80**.
[291] [2009] UKHL 26, [2008] 1 WLR 1299, HL.
[292] *Provision of Accommodation for 16 and 17 year old young people who may be homeless and/or require Accommodation*, (April 2010, CLG and Children, Schools and Families) and *Provision of Accommodation for 16 and 17 year old young people who may be homeless* (Welsh Assembly Government, September 2010). See also **13.151–13.164** (England) and **13.216–13.218** (Wales).

children in temporary accommodation have the opportunity to receive health and developmental checks from health visitors or other health professionals.[293]

Gypsies and travellers

18.162 Local housing authorities are advised to consider the needs and lifestyles of applicants who are gypsies and travellers when considering how to secure suitable accommodation. Where an applicant has a 'cultural aversion to the prospect of "bricks and mortar" accommodation', local housing authorities are advised that sites, or pitches, should be provided.[294] It is for the local housing authority to determine whether a particular applicant has 'a cultural aversion'.

18.163 In determining whether there is a 'cultural aversion', local housing authorities should:

'carefully … examine a gypsy's claim for such special consideration and, if satisfied that it is genuine, whether in all the circumstances of the case, it should attempt to meet it, and, if so, how. Those circumstances should, of course, include the likely duration of occupation in respect of which an offer is to be made.'[295]

18.164 In particular, they should consider:

(1)   whether the applicant and his or her family lived in a caravan; and

(2)   whether they subscribe to a gypsy culture; and

(3)   whether they are itinerant or nomadic for a substantial part of the year; and

(4)   whether itinerancy is linked to their livelihood; and

(5)   whether they subscribe to the relevant features of the gypsy life.[296]

18.165 The Codes add, drawing on decisions of the European Court of Human Rights,[297] that local housing authorities must also take into account

---

[293]   English Code, paras 4.16–4.18 and 16.10; Welsh Code, paras 18.12–18.14.

[294]   *R (Price) v Carmarthenshire County Council* [2003] EWHC 42 (Admin), (2003) March *Legal Action*, p 31, Admin Ct, and see *Codona v Mid-Bedfordshire District Council* [2004] EWCA Civ 925, [2005] HLR 1, CA. English Code, para 16.38; Welsh Code, para 18.46. See **18.135–18.137**.

[295]   *Codona v Mid-Bedfordshire District Council* [2004] EWCA Civ 925, [2005] HLR 1, CA, at [49], per Auld LJ.

[296]   *Codona v Mid-Bedfordshire District Council* [2004] EWCA Civ 925, [2005] HLR 1, CA, at [49]–[51], per Auld LJ.

[297]   For example, *Connors v United Kingdom* [2004] HLR 52, ECtHR.

their obligations to act consistently with the Human Rights Act 1998, and in particular the applicant's right to respect for his or her private and family life, and his or her home.[298]

18.166   Local housing authorities will have to address whether or not sites are available on four different occasions:

(1)   in determining whether or not they have 'reason to believe' that an applicant may be homeless, in that there is no place where the applicant is entitled or permitted to place and live in his or her mobile home or caravan – if so, and if they also have 'reason to believe' that an applicant may be eligible and may have a priority need, they have a duty to secure suitable interim accommodation pending notification of their decision;[299]

(2)   in determining whether or not the applicant is actually homeless according to the statutory test;[300]

(3)   in determining, if a main housing duty is owed to the applicant, what suitable accommodation could be offered to the applicant in performance of the main housing duty;[301] and

(4)   in determining whether the main housing duty has come to an end.[302]

18.167   If, during any part of this process, a place on an acceptable permanent site becomes available, is suitable for the applicant's needs, and has been secured for him or her to occupy, the applicant will no longer be 'homeless', as there will be somewhere where he or she is entitled or permitted to park his or her mobile home or caravan and to live in it. If this occurs while the applicant is occupying interim accommodation under HA 1996, s 188(1), the local housing authority will be able to notify him or her that he or she is no longer homeless, and no further duty is owed.

18.168   If no permanent site is available, the local housing authority's duty is to secure 'suitable' accommodation. The starting point is that, if the applicant is accepted as having a cultural aversion to bricks and mortar, a temporary site should be found, so that, at least, 'suitable' accommodation has been secured under either the interim accommodation duty or the main housing duty.[303]

---

[298]   English Code, para 16.38 and Welsh Code, para 18.46, referring to Art 8 of the European Convention on Human Rights and the Human Rights Act 1998, Sch 1.
[299]   HA 1996, s 188(1). See **16.12–16.28**.
[300]   HA 1996, s 175(2)(b). See Chapter 11 in general and in particular **11.70–11.74**.
[301]   HA 1996, s 193(2).
[302]   HA 1996, s 193(5)–(7F) as amended by LA 2011, s 148(3)–(9) for applicants whose applications for homelessness assistance were made on or after 9 November 2012 to local housing authorities in England. At the date of writing, the amendments to HA 1996 made by LA 2011, ss 148–149 had not been brought into effect in Wales. See **17.42–17.168**.
[303]   *Thompson v Mendip District Council* (2010) April 2011 *Legal Action*, p 31, Taunton County Court.

18.169 But, given the shortage of permanent and temporary sites for travellers, what if no site is available?

18.170 The Code of Appeal has held that:

> 'where land is not available, or cannot readily be made available, on which a gypsy applicant can station his or her caravan, it is open to a local authority to provide other accommodation of the conventional bricks and mortar kind, providing that it satisfies the *Wednesbury* minimum line of suitability.'[304]

18.171 The Codes reflect this advice.[305] It follows that 'bricks and mortar' can be provided in performance of the interim duty to secure accommodation pending inquiries,[306] and of the main housing duty,[307] only if no site is available and the conventional accommodation is suitable in all other aspects.

18.172 Although not fitting entirely happily with the statutory scheme in HA 1996, Part 7, in practice if a site were then to be offered to, and accepted by, the applicant, the understanding would be that the main housing duty had come to an end.[308]

ADVICE AND ASSISTANCE WHICH SECURES ACCOMMODATION

18.173 As already noted,[309] as an alternative to providing accommodation (or arranging for someone else to secure accommodation), a local housing authority may discharge its duty to secure that suitable accommodation is available for the applicant and his or her household by:

> '... giving him such advice and assistance as will secure that suitable accommodation is available from some other person.'[310]

---

[304] *Codona v Mid-Bedfordshire District Council* [2004] EWCA Civ 925, [2005] HLR 1, CA, at [47], per Auld LJ. Followed and applied in *Lee v Rhondda Cynon Taf CBC* [2008] EWCA Civ 1013, (2008) November *Legal Action*, p 20, CA and in *Sheridan v Basildon Borough Council* [2012] EWCA Civ 335, [2012] HLR 19, CA.

[305] English Code, para 16.38; Welsh Code, para 18.46.

[306] HA 1996, s 188(1). See **16.12–16.28**.

[307] HA 1996, s 193(2). See **17.23–17.168**.

[308] The provision of a suitable site would render the applicant no longer 'homeless'. This is not one of the events that can bring the main housing duty at HA 1996, s 193(2) to an end (HA 1996, s 193(5)–(7F)). However, assuming that the applicant moves from the HA 1996, s 193 accommodation to the site, he or she would 'voluntarily cease[s] to occupy as his only or principal home the accommodation made available' (HA 1996, s 193(6)(d)), and the main housing duty would come to an end. See **17.75–17.78**.

[309] See **18.8**.

[310] HA 1996, s 206(1)(c).

18.174 This is different from the distinct duties under HA 1996, Part 7 to provide advice and assistance to applicants who have no priority need, have become homeless intentionally, or are threatened with homelessness.[311]

18.175 If the advice and assistance provided under HA 1996, s 206(1)(c) enables the applicant to succeed in obtaining suitable accommodation, the local housing authority's HA 1996, Part 7 duty to him or her will have been performed. If suitable accommodation is not obtained, the local housing authority remains under that duty to secure accommodation for the applicant.

18.176 The Codes suggest, as examples of this method of performing the duty, the provision of advice on the financing of house purchases, advice on shared ownership schemes, financial assistance with rent deposits, or practical advice and assistance to obtain accommodation already identified by the applicants themselves.[312] So, if it is known that suitable accommodation is available to an applicant in a particular place, the duty may be performed by the provision of the information and assistance they need to get to that place (which might even be in another country).[313]

SUITABILITY: DECISIONS AND CHALLENGES

Decisions

18.177 Save in the exceptional cases mentioned at **18.19**, there is no strict requirement for a local housing authority to notify its decision that it considers particular accommodation secured in performance of a duty owed under HA 1996, Part 7 (or under an HA 1996, Part 7 power) to be 'suitable' for the applicant. Nor is there any duty to provide reasons for such a decision.[314]

18.178 Usually, however, such a decision will be notified in writing if:

(1) an applicant is being told that accommodation initially secured under an interim duty is subsequently being treated as suitable accommodation secured in performance of a different accommodation duty (if an applicant remains in the same accommodation during different stages of the local housing authority's handling of his or her application under HA 1996, Part 7), since the local housing authority is under a duty at each stage to consider whether the accommodation is suitable for an applicant's needs;[315] or

(2) if the applicant has raised a concern or complaint about the accommodation secured or offered; or

---

[311] HA 1996, ss 190(2)(b) and (3), 192(2) and 195(5). See **17.201–17.214**.
[312] English Code, paras 16.32–16.36; Welsh Code, paras 18.41–18.44.
[313] *R v Bristol City Council ex p Browne* [1979] 1 WLR 1437, DC.
[314] See **10.75–10.81**.
[315] *R v Lambeth London Borough Council ex p Touhey* (2000) 32 HLR 707, QBD.

(3)   if there is some other reason why it makes good administrative practice to give such a notice.

18.179   If such notice is given, it would be good practice for the applicant to be advised of any right to review and the time limit within which that right should be exercised.

Statutory reviews

18.180   As already noted,[316] the applicant has the right to request a statutory review of the local housing authority's decision that accommodation offered to him or her under HA 1996, ss 190(2), 193, or 195 is suitable. Additionally, the applicant may seek a review of the 'suitability' of a final offer of accommodation made under HA 1996, Part 6 where that is being relied upon to bring a main housing duty to an end.[317] Applicants whose applications are made to a local housing authority in England on or after 9 November 2012,[318] who are made private rented sector offers,[319] can request a review of the suitability of the private rented sector offer.[320] Applicants to local housing authorities in Wales[321] who are restricted cases[322] and who are made private accommodation offers intended to bring the main housing duty to an end[323] may also request a review of the suitability of the accommodation offered.[324] The Codes note that asking for a review of suitability of accommodation does not bring the main housing duty to an end.[325]

Informal reviews

18.181   Informally, an applicant can, at any time, request that the local housing authority reconsider its decision that the accommodation secured under HA 1996, Part 7 is suitable. An applicant might need to take that step if

---

[316]   See **18.19**.
[317]   HA 1996, s 202(1)(f). See **19.27–19.32**.
[318]   SI 2012/2599 (c 104). At the date of writing, the amendments to HA 1996 made by LA 2011, ss 148–149 had not been brought into effect in Wales.
[319]   HA 1996, s 193(7AC) as amended by LA 2011, s 148(7) for applicants whose applications for homelessness assistance was made on or after 9 November 2012 to a local housing authority in England. At the date of writing, the amendments to HA 1996 made by LA 2011, ss 148–149 had not been brought into effect in Wales. See **17.109–17.131**.
[320]   HA 1996, s 202(1)(g) as amended by LA 2011, s 149(9) for applicants whose applications for homelessness assistance was made to a local housing in England on or after 9 November 2012. At the date of writing, the amendments to HA 1996 made by LA 2011, ss 148–149 had not been brought into effect in Wales.
[321]   And applicants to local housing authorities in England whose applications for homelessness assistance were made before 9 November 2012.
[322]   HA 1996, s 193(3B), see **12.32–12.47**.
[323]   HA 1996, s 193(7AA)–(7AC) prior to amendment by LA 2011. See **17.165–17.168**.
[324]   HA 1996, s 202(1)(g) prior to amendment by LA 2011.
[325]   See English Code, para 17.45; Welsh Code, para 19.9.

accommodation that was originally suitable for the applicant when first occupied has become unsuitable as a result of a change in the applicant's circumstances.[326]

Offers which end duties

18.182   Four types of offer of 'suitable' accommodation raise special issues. If these offers are refused by an applicant, the making of the offer can bring to an end the main housing duty owed under HA 1996, Part 7. They are:

(1)   an offer of suitable accommodation in performance of the main housing duty;[327] or

(2)   a final offer of suitable accommodation made through the allocation arrangements in HA 1996, Part 6;[328] or

(3)   for applicants to local housing authorities in England whose applications for homelessness assistance were made on or after 9 November 2012,[329] a private rented sector offer;[330] or

(4)   for applicants to local housing authorities in Wales[331] who are 'restricted cases'[332] or 'restricted threatened homelessness cases'[333] only, a 'private accommodation offer'.[334]

---

[326]   *R v Southwark London Borough Council ex p Campisi* (1999) 31 HLR 560, CA; and *R v Newham London Borough Council ex p Mashuda Begum* (1999) 32 HLR 808, QBD. In *Muse v Brent London Borough Council* [2008] EWCA Civ 1447, (2009) February *Legal Action*, p 32, CA, the applicant refused to move from main housing duty accommodation which had become unsuitable to new accommodation offered to her which the local housing authority had decided was suitable for her and her household. As a result, the local housing authority's main housing duty to her came to an end under HA 1996, s 193(5) (see **17.55–17.66**).

[327]   HA 1996, s 193(5) as amended by LA 2011, s 148(3) for applicants whose applications for homelessness assistance were made on or after 9 November 2012 to local housing authorities in England. See **17.55–17.66**. For applicants to local housing authorities in Wales, or applicants to local housing authorities in England whose applications were made before 9 November 2012, see **17.136–17.137**.

[328]   HA 1996, s 193(7) as amended by LA 2011, s 148(4) or applicants whose applications for homelessness assistance were made on or after 9 November 2012 to local housing authorities in England. See **17.92–17.108**. For applicants to local housing authorities in Wales, or applicants to local housing authoritiesin England whose applications were made before 9 November 2012, see **17.138–17.146**.

[329]   SI 2012/2599 (c 104). At the date of writing, the amendments to HA 1996 made by LA 2011, ss 148–149 had not been brought into effect in Wales.

[330]   HA 1996, s 193(7AC) as amended by LA 2011, s 148(7).

[331]   And for applicants to local housing authorities in England whose applications for homelessness assistance were made before 9 November 2012.

[332]   HA 1996, s 193(3B). See **17.155–17.158**.

[333]   HA 1996, s 195(4B). See **17.196**.

[334]   HA 1996, s 193(7AA)–7AC) prior to amendment by LA 2011, s 148. See **17.165–17.168**.

18.183 Because these offers are of crucial importance, they are subject to special preconditions before they operate to bring the main housing duty to an end.[335]

18.184 They also, exceptionally, confer on the applicant the right to request a review of the suitability of the accommodation whilst simultaneously accepting it.[336] Given the serious consequences which may follow if an offer is refused but is later upheld as 'suitable', accepting the offer must usually be the advisable course of action.

18.185 Even if the applicant has not requested a review of a decision that accommodation offered in one of these two ways is suitable, he or she is still entitled to a review of any later decision (if one is made) that the duty on the local housing authority has ended by reason of the refusal of that accommodation.[337] If the applicant's reasons for refusing the offer are that the accommodation is not suitable, the local housing authority must consider his or her representations to that effect on review.

18.186 It should be noted that the general rules governing what facts, law and other circumstances the reviewing officer should consider are modified in relation to reviews of decisions to end duty as a result of the applicant having refused an offer of accommodation that the local housing authority has considered to be suitable for the applicant and his or her household. The reviewing officer is required to look at the facts that existed at the date of the applicant's refusal of the offer, albeit that some of those facts might only come to the local housing authority's attention after the refusal.[338]

Legal challenges

18.187 There is no explicit duty to assess the suitability of the accommodation in relation to the applicant's needs before making the offer of accommodation. It is expected that, if the accommodation appears to the applicant to be unsuitable, the applicant will have the opportunity to raise reasons why the accommodation is or was not suitable during the review process.[339] However, it makes good administrative sense for a local housing authority to satisfy itself as to the suitability of accommodation to be offered, *before* making the offer, not least in order to minimise dissatisfaction and the prospect of a review.

---

[335] See **17.55–17.66**, **17.92–17.108** and **17.109–17.131** (England), **17.136–17.137**, **17.138–17.146** and **17.165** and **17.168** (Wales).

[336] HA 1996, s 202(1A). See **19.41–19.49**.

[337] HA 1996, s 202(1)(b); and see *Warsame v Hounslow London Borough Council* (2000) 32 HLR 335, CA. See also **19.14–19.15**.

[338] *Osseily v Westminster City Council* [2007] EWCA Civ 1108, [2008] HLR 18, CA; and *Omar v Westminster City Council* [2008] EWCA Civ 421, [2008] HLR 36, CA. See **19.114**.

[339] *Abed v Westminster City Council* [2011] EWCA Civ 1406, (2012) January *Legal Action*, p 21, CA.

18.188   Where the local housing authority decides on review that the accommodation was suitable for the applicant, it has a duty to give reasons for that decision. Those reasons must be adequate and intelligible to the applicant.[340] Where a review decision is in the applicant's favour, the review officer is not required to give reasons for the decision that the accommodation was not suitable.[341]

18.189   If the review decision confirms that the accommodation offered was suitable, the applicant's remedy is to appeal to the county court on a point of law.[342]

18.190   An applicant can only seek to challenge a particular decision that the accommodation was suitable for his or her needs. The courts will not entertain a challenge to the local housing authority's policy on certain types of offers in abstract.[343]

18.191   If the local housing authority agrees that the accommodation is not suitable for the needs of the applicant and members of his or her household but does not secure any alternative accommodation, the applicant's remedy is to bring a claim in judicial review for a mandatory order requiring the local housing authority to secure suitable accommodation.[344]

18.192   If the dispute between the applicant and the local housing authority as to the suitability of accommodation does not attract a right to request a review,[345] the applicant's remedy is to bring a claim by way of judicial review proceedings arguing that the local housing authority's decision is wrong in law, or to invoke the local housing authority's complaints procedure.[346]

Handling 'suitability' disputes

18.193   The general conduct of reviews, appeals and court challenges is dealt with in Chapter 19, but several specific points can be made about the conduct of cases which concern 'suitability' issues.

18.194   Where an applicant pursuing a review raises new information as part of his or her argument that the accommodation is unsuitable, the reviewing officer must take that information into account. If the fact that the information was not previously raised causes the reviewing officer to disbelieve the applicant, the reviewing officer must put its concerns to the applicant and give

---

[340]   HA 1996, s 203(4). See **10.75–10.81**.
[341]   *Akhtar v Birmingham City Council* [2011] EWCA Civ 383, [2011] HLR 28, CA.
[342]   HA 1996, s 204. See **19.146–19.201**.
[343]   *R v Westminster City Council ex p Tansey* (1988) 21 HLR 57, CA.
[344]   *R v Newham London Borough Council ex p Mashuda Begum* (1999) 32 HLR 808, QBD. See also **18.25** and **19.224–19.250**.
[345]   See **18.19**.
[346]   See **19.224–19.250** for judicial review, and **19.251–19.258** for complaints.

him or her an opportunity to deal with them.[347] If the reviewing officer is relying on inconsistencies in the applicant's account, those too should be put to the applicant for explanation.[348] If a reviewing officer, in the course of its deliberations into whether or not accommodation offered was suitable, obtains information from a third party causing it to believe that the accommodation was suitable, it should put that information to the applicant and give him or her a chance to comment.[349]

18.195 Where both medical and non-medical considerations are raised as reasons for the refusal of an offer, the local housing authority must take an overall or composite view of those reasons as affecting the suitability of the accommodation for the individual applicant.[350] If there is conflicting medical evidence or opinion, the local housing authority is under a duty to act fairly and not merely to rely on the view of its medical adviser without explaining why it had rejected the contrary views of other medical practitioners.[351] It should also put to the applicant for comment any adverse medical views on which it is proposing to rely.[352] Where a consultant's report was rejected after referral to the local housing authority's medical adviser, the subsequent decision of the local housing authority was quashed because it had failed to give reasons for rejecting the report.[353] Where the local housing authority does not make its own investigations into the applicant's medical condition or obtain its own medical advice, it is bound by the medical evidence on suitability submitted by the applicant.[354]

18.196 Where an applicant has accepted the accommodation and simultaneously sought a review of the suitability, the reviewing officer should consider all the circumstances at the date of the review.[355] It follows that, if there have been any developments between the date of the request for a review and the reviewing officer's decision, and those developments might render the accommodation unsuitable, they should be considered.[356]

---

[347] *R v Hackney London Borough Council ex p Decordova* (1995) 27 HLR 108, QBD.

[348] *R v Camden London Borough Council ex p Mohammed* (1998) 30 HLR 315, QBD.

[349] *R v Southwark London Borough Council ex p Ryder* (1995) September *Legal Action*, p 15, CA (refusal of permission to appeal).

[350] *R v Lewisham London Borough Council ex p Dolan* (1993) 25 HLR 68, QBD.

[351] *R v Kensington and Chelsea Royal London Borough Council ex p Assister* (1996) September *Legal Action*, p 13, QBD.

[352] *R v Newham London Borough Council ex p Lumley* (2001) 33 HLR 124, QBD; and *R (Amirun Begum) v Tower Hamlets London Borough Council* [2002] EWHC 633 (Admin), (2003) 33 HLR 8, Admin Ct.

[353] *R v Kensington and Chelsea Royal London Borough Council ex p Campbell* (1996) 28 HLR 160, QBD.

[354] *R v Haringey London Borough Council ex p Karaman* (1997) 29 HLR 366, QBD.

[355] *Mohamed v Hammersmith & Fulham London Borough Council* [2001] UKHL 57, [2002] 1 AC 547, HL. See *Omar v Westminster City Council* [2008] EWCA Civ 421, [2008] HLR 36, CA, and **18.186** and **19.114** for the relevant considerations when an applicant has refused an offer of accommodation.

[356] *Omar v Westminster City Council* [2008] EWCA Civ 421, [2008] HLR 36, CA, at [25], per Waller LJ.

Chapter 19

REVIEWING AND APPEALING HOMELESSNESS DECISIONS

INTRODUCTION

19.1 Inevitably, some applicants are disappointed with the decisions made by local housing authorities on their applications for assistance under the Housing Act 1996 (HA 1996) Part 7 ('Homelessness'). Others may be concerned at the way in which they have been treated by a local housing authority or the way in which it has performed its obligations.

19.2 Disputes about the content of decisions were not addressed at all in the earliest versions of the statutory homelessness provisions. From 1977 onwards, those who were disappointed sought recourse to the courts, initially by ordinary civil claims in the county courts and in the Chancery and Queen's Bench Divisions of the High Court. But from the early 1980s, challenges to decisions could only be made by bringing judicial review proceedings in the Crown Office List of the High Court, now the Administrative Court. As a result, challenges were confined to claims alleging breach by the local housing authority of administrative law principles.

19.3 Only a modest number of judicial review applications were ever brought, but, partly at least to reduce the numbers of those challenges, later versions of the Codes of Guidance encouraged local housing authorities to establish and operate their own in-house mechanisms to review disputed decisions. Applicants who expressed concern about decisions on their applications could then request an extra-statutory, internal review of those decisions by the relevant local housing authority. The approach was widely adopted by local housing authorities, but in practice did little to diminish the numbers of judicial review applications to the courts.

19.4 The current regime in HA 1996, Part 7 built on both approaches (in-house reviews and access to the courts to challenge the contents of unlawful decisions). First, HA 1996, Part 7 contains a statutory scheme for internal review by a local housing authority of some of its own decisions. Second, most legal challenges are diverted away from the High Court to the county court, where there is a limited right of appeal against those decisions capable of being subject to statutory review. Third, judicial review remains available for a residual category of HA 1996, Part 7 disputes, in particular those relating to non-reviewable decisions. Concerns that this three-pronged arrangement for challenging decisions might not comply with the 'fair hearing' requirements of the European Convention on Human Rights were quickly put to rest by the House of Lords.[1] More recently, in February 2010, the Supreme Court held that decision-making on an application for homelessness assistance did not involve a determination of the applicant's 'civil rights' and therefore that Art 6(1) of the European Convention on Human Rights did not apply.[2]

---

[1] European Convention on Human Rights, Art 6; Human Rights Act 1998, Sch 1. *Runa Begum v Tower Hamlets London Borough Council* [2003] UKHL 5, [2003] 2 AC 430, HL.

[2] *Ali v Birmingham City Council* [2010] UKSC 8, [2010] 2 AC 39, SC.

19.5 Where the applicant's concern is over the way in which his or her application has been handled, or the way in which the duties owed have been performed, HA 1996, Part 7 provides no means of redress. For that, the applicant must look first to the local housing authority's own complaints procedure. That procedure is underscored by:

(1) a right of further complaint to the Local Commissioner for Administration;[3]

(2) the local housing authority's own monitoring officer, who deals with alleged maladministration or unlawful conduct;[4] and

(3) an enhanced statutory power permitting local authorities to give compensation to complainants.[5]

19.6 Of course, in the process of delivering its HA 1996, Part 7, service, the local housing authority may also infringe the applicant's rights under the European Convention on Human Rights (giving rise to a possible claim under the Human Rights Act 1998)[6] or be guilty of discrimination on grounds of one or more of the eight protected characteristics set out in the Equality Act 2010.[7] A full consideration of such specialist claims is beyond the scope of this book. However, if the local housing authority is not performing its acknowledged duty under HA 1996, Part 7, or is failing to consider exercising an available power, the Administrative Court can grant a mandatory order in judicial review proceedings, requiring it to perform its statutory obligations. Examples of such cases are given in this book.

19.7 Any particular application for homelessness assistance may trigger more than one of the different possibilities for redress. This Chapter considers each potential remedy in turn. The reader will need to consider the portfolio as a whole before deciding which remedy, or which selection of remedies, to pursue.

REVIEWS

Statutory reviews

An overview

19.8 Where an applicant is disappointed with a decision made by the local housing authority on his or her application for homelessness assistance, the statutory review process provided by HA 1996, Part 7 may give that applicant an opportunity to have all the relevant facts and the law reconsidered by the

---

[3] Commonly called 'the Local Government Ombudsman' (LGO) in England; or, in Wales, the Public Services Ombudsman for Wales.

[4] Local Government and Housing Act 1989, ss 5 and 5A.

[5] Local Government Act 2000, s 92.

[6] See **19.246–19.250** and **20.90–20.102**.

[7] Equality Act 2010, ss 5–12.

local housing authority.[8] In most cases, the reviewing officer must look at all the circumstances afresh, and as they exist at the date of the review decision. The process is not confined to considering matters as they stood when the applicant first applied or as at the date of the initial decision.[9] The statutory review is, therefore, the opportunity for the applicant to have his or her case completely re-examined by the local housing authority itself.[10]

19.9   There is no free-standing right to a review of *every* adverse decision made by a local housing authority under HA 1996, Part 7. The statutory review scheme applies only to a specific band of decisions.[11] However, nothing in HA 1996, Part 7 prevents a local housing authority from adopting its own informal arrangements enabling it to look again at any other decisions about which applicants express concern. Such informal reviews are no part of the statutory scheme, but can nevertheless help to reduce the number of formal complaints or claims for judicial review. HA 1996, Part 7 only permits one statutory review of any particular decision. A review decision cannot itself be the subject of a statutory review.[12]

19.10   When the scheme of statutory reviews was introduced by HA 1996, Part 7, it was hoped that this new regime would be monitored so as to establish its success or failure. Regrettably, there has been very little feedback on whether or not the scheme of statutory reviews has been a success.

19.11   The first government-commissioned research targeted a geographic area in which there had been relatively little review activity.[13] The little empirical information that is available has come mainly through independent academic

---

[8]   HA 1996, ss 202–203, as amended by Localism Act 2011, s 149(9) for applicants whose applications for homelessness assistance were made on or after 9 November 2012 to a local housing authority in England. At the date of writing, the amendments to HA 1996 made by LA Act 2011, ss 148–149 had not been brought into effect in Wales.

[9]   *Mohammed v Hammersmith and Fulham London Borough Council* [2001] UKHL 57, [2002] 1 AC 547, HL.

[10]   Case law has developed two exceptions to the general rule that a reviewing officer considers all the circumstances at the date of the review decision. The first exception is where the HA 1996, s 184 decision was unlawful, and had deprived the applicant of rights that he or she would have had if there had been a lawful decision, so the reviewing officer should restore those rights (*Robinson v Hammersmith & Fulham London Borough Council* [2006] EWCA Civ 1122, [2007] HLR 7, CA). See **13.132–13.139** and **19.113**. The second exception is where the review relates to a decision that the local housing authority's duty to the applicant has come to an end, because the applicant has refused an offer of suitable accommodation (HA 1996, s 193(5), (7) or (7AA)–(7AC) as amended by LA 2011, s 148(3)–(7) for applicants whose applications for homelessness assistance are made to a local housing authority in England on or after 9 November 2012, see **17.55–17.66**, **17.92–17.108** and **17.119–17.131** (England) and **17.136–17.137** and **17.138–17.146** (Wales)). In those circumstances, the reviewing officer should consider the facts and circumstances at the date of the refusal (*Omar v Westminster City Council* [2008] EWCA Civ 421, [2008] HLR 36, CA). See **17.52** and **19.114**.

[11]   See **19.12–19.37**.

[12]   HA 1996, s 202(2). See also **19.133–19.141**.

[13]   Atkinson et al *A Regional Study of Local Authority and Court Processes in Homelessness Cases* (Faculty of Law, University of Leicester, Department of Constitutional Affairs, 1999).

research.[14] In 2011, the magazine *Inside Housing* published the result of its own investigations, showing that on average 42% of initial decisions that reached the review stage were overturned by the reviewing officer.[15]

Which decisions can be reviewed?

19.12 An applicant who is dissatisfied with a local housing authority's decision in his or her case can only request a review if the decision falls into one of seven specified categories.[16] The final category of a right to request a review, at HA 1996, s 202(1)(f) contains different rights, depending on whether the applicant has made his or her application for homelessness assistance to a local housing authority in England on or after 9 November 2012[17] or to a local housing authority in Wales.[18] Between them, these categories encompass many of the most important decisions that a local housing authority is likely to make on an application. We consider each of the categories in turn.

(1) Any decision as to the applicant's 'eligibility' for assistance[19]

19.13 'Eligibility' is primarily a matter of immigration status and is fully discussed in Chapter 12. The decision capable of statutory review is the decision of the local housing authority, not any decision of the immigration or benefits authorities on essentially the same subject matter.

(2) Any decision as to what duty (if any) is owed to the applicant[20]

19.14 The right to a review is only available in respect of decisions as to whether a duty is owed under HA 1996, Part 7, ss 190, 191, 192, 193, 195 and 196.[21] The list of sections included here is a little odd. The references to ss 191

---

[14]   D Cowan, S Halliday and C Hunter 'Homelessness reviews – findings published' (2002) July *Legal Action*, p 6; and 'Homeless applicants and internal reviews' (2003) March *Legal Action*, p 8.

[15]   *Inside Housing*, 23 September 2011.

[16]   HA 1996, s 202(1). HA 1996, s 202(1)(f) was amended by LA 2011, s 149(9) for applicants whose applications for homelessness assistance were made on or after 9 November 2012 to a local housing authority in England. At the date of writing, the amendments to HA 1996 made by LA 2011, ss 148–149 had not been brought into effect in Wales.

[17]   Localism Act 2011 (Commencement No 2 and Transitional Provisions) (England) Order 2012, SI 2012/2599 (c 104). See Appendix 2.

[18]   At the date of writing, the amendments to HA 1996 made by LA 2011, ss 148–149 had not been brought into effect in Wales. The Welsh provisions are also relevant for applicants whose applications for homelessness assistance were made to a local housing authority in England before 9 November 2012.

[19]   HA 1996, s 202(1)(a).

[20]   HA 1996, s 202(1)(b).

[21]   HA 1996, s 190, duty to persons becoming homeless intentionally (see **17.182–17.189**); HA 1996, s 192, duty to persons not in priority need who have not become homeless intentionally (see **17.201–17.214**); HA 1996, s 193, duty to persons with priority need who have not become homeless intentionally (see **17.23–17.168**); HA 1996, s 195, duties in cases of threatened homelessness (see **17.190–17.200**).

and 196 are redundant, as they contain definitions,[22] not duties, and other sections of HA 1996, Part 7, which may also give rise to duties, are omitted. Several other sections carry separate rights to seek a review, but do not feature in this general right.[23] Moreover, the following sections all contain duties, yet are omitted from any right to request a review: ss 184,[24] 188,[25] 200,[26] 202,[27] 211[28] and 213A.[29]

19.15 This category is, however, broad enough to include a right to a review of any decision that a duty once owed (under one of the specified sections) is no longer owed.[30]

(3) Any decision to notify another local housing authority under HA 1996, s 198(1)[31]

19.16 Under HA 1996, s 198(1) ('conditions for referral'),[32] a local housing authority can initiate the procedure for the referral of an application for homelessness assistance to another local housing authority.[33] The procedure starts when the local housing authority that has received the application notifies the other local housing authority that it believes that one of the three conditions for a referral are made out.

19.17 The applicant must be given a notice by the notifying local housing authority that such a notification to another local housing authority is going to be made or has been made. That notice must also inform him or her of the right to seek a review of the decision to notify.[34]

19.18 The sequence of events here is important. The applicant has the right to request a review once the notifying local housing authority has made two decisions on his or her application:

---

[22] HA 1996, s 191 defines 'becoming homeless intentionally'; HA 1996, s 196 defines 'becoming threatened with homelessness intentionally'.
[23] For example, HA 1996, s 198, dealing with 'conditions for referral'.
[24] Duty to carry out inquiries and notify decisions. See Chapter 10.
[25] Duty to provide pre-decision accommodation. See **16.12–16.28**.
[26] Duty to accommodate in a referral situation. See **15.157–15.160** and **16.56–16.63**.
[27] Duty to carry out a review.
[28] Duty to protect possessions. See **17.233–17.254**.
[29] Duty to notify children's services. See **17.225–17.232**.
[30] *Warsame v Hounslow London Borough Council* (2000) 32 HLR 335, CA. Note the special rules regarding the scope of the review where the decision is that an accommodation duty has come to an end as a result of the applicant having refused an offer of accommodation. See **17.52** and **19.114**.
[31] HA 1996, s 202(1)(c).
[32] See Chapter 15.
[33] HA 1996, s 198(2)–(4) as amended by LA 2011, s 149(6)–(8) for applicants whose applications for homelessness assistance were made on or after 9 November 2012 to a local housing authority in England. At the date of writing, the amendments to HA 1996 made by LA 2011, ss 148–149 had not been brought into effect in Wales. Outlined at **15.155–15.156**.
[34] HA 1996, s 184(4) and (5).

(1)   that it considers that the conditions for referral are met; and

(2)   that it is going to exercise its discretion to notify the other local housing authority on that basis.

19.19 The applicant's request for a review can cause both or either of those decisions to be reconsidered.

19.20 It follows that the review request can be made before the notification is actually sent from the first to the second local housing authority. In those circumstances, it may be sensible for the first local housing authority to conduct and determine the review before it notifies the second local housing authority, as, if the review is successful and the decision set aside, there may be no need to notify. This is particularly true if the applicant is challenging a decision as to which (of several) local housing authorities he or she should be referred.[35]

19.21 Where the second local housing authority is notified before a review is requested, or concluded, any response it makes does not affect the applicant's right to a review or the conclusions of that review.

19.22 There is no right available, either under this category or any other, to review a decision *not* to notify another local housing authority under the referral provisions.[36]

(4) Any decision under HA 1996, s 198(5) as to whether the conditions for referral are met[37]

19.23 The right to request a review of the decision set out in the preceding category enables an applicant to challenge the opinion of the notifying local housing authority that the conditions for referral are made out. This additional category confers a right to a review of the *final decision* as to whether the referral conditions are actually made out.

19.24 The final decision arises *after* the first local housing authority has notified the second local housing authority. They may either agree between

---

[35]   In *Berhane v Lambeth London Borough Council* [2007] EWHC 2702 (QBD), (2008) March *Legal Action*, p 28, QBD, the High Court criticised a county court judge's decision to adjourn the applicant's appeal against a decision to notify another local housing authority until the two local housing authorities had resolved their dispute as to whether or not the conditions for referral were made out. Where there had been undue delay on the part of the notifying local housing authority, it was wrong, and deprived the applicant of effective access to the courts, to wait for the referee's decision. This decision emphasises that the applicant's right to challenge a decision to refer him or her to another local housing authority is entirely separate from the procedure used by two local housing authorities to resolve disputes between themselves. See **15.161–15.173** for disputes between two local housing authorities; **15.174–15.191** for challenges by the applicant.

[36]   *Sareen v Hackney London Borough Council* [2003] EWCA Civ 351, [2003] HLR 54, CA.

[37]   HA 1996, s 202(1)(d).

them that the conditions are made out (or that they are not), or, if they cannot agree, they may invite a referee to decide the matter under the disputes procedure.

19.25 There are special modifications made to the ordinary review procedures where the request for a review is in respect of either a joint decision or a referee's decision.[38]

(5) Any decision under HA 1996, s 200(3) or (4)[39]

19.26 In the light of amendments made to HA 1996, s 200(3) and (4) by the Homelessness Act 2002, this category is redundant. The only decision to which these two subsections now refer is the final decision that the conditions for referral are or are not met. That decision is the subject matter of the review category just described.

(6) Any decision as to the suitability of accommodation[40]

19.27 This category concerns decisions as to the suitability of accommodation offered to the applicant in performance of duties owed under HA 1996, ss 190, 191, 192, 193, 195, 196, 200(3) or (4), or as to the suitability of accommodation under HA 1996, Part 6 ('Allocation of Housing Accommodation') relied upon to release the local housing authority from the main housing duty under HA 1996, s 193(7).[41]

19.28 The meaning of 'suitability' in respect of the accommodation offered under the statutory provisions referred to in this category is considered in Chapter 18.

19.29 The selection of sections listed in this category is, again, a little odd. The references to HA 1996, ss 191 and 196 are redundant.[42] The references to subsections 200(3) and (4) are superfluous as they merely trigger the HA 1996, s 193 duty under which the offer will be made.

---

[38] HA 1996, s 202(4); Allocation of Housing and Homelessness (Review Procedures) Regulations 1999, SI 1999/71, regs 6–9, see Appendix 2. *Homelessness Code of Guidance for Local Authorities* (Communities and Local Government, Department for Education and Skills, Department of Health, July 2006) (the English Code), para 19.9, see Appendix 2. *Code of Guidance for Local Authorities Allocation of Accommodation and Homelessness 2012* (Welsh Government, August 2012) (the Welsh Code), paras 21.12–21.13, see CD-Rom; and see **15.178–15.180** and **15.182–15.191**.

[39] HA 1996, s 202(1)(e).

[40] HA 1996, s 202(1)(f).

[41] As amended by LA 2011, s 148(4) for applicants whose applications for homelessness assistance were made on or after 9 November 2012 to a local housing authority in England. At the date of writing, the amendments to HA 1996 made by LA 2011, ss 148–149 had not been brought into effect in Wales.

[42] They contain definitions and not duties. HA 1996, s 191 defines 'becoming homeless intentionally' and HA 1996, s 196 defines 'becoming threatened with homelessness intentionally'.

19.30 Those provisions of HA 1996, Part 7 giving the local housing authority *powers* to provide accommodation, or obliging the local housing authority to provide some form of *interim* accommodation, are omitted from this category.

19.31 As a result, there is no right to review a decision as to the suitability of accommodation provided:

(1)   under the duty to provide pre-decision accommodation;[43]

(2)   under the duty to provide accommodation pending the outcome of a local connection referral;[44]

(3)   under the power to accommodate pending review;[45]

(4)   under the power to accommodate the non-priority homeless who have not become homeless intentionally;[46]

(5)   under the power to accommodate the non-priority homeless who have not become threatened with homelessness intentionally;[47]

(6)   under the power to accommodate pending a referral review;[48] or

(7)   under the power to accommodate pending appeal.[49]

19.32 Finally, this review category does not give everyone made an offer of accommodation under HA 1996, Part 6 a right to a review of its suitability. The only HA 1996, Part 6 offer addressed here is a final offer made to an applicant owed the main housing duty under Part 7, where the refusal of that offer may bring that duty to an end.[50] If other offers, not expressed as 'final offers' of Part 6 accommodation, and therefore not bringing the s 193(2) duty to an end, have been made, there is no right to request a review of the suitability of the accommodation.

---

[43]   HA 1996, s 188(1) and 188(1A) as inserted by LA 2011, s 149(2) for applicants whose applications for homelessness assistance were made on or after 9 November 2012 to a local housing authority in England. At the date of writing, the amendments to HA 1996 made by LA 2011, ss 148–149 had not been brought into effect in Wales. See **16.12–16.35**.

[44]   HA 1996, s 200(1), See **15.157–15.160** and **16.63**.

[45]   HA 1996, s 188(3). See **16.36–16.48**.

[46]   HA 1996, s 192(3). See **17.23–17.168**.

[47]   HA 1996, s 195(9). See **17.215–17.222**.

[48]   HA 1996, s 200(5). See **15.157–15.160** and **16.63**.

[49]   HA 1996, s 204(4). See **16.49–16.55**.

[50]   HA 1996, s 193(7) as amended by LA 2011, s 148(4) for applicants whose applications for homelessness assistance were made on or after 9 November 2012 to a local housing authority in England. At the date of writing, the amendments to HA 1996 made by LA 2011, ss 148–149 had not been brought into effect in Wales. See **17.92–17.108** (England) and **17.138–17.146** (Wales) For rights to accept the offer of Part 6 accommodation and simultaneously request a review, see **19.41–19.49**.

(7) For applicants to local housing authorities in England,[51] any decision as to the suitability of accommodation contained in a private rented sector offer[52]

19.33 This provisions applies to applicants whose applications for homelessness assistance were made on or after 9 November 2012[53] to a local housing authority in England[54] and who have been made a private rented sector offer[55] in order to bring the main housing duty to an end. For 'private rented sector offer', see **17.109–17.131**. For 'suitability', see Chapter 18.

19.34 As with other disputes over the suitability of an offer of accommodation, the applicant has the right both to accept the offer and to request a review of its suitability.[56] This must always be the safest course of action. Here, the applicant is being required to enter into a fixed-term assured shorthold tenancy.[57] He or she will need a break clause to be contained in the tenancy, so as to permit the applicant to terminate the tenancy before the end of the fixed term upon notice to the landlord, if the outcome of the review (or any subsequent appeal) is a decision that the private rented sector offer was unsuitable.

(8) For restricted cases only, any decision as to the suitability of accommodation contained in a private accommodation offer[58]

19.35 This provision applies to an applicant whose application for homelessness assistance was made to a local housing authority in Wales, or to a local housing authority in England before 9 November 2012[59] and who is a

---

[51] For applicants whose applications for homelessness assistance were made on or after 9 November 2012 to a local housing authority in England. At the date of writing, the amendments to HA 1996 made by LA 2011, ss 148–149 had not been brought into effect in Wales.

[52] HA 1996, s 202(1)(g) as amended by LA 2011, s 149(9) for applicants whose applications for homelessness assistance were made on or after 9 November 2012 to a local housing authority in England. At the date of writing, the amendments to HA 1996 made by LA 2011, ss 148–149 had not been brought into effect in Wales.

[53] SI 2012/2599 (c 104).

[54] At the date of writing, the amendments to HA 1996 made by LA 2011, ss 148–149 had not been brought into effect in Wales.

[55] HA 1996, s 193(7AC) as amended by LA 2011, s 148(7) for applicants whose applications for homelessness assistance were made on or after 9 November 2012 to a local housing authority in England. At the date of writing, the amendments to HA 1996 made by LA 2011, ss 148–149 had not been brought into effect in Wales.

[56] HA 1996, s 202(1A).

[57] HA 1996, s 193(7AC) as amended by LA 2011, s 148(7) for applicants whose applications for homelessness assistance were made on or after 9 November 2012 to a local housing authority in England. At the date of writing, the amendments to HA 1996 made by LA 2011, ss 148–149 had not been brought into effect in Wales.

[58] HA 1996, s 202(1)(g) prior to amendment by LA 2011, s 149(9). This category applies to applicants whose applications for homelessness assistance were made to a local housing authority in Wales or were made before 9 November 2012 to a local housing authority in England.

[59] The date of commencement of the amendments to HA 1996 made by LA 2011, ss 148–149 in England. At the date of writing, the amendments had not been brought into effect in Wales.

restricted case.[60] If he or she is made 'a private accommodation offer',[61] there is a right to request a review of the suitability of the offer.[62]

19.36 As with private rented sector offers and other disputes over the suitability of an offer of accommodation, the applicant has the right both to accept the offer and to request a review of its suitability.[63] This must always be the safest course of action. Given that the private accommodation offer is an offer of a fixed-term assured shorthold tenancy, the same issues arise as with private rented sector offers if the reviewer agrees with the applicant that the accommodation is unsuitable.[64]

19.37 If a local housing authority's decision does not fall into one of the specified categories, there is no right to request a statutory review, and any legal challenge to the decision itself can only be by way of judicial review.[65]

Notifying review rights

19.38 It might be expected that, whenever a local housing authority takes *any* decision that carries a statutory right to a review, it should be required to notify the applicant not only of the decision, but also of the applicant's right to request a review and the time limit within which he or she should make the request.

19.39 However, that is only strictly true of decisions on an initial application for accommodation.[66] Even in those cases, there is no requirement that the applicant should also be informed of any advice or other help available to assist him or her in pursuing a review.

19.40 The Codes recommend that the local housing authority informs the applicant about the procedure involved in a review, if a request for review were to be made, but there is no statutory obligation to do so at this stage.[67] Nor is there any obligation to provide a pro-forma on which the applicant can request a review.[68] Notification can be given either directly to the applicant or, where the applicant has signed a form of authority appointing solicitors or other advisers as his or her agents, to those agents.[69]

---

[60]   HA 1996, s 193(3B). See **12.32–12.47** and **17.155–17.168**.
[61]   HA 1996, s 193(7AC) prior to amendment by LA 2011. See **17.165–17.168**.
[62]   For suitability, see Chapter 18.
[63]   HA 1996, s 202(1A).
[64]   See **19.34**.
[65]   See **19.224–19.250**.
[66]   HA 1996, s 184(5). See **10.66–10.81**.
[67]   English Code, para 19.3; Welsh Code, para 21.2.
[68]   Only when a review has been requested is the local housing authority obliged to notify the applicant of the procedure: Allocation of Housing and Homelessness (Review Procedures) Regulations 1999, SI 1999/71, reg 6(3)(b).
[69]   *Dharmaraj v Hounslow London Borough Council* [2011] EWCA Civ 312, [2011] HLR 18, CA.

Seeking a review and accepting accommodation

19.41 Where an applicant requests:[70]

- a review of the suitability of accommodation provided for him or her under the main housing duty;[71] or

- a review of the suitability of a final offer of accommodation made under HA 1996, Part 6;[72] or

- for applicants to local housing authorities in England whose applications for homelessness assistance were made on or after 9 November 2012,[73] a review of the suitability of a private rented sector offer;[74] or

- for applicants who are restricted cases, a review of the suitability of accommodation offered under a 'private accommodation offer',[75]

he or she has the right both to accept the offer and to request the review.[76]

19.42 Although it is not a statutory requirement, the Codes advise that where an offer is being made in these specific circumstances, the offer should be accompanied both by an explanation that the applicant has a right to request a review of suitability and by an indication that the applicant can both accept the offer and request such a review.[77]

---

[70] HA 1996, s 202(1)(f) and (g) as amended by LA 2011, s 149(9) for applicants whose applications for homelessness assistance were made on or after 9 November 2012 to a local housing authority in England. At the date of writing, the amendments to HA 1996 made by LA 2011, ss 148–149 had not been brought into effect in Wales.

[71] HA 1996, s 193(2) and (5) as amended by LA 2011, s 148(3) for applicants whose applications for homelessness assistance were made on or after 9 November 2012 to a local housing authority in England. At the date of writing, the amendments to HA 1996 made by LA 2011, ss 148–149 had not been brought into effect in Wales. See **17.55–17.66** (England) and **17.136–17.137** (Wales).

[72] HA 1996, s 193(7) as amended by LA 2011, s 148(4)for applicants whose applications for homelessness assistance were made on or after 9 November 2012 to a local housing authority in England. At the date of writing, the amendments to HA 1996 made by LA 2011, ss 148–149 had not been brought into effect in Wales. See **17.92–17.108** (England) and **17.138–17.146** (Wales).

[73] SI 2012/2599 (c 104). At the date of writing, the amendments to HA 1996 made by LA 2011, ss 148–149 had not been brought into effect in Wales.

[74] HA 1996, s 193(7AC) as amended by LA 2011, s 148(7) for applicants whose applications for homelessness assistance were made on or after 9 November 2012 to a local housing authority in England. At the date of writing, the amendments to HA 1996 made by LA 2011, ss 148–149 had not been brought into effect in Wales. See **17.119–17.131**.

[75] HA 1996, s 193(7AC), prior to amendment by LA 2011, s 148(7). For 'restricted cases', see s.193(3B), and **12.32–12.47**. For 'private accommodation offer', see **17.165–17.168**. Applicants whose applications for homelessness assistance were made to a local housing authority in England before 9 November 2012 and who are restricted cases will also fall into this category.

[76] HA 1996, s 202(1A), inserted by Homelessness Act 2002, overturning *Alghile v City of Westminster* [2001] EWCA Civ 363, (2001) 33 HLR 627, CA.

[77] English Code, para 19.3; Welsh Code, para 21.2.

19.43 The way in which the applicant's options might be put in the notification has been neatly summarised as follows:

> '[T]he choice which has to be presented to a person to whom an offer is made has to be in substance to this effect: you may accept or refuse a house. In either event you are entitled to seek a review of the decision to make this offer to you. If, though, you refuse to accept this accommodation you will not be able to retract your refusal, so that if the review goes against you, we shall be discharged of any duty towards you. On the other hand, if the review goes in your favour, we shall, in the light of the review decision, have to make you a different offer or reconsider our position.'[78]

19.44 If the local housing authority fails to provide this information, it risks a subsequent complaint that the whole procedure has been unfair.[79]

19.45 Since the consequences of refusing an offer of suitable accommodation in any of these cases will be that the local housing authority's main housing duty to provide accommodation for the applicant will end, acceptance of the accommodation whilst simultaneously requesting a review of its suitability must always be the cautiously correct approach. For private rented sector offers,[80] where the applicant is being required to enter into a fixed term assured shorthold tenancy,[81] the terms of the tenancy should contain a break clause, so as to permit the applicant to terminate the tenancy before the end of the fixed term upon notice to the landlord, if the outcome of the review (or any subsequent appeal) is a decision that that the private rented sector offer was unsuitable.[82] The same point applies to restricted cases who are made private accommodation offers.[83]

19.46 However, it is only in the case of these specific offers of accommodation[84] that the right to request a review whilst also accepting the

---

[78] *R v Tower Hamlets London Borough Council ex p Mbidi* (2000) April *Legal Action*, p 32, QBD, per Jowitt J.

[79] See *Akhtar & Naseem v Manchester City Council* (2003) April *Legal Action*, p 28, Manchester County Court, but also *Ali-Ahmed v Islington London Borough Council* [2004] EWCA Civ 128, (2004) April *Legal Action*, p 35, CA, where the process was not unfair, although the offer letter did not contain this information.

[80] HA 1996, s 193(7AC) amended by LA 2011, s 148(7) for applicants whose applications for homelessness assistance were made on or after 9 November 2012 to a local housing authority in England. At the date of writing, the amendments to HA 1996 made by LA 2011, ss 148–149 had not been brought into effect in Wales. See **17.119–17.131**.

[81] HA 1996, s 193(7AC)(c) amended by LA 2011, s 148(7) for applicants whose applications for homelessness assistance were made on or after 9 November 2012 to a local housing authority in England. At the date of writing, the amendments to HA 1996 made by LA 2011, ss 148–149 had not been brought into effect in Wales.

[82] See **19.34**.

[83] For 'restricted cases', see HA 1996, s 193(3B) and **12.32–12.47**. For 'private accommodation offer' see HA 1996, s 193(7AC) prior to amendment by LA 2011. Only applicants to local housing authorities in Wales, or applicants whose applications for homelessness assistance were made before 9 November 2012 to a local housing authority in England, will be restricted cases who are made private accommodation offers. See **17.165–17.168**.

[84] HA 1996, s 193(5), (7) and (7AA)–(7AC) as amended by LA 2011, s 148(3)–(7) for applicants

offer is available.[85] In the case of offers made under the other provisions[86] there is no statutory right both to accept the accommodation and request a review. It may be that a local housing authority will permit applicants who are offered the other categories of accommodation the right both to accept and to request a review, but that would be entirely a matter for the local housing authority.[87]

19.47 Where an applicant has rejected accommodation offered under the main housing duty,[88] as a final offer under HA 1996, Part 6,[89] or as a private rented sector offer[90] (or, for restricted cases, a private accommodation offer[91]), and has requested a review of its suitability and then subsequently sought to accept the offer, the decision whether to re-offer the accommodation or not is one for the local housing authority. There is no requirement on the local housing authority to keep the accommodation available for the applicant during the review process.[92]

19.48 What happens if an applicant accepts accommodation offered under the main housing duty, as a final offer under HA 1996, Part 6 or as a private rented sector offer, without requesting any review, and then subsequently decides to request a review of its suitability? HA 1996, s 193(6)(c) provides that the main housing duty has ended as a result of the acceptance of the HA 1996, Part 6 offer, which implies that the right to request a review would also have ended.[93] However, the present tense used in s 202(1A)[94] suggests that the

whose applications for homelessness assistance were made on or after 9 November 2012 to a local housing authority in England. At the date of writing, the amendments to HA 1996 made by LA 2011, ss 148–149 had not been brought into effect in Wales.

[85] HA 1996, s 202(1A).
[86] Referred to at **19.31**.
[87] English Code, para 17.45; Welsh Code, para 19.9.
[88] HA 1996, s 193(2) and (5) as amended by LA 2011, s 148(3) for applicants whose applications for homelessness assistance were made on or after 9 November 2012 to a local housing authority in England. At the date of writing, the amendments to HA 1996 made by LA 2011, ss 148–149 had not been brought into effect in Wales. See **17.55–17.66** (England) and **17.136–17.137** (Wales).
[89] HA 1996, s 193(7) and (7A) as amended by LA 2011, s 148(4) for applicants whose applications for homelessness assistance were made on or after 9 November 2012 to a local housing authority in England. At the date of writing, the amendments to HA 1996 made by LA 2011, ss 148–149 had not been brought into effect in Wales. See **17.92–17.108** (England) and **17.138–17.146** (Wales).
[90] HA 1996, s 193(7AA)–(7AC) as amended by LA 2011, s 148(5)–(7) for applicants whose applications for homelessness assistance were made on or after 9 November 2012 to a local housing authority in England. At the date of writing, the amendments to HA 1996 made by LA 2011, ss 148–149 had not been brought into effect in Wales. See **17.119–17.131**.
[91] For restricted cases, see HA 1996, s 193(3B) and **12.32–12.47**. For 'private accommodation offer', see HA 1996 s 193(7AC) prior to amendment by LA 2011. This category is for applicants whose applications for homelessness assistance have been to local housing authorities in Wales, or to local housing authorities in England, before 9 November 2012. See **17.165–17.168**.
[92] *Osseily v Westminster City Council* [2007] EWCA Civ 1108, [2008] HLR 18, CA.
[93] HA 1996, s 193(7AA)(a) as amended by LA 2011, s 148(5) deals with private rented sector offers and contains the same formulation, for applicants whose applications for homelessness assistance were made on or after 9 November 2012 to a local housing authority in England. At the date of writing, the amendments to HA 1996 made by LA 2011, ss 148–149 had not been

express statutory right to request a review, whilst also accepting the accommodation, remains open for the period of the statutory time limit in which to request a review.[95]

19.49 Where the applicant has accepted the offer of accommodation and also requested a review of its suitability, the reviewing officer should consider all the facts and circumstances as at the date of the review decision.[96]

Who may seek a review?

19.50 The statutory review rights are only available to 'an applicant'.[97] No member of the applicant's household has that statutory right. Nor can the review process be activated by others who may have an interest in challenging the local housing authority's decision, eg a different local housing authority, a private registered provider of social housing in England or a registered social landlord in Wales, or another homeless person.

19.51 An applicant's request for review does not need to be made personally. It may be made by someone else as the applicant's formal or informal agent (by a solicitor or anyone else asked to act on the applicant's behalf).[98]

How to seek a review

19.52 The obligation on a local housing authority to carry out a review is triggered 'on a request being duly made to them'.[99]

19.53 Beyond those words HA 1996, Part 7, says nothing about the form or content of the request. In particular:

- the request need not be in writing;

- there is no prescribed form;

---

brought into effect in Wales. HA 1996, s 193(7AA)(a) prior to amendment by LA 2011 also contains the same formulation, for restricted cases who accepted private accommodation offers and whose applications for homelessness assistance were made to a local housing authority in Wales or to a local housing authority in England before 9 November 2012.

94   HA 1996, s 202(1A): 'an applicant ... may'.

95   21 days beginning with the date on which the applicant is notified of the local housing authority's decision: HA 1996, s 202(3); and see **19.58–19.64**.

96   *Omar v Westminster City Council* [2008] EWCA Civ 421, [2008] HLR 36, CA, at [25], per Waller LJ.

97   HA 1996, s 202(1).

98   As happened in *R (Sederati) v Enfield London Borough Council* [2002] EWHC 2423 (Admin), (2003) January *Legal Action*, p 23, Admin Ct, where the manager of the applicant's temporary accommodation made the request on his behalf. If the person making the request is authorised by the applicant to act as his or her agent (usually by signing a form of authority to that effect), notification of the review decision can be given to that agent (*Dharmaraj v Hounslow London Borough Council* [2011] EWCA Civ 312, [2011] HLR 18, CA).

99   HA 1996, s 202(4).

- the applicant need not use a form provided by the local housing authority (even if a form is available);

- no grounds or reasons for requesting the review need be given;[100] and

- no particular office or officer is the specified recipient of the request.

19.54 However, it must be tolerably clear that the applicant is asking for a review of the decision made and not, for example, requesting a disciplinary investigation into the conduct of the officer(s) who took the decision.[101]

19.55 There are a number of examples of written review requests available as precedents.[102]

19.56 The use of the words 'made to them' suggests that the request must not only have been made to, but also received by, the local housing authority.[103] Simply posting a letter containing a written request for a review will probably not suffice (although a local housing authority might agree to extend the time limit for requesting a review if it was satisfied that the request had been posted in good time but not subsequently received in time or at all).[104]

19.57 The local housing authority to which the request is to be made is normally the local housing authority that made the decision sought to be reviewed.[105] Where review is sought under the fourth category,[106] the request is to be made to the 'notifying local housing authority' which made the referral.[107]

---

[100] English Code, para 19.10; Welsh Code, para 21.7.
[101] For example, *R (Taylor) v Commissioner for Local Administration* [2003] EWCA Civ 1088, (2003) September *Legal Action*, p 28, CA. In *Nzamy v Brent London Borough Council*, [2011] EWCA Civ 283, [2011] HLR 20, CA, a letter from an unrepresented applicant which set out reasons why an offer of main housing duty accommodation was unsuitable and concluded "I ask you please to offer us a permanent accommodation for us, but until that time we can wait in our current flat", was a request that the reviewing officer should look both at the issue of whether the accommodation offered was suitable and also at the question of the local housing authority had validly discharged its duty, see Black LJ at [19].
[102] For example, in Astin *Housing Law, an adviser's handbook* (Legal Action Group, 2nd edn, 2011).
[103] See *R (Lester) v London Rent Assessment Committee* [2003] EWCA Civ 319, [2003] 33 HLR 53, [2003] 1 WLR 1449, CA – a rent is not 'referred' to the RAC until notice of referral is received by it.
[104] HA 1996, s 202(3). See **19.61–19.64**.
[105] Allocation of Housing and Homelessness (Review Procedures) Regulations 1999, SI 1999/71, reg 6(1)(a).
[106] Of a decision made by a referee or by two local housing authorities jointly that the conditions for referral are met: HA 1996, s 202(1)(d); see **19.23–19.25**.
[107] SI 1999/71, reg 6(1)(b).

Time in which to request a review

19.58   The applicant has 21 days, 'beginning with the day on which he [or she] is notified of the authority's decision', in which to make the request to the local housing authority for a review.[108] Because it is relatively short, the time limit needs careful consideration.

19.59   The time limit begins with the day on which the original decision is 'notified'.[109] So, for example, if the local housing authority's decision is received by the applicant or his or her agents on 2 April, the review request must be made to the local housing authority by midnight on 22 April.[110] Provided that it is physically delivered to the local housing authority's offices before midnight, it will be in time, even if 22 April is not a working day, or if the office has already closed.[111]

19.60   The local housing authority may take the view that a particular request for review was not made in time and that it therefore has no duty to conduct a review. If it will not agree to extend the time, the applicant can apply for judicial review of the refusal to carry out the review. The issue of whether a request was made and, if so, whether it was made in time, will have to be resolved by the Administrative Court as a matter of fact.[112]

19.61   The local housing authority has a discretion to agree a longer period in which an applicant can request a review.[113] When a local housing authority receives a request to accept a review out of time, it should consider the explanation offered for the applicant's delay in making the request and the prospects of success on the review. The precise weight to be given to the balance between these two factors, and all other relevant considerations, is a matter for the local housing authority.[114] Nothing in HA 1996, Part 7, or in the regulations made under it, requires the decision on extending time to be taken by the person who would be conducting the review. As a matter of fairness and good practice, however, it probably should *not* be taken by the original decision-maker.[115]

---

[108]   HA 1996, s 202(3) and (4).

[109]   Which may be different from the day on which the decision was actually taken, and the day on which it was put in writing. See *Robinson v Hammersmith & Fulham London Borough Council* [2006] EWCA Civ 1122, [2007] HLR 7, CA, and **10.69–10.70**.

[110]   The phrase 'beginning with' includes the day of notification as the first day of the period: *Trow v Ind Coope (West Midlands) Ltd* [1967] 2 QB 899, CA, and *Zoan v Rouamba* [2000] 1 WLR 1509, CA.

[111]   *Van Aken v Camden London Borough Council* [2002] EWCA Civ 1724, (2003) 35 HLR 33, CA.

[112]   *R (Sederati) v Enfield London Borough Council* [2002] EWHC 2423 (Admin), (2003) January *Legal Action*, p 23, Admin Ct; and *R (Casey) v Restormel Borough Council* [2007] EWHC 2554 (Admin), (2008) January *Legal Action*, p 38, Admin Ct.

[113]   HA 1996, s 202(3).

[114]   *R (C) v Lewisham London Borough Council* [2003] EWCA Civ 927, [2004] HLR 4, CA; and *R (Slaiman) v Richmond upon Thames London Borough Council* [2006] EWHC 329 (Admin), [2006] HLR 20, Admin Ct.

[115]   It should be noted, however, that the Administrative Court, in *R (Abdi) v Lambeth London Borough Council* [2007] EWHC 1565 (Admin), [2008] HLR 5, Admin Ct, held that there was

19.62 Most (but not all) notifications of decisions carrying rights of review, will spell out the time limit.[116] A failure on the part of the local housing authority to comply with the obligation to notify the time limit (where it applies) would be a powerful factor in support of a request to extend time. The exact wording of HA 1996, s 184(5) need not be duplicated but the notification must contain the substance of the information required to be notified by HA 1996.[117] On the other hand, if the time limit was notified and emphasised in the notification letter, any request to extend time will be more difficult to sustain.

19.63 If the local housing authority accedes to the request to extend time, it must notify the applicant in writing accordingly.[118] This curious provision (not mirrored by any obligation to give written notice of a refusal to extend time) is presumably intended to avoid applicants suggesting that they were verbally given an indication that a late request would be allowed.

19.64 If the local housing authority refuses to extend the time limit for a review, where the request has been made late, the only challenge to that decision would be by way of judicial review.[119] A refusal to extend time is not itself a decision that can be subject to statutory review. If the decision to refuse to extend time was irrational, or for some other reason unlawful, it will be quashed and the local housing authority will be required to take the decision again on whether to extend time. In an exceptional case, the Administrative Court may even grant a mandatory order requiring the local housing authority to extend the time limit.[120]

Procedure on receipt of a request for a review

Procedure locally

19.65 Only the barest outline of the procedure to be followed on review is set out in HA 1996, Part 7 itself.[121] Little more detail is given in the current version

---

nothing in HA 1996, Part 7, the relevant regulations or the general law on issues of bias that prevented an original decision-maker from deciding a request for accommodation pending review.

[116] HA 1996, s 184(5).

[117] *Dharmaraj v Hounslow London Borough Council* [2011] EWCA Civ 312, [2011] HLR 18, CA.

[118] HA 1996, s 202(3).

[119] As happened in *R (Casey) v Restormel Borough Council* [2007] EWHC 2554 (Admin), (2008) January *Legal Action*, p 38, Admin Ct. See also *R (Dragic) v Wandsworth London Borough Council* [2012] EWHC 1241 (Admin), (2012) July *Legal Action*, p 42, Admin Ct, where the request for a review was two weeks' late and the judge held that 'two weeks in other contexts may not be regarded as very long, but in the context of a tight time limit of three weeks, two weeks has a different complexion'. She refused the claimant permission to apply for judicial review.

[120] *R v Newham London Borough Council ex p P* (2001) January *Legal Action*, p 28, QBD, reported as *R (Patrick) v Newham London Borough Council* (2001) 4 CCLR 48, QBD.

[121] HA 1996, ss 202–203 as amended by LA 2011, s 149(9) for applicants whose applications for homelessness assistance were made on or after 9 November 2012 to a local housing authority in England. At the date of writing, the amendments to HA 1996 made by LA 2011, ss 148–149 had not been brought into effect in Wales.

of the procedure regulations[122] which apply in both England and Wales. Accordingly, the day-to-day procedural operation of the review process is largely left to each local housing authority to determine with the benefit of the guidance given in HA 1996, Part 7, the regulations and in the respective Codes.[123]

19.66 The expectation is that each local housing authority will formulate and apply a written statement of its own procedure. Upon receipt of the review request the local housing authority must, if it has not earlier done so, notify the applicant of the 'procedure to be followed in connection with the review'.[124] Failure to comply with that obligation might undermine the fairness of the whole review process.

19.67 The Court of Appeal has recently considered the failure of two local housing authorities to comply with reg 6(2)[125] and, after the review request had been received, their failure to inform the applicant of the procedure to be followed and in particular of her right to make representations.[126] In both cases, the original decision letter had correctly notified the applicants that they had the right to request a review and had also notified them of their right to make representations and to provide new information, and that someone else could help them put their cases. It was also relevant that, in both cases, the applicants had solicitors representing them throughout the review process and that the solicitors were aware of their right to make representations on the review. Accordingly, the underlying purpose of reg 6(2) had been achieved in that the applicants knew about their right to make representations and so there was no breach of reg 6(2). The judge giving the leading judgment in one of those cases said:

> 'the self-evident purpose of imposing the duty to notify is not to inform an applicant who already had professional legal advisers about the right to make representations, but to protect those who did not have professional advisers, so that they can make representations themselves, or get someone else to do it for them'.[127]

---

[122] Allocation of Housing and Homelessness (Review Procedures) Regulations 1999, SI 1999/71, see Appendix 2.

[123] English Code, paras 19.2–19.19; Welsh Code, paras 21.1–21.14.

[124] Allocation of Housing and Homelessness (Review Procedures) Regulations 1999, SI 1999/71, reg 6(2)(b). See also English Code, para 19.11; Welsh Code, para 21.8.

[125] SI 1999/71, reg 6(2).

[126] *Maswaku v Westminster City Council* [2012] EWCA Civ 669, [2012] HLR 37, CA; and *El Goure v Kensington & Chelsea Royal London Borough Council* [2012] EWCA Civ 670, [2012] HLR 36, CA.

[127] *El Goure v Kensington & Chelsea Royal London Borough Council* [2012] EWCA Civ 670, [2012] HLR 36, CA, per Mummery LJ at [38].

19.68 If the review is being sought of a referee's decision,[128] the person appointed to conduct the review must notify the applicant of the procedure that he or she is going to follow.[129]

Inviting written representations

19.69 As already noted,[130] there is no requirement that the applicant should set out any grounds or reasons in the request for review. Accordingly, not least so that any particular issues can be drawn out, the regulations require that once the request for a review has been received, the local housing authority which received it must notify the applicant that he or she, or a representative, may make written representations to the local housing authority in connection with the review.[131] If the applicant has already been notified of the right to make representations, and particularly if he or she is represented by solicitors, there will be no error of law if the requirement is not strictly complied with after the request for the review has been received.[132]

19.70 This invitation must be issued in every case, either in the original decision or after the applicant has requested a review. The invitation to make written representations must be sent to either the applicant personally or to agents nominated by the applicant.[133]

19.71 If the review is being sought of a referee's decision,[134] the person appointed to conduct the review will notify the applicant of the right to make written representations direct to him or her and not to the local housing authority.[135]

19.72 There is no obligation on the applicant to respond to the invitation to make written representations. The review will take place whether or not a response is received. Neither HA 1996, Part 7 nor the regulations provide any deadline for the receipt of written representations, and therefore they can be submitted at any stage before the decision on review is actually made.

---

[128] HA 1996, s 202(1)(d). See **15.167–15.173** and **19.23–19.25**.
[129] Allocation of Housing and Homelessness (Review Procedures) Regulations 1999, SI 1999/71, reg 6(3)(b).
[130] See **19.53–19.54**.
[131] Allocation of Housing and Homelessness (Review Procedures) Regulations 1999, SI 1999/71, reg 6(2)(a). A notification which read 'you will be given an opportunity to make oral and/or written representations to the Panel' was described as wording which the local housing authority would be 'well advised' to reconsider, but was sufficient for the applicant to know that a review was under way and of his right to make representations (*Jama v Islington London Borough Council* [2006] EWCA Civ 45, (2006) June *Legal Action*, p 36, CA).
[132] *Maswaku v Westminster City Council* [2012] EWCA Civ 669, [2012] HLR 37, CA; and *El Goure v Kensington & Chelsea Royal London Borough Council* [2012] EWCA Civ 670, [2012] HLR 36, CA. See **19.67**.
[133] Allocation of Housing and Homelessness (Review Procedures) Regulations 1999, SI 1999/71, reg 6(2)(a).
[134] HA 1996, s 202(1)(d). See **15.167–15.173** and **19.23–19.25**.
[135] Allocation of Housing and Homelessness (Review Procedures) Regulations 1999, SI 1999/71, reg 6(3)(a).

19.73 Self-evidently, if the applicant has specific criticisms of the original decision, those criticisms should be set out in writing at the earliest possible stage so as to ensure that they are properly considered. The review process is the applicant's last opportunity to have the facts relevant to his or her application re-considered. The applicant, or his or her advisers, should therefore ensure that any fact that he or she believes might be relevant, and ought to be considered by the reviewing officer, is specifically brought to the reviewing officer's attention. It can often be helpful for the applicant, or his or her adviser, to ensure that the whole of the applicant's circumstances and representations are put together in one, full, letter, even if some or all of those representations have previously been put to the local housing authority in a more piecemeal fashion.

19.74 However, this does not mean that the reviewing officer is excused from considering points the applicant has not made. For example, even if the review request is primarily disputing whether an applicant did or did not personally do something that caused him or her to become homeless intentionally, and the reviewing officer is satisfied that the applicant did do the act in question, he or she must then go on, whether or not this point has been raised, to look at whether or not that act was 'deliberate'. That is true even if the applicant is professionally represented by experienced solicitors and has made detailed written representations which do not raise that point.[136]

19.75 A failure to inform the applicant of the right to make representations either in the original decision or subsequently would make the review process unfair, particularly if the applicant would have responded with representations. [137] The resultant review decision would be likely to be quashed on an appeal to the county court.

---

[136] *O'Connor v Kensington and Chelsea Royal London Borough Council* [2004] EWCA Civ 394, [2004] HLR 37, CA. A later Court of Appeal decision held that it was only those issues that fell within 'the circumstances of obviousness' that should be considered by the reviewing officer if they had not been raised by the applicant or his or her representatives (*Aw-Aden v Birmingham City Council* [2005] EWCA Civ 1834, (2005) July *Legal Action*, p 29, CA, at [12b], per Kay LJ). For another example, see *Black v Wandsworth London Borough Council* (2008) February *Legal Action*, p 41, Lambeth County Court, where the reviewing officer was obliged to consider the questions of causation and intervening settled accommodation, even though the applicant had not raised the issues, because those issues arose from the established facts before the reviewing officer.

[137] But see *Maswaku v Westminster City Council* [2012] EWCA Civ 669, [2012] HLR 37, CA; and *El Goure v Kensington & Chelsea Royal London Borough Council* [2012] EWCA Civ 670, [2012] HLR 36, CA where the applicants had been notified of their right to make representations in the original decision and were represented by solicitors during the review process. See **19.67**.

The identity of the reviewing officer

19.76 The review decision must be made by the local housing authority which made the original decision or, in the case of a review of a joint decision under the fourth category,[138] by the two or more local housing authorities which made that decision.[139]

19.77 Neither HA 1996, Part 7 nor the regulations prescribe that a particular officer or committee of the local housing authority (or authorities) should undertake the review. It is therefore for the local housing authority (or authorities) to decide whether:

- to delegate the task to an officer; or

- to devolve it to a committee or subcommittee of the council;[140] or

- to contract the function out.[141]

19.78 If the original decision (subject of the request for a review) was made by an officer of the local housing authority, and the local housing authority has decided that the review will also be carried out by an officer, then the local housing authority is required to ensure that the person conducting the review was not involved in the original decision and is senior to the original decision-maker.[142]

19.79 The original decision-maker is not excluded from assisting the reviewing officer or reviewing committee by, for example, writing and receiving letters, making further inquiries, or even attending a further interview or review hearing, but the review decision must be made by the reviewing officer or committee.[143]

19.80 If the decision subject to review was made in the fourth category,[144] that decision will have been made either by agreement between two local housing authorities or by a referee.[145] If the decision was one made by agreement

---

[138] HA 1996, s 202(1)(d); see **19.23–19.25**.

[139] HA 1996, s 202(4).

[140] But not to an individual councillor.

[141] *De-Winter Heald v Brent London Borough Council* [2009] EWCA Civ 930, [2010] HLR 8, CA. See **21.21–21.25**.

[142] HA 1996, s 203(2)(a); Allocation of Housing and Homelessness (Review Procedures) Regulations 1999, SI 1999/71, reg 2. See *Butt v Hounslow London Borough Council* [2011] EWCA Civ 1327, (2012) January *Legal Action*, p 22, CA, where the judge heard oral evidence as to which officer had taken the review decision.

[143] *Butler v Fareham Borough Council* (2001) May *Legal Action*, p 24, CA.

[144] Where the decision is whether the conditions are met for the referral of an applicant to another local housing authority under the conditions for referral: HA 1996, s 202(1)(d); see **19.23–19.25**.

[145] English Code, para 19.17; Welsh Code, para 21.6.

between two local housing authorities, then the review must be made by them jointly.[146] Presumably this will mean an arrangement for a joint committee or a joint panel of officers.

19.81 If a referee made the original decision,[147] then the reviewing officer should be a person jointly appointed by the local housing authorities within five working days from the day on which the review request was received by the notifying local housing authority.[148] This appointee could be anyone to whom both local housing authorities are prepared to entrust the review process.[149] If an appointment is not agreed within that time frame, the notifying local housing authority (which has received the review request) has a further five working days to ask the chair of the Local Government Association (LGA) or Welsh Local Government Association (WLGA) to appoint another referee.[150] The chair must then appoint a referee within a further seven (working or non-working) days[151] from among the membership of a panel appointed by the LGA.[152] That person then undertakes the review. Although this may appear to be a very tight time frame,[153] the membership of the panel comprises only a handful of referees, one of whom is already eliminated because he or she took the original decision.[154] Whether the reviewing officer is appointed by the local housing authorities or by the LGA or WLGA chairs, in this Chapter we will refer to that person as the 'appointed' reviewing officer.[155]

19.82 In some local housing authorities, all reviews are conducted by a single senior officer. This can cause difficulties. For example, where an earlier review decision has been quashed on appeal, the same officer would be taking the new review decision. Likewise, the review might be a second one in the history of a single application where the first review decision was withdrawn. An applicant may be aggrieved if the reviewing officer on the second review is the same officer who considered his or her case at an earlier stage and reached an adverse decision on a different issue. The courts have considered how fairness might be achieved in such circumstances. In *Feld v Barnet London Borough Council*[156] and *Poor v Westminster City Council*[157] it was decided that neither the regulations nor the need to avoid bias required that any second review be

---

[146] SI 1999/71, reg 1(2)(b)(i).
[147] See also **15.167–15.173**.
[148] SI 1999/71, reg 7(1) and (2).
[149] English Code, para 18.34; Welsh Code, para 21.12–21.13.
[150] SI 1999/71, reg 7(2) and (3).
[151] English Code, para 19.17; Welsh Code, para 21.12: both codes say five 'working days'. However, the current version of Local Authorities' Agreement (at English Code, Annex 18) refers to the five-day period as 'working days' and to the seven-day period simply as 'seven days', which suggests that seven non-working days is intended. See **15.169**.
[152] Allocation of Housing and Homelessness (Review Procedures) Regulations 1999, SI 1999/71, reg 7(2) and (3).
[153] The regulations even define 'working day': SI 1999/71, reg 7(7).
[154] SI 1999/71, reg 7(6).
[155] SI 1999/71, reg 7(4) refers to the reviewing officer appointed in these circumstances as 'the appointed person'.
[156] *Feld v Barnet London Borough Council* [2004] EWCA Civ 1307, [2005] HLR 9, CA.
[157] *Poor v Westminster City Council* [2004] EWCA 1307, [2005] HLR 9, CA.

conducted by a different reviewing officer. Applying the test of a 'fair-minded and intelligent observer', such an observer would conclude that reviewing officers were competent, conscientious, able to engage with issues on a reasonable and intelligent basis, and able to change their position on particular issues.[158]

Conduct of the review

The paper review

19.83 The reviewing officer's first task will be to gather together the relevant documents. These will consist of:

(1)   the original decision;

(2)   the request for review (if in writing);

(3)   the local housing authority's file relating to the application;

(4)   any written representations the applicant or his or her representative has made;

(5)   the Code of Guidance; and

(6)   the local homelessness strategy.

19.84   An 'appointed' reviewing officer[159] will, within five working days of his or her appointment, receive files from each of the local housing authorities involved containing the original decision and the 'information and evidence on which that decision was based'.[160] Presumably, if the 'appointed' reviewing officer is reviewing a referee's decision, she or he will ask for the documents that the referee had.

19.85   The reviewing officer is required by HA 1996, Part 7 and regulations to consider in every case:

(a)   any representations made;[161] and

(b)   the Code of Guidance;[162] and

---

[158]   *Feld v Barnet London Borough Council, Poor v Westminster City Council* [2004] EWC Civ 1307, [2005] HLR 9, CA, at [44]–[46], per Ward LJ. The test of a 'fair-minded and intelligent observer' is derived from *Porter v Magill* [2001] UKHL 67, [2002] 2 AC 257, [2002] HLR 16, HL.

[159]   See **19.81**.

[160]   Allocation of Housing and Homelessness (Review Procedures) Regulations 1999, SI 1999/71, reg 7(4).

[161]   SI 1999/71, reg 8(1).

[162]   HA 1996, s 182.

(c)   the local homelessness strategy.[163]

19.86 Additionally, an 'appointed' reviewing officer must distribute any representations received from the applicant to the two or more local housing authorities involved,[164] and must then consider any representations they make.[165]

The initial opinion and special procedure where there might be a deficiency or irregularity

19.87 A reviewing officer must consider, on review of this material, whether there was a deficiency or irregularity in the original decision or in the manner in which it was made.[166] If the reviewing officer decides that there was a deficiency or irregularity, special provisions apply.

19.88 If the reviewing officer is satisfied that there was a deficiency or irregularity in the original decision, but is minded to make a decision in favour of the applicant, the reviewing officer may immediately proceed to make that review decision.

19.89 If, however, the reviewing officer is satisfied that there was a deficiency or irregularity in the original decision or in the manner in which it was made, but is still minded to make a decision that is against the interests of the applicant, the reviewing officer must notify the applicant:

(1)   of his or her intention; and

(2)   the reasons why he or she is so minded; and

(3)   give the applicant an opportunity to make representations, either orally or in writing, or both.[167]

19.90 This preliminary notification ('minded-to') letter gives the applicant a final opportunity to persuade the reviewing officer away from an expressed intention to reach a substituted, but nevertheless unfavourable, decision.[168]

---

[163] Homelessness Act 2002, s 1(5).
[164] Allocation of Housing and Homelessness (Review Procedures) Regulations 1999, SI 1999/71, reg 7(5).
[165] SI 1999/71, reg 8(1)(a).
[166] *Lambeth London Borough Council v Johnston* [2008] EWCA Civ 690, [2009] HLR 10, CA.
[167] HA 1996, s 203(2)(b); Allocation of Housing and Homelessness (Review Procedures) Regulations 1999, SI 1999/71, reg 8(2).
[168] In one case, the reviewing officer had given the applicant a deadline for the submission of written representations of a week from the date of the letter inviting representations. That was held to be 'unreasonably short' a period by the judge, particularly since the letter took five days to arrive, so the two days' actual notice was 'manifestly too short': *Harman v Greenwich London Borough Council* (2010) January *Legal Action*, p 36, Lambeth County Court. In another case, seven days' notice was held to be too short: *Connors v Birmingham City Council* (2010) May *Legal Action*, p 25, Birmingham County Court.

When the applicant receives this notification, he or she could respond by requesting an oral hearing, or could choose simply to make further representations in writing.

19.91 This is a mandatory obligation on the reviewing officer. There is no room for the reviewing officer to decide, if these two circumstances apply, not to send a 'minded-to' letter because there is no apparent benefit to the applicant. The wording of the Regulations makes it clear that the duty must be complied with.[169] One Court of Appeal judge has said:

> 'The minded-to notice gives an opportunity to the applicant to try to persuade the review officer that his reasoning for his provisional conclusion is mistaken and is, at the very least, potentially of great benefit to an applicant, and to be deprived of that right is or may be seriously prejudicial.'[170]

19.92 The Codes provide some guidance as to the types of deficiencies or irregularities that a reviewing officer might consider render the original decision flawed. Examples given are:

(1) failure to take into account relevant considerations;

(2) taking into account irrelevant considerations;

(3) failure to base the decision on the facts;

(4) bad faith or dishonesty;

(5) a mistake of law;

(6) decisions that run contrary to the policy of HA 1996, Part 7;

(7) irrationality or unreasonableness; and

(8) procedural unfairness, e g where an applicant has not been given a chance to comment on relevant matters.[171]

19.93 In *Hall v Wandsworth London Borough Council*,[172] the Court of Appeal considered what was meant by 'deficiency'. It held that it meant 'something lacking' and was not limited to failings which would provide grounds for legal challenge, although it must be something sufficiently important to the fairness of the process to justify the operation of these special provisions and the 'minded-to' notification. In the two linked cases considered by the Court of

---

169 *Lambeth London Borough Council v Johnston* [2008] EWCA Civ 690, [2009] HLR 10, CA, at [51], per Rimer LJ.

170 *Banks v Royal Borough of Kingston-upon-Thames* [2008] EWCA Civ 1443, [2009] HLR 29, CA, per Lawrence Collins LJ at [67], following *Lambeth London Borough Council v Johnston* [2008] EWCA Civ 690, [2009] HLR 10, CA.

171 English Code, para 19.13; Welsh Code, para 21.9.

172 [2004] EWCA Civ 1740, [2005] HLR 23, CA.

Appeal, there was a deficiency in one (in that it was unclear whether the original decision-maker had applied the correct test for vulnerability). The reviewing officer should have understood that failing to be a 'deficiency' and should have applied the special provisions.

19.94 How significant should this flaw be? In *Hall v Wandsworth London Borough Council*,[173] the Court of Appeal had held that the 'something lacking' must be of sufficient importance to the fairness of the procedure to justify the extra procedural safeguard involved by application of reg 8(2).[174] In *Banks v Kingston upon Thames Royal London Borough Council*,[175] the Court of Appeal said that the test of 'sufficient importance' should be understood 'in the sense that further representations made in response could have made a difference to the decision that the reviewing officer had to make'.[176] A third Court of Appeal decision, *Bury Metropolitan Borough Council v Gibbons*,[177] relied upon the decision of *Hall v Wandsworth London Borough Council*, and the judge said: '[w]here the reviewer rejects the factual basis of the original decision and proposes to substitute a different factual basis leading to the same conclusion, it seems to me that the review has identified as "deficiency" within the meaning of regulation 8(2)'.[178]

19.95 In *Mitu v Camden London Borough Council*,[179] the local housing authority argued that a flaw in the original decision would only amount to a 'deficiency' if it was a flaw in the reasoning on an issue which the reviewing officer was minded to find against the applicant and if it was sufficiently serious. The Court of Appeal by a majority rejected that argument as entailing writing words into the regulation which are not there. The judge giving the leading judgment said:

> '[l]ooking at the matter broadly and untechnically, it seems to me that if the reviewing officer considers that the original decision maker was wrong on an important aspect of the case, then he has identified a deficiency in the original decision ... To hold otherwise means that the reviewing officer has the power to decide, in effect, that nothing the applicant can say will cause him to change his mind on the issue on which he has found against the applicant.'[180]

19.96 Both Codes, accordingly, advise that the reviewing officer must consider whether there is 'something lacking' in the decision under review. They suggest that significant issues which were not addressed, or addressed inadequately, which could have to led to unfairness, constitute 'something lacking'.[181]

---

[173] [2004] EWCA Civ 1740, [2005] HLR 23, CA.
[174] Carnwath LJ at [29].
[175] [2008] EWCA Civ 1443, [2009] HLR 29, CA.
[176] Lawrence Collins LJ at [72].
[177] [2010] EWCA Civ 327, [2010] HLR 33, CA.
[178] Per Jackson LJ at [45].
[179] [2011] EWCA Civ 1249, [2012] HLR 10, CA.
[180] Per Lewison LJ at [28].
[181] English Code, para 19.14; Welsh Code, para 21.9.

19.97   Examples from case law as to when there may have been 'something lacking' include:

- where it is unclear, from the wording of the original decision, whether or not the decision-maker had applied the correct legal test;[182]

- where the original decision-maker had failed to make adequate inquiries of the applicant's medical advisers and had failed to give a reasoned explanation for preferring the in-house medical advice against that of the applicant's advisers;[183]

- where the original decision had not mentioned the medical evidence that had been submitted by the applicant;[184]

- where the original decision had been made 11 months after the applicant had been interviewed, and by a different officer from the one who had interviewed the applicant;[185]

- on a 'broad reading' of the Regulations, where the original decision had become 'deficient' simply because it did not deal with a matter raised by a changed factual situation since the original decision was made;[186]

- where no reasons had been given in the original decision as to why offered accommodation had been suitable;[187]

- where both the applicant and the original decision maker had only viewed the accommodation, the suitability of which was subject to the request for a review, after the original decision had been made;[188]

- where the reviewing officer had rejected the factual basis of the original decision;[189]

- where the original decision had simply set out the statutory elements necessary for the ending of the main housing duty under HA 1996, s 193(5), and had not given any reasons for the decision;[190]

---

[182]   *Hall v Wandsworth London Borough Council* [2004] EWCA Civ 1740, [2005] HLR 23, CA.
[183]   *Benson v Lewisham London Borough Council* (2007) October *Legal Action*, p 26, Central London County Court.
[184]   *Al-Kabi v Southwark London Borough Council* (2008) March *Legal Action*, p 21, Lambeth County Court.
[185]   *Lambeth London Borough Council v Johnston* [2008] EWCA Civ 690, [2009] HLR 10, CA.
[186]   *Banks v Kingston upon Thames Royal London Borough Council* [2008] EWCA Civ 1443, [2009] HLR 29, CA.
[187]   *Connors v Birmingham City Council* (2010) *Legal Action* May, p 25, Birmingham County Court.
[188]   *Norris v Milton Keynes City Council* [2010] EWCA Civ 77, April *Legal Action*, p 26, CA.
[189]   *Bury Metropolitan Borough Council v Gibbons* [2010] EWCA Civ 327, [2010] HLR 33, CA.
[190]   *Makisi v Birmingham City Council* [2011] EWCA Civ 355, [2011] HLR 27, CA.

- where the original decision had concluded that the applicant had become homeless intentionally without giving reasons or explaining what that meant;[191] and

- where the decision as to whether or not the applicant had become homeless intentionally had been overturned by the reviewing officer even though the duty owed to the applicant had not changed.[192]

19.98   In *Banks v Kingston-upon-Thames Royal London Borough Council,*[193] the original decision had been that the applicant was not homeless. The applicant requested a review. Before the reviewing officer had completed the review, the applicant had been served with a notice to quit. The reviewing officer decided that the applicant was homeless but that he did not have a priority need. The Court of Appeal held that, once it was decided that the applicant was homeless, the original decision had become deficient because it had not addressed his priority need. As a result, where the reviewing officer is minded to decide the review against the interests of the applicant, reg 8(2) should operate so as to ensure that the applicant be given the opportunity to make representations.

Oral hearing

19.99   The reviewing officer must obviously adopt and apply a fair procedure at the review stage. There is, however, no general right for the applicant to have an oral hearing, or even to have a meeting or interview with the reviewing officer. It will generally be for the reviewing officer to determine whether the facts or circumstances of the particular case warrant an oral hearing.

19.100   There is one circumstance in which 'an oral hearing'[194] must be convened. That occurs when:

(1)   the reviewing officer has issued a 'minded-to' letter;[195] and

(2)   the applicant responds indicating that she or he wishes to make representations orally (either personally or through a representative).[196]

---

[191]   *Yosief v Birmingham City Council* [2011] EWCA Civ 355, [2011] HLR 27, CA, heard and reported at the same time as *Makisi v Birmingham City Council*. Note that in the third of these cases considered together by the Court of Appeal (*Nagi v Birmingham City Council*), the Court of Appeal found that there had not been a deficiency in the original decision even though the letter was 'poorly worded'. Despite that, the decision had addressed all the important aspects and could not have left a reasonable reader with any real doubt as to the basis of the decision (Etherton LJ at [77]).

[192]   *Mitu v Camden London Borough Council* [2011] EWCA 1249, [2012] HLR 10, CA.

[193]   [2008] EWCA Civ 1443, [2009] HLR 29, CA.

[194]   HA 1996, s 203(2)(b).

[195]   See **19.87–19.98**.

[196]   Allocation of Housing and Homelessness (Review Procedures) Regulations 1999, SI 1999/71, reg 8(2)(b); *Makisi v Birmingham City Council* [2011] EWCA Civ 355, [2011] HLR 27, CA.

19.101   Neither HA 1996, Part 7, nor the regulations specify how an oral hearing is to be conducted. The Court of Appeal considered this in *Makisi v Birmingham City Council*.[197] It held that, where an applicant requests the right to make oral representations, he or she must be given the option of a face to face meeting with the reviewing officer. However, the applicant does not have any right to insist that any witnesses are called, or that he or she may cross-examine them. The hearing should be 'a simple and relatively brief opportunity for the applicant to make oral representations to the review officer'.[198]

Fairness

19.102   The reviewing officer will consider not only the material originally before the decision-maker but also any further relevant material received. If a reviewing officer is minded to draw an adverse inference, or to call into question the applicant's credibility, or hold matters against the applicant, those should be put to the applicant for comment, especially if he or she has not already had an opportunity to comment prior to the original decision.[199]

19.103   Neither HA 1996, Part 7, nor the regulations specifically require or encourage the reviewing officer to make further inquiries at his or her own initiative. The reviewing officer should, however, be prepared to make further inquiries, if necessary, and to consider asking the applicant to agree to extend the time for a review to be completed if further inquiries need to be made, or an oral hearing needs to be arranged.[200] It is a decision for the reviewing officer as to what inquiries, if any, are necessary before the reviewing officer can take and notify the decision on the review.[201]

Independence in the conduct of the review

19.104   Review decisions are ultimately made by the very local housing authorities which made the original decisions and are usually made by staff or councillors of the local housing authorities concerned. Only where the review is conducted by an 'appointed' reviewing officer[202] will there be anything resembling independence in the review process.[203]

---

[197]   [2011] EWCA Civ 355, [2011] HLR 27, CA.
[198]   Etherton LJ at [70].
[199]   For general principles of fairness, see *Doody v Secretary of State for the Home Department* [1994] 1 AC 531, HL per Lord Mustill at 560. These principles have been applied in the context of homelessness law in *Feld v Barnet London Borough Council, Pour v Westminster City Council* [2004] EWCA Civ 1307, [2005] HLR 9, CA, and in *Akhtar v Birmingham City Council* [2011] EWCA Civ 383, [2011] HLR 28, CA.
[200]   English Code, para 19.16; Welsh Code, para 21.11.
[201]   *Cramp v Hastings Borough Council, Phillips v Camden London Borough Council* [2005] EWCA Civ 1005, [2005] HLR 48, CA. See Chapter 10 on inquiries.
[202]   See **19.81**.
[203]   In *Runa Begum v Tower Hamlets London Borough Council* [2003] UKHL 5, [2003] 2 AC 430, HL, the House of Lords held that reviewing officers employed by local housing authorities were not independent of the local housing authority. In *De-Winter Heald v Brent*

19.105 The review procedure itself is therefore not compliant with the requirements of Art 6 of the European Convention on Human Rights, which provides that:

> '... everyone is entitled to a fair and public hearing within a reasonable time by an independent and impartial tribunal established by law.'

19.106 However, the opportunity of an appeal to the county court on a point of law against the eventual review decision (and the judicial control exercisable within the appeal) safeguards the fairness of the proceedings and renders the overall process compliant with Art 6(1) of the Convention.[204] Indeed, the Supreme Court held in February 2010 that decision-making on an application for homelessness assistance did not involve a determination of an applicant's 'civil rights' and so the procedure at Art 6(1) did not apply.[205]

Scope of review

19.107 It is not possible for an applicant to restrict the scope of the review only to a specific part of the decision she or he has asked to be reviewed. This is particularly important where the original decision falls under the second category of reviewable decisions, ie a decision as to 'what duty, if any' is owed to the applicant.[206] The general rule is that the reviewing officer is charged with the task of considering the whole matter (of whether any duty is owed) afresh on the latest material available. There are two senses in which this can create difficulties for applicants.

19.108 First, an applicant owed the benefit of a duty as a result of the original decision may find that the reviewing officer concludes (on consideration of the same material) that he or she is owed not a higher but a lesser duty. For example, the original decision may have been that the applicant was eligible, homeless, and in priority need, but had become homeless intentionally. The reviewing officer on reconsideration may conclude that the applicant did not become homeless intentionally but has never had a priority need, and that therefore there is no accommodation duty at all. The 'minded-to' procedure ought to ensure that the applicant is not taken by surprise by such a decision.[207] Similarly, the original decision might find that an applicant does not have a

---

London Borough Council [2009] EWCA Civ 930, [2010] HLR 8, CA, the Court of Appeal held that a reviewing officer contracted by the local housing authority to carry out the review (instead of being employed by the local housing authority) was not necessarily any more or less independent of the local housing authority than its employees were (per Stanley Burnton LJ at [52]–[54]).

[204] *Runa Begum v Tower Hamlets London Borough Council* [2003] UKHL 5, [2003] 2 AC 430, HL. Subsequent to the House of Lords decision in *Begum*, the European Court of Human Rights held that local housing authorities' housing benefit review panels (as constituted to July 2001) were not independent or impartial and, despite the availability of judicial review, were therefore not compliant with Art 6(1) of the Convention: *Tsfayo v UK* [2007] HLR 19, ECHR.

[205] *Ali v Birmingham City Council* [2010] UKSC 8, [2010] 2 AC 39, SC.

[206] HA 1996, s 202(1)(b); see **19.14–19.15**.

[207] See **19.87–19.98**.

priority need and became homeless intentionally so that the only duty owed to him or her is a duty to provide advice and assistance. On review, the reviewing officer may uphold the decision that the applicant does not have a priority need but decide that he or she did not become homeless intentionally. The duty owed to the applicant is the same but there is an additional power available to the local housing authority to secure accommodation for the applicant.[208] Again, the 'minded to' procedure should apply.[209]

19.109 Second, the applicant may find that new information, or a change of circumstances between the original decision and the conclusion of the review, undermines the benefits of the original decision. For example, the original decision may have been that the applicant was eligible, homeless, and had a priority need but had become homeless intentionally. The reviewing officer may be satisfied (by either new information or a change of circumstances) that the applicant is not eligible or no longer has a priority need. Even if the original decision was correct on the facts available at the time, the new information or change of circumstances renders the original decision subject to a 'deficiency'. The reviewing officer should send a 'minded-to' letter inviting the applicant to make representations if the reviewing officer is minded to decide the review against the interests of the applicant.[210]

19.110 A difficult situation arises where the applicant is not provided with accommodation pending review[211] and therefore has obtained his or her own accommodation before the conclusion of the review. If the applicant has managed to obtain something better than emergency accommodation, the reviewing officer will be entitled – indeed required – to conclude that the applicant is not homeless as at the date of the review.[212] Another difficult situation is where the applicant has accepted a private rented sector offer[213] and simultaneously requested a review of its suitability.[214] The applicant will have entered into a fixed-term assured shorthold tenancy and so he or she will be liable to the landlord for the rent for the whole of the term. What happens if the reviewing officer agrees with the applicant that the accommodation is not suitable for the applicant? Arguably, in order to provide for this situation, all

---

[208] HA 1996, s 192(3).
[209] *Mitu v Camden London Borough Council* [2011] EWCA Civ 1249, [2012] HLR 10, CA.
[210] SI 1999/71, reg 8(2). *Banks v Kingston-upon-Thames Royal London Borough Council* [2008] EWCA Civ 1443, [2009] HLR 29, CA. See **19.87–19.98**.
[211] See **16.36–16.48**.
[212] See Chapter 11.
[213] HA 1996, s 193(7AA)–(7AC) as amended by LA 2011, s 148(5)–(7) for applicants whose applications for homelessness assistance were made on or after 9 November 2012 to local housing authorities in England. At the date of writing, the amendments to HA 1996 made by LA 2011, ss 148–149 had not been brought into effect in Wales. See **17.119–17.131**. The same point also applies to applicants who are restricted cases and who have been made private accommodation offers, see **17.165–17.168**. They will be applicants whose applications for homelessness assistance was made to a local housing authority in Wales or to a local housing authority before 9 November 2012.
[214] HA 1996, s 202(1)(g), as amended by LA 2011, s 149(9) for applicants whose applications for homelessness assistance were made on or after 9 November 2012 to local housing authorities in England, and HA 1996, s 202(1A). See **19.41–19.49**

private rented sector offers should contain break clauses, exercisable by the applicant. Otherwise, the applicant would either have to pay large sums of money to the landlord or would remain living in accommodation which is agreed not to be suitable.[215]

19.111 Obviously, any new information or change of circumstances could equally well work in an applicant's favour. Between the request for, and conclusion of, the review, he or she may have acquired priority need status, established a new local connection or had any other change of circumstance which could produce a more favourable review decision.[216] Provided that this material comes to the attention of the reviewing officer, it must be taken into account.

19.112 There are two exceptions to the general rule that the reviewing officer must consider the whole matter on the latest material available.

19.113 First, the Court of Appeal has held that, where the original decision was unlawful and had deprived the applicant of a benefit to which he or she would have been entitled had the original decision been lawfully taken, the reviewing officer should take a different approach from the normal course of considering all the facts and law at the date of the review decision. In those circumstances, the reviewing officer should restore to the applicant the rights he or she would have had if the decision had been lawful, even if the applicant's circumstances have changed such that he or she would normally not be entitled to that benefit.[217] The obvious example, and that considered by the Court of Appeal, is where a 17-year-old is notified that he or she does not have a priority need, requests a review and the review is decided after his or her eighteenth birthday.[218] These unusual circumstances apply where the original decision was unlawful, in this case because the 17-year-old could not have been anything other than in priority need at the date of the original decision. The position if, for example, the original decision had been that the 17-year-old had a priority need but had become homeless intentionally, and a reviewing officer is considering the position after the applicant's eighteenth birthday, is much more difficult. The original decision was not unlawful, certainly as far as the priority need part of the decision is concerned. Should the reviewing officer confine him- or herself to considering the part of the decision that did not relate to

---

[215] The implication being either that the main housing duty has not, in fact, come to an end because the applicant did not accept a suitable private rented sector offer (HA 1996, s 193(7AA) as amended by LA 2011, s 148(5) for applicants whose applications for homelessness assistance were made on or after 9 November 2012 to local housing authorities in England) or that the applicant is homeless because there is no accommodation that is reasonable for him or her and the members of his or her household to continue to occupy (HA 1996 s 175(3), see **11.75–11.120**).

[216] *Mohammed v Hammersmith and Fulham London Borough Council* [2001] UKHL 57, [2002] 1 AC 547, HL.

[217] *Robinson v Hammersmith & Fulham London Borough Council* [2006] EWCA Civ 1122, [2007] HLR 7, CA, at [32], per Waller LJ, drawing on dicta in *Crawley Borough Council v B* [2000] 32 HLR 636, CA, at 651, per Chadwick LJ.

[218] See **13.127–13.174** (England) and **13.214–13.218** (Wales).

priority need? The Court of Appeal's approach in *Crawley Borough Council v B*[219] suggests not and that all of the circumstances that go towards a decision as to what duty, if any, is owed to the applicant should be considered by the reviewing officer as at the date of the review. In those circumstances, reg 8(2)[220] requires the reviewing officer to send the applicant a 'minded-to' letter if he or she is minded to decide the review against the interests of the applicant.[221]

19.114 Second, where the reviewing officer is considering the applicant's reasons for refusing an offer of accommodation, the reviewing officer should consider the facts and circumstances that existed at the date of the refusal, not at the date of the review. Some of those facts may only come to the attention of the local housing authority after the date of the refusal, but the correct question for the reviewing officer is what facts existed at the date of the refusal.[222]

Notification of the review decision

19.115 Every review decision must be notified to the applicant or to his or her authorised agents by the local housing authority or authorities concerned, even if the review has been conducted by an 'appointed' reviewing officer.[223] That notice must be given in writing.[224] If the local housing authority is for some reason unable to give the applicant the written notice, it may make the review decision available for collection at its office for a reasonable period, and that can constitute notification.[225] It is important to establish the exact date of notification, because the very tight 21-day time-limit for the filing of an appeal to the county court runs from the date of notification. If there is any doubt as to the exact date of notification, the county court judge will have to determine the date for him or herself. In those circumstances, if there might be any doubt as to the deadline for issue, an applicant should be advised to apply for an extension of time when he or she issues his or her Appellant's Notice, in case the judge finds that the appeal has been issued out of time.[226]

19.116 If the review decision is:

- to confirm the original decision against the interests of the applicant on any issue; or

---

[219] (2000) 32 HLR 636, CA.
[220] SI 1999/71.
[221] *Banks v Kingston-upon-Thames Royal London Borough Council* [2008] EWCA Civ 1443, [2009] HLR 29, CA. See **19.87–19.98**.
[222] *Osseily v Westminster City Council* [2007] EWCA Civ 1108, [2008] HLR 18, CA; *Omar v Westminster City Council* [2008] EWCA Civ 421, [2008] HLR 36, CA. See **17.52** and **19.114**.
[223] HA 1996, s 203(3).
[224] HA 1996, s 203(8).
[225] HA 1996, s 203(8).
[226] HA 1996, s 204(2A). See **19.183**.

- to confirm the original decision to give a notice of referral under the conditions for referral;[227] or

- to confirm the original decision that the conditions are met for referral of the applicant's case,[228]

the local housing authority must notify the applicant of the reasons for the review decision.[229] In any other case, where applicants would be expected to be pleased with the review decision, reasons are not required to be given.[230] It might, however, be expected that an 'appointed' reviewing officer[231] would have given written reasons to the local housing authorities involved and that they would be passed on to the applicant.

19.117 If reasons are to be given, the same notice of the review decision must also inform the applicant of the right to appeal to the county court on a point of law and of the 21-day period in which the appeal must be made.[232]

19.118 A review decision notification that fails to provide either the reasons for the decision or the information about rights to appeal (where those are required) will not be effective as a review decision.[233] This will mean that the review has not been concluded.

19.119 The applicant's remedy in that case might be to appeal on a point of law against the original decision (because there is no review decision).[234] However, the better course might be to invite the reviewing officer to conclude the review properly by giving the required notice whilst seizing the opportunity to put forward any additional material before that notice is given.[235]

Time scale for completion of the review

19.120 There is no time scale for the completion of the review in HA 1996, Part 7 itself, but there is a provision allowing for regulations to be made to govern both the period for completion of the review and, separately, the period for notification of the decision on review.[236]

19.121 The regulations set a composite time limit, referring only to the overall period ending with the giving of the written notice of the review decision,

[227] See **19.16–19.22**.
[228] See **19.23–19.25**.
[229] HA 1996, s 203(4).
[230] *Akhtar v Birmingham City Council* [2011] EWCA Civ 383, [2011] HLR 28, CA.
[231] See **19.81**.
[232] HA 1996, s 203(5). The exact wording of this sub-section need not be set out so long as the substance is conveyed: *Dharmaraj v Hounslow London Borough Council* [2011] EWCA Civ 312, [2011] HLR 18, CA.
[233] HA 1996, s 203(6).
[234] HA 1996, s 204(1)(b). See **19.146–19.164**.
[235] See **19.127–19.130**.
[236] HA 1996, s 203(7).

rather than dividing the period up.[237] The importance of this approach is that it emphasises not only that the review must be concluded and the review decision notified within the prescribed time limit, but also that the review process is not completed until the review decision is actually given in writing.

19.122 As indicated, any representations made, new material received or changes of circumstance occurring before notification is given should be taken into account by the reviewing officer.

19.123 In most cases, the time limit is that the review must be completed within eight weeks from the receipt of the request for a review.[238]

19.124 Different time limits apply if the review has been sought under the fourth review category.[239] If the review is of a decision made by the two local housing authorities involved, the review period is 10 weeks.[240] If the review is of a decision made by a referee, the period is 12 weeks.[241] In the latter case, in order to give the local housing authorities concerned time to notify a review decision within the 12-week period, the 'appointed' reviewing officer must notify them of his or her decision within 11 weeks.[242]

19.125 The period for completion of a review can be longer than these prescribed periods if both the applicant and local housing authority agree in writing that the period should be extended.[243] This important provision allows flexibility. It also eliminates the possibility of the local housing authority unilaterally extending time, and ensures a written record of the agreement to extend time and of the period of that extension.

19.126 The time limit of 21 days for bringing an appeal to the county court against a review decision[244] runs from the date of written notification of the review decision to the applicant or to his or her agents.[245] That must mean the date on which the review decision is received if it is sent by post, and not the date of posting or the date on the letter itself.[246]

---

[237] Allocation of Housing and Homelessness (Review Procedures) Regulations 1999, SI 1999/71, reg 9(1).

[238] SI 1999/71, reg 9(1)(a).

[239] A review of a decision that the conditions for a referral to another local housing authority are met. See HA 1996, s 202(1)(d) and see **19.23–19.25**.

[240] Allocation of Housing and Homelessness (Review Procedures) Regulations 1999, SI 1999/71, reg 9(1)(b).

[241] SI 1999/71, reg 9(1)(c).

[242] SI 1999/71, reg 9(3).

[243] SI 1999/71, reg 9(2).

[244] See **19.174–19.182**.

[245] HA 1996, s 204(2). For review decisions notified to agents, see *Dharmaraj v Hounslow London Borough Council* [2011] EWCA Civ 312, [2011] HLR 18, CA

[246] *Demetri v Westminster City Council* (1999) 32 HLR 470, CA, at 471, in which the review decision was posted on 7 December but not received until 17 December. See *Lambeth London Borough Council v Namegembe* [2006] EWHC 3608 (Ch), (2007) February *Legal Action*, p 31, ChD, for an example of a judge having to determine a conflict of fact between the parties as to when the review decision had been received by the applicant.

Remedies if the local housing authority fails to complete the review in time

19.127 If no review decision is notified at the end of the prescribed (or any agreed extended) period, the applicant has 21 days from the end of that period in which to bring an appeal against the original decision on a point of law.[247]

19.128 It may be, however, that pursuing an appeal on a point of law against the original decision is not the most appropriate option available to the applicant. The original decision may have been one that the local housing authority was lawfully entitled to take. But the applicant may disagree with the factual conclusions or may have submitted new information within the course of the review process which might alter the local housing authority's approach. In these cases, what the applicant requires is a reconsideration of the facts relevant to his or her application, not an appeal on a point of law. The local housing authority's failure to complete the review will have prevented the applicant from having his or her case reconsidered on its facts.

19.129 The appropriate procedure in these circumstances would be for the applicant to apply by way of judicial review proceedings for a mandatory order requiring the local housing authority to complete the review and to notify the applicant of its decision on review.[248]

19.130 It may be sensible for the applicant to lodge an appellant's notice against the original decision in any event,[249] and then request that the appeal is adjourned until the judicial review application (seeking a review decision) has been determined.[250] If the applicant does not succeed in obtaining a review decision through the judicial review process, his or her appeal against the original decision will still have been issued at the court within the time limit.

Extra-statutory reviews

Preliminary reviews

19.131 As already noted,[251] prior to the introduction of HA 1996, Part 7, many local housing authorities had adopted informal local review procedures where decisions were disputed.

19.132 Since 1997, as the statutory review process has become more familiar, the operation of these informal preliminary reviews and of multi-layered reviewing has declined and, to the best of the authors' knowledge, no local housing authority in England or Wales operates a multi-staged scheme. Of

---

[247] HA 1996, s 204(1)(b) and (2).
[248] *R (Aguiar) v Newham London Borough Council* [2002] EWHC 1325 (Admin), (2002) September *Legal Action*, p 31, Admin Ct.
[249] HA 1996, s 204(1)(b).
[250] See **19.224–19.501**.
[251] See **19.3**.

course, local housing authorities may still offer informal extra-statutory reviews of those decisions which carry no right to a statutory review.[252]

Second reviews

19.133 There is no statutory provision for any further review of a review decision to be undertaken, and there is no right to request a statutory review of a review decision.[253]

19.134 Although the concept of a 're-review' is deployed in the case law, it has no statutory grounding. It is merely a convenient shorthand which refers to the exercise of the discretion enjoyed by any public authority to look again at a decision it has made.

19.135 A local housing authority is not precluded from reconsidering its decision on review, just as it is not precluded from reconsidering any other decision.[254] But if the review is reconsidered, the exercise is simply an extra-statutory reconsideration. It is not a review, and is not, and cannot be, a second statutory review.

19.136 The local housing authority may be prepared voluntarily to carry out an additional, extra-statutory reconsideration if, for example:

(1) new relevant information has come to light since the review decision; or

(2) an appeal against the review decision is likely to be mounted so that an early reconsideration would be a sensible opportunity to ensure the review decision is likely to survive judicial scrutiny; or

(3) there is some other good reason to justify looking at the matter again.

19.137 If the applicant is requesting that the local housing authority look again at the review decision, he or she should seek to dissuade the local housing authority from conducting only an informal or extra-statutory reconsideration. Instead, the applicant should ask the local housing authority to agree to treat the first review decision as withdrawn and the statutory review process as re-opened. The applicant should ask that the local housing authority confirms in writing that it is proceeding on this basis. That confirmation should also contain written agreement to any necessary extension of the time limit for completion of that review (if the original time limit has expired or is about to expire).

---

[252] See **19.12–19.37**.
[253] HA 1996, s 202(2).
[254] *R v Westminster City Council ex p Ellioua* (1998) 31 HLR 440, CA.

19.138 The applicant will need to take this course because only a true review decision, and not an extra-statutory reconsideration, can be subject to an appeal to the county court.[255]

19.139 If the local housing authority only agrees to an informal reconsideration, the applicant who wishes to preserve his or her position should bring an appeal against the statutory review decision. That appeal must be lodged within the normal 21-day period, even if the local housing authority has agreed to carry out an informal reconsideration of the review decision.

19.140 Theoretically, the decisions not to withdraw a review decision and/or not to undertake an extra-statutory reconsideration are amenable to judicial review. However, save in the most exceptional case, any such challenge is highly unlikely to be successful.[256] The better course would be to bring an appeal against the review decision or, if necessary, apply for an extension of time within which to bring that appeal.[257]

19.141 Of course, a review decision only affects the position between the applicant and the particular reviewing local housing authority. An applicant unable or unwilling to challenge an adverse review decision of a local housing authority in the county court is always free to apply to a different local housing authority.

Accommodation pending determination of the review

19.142 The local housing authority has a discretion, but not a duty, to provide accommodation for the applicant and the members of his or her household during the review process.[258] The discretion is available whether or not the applicant has been accommodated prior to the original decision.[259]

---

[255] *Demetri v Westminster City Council* (2000) 32 HLR 470, CA.
[256] Exceptionally, a claim for judicial review succeeded in quashing the local housing authority's informal reconsideration in *R (Van Der Stolk) v Camden London Borough Council* [2002] EWHC 1261 (Admin), (2002) July *Legal Action*, p 26, Admin Ct. In *R v Westminster City Council ex p Ellioua* (1999) 31 HLR 440, CA, the applicant's claim for judicial review of a refusal to reconsider did not succeed; the county court was the correct forum for an appeal against the statutory review decision. In *R (C) v Lewisham London Borough Council* [2003] EWCA Civ 927, (2004) 36 HLR 4, CA, the Court of Appeal held that the local housing authority's exercise of its extra-statutory discretion in considering an extension of time in which to request a review, a further reconsideration of a review decision or a further extension of time is close to being an absolute discretion and unlikely to be amenable to challenge by judicial review; and see *R (Slaiman) v Richmond upon Thames London Borough Council* [2006] EWHC 329 (Admin), [2006] HLR 20, Admin Ct, where a similar challenge failed.
[257] See **19.146–19.164** and **19.174–19.182**.
[258] HA 1996, ss 188(3) and 200(5). See also English Code, paras 15.12–15.20; Welsh Code, paras 21.15–21.18. See **16.36–16.48**.
[259] This important extension of the power was made by HA 1996, ss 188(3) and 200(5), amended by Homelessness Act 2002, Sch 1, para 8.

19.143 The local housing authority is under no obligation to consider, in every case, whether it should exercise the power. An applicant who wants accommodation pending the review should ask for it.[260]

19.144 If the local housing authority declines to exercise this power, a court will only intervene if the local housing authority has made an error of law in considering the exercise of its discretion (or has failed to consider the request for accommodation at all). Any challenge to the local housing authority's exercise or non-exercise of discretion can only be made by way of judicial review proceedings.[261]

19.145 A full description of the power to accommodate pending review, its various features and the scope for challenges to decisions is given in Chapter 16.[262]

APPEALS

Right to appeal

19.146 As already noted,[263] prior to HA 1996, Part 7 all legal challenges to local housing authority decisions made under the statutory homelessness provisions were brought by way of judicial review. Since 20 January 1997, challenges to most decisions are pursued instead by way of an appeal on a point of law to the county court.[264]

19.147 However, there is no free-standing or general right of appeal to the county court against every decision made under HA 1996, Part 7. The prerequisites (examined in more detail below) for a county court appeal against a substantive HA 1996, Part 7 decision are that:

(1)   the initial decision must have been a reviewable decision;[265] and

(2)   the applicant must have made a request for a review;[266] and

(3)   the review decision must have been properly notified;[267] or

(4)   the time limit for proper notification of a review decision must have expired;[268] and

---

[260]   *R (Ahmed) v Waltham Forest London Borough Council* [2001] EWHC 540 (Admin), (2001) October *Legal Action*, p 17, Admin Ct.

[261]   See **19.224–19.250**.

[262]   See **16.36–16.48**.

[263]   See **19.2–19.3**.

[264]   HA 1996, s 204(1). See also English Code, paras 19.21–19.24; Welsh Code, paras 21.19–21.26.

[265]   See **19.12–19.37**.

[266]   See **19.50–19.64**.

[267]   See **19.115–19.119**.

[268]   See **19.120–19.126**.

(5)   the appeal must be on a point of law;[269] and

(6)   the appeal must be brought within the prescribed time limit (or such extension of it as the court may allow).[270]

19.148   But there is no need for the applicant to first obtain permission to appeal from the court (or from anyone else).[271]

Was the initial decision a reviewable decision?

19.149   An appeal can only be brought against one of the decisions set out in the categories of decision conferring the right to request a review which are listed at HA 1996, s 202(1).[272]

19.150   If the decision does not fall into one of the categories specified, the applicant had no right to request a statutory review and has no right to bring a county court appeal. The appropriate challenge to any such decision is made by a claim for judicial review.[273]

Who can appeal?

19.151   The statutory appeal rights are only available to 'an applicant'.[274] No member of the applicant's household, however closely related, has that statutory right. In the case of *Lewis v Brent London Borough Council*,[275] one of two joint applicants appealed to the county court, relying on the strength of the other joint applicant's case (her husband). The appeal was dismissed and the Court of Appeal refused permission to appeal, holding that the husband was not a party to the proceedings and the wife could not rely, in her own case, on any error in the decision relating to her husband. Nor can the appeal process be activated by others who may have an interest in challenging the local housing authority's original or review decision, eg a different local housing authority, a private registered provider or registered social landlord, or another homeless person.

19.152   In addition, the applicant must actually have requested a statutory review in order to be able to bring an appeal.[276] If the applicant did not request a review of a reviewable decision, no appeal is available. The applicant in that situation could only reinstate his or her appeal rights by first asking the local

---

[269]   See **19.157–19.164**.

[270]   See **19.174–19.182**.

[271]   See *Buxton v Charnwood District Council* [2004] EWCA Civ 612, (2004) July *Legal Action*, p 19, CA, where the Court of Appeal made clear its disapproval of a local county court's practice of holding a preliminary consideration of the merits of HA 1996, s 204 appeals.

[272]   *Hackney London Borough Council v Sareen* [2003] EWCA Civ 351, (2003) 35 HLR 54, CA. See also **19.12–19.37**.

[273]   See **19.224–19.250**.

[274]   HA 1996, s 204(1).

[275]   [2005] EWCA Civ 605, (2005) July *Legal Action*, p 29, CA.

[276]   HA 1996, s 204(1).

housing authority to review its original decision. If the time limit for making a review request has expired, the local housing authority will also have to agree to extend the time limit for the making of the review request.[277]

Which decision to appeal?

19.153   Because the right of appeal is only available to an applicant who has sought a review, the appeal will normally be brought against the review decision.[278]

19.154   However, if the local housing authority has failed to notify the applicant of its review decision within the prescribed time limit (or any agreed extension of that time limit), the applicant can bring an appeal against the original decision, which was the subject of the request for the review.[279] This important provision prevents the applicant from being denied access to the courts by the local housing authority unduly prolonging the review procedure.

19.155   Even if the local housing authority has attempted to notify a review decision in time, a negative review decision is of no effect unless it has been communicated by written notice:

• containing reasons for the review decision; and

• informing the applicant of the right to appeal; and

• setting out the time limit for an appeal.[280]

19.156   Faced with a review decision which is invalid by reason of non-compliance with one or more of these provisions, the applicant can appeal against the original decision (although adding an appeal against the defective review decision in the alternative in the Appellant's Notice might be a sensible precaution).[281]

---

[277]   See **19.61–19.64**.
[278]   HA 1996, s 204(1)(a).
[279]   HA 1996, s 204(1)(b).
[280]   See **19.115–19.119**.
[281]   In *Bellamy v Hounslow London Borough Council* (reported under the name of *William v Wandsworth London Borough Council, Bellamy v Hounslow London Borough Council* [2006] EWCA Civ 535, [2006] HLR 42, CA), no review decision had been notified within the statutory time limits and the applicant appealed against the original decision. Before the appeal was heard in the county court, the local housing authority notified the applicant of its review decision. The appeal was then made against both the original and the review decision. The Court of Appeal, considering an appeal against the decision of the county court judge, doubted whether HA 1996, s 204 conferred a right of appeal against the original decision once the review decision had been notified (albeit late), and approved the first-instance judge's decision to treat the appeal as being against the review decision.

What is a 'point of law'?

19.157   Appeals can only be brought on a point of law 'arising from the decision' appealed against.[282]

19.158   Points of law include any of the grounds of challenge that would normally be available in judicial review proceedings. Traditionally those grounds for judicial review have been classified as 'illegality', 'irrationality' and 'procedural impropriety'.[283]

19.159   A point of law can be properly said to arise from any decision that:

- is based on a misconstruction of HA 1996, Part 7 or the regulations;

- is ultra vires the local housing authority's powers (ie beyond or in excess of its powers);

- is irrational;

- is taken in breach of natural justice;

- is the result of bias or bad faith;

- is reached without all necessary inquiries having been undertaken;

- is reached where there is no evidence to support factual findings made;

- is reached without regard to relevant factors;

- has failed to have regard to relevant factors; or

- gives inadequate reasons.[284]

19.160   Questions of fact, as distinct from questions of law, are for the local housing authority to decide,[285] unless the local housing authority's decision cannot be supported (in which case it will have made an error of law). Lord Millett in *Runa Begum v Tower Hamlets London Borough Council*[286] summarised the distinction between disputes of law and disputes of fact:

---

[282]   HA 1996, s 204(1).

[283]   *Council of Civil Service Unions v Minister for the Civil Service* [1985] AC 374, HL.

[284]   *Nipa Begum v Tower Hamlets London Borough Council,* (2000) 32 HLR 445, CA; see also *Runa Begum v Tower Hamlets* [2003] UKHL 5, [2006] AC 430, HL, at 439, per Lord Bingham, and at 426, per Lord Millett.

[285]   *Puhlhofer v Hillingdon London Borough Council* [1986] AC 484, HL.

[286]   [2003] UKHL 5, [2006] 2 AC 430, HL, at 462, per Lord Millett. See also Wall LJ in *Wandsworth London Borough Council v Allison* [2008] EWCA Civ 354, (2008) June *Legal Action,* p 33, CA, at [65].

'A decision may be quashed if it is based on a finding of fact or inference from the facts which is perverse or irrational; or there was no evidence to support it; or it was made by reference to irrelevant factors or without regard to relevant factors. It is not necessary to identify a specific error of law; if the decision cannot be supported the court will infer that the decision-making authority misunderstood or overlooked relevant evidence or misdirected itself in law. The court cannot substitute its own findings of fact for those of the decision-making authority if there was evidence to support them; and the questions as to the weight to be given to a particular piece of evidence and the credibility of witnesses are for the decision-making authority and not the court.'

19.161 Chadwick LJ put it succinctly in *Williams v Wandsworth London Borough Council*:[287]

'where what is alleged is a misconstruction of ascertained facts, "obvious perversity" is required before the court can properly interfere with the authority's findings of fact.'

19.162 What happens when the appellant is arguing that the review decision was based on a mistake of fact? In administrative law, there are two competing lines of authority. One argues that the issue of a mistaken fact should be absorbed into a traditional error of law approach, in that the decision-maker must have taken account of an irrelevant consideration, or failed to provide adequate or intelligible reasons, or failed to base the decision upon any evidence.[288] The other, more modern, approach holds that a mistake of fact giving rise to unfairness to the applicant can be a separate head of challenge in an appeal on a point of law. This latter view has recently prevailed in the context of asylum appeals.[289] Where there has been a mistake as to an existing 'established' fact,[290] that had not been brought about by the fault of the applicant or his or her advisers, and had played a material part in the decision-maker's decision, the decision-maker may have made an error of law.

19.163 There has been some litigation as to the extent to which the court should hear evidence as to factual issues that are contested between the parties. It is well-established that discretionary decisions, such as whether accommodation is suitable for the needs of the applicant and of his or her household, involve evaluative judgments and should be left to the local housing authority and its officers to determine (subject to the court ensuring that no errors of law were made).[291] However what about factual decisions that do not involve those evaluative judgments but instead require the local housing authority's officer to make a determination of hard fact, such as whether or not the applicant had been 'notified' as required by HA 1996, Part 7? The Supreme Court and the

---

[287] [2006] EWCA Civ 535, [2006] HLR 42, CA, at [20], per Chadwick LJ.
[288] *Wandsworth London Borough Council v A* [2000] 1 WLR 1246, CA, at 1255, per Buxton LJ; and *R v London Residuary Body ex p Inner London Education Authority* (1987) *The Times*, July 24, CA, per Watkins LJ.
[289] *E v Home Office* [2004] EWCA Civ 49, [2004] QB 1044, CA.
[290] 'Established' meaning 'uncontentious and objectively verifiable': *E v Home Office* [2004] EWCA Civ 49, [2004] QB 1044, CA, at [66], per Carnwath LJ.
[291] *Ali v Birmingham City Council* [2010] UKSC 8, [2010] 2 AC 39, SC.

Court of Appeal have held that there is no scope for a court hearing an appeal on a point of law, brought under HA 1996, s 204, to determine factual disagreements for itself. The judge should only decide whether or not the conclusion of a reviewing officer is wrong in law, and is not entitled to consider the factual issues.[292]

19.164 Procedural errors in the making of inquiries, or in the making of the decision or review decision, are errors of law and can render the relevant decision unlawful. However, procedural unfairness in the appeal process, such as a failure to provide a copy of the applicant's housing file until six days before the county court hearing, does necessarily not render the decision under appeal wrong in law.[293]

Fresh evidence

19.165 A local housing authority will not generally be said to have made an error of law if it failed to take into account information that was not put before it during its decision-making process, but is subsequently put, as new information, to the county court. Indeed, the starting-point is that a county court will not generally admit fresh evidence on an appeal at all. However, if an applicant is seeking to argue that the local housing authority made a mistake of fact or that it failed to carry out all necessary inquiries, he or she may have to present new information to the court in order to show that one of the local housing authority's factual conclusions was based on a mistake of fact, or a failure to carry out necessary inquiries.[294] The authorities on the presentation of new information have been described as 'unusually fact-sensitive' rather than laying down general propositions of law.[295] The traditional test for the submission of new information on an appeal is found in *Ladd v Marshall*,[296] which provides that the court will only permit new evidence to be produced at an appeal stage if:

(1)   it is evidence that could not have been obtained without reasonable diligence for use at trial (or, in a homelessness context, at the review or original decision stage); and

---

[292]   *Ali v Birmingham City Council* [2010] UKSC 8, [2010] 2 AC 39, SC and *Bubb v Wandsworth London Borough Council* [2011] EWCA Civ, 1285, [2012] HLR 13, CA. A judge retains the jurisdiction to consider whether, as a matter of fact, the applicant has complied with the procedural requirements of bringing an appeal under HA 1996, s 204, for example whether the appeal has been issued within the 21-day time limit, or the disputed identity of the reviewing officer, see *Butt v Hounslow London Borough Council* [2011] EWCA Civ 1327, (2012) January *Legal Action*, p 22, CA.

[293]   *Goodger v Ealing London Borough Council* [2002] EWCA Civ 751, (2003) 35 HLR 6, CA.

[294]   In *Cramp v Hastings Borough Council* [2005] EWCA Civ 1005, [2005] HLR 48, CA, the Court of Appeal overturned first-instance decisions that inadequate inquiries had been made, and noted that the inquiries said by the appellants' solicitors to be necessary in the grounds of appeal had not been suggested by those same solicitors during the review process.

[295]   *E v Home Office* [2004] EWCA Civ 49, [2004] QB 1044, CA, at [88], per Carnwath LJ.

[296]   [1954] 1 WLR 1489, CA.

(2)   the evidence would probably have an important (although it need not be decisive) influence on the outcome; and

(3)   the evidence is such as is presumably to be believed.

19.166   In *Cramp v Hastings Borough Council*,[297] the Court of Appeal warned that:

> 'judges in the county court need to be astute to ensure that evidential material over and above the contents of the housing file and the reviewing officer's decision is limited to that which is necessary to illuminate the points of law that are to be relied on in the appeal, or the issue of what, if any, relief ought to be granted. An undisciplined approach to the admission of new evidence may lead to the danger that the reviewing officer is found guilty of an error of law for not taking into account evidence that was never before her, notwithstanding the applicant's opportunity to make representations about the original decision.'[298]

Paying for an appeal

19.167   Taking cases to court is not cheap, and an appeal in the county court is no exception. The court fee alone is £135,[299] and the normal rule is that the unsuccessful party will pay the other party's legal costs, so there is a considerable financial risk.

19.168   Because appeals can only be pursued on a point of law, it is very unusual for an appeal to be brought by an individual acting in person. The services of solicitors and/or counsel will usually be required. Usually, appeals take a day, or half a day, of court time and require considerable preparation.

19.169   Some applicants will qualify for free preliminary advice from a lawyer or legal adviser under the Legal Help scheme. If an appeal is thought to have merit, application can be made for full public funding (Certificate for Legal Representation) to fund the appeal. Specialist housing solicitors and agencies with Legal Services Commission (LSC) or Legal Aid Agency (LAA) contracts will be able to grant emergency public funding so that work on an appeal can start quickly. The criteria under which the LSC will grant public funding for homelessness appeals is set out in the Funding Code (Section 7, 'Judicial Review') and in the Funding Code Decision-making Guidance (Section 16, 'Judicial Review').[300]

---

[297]   [2005] EWCA Civ 1005, [2005] HLR 48, CA.

[298]   At [71], per Brooke LJ.

[299]   At the time of writing, although it may increase. This can be waived where a litigant in person is in receipt of qualifying benefits: Civil Proceedings Fees Order 2008, SI 2008/1053, reg 5 and Sch 2. The up-to-date figures are at www.justice.gov.uk/guidance/courts-and-tribunals/courts/fees/index.htm.

[300]   Further information for lawyers and advisers on funding homelessness appeals is given in the Legal Services Commission Manual (Legal Services Commission). Note that considerable changes to public funding are likely to come into effect from April 2013 and the functions of the LSC are due to be provided by a new Legal Aid Agency.

19.170   As already noted, the normal rule is that the unsuccessful party will pay the other party's legal costs. This rule was applied in *Waltham Forest London Borough Council v Maloba*.[301]

19.171   It is not unusual for appeals brought under HA 1996, s 204, to be settled after the appeal has been issued, but before the hearing of the appeal. Usually the local housing authority will agree that the review decision should be quashed and therefore that a new review decision should be made. What should be the normal order as to costs in such circumstances? The principles can be found in the judicial review cases of *R (Boxall) v Waltham Forest London Borough Council*[302] and *R (Bahta & others) v Secretary of State for the Home Department*.[303] Those principles are:

- the court has the power to make a costs order when the substantive proceedings have been resolved without a hearing but the parties have not agreed about costs;

- it will ordinarily be irrelevant that the appellant is receiving public funding;

- the overriding objective is to do justice between the parties without incurring unnecessary court time and consequential additional cost;

- at each end of the spectrum there will be cases where it is obvious which side would have won had the substantive issues been fought to a conclusion; in between, the position will be less clear;

- how far the court will be prepared to look into the previously unresolved substantive issues will depend on the circumstances of the particular case not least the amount of costs at stake and the conduct of the parties;

- in the absence of a good reason to make any other order, the fall back is to make no order as to costs;[304] and

- the court should take care to ensure that it does not discourage parties from settling proceedings, for example by a local housing authority making a concession at an early stage.[305]

---

[301]   [2007] EWCA Civ 1281, [2008] HLR 26, CA, where the local housing authority argued unsuccessfully that there should be a general practice on HA 1996, s 204 appeals that any order for costs made against a local housing authority should be subject to a stay until after the re-determination of the decision under appeal and any subsequent appeal from that re-determination.

[302]   (2001) 4 CCLR 258, Admin Ct.

[303]   [2011] EWCA Civ 895, [2011] 5 Costs LR 857, CA.

[304]   Which has the effect that each party pays his or her own costs or, if a party is receiving public funding, the LSC will pay that party's costs: CPR PD 44, para 8.5.

[305]   Per Scott Baker J in *R (Boxall) v Waltham Forest London Borough Council* (2001) 4 CCLR 258, Admin Ct, at [22], quoted by Pill LJ in *R (Bahta) v SSHD* [2011] EWCA Civ 895, [2011] 5 Costs LR 857, CA at [7].

19.172 The practice has been that costs should be awarded where it is 'plain and obvious' that one party would have succeeded. If it is not 'plain and obvious', the usual order would be no order as to costs.[306] If agreement is reached between the parties as to most of the terms of a settlement, but not as to costs, the court has jurisdiction to hear submissions on the appropriate costs order. The court may be prepared to make an order having received written submissions from the parties (if both parties agree) or after an oral hearing.

19.173 These principles were applied in a HA 1996, Part 7 case by the Court of Appeal in *Harripaul v Lewisham London Borough Council*.[307] The applicant had been unsuccessful in her HA 1996, s 204 appeal before the first-instance judge. She had been given permission by the Court of Appeal to bring a second appeal.[308] Before the second appeal could be heard, the local housing authority informed the applicant that it would withdraw the review decision and carry out a fresh review. It was agreed between the parties that there would be no order as to costs in respect of the county court proceedings. Ms Harripaul pursued an application to the Court of Appeal that the local housing authority should pay the costs of her bringing the second appeal. The judge decided that:

(1)   the consequence of the local housing authority's decision to withdraw the review decision was that the applicant had succeeded;

(2)   the starting point was therefore that she should be entitled to her costs;

(3)   this was not a case in which it was obvious that the applicant would have won the appeal but she had at least a good arguable case that could well have resulted in success;

(4)   an early settlement of the appeal would make good practical sense; and

(5)   there were no factors justifying a departure from the general rule that the successful party should be entitled to her costs being paid by the other side.[309]

Time limit

19.174 If the appeal is being made against a decision reached on review, the appeal must be brought within 21 days of the appellant being notified of the review decision.[310] The time limit therefore begins to run on the date that the notice of review decision is actually received by the appellant or by his or her agents rather than the date on the review decision letter or the date it is sent.[311]

---

[306]   *R (Rahta) v SSHD*, [2011] EWCA Civ 895 [2011] 5 Costs LR 857, CA per Pill LJ at [7].
[307]   [2012] EWCA Civ 266, [2012] HLR 24, CA.
[308]   See **19.213–19.223**.
[309]   Rimer LJ at [10]–[12].
[310]   HA 1996, s 204(2).
[311]   *Aadan v Brent London Borough Council* (1999) 32 HLR 848, CA, at 851, per Chadwick LJ.

The last day of the 21-day period is the twenty-first day from the date of receipt, so that if a review decision is received on 4 July, the last day for bringing the appeal is 24 July.

19.175 If the appeal is being made in respect of an original decision, the appeal must be brought within 21 days of the date on which the review of that decision should have been notified. This time limit will therefore be calculated from the last day of the time limit for the conclusion of the review.[312] As already noted,[313] that will usually be a date eight weeks after the date on which the request for a review was made, meaning that an appeal against an original decision should be brought within 21 days after the end of the eight-week period.

19.176 An appeal is brought when an Appellant's Notice (court form N161) is filed at the county court.[314] 'Filing' means 'delivering it, by post or otherwise, to the court office'.[315] The form can be sent by fax or, in certain specified courts, by email or by online form.[316] Although criticised by the Court of Appeal,[317] Practice Directions 5A and 5B specify that, where a fax or email is received after 4pm on a working day, the document sent should not be recorded as 'filed' until the next working day.[318] However, documents physically posted through a court's letterbox after close of business on a working day, but before midnight, are 'filed' on that day, and not on the following working day.[319] Where the final day falls on a non-working day, the period in which the form must be filed ends on the next day on which the court office is open.[320]

19.177 If there is any dispute over the date on which the appellant was notified of the review decision (or as to the date on which the time limit for review expired), the court itself will have to decide the question of the correct date, and go on to decide whether or not the appeal was filed within the 21-day time limit.[321]

---

[312] HA 1996, s 204(2).

[313] See **19.127–19.130**.

[314] CPR, r 52.4(2) and PD 52D, para 28.

[315] CPR, r 2.3(1) and 5.5 and PD 5B.

[316] CPR, PD5B. The facility to file electronically is not available where a fee is payable. PD5C provides a procedure for filing electronically in the Court of Appeal, but not in the county court.

[317] *Van Aken v Camden London Borough Council* [2002] EWCA Civ 1724, (2003) 35 HLR 33, CA per Ward LJ at [60].

[318] PD 5A, para 5.3(3); PD 5B, para 8.4(2).

[319] *Van Aken v Camden London Borough Council* [2002] EWCA Civ 1724, (2003) 35 HLR 33, CA.

[320] CPR, r 2.8(5); *Aadan v Brent London Borough Council* (2000) 32 HLR 848, CA.

[321] See *Bakare v Waltham Forest London Borough Council* (1998) December *Legal Action*, p 27, Bow County Court, where the local housing authority put in evidence as to the method and likely date of delivery and the appellant had no contrary evidence, the court held that he had been notified more than 21 days before the appeal had been filed; and *Lambeth London Borough Council v Namegembe* [2006] EWHC 3608 (Ch), (2007) February *Legal Action*, p 31, ChD. These decisions are made under the county court's own jurisdiction to apply the Civil Procedure Rules and are different from the prohibition on courts making factual decisions in areas that were the province of the local housing authority's decision-maker, see

19.178 As already noted,[322] notification is treated as having occurred if the decision has been made available at the local housing authority's office for a reasonable period for collection.[323] However, this deeming provision only applies where the review decision has *not* been sent to the appellant.

Extending the time limit[324]

19.179 The county court may give permission for an appeal to be brought after the end of the 21-day period if it is satisfied that there was a good reason for the failure to bring the appeal in time and for any delay in applying for permission to extend time.[325] Permission may be applied for either during the 21-day period, or after it has ended.[326]

19.180 The court may give permission to extend time before the expiry of the 21-day period. This provision might be thought helpful where it is appreciated that the time limit is about to expire but an Appellant's Notice cannot be prepared in time. But if the applicant can manage to lodge an application to extend the time limit, it is a little difficult to envisage a case in which the applicant (or his or her advisers) could not have filed even a very basic Appellant's Notice. Indeed, a professional adviser may be in difficulties if no such Appellant's Notice is filed in time, because it is always possible that a time extension, for which an application is made instead, will be refused.

19.181 If the concern is that it is getting late on a working day, and that day is the last day of the 21-day time limit, some comfort can be taken from the Court of Appeal's decision in *Van Aken v Camden London Borough Council*.[327] The appellant's advisers, confronted with the imminent expiry of the 21-day period, should aim to file the notice of appeal by posting it through the letterbox of the court (if one exists) at any time until midnight of that twenty-first day, rather than apply for permission to extend time.

19.182 In *Short v Birmingham City Council*,[328] the High Court upheld the first-instance judge's approach to whether or not to grant permission to appeal out of time. The court should first consider the reasons for delay and only consider the merits of the appeal, and the hardship to the applicant, if there were good reasons for that delay. In *Barrett v Southwark London Borough*

19.160–19.163. A court can also hear evidence as to the local housing authority's compliance with the Regulations governing the review process, see *Butt v Hounslow London Borough Council* [2011] EWCA Civ 1327, (2012) January *Legal Action*, p 22, CA.

[322] See **19.115**.

[323] HA 1996, s 203(8).

[324] See Holbrook 'Appeals under the Homelessness Act 2002 – Part 2' (2002) December *Legal Action*, p 31.

[325] HA 1996, s 204(2A).

[326] HA 1996, s 204(2A).

[327] *Van Aken v Camden London Borough Council* [2002] EWCA Civ 1724, [2003] 35 HLR 33, CA. See also **19.176**.

[328] [2004] EWHC 2112 (QB), [2005] HLR 6, QBD.

Council,[329] the judge said 'good reason is a phrase in common parlance, which ... does not need elaboration'[330] and that all the circumstances were relevant.[331] Once it had been decided that there was 'good reason', permission should be given, unless the appeal is 'hopeless'.[332]

Procedure

19.183   The Civil Procedure Rules (CPR) and Practice Directions (PD) (particularly CPR 52 and PDs 52A–52E inclusive) govern the procedure for the county court appeal.[333] The appellant should file and serve the following documents:

- the Appellant's Notice on form N161 plus two additional copies for the court and a copy for the respondent;

- a copy of the decision subject to the appeal; and

- proposed case management directions.[334]

19.184   If the appellant is seeking permission to extend time, that application should be made in the Appellant's Notice and should be supported by a witness statement explaining the good reason for the failure to bring the appeal in time and for any delay since the time limit expired.[335]

19.185   As soon as practicable, and in any event within 35 days of the filing of the Appellant's Notice, the appellant should file an appeal bundle which contains:

- a copy of the Appellant's Notice;

- a copy of the appellant's skeleton argument and any skeleton argument filed at that stage by the respondent;

- a copy of the decision subject to the appeal;

---

[329]   [2008] EWHC 1568 (Comm), QBD.

[330]   *Barrett v Southwark London Borough Council* [2008] EWHC 1568 (Comm), (2008) September *Legal Action*, p 26, QBD, at [24], per Sir Thomas Morrison.

[331]   In *Barrett v Southwark London Borough Council* [2008] EWHC 1568 (Comm), (2008) September *Legal Action*, p 26, QBD, permission was given to bring an appeal four weeks late, where a profoundly deaf applicant had made diligent and wide attempts to obtain legal advice and had continued to try to find legal representation, even though she had received unfavourable advice.

[332]   *Barrett v Southwark London Borough Council* [2008] EWHC 1568 (Comm), (2008) September *Legal Action*, p 26, QBD, at [28], per Sir Thomas Morrison.

[333]   General procedure is at PD52A. Procedure for county court appeal is at PD 52B. Specific requirements for HA 1996, s 204 appeals are at para 28 of PD 52D.

[334]   PD 52B, paras 4.2 and 6.4 and PD 52D, para 28.1. There is an additional seven days from the date of filing in which to serve the documents (CPR 52.4(3)(b)).

[335]   CPR 52 and PD 52B, paras 3.1–3.3.

- any witness statements; and

- any other relevant documents such as extracts from the homelessness file
  if received from the local housing authority and any relevant
  correspondence.[336]

19.186 If the appellant has not received the whole of the homelessness file
from the local housing authority, then an application should be made in the
Appellant's Notice for a direction requiring the local housing authority (which
in the appeal will be described as 'the respondent') to disclose it. The
application can be made in the proposed case management directions which are
filed when the Appellant's Notice is issued.[337]

19.187 The respondent should consider the proposed case management
directions and either agree them or file and serve its own proposed directions
within 14 days of service of the Appellant's Notice on it. It should also disclose
any documents relevant to the appeal which had not previously been disclosed
within the same 14-day period. The appellant may then amend his or her
grounds of appeal if necessary, within 14 days of the documents being
disclosed to him or her.[338]

19.188 The usual practice is that witness statements need not be filed by either
party. If the points of law raised can be determined solely on contents of the
review letter and the relevant parts of the homelessness file, there will be no
need for any witness statement by the applicant. If, on the other hand, one of
the points of law is that the local housing authority has failed to make all
necessary inquiries, it can be helpful for the applicant to make a witness
statement in which he or she sets out what inquiries should have been made
and, if possible, what the results of those inquiries would have been. If the local
housing authority is satisfied that its review decision is correct, there will
normally be no need for a witness statement from the reviewing officer or any
other officer. Sometimes local housing authorities will want to put in witness
statements, usually by the decision-maker, to explain or elucidate the reasons
contained in the written decision. The purpose and admissibility of those
witness statements (formerly affidavits) was considered in detail by the Court of
Appeal in *R v Westminster City Council ex p Ermakov*.[339] Where the contents of

---

[336] PD 52B, para 6.4. In *Cramp v Hastings Borough Council* [2005] EWCA Civ 1005, [2005] HLR
48, CA, the Court of Appeal stated that it was 'thoroughly bad practice to state the barest
possible grounds in the original notice of appeal ... and then to delay formulating and serving
very substantial amended grounds of appeal for five months so that they surfaced for the first
time less than a week before the appeal hearing' (Brooke LJ at [72]). They also said that the
appeal bundle should be limited to the grounds of appeal, the decision being appealed and
only those documents which the appellant reasonably considers necessary to enable the appeal
court to reach its decision on the hearing. Documents extraneous to the issues to be considered
on appeal must be excluded, and it was quite wrong to photocopy the entire contents of a
bulky housing file regardless of whether it was necessary to do so.
[337] PD 52D, para 28.1 and **19.183**.
[338] PD 52D, para 28.1(5).
[339] *R v Westminster City Council ex p Ermakov* (1996) 28 HLR 819, [1996] 2 All ER 302, CA.

the witness statement serve to elucidate the reasons contained in the decision letter, they will be admissible. Examples of circumstances in which evidence might elucidate, rather than alter, the original decision were said to include where: 'an error has been made in transcription or expression, or a word or words inadvertently omitted, or where the language used may be in some way lacking in clarity.'[340] Where, however, the contents fundamentally alter the reasons in the decision letter, they should not be admitted.

19.189 In *Bellamy v Hounslow London Borough Council*,[341] the Court of Appeal made some cautionary remarks about the use of witness statements in second appeals,[342] which also hold true for first-instance appeals to the county court:

> 'Witness statements are a proper vehicle for relevant and admissible evidence going to the issue before the court, and for nothing else. Argument is for advocates. Innuendo has no place at all.'[343]

19.190 Once the homelessness file has been disclosed, any witness statements and skeleton arguments have been filed, and a bundle of documents has been prepared,[344] the appeal will generally be ready for hearing. The hearing itself will consist of oral argument, based on the skeleton arguments. Since the appeal is on a point of law, there is not generally any need for live evidence to be given.

19.191 Homelessness appeals may only be heard by a circuit judge, not a district judge.[345]

---

[340] *R v Westminster City Council ex p Ermakov* (1996) 28 HLR 819, [1996] 2 All ER 302, CA, at 315H, per Hutchison LJ; and see also *R v Westminster City Council ex p Khanam* (unreported) 9 May 1997, QBD, and *Hijazi v Kensington and Chelsea Royal London Borough Council* [2003] EWCA Civ 692, [2003] HLR 72, CA. In *Swords v Secretary of State for Communities and Local Government* [2007] EWCA Civ 795, [2008] HLR 17, CA, the Court of Appeal approved five reasons for admitting a witness statement into evidence, including '[i] it must, as a matter of common sense, be easier for a decision-maker to secure permission to make a belated assertion that she took into account a factor to which she had not previously referred but gave it no weight than that she gave weight to a factor to which she had not previously referred; for in the former case the lack of previous reference would be inherently less significant' (Wilson LJ at [47]).

[341] Reported under the name of *William v Wandsworth London Borough Council, Bellamy v Hounslow London Borough Council* [2006] EWCA Civ 535, [2006] HLR 42, CA.

[342] See **19.213–19.223.**

[343] *Bellamy v Hounslow London Borough Council* [2006] EWCA Civ 535, [2006] HLR 42, CA, at [80], per Sedley LJ.

[344] See **19.185.**

[345] CPR 2 and PD 2B, para 9.

Powers of the county court on an appeal

19.192 If the court concludes that there has been an error of law, it may confirm, quash or vary the decision which is the subject of the appeal;[346] if there is no error of law, it will dismiss the appeal.

Confirming the decision

19.193 The court is only entitled to confirm a decision that contains an error of law in one of two circumstances:

(1) if it is satisfied that a properly directed local housing authority, which did not make the same error of law, would inevitably have reached the same decision;[347] or

(2) if it is satisfied that the bringing of the appeal was an abuse of process in the sense that bringing the appeal was for practical purposes 'pointless', even though there was some irregularity in the decision appealed against.[348]

Quashing the decision

19.194 Normally, where there is an error of law, the court will simply quash the decision that has been the subject of the appeal.

19.195 If a review decision is quashed on appeal, then the review process will not have been concluded because no legally correct review decision has been reached. The reviewing officer will need to re-open the review and the applicant and the local housing authority will need to agree in writing a new deadline for the completion of the review (as the original prescribed time limit will inevitably have expired by this stage).[349]

---

[346] HA 1996, s 204(3).

[347] The test is one of inevitability; if there is any real possibility of a different conclusion being reached, it is wrong for the court to confirm the decision: *Ali and Nessa v Newham London Borough Council* [2001] EWCA Civ 73, [2002] HLR 20, CA.

[348] *O'Connor v Kensington and Chelsea Royal London Borough Council* [2004] EWCA Civ 394 [2004] HLR 37, CA, at [42]–[43], per Waller LJ and Carnwath LJ, giving majority judgments on this point (Sedley LJ dissenting). In *Ugiagbe v Southwark London Borough Council* [2009] EWCA Civ 31, [2009] HLR 35, CA, by the time the appeal reached the Court of Appeal the applicant had found herself accommodation. The Court of Appeal rejected the local housing authority's submission that the appeal was academic, and because there was a risk that the applicant might again become homeless, it quashed the review decision, see Lloyd LJ at [30]–[32].

[349] See **19.120–19.126**. If, however, the local housing authority has applied for permission to bring a second appeal, the Court of Appeal has suggested that both parties should agree that the new review decision should not be notified until the appeal process has been concluded: *William v Wandsworth London Borough Council* [2006] EWCA Civ 535, [2006] HLR 42, CA, at [42], per Chadwick LJ.

19.196 If the decision quashed on appeal is the original decision, then the local housing authority will have to take a fresh decision, having carried out such further inquiries as it considers necessary.

19.197 It is by no means inevitable that, following a successful appeal, the new decision reached will be different in effect from the one quashed. In either case the reviewing officer or the local housing authority must make the fresh decision on the basis of the facts and information as they stand at the date of that new decision, which may be very different from how they stood at the date of the quashed decision or even at the date of the quashing.

Varying the decision

19.198 It is unusual for the court to exercise its power to *vary* the decision appealed against. It may do so where it is satisfied on the evidence that there was only one lawful conclusion for the local housing authority to have reached, or, as Sedley LJ has put it: 'where the decision was erroneous in law and only a contrary decision was lawfully possible'.[350] In *Bond v Leicester City Council*,[351] the Court of Appeal held that, had the local housing authority asked itself the right question, it was 'more likely than not' that it would have found that the applicant was homeless and the court varied the decision accordingly. In *Ekwuru v Westminster City Council*,[352] the Court of Appeal held that, where the local housing authority had conceded that three successive statutory review decisions had been wrong in law, and there was no material which would entitle it to reach a conclusion other than that the applicant had not become homeless intentionally, it would exceptionally vary the latest decision rather than quash it.[353] It may also be appropriate to use this power where the behaviour of the local housing authority has been open to criticism, eg where it has repeatedly made and then withdrawn defective decisions.[354]

---

[350] *Ozbek v Ipswich Borough Council* [2006] EWCA Civ 534, [2006] HLR 41 CA, at [63], per Sedley LJ. See, as one example, *Mohammed v Waltham Forest London Borough Council* (2002) October *Legal Action*, p 30, Bow County Court.

[351] [2001] EWCA Civ 1544, [2002] HLR 6, CA.

[352] *Ekwuru v Westminster City Council* [2003] EWCA Civ 1293 [2004] HLR 13, CA.

[353] See also the following cases in which the power to vary was used: *Woodrow v Lewisham London Borough Council* (2000) November *Legal Action*, p 23, Woolwich County Court; *Yousif v Newham London Borough Council* (2002) December *Legal Action*, p 22, Bow County Court; *Bond v Leicester City Council* [2001] EWCA Civ 1544, [2002] HLR 6, CA; *Lane and Ginda v Islington London Borough Council* (2001) April *Legal Action*, p 21, Clerkenwell County Court; *Fetaj v Lambeth London Borough Council* (2002) September *Legal Action*, p 31, Lambeth County Court; *Houghton v Sheffield City Council* [2006] EWCA Civ 1799, (2007) March *Legal Action*, p 18, CA; *Benson v Lewisham London Borough Council* (2007) October *Legal Action*, p 26, Central London County Court; *Bolah v Croydon London Borough Council* (2008) February *Legal Action*, p 40, Central London County Court; *Quaid v Westminster City Council* (2008) February *Legal Action*, p 41, Central London County Court; *Adekunle v Islington London Borough Council* (2009) November *Legal Action*, p 25, Mayor's and City of London County Court; *Villiers v Lewisham London Borough Council* (2009) November *Legal Action*, p 26, Central London County Court; and *O'Callaghan v Southwark London Borough Council* (2010) May *Legal Action*, p 23, Lambeth County Court.

[354] *Mohamud v Lambeth London Borough Council* (2002) May *Legal Action*, p 30, Wandsworth County Court. In *Wandsworth London Borough Council v Brown* [2005] EWCA Civ 907, (2005)

19.199 More recently, the Court of Appeal has upheld two first-instance decisions where the judge had varied the review decision. In *Tower Hamlets London Borough Council v Deugi*,[355] the local housing authority had conceded that its decision that the applicant was not eligible was wrong, and the Court of Appeal held that varying the decision would provide some enduring benefit to the applicant, and so the first-instance judge was correct to vary it. In *Slater v Lewisham London Borough Council*,[356] the Court of Appeal agreed with the first-instance judge that there was no real prospect that the local housing authority, acting rationally and with the benefit of any further inquiries it might make, could conclude that it was reasonable for an offer of accommodation to be accepted, and it upheld the first-instance judge's decision to vary a review decision to a finding that the duty to provide accommodation had not been discharged.

19.200 The House of Lords varied a review decision in *Moran v Manchester City Council*,[357] having found that the applicant could not have become homeless intentionally from a women's refuge, because the refuge in that case had not been reasonable for the applicant to continue to occupy.[358]

19.201 The county court does not have any power to make a mandatory order to require that certain steps are taken or procedures are followed: in contrast to the power available to the Administrative Court on judicial review. So that where a county court judge had allowed an appeal and ordered that a further review be conducted by a different reviewing officer, he had exceeded his powers.[359] In any event, there should be no need for any additional order or direction. The statutory scheme makes it tolerably clear what should occur after a decision is confirmed, varied or quashed.

Accommodation pending appeal

19.202 The local housing authority has a power, but not a duty, to provide accommodation pending the making or determination of a county court appeal. The scope and exercise of the power is detailed in Chapter 16,[360] but a brief outline is given here for ease of reference.

Legal Action, p 16, CA, the first-instance judge varied a decision that the appellant was not 'vulnerable', which he held to be perverse, to a decision that he was 'vulnerable'. The local housing authority was refused permission to bring a second appeal, as no important point of principle was raised; see **19.213–19.223**.

[355] [2006] EWCA Civ 159, [2006] HLR 28, CA.

[356] [2006] EWCA Civ 394, [2006] HLR 37, CA. It should be noted that the issue under consideration in *Slater v Lewisham London Borough Council* is no longer applicable since the amendments to HA 1996, s 193(7F) inserted by LA 2011, s 148(9) for applicants whose applications for homelessness assistance were made on or after 9 November 2012 to a local housing authority in England. At the date of writing, the amendments to HA 1996 made by LA 2011, ss 148 149 had not been brought into effect in Wales. See **17.138–17.146**.

[357] *Ali & others v Birmingham City Council, Moran v Manchester City Council* [2009] UKHL 36, [2009] 1 WLR 1506, HL, at [65]–[66], per Baroness Hale.

[358] See **11.113**.

[359] *Adan v Newham London Borough Council* [2001] EWCA Civ 1916, (2002) 34 HLR 28, CA.

[360] See **16.49–16.55**.

19.203 The power is triggered as soon as the period for an appeal starts to run, so the applicant need not actually have lodged an appeal before inviting the local housing authority to provide accommodation (or to continue accommodation). The local housing authority can only exercise its discretion to provide accommodation,[361] if it previously owed the appellant a duty to provide accommodation under HA 1996, ss 188,[362] 190,[363] or 200,[364] or had the power to provide accommodation under HA 1996, s 195(8).[365] When considering whether or not to exercise its discretion to provide accommodation pending an appeal, the local housing authority should take into account the factors set out in *R v Camden London Borough Council ex p Mohammed*,[366] ie the prospects of success on appeal,[367] the appellant's personal circumstances, and any new information.[368]

19.204 If the local housing authority refuses to provide accommodation pending the determination of the appeal, or decides to provide accommodation only for a limited period, the appellant may appeal to the county court against that decision on a point of law.[369] This is a separate appeal from the main homelessness appeal and, for ease of reference, is referred to by the section number which contains the right to appeal: 'section 204A'. The principles to be applied in a HA 1996, s 204A appeal are the same as those applied in s 204 appeals and in judicial review.

19.205 Prior to 30 September 2002, any challenges to a refusal to provide accommodation pending appeal could only be brought by judicial review and the case law from that period is still instructive.[370] The Court of Appeal in *R v Brighton & Hove Council ex p Nacion*[371] held that where the local housing authority had followed the guidance in *Mohammed*,[372] any challenges arguing

[361] HA 1996, s 204(4).
[362] Interim accommodation duty pending decision or power to accommodate pending review. See **16.12–16.28**.
[363] Accommodation for those who have a priority need and have become homeless intentionally. See **17.182–17.189**.
[364] Duty to accommodate applicant pending referral. See **15.157–15.160** and **16.56–16.63**.
[365] Accommodation for those threatened with homelessness, pending review.
[366] *R v Camden London Borough Council ex p Mohammed* (1998) 30 HLR 315, QBD.
[367] *R v Newham London Borough Council ex p Lumley* (2001) 33 HLR 124, QBD.
[368] This power to provide accommodation pending appeal to the county court is not available to certain applicants from other EEA states, failed asylum-seekers, or people unlawfully present in the UK, unless the local housing authority considers it necessary in order to prevent a breach of rights under the European Convention on Human Rights or European Community law: Nationality, Immigration and Asylum Act 2002, s 54 and Sch 3, para 1, in force from 8 January 2003. For an example of an unsuccessful attempt to challenge a refusal to secure accommodation pending appeal (with complicated procedural points involved) see *R (Kondoyba) v Kensington & Chelsea Royal London Borough Council* [2011] EWHC 2653 (Admin), (2011) December *Legal Action*, p 30, Admin Ct. See **16.65**, **20.46–20.48** and **20.65–20.73**.
[369] HA 1996, s 204A.
[370] *Ali v Westminster City Council* (1999) 31 HLR 349, CA.
[371] (1999) 31 HLR 1095, CA.
[372] *R v Camden London Borough Council ex p Mohammed* (1998) 30 HLR 315, QBD. See **16.36–16.48**.

that the refusal to provide accommodation was wrong in law were likely to be futile, and applications should be strongly discouraged. The appropriate remedy for an appellant would normally be to apply to expedite the county court homelessness appeal, rather than bring judicial review proceedings.

19.206 After the HA 1996, s 204A appeal procedure was introduced,[373] the Court of Appeal considered the scope of those appeals in *Francis v Kensington and Chelsea Royal London Borough Council*.[374] In that case, the Court of Appeal applied its previous decision in *Nacion*[375] to appeals against the refusal of accommodation pending a homelessness appeal. It held that, unless the court considers that the local housing authority has failed to direct itself in accordance with *Mohammed*,[376] it should not intervene. Where the local housing authority has not properly directed itself, the decision should be quashed and the court should consider whether to exercise its power to order the local housing authority to provide accommodation pending the determination of the appeal.[377] The court should not embark on a review of the merits of the main appeal. The local housing authority is required to consider the applicant's grounds of appeal, as part of its consideration of the merits of the case, but would not normally be expected to refer to any of the grounds of appeal in its decision letter unless there is some important and striking ground which requires specific comment.[378]

19.207 In the light of the pronouncements made in these judicial review and Court of Appeal cases, if the local housing authority has considered the *Mohammed*[379] factors and applied them to the appellant's circumstances, an appeal against the refusal to accommodate pending appeal is unlikely to be successful. Indeed, where the appeal against the refusal to accommodate pending appeal was heard just one week before the date for hearing the full HA 1996, s 204 appeal, that in itself was a reason not to uphold the appeal. That is not to suggest that on a HA 1996, s 204A appeal in an appropriate case a court would not quash a decision to refuse to accommodate.[380] There must be proper consideration of the *Mohammed*[381] factors. Simply referring to them was described in one case as paying only 'lip-service', and a refusal to accommodate

---

[373] By Homelessness Act 2002, s 11, with effect from 30 September 2002.

[374] [2003] EWCA Civ 443, (2003) 35 HLR 50, CA.

[375] *R v Brighton & Hove Council ex p Nacion* (1999) 31 HLR 1095, CA.

[376] *R v Camden London Borough Council ex p Mohammed* (1998) 30 HLR 315, QBD. See **16.36–16.48**.

[377] Confirmed again by the Court of Appeal in *Brookes v Croydon London Borough Council* [2004] EWCA Civ 439, (2004) June *Legal Action*, p 31, CA and reviewed in *R (Kondoyba) v Kensington & Chelsea Royal London Borough Council* [2011] EWHC 2653 (Admin), (2011) December *Legal Action*, p 30, Admin Ct per HHJ Robinson at [44]–[45].

[378] *Lewis v Havering London Borough Council* [2006] EWCA Civ 1793, [2007] HLR 20, CA.

[379] *R v Camden London Borough Council ex p Mohammed* (1998) 30 HLR 315, QBD. See **16.36–16.48**.

[380] See *Onyaebor v Newham London Borough Council* (2004) May *Legal Action*, p 27, Bow County Court, and *Quadir v Tower Hamlets London Borough Council* (2011), (2012) April *Legal Action*, p 42, Central London Civil Justice Centre for examples of successful s 204A appeals.

[381] *R v Camden London Borough Council ex p Mohammed* (1998) 30 HLR 315, QBD.

pending review was quashed.[382] The HA 1996, s 204A appeal is only available in respect of a 'decision' not to accommodate pending an appeal. Where a local housing authority has failed altogether to make a decision on a request for accommodation pending appeal, the appropriate procedure is to seek a judicial review of the failure to make a decision. This has been described as a 'serious weakness' in the drafting of the section.[383]

Procedure[384]

19.208 There is no statutory time limit for the filing of an Appellant's Notice in a HA 1996, s 204A appeal against a refusal to accommodate pending appeal. The limit is therefore the 21-day period generally applied by the procedure rules to appeals.[385] If possible, the appellant should file one Appellant's Notice (form N161) containing both the main homelessness appeal and the s 204A appeal.[386] Otherwise, the s 204A appeal can be brought on a separate form N161.[387] The appellant should comply with CPR 52 and PDs 52A, 52B and 52D. See **19.183–19.185** for the documents required to be filed and served.

19.209 If a HA 1996, s 204A appeal is brought, the need for a speedy decision is obvious. The whole point is to provide accommodation urgently. An application can therefore be made for an interim injunction requiring that the local housing authority provide accommodation until the s 204A appeal is determined. The matters to be considered on the application for an interim injunction would include:

(1) the merits of the HA 1996, s 204A appeal itself and whether the applicant has a strong prima facie case;[388]

(2) whether or not the appellant's ability to pursue the main homelessness appeal would be substantially prejudiced if no interim order was made;[389] and

---

[382] *R (Paul-Coker) v Lewisham London Borough Council* [2006] EWHC 497 (Admin), [2006] HLR 32.

[383] Robert Duddridge 'House of Bricks or House of Sticks: Some thoughts on the new s 204A of the Housing Act 1996' [2003] JHL 11.

[384] See Jon Holbrook 'Appeals under the Homelessness Act 2002 – Part 1' (2002) November *Legal Action*, p 26.

[385] CPR 52.4(2).

[386] PD 52D, para 28.1(1).

[387] PD 52D, para 28.2.

[388] *Putans v Tower Hamlets London Borough Council* [2006] EWHC 1634 (Ch), [2007] HLR 10, ChD at [52], per Michael Briggs QC, applying the principles in *American Cyanamid Co v Ethicon Ltd* [1975] AC 396, HL to HA 1996, s 204A.

[389] HA 1996, s 204A(6)(a).

(3) the balance of convenience as between the appellant and the local housing authority as at the date of the hearing of the application for an interim injunction.[390]

19.210 An application can be made in the Appellant's Notice for an urgent injunction requiring the local housing authority to secure that accommodation is available for the applicant's occupation. If, exceptionally, the court were to make an order to that effect without giving the parties notice of any hearing, the appellant must serve his or her Appellant's Notice and a copy of the order on the respondent. The court would normally fix a hearing date when it will reconsider whether the order should continue.[391]

19.211 Appeals under HA 1996, s 204A can only be heard by a circuit judge.[392] The appeal may not be brought after the determination of the main homelessness appeal.[393]

19.212 At the final hearing of the HA 1996, s 204A appeal, the court may either confirm or quash the decision made by the local housing authority (refusing accommodation pending the main appeal). Variation is not a possibility. If the court quashes the decision, it may order that the local housing authority provides that accommodation is available for the appellant until the main appeal has been determined, or any earlier specified time. It can only order the local housing authority to provide accommodation if it is satisfied that the appellant's ability to pursue the main appeal would otherwise be substantially prejudiced.[394]

Appeal to the Court of Appeal

19.213 Any appeals against orders of the county court determining a main homelessness appeal or a HA 1996, s 204A appeal are *second* appeals and can only be made to the Court of Appeal.[395]

19.214 Such appeals require permission to appeal. Permission can be given only by the Court of Appeal itself and will only be given if the appeal raises 'an important point of principle or practice', or there is 'some other compelling reason' for the Court of Appeal to hear it.[396]

---

[390] See *R v Kensington & Chelsea Royal London Borough Council ex p Hammell* [1989] 1 QB 518, CA.

[391] PD 52D, paras 28.3 and 28.4.

[392] CPR 2 and PD 2B, para 9.

[393] HA 1996, s 204A(3).

[394] HA 1996, s 204A(5) and (6). For an example where the Court quashed the decision under appeal, but declined to make an injunction requiring the local housing authority to provide accommodation, see *Quadir v Tower Hamlets London Borough Council* (2011), (2012) April *Legal Action*, p 42, Central London Civil Justice Centre.

[395] *Azimi v Newham London Borough Council* (2001) 33 HLR 51, CA.

[396] CPR, r 52.13.

19.215 In *Uphill v BRB (Residuary) Ltd*,[397] the Court of Appeal considered the general principles to be applied when deciding whether to give permission to bring a second appeal.

19.216 It held that permission should only be granted in exceptional cases. When permission was sought under the first limb ('an important point of principle or practice'), it could be granted where such an important point had not yet been determined by a higher court, but would not be granted where the contention was merely that an established point of principle or practice had not been correctly applied. As far as the second limb was concerned ('some other compelling reason'), the starting point was that the prospects of success had to be very high. Even if they were very high, the decision against which the appellant sought permission to appeal had to be inconsistent with the authority of a higher court or tainted with some procedural irregularity leading to unfairness before permission would be given.[398]

19.217 The Court of Appeal considered the second limb of the test ('some other compelling reason') in *Cramp v Hastings Borough Council*.[399] It held that there was a good prospect of success on a second appeal because the first-instance judge had appeared to substitute his own view for that of the local housing authority. There was evidence before the Court of Appeal that the extent of inquiries needed to be undertaken by the local housing authority was a matter of great concern to it and had implications for its resources. Those two points together were 'compelling reasons' sufficient to justify a second appeal.[400]

19.218 In *Camden London Borough Council v Phillips*,[401] the Court of Appeal granted the local housing authority permission to appeal (having heard the full appeal in *Cramp v Hastings Borough Council*, which had been listed for hearing on the same day). It noted that the guidance in *Uphill v BRB Residuary Board Ltd*[402] was not exhaustive and should not require the Court of Appeal to feel that there is a:

> 'fetter on its power to put things right if it has occasion to believe that things are going wrong in an important way in the practical operation of the statutory scheme in Part 7 of the 1996 Act.'[403]

---

[397] [2005] EWCA Civ 60, [2005] I WLR 2070, CA.

[398] Another instance of the Court of Appeal considering whether or not to grant permission to bring a second appeal, outside of the homelessness context, is *Esure Insurance Ltd v Direct Line Insurance Ltd plc* [2008] EWCA Civ 842, [2009] Bus LR 438, CA, where the complexity of the case and the real prospect of showing that the first-instance judge had incorrectly exercised his appellate function were held to constitute 'compelling reasons' for permitting a second appeal.

[399] The permission hearing is at [2005] EWCA Civ 439, CA.

[400] Carnwath LJ quoted by Brooke LJ in the full appeal: *Cramp v Hastings Borough Council* [2005] EWCA Civ 1005, [2005] HLR 48, CA, at [34].

[401] Heard with the full appeal of *Cramp v Hastings Borough Council* [2005] EWCA Civ 1005, [2005] HLR 48, CA.

[402] [2005] EWCA Civ 60, [2005] 1 WLR 2070, CA.

[403] Brooke LJ at [66].

19.219 *Camden London Borough Council v Phillips* raised an important point of practice in that both it and *Cramp v Hastings Borough Council* evidenced:

> 'a worrying tendency in judges at that level to overlook the fact that it will never be easy for a judge to say that an experienced senior housing officer on a homelessness review, who has considered all the reports readily available, and all the representations made by the applicant's solicitors, has made an error of law when she considered that it was unnecessary to put in train further detailed inquiries, not suggested by the applicant's solicitors, before she could properly make a decision on the review. The need to correct that tendency raises an important point of practice.'[404]

19.220 In *William v Wandsworth London Borough Council*,[405] the Court of Appeal was concerned with a second appeal which had been brought by the local housing authority. Noting that the local housing authority had made a new review decision between the date of the county court appeal and the date on which permission to bring a second appeal was given, the Court of Appeal criticised the local housing authority's failure to inform the court that it had carried out a further review as 'verging on abuse' and doubted that permission would have been given, had the Court of Appeal been informed that a new review decision had been made. The new review decision had been made because both the applicant's lawyers and the local housing authority's lawyers believed that HA 1996, s 202(4) and the regulations required it to be made, once the previous review decision had been quashed by the county court judge. Chadwick LJ described this as an unsatisfactory position and said that:

> 'the parties should ... take the sensible and obvious course of agreeing that performance of the duty imposed on the authority by section 202(4) of the Act should await the outcome of the application [for permission], or the appeal (as the case may be).'[406]

19.221 An application for permission to bring a second appeal should be made within the Appellant's Notice, and must be filed at the Court of Appeal within 21 days of the judgment or order appealed from.[407] The county court does not have the power to grant or refuse permission to appeal, but does have the power to order that the time within which an Appellant's Notice is to be filed is extended.[408] Applications for permission do not need to be supported by witness statements, but if a witness statement is filed in support of the application for permission, or any other application, 'fairness requires it to be sent to the intended respondent' and, if it is the local housing authority which is seeking permission to appeal, it should bear in mind that the other party is likely to be without legal representation at the time and so those preparing a witness statement have a particular responsibility 'to ensure that it is relevant to

---

[404] Brooke LJ at [68].
[405] [2006] EWCA Civ 535, [2006] HLR 42, CA.
[406] *William v Wandsworth London Borough Council* [2006] EWCA Civ 535, [2006] HLR 42, CA, at [42]–[43], per Chadwick LJ.
[407] CPR, r 52.4. PD52C contains the procedure for a second appeal to the Court of Appeal.
[408] CPR, r 52.4(2)(a).

the specific question whether permission to appeal should be granted, and that it is not argumentative and so far as practicable not contentious'.[409]

19.222 Once permission has been granted, the issue for the Court of Appeal on hearing the appeal will be to consider errors of law in the review decision that was the original subject of the appeal, rather than confining itself to considering possible errors of law made by the county court judge on hearing the appeal.[410]

19.223 The local housing authority's power to provide accommodation for the appellant continues until any second appeal is finally determined, and so it may agree to provide accommodation until the determination of an appeal to the Court of Appeal.[411] If the local housing authority refuses to provide accommodation pending an appeal to the Court of Appeal, there is no power under HA 1996, s 204A for the county court to entertain an appeal against that refusal. Nor is there any other obvious power available to the county court or the Court of Appeal which would enable it to order the local housing authority to accommodate pending the Court of Appeal hearing. In the absence of such a power, the more straightforward course is for the applicant to challenge by way of judicial review the decision not to provide accommodation pending the second appeal to the Court of Appeal.

JUDICIAL REVIEW

Introduction

19.224 Local housing authority decisions made under HA 1996, Part 7 that do not carry with them a right to request a review can only be challenged (in the courts) in judicial review proceedings.

19.225 Complaints that the applicant has been treated unsatisfactorily, but where no error of law in the actual decision reached is alleged, should be raised within the local housing authority's internal complaints procedure.[412] If the treatment amounts to maladministration, the Local Government Ombudsman or Public Services Ombudsman for Wales can investigate, once the internal complaints procedure has been exhausted.[413]

---

[409] *William v Wandsworth London Borough Council* [2006] EWCA Civ 535, [2006] HLR 42, CA, at [80]–[81], per Sedley LJ; see **19.186–19.189** on contents of witness statements in general.

[410] *Abdullah v Westminster City Council* [2011] EWCA Civ 1171, [2012] HLR 5, CA per Mummery LJ at [15] and *Bubb v Wandsworth London Borough Council* [2011] EWCA Civ 1285, [2012] HLR 13, CA, per Neuberger MR at [31].

[411] HA 1996, s 204(4)(b).

[412] See **19.251–19.258**.

[413] See **19.254–19.258**.

Procedure

19.226 The procedure for judicial review is set out in the Civil Procedure Rules at CPR 54 and PDs 54A and 54D. Only a short summary of that procedure can be given here. Before the procedure is adopted, it will be expected that any applicant has complied with the Pre-Action Protocol for Judicial Review.

19.227 In order to bring a claim by way of judicial review, the applicant must obtain permission from the Administrative Court.[414] The application for permission[415] is first considered on the papers. The local housing authority has an opportunity to put its brief case to the judge on paper in an Acknowledgment of Service.[416] If permission is refused on the papers, the applicant has the right to renew his or her application for permission at an oral hearing.[417]

19.228 Claims should be brought promptly, and in any event within three months of the decision being challenged (although the court does have the discretion to extend time where there is a good reason for the delay).[418] Delay can be a reason in itself for refusing permission. Judicial review is not available, and permission will be refused, if there is an alternative avenue for redress available to the applicant.

19.229 If permission is granted, the local housing authority has the opportunity to put in its own evidence and submissions, and a full hearing will take place.

19.230 If the court finds that the decision was made in breach of the usual administrative law principles, it can:

(1) quash the decision and remit the matter back to the local housing authority for reconsideration; or

(2) make a mandatory order requiring the local housing authority to act in a certain way; or

(3) make a prohibitory order setting out how the local housing authority may not act; or

(4) make an injunction.[419]

---

[414] CPR 54.4.
[415] Made on claim form N461.
[416] Form N462.
[417] CPR 54.12(3).
[418] CPR, r 54.5 and CPR, r 3.1(2)(a).
[419] CPR, r 54.2.

19.231 Judicial review is a discretionary remedy and, even if the court finds that an error of law was made, it may still decide in all the circumstances not to make any order.

19.232 Since 2 October 2000, when the Human Rights Act 1998 came into force, it has also been possible to claim damages for breach of human rights within judicial review proceedings.[420] Judicial review proceedings cannot, however, be brought solely to claim damages.[421]

Obtaining interim relief

19.233 In many judicial review claims relating to a local housing authority's decisions under HA 1996, Part 7, the applicant will have an immediate need for accommodation. The judicial review claim is likely to wait months before a full hearing. Even the application for permission to bring the claim may not be considered for several weeks.

19.234 At all times during the progress of the judicial review claim, the Administrative Court has a discretion to grant an interim injunction requiring the local housing authority whose decision is under challenge to accommodate the applicant, and his or her household, until the judicial review claim has been heard or determined.[422] Indeed, in cases of extreme urgency, it is possible to obtain an interim injunction out-of-hours from the duty judge, upon the applicant and his or her legal advisers undertaking to issue the judicial review claim within a specified period (usually less than 24 hours).

19.235 The principles on which an Administrative Court judge will decide whether or not to make an interim injunction would include:

(1)   the merits of the judicial review claim itself and whether the claimant has made out a serious question to be tried;[423] and

(2)   the balance of convenience.[424]

19.236 Where the application for an interim injunction is made in an emergency, and without notice to the local housing authority, the following principles should be borne in mind:

---

[420]   See **19.246–19.250**.

[421]   CPR, r 54.3(2).

[422]   The power to make an injunction is at CPR 54.2. The Administrative Court's interim powers are at CPR 25.1(1) and include the power to make an interim injunction (CPR 25.1(1)(a)).

[423]   *R v Kensington & Chelsea Royal London Borough Council ex p Hammell* [1989] QB 518.

[424]   *American Cyanamid Co v Ethicon Ltd* [1975] AC 396, HL and *Zockoll Group Ltd v Mercury Communications Ltd* [1998] FSR 354, CA.

(1) that the granting of an injunction without notice is 'an exceptional remedy',[425] and normally appropriate only if the case is genuinely one of emergency or other great urgency;

(2) even then it should normally be possible to give some informal notice to the other party;

(3) the claimant applying for an injunction, and his or her legal representatives, are under a heavy duty to make full and frank disclosure of all matters relevant to the claim, whether matters of fact or of law;

(4) the duty to make full and frank disclosure includes a duty to make proper inquiries before making the application, so that the claimant, or his or her legal representatives, discloses all the material facts; and

(5) proper disclosure means identifying all relevant documents for the judge, taking the judge to the particular passages in those documents, and taking appropriate steps to ensure that the judge appreciates the significance of what he or she is being asked to read, or is being told.[426]

19.237 Legal representatives are also reminded of the importance of complying with the Pre-Action Protocol for Judicial Review, which requires that the claimant's representatives give notice of the intention to bring judicial review proceedings to the local housing authority's legal department. Even if the matter is too urgent to comply with the time limits required in the protocol, some warning to the legal department should be given.[427]

19.238 An interim injunction obtained without notice to the local housing authority will usually contain a provision permitting the local housing authority to apply to vary or discharge the injunction upon a short period of notice to the claimant or his or her legal representatives. Such applications should be considered relatively urgently by the Administrative Court.[428]

Judicial review as a substitute for a county court appeal

19.239 Where an appeal to the county court is available, it is only in really exceptional circumstances that the Administrative Court will give permission

---

[425] *R (Lawer) v Restormel Borough Council* [2007] EWHC 2299 (Admin), [2008] HLR 20, Admin Ct, at [62], per Munby J, quoting *Moat Housing Group South Ltd v Harris* [2005] EWCA Civ 287, [2006] QB 606, CA.

[426] *R (Lawer) v Restormel Borough Council* [2007] EWHC 2299 (Admin), [2008] HLR 20, Admin Ct, at [62]–[69], per Munby J. For another example where the claimant had failed to comply with the duty to make full and frank disclosure, see *R (Kondyba) v Kensington & Chelsea Royal London Borough Council* [2011] EWHC 2653 (Admin), (2011) December *Legal Action*, p 30, Admin Ct.

[427] *R (Lawer) v Restormel Borough Council* [2007] EWHC 2299 (Admin), [2008] HLR 20, Admin Ct, at [81]–[82], per Munby J.

[428] *R (Casey) v Restormel Borough Council* [2007] EWHC 2554 (Admin), (2008) January *Legal Action*, p 38, Admin Ct. The urgency application must be made on form N463.

for a judicial review claim to be brought.[429] Missing the 21-day deadline for the county court appeal[430] is not generally an exceptional circumstance,[431] and particularly so now that the county court has power to extend that deadline.

19.240 In one case, permission to bring a claim in judicial review was given where there was an arguable error of law and the applicant had unsuccessfully tried to issue a notice of appeal in the county court (but had wrongly made an application within possession proceedings instead).[432] In another case, permission was given, and the judicial review claim succeeded, where the local housing authority had refused to consider fresh information, produced after the review decision, concerning the applicant's mental health, which was relevant to the decision that he had become homeless intentionally.[433]

19.241 However, permission was refused to an applicant who had been found to have become homeless intentionally, had then withdrawn his request for a review, made a fresh application and then claimed that the local housing authority had failed to provide him with interim accommodation in accordance with the interim pre-decision duty.[434] Likewise, permission will be refused in cases where the applicant seeks to dispute the suitability of accommodation and where a right to a review of suitability is available under the sixth review category at HA 1996, s 202(1)(f).[435] An applicant also failed in a judicial review claim where she sought to challenge an original decision which contained inadequate reasons. The Administrative Court held that the proper route to challenge such deficiencies was by requesting a review and subsequently appealing to the county court.[436]

Judicial review where there can be no county court appeal

19.242 There may be several reasons why a county court appeal is not available and the applicant may need to bring a claim for judicial review. They include:

(1) where he or she wishes to challenge a decision which does not carry the right to request a statutory review; or

---

[429] *R v Brent London Borough Council ex p O'Connor* (1998) 31 HLR 923, QBD.
[430] See **19.174–19.182**.
[431] *R v Brent London Borough Council ex p O'Connor* (1999) 31 HLR 923, QBD; *R v Waltham Forest London Borough Council ex p Abdullahi* (1999) May *Legal Action*, p 29, QBD; and *R v Hillingdon London Borough Council ex p Rahim* (2000), (2000) May *Legal Action*, p 30, QBD.
[432] *R v Lambeth London Borough Council ex p Alleyne* (1999), (1999) June *Legal Action*, p 24, CA.
[433] *R (Van der Stolk) v Camden London Borough Council* [2002] EWHC 1261 (Admin), (2002) July *Legal Action*, p 26, Admin Ct.
[434] *R (Campbell) v Enfield London Borough Council* [2001] EWHC 357 (Admin), Admin Ct.
[435] *R (Cano) v Kensington and Chelsea Royal London Borough Council* [2002] EWHC 1922 (Admin), (2002) December *Legal Action*, p 22, Admin Ct. See also **19.27–19.32**.
[436] *R (Lynch) v Lambeth London Borough Council* [2006] EWHC 2737 (Admin), [2007] HLR 15, Admin Ct. Unusually, the claimant had also issued a HA 1996, s 204 appeal to the county court, which was transferred to the High Court and heard with the judicial review claim.

(2) if the local housing authority fails to comply with its acknowledged statutory duty, a judicial review claim can be brought for a mandatory order requiring the local housing authority to comply; or

(3) if the local housing authority simply fails to take a decision on a request or application made to it, a judicial review claim can be brought for a mandatory order requiring the local housing authority to make the decision.

19.243 Subjects for judicial review can therefore include:

(1) a local housing authority refusing to accept an application under HA 1996, Part 7;[437]

(2) a local housing authority's failure to make the necessary inquiries or to notify the applicant of the decision on those inquiries;[438]

(3) a local housing authority's refusal to provide interim accommodation pending an initial decision;[439]

(4) a local housing authority's decision not to provide accommodation pending a decision on review;[440]

(5) any dispute as to whether or not accommodation provided under an interim duty is suitable;[441]

(6) any failure to provide suitable accommodation in discharge of any of its statutory duties (where the local housing authority either fails to provide accommodation at all or provides accommodation that it is agreed is unsuitable for the needs of the applicant and his or her household);[442]

---

[437] HA 1996, s 183(1). For an example of a successful challenge to such a decision, see *R (G) v Haringey London Borough Council* [2009] EWHC 2699 (Admin), (2009) December *Legal Action*, p 17, Admin Ct.

[438] HA 1996, s 184. See **10.66–10.81**.

[439] HA 1996, s 188(1) or s 188(1A) as inserted by LA 2011, s 149(2) for applicants whose applications for homelessness assistance were made on or after 9 November 2012 to a local housing authority in England. At the date of writing, the amendments to HA 1996 made by LA 2011, ss 148–149 had not been brought into effect in Wales. See **16.12–16.28** and **16.29–16.35**.

[440] HA 1996, s 188(3). *R v Camden London Borough Council ex p Mohammed* (1998) 30 HLR 315, QBD. See **16.36–16.48**.

[441] *R (Sacupima) v Newham London Borough Council* (2001) 33 HLR 2, CA. See **16.66–16.69**.

[442] *R v Newham London Borough Council ex p Begum (Mashuda)* (2000) 32 HLR 808, QBD. See also *R (Dumbaya) v Lewisham London Borough Council* [2008] EWHC 1852 (Admin), (2008) September *Legal Action*, p 25, Admin Ct, where the local housing authority had failed to provide short-term accommodation under HA 1996, s 190(2)(a) to the claimant, whom it had found to have a priority need and to have become homeless intentionally. The local housing authority was ordered to pay the claimant's costs of bringing the judicial review. See **18.25**.

(7)   any dispute as to the length of the period that would provide an applicant who has a priority need and who had become homeless intentionally with 'a reasonable opportunity of securing accommodation';[443]

(8)   any failure to assess the applicant's housing needs before providing advice and assistance in discharge of the statutory duty;[444]

(9)   any challenge to the assessment of the applicant's housing needs;

(10) any decision not to provide accommodation for those homeless applicants who are not in priority need and did not become homeless intentionally;[445]

(11) any refusal to consider whether or not the conditions are met for the referral of the applicant's case to another local housing authority;[446]

(12) any decision not to allow the applicant to request a review outside the 21-day period;[447] and

(13) any failure to complete a statutory review or to notify the applicant of the decision on review.[448]

19.244   The last of these provides a good example of the usefulness of judicial review in the operation of HA 1996, Part 7. Where an applicant has requested a review, but the local housing authority has failed to complete the review or to notify him or her of the review decision, the applicant can appeal to the county court if there was an error of law in the original decision.[449] However, if there is no error of law in the original decision, but the applicant wants his or her case reconsidered, or has provided new information, then an appeal to the county court will not be the appropriate course. The applicant's remedy in those circumstances is to apply for a mandatory order in judicial review proceedings requiring the local housing authority to complete the review and notify him or her of the review decision.

---

[443]   HA 1996, s 190(2)(a). See *R (Conville) v Richmond upon Thames London Borough Council* [2006] EWCA Civ 718, [2006] HLR 45, CA, a decision of the Court of Appeal, containing, in the authors' opinion, the correct approach on forum; and *R (Nipyo) v Croydon London Borough Council* [2008] EWHC 847, [2008] HLR 37, Admin Ct. See **17.182–17.189**.
[444]   HA 1996, ss 190(4), 192(4) and 195(6). See **17.201–17.204**.
[445]   HA 1996, s 190(3). See **17.215-17.222**.
[446]   *Hackney London Borough Council v Sareen* [2003] EWCA Civ 351, [2003] HLR 54, CA. See **15.19-15.24**.
[447]   *R (C) v Lewisham London Borough Council* [2003] EWCA Civ 927, [2004] HLR 4, CA; *R (Slaiman) v Richmond upon Thames London Borough Council* [2006] EWHC 329 (Admin), [2006] HLR 20, Admin Ct; *R (Casey) v Restormel Borough Council* [2007] EWHC 2554 (Admin), (2008) January *Legal Action*, p 38, Admin Ct; and *R (Dragic) v Wandsworth London Borough Council* [2012] EWHC 1241(Admin) (2012) July *Legal Action*, p 42, Admin Ct. See **19.60–19.64**.
[448]   HA 1996, s 203.
[449]   HA 1996, s 204(1)(b).

19.245 Judicial review may also be available where the applicant is challenging the local housing authority's policy on some aspect of HA 1996, Part 7.[450] Although the court retains a discretion to consider disputes on policy matters that have become academic for the individual applicant (because matters have moved on, or the local housing authority has conceded the applicant's claim), it should only do so if that would be in the public interest and the appropriate procedural steps have been taken.[451]

Claims for damages

19.246 If an applicant for accommodation under HA 1996, Part 7 is not dealt with properly by a local housing authority, he or she may suffer considerable personal loss and hardship. Ordinarily, the law would provide a right to recompense through an award of financial compensation or damages at the suit of the individual who had suffered loss. That is *not* the case for applicants seeking assistance under HA 1996, Part 7.

19.247 The House of Lords decision in *O'Rourke v Camden London Borough Council*[452] established that damages were not available at common law for a local housing authority's breach of its statutory duty owed to a homeless person. The local housing authority, when dealing with an application for homelessness assistance, is implementing a scheme of social welfare that is intended to confer benefits at public expense on the grounds of public policy. To implement the scheme involves the local housing authority making discretionary decisions as to how to provide accommodation and the type of accommodation to be provided. The House of Lords decided that it was unlikely that Parliament had intended that any errors of judgment made by the local housing authority in those circumstances would give rise to an obligation to make financial reparation.

19.248 Since 2 October 2000, it has been possible for damages to be claimed for breach of an applicant's human rights where the court is satisfied that the award is necessary to afford 'just satisfaction' to the applicant.[453] This has been used to explore possible compensation claims in recent years. A failure to provide suitable accommodation does not breach the applicant's right to

---

[450] For example, *R (Khatun) v Newham London Borough Council* [2004] EWCA Civ 55, [2004] HLR 29, CA, where the applicants challenged the local housing authority's policy that offers of accommodation made under HA 1996, s 193 had to be accepted or rejected before they were viewed; *R (Calgin) v Enfield London Borough Council* [2005] EWHC 1716 (Admin), [2006] HLR 4, Admin Ct, where the challenge was to the local housing authority's policy of securing accommodation outside its district; and *Ali & others v Birmingham City Council* [2009] UKHL 36, [2009] 1 WLR 1506, HL, where the challenge was to the local housing authority's policy.

[451] *R (Tshikangu) v Newham London Borough Council* (2001) The Times, April 27, QBD. See *R (Morris) v Westminster City Council* [2004] EWHC 1199 (Admin) for an example of permission to continue a claim for judicial review which had become academic. The substantive point was subsequently decided by the Court of Appeal in *R (Morris) v Westminster City Council* [2005] EWCA Civ 1184, [2006] HLR 8, CA.

[452] *O'Rourke v Camden London Borough Council* [1998] AC 188, HL.

[453] Human Rights Act 1998, s 8(1) and (2). See J Compton 'Claiming Damages: a public law perspective' (2006) March *Legal Action*, p 23.

respect for his or her home.[454] It can, however, breach the applicant's right to respect for his or her family or private life under Art 8 of the European Convention on Human Rights.[455] Damages should be assessed on the basis that they should not be a lesser amount than damages that would be awarded for a claim in tort, and using the amount of compensation awarded by the Local Government Ombudsmen as a reference point.

19.249 The Court of Appeal in *Anufrijeva v Southwark London Borough Council*[456] considered the circumstances in which damages should be awarded for breach of an applicant's rights under Art 8. In considering the extent to which Art 8(1) imposed a positive obligation on states to provide public assistance, it concluded that generally a failure to provide welfare support was unlikely to infringe a single applicant's rights under Art 8 if it did not also infringe his or her rights under Art 3 not to be subjected to inhuman or degrading treatment. However, where families were involved, the applicant's right to respect for his or her family life might be more easily infringed. Before a local housing authority could be held to have failed to respect an applicant's private or family life, there had to be an element of culpability, involving at the very least knowledge by the local housing authority that the applicant's private or family life was at risk. For maladministration to infringe an applicant's Art 8 rights, the consequences (that the maladministration would lead to lack of respect for the applicant's private or family life) must be serious and foreseeable. Damages would be awarded, taking into account Judicial Studies Board Guidelines, Criminal Injuries Compensation awards, and awards by the Parliamentary and Local Government Ombudsmen for maladministration.

19.250 In a case relating to prisoners' rights, the House of Lords considered generally the principles under which damages for breach of Convention rights should be awarded. They held that in many cases, the finding that there had been a violation should be 'just satisfaction' for the applicant. Where the finding in itself was not sufficient for there to be 'just satisfaction', damages should be assessed in accordance with the amounts awarded by the European Court of Human Rights.[457]

COMPLAINTS

Local complaints procedures

19.251 Every local housing authority will have a procedure for entertaining complaints made by those using its services, including the homeless. A

---

[454] *R (Morris) v Newham London Borough Council* [2002] EWHC 1262 (Admin); and *Chapman v UK* (2001) 33 EHRR 18, ECHR.

[455] Human Rights Act 1998, Sch 1, art 8. See *R (Bernard) v Enfield London Borough Council* [2002] EWHC 2282 (Admin), (2003) 35 HLR 2, Admin Ct.

[456] *Anufrijeva v Southwark London Borough Council* [2003] EWCA Civ 1406, [2004] HLR 22, CA.

[457] *R (Greenfield) v Secretary of State for the Home Department* [2005] UKHL 14, [2005] 1 WLR 673, HL; and *Van Colle v Chief Constable of Hertfordshire Police* [2007] EWCA Civ 325, [2007] 1 WLR 1821, CA.

procedure leaflet and complaint form should be readily available on request. This process will enable the HA 1996, Part 7 applicant to log concerns which do not attack the merits of local housing authority decisions, but rather raise matters such as staff (mis)conduct, unfair treatment, delay, incompetence and the like.

19.252 Every local housing authority will have designated one of its most senior officials as the statutory monitoring officer.[458] That person is responsible for ensuring that the local housing authority's services are administered lawfully and without maladministration. Advisers assisting those who have been poorly dealt with under HA 1996, Part 7, should direct their complaints to the monitoring officer. For example, in one case a local housing authority reached an incorrect decision and resisted an appeal which had overwhelming merit. On receipt of a complaint from the trial judge, the local monitoring officer engaged an independent firm of solicitors to scrutinise what had gone wrong. As a result of their report, procedures were changed and the complainant received compensation.[459]

19.253 Since July 2001, every local housing authority has had a specific power to pay compensation, or provide some other suitable remedy, to any complainant who has been adversely affected by council action or inaction which may amount to maladministration.[460] In order to assist local housing authorities in determining how much to award, the Local Government Ombudsmen have published guidance.[461] This deals with both monetary and other redress.

Complaints to the Ombudsmen

19.254 Complaints can be made to the Local Government Ombudsmen (or Public Services Ombudsman for Wales) where it is alleged that the applicant has been subject to maladministration.[462] The complaint can be made informally, but the Local Government Ombudsman publishes a useful information booklet which contains a pro-forma complaint.

19.255 A complaint to the Local Government Ombudsman must be made within 12 months of the maladministration complained of, and the applicant should first complain through the local housing authority's internal complaints procedure.[463] If the applicant has not made an internal complaint before complaining to the Local Government Ombudsman, the Ombudsman will refer the complaint to the local housing authority's internal complaints procedure before investigating it.

---

[458] Local Government and Housing Act 1989, ss 5 and 5A.
[459] *Mohamud v Lambeth London Borough Council* (2003) March *Legal Action*, p 31.
[460] Local Government Act 2000, s 92.
[461] *Guidance on financial remedies* (LGO, July 2011) and *Homelessness: How councils can ensure justice for homeless people* (LGO Focus Report, July 2011).
[462] See English Code, paras 19.26–19.28; Welsh Code, paras 21.27–21.28.
[463] See **19.251–19.253**.

19.256 The Local Government Ombudsman has the power to make recommendations, if he or she concludes that maladministration has occurred, and can recommend that the local housing authority compensate the applicant. The level of compensation is usually modest, but the current rate for the 'distress' element alone in homelessness cases is in the general range of £500–£2000.[464]

19.257 Reports of individual investigations by the Local Government Ombudsmen can be found at the Local Government Ombudsman's website and many are noted in the monthly article Recent Developments in Housing Law in *Legal Action*. Each year the Local Government Ombudsmen gather a selection of homelessness cases in an Annual Digest. The housing Chapters of the digests for the last seven years are on the Local Government Ombudsman website.

19.258 For complaints involving local housing authorities in Wales, applicants should, having exhausted the local housing authority's internal complaints procedure, seek an investigation by the Public Services Ombudsman for Wales. In 2006, the Public Services Ombudsman for Wales produced a comprehensive report on the practices of local housing authorities in Wales relating to homelessness[465] and the Ombudsman has since published many investigation reports on homelessness complaints.

---

[464] Recent awards have included: £750 *Complaint against Hammersmith & Fulham London Borough Council*, 09 001 262, 13 January 2010, (2010) March *Legal Action*, p 31; £500 compensation plus £500 removal expenses *Complaint against Richmond upon Thames Royal London Borough Council*,10 009 269, 10 February 2011 (2011) April *Legal Action*, p 30; £500 *Complaint against Islington London Borough Council*, 10 013 025, 24 February 2011 (2011) April *Legal Action*, p 31; £500 plus an amount equivalent to a rent deposit *Complaint against Hounslow London Borough Council*, 10 019 388, 5 October 2011, (2011) December *Legal Action*, p 29; £300 *Complaint against Newham London Borough*, 11 000 383, 16 March 2012 (2012) May *Legal Action*, p 34; and £5,050 *Complaint against Dover District Council*, 09 017 510, 31 July 2012 (2012) October *Legal Action*, p 38.

[465] *Housing Allocations and Homelessness, a special report by the Local Government Ombudsman for Wales* (Public Services Ombudsman for Wales, 2006). See **7.29** and **8.75**.

Chapter 20

OTHER HELP WITH ACCOMMODATION FROM LOCAL AUTHORITIES

INTRODUCTION

20.1 The *homelessness* provisions in Housing Act 1996 ('HA 1996'), Part 7 are intended to ensure that local housing authorities provide short-term accommodation for those in the most urgent housing need. The *allocation* provisions in HA 1996, Part 6 are intended to facilitate the sensible distribution of longer-term homes in social housing by local housing authorities.

20.2 Taken together, the objective of these two Parts is to ensure that local housing authorities can help most people in housing need by providing them with temporary accommodation and/or by helping them find alternative homes.

20.3 Although these two Parts of HA 1996 are the primary statutory means by which local authorities meet housing need, they are not the only statutory provisions that allow local authorities to help with accommodation.

20.4 This Chapter focuses on help that local authorities (both local housing authorities and other authorities) can, and in some cases must, give to those needing accommodation, either by the local authorities providing accommodation themselves, or by helping applicants to find it. Initially, the Chapter outlines the general power to help (available in almost all cases) before turning separately to consider the special powers and duties that apply, in turn, to adults, young people and children. The Chapter concludes with a brief review of the duties to accommodate those displaced from their homes in emergencies, in other circumstances of involuntary displacement, and under the Human Rights Act 1998.

20.5 This Chapter cannot, however, cover all the help available to meet housing need. Apart from the powers and duties reviewed here, both central and local government departments have developed other arrangements to assist people in housing need.[1] Central government's housing policy in England is the responsibility of the Department for Communities and Local Government (DCLG). In Wales, the Welsh Government has responsibility for housing policy. Those in need of accommodation can also apply directly to other social sector providers such as private registered providers in England or registered social landlords in Wales, charitable trusts and co-operatives, and to private landlords.[2] For those on low incomes wishing to become tenants, housing benefit is available to help with the cost of renting.[3] On a more limited basis, the cost of mortgage interest can be claimed through the income support

---

[1] See *Homelessness Code of Guidance For Local Authorities* (Communities and Local Government, Department for Education and Skills, Department of Health, July 2006) (the English Code), Chapter 3.

[2] See English Code, Annex 5 and *Code of Guidance for Local Authorities Allocation of Accommodation and Homelessness 2012* (Welsh Government, August 2012) (the Welsh Code) at CD-Rom, Annex 13 on the duties on private registered providers and registered social landlords to co-operate with local housing authorities and see Chapter 6 of this book.

[3] There have been considerable changes to the availability and amount of housing benefit since

scheme, so that the poorest owner-occupiers can remain in their homes, and there are several schemes to assist those on low incomes with house purchase. There is also a wholly separate statutory scheme that provides accommodation for individuals seeking asylum in the UK.[4] It is not possible to set out here the details of all these different arrangements. Rather this Chapter concentrates on the powers and duties of local authorities to provide accommodation directly, or secure the provision of accommodation by others.

GENERAL POWER TO HELP WITH ACCOMMODATION FOR LOCAL AUTHORITIES

20.6 Because they are statutory bodies, local authorities can only undertake functions conferred on them by legislation. The legislative provision concerned with accommodation has developed incrementally for over a century. This has produced a veritable hotchpotch of powers and duties enabling local authorities to give help with housing and other social needs, including the provisions of what are now HA 1996, Parts 6 and 7. However, for cases falling outside the major provisions of those Parts, a local authority would have to scrabble about to identify some other discrete source of statutory power before it could know whether, when and how it could help to provide accommodation.[5]

20.7 Parliament adopted a wholly new approach when it enacted the Local Government Act 2000 ('LGA 2000'). This gave local authorities in both England and Wales wide-ranging statutory powers to meet local social needs, expressed as a power to promote economic, social and environmental 'well-being'.[6] The UK government's guidance suggested that this general power in LGA 2000, s 2, should be seen as a 'power of first resort' which could be 'wide ranging' and would lead to the abandonment of the 'traditionally cautious approach'.[7]

20.8 Since 4 April 2012, as a result of amendment by Localism Act 2011, this power has only been available to local authorities in Wales.[8]

2011 and prospective tenants should always obtain a pre-tenancy determination which will inform them how much housing benefit they will be entitled to.

[4] Immigration and Asylum Act 1999, Part 6, which set up the scheme formerly known as the National Asylum Support Service (NASS), now operated by the UK Border Agency (UKBA) on behalf of the Home Office. The extent of that scheme is outside the scope of this book, except in so far as there is an interplay with statutory powers and duties exercised by local housing authorities. A detailed guide can be found at Willman & Knafler *Support for Asylum Seekers and other Migrants, a guide to legal and welfare rights* (Legal Action Group, 3rd edn, 2009).

[5] There is now a useful summary of some (not all) of the statutory powers in Chapter 5 of the English Code.

[6] Local Government Act 2000, s 2.

[7] *Power to promote or improve economic, social or environmental well-being* (ODPM Guidance, 2000), Chapter 1, paras 6–7 and 10.

[8] Localism Act 2011, s 1 and Sch 1.

20.9 An individual who needs accommodation (or aid with obtaining accommodation), and is unable or unwilling to obtain help through HA 1996, Parts 6 or 7, can ask any local authority in Wales (including a local housing authority) to provide assistance under the general power in LGA 2000, s 2. There is no prescribed application process governing the request for help (no statutory form and not even a requirement that an application be made in writing). However, it makes good sense for any request for help to include a reference to it.

20.10 Under LGA 2000, s 2, local authorities in Wales have the power to do 'anything' that they consider is likely to achieve the improvement or promotion of the 'social well-being' of their area.[9] That includes 'anything' for the benefit of, or in relation to, any person resident in, or simply present in, the local authority's area.[10]

20.11 To put the scope for assistance with housing beyond doubt, LGA 2000, specifically provides that the power includes a power to give 'financial assistance to any person'[11] (so as to enable that person to find his or her own accommodation) and a power to provide 'accommodation to any person'.[12]

20.12 Local authorities in Wales can therefore be asked to exercise this power in order to provide accommodation either directly or indirectly, or to assist with financial help in obtaining accommodation, e g with the costs of rental deposits or rent-in-advance, etc. In *R (J) v Enfield London Borough Council*,[13] the court found that the power under LGA 2000, s 2 permitted the local authority to help with payments so that a family could obtain accommodation. The power has also been used to offer financial assistance for travel arrangements to an applicant who could not afford to fund those travel arrangements.[14] The power is by no means restricted to local housing authorities – others (e g county councils and local councils) have equal access to the power.[15]

---

9   LGA 2000, s 2(1)(b).

10   LGA 2000, s 2(2)(b).

11   LGA 2000, s 2(4)(b).

12   LGA 2000, s 2(4)(f).

13   *R (J) v Enfield London Borough Council* [2002] EWHC 432 (Admin), (2002) 34 HLR 38, Admin Ct.

14   *R (Grant) v Lambeth LBC* [2004] EWCA Civ 1171, [2005] HLR 27, CA. Providing financial assistance with travel costs usually arises in circumstances where the provisions of Nationality, Immigration and Asylum Act 2002, s 54 and Sch 3 exclude certain assistance to be given to people who fall within one of five classes of persons from abroad and who have approached a local authority asking for assistance under certain statutory powers and duties. For the restrictions on providing support to people who have asked for assistance under National Assistance Act 1948, s 21, see **20.46–20.48**. For the restriction on providing support to people who have asked for assistance meeting the needs of their children under Children Act 1989, s 17, see **20.65–20.73**. For restrictions on providing accommodation to an applicant for homelessness assistance pending review or pending appeal, under HA 1996, ss 188(3) and 204(4), see **16.47** and **16.54**.

15   LGA 2000, s 1, as amended by Local Government and Public Involvement in Health Act 2002, s 77, defines 'local authority'.

20.13 It must be emphasised that LGA 2000, s 2 contains only a power and not a duty. A local authority cannot be compelled to provide help under this section. The LGA 2000 contains no mechanism for statutory review or appeal against decisions about whether to exercise the power or how to exercise it. Nor does it provide any quality criteria, such as a requirement that any accommodation provided must be reasonable or suitable.

20.14 Anyone disappointed by the refusal to exercise the power, or a decision to exercise it in a particular way, can invoke the local authority's own complaints procedure and, if still dissatisfied, complain to the Public Services Ombudsman for Wales.[16] Alternatively, if the local authority is behaving irrationally, or in some other way unlawfully, a challenge could be brought in judicial review proceedings.[17]

20.15 However, there is an important qualification. Local authorities cannot use LGA 2000, s 2 to do anything that they are prevented from doing by a prohibition, restriction or limitation contained in some other enactment.[18] So, for example, a local housing authority in Wales cannot use the power to allocate an individual a secure tenancy if such an allocation would be outside the terms of the local housing authority's own allocation scheme, because to do so would breach a statutory prohibition.[19] Likewise, the power cannot be used by a local authority in Wales to assist with housing (or with the costs of housing) for an adult who is barred from help with accommodation under the National Assistance Act 1948.[20] Nor is it available to a children's authority in Wales to assist with accommodating a child or young person where the Children Act 1989 prohibits such assistance.[21]

POWERS AND DUTIES UNDER THE NATIONAL ASSISTANCE ACT 1948

The primary power/duty

20.16 Part 3 of the National Assistance Act 1948 (NAA 1948) originally gave a power to local authorities to make arrangements for providing residential accommodation for those who, 'by reason of':

• age;

• illness;

---

[16] See **19.254–19.258**.
[17] See *R (Theophilus) v Lewisham London Borough Council* [2002] EWHC 1371, [2002] 3 All ER 851, QBD as an example of a successful challenge to the refusal of an application for LGA 2000, s 2 assistance. And see **19.224–19.250** for judicial review.
[18] LGA 2000, s 3(1).
[19] The prohibition in HA 1996, s 167(8).
[20] *R (Khan) v Oxfordshire County Council* [2004] EWCA 309, [2004] HLR 41, CA. See also **20.43–20.48**.
[21] See **20.65–20.73**.

- disability; or

- any other circumstances,

were 'in need of care and attention which is not otherwise available to them'.[22]

20.17 NAA 1948 also contains a power to make arrangements for providing residential accommodation to pregnant women and breast-feeding mothers[23] who 'are in need of care and attention which is not otherwise available to them'.[24]

20.18 For historic reasons, and given the use of the terms 'age', 'illness' and 'disability', this power had been traditionally used to make places available in residential care homes and similar residential facilities (becoming colloquially known as 'Part 3 accommodation').

20.19 But the term 'residential accommodation', used in NAA 1948, Part 3, is also apt to describe a perfectly ordinary house, flat or any other form of housing provision. This is, therefore, a long-standing statutory power under which local authorities can meet ordinary housing needs for those who have unmet needs for care and attention.[25]

20.20 By direction of the Secretary of State, the power at NAA 1948, s 21(1)(a) has been converted into a duty.[26] So, provided that an individual is 'in need of care and attention which is not otherwise available' to him or her, by reason of one of the four matters prescribed,[27] residential accommodation must be provided by the local authority *either* if the applicant is ordinarily resident in its area *or* if he or she is in 'urgent need'.

20.21 Guidance on the exercise of the power/duty by local authorities in England is provided by the Secretary of State in *Prioritising Need in the context of Putting People First: A whole system approach to eligibility for social care*.[28] Local authorities are required to take account of the guidance when making decisions under NAA 1948, Part 3.[29]

---

[22] National Assistance Act 1948, s 21(1)(a).
[23] Described in NAA 1948, s 21(1)(b) as 'expectant and nursing mothers'.
[24] NAA 1948, s 21(1)(aa). For an example of the use of this power, see *R (AG) v Leeds City Council* [2007] EWHC 3275, (2008) March *Legal Action*, p 22, Admin Ct.
[25] *R (Wahid) v Tower Hamlets London Borough Council* [2002] EWCA Civ 287, [2003] HLR 2, CA.
[26] Local Authority Circular 93/10, para 2(1). It should be noted that the power to provide residential accommodation to expectant and nursing mothers who are in need of care and attention which is not otherwise available to them (NAA 1948, s 21(1)(aa)) remains a power and not a duty.
[27] See **20.16**.
[28] Department of Health, February 2010. There seems to be no equivalent Welsh guidance.
[29] *R v Islington London Borough Council ex p Rixon* (1998) 1 CCLR 119, QBD.

Restrictions on the power/duty

20.22 Prior to 6 December 1999, the duty to arrange accommodation under NAA 1948, s 21(1)(a) was owed to anyone who had the requisite 'need for care and attention'. Even people unlawfully in the UK could benefit from the duty if otherwise they risked serious injury to health.[30]

20.23 Since 6 December 1999, people subject to immigration control whose need for care and attention has arisen solely because of destitution or because of the physical effects or of the anticipated physical effects of destitution cannot be provided with residential accommodation under NAA 1948, Part 3.[31] Accommodation for those who are seeking asylum has become the responsibility of the United Kingdom Border Agency (UKBA). There is a further prohibition on providing residential accommodation to persons who fall within one of five specified classes of persons from abroad.[32]

20.24 Also the duty is now owed to adults only. The responsibility for arranging accommodation for children no longer falls under NAA 1948, Part 3, but is dealt with by the Children Act 1989.[33]

20.25 The duty does not extend to a requirement that a local authority should meet the needs of the applicant's family.[34] Family members should instead consider what other statutory provisions are available for their assistance.[35]

The duty to assess

20.26 Presented with an application for residential accommodation, the local authority's first task is to carry out an assessment of the applicant's needs.[36] The threshold triggering the obligation to assess is a very low one. The local authority is under a mandatory duty to assess the needs of anyone who 'may be in need' of any community care services (including the provision of

---

[30]   *R v Brent London Borough Council ex p D* (1998) 1 CCLR 234, QBD ; and *R v Lambeth London Borough Council ex p Sarhangi* (1999) 2 CCLR 145, QBD.
[31]   National Assistance Act 1948, s 21(1A), inserted by Immigration and Asylum Act 1999, s 116. See **20.43–20.45** for the legal test as to whether or not a 'need for care and assistance' is said to have arisen solely as a result of being destitute or of the anticipated physical effects of being destitute.
[32]   Nationality, Immigration and Asylum Act 2002, s 54 and Sch 3. See **20.46–20.48** and **20.65–20.73**.
[33]   See **20.74–20.82**.
[34]   *R (O) v Haringey London Borough Council* [2004] EWCA Civ 535, [2004] HLR 44, CA.
[35]   Such as Housing Act 1996; Children Act 1989; or Immigration and Asylum Act 1999.
[36]   National Health Service and Community Care Act 1990, s 47.

accommodation).[37] The local authority has a discretionary power to provide services while the assessment is being carried out.[38]

20.27   A failure to carry out an assessment, if the threshold is made out, is a breach of the local authority's statutory duty. It can be enforced by bringing a claim by way of judicial review seeking a mandatory order requiring the local authority to carry out an assessment.[39]

Which local authority?

20.28   The duty to assess is owed by the local authority in whose area the applicant is ordinarily resident.[40] Any dispute as to which local authority owes the duty to assess should be decided by the Secretary of State for Health.[41] If there is an urgent need for accommodation pending the resolution of the dispute as to which local authority is responsible, the local authority within whose area the applicant is physically present should provide the accommodation.[42] The same test of physical presence applies if the applicant has no settled residence.[43]

Assessing needs

20.29   Whether an applicant is 'in need of care and attention' by reason of one of the four statutory matters at NAA 1948, s 21(1)(a)[44] is a factual decision for the local authority to take. Local authorities should ensure that the circumstances of each individual applicant are separately considered, and not apply blanket policies. The House of Lords has held that a 'need for care and attention' occurs where a person needs 'looking after', or, in other words:

> 'doing something for the person being cared for which he cannot or should not be expected to do for himself: it might be household tasks which an old person can no longer perform or can only perform with great difficulty; it might be protection

---

[37]   *R v Bristol City Council ex p Penfold* (1998) 1 CCLR 315, QBD; *R (Patrick) v Newham London Borough Council* (2001) 4 CCLR 48, QBD; and *R (Bempoa) v Southwark London Borough Council* [2002] EWHC 153 (Admin). See also paras 68–89 of *Prioritising Need in the context of Putting People First: A whole system approach to eligibility for social care* (Department of Health, 2010).

[38]   National Health Service and Community Care Act 1990, s 47(5); *R (AA) v Lambeth London Borough Council* [2001] EWHC 471 (Admin), (2002) 5 CCLR 36, QBD.

[39]   See **19.224–19.250** on practice and procedure for judicial review claims.

[40]   NAA 1948, s 24(1). See *R (Sunderland City Council) v South Tyneside County Council* [2012] EWCA Civ 1232.

[41]   NAA 1948, s 32(3).

[42]   *R (Kromah) v Southwark London Borough Council CO/2032/2008* permission application (2008) August *Legal Action*, p 44, Admin Ct.

[43]   NAA 1948, s 24(3); *R (S) v Lewisham London Borough Council* [2008] EWHC 1290 (Admin), (2008) July *Legal Action*, p 23, Admin Ct.

[44]   See **20.16**.

from risks which a mentally disabled person cannot perceive; it might be personal care, such as feeding, washing or toileting.'[45]

20.30 NAA 1948, Part 3 does not establish a scheme for the accommodation of everyone who is short of housing or resources.[46]

20.31 The courts have held that a blind man, who received help with shopping, laundry, cooking and getting around, was 'in need of care and attention'.[47] A man who had weekly meetings with his social worker was 'in need of care and attention',[48] as was a man with advanced HIV, who was terminally ill and needed help with most domestic tasks.[49] Other applicants, one of whom required a 'low-level care package'[50] one who had medical needs,[51] and one who had a personality disorder giving rise to bizarre behaviour,[52] have been held not to fall within the definition of having a 'need for care and attention'.

20.32 Once it has been decided that a person has 'a need for care and attention', in what circumstances is he or she also entitled to accommodation under NAA 1984, s 21(1)? In *R (SL) v Westminster City Council*,[53] the Court of Appeal held that 'care and attention is not "otherwise available" unless it would be reasonably practicable and efficacious to supply it without the provision of accommodation'. If it would not be reasonably practical and efficacious to supply services to meet the need without the provision of accommodation, accommodation should be provided.

20.33 A person may have the requisite degree of 'need' for care and attention, even if he or she already has some accommodation.[54] Again, the question for the local authority is simply one as to whether the applicant has the requisite need. In one case, a secure tenant suffering from schizophrenia who occupied overcrowded accommodation was assessed not to be in need of care and

---

[45] *R (M) v Slough Borough Council* [2008] UKHL 52, [2008] 1 WLR 1808, HL, at [33], per Baroness Hale. This is not an exhaustive list of 'looking after' functions.

[46] *R v Hammersmith and Fulham London Borough Council ex p M* (1998) 30 HLR 10, CA, at [20]–[21].

[47] *R (Zarzour) v Hillingdon London Borough Council* [2009] EWCA Civ 1529, (2010) 13 CCLR 157, CA.

[48] *R (SL) v Westminster City Council* [2011] EWCA Civ 954, [2012] 1 All ER 935, CA.

[49] *R (De Almeida) v Royal Borough of Kensington & Chelsea Council* [2012] EWHC 1082 (Admin), (2012) June *Legal Action*, p 37, Admin Ct.

[50] *R (Walcott) v Lambeth London Borough Council* [2008] EWHC 2745 (Admin), (2009) March *Legal Action*, p 26, Admin Ct.

[51] *R (N) v Coventry City Council* [2008] EWHC 2786 (Admin), (2009) March *Legal Action*, p 26, Admin Ct. In *R (S) v Coventry City Council* [2009] EWHC 2191 (Admin), there was no error of law in the local authority's decision not to re-assess the needs of a person who was diagnosed with cancer, but was in remission and had no present need for services

[52] *R (Nassery) v Brent London Borough Council* [2011] EWCA Civ 539, (2011) July *Legal Action*, p 21, CA; see also *R (Okil) v Southwark London Borough Council* [2012] EWHC 1202 (Admin), (2012) July *Legal Action*, p 43, Admin Ct.

[53] [2011] EWCA Civ 954, [2012] 1 All ER 935, CA.

[54] *R v Newham London Borough Council ex p Gorenkin* (1998) 30 HLR 278, QBD.

attention, as support was available to address his mental health needs and the risk of the overcrowding causing a breakdown was relatively small.[55]

Services provided to meet the needs

20.34 If the applicant is assessed to be 'in need of care and attention' for one of the prescribed reasons, and no means of satisfying those needs is otherwise available, residential accommodation and any necessary ancillary services must be provided. The accommodation must be suitable to meet the applicant's needs.

20.35 The type of accommodation to be provided is not confined to institutions such as care homes. It can include bed and breakfast emergency type accommodation[56] or 'ordinary accommodation', if that is appropriate to meet the applicant's needs.[57] The restriction imposed by HA 1996, Part 7 on the use of bed and breakfast accommodation[58] does not apply here.

20.36 Many of the court decisions as to the extent of services to be provided under NAA 1948, Part 3 concern destitute asylum-seekers (who were eligible for NAA 1948, Part 3, services prior to 6 December 1999), but the principles they establish apply to anyone meeting the statutory criteria.[59]

20.37 It is not necessary that accommodation must be provided from the local authority's own stock or from specialist care accommodation providers. The local authority can give the applicant financial assistance to meet the costs of his or her own accommodation.[60]

20.38 The duty to provide accommodation and related services to those who meet the statutory criteria is an absolute and mandatory one. Local authorities may not rely on lack of funds to excuse them from fulfilling their duty and providing the relevant services to meet the applicant's needs.[61] Nor can they argue that they only have certain ways of providing accommodation, for example by only offering accommodation in residential care homes.

---

[55] *R (Wahid) v Tower Hamlets London Borough Council* [2002] EWCA Civ 287, (2003) 35 HLR 2, CA; see *R (Mooney) v Southwark London Borough Council* [2006] EWHC 1912 (Admin), (2006) September *Legal Action*, p 14, Admin Ct; and *Lambeth London Borough Council v Ireneschild* [2007] EWCA Civ 234, [2007] HLR 34, CA, for other cases involving secure tenants said to be in need of care and attention.

[56] *R v Newham London Borough Council ex p C* (1999) 31 HLR 567, QBD; and *R v Richmond London Borough Council ex p T* (2001) January *Legal Action*, p 28, QBD.

[57] *R (Wahid) v Tower Hamlets London Borough Council* [2002] EWCA Civ 287, (2003) 35 HLR 2, CA.

[58] See **18.114–18.128**.

[59] *R v Westminster City Council ex p M, P, A and X* (1997) 1 CCLR 85, CA.

[60] Health and Social Care Act 2001, s 57 as amended.

[61] *R v Sefton Metropolitan Borough Council ex p Help the Aged* (1997) 1 CCLR 57, CA; and *R v Islington London Borough Council ex p Batantu* (2001) 4 CCLR 445, QBD.

20.39 Once an applicant's needs have been assessed, local authorities should consider how best to meet those needs. This will involve reviewing options such as:

(1) supported or sheltered housing;

(2) helping the applicant to rent accommodation in the private sector;[62]

(3) paying an applicant's rent in his or her private or public sector accommodation so as to prevent his or her eviction; or

(4) moving the applicant from accommodation that does not meet his or her needs to accommodation that does.

20.40 The duty is a duty to meet the applicant's *needs*. It does not oblige the local authority to meet the applicant's preferences as to type or location of accommodation. Although the local authority is entitled to take the applicant's views as to his or her needs into account, its only duty is to provide those services that it has concluded meet the applicant's needs.[63] It is for the local authority to assess the extent of the applicant's needs and the services that will be provided to meet those needs.

20.41 As long as the need for care and attention remains, the local authority has a continuing obligation to provide accommodation to meet that need. A local authority is entitled to treat its duty as ended, and to decline to provide further accommodation, where the applicant refuses the accommodation offered, or has manifested by his or her conduct a persistent and unequivocal refusal to observe the reasonable requirements of the accommodation. However, even in those latter circumstances, there should be a reassessment of the applicant's needs and a careful consideration of the nature of his or her conduct before the local authority could decide that its duty had been discharged.[64]

Disputes

20.42 Any applicant disappointed by a local authority's response to his or her application can invoke the local authority's complaints procedure. But any legal challenge to the local authority's conclusions on the assessment, or as to the services provided, can only be brought in proceedings for judicial review.[65]

---

[62] For an example of where a local authority should have provided a detailed assessment of how it could use its power to help secure private rented accommodation in the context of Children Act 1989, see *R (S) v Plymouth City Council* [2009] EWHC 1499 (Admin), (2009) October *Legal Action,* p 26, Admin Ct and [2010] EWCA Civ 1490, (2010) March *Legal Action,* p 31, CA (refusal of permission to appeal).

[63] *R (Khana and Karim) v Southwark London Borough Council* [2001] EWCA Civ 999, (2002) 34 HLR 31, CA.

[64] *R v Kensington and Chelsea Royal London Borough Council ex p Kujtim* [1999] 4 All ER 161, CA; and *R (Patrick) v Newham London Borough Council* (2000) 4 CCLR 48, QBD.

[65] See **19.224–19.250** for practice and procedure in judicial review.

Damages are not available for breach of statutory duty, but where the authority's unlawful conduct has resulted in an infringement of an applicant's rights under the European Convention on Human Rights, Art 8(1), damages for breach of those Convention rights may be claimed within judicial review proceedings.[66]

Persons from abroad

Adults subject to immigration control

20.43   From 6 December 1999, people subject to immigration control who are excluded from benefits[67] cannot fall within the scope of NAA 1948, Part 3 if their need for care and attention arises solely from their being destitute, or from the physical effects or anticipated physical effects of being destitute.[68]

20.44   If such a person has a need for care and attention that has not arisen solely from being destitute, or the physical effects of being destitute, he or she remains entitled to a service under NAA 1948, Part 3. People in this position are colloquially referred to as experiencing 'destitution plus'. In *R (Westminster City Council) v National Asylum Support Service*,[69] an asylum-seeker suffering from cancer was not excluded from NAA 1948, Part 3 entitlement as her need for care and attention did not arise solely as a result of her being destitute. In *R v Wandsworth London Borough Council ex p O*[70] and in *R (Mani) v Lambeth London Borough Council*,[71] the Court of Appeal held that the exclusion did not apply where the applicant's need for care and attention had been rendered more acute by circumstances other than his or her destitution. Destitution can therefore contribute to the applicant having a need for care and attention, but if it is the sole cause, then a person subject to immigration control will be excluded from assistance under NAA 1948, Part 3 and reliant on support, if available, from the UKBA.

20.45   In *R (Khan) v Oxfordshire County Council*,[72] the local authority was held not to have misdirected itself in law when it took the view that a woman who was subject to immigration control, destitute and also fleeing domestic violence fell within the exclusion. The domestic violence could be a circumstance making her need for care and attention more acute, but the local authority had considered that and decided that it had not had that effect on her.

---

[66]   *R (Bernard) v Enfield London Borough Council* [2002] EWHC 2882 (Admin), (2003) 35 HLR 27, Admin Ct; and *Anufrijeva v Southwark London Borough Council* [2003] EWCA Civ 1406, [2004] 2 WLR 603, CA. See also discussion at **19.256–19.260** and **20.90–20.102**.

[67]   Under Immigration and Asylum Act 1999, s 115.

[68]   NAA 1948, s 21(1A) added by Immigration and Asylum Act 1999, s 116.

[69]   *R (Westminster City Council) v National Asylum Support Service* [2001] EWCA Civ 512, [2002] UKHL 38, [2002] 1 WLR 2956, HL.

[70]   *R v Wandsworth London Borough Council ex p O* [2000] 1 WLR 2539, CA.

[71]   *R (Mani) v Lambeth London Borough Council* [2003] EWCA Civ 836, [2004] HLR 5, CA.

[72]   *R (Khan) v Oxfordshire County Council* [2004] EWCA Civ 309, [2004] HLR 41, CA.

Certain classes of persons from abroad

20.46 From 8 January 2003, five additional classes of people have been excluded from accommodation provision under NAA 1948, Part 3:

- refugees granted refugee status by another state of the European Economic Area (EEA);[73]

- nationals of another state of the EEA;

- asylum-seekers whose claims for asylum have failed and who have failed to co-operate with removal directions;

- persons who are not asylum-seekers and are unlawfully present in the UK; and

- failed asylum-seekers with dependent children, where those families have been certified by the Secretary of State as not having taken reasonable steps to leave the UK.[74]

20.47 There is a general prohibition on providing support to *adults without dependent children* who fall into one of those classes. There are two exceptions to that general prohibition:

(1) where the support is necessary to prevent an interference with a person's human rights under the European Convention;[75] or

(2) for the first two classes of people, provision of support can be made only in the form of assistance with travel arrangements to their home countries.[76]

---

[73] For a list of EEA states, see **12.67**, Box 2.

[74] Nationality, Immigration and Asylum Act 2002, s 54 and Sch 3; Withholding and Withdrawal of Support (Travel Assistance and Temporary Accommodation) Regulations 2002, SI 2002/3078. The same exclusion applies to the discretionary powers to secure accommodation pending review or appeal. See **16.47** and **16.64** and **20.65–20.73**. For guidance on application of these restrictions, see *Practice Guidance for Local Authorities: Assessing and Supporting Adults with No Recourse to Public Funds* (No Recourse to Pubic Funds Network, April 2009).

[75] Nationality, Immigration and Asylum Act 2002, Sch 3, para 3. See *R (Limbuela) v Secretary of State for the Home Department* [2005] UKHL 66, [2006] 1 AC 396, HL, as to the operation of this threshold. For cases raising issues as to breach of Article 8 rights (which generally involve adults with dependent children), see **20.71–20.73**. The Court of Appeal held in *R (Clue) v Birmingham City Council* [2010] EWCA Civ 460, [2011] 1 WLR 99, CA, that where an applicant had made an application for leave to remain in the UK, that claim was not hopeless or abusive and that claim would be forfeited if he or she had to leave the UK before it was decided, it would be a breach of human rights to refuse support.

[76] SI 2002/3078, reg 3; there is no obligation to provide assistance with travel arrangements to the third and fourth classes, who are expected to comply with removal directions.

20.48 *Adults with dependent children* may receive limited temporary accommodation while they await implementation of the travel arrangements.[77] If a request is made for support by anyone falling within one of the third, fourth or fifth classes, the local authority is obliged to inform the UKBA.[78]

POWERS AND DUTIES UNDER THE MENTAL HEALTH ACT 1983

20.49 Special statutory provision is made to meet the accommodation needs of adults who are, or who have recently been, mentally ill. The Mental Health Act 1983, s 117 ('MHA 1983')[79] imposes a duty on local authorities to provide after-care services for any person who has left hospital, having been detained, or who has been subject to certain hospital orders made in criminal proceedings.[80] This duty rests jointly on the relevant primary care trust or local health board and on the local authority, and they are expected to co-operate in ensuring that services are provided. The local authority which owes the duty is the local authority for the area in which the person concerned is resident or to which he or she is sent on discharge from the hospital in which he or she was detained.[81] A patient is not 'resident' for these purposes in the hospital or other facility in which he or she was compulsorily detained.[82]

20.50 Guidance on this duty in England is provided in *After-Care Under the Mental Health Act 1983: section 117 after-care services*.[83]

20.51 It is unlawful for a primary care trust, health authority or local authority to fail to take steps to prepare a package of after-care services so as to enable discharge to take place from residential accommodation provided under the MHA 1983.[84] However, the duty at MHA 1983, s 117 is not absolute; all that local authorities are required to do is to use their best endeavours to provide after-care services. In those circumstances, if no package is set up despite the local authority using its best endeavours, and the consequence is that the patient remains detained rather than being released into the

---

[77] See **20.65–20.73**.

[78] Nationality, Immigration and Asylum Act 2002, Sch 3, para 14.

[79] As amended by Health and Social Care Act 2012, s 40.

[80] A description of the much broader provision in the Mental Health Act 1983, as amended by the Mental Capacity Act 2005 and Mental Health Act 2007, consolidating the health services to which mentally ill patients are entitled, is beyond the scope of this book.

[81] MHA 1983, s 117(3).

[82] *R (Hertfordshire County Council) v Hammersmith & Fulham London Borough Council & JM* [2011] EWCA Civ 77, (2011) 14 CCLR 224, CA. See also *R (Sunderland City Council) v South Tyneside County Council* [2012] EWCA Civ 1232.

[83] LAC (2000) 3, Department of Health and Chapter 27 of the *Code of Practice: Mental Health Act 1983* (Department of Heath, 2008). There is also LAC(96)8 *Guidance on supervised discharge (after-care under supervision) and related provisions* (Department of Heath 1996). In Wales, guidance is given in Chapter 31 of the *Mental Health Act 1983: Code of Practice for Wales* (Welsh Assembly Government, 2008).

[84] *R v Ealing London Borough Council ex p Fox* [1993] 3 All ER 170, QBD.

community, there is no illegality or breach of the patient's human rights.[85] Similarly, where there is a genuine inability to provide accommodation, because of the particular needs of the applicant and the absence of suitable accommodation, no unlawfulness or illegal detention will arise.[86]

20.52 The duty to provide after-care services is a duty to provide services that are necessary to meet any needs arising from the person's mental disorder.[87] Those services can include the provision of ordinary accommodation if accommodation is necessary to meet the person's needs.[88] Importantly, local authorities are not permitted to charge for after-care services provided under MHA 1983, s 117 and are not permitted to refuse to provide accommodation on the grounds of lack of resources.[89]

20.53 If the person has left hospital subject to supervised community treatment, the duty continues for the whole of the supervision period.[90] If he or she is not subject to supervision, the duty continues until the local authority is satisfied that he or she is no longer in need of MHA 1983, s 117, services.[91]

20.54 Voluntary patients and those patients detained for assessment under MHA 1983, s 2 are not entitled to the benefit of the MHA 1983, s 117 duty. If, on leaving hospital, they are in need of community care services and accommodation, they can require that the local authority assesses their needs under s 47 of the National Health Service and Community Care Act 1990 and that the local authority then provides community care services to meet those needs, which may include assistance with finding accommodation.[92]

ACCOMMODATION FOR CHILDREN AND YOUNG PEOPLE – POWERS AND DUTIES IN THE CHILDREN ACT 1989

20.55 Local children's services authorities have a duty, under s 17(1) of the Children Act 1989 ('CA 1989'), to safeguard and promote the welfare of children[93] within their area who are in need. So far as is consistent with that

[85] *R (K) v Camden and Islington Health Authority* [2001] EWCA Civ 240, (2001) 4 CCLR 170, CA.
[86] *R (W) v Doncaster Metropolitan Borough Council* [2004] EWCA Civ 378, CA.
[87] *R (Mwanza) v Greenwich London Borough Council & Bromley London Borough Council* [2010] EWHC 1462 (Admin), (2010) 13 CCLR 454, Admin Ct.
[88] *Clunis v Camden and Islington Health Authority* [1998] QB 978, (1998) 1 CCLR 215, CA.
[89] *R v Richmond London Borough Council ex p Watson, R v Manchester City Council ex p Stennett* [2002] UKHL 34, [2002] 2 AC 1127, HL.
[90] See Mental Health Act 1983, ss 17A–17G for provisions about supervised community treatment.
[91] *R (Mwanza) v Greenwich London Borough Council & Bromley London Borough Council* [2010] EWHC 1462 (Admin), (2010) 13 CCLR 454, Admin Ct.
[92] *R (B) v Camden London Borough Council and Camden & Islington Mental Health and Social Care Trust* [2005] EWHC 1366 (Admin), [2005] MHLR 258, Admin Ct. See **20.16–20.48**.
[93] Children Act 1989, s 105 defines a child as 'a person under the age of 18'.

duty, they must promote the upbringing of such children by their families by providing a range and level of services appropriate to those children's needs. This duty is a target duty, meaning that it is owed generally to children within the children's services authority's area. The children's services authority has a substantial discretion as to how it performs that duty.

Assessment

20.56 Children's services authorities must first assess whether or not a child is 'in need'. The children's services authority is under a duty to take reasonable steps to assess the needs of any child within its area who appears to be in need. If it fails to do so, a mandatory order can be sought in judicial review compelling it to do so.[94]

20.57 The concept of being 'in need' is defined at CA 1989, s 17(10). A child is in need if he or she is disabled or if, without the provision of local authority services, the child is unlikely to achieve or maintain a reasonable standard of health or development, or his or her health or development is likely to be significantly impaired. Guidance to children's services' authorities in England is provided in the *Framework for assessment of children in need and their families*.[95] It is well established that a child without accommodation can be a 'child in need' and that the provision of accommodation can be a service to meet that need.[96]

20.58 The duty imposed on a children's services authority by CA 1989, s 17(1) is to provide services appropriate to the needs of children within its area. 'Within their area' means that the child must be actually physically present. So the duty will be owed by the children's services authority for the area where the child lives or where he or she attends school.[97]

20.59 Where a homeless family with children is found not to be eligible for assistance under HA 1996, Part 7, or the adults are found to have become homeless intentionally or to have become threatened with homelessness

---

[94] *R (AB and SB) v Nottinghamshire County Council* (2001) 4 CCLR 295, QBD. See also *R (G) v Barnet London Borough Council* [2003] UKHL 57, [2004] 2 AC 208, HL, per Lord Nicholls at [32].

[95] *Framework for assessment of children in need and their families* (Department of Health, 2000) to be read along with *Assessing children in need and their families: Practice Guidance* (Department of Health, 2000). In Wales, the National Assembly for Wales issued the *Framework for the Assessment of Children in Need and their Families* (National Assembly for Wales, 2001) and *Assessing Children in need and their families: Practice Guidance* (National Assembly for Wales, 2001).

[96] CA 1989, s 17(6) and (10). See also *R v Northavon District Council ex p Smith* [1994] 2 AC 402, HL; and *R (G) v Barnet London Borough Council, R (W) v Lambeth London Borough Council, R (A) v Lambeth London Borough Council* [2003] UKHL 57, [2004] 2 AC 208, [2003] 3 WLR 1194, HL.

[97] *R (Stewart) v Wandsworth London Borough Council, Hammersmith & Fulham London Borough Council and Lambeth London Borough Council* [2001] EWHC 709 (Admin), (2001) 4 CCLR 446, Admin Ct. See also *R (M) v Barking & Dagenham London Borough Council* [2002] EWHC 2663 (Admin), (2003) 6 CCLR 87, Admin Ct.

intentionally so that there is no main housing duty on the local housing authority to provide accommodation, the local housing authority must ask the applicant to consent to the family being referred to the local children's services authority or department.[98] Even if the applicant refuses, the local housing authority must still make the referral if it considers that the child is, or may be, at risk of significant harm.[99] When a referral is received, the children's services authority is entitled to request advice and assistance from the local housing authority.[100] A local housing authority that has placed a homeless family outside its own district[101] should refer the family (if it is found to be ineligible or the adult members are found to have become homeless intentionally) to its own children's services department or authority.[102] It may, of course, also seek the assistance of the children's services authority for the district in which the family has been placed, under the general provisions for co-operation in HA 1996, s 213.

20.60 Once the children's services department is aware that the child may be in need, the child's needs *must* be assessed. If the child appears to be 'in need', there is a mandatory duty to assess, which should not be deferred.[103]

20.61 If a homeless applicant with dependent children has been found not to be 'eligible' for assistance under HA 1996, Part 7,[104] or there is no priority need because the dependent child or children are not 'eligible',[105] the children's services authority could consider using its powers under CA 1989, s 17 to provide accommodation.[106]

Services

20.62 After the assessment has been carried out, services to meet the child's identified needs must be provided. Services for the child's family or any member of his or her family may also be provided, with a view to safeguarding or promoting the child's welfare.[107] Those services can include drawing up and implementing plans to remedy inadequate accommodation,[108] or the provision of a roof over the child's head if he or she is facing literal homelessness. Cash

---

[98] HA 1996, s 213A. See **17.225–17.123**.
[99] HA 1996, s 213A(4). See also English Code, Chapter 13; Welsh Code, Chapter 17.
[100] HA 1996, s 213A(5).
[101] See **15.226–15.233**.
[102] *R (Ambrose) v Westminster City Council*, 13 May 2011 Admin Ct, July *Legal Action*, p 21, Admin Ct.
[103] *R (J) v Newham London Borough Council* [2001] EWHC 992 (Admin), (2002) 5 CCLR 303.
[104] See Chapter 12.
[105] See **12.24–12.31**.
[106] For examples of applicants who were found not to be eligible, see *R (Rekiouak) v Southwark LBC CO/4836/2005*, (2005) December *Legal Action*, p 22, Admin Ct; *R (Badu) v Lambeth London Borough Council* [2005] EWCA Civ 1184, [2006] HLR 8, CA. See also *R (Bangura) v Southwark London Borough Council* [2007] EWHC 1681 (Admin), (2007) September *Legal Action*, p 18.
[107] CA 1989, s 17(3).
[108] *R v Ealing London Borough Council ex p C (A Minor)* (2000) 3 CCLR 132, CA.

can, in exceptional circumstances, be provided.[109] Therefore, in practice, a child's need for accommodation with his or her family could result in the children's services authority assisting the family financially with a deposit or rent guarantee so that they can find accommodation in the private sector.[110] Other forms of assistance could include moving a child and his or her family from inadequate to adequate accommodation.[111] However, it is now not unusual for children's services' authorities to offer accommodation to the child, or children, alone under CA 1989, s 20[112] rather than offer assistance to the whole of the family. This practice was first considered by the House of Lords in *R (A) v Lambeth London Borough Council, R (W) v Lambeth London Borough Council and R (G) v Barnet London Borough Council*[113] and found, in principle, to be lawful.

20.63 The three cases considered by the House of Lords in *R (A) v Lambeth London Borough Council, R (W) v Lambeth London Borough Council and R (G) v Barnet London Borough Council*[114] illustrate the types of assistance with housing need that can be sought under CA 1989, s 17. In *A*, two severely disabled children, whose mother was a secure tenant, needed to move to larger and safer accommodation. In *W*, the child's mother had been found to have become homeless intentionally. She argued that her child was in need of emergency accommodation (and that it was in the child's best interests for the two of them to be accommodated together). In *G*, the child's mother was homeless and not eligible for homelessness assistance, as she was not habitually resident in the UK. The assessment of the child's needs had resulted in the local authority offering to pay for travel to the family's home country, which the mother had refused. The children in *W* and *G*, therefore, both had immediate needs for accommodation with (it was argued) their parents, and the children in *A* had a need for suitable long-term accommodation. In both *W* and *G*, the local authorities were offering accommodation to the children alone, without their mothers, pursuant to their duty under CA 1989, s 20.

20.64 The House of Lords confirmed that accommodation could be provided under CA 1989, s 17 powers, a position also legislated for by Parliament, which had amended s 17(6) to include specific reference to 'accommodation'.[115] It

---

[109]   CA 1989, s 17(6).

[110]   *R v Barking and Dagenham London Borough Council ex p Ebuki* (2001) March *Legal Action*, p 30, Admin Ct. For an example of where a children's services authority should have considered its powers to assist with rent in the private rented sector more carefully, see *R (S) v Plymouth City Council* [2009] EWHC 1499 (Admin) October *Legal Action*, p 26, Admin Ct and [2010] EWCA Civ 1490, (2010) March *Legal Action*, p 31, CA, (refusal of permission to appeal).

[111]   *R v Tower Hamlets London Borough Council ex p Bradford* (1997) 1 CCLR 294, CA. See also *R (Mooney) v Southwark London Borough Council* [2006] EWHC 1912 (Admin), (2006) September *Legal Action*, p 14, Admin Ct.

[112]   See **20.74–20.81**.

[113]   *R (G) v Barnet London Borough Council, R (W) v Lambeth London Borough Council, R (A) v Lambeth London Borough Council* [2003] UKHL 57, [2004] 2 AC 208, HL.

[114]   *R (G) v Barnet London Borough Council, R (W) v Lambeth London Borough Council, R (A) v Lambeth London Borough Council* [2003] UKHL 57, [2004] 2 AC 208, HL.

[115]   Adoption and Children Act 2002, s 116(1), in force from 7 November 2002 and enacted after

held, however, that the duty under CA 1989, s 17 was a 'target duty' and therefore there was no means by which an individual child could require that the local authority provide him or her with particular services under that section. In *A*'s case, there was no power for the court to order that the local authority obtain suitable accommodation for the children. The House of Lords also emphasised that the decisions, as to whether a child was in need and what services should be provided to meet those needs, were decisions for the local authority. In particular, local authorities are entitled to operate certain policies such as (in the case of *G*) offering to return the family to their home country and providing accommodation only for the child if the offer is refused. In *W*, the local authority had not been acting unreasonably when it decided that the child was not in need of accommodation (as her mother had relatives with whom they could stay) and that, if the mother failed to make her own arrangements for accommodation, it would provide accommodation for the child but not the family. Local authorities remain under an obligation to consider the individual circumstances of each applicant, but to operate a general policy normally providing accommodation for the children alone is not, in itself, unlawful.

Children of persons from abroad

20.65 There used to be no general prohibition on providing services under CA 1989, s 17 to children who were persons from abroad, or whose parents were persons from abroad. Prior to 6 December 1999, asylum-seekers whose families included dependent children were provided with accommodation and services by local authorities under CA 1989, s 17. As from 6 December 1999, the statutory basis for providing accommodation and services fell under the Asylum Support (Interim Provisions) Regulations 1999[116] and, from 3 April 2000, local authorities have been prevented from providing CA 1989, s 17 assistance to the children of asylum-seekers.[117] Even if the children have needs that would normally bring them within the scope of CA 1989, s 17(1) (eg disability), the provision of adequate accommodation and support for the family remains the responsibility of the Home Office.[118]

20.66 On 8 January 2003, s 54 and Sch 3 of the Nationality, Immigration and Asylum Act 2002 came into force, along with the Withholding and Withdrawal of Support (Travel Assistance and Temporary Accommodation) Regulations 2002.[119] These provisions apply to five classes of people:

---

the Court of Appeal decision in *R (A) v Lambeth London Borough Council* [2002] EWCA Civ 540, (2002) 34 HLR 13, CA, which had held that there was no such power and was subsequently overturned by the House of Lords.

[116] Asylum Support (Interim Provisions) Regulations 1999, SI 1999/3056.

[117] Immigration and Asylum Act 1999, s 122(5), to be substituted by s 122(3), but not yet in force (Nationality, Immigration and Asylum Act 2002, s 47).

[118] *R (A) v NASS and Waltham Forest London Borough Council* [2003] EWCA Civ 1473, [2004] HLR 24, CA.

[119] SI 2002/3078. However, where the only support that the family might be entitled to is support from the UKBA under Immigration and Asylum Act 1999, s 4 (commonly known as 'hard cases support'), the children's services authority should not take that possibility of support

(1) refugees given refugee status by another state of the EEA;

(2) nationals of another state of the EEA;

(3) asylum-seekers whose claims for asylum have failed and who have failed to co-operate with removal directions;

(4) persons who are not asylum-seekers and are unlawfully present in the UK; and

(5) failed asylum-seekers with dependent children where those families have been certified by the Secretary of State as not having taken reasonable steps to leave the UK.[120]

20.67 People in the first, second and fourth categories who have dependent children are entitled to limited support under CA 1989, s 17.[121] Children's services authorities can provide assistance with travel arrangements for families in the first two categories to return to their home countries and can provide support and accommodation until they travel.[122] They may also provide support and accommodation for families in the fourth category until those people make their own arrangements to travel. If the families do not leave the UK, accommodation and support will cease. The children will be entitled to accommodation and support under CA 1989, s 20, but their parents will not be entitled to any services. If a request is made for support by anyone falling within one of the third, fourth or fifth classes, the local children's services authority is obliged to inform the Home Office.[123]

20.68 When these restrictions were first enacted, guidance issued by the Secretary of State (to which children's services authorities must have regard)[124] stated that it was preferable that accommodation was only provided for a limited period, with maximum periods suggested of five days for families falling within the first two categories and ten days for families falling into the fourth category from the date when they first presented to the children's services authority for support. In the case of *R (M) v Islington London*

---

into account when assessing whether or not the child is a child 'in need': *R (VC) v Newcastle City Council & SSHD* [2011] EWHC 2673, Admin (2011) December *Legal Action,* p 30, Admin Ct.

[120] Nationality Immigration and Asylum Act 2002, s 54 and Sch 3; and SI 2002/3078. See also **20.46–20.48**. For a list of EEA states, see **12.67**, Box 2. The fifth category was added by s 9(1) of the Asylum and Immigration (Treatment of Claimants etc) Act 2004 and came into force on 1 December 2004.

[121] SI 2002/3078, reg 3(2) and (3). See *Practice Guidance for Local Authorities assessing and supporting children and families and former looked-after children who have No Recourse to Public Funds for Support from Local Authorities under Children Act 1989* (No Recourse to Public Funds Network, December 2011).

[122] SI 2002/3078, reg 3(1).

[123] Nationality Immigration and Asylum Act 2002, Sch 3, para 14.

[124] SI 2002/3078, reg 4(4).

Borough Council,[125] the majority of the Court of Appeal held that the periods of five and ten days suggested in the Secretary of State's guidance did not preclude a local authority from providing accommodation for a longer period.

20.69 Failed asylum-seeker families with dependent children (the fifth category) are the responsibility of the UKBA and remain eligible for support and accommodation from the UKBA until they are deported.[126]

20.70 Children's services authorities are not prevented from providing accommodation and support to anyone falling within one of these five categories if it is necessary to do so in order to prevent a breach of that individual's European Convention rights or European Union Treaty rights.[127] They should also take into account UKBA policy where the claimant might potentially be entitled to remain in the UK.

20.71 The possibility of a breach of an individual's European Convention rights usually relates to his or her rights under Art 6 (right to a fair trial) and/or Art 8 (right to respect for private and family life). In *R (Clue) v Birmingham City Council*,[128] the Court of Appeal held that children's services authorities should adopt the following approach:

- the first question is to ascertain the applicant's immigration status;

- if the applicant is a person in the UK in breach of immigration laws and is not an asylum-seeker, the next question is to decide whether the family is destitute; if so

- the next consideration is whether there is an impediment in the family returning to its country of origin (and if the only impediment is financial, the children's services authority can assist with funds);

- if it is said that there would be a breach of European Convention rights if the family were to return, and if the applicant has not applied to the UKBA for leave to remain in the UK, the children's services authority must consider whether the applicant enjoys a private or family life in the UK within the meaning of Art 8(1) and, if so, whether a return to the country of origin would constitute an interference with that right, relevant to that question is the length of time the family has spent in the UK and the degree to which the children may have spent their formative years in the UK;

- where an applicant has made an application for leave to remain in the UK, children's services authorities should not undertake their own assessment

---

[125] [2004] EWCA Civ 235, [2004] 4 All ER 709, CA.
[126] Immigration and Asylum Act 1999, s 94(5), to be repealed by the Nationality, Immigration and Asylum Act 2002, s 44(1) and (5).
[127] Nationality, Immigration and Asylum Act 2002, Sch 3, para 3.
[128] [2010] EWCA Civ 460, [2011] 1 WLR 99, CA.

of how the Secretary of State will determine the application for leave, unless the application is hopeless or abusive; and

- it follows that where a return to the country of origin would involve having to abandon the application for leave to remain, there is a legal impediment preventing the applicant from returning.

20.72 Earlier cases considered potential breach of the right to respect for family life. In *R (M) v Islington London Borough Council*,[129] the children's services authority's decision to provide support by returning the mother and child to the mother's home country of Guyana was held to be wrong in law because the children's services authority had failed to consider the child's right to respect for her family life, in that she might lose contact with her father, who was to remain in the UK and thus it might be necessary to provide support in order to prevent a breach of the child's European Convention rights.[130]

20.73 In *R (Conde) v Lambeth London Borough Council*,[131] the court considered the position of an EEA national who was seeking work, and held that children's services authorities considering applications from EEA nationals should always ensure that those applicants are not exercising any rights under European Union Treaties, although it was unlikely that work-seekers applying for housing or Children Act accommodation would be exercising European Union Treaty rights.

Individual children

20.74 By CA 1989, s 20, children's services authorities are required to provide accommodation for any children in need within their area who appear to them to require accommodation as a result of:

(1) there being no one who has parental responsibility for them; or

(2) their having been lost or abandoned; or

(3) the person who had been caring for them being prevented from providing suitable accommodation or care.

20.75 In *R (M) v Gateshead Metropolitan Borough Council*,[132] Dyson LJ described the duty as:

---

[129] *R (M) v Islington London Borough Council* [2004] EWCA Civ 235, [2004] 4 All ER 709, CA.
[130] In *R (K) v Lambeth London Borough Council* [2003] EWCA Civ 1150, [2004] HLR 15, CA, the Court of Appeal held that neither Art 3 nor Art 8 of the European Convention on Human Rights imposed a duty on the UK to provide support to foreign nationals who are permitted to enter the country but are in a position freely to return home. See also *R (Blackburn-Smith) v Lambeth London Borough Council* [2007] EWHC 767 (Admin), (2007) October *Legal Action*, p 27, Admin Ct.
[131] [2005] EWHC 62 (Admin), [2005] HLR 29, Admin Ct. See also **12.123–12.163** for EEA rights of residence and **12.181**.
[132] [2006] EWCA Civ 221, [2006] QB 650, CA.

'an absolute duty to provide accommodation for any child in need where one of the specified circumstances exists. It is a precise and specific duty. There is no scope of discretion as to whether or not to provide accommodation at all. Thus where it appears to the local authority that there is a child in need, for example, as a result of there being no person who has parental responsibility, the local authority has an absolute obligation to provide some accommodation for that child. Section 20, says nothing about the type of accommodation that must be provided: that is left to the discretion of the local authority.'[133]

20.76 CA 1989, s 20 poses a series of questions for the children's services authority to ask and answer:

(1) Is the applicant a child?

(2) If so, is the applicant a child in need, which might mean that he or she lacks accommodation?

(3) If so, is the child within the children's services authority's area?[134]

(4) If so, does he or she appear to the children's services authority to require accommodation?

(5) If so, is that because of one of the three statutory reasons, which can include the circumstance where a child is excluded from the parental home by his or her parent?

(6) If so, what are the child's wishes and feelings regarding the provision of accommodation for him or her?

(7) What consideration should be given to the child's wishes and feelings?[135]

20.77 If the answers to those questions indicate that the child falls within the statutory criteria at CA 1989, s 20(1), accommodation must be provided by the children's services authority. The children's services authority should not be 'side-stepping' its responsibilities, for example by simply advising a child to make a homelessness application.[136]

---

[133] *R (M) v Gateshead Metropolitan Borough Council* [2006] EWCA Civ 221, [2006] 1 QB 650, CA, at [33], per Dyson LJ.
[134] See *R (Liverpool City Council) v Hillingdon London Borough Council and AK* [2008] EWCA Civ 43, [2009] LGR 289, CA; and *R (A) v Leicester City Council and Hillingdon London Borough Council* [2009] EWHC 2351 (Admin), (2009) November *Legal Action*, p 26, Admin Ct, for examples of disputes between local authorities.
[135] *R (G) v Southwark London Borough Council* [2009] UKHL 26, [2009] 1 WLR 2399, HL, at [28], per Baroness Hale.
[136] A homeless child who has a priority need may also be a 'child in need' for the purposes of CA 1989 and local housing authorities should refer children who approach them for assistance with homelessness to children's services as well as complying with their duties under HA 1996, Part 7 but the primary responsibility is likely to fall on children's services authorities. See *R (M) v Hammersmith & Fulham London Borough Council* [2008] UKHL 14, 1 WLR 535, HL; *R (G) v Southwark London Borough Council* [2009] UKHL 26, [2009] 1 WLR 2399, HL; and

20.78   The duty is owed to the individual child, and for these purposes a child is defined as a person who is not yet 18 years old.[137] The children's services authority will initially assess whether or not a person claiming to be a child without parental support is in fact aged less than 18. Useful guidance on the assessment of the child's age is provided by *R (B) v Merton London Borough Council.*[138] However, if the child disagrees with the children's services authority's assessment of his or her age, he or she can bring judicial review proceedings and, unlike most claims in judicial review, ask the court to review the evidence available and make its own decision as to what age he or she is.[139]

20.79   There are no restrictions on the grounds of immigration status to providing CA 1989, s 20 accommodation to children. Asylum-seeking children who are unaccompanied are entitled to the same care and after-care duties as any other children.[140]

20.80   Children who are provided with accommodation under CA 1989, s 20 are entitled to certain assistance beyond their eighteenth birthday.[141] This is not the case for children provided with help with accommodation under CA 1989, s 17. In *R (H) v Wandsworth London Borough Council,*[142] the court held that where a local authority actually provided accommodation to a child whom it

---

R(TG) v Lambeth London Borough Council [2010] EWHC 907 (Admin), [2011] HLR 33, Admin Ct. Both the UK government and the Welsh Government have issued statutory guidance on the joint working relationship between local housing authorities and children's services authorities. See *Provision of Accommodation for 16 and 17 year old young people who may be homeless and/or require Accommodation* (CLG and Children, Schools and Families, April 2010) for guidance to children's services authorities in England and *Provision of Accommodation for 16 and 17 year old young people who may be homeless* (Welsh Assembly Government, September 2010). In January 2011, *Inside Housing* reported that many councils were still failing to assess the needs of vulnerable 16- and 17-year-olds: *Who Cares?* Inside Housing 17 January 2011). See *R (Liverpool City Council) v Hillingdon London Borough Council and AK* [2008] EWCA Civ 43, [2009] LGR 289, CA, on the extent to which the child's wishes and feelings should be taken into account. For one example where the local authority was guilty of maladministration, see *Complaint against Waltham Forest London Borough Council*, 08 016 986, 21 October 2009, (2010) February *Legal Action*, p 34, where £7,000 compensation was recommended in respect of the local authority's failure to assess and to provide a child with services under CA 1989, s 20 and then under the leaving-care provisions. See also **13.127–13.174** (England) and **13.214–13.218** (Wales).

[137]   CA 1989, s 105.

[138]   *R (B) v Merton London Borough Council* [2003] EWHC 1689 (Admin), [2003] 4 All ER 280, Admin Ct.

[139]   *R (A) v Croydon London Borough Council, R (M) v Lambeth London Borough Council* [2009] UKSC 8, [2009] 1 WLR 2557, SC. Since this important decision of the Supreme Court, there are various decisions of the Court of Appeal, Administrative Court and Upper Tribunal containing the court's own assessment of a claimant's age and guidance on how the courts should be carrying out that assessment. A detailed survey of those cases is beyond the scope of this book.

[140]   *R (Berhe) v Hillingdon London Borough Council* [2003] EWHC 2075 (Admin), [2004] 1 FLR 439, Admin Ct; and *R (SO) v Barking & Dagenham London Borough Council* [2010] EWCA Civ 1101, [2011] HLR 4, CA.

[141]   See **13.175–13.181** and **13.223** and **20.81–20.82**.

[142]   [2007] EWHC 1082 (Admin), [2007] 2 FCR 378, Admin Ct. See also *R (S) v Sutton London Borough Council* [2007] EWCA Civ 790, (2007) September *Legal Action*, p 19, CA.

had identified as a 'child in need', that accommodation was provided under CA 1989, s 20 and it was not for the children's services authority, or even the child, to characterise that accommodation as provided under CA 1989, s 17.[143] A child may have been provided with accommodation under CA 1989, s 20, even when he or she is assisted to live with relatives,[144] placed in respite care or in a residential specialist placement.

Young people

20.81 Children falling within the duties at CA 1989, s 20 are entitled to accommodation until the age of 18 and thereafter (subject to certain conditions) to the benefits of the amendments to CA 1989 made by the Children (Leaving Care) Act 2000 and the regulations and guidance made under CA 1989. As the child approaches 18, the children's services authority must prepare a pathway plan assessing the child's need for advice, assistance and support both before and after the authority ceases to look after the child.[145] That pathway plan should include consideration of the young person's needs for accommodation and how accommodation is to be provided.[146] The children's services authority must also provide a personal adviser and pay for certain education-related expenses.[147] The children's services authority continues to be under this obligation until the child reaches 21. Precisely because these young people, who have been in the care of the children's services authority, are owed continuing duties as care-leavers they are not entitled to priority need under the provisions of HA 1996, Part 7, on any application for homelessness assistance to a local housing authority in England, simply by virtue of their age.[148]

20.82 There are no restrictions on the grounds of immigration status to these services provided to young people.[149]

Performing obligations under the Children Act 1989

20.83 Once a children's services authority has identified a child's need for accommodation and has either acknowledged a duty to provide it (under CA

---

[143] See also *R (LW) v North Lincolnshire Council* [2008] EWHC 2299 (Admin), [2008] 2 FLR 2150, Admin Ct. For an example of where a children's services authority was correct to characterise the services provided as being pursuant to its duty under CA 1989, s 17, rather than under CA 1989, s 20, see *R (FL) v Lambeth London Borough Council* [2010] EWHC 49, (2010) March *Legal Action*, p 31, Admin Ct.

[144] *R (SA) v Kent County Council* [2010] EWHC 848 (Admin), (2012) February *Legal Action*, p 13, Admin Ct, also known as *S v A Local Authority*.

[145] CA 1989, s 23E.

[146] See *R (J) v Caerphilly County Borough Council* [2005] EWHC 586, [2005] 2 FCR 157, Admin Ct.

[147] CA 1989, ss 23C–23D.

[148] See **13.175–13.181** for English Priority Need Order; and see **13.219–13.227** for Welsh Priority Need Order, where they will have a priority need.

[149] *R (Binomughisa) v Southwark London Borough Council* [2006] EWHC 2254 (Admin), [2007] 1 FLR 916.

1989, s 20) or decided to exercise a power to provide it (under CA 1989, s 17) the crucial next step is to find that accommodation. The children's services authority is most unlikely to have units of residential accommodation simply standing ready to meet demand.

20.84 Where what is needed is ordinary housing provision, the children's services authority (or department) needs to be able to call upon others. Co-operation can be expected from the local housing authority (or department) as a result of the statutory requirement upon local housing authorities to assist, on request.[150] Similar expectations as to co-operation are imposed on local private registered providers or registered social landlords, not least by the requirements of their regulatory bodies.[151] Beyond assistance from local housing authorities and private registered providers or registered social landlords, a children's services authority will either need to pay for housing itself (by purchase or renting from the private sector) or help to finance the acquisition by the child, or his or her family, of suitable accommodation, usually by assisting with a deposit and rent guarantee.[152]

DISPLACED OCCUPIERS

20.85 Quite apart from the requirements of HA 1996, Parts 6 and 7, local housing authorities can be required, in certain circumstances, to provide accommodation to existing tenants, or owner-occupiers who are faced with loss of their homes.

20.86 If the local housing authority is the landlord of a secure tenant, and is bringing possession proceedings against that tenant under statutory grounds 9–16 inclusive,[153] it must make suitable alternative accommodation available for the tenant and his or her family in order to obtain an order for possession from the court. The accommodation need not be provided by that, or any, local housing authority landlord; it may be provided by a private registered provider or registered social landlord or even by a private landlord on an assured tenancy. What is 'suitable' accommodation for these purposes is determined by Sch 2, Part 4 of the Housing Act 1985. If no suitable accommodation is available from another provider, the local housing authority itself will have to provide the accommodation if it wishes to obtain possession.

20.87 More generally, where any person is 'displaced from residential accommodation' as a result of a local housing authority compulsorily purchasing land, making a housing order or making improvements to or redeveloping land, the local housing authority will be under a duty to provide

---

[150] CA 1989, s 27.
[151] See English Code, Annex 5; Welsh Code Annex 9.
[152] See *R (S) v Plymouth City Council* [2009] EWHC 1499 (Admin), (2009) October *Legal Action*, p 26, Admin Ct and [2010] EWCA Civ 1490, (2010) March *Legal Action*, p 31, CA, (refusal of permission to appeal).
[153] Housing Act 1985, Sch 2.

suitable alternative residential accommodation on reasonable terms, if no such accommodation is otherwise available to the person displaced.[154] That duty does not require the local housing authority to put the displaced person to the top of its allocation scheme, thereby achieving priority over those who may have been waiting some considerable time. The provision of temporary accommodation until more permanent housing becomes available is sufficient to comply with the duty.[155] In order to give local housing authorities maximum flexibility, suitable alternative accommodation provided under this duty does not constitute an 'allocation', and the local housing authority does not have to comply with the requirements of HA 1996, Part 6 or its own allocation scheme.[156]

DEFECTIVE DWELLING-HOUSES

20.88 Special statutory provision is made for the re-housing of those who currently occupy, but need to leave, defective homes which were purchased from local housing authorities under right-to-buy arrangements. Local housing authorities have to take responsibility for those defective dwelling-houses in their areas,[157] including the re-purchase of a defective dwelling-house where an individual is entitled to that assistance.[158] Where such a property is occupied, the local housing authority will then become subject to housing obligations towards that occupier. If the property is occupied by its owner or by a statutory Rent Act 1977 tenant, the local housing authority is required to grant the occupier a secure tenancy of that property or, if the dwelling-house is not safe for occupation or the local housing authority intends to demolish or reconstruct it within a reasonable time, a different property.[159] If the property is occupied by a contractual tenant, who is either protected under the Rent Act 1977 or an assured tenant protected by the Housing Act 1988, the local housing authority acquires the landlord's interest under the tenancy and the status of the tenancy changes to that of a secure tenancy.[160] Again, if there is to be reconstruction or the house is unsafe, the tenant must be re-housed.

20.89 The grant of a secure tenancy to a former owner-occupier or statutory tenant in these circumstances does not constitute an 'allocation' for the purposes of HA 1996, Part 6, and so the local housing authority is not obliged

---

[154] Land Compensation Act 1973, s 39(1).

[155] *R v Bristol Corporation ex p Hendy* [1974] 1 All ER 1047, CA; *R v East Hertfordshire District Council ex p Smith* (1990) 23 HLR 26, CA.

[156] Allocation of Housing (England) Regulations 2002, SI 2002/3264, reg 3(2); and Allocation of Housing (Wales) Regulations 2003, SI 2003/239 (W 36), reg 3(a), both made under HA 1996, s 160(4). See also **1.43**.

[157] Housing Act 1985, Part XVI, 'Assistance for Owners of Defective Housing'.

[158] Housing Act 1985, ss 547–553 and Sch 20.

[159] These provisions only apply if the occupier makes a written request for the grant of a tenancy: Housing Act 1985, ss 554–557.

[160] Housing Act 1985, s 553.

to offer the accommodation to those applicants entitled to reasonable preference under the HA 1996, Part 6 or its allocation scheme.[161]

HELP WITH HOUSING UNDER THE HUMAN RIGHTS ACT 1998

20.90   Since 2 October 2000, all local housing authorities, along with all other public authorities, have had to refrain from acting in a way which is incompatible with the main provisions of the European Convention on Human Rights. Private registered providers and registered social landlords may constitute public authorities for the purposes of allocating and terminating tenancies of social housing.[162]

20.91   Two Articles of the European Convention are particularly relevant to the subject of this book: an individual's absolute right not to be subjected to inhuman or degrading treatment (Art 3) and the qualified right to respect for his or her home, family life, private life and correspondence (Art 8).[163]

20.92   Each of these Articles may give an individual the right to insist on a local authority or other public authority providing adequate accommodation where he or she has none.

Article 3

20.93   For a breach of Art 3 of the European Convention to be made out, there must be either:

'... ill-treatment that attains a minimum level of severity and involves actual bodily injury or intense physical or mental suffering',

or treatment that:

'... humiliates or debases an individual showing lack of respect for, or diminishing, his or her human dignity or arouses feelings of fear, anguish or inferiority capable of breaking an individual's moral and physical resistance.'[164]

20.94   If the failure to provide accommodation would reduce an individual to this condition, then public authorities may have to take measures to avoid that situation arising.[165]

20.95   Prior to the implementation of the Human Rights Act 1998, the European Court of Human Rights considered the application of Art 3 in the

---

[161]   SI 2003/3264, reg 3(3); SI 2003/239, reg 3(b), both made under HA 1996, s 160(4).
[162]   *R (Weaver) v London & Quadrant Housing Trust* [2009] EWCA Civ 587, [2009] HLR 40, CA.
[163]   Human Rights Act 1998, s 6 and Sch 1.
[164]   *Pretty v UK* (2002) 35 EHRR 1, ECtHR.
[165]   But see **20.98**.

case of a homeless person who was entitled to work and to claim benefits. He had been evicted from a night shelter due to his behaviour and had thereafter spent 14 months on the streets (essentially by his own choice). It was held that he had not demonstrated a minimum level of suffering sufficient to breach Art 3.[166]

20.96 An attempt, in *R (Bernard) v Enfield London Borough Council*,[167] to establish that the provision of grossly unsuitable temporary accommodation which failed to meet the assessed needs of a disabled woman was in breach of Art 3 was not successful.

20.97 The courts have considered the extent to which the failure of public authorities to provide shelter and subsistence can infringe Art 3 (in the context of destitute asylum-seekers).[168] It is not enough for there to be a risk, or even a real risk, of Art 3, suffering occurring; it must actually be occurring or be about to occur.[169] Physical ill health or psychological disturbance arising from a lack of a roof over the individual's head can constitute a condition that amounts to inhuman or degrading treatment.[170] Public authorities have to ask whether the entire package of deprivation is so severe that it can properly be described as inhuman or degrading treatment. The threshold of severity would, in the ordinary way, be crossed where a person deprived of subsistence and restricted from work is obliged to sleep in the street, or is seriously hungry, or is unable to sustain the most basic level of hygiene.[171]

20.98 Since local authorities, as public authorities, are subject to the obligation not to submit an individual to inhuman or degrading treatment, arguably they have a responsibility to provide accommodation to anyone in their area whose suffering is verging on being inhuman or degrading treatment.[172] It is important to note, however, that the threshold is a strict one. A person must have no access to any form of support (including welfare

---

[166] *O'Rourke v UK (Application No 39022/97)* (2001), ECtHR.

[167] *R (Bernard) v Enfield London Borough Council* [2002] EWHC 2282 (Admin), (2003) 35 HLR 27, Admin Ct.

[168] *R (Limbuela) v Secretary of State for the Home Department* [2005] UKHL 66, [2006] 1 AC 396, HL.

[169] *R (Q) v Secretary of State for the Home Department* [2003] EWCA Civ 364, [2004] QB 36, CA.

[170] *R (T) v Secretary of State for the Home Department* [2003] EWCA Civ 1285, (2003) 7 CCLR 53, CA, at [17], per Kennedy LJ, referring to the condition of S, an applicant in the first instance decision.

[171] *R (Limbuela) v Secretary of State for the Home Department* [2005] UKHL 66, [2006] 1 AC 396, HL.

[172] However, in *R (Limbuela) v Secretary of State for the Home Department* [2005] UKHL 66, [2006] 1 AC 396, HL, the Secretary of State was under a statutory duty to provide support to an asylum-seeker in order to avoid a breach of his or her European Convention rights. The issue was therefore whether destitution constituted a breach of Art 3 and the House of Lords held that it did so. In *R (EW) v Secretary of State for the Home Department* [2009] EWHC 2957, (2010) January *Legal Action*, p 35, Admin Ct, at [90] Hickinbottom J said (relying on *R (Limbuela)*) that Art 3 does 'not require a member state to provide accommodation for all within its jurisdiction, nor provide a minimum standard of living ... and it required more than a state's passivity for breach'.

benefits) and not be able to work, whether through physical or legal incapacity. The human rights obligation to support destitute asylum-seekers is undertaken by the Secretary of State; a local authority's obligation, therefore, would only extend to a destitute person in its area who was not entitled to asylum support or any other statutory scheme providing support, was prohibited from claiming welfare benefits, who had no access to employment, and was without any form of shelter or private means of subsistence.[173]

Article 8

20.99 Claims centering on a public authority's obligation not to interfere with an individual's right to respect for his or her home, family, private life and correspondence under Art 8 of the European Convention have had rather more success since the introduction of the Human Rights Act 1998. Art 8:

> '... concerns rights of central importance to the individual's identity, self-determination, physical and moral integrity, maintenance of relationships with others and a settled and secure place in the community.'[174]

20.100 It is well established in European human rights law that Art 8 does not contain a positive general obligation on central or local government to provide every individual with a home.[175] But where accommodation is provided by public authorities it must not be of such standard or condition as to amount to a lack of respect within Art 8. Nor must it be allowed to fall to such a standard once occupied.[176] Furthermore, if an individual is left without any accommodation, with the result that his or her family is fractured or private life is adversely affected, Art 8 may be engaged. This possibility has already been explored by the European Court of Human Rights in relation to a severely disabled individual.[177]

---

[173] It would be surprising if this level of destitution were to be experienced by a British national, or a person with leave to remain in the UK and whose leave permitted him or her to claim welfare benefits. The scenario might be more likely to arise in the case of a person who does not have leave to remain in the UK, or whose leave is dependent upon him or her having no recourse to public funds. In those circumstances, local authorities might in any event have statutory duties to assist an adult applicant and certainly have powers and duties to assist and accommodate children (Children Act 1989, ss 17 and 20). See **20.16–20.48** for adult care and **20.55–20.84** for children's services. If an adult applicant is seeking help from a local authority in order to avoid destitution, it is a matter for the local authority how it provides that help. In the case of a person without leave to remain in the UK, that help might consist of assisting him or her to return to his or her country of origin or making those arrangements with the UKBA.

[174] *Connors v UK* [2004] HLR 52, ECHR, at 82.

[175] See, among others, *Marzari v Italy* [1999] 28 EHRR CD 175, ECHR; *O'Rourke v UK* (*Application No 00039022/97*), ECtHR.

[176] *Lee v Leeds City Council* [2002] 1 WLR 1488, [2002] HLR 17, CA.

[177] *Marzari v Italy* [1999] 28 EHRR CD 175, ECtHR.

20.101 The conditions of the accommodation provided by the local authority in *R (Bernard) v Enfield London Borough Council*[178] were sufficiently demeaning to breach the applicant's right to respect for her private and family life under Art 8. However, in *R (Anufrijeva) v Southwark London Borough Council*,[179] a local authority was found not to have interfered with an elderly woman's right to respect for her home, or for her family and private life, by virtue of the nature of temporary accommodation it had provided. The court held that before a public authority could be held to have failed to respect an applicant's private or family life, there had to be an element of culpability, involving (at the very least) knowledge by the public authority that the applicant's private or family life was at risk.

20.102 The right to respect for an applicant's home, protected by Art 8(1), can be relevant in a separate context. Where an occupier faces possession proceedings in respect of his or her home, the court has a duty to consider whether the making of a possession order is proportionate if that point is taken by the occupier.[180]

---

[178] *R (Bernard) v Enfield London Borough Council* [2002] EWHC Admin 2282, (2003) 35 HLR 27, Admin Ct.

[179] *R (Anufrijeva) v Southwark London Borough Council* [2003] EWCA Civ 1406, [2004] 2 WLR 603, CA.

[180] *Manchester City Council v Pinnock* [2010] UKSC 45, [2011] 2 AC 104, SC.

Chapter 21

CONTRACTING OUT OF HOMELESSNESS AND ALLOCATION FUNCTIONS

INTRODUCTION

21.1 The major duties and powers discussed in this book are those which are the responsibility of local housing authorities under the provisions of the Housing Act 1996 (HA 1996), Parts 6 ('Allocation of Housing Accommodation') and 7 ('Homelessness'). Those local housing authorities must ensure that:

(1) they comply with the law;

(2) they perform those duties required by HA 1996; and

(3) they lawfully exercise the powers given to them by HA 1996.

21.2 If a local housing authority refuses to carry out its duties or to exercise its powers, or if there is a dispute as to the lawfulness of how it has carried out a duty or exercised a power, it will be the local housing authority itself that is answerable to the courts or the Ombudsmen.[1] The local housing authority cannot escape that responsibility by reference to, or reliance upon, some other body.

THE MOVE TOWARDS CONTRACTING OUT

21.3 A local housing authority is free to decide for itself how it wishes to organise the performance of its duties and the exercise of its powers. Traditionally, staff directly employed by the local housing authority would carry out those functions on behalf of the local housing authority.

21.4 In recent years, however, more and more local housing authorities have chosen to employ private contractors, frequently local private registered providers in England or registered social landlords in Wales, to carry out those functions for them. Even when they engage contractors, local housing authorities remain responsible for those contractors' actions and also remain responsible to applicants for homelessness assistance, and to applicants for social housing, for any lapses made either by their own staff or by the contractors' staff. Therefore, in order to protect their position, local housing authorities are sensibly advised to build into the contracts between themselves and the private contractors robust penalty and escape clauses, in case of poor performance by the contractors.[2] So assured, more and more local housing authorities have been contracting out their homelessness and allocation functions.

---

[1] In England, the Local Government Ombudsman. In Wales, the Public Services Ombudsman for Wales.

[2] *Homelessness Code of Guidance for Local Authorities* (Communities and Local Government, Department of Education and Skills, Department of Health, July 2006) (the English Code), para 21.10; *Code of Guidance for Local Authorities Allocation of Accommodation and Homelessness 2012* (Welsh Government, August 2012) (the Welsh Code), Annex 9.

THE RELEVANCE OF STOCK TRANSFER

21.5 Over 150 local housing authorities have chosen (with the consent of their tenants and the approval of the Secretary of State) to transfer all of their own housing stock to private registered providers or registered social landlords.[3] The law and guidance governing stock transfer itself is complex and outside the scope of this book. However, three particular points arise concerning homelessness and allocation of social housing following such a stock transfer.

21.6 *First,* even though a local housing authority no longer has any housing stock, and therefore cannot grant secure or introductory tenancies, it is still responsible for receiving and determining applications for homelessness assistance and for deciding (in response to an application for an allocation) who is to be nominated to private registered providers or registered social landlords for the granting of any assured tenancies (including nominations to any landlords who have acquired the local housing authority's own stock). It must, therefore, still have an allocation scheme and make those nominations in accordance with that scheme.

21.7 *Second,* some local housing authorities, having transferred the whole of their housing stock, have also contracted out their homelessness and/or allocation functions, usually to the transferee private registered provider or registered social landlord. Applicants may find that, for all intents and purposes, they appear to be dealing exclusively with staff working for a private registered provider or registered social landlord, from the moment that they apply (for homelessness assistance or under the local housing authority's allocation scheme), up to receiving an offer of accommodation from that same private registered provider or registered social landlord. Despite that appearance, decisions that are made under one of the local housing authority's statutory functions remain the responsibility of the local housing authority.

21.8 *Third,* the statutory duties on a private registered provider or registered social landlord to co-operate with a local housing authority from which it has acquired housing stock[4] do not mean that the purchasing private registered provider or registered social landlord is itself obliged to operate an allocation scheme in the same terms as that which would have been operated by the local housing authority. A private registered provider or registered social landlord will normally be required by the terms of the stock transfer contract to ensure that a certain proportion of its housing stock is available for the local housing authority to nominate applicants to. However, the private registered provider or registered social landlord may also operate its own policies governing which applicants it will accept in relation to the rest of its stock.[5]

---

[3]   H Pawson et al *The impacts of housing stock transfers in urban Britain* (Joseph Rowntree Press, 2009).

[4]   For example, Housing Act 1996, s 213.

[5]   English Code, Annex 5; Welsh Code Annex 9. Paragraph 9 of the English Code, Annex 5 refers to private registered providers being required to offer at least 50% of vacancies in their stock to local housing authority nominations. This is out of date. Of course, many local housing

21.9 The guidance in the current Regulatory Code for private registered providers in England states:

> '[r]egistered providers shall co-operate with local authorities' strategic housing functions, and their duties to meet identified local housing needs. This includes assistance with local authorities' homelessness duties, and through meeting obligations in nominations agreements. Where, in exceptional circumstances, registered providers choose not to participate in choice-based lettings schemes in areas where they own homes, they shall publish their reasons for doing so.'[6]

THE DIFFERENT LEGAL STRUCTURES GOVERNING CONTRACTING OUT

21.10 When local housing authorities deliver their own homelessness and allocation services, they do so under HA 1996, Parts 6 and 7 and the Codes of Guidance issued by the Secretary of State and the Welsh Government pursuant to those statutory provisions. The legal basis for contracting out to any contractor is explained below under sub-headings that deal separately with allocation and homelessness functions. In practice, most of the contractors engaged by local housing authorities (for either or both of the functions) are private registered providers or registered social landlords.

21.11 Private registered providers and registered social landlords do not have the same statutory powers and duties as local housing authorities. They are simply required by HA 1996 to 'co-operate' in the delivery of the local housing authority's homelessness and allocation functions 'to such extent as is reasonable in the circumstances', if requested to do so by the local housing authority.[7] That requirement is amplified by the Regulatory Codes,[8] which emphasise that private registered providers and registered social landlords should be working with local housing authorities to enable the local housing authorities' statutory duties to be fulfilled.

21.12 Whether or not the local housing authority has disposed of its stock, if it has contracted out the HA 1996, Part 6 and/or HA 1996, Part 7 functions, the instrument regulating each private registered provider's or registered social landlord's (or other contractor's) relationship with the local housing authority

---

authorities will make provision for a certain proportion, often 50%, of private registered provider or registered social landlord stock to be made available to them in their contractual arrangements. See **6.32–6.59**.

[6]   *Regulatory Framework for social housing in England 2012* (Homes and Community Agency, April 2012), para 1.1. The guidance for registered social landlords in Wales is *The Regulatory Framework for Housing Associations Registered in Wales* (Welsh Government, December 2011). At Part B it states that registered social landlords should 'work with other organisations to prevent and alleviate homelessness'.

[7]   HA 1996, ss 170 and 213(1).

[8]   *Regulatory Framework for social housing in England 2012* (Homes and Community Agency, April 2012), para 1.1 The guidance for registered social landlords in Wales is *The Regulatory Framework for Housing Associations Registered in Wales* (Welsh Government, December 2011).

is the contract by which the private registered provider, registered social landlord or other contractor agrees to deliver the local housing authority's homelessness or allocation service (or both) at a price. Again, guidance is provided by government on the contents of that contract, particularly where it forms part of an overall arrangement for stock transfer.[9] Clearly, the terms of the contract will govern the standard of the service to be provided and, in cases of stock transfer, the extent to which the private registered provider or registered social landlord must make its vacancies available for nomination by the local housing authority.

21.13 Where, exceptionally, the local housing authority contracts out its HA 1996, Part 6 or Part 7 functions to another local authority, the legal basis for that process is given by the Local Government Act 1972, s 101 and the exact scope of the functions contracted out will be shown in the contract itself.

21.14 Any complaints by members of the public about the services provided by contractors acting on behalf of local housing authorities in respect of HA 1996 functions are made against the local housing authorities themselves, not the contractors. Accordingly, any member of the public wishing to complain should use first the local housing authority's complaints procedure[10] and then complain to the Ombudsmen.[11]

HOMELESSNESS (HOUSING ACT 1996, PART 7)

The statutory basis governing contracting out of homelessness functions

Background to the present arrangements

21.15 As a matter of strict law, a local housing authority consists only of its elected councillors. In practice, no local housing authority, whatever its size, expects the majority of its functions (except general policy-making) to be carried out by its elected councillors. The Local Government Act 1972 permits the elected councillors to delegate the performance of the local housing authority's duties to its own officers (staff employed directly by the local housing authority) and to other local authorities.[12]

---

[9]   There is no current guidance to local housing authorities in England on stock transfers. The Welsh Assembly Government published *Housing Transfer Guidance* (Welsh Assembly Government, 2009).

[10]   See **19.251–19.253**.

[11]   See **19.254–19.258**. Note that a local housing authority was found guilty of serious maladministration by the Ombudsman when a housing association to whom it had contracted out some of its homelessness responsibilities advised an applicant that complaints should be made to the Independent Housing Ombudsman and not to the Local Government Ombudsman (*Complaint against East Dorset District Council*, 05/B/08409, 22 June 2006).

[12]   Local Government Act 1972, s 101.

21.16   In the homelessness context, by 1985 the statutory regime recognised a form of quasi-delegation.[13] The legislation provided that where a local housing authority requested a registered housing association to assist it with the discharge of its homelessness functions, the association should co-operate in rendering such assistance as was reasonable in the circumstances.

21.17   However, in recent years, many local housing authorities have actually employed private registered providers, registered social landlords or other private contractors to assist with the performance of their duties (and some have gone so far as to transfer the whole or part of their housing stock to the same or different contractors).[14]

21.18   In 1994 and 1995, the High Court considered the extent to which a local housing authority could contract out its homelessness functions. In *R v West Dorset District Council and West Dorset Housing Association ex p Gerrard*,[15] the local housing authority had transferred all its stock to the housing association with which it also contracted for the provision of a homelessness advice and investigation service. On receipt of a summary report from the association, a local housing authority officer decided that the applicant in that case was not homeless. A deputy High Court judge held that the local housing authority remained responsible for taking 'an active and dominant part in the investigative process' even after contracting out. Since the local housing authority had not itself carried out any part of the inquiries into the applicant's application for homelessness assistance (and, in addition, relevant representations made by the applicant's solicitor had not been brought to the officer's attention), the decision was quashed. Indeed, the whole administration of the local housing authority's homelessness duties was held to be unlawful. A subsequent appeal against that judgment was dismissed by consent in the Court of Appeal.

21.19   Some 10 months later, another deputy High Court judge considered the same issue in *R v Hertsmere Borough Council ex p Woolgar*.[16] That local housing authority had transferred its stock to two housing associations. A different decision (the suitability of accommodation offered) was under scrutiny, but the judge held that the same statutory framework applied. He went on to consider Housing Act 1985, s 72,[17] the guidance offered in the Code,[18] and government guidelines on transfer of housing stock,[19] all of which clearly envisaged that:

- both the homelessness functions and a local housing authority's housing stock could be transferred;

---

[13]   Housing Act 1985, s 72, repealed by HA 1996, s 227, Sch 19 (with effect from 20 January 1997).
[14]   Governed by separate statutory powers: see **21.39–21.42**.
[15]   (1995) 27 HLR 150, QBD.
[16]   (1995) 27 HLR 703, QBD.
[17]   See **21.16**.
[18]   At that time Department of Environment's *Code of Guidance*, para 11.7.
[19]   *Large Scale Voluntary Transfers Guidelines* (Department of the Environment, December 1993).

- that the local housing authority should retain responsibility for decisions made under its homelessness duties; and

- that the local housing authority should retain at least some nomination rights to its former housing.

21.20 Having considered those materials, he held that the decision in *Gerrard* had been made without any scrutiny of the government's guidelines and was therefore made *per incuriam*.[20] As a result, Hertsmere Borough Council's scheme for delivering its homelessness duties, which amounted to its homelessness functions being carried out by a registered social landlord (now a private registered provider) and the accommodation offered being provided by that same landlord, was held to be lawful.

The modern framework

21.21 The judicial uncertainty created by these two conflicting decisions was soon resolved by Parliament. The modern legislative framework permitting a local housing authority to contract out its homelessness functions is found in the Deregulation and Contracting Out Act 1994, s 70. Under that Act, the Secretary of State has made the Local Authorities (Contracting Out of Allocation of Housing and Homelessness Functions) Order 1996.[21] Local housing authorities are now permitted to contract out the bulk of their homelessness functions.[22]

21.22 Particular conditions related to the carrying out of those functions can be (and should be) included in the contract itself, so that standards of performance are prescribed. The Deregulation and Contracting Out Act 1994 provides that the contract cannot be for a period of more than 10 years, and may be for any shorter period.[23] The contract must also provide that it can be revoked at any time by the Minister or by the local housing authority.[24] The local housing authority remains responsible for any acts or omissions made by the contractor in the performance of the local housing authority's homelessness functions, unless the contractor is in breach of the conditions specified in the contract or the contractor has committed a criminal offence.

21.23 In *Runa Begum v Tower Hamlets London Borough Council*,[25] the House of Lords considered whether such a contractor could be considered 'independent' of the local housing authority for the purposes of the European Convention on Human Rights, Art 6(1).[26] If contractors were held to be

---

[20] Without awareness of authority that might have made a difference to the court's decision.
[21] SI 1996/3205, reproduced in Appendix 2 of this book. See also English Code, Chapter 21; Welsh Code, Annex 9 for guidance.
[22] Except those listed at **21.24**.
[23] Deregulation and Contracting Out Act 1994, s 69(5)(a).
[24] Deregulation and Contracting Out Act 1994, s 69(5)(b).
[25] *Runa Begum v Tower Hamlets London Borough Council* [2003] UKHL 5, [2003] 2 AC 430, HL.
[26] Which provides that civil rights are to be determined by a body independent of the parties. In

'independent' for those purposes, review decisions that were being taken by officers employed by the local housing authority (who were obviously not independent) could, instead, be taken by contracted individuals or organisations in order to obtain the necessary measure of independence. The House of Lords held that a contractor, whose services could be dispensed with, was probably no more independent than an officer employed directly by the local housing authority. However, Lord Bingham, in an *obiter* paragraph, added that he had very considerable doubt whether the resolution of applications for review fell within a local housing authority's relevant functions and therefore could be contracted out at all.[27] Since then, the Court of Appeal has held that the making of review decisions *is* a function that can be contracted by a local housing authority in *De-Winter Heald v Brent London Borough Council.*[28]

21.24 The local housing authority may *not* contract out four specified functions:

(1)   its power to provide finance to a person or organisation so that housing advice and information is provided on the local housing authority's behalf;[29]

(2)   its power to assist such a person or organisation by providing premises, furniture, or its own housing staff;[30]

(3)   its power to finance, or provide premises, furniture or the services of its staff, to a voluntary organisation concerned with homelessness or matters relating to homelessness;[31]

(4)   its obligation to render such assistance as is reasonable if asked by another local housing authority to assist it in the discharge of that local housing authority's HA 1996, Part 7 functions.[32]

21.25 Where a local housing authority has contracted out its function of making review decisions, the review decision is only lawful if the process of contracting out complied with the statutory obligations. In *Shacklady v Flintshire County Council,*[33] the local housing authority could not produce any written authorisation in respect of the contract. In addition, the only document that it could trace contained no time-limited authorisation or any indication of

---

February 2010, the Supreme Court decided that decision-making on applications for homelessness assistance does not involve a determination of an applicant's 'civil rights' and so Art 6(1) does not apply (*Ali v Birmingham City Council* [2010] UKSC 8, [2010] 2 AC 39, SC).

27   [2003] UKHL 5, [2003] 2 AC 430, HL, at [10], per Lord Bingham.

28   [2009] EWCA Civ 930, [2010] HLR 8, CA.

29   HA 1996, s 179(2); Local Authorities (Contracting Out of Allocation of Housing and Homelessness Functions) Order 1996, SI 1996/3205, art 3 and Sch 2.

30   HA 1996, s 179(3); SI 1996/3205, art 3 and Sch 2.

31   HA 1996, s 180; SI 1996/3205, art 3 and Sch 2.

32   HA 1996, s 213; SI 1996/3205, art 3 and Sch 2.

33   (2010) November *Legal Action*, p 26, Mold County Court.

a 10-year maximum period of appointment. The judge found that the absence of any written record containing a period of appointment was a serious departure from the statutory requirements and could not be waived. The authorisation to the contractor was therefore invalid and the review decision a nullity. In *Karaj v Three Rivers District Council*,[34] the applicant was granted permission to appeal to the Court of Appeal on a point concerning the lawfulness of the appointment of a reviewing officer under the Deregulation and Contracting Out Act 1994.[35] However, in *England v Westminster City Council*,[36] the courts found that the review decision had not been contracted out. The private registered provider involved had provided information to the reviewing officer but had not made the decision.

Contracting to use a contractor's accommodation for the homeless

21.26   Different statutory provisions govern a local housing authority's ability to use accommodation from other sectors in order to perform its HA 1996, Part 7 duties to applicants for homelessness assistance. As an alternative to providing the applicant with its own accommodation, the HA 1996, Part 7[37] permits a local housing authority to perform its duty to provide accommodation for an applicant and members of his or her household, by securing that the applicant obtains suitable accommodation 'from some other person' or, even, merely by 'giving him such advice and assistance as will secure that suitable accommodation is available from some other person'.[38] If the latter course is taken, then the local housing authority must ensure that the advice and assistance does actually secure that suitable accommodation is obtained. If not, the local housing authority's duty to secure accommodation from its own stock or from some other person remains.[39] These provisions have given local housing authorities considerable flexibility to arrange for accommodation for the homeless to be supplied, under contract, by private registered providers, registered social landlords and other private contractors.

21.27   The ability to secure accommodation 'from some other person' allows a local housing authority to arrange for a private landlord, a private registered provider or registered social landlord to grant a tenancy directly to an applicant in performance of any duty to accommodate the applicant.[40] HA 1996, s 193 also allows the local housing authority to bring the main housing duty to an end when an applicant accepts an offer of an assured tenancy from a private

---

34   [2011] EWCA Civ 768, (2011) August *Legal Action*, p 41, CA.
35   The transcript from the Court of Appeal does not set out the exact issue and the case was subsequently settled.
36   [2010] EWCA Civ 106, (2010) April *Legal Action*, p 26, CA.
37   HA 1996, s 206.
38   HA 1996, s 206(1)(b) and (c).
39   See **18.8–18.10**.
40   HA 1996, s 206(1)(b) and see *R (on the application of Khatun) v Newham London Borough Council* [2004] EWCA Civ 55, [2004] HLR 29, CA, at [91], per Laws LJ.

registered provider or registered social landlord[41] or accepts or refuses a private rented offer of suitable accommodation from a private landlord.[42]

Ensuring that the private contractor maintains the appropriate level of service

21.28 Given that the local housing authority remains responsible for the calibre and correctness of its homelessness decisions, even when the inquiries and recommendations leading to those decisions have been made by a private contractor, it is vital for a local housing authority to be able to rely upon the quality of the service provided by the contractor. That safeguard should be contained in the contract between the local housing authority and the contractor. The Audit Commission noted (in the context of stock transfer):

> '... few [authorities] have experience of contracting out these services, and there is rarely time during the hectic [stock] transfer process to review them, decide their best location and draw up a good contract. As a result, some contracts are poorly written or difficult to monitor. Attention can focus on "maintaining" minimum service rather than improvement.'[43]

21.29 The Audit Commission recommended that, before a decision to contract out the service is made, the local housing authority should:

(1) undertake a scrutiny report or best value review;

(2) consult users;

(3) consider more than one provider; and

(4) take into account the impact that contracting out the service will have on retained housing services.

21.30 The contract should include targets for improvements in the service, quality control and workable monitoring arrangements.[44]

21.31 In 2004, the Office of the Deputy Prime Minister (ODPM)[45] provided non-statutory guidance in *Housing Allocation, Homelessness and Stock Transfer: A guide to key issues*.[46] Particular guidance was provided on drafting

---

[41]   HA 1996, s 193(6)(cc). See **17.88–17.91**.

[42]   HA 1996, s 193(7AA)–(7AC) as amended by Localism Act 2011, s 148(5)–(7) for applicants whose applications for homelessness assistance were made on or after 9 November 2012 to local housing authorities in England. At the date of writing the amendments to HA 1996 made by LA 2011, ss 148–149 had not been brought into effect in Wales. See **17.109–17.131**.

[43]   *Housing after Transfer, the Local Authority Role* (The Audit Commission, 2002), Chapter 3, para 64.

[44]   *Housing after Transfer, the Local Authority Role* (The Audit Commission, 2002), Chapter 3.

[45]   At that time the government department responsible for housing and homelessness.

[46]   *Housing Allocation, Homelessness and Stock Transfer: A guide to key issues* (ODPM, January 2004).

the contract. Detailed service standards, monitoring of those standards, performance indicators and targets need to be specified, along with a procedure for reviewing and altering the contract. Power should be reserved for the local housing authority to terminate the contract for poor performance.

ALLOCATION OF ACCOMMODATION (HOUSING ACT 1996, PART 6)

21.32 The same statutory framework applies to the contracting out of the functions of the allocation of social housing. The Local Authorities (Contracting Out of Allocation of Housing and Homelessness Functions) Order 1996,[47] made by the Secretary of State under Deregulation and Contracting Out Act 1994, s 70, permits local housing authorities to contract out the bulk of their functions involved in the allocation of social housing under HA 1996, Part 6. Many local housing authorities have disposed of the whole of their housing stock to local private registered providers or registered social landlords, so that the local housing authority's allocations are made by nomination to private registered providers or registered social landlords for assured tenancies.

21.33 The overall policy of the allocation scheme is for the local housing authority to decide, subject to complying with HA 1996, Part 6, the regulations and the Codes. The House of Lords has noted that '[h]ousing allocation policy is a difficult exercise which requires not only social and political sensitivity and judgment, but also local expertise and knowledge'.[48] The overall policy decisions are political decisions.

21.34 It follows that the local housing authority is responsible for general policy decisions on:

(1) whether or not it will offer 'choice' in its allocation scheme, or provide applicants with the opportunity to express preferences;[49]

(2) whether it will frame the scheme so as to give additional preferences within the reasonable preference categories and, if so, on what criteria;[50]

(3) on what principles it will prioritise different applicants within the reasonable preference categories;[51] and

---

[47] SI 1996/3205, reproduced in Appendix 1 of this book.

[48] *Ahmad v Newham London Borough Council* [2009] UKHL 14, [2009] HLR 41, HL, at [47], per Lord Neuberger.

[49] HA 1996, s 166A(2) for local housing authorities in England; HA 1996, s 167(1A) for local housing authorities in Wales. See **5.51–5.65**.

[50] HA 1996, s 166A(3) for local housing authorities in England; HA 1996, s 167(2) for local housing authorities in Wales. See **4.123–4.151**.

[51] HA 1996, s 166A(3) for local housing authorities in England; HA 1996, s 167(2) for local housing authorities in Wales. See **4.28–4.169**.

(4)   whether it will provide for the allocation of accommodation to persons of a particular description and, if so, what accommodation, and to whom.[52]

Functions

21.35   Having drawn up its allocation scheme, the local housing authority may contract out nearly all of its *functions* under HA 1996, Part 6 to a contractor. The contractor's staff, therefore, could receive an application, ensure that the applicant is given the information to which he or she is entitled, provide advice and assistance with the making of an application, process the application, make any decisions required to be made in respect of the application and, in accordance with the policy, arrange for the grant of a secure or introductory tenancy, or nominate the applicant to a private registered provider or registered social landlord for an assured tenancy. At each stage the contractor will be taking the practical steps, but the local housing authority remains liable for the decisions.

21.36   The local housing authority cannot contract out the duties:

(1)   to determine the terms of its allocation scheme;

(2)   to allocate in accordance with that scheme; and

(3)   to make the scheme available for inspection.[53]

21.37   If the contractor's staff fail to treat an applicant in accordance with the local housing authority's scheme, it is the local housing authority that will be answerable for that failure.

21.38   In the unreported case of *R (Uddin) v Tower Hamlets London Borough Council*,[54] Mr Uddin was a tenant of a private registered provider who needed a transfer to larger accommodation. The local housing authority and private registered provider operated a common housing register and it was the private registered provider which made the decisions on his application for a transfer. The applicant argued that the private registered provider was not authorised by the local housing authority to make the decision. It appears that the local housing authority did not have any contemporaneous documents authorising the private registered provider to make the decision. It sought to ratify previous

---

[52]   HA 1996, s 166A(6)(b) for local housing authorities in England; HA 1996, s 167(2E)(b) for local housing authorities in Wales. See **4.170–4.176**.

[53]   HA 1996, s 166A(13) for local housing authorities in England; HA 1996, s 167(7) for local housing authorities in Wales. See **4.1–4.27**. These sections refer to adopting or altering an allocation scheme and to consulting private registered providers and registered social landlords. See also HA 1996, s 168(2); SI 1996/3205, art 2 and Sch 1.

[54]   CO/8098/2008.

decisions retrospectively and made a resolution authorising future contracting out of decision-making under its allocation scheme. The case was subsequently settled.[55]

Stock transfers and nominations to private registered providers or registered social landlords[56]

21.39 Where a local housing authority is proposing a large scale voluntary transfer of its own stock, so that there will no longer be any council-owned accommodation in its district, any future allocation made under its allocation scheme will be by way of a nomination to a private registered provider or registered social landlord for an assured tenancy. In order to ensure that it can continue to comply with its statutory duty to maintain an allocation scheme, and to allocate accommodation, the local housing authority must ensure that the purchasing private registered provider(s) or registered social landlord(s) will accept its nominations.

21.40 There are statutory duties, contractual obligations, and Homes and Communities Agency and government guidance requiring that private registered providers and registered social landlords co-operate with local housing authorities to ensure that a certain amount of their available accommodation is provided to people nominated by local housing authorities. If a local housing authority requests that a private registered provider or registered social landlord co-operates with it by offering accommodation to people on the local housing authority's allocation scheme, the private registered provider or registered social landlord is under a statutory duty to co-operate 'to such extent as is reasonable in the circumstances'.[57] In addition, when the local housing authority has transferred its own stock to the private registered provider or registered social landlord, after the process of government approval, consultation and balloting, it will have done so in a contract. The local housing authority should ensure that the terms of the contract provide that the private registered provider or registered social landlord will make a certain proportion of its empty properties available for people nominated by the local housing authority under its allocation scheme.[58] Any proposed transfer that does not include a contractual obligation on the private registered provider or registered social landlord to make a specified proportion of empty accommodation available for allocation is unlikely to receive government approval. In addition, the Homes and Communities Agency expects private registered providers to assist local housing authorities in the performance of their homelessness duties and through meeting obligations in nominations agreements.[59]

---

[55] See 'Contracting out Decision-making: Unanswered Questions', David Cowan [2010] 13 JHL 24.

[56] See Chapter 6 of this book.

[57] HA 1996, s 170.

[58] *Housing Allocation, Homelessness and Stock Transfer: A guide to key issues* (ODPM, January 2004).

[59] See **6.32–6.69**.

21.41 Private registered providers and registered social landlords, including stock transfer associations, can therefore operate quotas under which a proportion (which can be up to 100%) of their vacancies will be allocated on the basis of the local housing authority's nominations. The remaining part of their vacancies will be allocated by the private registered provider or registered social landlord itself, either to its own tenants seeking transfers or to people who have applied directly to the private registered provider or registered social landlord for accommodation.

21.42 Generally, if a private registered provider or registered social landlord gives over a proportion of its empty stock to local housing authority nominations, it should not impose its own conditions on the type of applicant nominated, and should be contractually obliged to accept whoever the authority nominates. However, when it comes to the remainder of the vacancies, private registered providers and registered social landlords will make their own decisions as to who is to be offered each vacancy. Each private registered provider and registered social landlord, therefore, must have its own policy governing transfer applications (from its own tenants) and any applications made to it directly rather than through the local housing authority. The Regulatory Codes require private registered providers and registered social landlords to let their stock in a fair and transparent way and to develop allocations processes in a way which supports their effective use by the full range of actual and potential tenants including those with support needs, those who do not speak English as a first language and those who have difficulties with written English.[60] They are also required to work with local housing authorities to assist them to fulfil their statutory duties to applicants for homelessness assistance.

---

[60] *Regulatory Framework for social housing in England 2012* (Homes and Community Agency, April 2012), paras 1.1–1.3. The guidance for registered social landlords in Wales is *The Regulatory Framework for Housing Associations Registered in Wales* (Welsh Government, December 2011. In Wales the Regulatory Framework requires registered social landlords to give reasonable preference to those who are in greatest housing need or who are homeless (Part B).

Appendix 1

ENGLAND: ALLOCATION

Housing Act 1996

1996 c 52

CONTENTS

PART 6
ALLOCATION OF HOUSING ACCOMMODATION

Introductory

PART 8
MISCELLANEOUS AND GENERAL PROVISIONS

General

PART 6
ALLOCATION OF HOUSING ACCOMMODATION

Introductory

159 Allocation of housing accommodation

(1) A local housing authority shall comply with the provisions of this Part in allocating housing accommodation.

(2) For the purposes of this Part a local housing authority allocate housing accommodation when they –

(a) select a person to be a secure or introductory tenant of housing accommodation held by them,

(b) nominate a person to be a secure or introductory tenant of housing accommodation held by another person, or

(c) nominate a person to be an assured tenant of housing accommodation held by [a private registered provider of social housing or]² a registered social landlord.

(3) The reference in subsection (2)(a) to selecting a person to be a secure tenant includes deciding to exercise any power to notify an existing tenant or licensee that his tenancy or licence is to be a secure tenancy.

(4) The references in subsection (2)(b) and (c) to nominating a person include nominating a person in pursuance of any arrangements (whether legally enforceable or not) to require that housing accommodation, or a specified amount of housing accommodation, is made available to a person or one of a number of persons nominated by the authority.

[(4A) Subject to subsection (4B), the provisions of this Part do not apply to an allocation of housing accommodation by a local housing authority in England to a person who is already –

(a) a secure or introductory tenant, or

(b) an assured tenant of housing accommodation held by a private registered provider of social housing or a registered social landlord.

(4B) The provisions of this Part apply to an allocation of housing accommodation by a local housing authority in England to a person who falls within subsection (4A)(a) or (b) if –

(a) the allocation involves a transfer of housing accommodation for that person,

(b) the application for the transfer is made by that person, and

(c) the authority is satisfied that the person is to be given reasonable preference under section 166A(3).]³

[(5) The provisions of this Part do not apply to an allocation of housing accommodation [by a local housing authority in Wales]⁴ to a person who is already a secure or introductory tenant unless the allocation involves a transfer of housing accommodation for that person and is made on his application.

(6) ...]¹

(7) Subject to the provisions of this Part, a local housing authority may allocate housing accommodation in such manner as they consider appropriate.

AMENDMENT

[1] Sub-sections substituted: Homelessness Act 2002, s 13.

[2] Words inserted: Housing and Regeneration Act 2008 (Consequential Provisions) Order 2010, SI 2010/866, art 5, Sch 2, paras 81, 100.

[3] Sub-sections inserted: Localism Act 2011, s 145(1), (2), with effect from 15 January 2012 for certain purposes (SI 2012/57), for remaining purposes with effect from 18 June 2012 (SI 2012/1463).

[4] Words inserted: Localism Act 2011, s 145(1), (3), with effect from 15 January 2012 for certain purposes (SI 2012/57), for remaining purposes with effect from 18 June 2012 (SI 2012/1463).

160 Cases where provisions about allocation do not apply

(1) The provisions of this Part about the allocation of housing accommodation do not apply in the following cases.

(2) They do not apply where a secure tenancy –

    (a)   vests under section 89 of the Housing Act 1985 (succession to periodic secure tenancy on death of tenant),

    (b)   remains a secure tenancy by virtue of section 90 of that Act (devolution of term certain of secure tenancy on death of tenant),

    (c)   is assigned under section 92 of that Act (assignment of secure tenancy by way of exchange),

    (d)   is assigned to a person who would be qualified to succeed the secure tenant if the secure tenant died immediately before the assignment,

  [(da) is granted in response to a request under section 158 of the Localism Act 2011 (transfer of tenancy), or][5]

    (e)   vests or is otherwise disposed of in pursuance of an order made under –

        (i)   section 24 of the Matrimonial Causes Act 1973 (property adjustment orders in connection with matrimonial proceedings),

        (ii)   section 17(1) of the Matrimonial and Family Proceedings Act 1984 (property adjustment orders after overseas divorce, &c), ...[1]

        (iii) paragraph 1 of Schedule 1 to the Children Act 1989 (orders for financial relief against parents)[, or

        (iv) Part 2 of Schedule 5, or paragraph 9(2) or (3) of Schedule 7, to the Civil Partnership Act 2004 (property adjustment orders in connection with civil partnership proceedings or after overseas dissolution of civil partnership, etc)][2].

(3) They do not apply where an introductory tenancy –

    (a)   becomes a secure tenancy on ceasing to be an introductory tenancy,

    (b)   vests under section 133(2) (succession to introductory tenancy on death of tenant),

(c)   is assigned to a person who would be qualified to succeed the introductory tenant if the introductory tenant died immediately before the assignment, or

(d)   vests or is otherwise disposed of in pursuance of an order made under –

    (i)   section 24 of the Matrimonial Causes Act 1973 (property adjustment orders in connection with matrimonial proceedings),

    (ii)   section 17(1) of the Matrimonial and Family Proceedings Act 1984 (property adjustment orders after overseas divorce, &c), ...³

    (iii)   paragraph 1 of Schedule 1 to the Children Act 1989 (orders for financial relief against parents)[, or

    (iv)   Part 2 of Schedule 5, or paragraph 9(2) or (3) of Schedule 7, to the Civil Partnership Act 2004 (property adjustment orders in connection with civil partnership proceedings or after overseas dissolution of civil partnership, etc)]⁴.

(4) They do not apply in such other cases as the Secretary of State may prescribe by regulations.

(5) The regulations may be framed so as to make the exclusion of the provisions of this Part about the allocation of housing accommodation subject to such restrictions or conditions as may be specified.

In particular, those provisions may be excluded –

(a)   in relation to specified descriptions of persons, or

(b)   in relation to housing accommodation of a specified description or a specified proportion of housing accommodation of any specified description.

AMENDMENT

¹ Word repealed: Civil Partnership Act 2004, s 261(4), Sch 30.

² Paragraph inserted: Civil Partnership Act 2004, s 81, Sch 8, para 60.

³ Word repealed: Civil Partnership Act 2004, s 261(4), Sch 30.

⁴ Paragraph inserted: Civil Partnership Act 2004, s 81, Sch 8, para 60.

⁵ Sub-section inserted: Localism Act 2011, s 159(7).

[Eligibility for allocation of housing accommodation]¹

[160ZA   Allocation only to eligible and qualifying persons: England

(1) A local housing authority in England shall not allocate housing accommodation –

(a)   to a person from abroad who is ineligible for an allocation of housing accommodation by virtue of subsection (2) or (4), or

(b)   to two or more persons jointly if any of them is a person mentioned in paragraph (a).

(2) A person subject to immigration control within the meaning of the Asylum and Immigration Act 1996 is ineligible for an allocation of housing accommodation by a local housing authority in England unless he is of a class prescribed by regulations made by the Secretary of State.

(3) No person who is excluded from entitlement to housing benefit by section 115 of the Immigration and Asylum Act 1999 (exclusion from benefits) shall be included in any class prescribed under subsection (2).

(4) The Secretary of State may by regulations prescribe other classes of persons from abroad who are ineligible to be allocated housing accommodation by local housing authorities in England.

(5) Nothing in subsection (2) or (4) affects the eligibility of a person who falls within section 159(4B).

(6) Except as provided by subsection (1), a person may be allocated housing accommodation by a local housing authority in England (whether on his application or otherwise) if that person –

(a)   is a qualifying person within the meaning of subsection (7), or
(b)   is one of two or more persons who apply for accommodation jointly, and one or more of the other persons is a qualifying person within the meaning of subsection (7).

(7) Subject to subsections (2) and (4) and any regulations under subsection (8), a local housing authority may decide what classes of persons are, or are not, qualifying persons.

(8) The Secretary of State may by regulations –

(a)   prescribe classes of persons who are, or are not, to be treated as qualifying persons by local housing authorities in England, and
(b)   prescribe criteria that may not be used by local housing authorities in England in deciding what classes of persons are not qualifying persons.

(9) If a local housing authority in England decide that an applicant for housing accommodation –

(a)   is ineligible for an allocation by them by virtue of subsection (2) or (4), or
(b)   is not a qualifying person,

they shall notify the applicant of their decision and the grounds for it.

(10) That notice shall be given in writing and, if not received by the applicant, shall be treated as having been given if it is made available at the authority's office for a reasonable period for collection by him or on his behalf.

(11) A person who is not being treated as a qualifying person may (if he considers that he should be treated as a qualifying person) make a fresh application to the authority for an allocation of housing accommodation by them.][1]

AMENDMENT

[1] Section inserted: Localism Act 2011, s 146(1), with effect from 15 January 2012 for certain purposes (SI 2012/57), for remaining purposes with effect from 18 June 2012 (SI 2012/1463).

160A Allocation only to eligible persons [: Wales][2]

[(1) A local housing authority [in Wales][2] shall not allocate housing accommodation –

    (a)   to a person from abroad who is ineligible for an allocation of housing accommodation by virtue of subsection (3) or (5);

    (b)   to a person who the authority have decided is to be treated as ineligible for such an allocation by virtue of subsection (7); or

    (c)   to two or more persons jointly if any of them is a person mentioned in paragraph (a) or (b).

(2) Except as provided by subsection (1), any person may be allocated housing accommodation by a local housing authority [in Wales][2] (whether on his application or otherwise).

(3) A person subject to immigration control within the meaning of the Asylum and Immigration Act 1996 (c 49) is (subject to subsection (6)) ineligible for an allocation of housing accommodation by a local housing authority [in Wales][2] unless he is of a class prescribed by regulations made by the Secretary of State.

(4) No person who is excluded from entitlement to housing benefit by section 115 of the Immigration and Asylum Act 1999 (c 33) (exclusion from benefits) shall be included in any class prescribed under subsection (3).

(5) The Secretary of State may by regulations prescribe other classes of persons from abroad who are (subject to subsection (6)) ineligible for an allocation of housing accommodation, either in relation to local housing authorities [in Wales][2] generally or any particular local housing authority [in Wales][2].

(6) Nothing in subsection (3) or (5) affects the eligibility of a person who is already –

    (a)   a secure or introductory tenant;

    (b)   an assured tenant of housing accommodation allocated to him by a local housing authority [in Wales][2].

(7) A local housing authority [in Wales][2] may decide that an applicant is to be treated as ineligible for an allocation of housing accommodation by them if they are satisfied that –

    (a)   he, or a member of his household, has been guilty of unacceptable behaviour serious enough to make him unsuitable to be a tenant of the authority; and

    (b)   in the circumstances at the time his application is considered, he is unsuitable to be a tenant of the authority by reason of that behaviour.

(8) The only behaviour which may be regarded by the authority as unacceptable for the purposes of subsection (7)(a) is –

(a) behaviour of the person concerned which would (if he were a secure tenant of the authority) entitle the authority to a possession order under section 84 of the Housing Act 1985 (c 68) on any ground mentioned in Part 1 of Schedule 2 to that Act (other than ground 8); or

(b) behaviour of a member of his household which would (if he were a person residing with a secure tenant of the authority) entitle the authority to such a possession order.

(9) If a local housing authority [in Wales]² decide that an applicant for housing accommodation –

(a) is ineligible for an allocation by them by virtue of subsection (3) or (5); or

(b) is to be treated as ineligible for such an allocation by virtue of subsection (7),

they shall notify the applicant of their decision and the grounds for it.

(10) That notice shall be given in writing and, if not received by the applicant, shall be treated as having been given if it is made available at the authority's office for a reasonable period for collection by him or on his behalf.

(11) A person who is being treated by a local housing authority [in Wales]² as ineligible by virtue of subsection (7) may (if he considers that he should no longer be treated as ineligible by the authority) make a fresh application to the authority for an allocation of housing accommodation by them.]¹

AMENDMENT

¹ Heading and section inserted: Homelessness Act 2002, s 14(2); for transitional provisions see s 14(3), (4) thereof.

² Words inserted: Localism Act 2011, s 146(2), with effect from 15 January 2012 for certain purposes (SI 2012/57), for remaining purposes with effect from 18 June 2012 (SI 2012/1463).

161–165 ...¹

AMENDMENT

¹ Sections repealed: Homelessness Act 2002, ss 14(1), 18(2), Sch 2; for transitional provisions see s 14(3), (4) thereof.

[Applications for housing accommodation]¹

166 Applications for housing accommodation

[(1) A local housing authority shall secure that –

(a) advice and information is available free of charge to persons in their district about the right to make an application for an allocation of housing accommodation; and

(b) any necessary assistance in making such an application is available free of charge to persons in their district who are likely to have difficulty in doing so without assistance.

[(1A) A local housing authority in England shall secure that an applicant for an allocation of housing accommodation is informed that he has the rights mentioned in section 166A(9).]²

(2) A local housing authority [in Wales]³ shall secure that an applicant for an allocation of housing accommodation is informed that he has the rights mentioned in section 167(4A).

(3) Every application made to a local housing authority for an allocation of housing accommodation shall (if made in accordance with the procedural requirements of the authority's allocation scheme) be considered by the authority.

(4) The fact that a person is an applicant for an allocation of housing accommodation shall not be divulged (without his consent) to any other member of the public.

(5) In this Part 'district' in relation to a local housing authority has the same meaning as in the Housing Act 1985 (c 68).]¹

AMENDMENT

¹ Heading and section substituted: Homelessness Act 2002, s 15.

² Sub-section inserted: Localism Act 2011, s 147(1), (2)(a), with effect from 15 January 2012 for certain purposes (SI 2012/57), for remaining purposes with effect from 18 June 2012 (SI 2012/1463).

³ Words inserted: Localism Act 2011, s 147(1), (2)(b), with effect from 15 January 2012 for certain purposes (SI 2012/57), for remaining purposes with effect from 18 June 2012 (SI 2012/1463).

[Allocation schemes]¹

166A Allocation in accordance with allocation scheme: England

(1) Every local housing authority in England must have a scheme (their 'allocation scheme') for determining priorities, and as to the procedure to be followed, in allocating housing accommodation.

For this purpose 'procedure' includes all aspects of the allocation process, including the persons or descriptions of persons by whom decisions are taken.

(2) The scheme must include a statement of the authority's policy on offering people who are to be allocated housing accommodation –

    (a)   a choice of housing accommodation; or

    (b)   the opportunity to express preferences about the housing accommodation to be allocated to them.

(3) As regards priorities, the scheme shall, subject to subsection (4), be framed so as to secure that reasonable preference is given to –

    (a)   people who are homeless (within the meaning of Part 7);

    (b)   people who are owed a duty by any local housing authority under section 190(2), 193(2) or 195(2) (or under section 65(2) or 68(2) of the Housing Act 1985) or who are occupying accommodation secured by any such authority under section 192(3);

(c)   people occupying insanitary or overcrowded housing or otherwise living in unsatisfactory housing conditions;

(d)   people who need to move on medical or welfare grounds (including any grounds relating to a disability); and

(e)   people who need to move to a particular locality in the district of the authority, where failure to meet that need would cause hardship (to themselves or to others).

The scheme may also be framed so as to give additional preference to particular descriptions of [people within one or more of paragraphs (a) to (e)][3] (being descriptions of people with urgent housing needs). [The scheme must be framed so as to give additional preference to a person with urgent housing needs who falls within one or more of paragraphs (a) to (e) and who –

(i)   is serving in the regular forces and is suffering from a serious injury, illness or disability which is attributable (wholly or partly) to the person's service,

(ii)   formally served in the regular forces,

(iii)   has recently ceased, or will cease to be entitled, to reside in accommodation provided by the Ministry of Defence following the death of that person's spouse or civil partner who has served in the regular forces and who's death was attributable (wholly or partly) to that service, or

(iv)   is serving or has served in the reserve forces and is suffering from a serious injury, illness or disability which is attributable (wholly or partly) to the person's service.

For this purpose 'the regular forces' and 'the reserve forces' have the meanings given by section 374 of the Armed Forces Act 2006.][3]

(4) People are to be disregarded for the purposes of subsection (3) if they would not have fallen within paragraph (a) or (b) of that subsection without the local housing authority having had regard to a restricted person (within the meaning of Part 7).

(5) The scheme may contain provision for determining priorities in allocating housing accommodation to people within subsection (3); and the factors which the scheme may allow to be taken into account include –

(a)   the financial resources available to a person to meet his housing costs;

(b)   any behaviour of a person (or of a member of his household) which affects his suitability to be a tenant;

(c)   any local connection (within the meaning of section 199) which exists between a person and the authority's district.

(6) Subject to subsection (3), the scheme may contain provision about the allocation of particular housing accommodation –

(a)   to a person who makes a specific application for that accommodation;

(b)   to persons of a particular description (whether or not they are within subsection (3)).

(7) The Secretary of State may by regulations –

(a)   specify further descriptions of people to whom preference is to be given as mentioned in subsection (3), or

(b)   amend or repeal any part of subsection (3).

(8) The Secretary of State may by regulations specify factors which a local housing authority in England must not take into account in allocating housing accommodation.

(9) The scheme must be framed so as to secure that an applicant for an allocation of housing accommodation –

(a)   has the right to request such general information as will enable him to assess –

   (i)   how his application is likely to be treated under the scheme (including in particular whether he is likely to be regarded as a member of a group of people who are to be given preference by virtue of subsection (3)); and

   (ii)   whether housing accommodation appropriate to his needs is likely to be made available to him and, if so, how long it is likely to be before such accommodation becomes available for allocation to him;

(b)   has the right to request the authority to inform him of any decision about the facts of his case which is likely to be, or has been, taken into account in considering whether to allocate housing accommodation to him; and

(c)   has the right to request a review of a decision mentioned in paragraph (b), or in section 160ZA(9), and to be informed of the decision on the review and the grounds for it.

(10) As regards the procedure to be followed, the scheme must be framed in accordance with such principles as the Secretary of State may prescribe by regulations.

(11) Subject to the above provisions, and to any regulations made under them, the authority may decide on what principles the scheme is to be framed.

(12) A local housing authority in England must, in preparing or modifying their allocation scheme, have regard to –

(a)   their current homelessness strategy under section 1 of the Homelessness Act 2002,

(b)   their current tenancy strategy under section 150 of the Localism Act 2011, and

(c)   in the case of an authority that is a London borough council, the London housing strategy.

(13) Before adopting an allocation scheme, or making an alteration to their scheme reflecting a major change of policy, a local housing authority in England must –

(a) send a copy of the draft scheme, or proposed alteration, to every private registered provider of social housing and registered social landlord with which they have nomination arrangements (see section 159(4)), and

(b) afford those persons a reasonable opportunity to comment on the proposals.

(14) A local housing authority in England shall not allocate housing accommodation except in accordance with their allocation scheme.]²

AMENDMENT

¹ Cross head substituted: Localism Act 2011, s 147(1), (3) with effect from 15 January 2012 for certain purposes (SI 2012/57), for remaining purposes with effect from 18 June 2012 (SI 2012/1463).

² Section inserted: Localism Act 2011, s 147(1), (4) with effect from 15 January 2012 for certain purposes (SI 2012/57), for remaining purposes with effect from 18 June 2012 (SI 2012/1463).

3 Words inserted: Housing Act 1996 (Additional Preference for Armed Forces) (England) Regulations 2012, SI 2012/****, reg 3 with effect from the day on which the Regulations are made.

167 Allocation in accordance with allocation scheme [: Wales]⁸

(1) Every local housing authority [in Wales]⁸ shall have a scheme (their 'allocation scheme') for determining priorities, and as to the procedure to be followed, in allocating housing accommodation.

For this purpose 'procedure' includes all aspects of the allocation process, including the persons or descriptions of persons by whom decisions are to be taken.

[(1A) The scheme shall include a statement of the authority's policy on offering people who are to be allocated housing accommodation –

(a) a choice of housing accommodation; or

(b) the opportunity to express preferences about the housing accommodation to be allocated to them.]¹

[(2) As regards priorities, the scheme shall[, subject to subsection (2ZA),]² be framed so as to secure that reasonable preference is given to –

(a) people who are homeless (within the meaning of Part 7);

(b) people who are owed a duty by any local housing authority under section 190(2), 193(2) or 195(2) (or under section 65(2) or 68(2) of the Housing Act 1985) or who are occupying accommodation secured by any such authority under section 192(3);

(c) people occupying insanitary or overcrowded housing or otherwise living in unsatisfactory housing conditions;

(d) people who need to move on medical or welfare grounds [(including grounds relating to a disability)]³; and

(e) people who need to move to a particular locality in the district of the authority, where failure to meet that need would cause hardship (to themselves or to others).

The scheme may also be framed so as to give additional preference to particular descriptions of people within this subsection (being descriptions of people with urgent housing needs).

[(2ZA) People are to be disregarded for the purposes of subsection (2) if they would not have fallen within paragraph (a) or (b) of that subsection without the local housing authority having had regard to a restricted person (within the meaning of Part 7).]⁴

(2A) The scheme may contain provision for determining priorities in allocating housing accommodation to people within subsection (2); and the factors which the scheme may allow to be taken into account include –

(a)   the financial resources available to a person to meet his housing costs;
(b)   any behaviour of a person (or of a member of his household) which affects his suitability to be a tenant;
(c)   any local connection (within the meaning of section 199) which exists between a person and the authority's district.

(2B) Nothing in subsection (2) requires the scheme to provide for any preference to be given to people the authority have decided are people to whom subsection (2C) applies.

(2C) This subsection applies to a person if the authority are satisfied that –

(a)   he, or a member of his household, has been guilty of unacceptable behaviour serious enough to make him unsuitable to be a tenant of the authority; and
(b)   in the circumstances at the time his case is considered, he deserves by reason of that behaviour not to be treated as a member of a group of people who are to be given preference by virtue of subsection (2).

(2D) Subsection (8) of section 160A applies for the purposes of subsection (2C)(a) above as it applies for the purposes of subsection (7)(a) of that section.

(2E) Subject to subsection (2), the scheme may contain provision about the allocation of particular housing accommodation –

(a)   to a person who makes a specific application for that accommodation;
(b)   to persons of a particular description (whether or not they are within subsection (2)).]⁵

(3) The Secretary of State may by regulations –

(a)   specify further descriptions of people to whom preference is to be given as mentioned in subsection (2), or
(b)   amend or repeal any part of subsection (2).

(4) The Secretary of State may by regulations specify factors which a local housing authority [in Wales]⁸ shall not take into account in allocating housing accommodation.

[(4A) The scheme shall be framed so as to secure that an applicant for an allocation of housing accommodation –

(a) has the right to request such general information as will enable him to assess –
    (i) how his application is likely to be treated under the scheme (including in particular whether he is likely to be regarded as a member of a group of people who are to be given preference by virtue of subsection (2)); and
    (ii) whether housing accommodation appropriate to his needs is likely to be made available to him and, if so, how long it is likely to be before such accommodation becomes available for allocation to him;

(b) is notified in writing of any decision that he is a person to whom subsection (2C) applies and the grounds for it;

(c) has the right to request the authority to inform him of any decision about the facts of his case which is likely to be, or has been, taken into account in considering whether to allocate housing accommodation to him; and

(d) has the right to request a review of a decision mentioned in paragraph (b) or (c), or in section 160A(9), and to be informed of the decision on the review and the grounds for it.][6]

(5) As regards the procedure to be followed, the scheme shall be framed in accordance with such principles as the Secretary of State may prescribe by regulations.

(6) Subject to the above provisions, and to any regulations made under them, the authority may decide on what principles the scheme is to be framed.

(7) Before adopting an allocation scheme, or making an alteration to their scheme reflecting a major change of policy, a local housing authority [in Wales][8] shall –

(a) send a copy of the draft scheme, or proposed alteration, to every [private registered provider of social housing and][7] registered social landlord with which they have nomination arrangements (see section 159(4)), and

(b) afford those persons a reasonable opportunity to comment on the proposals.

(8) A local housing authority [in Wales][8] shall not allocate housing accommodation except in accordance with their allocation scheme.

AMENDMENT

[1] Sub-section inserted: Homelessness Act 2002, s 16(1), (2).

[2] Words inserted: Housing and Regeneration Act 2008, s 314, Sch 15, Pt 1, paras 1, 2(1), (2), with effect from 2 March 2009 (except in relation to applications for an allocation of social housing or housing assistance (homelessness) or for accommodation made before that date) (SI 2009/415, art 2).

[3] Words inserted: Housing Act 2004, s 223, with effect from 27 April 2005 in England (SI 2005/1120), and as from a date to be appointed in Wales.

Appendix 1
England: Allocation

[4] Sub-section inserted: Housing and Regeneration Act 2008, s 314, Sch 15, Pt 1, paras 1, 2(1), (3), with effect from 2 March 2009 (except in relation to applications for an allocation of social housing or housing assistance (homelessness) or for accommodation made before that date) (SI 2009/415, art 2).

[5] Sub-sections substituted: Homelessness Act 2002, s 16(1), (3).

[6] Sub-section inserted: Homelessness Act 2002, s 16(1), (4).

[7] Words inserted: Housing and Regeneration Act 2008 (Consequential Provisions) Order 2010, SI 2010/866, art 5, Sch 2, paras 81, 101.

[8] Words inserted: Localism Act 2011, s 147(1), (5) with effect from 15 January 2012 for certain purposes (SI 2012/57), for remaining purposes with effect from 18 June 2012 (SI 2012/1463).

168 Information about allocation scheme

(1) A local housing authority shall publish a summary of their allocation scheme and provide a copy of the summary free of charge to any member of the public who asks for one.

(2) The authority shall make the scheme available for inspection at their principal office and shall provide a copy of the scheme, on payment of a reasonable fee, to any member of the public who asks for one.

(3) When the authority make an alteration to their scheme reflecting a major change of policy, they shall within a reasonable period of time [take such steps as they consider reasonable to bring the effect of the alteration to the attention of those likely to be affected by it][1].

AMENDMENT

[1] Words substituted: Homelessness Act 2002, s 18(1), Sch 1, paras 2, 4.

Supplementary

169 Guidance to authorities by the Secretary of State

(1) In the exercise of their functions under this Part, local housing authorities shall have regard to such guidance as may from time to time be given by the Secretary of State.

(2) The Secretary of State may give guidance generally or to specified descriptions of authorities.

170 Co-operation between [certain][2] social landlords and local housing authorities

Where a local housing authority so request, a [private registered provider of social housing or][3] registered social landlord shall co-operate to such extent as is reasonable in the circumstances in offering accommodation to [people with priority under the authority's allocation scheme][1].

AMENDMENT

[1] Words substituted: Homelessness Act 2002, s 18(1), Sch 1, paras 2, 5.

² Word substituted: Housing and Regeneration Act 2008 (Consequential Provisions) Order 2010, SI 2010/866, art 5, Sch 2, paras 81, 102(a).

³ Words inserted: Housing and Regeneration Act 2008 (Consequential Provisions) Order 2010, SI 2010/866, art 5, Sch 2, paras 81, 102(b).

171 False statements and withholding information

(1) A person commits an offence if, in connection with the exercise by a local housing authority of their functions under this Part –

    (a)   he knowingly or recklessly makes a statement which is false in a material particular, or

    (b)   he knowingly withholds information which the authority have reasonably required him to give in connection with the exercise of those functions.

(2) A person guilty of an offence under this section is liable on summary conviction to a fine not exceeding level 5 on the standard scale.

172 Regulations

(1) Regulations under this Part shall be made by statutory instrument.

(2) No regulations shall be made under section [166A(7) or]¹ 167(3) (regulations amending provisions about priorities in allocating housing accommodation) unless a draft of the regulations has been laid before and approved by a resolution of each House of Parliament.

(3) Any other regulations under this Part shall be subject to annulment in pursuance of a resolution of either House of Parliament.

(4) Regulations under this Part may contain such incidental, supplementary and transitional provisions as appear to the Secretary of State appropriate, and may make different provision for different cases including different provision for different areas.

AMENDMENT

¹ Words inserted: Localism Act 2011, s 147(1), (6), with effect from 15 January 2012 (SI 2012/57).

173 Consequential amendments: Part 6

The enactments mentioned in Schedule 16 have effect with the amendments specified there which are consequential on the provisions of this Part.

174 Index of defined expressions: Part 6

The following Table shows provisions defining or otherwise explaining expressions used in this Part (other than provisions defining or explaining an expression used in the same section) –

allocation (of housing)	section 159(2)
allocation scheme	section [166A and]⁴ 167

assured tenancy	section 230
[district (of local housing authority)	section 166(5)][1]
...	...[2]
introductory tenancy and introductory tenant	section 230 and 124
local housing authority	section 230
...	...[3]
registered social landlord	section 230 and 2
secure tenancy and secure tenant	section 230

AMENDMENT

[1] Entry inserted: Homelessness Act 2002, s 18(1), Sch 1, paras 2, 6.

[2] Entry repealed: Homelessness Act 2002, s 18(2), Sch 2.

[3] Entry repealed: Homelessness Act 2002, s 18(2), Sch 2.

[4] Words inserted: Localism Act 2011, s 147(1), (7), with effect from 18 June 2012 (SI 2012/1463).

PART 8
MISCELLANEOUS AND GENERAL PROVISIONS

General

****

230 Minor definitions: general

In this Act –

'assured tenancy', 'assured shorthold tenancy' and 'assured agricultural occupancy' have the same meaning as in Part I of the Housing Act 1988;

'enactment' includes an enactment comprised in subordinate legislation (within the meaning of the Interpretation Act 1978);

'housing action trust' has the same meaning as in the Housing Act 1988;

'housing association' has the same meaning as in the Housing Associations Act 1985;

'introductory tenancy' and 'introductory tenant' have the same meaning as in Chapter I of Part V of this Act;

'local housing authority' has the same meaning as in the Housing Act 1985;

'registered social landlord' has the same meaning as in Part I of this Act;

'secure tenancy' and 'secure tenant' have the same meaning as in Part IV of the Housing Act 1985.

Appendix 1
England: Allocation

Allocation of Accommodation: Guidance for Local Housing Authorities in England (2012)

MINISTERIAL FOREWORD

Social housing is of enormous importance – for the millions who live in it now, and the many more who look to it to provide the support they need in future – and the way it is allocated is key to creating communities where people choose to live and are able to prosper.

Under the previous Government housing waiting lists almost doubled, with many people left languishing on waiting lists for years. That is why we have taken decisive steps to tackle this problem, including an affordable homes programme set to exceed expectations and deliver up to 170,000 new homes and lever in £19.5 billion of new investment – in stark contrast to the net reduction of 421,000 affordable homes for rent from 1997 to 2010. Through the Localism Act 2011 we have introduced the most radical reform to social housing for a generation.

The new freedoms in the Localism Act which allow councils to better manage their waiting lists and promote mobility for existing social tenants came into force on 18 June. This guidance will assist councils to make full use of these new freedoms – and the existing flexibilities within the allocation legislation – to encourage work and mobility, and to tailor their allocation priorities to meet local needs and local circumstances.

The guidance makes clear that we expect social homes to go to people who genuinely need them, such as hard working families and those who are looking to adopt or foster a child in need of a stable family; and not to those who do not, such as people who already own a home that is suitable for them to use.

Through the Military Covenant, the Government has made clear its responsibility to support our Armed Forces in return for the important contribution they make to the country. This guidance will assist councils to ensure that Service families get the priority for social housing they deserve.

The guidance encourages councils to adopt a modern measure of overcrowding and encourages them to give appropriate priority to tenants who want to downsize, helping them move to smaller, more manageable properties and freeing up precious social housing for crowded families.

I know that an increasing number of councils are already starting to think creatively about how social housing can change people's lives. This guidance will help others follow suit.

It is half the size of the previous guidance it replaces and is evidence of the Government's commitment to 'cutting red tape'. It is also an important part of the

Government's commitment to make the social housing system more flexible and responsive, to get the best out of our four million social homes, and to make the system fairer for all.

Rt Hon Grant Shapps, MP

CHAPTER 1

Scope of guidance and definition of an allocation

1.1 This guidance is issued to local housing authorities ('housing authorities') in England under s.169 of the Housing Act 1996 ('the 1996 Act'). Housing authorities are required to have regard to it in exercising their functions under Part 6 of the 1996 Act ('Part 6'). In so far as this guidance comments on the law, it can only reflect the Department's understanding at the time of issue.

1.2 This guidance replaces all previous guidance on social housing allocations.

Definition of an 'allocation'

1.3 For the purposes of Part 6, a housing authority allocates accommodation when it:

- selects a person to be a secure or introductory tenant of accommodation held by that authority

- nominates a person to be a secure or introductory tenant of accommodation held by another housing authority

- nominates a person to be an assured tenant of accommodation held by a Private Registered Provider (or Registered Social Landlord in Wales) (s.159(2))

1.4 The term 'assured tenant' includes a person with an assured shorthold tenancy, including of an Affordable Rent property[1]. 'Secure tenant' includes a person with a flexible tenancy granted under s.107A of the Housing Act 1985[2].

Allocations to existing tenants

1.5 Provisions in relation to existing tenants are contained in s.159(4A) and (4B). These provide that Part 6 does not apply to an allocation of accommodation by a housing authority to a tenant of a local authority or Private Registered Provider unless:

- the allocation involves a transfer made at the tenant's request, and

- the authority is satisfied that the tenant has reasonable preference.

Accordingly, social tenants applying to the housing authority for a transfer who are considered to have reasonable preference for an allocation must be treated on the same basis as new applicants in accordance with the requirements of s.166A(3).

1.6 Transfers at the tenant's request, where the authority is satisfied the tenant does not have reasonable preference, do not fall within Part 6 and housing authorities may set their own transfer policies in relation to these tenants. Authorities should consider how to make the best use of this flexibility. Providing tenants with greater opportunities to move within the social sector can help promote social and economic mobility and make the best use of social housing stock.

1.7 Authorities should consider the importance of giving social tenants who under-occupy their accommodation appropriate priority for a transfer. This will be important in light of the measure in the Welfare Reform Act 2012 which will reduce Housing Benefit entitlement for working age social sector tenants who under-occupy their property (measured in accordance with the Local

---

[1] Affordable Rent is not subject to the national rent regime but is subject to other rent controls that require a rent (including service charges, where applicable) of no more than 80% of the local market rent.
[2] Inserted by s.154 of the Localism Act 2011.

Housing Allowance size criteria) from April 2013[3]. Authorities should also consider whether there are other provisions that might make it more difficult for under-occupiers to move, such as a prohibition against tenants with minor rent arrears transferring, and the scope for removing or revising these in relation to under-occupiers.

1.8 Housing authorities may decide to operate a separate allocation system for transferring tenants who are not in the reasonable preference categories (with a separate waiting list and lettings policy) or to continue with a single allocation system which covers all applicants but which, for example, rewards transferring tenants with a good tenancy record, or gives a degree of priority to those who want to move for work.

1.9 Transfers that the housing authority initiates for management purposes do not fall within Part 6. These would include a temporary decant to allow repairs to a property to be carried out. The renewal of a flexible tenancy in the same property also does not fall within Part 6; neither do mutual exchanges between existing tenants, including exchanges between secure and assured tenants and those with flexible tenancies (under s.107A of the Housing Act 1985). Other specific exemptions from the provisions of Part 6 are set out in s.160 of the 1996 Act and the Allocation of Housing (England) Regulations 2002 (SI 2002/3264).

CHAPTER 2

Overview of the amendments to Part 6 made by the Localism Act 2011

2.1 The Localism Act 2011 introduces significant amendments to Part 6. The main policy objectives behind these amendments are to:

- enable housing authorities to better manage their housing waiting list by giving them the power to determine which applicants do or do not qualify for an allocation of social housing. Authorities will be able to operate a more focused list which better reflects local circumstances and can be understood more readily by local people. It will also be easier for authorities to manage unrealistic expectations by excluding people who have little or no prospect of being allocated accommodation

- make it easier for existing social tenants to move by removing the constraints of Part 6 from those social tenants who apply to the housing authority for a transfer, unless they have reasonable preference. Housing authorities will be able to strike a balance between meeting the needs of

---

[3]   The LHA size criteria allow one bedroom for each: adult couple; any other adult (aged 16 or over); two children of the same sex aged 10 or over; two children under 10 regardless of sex; any other child.

existing tenants and new applicants for social housing, while making best use of their stock. Part 6 continues to apply to transferring tenants with reasonable preference, ensuring they continue to receive priority under the authority's allocation scheme

- maintain the protection provided by the statutory reasonable preference criteria – ensuring that priority for social housing goes to those in the greatest need.

2.2 The detailed changes to Part 6 contained in the Localism Act 2011 are set out in the following paragraphs.

2.3 By virtue of new s.159(4B) the term 'allocation' continues to apply to a transfer at the request of an existing secure, introductory or assured tenant where the authority is satisfied that he or she has 'reasonable preference' for an allocation. Existing secure, introductory and assured tenants seeking a transfer who are not considered to have reasonable preference are now outside the scope of Part 6 (s.159(4A).

2.4 New s.160ZA replaces s.160A in relation to allocations by housing authorities in England. Social housing may only be allocated to 'qualifying persons' and housing authorities are given the power to determine what classes of persons are or are not qualified to be allocated housing (s.160ZA(6) and (7)). These requirements are in addition to the provisions on eligibility in respect of persons from abroad (s.160ZA(2) and (4)) which continue to be set centrally. The power for a housing authority to decide that an applicant is to be treated as ineligible by reason of unacceptable behaviour serious enough to make him unsuitable to be a tenant is redundant and has therefore been repealed.

2.5 New s.166A requires housing authorities in England to allocate accommodation in accordance with a scheme which must be framed to ensure that certain categories of applicants are given reasonable preference. With certain exceptions, s.166A replicates the provisions in s.167 which continues to apply to allocations by housing authorities in Wales. Section 166A(9) includes a new requirement for an allocation scheme to give a right to review a decision on qualification in s.160AZ(9), and to be informed of the decision on the review and the grounds for it. This is in addition to the existing right to review a decision on eligibility. Section 166A(12) is new and provides that authorities must have regard to their homelessness and tenancy strategies when framing their allocation scheme.

2.6 The provisions in s.167 which allow for no preference to be given to a person guilty of serious unacceptable behaviour (s.167(2B) – (2D)) are not reproduced in s.166A. However, the power to take behaviour – whether good or poor – into account in determining priorities between people in the reasonable preference categories remains (new s.166A(5)(b)).

2.7 The requirement for an allocation scheme to contain a statement of the authority's policy on offering a choice of accommodation or the opportunity to express preferences about their accommodation is retained (s.166A(2)). However, the requirement to provide a copy of this statement to people to whom they owe a homelessness duty (under s.193(3A) or s.195(3A) of the 1996 Act) is repealed[4].

CHAPTER 3

Eligibility and qualification

3.1 Housing authorities must consider all applications made in accordance with the procedural requirements of the authority's allocation scheme (s.166(3)). In considering applications, authorities must ascertain:

- if an applicant is eligible for an allocation of accommodation, and

- if he or she qualifies for an allocation of accommodation.

Eligibility

3.2 An applicant may be ineligible for an allocation of accommodation under s.160ZA(2) or (4). Authorities are advised to consider applicants' eligibility at the time of the initial application and again when considering making an allocation to them, particularly where a substantial amount of time has elapsed since the original application.

Joint Tenancies

3.3 Under s.160ZA(1)(b), a housing authority must not grant a joint tenancy to two or more people if any one of them is a person from abroad who is ineligible. However, where two or more people apply and one of them is eligible, the authority may grant a tenancy to the person who is eligible. In addition, while ineligible family members must not be granted a tenancy, they may be taken into account in determining the size of accommodation which is to be allocated.

Existing Tenants

3.4 The eligibility provisions do not apply to applicants who are already secure or introductory tenants or assured tenants of a Private Registered Provider. Most transferring tenants fall outside the scope of the allocation legislation (s.159(4A)); while those who are considered to have reasonable preference for an allocation are specifically exempted from the eligibility provisions by virtue of s.160ZA(5).

---

4   Section 148(2) and s.149(3) of the Localism Act 2011.

Persons from abroad

3.5 A person may not be allocated accommodation under Part 6 if he or she is a person from abroad who is ineligible for an allocation under s.160ZA of the 1996 Act. There are two categories for the purposes of s.160ZA:

(i)   *a person subject to immigration control* – such a person is not eligible for an allocation of accommodation unless he or she comes within a class prescribed in regulations made by the Secretary of State (s.160ZA(2)), and

(ii) *a person from abroad other than a person subject to immigration control* – regulations may provide for other descriptions of persons from abroad who, although not subject to immigration control, are to be treated as ineligible for an allocation of accommodation (s.160ZA(4)).

3.6 The regulations setting out which classes of persons from abroad are eligible or ineligible for an allocation are the Allocation of Housing and Homelessness (Eligibility) (England) Regulations 2006 (SI 2006 No.1294) ('the Eligibility Regulations').

Persons subject to immigration control

3.7 The term 'person subject to immigration control' is defined in s.13(2) of the Asylum and Immigration Act 1996 as a person who under the Immigration Act 1971 requires leave to enter or remain in the United Kingdom (whether or not such leave has been given).

3.8 The following categories of persons do not require leave to enter or remain in the UK:

(i)   British citizens

(ii) certain Commonwealth citizens with a right of abode in the UK

(iii) Irish citizens, who are not subject to immigration control in the UK because the Republic of Ireland forms part of the Common Travel Area (see paragraph 3.11 (iii) below) with the UK which allows free movement

(iv) EEA nationals[5], and their family members, who have a right to reside in the UK that derives from EU law. Whether an EEA national (or family member) has a particular right to reside in the UK (or another Member State) will depend on the circumstances, particularly their economic status (e.g. whether he or she is a worker, self-employed, a student, or economically inactive)

---

[5]   European Economic Area nationals are nationals of any EU member state (except the UK), and nationals of Iceland, Norway, Liechtenstein and Switzerland.

(v)   persons who are exempt from immigration control under the Immigration Acts, including diplomats and their family members based in the UK, and some military personnel.

3.9 Any person who does not fall within one of the four categories in paragraph 3.11 will be a person subject to immigration control and will be ineligible for an allocation of accommodation unless they fall within a class of persons prescribed by regulation 3 of the Eligibility Regulations (see further below).

3.10 If there is any uncertainty about an applicant's immigration status, housing authorities are recommended to contact the UK Border Agency (UKBA). UKBA provides a service to housing authorities to confirm the immigration status of an applicant from abroad (non asylum seekers) by email at LA@UKBA.gsi.gov.uk. Where UKBA indicates the applicant may be an asylum seeker, enquiries of their status can be made to the Immigration Enquiry Bureau helpline on 0870 606 7766.

3.11 Regulation 3 of the Eligibility Regulations provides that the following classes of persons subject to immigration control are eligible for an allocation of accommodation:

i)   *a person granted refugee status*: granted 5 years' limited leave to remain in the UK

ii)   *a person granted exceptional leave to enter or remain in the UK without condition that they and any dependants should make no recourse to public funds*: granted for a limited period where there are compelling humanitarian or compassionate circumstances for allowing them to stay. However, if leave is granted on condition that the applicant and any dependants are not a charge on public funds, the applicant will not be eligible for an allocation of accommodation. Exceptional leave to remain (granted at the Secretary of State's discretion outside the Immigration Rules) now takes the form of 'discretionary leave'.

iii) *a person with current leave to enter or remain in the UK with no condition or limitation, and who is habitually resident in the UK, the Channel Islands, the Isle of Man or the Republic of Ireland* (the Common Travel Area): such a person will have indefinite leave to enter (ILE) or remain (ILR) and is regarded as having settled status. However, where ILE or ILR status is granted as a result of an undertaking that a sponsor will be responsible for the applicant's maintenance and accommodation, the person must have been resident in the Common Travel Area for five years since the date of entry – or the date of the sponsorship undertaking, whichever is later – to be eligible. Where all sponsors have died within the first five years, the applicant will be eligible for an allocation of accommodation.

iv) *a person who has humanitarian protection granted under the Immigration Rules*[6]: a form of leave granted to persons who do not qualify for refugee status but would face a real risk of suffering serious harm if returned to their state of origin (see paragraphs 339C–344C of the Immigration Rules (HC 395))

Other persons from abroad who may be ineligible for an allocation

3.12 By virtue of regulation 4 of the Eligibility Regulations, a person who is not subject to immigration control and who falls within one of the following descriptions is to be treated as a person from abroad who is ineligible for an allocation of accommodation:

(i) a person who is not habitually resident in the Common Travel Area (subject to certain exceptions – see paragraph 3.14 below)

(ii) a person whose only right to reside in the UK is derived from his status as a jobseeker (or his status as the family member of a jobseeker). 'Jobseeker' has the same meaning as in regulation 6(1) of the Immigration (European Economic Area) Regulations 2006 (SI 2006/1003) ('the EEA Regulations')

(iii) a person whose only right to reside in the UK is an initial right to reside for a period not exceeding three months under regulation 13 of the EEA Regulations

(iv) a person whose only right to reside in the Common Travel Area is a right equivalent to one of the rights mentioned in (ii) or (iii) above and which is derived from EU Treaty rights.

3.13 See annex 2 for guidance on rights to reside in the UK derived from EU law.

3.14 The following persons from abroad are eligible for an allocation of accommodation even if they are not habitually resident in the Common Travel Area:

a) an EEA national who is in the UK as a worker (which has the same meaning as in regulation 6(1) of the EEA Regulations)

b) an EEA national who is in the UK as a self-employed person (which has the same meaning as in regulation 6(1) of the EEA Regulations)

c) a person who is treated as a worker for the purposes of regulation 6(1) of the EEA Regulations, pursuant to the Accession (Immigration and Worker Authorisation) Regulations 2006 (ie nationals of Bulgaria and

---

[6] Inserted by the Allocation of Housing and Homelessness (Miscellaneous Provisions) (England) Regulations 2006.

Romania required to be authorised by the Home Office to work until they have accrued 12 months uninterrupted authorised work)[7]

d) a person who is a family member of a person referred to in (a) to (c) above

e) a person with a right to reside permanently in the UK by virtue of regulation 15(c), (d) or (e) of the EEA Regulations

f) a person who left Montserrat after 1 November 1995 because of the effect of volcanic activity there

g) a person who is in the UK as a result of his deportation, expulsion or other removal by compulsion of law from another country to the UK. This could include EEA nationals, if the person was settled in the UK and exercising EU Treaty rights prior to deportation from the third country. Where deportation occurs, most countries will signal this in the person's passport.

3.15 A person who is no longer working or no longer in self-employment will retain his or her status as a worker or self-employed person in certain circumstances. However, accession state workers requiring authorisation will generally only be treated as a worker when they are actually working as authorised and will not retain 'worker' status between jobs until they have accrued 12 months continuous authorised employment. 'Family member' does not include a person who is an extended family member who is treated as a family member by virtue of regulation 7(3) of the EEA Regulations (see annexes 2 and 3 for further guidance).

3.16 The term 'habitual residence' is intended to convey a degree of permanence in the person's residence in the Common Travel Area; it implies an association between the individual and the place of residence and relies substantially on fact.

3.17 Applicants who have been resident in the Common Travel Area continuously during the two year period prior to their housing application are likely to be habitually resident (periods of temporary absence, e.g. visits abroad for holidays or to visit relatives may be disregarded). Where two years' continuous residency has not been established, housing authorities will need to conduct further enquiries to determine whether the applicant is habitually resident (see annex 4 for further guidance).

---

[7] As of 1 May 2011, nationals of the 8 Eastern European countries (A8 nationals) which acceded to the EU in 2004 are no longer required to register with the Workers Registration Scheme in order to work in the UK. Regulation 4(2)(c) of the Eligibility Regulations no longer applies to applications from A8 workers as of that date. Rather applications from A8 workers should be considered on the same basis as those from other EU workers under regulation 4(2)(a).

Appendix 1 England: Allocation

Qualification

3. 18 Housing authorities may only allocate accommodation to people who are defined as 'qualifying persons' (s.160ZA(6)(a)). Subject to the requirement not to allocate to persons from abroad who are ineligible and the exception for members of the Armed and Reserve Forces in paragraph 3.27 below, a housing authority may decide the classes of people who are, or are not, qualifying persons.

3.19 Housing authorities are encouraged to adopt a housing options approach as part of a move to a managed waiting list. A strong and pro-active housing options approach brings several benefits: people are offered support to access the housing solution which best meets their needs (which might be private rented housing, low cost home ownership or help to stay put); expectations about accessing social housing are properly managed; and social housing is focused on those who need it most. A lower waiting list can also be a by-product.

3.20 In framing their qualification criteria, authorities will need to have regard to their duties under the equalities legislation, as well as the requirement in s.166A(3) to give overall priority for an allocation to people in the reasonable preference categories.

3.21 Housing authorities should avoid setting criteria which disqualify groups of people whose members are likely to be accorded reasonable preference for social housing, for example on medical or welfare grounds. However, authorities may wish to adopt criteria which would disqualify individuals who satisfy the reasonable preference requirements. This could be the case, for example, if applicants are disqualified on a ground of anti-social behaviour.

3.22 When deciding what classes of people do not qualify for an allocation, authorities should consider the implications of excluding all members of such groups. For instance, when framing residency criteria, authorities may wish to consider the position of people who are moving into the district to take up work or to escape violence, or homeless applicants or children in care who are placed out of borough.

3.23 The Government believes that authorities should avoid allocating social housing to people who already own their own homes. Where they do so, this should only be in exceptional circumstances; for example, for elderly owner occupiers who cannot stay in their own home and need to move into sheltered accommodation.

3.24 There may be sound policy reasons for applying different qualification criteria in relation to existing tenants from those which apply to new applicants. For example, where residency requirements are imposed, authorities may wish to ensure they do not restrict the ability of existing social tenants to move to take up work or to downsize to a smaller home. Authorities may decide to apply different qualification criteria in relation to particular types of stock, for example properties which might otherwise be hard to let.

3.25 Whatever general criteria housing authorities use to define the classes of persons who do not qualify for social housing, there may be exceptional circumstances where it is necessary to disapply these criteria in the case of individual applicants. An example might be an intimidated witness[8] who needs to move quickly to another local authority district. Authorities are encouraged to make explicit provision for dealing with exceptional cases within their qualification rules.

3.26 As with eligibility, authorities are advised to consider whether an applicant qualifies for an allocation at the time of the initial application and when considering making an allocation, particularly where a long time has elapsed since the original application.

Members of the Armed Forces and the Reserve Forces

3.27 Subject to Parliamentary scrutiny, we will regulate to provide that authorities must not disqualify the following applicants on the grounds that they do not have a local connection[9] with the authority's district:

(a) members of the Armed Forces and former Service personnel, where the application is made within five[10] years of discharge

(b) bereaved spouses and civil partners of members of the Armed Forces leaving Services Family Accommodation following the death of their spouse or partner

(c) serving or former members of the Reserve Forces who need to move because of a serious injury, medical condition or disability sustained as a result of their service.

3.28 These provisions recognise the special position of members of the Armed Forces (and their families) whose employment requires them to be mobile and who are likely therefore to be particularly disadvantaged by local connection requirements; as well as those injured reservists who may need to move to another local authority district to access treatment, care or support.

---

[8] 'Intimidated witnesses include Protected Persons as specified in Section 82 and schedule 5 of the Serious Organised Crime and Police Act 2005.'

[9] As defined by s.199 of the 1996 Act.

[10] 5 years reflects guidelines issued by the local authorities associations which propose a working definition of normal residence for the purposes of establishing a local connection (see paragraph 4.1(i) to Annex 18 of the Homelessness Code of Guidance 2006).

Joint tenants

3.29 In the case of an allocation to two or more persons jointly, at least one of the persons must be a qualifying person (s.160ZA(6)(b)) and all of them must be eligible.

Fresh applications

3.30 Applicants who have previously been deemed not to qualify may make a fresh application if they consider they should now be treated as qualifying, but it will be for the applicant to show that his or her circumstances have changed (s.160ZA(11)).

Reviews of decisions on eligibility and qualification

3.31 For guidance on decisions and reviews see chapter 5.

CHAPTER 4

Framing an allocation scheme

4.1 Housing authorities are required by s.166A(1) to have an allocation scheme for determining priorities, and for defining the procedures to be followed in allocating housing accommodation; and they must allocate in accordance with that scheme (s.166A(14)). All aspects of the allocation process must be covered in the scheme, including the people by whom decisions are taken. In the Secretary of State's view, qualification criteria form part of an allocation scheme.

4.2 All housing authorities must have an allocation scheme, regardless of whether they own housing stock and whether they contract out the delivery of any of their allocation functions (see further chapter 6). When framing or modifying their scheme, authorities must have regard to their current tenancy and homelessness strategies (s.166A(12)).

Choice and preference options

4.3 An allocation scheme must include a statement as to the housing authority's policy on offering people a choice of accommodation or the opportunity to express preferences about the accommodation to be allocated to them (s.166A). It is for housing authorities to determine their policy on providing choice or the ability to express preferences.

Reasonable preference

4.4 In framing their allocation scheme to determine allocation priorities, housing authorities must ensure that reasonable preference is given to the following categories of people (s.166A(3):

(a)   people who are homeless within the meaning of Part 7 of the 1996 Act (including those who are intentionally homeless and those not in priority need)

(b)   people who are owed a duty by any housing authority under section 190(2), 193(2) or 195(2) of the 1996 Act (or under section 65(2) or 68(2) of the Housing Act 1985) or who are occupying accommodation secured by any housing authority under s.192(3)

(c)   people occupying insanitary or overcrowded housing or otherwise living in unsatisfactory housing conditions

(d)   people who need to move on medical or welfare grounds, including grounds relating to a disability[11], and

(e)   people who need to move to a particular locality in the district of the housing authority, where failure to meet that need would cause hardship (to themselves or others).

4.5 In framing their allocation scheme to give effect to s.166A(3), housing authorities should have regard to the following considerations:

•   the scheme must be framed so as to give reasonable preference to applicants who fall within the categories set out in s.166A(3), over those who do not

•   although there is no requirement to give equal weight to each of the reasonable preference categories, authorities will need to demonstrate that, overall, reasonable preference has been given to all of them

•   there is no requirement for housing authorities to frame their scheme to afford greater priority to applicants who fall within more than one reasonable preference category (cumulative preference) over those who have reasonable preference on a single, non-urgent basis[12].

Otherwise, it is for housing authorities to decide how to give effect to the provisions of s.166A(3) in their allocation scheme.

---

[11]   The words 'including grounds relating to a disability' were added by the Housing Act 2004.

[12]   *R (on application of Ahmad) v London Borough of Newham* [2009] UKHL 14, [2009] HLR 31.

Restricted persons

4.6 Applicants should not be given reasonable preference under paragraph (a) or (b) of s.166A(3) if they would only qualify for reasonable preference by taking into account a 'restricted person' within the meaning of Part 7 (s.166A(4)). A restricted person is a person subject to immigration control who is not eligible for homelessness assistance because he or she does not have leave to enter or remain in the UK or has leave which is subject to a 'no recourse to public funds' condition (s.184(7) of the 1996 Act).

Homeless or owed a homelessness duty

4.7 The requirement for housing authorities to frame their allocation scheme to give reasonable preference to people who are owed certain homeless duties remains the case, notwithstanding the amendments to Part 7 made by the Localism Act which give authorities the power to end the main homelessness duty with an offer of private rented accommodation, without requiring the applicant's consent.

Overcrowding

4.8 The Secretary of State takes the view that the bedroom standard is an appropriate measure of overcrowding for allocation purposes, and recommends that all housing authorities should adopt this as a minimum. The bedroom standard allocates a separate bedroom to each:

- married or cohabiting couple

- adult aged 21 years or more

- pair of adolescents aged 10–20 years of the same sex

- pair of children aged under 10 years regardless of sex.

Medical and welfare grounds

4.9 The medical and welfare reasonable preference category includes people who need to move because of their disability or access needs, and this includes people with a learning disability as well as those with a physical disability.

4.10 'Welfare grounds' would encompass a wide range of needs, including, but not limited to, the need to:

- provide a secure base from which a care leaver, or a person who is moving on from a drug or alcohol recovery programme, can build a stable life

- provide accommodation, with appropriate care and support, for those who could not be expected to find their own accommodation, such as young adults with learning disabilities who wish to live independently in the community

- provide or receive care or support. This would include foster carers, those approved to adopt, or those being assessed for approval to foster or adopt, who need to move to a larger home in order to accommodate a looked after child or a child who was previously looked after by a local authority. It would also include special guardians, holders of a residence order and family and friends carers who are not foster carers but who have taken on the care of a child because the parents are unable to provide care.

Hardship grounds

4.11 This would include, for example, a person who needs to move to a different locality in order to give or receive care, to access specialised medical treatment, or to take up a particular employment, education or training opportunity.

4.12 Possible indicators of the criteria which apply to reasonable preference categories (c) and (d) are given in annex 1.

Additional preference

4.13 Section 166A(3) gives housing authorities the power to frame their allocation scheme to give additional preference to particular descriptions of people who fall within the statutory reasonable preference categories and have urgent housing needs. All housing authorities must consider, in the light of local circumstances, the need to give effect to this provision. Examples of people with urgent housing needs to whom housing authorities should consider giving additional preference within their allocation scheme include:

- those who need to move urgently because of a life threatening illness or sudden disability

- families in severe overcrowding which poses a serious health hazard

- those who are homeless and require urgent re-housing as a result of violence or threats of violence, including intimidated witnesses, and those escaping serious anti-social behaviour or domestic violence.

Members of the Armed and Reserve Forces

4.14 Subject to parliamentary approval, we will regulate to require authorities to frame their allocation scheme to give additional preference to the following categories of people who fall within one or more of the reasonable preference categories and who have urgent housing needs:

(a)   former members of the Armed Forces

(b)   serving members of the Armed Forces who need to move because of a
      serious injury, medical condition or disability sustained as a result of their
      service

(c)   bereaved spouses and civil partners of members of the Armed Forces
      leaving Services Family Accommodation following the death of their
      spouse or partner

(d)   serving or former members of the Reserve Forces who need to move
      because of a serious injury, medical condition or disability sustained as a
      result of their service.

Determining priorities between households with a similar level of need

4.15 Authorities may frame their allocation scheme to take into account factors
in determining relative priorities between applicants in the reasonable (or
additional) preference categories (s.166A(5)). Examples of such factors are
given in the legislation: financial resources, behaviour and local connection.
However, these examples are not exclusive and authorities may take into
account other factors instead or as well as these.

Financial resources available to a person to meet his housing costs

4.16 This would enable a housing authority, for example, to give less priority to
owner occupiers (wherever the property is situated).

Behaviour

4.17 This would allow for greater priority to be given to applicants who have
been model tenants or have benefited the community, for example.

Local connection

4.18 Local connection is defined by s.199 of the 1996 Act. A person has a local
connection because of normal residence (current or previous) of their own
choice, employment, family associations, or special circumstances. Residence is
not of a person's choice if it is the consequence of being detained in prison or
in hospital under the Mental Health Act. As a result of changes to s.199
introduced in 2008[13] a person serving in the Armed Forces can establish a local
connection with a local authority district through residence or employment
there, in the same way as a civilian.

---

[13]   Amendment to s.199 of the 1996 Act made by s.315 of the Housing and Regeneration
       Act 2008.

Including local priorities alongside the statutory reasonable preference categories

4.19 As the House of Lords made clear in the case of *R (on application of Ahmad) v Newham LBC*[14], s.166A(3)[15] only requires that the people encompassed within that section are given 'reasonable preference'. It 'does not require that they should be given absolute priority over everyone else'[16]. This means that an allocation scheme may provide for other factors than those set out in s.166A(3) to be taken into account in determining which applicants are to be given preference under a scheme, provided that:

- they do not dominate the scheme, and

- overall, the scheme operates to give reasonable preference to those in the statutory reasonable preference categories over those who are not.

The Secretary of State would encourage authorities to consider the scope to take advantage of this flexibility to meet local needs and local priorities.

4.20 The House of Lords also made clear that, where an allocation scheme complies with the reasonable preference requirements and any other statutory requirements, the courts should be very slow to interfere on the ground of alleged irrationality[17].

Local lettings policies

4.21 Section 166A(6)(b) of the 1996 Act enables housing authorities to allocate particular accommodation to people of a particular description, whether or not they fall within the reasonable preference categories, provided that overall the authority is able to demonstrate compliance with the requirements of s.166A(3). This is the statutory basis for so-called 'local lettings policies' which may be used to achieve a wide variety of housing management and policy objectives.

Households affected by the under-occupation measure

4.22 When framing the rules which determine the size of property to allocate to different households and in different circumstances, housing authorities are free to set their own criteria, provided they do not result in a household being statutorily overcrowded. However, in setting these criteria, authorities will want to take account of the provision in the Welfare Reform Act 2012 which will reduce Housing Benefit to under-occupiers.

---

[14] [2009] UKHL 14.
[15] Previously s.167(2), which continues to apply to allocations by housing authorities in Wales.
[16] Baroness Hale at para [18].
[17] Lord Neuberger at para [55].

Appendix 1
England: Allocation

4.23 Social tenants affected by the under-occupation measure may choose to move to more suitably sized accommodation in the private rented sector. One way to encourage tenants to consider this option might be to ensure they are given some degree of preference for an allocation if they apply for a new social tenancy at a later date.

Members of the Armed Forces

4.24 Authorities are also strongly encouraged to take into account the needs of all serving or former Service personnel when framing their allocation schemes, and to give sympathetic consideration to the housing needs of family members of serving or former Service personnel who may themselves have been disadvantaged by the requirements of military service and, in particular, the need to move from base to base. This would be in line with terms of the Government's Armed Forces Covenant published in May 2011.

4.25 Examples of ways in which authorities can ensure that Service personnel and their families are given appropriate priority, include:

• using the flexibility within the allocation legislation to set local priorities alongside the statutory reasonable preference categories so as to give preference, for example, to those who have recently left, or are close to leaving, the Armed Forces[18] (see paragraph 4.19 above)

• using the power to determine priorities between applicants in the reasonable preference categories, so that applicants in housing need who have served in the Armed Forces are given greater priority for social housing over those who have not (see paragraph 4.15 above)

• if taking into account an applicant's financial resources in determining priorities between households with a similar level of need (see paragraph 4.16 above), disregarding any lump sum received by a member of the Armed Forces as compensation for an injury or disability sustained on active service

• setting aside a proportion of properties for former members of the Armed Forces under a local lettings policy (see paragraph 4.21 above).

4.26 A number of organisations provide specialist housing and support for veterans, such as the Royal British Legion, Stoll, Haig Homes, Alabare and Norcare, and housing authorities are encouraged to liaise with them to ensure that former Service personnel are able to access the housing option which best suits their needs.

---

[18] MoD issues a Certificate of Cessation of Entitlement to Occupy Service Living Accommodation 6 months before discharge.

Households in work or seeking work

4.27 Local authorities are urged to consider how they can use their allocation policies to support those households who want to work, as well as those who – while unable to engage in paid employment – are contributing to their community in other ways, for example, through voluntary work. The flexibilities which authorities are encouraged to make use of to meet the needs of Service personnel would apply equally here. This might involve, for example, framing an allocation scheme to give some preference to households who are in low paid work or employment-related training, even where they are not in the reasonable preference categories; or to give greater priority to those households in the reasonable preference categories who are also in work or who can demonstrate that they are actively seeking work. Alternatively, it might involve using local lettings policies to ensure that specific properties, or a specified proportion of properties, are allocated to households in particular types of employment where, for example, skills are in short supply.

4.28 Authorities should also consider how best they can make use of the new power to offer flexible tenancies to support households who are in low paid work, and incentivise others to take up employment opportunities.

Carers

4.29 In making accommodation offers to applicants who receive support from carers who do not reside with them but may need to stay overnight, housing authorities should, wherever possible, take account of the applicant's need for a spare bedroom.

Prospective adopters and foster carers

4.30 When considering housing applications from prospective foster carers or adopters who would require an extra bedroom to accommodate a foster or adoptive child, authorities will wish to weigh up the risk that the application to foster or adopt may be unsuccessful (leading to the property being under-occupied), against the wider benefits which would be realised if the placement was successful.

4.31 Children's services have a duty under s.22G of the Children Act 1989 to ensure sufficient accommodation to meet the needs of the looked after children in their area. Authorities should work together with children's services to best meet the needs of prospective and approved foster carers and adopters, so that children's services can meet their s.22G duty. One way to strike an appropriate balance would be to set aside a quota of properties each year for people who need to move to larger accommodation in order to foster or adopt a child on the recommendation of children's services.

4.32 The advice in paragraph 4.22 is particularly relevant in relation to prospective foster carers, as foster children are not taken into account in

Appendix 1
England: Allocation

determining the household size for the purposes of the under-occupation measure in the Welfare Reform Act. However, current and prospective foster carers affected by the measure may be eligible to apply for a Discretionary Housing Payment.

General information about particular applications

4.33 Under s166A(9), allocation schemes must be framed so as to give applicants the right to request from housing authorities general information that will enable them to assess:

(a) how their application is likely to be treated under the scheme and, in particular, whether they are likely to have reasonable preference

(b) whether accommodation appropriate to their needs is likely to be made available and, if so, how long it is likely to be before such accommodation becomes available.

Notification about decisions and the right to a review of a decision

4.34 An allocation scheme must be framed so as to give applicants the right to be informed of certain decisions and the right to review certain decisions (s.166A(9)). For further advice on decisions and reviews, see chapter 5.

CHAPTER 5

Allocation scheme management

Publishing and consulting on allocation schemes

5.1 Housing authorities must publish a summary of their allocation scheme and, if requested, provide a free copy of it (s.168(1)). They must also make the full scheme available for inspection at their principal office and, if requested, provide a copy of it on payment of a reasonable fee (s.168(2)).

5.2 When an alteration is made to a scheme reflecting a major change of policy, an authority must ensure within a reasonable time that those likely to be affected by the change have the effect brought to their attention, taking such steps as the housing authority considers reasonable (s.168(3)). A major policy change would include, for example, any amendment affecting the relative priority of a large number of applicants or a significant alteration to procedures. Housing authorities should be aware that they still have certain duties under s.106 of the Housing Act 1985.

5.3 Section 166A(13) requires authorities, before adopting an allocation scheme, or altering a scheme to reflect a major change of policy, to:

- send a copy of the draft scheme, or proposed alteration, to every Private Registered Provider[19] with which they have nomination arrangements, and

- ensure they have a reasonable opportunity to comment on the proposals.

Advice and information

5.4 Housing authorities must ensure that advice and information is available free of charge to everyone in their district about the right to apply for an allocation of accommodation (s.166(1)(a)). This would include general information about application procedures; as well as information about qualification and prioritisation criteria.

5.5 If a person is likely to have difficulty making an application without assistance, the authority must secure that any necessary assistance is available free of charge (s.166(1)(b)).

5.6 Housing authorities must inform applicants that they have the right to the following general information (s.166(1A)):

- information that will enable them to assess how their application is likely to be treated under the authority's allocation scheme, and, in particular, whether they are likely to fall within the reasonable preference categories, and

- information about whether accommodation appropriate to their needs is likely to be made available to them and, if so, how long it is likely to be before such accommodation becomes available. Maintaining a database of housing suitable for applicants with access needs would assist with this.

5.7 Section 166(4) prohibits housing authorities from divulging to other members of the public that a person is an applicant for social housing, unless they have the applicant's consent. Furthermore, authorities should process any personal data they hold about applicants consistently with the Data Protection Act 1998. If authorities are unclear about their obligations and responsibilities under the Data Protection Act they should contact the Information Commissioner.

Elected Members' Involvement in Allocation Decisions

5.8 The Allocation of Housing (Procedure) Regulations 1997 (SI 1997/483) prevent an elected Member from being part of a decision-making body at the time an allocation decision is made, when either:

---

[19]   And, where relevant, every Registered Social Landlord in Wales with which they have nomination arrangements.

- the accommodation concerned is situated in their division or electoral ward, or

- the person subject to the decision has their sole or main residence there

5.9 The regulations do not prevent an elected Member from representing their constituents in front of the decision making body, or from participating in the decision making body's deliberations prior to its decision. The regulations also do not prevent elected Members' involvement in policy decisions that affect the generality of housing accommodation in their division or electoral ward rather than individual allocations; for example, a decision that certain types of property should be prioritised for older people.

Offences related to information given or withheld by applicants

5.10 Section 171 makes it an offence for anyone, in connection with the exercise by a housing authority of its functions under Part 6, to:

- knowingly or recklessly give false information

- knowingly withhold information which the housing authority has reasonably required the applicant to give in connection with the exercise of those functions.

5.11 The circumstances in which an offence is committed could include providing false information:

- on an application form for social housing

- in response to a request for further information in support of the application

- during review proceedings.

5.12 Ground 5 in Schedule 2 to the Housing Act 1985 (as amended by s.146 of the 1996 Act) enables a housing authority to seek possession of a tenancy granted as a result of a false statement by the tenant or a person acting at the tenant's instigation.

Fraudulent or incorrect allocations

5.13 Authorities may also wish to take action to minimise the risk of staff allocating incorrectly or even fraudulently, for example to applicants who do not have sufficient priority under the allocation scheme or do not meet the authority's qualification criteria. Appropriate steps might include vetting staff who take allocation decisions or providing for decisions to be validated by employing senior staff to undertake random checks.

Decisions and reviews

Information about decisions and reviews

5.14 Housing authorities must inform applicants that they have the right to information about certain decisions which are taken in respect of their application and the right to review those decisions (s.166(1A)).

5.15 By virtue of s.160ZA (9) and (10) housing authorities must notify an applicant in writing of any decision that he or she:

- is ineligible for an allocation of accommodation under s.160ZA(2) or (4), or

- is not a qualifying person under s.160ZA(7).

5.16 The notification must give clear grounds for the decision based on the relevant facts of the case. Section 160ZA(10) provides that, where a notification is not received by an applicant, it can be treated as having been given to him or her, if it is made available at the housing authority's office for a reasonable period. Where an authority considers that an applicant may have difficulty in understanding the implications of a decision on ineligibility or disqualification, it would be good practice to make arrangements for the information to be explained verbally in addition to providing a written notice.

5.17 Applicants also have the right, on request, to be informed of any decision about the facts of their case which has been, or is likely to be, taken into account in considering whether to make an allocation to them (s.166A(9)(b)).

5.18 Under s.166A(9)(c) applicants have the right to request a review of any of the decisions mentioned in paragraphs 5.15 and 5.17 above and to be informed of the decision on the review and the grounds for it.

Procedures on review

5.19 Review procedures should be clearly set out, including timescales for each stage of the process, and must accord with the principles of transparency and fairness. Failure to put in place a fair procedure for reviews, which allows for all relevant factors to be considered, could result in a judicial review of any decision reached. The following are general principles of good administrative practice:

i. Applicants should be notified of the timescale within which they must request a review. 21 days from the date the applicant is notified of the decision is well-established as a reasonable timescale. A housing authority should retain the discretion to extend this time limit in exceptional circumstances.

ii. Applicants should be notified that the request for review should be made in writing, and that it would also be acceptable for the request to be submitted by a representative on their behalf. Applicants should also be advised of the information which should accompany the request.

iii. Authorities should consider whether to advise that provision can be made for verbal representations, as well as written submissions, to be made.

iii. The review should be carried out by an officer who is senior to the person who made the original decision. Alternatively, authorities may wish to appoint a panel to consider the review. If so, it should not include any person involved in the original decision.

v. The review should be considered on the basis of the authority's allocation scheme, any legal requirements and all relevant information. This should include information provided by the applicant on any relevant developments since the original decision was made – for instance, the settlement of arrears or establishment of a repayment plan, or departure of a member of the household responsible for anti-social behavior.

vi. Reviews should be completed wherever practicable within a set deadline. Eight weeks is suggested as a reasonable timescale. The applicant should be notified of any extension to this deadline and the reasons for this.

viii. Applicants must be notified in writing of the outcome of the review. The notification must set out the reasons for the decision. This will assist the applicant and the authority if, for example, the applicant is not satisfied with the outcome and decides to seek a judicial review or to take their case to the Local Government Ombudsman.

CHAPTER 6

Private Registered Providers and contracting out

Working with Private Registered Providers

6.1 Private Registered Providers have a duty under s.170 to cooperate with housing authorities – where the authority requests it – to such extent as is reasonable in the circumstances in offering accommodation to people with priority under the authority's allocation scheme. Similarly, s.213 provides that, where a Private Registered Provider has been requested by a housing authority to assist them in the discharge of their homelessness functions under Part 7, it must cooperate to the same extent.

6.2 Housing authorities must comply with the requirements of Part 6 when they nominate an applicant to be the tenant of a Private Registered Provider. A housing authority nominates for these purposes when it does so 'in pursuance of any arrangements (whether legally enforceable or not) to require that housing accommodation, or a specified amount of housing accommodation, is made available to a person or one of a number of persons nominated by the authority' (s.159(4)).

6.3 Nomination agreements should set out the proportion of lettings that will be made available; any criteria which the Private Registered Provider has adopted for accepting or rejecting nominees; and how any disputes will be resolved. Housing authorities will want to put in place arrangements to monitor effective delivery of the nomination agreement so they can demonstrate they are meeting their obligations under Part 6.

6.4 The Secretary of State expects that Affordable Rent homes will be allocated in the same way as social rent properties and that existing lettings arrangements operated by housing authorities and Private Registered Providers will continue to apply. The statutory and regulatory framework for allocations provides scope for local flexibility, and authorities and Private Registered Providers may wish to exercise this discretion in relation to Affordable Rent in order to meet local needs and priorities effectively.

Contracting Out

6.5 The *Local Authorities (Contracting Out of Allocation of Housing and Homelessness Functions) Order 1996* (SI 1996/3205) – made under s.70 of the Deregulation and Contracting Out Act 1994 ('the 1994 Act') – enables housing authorities to contract out certain functions under Part 6. In essence, it allows the contracting out of administrative functions, leaving the responsibility for strategic decisions with the housing authority.

6.6 Schedule 1 to the Order lists allocation functions which may not be contracted out:

- adopting or altering the allocation scheme, including the principles on which the scheme is framed, and consulting Private Registered Providers,

- making the allocation scheme available at the authority's principal office.

6.7 The Order therefore provides that the majority of functions under Part 6 may be contracted out. These include:

i) making enquiries about and deciding a person's eligibility for an allocation

ii) carrying out reviews of decisions

iii) securing that advice and information is available free of charge on how to apply for housing

iv) securing that assistance is available free of charge to people likely to have difficulty in making a housing application without such assistance, and

v) making individual allocations in accordance with the allocation scheme.

6.8 The 1994 Act provides that a contract:

i) may authorise a contractor to carry out only part of the function concerned

ii) may specify that the contractor is authorised to carry out functions only in certain cases or areas specified in the contract

iii) may include conditions relating to the carrying out of the functions, for example prescribing standards of performance

iv) shall be for a period not exceeding 10 years and may be revoked at any time by the Minister or the housing authority. Any subsisting contract is to be treated as having been repudiated in these circumstances

v) shall not prevent the authority from exercising the functions to which the contract relates.

6.9 The 1994 Act also provides that the authority is responsible for any act or omission of the contractor in exercising functions under the contract, except where:

- the contractor fails to fulfil conditions specified in the contract relating to the exercise of the function

- criminal proceedings are brought in respect of the contractor's act or omission.

6.10 Where a housing authority has delegated or contracted out the operation of its allocation functions to an external contractor, the contractor must be made aware of the provisions of Part 6 and advised how the legislation and this guidance apply to them.

6.11 Where there is an arrangement in force under s.101 of the Local Government Act 1972 by virtue of which one authority exercises the functions of another, the 1994 Act provides that the authority exercising the function is not allowed to contract it out without the principal authority's consent.

ANNEX 1

Indicators of criteria in reasonable preference categories (c) & (d)

Housing authorities may devise their own indicators of the criteria in the reasonable preference categories. The following list is included for illustrative purposes and to assist housing authorities in this task. It is by no means comprehensive or exhaustive, and housing authorities may have other, local factors to consider and include as indicators of the categories.

Insanitary, overcrowded and unsatisfactory housing conditions

Lacking bathroom or kitchen

Lacking inside WC

Lacking cold or hot water supplies, electricity, gas, or adequate heating

Lack of access to a garden for young children

Sharing living room, kitchen, bathroom/WC

Property in disrepair Poor internal or external arrangements

Young children in flats above ground floor

People who need to move on medical or welfare grounds (criteria may apply to any member of the household)

A mental illness or disorder A physical or learning disability

Chronic or progressive medical conditions (e.g. MS, HIV/AIDS)

Infirmity due to old age

The need to give or receive care

The need to recover from the effects of violence or threats of violence, or physical, emotional or sexual abuse

Ability to fend for self restricted for other reasons Young people at risk

People with behavioural difficulties

Need for adapted housing and/or extra facilities, bedroom or bathroom

Need for improved heating (on medical grounds)

Need for sheltered housing (on medical grounds) Need for ground floor accommodation (on medical grounds)

Need to be near friends/relatives or medical facility on medical grounds

Need to move following hospitalisation or long term care

ANNEX 2

Rights to reside in the UK derived from EU Law

1. EEA nationals and their family members who have a right to reside in the UK that derives from EU law are not persons subject to immigration control. This means that they will be eligible for an allocation of accommodation under Part 6 unless they fall within one of the categories of persons to be treated as a person from abroad who is ineligible for an allocation of accommodation by virtue of regulation 4 of the Eligibility Regulations.

General

Nationals of EU countries

2. Nationals of EU countries enjoy a number of different rights to reside in other Member States, including the UK. These rights derive from the EU Treaties, EU secondary legislation (in particular *Directive 2004/38*), and the case law of the European Court of Justice.

3. Whether an individual EU national has a right to reside in the UK will depend on his or her circumstances, particularly his or her economic status (e.g. whether employed, self-employed, seeking work, a student, or economically inactive etc).

Nationals of Bulgaria and Romania – the A2 accession states

4. A slightly different regime applies to EU nationals who are nationals of Bulgaria and Romania which acceded to the EU on 1 January 2007. Bulgaria and Romania are referred to in this guidance as the A2 accession states.

The Immigration (European Economic Area) Regulations 2006

5. The *Immigration (European Economic Area) Regulations 2006* ('the EEA Regulations' – SI 2006/1003) implement into UK domestic law *Directive 2004/38*. Broadly, the EEA Regulations provide that EU nationals have the right to reside in the UK without the requirement for leave to remain under the Immigration Act 1971 for the first 3 months of their residence, and for longer, if they are a 'qualified person' or they have acquired a permanent right of residence.

Nationals of Iceland, Liechtenstein and Norway, and Switzerland

6. The EEA Regulations extend the same rights to reside in the UK to nationals of Iceland, Liechtenstein and Norway as those afforded to EU nationals. (The EU countries plus Iceland, Liechtenstein and Norway together comprise the EEA.) The EEA Regulations also extend the same rights to reside in the UK to nationals of Switzerland. For the purposes of this guidance, 'EEA nationals' means nationals of any of the EU member states (excluding the UK), and nationals of Iceland, Norway, Liechtenstein and Switzerland.

Initial 3 months residence

7. Regulation 13 of the EEA Regulations provides that EEA nationals have the right to reside in the UK for a period of up to 3 months without any conditions or formalities other than holding a valid identity card or passport. Therefore, during their first 3 months of residence in the UK, EEA nationals will not be subject to immigration control (unless the right to reside is lost following a decision by an immigration officer in accordance with regulation 13(3) of the EEA Regulations).

8. However, regulations 4(1)(b)(ii) and (c) of the Eligibility Regulations provide that a person who is not subject to immigration control is not eligible for an allocation of accommodation if:

(i)   his or her **only** right to reside in the UK is an initial right to reside for a period not exceeding 3 months under regulation 13 of the EEA Regulations, or

(ii) his or her **only** right to reside in the Channel Islands, the Isle of Man or the Republic of Ireland (the Common Travel Area) is a right equivalent to the right mentioned in (i) above which is derived from the EU Treaty

Rights of residence for 'qualified persons'

9. Regulation 14 of the EEA Regulations provides that 'qualified persons' have the right to reside in the UK so long as they remain a qualified person. Under regulation 6 of the EEA Regulations, 'qualified person' means:

a)   a jobseeker

b)   a worker

c)   a self-employed person

d)   a self-sufficient person

e)   a student

Jobseekers

10. For the purposes of regulation 6(1)(a) of the EEA Regulations, 'jobseeker' means a person who enters the UK in order to seek employment and can provide evidence that he or she is seeking employment and has a genuine chance of being employed.

11. Nationals of Bulgaria and Romania who need to be authorised to work do not have a right to reside in the UK as a jobseeker[20]. However, they may have a right to reside by virtue of another status, e.g. as a self-sufficient person.

12. Although a person who is a jobseeker is not subject to immigration control, regulation 4 of the Eligibility Regulations provides that a person is not eligible for an allocation of accommodation if:

(i)   his or her **only** right to reside in the UK is derived from his or her status as a jobseeker or the family member of a jobseeker, or

(ii)   his or her **only** right to reside in the Channel Islands, the Common Travel Area is a right equivalent to the right mentioned in (i) above which is derived from the Treaty establishing the European Community.

Workers

13. In order to be a worker for the purposes of the EEA Regulations, a person must be employed. That is to say, he or she is obliged to provide services for another person in return for monetary reward and is subject to the control of that other person as regards the way in which the work is to be done.

14. Activity as an employed person may include part time work, seasonal work and cross-border work (ie. where a worker is established in another Member State and travels to work in the UK). However, case law provides that the employment must be effective and genuine economic activity, and not on such a small scale as to be regarded as purely marginal and ancillary.

15. Provided the employment is effective and genuine economic activity, the fact that a person's level of remuneration may be below the level of subsistence or below the national minimum wage, or the fact that a person may be receiving financial assistance from public benefits, would not exclude that person from being a 'worker'.

16. A person who is a worker is not subject to immigration control, and is eligible for an allocation of accommodation whether or not he or she is habitually resident in the Common Travel Area.

---

[20]   Regulation 6(2) of the *Accession (Immigration and Worker Authorisation) Regulations 2006* (SI 2006/3317).

Retention of worker status

17. A person who is no longer working does not cease to be treated as a 'worker' for the purpose of regulation 6(1)(b) of the EEA Regulations, if he or she:

(a)   is temporarily unable to work as the result of an illness or accident; or

(b)   is recorded as involuntarily unemployed after having being employed in the UK, provided that he or she has registered as a jobseeker with the relevant employment office, and:
       (i)   was employed for one year or more before becoming unemployed, or
       (ii)   has been unemployed for no more than 6 months, or
       (iii) can provide evidence that he or she is seeking employment in the UK and has a genuine chance of being engaged; or

(c)   is involuntarily unemployed and has embarked on vocational training; or

(d)   has voluntarily ceased working and embarked on vocational training that is related to his or her previous employment.

A2 state workers requiring authorisation who are treated as workers

18. By virtue of the *Accession (Immigration and Worker Authorisation) Regulations 2006* ('the Accession Regulations'), nationals of the A2 states (with certain exceptions) must obtain authorisation to work in the UK until they have accrued a period of 12 months continuous employment.

19. An A2 national requiring authorisation is only treated as a worker if he or she is actually working and:

(i)   holds an accession worker authorisation document, and

(ii)   is working in accordance with the conditions set out in that document (regulation 9(1) of the Accession Regulations).

20. Authorities may need to contact the employer named in the authorisation document, to confirm that the applicant continues to be employed.

Self-employed persons

21. 'Self-employed person' means a person who establishes himself in the UK in order to pursue activity as a self-employed person in accordance with Article 49 of the Treaty on the Functioning of the European Union.

22. A self-employed person should be able to confirm that he or she is pursuing activity as a self-employed person by providing documents relating to their business. A person who is no longer in self-employment does not cease to be

Appendix 1
England: Allocation

treated as a self-employed person for the purposes of regulation 6(1)(c) of the EEA regulations, if he or she is temporarily unable to pursue his or her activity as a self-employed person as the result of an illness or accident.

23. A2 nationals are not required to be authorised in order to establish themselves in the UK as a self-employed person.

24. A person who is a self-employed is not subject to immigration control and is eligible for an allocation of accommodation whether or not he or she is habitually resident in the Common Travel Area.

Self-sufficient persons

25. Regulation 4(1)(c) of the EEA regulations defines 'self-sufficient person' as a person who has:

(i)   sufficient resources not to become a burden on the social assistance system of the UK during his or her period of residence, and

(ii)   comprehensive sickness insurance cover in the UK.

26. By regulation 4(4) of the EEA Regulations, the resources of a person who is a self-sufficient person (or a student – see below) and, where applicable, any family members, are to be regarded as sufficient if (a) they exceed the maximum level of resources which a UK national and his or her family members may possess if he or she is to become eligible for social assistance under the UK benefit system or, if (a) does not apply, (b) taking into account the personal situation of the person concerned and, where applicable, any family members, it appears to the decision maker that the resources of the person or persons concerned should be regarded as sufficient.

27. Where an EEA national applies for an allocation of accommodation as a self-sufficient person and does not appear to meet the conditions of regulation 4(1)(c) of the EEA regulations, the housing authority will need to consider whether he or she may have some other right to reside in the UK.

28. Where the applicant does not meet the conditions of regulation 4(1)(c) but has previously done so during his or her residence in the UK, the case should be referred to the Home Office for clarification of their status.

29. A person who is a self-sufficient person is not subject to immigration control, but must be habitually resident in the Common Travel Area to be eligible for an allocation of accommodation.

Students

30. Regulation 4(1)(d) of the EEA regulations defines 'student' as a person who:

(a) is enrolled at a private or public establishment included on the Register of Education and Training Providers[21], or is financed from public funds, for the principal purpose of following a course of study, including vocational training, and

(b) has comprehensive sickness insurance cover in the UK, and

(c) assures the Secretary of State, by means of a declaration or such equivalent means as the person may choose, that he or she (and if applicable his or her family members) has sufficient resources not to become a burden on the social assistance system of the UK during his or her period of residence.

31. A person who is a student is not subject to immigration control but must be habitually resident in the Common Travel Area to be eligible for an allocation of accommodation.

Permanent right of residence

32. Regulation 15 of the EEA Regulations provides that the following persons shall acquire the right to reside in the UK permanently:

(a) an EEA national who has resided in the UK in accordance with the EEA regulations for a continuous period of 5 years

(b) a non-EEA national who is a family member of an EEA national and who has resided in the UK with the EEA national in accordance with the EEA regulations for a continuous period of 5 years

(c) a worker or self-employed person who has ceased activity (see regulation 5 of the EEA Regulations for the definition of worker or self-employed person who has ceased activity)

(d) the family member of a worker or self-employed person who has ceased activity

(e) a person who was the family member of a worker or self-employed person who has died, where the family member resided with the worker or self-employed person immediately before the death and the worker or self-employed person had resided continuously in the UK for at least 2 years before the death (or the death was the result of an accident at work or an occupational disease)

(f) a person who has resided in the UK in accordance with the EEA regulations for a continuous period of 5 years, and at the end of that period was a family member who has retained the right of residence (see

---

[21]   Now known as the Register of Sponsors and held by UKBA.

regulation 10 of the EEA Regulations for the definition of a family member who has retained the right of residence).

Once acquired, the right of permanent residence can be lost through absence from the UK for a period exceeding two consecutive years.

33. A person with a right to reside permanently in the UK arising from (c), (d) or (e) above is eligible for an allocation of accommodation whether or not he or she is habitually resident in the Common Travel Area. Persons with a permanent right to reside by virtue of (a), (b), or (f) must be habitually resident to be eligible.

Rights of residence for certain family members

The right to reside

34. Regulation 14 of the EEA Regulations provides that the following family members are entitled to reside in the UK:

(i)   a family member of a qualified person residing in the UK

(ii)   a family member of an EEA national with a permanent right of residence under regulation 15

(iii)   a family member who has retained the right of residence (see regulation 10 of the EEA Regulations for the definition).

35. A person who has a right to reside in the UK as the family member of an EEA national under the EEA Regulations will not be subject to immigration control. The eligibility of such a person for an allocation of accommodation should therefore be considered in accordance with regulation 4 of the Eligibility Regulations.

36. When considering the eligibility of a family member, housing authorities should consider whether the person has acquired a right to reside in their own right, for example a permanent right to reside under regulation 15 of the EEA Regulations.

Who is a 'family member'?

37. Regulation 7 of the EEA regulations provides that the following persons are treated as the family members of another person (with certain exceptions for students – see below):

(a)   the spouse of the person

(b)   the civil partner of the person

(c)   a direct descendant of the person, or of the person's spouse or civil partner, who is under the age of 21

(d)   a direct descendant of the person, or of the person's spouse or civil partner, who is over 21 and dependent on the person, or the spouse or civil partner

(e)   an ascendant relative of the person, or of the person's spouse or civil partner, who is dependent on the person or the spouse or civil partner

(f)   a person who is an extended family member and is treated as a family member by virtue of regulation 7(3) of the EEA regulations (see below).

Family members of students

38. Regulation 7(2) of the EEA regulations provides that a person who falls within (c), (d) or (e) above shall not be treated as a family member of a student residing in the UK after the period of 3 months beginning on the date the student is admitted to the UK unless:

(i)   in the case of paragraph 37(c) and (d) above, the person is the dependant child of the student, or of the spouse or civil partner, or

(ii)   the student is also a qualified person (for the purposes of regulation 6(1) of the EEA regulations) other than as a student.

Extended family members

39. Broadly, extended family members will be persons who:

(a)   do not fall within any of the categories (a) to (e) in paragraph 37 above, and

(b)   are either a relative of an EEA national (or of the EEA national's spouse or civil partner) or the partner of an EEA national, and

(c)   have been issued with an EEA family permit, a registration certificate or a residence card which is valid and has not been revoked.

Family members' eligibility for an allocation of accommodation

Relationship with other rights to reside

40. This section concerns the eligibility of an applicant for an allocation of accommodation whose right to reside is derived from his or her status as the family member of an EEA national with a right to reside. In some cases, a family member will have acquired a right to reside in his or her own right. In particular, a person who arrived in the UK as the family member of an EEA national may have subsequently acquired a permanent right of residence under

regulation 15 of the EEA Regulations, as outlined in paragraph 32 (a) – (f) above. The eligibility for an allocation of accommodation of those with a permanent right of residence is discussed at paragraphs 32 and 33.

Family members who must be habitually resident

41. For family members with a right to reside under regulation 14 of the EEA Regulations, the following categories of persons must be habitually resident in the UK, the Channel Islands, the Isle of Man or the Republic of Ireland in order to be eligible for an allocation of accommodation:

a)   a person whose right to reside derives from their status as a family member of an EEA national who is a self-sufficient person for the purposes of regulation 6(1)(d) of the EEA regulations

b)   a person whose right to reside derives from their status as a family member of an EEA national who is a student for the purposes of regulation 6(1)(e) of the EEA regulations

c)   a person whose right to reside is dependent on their status as a family member of an EEA national with a permanent right to reside

d)   a person whose right to reside is dependent on their status as a family member who has retained the right of residence.

Family members who are exempt from the habitual residence requirement

42. A person with a right to reside under regulation 14 as a family member of an EEA national who is a worker or a self-employed person for the purposes of regulation 6(1) of the EEA regulations is exempted from the requirement to be habitually resident by regulation 4(2)(d) of the Eligibility Regulations. However, authorities should note that an extended family member (see above) is not counted as a family member for the purposes of regulation 4(2)(d) of the Eligibility Regulations (see regulation 2(3) of the Eligibility Regulations).

Family members of UK nationals exercising rights under the EU Treaty

43. There are some limited cases in which the non-EEA family member of a UK national may have a right to reside under EU law. Under regulation 9 of the EEA Regulations, the family member of a UK national should be treated as an EEA family member where the following conditions are met:

(i)   the UK national is residing in an EEA State as a worker or self-employed person, or was so residing before returning to the UK, and

(ii) if the family member of the UK national is his spouse or civil partner, the parties are living together in the EEA State, or had entered into a marriage or civil partnership and were living together in that State before the UK national returned to the UK.

44. Where the family member of a UK national is to be treated as an EEA family member by virtue of regulation 9 of the EEA Regulations, that person is not subject to immigration control, and his or her eligibility for an allocation of accommodation should therefore be determined in accordance with regulation 4 of the Eligibility Regulations.

ANNEX 3

Worker authorisation scheme

1. Bulgaria and Romania ('the A2') acceded to the European Union on 1 January 2007. A2 nationals have the right to move freely among all EU Member States. However, under the EU Accession Treaty for Bulgaria and Romania existing Member States can impose limitations on the rights of A2 nationals to access their labour markets (and the associated rights of residence) for a transitional period.

The Accession (Immigration and Worker Authorisation) Regulations 2006

2. Under the *Accession (Immigration and Worker Authorisation) Regulations 2006* (SI 2006/3317) ('the Accession Regulations'), nationals of the A2 States (with certain exceptions set out in paragraph 9 below) are required to be authorised to work by the Home Office if they work in the UK during the transitional period. While looking for work (or between jobs) their right to reside will be conditional on them being self-sufficient and not imposing an unreasonable burden on the UK social assistance system. These conditions cease to apply once they have worked in the UK continuously and legally for 12 months.

3. The Accession Regulations also give workers from the A2 states the right to reside in the UK. This means that workers from the A2 states have the same right to equal treatment as other EEA workers while they are working in accordance with work authorisation requirements or are exempt from those requirements.

The worker authorisation scheme

4. Nationals of A2 states who wish to work in the UK (except those who are exempt from the requirement) must have an accession worker authorisation document and must be working in accordance with the conditions set out in that document.

5. Nationals of the A2 states who are self-employed are not required to be authorised if they are working that capacity.

6. The following constitute worker authorisation documents:

i.   a passport or other travel document endorsed to show that the person was given leave to enter or remain in the UK before 1 January 2007, subject to a condition restricting his or her employment in the UK to a particular employer or category of employment

   If the leave to enter or remain expires before the person qualifies to be exempt from the work authorisation requirements, or they wish to engage in employment other than the job for which the leave was granted, they will need to obtain an accession worker card

ii.   a seasonal agricultural work card issued by the Home Office under the Seasonal Agricultural Workers Scheme. The card is valid for 6 months from the date the person starts work for the agricultural employer specified in the card

iii.   an accession worker card issued by the Home Office.

7. The accession worker card is valid for as long as the person continues to work for the employer specified in the card. If the person changes employer, he or she must apply for a new accession worker card.

8. The worker authorisation scheme is a transitional measure. The Accession Regulations provide for the scheme to operate for up to five years from 1 January 2007 (i.e. until 31 December 2011). However, there is provision for the scheme to be extended for a further two years in the event of a serious disturbance to the labour market. The decision was taken on 23 November 2011 to maintain transitional controls on Romanian and Bulgarian workers until the end of 2013.

A2 nationals exempt from worker authorisation

9. The following are the categories of A2 nationals who are not required to obtain authorisation to work:

- those who are classified as highly skilled persons and hold a registration certificate allowing them unconditional access to the UK labour market

- those working legally, and without interruption, in the UK for a period of 12 months or more ending on 31 December 2006 (for example, they may have been already present in the UK as a work permit holder before accession)

- those who had leave to enter the UK under the Immigration Act 1971 on 31 December 2006 and that leave does not place any restrictions on taking employment in the United Kingdom (for example, a person may have been given leave to remain as the spouse of a British citizen or as the dependant of a work permit holder)

- those who are providing services in the UK on behalf of an employer established elsewhere in the EEA

- those who are also a national of the UK or another EEA state (other than an A2 state)

- those who are a spouse or civil partner of a national of the UK or a person settled in the UK

- those who are the spouse, civil partner or child under 18 of a person who has limited leave to enter or remain in the UK and that leave allows that person to work in the UK

- those who are a family member (spouse, civil partner or dependant child) of an EEA national who has a right to reside in the UK under the EEA Regulations, including those who are the family member (spouse, civil partner or descendant (under 21 or dependant)) of an A2 national who is working in accordance with worker authorisation requirements

- those who have a permanent right to reside in the UK under regulation 15 of the EEA Regulations

- those who are in the UK as a student and are permitted to work for 20 hours a week, provided they are in possession of a registration certificate confirming that they are exercising a Treaty right as a student.

10. In addition, where a person has worked legally in the UK without interruption for a 12 month period falling wholly or partly after 31 December 2006, they will be free from the requirement to seek authorisation. At that stage, they will be able to apply to the Home Office for an EEA residence permit to confirm their right to equal treatment on the same basis as other EEA nationals.

12 months' uninterrupted work

11. In order to establish '12 months' uninterrupted work' an A2 worker must have been working legally in the UK at the beginning and end of the 12 month period. The 12 month period does not have to run continuously. However, any intervening period in which an A2 national is not legally working must not exceed 30 days in total. If more than 30 days between periods of employment occur before a 12-month period of uninterrupted employment is established, a fresh period of 12 months' uninterrupted employment would need to commence from that point.

12. There is no restriction on the number of different authorised jobs (or employers) that a worker can have during a 12-month period of continuous employment.

Highly skilled workers

13. A national of an A2 state is not required to be authorised under the worker authorisation scheme, if he is a highly skilled worker who has been given a registration certificate by the Home Office which includes a statement that he or she has unconditional access to the UK labour market.

ANNEX 4

Habitual residence

1. In practice, when considering housing applications from persons subject to the habitual residence test, it is only necessary to investigate habitual residence if the applicant has arrived or returned to live in the UK during the two year period prior to making the application.

Definition of habitual residence

2. The term 'habitual residence' is not defined in legislation. Housing authorities should always consider the overall circumstances of a case to determine whether someone is habitually resident in the Common Travel Area.

General principles

3. When deciding whether a person is habitually resident, consideration must be given to all the facts of each case in a common sense way. It should be remembered that:

- the test focuses on the fact and nature of residence

- a person who is not resident somewhere cannot be habitually resident there

- residence is a more settled state than mere physical presence in a country. To be resident a person must be seen to be making a home. It need not be the only home or a permanent home but it must be a genuine home for the time being. For example, a short stay visitor or person receiving short term medical treatment is not resident

- the most important factors for habitual residence are length, continuity and general nature of actual residence rather than intention

- the practicality of a person's arrangements for residence is a necessary part of determining whether it can be described as settled and habitual

- established habitual residents who have periods of temporary or occasional absence of long or short duration may still be habitually resident during such absences.

Action on receipt of an application

Applicant came to live in the UK during the previous two years

4. If it appears that the applicant came to live in the UK during the previous two years, authorities should make further enquiries to decide if the applicant is habitually resident, or can be treated as such.

Factors to consider

5. The applicant's stated reasons and intentions for coming to the UK will be relevant to the question of whether he or she is habitually resident. If the applicant's stated intention is to live in the UK, and not return to the country from which they came, that intention must be consistent with their actions.

6. To decide whether an applicant is habitually resident in the UK, authorities should consider the factors set out below. However, these do not provide an exhaustive check list of the questions or factors that need to be considered. Further enquiries may be needed. The circumstances of each case will dictate what information is needed, and all relevant factors should be taken into account.

Why has the applicant come to the UK?

7. If the applicant is returning to the UK after a period spent abroad, and it can be established that the applicant was previously habitually resident in the UK and is returning to resume his or her former period of habitual residence, he or she will be immediately habitually resident.

8. In determining whether an applicant is returning to resume a former period of habitual residence authorities should consider:

- when the applicant left the UK

- how long the applicant lived in the UK before leaving

- why the applicant left the UK

- how long the applicant intended to remain abroad

- why the applicant returned

- whether the applicant's partner and children, if any, also left the UK

- whether the applicant kept accommodation in the UK

- if the applicant owned property, whether it was let, and whether the lease was timed to coincide with the applicant's return to the UK

- what links the applicant kept with the UK

- whether there have been other brief absences

- why the applicant has come back to the UK.

9. If the applicant has arrived in the UK within the previous two years and is not resuming a period of habitual residence, consideration should be given to his or her reasons for coming to the UK, and in particular to the factors set out below.

Applicant is joining family or friends

10. If the applicant has come to the UK to join or rejoin family or friends, authorities should consider:

- whether the applicant has sold or given up any property abroad

- whether the applicant has bought or rented accommodation or is staying with friends

- whether the move to the UK is intended to be permanent.

Applicant's plans

11. Authorities should consider the applicant's plans, e.g:

- if the applicant plans to remain in the UK, whether their stated plan is consistent with their actions

- whether any arrangements were made for employment and accommodation (even if unsuccessful) before the applicant arrived in the UK

- whether the applicant bought a one-way ticket

- whether the applicant brought all their belongings

- whether there is evidence of links with the UK, e.g. membership of clubs.

12. The fact that a person may intend to live in the UK for the foreseeable future does not, of itself, mean that habitual residence has been established.

However, the applicant's intentions along with other factors, for example the disposal of property abroad, may indicate that the applicant is habitually resident in the UK.

13. An applicant who intends to reside in the UK for only a short period, for example for a holiday or to visit friends is unlikely to be habitually resident in the UK.

Length of residence in another country

14. Authorities should consider the length and continuity of an applicant's residence in another country:

- whether the applicant has any remaining ties with his or her former country of residence

- whether the applicant stayed in different countries outside the UK.

15. It is possible that a person may own a property abroad but still be habitually resident in the UK. A person who has a home or close family in another country would normally retain habitual residence in that country. A person who has previously lived in several different countries but has now moved permanently to the UK may be habitually resident here.

Centre of interest

16. An applicant is likely to be habitually resident in the Common Travel Area despite spending time abroad, if his or her centre of interest is located in one of these places.

17. People who maintain their centre of interest in the Common Travel Area for example a home, a job, friends, membership of clubs, are likely to be habitually resident there. People who have retained their centre of interest in another country and have no particular ties with the Common Travel Area are unlikely to be habitually resident.

18. Authorities should take the following into account when deciding the centre of interest:

- home

- family ties

- club memberships

- finance accounts

19. If the centre of interest appears to be in the Common Travel Area but the applicant has a home somewhere else, authorities should consider the applicant's intentions regarding the property.

20. It is not uncommon for a person to live in one country but have property abroad that they do not intend to sell. Where such a person has lived in the Common Travel Area for many years, the fact that they have property elsewhere does not necessarily mean that they intend to leave, or that the applicant's centre of interest is elsewhere.

Local Authorities (Contracting Out of Allocation of Housing and Homelessness Functions) Order 1996

SI 1996/3205

Made	*20th December 1996*
Coming into force	
Articles 1 and 3	*20th January 1997*
Article 2	*1st April 1997*

The Secretary of State for the Environment, as respects England, and the Secretary of State for Wales, as respects Wales, in exercise of the powers conferred on them by sections 70(2) and (4) and 77(1) of the Deregulation and Contracting Out Act 1994 and of all other powers enabling them in that behalf, after consultation with such representatives of local government as they consider appropriate, hereby make the following Order, a draft of which has been laid before and approved by resolution of each House of Parliament:

1 Citation, commencement and interpretation

(1) This Order may be cited as the Local Authorities (Contracting Out of Allocation of Housing and Homelessness Functions) Order 1996.

(2) This article and article 3 of this Order shall come into force on 20th January 1997 and article 2 of this Order shall come into force on 1st April 1997.

(3) In this Order –

'the Act' means the Housing Act 1996;
'an authority' means a local housing authority as defined in the Housing Act 1985.

(4) Any expressions used in this Order which are also used in the Act have the same meaning as they have in the Act.

2 Contracting out of allocation of housing functions

Any function of an authority which is conferred by or under Part 6 of the Act (allocation of housing accommodation), except one which is listed in Schedule 1 to this Order, may be exercised by, or by employees of, such person (if any) as may be authorised in that behalf by the authority whose function it is.

3 Contracting out of homelessness functions

Any function of an authority which is conferred by or under Part 7 of the Act (homelessness), except one which is listed in Schedule 2 to this Order, may be exercised by, or by employees of, such person (if any) as may be authorised in that behalf by the authority whose function it is.

Schedule 1
Allocation of Housing Functions of a Local Housing Authority Excluded from Contracting Out

Article 2

Functions conferred by or under any of the following provisions of the Act:

(a)   section 161(4) (classes of persons qualifying for allocations);
(b)   section 162 (the housing register) so far as they relate to any decision about the form of the register;
(c)   section 167 (allocation in accordance with allocation scheme) so far as they relate to adopting or altering an allocation scheme (including decisions on what principles the scheme is to be framed) and to the functions in subsection (7) of that section;
(d)   section 168(2) (information about allocation scheme) so far as they relate to making the allocation scheme available for inspection at the authority's principal office.

Schedule 2
Homelessness Functions of a Local Housing Authority Excluded from Contracting Out

Article 3

Functions conferred by or under any of the following provisions of the Act:

(a)   section 179(2) and (3) (duty of local housing authority to provide advisory services);
(b)   section 180 (assistance for voluntary organisations);
(c)   section 213 (co-operation between relevant housing authorities and bodies).

Allocation of Housing (Procedure) Regulations 1997

SI 1997/483

Made	*26th February 1997*
Laid before Parliament	*27th February 1997*
Coming into force	*1st April 1997*

The Secretary of State, in exercise of the powers conferred on him by sections 167(5) and 172(4) of the Housing Act 1996 and of all other powers enabling him in that behalf, hereby makes the following Regulations:

1 Citation and commencement

These Regulations may be cited as the Allocation of Housing (Procedure) Regulations 1997 and shall come into force on 1st April 1997.

2 Interpretation

In these Regulations –

'allocation decision' means a decision to allocate housing accommodation;
'authority' means a local housing authority in England;
'decision-making body' means an authority or a committee or sub-committee of an authority.

3 Allocation scheme procedure

(1) As regards the procedure to be followed, an authority's allocation scheme shall be framed in accordance with the principle prescribed in this regulation.

(2) A member of an authority who has been elected for the electoral division or ward in which –

(a)   the housing accommodation in relation to which an allocation decision falls to be made is situated, or

(b)   the person in relation to whom that decision falls to be made has his sole or main residence,

shall not, at the time the allocation decision is made, be included in the persons constituting the decision-making body.

Appendix 1
England: Allocation

Allocation of Housing (England) Regulations 2002

SI 2002/3264

Made	*18th December 2002*
Laid before Parliament	*10th January 2003*
Coming into force	*31st January 2003*

The Secretary of State, in exercise of the powers conferred upon him by sections 160(4), 160A(3) and (5) and 172(4) of the Housing Act 1996 hereby makes the following Regulations:

1 Citation, commencement and application

(1) These Regulations may be cited as the Allocation of Housing (England) Regulations 2002 and shall come into force on 31st January 2003.

(2) These Regulations apply in England only.

2 Interpretation

In these Regulations–

'the Act' means the Housing Act 1996;

'the Common Travel Area' means the United Kingdom, the Channel Islands, the Isle of Man and the Republic of Ireland collectively; and

'the immigration rules' means the rules laid down as mentioned in section 3(2) of the Immigration Act 1971 (general provisions for regulation and control).

['family intervention tenancy' –

(a) in relation to a tenancy granted by a local housing authority, has the meaning given by paragraph 4ZA(3) of Schedule 1 to the Housing Act 1985;

(b) in relation to a tenancy granted by a registered social landlord [or a private registered provider of social housing][1], has the meaning given by paragraph 12ZA(3) of Part 1 of Schedule 1 to the Housing Act 1988;][2]

'the immigration rules' means the rules laid down as mentioned in section 3(2) of the Immigration Act 1971 (general provisions for regulation and control).

AMENDMENT

[1] Words inserted: Housing and Regeneration Act 2008 (Consequential Provisions) (No 2) Order 2010, SI 2010/671, art 4, Sch 1, para 29.

[2] Words inserted: Allocation of Housing (England) (Amendment) (Family Intervention Tenancies) Regulations 2008, SI 2008/3015, reg 2(1), (2).

3 Cases where the provisions of Part 6 of the Act do not apply

(1) The provisions of Part 6 of the Act about the allocation of housing accommodation do not apply in the following cases.

(2) They do not apply where a local housing authority secures the provision of suitable alternative accommodation under section 39 of the Land Compensation Act 1973 (duty to rehouse residential occupiers).

(3) They do not apply in relation to the grant of a secure tenancy under sections 554 and 555 of the Housing Act 1985 (grant of tenancy to former owner-occupier or statutory tenant of defective dwelling-house).

[(4) They do not apply in relation to the allocation of housing accommodation by a local housing authority to a person who lawfully occupies accommodation let on a family intervention tenancy.][1]

[1] Words inserted: SI 2008/3015, reg 2(1), (3).

4 Classes prescribed under section 160A(3) who are eligible persons

AMENDMENT

Regulation revoked: SI 2006/1294, reg 7, Sch, with effect from 1 June 2006, subject to transitional provisions see SI 2006/1294, reg 8 (see Appendix 2).

5 Classes prescribed under section 160A(5) who are ineligible persons

AMENDMENT

Regulation revoked: SI 2006/1294, reg 7, Sch, with effect from 1 June 2006, subject to transitional provisions see SI 2006/1294, reg 8 (see Appendix 2).

6 Revocation

The Allocation of Housing (England) Regulations 2000 are revoked.

Allocation of Housing (Qualification Criteria for Armed Forces) (England) Regulations 2012

SI 2012/1869

Made	*16th July 2012*
Laid before Parliament	*19th July 2012*
Coming into force	*24th August 2012*

1 Citation and commencement

(1) These Regulations may be cited as the Allocation of Housing (Qualification Criteria for Armed Forces) (England) Regulations 2012.

(2) These Regulations come into force on 24th August 2012.

2 Interpretation

In these Regulations –

"the 1996 Act" means the Housing Act 1996;
"local connection" has the meaning given by section 199 of the 1996 Act; and
"regular forces" and "reserve forces" have the meanings given by section 374 of the Armed Forces Act 2006.

3 Criterion that may not be used in deciding what classes of persons are not qualifying persons

(1) In deciding what classes of persons are not qualifying persons under section 160ZA(7) of the 1996 Act, a local housing authority in England may not use the criterion set out in paragraph (2).

(2) The criterion is that a relevant person must have a local connection to the district of a local housing authority.

(3) A relevant person is a person who –

(a) is serving in the regular forces or who has served in the regular forces within five years of the date of their application for an allocation of housing under Part 6 of the 1996 Act;

(b) has recently ceased, or will cease to be entitled, to reside in accommodation provided by the Ministry of Defence following the death of that person's spouse or civil partner where –
(i) the spouse or civil partner has served in the regular forces; and
(ii) their death was attributable (wholly or partly) to that service; or

(c) is serving or has served in the reserve forces and who is suffering from a serious injury, illness or disability which is attributable (wholly or partly) to that service.

Housing Act 1996 (Additional Preference for Armed Forces) (England) Regulations 2012

SI 2012/****

Made   2012

Coming into force in accordance
with regulation 1

Appendix 1
England: Allocation

The Secretary of State makes the following Regulations in exercise of the powers conferred by section 166A(7) of the Housing Act 1996.

In accordance with section 172(2) of the Housing Act 1996 a draft of this instrument has been laid before and approved by a resolution of each House of Parliament.

1. Citation and commencement

These Regulations may be cited as the Housing Act 1996 (Additional Preference for Armed Forces) (England) Regulations 2012 and come into force on the day after the day on which they are made.

2. Amendment of section 166A(3) of the Housing Act 1996

Section 166A(3) of the Housing Act 1996 (Allocation in accordance with allocation scheme: England) is amended as follows–

(a) in the sentence following the end of paragraph (e) (beginning with "The scheme may also be framed") for "people within this subsection" substitute "people within one or more of paragraphs (a) to (e)";

(b) at the end of that sentence, insert –

'The scheme must be framed so as to give additional preference to a person with urgent housing needs who falls within one or more of paragraphs (a) to (e) and who –

(i)   is serving in the regular forces and is suffering from a serious injury, illness or disability which is attributable (wholly or partly) to the person's service,

(ii) formerly served in the regular forces,

(iii) has recently ceased, or will cease to be entitled, to reside in accommodation provided by the Ministry of Defence following the death of that person's spouse or civil partner who has served in the regular forces and whose death was attributable (wholly or partly) to that service, or

(iv) is serving or has served in the reserve forces and is suffering from a serious injury, illness or disability which is attributable (wholly or partly) to the person's service.

For this purpose "the regular forces" and "the reserve forces" have the meanings given by section 374 of the Armed Forces Act 2006.'

Appendix 2

ENGLAND: HOMELESSNESS

Housing Act 1996

1996 c 52

CONTENTS

PART 7
HOMELESSNESS

Homelessness and threatened homelessness

Appendix 2
England: Homelessness

PART 7
HOMELESSNESS

Homelessness and threatened homelessness

175 Homelessness and threatened homelessness

(1)   A person is homeless if he has no accommodation available for his occupation, in the United Kingdom or elsewhere, which he –

(a)   is entitled to occupy by virtue of an interest in it or by virtue of an order of a court,

(b)   has an express or implied licence to occupy, or

(c)   occupies as a residence by virtue of any enactment or rule of law giving him the right to remain in occupation or restricting the right of another person to recover possession.

(2)   A person is also homeless if he has accommodation but –

(a)   he cannot secure entry to it, or

(b)   it consists of a moveable structure, vehicle or vessel designed or adapted for human habitation and there is no place where he is entitled or permitted both to place it and to reside in it.

(3)   A person shall not be treated as having accommodation unless it is accommodation which it would be reasonable for him to continue to occupy.

(4)   A person is threatened with homelessness if it is likely that he will become homeless within 28 days.

176 Meaning of accommodation available for occupation

Accommodation shall be regarded as available for a person's occupation only if it is available for occupation by him together with –

(a)   any other person who normally resides with him as a member of his family, or

(b)   any other person who might reasonably be expected to reside with him.

References in this Part to securing that accommodation is available for a person's occupation shall be construed accordingly.

177 Whether it is reasonable to continue to occupy accommodation

(1)   It is not reasonable for a person to continue to occupy accommodation if it is probable that this will lead to domestic violence [or other violence][1] against him, or against –

(a)   a person who normally resides with him as a member of his family, or

(b)   any other person who might reasonably be expected to reside with him.

[(1A)   For this purpose 'violence' means

(a)   violence from another person; or

(b)   threats of violence from another person which are likely to be carried out;

and violence is 'domestic violence' if it is from a person who is associated with the victim.]²

(2)   In determining whether it would be, or would have been, reasonable for a person to continue to occupy accommodation, regard may be had to the general circumstances prevailing in relation to housing in the district of the local housing authority to whom he has applied for accommodation or for assistance in obtaining accommodation.

(3)   The Secretary of State may by order specify –

(a)   other circumstances in which it is to be regarded as reasonable or not reasonable for a person to continue to occupy accommodation, and

(b)   other matters to be taken into account or disregarded in determining whether it would be, or would have been, reasonable for a person to continue to occupy accommodation.

AMENDMENT

¹ Words inserted: Homelessness Act 2002, s 10(1)(a).

² Sub-section substituted: Homelessness Act 2002, s 10(1)(b).

178 Meaning of associated person

(1)   For the purposes of this Part, a person is associated with another person if –

(a)   they are or have been married to each other;
[(aa) they are or have been civil partners of each other;]¹
(b)   they are cohabitants or former cohabitants;
(c)   they live or have lived in the same household;
(d)   they are relatives;
(e)   they have agreed to marry one another (whether or not that agreement has been terminated);
[(ea) they have entered into a civil partnership agreement between them (whether or not that agreement has been terminated);]²
(f)   in relation to a child, each of them is a parent of the child or has, or has had, parental responsibility for the child.

(2)   If a child has been adopted or [falls within subsection (2A)]³, two persons are also associated with each other for the purposes of this Part if –

(a)   one is a natural parent of the child or a parent of such a natural parent, and
(b)   the other is the child or a person –
(i)   who has become a parent of the child by virtue of an adoption order or who has applied for an adoption order, or
(ii)   with whom the child has at any time been placed for adoption.

[(2A)   A child falls within this subsection if –

(a)   an adoption agency, within the meaning of section 2 of the Adoption and Children Act 2002, is authorised to place him for adoption under section 19 of that Act (placing children with parental consent) or he has become the subject of an order under section 21 of that Act (placement orders), or

(b)   he is freed for adoption by virtue of an order made –

    (i)   in England and Wales, under section 18 of the Adoption Act 1976,

    (ii)   in Scotland, under section 18 of the Adoption (Scotland) Act 1978, or

    (iii)   in Northern Ireland, under Article 17(1) or 18(1) of the Adoption (Northern Ireland) Order 1987.][4]

(3)   In this section –

['adoption order' means an adoption order within the meaning of section 72(1) of the Adoption Act 1976 or section 46(1) of the Adoption and Children Act 2002;][5]

'child' means a person under the age of 18 years;

['civil partnership agreement' has the meaning given by section 73 of the Civil Partnership Act 2004;][6]

['cohabitants' means –

(a)   a man and a woman who, although not married to each other, are living together as husband and wife, or

(b)   two people of the same sex who, although not civil partners of each other, are living together as if they were civil partners;

and 'former cohabitants' shall be construed accordingly;][7]

'parental responsibility' has the same meaning as in the Children Act 1989; and

'relative', in relation to a person, means –

(a)   the father, mother, stepfather, stepmother, son, daughter, stepson, stepdaughter, grandmother, grandfather, grandson or grand-daughter of that person or of that person's [spouse, civil partner, former spouse or former civil partner],[8] or

(b)   the brother, sister, uncle, aunt, niece or nephew (whether of the full blood or of the half blood or by [marriage or civil partnership])[9] of that person or of that person's [spouse, civil partner, former spouse or former civil partner],[10]

and includes, in relation to a person who is living or has lived with another person as husband and wife, a person who would fall within paragraph (a) or (b) if the parties were married to each other.

AMENDMENT

[1] Sub-section inserted: Civil Partnership Act 2004, s 81, Sch 8, para 61(1), (2).

[2] Sub-section inserted: Civil Partnership Act 2004, s 81, Sch 8, para 61(1), (3).

[3] Words substituted: Adoption and Children Act 2002, s 139(1), Sch 3, paras 89, 90.

[4] Sub-section inserted: Adoption and Children Act 2002, s 139(1), Sch 3, paras 89, 91.

[5] Definition substituted: Adoption and Children Act 2002, s 139(1), Sch 3, paras 89, 92.

Appendix 2
England: Homelessness

[6] Definition inserted: Civil Partnership Act 2004, s 81, Sch 8, para 61(1), (4).

[7] Definition substituted: Civil Partnership Act 2004, s 81, Sch 8, para 61(1), (5).

[8] Words substituted: Civil Partnership Act 2004, s 81, Sch 8, para 61(1), (6).

[9] Words substituted: Civil Partnership Act 2004, s 81, Sch 8, para 61(1), (7).

[10] Words substituted: Civil Partnership Act 2004, s 81, Sch 8, para 61(1), (6).

General functions in relation to homelessness or threatened homelessness

179 Duty of local housing authority to provide advisory services

(1) Every local housing authority shall secure that advice and information about homelessness, and the prevention of homelessness, is available free of charge to any person in their district.

(2) The authority may give to any person by whom such advice and information is provided on behalf of the authority assistance by way of grant or loan.

(3) A local housing authority may also assist any such person –

    (a) by permitting him to use premises belonging to the authority,

    (b) by making available furniture or other goods, whether by way of gift, loan or otherwise, and

    (c) by making available the services of staff employed by the authority.

180 Assistance for voluntary organisations

(1) The Secretary of State or a local housing authority may give assistance by way of grant or loan to voluntary organisations concerned with homelessness or matters relating to homelessness.

(2) A local housing authority may also assist any such organisation –

    (a) by permitting them to use premises belonging to the authority,

    (b) by making available furniture or other goods, whether by way of gift, loan or otherwise, and

    (c) by making available the services of staff employed by the authority.

(3) A 'voluntary organisation' means a body (other than a public or local authority) whose activities are not carried on for profit.

181 Terms and conditions of assistance

(1) This section has effect as to the terms and conditions on which assistance is given under section 179 or 180.

(2) Assistance shall be on such terms, and subject to such conditions, as the person giving the assistance may determine.

(3) No assistance shall be given unless the person to whom it is given undertakes –

(a)   to use the money, furniture or other goods or premises for a specified purpose, and

(b)   to provide such information as may reasonably be required as to the manner in which the assistance is being used.

The person giving the assistance may require such information by notice in writing, which shall be complied with within 21 days beginning with the date on which the notice is served.

(4)   The conditions subject to which assistance is given shall in all cases include conditions requiring the person to whom the assistance is given –

(a)   to keep proper books of account and have them audited in such manner as may be specified,

(b)   to keep records indicating how he has used the money, furniture or other goods or premises, and

(c)   to submit the books of account and records for inspection by the person giving the assistance.

(5)   If it appears to the person giving the assistance that the person to whom it was given has failed to carry out his undertaking as to the purpose for which the assistance was to be used, he shall take all reasonable steps to recover from that person an amount equal to the amount of the assistance.

(6)   He must first serve on the person to whom the assistance was given a notice specifying the amount which in his opinion is recoverable and the basis on which that amount has been calculated.

182 Guidance by the Secretary of State

(1)   In the exercise of their functions relating to homelessness and the prevention of homelessness, a local housing authority or social services authority shall have regard to such guidance as may from time to time be given by the Secretary of State.

(2)   The Secretary of State may give guidance either generally or to specified descriptions of authorities.

Application for assistance in case of homelessness or threatened homelessness

183 Application for assistance

(1)   The following provisions of this Part apply where a person applies to a local housing authority for accommodation, or for assistance in obtaining accommodation, and the authority have reason to believe that he is or may be homeless or threatened with homelessness.

(2)   In this Part –

'applicant' means a person making such an application,

'assistance under this Part' means the benefit of any function under the following provisions of this Part relating to accommodation or assistance in obtaining accommodation, and 'eligible for assistance' means not excluded from such assistance by section 185 (persons from abroad not eligible for housing assistance) [or section 186 (asylum seekers and their dependants)][1].

(3)   Nothing in this section or the following provisions of this Part affects a person's entitlement to advice and information under section 179 (duty to provide advisory services).

AMENDMENT

[1] Words repealed: Immigration and Asylum Act 1999, s 169(1), (3), Sch 14, para 116, Sch 16, as from a date to be appointed.

184 Inquiry into cases of homelessness or threatened homelessness

(1)   If the local housing authority have reason to believe that an applicant may be homeless or threatened with homelessness, they shall make such inquiries as are necessary to satisfy themselves –

   (a)   whether he is eligible for assistance, and
   (b)   if so, whether any duty, and if so what duty, is owed to him under the following provisions of this Part.

(2)   They may also make inquiries whether he has a local connection with the district of another local housing authority in England, Wales or Scotland.

(3)   On completing their inquiries the authority shall notify the applicant of their decision and, so far as any issue is decided against his interests, inform him of the reasons for their decision.

[(3A)   If the authority decide that a duty is owed to the applicant under section 193(2) or 195(2) but would not have done so without having had regard to a restricted person, the notice under subsection (3) must also –

   (a)   inform the applicant that their decision was reached on that basis,
   (b)   include the name of the restricted person,
   (c)   explain why the person is a restricted person, and
   (d)   explain the effect of section 193(7AD) or (as the case may be) section 195(4A).][1]

(4)   If the authority have notified or intend to notify another local housing authority under section 198 (referral of cases), they shall at the same time notify the applicant of that decision and inform him of the reasons for it.

(5)   A notice under subsection (3) or (4) shall also inform the applicant of his right to request a review of the decision and of the time within which such a request must be made (see section 202).

(6)   Notice required to be given to a person under this section shall be given in writing and, if not received by him, shall be treated as having been given to him if it is made available at the authority's office for a reasonable period for collection by him or on his behalf.

[(7)   In this Part 'a restricted person' means a person –

   (a)   who is not eligible for assistance under this Part,

(b)   who is subject to immigration control within the meaning of the Asylum and Immigration Act 1996, and

(c)   either –

    (i)   who does not have leave to enter or remain in the United Kingdom, or

    (ii)   whose leave to enter or remain in the United Kingdom is subject to a condition to maintain and accommodate himself, and any dependants, without recourse to public funds.][2][1]

AMENDMENT

[1] Paragraph inserted: Housing and Regeneration Act 2008, s 314, Sch 15, Pt 1, paras 1, 3(1), (2), with effect from 2 March 2009 (except in relation to applications for an allocation of social housing or housing assistance (homelessness) or for accommodation made before that date) (SI 2009/415, art 2).

[2] Paragraph inserted: Housing and Regeneration Act 2008, s 314, Sch 15, Pt 1, paras 1, 3(1), (3), with effect from 2 March 2009 (except in relation to applications for an allocation of social housing or housing assistance (homelessness) or for accommodation made before that date) (SI 2009/415, art 2).

Eligibility for assistance

185 Persons from abroad not eligible for housing assistance

(1)   A person is not eligible for assistance under this Part if he is a person from abroad who is ineligible for housing assistance.

(2)   A person who is subject to immigration control within the meaning of the Asylum and Immigration Act 1996 is not eligible for housing assistance unless he is of a class prescribed by regulations made by the Secretary of State.

[(2A)   No person who is excluded from entitlement to housing benefit by section 115 of the Immigration and Asylum Act 1999 (exclusion from benefits) shall be included in any class prescribed under subsection (2).][1]

(3)   The Secretary of State may make provision by regulations as to other descriptions of persons who are to be treated for the purposes of this Part as persons from abroad who are ineligible for housing assistance.

(4)   A person from abroad who is not eligible for housing assistance shall be disregarded in determining for the purposes of this Part whether [a person falling within subsection (5)][2] –

(a)   is homeless or threatened with homelessness, or

(b)   has a priority need for accommodation.

[(5)   A person falls within this subsection if the person –

(a)   falls within a class prescribed by regulations made under subsection (2); but

(b)   is not a national of an EEA State or Switzerland][3]

AMENDMENT

[1] Sub-section: substituted by the Homelessness Act 2002, s 18(1), Sch 1, paras 2, 7(1).

[2] Words substituted: Housing and Regeneration Act 2008, s 314, Sch 15, Pt 1, paras 1, 4(1), (2), with effect from 2 March 2009 (except in relation to applications for an allocation of social housing or housing assistance (homelessness) or for accommodation made before that date) (SI 2009/415, art 2).

[3] Sub-section inserted: Housing and Regeneration Act 2008, s 314, Sch 15, Pt 1, paras 1, 4(1), (3), with effect from 2 March 2009 (except in relation to applications for an allocation of social housing or housing assistance (homelessness) or for accommodation made before that date) (SI 2009/415, art 2).

[186 Asylum-seekers and their dependants

(1) An asylum-seeker, or a dependant of an asylum-seeker who is not by virtue of section 185 a person from abroad who is ineligible for housing assistance, is not eligible for assistance under this Part if he has any accommodation in the United Kingdom, however temporary, available for his occupation.

(2) For the purposes of this section a person who makes a claim for asylum –

(a) becomes an asylum-seeker at the time when his claim is recorded by the Secretary of State as having been made, and
(b) ceases to be an asylum-seeker at the time when his claim is recorded by the Secretary of State as having been finally determined or abandoned.

(3) For the purposes of this section a person –

(a) becomes a dependant of an asylum-seeker at the time when he is recorded by the Secretary of State as being a dependant of the asylum-seeker, and
(b) ceases to be a dependant of an asylum-seeker at the time when the person whose dependant he is ceases to be an asylum-seeker or, if it is earlier, at the time when he is recorded by the Secretary of State as ceasing to be a dependant of the asylum-seeker.

(4) In relation to an asylum-seeker, 'dependant' means a person –

(a) who is his spouse or a child of his under the age of eighteen, and
(b) who has neither a right of abode in the United Kingdom nor indefinite leave under the Immigration Act 1971 to enter or remain in the United Kingdom.

(5) In this section a 'claim for asylum' means a claim made by a person that it would be contrary to the United Kingdom's obligations under the Convention relating to the Status of Refugees done at Geneva on 28th July 1951 and the Protocol to that Convention for him to be removed from, or required to leave, the United Kingdom.][1]

AMENDMENT

[1] Section repealed: Immigration and Asylum Act 1999, ss 117(5), 169(3), Sch 16, as from a date to be appointed.

187 Provision of information by Secretary of State

(1)   The Secretary of State shall, at the request of a local housing authority, provide the authority with such information as they may require –

   (a)   as to whether a person is [a person to whom section 115 of the Immigration and Asylum Act 1999 (exclusion from benefits) applies][1], and

   (b)   to enable them to determine whether such a person is eligible for assistance under this Part under section 185 (persons from abroad not eligible for housing assistance).

(2)   Where that information is given otherwise than in writing, the Secretary of State shall confirm it in writing if a written request is made to him by the authority.

(3)   If it appears to the Secretary of State that any application, decision or other change of circumstances has affected the status of a person about whom information was previously provided by him to a local housing authority under this section, he shall inform the authority in writing of that fact, the reason for it and the date on which the previous information became inaccurate.

AMENDMENT

[1] Words substituted: Immigration and Asylum Act 1999, s 117(6).

Interim duty to accommodate

188 Interim duty to accommodate in case of apparent priority need

(1)   If the local housing authority have reason to believe that an applicant may be homeless, eligible for assistance and have a priority need, they shall secure that accommodation is available for his occupation pending a decision as to the duty (if any) owed to him under the following provisions of this Part.

[(1A) But if the local housing authority have reason to believe that the duty under section 193(2) may apply in relation to an applicant in the circumstances referred to in section 195A(1), they shall secure that accommodation is available for the applicant's occupation pending a decision of the kind referred to in subsection (1) regardless of whether the applicant has a priority need.][2]

(2)   The duty under this section arises irrespective of any possibility of the referral of the applicant's case to another local housing authority (see sections 198 to 200).

(3)   The duty ceases when the authority's decision is notified to the applicant, even if the applicant requests a review of the decision (see section 202).

The authority may [secure][1] that accommodation is available for the applicant's occupation pending a decision on a review.

AMENDMENT

[1] Word substituted: Homelessness Act 2002, s 18(1), Sch 1, paras 2, 8.

Appendix 2
England: Homelessness

[2] Sub-section inserted: Localism Act 2011, s 149(1), (2), with effect from 9 November 2012 in relation to England (not yet Wales), Localism Act 2011 (Commencement No 2 and Transitional Provisions) (England) Order 2012. SI 2012/2599.

For England only: Transitional provisions, SI 2012/2599; The amendments made by sections 148 and 149 of the Act do not apply to a case where—(a) a person ('the applicant') has applied to a local housing authority for accommodation, or for assistance in obtaining accommodation, under Part 7 of the 1996 Act; and (b) a duty of the local housing authority to secure that accommodation is available for the applicant's occupation under Part 7 of the 1996 Act including on an interim or temporary basis has arisen and has not ceased, before the commencement date.

189 Priority need for accommodation

(1)   The following have a priority need for accommodation –

- (a)   a pregnant woman or a person with whom she resides or might reasonably be expected to reside;
- (b)   a person with whom dependent children reside or might reasonably be expected to reside;
- (c)   a person who is vulnerable as a result of old age, mental illness or handicap or physical disability or other special reason, or with whom such a person resides or might reasonably be expected to reside;
- (d)   a person who is homeless or threatened with homelessness as a result of an emergency such as flood, fire or other disaster.

(2)   The Secretary of State may by order –

- (a)   specify further descriptions of persons as having a priority need for accommodation, and
- (b)   amend or repeal any part of subsection (1).

(3)   Before making such an order the Secretary of State shall consult such associations representing relevant authorities, and such other persons, as he considers appropriate.

(4)   No such order shall be made unless a draft of it has been approved by resolution of each House of Parliament.

Duties to persons found to be homeless or threatened with homelessness

190 Duties to persons becoming homeless intentionally

(1)   This section applies where the local housing authority are satisfied that an applicant is homeless and is eligible for assistance but are also satisfied that he became homeless intentionally.

(2)   If the authority are satisfied that the applicant has a priority need, they shall –

- (a)   secure that accommodation is available for his occupation for such period as they consider will give him a reasonable opportunity of securing accommodation for his occupation, and
- (b)   provide him with [(or secure that he is provided with) advice and assistance][1] in any attempts he may make to secure that accommodation becomes available for his occupation.

(3)   If they are not satisfied that he has a priority need, they shall provide him with [(or secure that he is provided with) advice and assistance][2] in any attempts he may make to secure that accommodation becomes available for his occupation.

[(4)   The applicant's housing needs shall be assessed before advice and assistance is provided under subsection (2)(b) or (3).

(5)   The advice and assistance provided under subsection (2)(b) or (3) must include information about the likely availability in the authority's district of types of accommodation appropriate to the applicant's housing needs (including, in particular, the location and sources of such types of accommodation).][3]

AMENDMENT

[1] Words substituted: Homelessness Act 2002, s 18(1), Sch 1, paras 2, 9.

[2] Words substituted: Homelessness Act 2002, s 18(1), Sch 1, paras 2, 9.

[3] Sub-sections inserted: Homelessness Act 2002, s 18(1), Sch 1, paras 2, 10.

191   Becoming homeless intentionally

(1)   A person becomes homeless intentionally if he deliberately does or fails to do anything in consequence of which he ceases to occupy accommodation which is available for his occupation and which it would have been reasonable for him to continue to occupy.

(2)   For the purposes of subsection (1) an act or omission in good faith on the part of a person who was unaware of any relevant fact shall not be treated as deliberate.

(3)   A person shall be treated as becoming homeless intentionally if –

(a)   he enters into an arrangement under which he is required to cease to occupy accommodation which it would have been reasonable for him to continue to occupy, and

(b)   the purpose of the arrangement is to enable him to become entitled to assistance under this Part,

and there is no other good reason why he is homeless.

(4)   ...[1]

AMENDMENT

[1] Sub-section repealed: Homelessness Act 2002, s 18(2), Sch 2.

192   Duty to persons not in priority need who are not homeless intentionally

(1)   This section applies where the local housing authority –

(a)   are satisfied that an applicant is homeless and eligible for assistance, and

(b)   are not satisfied that he became homeless intentionally, but are not satisfied that he has a priority need.

(2) The authority shall provide the applicant with [(or secure that he is provided with) advice and assistance]¹ in any attempts he may make to secure that accommodation becomes available for his occupation.

[(3) The authority may secure that accommodation is available for occupation by the applicant.]²

[(4) The applicant's housing needs shall be assessed before advice and assistance is provided under subsection (2).

(5) The advice and assistance provided under subsection (2) must include information about the likely availability in the authority's district of types of accommodation appropriate to the applicant's housing needs (including, in particular, the location and sources of such types of accommodation).]³

AMENDMENT

¹ Words substituted by the Homelessness Act 2002, s 18(1), Sch 1, paras 2, 11.

² Sub-section inserted: Homelessness Act 2002, s 5(1).

³ Sub-sections inserted: Homelessness Act 2002, s 18(1), Sch 1, paras 2, 12.

193 Duty to persons with priority need who are not homeless intentionally

(1) This section applies where the local housing authority are satisfied that an applicant is homeless, eligible for assistance and has a priority need, and are not satisfied that he became homeless intentionally.

...¹

(2) Unless the authority refer the application to another local housing authority (see section 198), they shall secure that accommodation is available for occupation by the applicant.

[(3) The authority are subject to the duty under this section [in a case which is not a restricted case]² until it ceases by virtue of any of the following provisions of this section.]³

*[(3A) The authority shall, on becoming subject to the duty under this section, give the applicant a copy of the statement included in their allocation scheme by virtue of section 167(1A) (policy on offering choice to people allocated housing accommodation under Part 6).]*⁴, ¹⁵

[(3B) In this section 'a restricted case' means a case where the local housing authority would not be satisfied as mentioned in subsection (1) without having had regard to a restricted person.]⁵

(4) ...⁶

(5) The local housing authority shall cease to be subject to the duty under this section if the applicant, having been informed by the authority of the possible consequence of refusal [and of his right to request a review of the suitability of the accommodation],⁷ refuses an offer of accommodation which the authority are

satisfied is suitable for him and the authority notify him that they regard themselves as having discharged their duty under this section.

[(5) The local housing authority shall cease to be subject to the duty under this section if –

    (a)   the applicant, having been informed by the authority of the possible consequence of refusal or acceptance and of the right to request a review of the suitability of the accommodation, refuses an offer of accommodation which the authority are satisfied is suitable for the applicant,

    (b)   that offer of accommodation is not an offer of accommodation under Part 6 or a private rented sector offer, and

    (c)   the authority notify the applicant that they regard themselves as ceasing to be subject to the duty under this section.][16]

(6)   The local housing authority shall cease to be subject to the duty under this section if the applicant –

    (a)   ceases to be eligible for assistance,

    (b)   becomes homeless intentionally from the accommodation made available for his occupation,

    (c)   accepts an offer of accommodation under Part 6 (allocation of housing), or

    [(cc) accepts an offer of an assured tenancy (other than an assured shorthold tenancy) from a private landlord,][8]

    (d)   otherwise voluntarily ceases to occupy as his only or principal home the accommodation made available for his occupation.

[(7)   The local housing authority shall also cease to be subject to the duty under this section if the applicant, having been informed of the possible consequence of refusal [or acceptance][17] and of his right to request a review of the suitability of the accommodation, refuses a final offer of accommodation under Part 6.

(7A)   An offer of accommodation under Part 6 is a final offer for the purposes of subsection (7) if it is made in writing and states that it is a final offer for the purposes of subsection (7).][9]

[(7AA)   *In a restricted case*[18] the authority shall also cease to be subject to the duty under this section if the applicant, having been informed [in writing][19] of the matters mentioned in subsection (7AB) –

    (a)   accepts a *private accommodation offer* [private rented sector offer],[20] or

    (b)   refuses such an offer.

(7AB)   The matters are –

    (a)   the possible consequence of refusal [or acceptance][21] of the offer, and

    (b)   that the applicant has the right to request a review of the suitability of the accommodation[, and

(c)   in a case which is not a restricted case, the effect under section 195A of a further application to a local housing authority within two years of acceptance of the offer.][22]

(7AC)   For the purposes of this section an offer is a *private accommodation offer* [private rented sector offer][23] if –

(a)   it is an offer of an assured shorthold tenancy made by a private landlord to the applicant in relation to any accommodation which is, or may become, available for the applicant's occupation,

(b)   it is made, with the approval of the authority, in pursuance of arrangements made by the authority with the landlord with a view to bringing the authority's duty under this section to an end, and

(c)   the tenancy being offered is a fixed term tenancy (within the meaning of Part 1 of the Housing Act 1988) for a period of at least 12 months.

(7AD)   In a restricted case the authority shall, so far as reasonably practicable, bring their duty under this section to an end as mentioned in subsection (7AA).][10]

[(7B)   The authority shall also cease to be subject to the duty under this section if the applicant accepts a qualifying offer of an assured shorthold tenancy which is made by a private landlord in relation to any accommodation which is, or may become, available for the applicant's occupation.

(7C)   The applicant is free to reject a qualifying offer without affecting the duty owed to him under this section by the authority.

(7D)   For the purposes of subsection (7B) an offer of an assured shorthold tenancy is a qualifying offer if –

(a)   it is made, with the approval of the authority, in pursuance of arrangements made by the authority with the landlord with a view to bringing the authority's duty under this section to an end;

(b)   the tenancy being offered is a fixed term tenancy (within the meaning of Part 1 of the Housing Act 1988 (c 50)); and

(c)   it is accompanied by a statement in writing which states the term of the tenancy being offered and explains in ordinary language that –

(i)   there is no obligation to accept the offer, but

(ii)   if the offer is accepted the local housing authority will cease to be subject to the duty under this section in relation to the applicant.

(7E)   An acceptance of a qualifying offer is only effective for the purposes of subsection (7B) if the applicant signs a statement acknowledging that he has understood the statement mentioned in subsection (7D).[24]

(7F)   The local housing authority shall not –

(a)   make a final offer of accommodation under Part 6 for the purposes of subsection (7); [or][25]

[(ab) approve a *private accommodation offer* [private rented sector offer][26];][11] *or*

(b)   approve an offer of an assured shorthold tenancy for the purposes of subsection (7B),[27]

unless they are satisfied that the accommodation is suitable for the applicant and that *it is reasonable for him to accept the offer* [subsection (8) does not apply to the applicant][28].][12]

(8)   For the purposes of [subsection (7F)][13] *an applicant may reasonably be expected to accept an offer ...*[14] *even though he is under contractual or other obligations in respect of his existing accommodation, provided he is able to bring those obligations to an end before he is required to take up the offer.*

[(8) This subsection applies to an applicant if –

(a)   the applicant is under contractual or other obligations in respect of the applicant's existing accommodation, and
(b)   the applicant is not able to bring those obligations to an end before being required to take up the offer.][29]

(9)   A person who ceases to be owed the duty under this section may make a fresh application to the authority for accommodation or assistance in obtaining accommodation.

[(10) The appropriate authority may provide by regulations that subsection (7AC)(c) is to have effect as if it referred to a period of the length specified in the regulations.

(11) Regulations under subsection (10) –

(a)   may not specify a period of less than 12 months, and
(b)   may not apply to restricted cases.

(12) In subsection (10) 'the appropriate authority' –

(a)   in relation to local housing authorities in England, means the Secretary of State;
(b)   in relation to local housing authorities in Wales, means the Welsh Ministers.][30]

AMENDMENT

[1] Words repealed: Homelessness Act 2002, s 18(2), Sch 2.

[2] Words inserted: Housing and Regeneration Act 2008, s 314, Sch 15, Pt 1, paras 1, 5(1), (2), with effect from 2 March 2009 (except in relation to applications for an allocation of social housing or housing assistance (homelessness) or for accommodation made before that date) (SI 2009/415, art 2).

[3] Sub-section substituted: Homelessness Act 2002, s 6(1); for transitional provision see s 6(2) thereof.

[4] Sub-section inserted: Homelessness Act 2002, s 18(1), Sch 1, paras 2, 13.

[5] Sub-section inserted: Housing and Regeneration Act 2008, s 314, Sch 15, Pt 1, paras 1, 5(1), (3), with effect from 2 March 2009 (except in relation to applications for an allocation of social housing or housing assistance (homelessness) or for accommodation made before that date) (SI 2009/415, art 2).

⁶ Sub-section substituted (by sub-section (3)): Homelessness Act 2002, s 6(1); for transitional provision see s 6(2) thereof.

⁷ Words inserted: Homelessness Act 2002, s 8(1).

⁸ Sub-section inserted: Homelessness Act 2002, s 7(1), (2); for transitional provision see s 7(6) thereof.

⁹ Sub-sections substituted: Homelessness Act 2002, s 7(1), (3); for transitional provision see s 7(6) thereof.

¹⁰ Sub-sections inserted: Housing and Regeneration Act 2008, s 314, Sch 15, Pt 1, paras 1, 5(1), (4), with effect from 2 March 2009 (except in relation to applications for an allocation of social housing or housing assistance (homelessness) or for accommodation made before that date) (SI 2009/415, art 2).

¹¹ Words inserted: by the Housing and Regeneration Act 2008, s 314, Sch 15, Pt 1, paras 1, 5(1), (6). Date in force: 2 March 2009 (except in relation to applications for an allocation of social housing or housing assistance (homelessness) or for accommodation made before that date): see SI 2009/415, art 2

¹² Sub-sections inserted: Homelessness Act 2002, s 7(1), (4); for transitional provision see s 7(6) thereof.

¹³ Words substituted: Homelessness Act 2002, s 7(1), (5); for transitional provision see s 7(6) thereof.

¹⁴ Words repealed: Homelessness Act 2002, ss 7(1), (5), 18(2), Sch 2; for transitional provision see s 7(6) thereof.

¹⁵ Sub-section (3A) repealed: Localism Act 2011, ss 148(1), (2), 237, Sch 25, Pt 22, with effect from 9 November 2012 in relation to England (not yet Wales), Localism Act 2011 (Commencement No 2 and Transitional Provisions) (England) Order 2012. SI 2012/2599.

¹⁶ Sub-section (5) in italics substituted by subsection (5) in square brackets: Localism Act 2011, s 148(1), (3), with effect from 9 November 2012 in relation to England (not yet Wales), Localism Act 2011 (Commencement No 2 and Transitional Provisions) (England) Order 2012. SI 2012/2599.

¹⁷ Words inserted: Localism Act 2011, s 148(1), (4), with effect from 9 November 2012 in relation to England (not yet Wales), Localism Act 2011 (Commencement No 2 and Transitional Provisions) (England) Order 2012 (SI 2012/2599).

¹⁸ Words repealed: Localism Act 2011, ss 148(1), (5)(a), 237, Sch 25, Pt 22, with effect from 9 November 2012 in relation to England (not yet Wales), Localism Act 2011 (Commencement No 2 and Transitional Provisions) (England) Order 2012 (SI 2012/2599).

¹⁹ Words inserted: Localism Act 2011, s 148(1), (5)(b), with effect from 9 November 2012 in relation to England (not yet Wales), Localism Act 2011 (Commencement No 2 and Transitional Provisions) (England) Order 2012 (SI 2012/2599).

²⁰ Words in italics substituted by those in square brackets: Localism Act 2011, s 148(1), (5)(c), with effect from 9 November 2012 in relation to England (not yet Wales), Localism Act 2011 (Commencement No 2 and Transitional Provisions) (England) Order 2012 (SI 2012/2599).

²¹ Words inserted: Localism Act 2011, s 148(1), (6)(a), with effect from 9 November 2012 in relation to England (not yet Wales), Localism Act 2011 (Commencement No 2 and Transitional Provisions) (England) Order 2012 (SI 2012/2599).

²² Paragraph inserted: Localism Act 2011, s 148(1), (6)(b), with effect from 9 November 2012 in relation to England (not yet Wales), Localism Act 2011 (Commencement No 2 and Transitional Provisions) (England) Order 2012 (SI 2012/2599).

[23] Words in italics substituted by those in square brackets: Localism Act 2011, s 148(1), (7), with effect from 9 November 2012 in relation to England (not yet Wales), Localism Act 2011 (Commencement No 2 and Transitional Provisions) (England) Order 2012 (SI 2012/2599).

[24] Sub-sections (7B) to (7E) repealed: Localism Act 2011, ss 148(1), (8), 237, Sch 25, Pt 22, with effect from 9 November 2012 in relation to England (not yet Wales), Localism Act 2011 (Commencement No 2 and Transitional Provisions) (England) Order 2012 (SI 2012/2599).

[25] Word inserted: Localism Act 2011, ss 148(1), (9)(a), with effect from 9 November 2012 in relation to England (not yet Wales), Localism Act 2011 (Commencement No 2 and Transitional Provisions) (England) Order 2012 (SI 2012/2599).

[26] Words in italics substituted by words in square brackets: Localism Act 2011, ss 148(1), (9)(b), with effect from 9 November 2012 in relation to England (not yet Wales), Localism Act 2011 (Commencement No 2 and Transitional Provisions) (England) Order 2012 (SI 2012/2599).

[27] Paragraph and the word 'or' repealed: Localism Act 2011, ss 148(1), (8), 237, Sch 25, Pt 22, with effect from 9 November 2012 in relation to England (not yet Wales), Localism Act 2011 (Commencement No 2 and Transitional Provisions) (England) Order 2012 (SI 2012/2599).

[28] Words in italics substituted by words in square brackets: Localism Act 2011, ss 148(1), (9)(d), with effect from 9 November 2012 in relation to England (not yet Wales), Localism Act 2011 (Commencement No 2 and Transitional Provisions) (England) Order 2012 (SI 2012/2599).

[29] Sub-section (8) in italics substituted for that in square brackets: Localism Act 2011, ss 148(1), (10), with effect from 9 November 2012 in relation to England (not yet Wales), Localism Act 2011 (Commencement No 2 and Transitional Provisions) (England) Order 2012 (SI 2012/2599).

[30] Sub-sections inserted: Localism Act 2011, ss 148(1), (11), with effect from 9 November 2012 in relation to England (not yet Wales), Localism Act 2011 (Commencement No 2 and Transitional Provisions) (England) Order 2012 (SI 2012/2599).

For England only: Transitional provisions, SI 2012/2599; The amendments made by sections 148 and 149 of the Act do not apply to a case where—(a) a person ('the applicant') has applied to a local housing authority for accommodation, or for assistance in obtaining accommodation, under Part 7 of the 1996 Act; and (b) a duty of the local housing authority to secure that accommodation is available for the applicant's occupation under Part 7 of the 1996 Act including on an interim or temporary basis has arisen and has not ceased, before the commencement date.

194 ...[1]

AMENDMENT

[1] Section repealed: Homelessness Act 2002, ss 6(3), 18(2), Sch 2; for transitional provision see s 6(4) thereof.

195 Duties in case of threatened homelessness

(1) This section applies where the local housing authority are satisfied that an applicant is threatened with homelessness and is eligible for assistance.

(2) If the authority –

(a) are satisfied that he has a priority need, and
(b) are not satisfied that he became threatened with homelessness intentionally,

they shall take reasonable steps to secure that accommodation does not cease to be available for his occupation.

...¹

(3)   Subsection (2) does not affect any right of the authority, whether by virtue of a contract, enactment or rule of law, to secure vacant possession of any accommodation.

[(3A)   The authority shall, on becoming subject to the duty under this section [in a case which is not a restricted threatened homelessness case]², give the applicant a copy of the statement included in their allocation scheme by virtue of section 167(1A) (policy on offering choice to people allocated housing accommodation under Part 6).]³, ¹²

(4)   Where[, in a case which is not a restricted threatened homelessness case,]⁴ in pursuance of the duty under subsection (2) the authority secure that accommodation other than that occupied by the applicant when he made his application is available for occupation by him, the provisions of section 193(3) to (9) (period for which duty owed) ...⁵ apply, with any necessary modifications, in relation to the duty under this section as they apply in relation to the duty under section 193 [in a case which is not a restricted case (within the meaning of that section)]⁶.

[(4A)   Where, in a restricted threatened homelessness case, in pursuance of the duty under subsection (2) the authority secure that accommodation other than that occupied by the applicant when he made his application is available for occupation by him, the provisions of section 193(3) to (9) (period for which duty owed) apply, with any necessary modifications, in relation to the duty under this section as they apply in relation to the duty under section 193 in a restricted case (within the meaning of that section).

(4B)   In subsections *(3A)   to* [(4) and]¹³ (4A) 'a restricted threatened homelessness case' means a case where the local housing authority would not be satisfied as mentioned in subsection (1) without having had regard to a restricted person.]⁷

(5)   If the authority –

  (a)   are not satisfied that the applicant has a priority need, or
  (b)   are satisfied that he has a priority need but are also satisfied that he became threatened with homelessness intentionally,

they shall [provide him with (or secure that he is provided with) advice and assistance]⁸ in any attempts he may make to secure that accommodation does not cease to be available for his occupation.

[(6)   The applicant's housing needs shall be assessed before advice and assistance is provided under subsection (5).

(7)   The advice and assistance provided under subsection (5) must include information about the likely availability in the authority's district of types of accommodation appropriate to the applicant's housing needs (including, in particular, the location and sources of such types of accommodation).]⁹

[(8) If the authority decide that they owe the applicant the duty under subsection (5) by virtue of paragraph (b) of that subsection, they may, pending a decision on a review of that decision –

(a)   secure that accommodation does not cease to be available for his occupation; and

(b)   if he becomes homeless, secure that accommodation is so available.][10]

[(9)   If the authority –

(a)   are not satisfied that the applicant has a priority need; and

(b)   are not satisfied that he became threatened with homelessness intentionally,

the authority may take reasonable steps to secure that accommodation does not cease to be available for the applicant's occupation.][11]

AMENDMENT

[1] Words repealed: Homelessness Act 2002, s 18(2), Sch 2.

[2] Words inserted: Housing and Regeneration Act 2008, s 314, Sch 15, Pt 1, paras 1, 6(1), (2), with effect from 2 March 2009 (except in relation to applications for an allocation of social housing or housing assistance (homelessness) or for accommodation made before that date) (SI 2009/415, art 2).

[3] Sub-section inserted: Homelessness Act 2002, s 18(1), Sch 1, paras 2, 14(a).

[4] Words inserted: Housing and Regeneration Act 2008, s 314, Sch 15, Pt 1, paras 1, 6(1), (3)(a), with effect from 2 March 2009 (except in relation to applications for an allocation of social housing or housing assistance (homelessness) or for accommodation made before that date) (SI 2009/415, art 2).

[5] Words repealed: Homelessness Act 2002, s 18(2), Sch 2.

[6] Words inserted: Housing and Regeneration Act 2008, s 314, Sch 15, Pt 1, paras 1, 6(1), (3)(b), with effect from 2 March 2009 (except in relation to applications for an allocation of social housing or housing assistance (homelessness) or for accommodation made before that date) (SI 2009/415, art 2).

[7] Words inserted: Housing and Regeneration Act 2008, s 314, Sch 15, Pt 1, paras 1, 6(1), (4), with effect from 2 March 2009 (except in relation to applications for an allocation of social housing or housing assistance (homelessness) or for accommodation made before that date) (SI 2009/415, art 2).

[8] Words substituted: Homelessness Act 2002, s 18(1), Sch 1, paras 2, 14(b).

[9] Sub-sections inserted: Homelessness Act 2002, s 18(1), Sch 1, paras 2, 14(c).

[10] Sub-section inserted: Homelessness Act 2002, s 18(1), Sch 1, paras 2, 14(d).

[11] Sub-section inserted: Homelessness Act 2002, s 5(2).

[12] Sub-section repealed: Localism Act 2011, ss 149(1), (3)(a), 237, Sch 25, Pt 22, with effect from 9 November 2012 in relation to England (not yet Wales), Localism Act 2011 (Commencement No 2 and Transitional Provisions) (England) Order 2012 (SI 2012/2599).

[13] Words in italics substituted by words in square brackets: Localism Act 2011, s 149(1), (3)(b), with effect from 9 November 2012 in relation to England (not yet Wales), Localism Act 2011 (Commencement No 2 and Transitional Provisions) (England) Order 2012 (SI 2012/2599).

Appendix 2
England: Homelessness

For England only: Transitional provisions, SI 2012/2599; The amendments made by sections 148 and 149 of the Act do not apply to a case where—(a) a person ('the applicant') has applied to a local housing authority for accommodation, or for assistance in obtaining accommodation, under Part 7 of the 1996 Act; and (b) a duty of the local housing authority to secure that accommodation is available for the applicant's occupation under Part 7 of the 1996 Act including on an interim or temporary basis has arisen and has not ceased, before the commencement date.

[195A   Re-application after private rented sector offer

(1) If within two years beginning with the date on which an applicant accepts an offer under section 193(7AA) (private rented sector offer), the applicant re-applies for accommodation, or for assistance in obtaining accommodation, and the local housing authority –

(a)   is satisfied that the applicant is homeless and eligible for assistance, and

(b)   is not satisfied that the applicant became homeless intentionally,

the duty under section 193(2) applies regardless of whether the applicant has a priority need.

(2) For the purpose of subsection (1), an applicant in respect of whom a valid notice under section 21 of the Housing Act 1988 (orders for possession on expiry or termination of assured shorthold tenancy) has been given is to be treated as homeless from the date on which that notice expires.

(3) If within two years beginning with the date on which an applicant accepts an offer under section 193(7AA), the applicant re-applies for accommodation, or for assistance in obtaining accommodation, and the local housing authority –

(a)   is satisfied that the applicant is threatened with homelessness and eligible for assistance, and

(b)   is not satisfied that the applicant became threatened with homelessness intentionally,

the duty under section 195(2) applies regardless of whether the applicant has a priority need.

(4) For the purpose of subsection (3), an applicant in respect of whom a valid notice under section 21 of the Housing Act 1988 has been given is to be treated as threatened with homelessness from the date on which that notice is given.

(5) Subsection (1) or (3) does not apply to a case where the local housing authority would not be satisfied as mentioned in that subsection without having regard to a restricted person.

(6) Subsection (1) or (3) does not apply to a re-application by an applicant for accommodation, or for assistance in obtaining accommodation, if the immediately preceding application made by that applicant was one to which subsection (1) or (3) applied.][1]

AMENDMENT

[1] Section inserted: Localism Act 2011, s 149(1), (4) with effect from 9 November 2012 in relation to England (not yet Wales), Localism Act 2011 (Commencement No 2 and Transitional Provisions) (England) Order 2012. SI 2012/2599.

For England only:Transitional provisions, SI 2012/2599; The amendments made by sections 148 and 149 of the Act do not apply to a case where—(a) a person ('the applicant') has applied to a local housing authority for accommodation, or for assistance in obtaining accommodation, under Part 7 of the 1996 Act; and (b) a duty of the local housing authority to secure that accommodation is available for the applicant's occupation under Part 7 of the 1996 Act including on an interim or temporary basis has arisen and has not ceased, before the commencement date.

196 Becoming threatened with homelessness intentionally

(1) A person becomes threatened with homelessness intentionally if he deliberately does or fails to do anything the likely result of which is that he will be forced to leave accommodation which is available for his occupation and which it would have been reasonable for him to continue to occupy.

(2) For the purposes of subsection (1) an act or omission in good faith on the part of a person who was unaware of any relevant fact shall not be treated as deliberate.

(3) A person shall be treated as becoming threatened with homelessness intentionally if –

    (a)   he enters into an arrangement under which he is required to cease to occupy accommodation which it would have been reasonable for him to continue to occupy, and

    (b)   the purpose of the arrangement is to enable him to become entitled to assistance under this Part,

and there is no other good reason why he is threatened with homelessness.

(4) ...[1]

AMENDMENT

[1] Sub-section repealed: Homelessness Act 2002, s 18(2), Sch 2.

197 ...[1]

AMENDMENT

[1] Section repealed: Homelessness Act 2002, ss 9(1), 18(2), Sch 2; for transitional provision see s 9(2), (3) thereof.

Referral to another local housing authority

198 Referral of case to another local housing authority

(1) If the local housing authority would be subject to the duty under section 193 (accommodation for those with priority need who are not homeless intentionally) but consider that the conditions are met for referral of the case to another local housing authority, they may notify that other authority of their opinion.

...¹

(2) The conditions for referral of the case to another authority are met if –

 (a) neither the applicant nor any person who might reasonably be
      expected to reside with him has a local connection with the district of
      the authority to whom his application was made,
 (b) the applicant or a person who might reasonably be expected to reside
      with him has a local connection with the district of that other
      authority, and
 (c) neither the applicant nor any person who might reasonably be
      expected to reside with him will run the risk of domestic violence in
      that other district.

[(2ZA) The conditions for referral of the case to another authority are also
met if –

 (a) the application is made within the period of two years beginning with
      the date on which the applicant accepted an offer from the other
      authority under section 193(7AA) (private rented sector offer), and
 (b) neither the applicant nor any person who might reasonably be
      expected to reside with the applicant will run the risk of domestic
      violence in the district of the other authority.]³

[(2A) But the conditions for referral mentioned in subsection (2) [or (2ZA)]⁴
are not met if –

 (a) the applicant or any person who might reasonably be expected to
      reside with him has suffered violence (other than domestic violence) in
      the district of the other authority; and
 (b) it is probable that the return to that district of the victim will lead to
      further violence of a similar kind against him.

(3) For the purposes of subsections (2)[, (2ZA)]⁵ and (2A)[, *and for the
purpose of subsection (4A)(c)*]⁶ 'violence' means –

 (a) violence from another person; or
 (b) threats of violence from another person which are likely to be carried
      out;

and violence is 'domestic violence' if it is from a person who is associated with
the victim.]²

(4) The conditions for referral of the case to another authority are also met
if –

 (a) the applicant was on a previous application made to that other
      authority placed (in pursuance of their functions under this Part) in
      accommodation in the district of the authority to whom his
      application is now made, and
 (b) the previous application was within such period as may be prescribed
      of the present application.

[*(4A)* The conditions for referral of the case to another authority are also met if –

   (a) the local housing authority to whom the application has been made and another housing authority have agreed that the case should be referred to that other authority;

   (b) that other authority has provided written confirmation of the agreement to the local housing authority; and

   (c) neither the applicant nor any person who might reasonably be expected to reside with him will run the risk of domestic violence in the district of that other authority.

(4B) When reaching the agreement referred to in subsection *(4A)(a)*, the local housing authority to whom the application was made and the other authority need not have regard to –

   (a) any preference that the applicant, or any person who might reasonably be expected to reside with him, may have as to the locality in which the accommodation is to be secured; or

   (b) whether the applicant, or any person who might reasonably be expected to reside with him, has a local connection with the district of any local housing authority.][7]

(5) The question whether the conditions for referral of a case are satisfied shall be decided by agreement between the notifying authority and the notified authority or, in default of agreement, in accordance with such arrangements as the Secretary of State may direct by order.

(6) An order may direct that the arrangements shall be –

   (a) those agreed by any relevant authorities or associations of relevant authorities, or

   (b) in default of such agreement, such arrangements as appear to the Secretary of State to be suitable, after consultation with such associations representing relevant authorities, and such other persons, as he thinks appropriate.

(7) No such order shall be made unless a draft of the order has been approved by a resolution of each House of Parliament.

AMENDMENT

[1] Words repealed: Homelessness Act 2002, s 18(2), Sch 2.

[2] Sub-sections substituted: Homelessness Act 2002, s 10(2).

[3] Sub-section inserted: Localism Act 2011, s 149(1), (5), (6) with effect from 9 November 2012 in relation to England (not yet Wales), Localism Act 2011 (Commencement No 2 and Transitional Provisions) (England) Order 2012 (SI 2012/2599).

[4] Words inserted. Localism Act 2011, s 149(1), (5), (7) with effect from 9 November 2012 in relation to England (not yet Wales), Localism Act 2011 (Commencement No 2 and Transitional Provisions) (England) Order 2012 (SI 2012/2599).

Appendix 2
England: Homelessness

[5] Words inserted: Localism Act 2011, s 149(1), (5), (8) with effect from 9 November 2012 in relation to England (not yet Wales), Localism Act 2011 (Commencement No 2 and Transitional Provisions) (England) Order 2012 (SI 2012/2599).

For England only: Transitional provisions, SI 2012/2599; The amendments made by sections 148 and 149 of the Act do not apply to a case where—(a) a person ('the applicant') has applied to a local housing authority for accommodation, or for assistance in obtaining accommodation, under Part 7 of the 1996 Act; and (b) a duty of the local housing authority to secure that accommodation is available for the applicant's occupation under Part 7 of the 1996 Act including on an interim or temporary basis has arisen and has not ceased, before the commencement date.

MODIFICATION

[6] Original sub-section (3) as modified: SI 1999/3126, art 1(2), 2, 3(a).

[7] Modifying sub-sections 4A and 4B: SI 1999/3126, art 1(2), 2, 3(b).

For England only, this section is modified in relation to asylum-seekers who are eligible for housing assistance as a result of regulations made under s 185(2) of the Housing Act 1996, and who are not made ineligible by s 186 (or any other provision) of that Act: Homelessness (Asylum-Seekers) (Interim Period) (England) Order 1999, SI 1999/3126, arts 1(2), 2, 3. That Order shall cease to have effect on the date on which s 186 of the Housing Act 1996 is repealed by the Immigration and Asylum Act 1999, s 117(5).

199 Local connection

(1) A person has a local connection with the district of a local housing authority if he has a connection with it –

    (a)   because he is, or in the past was, normally resident there, and that residence is or was of his own choice,

    (b)   because he is employed there,

    (c)   because of family associations, or

    (d)   because of special circumstances.

(2) ...[1]

(3) Residence in a district is not of a person's own choice if –

    (a) ...[2]

    (b)   he, or a person who might reasonably be expected to reside with him, becomes resident there because he is detained under the authority of an Act of Parliament.

(4) [In subsections (2) and (3) 'regular armed forces of the Crown' means *the Royal Navy, the regular forces as defined by section 225 of the Army Act 1955* [*or the regular air force as defined by section 223 of the Air Force Act 1955.*][3] [the regular forces as defined by section 374 of the Armed Forces Act 2006.][4]][5]

(5) The Secretary of State may by order specify *other*[6] circumstances in which –

    (a)   a person is not to be treated as employed in a district, or

    (b)   residence in a district is not to be treated as of a person's own choice.

[(6)   A person has a local connection with the district of a local housing authority if he was (at any time) provided with accommodation in that district under section 95 of the Immigration and Asylum Act 1999 (support for asylum-seekers).

(7)   But subsection (6) does not apply –

(a)   to the provision of accommodation for a person in a district of a local housing authority if he was subsequently provided with accommodation in the district of another local housing authority under section 95 of that Act, or

(b)   to the provision of accommodation in an accommodation centre by virtue of section 22 of the Nationality, Immigration and Asylum Act 2002 (c 41) (use of accommodation centres for section 95 support).][7]

AMENDMENT

[1] Sub-section repealed: Housing and Regeneration Act 2008, s 315(a), 321(1), Sch 16. Date in force (in relation to England): 1 December 2008; SI 2008/3068, arts 1(2), 4(2), (10), 5, Schedule; for transitional provisions and savings see arts 6, 9, 10 thereof. Date in force (in relation to Wales): 30 March 2009: see SI 2009/773, art 2.

[2] Paragraph repealed by Housing and Regeneration Act 2008, s 315(b), 321(1), Sch 16. Date in force (in relation to England): 1 December 2008; SI 2008/3068, arts 1(2), 4(2), (10), 5, Schedule; for transitional provisions and savings see arts 6, 9, 10 thereof. Date in force (in relation to Wales): see SI 2009/773, art 2.

[3] Words substituted: Armed Forces Act 2001, s 34, Sch 6, Pt 5, para 30.

[4] Words from 'the Royal Navy' to the end in italics substituted by words in square brackets: Armed Forces Act 2006, s 378(1), Sch 16, para 139, as from a date to be appointed.

[5] Sub-section repealed by Housing and Regeneration Act 2008, s 315(c), 321(1), Sch 16. Date in force (in relation to England for certain purposes): 1 December 2008; SI 2008/3068, arts 1(2), 4(2), (10), 5, Schedule; for transitional provisions and savings see arts 6, 9, 10 thereof. Date in force (in relation to Wales for certain purposes): 30 March 2009: see SI 2009/773, art 2. Date in force (for remaining purposes): to be appointed: see the Housing and Regeneration Act 2008, s 325(3)(b), (4), s 315(b), 321(1), Sch 16.

[6] Word repealed by Housing and Regeneration Act 2008, s 315(d), 321(1), Sch 16. Date in force (in relation to England): 1 December 2008; SI 2008/3068, arts 1(2), 4(2), (10), 5, Schedule; for transitional provisions and savings see arts 6, 9, 10 thereof. Date in force (in relation to Wales): 30 March 2009: see SI 2009/773, art 2.

[7] Sub-sections inserted: Asylum and Immigration (Treatment of Claimants, etc) Act 2004, s 11(1).

200   Duties to the applicant whose case is considered for referral or referred

(1)   Where a local housing authority notify an applicant that they intend to notify or have notified another local housing authority of their opinion that the conditions are met for the referral of his case to that other authority –

(a)   they cease to be subject to any duty under section 188 (interim duty to accommodate in case of apparent priority need), and

(b)   they are not subject to any duty under section 193 (the main housing duty), but they shall secure that accommodation is available for occupation by the applicant until he is notified of the decision whether the conditions for referral of his case are met.

(2) When it has been decided whether the conditions for referral are met, the notifying authority shall notify the applicant of the decision and inform him of the reasons for it.

The notice shall also inform the applicant of his right to request a review of the decision and of the time within which such a request must be made.

[(3) If it is decided that the conditions for referral are not met, the notifying authority are subject to the duty under section 193 (the main housing duty).

(4) If it is decided that those conditions are met, the notified authority are subject to the duty under section 193 (the main housing duty).]¹

(5) The duty under subsection (1), ...² ceases as provided in that subsection even if the applicant requests a review of the authority's decision (see section 202).

The authority may [secure]³ that accommodation is available for the applicant's occupation pending the decision on a review.

(6) Notice required to be given to an applicant under this section shall be given in writing and, if not received by him, shall be treated as having been given to him if it is made available at the authority's office for a reasonable period for collection by him or on his behalf.

AMENDMENT

¹ Sub-sections substituted: Homelessness Act 2002, s 18(1), Sch 1, paras 2, 15(a).

² Words repealed: Homelessness Act 2002, s 18(2), Sch 2.

³ Word substituted: Homelessness Act 2002, s 18(1), Sch 1, paras 2, 15(b).

201 Application of referral provisions to cases arising in Scotland

Sections 198 and 200 (referral of application to another local housing authority and duties to applicant whose case is considered for referral or referred) apply –

  (a) to applications referred by a local authority in Scotland in pursuance of sections 33 and 34 of the Housing (Scotland) Act 1987, and

  (b) to persons whose applications are so transferred,

as they apply to cases arising under this Part (the reference in section 198 to this Part being construed as a reference to Part II of that Act).

Right to request review of decision

202 Right to request review of decision

(1) An applicant has the right to request a review of –

  (a) any decision of a local housing authority as to his eligibility for assistance,

(b)   any decision of a local housing authority as to what duty (if any) is owed to him under sections 190 to 193 and 195 [and 196]¹ (duties to persons found to be homeless or threatened with homelessness),

(c)   any decision of a local housing authority to notify another authority under section 198(1) (referral of cases),

(d)   any decision under section 198(5) whether the conditions are met for the referral of his case,

(e)   any decision under section 200(3) or (4) (decision as to duty owed to applicant whose case is considered for referral or referred), ...²

(f)   any decision of a local housing authority as to the suitability of accommodation offered to him in discharge of their duty under any of the provisions mentioned in paragraph (b) or (e) [or as to the suitability of accommodation offered to him as mentioned in section 193(7)]³ [, or

(g)   any decision of a local housing authority as to the suitability of accommodation offered to him by way of a *private accommodation offer* [private rented sector offer]⁸ (within the meaning of section 193)]⁴.

[(1A) An applicant who is offered accommodation as mentioned in section 193(5)[, (7) or (7AA)]⁵ may under subsection (1)(f) [or (as the case may be) (g)]⁶ request a review of the suitability of the accommodation offered to him whether or not he has accepted the offer.]⁷

(2)   There is no right to request a review of the decision reached on an earlier review.

(3)   A request for review must be made before the end of the period of 21 days beginning with the day on which he is notified of the authority's decision or such longer period as the authority may in writing allow.

(4)   On a request being duly made to them, the authority or authorities concerned shall review their decision.

AMENDMENT

¹ Words substituted: Homelessness Act 2002, s 18(1), Sch 1, paras 2, 16.

² Word repealed: Housing and Regeneration Act 2008, s 321(1), Sch 16.

³ Words inserted: Homelessness Act 2002, s 8(2)(a).

⁴ Sub-section inserted: Housing and Regeneration Act 2008, s 314, Sch 15, Pt 1, paras 1, 7(1), (2). Date in force: 2 March 2009 (except in relation to applications for an allocation of social housing or housing assistance (homelessness) or for accommodation made before that date): see SI 2009/415, art 2.

⁵ Words substituted: Housing and Regeneration Act 2008, s 314, Sch 15, Pt 1, paras 1, 7(1), (3)(a). Date in force: 2 March 2009 (except in relation to applications for an allocation of social housing or housing assistance (homelessness) or for accommodation made before that date): see SI 2009/415, art 2.

[6] Words inserted: Housing and Regeneration Act 2008, Sch 15, Pt 1, paras 1, 7(1), (3)(b). Date in force: 2 March 2009 (except in relation to applications for an allocation of social housing or housing assistance (homelessness) or for accommodation made before that date): see SI 2009/415, art 2.

[7] Sub-section inserted: Homelessness Act 2002, s 8(2)(b).

[8] Words in italics substituted by words in square brackets: Localism Act 2011, s 149(1), (5), (9) with effect from 9 November 2012 in relation to England (not yet Wales), Localism Act 2011 (Commencement No 2 and Transitional Provisions) (England) Order 2012 (SI 2012/2599).

For England only: Transitional provisions, SI 2012/2599; The amendments made by sections 148 and 149 of the Act do not apply to a case where—(a) a person ('the applicant') has applied to a local housing authority for accommodation, or for assistance in obtaining accommodation, under Part 7 of the 1996 Act; and (b) a duty of the local housing authority to secure that accommodation is available for the applicant's occupation under Part 7 of the 1996 Act including on an interim or temporary basis has arisen and has not ceased, before the commencement date.

203 Procedure on a review

(1)   The Secretary of State may make provision by regulations as to the procedure to be followed in connection with a review under section 202.

Nothing in the following provisions affects the generality of this power.

(2)   Provision may be made by regulations –

(a)   requiring the decision on review to be made by a person of appropriate seniority who was not involved in the original decision, and

(b)   as to the circumstances in which the applicant is entitled to an oral hearing, and whether and by whom he may be represented at such a hearing.

(3)   The authority, or as the case may be either of the authorities, concerned shall notify the applicant of the decision on the review.

(4)   If the decision is –

(a)   to confirm the original decision on any issue against the interests of the applicant, or

(b)   to confirm a previous decision –

(i)   to notify another authority under section 198 (referral of cases), or

(ii)   that the conditions are met for the referral of his case,

they shall also notify him of the reasons for the decision.

(5)   In any case they shall inform the applicant of his right to appeal to a county court on a point of law, and of the period within which such an appeal must be made (see section 204).

(6)   Notice of the decision shall not be treated as given unless and until subsection (5), and where applicable subsection (4), is complied with.

(7)   Provision may be made by regulations as to the period within which the review must be carried out and notice given of the decision.

(8)   Notice required to be given to a person under this section shall be given in writing and, if not received by him, shall be treated as having been given if it is made available at the authority's office for a reasonable period for collection by him or on his behalf.

204   Right of appeal to county court on point of law

(1)   If an applicant who has requested a review under section 202 –

(a)   is dissatisfied with the decision on the review, or
(b)   is not notified of the decision on the review within the time prescribed under section 203,

he may appeal to the county court on any point of law arising from the decision or, as the case may be, the original decision.

(2)   An appeal must be brought within 21 days of his being notified of the decision or, as the case may be, of the date on which he should have been notified of a decision on review.

[(2A)   The court may give permission for an appeal to be brought after the end of the period allowed by subsection (2), but only if it is satisfied –

(a)   where permission is sought before the end of that period, that there is a good reason for the applicant to be unable to bring the appeal in time; or
(b)   where permission is sought after that time, that there was a good reason for the applicant's failure to bring the appeal in time and for any delay in applying for permission.]¹

(3)   On appeal the court may make such order confirming, quashing or varying the decision as it thinks fit.

(4)   Where the authority were under a duty under section 188, 190 or 200 to secure that accommodation is available for the applicant's occupation[, or had the power under section 195(8) to do so, they may]² secure that accommodation is so available –

(a)   during the period for appealing under this section against the authority's decision, and
(b)   if an appeal is brought, until the appeal (and any further appeal) is finally determined.

AMENDMENT

¹ Sub-section inserted: Homelessness Act 2002, s 18(1), Sch 1, paras 2, 17(a).

² Words substituted: Homelessness Act 2002, s 18(1), Sch 1, paras 2, 17(b).

[204A   Section 204(4): appeals

(1)   This section applies where an applicant has the right to appeal to the county court against a local housing authority's decision on a review.

(2)   If the applicant is dissatisfied with a decision by the authority –

   (a)   not to exercise their power under section 204(4) ('the section 204(4) power') in his case;

   (b)   to exercise that power for a limited period ending before the final determination by the county court of his appeal under section 204(1) ('the main appeal'); or

   (c)   to cease exercising that power before that time,

he may appeal to the county court against the decision.

(3) An appeal under this section may not be brought after the final determination by the county court of the main appeal.

(4) On an appeal under this section the court –

   (a)   may order the authority to secure that accommodation is available for the applicant's occupation until the determination of the appeal (or such earlier time as the court may specify); and

   (b)   shall confirm or quash the decision appealed against,

and in considering whether to confirm or quash the decision the court shall apply the principles applied by the High Court on an application for judicial review.

(5) If the court quashes the decision it may order the authority to exercise the section 204(4) power in the applicant's case for such period as may be specified in the order.

(6) An order under subsection (5) –

   (a)   may only be made if the court is satisfied that failure to exercise the section 204(4) power in accordance with the order would substantially prejudice the applicant's ability to pursue the main appeal;

   (b)   may not specify any period ending after the final determination by the county court of the main appeal.][1]

AMENDMENT

[1] Section inserted: Homelessness Act 2002, s 11.

Supplementary provisions

205 Discharge of functions: introductory

(1) The following sections have effect in relation to the discharge by a local housing authority of their functions under this Part to secure that accommodation is available for the occupation of a person –

section 206 (general provisions),
   …[1]
section 208 (out-of-area placements),
section 209 (arrangements with private landlord).

(2) In [sections 206 and 208][2] those functions are referred to as the authority's 'housing functions under this Part'.

AMENDMENT

¹ Words repealed: Homelessness Act 2002, s 18(2), Sch 2.

² Words substituted: Homelessness Act 2002, s 18(1), Sch 1, paras 2, 18.

206 Discharge of functions by local housing authorities

(1) A local housing authority may discharge their housing functions under this Part only in the following ways –

    (a)   by securing that suitable accommodation provided by them is available,

    (b)   by securing that he obtains suitable accommodation from some other person, or

    (c)   by giving him such advice and assistance as will secure that suitable accommodation is available from some other person.

[*(1A   In discharging their housing functions under this Part, a local housing authority shall have regard to the desirability, in general, of securing accommodation in areas in which there is a ready supply of accommodation.*]¹

(2) A local housing authority may require a person in relation to whom they are discharging such functions –

    (a)   to pay such reasonable charges as they may determine in respect of accommodation which they secure for his occupation (either by making it available themselves or otherwise), or

    (b)   to pay such reasonable amount as they may determine in respect of sums payable by them for accommodation made available by another person.

MODIFICATION

¹ For England only, this section is modified in relation to asylum-seekers who are eligible for housing assistance as a result of regulations made under s 185(2) of the Housing Act 1996, and who are not made ineligible by s 186 (or any other provision) of that Act: Homelessness (Asylum-Seekers) (Interim Period) (England) Order 1999, SI 1999/3126, arts 1(2), 2, 4. That Order shall cease to have effect on the date on which s 186 of the Housing Act 1996 is repealed by the Immigration and Asylum Act 1999, s 117(5).

207 ...¹

AMENDMENT

¹ Section repealed: Homelessness Act 2002, s 18(2), Sch 2.

208 Discharge of functions: out-of-area placements

(1) So far as reasonably practicable a local housing authority shall in discharging their housing functions under this Part secure that accommodation is available for the occupation of the applicant in their district.

(1A)   Subsection (1) shall not apply where

    (a)   the local housing authority and another housing authority have agreed that the local housing authority may secure that accommodation is

available for the occupation of all or an agreed number of asylum-seekers who are section 185(2) persons in that other authority's district; and

(b)   that other authority has provided written confirmation of the agreement to the local housing authority.][1]

(2)   If they secure that accommodation is available for the occupation of the applicant outside their district, they shall give notice to the local housing authority in whose district the accommodation is situated.

(3)   The notice shall state –

(a)   the name of the applicant,
(b)   the number and description of other persons who normally reside with him as a member of his family or might reasonably be expected to reside with him,
(c)   the address of the accommodation,
(d)   the date on which the accommodation was made available to him, and
(e)   which function under this Part the authority was discharging in securing that the accommodation is available for his occupation.

(4)   The notice must be in writing, and must be given before the end of the period of 14 days beginning with the day on which the accommodation was made available to the applicant.

MODIFICATION

[1] For England only, this section is modified in relation to asylum-seekers who are eligible for housing assistance as a result of regulations made under s 185(2) of the Housing Act 1996, and who are not made ineligible by s 186 (or any other provision) of that Act: Homelessness (Asylum-Seekers) (Interim Period) (England) Order 1999, SI 1999/3126, arts 1(2), 2, 5. That Order shall cease to have effect on the date on which s 186 of the Housing Act 1996 is repealed by the Immigration and Asylum Act 1999, s 117(5).

[209 Discharge of interim duties: arrangements with private landlord]

[(1)   This section applies where in pursuance of any of their housing functions under section 188, 190, 200 or 204(4) (interim duties) a local housing authority make arrangements with a private landlord to provide accommodation.

(2)   A tenancy granted to the applicant in pursuance of the arrangements cannot be an assured tenancy before the end of the period of twelve months beginning with –

(a)   the date on which the applicant was notified of the authority's decision under section 184(3) or 198(5); or
(b)   if there is a review of that decision under section 202 or an appeal to the court under section 204, the date on which he is notified of the decision on review or the appeal is finally determined,

unless, before or during that period, the tenant is notified by the landlord (or in the case of joint landlords, at least one of them) that the tenancy is to be regarded as an assured shorthold tenancy or an assured tenancy other than an assured shorthold tenancy.][1]

AMENDMENT

[1] Section substituted: Homelessness Act 2002, s 18(1), Sch 1, paras 2, 19.

210 Suitability of accommodation

(1) In determining for the purposes of this Part whether accommodation is suitable for a person, the local housing authority shall have regard to *Parts IX, X and XI* [Parts 9 and 10][1] of the Housing Act 1985 (slum clearance; *overcrowding; houses in multiple occupation* [and overcrowding) and Parts 1 to 4 of the Housing Act 2004][2].

[*(1A)   In determining for the purposes of this Part whether accommodation is suitable for an applicant, or any person who might reasonably be expected to reside with him, the local housing authority –*

(*a*)   *shall also have regard to the fact that the accommodation is to be temporary pending the determination of the applicant's claim for asylum; and*

(*b*)   *shall not have regard to any preference that the applicant, or any person who might reasonably be expected to reside with him, may have as to the locality in which the accommodation is to be secured.*][3]

(2)   The Secretary of State may by order specify –

(a)   circumstances in which accommodation is or is not to be regarded as suitable for a person, and

(b)   matters to be taken into account or disregarded in determining whether accommodation is suitable for a person.

AMENDMENT

[1] Words in italics repealed and words in square brackets substituted: Housing Act 2004, s 265(1), Sch 15, paras 40, 43(a).

[2] Words in italics repealed and words in square brackets substituted: Housing Act 2004, s 265(1), Sch 15, paras 40, 43(b).

MODIFICATION

[3] For England only, this section is modified in relation to asylum-seekers who are eligible for housing assistance as a result of regulations made under s 185(2) of the Housing Act 1996, and who are not made ineligible by s 186 (or any other provision) of that Act: Homelessness (Asylum-Seekers) (Interim Period) (England) Order 1999, SI 1999/3126, arts 1(2), 2, 6. That Order shall cease to have effect on the date on which s 186 of the Housing Act 1996 is repealed by the Immigration and Asylum Act 1999, s 117(5).

211 Protection of property of homeless persons and persons threatened with homelessness

(1)   This section applies where a local housing authority have reason to believe that -

(a)   there is danger of loss of, or damage to, any personal property of an applicant by reason of his inability to protect it or deal with it, and

(b)   no other suitable arrangements have been or are being made.

(2)   If the authority have become subject to a duty towards the applicant under –

section 188 (interim duty to accommodate),
section 190, 193 or 195 (duties to persons found to be homeless or threatened with homelessness), or
section 200 (duties to applicant whose case is considered for referral or referred),

then, whether or not they are still subject to such a duty, they shall take reasonable steps to prevent the loss of the property or prevent or mitigate damage to it.

(3)   If they have not become subject to such a duty, they may take any steps they consider reasonable for that purpose.

(4)   The authority may decline to take action under this section except upon such conditions as they consider appropriate in the particular case, which may include conditions as to –

(a)   the making and recovery by the authority of reasonable charges for the action taken, or
(b)   the disposal by the authority, in such circumstances as may be specified, of property in relation to which they have taken action.

(5)   References in this section to personal property of the applicant include personal property of any person who might reasonably be expected to reside with him.

(6)   Section 212 contains provisions supplementing this section.

212 Protection of property: supplementary provisions

(1)   The authority may for the purposes of section 211 (protection of property of homeless persons or persons threatened with homelessness) –

(a)   enter, at all reasonable times, any premises which are the usual place of residence of the applicant or which were his last usual place of residence, and
(b)   deal with any personal property of his in any way which is reasonably necessary, in particular by storing it or arranging for its storage.

(2)   Where the applicant asks the authority to move his property to a particular location nominated by him, the authority –

(a)   may, if it appears to them that his request is reasonable, discharge their responsibilities under section 211 by doing as he asks, and
(b)   having done so, have no further duty or power to take action under that section in relation to that property.

If such a request is made, the authority shall before complying with it inform the applicant of the consequence of their doing so.

(3)   If no such request is made (or, if made, is not acted upon) the authority cease to have any duty or power to take action under section 211 when, in their

opinion, there is no longer any reason to believe that there is a danger of loss of or damage to a person's personal property by reason of his inability to protect it or deal with it.

But property stored by virtue of their having taken such action may be kept in store and any conditions upon which it was taken into store continue to have effect, with any necessary modifications.

(4)   Where the authority –

(a)   cease to be subject to a duty to take action under section 211 in respect of an applicant's property, or

(b)   cease to have power to take such action, having previously taken such action,

they shall notify the applicant of that fact and of the reason for it.

(5)   The notification shall be given to the applicant –

(a)   by delivering it to him, or

(b)   by leaving it, or sending it to him, at his last known address.

(6)   References in this section to personal property of the applicant include personal property of any person who might reasonably be expected to reside with him.

213 Co-operation between relevant housing authorities and bodies

(1)   Where a local housing authority –

(a)   request another relevant housing authority or body, in England, Wales or Scotland, to assist them in the discharge of their functions under this Part, or

(b)   request a social services authority, in England, Wales or Scotland, to exercise any of their functions in relation to a case which the local housing authority are dealing with under this Part,

the authority or body to whom the request is made shall co-operate in rendering such assistance in the discharge of the functions to which the request relates as is reasonable in the circumstances.

(2)   In subsection (1)(a) 'relevant housing authority or body' means –

(a)   in relation to England and Wales, a local housing authority, a new town corporation, [a private registered provider of social housing][1] a registered social landlord or a housing action trust;

(b)   in relation to Scotland, a local authority, a development corporation, a registered housing association or Scottish Homes.

Expressions used in paragraph (a) have the same meaning as in the Housing Act 1985; and expressions used in paragraph (b) have the same meaning as in the Housing (Scotland) Act 1987.

(3)   Subsection (1) above applies to a request by a local authority in Scotland under section 38 of the Housing (Scotland) Act 1987 as it applies to a request

Appendix 2
England: Homelessness

by a local housing authority in England and Wales (the references to this Part being construed, in relation to such a request, as references to Part II of that Act).

AMENDMENT

¹ Words inserted: Housing and Regeneration Act 2008 (Consequential Provisions) Order 2010, SI 2010/886, art 5, Sch 2, paras 81, 103, with effect from 1 April 2010.

[213A Co-operation in certain cases involving children

(1)   This section applies where a local housing authority have reason to believe that an applicant with whom a person under the age of 18 normally resides, or might reasonably be expected to reside –

(a)   may be ineligible for assistance;
(b)   may be homeless and may have become so intentionally; or
(c)   may be threatened with homelessness intentionally.

(2)   A local housing authority shall make arrangements for ensuring that, where this section applies –

(a)   the applicant is invited to consent to the referral of the essential facts of his case to the social services authority for the district of the housing authority (where that is a different authority); and
(b)   if the applicant has given that consent, the social services authority are made aware of those facts and of the subsequent decision of the housing authority in respect of his case.

(3)   Where the local housing authority and the social services authority for a district are the same authority (a 'unitary authority'), that authority shall make arrangements for ensuring that, where this section applies –

(a)   the applicant is invited to consent to the referral to the social services department of the essential facts of his case; and
(b)   if the applicant has given that consent, the social services department is made aware of those facts and of the subsequent decision of the authority in respect of his case.

(4)   Nothing in subsection (2) or (3) affects any power apart from this section to disclose information relating to the applicant's case to the social services authority or to the social services department (as the case may be) without the consent of the applicant.

(5)   Where a social services authority –

(a)   are aware of a decision of a local housing authority that the applicant is ineligible for assistance, became homeless intentionally or became threatened with homelessness intentionally, and
(b)   request the local housing authority to provide them with advice and assistance in the exercise of their social services functions under Part 3 of the Children Act 1989,

the local housing authority shall provide them with such advice and assistance as is reasonable in the circumstances.

(6) A unitary authority shall make arrangements for ensuring that, where they make a decision of a kind mentioned in subsection (5)(a), the housing department provide the social services department with such advice and assistance as the social services department may reasonably request.

(7) In this section, in relation to a unitary authority –

'the housing department' means those persons responsible for the exercise of their housing functions; and

'the social services department' means those persons responsible for the exercise of their social services functions under Part 3 of the Children Act 1989.]¹

AMENDMENT

¹ Section inserted: Homelessness Act 2002, s 12.

General provisions

214 False statements, withholding information and failure to disclose change of circumstances

(1) It is an offence for a person, with intent to induce a local housing authority to believe in connection with the exercise of their functions under this Part that he or another person is entitled to accommodation or assistance in accordance with the provisions of this Part, or is entitled to accommodation or assistance of a particular description –

(a) knowingly or recklessly to make a statement which is false in a material particular, or

(b) knowingly to withhold information which the authority have reasonably required him to give in connection with the exercise of those functions.

(2) If before an applicant receives notification of the local housing authority's decision on his application there is any change of facts material to his case, he shall notify the authority as soon as possible.

The authority shall explain to every applicant, in ordinary language, the duty imposed on him by this subsection and the effect of subsection (3).

(3) A person who fails to comply with subsection (2) commits an offence unless he shows that he was not given the explanation required by that subsection or that he had some other reasonable excuse for non-compliance.

(4) A person guilty of an offence under this section is liable on summary conviction to a fine not exceeding level 5 on the standard scale.

215 Regulations and orders

(1) In this Part 'prescribed' means prescribed by regulations of the Secretary of State.

(2) Regulations or an order under this Part may make different provision for different purposes, including different provision for different areas.

Appendix 2
England: Homelessness

(3) Regulations or an order under this Part shall be made by statutory instrument.

(4) Unless required to be approved in draft, regulations or an order under this Part shall be subject to annulment in pursuance of a resolution of either House of Parliament.

216 Transitional and consequential matters

(1) The provisions of this Part have effect in place of the provisions of Part III of the Housing Act 1985 (housing the homeless) and shall be construed as one with that Act.

(2) Subject to any transitional provision contained in an order under section 232(4) (power to include transitional provision in commencement order), the provisions of this Part do not apply in relation to an applicant whose application for accommodation or assistance in obtaining accommodation was made before the commencement of this Part.

(3) The enactments mentioned in Schedule 17 have effect with the amendments specified there which are consequential on the provisions of this Part.

217 Minor definitions: Part 7

(1) In this Part, subject to subsection (2) –

['private landlord' means a landlord who is not within section 80(1) of the Housing Act 1985 (c 68) (the landlord condition for secure tenancies);]¹
'relevant authority' means a local housing authority or a social services authority; and
'social services authority' means a local authority for the purposes of the Local Authority Social Services Act 1970, as defined in section 1 of that Act.

(2) In this Part, in relation to Scotland –

(a) 'local housing authority' means a local authority within the meaning of the Housing (Scotland) Act 1988, and
(b) 'social services authority' means a local authority for the purposes of the Social Work (Scotland) Act 1968.

(3) References in this Part to the district of a local housing authority –

(a) have the same meaning in relation to an authority in England or Wales as in the Housing Act 1985, and
(b) in relation to an authority in Scotland, mean the area of the local authority concerned.

AMENDMENT

¹ Definition: inserted: Homelessness Act 2002, s 18(1), Sch 1, paras 2, 20.

218 Index of defined expressions: Part 7

The following Table shows provisions defining or otherwise explaining expressions used in this Part (other than provisions defining or explaining an expression used in the same section) –

accommodation available for occupation	section 176
applicant	section 183(2)
assistance under this Part	section 183(2)
associated (in relation to a person)	section 178
assured tenancy and assured shorthold tenancy	section 230
district (of local housing authority)	section 217(3)
eligible for assistance	section 183(2)
homeless	section 175(1)
housing functions under this Part (in sections [206 and 208][1])	section 205(2)
intentionally homeless	section 191
intentionally threatened with homelessness	section 196
local connection	section 199
local housing authority–	
– in England and Wales	section 230
– in Scotland	section 217(2)(a)
...	...[2]
Prescribed	section 215(1)
priority need	section 189
[private landlord	section 217(1)][3]
Reasonable to continue to occupy accommodation	section 177
registered social landlord	section 230
relevant authority	section 217(1)
[restricted person	section 184 (7)][4]
social services authority	section 217(1) and (2)(b)
threatened with homelessness	section 175(4)

AMENDMENT

[1] Words substituted: Homelessness Act 2002, s 18(1), Sch 1, paras 2, 21(a).

[2] Entry repealed: Homelessness Act 2002, s 18(2), Sch 2.

[3] Entry inserted: Homelessness Act 2002, s 18(1), Sch 1, paras 2, 21(b).

Appendix 2
England: Homelessness

[4] Entry inserted: Housing and Regeneration Act 2008, s 314, Sch 15, Pt 1, paras 1, 8. Date in force: 2 March 2009 (except in relation to applications for an allocation of social housing or housing assistance (homelessness) or for accommodation made before that date): see SI 2009/415, art 2.

PART 8
MISCELLANEOUS AND GENERAL PROVISIONS

General

****

230 Minor definitions: general

In this Act –

'assured tenancy', 'assured shorthold tenancy' and 'assured agricultural occupancy' have the same meaning as in Part I of the Housing Act 1988;

'enactment' includes an enactment comprised in subordinate legislation (within the meaning of the Interpretation Act 1978);

'housing action trust' has the same meaning as in the Housing Act 1988;

'housing association' has the same meaning as in the Housing Associations Act 1985;

'introductory tenancy' and 'introductory tenant' have the same meaning as in Chapter I of Part V of this Act;

'local housing authority' has the same meaning as in the Housing Act 1985;

'registered social landlord' has the same meaning as in Part I of this Act;

'secure tenancy' and 'secure tenant' have the same meaning as in Part IV of the Housing Act 1985.

Homelessness Act 2002

2002 c 7

CONTENTS

Homelessness reviews and strategies

1 Duty of local housing authority to formulate a homelessness strategy

(1) A local housing authority ('the authority') may from time to time –

    (a) carry out a homelessness review for their district; and

    (b) formulate and publish a homelessness strategy based on the results of that review.

(2) The social services authority for the district of the authority (where that is a different local authority) shall give such assistance in connection with the exercise of the power under subsection (1) as the authority may reasonably require.

(3) The authority shall exercise that power so as to ensure that the first homelessness strategy for their district is published within the period of twelve months beginning with the day on which this section comes into force.

(4) The authority shall exercise that power so as to ensure that a new homelessness strategy for their district is published within the period of five years beginning with the day on which their last homelessness strategy was published.

(5) A local housing authority shall take their homelessness strategy into account in the exercise of their functions.

(6) A social services authority shall take the homelessness strategy for the district of a local housing authority into account in the exercise of their functions in relation to that district.

(7) Nothing in subsection (5) or (6) affects any duty or requirement arising apart from this section.

MODIFICATION

Article 3 of the Local Authorities' Plans and Strategies (Disapplication) (England) Order 2005, SI 2005/157, as amended by the Local Authorities' Plans and Strategies (Disapplication) (England) (Amendment) Order 2009, SI 2009/714, arts 2 and 4, disapplies the requirement to publish homelessness strategies under s 1(4) above for those local housing authorities in England which are categorised as excellent, 4 stars or 3 stars authorities.

2 Homelessness reviews

(1)   For the purposes of this Act 'homelessness review' means a review by a local housing authority of –

    (a)   the levels, and likely future levels, of homelessness in their district;

    (b)   the activities which are carried out for any purpose mentioned in subsection (2) (or which contribute to their achievement); and

    (c)   the resources available to the authority, the social services authority for their district, other public authorities, voluntary organisations and other persons for such activities.

(2)   Those purposes are –

    (a)   preventing homelessness in the district of the authority;

    (b)   securing that accommodation is or will be available for people in the district who are or may become homeless;

    (c)   providing support for people in the district –

        (i)   who are or may become homeless; or

        (ii)   who have been homeless and need support to prevent them becoming homeless again.

(3)   A local housing authority shall, after completing a homelessness review –

    (a)   arrange for the results of the review to be available at its principal office for inspection at all reasonable hours, without charge, by members of the public; and

    (b)   provide (on payment if required by the authority of a reasonable charge) a copy of those results to any member of the public who asks for one.

3 Homelessness strategies

(1)   For the purposes of this Act 'homelessness strategy' means a strategy formulated by a local housing authority for –

    (a)   preventing homelessness in their district;

    (b)   securing that sufficient accommodation is and will be available for people in their district who are or may become homeless;

    (c)   securing the satisfactory provision of support for people in their district –

        (i)   who are or may become homeless; or

        (ii)   who have been homeless and need support to prevent them becoming homeless again.

(2) A homelessness strategy may include specific objectives to be pursued, and specific action planned to be taken, in the course of the exercise of –

(a) the functions of the authority as a local housing authority; or

(b) the functions of the social services authority for the district.

(3) A homelessness strategy may also include provision relating to specific action which the authority expects to be taken –

(a) by any public authority with functions (not being functions mentioned in subsection (2)) which are capable of contributing to the achievement of any of the objectives mentioned in subsection (1); or

(b) by any voluntary organisation or other person whose activities are capable of contributing to the achievement of any of those objectives.

(4) The inclusion in a homelessness strategy of any provision relating to action mentioned in subsection (3) requires the approval of the body or person concerned.

(5) In formulating a homelessness strategy the authority shall consider (among other things) the extent to which any of the objectives mentioned in subsection (1) can be achieved through action involving two or more of the bodies or other persons mentioned in subsections (2) and (3).

(6) The authority shall keep their homelessness strategy under review and may modify it from time to time.

(7) If the authority modify their homelessness strategy, they shall publish the modifications or the strategy as modified (as they consider most appropriate).

[(7A) In formulating or modifying a homelessness strategy, a local housing authority in England shall have regard to –

(a) its current allocation scheme under section 166A of the Housing Act 1996,

(b) its current tenancy strategy under section 150 of the Localism Act 2011, and

(c) in the case of an authority that is a London borough council, the current London housing strategy.][3]

(8) Before adopting or modifying a homelessness strategy the authority shall consult such public or local authorities, voluntary organisations or other persons as they consider appropriate.

(9) The authority shall –

(a) make a copy of [everything published under section 1 or][1] this section available at its principal office for inspection at all reasonable hours, without charge, by members of the public; and

(b) provide (on payment if required by the authority of a reasonable charge) a copy of [anything][2] so published to any member of the public who asks for one.

AMENDMENT

[1] Words substituted: Local Government Act 2003, s 127(1), Sch 7, para 81(a).

[2] Word substituted: Local Government Act 2003, s 127(1), Sch 7, para 81(b).

[3] Sub-section inserted: Localism Act 2011, s 153, with effect from 15 January 2012, for certain purposes (SI 2012/57) and 7 June 2012 for remaining purposes (SI 2012/1463).

4 Sections 1 to 3: interpretation

In sections 1 to 3 –

'homeless' and 'homelessness' have the same meaning as in Part 7 of the Housing Act 1996 (c 52) (in this Act referred to as 'the 1996 Act');
'local housing authority' and 'district' have the same meaning as in the Housing Act 1985 (c 68);
'social services authority' means a local authority for the purposes of the Local Authority Social Services Act 1970 (c 42);
'support' means advice, information or assistance; and
'voluntary organisation' has the same meaning as in section 180(3) of the 1996 Act.

****

Supplementary

17 Wales

(1)   The reference to the 1996 Act in Schedule 1 to the National Assembly for Wales (Transfer of Functions) Order 1999 (SI 1999/672) is to be treated as referring to that Act as amended by this Act.

(2)   Subsection (1) does not affect the power to make further Orders varying or omitting that reference.

18 Minor and consequential amendments and repeals

(1)   Schedule 1 (which contains minor and consequential amendments) has effect.

(2)   Schedule 2 (which contains repeals) has effect.

19 Financial provision

There shall be paid out of money provided by Parliament any increase attributable to this Act in the sums payable out of money so provided under any other Act.

20 Commencement, transitional provision and general saving

(1)   The preceding provisions of this Act (and the Schedules), other than section 8 and paragraphs 3 and 7 of Schedule 1, come into force on such day as the Secretary of State may by order made by statutory instrument appoint; and different days may be appointed for different purposes.

(2)   The Secretary of State may by order made by statutory instrument make such transitional provisions and savings as he considers appropriate in connection with the coming into force of any provision of this Act.

(3)   The powers conferred by subsection (1) and (2) are exercisable as respects Wales by the National Assembly for Wales (and not the Secretary of State).

(4)   Nothing in this Act affects the operation of section 216(2) of the 1996 Act in relation to persons who applied for accommodation or assistance in obtaining accommodation before the commencement of Part 7 of that Act.

21 Short title, extent and application to Isles of Scilly

(1)   This Act may be cited as the Homelessness Act 2002.

(2)   This Act extends to England and Wales only.

(3)   This Act applies to the Isles of Scilly subject to such exceptions, adaptations and modifications as the Secretary of State may by order direct.

(4)   The power to make such an order is exercisable by statutory instrument subject to annulment in pursuance of a resolution of either House of Parliament.

****

Homelessness Code of Guidance for Local Authorities (July 2006)

CONTENTS

Appendix 2
England: Homelessness

OVERVIEW OF THE HOMELESSNESS LEGISLATION

This overview provides a summary of the homelessness legislation and the duties, powers and obligations on housing authorities and others towards people who are homeless or at risk of homelessness. This overview does not form part of the statutory code of guidance and is not a legal commentary.

Introduction

1. The homelessness legislation – that is, Part 7 of *the Housing Act 1996* – provides the statutory under-pinning for action to tackle homelessness.

2. The Government's strategy for tackling homelessness is outlined in *Sustainable Communities: Homes for All* and *Sustainable Communities: settled homes; changing lives*, published in 2005. The strategy aims to expand housing opportunities, including for those who need additional support, and for disadvantaged sections of society by offering a wider range of preventative measures and increasing access to settled homes.

The homelessness legislation

3. The homelessness legislation places a general duty on housing authorities to ensure that advice and information about homelessness, and preventing homelessness, is available to everyone in their district free of charge. The legislation also requires authorities to assist individuals and families who are homeless or threatened with homelessness and apply for help.

4. In 2002, the Government amended the homelessness legislation through the *Homelessness Act 2002* and the *Homelessness (Priority Need for Accommodation) (England) Order 2002* to:

- ensure a more strategic approach to tackling and preventing homelessness, in particular by requiring a homelessness strategy for every housing authority district, and
- strengthen the assistance available to people who are homeless or threatened with homelessness by extending the priority need categories to homeless 16 and 17 year olds; care leavers aged 18, 19 and 20; people who are vulnerable as a result of time spent in care, the armed forces, prison or custody, and people who are vulnerable because they have fled their home because of violence.

5. The legislation places duties on housing authorities, and gives them powers, to meet these aims. But it also emphasises the need for joint working between housing authorities, social services and other statutory, voluntary and private sector partners in tackling homelessness more effectively.

6. The Government continues to supplement housing authorities' resources with specific programmes to help them deliver effective homelessness strategies and services, prevent homelessness, reduce use of temporary accommodation and end the worst manifestations of homelessness such as people sleeping rough and families with children living in bed and breakfast hotels.

The homelessness review and strategy

7. Under the *Homelessness Act 2002* all housing authorities must have in place a homelessness strategy based on a review of all forms of homelessness in their district. The first strategy was required by July 2003 and it must be renewed at least every 5 years (unless this duty has been disapplied by the *Local Authorities Plans and Strategies (Disapplication) (England) Order 2005*). The social services authority must provide all reasonable assistance.

8. The strategy must set out the local authority's plans for the prevention of homelessness and for securing that sufficient accommodation and support are or will be available for people who become homeless or who are at risk of becoming so. Housing authorities will therefore need to ensure that all organisations, within all sectors, whose work can help to prevent homelessness and/or meet the needs of homeless people in their district are involved in the strategy. This will need to include not just housing providers (such as housing associations and private landlords) but also other statutory bodies such as social services, the probation service, the health service and the wide range of organisations in the private and voluntary sectors whose work helps prevent homelessness or meet the needs of people who have experienced homelessness.

9. Housing authorities will also need to give careful consideration to the scope for joint working between social services and the many other key players in the district who are working to meet the needs of people who are homeless or have experienced homelessness.

General duty to provide advice on homelessness

10. The housing authority can provide advice and information about homelessness – and the prevention of homelessness – themselves or arrange for another agency to do it on their behalf. Either way, the advice and assistance provided will need to be up to date and robust if it is to be effective and help achieve the housing authority's strategic aim of preventing homelessness. The service will need to be wide-ranging so that it offers advice and information about not only housing options but also the broad range of factors that can contribute to homelessness. This might include, for example, advice on social security benefits, household budgeting, tenancy support services and family mediation services. The advice provided should also act as a signpost to other, more specialist advice such as debt management, health care and coping with drug and alcohol misuse, where this is needed.

The main homelessness duty

11. Under the legislation, certain categories of household, such as families with children and households that include someone who is vulnerable, for example because of pregnancy, old age, or physical or mental disability, have a priority need for accommodation. Housing authorities must ensure that suitable accommodation is available for people who have priority need, if they are eligible for assistance and unintentionally homeless (certain categories of persons from abroad are ineligible.) This is known as the main homelessness duty. The housing authority can provide accommodation in their own stock or arrange for it to be provided by another landlord, for example, a housing association or a landlord in the private rented sector.

12. If settled accommodation is not immediately available, accommodation must be made available in the short term until the applicant can find a settled home, or until some other circumstance brings the duty to an end, for example, where the household voluntarily leaves the temporary accommodation provided by the housing authority. A settled home to bring the homelessness duty to an end could include the offer of a suitable secure or introductory tenancy in a local authority's housing stock (or nomination for a housing association assured tenancy) allocated under Part 6 of the 1996 Act or the offer of a suitable tenancy from a private landlord made by arrangement with the local authority.

13. Under the *Homelessness (Suitability of Accommodation) (England) Order 2003*, housing authorities can no longer discharge a homelessness duty to secure suitable accommodation by placing families with children, and households that include a pregnant woman, in Bed & Breakfast accommodation for longer than six weeks – and then only if more suitable accommodation is not available.

Applications and inquiries

14. Housing authorities must give proper consideration to all applications for housing assistance, and if they have reason to believe that an applicant may be homeless or threatened with homelessness, they must make inquiries to see whether they owe them any duty under Part 7 of the 1996 Act. This assessment process is important in enabling housing authorities to identify the assistance which an applicant may need either to prevent them from becoming homeless or to help them to find another home. In each case, the authority will need to decide whether the applicant is eligible for assistance, actually homeless, has a priority need, and whether the homelessness was intentional (see below). If they wish, housing authorities can also consider whether applicants have a local connection with the local district, or with another district. Certain applicants who are persons from abroad are not eligible for any assistance under Part 7 except free advice and information about homelessness and the prevention of homelessness.

Interim duty to accommodate

15. If an authority have reason to believe that an applicant may be homeless or threatened with homelessness, they must also decide if they also have reason to believe that the applicant may be eligible for assistance and have a priority need for accommodation. They must do this even before they have completed their inquiries. If there is reason to believe the applicant meets these criteria, the housing authority have an immediate duty to ensure that suitable accommodation is available until they complete their inquiries and decide whether a substantive duty is owed under Part 7. This is an important part of the safety net for people who have a priority need for accommodation and are unintentionally homeless.

When is someone homeless?

16. Broadly speaking, somebody is statutorily homeless if they do not have accommodation that they have a legal right to occupy, which is accessible and physically available to them (and their household) and which it would be reasonable for them to continue to live in. It would not be reasonable for someone to continue to live in their home, for example, if that was likely to lead to violence against them (or a member of their family).

Intentional homelessness

17. A person would be homeless intentionally where homelessness was the consequence of a deliberate action or omission by that person (unless this was made in good faith in ignorance of a relevant fact). A deliberate act might be a decision to leave the previous accommodation even though it would have been reasonable for the person (and everyone in the person's household) to continue to live there. A deliberate omission might be non-payment of rent that led to rent arrears and eviction.

Local connection and referrals to another authority

18. Broadly speaking, for the purpose of the homelessness legislation, people may have a local connection with a district because of residence, employment or family associations in the district, or because of special circumstances. (There are exceptions, for example residence in a district while serving a prison sentence there does not establish a local connection.) Where applicants are found to be eligible for assistance, unintentionally homeless and in priority need (ie they meet the criteria for the main homelessness duty) and the authority consider the applicant does not have a local connection with the district but does have one somewhere else, the housing authority dealing with the application can ask the housing authority in that other district to take responsibility for the case. However, applicants cannot be referred to another housing authority if they, or any member of their household, would be at risk of violence in the district of the other authority.

Other homelessness duties

19. If applicants are homeless but do not have a priority need, or if they have brought homelessness on themselves, the housing authority must ensure that they are provided with advice and assistance to help them find accommodation for themselves – but the authority does not have to ensure that accommodation becomes available for them. The housing authority can provide advice and assistance itself or arrange for another agency to do this. The housing authority must ensure that this includes a proper assessment of their housing

Appendix 2
England: Homelessness

needs and information about where they are likely to find suitable accommodation. Again, it will be crucial that the advice and assistance is effective and up to date if the housing authority's strategic aim of preventing homelessness is to be achieved.

20. Where people have a priority need but have brought homelessness on themselves, the housing authority must also ensure they have suitable accommodation available for a period that will give them a reasonable chance of finding accommodation for themselves. Sometimes, this may be for only a few weeks.

Intentionally homeless families with children

21. So, families with children who have been found intentionally homeless will not be owed a main homelessness duty; they will be entitled to advice and assistance and temporary accommodation for a short period only. If homelessness persists, any children in the family could be in need and the family could seek assistance from the social services authority under the *Children Act 1989*. It is therefore important that social services are made aware of such cases as soon as possible. Consequently, where a housing authority are dealing with a family that includes a child under 18 and they consider the family may be found intentionally homeless, they must make social services aware of the case. Where the family are found to be intentionally homeless by the housing authority, and social services decide the child's needs would best be met by helping the family to obtain accommodation, social services can ask the housing authority for reasonable assistance and the housing authority must respond.

Notifications/reviews of decisions/appeals to county court

22. Where authorities have reason to believe an applicant may be homeless or threatened with homelessness and make inquiries into the case, they must give the applicant written notification of their decision on the case, and the reasons for it insofar as it goes against the applicant's interests. Applicants can ask the housing authority to review most aspects of their decisions, and, if still dissatisfied, can appeal to the county court on a point of law. The county court can confirm or quash a housing authority's decision.

Power to accommodate pending a review or appeal

23. Housing authorities have the power to accommodate applicants pending a review or appeal to the county court, and they must consider whether to exercise this power in all cases. If the housing authority decide not to exercise this power pending a review, and the applicant wishes to appeal to the courts, he or she would need to seek permission to ask the High Court to judicially review the decision. If the housing authority decide not to exercise this power pending an appeal to the county court, the applicant can appeal to the county court to review the decision not to accommodate, and the court can require the housing authority to accommodate the applicant, pending the appeal on the substantive homelessness decision if the court considers this is necessary.

INTRODUCTION

Purpose of the code

1. The Secretary of State for Communities and Local Government is issuing this Code of Guidance to local housing authorities (referred to as housing authorities) in England under s 182 of the *Housing Act 1996* ('the 1996 Act'). Under s 182(1) of the 1996 Act, housing authorities are required to have regard to this guidance in exercising their functions under Part 7 of the 1996 Act and under the *Homelessness Act 2002* ('the 2002 Act'). This Code of Guidance replaces the previous version published in 2002.

2. Under s 182(1), social services authorities in England are also required to have regard to the guidance when exercising their functions relating to homelessness and the prevention of homelessness. The guidance applicable to social services authorities is issued jointly with the Secretary of State for Health and the Secretary of State for Education and Skills.

3. The Code gives guidance on how local authorities should exercise their homelessness functions and apply the various statutory criteria in practice. It is not a substitute for legislation and in so far as it comments on the law can only reflect the Department's understanding at the time of issue. Local authorities will still need to keep up to date on any developments in the law in these areas.

4. In addition to this Code, there is issued a range of good practice publications to assist local authorities in exercising their functions relating to homelessness and the prevention of homelessness (see Annex 1).

Who is the code for?

5. The Code is issued specifically for local authority members and staff. It is also of direct relevance to registered social landlords (RSLs). RSLs have a duty under the 1996 Act to co-operate with housing authorities in exercising their homelessness functions. RSLs are subject to the Housing Corporation's Regulatory Code and guidance and they need to take this into account when assisting housing authorities. Many of the activities discussed in the Code require joint planning and operational co-operation between housing authorities and social services authorities, health authorities, other referral agencies, voluntary sector organisations and the diverse range of bodies working in the rented sectors – so the Code is also relevant to these agencies.

The homelessness legislation

6. Part 7 of the 1996 Act sets out the powers and duties of housing authorities where people apply to them for accommodation or assistance in obtaining accommodation. The 2002 Act places a requirement on housing authorities to formulate and publish a homelessness strategy based on a review of homelessness in their district. The 2002 Act also amends a number of provisions in Part 7 of the 1996 Act to strengthen the safety net for vulnerable people.

Equality and diversity

7. When exercising their functions relating to homelessness and the prevention of homelessness, local authorities are under a statutory duty to ensure that their polices and procedures do not discriminate, directly or indirectly, on grounds of race, sex or gender, or disability. Authorities should also ensure that their policies and procedures do not discriminate on the basis of any other ground which is not material to a person's housing application, including grounds of sexual orientation or religion or belief. Authorities should observe relevant codes of practice and adopt a formal equality and diversity policy relating to all aspects of their homelessness service, to ensure equality of access and treatment for all applicants. Appropriate provision will need to be made to ensure accessibility for people with particular needs, including those with mobility difficulties, sight or hearing loss and learning difficulties, as well as those for whom English is not their first language.

8. The Race Relations Act 1976 now places a general duty on local authorities to promote race equality. This means that they must have due regard to the need to:

- eliminate unlawful racial discrimination; and
- promote equality of opportunity and good relations between people of difference racial groups.

In practice, this means building racial equality considerations into the day-to-day work of policy-making, service delivery, employment practice and other functions. The duty is a positive rather than a reactive one.

9. There are also specific duties relating to policy and service delivery. One of these concerns publishing a Race Equality Scheme every three years. Authorities' Race Equality Schemes should include their arrangements for:

- assessing and consulting on the likely impact of homelessness strategies on the promotion of race equality;
- monitoring homelessness policies for any adverse impact on the promotion of race equality;
- publishing the results of assessments, consultations and monitoring;
- ensuring access to homelessness information, advice and services.

The Commission for Racial Equality will publish a statutory Code of Practice on Racial Equality in Housing later this year (see Annex 1).

10. People from ethnic minority groups are around three times more likely than other households to be accepted as unintentionally homeless and in priority need.[1] Housing authorities need to ensure that their homelessness

---

[1] Source: ODPM data based on the P1E statistical returns completed by local authorities.

strategies and homelessness services pay particular attention to the needs of the ethnic minority communities they serve, for example, by ensuring that advice and information about homelessness and the prevention of homelessness is available in a range of ethnic languages appropriate to the district. ODPM published a Development Guide for local authorities on *Tackling Homelessness Amongst Ethnic Minority Households* (see Annex 1).

11. Section 49A of the *Disability Discrimination Act 1995* (added by the *Disability Discrimination Act 2005*) introduces a new duty to promote equality for disabled people. It requires public authorities to exercise their functions with due regard to the need to:

- eliminate unlawful discrimination against disabled people;
- eliminate harassment of disabled people that is related to their disabilities;
- promote equality of opportunity between disabled people and other persons;
- take steps to take account of disabled people's disabilities (even where that involves treating disabled people more favourably than other persons);
- promote positive attitudes towards disabled people; and
- encourage participation by disabled people in public life.

Authorities will be required to publish a Disability Equality Scheme every three years setting out how they will implement the duty to promote equality in their own context.

As with the duty to promote race equality, this is a positive duty rather than a reactive one and authorities will need to consider the implications for the delivery of their homelessness services.

The Disability Rights Commission has published a statutory Code of Practice on the Duty to Promote Disability Equality which will come into force in December 2006 (see Annex 1).

12. Authorities should also inform themselves of the provisions of Council Directives 2000/43/EC (the Race Directive) and 2000 78/EC (the Equality Directive). Under the *Equalities Act 2006* the Commission for Equality and Human Rights (CEHR) will bring together the Disability Rights Commission and the Equal Opportunities Commission from October 2007. The Act imposes a positive duty on public authorities to promote equality of opportunity and the elimination of discrimination on grounds of age; colour; race, nationality or ethnic origins; disability; family status; gender reassignment; marital status; pregnancy; religion or belief; sex; and sexual orientation. Discrimination on any such grounds in the carrying out by a public authority of its functions would be made unlawful. The *Gender Recognition Act 2004*, the *Employment Equality (Sexual Orientation) (Amendment) Regulations 2003* and the *Employment Equality (Religion or Belief) Regulations 2003* outlaw discrimination on the grounds of gender reassignment, sexual orientation or religion in the fields of employment and vocational training. In addition, the *Employment*

Equality (Age) Regulations, which are due to come into force in October 2006, will outlaw discrimination on the grounds of age in the fields of employment and vocational training.

13. Housing authorities should ensure that their homelessness strategies and homelessness services comply with existing equality and diversity legislation and new legislation as it comes into force.

Definitions

Throughout the Code,

'the 1996 Act' means the Housing Act 1996;

'the 2002 Act' means the Homelessness Act 2002;

'the housing authority' means the local housing authority.

CHAPTER 1: HOMELESSNESS REVIEWS & STRATEGIES

This chapter provides guidance on housing authorities' duties to carry out a homelessness review and to formulate and publish a strategy based on the results of that review.

Duty to formulate a homelessness strategy

1.1. Section 1(1) of the *Homelessness Act 2002* ('the 2002 Act') gives housing authorities the power to carry out a homelessness review for their district and formulate and publish a homelessness strategy based on the results of the review. This power can be exercised from time to time, however s 1(3) required housing authorities to publish their first homelessness strategy by 31 July 2003. Section 1(4) requires housing authorities to publish a new homelessness strategy, based on the results of a further homelessness review, within the period of five years beginning with the day on which their last homelessness strategy was published (there is an exemption from this requirement for local authorities categorised as an 'excellent authority', see paragraph 1.42). However, it is open to a housing authority to conduct homelessness reviews and strategies more frequently, if they wish.

1.2. For a homelessness strategy to be effective housing authorities need to ensure that it is consistent with other local plans and strategies and takes into account any wider relevant sub-regional or regional plans and strategies. There will be a lot of common ground between an authority's housing strategy (whether its own or a sub-regional one produced with neighbouring authorities) and its homelessness strategy. It is open to authorities to produce either separate housing and homelessness strategies or combine these in a single document where it is consistent to do so. It is also open to authorities, again where it would be consistent to do so, to consider producing a wider composite plan that includes not only the housing and homelessness strategies but also their Housing Revenue Account Business Plans and Home Energy Conservation Act report. The homelessness strategy should also link with other strategies and programmes that address the wide range of problems that can cause homelessness (see indicative list at Annex 2). It will be important to consider how these strategies and programmes can help achieve the objectives of the homelessness strategy and vice-versa.

1.3. Housing authorities are encouraged to take a broad view and consider the benefits of cross-boundary, sub-regional and regional co-operation. A county-wide approach will be particularly important in non-unitary authorities, where housing and homelessness services are provided by the district authority whilst other key services, such as social services and Supporting People, are delivered at the county level. Housing authorities should ensure that the homelessness strategy for their district forms part of a coherent approach to tackling homelessness with neighbouring authorities. Authorities may wish to collaborate with neighbouring housing authorities to produce a joint homelessness strategy covering a sub-regional area. London

Appendix 2
England: Homelessness

boroughs are encouraged to work closely with the Greater London Authority when formulating their homelessness strategies.

1.4. When carrying out a review and formulating a strategy, housing authorities are encouraged to refer to *Homelessness Strategies: A good practice handbook, Local Authorities' Homelessness Strategies: Evaluation and Good Practice* and other relevant good practice documents published by the Office of the Deputy Prime Minister (see list of publications at Annex 1).

1.5. Housing authorities are reminded that when drawing up their strategies for preventing and tackling homelessness, they must consider the needs of all groups of people in their district who are homeless or likely to become homeless, including Gypsies and Travellers. Under s 225 of the *Housing Act 2004*, which supplements s 8 of the *Housing Act 1985*, when undertaking a review of housing needs in their district, local authorities are required to carry out an assessment of the accommodation needs of Gypsies and Travellers residing in or resorting to their district. Draft guidance on accommodation needs assessment for Gypsies and Travellers is available on the DCLG website, and will be finalised after further consultation in 2006.

Assistance from social services

1.6. In non-unitary districts, where the social services authority and the housing authority are different authorities, section 1(2) of the 2002 Act requires the social services authority to give the housing authority such assistance as may be reasonably required in carrying out a homelessness review and formulating and publishing a homelessness strategy. **Since a number of people who are homeless or at risk of homelessness will require social services support, it is unlikely that it would be possible for a housing authority to formulate an effective homelessness strategy without assistance from the social services authority. It will be necessary therefore in all cases for housing authorities to seek assistance from the social services authority.** In unitary authorities the authority will need to ensure that the social services department assists the housing department in carrying out a homelessness review and formulating and publishing a homelessness strategy.

1.7. The social services authority must comply with all requests for assistance from housing authorities within their district which are reasonable. Examples of the type of assistance that a housing authority may reasonably require from the social services authority when carrying out a review and formulating a strategy may include:

- information about current and likely future numbers of social services client groups who are likely to be homeless or at risk of homelessness e g young people in need, care leavers and those with community care needs;
- details of social services' current programme of activity, and the resources available to them, for meeting the accommodation needs of these groups;

- details of social services' current programme of activity, and the resources available to them, for providing support for vulnerable people who are homeless or likely to become homeless (and who may not currently be social services clients).

1.8. Effective co-operation will benefit both housing and social services authorities. See Chapter 5 for guidance on joint working with other agencies and Chapter 13 for guidance on co-operation in cases involving children.

Taking the strategy into account

1.9. Sections 1(5) and (6) of the 2002 Act require housing and social services authorities to take the homelessness strategy into account when exercising their functions.

1.10. For a homelessness strategy to be effective it will need to be based on realistic assumptions about how it will be delivered in practice. Whilst this will apply in respect of all the agencies and organisations involved, the key players will be the housing authority and the social services authority. Both authorities will therefore need to ensure that, on the one hand, the assumptions in the strategy about their future activities are realistic and, on the other, that in practice these activities are actually delivered through the operation of their statutory functions. When the strategy is formulated, the social services authority (or social services department within a unitary authority) will need to work closely with the housing authority (or department) to ensure that this can be achieved. All contributors will need to take ownership of the strategy if it is to be effective. Again, because of its crucial role in delivering the strategy, this will be particularly important in the case of the social services authority (or department).

Homelessness reviews

1.11. Under section 2(1) of the 2002 Act a homelessness review means a review by a housing authority of:

a) the levels, and likely future levels, of homelessness in their district;

b) the activities which are carried out for any the following purposes (or which contribute to achieving any of them):
   i) preventing homelessness in the housing authority's district;
   ii) securing that accommodation is or will be available for people in the district who are or may become homeless; and
   iii) providing support for people in the district:
      – who are or may become homeless; or
      – who have been homeless and need support to prevent them becoming homeless again;

c) the resources available to the housing authority, the social services authority for the district, other public authorities, voluntary organisations and other persons for the activities outlined in (b) above.

Appendix 2
England: Homelessness

1.12. The purpose of the review is to establish the extent of homelessness in the district, assess its likely extent in the future, and identify what is currently being done, and by whom, and what level of resources are available, to prevent and tackle homelessness.

a)   current levels, and likely future levels, of homelessness

1.13. Homelessness is defined by sections 175 to 178 of the 1996 Act (see Chapter 8 for guidance). The review must take account of **all** forms of homelessness within the meaning of the 1996 Act, not just people who are unintentionally homeless and have a priority need for accommodation under Part 7. The review should therefore consider a wide population of households who are homeless or at risk of homelessness, including those who might be more difficult to identify, including people sleeping rough, or those whose accommodation circumstances make them more likely than others to become homeless or to resort to sleeping rough.

1.14. The housing authority's own records of its activity under the homelessness legislation (Part 7 of the 1996 Act) will provide a baseline for assessing the number of people who are likely to become homeless and seek help directly from the housing authority. These records should give some indication as to why those accepted as statutorily homeless became homeless. Other useful sources of data on potential homelessness in the district may include:

- records on rough sleeping;
- estimates of people staying with friends/family on an insecure basis;
- court records on possession orders;
- records of evictions by the local authority and registered social landlords (RSLs);
- local advice service records on homelessness cases;
- hospital records of people homeless on discharge;
- armed forces records of those homeless on discharge;
- prison/probation service records of ex-prisoners homeless on discharge;
- social services records of homeless families with children;
- social services records of young people leaving care and children in need requiring accommodation;
- records of Supporting People clients;
- records available from hostels and refuges;
- voluntary sector records, e g day centres, advice services;
- records of asylum seekers being accommodated in the district by the National Asylum Support Service;
- data from the national population census and housing authorities' own household surveys.

1.15. Some groups of people are likely to be more at risk of homelessness than others. These may include:

- young people who have become estranged from their family; have been in care; have a history of abuse, running away or school exclusions; or whose parents have had mental health, alcohol or drug problems; (see Chapter 12)
- people from ethnic minority groups;
- people with an institutionalised background, for example where they have spent time in prison or the armed forces;
- former asylum seekers who have been given permission to stay in the UK and are no longer being accommodated by the National Asylum Support Service;
- people who have experienced other problems that may increase the risk of homelessness including family/relationship breakdowns; domestic, racial or other violence; poor mental or physical health; drug and alcohol abuse; age-related problems and debt.

1.16. As part of the process of mapping and understanding the extent of current homelessness in the district, housing authorities may wish to develop a profile of those who have experienced homelessness. Elements within a profile may include:

- location of homelessness;
- reason(s) for homelessness;
- housing history including previous tenures and length of homelessness;
- ethnic background;
- other background (eg care provided by the local authority or other institution);
- age;
- gender and sexuality;
- disabilities;
- levels and types of debts;
- employment/benefits history;
- composition of household;
- vulnerability of applicant (or household members);
- support needs (housing-related or other);
- health/drug problems;
- immigration status;
- trends in any of these elements.

1.17. Housing authorities will also need to consider the range of factors which could affect future levels of homelessness in their district. Many of these will be similar to factors taken into account for the purpose of assessing housing needs in the district (eg as part of a broader housing strategy). Relevant factors in the district may include:

- the availability of affordable accommodation including housing provided by the housing authority and by RSLs;
- housing market analyses, including property prices and rent levels;
- the supply of accommodation in the private rented sector;
- the provision and effectiveness of housing advice;

Appendix 2
England: Homelessness

- local voluntary and community sector services;
- the allocation policy of the housing authority;
- the lettings policies of RSLs;
- the effectiveness of nomination agreements between the housing authority and RSLs;
- the policy of the housing authority and RSLs on management of tenants' rent arrears and on seeking repossession;
- the efficiency of the housing authority's administration of housing benefit;
- the provision and effectiveness of housing-related support services;
- redevelopment and regeneration activity;
- unemployment;
- strength of the local economy;
- the local population (and demographic trends);
- the level of overcrowding;
- the rate of new household formation in the district;
- the level of inward migration (both national and international);
- the flow of itinerant population (ie Gypsies and Travellers) and availability of authorised sites;
- the number of people likely to be in housing need on leaving:
  - the armed forces,
  - residential care,
  - local authority care,
  - prison,
  - hospital or
  - accommodation provided by the National Asylum Support Service.

1.18. Individual cases of homelessness are often the result of a complex matrix of problems that may develop over time. In many cases homelessness may be triggered by individual circumstances (for example, relationship breakdown or unemployment) but it can also be the result of a failure in the housing market (for example, high rents in the private sector and a shortage of accommodation in the social sector) or a failure of the administrative system (for example, delays in the payment of housing benefit). In districts where the housing market and administrative systems are functioning well, the levels of homelessness are likely to be lower. All these factors will need to be taken into account when assessing the likely future levels of homelessness in the district.

b)   activities which are carried out

1.19. The public, private and voluntary sectors can all contribute, directly or indirectly, to the prevention of homelessness, the provision of accommodation and the provision of support for homeless people. When reviewing the activities which are being carried out for these purposes, the housing authority should consider the activities of all the various agencies and organisations, across all sectors, which are providing, or contributing to the provision of accommodation, support or relevant services in the district (Annex 3 provides an indicative list).

1.20. Having mapped all the current activities, the housing authority should consider whether these are appropriate and adequate to meet the aims of the strategy, and whether any changes or additional provision are needed.

Preventing homelessness

1.21. Gaining a good understanding of the causes of homelessness during the homelessness review process will help to inform the range of preventative measures that need to be put in place. Many statutory and non-statutory services can contribute to preventing homelessness. Housing authorities should adopt an open approach and recognise that there will be a broad range of organisations operating in fields other than housing, including, for example, health, education and employment, whose activities may help to prevent homelessness. Activities that contribute to preventing homelessness may include:

- advice services;
- mediation and reconciliation services;
- tenancy support schemes;
- proactive liaison with private sector landlords;
- rent deposit/guarantee schemes;
- management of social housing by the housing authority and by RSLs;
- debt counselling;
- Supporting People programme;
- social services support for vulnerable people;
- housing benefit administration;
- benefit liaison to young people delivered through Connexions;
- 'Sanctuary Schemes' to enable victims of domestic violence to stay in their homes;
- planning for the housing needs of people leaving institutions – e g local authority care, prison and the armed services.

Further guidance on preventing homelessness is provided in Chapter 2.

Securing accommodation

1.22. Housing authorities need to consider that a range of accommodation is likely to be required for people who are, or may become, homeless. Landlords, accommodation providers and housing developers across all sectors can contribute to the provision of accommodation in the district. Activities that contribute to securing that accommodation will be available for people who are homeless, or at risk of becoming homeless, may include:

- initiatives to increase the supply of new affordable accommodation in the district (eg: affordable housing secured through the planning system);
- provision of new housing for owner occupation;
- initiatives to increase the supply of specialist and/or supported accommodation;
- provision of accommodation from the housing authority's own stock;

Appendix 2
England: Homelessness

- the proportion of lettings RSLs make available to the housing authority and to homeless people generally;
- programmes for the provision of hostel, foyer and refuge spaces;
- initiatives for maximising use of the private rented sector (eg rent deposit guarantee schemes and landlord/tenant mediation services);
- schemes for maximising access to affordable accommodation (eg rent guarantee schemes);
- local, regional and national mobility schemes (eg to assist tenants or homeless households to move to other areas, incentives to reduce under-occupation, and assistance to move into home ownership).

Further guidance on ensuring a sufficient supply of accommodation is provided in Chapter 3.

Providing support

1.23. As part of the review housing authorities should consider all the current activities which contribute to the provision of support for people in the district who are, or may become, homeless and people in the district who have been homeless and need support to prevent them becoming homeless again. The range of providers whose activities will be making a contribution to this area are likely to embrace the public, private and voluntary sectors.

1.24. As a starting point, the housing authority may wish to consider the level of services being provided under the Supporting People programme. Other activities which may be relevant are:

- social services support under the community care programme;
- social services support for children in need who require accommodation;
- social services support for young people at risk;
- housing advice services;
- tenancy support services;
- schemes which offer practical support for formerly homeless people (eg furniture schemes);
- day centres for homeless people;
- supported hostel provision;
- women's refuges;
- support for people to access health care services (eg registration with a GP practice);
- support for people with problems of alcohol or substance abuse;
- support for people with mental health problems;
- support for people with learning disabilities;
- support for people seeking employment, eg personal adviser through Connexions, Jobcentre Plus, voluntary sector organisations dealing with homelessness and worklessness;
- advocacy support.

Further guidance on securing support services is provided in Chapter 4.

c) resources available for activities

1.25. As part of the homelessness review, the housing authority should consider the resources available for the activities set out in paragraph 1.11. The housing authority should consider not only its own resources (ie housing funding whether provided by central government or from authorities' own sources) but also those available for these purposes to the social services authority for their district, other public authorities, voluntary organisations and other persons. Annex 3 provides an indicative list of other authorities, organisations and persons whose activities may contribute to preventing and tackling homelessness.

Preventing homelessness

1.26. Housing authorities should invest their own resources in prevention services and measures since these are likely to produce direct net savings for the authority, for example through reduced processing of repeat homelessness applications, lower use of temporary accommodation and fewer social services interventions. Resources allocated to preventing homelessness will also help to reduce pressures on wider services, such as housing, health and employment, in the longer-term.

1.27. Resources available for the prevention of homelessness may include:

- staff or administrative budgets and resources available to the housing authority (eg related to the homeless persons unit, the housing advice service, the Supporting People programme, tenancy support etc);
- the resources allocated within the housing authority for rent guarantee schemes and other preventative measures;
- the availability and quality of housing and homelessness advice in the district (eg number and location of advice centres);
- staff or administrative budgets and resources within other public bodies (eg social services authority, Primary Care Trust, local education authority) dedicated to activities that help prevent/tackle homelessness; and
- staff or administrative budgets and resources available to other agencies working to prevent homelessness in the district (eg housing advice services in the voluntary sector and agencies working with young people).

Securing accommodation

1.28. Resources available for securing that accommodation is, or will be, available may include:

- initiatives to increase the supply of new affordable accommodation in the district (eg bids for resources through the Regional Housing Strategy and Housing Corporation Approved Development Programme, cash incentive schemes, affordable housing secured through the planning system, other RSL developments, Private Finance

Appendix 2
England: Homelessness

Initiative or regeneration developments, self-funded developments, self build schemes, shared ownership schemes, Homebuy);

- initiatives to increase the supply of specialist and/or supported accommodation;
- staff or administrative budgets and resources to make better use of the existing social housing stock (eg working with RSLs, managing own housing stock, mobility schemes);
- staff or administrative budgets and resources for maximising use of the private rented sector (eg landlord fora and accreditation schemes, rent deposit/guarantee schemes);
- initiatives to enable people to remain in their homes (eg through housing renewal assistance and disabled facilities grants).

Providing support

1.29.   Resources available for providing support may include:

- staff or administrative budgets and resources available through the Supporting People programme;
- other staff or administrative budgets and resources available to the housing authority, for example through general fund expenditure or the Housing Revenue Account;
- staff or administrative budgets and resources available to the social services authority (eg personnel working to meet the support needs of homeless people);
- staff or administrative budgets and resources available to other public authorities and voluntary and community sector agencies (eg Primary Care Trusts, Drug Action Teams, Sure Start, Connexions and others listed at Annex 3); and
- availability of supported accommodation units and floating support for homeless people.

Results of the review

1.30.   Having completed a homelessness review, housing authorities must arrange for a copy of the results of the review to be made available at their principal office; these must be available to the public for inspection at all reasonable hours without charge. A copy of the results must also be made available to any member of the public, on request (for which a reasonable charge can be made).

Homelessness strategies

1.31.   Having carried out a homelessness review the housing authority will be in a position to formulate its homelessness strategy based on the results of that review as required by s 1(1)(b) of the 2002 Act. In formulating its strategy a housing authority will need to consider the necessary levels of activity required to achieve the aims set out in the paragraph below and the sufficiency of the resources available to them as revealed by the review.

1.32. Under s 3(1) of the 2002 Act a homelessness strategy means a strategy for:

i) preventing homelessness in the district (see Chapter 2 for further guidance);

ii) securing that sufficient accommodation is and will be available for people in the district who are or may become homeless (see Chapter 3 for further guidance);

iii) securing the satisfactory provision of support for people in the district who are or may become homeless or who have been homeless and need support to prevent them becoming homeless again (see Chapter 4 for further guidance).

Specific objectives and actions for housing and social services authorities

1.33. A homelessness strategy may include specific objectives to be achieved and actions planned to be taken in the course of the exercise of the functions of the housing authority and the social services authority. This will apply equally in areas where the social services authority is not also the housing authority (for example, in district councils in county areas). Examples of specific objectives and actions for housing and social services authorities that might be included in a strategy are set out in Annex 4.

Specific action by others

1.34. A homelessness strategy can also include specific action which the housing authority expects to be taken by:

i) other public authorities;

ii) voluntary organisations; and

iii) other persons whose activities could contribute to achieving the strategy's objectives.

1.35. In all housing authority districts there will be a significant number of agencies whose activities address the wide range of needs and problems that can be linked to homelessness. These will be found across all sectors: public, private and voluntary. Housing authorities will need to seek the participation of all relevant agencies in the district in order to assist them in formulating and delivering an effective homelessness strategy that includes specific action that the housing authority expects to be taken by others.

1.36. In particular, housing authorities should enter into constructive partnerships with RSLs operating in their district. See Annex 5 for guidance on co-operation between housing authorities and RSLs.

1.37. An indicative list of the other public authorities, voluntary organisations and persons whose activities could contribute to achieving the strategy's objectives is at Annex 3. However, s 3(4) provides that a housing authority cannot include in a homelessness strategy any specific action expected to be taken by another body or organisation without their approval.

1.38. Examples of specific action that the housing authority might expect to be taken by others are provided at Annex 6.

Joint action

1.39. Section 3(5) of the 2002 Act requires housing authorities, when formulating a homelessness strategy, to consider (among other things) the extent to which any of the strategy's objectives could be achieved through joint action involving two or more of the persons or other bodies tackling homelessness in the district. This could include the housing authority, the social services authority, neighbouring housing authorities and any other public bodies working to alleviate homelessness within the district, for example, the National Offender Management Service. It might also include any other organisation or person whose activities could contribute to achieving the objectives of the homelessness strategy, for example, voluntary sector organisations working with homeless people, registered social landlords, and private landlords. The most effective strategies will be those which harness the potential of all the organisations and persons working to prevent and alleviate homelessness in the district, and which ensure that all the activities concerned are consistent and complementary. It will be important for all such organisations to take ownership of the strategy if they strive to help meet its objectives. See Chapter 5 for guidance on joint working with other agencies.

Action plans

1.40. As part of the homelessness strategy housing authorities should develop effective action plans, to help ensure that the objectives set out in the homelessness strategy are achieved. Action plans could include, for example, targets, milestones and arrangements for monitoring and evaluation. Good practice guidance on developing action plans is provided in the ODPM publication *'Local Authorities' Homelessness Strategies: Evaluation and Good Practice (2004)'*.

Need to consult on a strategy

1.41. Housing authorities must consult such public or local authorities, voluntary organisations or other persons as they consider appropriate before adopting or modifying a homelessness strategy. For a strategy to be effective it will need to involve every organisation and partnership whose activities contribute, or could contribute, in some way to achieving its objectives. As a minimum, therefore, it will be appropriate for all such organisations to be consulted on the strategy before it is adopted. It will be important to consult service users and homeless people themselves, or organisations representing their interests. Consultation with ethnic minority and faith-based groups will also be important in addressing the disproportionate representation of people from ethnic minority communities amongst homeless households. Annex 3 provides an indicative list of the types of authorities, organisations and people that the housing authority may wish to consult about a strategy.

Publishing a strategy

1.42. Under s 1(3) of the 2002 Act, housing authorities were required to publish their first homelessness strategy by 31 July 2003. Section 1(4) requires housing authorities to publish a new homelessness strategy, based on the results of a further homelessness review, within the period of five years beginning with the day on which their last homelessness strategy was published. However, those authorities which are categorised as an 'excellent authority' by the Secretary of State by virtue of the *Local Authorities' Plans and Strategies (Disapplication) (England) Order 2005* are exempt from this requirement. Housing authorities must make a copy of the strategy available to the public at their principal office, and this is to be available for inspection at all reasonable hours without charge. A copy must also be made available to any member of the public, on request (for which a reasonable charge can be made).

Keeping a strategy under review and modifying it

1.43. Housing authorities must keep their homelessness strategy under review and may modify it from time to time. Before modifying the strategy, they must consult on the same basis as required before adopting a strategy (see paragraph 1.41). If a strategy is modified, the housing authority must publish the modifications or the modified strategy and make copies available to the public on the same basis as required when adopting a strategy (see paragraph 1.42).

1.44. Circumstances that might prompt modification of a homelessness strategy include: transfer of the housing authority's housing stock to an RSL; the setting up of an Arms Length Management Organisation; a review of other, relevant local plans or strategies; new data sources on homelessness becoming available; a significant change in the levels or causes of homelessness; changes in either housing/homelessness/social security policy or legislation, or new factors that could contribute to a change in the levels or nature of homelessness in the district such as significant changes to the local economy (eg housing markets or levels of employment).

CHAPTER 2: PREVENTING HOMELESSNESS

2.1. This chapter provides guidance on housing authorities' duties to have a strategy to prevent homelessness in their district and to ensure that advice and information about homelessness, and the prevention of homelessness, are available free of charge to anyone in their district. The chapter also provides some examples of the action housing authorities and their partners can take to tackle the more common causes of homelessness and to prevent homelessness recurring.

2.2. Preventing homelessness means providing people with the ways and means to meet their housing, and any housing-related support, needs in order to avoid experiencing homelessness. Effective prevention will enable a person to remain in their current home, where appropriate, to delay a need to move out of current accommodation so that a move into alternative accommodation can be planned in a timely way; to find alternative accommodation, or to sustain independent living.

2.3. The prevention of homelessness should be a key strategic aim which housing authorities and other partners pursue through the homelessness strategy. It is vital that individuals are encouraged to seek assistance at the earliest possible time when experiencing difficulties which may lead to homelessness. In many cases early, effective intervention can prevent homelessness occurring. Housing authorities are reminded that they must not avoid their obligations under Part 7 of the 1996 Act (including the duty to make inquiries under s 184, if they have reason to believe that an applicant may be homeless or threatened with homelessness), but it is open to them to suggest alternative solutions in cases of potential homelessness where these would be appropriate and acceptable to the applicant.

2.4. The Secretary of State considers that housing authorities should take steps to prevent homelessness wherever possible, offering a broad range of advice and assistance for those in housing need. It is also important that, where homelessness does occur and is being tackled, consideration is given to the factors which may cause repeat homelessness and action taken to prevent homelessness recurring.

2.5. Homelessness can have significant negative consequences for the people who experience it. At a personal level, homelessness can have a profound impact on health, education and employment prospects. At a social level, homelessness can impact on social cohesion and economic participation. Early intervention to prevent homelessness can therefore bring benefits for those concerned, including being engaged with essential services and increasing the likelihood that children will live in a more secure environment. Investment in prevention services can also produce direct cost savings for local authorities, for example through lower use of temporary accommodation and fewer social services interventions. Furthermore, measures to prevent homelessness will also help to reduce longer-term pressures on wider services, such as health and employment.

2.6. There are three stages where intervention can prevent homelessness:

early identification – by identifying categories of people who are at risk of homelessness and ensuring that accommodation and any necessary support are available to them in time to prevent homelessness. Early identification can target people who fall within known indicator groups (eg those leaving local authority care, prison, secure accommodation or the armed forces, or people at known or observed risk due to mental or physical health problems) even though they may not currently have a need for housing but for whom timely intervention can avoid homelessness when they leave their institutional environment and before they reach a crisis point;

pre-crisis intervention – this can take the form of: advice services and proactive intervention such as negotiation with landlords to enable people to retain their current tenancies. Such intervention is important even if it only delays the date when a person has to leave their home, as this may allow time to plan and manage a move to alternative accommodation;

preventing recurring homelessness – ensuring tenancy sustainment can be central to preventing repeat homelessness where there is an underlying need for support and the provision of accommodation by itself is insufficient to prevent homelessness.

Strategy to prevent homelessness

2.7. Under s 1 of the 2002 Act, local housing authorities must formulate and publish a homelessness strategy based on a review of homelessness for their district, and they must take the strategy into account when exercising their functions. (See Chapter 1 for guidance.) Under section 3(1)(a) of the 2002 Act a homelessness strategy must include, among other things, a strategy for preventing homelessness in the district. Gaining a thorough understanding of the causes of homelessness in a local area through the review process will help to inform the range of measures required to prevent homelessness. As part of the review, housing authorities must consider all the current activities in their area that contribute to the prevention of homelessness. They must also consider the resources available. Both activities and resources are likely to involve a wide range of providers working in the public, private and voluntary sectors.

2.8. In developing their homelessness strategies, housing authorities should consider the range of measures that need to be put in place to prevent homelessness. These will depend on local circumstances. Housing authorities are advised to adopt an open approach and recognise that there will be a broad range of organisations operating in fields other than housing, for example, in education, health and employment, whose activities may help to prevent homelessness. (See Chapter 1 for further guidance on carrying out a homelessness review and formulating a homelessness strategy).

Appendix 2
England: Homelessness

Advice and information about homelessness and the prevention of homelessness

2.9.   Under s 179(1) of the 1996 Act, housing authorities have a duty to secure that advice and information about homelessness, and the prevention of homelessness, are available free of charge to **any person** in their district. The provision of comprehensive advice will play an important part in delivering the housing authority's strategy for preventing homelessness in their district.

2.10.   There is an enormous variety of reasons why people become homeless or find themselves threatened with homelessness. And, in many cases, there can be multiple reasons, and a complex chain of circumstances, that lead to homelessness. Some of these may relate to the housing market, for example, high rents and a shortage of affordable accommodation in the area, or to administrative systems, for example delays in the payment of benefits. Others may relate to personal circumstances, for example, relationship breakdown, a bereavement, long-term or acute ill health or loss of employment. The provision of advice and information to those at risk of homelessness will need to reflect this. It will need to be wide-ranging and comprehensive in its coverage and may require a full multi-disciplinary assessment.

2.11.   Many people who face the potential loss of their current home will be seeking practical advice and assistance to help them remain in their accommodation or secure alternative accommodation. Some may be seeking to apply for assistance under the homelessness legislation without being aware of other options that could help them to secure accommodation. Advice services should provide information on the range of housing options that are available in the district. This might include options to enable people to stay in their existing accommodation, delay homelessness for long enough to allow a planned move, or access alternative accommodation in the private or social sectors. This 'housing options' approach is central to addressing housing need as a means of preventing homelessness.

2.12.   Advice on the following issues may help to prevent homelessness:

- tenants' rights and rights of occupation;
- leaseholders' rights and service charges;
- what to do about harassment and illegal eviction;
- how to deal with possession proceedings;
- rights to benefits (eg housing benefit) including assistance with making claims as required;
- current rent levels;
- how to retrieve rent deposits;
- rent and mortgage arrears;
- how to manage debt;
- grants available for housing repair and/or adaptation;
- how to obtain accommodation in the private rented sector – eg details of landlords and letting agents within the district, including any accreditation schemes, and information on rent guarantee and deposit schemes;

- how to apply for an allocation of accommodation through the social housing waiting list or choice-based lettings scheme;
- how to apply to other social landlords for accommodation.

The advisory service might also include an advocacy service, which may include providing legal representation for people facing the loss of their home.

2.13. Housing authorities will need to ensure that the implications and likely outcomes of the available housing options are made clear to all applicants, including the distinction between having priority need for accommodation under Part 7 and having priority for an allocation of social housing under Part 6.

2.14. Advice services will need to be effectively linked to other relevant statutory and non-statutory service providers. As noted in paragraph 2.10 above, it is often a combination of factors that lead to homelessness, and housing authorities are advised to ensure that people who require advice of a wider or more specialist nature, for example, to address family and relationship breakdown, mental or physical health problems, drug and alcohol abuse, or worklessness are directed to other agencies who can provide the service they need. In situations where there is a history of child abuse or where there are child protection concerns, homelessness and housing organisations will need to work closely with the Local Safeguarding Children Board (LSCB).

2.15. The effectiveness of authorities' housing advice in preventing homelessness or the threat of homelessness is measured by Best Value Performance Indicator BVPI 213. Guidance on BVPI 213 is available at www.communities.gov.uk.

Accessibility

2.16. It is recommended that advisory services are well publicised and accessible to everyone in the district. Appropriate provision will need to be made to ensure accessibility for people with particular needs, including those with mobility difficulties, sight or hearing loss and learning difficulties, as well as those for whom English is not their first language.

Who provides the advice and information?

2.17. The legislation does not specify how housing authorities should ensure that advice and information on homelessness and the prevention of homelessness are made available. They could do this in a number of ways, for example:

i) provide the service themselves;
ii) ensure that it is provided by another organisation; or
iii) ensure that it is provided in partnership with another organisation.

2.18. The housing authority must ensure that the service is free of charge and available and accessible to everyone in their district. Securing the provision of an independent advisory service may help to avoid conflicts of interest. Private

Appendix 2
England: Homelessness

sector tenants may not naturally look to the housing authority for advice. Some young people may be reluctant to approach a statutory authority for advice, but they may feel more at ease in dealing with a more informal advisory service provided by the voluntary sector. People from different ethnic minority groups might also find advice more accessible if it is delivered through community or faith organisations. (See Chapter 21 for guidance on contracting out homelessness functions).

2.19. Under s 179(2), housing authorities may give grants or loans to other persons who are providing advice and information about homelessness and the prevention of homelessness on behalf of the housing authority. Under s 179(3), housing authorities may also assist such persons (eg voluntary organisations) by:

i)   allowing them to use premises belonging to the housing authority,

ii)   making available furniture or other goods, by way of gift, loan or some other arrangement, and

iii)   making available the services of staff employed by the housing authority.

Standards of advice

2.20. Housing authorities should ensure that information provided is current, accurate and appropriate to the individual's circumstances. To ensure they are providing an effective service to a high standard, housing authorities may wish to refer to the quality assurance systems applied by the National Association of Citizens Advice Bureaux, the Shelter network of housing advice centres, the National Disabled Housing Services Ltd (HoDis) accreditation scheme and the Community Legal Service Quality Mark. Housing authorities are also advised to monitor the provision of advisory services to ensure they continue to meet the needs of all sections of the community and help deliver the aims of their homelessness strategy.

Preventing homelessness in specific circumstances

2.21. Some groups of people are likely to be more at risk of homelessness than others. These may include:

- young people who have become estranged from their family; have been in care and/or secure accommodation; have a history of abuse, running away or school exclusions; or whose parents have had mental health, alcohol or drug problems (see Chapter 12 for further guidance on 16 and 17 year olds);

- people from ethnic minority groups;

- people with an institutionalised background, for example where they have spent time in care, in prison or in the armed forces;

- former asylum seekers who have been given permission to stay in the UK and are no longer being accommodated by the National Asylum Support Service;

- people who have experienced other problems that may increase the risk of homelessness including family/relationship breakdowns; domestic, racial or other violence; poor mental or physical health; drug and alcohol misuse; age-related problems and debt.

2.22. In many cases homelessness can be prevented by identifying people who are in circumstances which put them at risk of homelessness, and by providing services which can enable them to remain in their current home. Homelessness can also be prevented by ensuring assistance is available at known risk points such as discharge from prison or hospital. Table 2.1 below gives examples of some of the measures that may help tackle some of the more common causes of homelessness. More detailed guidance is provided in Annex 7.

2.23. Housing authorities should also work with housing providers to encourage them to seek to maintain and sustain tenancies by employing effective strategies for the prevention and management of rent arrears. Landlords should be encouraged to make early and personal contact with tenants in arrears and to assess whether there are any additional support needs and, where relevant, to establish that all benefits to which tenants are entitled are being claimed. Landlords should offer assistance and advice on welfare benefits and in making a claim, debt counselling and money advice either in-house or through a referral to an external agency and implement ways for recovering the money such as debt management plans or attachment to benefits or earnings orders. Possession action should only be taken as a last resort. See Annex 1 for ODPM guidance on *Improving the Effectiveness of Rent Arrears Management*.

Table 2.1: Tackling common causes of homelessness

Cause	Action
Parents, relatives or friends not being able or willing to provide accommodation	Mediation services, usually contracted out by local authority to, for example, Relate, Youth Crime prevention and parenting programmes.
Relationship breakdown, including domestic violence	'Sanctuary' schemes, which allow domestic violence victims to remain in their homes where they choose to do so once security measures are in place.

Appendix 2
England: Homelessness

Cause	Action
Discharge from an institutional situation eg hospital, custody, residential treatment/care	Early planning for discharge between institutional staff and local housing providers, including assessing support needs. Proactive provision of advice by local housing authority on housing options (prior to discharge).
End of assured shorthold tenancy	Housing advice. Rent deposit or bond schemes to encourage landlords to let to potentially homeless people. Landlord-tenant mediation services, to resolve disputes about behaviour or repairs.
Mortgage and rent arrears	Debt counselling. Advocacy services in county court. Fast tracking housing benefit claims.
Person ill-equipped to sustain a tenancy	Advice and support under the Supporting People programme for vulnerable people at risk of homelessness, for example improving budgeting and 'life' skills.
Lack of information	Early and proactive intervention from local authority homelessness services to discuss options and offer assistance and advice.

Preventing homelessness recurring

2.24.   The underlying problems which led to homelessness in the first place have to be addressed in order to provide long-term solutions. Failure to address these root causes can lead to repeated episodes of homelessness. Recurring homelessness may be indicative of problems that are not being resolved by the provision of accommodation alone.

2.25.   An effective approach to tackling recurring homelessness is likely to be based on:

- effective monitoring that identifies housing applicants who are homeless or threatened with homelessness and who have previously been secured accommodation under the homelessness legislation (either by the same authority or another authority in a different area);
- an analysis of the main causes of homelessness among housing applicants who have experienced homelessness more than once; and

- the existence of support services (and, in particular, strong links with the local Supporting People strategy and services) for housing applicants who have experienced homelessness more than once, which tackle these causes and help the applicants to sustain tenancies or other forms of settled accommodation in the longer term.

2.26. Tenancy sustainment is central to preventing repeat homelessness and can include a range of interventions. It is closely linked with good housing management and the Supporting People programme. See Chapter 4 for further guidance on securing support services and the housing-related support services that can be funded through Supporting People.

2.27. Whilst tenancy sustainment is the eventual objective, there are some individuals who may not be able to sustain accommodation due to personal circumstances, for example mental health or substance misuse difficulties. Support will need to be provided to progress towards the time when they are able to maintain accommodation.

Appendix 2
England: Homelessness

CHAPTER 3: ENSURING A SUFFICIENT SUPPLY OF ACCOMMODATION

3.1. This chapter provides guidance on options available to housing authorities to help increase the supply of new housing and maximise the use of the housing stock in their district.

3.2. Section 3(1)(b) of the *Homelessness Act 2002* provides that a homelessness strategy is a strategy for, amongst other things, securing that sufficient accommodation is and will be available for people who are or may become homeless. Chapter 16 provides guidance on the different ways in which housing authorities can ensure that suitable accommodation is available for applicants, for example by providing the accommodation themselves or by securing it from a private landlord or a registered social landlord.

3.3. Homelessness is significantly influenced by the availability of housing, and in particular affordable housing. A shortage of affordable housing can lead to increasing numbers of people being accommodated in temporary accommodation whilst waiting for settled housing to bring the main homelessness duty to an end. 'Settled housing' in this context will primarily be social housing and good quality private sector accommodation (see Chapter 14 for further guidance on bringing the main homelessness (s 193(2)) duty to an end.)

3.4. Although, in 2005, over 80% of people living in temporary accommodation were in self-contained homes they often lack certainty over how long they will live there. This can cause disruption to their lives, make it hard for them to put roots down in the community or to access important services. For example, they may face real difficulties in gaining access to a local GP or in enrolling their children in a local school. Many may already have faced disruption and become disconnected or moved away from existing services and support networks as a result of homelessness.

3.5. The Government's current target is to halve the number of households living in temporary accommodation by 2010. Increasing the supply of new affordable housing and making better use of existing social and private rented stock to provide settled homes will be critical for achieving this target, as will measures to prevent homelessness.

Increase supply of new housing

3.6. The *Sustainable Communities Plan* and *Sustainable Communities: Homes for All* set out how the Government is creating new communities and expanding existing communities in four areas in the wider South East. Taken together, these areas are expected to deliver an extra 200,000 homes above current planning totals.

3.7. At a regional level, local authorities have a key role to play to identify the priorities for housing in their region, to ensure these are reflected in regional housing strategies and to secure funding for their plans. Housing authorities will also need to ensure that housing strategies are aligned with regional economic and planning strategies.

3.8. There are a number of ways housing authorities can increase the supply of new housing. The main source of funding for the provision of affordable housing is the Housing Corporation's national Affordable Housing Programme (AHP), known formerly as the Approved Development Programme (ADP). From the 2006–2008 biannual bidding round, the AHP is open to both registered social landlords and non-registered bodies (eg developers). Bids continue to be assessed against a range of criteria including housing quality and value for money, and against regional and local priorities. Housing authorities will need to work closely with RSLs and others to make best use of this funding.

3.9. Another important means of providing affordable housing is through planning obligations, which are usually negotiated in the context of granting planning permission for new housing development. Planning obligations are generally secured by agreements made between a local authority and a developer under s 106 of the *Town and Country Planning Act 1990* and they are commonly referred to as 's 106 agreements'. Obligations may be appropriate where, for example, a planning objection to a proposed development cannot be overcome by the imposition of a condition. More detailed guidance on the use of s 106 agreements is contained in ODPM Circular 05/2005: Planning Obligations.

3.10. National guidance on planning and affordable housing is currently contained in Planning Policy Guidance Note 3 (PPG3): Housing, as supplemented by Circular 06/98. These documents provide advice to planning authorities about securing the provision of affordable housing either in kind or by financial contribution. They also remind local authorities when formulating local policy or determining planning applications to take account of the need to cater for a range of housing needs and to encourage the development of mixed and balanced communities in order to avoid areas of social exclusion.

3.11. PPG3 and Circular 06/98 are presently under review and a draft Planning Policy Statement 3 (PPS3): Housing was issued for consultation in December 2005. Following the publication of final PPS3, local planning authorities will be expected to ensure that policies in their Local Development Frameworks take into account the updated national planning policy framework for delivering the Government's housing objectives.

3.12. Planning authorities will need to ensure that their affordable housing policies are evidence-based, kept up to date over time, and applied consistently across developments to ensure that affordable housing is effectively and fairly delivered through this route.

Maximising the use of existing housing stock

3.13. A number of options are discussed below for how housing authorities might maximise the use of current housing stock.

The private rented sector

3.14. Some people living in the private rented sector can experience homelessness, but this sector can also provide solutions to homelessness. Homelessness statistics routinely show that the end of an assured shorthold tenancy (AST) is one of the top three reasons for loss of a settled home. Authorities are encouraged to work with landlords in their area to see how this can be addressed, for example, by offering mediation between landlord and tenant where relations have broken down, and negotiating to extend or renew ASTs where appropriate.

3.15. For many, renting in the private sector may offer a practical solution to their housing need (for example, it may offer more choice over location and type of property). Authorities are therefore encouraged to consider providing rent deposits, guarantees or rent in advance, to help households access this sector. They may also consider establishing Accreditation Schemes, whereby landlords voluntarily agree to a set of standards relating to the management or physical condition of privately rented accommodation to help increase the supply of private rented accommodation.

3.16. Many local authorities have used the private rented sector as a source of good quality, self-contained temporary accommodation. However, the private rented sector can also provide a source of settled accommodation, where qualifying offers of ASTs are accepted by households who are owed the main homelessness duty.

3.17. There is scope to make greater use of the private rented sector, either to help households avoid homelessness or to provide more settled homes for people living in temporary accommodation. Authorities are recommended to establish and maintain good relations with private sector landlords, for example through landlord fora. This can be effective in securing an improved supply of properties in the private rented sector for homeless, or potentially homeless, households.

3.18. It is also recommended that authorities review the extent to which qualifying offers of ASTs are being made to households in temporary accommodation in their area; whether there are any barriers to such offers being made or accepted and, if so, what additional steps would need to be taken to address those barriers.

Social housing

3.19. The Secretary of State considers that, generally, it is inappropriate for general needs social housing to be used as temporary accommodation for long periods, especially where such properties are able to be let as settled homes.

3.20. It is important that housing authorities work effectively with RSLs to help them prevent and tackle homelessness in the district. RSLs have a key role to play in sustaining tenancies, reducing evictions and abandonment, and preventing homelessness through their housing management functions. To ensure effective collaboration between themselves and partner RSLs operating in their district housing authorities are advised to consider establishing a nominations agreement. This would include the proportion of lettings that will be made available, any conditions that will apply, and how any disputes about suitability or eligibility will be resolved. Housing authorities are also advised to aim for any exclusion criteria (that may be applied to nominees by the RSL) to be kept to a minimum. Further guidance on co-operation between RSLs and housing authorities is at Annex 5.

3.21. There are a number of schemes and policies that social housing providers can implement to facilitate the effective management and use of the existing housing stock and to keep voids and re-let times to a minimum.

- **Mobility**: 'moveUK' (formerly Housing Employment and Mobility Services) has been developed to offer social housing tenants and jobseekers more choice about where they live and work around the UK. Its services will open up new opportunities for people who wish to move. 'moveUK' will have three main service components:
  (i)   facilitated mobility services to social landlords and their tenants and applicants to help tenants and applicants to find new homes. This will continue and enhance the provision of the grant funded mobility previously provided by Housing Mobility and Exchange Services (HOMES) and LAWN (the Association of London Government scheme that helps tenants who want to, move out of London to areas of low demand);
  (ii) 'one stop shop' web-based information about available housing, neighbourhoods and job vacancies;
  (iii) web access to information on vacancies in social housing.

- **Cash Incentive Scheme** (CIS): although there is no obligation for a housing authority to provide a scheme, the main objectives of the Cash Incentive Scheme (CIS) are to release local authority accommodation required for letting to those in housing need, and to encourage sustainable home ownership. This is achieved by the payment of a grant to a local authority tenant to assist them in buying a property in the private sector.

- **The new HomeBuy scheme**: this scheme, which commenced on 1st April 2006, provides people with the opportunity to own a home based on equity sharing, whilst protecting the supply of social housing. Existing social tenants are one of the priority groups helped under the scheme, and any rented housing association/local authority home vacated by them will then be made available to others in priority housing need. The Social HomeBuy option, which allows housing association and local authority tenants to purchase a share in their rented home, will be voluntary. Landlords will be able to reinvest the proceeds in replacement social homes.

3.22. The Secretary of State also considers that where local authority or RSL stock is provided as temporary accommodation to discharge a main homelessness duty (owed under section 193(2)) the housing authority should give very careful consideration to the scope for allocating the accommodation as a secure or assured tenancy, as appropriate, especially where a household has been living in a particular property for anything other than a short-term emergency stay.

Choice-based Lettings schemes

3.23. The expansion of choice-based lettings policy aims to achieve nationwide coverage by 2010. Local authorities are encouraged to work together, and with RSL partners, to develop sub-regional and regional choice-based lettings schemes which provide maximum choice and flexibility. Local authorities are encouraged to offer choice to homeless households, while ensuring that their schemes are designed so as not to provide a perverse incentive to applicants to make a homelessness application in order to increase their priority for housing. Housing authorities should also consider involving the private rented sector in their choice-based lettings schemes in order to maximise the housing options available.

Empty homes

3.24. Housing authorities are encouraged to adopt positive strategies for minimising empty homes, and other buildings that could provide residential accommodation, across all housing sectors and tenures within their district. A strategy for minimising empty homes might include schemes for tackling low demand social housing, bringing empty private sector properties back into use and bringing flats over shops into residential use.

3.25. Under the *Housing Act 2004* new provisions on Empty Dwelling Management Orders (EDMOs) are expected to be brought into force. EDMOs are a discretionary power for local authorities to use as part of their empty homes strategy. The new powers will allow local authorities to apply to a residential property tribunal for approval to make an interim EDMO lasting for up to 12 months. During this interim period, the authority may only place tenants in the house with the consent of the owner.

3.26. Local authorities also have the discretion to set the council tax discount on long term empty properties at any point between 50% and 0%, as well as at any point between 50% and 10% on second homes, taking into account local conditions.

Housing renewal

3.27. Housing renewal assistance can also assist in meeting the aims of the homelessness strategy. Under the *Regulatory Reform (Housing Assistance) (England and Wales) Order 2002*, local authorities have power to promote housing renewal assistance to landlords, private homeowners and others to increase the supply of a particular type of accommodation through converting under-utilised accommodation to meet identified housing need within the district. Empty homes, vacant accommodation above shops or commercial buildings can be targeted for assistance. Housing renewal assistance can also enable private homeowners to carry out essential repairs or improvements, and remain in their home.

Disabled facilities grant

3.28. Uptake of the Disabled Facilities Grant – a mandatory entitlement administered by housing authorities for eligible disabled people in all housing tenures – can enable homeowners to remain living an independent life at home, and should be considered as part of an effective homelessness strategy. Authorities are required to give a decision within six months of receiving an application. The grant is subject to a maximum limit and is means tested to ensure that funding goes to those most in need.

CHAPTER 4: SECURING SUPPORT SERVICES

4.1. **This chapter provides guidance on the importance of support services in preventing and tackling homelessness and outlines the types of housing-related and other support services that might be required.**

4.2. A homelessness strategy is defined in section 3(1)(c) of the 2002 Act as (among other things) a strategy for securing the satisfactory provision of support for people in their district:

i)   who are or may become homeless; or
ii) who have been homeless and need support to prevent them from becoming homeless again.

4.3. In formulating their homelessness strategies, housing authorities need to recognise that for some households, homelessness cannot be tackled, or prevented, solely through the provision of accommodation. Some households will require a range of support services, which may include housing-related support to help them sustain their accommodation, as well as personal support relating to factors such as relationship breakdown, domestic violence, mental health problems, drug and alcohol addiction, poverty, debt and unemployment.

4.4. Support can help to prevent people who are at risk of homelessness from becoming homeless at all. In other cases, where people have experienced homelessness and been placed in temporary accommodation, the provision of support may be essential to ensure that they are able to continue to enjoy a reasonable quality of life and access the range of services they need to rebuild their lives. The provision of support can also be important in helping formerly homeless households to sustain settled housing and prevent homelessness from recurring.

4.5. Solutions to homelessness should be based on a thorough assessment of the household's needs, including support needs. Housing authorities will need to establish effective links with the Supporting People team, the social services authority and other agencies (for example, Primary Care Trusts, the Criminal Justice Service, and voluntary and community organisations) to ensure that a joint assessment of an applicant's housing and support needs can be made where necessary. Such assessments should inform decisions on intervention to enable a household to remain in their home, placements in temporary accommodation and options for the provision of more settled accommodation that will bring the main homelessness duty to an end.

4.6. Where children and young people are involved, it is important that any solutions to homelessness address the issues they are facing and do not undermine any support they may already be receiving. In particular, housing authorities will need to establish effective links with children's services authorities[2] and establish whether a Common Assessment Framework has been undertaken, and, if so, which agency will have relevant information about the child's or young person's needs.

---

[2]   All authorities should have a children's services authority, delivering through a children's trust, by April 2008. All Directors of Children's Services will be in post by 2008.

Strategy to secure provision of support services

4.7. Section 1 of the 2002 Act requires housing authorities to carry out a homelessness review for their district. Gaining a thorough understanding of the causes of homelessness through the review process will help to inform the range of support provision required. As part of the review, housing authorities must consider all the current activities in their area which contribute to the provision of support for households who are, or may become, homeless, as well as people in the district who have been homeless and need support to prevent them becoming homeless again. They must also consider the resources available. Both activities and resources are likely to involve a range of providers working in the public, private and voluntary sectors. (See Chapter 1 for further guidance on carrying out a homelessness review and formulating a homelessness strategy).

4.8. In formulating their homelessness strategies housing authorities will need to consider the different types and level of support that households may require. Households who have experienced homelessness or who are at risk of homelessness may have diverse needs. Some households may only need information and advice in order to avoid experiencing homelessness, or becoming homeless again. Others, however, will need greater assistance including housing-related support and in some cases may require intensive support from a range of services.

Individuals at risk of homelessness

4.9. Housing authorities should be aware that some individuals may be at particular risk of homelessness, for example young people leaving care, ex-offenders, former members of the armed forces, refugees, people with mental health problems or individuals leaving hospital, and may require a broader package of resettlement support. When developing their homelessness strategies, housing authorities should consider carefully how to work effectively to prevent homelessness amongst these groups and ensure that appropriate support is available. Early identification of people at risk will be crucial to preventing homelessness. Housing authorities should consider agreeing protocols for joint action with local agencies in order to assist with early identification and prevention measures.

4.10. Individuals at risk of homelessness may also include those who have never experienced homelessness in the past and for whom, with the appropriate support, homelessness can be avoided. These individuals may be at risk of homelessness due to specific problems such as managing debt or accessing benefits and require specialist advice which may be delivered through partner agencies such as Citizens Advice Bureaux or Jobcentre Plus. See Chapter 2 for guidance on preventing homelessness.

Young people

4.11. Many young people who have experienced homelessness may lack skills in managing their affairs and require help with managing a tenancy and operating a household budget. Those estranged from their family, particularly care leavers, may lack the advice and support normally available to young people from family, friends and other mentors. 16 and 17 year olds who are homeless and estranged from their family will be particularly vulnerable and in need of support. See Chapter 12 for further guidance on 16 and 17 year olds.

Housing-related support services

4.12. Housing-related support services have a key role in preventing homelessness occurring or recurring. The types of housing-related support that households who have experienced homelessness may need include:

- *support in establishing a suitable home* – help, advice and support in finding and maintaining suitable accommodation for independent living in the community;
- *support with daily living skills* – help, advice and training in the day-to-day skills needed for living independently, such as budgeting and cooking;
- *support in accessing benefits, health and community care services* – information, advice and help in claiming benefits or accessing community care or health services;
- *help in establishing and maintaining social support* – help in rebuilding or establishing social networks that can help counter isolation and help support independent living.

4.13. Services might be delivered through:

- **floating support services** – using support workers who travel to clients' accommodation in order to provide support. These services can operate across all tenures and generally provide time-limited and low intensity support;
- **short and medium stay housing with support** – including direct access schemes, night shelters, hostels, transitional housing and supported lodgings. Some of these services may specialise in supporting particular groups of individuals at risk of homelessness, such as vulnerable young people;
- **long-stay supported housing services** – to provide ongoing support to those who are unable to live independently in the community.

4.14. Housing-related support can be funded through the Supporting People programme, and close co-operation between housing authorities and the Supporting People team will be essential for ensuring effective support for households who have experienced homelessness, particularly through the local Commissioning Body and Core Strategy Group. Further information on housing-related support services is provided in separate guidance, *Supporting People – Guide to Accommodation and Support Options for Homeless Households* (ODPM, 2003).

Other support services

4.15. Households who have experienced homelessness may need additional support services which are not directly housing-related and fall outside the scope of the Supporting People programme funding. Housing authorities will need to co-operate and work collaboratively with other departments within the authority and a wide range of statutory, voluntary and private sector agencies in order to ensure that the support which is required is provided. Joint working with commissioners/planners and providers of the following services will be particularly important:

- health services;
- drug/alcohol services including Drug Action Teams;
- social services;
- children's and young persons' services (eg Connexions, Sure Start children's centres, child care services);
- voluntary and community sector service providers;
- National Offender Management Service (incorporating the Prison Service and the Probation Service);
- Youth Offending Teams;
- Crime and Disorder Reduction Partnerships;
- the Police;
- education and training services;
- the Employment Service (Jobcentre Plus);
- grant making charities and trusts;
- local strategic partnerships.

Support for households in temporary accommodation

4.16. The provision of support to households placed in temporary accommodation is essential to ensure that they are able to continue to enjoy a reasonable quality of life and access the range of services they need. In formulating their homelessness strategies, housing authorities should consider what arrangements need to be in place to ensure that households placed in temporary accommodation, within their district or outside, are able to access relevant support services. In particular households will need to be able to access:

- primary care services such as health visitors and GPs;
- appropriate education services;
- relevant social services; and
- employment and training services.

4.17. Housing authorities will need to liaise and work collaboratively with the relevant service providers to ensure that appropriate arrangements are put in place and monitored. When households are placed in temporary accommodation, it is recommended that housing authorities offer to liaise with the relevant health, education and social services departments in the area in which the households are temporarily housed. Liaison will be particularly important in cases where households have to be accommodated in the district of another housing authority.

4.18. The Secretary of State recommends that housing authorities offer to liaise with the appropriate Primary Care Trust of all families with babies or young children who are placed in temporary accommodation, to ensure that they have the opportunity to receive health and developmental checks from health visitors and/or other primary health care professionals and can participate in vaccination programmes. It would be insufficient for an authority simply to provide such a family with details of health centres and GP practices in the area.

Notify

4.19. Authorities are encouraged to participate in any regional or sub-regional arrangements which facilitate the notification of other authorities and agencies about the location and support needs of households in temporary accommodation. When considering procedures for notifying the relevant agencies of placements in temporary accommodation, housing authorities may wish to have regard to NOTIFY – a web-based notification and information system administered by the Greater London Authority (GLA).

4.20. NOTIFY is designed to improve access to services for households placed in temporary accommodation. Its primary role is to notify relevant services of the placement or movement of households placed in temporary accommodation by London boroughs under the homelessness legislation. The system uses information provided by London borough housing departments to notify housing, education, social services and Primary Care Trusts about households placed in, moving between or leaving temporary accommodation. Information is contained in a database and updated weekly. Authorised users of the NOTIFY notifications website can view information held on NOTIFY at any time, by accessing that website. Relevant services receive a weekly email alert from NOTIFY, informing them of any unviewed notifications and reminding them to access the website. NOTIFY will also shortly provide access for each borough to its own operational management data. The system also has the capacity to analyse aggregated data both at borough and London level. For further information on NOTIFY see notifylondon.gov.uk or contact notify@london.gov.uk.

CHAPTER 5: WORKING WITH OTHERS

5.1. This chapter provides guidance to housing authorities on working in partnership with other agencies to deliver co-ordinated and effective services to tackle homelessness. It considers the range of organisations and people that contribute to preventing and tackling homelessness and provides examples of types of joint working. It also sets out the statutory provisions that require co-operation between various authorities.

5.2. Under s 3(5) of the 2002 Act, when formulating a homelessness strategy the housing authority must consider, among other things, the extent to which any of the strategy's objectives could be achieved through joint action involving two or more of the organisations tackling homelessness in the district. Whilst housing authorities are best placed to take the strategic lead in tackling homelessness, it is vital that as part of their homelessness strategies effective partnerships are developed with other organisations to deliver co-ordinated and more effective approaches to tackling homelessness locally that address not only housing need but all aspects of social need.

Why joint working?

5.3. At its best, joint working can result in higher quality and more efficient and cost-effective services. Joint working can:

- expand the knowledge and expertise of partner agencies;
- help to provide higher quality integrated services to clients with multiple needs;
- help to ensure people who are homeless or at risk of homelessness do not fall through the net because no one agency can meet all their needs;
- reduce wasteful referrals and duplicated work between agencies. For example, common procedures for assessing clients and exchanging information mean homeless people do not have to be repeatedly assessed by different agencies.

Organisations/people working to prevent and tackle homelessness

5.4. The most effective homelessness strategies will be those which harness the potential of all the organisations and persons working to prevent and tackle homelessness in the district, and which ensure that all the activities concerned are consistent and complementary. Joint working could involve the social services authority, the Primary Care Trust, other public bodies such as the National Offender Management Service, voluntary and community sector organisations, registered social landlords, private landlords, and any other relevant organisations. Housing authorities should also consider joint working with other agencies, for example, the Police and voluntary and community sector organisations, to tackle issues related to homelessness such as street drinking, begging, drug misuse and anti-social behaviour. Such collaborative working can help reduce the numbers of people sleeping rough and provide effective services targeted at those who are homeless or at risk of becoming homeless. Annex 3 provides an indicative list of other authorities, organisations and persons whose activities may contribute to preventing and tackling homelessness. Chapter 2 provides guidance on the range of activities that housing authorities might undertake in conjunction with other bodies in order to prevent homelessness.

5.5. Housing authorities should also consider developing cross-boundary partnerships to help tackle homelessness, for example with neighbouring local authorities and local strategic partnerships. Initiatives at regional, cross-regional and sub-regional level that address issues which cut across administrative boundaries may also be relevant – for example regional strategies for refugee integration or reducing re-offending.

Types of joint working

5.6. Joint working can take many forms. Examples of types of collaborative working that could help to achieve the objectives of a homelessness strategy might include:

- establishment of a multi-agency forum for key practitioners and providers to share knowledge, information, ideas and complementary practices;
- clear links between the homelessness strategy and other key strategies such as Supporting People, and the NHS Local Delivery Plan;
- protocols for the referral of clients between services and sharing information between services – for example a joint protocol between hospital-based social workers and housing officers to address the housing needs of patients to be discharged from hospital;
- joint consideration of the needs of homeless people by housing and social services authorities under Part 7, the *Children Act 1989* and community care legislation;
- establishment of formal links with other services – for example with those provided by voluntary and community sector organisations;
- joint planning and commissioning of services;
- joint training;
- funding of joint posts, for example with the social services authority;
- senior housing representation on key corporate groups such as the Local Strategic Partnership (LSP) and the Crime and Disorder Reduction Partnership (CDRP);
- senior commitment from all stakeholders to joined-up working to ensure the homelessness strategy action plan is carried out;
- appropriate user involvement and consultation.

5.7. When offering housing advice and assistance, housing authorities should consider devising screening procedures that identify at an early stage those cases where there is a need for case-specific joint working. Authorities may also wish to encourage their partner agencies to develop similar procedures. Where there is a need for such an approach, authorities are encouraged to adopt agreed protocols to ensure that appropriate action can be quickly initiated.

Early appraisal of all clients who may require multiple assessments, by whichever authority is first approached, with agreed triggers and procedures for further action, may help to prevent duplication of enquiries.

5.8. *Homelessness Strategies – A good practice handbook* (DTLR, March 2002) provides advice on successful joint working and the establishment of good links between different agencies and programmes that can prevent and alleviate homelessness. The handbook also signposts to other sources of guidance, for example, on joint protocols, joint commissioning and joint assessments.

The statutory framework

5.9. The need for co-operation between statutory authorities is recognised in legislation:

- s 213, s 213A and s 170 of the *Housing Act 1996*;
- s 1 of the *Homelessness Act 2002*;
- s 2 of the *Local Government Act 2000*;
- s 27 of the *Children Act 1989*;
- s 10, s 11 and s 13 of the *Children Act 2004*;
- s 47 of the *National Health Service and Community Care Act 1990*;
- s 27 and s 31 of the *Health Act 1999*.

These provisions are outlined in more detail below. However, the absence of a formal legal duty should not act as a barrier to joint working. Rather this should be predicated on meeting local needs and effectively implementing the homelessness strategy.

Housing Act 1996

Section 213

5.10. Where housing or inquiry duties arise under the 1996 Act a housing authority may seek co-operation from another relevant housing authority or body or a social services authority in England, Scotland or Wales. The authority or body to whom the request is made must co-operate to the extent that is reasonable in the circumstances. For this purpose, 'relevant housing authority or body' will include:

in England and Wales:

– another housing authority,

– a registered social landlord,

– a housing action trust, and

in Scotland:

– a local authority,

– a registered social landlord, and

– Scottish Homes.

5.11. The duty on the housing authority, body or social services authority receiving such a request to co-operate will depend on their other commitments and responsibilities. However, they cannot adopt a general policy of refusing such requests, and each case will need to be considered in the circumstances at the time.

5.12. Section 170 of the 1996 Act also provides that where a registered social landlord (RSL) has been requested by a housing authority to offer accommodation to people with priority under its allocation scheme, the RSL must co-operate to such extent as is reasonable in the circumstances. RSLs have a key role to play in preventing and tackling homelessness. See Annex 5 for guidance on co-operation between RSLs and housing authorities.

Section 213A

5.13. Section 213A applies where the housing authority has reason to believe than an applicant with whom a person under the age of 18 resides, or might normally be expected to reside, may be ineligible for assistance, or homeless, or threatened with homelessness, intentionally. Housing authorities are required to have arrangements in place to ensure that all such applicants are invited to agree to the housing authority notifying the social services authority of the essential facts of their case. This will give social services the opportunity to consider the circumstances of the child(ren) and family and plan any response that may be deemed by them to be appropriate. See Chapter 13 for further guidance on s 213A.

Local Government Acts

5.14. The promotion of well-being power contained in s 2 of the *Local Government Act 2000* gives local authorities substantial capacity for cross-boundary partnership working with other authorities and partners, such as the health and social services sectors. In particular, the power provides local authorities with increased scope to improve the social, economic and environmental well-being of their communities. Section 2(5) of the *Local Government Act 2000* makes it clear that local authorities may act in relation to and for the benefit of any person or area outside their own area if they consider that to do so is likely to promote or improve the social, economic or environmental well-being of their own area. This, therefore, provides scope for:

- co-operation between neighbouring local authorities and local strategic partnerships; and
- initiatives at regional, cross-regional and sub-regional level that address issues which cut across administrative boundaries.

It should be noted, however, that the s 2 power cannot be used by authorities to delegate, or contract out their functions. In order to do this, authorities will need to make use of specific powers such as those in s 101 of the *Local Government Act 1972* which provides for the joint exercise of functions between local authorities.

Children Act 1989

5.15. Under s 27 of the *Children Act 1989* ('the 1989 Act'), a local authority can ask a range of other statutory authorities, including a housing authority, to help them in delivering services for children and families, under their functions in Part 3 of the 1989 Act. Authorities must comply with such a request to the extent that it is compatible with their own statutory duties and other obligations, and does not unduly prejudice the discharge of any of their own functions. They cannot adopt a general policy of refusing such requests, and each case will need to be considered according to the circumstances at the time.

5.16. Children and young people should not be sent to and fro between different authorities (or between different departments within authorities). To provide an effective safety net for vulnerable young people who are homeless or at risk of homelessness, housing and social services will need to work together. Effective collaborative working will require clear corporate policies and departmental procedures agreed between the relevant departments. These should make provision for speedy resolution of any dispute as to which department should take responsibility for a particular case. Joint agreements should cover not only the assessment of clients, but should also reflect the strategic planning and delivery of provision to be set out in the local Children and Young People's Plan. Local Safeguarding Children Boards, which will co-ordinate and ensure the effectiveness of local work to safeguard and promote the welfare of children, may also be involved in drawing up policies and procedures to ensure effective inter-agency co-operation (see also paragraphs 5.17–5.20 below) and Chapter 13.

5.17. Under the 1989 Act, young people leaving care and 16/17 year old children assessed as in need are owed duties which may extend to the provision of accommodation. Where social services approach a housing authority for assistance in housing a young person, the housing authority must co-operate subject to the conditions referred to above in para 5.16. Whether a young person is accommodated under the auspices of the social services authority or the housing authority is a matter for individual authorities to determine in each case. Ideally the relationship of the two authorities should be symbiotic, with jointly agreed protocols in place in respect of the assessment of needs. In many cases the social services authority will have a continuing responsibility for the welfare of vulnerable young people and for assisting them in the transition to adulthood and independent living. Under the 1989 Act, these responsibilities can extend until the young person is aged 18 and in the case of care leavers until the age of 21 (or beyond that age if they are in an agreed programme of education and training). Thus, social services authorities can request assistance from housing authorities in meeting their obligations to provide accommodation for a young person and housing authorities can look to social services authorities to provide the support that young homeless applicants may require. In some cases, housing and social services authorities will both have responsibilities towards young people and will need to work together in order to ensure that an appropriate combination of housing and support is arranged to help the young person to live independently successfully.

Children Act 2004

5.18. The *Children Act 2004* ('the 2004 Act') provides the legislative support for the *Every Child Matters: Change for Children* programme which sets out a national framework for local change programmes to build services around the needs of children and young people. Improved outcomes for children will be driven by an analysis of local priorities and secured through more integrated front-line delivery such as multi-agency working, integrated processes such as the Common Assessment Framework, integrated strategy with joint planning and commissioning, and governance arrangements such as the creation of a Director of Children's Services and lead member for children's services.

5.19. To support the integration of systems to improve outcomes for children and young people by the creation of children's trusts, s 10 of the 2004 Act establishes a duty on county level and unitary authorities[3] to make arrangements to promote co-operation between the authority, relevant partners (including district councils) and other persons or bodies engaged in activities in relation to children, to improve the well-being of children and young people in the authority's area. Relevant partners are required to co-operate with the authority. Section 11 of the 2004 Act requires a range of agencies – including county level and unitary authorities and district authorities where there are two tiers of local government – to make arrangements for ensuring that their functions are discharged having regard to the need to safeguard and promote the welfare of children. Section 13 of the 2004 Act requires county level and unitary authorities to set up a Local Safeguarding Children Board (LSCB) incorporating key organisations including district councils where relevant. As set out in s 14, the objective of the LSCB is to co-ordinate and ensure the effectiveness of what is done by each person or body represented on the board to safeguard and promote the welfare of children in that area.

5.20. The 2004 Act also makes provision for indexes containing basic information about children and young people to enable better sharing of information. In addition, each local authority is required to draw up a Children and Young People's Plan (CYPP) by April 2006. The CYPP will be a single, strategic, over-arching plan for all services affecting children and young people. The CYPP and the process of joint planning should support local authorities and their partners as they work together. An integrated inspection framework is also being created with Joint Area Reviews assessing local areas' progress in improving outcomes.

The Department for Education and Skills has produced statutory guidance on the *Children Act 2004* which is available from **www.everychildmatters.gov.uk**.

---

[3] Section 65 of the Children Act 2004 uses the term 'children's services authority' to define these authorities as: a county council in England; a metropolitan district council; a non-metropolitan district council for an area where there is no county council; a London borough council; the Common Council of the City of London and the Council of the Isles of Scilly.

National Health Service and Community Care Act 1990

5.21. Under the National Health Service (NHS) and Community Care Act 1990 ('the 1990 Act'), social services authorities are required to carry out an assessment of any person who may have a need for community care services. The purpose of the legislation is to ensure that the planning and assessment processes identify a person's full range of needs, including housing needs. Section 47 of the 1990 Act requires social service authorities to notify the housing authority if there appears to be a housing need when the assessment is carried out. The 'housing need', for example, may be for renovation or adaptation of the person's current accommodation or for alternative accommodation.

5.22. An assessment of vulnerability under the homelessness legislation will not necessarily mean that a client is eligible for social care services. Policy guidance on fair access to care services (FACS) was published on 2 June 2002 under guidance of local authority circular (LAC) (2002) 13. The guidance provides authorities with an eligibility framework for adult social care for them to use when setting and applying their eligibility criteria.

Health Act 1999

5.23. Section 27 of the Health Act 1999 ('the 1999 Act') requires NHS bodies and local authorities to co-operate with one another in exercising their respective functions in order to secure and advance the health and welfare of the people of England and Wales.

5.24. Under s 31 of the 1999 Act, partnership arrangements can be designed to help break down the barriers between NHS and local authority services by removing existing constraints in the system and increasing flexibility in the provision and commissioning of services. The legislation introduces three flexibilities: pooled budgets, lead commissioning and integrated provision. Any health-related local authority function can be included in these partnerships, for example, housing, social services, education and leisure services.

National Standards, Local Action: Health and Social Care Standards and Planning Framework 2005/06–2007/08

5.25. This document sets out the framework for all NHS organisations and social services authorities to use in planning over the financial years 2005/06–2007/08. It looks to Primary Care Trusts (PCTs) and local authorities to lead community partnership by even closer joint working to take forward the NHS Improvement Plan. Building on joint work on Local Strategic Partnerships (LSPs), they will need to work in partnership with other NHS organisations in preparing Local Delivery Plans (LDPs) for the period 2005/06 to 2007/08.

Appendix 2
England: Homelessness

Mental health

5.26. The Mental Health National Service Framework (NSF 30/09/1999) addresses the mental health needs of working age adults up to 65. It sets out national standards; national service models; local action and national underpinning programmes for implementation; and a series of national milestones to assure progress, with performance indicators to support effective performance management. An organisational framework for providing integrated services and for commissioning services across the spectrum is also included.

5.27. The Government wants to ensure that people suffering from mental illness receive appropriate care and assistance, particularly those whose illness is severe and enduring. Research has shown that provision of suitable, settled housing is essential to the well-being of this vulnerable group. A key element in the spectrum of care and support is the development of a care plan under the Care Programme Approach (CPA). The initial assessment and ongoing reviews under the CPA must include an assessment of an individual's housing needs. It is essential that housing authorities liaise closely with social services authorities so that any provision of housing is appropriate to the needs of the individual, and meshes with the social and health care support that may be an essential part of the person's care programme.

5.28. This is equally important for young people up to the age of 18. Chapter 9 of the National Service Framework for Children, Young People and Maternity Services published in 2004 makes clear that use of the CPA is also a key marker of good practice for child and adolescent mental health services working with young people with high levels of mental health need.

CHAPTER 6: APPLICATIONS, INQUIRIES, DECISIONS AND NOTIFICATIONS

6.1. This chapter provides guidance on dealing with applications for accommodation or assistance in obtaining accommodation; a housing authority's duty to carry out inquiries (where it has reason to believe an applicant may be homeless or threatened with homelessness); and, following inquiries, an authority's duty to notify an applicant of its decision.

Applications for assistance

6.2. Under s 184 of the 1996 Act, if a housing authority has reason to believe that a person applying to the authority for accommodation or assistance in obtaining accommodation may be homeless or threatened with homelessness, the authority must make such inquiries as are necessary to satisfy itself whether the applicant is eligible for assistance and if so, whether any duty, and if so what duty, is owed to that person under Part 7 of the 1996 Act. The definitions of 'homeless' and 'threatened with homelessness' are discussed in Chapter 8.

Preventing homelessness

6.3. Under s 179, housing authorities have a duty to ensure that advice and information about homelessness and the prevention of homelessness are available free of charge to anyone in their district (see Chapter 2 for further guidance on providing advice and information to prevent homelessness). In many cases early, effective intervention can prevent homelessness occurring. Many people who face the potential loss of their current home will be seeking practical advice and assistance to help them remain in their accommodation or secure alternative accommodation. Some may be seeking to apply for assistance under the homelessness legislation without being aware of other options that could help them to secure accommodation. Authorities should explain the various housing options that are available. These might include:

- advice and assistance (eg legal advice or mediation with a landlord) to enable them to remain in their current home;
- assistance (eg rent deposit or guarantee) to obtain accommodation in the private rented sector;
- an application for an allocation of long term social housing accommodation through a social housing waiting list or choice-based lettings scheme; or
- advice on how to apply to another social landlord for accommodation.

6.4. Housing authorities should ensure that the implications and likely outcomes of the available housing options are made clear to all applicants, including the distinction between having a priority need for accommodation under Part 7 and being in a 'reasonable preference' category for an allocation of housing under Part 6. Authorities must not avoid their obligations under Part 7 (especially the duty to make inquiries under s 184), but it is open to them to suggest alternative solutions in cases of potential homelessness where these would be appropriate and acceptable to the applicant.

Interim duty to accommodate

6.5. If a housing authority has reason to believe that an applicant may be eligible for assistance, homeless and have a priority need, the authority will have **an immediate duty under s 188 to ensure that suitable accommodation is available for the applicant** (and his or her household) pending the completion of the authority's inquiries and its decision as to what duty, if any, is owed to the applicant under Part 7 of the Act. Chapter 7 provides guidance on the interim duty to accommodate. Authorities are reminded that 'having reason to believe' is a lower test than 'being satisfied'.

Form of the application

6.6. Applications can be made by any adult to any department of the local authority and expressed in any particular form; they need not be expressed as explicitly seeking assistance under Part 7. Applications may also be made by a person acting on behalf of the applicant, for example, by a social worker or solicitor acting in a professional capacity, or by a relative or friend in circumstances where the applicant is unable to make an application themselves.

Applications to more than one housing authority

6.7. In some cases applicants may apply to more than one housing authority simultaneously and housing authorities will need to be alert to cases where an applicant is doing this. In such cases, where a housing authority has reason to believe that the applicant may be homeless or threatened with homelessness, it may wish to contact the other housing authorities involved, to agree which housing authority will take responsibility for conducting inquiries. Where another housing authority has previously made decisions about an applicant's circumstances, a housing authority considering a fresh application may wish to have regard to those decisions. However, housing authorities should not rely solely on decisions made by another housing authority and will need to make their own inquiries in order to reach an independent decision on whether any duty, and if so which duty, is owed under Part 7. Any arrangements for the discharge of any of their functions by another housing authority must comply with s 101 of the *Local Government Act 1972*.

Service provision

6.8. A need for accommodation or assistance in obtaining accommodation can arise at any time. Housing authorities will therefore need to provide access to advice and assistance at all times during normal office hours, and have arrangements in place for 24-hour emergency cover, e g by enabling telephone access to an appropriate duty officer. The police and other relevant services should be provided with details of how to access the service outside normal office hours.

6.9. In the interests of good administration, it is recommended that housing authorities should give proper consideration to the location of, and accessibility to, advice and information about homelessness and the prevention of homelessness, including the need to ensure privacy during interviews. Details of the service including the opening hours, address, telephone numbers and the 24-hour emergency contact should be well publicised within the housing authority's district.

6.10. Housing authorities should provide applicants with a clear and simple explanation of their procedures for handling applications and making decisions. It is recommended that this is provided in written form, for example as a leaflet, as well as orally. In order to ensure advice and assistance are accessible to everyone in the district, it is recommended that information is made available in the main languages spoken in the area, and that for languages less frequently spoken there is access to interpreters. Applicants should be kept informed of the progress of their application and the timescales involved for making a decision on their case. They should also be given a realistic expectation of the assistance to which they may be entitled.

6.11. Under s 214, it is an offence for a person, knowingly or recklessly to make a false statement, or knowingly to withhold information, with intent to induce the authority to believe that he or she, or another person, is entitled to accommodation under Part 7. If, before the applicant receives notification of a decision, there is any change of facts material to his or her case, he or she must inform the housing authority of this as soon as possible. Housing authorities must ensure that all applicants are made aware of these obligations and that they are explained in ordinary language. Housing authorities are advised to ensure that the obligations are conveyed sensitively to avoid intimidating applicants.

Inquiries

6.12. Under s 184, where a housing authority has reason to believe that an applicant may be homeless or threatened with homelessness, it must make inquiries to satisfy itself whether the applicant is eligible for assistance (see Chapter 9) and, if so, whether any duty and if so what duty is owed to him or her under Part 7. In order to determine this, the authority will need to establish whether the applicant is homeless or threatened with homelessness (see Chapter 8), whether he or she became homeless, or threatened with homelessness, intentionally (see Chapter 11) and whether he or she has a priority need for accommodation (see Chapter 10).

6.13. In addition to determining whether an applicant is owed any duty under Part 7, housing authorities are reminded that they have a **power** to provide further assistance to applicants who are eligible for assistance, homeless (or threatened with homelessness) unintentionally and do not have a priority need.

Under s 192(3), housing authorities may secure that accommodation is available for applicants who are eligible, unintentionally homeless and do not have a priority need (see Chapter 15 for further guidance). Under s 195(9), housing authorities may take reasonable steps to secure that accommodation does not cease to be available for applicants who are eligible for assistance, unintentionally threatened with homelessness and do not have a priority need for accommodation (see paragraph 14.7 for guidance on steps to secure that accommodation does not cease to be available).

6.14. Under s 184(2), housing authorities may also make inquiries to decide whether the applicant has a local connection with another housing authority district in England, Wales or Scotland, but they are not required to do so. The possibility of a referral of an applicant to another housing authority can only arise where the applicant has been accepted as eligible for assistance, unintentionally homeless and having a priority need for accommodation (see Chapter 18 for guidance on local connection and referrals).

6.15. The obligation to make inquiries, and satisfy itself whether a duty is owed, rests with the housing authority and it is not for applicants to 'prove their case'. Applicants should always be given the opportunity to explain their circumstances fully, particularly on matters that could lead to a decision against their interests, for example, a decision that an applicant is intentionally homeless.

6.16. Housing authorities should deal with inquiries as quickly as possible, whilst ensuring that they are thorough and, in any particular case, sufficient to enable the housing authority to satisfy itself what duty, if any, is owed or what other assistance can be offered. Housing authorities are obliged to begin inquiries as soon as they have reason to believe that an applicant may be homeless or threatened with homelessness and should aim to carry out an initial interview and preliminary assessment on the day an application is received. An early assessment will be vital to determine whether the housing authority has an immediate duty to secure accommodation under s 188 (see Chapter 7 for guidance on the interim duty to accommodate). Wherever possible, it is recommended that housing authorities aim to complete their inquiries and notify the applicant of their decision within 33 working days of accepting a duty to make inquiries under s 184. In many cases it should be possible for authorities to complete the inquiries significantly earlier.

Violence

6.17. Under s 177, it is not reasonable for a person to continue to occupy accommodation if it is probable that this will lead to domestic or other violence against him or her, or against a person who normally resides with him or her as a member of his or her family, or any other person who might reasonably be expected to reside with him or her. Violence includes threats of violence from another person which are likely to be carried out. Inquiries into cases where violence is alleged will need careful handling. It is essential that inquiries do not provoke further violence. It is not advisable for the housing authority to approach the alleged perpetrator, since this could generate further violence, and may delay the assessment. Housing authorities may, however, wish to seek information from friends and relatives of the applicant, social services and the police, as appropriate. In some cases, corroborative evidence of actual or threatened violence may not be available, for example, because there were no adult witnesses and/or the applicant was too frightened or ashamed to report incidents to family, friends or the police. In many cases involving violence, the applicant may be in considerable distress and an officer trained in dealing with the particular circumstances should conduct the interview. Applicants should be given the option of being interviewed by an officer of the same sex if they so wish.

6.18. In cases where violence is a feature and the applicant may have a local connection elsewhere, the housing authority, in considering whether to notify another housing authority about a possible referral of the case, must be aware that s 198 provides that an applicant cannot be referred to another housing authority if he or she, or any person who might reasonably be expected to reside with him or her, would be at risk of violence in the district of the other housing authority (see Chapter 18 for guidance on referrals to another housing authority).

Support needs

6.19. 16 and 17 year olds (including lone parents) who apply for housing assistance may also have care and support needs that need to be assessed. The Secretary of State recommends that housing authorities and social services authorities (and the relevant departments within unitary authorities) have arrangements in place for joint consideration of such young people's needs, whether the application is made initially to the housing department or social services department. See Chapter 12 for further guidance on 16 and 17 year olds.

Assistance from another authority or body

6.20. Under s 213, a housing authority may request another relevant housing authority or body to assist them in the discharge of their functions under Part 7. In such cases the authority or body must co-operate in rendering such assistance in the discharge of the functions to which the request relates as is reasonable in the circumstances. For example, a housing authority may request another housing authority to co-operate in providing information about a previous application. See paragraph 5.10 for further guidance on s 213.

Decisions/notifications

6.21. When a housing authority has completed its inquiries under s 184 it must notify the applicant in writing of its decision on the case. Where the decision is against the applicant's interests, eg a decision that he or she is ineligible for assistance, not homeless, not in priority need or homeless intentionally, the notification must explain clearly and fully the reasons for the decision. If the housing authority has decided that the conditions for referring the applicant's homelessness case to another housing authority have been met, they must notify the applicant of this and give their reasons for doing so.

6.22. All notifications must inform applicants of their right to request a review of the housing authority's decision and the time within which such a request must be made. At this stage, it is also recommended that housing authorities explain the review procedures. (See Chapter 19 for guidance on reviews of decisions and appeals to the county court).

6.23. It will be important to ensure that the applicant fully understands the decision and the nature of any housing duty that is owed. In cases where the applicant may have difficulty understanding the implications of the decision, it is recommended that housing authorities consider arranging for a member of staff to provide and explain the notification in person.

6.24. Under s 193(3A), where the housing authority accepts a duty to secure accommodation for an applicant under s 193(2), they must give the applicant a copy of the statement included in their allocation scheme of the housing authority's policy on offering people a choice of housing or the opportunity to express their preferences about the accommodation to be allocated to them. This statement is required to be included in the allocation scheme under s 167(1A).

6.25. Section 184(6) provides that where a notification is not received by an applicant, it can be treated as having been given to him or her, if it is made available at the housing authority's office for a reasonable period that would allow it to be collected by the applicant or by someone acting on his or her behalf.

Withdrawn applications

6.26. It is recommended that housing authorities have procedures in place for dealing with applications that are withdrawn or where someone fails to maintain contact with the housing authority after making an application. The Secretary of State considers that it would be reasonable to consider an application closed where there has been no contact with the applicant for three months or longer. Any further approach from the applicant after this time may need to be considered as a fresh application. Where an applicant renews contact within three months the housing authority will need to consider any change of circumstances that may affect the application.

Further applications

6.27. There is no period of disqualification if someone wants to make a fresh application. Where a person whose application has been previously considered and determined under Part 7 makes a fresh application, the authority will need to decide whether there are any new facts in the fresh application which render it different from the earlier application. If no new facts are revealed, or any new facts are of a trivial nature, the authority would not be required to consider the new application. However, where the fresh application does reveal substantive new facts, the authority must treat the fresh application in the same way as it would any other application for accommodation or assistance in obtaining accommodation. Therefore, if the authority has reason to believe that the person is homeless, or threatened with homelessness, the authority should make inquiries under s 184 and decide whether any duty is owed under s 188(1).

CHAPTER 7: INTERIM DUTY TO ACCOMMODATE

7.1. This chapter provides guidance on housing authorities' interim duty to secure that accommodation is available for an applicant if they have reason to believe that the applicant may be homeless, eligible for assistance and has a priority need.

7.2. Section 188(1) imposes an interim duty on housing authorities to secure that accommodation is available for an applicant (and his or her household) pending their decision as to what duty, if any, is owed to the applicant under Part 7 of the Act if they have reason to believe that the applicant may:

a)   be homeless,
b)   be eligible for assistance, and
c)   have a priority need.

7.3.   The threshold for the duty is low as the local authority only has to have a reason to believe that the applicant **may** be homeless, eligible for assistance and have a priority need. (See paragraph 6.5 for guidance on the 'reason to believe' test.)

7.4.   The s 188(1) duty applies even where the authority considers the applicant may not have a local connection with their district and may have one with the district of another housing authority (s 188(2)). Applicants cannot be referred to another housing authority unless the housing authority dealing with the application is satisfied that s 193 applies (ie the applicant is eligible for assistance, unintentionally homeless and has a priority need). (See Chapter 18 for guidance on referrals to other housing authorities.)

Suitability of accommodation

7.5.   The accommodation provided under s 188(1) must be suitable for the applicant and his or her household and the suitability requirements under s 206(1) and s 210(1) apply (see Chapter 17 for guidance on the suitability of accommodation). The applicant does not have the right to ask for a review of the housing authority's decision as to the suitability of accommodation secured under the interim duty, but housing authorities are reminded that such decisions could be subject to judicial review.

7.6.   Housing authorities should avoid using Bed & Breakfast (B&B) accommodation wherever possible. Where B&B accommodation has been used in an emergency situation, applicants should be moved to more suitable accommodation as soon as possible. The *Homelessness (Suitability of Accommodation) (England) Order 2003* provides that B&B accommodation is not suitable accommodation for families with children and households that include a pregnant woman unless there is no alternative accommodation available and then only for a maximum of six weeks.

Discharging the interim duty

7.7. Where the s 188(1) interim duty is being discharged, inquiries should be completed as quickly as possible to minimise uncertainty for the applicant and the period for which accommodation needs to be secured by the housing authority. (See Chapter 6 for guidance on inquiries).

7.8. Housing authorities can discharge their interim duty to secure accommodation by providing their own accommodation or by arranging that it is provided by some other person, or by providing advice and assistance so that it will be provided by some other person. (See Chapter 16 for more information on discharging the duty to secure accommodation).

Ending the interim duty

7.9. The s 188(1) interim duty ends once the housing authority has notified the applicant of its decision as to what duty, if any, is owed to him or her under Part 7, even if the applicant requests a review of the decision.

7.10. Where, having completed their inquiries, the housing authority is satisfied that they are under no further duty to secure accommodation, they should give the applicant a reasonable period of notice to vacate the accommodation to enable him or her to make alternative accommodation arrangements for him/herself. The time allowed should be reasonable when judged against the circumstances of the applicant. Housing authorities should give the applicant time to consider whether to request a review of their decision and, if a review is requested, will need to consider whether to exercise their discretionary power under s 188(3) to secure that accommodation is available (see paragraph 7.13 below).

7.11. It has been established that, as a general rule, accommodation provided pending inquiries under s 184 does not create a tenancy or a licence under the *Protection from Eviction Act 1977*. The courts have applied this principle in cases where the accommodation provided was B&B accommodation in a hotel and where it was a self-contained flat. Consequently, where this general rule applies, housing authorities are required only to provide an applicant with reasonable notice to vacate accommodation provided under the interim duty, and do not need to apply for a possession order from the court. Authorities should note, however, that this general rule may be displaced by an agreement between the housing authority and the applicant, or if the occupation of the accommodation is allowed to continue on more than a transient basis.

7.12. In cases involving applicants who have children under 18 where the housing authority are satisfied that the applicant is ineligible for assistance, the housing authority must alert the social services authority, or social services department, as appropriate, to the case (see Chapter 13 for further guidance on co-operation with social services). Applicants should be invited to consent to social services being notified of the case, but in certain circumstances, for example where the housing authority are concerned about the welfare of the child, they should disclose information about the case even where consent has not been given.

Accommodation pending a review

7.13. Where a review of a decision of a housing authority is requested under s 202, although there is no duty under s 188(1), under s 188(3) the housing authority has a discretionary power to provide accommodation pending the outcome of the review. Failure to consider exercising this discretionary power could be the subject of challenge by judicial review proceedings. Housing authorities are reminded that applicants have 21 days in which to request a review of a decision. (See Chapter 19 for guidance on review of decisions and Chapter 15 for guidance on powers to accommodate pending a review).

CHAPTER 8: HOMELESS OR THREATENED WITH HOMELESSNESS

8.1. This chapter provides guidance on how to determine whether a person is 'homeless' or 'threatened with homelessness' for the purposes of Part 7.

8.2. Under s 184 of the 1996 Act, if a housing authority has reason to believe that a person applying to the housing authority for accommodation, or assistance in obtaining accommodation, may be homeless or threatened with homelessness, the housing authority must make inquiries to satisfy itself whether the applicant is eligible for assistance and if so, whether a duty is owed to that person under Part 7 of the 1996 Act (see Chapter 6 for guidance on applications for assistance).

Threatened with homelessness

8.3. Under s 175(4), a person is 'threatened with homelessness' if he or she is likely to become homeless within 28 days. In many cases, effective intervention can enable homelessness to be prevented or the loss of the current home to be delayed sufficiently to allow for a planned move. The Secretary of State considers that housing authorities should take steps to prevent homelessness wherever possible, offering a broad range of advice and assistance for those in housing need. Authorities should not wait until homelessness is a likelihood or is imminent before providing advice and assistance. (See Chapter 2 for guidance on preventing homelessness).

Homeless

8.4. There are a number of different factors that determine whether a person is homeless. Under s 175, a person is homeless if he or she has no accommodation in the UK or elsewhere which is available for his or her occupation and which that person has a legal right to occupy. A person is also homeless if he or she has accommodation but cannot secure entry to it, or the accommodation is a moveable structure, vehicle or vessel designed or adapted for human habitation (such as a caravan or house boat) and there is no place where it can be placed in order to provide accommodation. A person who has accommodation is to be treated as homeless where it would not be reasonable for him or her to continue to occupy that accommodation.

Available for occupation

8.5. Section 176 provides that accommodation shall be treated as available for a person's occupation only if it is available for occupation by him or her together with:

   i)   any other person who normally resides with him or her as a member of the family, or

   ii)   any other person who might reasonably be expected to reside with him or her.

The first group covers those members of the family who normally reside with the applicant. The phrase 'as a member of the family' although not defined, will include those with close blood or marital relationships and cohabiting partners (including same sex partners), and, where such a person is an established member of the household, the accommodation must provide for him or her as well. The second group relates to any other person, and includes those who may not have been living as part of the household at the time of the application, but whom it would be reasonable to expect to live with the applicant as part of his or her household. Persons in the second group might include a companion for an elderly or disabled person, or children who are being fostered by the applicant or a member of his or her family. The second group will also include those members of the family who were not living as part of the household at the time of the application but who nonetheless might reasonably be expected to form part of it.

8.6. It is for the housing authority to assess whether any other person might reasonably be expected to live with the applicant and there will be a range of situations that the authority will need to consider. Persons who would normally live with the applicant but who are unable to do so because there is no accommodation in which they can all live together should be included in the assessment. When dealing with a family which has split up, housing authorities will need to take a decision as to which members of the family normally reside, or might be expected to reside, with the applicant. A court may have made a residence order indicating with whom the children are to live, but in many cases it will be a matter of agreement between the parents and a court will not have been involved.

Legal right to occupy accommodation

8.7. Under s 175(1), a person is homeless if he or she has no accommodation which he or she can legally occupy by virtue of:

i) an interest in it (eg as an owner, lessee or tenant) or by virtue of a court order;

ii) an express or implied licence to occupy it (eg as a lodger, as an employee with a service occupancy, or when living with a relative); or

iii) any enactment or rule of law giving him or her the right to remain in occupation or restricting the right of another person to recover possession (eg a person retaining possession as a statutory tenant under the Rent Acts where that person's contractual rights to occupy have expired or been terminated).

8.8. A person who has been occupying accommodation as a licensee whose licence has been terminated (and who does not have any other accommodation available for his or her occupation) is homeless because he or she no longer has a legal right to continue to occupy, despite the fact that that person may continue to occupy but as a trespasser. This may include, for example:

i) those required to leave hostels or hospitals; or

ii)   former employees occupying premises under a service occupancy which is dependent upon contracts of employment which have ended.

People asked to leave accommodation by family or friends

8.9. Some applicants may have been asked to leave their current accommodation by family or friends with whom they have been living. In such cases, the housing authority will need to consider carefully whether the applicant's licence to occupy the accommodation has in fact been revoked. Housing authorities may need to interview the parents or friends to establish whether they are genuinely revoking the licence to occupy and rendering the applicants homeless. Authorities are encouraged to be sensitive to situations where parents or carers may have been providing a home for a family member with support needs (for example a person with learning difficulties) for a number of years and who are genuinely finding it difficult to continue with that arrangement, but are reluctant to revoke their licence to occupy formally until alternative accommodation can be secured.

8.10. In some cases the applicant may be unable to stay in his or her accommodation and in others there may be scope for preventing or postponing homelessness, and providing the applicant with an opportunity to plan their future accommodation and pursue various housing options with assistance from the housing authority. However, housing authorities will need to be sensitive to the possibility that for some applicants it may not be safe for them to remain in, or return to, their home because of a risk of violence or abuse.

8.11. In areas of high demand for affordable housing, people living with family and friends may have genuine difficulties in finding alternative accommodation that can lead to friction and disputes within their current home, culminating in a threat of homelessness. In some cases external support, or the promise of assistance with alternative housing, may help to reduce tension and prevent homelessness. The use of family mediation services may assist here.

8.12. Housing authorities will also need to be alert to the possibility of collusion where family or friends agree to revoke a licence to occupy accommodation as part of an arrangement whose purpose is to enable the applicant to be entitled to assistance under Part 7. Some parents and children, for example, may seek to take advantage of the fact that 16 and 17 year old applicants have a priority need for accommodation (see also Chapter 11 on intentional homelessness).

16 and 17 year olds

8.13. The Secretary of State considers that, generally, it will be in the best interests of 16 and 17 year olds to live in the family home, unless it would be unsafe or unsuitable for them to do so because they would be at risk of violence or abuse. See Chapter 12 for further guidance on 16 and 17 year olds.

Appendix 2
England: Homelessness

Tenant given notice

8.14. With certain exceptions, a person who has been occupying accommodation as a tenant and who has received a valid notice to quit, or notice that the landlord requires possession of the accommodation, would have the right to remain in occupation until a warrant for possession was executed (following the granting of an order for possession by the court). The exceptions are tenants with resident landlords and certain other tenants who do not benefit from the *Protection from Eviction Act 1977*. **However, authorities should note that the fact that a tenant has a right to remain in occupation does not necessarily mean that he or she is not homeless.** In assessing whether an applicant is homeless in cases where he or she is a tenant who has a right to remain in occupation pending execution of a warrant for possession, the housing authority will also need to consider whether it would be reasonable for him or her to continue to occupy the accommodation in the circumstances (see paragraphs 8.30–8.32 below).

8.15. Some tenants may face having to leave their accommodation because their landlord has defaulted on the mortgage of the property they rent. Where a mortgage lender starts possession proceedings, the lender is obliged to give written notice of the proceedings to the occupiers of the property before an order for possession is granted. The notice must be given after issue of the possession summons and at least 14 days before the court hearing. As for tenants given notice that the landlord requires possession of the accommodation (see paragraph 8.14 above), authorities will need to consider whether it would be reasonable for a tenant to continue to occupy the accommodation after receiving notice of possession proceedings from the lender.

Inability to secure entry to accommodation

8.16. Under s 175(2), a person is homeless if he or she has a legal entitlement to accommodation, but is unable to secure entry to it, for example:

- those who have been evicted illegally, or
- those whose accommodation is being occupied illegally by squatters.

Although legal remedies may be available to the applicant to regain possession of the accommodation, housing authorities cannot refuse to assist while he or she is actually homeless.

Accommodation consisting of a moveable structure

8.17. Section 175(2)(b) provides that a person is homeless if he or she has accommodation available for his or her occupation which is a moveable structure, vehicle or vessel designed or adapted for human habitation (eg a caravan or houseboat), and there is nowhere that he or she is entitled or permitted to place it and reside in it. The site or mooring for the moveable structure need not be permanent in order to avoid homelessness. In many cases the nature of the structure may reflect the itinerant lifestyle of the applicant, who may not be looking for a permanent site but somewhere to park or moor on a temporary basis.

Reasonable to continue to occupy

8.18. Section 175(3) provides that a person shall not be treated as having accommodation unless it is accommodation which it would be reasonable for him or her to continue to occupy. There are a number of provisions relating to whether or not it is reasonable for someone to continue to occupy accommodation and these are discussed below. There is no simple test of reasonableness. It is for the housing authority to make a judgment on the facts of each case, taking into account the circumstances of the applicant.

Domestic violence or other violence

8.19. Section 177(1) provides that it is not reasonable for a person to continue to occupy accommodation if it is probable that this will lead to domestic violence or other violence against:

i) the applicant;
ii) a person who normally resides as a member of the applicant's family; or
iii) any other person who might reasonably be expected to reside with the applicant.

Section 177(1A) provides that violence means violence from another person or threats of violence from another person which are likely to be carried out. Domestic violence is violence from a person who is associated with the victim and also includes threats of violence which are likely to be carried out. Domestic violence is not confined to instances within the home but extends to violence outside the home.

8.20. Section 178 provides that, for the purposes of defining domestic violence, a person is associated with another if:

(a) they are, or have been, married to each other;
(b) they are or have been civil partners of each other;
(c) they are, or have been, cohabitants (including same sex partners);
(d) they live, or have lived, in the same household;
(e) they are relatives, ie father, mother, stepfather, stepmother, son, daughter, stepson, stepdaughter, grandmother, grandfather, grandson, granddaughter, brother, sister, uncle, aunt, niece or nephew (whether of full blood, half blood or by affinity) of that person or of that person's spouse or former spouse. A person is also included if he or she would fall into any of these categories in relation to cohabitees or former cohabitees if they were married to each other;
(f) they have agreed to marry each other whether or not that agreement has been terminated;
(g) they have entered into a civil partnership agreement between them whether or not that agreement has been terminated;

(h)   in relation to a child, each of them is a parent of the child or has, or has had, parental responsibility for the child (within the meaning of the *Children Act 1989*). A child is a person under 18 years of age;

(i)   if a child has been adopted or freed for adoption (s 16(1) *Adoption Act 1976*), two persons are also associated if one is the natural parent or grandparent of the child and the other is the child of a person who has become the parent by virtue of an adoption order (s 72(1) *Adoption Act 1976*) or has applied for an adoption order or someone with whom the child has been placed for adoption.

8.21.   The Secretary of State considers that the term 'violence' should not be given a restrictive meaning, and that 'domestic violence' should be understood to include threatening behaviour, violence or abuse (psychological, physical, sexual, financial or emotional) between persons who are, or have been, intimate partners, family members or members of the same household, regardless of gender or sexuality.

8.22.   An assessment of the likelihood of a threat of violence being carried out should not be based on whether there has been actual violence in the past. An assessment must be based on the facts of the case and devoid of any value judgments about what an applicant should or should not do, or should or should not have done, to mitigate the risk of any violence (eg seek police help or apply for an injunction against the perpetrator). Inquiries into cases where violence is alleged will need careful handling. See Chapter 6 for further guidance.

8.23.   In cases involving violence, housing authorities may wish to inform applicants of the option of seeking an injunction, but should make clear that there is no obligation on the applicant to do so. Where applicants wish to pursue this option, it is advisable that they obtain independent advice as an injunction may be ill-advised in some circumstances. Housing authorities should recognise that injunctions ordering a person not to molest, or enter the home of, an applicant may not be effective in deterring perpetrators from carrying out further violence or incursions, and applicants may not have confidence in their effectiveness. Consequently, applicants should not be expected to return home on the strength of an injunction. To ensure applicants who have experienced actual or threatened violence get the support they need, authorities should inform them of appropriate organisations in the area such as agencies offering counselling and support as well as specialist advice.

8.24.   When dealing with cases involving violence, or threat of violence, from outside the home, housing authorities should consider the option of improving the security of the applicant's home to enable him or her to continue to live there safely, where that is an option that the applicant wishes to pursue. In some cases, immediate action to improve security within the victim's home may prevent homelessness. A fast response combined with support from the housing authority, police and the voluntary sector may provide a victim with the confidence to remain in their home. When dealing with domestic violence within the home, where the authority is the landlord, housing authorities should consider the scope for evicting the perpetrator and allowing the victim to remain in their home. **However, where there would be a probability of violence if the applicant continued to occupy his or her present accommodation, the housing authority must treat the applicant as homeless and should not expect him or her to remain in, or return to, the accommodation. In all cases involving violence the safety of the applicant and his or her household should be the primary consideration at all stages of decision making as to whether or not the applicant remains in their own home.**

8.25. The effectiveness of housing authorities' services to assist victims of domestic violence and prevent further domestic violence is measured by Best Value Performance Indicator BVPI 225. Guidance on BVPI 225 is available at www.communities.gov.uk.

General housing circumstances in the district

8.26. Section 177(2) provides that, in determining whether it is reasonable for a person to continue to occupy accommodation, housing authorities may have regard to the general housing circumstances prevailing in the housing authority's district.

8.27. This would apply, for example, where it was suggested that an applicant was homeless because of poor physical conditions in his or her current home. In such cases it would be open to the authority to consider whether the condition of the property was so bad in comparison with other accommodation in the district that it would not be reasonable to expect someone to continue to live there.

8.28. Circumstances where an applicant may be homeless as a result of his or her accommodation being overcrowded should also be considered in relation to the general housing circumstances in the district. Statutory overcrowding, within the meaning of Part 10 of the *Housing Act 1985*, may not by itself be sufficient to determine reasonableness, but it can be a contributory factor if there are other factors which suggest unreasonableness.

Affordability

8.29. One factor that **must** be considered in all cases is affordability. The *Homelessness (Suitability of Accommodation) Order 1996* (SI 1996 No 3204) requires the housing authority to consider the affordability of the accommodation for the applicant. The Order specifies, among other things, that in determining whether it would be (or would have been) reasonable for a person to continue to occupy accommodation, a housing authority must take into account whether the accommodation is affordable for him or her and must, in particular, take account of:

(a)   the financial resources available to him or her;

(b)   the costs in respect of the accommodation;

(c)   maintenance payments (to a spouse, former spouse or in respect of a child); and

(d)   his or her reasonable living expenses.

Tenant given notice of intention to recover possession

8.30. In cases where the applicant has been occupying accommodation as a tenant and has received a valid notice to quit, or a notice that the landlord intends to recover possession, housing authorities should consider the scope for preventing homelessness through consulting the landlord at an early stage to explore the possibility of the tenancy being allowed to continue or the tenant being allowed to remain for a reasonable period to provide an opportunity for alternative accommodation to be found. If the landlord is not persuaded to agree, the authority will need to consider whether it would be reasonable for the applicant to continue to occupy the accommodation once the valid notice has expired.

8.31. In determining whether it would be reasonable for an applicant to continue to occupy accommodation, the housing authority will need to consider all the factors relevant to the case and decide the weight that individual factors should attract. As well as the factors set out elsewhere in this chapter, other factors which may be relevant include the general cost to the housing authority, the position of the tenant, the position of the landlord, the likelihood that the landlord will actually proceed with possession proceedings, and the burden on the courts of unnecessary proceedings where there is no defence to a possession claim (see paragraphs 8.14 and 8.15 above for guidance on the right to occupy where notice of possession proceedings has been given).

8.32. Each case must be decided on its facts, so **housing authorities should not adopt a general policy of accepting – or refusing to accept – applicants as homeless or threatened with homelessness when they are threatened with eviction but a court has not yet made an order for possession or issued a warrant of execution**. In any case where a housing authority decides that it would be reasonable for an applicant to continue to occupy their accommodation after a valid notice has expired – and therefore decides that he or she is not yet homeless or threatened with homelessness – that decision will need to be based on sound reasons which should be made clear to the applicant in writing (see Chapter 6 for guidance on housing authorities' duties to inform applicants of their decisions). **The Secretary of State considers that where a person applies for accommodation or assistance in obtaining accommodation, and:**

(a)   **the person is an assured shorthold tenant who has received proper notice in accordance with s 21 of the** *Housing Act 1988*;

(b)   **the housing authority is satisfied that the landlord intends to seek possession; and**

(c)   **there would be no defence to an application for a possession order;**

then it is unlikely to be reasonable for the applicant to continue to occupy the accommodation beyond the date given in the s 21 notice, unless the housing authority is taking steps to persuade the landlord to withdraw the notice or allow the tenant to continue to occupy the accommodation for a reasonable period to provide an opportunity for alternative accommodation to be found.

8.32a. Authorities are reminded that an applicant cannot be treated as intentionally homeless unless it would have been reasonable for him or her to have continued to occupy the accommodation. Guidance on 'intentional homelessness' is provided in Chapter 11.

Former armed forces personnel required to leave service accommodation

8.33. The Ministry of Defence recognises that housing authorities will need to be satisfied that entitlement to occupy service accommodation will end on a certain date, in order to determine whether applicants who are service personnel and who are approaching their date of discharge may be homeless or threatened with homelessness. For this purpose, the MOD issues a *Certificate of Cessation of Entitlement to Occupy Service Living Accommodation* six months before discharge (see examples at Annexes 14 and 15). These certificates indicate the date on which entitlement to occupy service accommodation ends, and the Secretary of State considers that housing authorities should not insist upon a court order for possession to establish that entitlement to occupy has ended. Authorities should take advantage of the six-month period of notice of discharge to ensure that service personnel receive timely and comprehensive advice on the housing options available to them when they leave the armed forces.

Other relevant factors

8.34. Other factors which may be relevant in determining whether it would be reasonable for an applicant to continue to occupy accommodation include:

physical characteristics: it would not be reasonable for an applicant to continue to occupy accommodation if the physical characteristics of the accommodation were unsuitable for the applicant because, for example, he or she was a wheelchair user and access was limited.

type of accommodation: some types of accommodation, for example women's refuges, direct access hostels, and night shelters are intended to provide very short-term, temporary accommodation in a crisis and it should not be regarded as reasonable to continue to occupy such accommodation in the medium and longer-term.

people fleeing harassment: in some cases severe harassment may fall short of actual violence or threats of violence likely to be carried out. Housing authorities should consider carefully whether it would be, or would have been, reasonable for an applicant to continue to occupy accommodation in circumstances where they have fled, or are seeking to leave, their home because of non-violent forms of harassment, for example verbal abuse or damage to property. Careful consideration should be given to applicants who may be at risk of witness intimidation. In some criminal cases the police may provide alternative accommodation for witnesses, but usually this will apply for the duration of the trial only. Witnesses may have had to give up their home or may feel unable to return to it when the trial has finished.

This is not an exhaustive list and authorities will need to take account of all relevant factors when considering whether it is reasonable for an applicant to continue to occupy accommodation.

CHAPTER 9: ELIGIBILITY FOR ASSISTANCE

General

9.1. Part 7 of the 1996 Act includes provisions that make certain persons from abroad ineligible for housing assistance. Housing authorities will therefore need to satisfy themselves that applicants are eligible before providing housing assistance. The provisions on eligibility are complex and housing authorities will need to ensure that they have procedures in place to carry out appropriate checks on housing applicants.

9.2. Housing authorities should ensure that staff who are required to screen housing applicants about eligibility for assistance are given training in the complexities of the housing provisions, the housing authority's duties and responsibilities under the race relations legislation and how to deal with applicants in a sensitive manner.

9.3. Local authorities are reminded that Schedule 3 to the *Nationality, Immigration and Asylum Act 2002* provides that certain persons shall not be eligible for support or assistance provided through the exercise of local housing authorities' powers to secure accommodation pending a review (s 188(3)) or pending an appeal to the county court (s 204(4)). See paragraph 9.22 below.

Persons from abroad

9.4. A person will not be eligible for assistance under Part 7 if he or she is a person from abroad who is ineligible for housing assistance under s 185 of the 1996 Act. There are two categories of 'person from abroad' for the purposes s 185:

(i) *a person subject to immigration control* – such a person is not eligible for housing assistance unless he or she comes within a class prescribed in regulations made by the Secretary of State, and

(ii) *a person from abroad other than a person subject to immigration control* – the Secretary of State can make regulations to provide for other descriptions of person from abroad who, although they are not subject to immigration control, are to be treated as ineligible for housing assistance.

9.5. The regulations that set out which classes of persons from abroad are eligible or ineligible for housing assistance are the *Allocation of Housing and Homelessness (Eligibility) (England) Regulations 2006* (SI 2006 No 1294) ('the Eligibility Regulations'). Persons subject to immigration control are not eligible for housing assistance unless they fall within a class of persons prescribed in **regulation 5** of the Eligibility Regulations. Persons who are not subject to immigration control will be eligible for housing assistance unless they fall within a description of persons who are to be treated as persons from abroad who are ineligible for assistance by virtue of **regulation 6** of the Eligibility Regulations.

Persons subject to immigration control

9.6. The term 'person subject to immigration control' is defined in s 13(2) of the *Asylum and Immigration Act 1996* as a person who requires leave to enter or remain in the United Kingdom (whether or not such leave has been given).

9.7. Only the following categories of person do **not** require leave to enter or remain in the UK:

(i)   British citizens;

(ii) certain Commonwealth citizens with a right of abode in the UK;

(iii) citizens of an EEA country, ('EEA nationals') and their family members, who have a right to reside in the UK that derives from EC law. The question of whether an EEA national (or family member) has a particular right to reside in the UK (or in another Member State eg the Republic of Ireland) will depend on the circumstances, particularly the economic status of the EEA national (eg whether he or she is a worker, self-employed, a student, or economically inactive etc). See Annex 12 for further guidance on rights to reside;

(iv) persons who are exempt from immigration control under the Immigration Acts, including diplomats and their family members based in the United Kingdom, and some military personnel.

For the purposes of this guidance, 'EEA nationals' means nationals of any of the EU member states (excluding the UK), and nationals of Iceland, Norway, Liechtenstein and Switzerland.

9.8. Any person who **does not** fall within one of the 4 categories in paragraph 9.7 above will be a person subject to immigration control and will be ineligible for housing assistance unless they fall within a class of persons prescribed by regulation 5 of the Eligibility Regulations (see paragraph 9.10 below).

9.9. If there is any uncertainty about an applicant's immigration status, it is recommended that authorities contact the Home Office Immigration and Nationality Directorate, using the procedures set out in Annex 8. In some circumstances, local authorities may be under a duty to contact the Immigration and Nationality Directorate (see paragraph 9.24).

Persons subject to immigration control who are eligible for housing assistance

9.10. Generally, persons subject to immigration control are not eligible for housing assistance. However, by virtue of regulation 5 of the Eligibility Regulations, the following classes of person subject to immigration control are eligible for housing assistance:

(i)   *a person granted refugee status*: a person is granted refugee status when his or her request for asylum is accepted. Persons granted refugee status are granted 5 years' limited leave to remain in the UK. (Prior to

30 August 2005, it was the policy to provide immediate settlement (indefinite leave to remain) for persons granted refugee status.)

(ii)   *a person granted exceptional leave to enter or remain in the UK without condition that they and any dependants should make no recourse to public funds*: this status is granted to persons, including some persons whose claim for asylum has been refused, for a limited period where there are compelling humanitarian and/or compassionate circumstances for allowing them to stay. However, if leave was granted on condition that the applicant and any dependants should not be a charge on public funds, the applicant will not be eligible for homelessness assistance. Since April 2003, exceptional leave to remain (which is granted at the Secretary of State's discretion outside the Immigration Rules) has taken the form of either humanitarian protection or discretionary leave.

(iii)   *a person with current leave to enter or remain in the UK with no condition or limitation, and who is habitually resident in the UK, the Channel Islands, the Isle of Man or the Republic of Ireland*: such a person will have indefinite leave to enter (ILE) or remain (ILR) and will be regarded as having settled status. However, where ILE or ILR status was granted as a result of an undertaking that a sponsor would be responsible for the applicant's maintenance and accommodation, the person must have been resident in the UK, the Channel Islands, the Isle of Man or the Republic of Ireland for five years since the date of entry – or the date of the sponsorship undertaking, whichever is later – for the applicant to be eligible. Where a sponsor has (or, if there was more than one sponsor, all of the sponsors have) died within the first five years, the applicant will be eligible for housing assistance;

(iv)   *a person who left the territory of Montserrat after 1 November 1995 because of the effect on that territory of a volcanic eruption.* (See paragraph 9.19 below.)

Asylum seekers

9.11.   Asylum seekers will almost always be persons subject to immigration control.

Asylum seekers who are persons subject to immigration control and whose claim for asylum was made after 2 April 2000 are not eligible for assistance under Part 7 of the 1996 Act. Some asylum seekers whose claim for asylum was made before 3 April 2000 would be eligible for assistance under Part 7 in certain limited circumstances, but the number of persons who fall in these classes is likely to be very small (if any). Annex 9 provides guidance on the limited categories of asylum seekers eligible for assistance under Part 7 of the 1996 Act.

9.12.   Under s 186 of the 1996 Act, an asylum seeker who would otherwise be eligible for assistance under the Eligibility Regulations, will be ineligible, if he or she has any accommodation available in the UK for his or her occupation, however temporary.

Other persons from abroad who may be ineligible for assistance

9.13. By virtue of regulation 6 of the Eligibility Regulations, a person who is not subject to immigration control and who falls within one of the following descriptions of persons is to be treated as a person from abroad who is ineligible for housing assistance:

(i) a person who is not habitually resident in the UK, the Channel Islands, the Isle of Man or the Republic of Ireland (subject to certain exceptions – see paragraph 9.14 below);

(ii) a person whose only right to reside in the UK is derived from his status as a jobseeker (or his status as the family member of a jobseeker). For this purpose, 'jobseeker' has the same meaning as for the purpose of regulation 6(1)(a) of the *Immigration (European Economic Area) Regulations 2006* (SI 2006 No 1003) ('the EEA Regulations');

(iii) a person whose only right to reside in the UK is an initial right to reside for a period not exceeding three months under regulation 13 of the EEA Regulations;

(iv) a person whose only right to reside in the Channel Islands, the Isle of Man or the Republic of Ireland is a right equivalent to one of the rights mentioned in (ii) or (iii) above and which is derived from the Treaty establishing the European Community ('the EC Treaty').

See Annex 12 for guidance on rights to reside in the UK derived from EC law.

Persons exempted from the requirement to be habitually resident

9.14. Certain persons from abroad (not being persons subject to immigration control) will be eligible for housing assistance even though they are not habitually resident in the UK, the Channel Islands, the Isle of Man or the Republic of Ireland. Such a person will be eligible for assistance even if not habitually resident, if he or she is:

(a) an EEA national who is in the UK as a worker (which has the same meaning as it does for the purposes of regulation 6(1) of the EEA Regulations);

(b) an EEA national who is in the UK as a self-employed person (which has the same meaning as it does for the purposes of regulation 6(1) of the EEA Regulations);

(c) a person who is an accession state worker requiring registration who is treated as a worker for the purposes of regulation 6(1) of the EEA Regulations, pursuant to the *Accession (Immigration and Worker Registration) Regulations 2004*, as amended;

(d) a person who is a family member of a person referred to in (a) to (c) above;

(e) a person with a right to reside permanently in the UK by virtue of regulation 15(c), (d) or (e) of the EEA Regulations (see Annex 12);

(f) a person who left Montserrat after 1 November 1995 because of the effect of volcanic activity there (see paragraph 9.19 below);

(g)   a person who is in the UK as a result of his or her deportation, expulsion or other removal by compulsion of law from another country to the UK (see paragraph 9.21 below).

On (a) and (b), authorities should note that a person who is no longer working or no longer in self-employment will retain his or her status as a worker or self-employed person in certain circumstances. (See Annex 12 for further guidance.) On (c), authorities should note that accession state workers requiring registration will generally only be treated as a worker when they are actually working and will not retain 'worker' status in the circumstances referred to above. (See annexes 12 and 13 for further guidance.) On (d), authorities should note that 'family member' does not include a person who is an extended family member who is treated as a family member by virtue of regulation 7(3) of the EEA Regulations (see Annex 12 for further guidance).

The habitual residence test

9.15.   The term 'habitual residence' is intended to convey a degree of permanence in the person's residence in the UK, the Channel Islands, the Isle of Man or the Republic of Ireland; it implies an association between the individual and the place of residence and relies substantially on fact.

9.16.   The Secretary of State considers that it is likely that applicants who have been resident in the UK, Channel Islands, the Isle of Man or the Republic of Ireland continuously during the 2-year period prior to their housing application will be habitually resident. In such cases, therefore, housing authorities may consider it unnecessary to make further enquiries to determine whether the person is habitually resident, unless there are other circumstances that need to be taken into account. A period of continuous residence in the UK, Channel Islands, the Isle of Man or the Republic of Ireland might include periods of temporary absence, e g visits abroad for holidays or to visit relatives. Where two years' continuous residency has not been established, housing authorities will need to conduct further enquiries to determine whether the applicant is habitually resident.

9.17.   A person will not generally be habitually resident anywhere unless he or she has taken up residence and lived there for a period. There will be cases where the person concerned is not coming to the UK for the first time, and is resuming a previous period of habitual residence.

9.18.   Annex 10 provides guidance on the factors that a housing authority should consider in determining whether an applicant is habitually resident.

Persons from Montserrat

9.19.   The classes of persons (not being persons subject to immigration control) who are not required to be habitually resident in order to be eligible for assistance under Part 7 include a person who left Montserrat after 1 November 1995 because of the effect of volcanic activity there.

9.20. On 21 May 2002 most British overseas territories citizens, including those from Montserrat, became British Citizens. Since their new EU-style passport will not identify that they are from Montserrat, it has been recommended that they should also retain their old British Overseas Citizen passport, to help them demonstrate eligibility for, among other things, housing assistance in the UK.

Persons deported, expelled or removed to the UK from another country

9.21. Persons who are in the UK as a result of their deportation, expulsion or other removal by compulsion of law from another country to the UK will generally be UK nationals. (However, such persons could include EEA nationals, where the UK immigration authorities were satisfied that the person was settled in the UK and exercising EC Treaty rights prior to deportation from the third country.) Where deportation occurs, most countries will signal this in the person's passport and provide them with reasons for their removal. This should enable such persons to identify their circumstances when making an application for housing assistance.

Persons ineligible under certain provisions by virtue of Schedule 3 to the Nationality, Immigration and Asylum Act 2002

9.22. Section 54 of, and Schedule 3 to, the *Nationality, Immigration and Asylum Act 2002* have the effect of making certain applicants for housing assistance ineligible for accommodation under s 188(3) (*power to accommodate pending a review*) or s 204(4) (*power to accommodate pending an appeal to the county court*) of the 1996 Act. The following classes of person will be ineligible for assistance under those powers:

(i) *a person who has refugee status abroad*, ie a person:
  – who does not have the nationality of an EEA State, and
  – who the government of an EEA State other than the UK has determined is entitled to protection as a refugee under the Refugee Convention;

(ii) *a person who has the nationality of an EEA State other than the UK* (but see paragraph 9.23 below);

(iii) *a person who was (but is no longer) an asylum seeker and who fails to cooperate with removal directions* issued in respect of him or her;

(iv) *a person who is in the UK in breach of the immigration laws* (within the meaning of s 11 of the *Nationality, Immigration and Asylum Act 2002*) *and is not an asylum seeker*;

(v) *certain persons who are failed asylum seekers with dependent children*, where the Secretary of State has certified that, in his opinion, such a person has failed without reasonable excuse to take reasonable steps to leave the UK voluntarily or place himself or herself in a position where he or she is able to leave the UK voluntarily, and that person has received the Secretary of State's certificate more than 14 days previously;

(vi) *a person who is the dependant of a person who falls within class (i), (ii), (iii) or (v) above.*

9.23. However, s 54 and Schedule 3 do not prevent the exercise of an authority's powers under s 188(3) and s 204(4) of the 1996 Act to the extent that such exercise is necessary for the purpose of avoiding a breach of a person's rights under the European Convention of Human Rights or rights under the EC Treaties. Among other things, this means that a local authority can exercise these powers to accommodate an EEA national who has a right to reside in the UK under EC law (see Annex 12).

9.24. Paragraph 14 of Schedule 3 provides, among other things, that authorities must inform the Secretary of State where the powers under s 188(3) or s 204(4) apply, or may apply, to a person who is, or may come, within classes (iii), (iv) or (v) in paragraph 9.22 (by contacting the Home Office Immigration and Nationality Directorate).

9.25. For further guidance, local authorities should refer to Guidance to Local Authorities and Housing Authorities about the *Nationality, Immigration and Asylum Act*, Section 54 and Schedule 3, and the *Withholding and Withdrawal of Support (Travel Assistance and Temporary Accommodation) Regulations 2002*, issued by the Home Office.

Eligibility – List of related Annexes:

Annex 8   How to contact the Home Office Immigration and
             Nationality Directorate

Annex 9   Asylum seekers

Annex 10   The habitual residence test

Annex 11   European groupings (EU, A8, EEA, Switzerland)

Annex 12   Rights to reside in the UK derived from EC law

Annex 13   Worker registration scheme

CHAPTER 10: PRIORITY NEED

This chapter provides guidance on the categories of applicant who have a priority need for accommodation under the homelessness legislation.

10.1. Under the homelessness legislation, housing authorities must have a strategy for preventing homelessness and ensuring that accommodation and support are available to **anyone** in their district who is homeless or at risk of homelessness. They must also provide advice and assistance on housing and homelessness prevention to anyone in their district, free of charge. Stronger duties to secure accommodation exist for households who have a priority need for accommodation. Since 2002, the priority need categories have embraced a wider range of people whose age or background puts them at greater risk when homeless, including more single people.

10.2. The main homelessness duties in s 193(2) and s 195(2) of the 1996 Act (to secure accommodation or take reasonable steps to prevent the loss of accommodation) apply only to applicants who have a priority need for accommodation. Section 189(1) and the *Homelessness (Priority Need for Accommodation) (England) Order 2002* provide that the following categories of applicant have a priority need for accommodation:

i)   a pregnant woman or a person with whom she resides or might reasonably be expected to reside (see paragraph 10.5);

ii) a person with whom dependent children reside or might reasonably be expected to reside (see paragraphs 10.6–10.11);

iii) a person who is vulnerable as a result of old age, mental illness or handicap or physical disability or other special reason, or with whom such a person resides or might reasonably be expected to reside (see paragraphs 10.12–10.18);

iv) a person aged 16 or 17 who is not a 'relevant child' or a child in need to whom a local authority owes a duty under section 20 of the *Children Act 1989* (see paragraphs 10.36–10.39);

v)   a person under 21 who was (but is no longer) looked after, accommodated or fostered between the ages of 16 and 18 (except a person who is a 'relevant student') (see paragraphs 10.40–10.41);

vi) a person aged 21 or more who is vulnerable as a result of having been looked after, accommodated or fostered (except a person who is a 'relevant student') (see paragraphs 10.19–10.20);

vii) a person who is vulnerable as a result of having been a member of Her Majesty's regular naval, military or air forces (see paragraphs 10.21–10.23);

viii) a person who is vulnerable as a result of:
(a) having served a custodial sentence,
(b) having been committed for contempt of court or any other kindred offence, or
(c) having been remanded in custody;
(see paragraphs 10.24–10.27 [of this Code])

ix) a person who is vulnerable as a result of ceasing to occupy accommodation because of violence from another person or threats of violence from another person which are likely to be carried out (see paragraphs 10.28–10.29);

x) a person who is vulnerable for any other special reason, or with whom such a person resides or might reasonably be expected to reside (see paragraphs 10.30–10.35);

xi) a person who is homeless, or threatened with homelessness, as a result of an emergency such as flood, fire or other disaster (see paragraph 10.42).

10.3. Inquiries as to whether an applicant has a priority need must be carried out in all cases where the housing authority has reason to believe that an applicant may be homeless or threatened with homelessness, and is eligible for assistance (s 184). Moreover, where the housing authority has reason to believe that the applicant is homeless, eligible for assistance and in priority need, they will have an immediate duty to secure interim accommodation, pending a decision on the case (see Chapter 7).

10.4. Once a housing authority has notified an applicant that he or she has a priority need and has been accepted as owed the main homelessness duty (s 193(2)) it cannot – unless the decision is subject to a request for a review – change the decision if the applicant subsequently ceases to have a priority need (eg because a dependent child leaves home). Any change of circumstance prior to the decision on the homelessness application should be taken into account. However, once all the relevant inquiries are completed, the housing authority should not defer making a decision on the case in anticipation of a possible change of circumstance. (See Chapter 19 for guidance on reviews.)

Pregnant women

10.5. A pregnant woman, and anyone with whom she lives or might reasonably be expected to live, has a priority need for accommodation. This is regardless of the length of time that the woman has been pregnant. Housing authorities should seek normal confirmation of pregnancy, eg a letter from a medical professional, such as a midwife, should be adequate evidence of pregnancy. If a pregnant woman suffers a miscarriage or terminates her pregnancy during the assessment process the housing authority should consider whether she continues to have a priority need as a result of some other factor (eg she may be vulnerable as a result of an other special reason – see paragraph 10.30).

Dependent children

10.6. Applicants have a priority need if they have one or more dependent children who normally live with them or who might reasonably be expected to live with them. There must be actual dependence on the applicant, although the child need not be wholly and exclusively dependent on him or her. There must also be actual residence (or a reasonable expectation of residence) with some degree of permanence or regularity, rather than a temporary arrangement whereby the children are merely staying with the applicant for a limited period (see paragraphs 10.9 and 10.10). Similarly, the child need not be wholly and exclusively resident (or expected to reside wholly and exclusively) with the applicant.

10.7. The 1996 Act does not define dependent children, but housing authorities may wish to treat as dependent all children under 16, and all children aged 16–18 who are in, or are about to begin, full-time education or training or who for other reasons are unable to support themselves and who live at home. The meaning of dependency is not, however, limited to financial dependency. Thus, while children aged 16 and over who are in full-time employment and are financially independent of their parents would not normally be considered to be dependants, housing authorities should remember that such children may not be sufficiently mature to live independently of their parents, and there may be sound reasons for considering them to be dependent. Each case will need to be carefully considered according to the circumstances.

10.8. Dependent children need not necessarily be the applicant's own children but could, for example, be related to the applicant or his or her partner or be adopted or fostered by the applicant. There must, however, be some form of parent/child relationship.

10.9. Housing authorities may receive applications from a parent who is separated from his or her former spouse or partner. In some cases where parents separate, the court may make a residence order indicating with which parent the child normally resides. In such cases, the child may be considered to reside with the parent named in the order, and would not normally be expected to reside with the other parent. However, in many cases the parents come to an agreement themselves as to how the child is to be cared for, and a court order will not be made or required.

10.10. Residence does not have to be full-time and a child can be considered to reside with either parent even where he or she divides his or her time between both parents. However, as mentioned above, there must be some regularity to the arrangement. If the child is not currently residing with the applicant, the housing authority will need to decide whether, in the circumstances, it would be reasonable for the child to do so. An agreement between a child's parents, or a joint residence order by a court, may not automatically lead to a conclusion that it would be reasonable for the child to reside with the parent making the application, and housing authorities will need to consider each case individually. However, housing authorities should remember that where parents separate, it will often be in the best interests of the child to maintain a relationship with both parents.

10.11. Where the applicant's children are being looked after by a social services authority – for example, they are subject to a care order or are being accommodated under a voluntary agreement – and they are not currently living with the applicant, liaison with the social services authority will be essential. Joint consideration with social services will ensure that the best interests of the applicant and the children are served. This may, for example, enable a family to be reunited subject to suitable accommodation being available.

Vulnerability

10.12. A person has a priority need for accommodation if he or she is vulnerable as a result of:

i)   old age;

ii)   mental illness or learning disability (mental handicap) or physical disability;

iii) having been looked after, accommodated or fostered and is aged 21 or more;

iv)   having been a member of Her Majesty's regular naval, military or air forces;

v)   having been in custody or detention;

vi)   ceasing to occupy accommodation because of violence from another person or threats of violence from another person which are likely to be carried out; or

vii) any other special reason.

In the case of i), ii) and vii) only, a person with whom a vulnerable person lives or might reasonably be expected to live also has a priority need for accommodation and can therefore make an application on behalf of themselves and that vulnerable person.

10.13.   It is a matter of judgment whether the applicant's circumstances make him or her vulnerable. When determining whether an applicant in any of the categories set out in paragraph 10.12 is vulnerable, the local authority should consider whether, when homeless, the applicant would be less able to fend for him/herself than an ordinary homeless person so that he or she would suffer injury or detriment, in circumstances where a less vulnerable person would be able to cope without harmful effects.

10.14.   Some of the factors which may be relevant to determining whether a particular category of applicant is vulnerable are set out below. The assessment of an applicant's ability to cope is a composite one taking into account all of the circumstances. The applicant's vulnerability must be assessed on the basis that he or she is or will become homeless, and not on his or her ability to fend for him or herself while still housed.

Old age

10.15. Old age alone is not sufficient for the applicant to be deemed vulnerable. However, it may be that as a result of old age the applicant would be less able to fend for him or herself as provided in paragraph 10.13 above. All applications from people aged over 60 need to be considered carefully, particularly where the applicant is leaving tied accommodation. However, housing authorities should not use 60 (or any other age) as a fixed age beyond which vulnerability occurs automatically (or below which it can be ruled out); each case will need to be considered in the light of the individual circumstances.

Mental illness or learning disability or physical disability

10.16. Housing authorities should have regard to any advice from medical professionals, social services or current providers of care and support. In cases where there is doubt as to the extent of any vulnerability authorities may also consider seeking a clinical opinion. However, the final decision on the question of vulnerability will rest with the housing authority. In considering whether such applicants are vulnerable, authorities will need to take account of all relevant factors including:

  i)   the nature and extent of the illness and/or disability which may render the applicant vulnerable;
  ii)   the relationship between the illness and/or disability and the individual's housing difficulties; and
  iii)   the relationship between the illness and/or disability and other factors such as drug/alcohol misuse, offending behaviour, challenging behaviours, age and personality disorder.

10.17. Assessment of vulnerability due to mental health will require close co-operation between housing authorities, social services authorities and mental health agencies. Housing authorities should consider carrying out joint assessments or using a trained mental health practitioner as part of an assessment team. Mental Health NHS Trusts and local authorities have an express duty to implement a specifically tailored care programme (the Care Programme Approach – CPA) for all patients considered for discharge from psychiatric hospitals and all new patients accepted by the specialist psychiatric services (see *Effective care co-ordination in mental health services: modernising the care programme approach*, DH, 1999). **People discharged from psychiatric hospitals and local authority hostels for people with mental health problems are likely to be vulnerable.** Effective, timely, liaison between housing, social services and NHS Trusts will be essential in such cases but authorities will also need to be sensitive to direct approaches from former patients who have been discharged and may be homeless.

10.18. Learning or physical disabilities or long-term acute illnesses, such as those defined by the *Disability Discrimination Act 1995*, which impinge on the applicant's housing situation and give rise to vulnerability may be readily discernible, but advice from health or social services staff should be sought, wherever necessary.

Having been looked after, accommodated or fostered and aged 21 or over

10.19. A person aged 21 or over who is vulnerable as a result of having been looked after, accommodated or fostered has a priority need (other than a person who is a 'relevant student'). The terms 'looked after, accommodated or fostered' are set out in the *Children Act 1989* (s 24) and include any person who has been:

i)   looked after by a local authority (ie has been subject to a care order or accommodated under a voluntary agreement);

ii)   accommodated by or on behalf of a voluntary organisation;

iii)   accommodated in a private children's home;

iv)   accommodated for a consecutive period of at least three months:

–   by a health authority, special health authority, primary care trust or local education authority, or

–   in any care home or independent hospital or in any accommodation provided by a National Health Service trust; or

v)   privately fostered.

A 'relevant student' means a care leaver under 24 to whom section 24B(3) of the *Children Act 1989* applies, and who is in full-time further or higher education and whose term-time accommodation is not available during a vacation. Under s 24B(5), where a social services authority is satisfied that a person is someone to whom section 24B(3) applies and needs accommodation during a vacation they must provide accommodation or the means to enable it to be secured.

10.20. Housing authorities will need to make enquiries into an applicant's childhood history to establish whether he or she has been looked after, accommodated or fostered in any of these ways. If so, they will need to consider whether he or she is vulnerable as a result. In determining whether there is vulnerability (as set out in paragraph 10.13 above), factors that a housing authority may wish to consider are:

i)   the length of time that the applicant was looked after, accommodated or fostered;

ii)   the reasons why the applicant was looked after, accommodated or fostered;

iii)   the length of time since the applicant was looked after, accommodated or fostered, and whether the applicant had been able to obtain and/or maintain accommodation during any of that period;

iv)   whether the applicant has any existing support networks, particularly including family, friends or mentor.

Having been a member of the armed forces

10.21. A person who is vulnerable as a result of having been a member of Her Majesty's regular armed forces has a priority need for accommodation. Former members of the armed forces will include a person who was previously a member of the regular naval, military or air forces, including a person who has been released following detention in a military corrective training centre.

10.22. The principal responsibility for providing housing information and advice to Service personnel lies with the armed forces up to the point of discharge and these services are delivered through the Joint Service Housing

Advice Office (telephone: 01722 436575). Some people, who have served in the armed forces for a long period, and those who are medically discharged, may be offered assistance with resettlement by Ministry of Defence (MOD) resettlement staff. The MOD issues a *Certificate of Cessation of Entitlement to Occupy Service Living Accommodation* (see examples at Annexes 14 and 15) six months before discharge. Applications from former members of the armed forces will need to be considered carefully to assess whether the applicant is vulnerable as a result of having served in the armed forces.

10.23. In considering whether former members of the armed forces are vulnerable (as set out in paragraph 10.13 above) as a result of their time spent in the forces, a housing authority may wish to take into account the following factors:

i) the length of time the applicant spent in the armed forces (although authorities should not assume that vulnerability could not occur as a result of a short period of service);

ii) the type of service the applicant was engaged in (those on active service may find it more difficult to cope with civilian life);

iii) whether the applicant spent any time in a military hospital (this could be an indicator of a serious health problem or of post-traumatic stress);

iv) whether HM Forces' medical and welfare advisers have judged an individual to be particularly vulnerable in their view and have issued a Medical History Release Form (F Med 133) giving a summary of the circumstances causing that vulnerability;

v) the length of time since the applicant left the armed forces, and whether he or she had been able to obtain and/or maintain accommodation during that time;

vi) whether the applicant has any existing support networks, particularly by way of family or friends.

Having been in custody or detention

10.24. A person who is vulnerable as a result of having served a custodial sentence, been committed for contempt of court or remanded in custody has a priority need for accommodation. This category applies to applicants who are vulnerable as a result of having:

i) served a custodial sentence within the meaning of the *Powers of Criminal Courts (Sentences) Act 2000*, s 76. (This includes sentences of imprisonment for those aged 21 or over and detention for those aged under 21, including children.);

ii) been committed for contempt of court or any other kindred offence (kindred offence refers to statutory provisions for contempt as opposed to the inherent jurisdiction of the court, eg under the *Contempt of Court Act 1981*, s 12 (magistrates' court) and *County Court Act 1984*, s 118 (county court)). (Committal may arise, eg where an applicant has breached a civil injunction.);

iii) been remanded in custody within the meaning of the *Powers of Criminal Courts (Sentencing) Act 2000*, s 88(1)(b), (c) or (d), ie remanded in or committed to custody by an order of a court; remanded or committed to housing authority accommodation under the *Children and Young Persons Act 1969* and placed and kept in secure accommodation; or, remanded, admitted or removed to hospital under the *Mental Health Act 1983*, ss 35, 36, 38 or 48.

10.25. Applicants have a priority need for accommodation only if they are vulnerable (see paragraph 10.13 above) as a result of having been in custody or detention. In determining whether applicants who fall within one of the descriptions in paragraph 10.24 are vulnerable as a result of their period in custody or detention, a housing authority may wish to take into account the following factors:

i) the length of time the applicant served in custody or detention (although authorities should not assume that vulnerability could not occur as a result of a short period in custody or detention);

ii) whether the applicant is receiving supervision from a criminal justice agency eg the Probation Service, Youth Offending Team or Drug Intervention Programme. Housing authorities should have regard to any advice from criminal justice agency staff regarding their view of the applicant's general vulnerability, but the final decision on the question of vulnerability for the purposes of the homelessness legislation will rest with the housing authority;

iii) the length of time since the applicant was released from custody or detention, and the extent to which the applicant had been able to obtain and/or maintain accommodation during that time;

iv) whether the applicant has any existing support networks, for example family or friends, and how much of a positive influence these networks are likely to be in the applicant's life.

10.26. In many cases a housing needs assessment may have been completed in respect of offenders by the Probation Service, Prison Services, Youth Offending Team, Criminal Justice Intervention Team or a voluntary organisation acting on behalf of one of these agencies. Where such an assessment identifies an individual as needing help in finding accommodation and judges the individual to be particularly vulnerable and the applicant makes an application for housing assistance, this information will be made available to the relevant housing authority.

10.27. In addition to the question of priority need, when assessing applicants in this client group difficult issues may arise as to whether the applicant has become homeless intentionally. Housing authorities must consider each case in the light of all the facts and circumstances. **Housing authorities are reminded that they cannot adopt a blanket policy of assuming that homelessness will be intentional or unintentional in any given circumstances** (see Chapter 11 for guidance on intentional homelessness).

Having left accommodation because of violence

10.28. A person has a priority need if he or she is vulnerable (as set out in paragraph 10.13 above) as a result of having to leave accommodation because of violence from another person, or threats of violence from another person that are likely to be carried out. It will usually be apparent from the assessment of the reason for homelessness whether the applicant has had to leave accommodation because of violence or threats of violence (see Chapter 8 for further guidance on whether it is reasonable to continue to occupy accommodation). **In cases involving violence, the safety of the applicant and ensuring confidentiality must be of paramount concern.** It is not only domestic violence that is relevant, but all forms of violence, including racially motivated violence or threats of violence likely to be carried out. Inquiries of the perpetrators of violence should not be made. In assessing whether it is likely that threats of violence are likely to be carried out, a housing authority should only take into account the probability of violence, and not actions which the applicant could take (such as injunctions against the perpetrators). See Chapter 6 for further guidance on dealing with cases involving violence.

10.29. In considering whether applicants are vulnerable as a result of leaving accommodation because of violence or threats of violence likely to be carried out, a housing authority may wish to take into account the following factors:

i) the nature of the violence or threats of violence (there may have been a single but significant incident or a number of incidents over an extended period of time which have had a cumulative effect);

ii) the impact and likely effects of the violence or threats of violence on the applicant's current and future well being;

iii) whether the applicant has any existing support networks, particularly by way of family or friends.

Other special reason

10.30. Section 189(1)(c) provides that a person has a priority need for accommodation if he or she is vulnerable for any 'other special reason'. A person with whom such a vulnerable person normally lives or might reasonably be expected to live also has a priority need. The legislation envisages that vulnerability can arise because of factors that are not expressly provided for in statute. Each application must be considered in the light of the facts and circumstances of the case. Moreover, other special reasons giving rise to vulnerability are not restricted to the physical or mental characteristics of a person. Where applicants have a need for support but have no family or friends on whom they can depend they may be vulnerable as a result of another special reason.

10.31. Housing authorities must keep an open mind and should avoid blanket policies that assume that particular groups of applicants will, or will not, be vulnerable for any 'other special reason'. Where a housing authority considers that an applicant may be vulnerable, it will be important to make an in-depth assessment of the circumstances of the case. Guidance on certain categories of applicants who may be vulnerable as a result of any 'other special reason' is given below. The list below is not exhaustive and housing authorities must ensure that they give proper consideration to every application on the basis of the individual circumstances. In addition, housing authorities will need to be aware that an applicant may be considered vulnerable for any 'other special reason' because of a combination of factors which taken alone may not necessarily lead to a decision that they are vulnerable (eg drug and alcohol problems, common mental health problems, a history of sleeping rough, no previous experience of managing a tenancy).

10.32. *Chronically sick people, including people with AIDS and HIV-related illnesses.* People in this group may be vulnerable not only because their illness has progressed to the point of physical or mental disability (when they are likely to fall within one of the specified categories of priority need) but also because the manifestations or effects of their illness, or common attitudes to it, make it very difficult for them to find and maintain stable or suitable accommodation. Whilst this may be particularly true of people with AIDS, it could also apply in the case of people infected with HIV (who may not have any overt signs or symptoms) if the nature of their infection is known.

10.33. *Young people.* The 2002 Order makes specific provision for certain categories of young homeless people (see paragraph 10.2). However, there are many other young people who fall outside these categories but who could become homeless and be vulnerable in certain circumstances. When assessing applications from young people under 25 who do not fall within any of the specific categories of priority need, housing authorities should give careful consideration to the possibility of vulnerability. Most young people can expect a degree of support from families, friends or an institution (eg a college or university) with the practicalities and costs of finding, establishing, and managing a home for the first time. But some young people, particularly those who are forced to leave the parental home or who cannot remain there because they are being subjected to violence or sexual abuse, may lack this back-up network and be less able than others to establish and maintain a home for themselves. Moreover, a young person on the streets without adequate financial resources to live independently may be at risk of abuse or prostitution. See Chapter 12 for further guidance on 16 and 17 year olds.

10.34. *People fleeing harassment.* Authorities should consider whether harassment falls under the general definition of domestic violence (see definition in Chapter 8 and paragraphs 10.28–10.29 above which give guidance on vulnerability as a result of violence). In some cases, however, severe harassment may fall short of actual violence or threats of violence likely to be carried out. Housing authorities should consider carefully whether applicants who have fled their home because of non-violent forms of harassment, for example verbal abuse or damage to property, are vulnerable as a result. Careful consideration should be given to applicants who may be at risk of witness intimidation. In some criminal cases the police may provide alternative accommodation for witnesses, but usually this will apply for the duration of the trial only. Witnesses may have had to give up their home or may feel unable to return to it when the trial has finished.

10.35. *Former asylum seekers.* Former asylum seekers who have been granted refugee status or exceptional leave to remain, humanitarian protection, or discretionary leave will be eligible for homelessness assistance and may be at risk of homelessness as a result of having to leave accommodation that had been provided for them (eg by the National Asylum Support Service) in the period before a decision was reached on their asylum claim. They may well have experienced persecution or trauma in their country of origin or severe hardship in their efforts to reach the UK and may be vulnerable as a result. In assessing applications from this client group, housing authorities should give careful consideration to the possibility that they may be vulnerable as a result of another special reason. Authorities should be sensitive to the fact that former asylum seekers may be reluctant to discuss, or have difficulty discussing, their potential vulnerability, if, for example, they have experienced humiliating, painful or traumatic circumstances such as torture, rape or the killing of a family member.

16 and 17 year olds

10.36. All 16 and 17 year old homeless applicants have a priority need for accommodation except those who are:

i)   a relevant child, or
ii)   a child in need who is owed a duty under s 20 of the *Children Act 1989*.

Relevant child or child in need owed a duty under s 20 of the 1989 Act

10.37. A relevant child is a child aged 16 or 17 who has been looked after by a local authority for at least 13 weeks since the age of 14 and has been looked after at some time while 16 or 17 and who is not currently being looked after (ie an 'eligible child' for the purposes of paragraph 19B of Schedule 2 to the *Children Act 1989*). In addition, a child is also a relevant child if he or she would have been looked after by the local authority as an eligible child but for the fact that on his or her 16th birthday he or she was detained through the criminal justice system, or in hospital, or if he or she has returned home on family placement and that has broken down (see the *Children Act 1989*, s 23A and the *Children (Leaving Care) Regulations 2001* regulation 4).

10.38. The *Children Act 1989* (s 20(3)) places a duty on children's services authorities to provide accommodation for a child in need aged 16 or over whose welfare is otherwise likely to be seriously prejudiced if they do not provide accommodation; and s 20(1) places a duty on children's services authorities to provide accommodation for children in need in certain other circumstances.

10.39. Responsibility for providing suitable accommodation for a relevant child or a child in need to whom a local authority owes a duty under s 20 of the *Children Act 1989* rests with the children's services authority. In cases where a housing authority considers that a section 20 duty is owed, they should verify this with the relevant children's services authority. In all cases of uncertainty as to whether a 16 or 17 year old applicant may be a relevant child or a child in need, the housing authority should contact the relevant children's services authority and, where necessary, should provide interim accommodation under s 188, pending clarification. A framework for joint assessment of 16 and 17 year olds will need to be established by housing and children's services authorities (and housing and children's services departments within unitary authorities) to facilitate the seamless discharge of duties and appropriate services to this client group.

See Chapter 12 for more detailed guidance on 16 and 17 year olds.

Having been looked after, accommodated or fostered and aged under 21

10.40. A person under 21 who was (but is no longer) looked after, accommodated or fostered between the ages of 16 and 18 has a priority need for accommodation (other than a person who is a 'relevant student'). The terms 'looked after', 'accommodated' or 'fostered' are set out in the *Children Act 1989* (s 24) and include any person who has been:

 i) looked after by a local authority (ie has been subject to a care order or accommodated under a voluntary agreement);

 ii) accommodated by or on behalf of a voluntary organisation;

 iii) accommodated in a private children's home;

 iv) accommodated for a consecutive period of at least three months:

  – by a health authority, special health authority, primary care trust or local education authority, or

  – in any care home or independent hospital or in any accommodation provided by a National Health Service trust; or

 v) privately fostered.

A 'relevant student' means a care leaver under 24 to whom section 24B(3) of the *Children Act 1989* applies, and who is in full-time further or higher education and whose term-time accommodation is not available during a vacation. Under s 24B(5), where a social services authority is satisfied that a person is someone to whom s 24B(3) applies and needs accommodation during a vacation they must provide accommodation or the means to enable it to be secured.

10.41. Housing authorities will need to liaise with the social services authority when dealing with homeless applicants who may fall within this category of priority need.

Homeless as a result of an emergency

10.42. Applicants have a priority need for accommodation if they are homeless or threatened with homelessness as a result of an emergency such as fire, flood or other disaster. To qualify as an 'other disaster' the disaster must be in the nature of a flood or fire, and involve some form of physical damage or threat of damage. Applicants have a priority need by reason of such an emergency whether or not they have dependent children or are vulnerable for any reason.

CHAPTER 11: INTENTIONAL HOMELESSNESS

11.1. **This chapter provides guidance on determining whether an applicant became homeless, or threatened with homelessness, *intentionally* or *unintentionally*.**

11.2. The duty owed towards those who are homeless, or threatened with homelessness, and who have a priority need for accommodation will depend upon whether they became homeless, or threatened with homelessness, intentionally or unintentionally. Section 191 defines the circumstances in which an applicant is to be regarded as having become homeless intentionally. Section 196 frames the same definitions in regard to someone who is threatened with homelessness.

11.3. The duty owed to applicants who have a priority need for accommodation but have become homeless, or threatened with homelessness, intentionally is less than the duty owed to those who have a priority need for accommodation and have become homeless, or threatened with homelessness, unintentionally. This recognises the general expectation that, wherever possible, people should take responsibility for their own accommodation needs and ensure that they do not behave in a way which might lead to the loss of their accommodation.

11.4. Where a housing authority finds an applicant to be homeless, or threatened with homelessness, intentionally they have a duty to provide the applicant (or secure that the applicant is provided) with advice and assistance in any attempts he or she may make to secure that accommodation becomes available (or does not cease to be available) for his or her occupation. Before this advice and assistance is given, the authority must assess the applicant's housing needs. The advice and assistance must include information about the likely availability in the authority's district of types of accommodation appropriate to the applicant's housing needs (including, in particular, the location and sources of such types of accommodation). Authorities should consider what best advice and assistance the authoritiy could provide, for example, providing information about applying for social housing, local lettings in the private rented sector, rent deposit schemes or housing benefit eligibility – to help the applicant avoid homelessness or secure accommodation (see Chapter 2 for further guidance on preventing homelessness). Where such an applicant also has a priority need for accommodation the authority will also have a duty to secure accommodation for such period as will give the applicant a reasonable opportunity of securing accommodation for his or her occupation. See Chapter 14 for guidance on the main duties owed to applicants on completion of inquiries.

11.5. It is for housing authorities to satisfy themselves in each individual case whether an applicant is homeless or threatened with homelessness intentionally. Generally, it is not for applicants to 'prove their case'. The exception is where an applicant seeks to establish that, as a member of a household previously found to be homeless intentionally, he or she did not acquiesce in the behaviour that led to homelessness. In such cases, the applicant will need to demonstrate that he or she was not involved in the acts or omissions that led to homelessness, and did not have control over them.

11.6. Housing authorities must not adopt general policies which seek to pre-define circumstances that do or do not amount to intentional homelessness or threatened homelessness (for example, intentional homelessness should not be assumed in cases where an application is made following a period in custody – see paragraph 11.14). In each case, housing authorities must form a view in the light of all their inquiries about that particular case. Where the original incident of homelessness occurred some years earlier and the facts are unclear, it may not be possible for the housing authority to satisfy themselves that the applicant became homeless intentionally. In such cases, the applicant should be considered to be unintentionally homeless.

Definitions of intentional homelessness

11.7. Sections 191(1) and 196(1) provide that a person becomes homeless, or threatened with homelessness, intentionally if:

i) he or she deliberately does or fails to do anything in consequence of which he or she ceases to occupy accommodation (or the likely result of which is that he or she will be forced to leave accommodation),

ii) the accommodation is available for his or her occupation, and

iii) it would have been reasonable for him or her to continue to occupy the accommodation.

However, for this purpose, an act or omission made in good faith by someone who was unaware of any relevant fact must not be treated as deliberate (see paragraph 11.20).

11.8. Sections 191(3) and 196(3) provide that a person must be treated as homeless, or threatened with homelessness, intentionally if:

i) the person enters into an arrangement under which he or she is required to cease to occupy accommodation which it would have been reasonable for the person to continue to occupy,

ii) the purpose of the arrangement is to enable the person to become entitled to assistance under Part 7, and

iii) there is no other good reason why the person is homeless or threatened with homelessness.

Whose conduct results in intentional homelessness?

11.9. Every applicant is entitled to individual consideration of his or her application. This includes applicants where another member of their family or household has made, or is making, a separate application. It is the **applicant** who must deliberately have done or failed to do something which resulted in homelessness or threatened homelessness. Where a housing authority has found an applicant to be homeless intentionally, nothing in the 1996 Act prevents another member of his or her household from making a separate application. Situations may arise where one or more members of a household found to be intentionally homeless were not responsible for the actions or omissions that led to the homelessness. For example, a person may have deliberately failed to pay the rent or defaulted on the mortgage payments, which resulted in homelessness or threatened homelessness, against the wishes or without the knowledge of his or her partner. However, where applicants were not directly responsible for the act or omission which led to their family or household becoming homeless, but they acquiesced in that behaviour, then they may be treated as having become homeless intentionally themselves. In considering whether an applicant has acquiesced in certain behaviour, the Secretary of State recommends that the housing authority take into account whether the applicant could reasonably be expected to have taken that position through a fear of actual or probable violence.

Cessation of occupation

11.10.   For intentional homelessness to be established there must have been actual occupation of accommodation which has ceased. However, occupation need not necessarily involve continuous occupation at all times, provided the accommodation was at the disposal of the applicant and available for his or her occupation. The accommodation which has been lost can be outside the UK.

Consequence of a deliberate act or omission

11.11.   For homelessness, or threatened homelessness, to be intentional it must be a consequence of a deliberate act or omission. Having established that there was a deliberate act or omission, the housing authority will need to decide whether the loss of the applicant's home, or the likelihood of its loss, is the reasonable result of that act or omission. This is a matter of cause and effect. An example would be where a person voluntarily gave up settled accommodation that it would have been reasonable for them to continue to occupy, moved into alternative accommodation of a temporary or unsettled nature and subsequently became homeless when required to leave the alternative accommodation. Housing authorities will, therefore, need to look back to the last period of settled accommodation and the reasons why the applicant left that accommodation, to determine whether the current incidence of homelessness is the result of a deliberate act or omission.

11.12.   Where a person becomes homeless intentionally, that condition may persist until the link between the causal act or omission and the intentional homelessness has been broken. It could be broken, for example, by a period in settled accommodation which follows the intentional homelessness. Whether accommodation is settled will depend on the circumstances of the particular case. Factors such as security of tenure and length of residence will be relevant. It has been established that a period in settled accommodation after an incidence of intentional homelessness would make the deliberate act or omission which led to that homelessness irrelevant in the event of a subsequent application for housing assistance. Conversely, occupation of accommodation that was merely temporary rather than settled, for example, staying with friends on an insecure basis, may not be sufficient to break the link with the earlier intentional homelessness. However, a period in settled accommodation is not necessarily the only way in which a link with the earlier intentional homelessness may be broken: some other event, such as the break-up of a marriage, may be sufficient.

Probability of violence

11.13. In cases where there is a probability of violence against an applicant if they continue, or had continued, to occupy their accommodation, and the applicant was aware of measures that could have been taken to prevent or mitigate the risk of violence but decided not to take them, their decision cannot be taken as having caused the probability of violence, and thus, indirectly, having caused the homelessness. Authorities must not assume that measures which could have been taken to prevent actual or threatened violence would necessarily have been effective.

Ex-offenders

11.14. Some ex-offenders may apply for accommodation or assistance in obtaining accommodation following a period in custody or detention because they have been unable to retain their previous accommodation, due to that period in custody or detention. In considering whether such an applicant is homeless intentionally, the housing authority will have to decide whether, taking into account all the circumstances, there was a likelihood that ceasing to occupy the accommodation could reasonably have been regarded at the time as a likely consequence of committing the offence.

Former members of the armed forces

11.15. Where service personnel are required to vacate service quarters as a result of taking up an option to give notice to leave the service, and in so doing are acting in compliance with their contractural engagement, the Secretary of State considers that they should not be considered to have become homeless intentionally.

Deliberate act or omission

11.16. For homelessness to be intentional, the act or omission that led to homelessness must have been deliberate, and applicants must always be given the opportunity to explain such behaviour. An act or omission should not generally be treated as deliberate, even where deliberately carried out, if it is forced upon the applicant through no fault of their own. Moreover, an act or omission made in good faith where someone is genuinely ignorant of a relevant fact must not be treated as deliberate (see paragraph 11.24).

11.17. Generally, an act or omission should not be considered deliberate where:

i)   the act or omission was non-payment of rent which was the result of housing benefit delays, or financial difficulties which were beyond the applicant's control;

ii)   the housing authority has reason to believe the applicant is incapable of managing his or her affairs, for example, by reason of age, mental illness or disability;

iii)   the act or omission was the result of limited mental capacity; or a temporary aberration or aberrations caused by mental illness, frailty, or an assessed substance abuse problem;

iv)   the act or omission was made when the applicant was under duress;

v)   imprudence or lack of foresight on the part of an applicant led to homelessness but the act or omission was in good faith.

11.18.   An applicant's actions would not amount to intentional homelessness where he or she has lost his or her home, or was obliged to sell it, because of rent or mortgage arrears resulting from significant financial difficulties, and the applicant was genuinely unable to keep up the rent or mortgage payments even after claiming benefits, and no further financial help was available.

11.19.   Where an applicant has lost a former home due to rent arrears, the reasons why the arrears accrued should be fully explored. Similarly, in cases which involve mortgagors, housing authorities will need to look at the reasons for mortgage arrears together with the applicant's ability to pay the mortgage commitment when it was taken on, given the applicant's financial circumstances at the time.

11.20.   Examples of acts or omissions which may be regarded as deliberate (unless any of the circumstances set out in paragraph 11.17 apply) include the following, where someone:

i)   chooses to sell his or her home in circumstances where he or she is under no risk of losing it;

ii)   has lost his or her home because of wilful and persistent refusal to pay rent or mortgage payments;

iii)   could be said to have significantly neglected his or her affairs having disregarded sound advice from qualified persons;

iv)   voluntarily surrenders adequate accommodation in this country or abroad which it would have been reasonable for the applicant to continue to occupy;

v)   is evicted because of his or her anti-social behaviour, for example by nuisance to neighbours, harassment etc;

vi)   is evicted because of violence or threats of violence by them towards another person;

vii)   leaves a job with tied accommodation and the circumstances indicate that it would have been reasonable for him or her to continue in the employment and reasonable to continue to occupy the accommodation (but note paragraph 11.15).

Available for occupation

11.21.   For homelessness to be intentional the accommodation must have been available for the applicant and anyone reasonably expected to live with him or her. Further guidance on 'availability for occupation' is provided in Chapter 8.

Reasonable to continue to occupy the accommodation

11.22.   An applicant cannot be treated as intentionally homeless unless it would have been reasonable for him or her to have continued to occupy the accommodation. Guidance on 'reasonable to continue to occupy' is provided in Chapter 8. It will be necessary for the housing authority to give careful consideration to the circumstances of the applicant and the household, in each case, and with particular care in cases where violence has been alleged.

11.23.   Authorities are reminded that, where the applicant has fled his or her home because of violence or threats of violence likely to be carried out, and has failed to pursue legal remedies against the perpetrator(s) which might have prevented the violence or threat of violence, although these decisions (to leave the home and not pursue legal remedies) may be deliberate, the homelessness would not be intentional if it would not have been reasonable for the applicant to continue to occupy the home.

Acts or omissions in good faith

11.24.   Acts or omissions made in good faith where someone was genuinely unaware of a relevant fact must not be regarded as deliberate. Provided that the applicant has acted in good faith, there is no requirement that ignorance of the relevant fact be reasonable.

11.25.   A general example of an act made in good faith would be a situation where someone gave up possession of accommodation in the belief that they had no legal right to continue to occupy the accommodation and, therefore, it would not be reasonable for them to continue to occupy it. This could apply where someone leaves rented accommodation in the private sector having received a valid notice to quit or notice that the assured shorthold tenancy has come to an end and the landlord requires possession of the property, and the former tenant was genuinely unaware that he or she had a right to remain until the court granted an order and warrant for possession.

11.26.   Where there was dishonesty there could be no question of an act or omission having been made in good faith.

11.27.   Other examples of acts or omissions that could be made in good faith might include situations where:

  i)   a person gets into rent arrears, being unaware that he or she may be entitled to housing benefit or other social security benefits;

ii)   an owner-occupier faced with foreclosure or possession proceedings to which there is no defence, sells before the mortgagee recovers possession through the courts or surrenders the property to the lender; or

iii) a tenant, faced with possession proceedings to which there would be no defence, and where the granting of a possession order would be mandatory, surrenders the property to the landlord.

In (iii) although the housing authority may consider that it would have been reasonable for the tenant to continue to occupy the accommodation, the act should not be regarded as deliberate if the tenant made the decision to leave the accommodation in ignorance of material facts, eg the general pressure on the authority for housing assistance.

Applicant enters into an arrangement

11.28.   Housing authorities will need to be alert to the possibility of collusion by which a person may claim that he or she is obliged to leave accommodation in order to take advantage of the homelessness legislation. Some parents and children, for example, may seek to take advantage of the fact that 16 and 17 year old applicants have a priority need for accommodation. Collusion is not confined to those staying with friends or relatives but can also occur between landlords and tenants. Housing authorities, while relying on experience, nonetheless need to be satisfied that collusion exists, and must not rely on hearsay or unfounded suspicions. For collusion to amount to intentional homelessness, s 191(3) specifies that there should be no other good reason for the applicant's homelessness. Examples of other good reasons include overcrowding or an obvious breakdown in relations between the applicant and his or her host or landlord. In some cases involving collusion the applicant may not actually be homeless, if there is no genuine need for the applicant to leave the accommodation. See paragraphs 8.9–8.12 for further guidance on applicants asked to leave by family or friends.

Families with children under 18

11.29.   It is important that social services are alerted as quickly as possible to cases where the applicant has children under 18 and the housing authority considers the applicant may be homeless, or threatened with homelessness, intentionally. Section 213A(2) therefore requires housing authorities to have arrangements in place to ensure that all such applicants are invited to agree to the housing authority notifying the social services authority of the essential facts of their case. The arrangements must also provide that, where consent is given, the social services authority are made aware of the essential facts and, in due course, of the subsequent decision on the homelessness case. See Chapter 13 for further guidance on section 213A.

Further applications for assistance

11.30. There is no period of disqualification if someone wants to make a fresh application after being found intentionally homeless. Where a person whose application has just been decided makes a fresh application, the authority will need to decide whether there are any new facts in the fresh application which render it different from the earlier application. If no new facts are revealed, or any new facts are of a trivial nature, the authority would not be required to consider the new application. However, where the fresh application does reveal substantive new facts, the authority must treat the fresh application in the same way as it would any other application for accommodation or assistance in obtaining accommodation. Therefore, if the authority have reason to believe that the person is homeless or threatened with homelessness, the authority must make inquiries under s 184 and decide whether any interim duty is owed under s 188(1). See Chapter 6 for guidance on inquiries and Chapter 7 for guidance on the interim duty.

Appendix 2
England: Homelessness

CHAPTER 12: 16 & 17 YEAR OLDS

12.1. This chapter provides guidance on specific duties towards 16 and 17 year old applicants.

Priority need

12.2. All 16 and 17 year old homeless applicants have a priority need for accommodation except those who are:

i) a relevant child, or

ii) a child in need who is owed a duty under s 20 of the *Children Act 1989*.

See Chapter 10 for more detailed guidance on priority need.

Relevant child or child in need owed a duty under s 20 of the 1989 Act

12.3. A relevant child is a child aged 16 or 17 who has been looked after by a local authority for at least 13 weeks since the age of 14 and has been looked after at some time while 16 or 17 and who is not currently being looked after (ie an 'eligible child' for the purposes of paragraph 19B of Schedule 2 to the *Children Act 1989*). In addition, a child is also a relevant child if he or she would have been looked after by the local authority as an eligible child but for the fact that on his or her 16th birthday he or she was detained through the criminal justice system, or in hospital, or if he or she has returned home on family placement and that has broken down (see the *Children Act 1989*, s 23A and the *Children (Leaving Care) Regulations 2001*, Regulation 4).

12.4. The *Children Act 1989* (s 20(3)) places a duty on children's services authorities to provide accommodation for a child in need aged 16 or over whose welfare is otherwise likely to be seriously prejudiced if they do not provide accommodation; and s 20(1) places a duty on children's services authorities to provide accommodation for children in need in certain other circumstances.

12.5. Responsibility for providing suitable accommodation for a relevant child or a child in need to whom a local authority owes a duty under s 20 of the *Children Act 1989* rests with the children's services authority. In cases where a housing authority considers that a s 20 duty is owed, they should verify this with the relevant children's services authority.

12.6. In all cases of uncertainty as to whether a 16 or 17 year old applicant may be a relevant child or a child in need, the housing authority should contact the relevant children's services authority and, where necessary, should provide interim accommodation under s 188, pending clarification. A framework for joint assessment of 16 and 17 year olds will need to be established by housing and children's services authorities (and housing and children's services departments within unitary authorities) to facilitate the seamless discharge of duties and appropriate services to this client group.

Family relationships

12.7. The Secretary of State considers that, generally, it will be in the best interests of 16 and 17 year olds to live in the family home, unless it would be unsafe or unsuitable for them to do so because they would be at risk of violence or abuse. It is not unusual for 16 and 17 year olds to have a turbulent relationship with their family and this can lead to temporary disagreements and even temporary estrangement. Where such disagreements look likely to lead to actual or threatened homelessness the housing authority should consider the possibility of reconciliation with the applicant's immediate family, where appropriate, or the possibility of him or her residing with another member of the wider family.

Reconciliation

12.8. In all cases involving applicants who are 16 or 17 years of age a careful assessment of the young person's circumstances and any risk to them of remaining at home should be made at the first response. Some 16 and 17 year olds may be at risk of leaving home because of a temporary breakdown in their relationship with their family. In such cases, the housing authority may be able to effect a reconciliation with the family. In some cases, however, relationships may have broken down irretrievably, and in others it may not be safe or desirable for the applicant to remain in the family home, for example, in cases involving violence or abuse.

12.9. Therefore, any mediation or reconciliation will need careful brokering and housing authorities may wish to seek the assistance of social services in all such cases.

Collusion

12.10. Where homelessness can not be avoided, local authorities should work with 16 and 17 year olds, and their families where appropriate, to explore alternative housing options. Where the main homelessness duty is owed young people need to be given the chance to consider a range of housing options including but not limited to any accommodation to be offered under s 193. Clear and accurate information is essential to allow young people to identify the right housing solution for them.

12.11. Some parents and children may seek to take advantage of the fact that 16 and 17 year old applicants have a priority need for accommodation. Housing authorities will therefore need to be alive to the possibility of collusion when assessing applications from this client group. Section 191(3) (intentional homelessness) will apply in cases where there is no genuine basis for homelessness and parents have colluded with a child and fabricated an arrangement under which the child has been asked to leave the family home (see Chapter 11 for guidance on intentional homelessness).

Appendix 2
England: Homelessness

Care and support needs

12.12. Where young people actually become homeless and are provided with accommodation, local authorities should consider whether they have any care or support needs. Many young people who have experienced homelessness may lack skills in managing their affairs and require help with managing a tenancy and operating a household budget. Those estranged from their family, particularly care leavers, may lack the advice and support normally available to young people from family, friends and other mentors. 16 and 17 year olds who are homeless and estranged from their family will be particularly vulnerable and in need of support.

12.13. Housing authorities will need to recognise that accommodation solutions for this client group are likely to be unsuccessful if the necessary support is not provided. Close liaison with social services, the Supporting People team and agencies working with young people will be essential. Most 16 and 17 year old applicants are likely to benefit from a period in supported accommodation before moving on to a tenancy of their own, but housing authorities should consider the circumstances of each case.

12.14. Housing authorities are reminded that Bed and Breakfast (B&B) accommodation is unlikely to be suitable for 16 and 17 year olds who are in need of support. Where B&B accommodation is used for this group it ought to be as a last resort for the shortest time possible and housing authorities will need to ensure that appropriate support is provided where necessary. See Chapter 17 on the suitability of accommodation for further guidance on the use of B&B accommodation.

12.15. 16 and 17 year olds (including lone parents) who apply for housing assistance may also have care and support needs that need to be assessed. **The Secretary of State recommends that housing authorities and social services authorities (and the relevant departments within unitary authorities) have arrangements in place for joint assessments of such young people's needs, whether the application is made initially to the housing department or social services department.** In all cases where an applicant may have care, health or other support needs, it is recommended that the housing authority liaise with the social services authority, the Supporting People team and other agencies (for example, the Primary Care Trust, Criminal Justice Services, and voluntary and community organisations), as appropriate, as part of their inquiries. A joint consideration of an applicant's housing and support needs may be crucial to assist the authority in establishing whether the applicant has a priority need for accommodation and any non-housing support needs (see Chapter 4 for guidance on securing support services and Chapter 5 for guidance on joint working).

Lone teenage parents under 18

12.16. The provision of suitable accommodation with support for lone parents under 18 is a key part of the Government's Teenage Pregnancy Strategy. Providing accommodation with support for 16 and 17 year old lone parents is important for a very vulnerable group at risk of social isolation. It increases the likelihood of them making a successful transition to an independent tenancy and reduces the risk of subsequent homelessness.

12.17. The Government's objective is that all 16 and 17 year old lone parents who cannot live with their parents or partner should be offered accommodation with support. Housing authorities should work with social services, RSLs, the local teenage pregnancy co-ordinator and relevant voluntary organisations in their district to ensure that the Government's objective is met. The allocation of appropriate housing and support should be based on consideration of the young person's housing and support needs, their individual circumstances and their views and preferences. Young parents under the age of 16 must always be referred to social services so that their social care needs may be assessed. Housing authorities may find it helpful to refer to *Guidelines for Good Practice in Supported Accommodation for Young Parents*, separate guidance published jointly by DTLR and the Teenage Pregnancy Unit in September 2001 (available from **www.teenagepregnancyunit.gov.uk**).

CHAPTER 13: CO-OPERATION IN CERTAIN CASES INVOLVING CHILDREN

13.1. This chapter provides guidance on the duty housing authorities and social services authorities have to co-operate in certain cases involving children.

13.2. Section 10 of the *Children Act 2004* establishes a duty on county level and unitary authorities[4] to make arrangements to promote co-operation between the authority, relevant partners (including district authorities) and other persons or bodies engaged in activities in relation to children, to improve the well-being of children and young people in the authority's area. Relevant partners are required to co-operate with the authority. Section 11 of the 2004 Act requires a range of agencies – including county level and unitary authorities and district authorities where there are two tiers of local government – to make arrangements for ensuring that their functions are discharged having regard to the need to safeguard and promote the welfare of children. See Chapter 5 for guidance on joint working.

13.3. Where an applicant is eligible for assistance and unintentionally homeless, and has a priority need because there is one or more dependent child in his or her household, the housing authority will owe a main homelessness duty to secure that accommodation is available to them. However, not all applicants with dependent children will be owed a main homelessness duty. Applicants who are found to be ineligible for assistance are not entitled to homelessness assistance under Part 7 of the 1996 Act. Where an applicant with a priority need is found to be eligible but homeless intentionally, s 190(2) requires the housing authority to secure accommodation for such period as will give the applicant a reasonable opportunity to secure accommodation for him/herself and to ensure that the applicant is provided with advice and assistance in any attempts he or she may make to secure accommodation for his or her occupation. Where an applicant with a priority need is found to be eligible but threatened with homelessness intentionally, s 195(5) requires the housing authority to ensure that the applicant is provided with advice and assistance in any attempts he or she may make to secure that accommodation does not cease to be available for his or her occupation. See Chapter 14 for guidance on the main duties owed to applicants on completion of inquiries, including the duty to provide advice and assistance.

13.4. In each of the above cases, there is a possibility that situations could arise where families may find themselves without accommodation and any prospect of further assistance from the housing authority. This could give rise to a situation in which the children of such families might become children in need, within the meaning of the term as set out in s 17 of the *Children Act 1989*.

---

[4] Section 65 of the *Children Act 2004* uses the term 'children's services authority' to define these authorities as: a county council in England; a metropolitan district council; a non-metropolitan district council for an area where there is no county council; a London borough council; the Common Council of the City of London and the Council of the Isles of Scilly.

13.5. In such cases, it is important that local authority children's services are alerted as quickly as possible because the family may wish to seek assistance under Part 3 of the *Children Act 1989*, in circumstances in which they are owed no, or only limited, assistance under the homelessness legislation. This will give local authority children's services the opportunity to consider the circumstances of the child(ren) and family, and plan any response that may be deemed by them to be appropriate.

13.6. Section 213A of the 1996 Act applies where a housing authority has reason to believe that an applicant for assistance under Part 7 with whom a person under the age of 18 normally resides, or might reasonably be expected to reside:

a)   may be ineligible for assistance;
b)   may be homeless and may have become so intentionally; or
c)   may be threatened with homelessness intentionally.

In these circumstances, a housing authority is required to have arrangements in place to ensure that the applicant is invited to consent to the referral of the essential facts of his or her case to the social services authority[5] for the district (or, in the case of a unitary authority, the social services department of the authority). The arrangements must also provide that, where consent is given, the social services authority or department is made aware of the essential facts and, in due course, of the subsequent decision in relation to the homelessness case.

13.7. The requirement to obtain the applicant's consent to the referral of the essential facts of his or her case under section 213A(2) or (3) does not affect any other power for the housing authority to disclose information about a homelessness case to the social services authority or department. For example, even where consent is withheld, the housing authority should disclose information about a homelessness case to the social services authority, if they have reason to believe that a child is, or may be, at risk of significant harm, as laid out in Chapter 5 of *Working Together to Safeguard Children: A guide to inter-agency working to safeguard and promote the welfare of children* (2006). *Working Together* was recently revised to reflect developments in legislation, policy and practice. It was published in April 2006 and can be found on the *Every Child Matters* website at http://www.everychildmatters.gov.uk/socialcare/safeguarding/workingtogether/

13.8. Where a family with one or more children has been found ineligible for assistance under Part 7 or homeless, or threatened with homelessness, intentionally and approaches the social services authority, that authority will need to decide whether the child is a 'child in need' under the terms of the *Children Act 1989*, by carrying out an assessment of their needs in accordance with the *Framework for the Assessment of Children in Need and their Families* (2000), Department of Health. The findings of the assessment should provide

Appendix 2
England: Homelessness

---

[5]   'Social services authority' is the term used in s 213A of the *Housing Act 1996*, and defined in s 217 of the *Housing Act 1996*. Such authorities are often now referred to as 'children's services authorities'. See footnote [4].

the basis for the decision as to whether the child is a 'child in need' and what, if any, services should be offered to the child in order to safeguard and promote his/her welfare. Section 17 of the *Children Act 1989* requires a local authority to promote the upbringing of children within their family, in so far as this is consistent with their general duty to safeguard and promote their welfare. The social services authority might wish to consider, for example, whether the best way of meeting the child's needs would be by assisting the family to obtain accommodation, for example by providing temporary accommodation or a rent deposit, as part of the exercise of its duty set out in s 17 of the *Children Act 1989. Local Authority Circular 2003(13): Guidance on accommodating children in need and their families* provides further guidance to social services authorities on the effect of s 17.

13.9. Where a social services authority has been made aware of a family found to be ineligible for assistance or homeless, or threatened with homelessness, intentionally by the housing authority, and they consider the needs of a child or children could best be met by helping the family to obtain accommodation, they can request the housing authority to provide them with such advice and assistance as is reasonable in the circumstances. Under s 213A(5), the housing authority must comply with such a request. Advice and assistance as is reasonable in the circumstances might include, for example, help with locating suitable accommodation and making an inspection of the property to ensure that it meets adequate standards of fitness and safety. However, the housing authority is not under a duty to provide accommodation for the family in these circumstances.

13.10. Section 213A(6) requires unitary authorities to have similar arrangements in place so that the housing department provide the social services department with such advice and assistance as they may reasonably request.

13.11. Housing authorities may also wish to consider alerting social services authorities to cases where an applicant whose household includes a child has refused an offer of accommodation which the authority is satisfied is suitable, and the authority has made a decision that it has discharged its homelessness duty under Part 7. In such cases the household could find itself without accommodation and any prospect of further assistance from the housing authority. The applicant would, however, need to consent to the housing authority notifying the social services authority of the essential facts of his or her case (unless the housing authority has any other powers to disclose the information without consent).

CHAPTER 14: MAIN DUTIES OWED TO APPLICANTS ON COMPLETION OF INQUIRIES

14.1. This chapter provides guidance on the main duties owed to applicants where the housing authority has completed its inquiries and is satisfied that an applicant is eligible for assistance and homeless or threatened with homelessness. The chapter also provides guidance on the circumstances that will bring the s 193(2) duty ('the main homelessness duty') to an end.

14.2. In many cases early, effective intervention can prevent homelessness occurring. The Secretary of State considers that housing authorities should take steps to prevent homelessness wherever possible, and offer a broad range of advice and assistance to those who face the prospect of losing their current home. However, where a housing authority has completed inquiries made under s 184 (see Chapter 6 for guidance on applications) and is satisfied that an applicant is eligible for assistance and homeless or threatened with homelessness, then one or more of the duties outlined in this chapter will apply under Part 7.

14.3. No duty is owed under Part 7 to applicants who are ineligible for assistance or not homeless or threatened with homelessness. However, homelessness strategies should aim to prevent homelessness amongst all households in the district and under s 179 advice and information about homelessness and the prevention of homelessness must be available free of charge to any person in the district, including these applicants. Housing authorities may also choose to offer other assistance to help them obtain accommodation, such as a rent deposit.

Duties to provide advice and assistance

14.4. Housing authorities have a duty to ensure that the applicant is provided with advice and assistance in a number of different circumstances, and these are dealt with below. These duties require an assessment to be made of the housing needs of the applicant before advice and assistance is provided. This assessment may need to range wider than the housing authority's inquiries into the applicant's homelessness carried out for the purpose of s 184, and should inform the provision of appropriate advice and assistance for that particular applicant. Among other things, the Secretary of State considers the assessment should identify any factors that may make it difficult for the applicant to secure accommodation for him or herself, for example, poverty, outstanding debt, health problems, disabilities and whether English is not a first language. In particular, housing authorities are advised to take account of the circumstances that led to the applicant's homelessness, or threatened homelessness, since these may impact on his or her ability to secure and maintain accommodation and may indicate what types of accommodation would be appropriate.

Duties owed to applicants who are threatened with homelessness

14.5.   Under s 175(4), a person is 'threatened with homelessness' if he or she is likely to become homeless within 28 days. However, the Secretary of State considers that housing authorities should not wait until homelessness is a likelihood or is imminent before providing advice and assistance. Early intervention may enable homelessness to be prevented, or delayed sufficiently to allow for a planned move to be arranged. However, where a housing authority has completed its inquiries under s 184 and is satisfied that an applicant is eligible for assistance and threatened with homelessness, then the specific duties outlined in paragraphs 14.6–14.9 below will apply.

Unintentionally threatened with homelessness and has priority need (s 195(2))

14.6.   Where the authority are satisfied that an applicant is threatened with homelessness unintentionally, eligible for assistance and has a priority need for accommodation, it has a **duty** under s 195(2) *to take reasonable steps to secure that accommodation does not cease to be available for the applicant's occupation.*

14.7.   Such reasonable steps may include for example, negotiation with the applicant's landlord or, in cases where the applicant has been asked to leave by family and friends, by exploring the scope for mediation and the provision of support to the household in order to ease any pressures that may have led to the applicant being asked to leave. Where a housing authority is able to identify the precise reasons why the applicant is being required to leave his or her current accommodation – for example, by interviewing the applicant and visiting his or her landlord or family or friends (as appropriate) – there may be specific actions that the housing authority or other organisations can take, for example, addressing rent arrears due to delays in housing benefit payments or providing mediation services through the voluntary sector, that can prevent the threat of homelessness being realised. See Chapter 2 for further guidance on preventing homelessness.

14.8.   Under s 195(3A), as soon as an authority has become subject to a duty under s 195(2), the authority must give the applicant a copy of the statement included in their allocation scheme about their policy on offering choice to people allocated housing accommodation under Part 6. Authorities are required to include such a statement in their allocation scheme by virtue of s 167(1A) of the 1996 Act.

14.9.   Where the housing authority is under a duty under s 195(2) and they are unable to prevent the applicant losing his or her current accommodation, the authority will need to secure alternative suitable accommodation for the applicant. Authorities should not delay; arrangements to secure alternative accommodation should begin as soon as it becomes clear that it will not be possible to prevent the applicant from losing their current home. Section 195(4) provides that, where alternative suitable accommodation is secured, the provisions of s 193(3) to (9) will apply in relation to the duty under s 195(2) as they apply in relation to the duty under s 193(2) (see paragraphs 14.17 to 14.24 below).

Unintentionally threatened with homelessness, no priority need (s 195(5) and s 195(9))

14.10. Where the housing authority are satisfied that an applicant is threatened with homelessness, eligible for assistance and does not have a priority need for accommodation, it has a **duty** under s 195(5) *to ensure that the applicant is provided with advice and assistance in any attempts he or she may make to secure that accommodation does not cease to be available for his or her occupation.*

14.11. In addition, where the housing authority are satisfied that an applicant is threatened with homelessness unintentionally, it has a **power** under s 195(9) *to take reasonable steps to secure that accommodation does not cease to be available for the applicant's occupation.* See Chapter 2 for guidance on preventing homelessness and paragraph 14.7 above.

Intentionally threatened with homelessness and has priority need (s 195(5))

14.12. Where the authority are satisfied that an applicant is threatened with homelessness intentionally, eligible for assistance and has a priority need for accommodation, the housing authority has a **duty** under s 195(5) *to ensure that the applicant is provided with advice and assistance in any attempts he or she may make to secure that accommodation does not cease to be available for his or her occupation.* See Chapter 2 for guidance on preventing homelessness.

Duties owed to applicants who are homeless

14.13. Under s 175 a person is 'homeless' if he or she has no accommodation in the UK or elsewhere which is available for his or her occupation and which that person has a legal right to occupy. Where a housing authority has completed its inquiries under s 184 and is satisfied that an applicant is eligible for assistance and homeless then the specific duties outlined below will apply.

Unintentionally homeless and has priority need (s 193(2))

14.14. Where an applicant is unintentionally homeless, eligible for assistance and has a priority need for accommodation, the housing authority has a **duty** under s 193(2) *to secure that accommodation is available for occupation by the applicant* (unless it refers the application to another housing authority under s 198). This is commonly known as 'the main homelessness duty'. In all cases, the accommodation secured must be available for occupation by the applicant together with any other person who normally resides with him or her as a member of his or her family, or any other person who might reasonably be expected to reside, with him or her, and must be suitable for their occupation. See Chapter 16 for guidance on discharging the duty to secure accommodation and Chapter 17 for guidance on suitability of accommodation.

14.15. Acceptance of a duty under s 193(2) does not prevent an immediate allocation of accommodation under Part 6 of the 1996 Act if the applicant has the necessary priority under the housing authority's allocation scheme. Under s 193(3A), as soon as an authority has become subject to a duty under s 193(2), the authority must give the applicant a copy of the statement included in their allocation scheme about their policy on offering choice to people allocated housing accommodation under Part 6. Authorities are required to include such a statement in their allocation scheme by virtue of s 167(1A) of the 1996 Act.

14.16. If the housing authority has notified the applicant that it proposes to refer the case to another housing authority, the authority has a duty under s 200(1) to secure that accommodation is available for the applicant until he or she is notified of the decision whether the conditions for referral of his case are met. The duty under s 200(1) is therefore an interim duty only. Once it has been established whether or not the conditions for referral are met, a duty under s 193(2) will be owed by either the notified housing authority or the notifying housing authority. See Chapter 18 for guidance on referrals to another housing authority.

How the s 193(2) duty ends (this also applies where alternative accommodation has been secured under s 195(2))

14.17. The housing authority will cease to be subject to the duty under s 193(2) (the main homelessness duty) in the following circumstances:

i) *the applicant accepts an offer of accommodation under Part 6 (an allocation of long term social housing)* (s 193(6)(c)): this would include an offer of an assured tenancy of a registered social landlord property via the housing authority's allocation scheme (see current guidance on the allocation of accommodation issued under s 169 of the 1996 Act);

ii) *the applicant accepts an offer of an assured tenancy (other than an assured shorthold tenancy) from a private landlord* (s 193(6)(cc)): this could include an offer of an assured tenancy made by a registered social landlord;

iii) *the applicant accepts a qualifying offer of an assured shorthold tenancy from a private landlord* (s 193(7B)). The local authority must not approve an offer of an assured shorthold tenancy for the purposes of s 193(7B), unless they are satisfied that the accommodation is suitable and that it would be reasonable for the applicant to accept it (s 193(7F)) (see paragraph 14.25 below);

iv) *the applicant refuses a final offer of accommodation under Part 6 (an allocation of long term social housing)*: the duty does not end unless the applicant is informed of the possible consequences of refusal and of his or her right to ask for a review of the suitability of the accommodation (s 193(7)), the offer is made in writing and states that it is a final offer (s 193(7A)), and the housing authority is satisfied that the accommodation is suitable and that it would be reasonable for the applicant to accept it (s 193(7F)) (see paragraph 14.25 below);

v) *the applicant refuses an offer of accommodation to discharge the duty which the housing authority is satisfied is suitable for the applicant* (s 193(5)): the duty does not end unless the applicant is informed of the possible consequences of refusal and of his or her right to ask for a review of the suitability of the accommodation. The housing authority must also notify the applicant that it regards itself as having discharged its duty, before it can end;

vi) *the applicant ceases to be eligible for assistance as defined in s 185 of the 1996 Act*;

vii) *the applicant becomes homeless intentionally from accommodation made available to him or her under s 193 or s 195*; see Chapter 11 for guidance on determining whether an applicant became homeless intentionally;

viii) *the applicant otherwise voluntarily ceases to occupy as his or her principal home accommodation made available under s 193 or s 195.*

14.18. The Secretary of State recommends that applicants are given the chance to view accommodation before being required to decide whether they accept or refuse an offer, and before being required to sign any written agreement relating to the accommodation (eg a tenancy agreement). Under s 202(1A), an applicant who is offered accommodation can request a review of its suitability whether or not he or she has accepted the offer. See Chapter 17 for guidance on suitability and Chapter 19 for guidance on reviews.

Qualifying offer of an assured shorthold tenancy

14.19. An offer of an assured shorthold tenancy is a qualifying offer if:

i) it is made, with the approval of the authority, in pursuance of arrangements made by the authority with the landlord with a view to bringing the authority's duty under s 193 to an end;

ii) it is for a fixed term within the meaning of Part 1 of the *Housing Act 1988* (ie not a periodic tenancy); and

iii) it is accompanied by a written statement that states the term of the tenancy being offered and explains in ordinary language that there is no obligation on the applicant to accept the offer, but if the offer is accepted the housing authority will cease to be subject to the s 193 duty.

14.20. The s 193 duty will not end with acceptance of an offer of a qualifying tenancy unless the applicant signs a statement acknowledging that he or she has understood the written statement accompanying the offer.

Reasonable to accept an offer

14.21. Housing authorities must not make a final offer under Part 6 or approve a qualifying offer of an assured shorthold tenancy unless they are satisfied that the accommodation is suitable for the applicant and that it is reasonable for him or her to accept the offer (s 193(7F)) (see Chapter 17 for guidance on suitability). Where an applicant has contractual or other

Appendix 2
England: Homelessness

obligations in respect of his or her existing accommodation (eg a tenancy agreement or lease), the housing authority can reasonably expect the offer to be taken up only if the applicant is able to bring those obligations to an end before he is required to take up the offer (s 193(8)).

14.22. Housing authorities must allow applicants a reasonable period for considering offers of accommodation made under Part 6 that will bring the homelessness duty to an end whether accepted or refused. There is no set reasonable period; some applicants may require longer than others depending on their circumstances, whether they wish to seek advice in making their decision and whether they are already familiar with the property in question. Longer periods may be required where the applicant is in hospital or temporarily absent from the district. In deciding what is a reasonable period, housing authorities must take into account the applicant's circumstances in each case.

Other circumstances that bring the s 193(2) duty to an end

14.23. Under s 193(6) the housing authority will also cease to be subject to the duty under s 193 in the following circumstances:

i)   *the applicant ceases to be eligible for assistance as defined in s 185 of the 1996 Act*;

ii)   *the applicant becomes homeless intentionally from accommodation made available to him or her under s 193 or s 195*: see Chapter 11 for guidance on determining whether an applicant became homeless intentionally;

iii) *the applicant otherwise voluntarily ceases to occupy as his or her only or principal home accommodation made available under s 193 or s 195.*

Further applications

14.24. Under s 193(9) a person who ceases to be owed a duty under s 193(2) can make a fresh application for accommodation or assistance in obtaining accommodation (see Chapter 6 for guidance on applications).

Unintentionally homeless and has no priority need (s 192(2) and s 192(3))

14.25. Where an applicant is unintentionally homeless, eligible for assistance and does not have a priority need for accommodation, the housing authority has a **duty** under s 192(2) *to ensure that the applicant is provided with advice and assistance in any attempts he or she may make to secure that accommodation becomes available for his or her occupation.* The housing authority might, for example, provide assistance with a rent deposit or guarantee to help the applicant to obtain accommodation in the private rented sector, or advice on applying for an allocation of accommodation through the social housing waiting list or through another social landlord (see Chapter 2 for guidance on advisory services).

14.26. In addition, housing authorities have a **power** under s 192(3) *to secure that accommodation is available for occupation by the applicant.* Authorities should consider whether to use this power in all relevant cases.

Intentionally homeless and has priority need (s 190(2))

14.27. Where an applicant is intentionally homeless, eligible for assistance and has a priority need for accommodation, the housing authority has a **duty** under s 190(2) to:

a) *secure that accommodation is available for the applicant's occupation for such period as it considers will give him or her a reasonable opportunity of securing accommodation for his or her occupation (s 190(2)(a)); and*

b) *provide the applicant, or secure that the applicant is provided with, advice and assistance in any attempts he or she may make to secure that accommodation becomes available for his or her occupation (s 190(2)(b)).*

14.28. The accommodation secured must be suitable. Housing authorities must consider each case on its merits when determining the period for which accommodation will be secured. A few weeks may provide the applicant with a reasonable opportunity to secure accommodation for him or herself. However, some applicants might require longer, and others, particularly where the housing authority provides pro-active and effective advice and assistance, might require less time. In particular, housing authorities will need to take account of the housing circumstances in the local area, including how readily other accommodation is available in the district, and have regard to the particular circumstances of the applicant, including the resources available to him or her to provide rent in advance or a rent deposit where this may be required by private landlords.

14.29. In addition to securing accommodation, the housing authority must ensure the applicant is provided with advice and assistance to help him or her secure accommodation for him/herself. This might include, for example, assistance with a rent deposit or guarantee to help the applicant to obtain accommodation in the private rented sector, or advice on applying for an allocation of long term social housing or accommodation through another social landlord. See Chapter 2 for guidance on advisory services.

Intentionally homeless and has no priority need (s 190(3))

14.30. Where an applicant is intentionally homeless, eligible for assistance and does not have a priority need for accommodation, the housing authority has a **duty** under s 190(3) *to ensure that the applicant is provided with advice and assistance in any attempts he or she may make to secure that accommodation becomes available for his or her occupation.* This might include, for example, assistance with a rent deposit or guarantee to help the applicant to obtain accommodation in the private rented sector, or advice on applying for an allocation of long term social housing accommodation or through another social landlord. See Chapter 2 for guidance on advisory services.

CHAPTER 15: DISCRETIONARY POWERS TO SECURE ACCOMMODATION

15.1. This chapter provides guidance on the discretionary *powers* housing authorities have to secure accommodation for a household where they do not have a *duty* to secure accommodation for that household (see Chapter 16 for guidance on discharge of duties to secure accommodation).

15.2. Housing authorities have powers to secure accommodation for:

i) applicants who are eligible for assistance, unintentionally homeless and do not have a priority need for accommodation;

ii) applicants who request a review of the housing authority's decision on their case and who satisfy the relevant conditions, pending a decision on the review; and

iii) applicants who appeal to the county court against the housing authority's decision and who satisfy the relevant conditions, pending the determination of the appeal.

15.3. The fact that a housing authority has decided that an applicant is ineligible for housing assistance under Part 7 does not preclude it from exercising its powers to secure accommodation pending a review or appeal. However, housing authorities should note that s 54 of, and Schedule 3 to, the *Nationality, Immigration and Asylum Act 2002* prevent them from exercising their powers to accommodate an applicant pending a review or appeal to the county court, where the applicant is a person who falls within one of a number of classes of person specified in Schedule 3. See paragraphs 9.20–9.23 in Chapter 9 on eligibility for assistance for further details.

Ways of securing accommodation

15.4. A housing authority may only discharge its housing functions under Part 7 in the following ways:

a) by securing that suitable accommodation provided by them is available for the applicant (s 206(1)(a));

b) by securing that the applicant obtains suitable accommodation from some other person (s 206(1)(b)); or

c) by giving the applicant such advice and assistance as will secure that suitable accommodation is available from some other person (s 206(1)(c)).

See Chapter 17 for guidance on the suitability of accommodation and Chapter 8 for guidance on when accommodation is available for occupation. In so far as is reasonably practicable, accommodation should be secured within the authority's own district (s 208(1)).

Power to secure accommodation for applicants who are unintentionally homeless and do not have priority need

15.5. Under s 192(3), housing authorities may secure that accommodation is made available for applicants who are eligible for assistance, unintentionally homeless and do not have a priority need for accommodation. Where a housing authority decides to exercise this power it will still have a duty under s 192(2) to provide advice and assistance to the applicant in any attempts that he or she may make to secure accommodation for him/herself. See Chapter 14 for guidance on this duty.

15.6. By virtue of paragraph 4 of Schedule 1 to the *Housing Act 1985*, a tenancy granted under the power in s 192(3) will not be a secure tenancy. Housing authorities are reminded that all secure and introductory tenancies must be allocated in accordance with their allocation scheme, as framed under Part 6.

15.7. Housing authorities should consider using this power in all relevant cases. Any exercise of, or decision not to exercise, a power may be open to challenge by way of judicial review. In considering the use of this power, housing authorities must have regard to the legitimate expectations of others in housing need who have applied for an allocation of housing under Part 6, and to any need for accommodation to meet their obligations under Part 7.

15.8. Housing authorities should, in particular, consider exercising the s 192(3) power in circumstances where to do so would enable compliance with the obligations imposed on them by virtue of s 6 of the *Human Rights Act 1998* and where not doing so would mean acting in a way that may be incompatible with the applicant's Convention rights. The same is true of the power in s 195(8) (see paragraph 15.17 below).

15.9. Housing authorities may also wish to consider exercising the s 192(3) power to provide accommodation for a limited period to applicants such as key workers who are unintentionally homeless but do not have priority need under Part 7, or priority for an allocation under Part 6. This would be particularly appropriate where it would be in the interests of the local community for such persons to be accommodated in the district.

15.10. Non-secure tenancies will generally be suitable for a limited period only. They should be provided as part of a managed programme of accommodation to give the applicant an opportunity to secure a more settled housing solution in due course. This should be explained to the applicant from the outset and the housing authority should assist him or her to secure alternative accommodation. Reasonable notice should be given of a decision to stop exercising the power.

15.11. Housing authorities should not provide accommodation under s 192(3) as an alternative to allocating accommodation under Part 6 and should not allow non-secure tenancies to continue over the long-term.

Powers to accommodate pending a review

15.12. Under s 202, applicants have the right to ask for a review of a housing authority's decision on a number of issues relating to their case (see Chapter 19 for guidance on reviews). Housing authorities have three powers to accommodate applicants pending a decision on the review. The relevant powers are found in s 188(3), s 195(8)(b) and s 200(5).

15.13. Under s 188(1), housing authorities must secure that accommodation is available for occupation by an applicant who they have reason to believe is:

(a) homeless,
(b) eligible for assistance, and
(c) in priority need,

pending their decision as to what duty, if any, is owed to that applicant under Part 7. See Chapter 7 for further guidance on this interim duty. Under s 188(3), if the applicant requests a review of the housing authority's decision on the duty owed to them under Part 7, the authority has the power to secure that accommodation is available for the applicant's occupation pending a decision on the review.

15.14. Section 188(3) includes a power to secure that accommodation is available where the applicant was found to be intentionally homeless and in priority need and:

(a) a duty was owed under s 190(2)(a);
(b) the s 190(2)(a) duty has been fully discharged; and
(c) the applicant is awaiting a decision on a review.

15.15. In considering whether to exercise their s 188(3) power, housing authorities will need to balance the objective of maintaining fairness between homeless persons in circumstances where they have decided that no duty is owed to them against proper consideration of the possibility that the applicant might be right. The Secretary of State is of the view that housing authorities should consider the following, although other factors may also be relevant:

(a) the merits of the applicant's case that the original decision was flawed and the extent to which it can properly be said that the decision was one which was either contrary to the apparent merits or was one which involved a very fine balance of judgment;
(b) whether any new material, information or argument has been put to them which could alter the original decision; and
(c) the personal circumstances of the applicant and the consequences to him or her of a decision not to exercise the discretion to accommodate.

The Secretary of State considers that when determining the merits of the applicant's case that the original decision was flawed, housing authorities should take account of whether there may have been procedural irregularities in making the original decision which could have affected the decision taken.

15.16. Housing authorities should give applicants reasonable notice to vacate accommodation provided under s 188(3) following an unsuccessful s 202

Appendix 2
England: Homelessness

review. The Secretary of State considers that reasonableness should be judged against the particular applicant's circumstances. The applicant will require time to enable him or her to make alternative accommodation arrangements and housing authorities should take account of the fact that this may be easier for some applicants than others. Housing authorities may also require time to consider whether they should exercise their discretion under s 204(4) where the applicant appeals to the county court under s 204(1) (see paragraph 15.21).

15.17. Under s 195(5)(b), where a housing authority is satisfied that an applicant is:

(a)   threatened with homelessness,
(b)   eligible for assistance, and
(c)   has a priority need, but
(d)   became threatened with homelessness intentionally,

the authority is under a duty to provide the applicant (or secure that he or she is provided with) advice and assistance so that accommodation does not cease to be available for his or her occupation. Under s 195(8)(b), if the applicant requests a review of the housing authority's decision and, pending a decision on the review, becomes homeless, the housing authority may secure that accommodation is available for his or her occupation.

15.18. Under s 200(1), where a housing authority notifies another authority of its opinion that the conditions for the referral of an applicant's case to that authority are met, the authority has a duty to secure that accommodation is available for occupation by the applicant until a decision on the referral is reached. See Chapter 18 for guidance on local connection and referrals. If the applicant subsequently requests a review of the decision reached on the referral of his or her case, the notifying authority has the power under s 200(5) to secure that accommodation is available for the applicant's occupation pending the decision on that review.

15.19. Where, generally, only a small proportion of requests for a review are successful, it may be open to housing authorities to adopt a policy of deciding to exercise their powers to accommodate pending a review only in exceptional circumstances. However, such a policy would need to be applied flexibly and each case would need to be considered on its particular facts. In deciding whether there were exceptional circumstances, the housing authority would need to take account of all material considerations and disregard all those which were immaterial.

15.20. Where an applicant is refused accommodation pending a review, he or she may seek to challenge the decision by way of judicial review.

Power to accommodate pending an appeal to the county court

15.21. Applicants have the right to appeal to the county court on a point of law against a housing authority's decision on a review or, if they are not notified of the review decision, against the original homelessness decision (see

Chapter 19 for guidance on appeals). Under s 204(4), housing authorities have the power to accommodate certain applicants:

(a) during the period for making an appeal against their decision, and

(b) if an appeal is brought, until it and any subsequent appeals are finally determined.

This power may be exercised where the housing authority was previously under a duty to secure accommodation for the applicant's occupation under s 188 (interim duty pending initial inquiries), s 190 (duty owed to applicants intentionally homeless and in priority need), or s 200 (interim duty owed pending decision on a referral). The power may also be exercised in a case where the applicant was owed a duty under s 195(5)(b) (intentionally threatened with homelessness and in priority need), the applicant requested a review and subsequently become homeless, and, in consequence, the housing authority had a power under s 195(8)(b) to secure accommodation pending the decision on the review.

15.22. The power under s 204(4) may be exercised whether or not the housing authority has exercised its powers to accommodate the applicant pending a review.

15.23. In deciding whether to exercise this power, housing authorities will need to adopt the same approach, and consider the same factors, as for a decision whether to exercise their power to accommodate pending a review (see paragraph 15.12).

15.24. Under s 204A, applicants have a right to appeal to the county court against a decision not to secure accommodation for them pending their main appeal. In deciding a s 204A appeal, the court must apply the principles that would be applied by the High Court on an application for judicial review. The county court cannot substitute its own decision as such. However, where the court quashes the decision of the housing authority, it may order the housing authority to accommodate the applicant, but only where it is satisfied that failure to do so would substantially prejudice the applicant's ability to pursue the main appeal on the homelessness decision.

Appendix 2
England: Homelessness

CHAPTER 16: SECURING ACCOMMODATION

16.1. **This chapter provides guidance on the different ways in which housing authorities can ensure that suitable accommodation is available for applicants. In the case of the main homelessness duty the obligation to secure such accommodation will continue until such time as the duty ends in accordance with s 193.**

Ways of securing accommodation

16.2. Section 206(1) provides that a housing authority may only discharge its housing functions under Part 7 in the following ways:

(a)　by securing that suitable accommodation provided by them is available for the applicant (s 206(1)(a));

(b)　by securing that the applicant obtains suitable accommodation from some other person (s 206(1)(b)); or

(c)　by giving the applicant such advice and assistance as will secure that suitable accommodation is available from some other person (s 206(1)(c)).

16.3. Accommodation secured must be available for occupation by the applicant and any other person who normally resides with them as a member of their family, or might reasonably be expected to reside with them. The accommodation must also be suitable for their occupation. See Chapter 8 for guidance on when accommodation is available for occupation and Chapter 17 for guidance on the suitability of accommodation.

16.4. In deciding what accommodation needs to be secured housing authorities will need to consider whether the applicant has any support needs. Housing authorities will therefore need to make arrangements for effective links with the Supporting People team, the social services authority or other bodies (for example, Primary Care Trusts, Criminal Justice Services, RSLs and voluntary and community organisations) to ensure that a joint assessment of an applicant's housing and support needs can be made where necessary. See Chapter 4 for guidance on securing support services.

16.5. Where a housing authority has a duty under s 193(2) to secure accommodation for an applicant ('the main homelessness duty'), the Secretary of State recommends that the authority considers, where availability of suitable housing allows, securing settled (rather than temporary) accommodation that will bring the duty to an end in the immediate or short term. For example, an offer of accommodation under the housing authority's allocation scheme or a qualifying offer of an assured shorthold tenancy from a private landlord. See Chapter 14 for guidance on bringing the s 193(2) duty to an end.

16.6. The Secretary of State considers that, generally, it is inappropriate for social housing to be used as temporary accommodation for applicants other than for short periods (see paragraph 16.18 below). Except in limited circumstances where social housing is only going to be available for use for a short period, where an authority has placed a household in social housing as a temporary arrangement to fulfil a duty under s 193(2), the Secretary of State recommends that the authority considers offering the household a settled home under the terms of its allocation scheme as soon as possible.

Accommodation secured out of district

16.7. Section 208(1) requires housing authorities to secure accommodation within their district, in so far as is reasonably practicable. Housing authorities should, therefore, aim to secure accommodation within their own district wherever possible, except where there are clear benefits for the applicant of being accommodated outside of the district. This could occur, for example, where the applicant, and/or a member of his or her household, would be at risk of domestic or other violence in the district and need to be accommodated elsewhere to reduce the risk of further contact with the perpetrator(s) or where ex-offenders or drug/alcohol users would benefit from being accommodated outside the district to help break links with previous contacts which could exert a negative influence.

16.8. Where it is not reasonably practicable for the applicant to be placed in accommodation within the housing authority's district, and the housing authority places the applicant in accommodation elsewhere, s 208(2) requires the housing authority to notify the housing authority in whose district the accommodation is situated of the following:

i)   the name of the applicant;
ii)   the number and description of other persons who normally reside with the applicant as a member of his or her family or might reasonably be expected to do so;
iii)   the address of the accommodation;
iv)   the date on which the accommodation was made available;
v)   which function the housing authority is discharging in securing the accommodation.

The notice must be given in writing within 14 days of the accommodation being made available to the applicant.

16.9. The Secretary of State considers that applicants whose household has a need for social services support or a need to maintain links with other essential services within the borough, for example specialist medical services or special schools, should be given priority for accommodation within the housing authority's own district. In particular, careful consideration should be given to applicants with a mental illness or learning disability who may have a particular need to remain in a specific area, for example to maintain links with health service professionals and/or a reliance on existing informal support networks and community links. Such applicants may be less able than others to adapt to any disruption caused by being placed in accommodation in another district.

Access to support services

16.10.   The Secretary of State recommends that housing authorities consider what arrangements need to be in place to ensure that households placed in temporary accommodation, within their district or outside, are able to access relevant support services, including health, education and social services. The Secretary of State considers that all babies and young children placed in temporary accommodation, for example, should have the opportunity to receive health and developmental checks from health visitors and/or other primary health care professionals. See Chapter 4 for further guidance on securing support services.

Accommodation provided by the housing authority

16.11.   Housing authorities may secure accommodation by providing suitable accommodation for the applicant themselves (s 206(1)(a)), in which case the housing authority will be the immediate landlord of the applicant, for example, where the housing authority place the applicant in:

i)   a house or flat from its own stock (ie held under Part 2 of the *Housing Act 1985*);
ii)   a hostel owned by the housing authority; or
iii)   accommodation leased by the housing authority from another landlord (eg under a private sector leasing agreement) and sub-let to the applicant.

Housing authority's own stock

16.12.   In considering whether to provide accommodation from their own stock, housing authorities will need to balance the requirements of applicants owed a duty under Part 7 against the need to provide accommodation for others who have priority for an allocation under Part 6 of the 1996 Act. **The Secretary of State considers that, generally, it is inappropriate for social housing to be used as temporary accommodation for applicants other than for short periods.**

16.13.   Paragraph 4 of Schedule 1 to the *Housing Act 1985* provides that a tenancy granted by a housing authority in pursuance of any function under Part 7 is not a secure tenancy unless the housing authority notifies the tenant that it is such. Housing authorities are reminded that the allocation of secure and introductory tenancies must be made in accordance with their allocation scheme framed under the provisions of Part 6.

Housing authority hostels

16.14.   Some housing authorities operate their own hostels and may wish to use these to accommodate certain applicants, particularly where they consider an applicant would benefit from a supported environment. See paragraphs 16.25 and 16.26 for further guidance on the use of hostel accommodation.

Accommodation leased from a private landlord

16.15.   Accommodation leased from a private landlord can provide housing authorities with a source of good quality, self-contained accommodation which can be let to applicants. Where there is a need for temporary accommodation, housing authorities are encouraged to maximise their use of this type of leasing, in so far as they can secure cost-effective arrangements with landlords.

16.16.   Under the prudential capital finance system (introduced by the *Local Government Act 2003* on 1 April 2004) local authorities are free to borrow without Government consent, provided that they can service the debts without extra Government support. The authority must determine how much it can afford to borrow. The new system ended the former financial disincentives to use leasing (and other forms of credit). Consequently, there is no longer any need for special concessions relating to leases of property owned by private landlords where that property is used to accommodate households owed a duty under Part 7. When entering into leases, as when borrowing, the capital finance rules simply require authorities to be satisfied that the associated liabilities are affordable.

Accommodation secured from another person

16.17.   Housing authorities may secure that the applicant obtains suitable accommodation from some other person (s 206(1)(b)). Housing authorities can make use of a wide range of accommodation, including housing in the private rented sector and accommodation held by RSLs. The following paragraphs outline a number of options for securing accommodation from another landlord, which are available to housing authorities.

Registered social landlords

16.18.   As the proportion of housing stock in the social sector held by RSLs increases, housing authorities should ensure that they maximise the opportunities for securing housing from RSLs. Under s 213 of the 1996 Act, where requested by a housing authority, an RSL must assist the housing authority in carrying out their duties under the homelessness legislation by co-operating with them as far as is reasonable in the circumstances. Housing Corporation regulatory guidance, issued with the consent of the Secretary of State under s 36 of the 1996 Act, requires RSLs, on request, to provide a proportion of their stock for nominations and as temporary accommodation for people owed a homelessness duty under Part 7 of the 1996 Act – to such extent as is reasonable in the circumstances. **The Secretary of State considers that, generally, it is inappropriate for social housing to be used as temporary accommodation other than for short periods** (see paragraph 16.6 above). Where a longer-term stay occurs or seems likely, the authority and RSL should consider offering an assured tenancy to bring the main homelessness duty to an end. See Annex 5 for further guidance on RSL co-operation with housing authorities.

16.19. Housing authorities may wish to consider contracting with RSLs for assistance in discharging their housing functions under arrangements whereby the RSL lease and/or manage accommodation owned by private landlords, which can be let to households owed a homelessness duty and nominated by the housing authority. A general consent under s 25 of the *Local Government Act 1988* (*The General Consent under Section 25 of the Local Government Act 1988 for Financial Assistance to Registered Social Landlords or to Private Landlords to Relieve or Prevent Homelessness 2005*) allows housing authorities to provide RSLs with financial assistance in connection with such arrangements. Housing authorities must reserve the right to terminate such agreements, without penalty, after 3 years.

Private lettings

16.20. Housing authorities may seek the assistance of private sector landlords in providing suitable accommodation direct to applicants. A general consent under s 25 of the *Local Government Act 1988* (*The General Consent under Section 25 of the Local Government Act 1988 for Financial Assistance to Registered Social Landlords or to Private Landlords to Relieve or Prevent Homelessness 2005*) allows housing authorities to provide financial assistance to private landlords in order to secure accommodation for people who are homeless or at risk of homelessness. This could involve, for example, the authority paying the costs of leases; making small one-off grants ('finders' fees') to landlords to encourage them to let dwellings to households owed a homelessness duty; paying rent deposits or indemnities to ensure accommodation is secured for such households; and making one-off grant payments which would prevent an eviction. There is no limit set on the amount of financial assistance that can be provided, however authorities are obliged to act reasonably and in accordance with their fiduciary duty to local tax and rent payers. Housing authorities may also make Discretionary Housing Payments (DHP) to a private landlord to meet a shortfall between the rent and the amount of housing benefit payable to a person who is homeless or at risk of homelessness. DHPs are intended to provide extra financial assistance where there is a shortfall in a person's eligible rent and the housing authority consider that the claimant is in need of further financial assistance. They are governed by the *Discretionary Housing Payment (Grant) Order 2001*. Housing authorities should also consider working with private landlords to arrange qualifying offers of assured shorthold tenancies which would bring the main homelessness duty to an end if accepted by the applicant. See paragraph 14.19 for guidance on qualifying offers.

Tenancies granted by private landlords and registered social landlords to assist with interim duties

16.21. Section 209 governs security of tenure where a private landlord provides accommodation to assist a housing authority discharge an **interim** duty, for example, a duty under s 188(1), s 190(2), s 200(1) or 204(4). Any such accommodation is exempt from statutory security of tenure until 12 months from the date on which the applicant is notified of the authority's decision under s 184(3) or s 198(5) or from the date on which the applicant is notified of the decision of any review under s 202 or an appeal under s 204, unless the landlord notifies the applicant that the tenancy is an assured or assured shorthold tenancy.

16.22. Where a private landlord or RSL lets accommodation directly to an applicant to assist a housing authority discharge any other homelessness duty, the tenancy granted will be an assured shorthold tenancy unless the tenant is notified that it is to be regarded as an assured tenancy.

Other social landlords

16.23. Under s 213 other social landlords, ie new town corporations and housing action trusts, have a duty to co-operate, as far as is reasonable in the circumstances, with a housing authority in carrying out their housing functions under Part 7 of the 1996 Act, if asked to do so.

Lodgings

16.24. Lodgings provided by householders may be suitable for some young and/or vulnerable single applicants. Housing authorities may wish to establish a network of such landlords in their district, and to liaise with social services who may operate supported lodgings schemes for people with support needs.

Hostels

16.25. Some applicants may benefit from the supportive environment which managed hostels can provide. Hostels can offer short-term support to people who are experiencing a temporary crisis, and provide an opportunity for them to regain their equilibrium and subsequently move on to live independently. Where an applicant appears to need support, particularly on-going support, and there is no social worker or support worker familiar with their case, the housing authority should request a community care assessment by the social services authority. However, housing authorities should not assume that a hostel will automatically be the most appropriate form of accommodation for vulnerable people, particularly in relation to young people, people with mental health problems and those who have experienced violence and/or abuse. In addition, where hostel accommodation is used to accommodate vulnerable young people or families with children, the Secretary of State considers that it would be inappropriate to accommodate these groups alongside adults with chaotic behavioural problems.

Appendix 2
England: Homelessness

16.26. Housing authorities will need to take into account that some hostels are designed to meet short-term needs only. In addition to the question of whether the hostel accommodation would be suitable for the applicant for other than a short period, housing authorities should have regard to the need to ensure that bed spaces continue to be available in hostels for others who need them.

Women's refuges

16.27. Housing authorities should develop close links with women's refuges within their district, and neighbouring districts, to ensure they have access to emergency accommodation for women applicants who are fleeing domestic or other violence or who are at risk of such violence. However, housing authorities should recognise that placing an applicant in a refuge will generally be a temporary expedient only, and a prolonged stay could block a bed space that was urgently needed by someone else at risk. Refuges should be used to provide accommodation for the minimum period necessary before alternative suitable accommodation is secured elsewhere. Housing authorities should not delay in securing alternative accommodation in the hope that the applicant might return to her partner.

Bed and breakfast accommodation

16.28. Bed and Breakfast (B&B) accommodation caters for very short-term stays only and generally will afford residents only limited privacy and may lack certain important amenities, such as cooking and laundry facilities. Consequently, where possible, housing authorities should avoid using B&B hotels to discharge a duty to secure accommodation for applicants, unless, in the very limited circumstances where it is likely to be the case, it is the most appropriate option for an applicant. The Secretary of State considers B&B hotels as particularly unsuitable for accommodating applicants with family commitments and applicants aged 16 or 17 years who need support. See paragraphs 17.23 et seq in Chapter 17 for guidance on suitability and Chapter 12 for more detailed guidance on 16 and 17 year olds.

Accommodation provided by other housing authorities

16.29. Other housing authorities experiencing less demand for housing may be able to assist a housing authority by providing temporary or settled accommodation for homeless applicants. This could be particularly appropriate in the case of applicants who would be at risk of violence or serious harassment in the district of the housing authority to whom they have applied for assistance. Other housing authorities may also be able to provide accommodation in cases where the applicant has special housing needs and the other housing authority has accommodation available which is appropriate to those needs. Under s 213(1), where one housing authority requests another to help them discharge a function under Part 7, the other housing authority must co-operate in providing such assistance as is reasonable in the circumstances.

Housing authorities are encouraged to consider entering into reciprocal and co-operative arrangements under these provisions. See Chapter 5 for guidance on the statutory provisions on co-operation between authorities.

Mobile homes

16.30. Although mobile homes may sometimes provide emergency or short-term accommodation, eg to discharge an interim duty, housing authorities will need to be satisfied that the accommodation is suitable for the applicant and his or her household, paying particular regard to their needs, requirements and circumstances and the conditions and facilities on the site. Caravans designed primarily for short-term holiday use should not be regarded as suitable as temporary accommodation for applicants.

Tenancies for minors

16.31. There are legal complications associated with the grant of a tenancy to a minor because a minor cannot hold a legal estate in land. However, if a tenancy is granted it is likely to be enforceable as a contract for necessaries (ie the basic necessities of life) under common law. In some circumstances, social services authorities may consider it appropriate to underwrite a tenancy agreement for a homeless applicant who is under 18.

Advice and assistance that will secure accommodation from another person

16.32. Housing authorities may secure accommodation by giving advice and assistance to an applicant that will secure that accommodation becomes available for him or her from another person (s 206(1)(c)). However, where an authority has a duty to secure accommodation, they will need to ensure that the advice and assistance provided results in suitable accommodation actually being secured. Merely assisting the applicant in any efforts that he or she might make to find accommodation would not be sufficient if suitable accommodation did not actually become available.

16.33. One example of securing accommodation in this way is where house purchase is a possibility for the applicant. Advice on all options for financing house purchase should be made available, especially those financial packages which may be suited to people on lower incomes.

16.34. One option to help people into home ownership is shared equity schemes (eg part buy/part rent or equity loans to assist with purchase). These schemes are mainly funded by the Housing Corporation and generally offered by RSLs. The Housing Corporation publishes booklets (available from their publication section) giving further details of the existing shared ownership and Homebuy schemes. A new HomeBuy scheme offering further opportunities for home ownership and building on the current schemes commenced on 1st April 2006.

Appendix 2
England: Homelessness

16.35. In other cases, applicants may have identified suitable accommodation but need practical advice and assistance to enable them to secure it, for example the applicant may require help with understanding a tenancy agreement or financial assistance with paying a rent deposit.

16.36. Housing authorities should bear in mind that the advice and assistance must result in suitable accommodation being secured, and that applicants who wish to pursue this option may need alternative accommodation until this result is achieved.

Applicants who normally occupy moveable accommodation (eg caravans, houseboats)

16.37. Under s 175(2) applicants are homeless if the accommodation available for their occupation is a caravan, houseboat, or other movable structure and they do not have a place where they are entitled, or permitted, to put it and live in it. If a duty to secure accommodation arises in such cases, the housing authority is not required to make equivalent accommodation available (or provide a site or berth for the applicant's own accommodation). However, the authority must consider whether such options are reasonably available, particularly where this would provide the most suitable solution to the applicant's accommodation needs.

Gypsies and Travellers

16.38. The circumstances described in paragraph 16.37 will be particularly relevant in the case of Gypsies and Travellers. Where a duty to secure accommodation arises but an appropriate site is not immediately available, the housing authority may need to provide an alternative temporary solution until a suitable site, or some other suitable option, becomes available. Some Gypsies and Travellers may have a cultural aversion to the prospect of 'bricks and mortar' accommodation. In such cases, the authority should seek to provide an alternative solution. However, where the authority is satisfied that there is no prospect of a suitable site for the time being, there may be no alternative solution. Authorities must give consideration to the needs and lifestyle of applicants who are Gypsies and Travellers when considering their application and how best to discharge a duty to secure suitable accommodation, in line with their obligations to act consistently with the *Human Rights Act 1998*, and in particular the right to respect for private life, family and the home.

Temporary to settled accommodation

16.39. Housing authorities are encouraged to test new approaches that would enable temporary accommodation to become settled accommodation. This would reduce the uncertainty and lack of security that households in temporary accommodation can face, and provide them with a settled home more quickly. Such approaches could be developed with housing associations through a range of 'temporary to settled' housing initiatives.

16.40. Each year approximately a quarter to a third of all leases of private sector accommodation held by social landlords expire. This presents an opportunity for the leased accommodation to be converted from use as temporary accommodation to the provision of settled housing, through negotiation with the landlord and the tenant during the final months of the lease. Where the household would be content to remain in the accommodation when the lease ends if it could be provided on a more settled basis, and the landlord would be prepared to let directly to the household, the local authority may wish to arrange for the landlord to make a 'qualifying offer' of an assured shorthold tenancy, for the purposes of s 193(7B). See paragraph 14.19 for guidance on 'qualifying offer'.

16.41. Where scope for conversion of temporary accommodation to settled accommodation is explored, the interests of the household must take priority, and the household should not be pressured to accept offers of accommodation that would bring the homelessness duty to an end.

16.42. There may also be limited potential for converting temporary accommodation leased from the private sector to a qualifying offer of an assured shorthold tenancy at the beginning or mid-point of a lease. However, this would probably require the lease to include a break clause to facilitate early termination.

16.43. While the local authority holds the lease of accommodation owned by a private sector landlord, the accommodation would not be capable of being offered to a household as a qualifying offer of an assured shorthold tenancy under s 193(7B). However, where a registered social landlord held such a lease, the accommodation may be capable of being offered to a household as a qualifying offer of an assured shorthold tenancy under s 193(7B) during the period of the lease, if all the parties agreed and the qualifying offer met the terms of s 193(7D).

CHAPTER 17: SUITABILITY OF ACCOMMODATION

17.1. This chapter provides guidance on the factors to be taken into account when determining the suitability of temporary accommodation secured under the homelessness legislation. Key factors include: the needs, requirements and circumstances of each household; space and arrangement; health and safety considerations; affordability, and location. Annex 16 sets out the statutory definition of overcrowding and Annex 17 sets out the minimum recommended standards for Bed and Breakfast accommodation.

17.2. Section 206 provides that where a housing authority discharges its functions to secure that accommodation is available for an applicant the accommodation must be suitable. This applies in respect of all powers and duties to secure accommodation under Part 7, including interim duties such as those under s 188(1) and s 200(1). The accommodation must be suitable in relation to the applicant and to all members of his or her household who normally reside with him or her, or who might reasonably be expected to reside with him or her.

17.3. Suitability of accommodation is governed by s 210. Section 210(2) provides for the Secretary of State to specify by order the circumstances in which accommodation is or is not to be regarded as suitable for someone, and matters to be taken into account or disregarded in determining whether accommodation is suitable for someone.

17.4. Space and arrangement will be key factors in determining the suitability of accommodation. However, consideration of whether accommodation is suitable will require an assessment of all aspects of the accommodation in the light of the relevant needs, requirements and circumstances of the homeless person and his or her family. The location of the accommodation will always be a relevant factor (see paragraph 17.41).

17.5. Housing authorities will need to consider carefully the suitability of accommodation for applicants whose household has particular medical and/or physical needs. The Secretary of State recommends that physical access to and around the home, space, bathroom and kitchen facilities, access to a garden and modifications to assist sensory loss as well as mobility need are all taken into account. These factors will be especially relevant where a member of the household is disabled.

17.6. Account will need to be taken of any social considerations relating to the applicant and his or her household that might affect the suitability of accommodation. Any risk of violence or racial harassment in a particular locality must also be taken into account. Where domestic violence is involved and the applicant is not able to stay in the current home, housing authorities may need to consider the need for alternative accommodation whose location can be kept a secret and which has security measures and staffing to protect the occupants. For applicants who have suffered domestic violence who are accommodated temporarily in hostels or bed and breakfast accommodation, the accommodation may need to be gender-specific as well as have security measures.

17.7. Accommodation that is suitable for a short period, for example bed and breakfast or hostel accommodation used to discharge an interim duty pending inquiries under s 188, may not necessarily be suitable for a longer period, for example to discharge a duty under s 193(2).

17.8. As the duty to provide suitable accommodation is a continuing obligation, housing authorities must keep the issue of suitability of accommodation under review. If there is a change of circumstances of substance the authority is obliged to reconsider suitability in a specific case.

Standards of accommodation

17.9. Section 210(1) requires a housing authority to have regard to the following provisions when assessing the suitability of accommodation for an applicant:

- Parts 9 and 10 of the *Housing Act 1985* (the '1985 Act') (slum clearance and overcrowding), and
- Parts 1 to 4 of the *Housing Act 2004* (the '2004 Act') (housing conditions, licensing of houses in multiple occupation, selective licensing of other residential accommodation and additional control provisions in relation to residential accommodation.)

Fitness for habitation

17.10. Part 1 of the *Housing Act 2004* (the '2004 Act') contains provisions that replace the housing fitness regime in s 604 of the 1985 Act. From 6th April 2006, the fitness standard in the 1985 Act is replaced by a new evidence-based assessment of risks to health and safety in all residential premises (including HMOs), carried out using the Housing Health and Safety Rating System (HHSRS). Part 9 of the 1985 Act is retained, with amendments, to deal with hazards for which demolition or area clearance is the most appropriate option.

Housing Health and Safety Rating System (HHSRS)

17.11. Action by local authorities is based on a three-stage consideration: (a) the hazard rating determined under HHSRS; (b) whether the authority has a duty or power to act, determined by the presence of a hazard above or below a threshold prescribed by Regulations (Category 1 and Category 2 hazards); and (c) the authority's judgment as to the most appropriate course of action to deal with the hazard.

17.12. The purpose of the HHSRS assessment is to generate objective information in order to determine and inform enforcement decisions. HHSRS allows for the assessment of twenty nine categories of housing hazard and provides a method for rating each hazard. It does *not* provide a single rating for the dwelling as a whole or, in the case of HMOs, for the building as a whole. A hazard rating is expressed through a numerical score which falls within a band, ranging from Band A to J. Scores in Bands A to C are Category 1 hazards. Scores in Bands D to J are Category 2 hazards. If a housing authority considers that a Category 1 hazard exists on any residential premises, they have a duty under the 2004 Act to take appropriate enforcement action in relation to the hazard. They also have a power to take particular kinds of enforcement action in cases where they consider that a Category 2 hazard exists.

17.13.   The HHSRS assessment is based on the risk to the *potential occupant who is most vulnerable to that hazard.* For example, stairs constitute a greater risk to the elderly, so for assessing hazards relating to stairs they are considered the most vulnerable group. The very young as well as the elderly are susceptible to low temperatures. A dwelling that is safe for those most vulnerable to a hazard is safe for all.

17.14.   Housing authorities should be familiar with the principles of the HHSRS and with the operational guidance issued under s 9 of the 2004 Act.

17.15.   The Secretary of State recommends that when determining the suitability of accommodation secured under the homelessness legislation, local authorities should, as a minimum, ensure that all accommodation is free of Category 1 hazards. In the case of an out of district placement it is the responsibility of the placing authority to ensure that accommodation is free of Category 1 hazards.

Overcrowding

17.16.   Part 10 of the 1985 Act is intended to tackle the problems of overcrowding in dwellings. Section 324 provides a definition of overcrowding which in turn relies on the room standard specified in s 325 and the space standard in s 326 (the standards are set out in Annex 17).

17.17.   A room provided within an HMO may be defined as a 'dwelling' under Part 10 of the 1985 Act and the room and space standards will therefore apply. Housing authorities should also note that 'crowding and space' is one of the hazards assessed by the HHSRS. Any breach of the room and space standards under Part 10 is likely to constitute a Category 1 hazard.

Houses in Multiple Occupation (HMOs)

17.18.   Parts 2, 3 and 4 of the 2004 Act – which came into force on 6 April 2006 – contain provisions to replace Part 11 of the 1985 Act which relates to HMOs.

17.19.   The 2004 Act introduces a new definition of an HMO. A property is an HMO if it satisfies the conditions set out in sections 254(2) to (4), has been declared an HMO under s 255 or is a converted block of flats to which s 257 applies.

17.20.   Privately owned Bed and Breakfast or hostel accommodation that is used to accommodate a household pursuant to a homelessness function, and which is the household's main residence, will fall within this definition of an HMO. Buildings managed or owned by a public body (such as the police or the NHS), local housing authority, registered social landlord or buildings which are already regulated under other legislation (such as care homes or bail hostels) will be exempt from the HMO definition. Buildings which are occupied entirely by freeholders or long leaseholders, those occupied by only two people, or by a resident landlord with up to two tenants will also be exempt. Most student accommodation (housing students undertaking a course in higher or further education) will also be exempt if it is managed and controlled by the establishment in accordance with a code of management practice.

17.21. From 6 April 2006, local authorities have been required to undertake the mandatory licensing of all privately rented HMOs (except converted blocks of flats to which s 257 applies) of three or more storeys and occupied by five or more people who form two or more households. Local authorities will also have discretionary powers to introduce additional licensing schemes covering smaller HMOs. In order to be a licence holder, a landlord will have to be a 'fit and proper' person, as defined in s 89 of the Act and demonstrate that suitable management arrangements are in place in their properties.

17.22. In addition a local authority will have to be satisfied that the HMO is suitable for the number of occupants it is licensed for and meets statutory standards relating to shared amenities and facilities, e g that it has an adequate number, type and quality of shared bathrooms, toilets and cooking facilities. These standards are set out in Schedule 3 to the *Licensing and Management of Houses in Multiple Occupation and Other Houses (Miscellaneous Provisions) (England) Regulations 2006* (SI No 2006/373). These 'amenity standards' will run alongside the consideration of health and safety issues under HHSRS. The *Housing (Management of Houses in Multiple Occupation) Regulations 1990* are to be replaced by the *Management of Houses in Multiple Occupation (England) Regulations 2006* (SI 2006/372). Neither the amenity standards nor the new management regulations apply to HMOs that are converted blocks of flats to which s 257 applies. It is intended that separate regulations will be made by July 6th to modify Part 2 of the 2004 Act (which deals with mandatory licensing) in so far as it relates to these types of HMO, and to extend, with modifications, the application of the new amenity standards and management regulations to these types of HMO. Until then they will continue to be subject to the registration schemes made under Part 11 of the 1985 Act. Transitional arrangements have been in place since April 2006 so that most HMOs that are registered in a 1985 scheme will automatically be licensed under the 2004 Act.

17.23. Local authorities also have discretion to extend licensing to privately rented properties in all, or part of, their area to address particular problems, such as low housing demand or significant incidence of anti-social behaviour. However, licensing in these selective circumstances is concerned only with property management and not the condition of the property.

Bed and breakfast accommodation

17.24. Bed and Breakfast (B&B) accommodation caters for very short-term stays only and generally will afford residents only limited privacy and may lack certain important amenities, such as cooking and laundry facilities. Consequently, where possible, housing authorities should avoid using B&B

hotels to discharge a duty to secure accommodation for homeless applicants, unless, in the very limited circumstances where it is likely to be the case, it is the most appropriate option for the applicant.

17.25. Living in B&B accommodation can be particularly detrimental to the health and development of children. Under s 210(2), the Secretary of State has made the *Homelessness (Suitability of Accommodation) (England) Order 2003* (SI 2003 No 3326) ('the Order'). The Order specifies that when accommodation is made available for occupation under certain functions in Part 7, B&B accommodation is not to be regarded as suitable for applicants with family commitments.

17.26. Housing authorities should, therefore, use B&B hotels to discharge a duty to secure accommodation for applicants with family commitments only as a last resort. Applicants with family commitments means an applicant –

(a) who is pregnant;
(b) with whom a pregnant woman resides or might reasonably be expected to reside; or
(c) with whom dependent children reside or might reasonably be expected to reside.

17.27. For the purpose of the Order, B&B accommodation means accommodation (whether or not breakfast is included):

(a) which is not separate and self-contained premises; and
(b) in which any of the following amenities is shared by more than one household:
   (i)   a toilet;
   (ii)   personal washing facilities;
   (iii) cooking facilities.

B&B accommodation does not include accommodation which is owned or managed by a local housing authority, a registered social landlord or a voluntary organisation as defined in section 180(3) of the *Housing Act 1996*.

17.28. B&B accommodation is not to be regarded as suitable for applicants with family commitments (except as specified in paragraph 17.29 below) for the purpose of discharging a duty under the following duties:

* section 188(1) (interim duty to accommodate in case of apparent priority need);
* section 190(2)(a) (duties to persons becoming homeless intentionally);
* section 193(2) (duty to persons with priority need who are not homeless intentionally);
* section 200(1) (duty to applicant whose case is considered for referral or referred); and
* section 195(2) (duties in cases of threatened homelessness) where the accommodation is other than that occupied by the applicant at the time of making his or her application.

17.29. The Order provides that if no alternative accommodation is available for the applicant the housing authority may accommodate the family in B&B

for a period, or periods, not exceeding six weeks in result of a single homelessness application. **Where B&B accommodation is secured for an applicant with family commitments, the Secretary of State considers that the authority should notify the applicant of the effect of the Order, and, in particular, that the authority will be unable to continue to secure B&B accommodation for such applicants any longer than 6 weeks, after which they must secure alternative, suitable accommodation.**

17.30. When determining whether accommodation other than B&B accommodation is available for use, housing authorities will need to take into account, among other things, the cost to the authority of securing the accommodation, the affordability of the accommodation for the applicant and the location of the accommodation. An authority is under no obligation to include in its considerations accommodation which is to be allocated in accordance with its allocation scheme, published under s 167 of the 1996 Act.

17.31. If there is a significant change in an applicant's circumstances that would bring the applicant within the scope of the Order (eg a new pregnancy), the six week period should start from the date the authority was informed of the change of circumstances not the date the applicant was originally placed in B&B accommodation.

17.32. If the conditions for referring a case are met and another housing authority accepts responsibility for an applicant under s 200(4), any time spent in B&B accommodation before this acceptance should be disregarded in calculating the six week period.

17.33. B&B accommodation is also unlikely to be suitable for 16 and 17 year olds who are in need of support. Where B&B accommodation is used for this group it ought to be as a last resort for the shortest time possible and housing authorities will need to ensure that appropriate support is provided where necessary. See Chapter 12 for guidance on the use of B&B for 16 and 17 year olds.

17.34. The Secretary of State considers that the limited circumstances in which B&B hotels may provide suitable accommodation could include those where:

    (a)   emergency accommodation is required at very short notice (for example to discharge the interim duty to accommodate under s 188); or

    (b)   there is simply no better alternative accommodation available and the use of B&B accommodation is necessary as a last resort.

17.35. The Secretary of State considers that where housing authorities are unable to avoid using B&B hotels to accommodate applicants, they should ensure that such accommodation is of a good standard (see paragaphs 17.36–17.38 below) and is used for the shortest period possible. The Secretary of State considers that where a lengthy stay seems likely, the authority should consider other accommodation more appropriate to the applicant's needs.

Standards of B&B accommodation

17.36. Where housing authorities are unable to avoid using B&B hotels to accommodate applicants they should ensure that such accommodation is of a suitable standard. Where a B&B hotel is used to accommodate an applicant and is their main residence, it falls within the definition of an HMO. Paragraphs 17.18–17.23 above explain the legislation that applies to HMOs with regard to health and safety and overcrowding. Since April 2006, local authorities have a power under the 2004 Act to issue an HMO Declaration confirming HMO status where there is uncertainty about the status of a property.

17.37. The Government recognises that living conditions in HMOs should not only be healthy and safe but should also provide acceptable, decent standards for people who may be unrelated to each other and who are sharing basic facilities. As noted at paragraph 17.22 above, the Government has set out in regulation the minimum 'amenity standards' required for a property to be granted an HMO licence. These standards will only apply to 'high-risk' HMOs covered by mandatory licensing or those HMOs that will be subject to additional licensing, and will not apply to the majority of HMOs. However, housing authorities (or groups of authorities) can adopt their own local classification, amenity specification or minimum standards for B&B and other shared accommodation provided as temporary accommodation under Part 7. In London, for example, boroughs have, since 1988, had a code of practice on the use of B&B and other shared temporary accommodation used to accommodate households under Part 7. This establishes clear benchmarks for standards across the Capital. Under the code of practice, properties are graded from A to E, with the grading dependent upon a wide range of considerations and factors relating to the facilities and services provided by an establishment. Placements are expected to be made only in those properties that meet the required standard. Setting the Standard (STS), a new automated system administered by the Greater London Authority (GLA), assists boroughs to comply with the code of practice. It collects and collates information from environmental health officers' annual inspections of properties and then makes this easily accessible to relevant borough officers across London. For further information on STS contact STS@london.gov.uk. The Secretary of State welcomes these arrangements and encourages other housing authorities to consider adopting similar systems to support the exchange of information and improve standards of temporary accommodation.

17.38. The Government considers that the size and occupancy levels of rooms, the provision and location of cooking, toilet and bathing facilities, and management standards are particularly important factors for determining whether B&B accommodation is suitable for accommodating households under Part 7. The Secretary of State therefore recommends that housing authorities have regard to the recommended minimum standards set out in Annex 17 when assessing whether B&B accommodation is suitable.

Affordability

17.39. Under s 210(2), the Secretary of State has made the *Homelessness (Suitability of Accommodation) Order 1996* (SI 1996 No 3204). The 1996 Order specifies that in determining whether it would be, or would have been, reasonable for a person to occupy accommodation that is considered suitable, a housing authority must take into account whether the accommodation is affordable by him or her, and in particular must take account of:

(a) the financial resources available to him or her *(ie all forms of income)*, including, but not limited to:

   i)   salary, fees and other remuneration *(from such sources as investments, grants, pensions, tax credits etc)*;

   ii) social security benefits *(such as housing benefit, income support, income-based Jobseekers Allowances or Council Tax benefit etc)*;

   iii) payments due under a court order for the making of periodical payments to a spouse or a former spouse, or to, or for the benefit of, a child;

   iv) payments of child support maintenance due under the *Child Support Act 1991*;

   v)   pensions;

   vi) contributions to the costs in respect of the accommodation which are or were made or which might reasonably be expected to be, or have been, made by other members of his or her household *(most members can be assumed to contribute, but the amount depends on various factors including their age and income. Other influencing factors can be drawn from the parallels of their entitlement to housing benefit and income support in relation to housing costs. Current rates should be available from housing authority benefit sections)*;

   vii) financial assistance towards the costs in respect of the accommodation, including loans, provided by a local authority, voluntary organisation or other body;

   viii) benefits derived from a policy of insurance *(such as cover against unemployment or sickness)*;

   ix) savings and other capital sums *(which may be a source of income or might be available to meet accommodation expenses. However, it should be borne in mind that, again drawing from the parallel social securities assistance, capital savings below a threshold amount are disregarded for the purpose of assessing a claim)*;

(b) the costs in respect of the accommodation, including, but not limited to:

   i)   payments of, or by way of, rent *(including rent default/property damage deposits)*;

   ii) payments in respect of a licence or permission to occupy the accommodation;

   iii) mortgage costs *(including an assessment of entitlement to Income Support Mortgage Interest (ISMI))*;

iv) payments of, or by way of, service charges *(eg maintenance or other costs required as a condition of occupation of the accommodation)*;

v) mooring charges payable for a houseboat;

vi) where the accommodation is a caravan or a mobile home, payments in respect of the site on which it stands;

vii) the amount of council tax payable in respect of the accommodation;

viii) payments by way of deposit or security in respect of the accommodation;

ix) payments required by an accommodation agency;

(c) payments which that person is required to make under a court order for the making of periodical payments to a spouse or former spouse, or to, or for the benefit of, a child and payments of child support maintenance required to be made under the *Child Support Act 1991*; and

(d) his or her other reasonable living expenses.

17.40. In considering an applicant's residual income after meeting the costs of the accommodation, the Secretary of State recommends that housing authorities regard accommodation as not being affordable if the applicant would be left with a residual income which would be less than the level of income support or income-based jobseekers allowance that is applicable in respect of the applicant, or would be applicable if he or she was entitled to claim such benefit. This amount will vary from case to case, according to the circumstances and composition of the applicant's household. A current tariff of applicable amounts in respect of such benefits should be available within the authority's housing benefit section. Housing authorities will need to consider whether the applicant can afford the housing costs without being deprived of basic essentials such as food, clothing, heating, transport and other essentials. The Secretary of State recommends that housing authorities avoid placing applicants who are in low paid employment in accommodation where they would need to resort to claiming benefit to meet the costs of that accommodation, and to consider opportunities to secure accommodation at affordable rent levels where this is likely to reduce perceived or actual disincentives to work.

Location of accommodation

17.41. The location of the accommodation will be relevant to suitability and the suitability of the location for all the members of the household will have to be considered. Where, for example, applicants are in paid employment account will need to be taken of their need to reach their normal workplace from the accommodation secured. The Secretary of State recommends that local authorities take into account the need to minimise disruption to the education of young people, particularly at critical points in time such as close to taking GCSE examinations. Housing authorities should avoid placing applicants in isolated accommodation away from public transport, shops and other facilities, and, wherever possible, secure accommodation that is as close as possible to where they were previously living, so they can retain established links with schools, doctors, social workers and other key services and support essential to the well-being of the household.

Households with pets

17.42. Housing authorities will need to be sensitive to the importance of pets to some applicants, particularly elderly people and rough sleepers who may rely on pets for companionship. Although it will not always be possible to make provision for pets, the Secretary of State recommends that housing authorities give careful consideration to this aspect when making provision for applicants who wish to retain their pet.

Asylum seekers

17.43. Since April 2000 the National Asylum Support Service (NASS) has had responsibility for providing support, including accommodation, to asylum seekers who would otherwise be destitute, whilst their claims and appeals are being considered. Some local authorities may still be providing accommodation to asylum seekers who applied for asylum prior to April 2000 and whose cases have not yet been resolved. However, the number of these cases, if any, will be small and declining.

17.44. Section 210(1A) provides that, in considering whether accommodation is suitable for an applicant who is an asylum seeker, housing authorities:

(a) shall also have regard to the fact that the accommodation is to be temporary pending the determination of the applicant's claim for asylum; and

(b) shall not have regard to any preference that the applicant, or any person who might reasonably be expected to reside with him or her, may have as to the locality of the accommodation secured.

Right to request a review of suitability

17.45. Applicants may ask for a review on request of the housing authority's decision that the accommodation offered to them is suitable under s 202(1)(f), although this right does not apply in the case of accommodation secured under s 188, the interim duty to accommodate pending inquiries, or s 200(1), the interim duty pending the decision on a referral. Under s 202(1A) an applicant may request a review as to suitability regardless of whether or not he or she accepts the accommodation. This applies equally to offers of accommodation made under s 193(5) to discharge the s 193(2) duty and to offers of an allocation of accommodation made under s 193(7) that would bring the s 193(2) duty to an end. This means that the applicant is able to ask for a review of suitability without inadvertently bringing the housing duty to an end (see Chapter 19 for guidance on reviews). Housing authorities should note that although there is no right of review of a decision on the suitability of accommodation secured under s 188 or s 200(1), such decisions could nevertheless be subject to judicial review in the High Court.

CHAPTER 18: LOCAL CONNECTION AND REFERRALS TO ANOTHER HOUSING AUTHORITY

18.1. **This chapter provides guidance on the provisions relating to an applicant's 'local connection' with an area and explains the conditions and procedures for referring an applicant to another housing authority.**

18.2. Where a housing authority ('the notifying authority') decide that s 193 applies to an applicant (ie the applicant is eligible for assistance, unintentionally homeless and has a priority need) but it considers that the conditions for referral of the case to another housing authority are met, they may notify the other housing authority ('the notified authority') of their opinion.

18.3. Notwithstanding that the conditions for a referral are apparently met, it is the responsibility of the notifying authority to determine whether s 193 applies before making a reference. **Applicants can only be referred to another authority if the notifying authority is satisfied that the applicant is unintentionally homeless, eligible for assistance and has a priority need.** Applicants cannot be referred while they are owed only the interim duty under s 188, or any duty other than the s 193 duty (eg where they are threatened with homelessness or found to be homeless intentionally).

18.4. **Referrals are discretionary only: housing authorities are not required to refer applicants to other authorities. Nor are they, generally, required to make any inquiries as to whether an applicant has a local connection with an area.** However, by virtue of s 11 of the *Asylum and Immigration (Treatment of Claimants, etc) Act 2004*, housing authorities will need to consider local connection in cases where the applicant is a former asylum seeker:

    i)   who was provided with accommodation in Scotland under s 95 of the *Immigration and Asylum Act 1999*, and

    ii)   whose accommodation was not provided in an accommodation centre by virtue of s 22 of the *Nationality, Immigration and Asylum Act 2002*.

In such cases, by virtue of s 11(2)(d) and (3) of the A*sylum and Immigration (Treatment of Claimants, etc) Act 2004*, local connection to a district in England, Wales or Scotland will be relevant to what duty is owed under s 193. (See paragraph 18.21 below.)

18.5. Housing authorities may have a policy about how they may exercise their discretion to refer a case. This must not, however, extend to deciding in advance that in all cases where there is a local connection to another district the case should be referred.

18.6. The Local Government Association (LGA) has issued guidelines for housing authorities about procedures for referring a case. These include guidance on issues such as local connection and invoking the disputes procedure when two housing authorities are unable to agree whether the conditions for referral are met. (A copy of the LGA guidelines is at Annex 18 for information).

Conditions for referral

18.7. Sections 198(2) and (2A) describe the conditions which must be satisfied before a referral may be made. A notifying authority may refer an applicant to whom s 193 applies to another housing authority if all of the following are met:

i)   neither the applicant nor any person who might reasonably be expected to live with him or her has a local connection with its district; and

ii)   at least one member of the applicant's household has a local connection with the district of the authority to be notified; and

iii)   none of them will be at risk of domestic or non-domestic violence, or threat of domestic or non-domestic violence which is likely to be carried out, in the district of the authority to be notified.

Local connection

18.8. When a housing authority makes inquiries to determine whether an applicant is eligible for assistance and owed a duty under Part 7, it may also make inquiries under s 184(2) to decide whether the applicant has a local connection with the district of another housing authority in England, Wales or Scotland.

18.9. Section 199(1) provides that a person has a local connection with the district of a housing authority if he or she has a connection with it:

i)   because he or she is, or was in the past, normally resident there, and that residence was of his or her own choice; or

ii)   because he or she is employed there; or

iii)   because of family associations there; or

iv)   because of any special circumstances.

18.10. For the purposes of (i), above, residence in temporary accommodation provided by a housing authority under s 188 can constitute normal residence of choice and therefore contribute towards a local connection. With regard to (ii) the applicant should actually work in the district: it would not be sufficient that his or her employers' head office was located there. For the purposes of (iii), where the applicant raises family associations, the Secretary of State considers that this may extend beyond parents, adult children or siblings. They may include associations with other family members such as step-parents, grandparents, grandchildren, aunts or uncles provided there are sufficiently close links in the form of frequent contact, commitment or dependency. Family associations may also extend to unmarried couples, provided that the relationship is sufficiently enduring, and to same sex couples. With regard to (iv), special circumstances might include the need to be near special medical or support services which are available only in a particular district.

18.11. The grounds in s 199(1) should be applied in order to establish whether the applicant has the required local connection. However, the fact that an applicant may satisfy one of these grounds will not necessarily mean that he or she has been able to establish a local connection. For example, an applicant may be 'normally resident' in an area even though he or she does not intend to settle there permanently or indefinitely, and the local authority could therefore determine that he or she does not have a local connection. The overriding consideration should always be whether the applicant has a real local connection with an area – the specified grounds are subsidiary to that overriding consideration.

18.12. In assessing whether an applicant's household has a local connection with either its district or a district to which the case might be referred, a housing authority should also consider whether any person who might reasonably be expected to live with the applicant has such a connection.

18.13. A housing authority may not seek to transfer responsibility to another housing authority where the applicant has a local connection with their district but they consider there is a stronger local connection elsewhere. However, in such a case, it would be open to a housing authority to seek assistance from the other housing authority in securing accommodation, under s 213.

18.14. Where a person has a local connection with the districts of more than one other housing authority, the referring housing authority will wish to take account of the applicant's preference in deciding which housing authority to notify.

Ex-service personnel

18.15. Under s 199(2) and (3), serving members of the armed forces, and other persons who normally live with them as part of their household, do not establish a local connection with a district by virtue of serving, or having served, there while in the forces.

Ex-prisoners and detainees under the Mental Health Act 1983

18.16. Similarly, detention in prison (whether convicted or not) does not establish a local connection with the district the prison is in. However, any period of residence in accommodation prior to imprisonment may give rise to a local connection under s 199(1)(a). The same is true of those detained under the *Mental Health Act 1983*.

Former asylum seekers

18.17. Sections 199(6) and (7) were inserted by section 11 of the *Asylum and Immigration (Treatment of Claimants, etc) Act 2004*. Section 199(6) provides that a person has a local connection with the district of a housing authority if he or she was (at any time) provided with accommodation there under s 95 of the *Immigration and Asylum Act 1999* ('s 95 accommodation').

18.18. Under s 199(7), however, a person does not have a local connection by virtue of s 199(6):

    (a)   if he or she has been subsequently provided with s 95 accommodation in a different area. Where a former asylum seeker has been provided with s 95 accommodation in more than one area, the local connection is with the area where such accommodation was last provided; or

(b) if they have been provided with s 95 accommodation in an accommodation centre in the district by virtue of s 22 of the *Nationality, Immigration and Asylum Act 2002*.

18.19. A local connection with a district by virtue of s 199(6) does not override a local connection by virtue of s 199(1). Thus, a former asylum seeker who has a local connection with a district because he or she was provided with accommodation there under s 95 may also have a local connection elsewhere for some other reason, for example, because of employment or family associations.

Former asylum seekers provided with s 95 accommodation in Scotland

18.20. Under Scottish legislation, a person does not establish a local connection with a district in Scotland if he or she is resident there in s 95 accommodation. Consequently, if such a person made a homelessness application to a housing authority in England, and he or she did not have a local connection with the district of that authority, the fact that he or she had been provided with s 95 accommodation in Scotland would not establish conditions for referral to the relevant local authority in Scotland.

18.21. Sections 11(2) and (3) of the *Asylum and Immigration (Treatment of Claimants, etc) Act 2004* provides that where a housing authority in England or Wales is satisfied that an applicant is eligible for assistance, unintentionally homeless and in priority need and:

i) the applicant has been provided with s 95 accommodation in Scotland at any time;

ii) the s 95 accommodation was not provided in an accommodation centre by virtue of s 22 of the *Nationality, Immigration and Asylum Act 2002*;

iii) the applicant does not have a local connection anywhere in England and Wales (within the meaning of s 199 of the 1996 Act); and

iv) the applicant does not have a local connection anywhere in Scotland (within the meaning of s 27 of the *Housing (Scotland) Act 1987*);

then the duty to the applicant under s 193 (the main homelessness duty) shall not apply. However, the authority:

(a) may secure that accommodation is available for occupation by the applicant for a period giving him or her a reasonable opportunity of securing accommodation for his or her occupation; and

(b) may provide the applicant (or secure that he or she is provided with) advice and assistance in any attempts he or she may make to secure accommodation for his or her occupation.

When dealing with an applicant in these circumstances, authorities will need to take into account the wishes of the applicant but should consider providing such advice and assistance as would enable the applicant to make an application for housing to the Scottish authority in the district where the s 95 accommodation was last provided, or to another Scottish authority of the applicant's choice. If such a person was unintentionally homeless and in priority need, it would be open to them to apply to any Scottish housing authority and a main homelessness duty would be owed to them.

No local connection anywhere

18.22. If an applicant, or any person who might reasonably be expected to live with the applicant, has no local connection with any district in Great Britain, the duty to secure accommodation will rest with the housing authority that has received the application.

Risk of violence

18.23. A housing authority cannot refer an applicant to another housing authority if that person or any person who might reasonably be expected to reside with him or her would be at risk of violence. The housing authority is under a positive duty to enquire whether the applicant would be at such a risk and, if he or she would, it should not be assumed that the applicant will take steps to deal with the threat.

18.24. Section 198(3) defines violence as violence from another person or threats of violence from another person which are likely to be carried out. This is the same definition as appears in s 177 in relation to whether it is reasonable to continue to occupy accommodation and the circumstances to be considered as to whether a person runs a risk of violence are the same.

18.25. Housing authorities should be alert to the deliberate distinction which is made in s 198(3) between actual violence and threatened violence. A high standard of proof of actual violence in the past should not be imposed. The threshold is that there must be:

(a) no risk of domestic violence (actual or threatened) in the other district; and
(b) no risk of non-domestic violence (actual or threatened) in the other district.

Nor should 'domestic violence' be interpreted restrictively (see definitions in the introduction to this Code).

Duties where case referred to another housing authority

18.26. If a housing authority decide to refer a case to another housing authority, they will need to notify the other housing authority that they believe the conditions for referral are met (s 198(1)). They must also notify the applicant that they have notified, or intend to notify, another housing authority that they consider that the conditions for referral are met (s 184(4)). At that point, the notifying authority would cease to be subject to the interim duty to accommodate under s 188(1) but will owe a duty under s 200(1) to secure that accommodation is available for the applicant until the question of whether the conditions for referral are met is decided.

18.27. Under s 200(4), if the referral is accepted by the notified authority they will be under a duty to secure accommodation for the applicant under s 193(2). Regardless of whether the notified authority had reached a different decision on a previous application, it is not open to it to re-assess the notifying authority's decision that the applicant is eligible, unintentionally homeless and in priority need. Nor may the notified authority rely on an offer of accommodation which was refused having been made in pursuance of a previous application to it.

18.28. Under s 200(3), if it is decided that the conditions for referral are not met, the notifying authority will be under a duty to secure accommodation for the applicant under s 193(2).

18.29. When the question of whether the conditions for referral to the notified authority are met has been decided, the notifying housing authority must notify the applicant of the decision and the reasons for it (s 200(2)). The notification must also advise the applicant of his or her right to request a review of the decision, and the timescale within which such a request must be made. The interim duty to accommodate under s 200(1) ends regardless of whether the applicant requests a review of the decision. However, where the applicant does request a review the notifying authority has a power under s 200(5) to secure that accommodation is available pending the review decision. (See Chapter 15 for guidance on powers to secure accommodation.)

18.30. Notifications to the applicant must be provided in writing and copies made available at the housing authority's office for collection by the applicant, or his or her representative, for a reasonable period.

Disputes

18.31. Applicants have the right to request a review of various decisions relating to local connection and referrals (see Chapter 19 for further guidance). There is not a right to request a review of a housing authority's decision not to refer a case, although a failure by a housing authority to consider whether it has the discretion to refer an applicant may be amenable to challenge by way of judicial review. The same is true of an unreasonable use of the discretion.

18.32. The question of whether the conditions for referral are met in a particular case should be decided by agreement between the housing authorities concerned. If they cannot agree, the decision should be made in accordance with such arrangements as may be directed by order of the Secretary of State (s 198(5)).

18.33. The *Homelessness (Decisions on Referrals) Order 1998* (SI 1998 No 1578) directs that the arrangements to be followed in such a dispute are the arrangements agreed between the local authority associations (ie the Local

Government Association, the Convention of Scottish Local Authorities, the Welsh Local Government Association and the Association of London Government).

18.34.   The arrangements are set out in the Schedule to the Order. Broadly speaking, they provide that in the event of two housing authorities being unable to agree whether the conditions for referral are met, they must agree on a person to be appointed to make the decision for them. If unable to agree on that, they should agree to request the LGA to appoint someone. In default of this, the notifying housing authority must make such a request of the LGA. In all cases the appointed person must be drawn from a panel established by the LGA for the purpose. The Local Government Association has issued guidelines for housing authorities on invoking the disputes procedure (a copy is at Annex 18 for information).

18.35.   The arrangements set out in the Schedule to SI 1998 No 1578 apply where a housing authority in England, Wales or Scotland seek to refer a homelessness case to another housing authority in England or Wales, and they are unable to agree whether the conditions for referral are met. A similar Order, the *Homelessness (Decisions on Referrals) (Scotland) Order 1998*, SI 1998 No 1603 applies under the Scottish homelessness legislation. The arrangements in the latter apply in cases where a housing authority in England, Wales or Scotland refer a homelessness case to a housing authority in Scotland, and they are unable to agree whether the conditions for referral are met.

18.36.   Where an English or Welsh housing authority seek to refer a case to a Scottish housing authority, a request to the local authority association to appoint an arbitrator should be made to the Convention of Scottish Local Authorities.

18.37.   A notified authority which wishes to refuse a referral because it disagrees on a finding as to the application of s 193 to the applicant must challenge the notifying authority's finding (for example as to intentionality) by way of judicial review.

Appendix 2
England: Homelessness

CHAPTER 19: REVIEW OF DECISIONS AND APPEALS TO THE COUNTY COURT

19.1.   **This chapter provides guidance on the procedures to be followed when an applicant requests the housing authority to review their decision on the homelessness case.**

Right to request a review

19.2.   Applicants have the right to request the housing authority to review their decisions on homelessness cases in some circumstances. If the request is made in accordance with s 202 the housing authority must review the relevant decision.

19.3.   When a housing authority have completed their inquiries into the applicant's homelessness case they must notify the applicant of:

  (a)   their decision and, if any decision is against the applicant's interest, the reasons for it;
  (b)   the applicant's right to request a review; and
  (c)   the time within which such a request must be made.

Housing authorities should also advise the applicant of his or her right to request a review of the suitability of any accommodation offered as a discharge of a homelessness duty, whether or not the offer is accepted. Authorities should also advise the applicant of the review procedures.

19.4.   Under s 202 an applicant has the right to request a review of:

  (a)   any decision of a housing authority about his or her eligibility for assistance (ie whether he or she is considered to be a person from abroad who is ineligible for assistance under Part 7);
  (b)   any decision of a housing authority as to what duty (if any) is owed to him or her under s 190, s 191, s 192, s 193, s 195 and s 196 (duties owed to applicants who are homeless or threatened with homelessness);
  (c)   any decision of a housing authority to notify another housing authority under s 198(1) (ie a decision to refer the applicant to another housing authority because they appear to have a local connection with that housing authority's district and not with the district where they have made the application);
  (d)   any decision under s 198(5) whether the conditions are met for the referral of the applicant's case (including a decision taken by a person appointed under the *Homelessness (Decisions on Referrals) Order 1998* (SI 1998 No 1578));
  (e)   any decision under s 200(3) or (4) (ie a decision as to whether the notified housing authority or the notifying housing authority owe the duty to secure accommodation in a case considered for referral or referred);
  (f)   any decision of a housing authority as to the suitability of accommodation offered to the applicant under any of the provisions in (b) or (e) above or the suitability of accommodation offered under

s 193(7) (allocation under Part 6). Under s 202(1A), applicants can request a review of the suitability of accommodation whether or not they have accepted the offer.

19.5. An applicant must request a review before the end of the period of 21 days beginning with the day on which he or she is notified of the housing authority's decision. The housing authority may specify, in writing, a longer period during which a review may be requested. Applicants do not have a right to request a review of a decision made on an earlier review.

19.6. In reviewing a decision, housing authorities will need to have regard to any information relevant to the period before the decision (even if only obtained afterwards) as well as any new relevant information obtained since the decision.

The review regulations

19.7. The *Allocation of Housing and Homelessness (Review Procedures) Regulations 1999* (SI 1999 No 71) set out the procedures to be followed by housing authorities in carrying out reviews under Part 7.

Who may carry out the review

19.8. A review may be carried out by the housing authority itself or by someone acting as an agent of the housing authority (see Chapter 21 on contracting out homelessness functions). Where the review is to be carried out by an officer of the housing authority, the officer must not have been involved in the original decision, and he or she must be senior to the officer (or officers) who took that decision. Seniority for these purposes means seniority in rank or grade within the housing authority's organisational structure. The seniority provision does not apply where a committee or sub-committee of elected members took the original decision.

19.9. Where the decision under review is a joint decision by the notifying housing authority and the notified housing authority as to whether the conditions of referral of the case are satisfied, s 202(4) requires that the review should be carried out jointly by the two housing authorities. Where the decision under review was taken by a person appointed pursuant to the arrangements set out in the Schedule to the *Homelessness (Decisions on Referrals) Order 1998* (SI 1998 No 1578), the review must be carried out by another person appointed under those arrangements (see paragraph 19.15).

Written representations

19.10. The applicant should be invited to make representations in writing in connection with his or her request for a review. The relevant provisions in Part 7 give a person an unfettered right to request a review of a decision, so he or she is not required to provide grounds for challenging the housing authority's decision. The purpose of the requirement is to invite the applicant to state his or her grounds for requesting a review (if he or she has not already done so) and to elicit any new information that the applicant may have in relation to his or her request for a review.

19.11. Regulation 6 requires the housing authority to notify the applicant that he or she, or someone acting on his or her behalf, may make written representations in connection with the request for a review. The notice should also advise the applicant of the procedure to be followed in connection with the review (if this information has not been provided earlier). Regulation 6 also provides that:

i) where the original decision was made jointly by the notifying and notified housing authorities under s 198(5), the notification should be made by the notifying housing authority; and

ii) where the original decision was made by a person appointed pursuant to the *Homelessness (Decisions on Referrals) Order 1998* (SI 1998 No 1578), the notification should be made by the person appointed to carry out the review.

Oral hearings

19.12. Regulation 8 provides that in cases where a review has been requested, if the housing authority, authorities or person carrying out the review consider that there is a deficiency or irregularity in the original decision, or in the manner in which it was made, but they are minded nonetheless to make a decision that is against the applicant's interests on one or more issues, they should notify the applicant:

(a) that they are so minded and the reasons why; and,

(b) that the applicant, or someone acting on his or her behalf, may, within a reasonable period, make oral representations, further written representations, or both oral and written representations.

19.13. Such deficiencies or irregularities would include:

i) failure to take into account relevant considerations and to ignore irrelevant ones;

ii) failure to base the decision on the facts;

iii) bad faith or dishonesty;

iv) mistake of law;

v) decisions that run contrary to the policy of the 1996 Act;

vi) irrationality or unreasonableness;

vii) procedural unfairness, eg where an applicant has not been given a chance to comment on matters relevant to a decision.

19.14. The reviewer must consider whether there is 'something lacking' in the decision, ie were any significant issues not addressed or addressed inadequately, which could have led to unfairness.

Period during which review must be completed

19.15.   Regulation 9 provides that the period within which the applicant must be notified of the decision on review is:

   i)   eight weeks from the day of the request for a review, where the original decision was made by the housing authority;

   ii)   ten weeks, where the decision was made jointly by two housing authorities under s 198(5) (a decision whether the conditions for referral are met);

   iii)   twelve weeks, where the decision is taken by a person appointed pursuant to the *Schedule to the Homelessness (Decisions on Referrals) Order* (SI 1998 No 1578).

The regulations provide that in all of these cases it is open to the reviewer to seek the applicant's agreement to an extension of the prescribed period; any such agreement must be given in writing.

Late representations

19.16.   The regulations require the reviewer(s) to consider any written representations received subject to compliance with the requirement to notify the applicant of the decision on review within the period of the review, ie the period prescribed in the regulations or any extended period agreed in writing by the applicant. It may in some circumstances be necessary to make further enquiries of the applicant about information he or she has provided. The reviewer(s) should be flexible about allowing such further exchanges, having regard to the time limits for reviews prescribed in the regulations. If this leads to significant delays, the applicant may be approached to agree an extension in the period for the review. Similarly, if an applicant has been invited to make oral representations and this requires additional time to arrange, the applicant should be asked to agree an appropriate extension.

Procedures for review of decisions made under the decisions on referrals order

19.17.   Where the original decision under s 198(5) was made by a person appointed pursuant to the Schedule to the *Homelessness (Decisions on Referrals) Order 1998* (SI 1998 No 1578), regulation 7 provides that a review should be carried out by another person appointed by the notifying housing authority and the notified housing authority. This requirement applies even where the original decision was carried out by a person appointed from the panel by the chairman of the Local Government Association, or his or her nominee. If, however, the two housing authorities fail to appoint a person to carry out the review within five working days of the date of the request for a review, the notifying housing authority must request the chairman of the Local Government Association to appoint a person from the panel. The chairman, in turn, must within seven working days of that request appoint a person from the panel to undertake the review. The housing authorities are required to provide the reviewer with the reasons for the original decision, and the information on which that decision is based, within five working days of his or her appointment.

19.18. Any person thus appointed must comply with the procedures set out in regulations 6, 7, 8 and 9. Specifically, he or she must invite written representations from the applicant and send copies of these to the two housing authorities, inviting them to respond. The reviewer is also required to notify in writing the two housing authorities of his or her decision on review and the reasons for it at least a week before the end of the prescribed period of twelve weeks (or of any extended period agreed by the applicant). This allows the housing authorities adequate time to notify the applicant of the decision before expiry of the period.

Notification of decision on review

19.19. Section 203 requires a housing authority to notify the applicant in writing of their decision on the review. The authority must also notify the applicant of the reasons for their decision where it:

i) confirms the original decision on any issue against the interests of the applicant;

ii) confirms a previous decision to notify another housing authority under s 198; or,

iii) confirms a previous decision that the conditions for referral in s 198 are met in the applicant's case.

Where the review is carried out jointly by two housing authorities under s 198(5), or by a person appointed pursuant to the *Homelessness (Decisions on Referrals) Order 1998* (SI 1998 No 1578), the notification may be made by either of the two housing authorities concerned.

At this stage, the authority making the notification should advise the applicant of his or her right to appeal to the County Court against a review decision under s 204 and of the period in which to appeal.

Powers to accommodate pending a review

19.20. Sections 188(3) and 200(5) give housing authorities powers to secure accommodation for certain applicants pending the decision on a review. See Chapter 15 for guidance on powers to secure accommodation.

Appeals to the county court

19.21. Section 204 provides an applicant with the right of appeal on a point of law to the County Court if:

(a) he or she is dissatisfied with the decision on a review; or

(b) he or she is not notified of the decision on the review within the time prescribed in regulations made under s 203.

In the latter case, an applicant will be entitled to appeal against the original decision.

19.22.   An appeal must be brought by an applicant within 21 days of:

(a)   the date on which he or she is notified of the decision on review; or

(b)   the date on which he or she should have been notified (ie the date marking the end of the period for the review prescribed in the regulations, or any extended period agreed in writing by the applicant).

19.23.   The court may give permission for an appeal to be brought after 21 days, but only where it is satisfied that:

(a)   (where permission is sought within the 21-day period), there is good reason for the applicant to be unable to bring the appeal in time; or

(b)   (where permission is sought after the 21-day period has expired), there was a good reason for the applicant's failure to bring the appeal in time and for any delay in applying for permission.

19.24.   On an appeal, the County Court is empowered to make an order confirming, quashing or varying the housing authority's decision as it thinks fit. It is important, therefore, that housing authorities have in place review procedures that are robust, fair, and transparent.

Power to accommodate pending an appeal to the county court

19.25.   Section 204(4) gives housing authorities the power to accommodate certain applicants during the period for making an appeal, and pending the appeal and any subsequent appeal. Applicants have a right to appeal against a housing authority's decision not to secure accommodation for them pending an appeal to the County Court (s 204A). Applicants can also appeal against a housing authority's decision to secure accommodation for them for only a limited period which ends before final determination of the appeal. See Chapter 15 for guidance on powers to secure accommodation.

Local Government Ombudsman

19.26.   Applicants may complain to a Local Government Ombudsman if they consider that they have been caused injustice as a result of maladministration by a housing authority. The Ombudsman may investigate the way a decision has been made, but may not question the merits of a decision properly reached. For example, maladministration would occur where a housing authority:

i)   took too long to do something;

ii)   did not follow their own rules or the law;

iii)   broke their promises;

iv)   treated the applicant unfairly;

v)   gave the applicant the wrong information.

19.27.   There are some matters an Ombudsman cannot investigate. These include:

i)   matters the applicant knew about more than twelve months before he or she wrote to the Ombudsman or to a councillor, unless the Ombudsman considers it reasonable to investigate despite the delay;

ii)   matters about which the applicant has already taken court action against the housing authority, for example, an appeal to the County Court under s 204;

iii)   matters about which the applicant could go to court, unless the Ombudsman considers there are good reasons why the applicant could not reasonably be expected to do so.

19.28. Where there is a right of review the Ombudsman would expect an applicant to pursue the right before making a complaint. If there is any doubt about whether the Ombudsman can look into a complaint, the applicant should seek advice from the Ombudsman's office.

CHAPTER 20: PROTECTION OF PERSONAL PROPERTY

20.1. This chapter provides guidance on the duty and powers housing authorities have to protect the personal property of an applicant.

20.2. Under s 211(1) and (2), where a housing authority has become subject to a duty to an applicant under specified provisions of Part 7 and it has reason to believe that:

i) there is a danger of loss of, or damage to, the applicant's personal property because the applicant is unable to protect it or deal with it, and

ii) no other suitable arrangements have been, or are being, made, then, whether or not the housing authority is still subject to such a duty, it must take reasonable steps to prevent the loss of, or to prevent or mitigate damage to, any personal property of the applicant.

20.3. The specified provisions are:

- s 188 (interim duty to accommodate);
- s 190, s 193 or s 195 (duties to persons found to be homeless or threatened with homelessness); or
- s 200 (duties to applicant whose case is considered for referral or referred).

20.4. In all other circumstances, housing authorities have a power to take any steps they consider reasonable to protect in the same ways an applicant's personal property (s 211(3)).

20.5. Section 212 makes provisions supplementing s 211. For the purposes of both s 211 and s 212, the personal property of an applicant includes the personal property of any person who might reasonably be expected to reside with him or her (s 211(5) and s 212(6)).

20.6. A danger of loss or damage to personal property means that there is a likelihood of harm, not just that harm is a possibility. Applicants may be unable to protect their property if, for example, they are ill or are unable to afford to have it stored themselves.

20.7. Under s 212(1), in order to protect an applicant's personal property, a housing authority can enter, at all reasonable times, the applicant's current or former home, and deal with the property in any way which seems reasonably necessary. In particular, it may store the property or arrange for it to be stored; this may be particularly appropriate where the applicant is accommodated by the housing authority in furnished accommodation for a period. In some cases, where the applicant's previous home is not to be occupied immediately, it may be possible for the property to remain there, if it can be adequately protected.

20.8. Where a housing authority does take steps to protect personal property, whether by storing it or otherwise, it must take reasonable care of it and deliver it to the owner when reasonably requested to do so.

Appendix 2
England: Homelessness

20.9.   The applicant can request the housing authority to move his or her property to a particular location. If the housing authority considers that the request is reasonable, they may discharge their responsibilities under s 211 by doing as the applicant asks. Where such a request is met, the housing authority will have no further duty or power to protect the applicant's property, and it must inform the applicant of this consequence before complying with the request (s 212(2)).

20.10.   Housing authorities may impose conditions on the assistance they provide where they consider these appropriate to the particular case. Conditions may include making a reasonable charge for storage of property and reserving the right to dispose of property in certain circumstances specified by the housing authority – eg if the applicant loses touch with them and cannot be traced after a certain period (s 211(4)).

20.11.   Where a request to move personal property to another location is either not made or not carried out, the duty or power to take any action under s 211 ends when the housing authority believes there is no longer any danger of loss or damage to the property because of the applicant's inability to deal with or protect it (s 212(3)). This may be the case, for example, where an applicant recovers from illness or finds accommodation where he or she is able to place his or her possessions, or becomes able to afford the storage costs him/herself. However, where the housing authority has discharged the duty under s 211 by placing property in storage, it has a discretionary power to continue to keep the property in storage. Where it does so, any conditions imposed by the housing authority continue to apply and may be modified as necessary.

20.12.   Where the housing authority ceases to be under a duty, or ceases to have a power, to protect an applicant's personal property under s 211, it must notify the applicant of this and give the reasons for it. The notification must be delivered to the applicant or sent to his or her last known address (s 212(5)).

CHAPTER 21: CONTRACTING OUT HOMELESSNESS FUNCTIONS

21.1. **This chapter provides guidance on contracting out homelessness functions and housing authorities' statutory obligations with regard to the discharge of those functions.**

21.2. The *Local Authorities (Contracting Out of Allocation of Housing and Homelessness Functions) Order 1996* (SI 1996 No 3215) ('the Order') enables housing authorities to contract out certain functions under Parts 6 and 7 of the 1996 Act. The Order is made under s 70 of the *Deregulation and Contracting Out Act 1994* ('the 1994 Act'). In essence, the Order allows the contracting out of executive functions while leaving the responsibility for making strategic decisions with the housing authority.

21.3. The Order provides that the majority of functions under Part 7 can be contracted out. These include:

- making arrangements to secure that advice and information about homelessness, and the prevention of homelessness, is available free of charge within the housing authority's district;
- making inquiries about and deciding a person's eligibility for assistance;
- making inquiries about and deciding whether any duty, and, if so, what duty is owed to a person under Part 7;
- making referrals to another housing authority;
- carrying out reviews of decisions;
- securing accommodation to discharge homelessness duties.

21.4. Where decision-making in homelessness cases is contracted out, authorities may wish to consider retaining the review function under s 202 of the 1996 Act. This may provide an additional degree of independence between the initial decision and the decision on review.

21.5. The 1994 Act provides that a contract made:

i) may authorise a contractor to carry out only part of the function concerned;

ii) may specify that the contractor is authorised to carry out functions only in certain cases or areas specified in the contract;

iii) may include conditions relating to the carrying out of the functions, eg prescribing standards of performance;

iv) shall be for a period not exceeding 10 years and may be revoked at any time by the Minister or the housing authority. Any subsisting contract is to be treated as having been repudiated in these circumstances;

v) shall not prevent the housing authority from exercising themselves the functions to which the contract relates.

21.6. Schedule 2 to the Order lists the homelessness functions in Part 7 that may **not** be contracted out. These are:

- s 179(2) and (3): the provision of various forms of assistance to anyone providing advice and information about homelessness and the prevention of homelessness to people in the district, on behalf of the housing authority;
- s 180: the provision of assistance to voluntary organisations concerned with homelessness; and
- s 213: co-operation with relevant housing authorities and bodies by rendering assistance in the discharge of their homelessness functions.

21.7. Local authorities also **cannot** contract out their functions under the *Homelessness Act 2002* which relate to homelessness reviews and strategies. Chapter 1 provides guidance on homelessness reviews and strategies and outlines the main functions. These include:

- s 1(1): carry out a homelessness review for the district, and formulate and publish a homelessness strategy based on the results of that review;
- s 1(4): publish a new homelessness strategy within 5 years from the day on which their last homelessness strategy was published; and
- s 3(6): keep their homelessness strategy under review and modify it from time to time.

Reviews and the formulation of strategies can, however, be informed by research commissioned from external organisations.

21.8. The 1994 Act also provides that the housing authority is responsible for any act or omission of the contractor in exercising functions under the contract, except:

i) where the contractor fails to fulfil conditions specified in the contract relating to the exercise of the function; or,
ii) where criminal proceedings are brought in respect of the contractor's act or omission.

21.9. Where there is an arrangement in force under s 101 of the *Local Government Act 1972* by virtue of which one local authority exercises the functions of another, the 1994 Act provides that the authority exercising the function is not allowed to contract it out without the principal authority's consent.

21.10. Where a housing authority has contracted out the operation of any homelessness functions the authority remains statutorily responsible and accountable for the discharge of those functions. This is the case whether a housing authority contracts with a Large Scale Voluntary Transfer registered social landlord, an Arms Length Management Organisation or any other organisation. The authority will therefore need to ensure that the contract provides for delivery of the homelessness functions in accordance with both the statutory obligations and the authority's own policies on tackling and preventing homelessness. The performance of a housing authority's homelessness functions will continue to be part of its Comprehensive Performance Assessment and will need to be covered by Best Value reviews, whether or not it discharges the homelessness functions directly.

21.11. When contracting out homelessness functions, housing authorities will need to ensure that:

- proposed arrangements are consistent with their obligations under the 2002 Act to have a strategy for preventing homelessness and ensuring that accommodation and any necessary support will be available to everyone in their district who is homeless or at risk of homelessness;
- a high quality homelessness service will be provided, in particular the assessment of applicants and the provision of advice and assistance; and
- both short-term and settled accommodation services will be available for offer to all applicants owed the main homelessness duty.

21.12. Housing authorities should also ensure they have adequate contractual, monitoring and quality assurance mechanisms in place to ensure their statutory duties are being fully discharged.

21.13. In deciding whether to contract out homelessness functions, housing authorities are encouraged to undertake an options appraisal of each function to decide whether it would best be provided in-house or by another organisation. *Housing Allocation, Homelessness and Stock Transfer – A guide to key issues (ODPM 2004)* provides guidance on the key issues that housing authorities need to consider when deciding whether to retain or contract out the delivery of their homelessness functions.

ANNEX 1
GOOD PRACTICE/GUIDANCE PUBLICATIONS

Department for Communities and Local Government

Homelessness prevention: a guide to good practice (2006)

Office of the Deputy Prime Minister

Homelessness publications

www.communities.gov.uk/index.asp?id=1162505

Sustainable Communities: settled homes, changing lives. A strategy for tackling homelessness (2005)

Tackling homelessness amongst ethnic minority households – a development guide (2005)

Resources for homeless ex-service personnel in London (2004)

Effective Co-operation in Tackling Homelessness: Nomination Agreements and Exclusions (2004)

Achieving Positive Shared Outcomes in Health and Homelessness (2004)

Appendix 2
England: Homelessness

Local Authorities' Homelessness Strategies: Evaluation and Good Practice (2004)

Reducing B&B use and tackling homelessness – What's working: A Good Practice Handbook (2003)

Housing Associations and Homelessness Briefing (2003)

Achieving Positive Outcomes on Homelessness – A Homelessness Directorate Advice Note to Local Authorities (2003)

Addressing the health needs of rough sleepers (2002)

Care leaving strategies – a good practice handbook (2002)

Drugs services for homeless people – a good practice handbook (2002)

Homelessness Strategies: A Good Practice Handbook (2002)

More than a roof: a report into tackling homelessness (2002)

Helping rough sleepers off the streets: A report to the Homelessness Directorate – Randall, G and Brown, S (2002)

Preventing tomorrow's rough sleepers – Rough Sleepers Unit (2001)

Blocking the fast track from prison to rough sleeping – Rough Sleepers Unit (2000)

Homelessness and Housing Support Directorate Policy Briefings

Briefing 15: *Summary of Homelessness Good Practice Guidance* (June 2006)

Briefing 14: *Sustainable Communities: settled homes; changing lives – one year on* (March 2006)

Briefing 13: *Survey of English local authorities about homelessness* (December 2005)

Briefing 12: *Hostels Capital Improvement Programme (HCIP)* (September 2005)

Briefing 11: *Providing More Settled Homes* (June 2005)

Briefing 10: *Delivering on the Positive Outcomes* (December 2004)

Briefing 9: *Homelessness Strategies: Moving Forward* (November 2004)

Briefing 8: *Improving the Quality of Hostels and Other Forms of Temporary Accommodation* (June 2004)

Briefing 7: *Addressing the Health Needs of Homeless People Policy* (April 2004)

Briefing 6: *Repeat Homelessness Policy* (January 2004)

Briefing 5: *Improving Employment Options for Homeless People* (September 2003)

Briefing 4: *Prevention of Homelessness Policy* (June 2003)

Briefing 3: *Bed and Breakfast Policy* (March 2003)

Briefing 2: *Domestic Violence Policy* (December 2002)

Briefing 1: *Ethnicity and Homelessness Policy* (September 2002)

Supporting People publications

www.spkweb.org.uk

Supporting People: Guide to Accommodation and Support Options for People with Mental Health Problems (2005)

Guide to Housing and Housing Related Support Options for Offenders and People at Risk of Offending (2005)

Supporting People: Guide to Accommodation and Support Options for Homeless Households (2003)

Supporting People: The Support Needs of Homeless Households (2003)

Supporting People: Guide to Accommodation and Support Options for Households Experiencing Domestic Violence (2002)

Reflecting the Needs and Concerns of Black and Minority Ethnic Communities in Supporting People (2002)

Other ODPM publications

www.communities.gov.uk

Sustainable Communities: Homes for All. A Five Year Plan (2005)

Improving the Effectiveness of Rent Arrears Management (2005)

Housing Allocation, Homelessness and Stock Transfer – A guide to key issues (2004)

Guidance on Arms Length Management of Local Authority Housing (2004)

Allocation of Accommodation – Code of Guidance for local housing authorities (2002)

Working together, Connexions and youth homelessness agencies, London, Department for Transport, Local Government and the Regions (DTLR) and Connexions (2001)

Other Government publications

Audit Commission

www.audit-commission.gov.uk

Homelessness: Responding to the New Agenda (2003)

Appendix 2
England: Homelessness

ALMO Inspections. The Delivery of Excellent Housing Management Services (2003)

Housing Services After Stock Transfer (2002)

Department for Education and Skills

www.dfes.gov.uk

Safeguarding Children, The second joint Chief Inspectors' Report on arrangements to Safeguard Children, Commission for Social Care Inspection (2005)

Every Child Matters: Change for Children (2004)

Working with Voluntary and Community Organisations to Deliver Change for Children and Young People (2004)

Department of Health

www.dh.gov.uk/Home/fs/en

Our health, our care, our say: a new direction for community (2006)

Working together to safeguard children (2005)

Government response to Hidden Harm: the Report of an inquiry by the Advisory Council on the Misuse of Drugs (2005)

Making a Difference: Reducing Bureaucracy in Children, Young People and Family Services (2005)

Independence, well-being and choice: Our vision for the future of social care for adults in England (2005)

Commissioning a patient-led NHS (2005)

Health reform in England: update and next steps (2005)

National service framework for mental health: modern standards and service models (1999)

National service framework for children, young people and maternity services (2004)

From Vision to Reality: Transforming Outcomes for Children and Families (2004)

What to do if you're worried a child is being abused (2003)

Tackling Health Inequalities: a programme for action (2003)

Guidance on accommodating children in need and their families – Local Authority Circular 13 (2003)

Children Missing from Care and Home – a guide for good practice published in tandem with the Social Exclusion Unit's report *Young Runaways* (2002)

Getting it Right: good practice in leaving care resource pack (2000)

The framework for assessment of children in need and their families (2000)

Valuing People: A New Strategy for Learning Disability for the 21st Century (2000)

Working Together to Safeguard Children: a guide to interagency working to safeguard and promote the welfare of children (1999) Department of Health, Home Office and Department for Education and Employment

Home Office

www.homeoffice.gov.uk

Advice note on accommodation for vulnerable young people (2001)

Housing Corporation

www.housingcorp.gov.uk

Tenancy management: eligibility and evictions (2004)

Local Authority Nominations. Circular 02/03/Regulation (2003)

Non-Government publications

Centrepoint

www.centrepoint.org.uk

Joint protocols between housing and social services departments: a good practice guide for the assessment and assistance of homeless young people aged 16 and 17 years, Bellerby, N. London (2000)

Chartered Institute of Housing

www.cih.org

The Housing Manual (2005)

Housing and Support Services for asylum seekers and refugees: a good practice guide, John Perry (2005)

Strategic Approaches to Homelessness; Good Practice Briefing 24 (2002)

Commission for Racial Equality

www.cre.gov.uk

CRE Code of Practice on Racial Equality in Housing (2006)

Disability Rights Commission

www.drc-gb.org/

The Duty to Promote Disability Equality: Statutory Code of Practice (2005)

National Housing Federation

www.housing.org.uk

Level threshold: towards equality in housing for disabled people: good practice guide (2005)

Flexible allocation and local letting schemes (2000)

Homeless Link

www.homeless.org.uk

Hospital admission and discharge: Guidelines for writing a protocol for the hospital admission and discharge of people who are homeless (2006)

Shelter

http://england.shelter.org.uk/home/index.cfm

Sexual exclusion: issues and best practice in lesbian, gay and bisexual housing and homelessness (2005)

Youth housing: a good practice guide (2004)

Local authorities and registered social landlords – best practice on joint working (2002)

ANNEX 2
OTHER STRATEGIES AND PROGRAMMES THAT MAY ADDRESS HOMELESSNESS

- Local and Regional Housing Strategy
- Regional Homelessness Strategy
- Regional Economic Development Plan
- Local Strategic Partnership and Community Strategy
- Local Area Agreements
- Supporting People Strategy
- Children and Young People's Plan
- Sure Start
- Connexions
- Education and Employment programmes (eg The Princes Trust, New Deal, The Careers Service)
- Progress2work, for drug misusers, and where available, Progress2work-LinkUp for alcohol misusers, offenders and homeless people

- Local health schools programme
- Quality Protects
- NHS Local Delivery Plan
- Teenage Pregnancy Strategy
- Drug Action Team Plan
- Crime and Disorder Strategy
- Regional Reducing Reoffending Strategy
- Domestic Violence Strategy
- Anti-Social Behaviour Strategy
- Anti-Poverty Strategy
- Social Inclusion Strategy
- Valuing People Plan
- Town Centre Management Strategy
- Voluntary and community sector plans
- Gypsy and Traveller Accommodation Strategy (where required by s 225 *Housing Act 2004*)

ANNEX 3
OTHER AUTHORITES, ORGANISATIONS AND PERSONS WHOSE ACTIVITIES MAY CONTRIBUTE TO PREVENTING/TACKLING HOMELESSNESS

- Registered social landlords
- Private landlords
- Lettings agencies
- Self build groups
- Housing Co-operatives
- Housing Corporation
- Supported housing providers
- Home improvement agencies
- Primary Care Trusts, health centres and GP practices
- NHS Trusts – Acute and Mental Health
- Local mental health organisations (e.g. Mind)
- Local disability groups
- Care Services Improvement Partnership Regional Development Centres
- Learning Disability Partnership Boards
- Children's Trusts
- Youth Services and youth advice groups
- Education Welfare Services
- LEA Pupil Referral Units
- Schools
- Sure Start
- Connexions
- Youth Offending Team
- Police
- Crime and Disorder Reduction Partnerships

- Drug Action Teams
- National Offender Management Service (incorporating The Prison and Probation Services)
- Victim support groups
- Anti-Social Behaviour Team
- Street Wardens
- Jobcentre Plus
- Learning and Skills Councils
- Environmental Health Team
- Housing Management Team
- Housing Benefits Team
- Armed Forces resettlement services
- National Asylum Support Service
- Refugee Community Organisations
- Law Centres
- Advice/advocacy services (eg Citizens Advice Bureaux and Shelter)
- Local voluntary sector infrastructure bodies (eg CVS)
- Faith groups
- Women's groups
- Local domestic violence fora
- Ethnic minority groups
- Age groups (eg Age Concern, Help the Aged)
- Lesbian, gay and bisexual groups
- Emergency accommodation providers (such as the Salvation Army)
- Day centres for homeless people
- Refuges
- The Samaritans
- Mediation Services
- Local Strategic Partnerships
- Local businesses/Chambers of Commerce
- Regional Housing Board
- Regional planning bodies
- People living in insecure accommodation (and their representative bodies)
- Rough sleepers (and their representative bodies)
- Residents/tenants organisations
- Self help/user groups
- Services supporting sex workers

ANNEX 4
SPECIFIC OBJECTIVES AND ACTIONS FOR LOCAL AUTHORITIES THAT MIGHT BE INCLUDED IN A HOMELESSNESS STRATEGY

This Annex provides suggestions for objectives and actions that local authorities may wish to consider including in their homelessness strategies.

Housing authority

- **Facilitate the effective co-ordination of all service providers, across all sectors in the district, whose activities contribute to preventing homelessness and/or meeting the accommodation and support needs of people who are homeless or at risk of homelessness (objective).**
  - establish a homelessness forum to co-ordinate the activities of all the key players, across all sectors, who are contributing to meeting the aims of the homelessness strategy.
  - ensure the homelessness strategy is consistent with other relevant local plans and strategies and that all relevant stakeholders are aware of how they work together.
- **Ensure that people who are at risk of homelessness are aware of, and have access to, the services they may need to help them prevent homelessness (objective).**
  - provide comprehensive advice and information about homelessness and the prevention of homelessness, free to everyone in the district.
  - provide mediation and reconciliation services (eg to tackle neighbour disputes and family relationship breakdown).
  - implement an effective tenancy relations service (and good liaison with private landlords).
- **Ensure that the supply of accommodation, including affordable accommodation, in the district reflects estimated housing need (objective).**
  - in conjunction with RSLs operating in the district, maximise the number of social lettings available for people who have experienced homelessness or at risk of homelessness, consistent with the need to meet the reasonable aspirations of other groups in housing need.
  - ensure that provision of specialised and supported accommodation for people who have experienced homelessness or at risk of homelessness (eg refuges and wet hostels) reflects estimated need.
  - maximise the provision of affordable housing through planning requirements for new private developments.
- **Work with the social services authority to ensure that the needs of clients who have both housing and social services support needs are fully assessed and taken into account (objective).**
  - develop a framework for effective joint working with the social services authority, including screening procedures to identify at an early stage where there is a need for case specific joint working.
  - put in place arrangements for carrying out joint assessments of people with support needs who are homeless or have experienced homelessness.
  - establish a protocol for the referral of clients and the sharing information between services.

Appendix 2
England: Homelessness

Social services authority

- **Work with the housing authority to ensure that the needs of clients who have both housing and social services support needs are fully assessed and taken into account (objective).**
  - develop a framework for effective joint working with the housing authority, including screening procedures, to identify at an early stage where there is a need for case specific joint working.
  - put in place arrangements for carrying out joint assessments of people with support needs who are homeless or have experienced homelessness.
  - establish a protocol for the referral of clients and the sharing information between services.
- **Ensure that, subject to relevant eligibility criteria, vulnerable people who are homeless, or at risk of homelessness, receive the support they need to help them sustain a home and prevent homelessness recurring (objective).**
  - provide a reconciliation service for young people estranged from their families.
  - exercise powers under the *Children Act 1989* to make payments to assist young people who are homeless or at risk of homelessness to sustain/find accommodation.
  - operate a supported lodgings scheme for homeless 16 and 17 year olds who need a supportive environment.
  - provide assistance to enable families with children who have become homeless intentionally (or are ineligible for housing assistance) to secure accommodation for themselves (e g financial assistance with rent deposit/guarantees).

ANNEX 5
CO-OPERATION BETWEEN REGISTERED SOCIAL LANDLORDS AND HOUSING AUTHORITIES

Housing: the strategic context

1. Housing authorities have a statutory obligation to consider the housing needs of their district (s 8 Housing Act 1985). Under the *Homelessness Act 2002* ('the 2002 Act'), they also have a statutory duty to formulate a strategy for preventing homelessness and ensuring that accommodation and support are available for people who are homeless or at risk of homelessness in their district. A homelessness strategy may include actions which the authority expects to be taken by various other organisations, with their agreement.

2. Most social housing is provided by housing authorities and by Registered Social Landlords (RSLs). Virtually all provision of new social housing is delivered through RSLs and, under the transfer programme, ownership of a significant proportion of housing authority stock is being transferred from housing authorities to RSLs, subject to tenants' agreement. This means that, increasingly, RSLs will become the main providers of social housing.

Consequently, it is essential that housing authorities work closely with RSLs, as well as all other housing providers, in order to meet the housing needs in their district and ensure that the aims and objectives of their homelessness strategy are achieved.

Statutory framework for co-operation

3. Section 170 of the *Housing Act 1996* ('the 1996 Act') provides that where an RSL has been requested by a housing authority to offer accommodation to people with priority under its allocation scheme, the RSL must co-operate to such extent as is reasonable in the circumstances. Similarly, s 213 provides that where an RSL has been requested by a housing authority to assist them in the discharge of their homelessness functions under Part 7, it must also co-operate to the same extent. Section 3 of the 2002 Act requires housing authorities to consult appropriate bodies and organisations before publishing a homelessness strategy, and this will inevitably need to include RSLs.

Housing corporation regulatory guidance

4. RSLs are regulated by the Housing Corporation which, under s 36 of the 1996 Act, and with the approval of the Secretary of State, has issued guidance to RSLs with respect to their management of housing accommodation. The Housing Corporation's Regulatory Code and guidance requires housing associations to work with local authorities to enable them to fulfil their statutory duties to, among others, homeless people and people who have priority for an allocation of housing. In particular, RSLs must ensure that:

- their lettings policies are flexible, non-discriminatory and responsive to demand while contributing to inclusivity and sustainable communities;
- they can demonstrate their co-operation with local authorities on homelessness reviews, homelessness strategies and the delivery of authorities' homelessness functions;
- when requested, and to such extent as is reasonable in the circumstances, they provide a proportion of their stock (at least 50% – see paragraph 9 below) to housing authority nominations and as temporary accommodation for people owed a homelessness duty;
- following consultation with local authorities, criteria are adopted for accepting or rejecting nominees and other applicants for housing;
- applicants are excluded from consideration for housing only if their unacceptable behaviour is serious enough to make them unsuitable to be a tenant; and
- their lettings policies are responsive to authorities' housing duties, take account of the need to give reasonable priority to transfer applicants, are responsive to national, regional and local mobility and exchange schemes, and are demonstrably fair and effectively controlled.

5. Therefore, the overriding requirement for RSLs in relation to homelessness is to demonstrate that they are co-operating with local authorities to enable them to fulfil their statutory duties.

Appendix 2
England: Homelessness

Co-operation and partnerships

6. Housing authorities need to draw on these regulatory requirements to form constructive partnerships with RSLs. It is also recommended that authorities refer to the strategic document 'A Framework for Partnership' published jointly by the Local Government Association, the National Housing Federation and the Housing Corporation and available at www.lga.gov.uk/Documents/ Briefing/framework.pdf.

7. Where RSLs participate in choice-based lettings schemes, the Corporation will expect any protocols for joint working with housing authorities to make proper provision to meet the needs of vulnerable groups, and ensure that support is available to enable tenants and applicants to exercise choice. Housing authorities should involve RSLs in the implementation of choice-based lettings schemes at an early stage.

Nomination agreements

8. Whilst legislation provides the framework for co-operation between housing authorities and RSLs, nomination agreements set out the way in which this co-operation is given effect. It is crucial that a housing authority has a comprehensive nomination agreement with each of its partner RSLs to ensure that both sides know what is expected of them. The need for a robust nomination agreement applies in all circumstances, but will be particularly important where the housing authority has transferred ownership of its housing stock and is reliant on the transfer RSL (and any other partner RSLs) to provide housing for their applicants. ODPM guidance on *Housing Allocation, Homelessness and Stock Transfer – A Guide to Key Issues (2004)* sets out the policy and operational matters which the nomination agreement between the housing authority and their transfer RSL should cover.

9. RSLs are required to offer at least 50% of vacancies in their stock (net of internal transfers) to housing authority nominations, unless some lower figure is agreed between the two bodies.[6] In some circumstances, they may agree a substantially higher figure. However, housing authorities should bear in mind that RSLs are required to retain their independence. They must honour their constitutional obligations under their diverse governing instruments, and will make the final decision on the allocation of their housing, within their regulatory framework.

10. Where requested by a housing authority, RSLs should consider the possible use of a proportion of their own stock to provide temporary accommodation for people owed a homelessness duty under Part 7 of the 1996 Act. This may be necessary in some areas, particularly those where demand for housing is very high and there is a significant number of homeless families with children who need to be placed in temporary accommodation. RSLs and housing authorities will have joint responsibility for determining the appropriate use of settled housing stock for temporary lettings, taking into

---

[6]   Housing Corporation Regulatory Circular, 02/03 Regulation, February 2003.

account that such use will reduce the volume of RSL housing stock available for nominations into long-term tenancies. Housing authorities should ensure that their partnerships take maximum advantage of the flexibility that such arrangements can provide. The Secretary of State expects that, wherever possible, social housing should be allocated on a settled basis rather than used to provide temporary accommodation in the medium to long term. Where medium to long term accommodation is required, the authority and RSL should consider whether it is possible to offer a secure or an assured tenancy under the terms of the authority's allocations scheme.

11. Housing authorities should ensure that the details of nominated households given to RSLs are accurate and comprehensive. Details should include information about the applicant's priority status under the housing authority's policy, as well as indications of vulnerability, support needs and arrangements for support.

12. The Corporation expects that RSLs' approach to exclusions and evictions will generally reflect the principles to which housing authorities work. Housing Corporation Circular 07/04 *Tenancy management: eligibility and evictions* sets out the Corporation's expectations of RSLs when assessing the eligibility of applicants and when working to prevent or respond to breaches of tenancy.

Effective collaboration

13. It is important that housing authorities foster good partnership working with RSLs, to help them prevent and tackle homelessness in the district. The housing management and care and support approaches undertaken by RSLs are key to sustaining tenancies, reducing evictions and abandonment, and preventing homelessness. To ensure effective collaboration between themselves and partner RSLs operating in their district, housing authorities should consider the following:

nominations agreements: housing authorities should ensure that they have a formal nominations agreement with all partner RSLs and that there are robust arrangements in place to monitor effective delivery of the terms of the agreement. These should be clearly set out, and should include the proportion of lettings that will be made available, any conditions that will apply, and how any disputes about suitability or eligibility will be resolved. Housing authorities should negotiate for the maximum number of lettings that will be required to enable them to discharge their housing functions and which would be reasonable for the RSL to deliver.

exclusion criteria: when negotiating nominations agreements housing authorities should aim for any exclusion criteria (that may be applied to nominees by the RSL) to be kept to a minimum. To prevent new tenancies from failing and to minimise the likelihood of exclusion, housing authorities should also ensure that adequate support packages are in place for vulnerable applicants before a nominee is expected to take up their tenancy.

eviction policies: to help prevent homelessness, housing authorities should encourage RSLs to seek to minimise any need for eviction of their tenants by employing preventative strategies and taking early positive action where breaches of tenancy agreement have occurred. Associations should act to support and sustain, rather than terminate, a tenancy.

In cases involving anti-social behaviour eviction should, where possible, be used as a last resort, although in particularly serious cases or where perpetrators refuse to co-operate it may be necessary. A number of measures have been introduced which may be used to tackle anti-social behaviour without removing the perpetrator from their home and moving the problem to somewhere else. These include Acceptable Behaviour Contracts, Anti-Social Behaviour Orders, housing injunctions and demotion. Further information on the tools and powers available to tackle anti-social behaviour can be found on the TOGETHER website, a resource for practitioners working to tackle anti-social behaviour (www.together.gov.uk).

Similarly, in cases involving rent arrears eviction should, where possible, be used as a last resort. RSLs should employ strategies to maximise their income and to prevent and manage rent arrears. Where arrears have accrued they should seek early intervention through personal contact with the tenant(s) offering support and advice. They should offer practical ways for recovering the arrears through debt management plans, referrals to debt advice agencies and ensuring that tenants are claiming all the benefits to which they are entitled. ODPM published guidance for local authorities and RSLs on *Improving the Effectiveness of Rent Arrears Management* (June 2005).

Supporting People programme: housing authorities should ensure they work closely with RSLs in implementing the Supporting People programme to ensure that housing-related support can be delivered, where appropriate, for people who would be at risk of homelessness without such support.

mobility: housing authorities should work with RSLs in considering the scope for mobility – including moves to other areas, moves to other tenures, and joint action to reduce under-occupation and over-crowding – in meeting housing need and reducing homelessness. Larger RSLs, which operate in a number of different areas, may be uniquely placed to facilitate cross-boundary moves, including voluntary moves from high demand areas to areas of lower demand.

ODPM, in conjunction with the Housing Corporation, National Housing Federation and Local Government Association, published a good practice guide for local authorities and housing associations on *Effective Co-operation in Tackling Homelessness: Nomination Agreements and Exclusions (2004)*.

ANNEX 6
HOMELESSNESS STRATEGY: SPECIFIC ACTION THAT MIGHT BE EXPECTED TO BE TAKEN BY OTHERS

Public sector

Registered social landlords

- ensure allocation policies meet the needs of people accepted as homeless including specialist provision for vulnerable groups, eg drug misusers;
- ensure allocation policies are inclusive, defensible and do not operate 'blanket bans' for particular groups;
- ensure arrears policies take into account the aims of the homelessness strategy (and facilitate early access to money and housing advice).

Primary Care Trusts

- develop health services for homeless people, (eg Personal Medical Service pilots, walk-in centres, GP service that visits hostels and day centres);
- ensure access to primary health care for all homeless people including rough sleepers and those using emergency access accommodation;
- liaise with social services and special needs housing providers to ensure access to dependency and multiple needs services where needed;
- ensure that hospital discharge policies and protocols are developed and put in place for those leaving hospital who are in housing need;
- ensure access to mental health services, including counselling and therapy where needed.

Children's Trusts

- ensure children's services and housing strategies are integrated to achieve better outcomes for children.

Youth and Community Services

- develop peer support schemes;
- raise awareness of homelessness issues with young people at risk.

National Offender Management Service

- complete a basic housing needs assessment on entry to custody in all local establishments;
- share information with other agencies on risk of harm, potential homelessness and vulnerability;
- develop local protocols regarding dealing with potentially homeless offenders and information sharing;

Appendix 2
England: Homelessness

- as part of the local Supporting People Commissioning bodies, provide specialist knowledge to help commission new services for vulnerable offender and victim groups.

Regional Offender Managers

- ensure regional strategic representation of the needs of offenders in custody and the community.

Community Safety Team/Anti-social Behaviour Team

- develop steps/interventions to reduce anti-social behaviour and therefore reduce the risk of evictions.

Youth Offending Team

- work with children and young people to prevent their offending, effectively integrate them and their families within the community and ultimately prevent evictions.

Drug Action Team

- consider the need to commission treatment for homeless people, or whether mainstream services can be extended to meet their needs;
- develop accommodation options for substance misusers including such provision as Rent Deposit Schemes;
- develop, in collaboration with Supporting People teams, specialist housing provision for substance misusers;
- ensure that the children of adults with substance misuse problems are taken into account when planning services.

Jobcentre Plus

- ensure that clients are helped to find and keep a job;
- ensure that clients claim and receive the benefits they are entitled to.

Connexions Service

- provide advice and information on housing and related benefits (or referral to other agencies where appropriate) to all 13 to 19 year olds who need it;
- ensure vulnerable young people have access to a personal adviser with the aim of preventing those young people becoming homeless.

National Asylum Support Service (NASS)

- ensure NASS accommodation providers notify local authorities of the planned withdrawal of NASS accommodation within two days of a positive asylum decision;
- encourage NASS accommodation providers to help prevent homelessness amongst new refugees (eg via tenancy conversion or delaying evictions);
- ensure that homelessness and housing pressures are taken into account by Regional Strategic Co-ordination Meetings when decisions are taken on future asylum seeker dispersal areas.

Voluntary sector

- Provision of a range of services including:
  - Rent in advance/deposit bond schemes;
  - Night stop schemes;
  - Supported lodgings schemes;
  - Homelessness awareness/preventative input to schools;
  - Advice services (housing/debt/benefits etc);
  - Counselling, mediation, reconciliation services;
  - Provision of floating support;
  - Lay advocacy services;
  - Dependency services;
  - Hospital discharge services;
  - Women's refuges;
  - Day Centres;
  - Outreach to those sleeping rough;
  - Provision of emergency accommodation (eg night shelters);
  - Hostels;
  - Foyers;
  - Resettlement services (including pre-tenancy, move-on accommodation and tenancy sustainment);
  - Mental health services;
  - Peer support, self-help and user groups;
  - Meaningful occupation/personal development work/job training/ skills for employment/work placements;
  - Support for parents of young people at risk of homelessness;
  - Support for victims of crime.

Private sector

- provision of hostels;
- making lettings available to people who are homeless or at risk of homelessness (eg through landlord accreditation schemes);
- working with tenants to address rent arrears.

Appendix 2
England: Homelessness

ANNEX 7
TACKLING COMMON CAUSES OF HOMELESSNESS

1. This annex provides guidance on how authorities might tackle some of the more common causes of homelessness at an early stage.

Parents, relatives or friends not being able to provide accommodation

2. Housing authorities are advised to consider a range of approaches aimed at avoiding the crisis of homelessness, resolving problems in the long-term or providing respite and time for a planned, and often more sustainable move. Home visits and mediation services can play an important role in delaying or preventing homelessness by helping people find solutions and resolve difficulties.

3. Family tensions can make living conditions intolerable for young people and their parents. Housing authorities are advised to work closely with children's trusts at strategic level to ensure that housing need and homelessness prevention are included in the strategic planning process through the Children and Young People's Plan. They are also advised to work closely with children's trusts at delivery level as part of local multi-agency teams that provide joined up services focusing on improving outcomes for children and young people. As part of this work, they may consider developing partnerships with key agencies in the voluntary sector who work with young people at risk of homelessness. Trained staff and peer mentors can often help young people in difficult relationships restore some links to their families or supporters, resolve family conflict or facilitate planned moves into alternative accommodation.

Relationship breakdown

4. Relationships may often be strained or break down due to periods of separation, eg long-term hospital or drug treatment or because of the behaviour of family members, eg offending or violence. Local authorities should develop systems for assessing appropriate forms of intervention and the assessment of risks to vulnerable family members to inform decisions about intervention, eg where domestic violence or child safety is involved.

5. Local authorities should consider the use of home visits, mediation and counselling services to help couples and families reconcile their differences or facilitate planned moves to alternative accommodation.

6. Housing authorities are advised to consider the provision of specialist advice targeted at young people at risk of homelessness. Local Connexions services, for example, can play a key role in reaching vulnerable young people; helping them access information and advice, providing one-to-one support or brokering appropriate specialist support from key services such as welfare, health, substance and/or alcohol misuse services, education and employment. Housing authorities might also consider working with local schools in order to provide young people with information about the implications of leaving home and the housing choices available to them.

Domestic violence

7. As well as being a direct and underlying cause of homelessness, it is becoming increasingly apparent that domestic violence is a major factor among people who experience 'repeat' homelessness. In many cases, the provision of advice and outreach services to support people who experience domestic violence before they reach crisis point, for example on ex-partner rent arrears, tenancy agreements and property rights, can help to prevent homelessness.

8. Housing authorities are encouraged to offer people who have experienced domestic violence a range of accommodation and support options. For some, escaping domestic violence will involve leaving their home, often as a last resort, and those who have experienced domestic violence may be placed in a refuge or another form of appropriate temporary accommodation where necessary. Many people who have experienced domestic violence would, however, prefer to remain in their own homes with their social and support networks around them. From 1 April 2005 local authorities have been strongly encouraged to develop, launch and promote a sanctuary type scheme in order to meet part of the revised domestic violence Best Value Performance Indicator 225. The scheme provides security measures to allow those experiencing domestic violence to remain in their own homes where they choose to do so, where safety can be assured and where the perpetrator no longer lives within the accommodation.

9. It is important that when developing policies, strategies and practice-based interventions, housing authorities work with all relevant bodies. For example, when considering the safety, security and confidentiality of people who have experienced domestic violence and their children, especially those children who may be vulnerable and/or at risk, housing authorities will need to work with Crime and Disorder Reduction Partnerships, the Local Domestic Violence Fora and with the Local Safeguarding Children Board. BVPI 225 encourages further work in this area.

End of an assured shorthold tenancy

10. The use of home visits, landlord-tenant mediation services and tenancy sustainment services may enable tenants who have been asked to leave their home to remain with their existing private landlords, through negotiation, mediation and the offer of practical solutions, such as clearing a debt, providing the tenant with advice on managing budgets or fast-tracking a Housing Benefit claim.

11. Housing authorities should also establish services to provide tenants in housing difficulties with advice and information about available housing options and, where necessary, assistance to help them access alternative accommodation. Advice might include, for example, advice about private landlords and letting agents, including any accreditation schemes, within the district; the availability of rent guarantee or rent deposit schemes; or how to apply for social housing through the local authority housing waiting list or from other social landlords).

Rent and mortgage arrears

12. Early intervention by the housing authority could help prevent difficulties with rent or mortgage arrears from triggering a homelessness crisis for tenants or home owners.

Options might include:

- personal contact with tenants or homeowners to offer support and advice;
- mediation with private landlords;
- welfare benefits advice and assistance with making claims;
- debt counselling and money advice (either in-house or through referrals to specialist advice agencies);
- advice on practical ways of recovering rent arrears through debt management plans, attachment to earnings or benefits orders or by referrals to a debt advice agencies.

13. Many approaches to the prevention and management of rent arrears among tenants can apply equally whether the landlord is a social sector or a private sector landlord. ODPM published guidance for local authorities and RSLs on *Improving the Effectiveness of Rent Arrears Management (June 2005)*.

14. In some cases rent arrears may be the result of an underlying problem such as alcohol or drug misuse, death of a partner, relationship breakdown, change in employment status, or physical or mental health problems. In such cases the housing authority may wish to contact the appropriate health and social services departments and other relevant agencies for advice, assistance and specialist support. The Secretary of State considers that housing authorities should always consult the Children's Trust before considering the eviction of a family with children. Vital work helping vulnerable children can be affected if families with children are forced to move out of the local area. Effective, ongoing liaison arrangements and collaborative working will be important in such instances.

Housing Benefit administration

15. Rent arrears can arise from delays in the calculation and payment of housing benefit. It is therefore in housing authorities' interests to develop prompt and efficient systems for the payment of benefit in order to avoid a risk of homelessness arising as a result of such delays. Where the administration of housing benefit and the provision of housing assistance are dealt with by different departments of the local authority, it will be necessary for the authority to ensure that effective liaison arrangements are in place. Efficient housing benefit payments systems can also help to increase the confidence of private sector landlords in letting accommodation to tenants who may rely on benefits to meet their rent costs.

Anti-Social Behaviour and Offending

16. Tenants may be at risk of becoming homeless as a result of their own or others' anti-social or offending behaviour. Housing authorities are urged to contact tenants in these circumstances at the earliest possible stage where they have received a complaint or where it has been brought to their attention that a tenant is causing a nuisance or annoyance. This will enable them to inform such tenants of the possible consequences of continuing with the reported behaviour and may prevent homelessness resulting in some instances. Authorities will need to be aware of the need for discretion about the source of any complaint, particularly where there is concern about threatening or aggressive behaviour.

17. In cases where a housing authority is satisfied that there is a substantive complaint of anti-social behaviour they will need to consider a range of options to address the problem with the tenant before embarking on action to terminate the tenancy. Housing authorities are advised, where possible, to use eviction as a last resort, although in particularly serious cases or where perpetrators refuse to co-operate it may be necessary.

18. Mediation services may help to resolve neighbour disputes which have led to complaints of anti-social behaviour. A number of measures have been introduced which may be used to tackle anti-social behaviour without removing the perpetrator from their home and simply moving the problem somewhere else. These include: Acceptable Behaviour Contracts, Anti-Social Behaviour Orders, housing injunctions and demotion. Further information can be found on the TOGETHER website, a resource for practitioners working to tackle anti-social behaviour (www.together.gov.uk).

19. Where local authority tenants are at risk of homelessness as a result of other tenants' anti-social behaviour, authorities should be aware of the powers they have to take action against the perpetrators and make urgent housing transfers to protect victims of violence or harassment, where requested.

20. Housing authorities will need to work closely with the National Offender Management Service (NOMS) and their partners in the voluntary and community sector to manage the housing arrangements of offenders in the community, and ensure they receive any support necessary to avoid a risk of homelessness. Where an authority may be considering the eviction of an offender, it will need to consult closely with NOMS to ensure this can be avoided wherever possible. This will also help reduce re-offending and promote community safety.

Leaving an institutional environment

21. People leaving an institutional environment can be particularly at risk of homelessness and may seek assistance from the housing authority to obtain

Appendix 2
England: Homelessness

accommodation when they move on. Authorities should have systems in place to ensure that they have advance notice of such people's needs for accommodation in such circumstances to allow them to take steps well in advance to ensure that arrangements are in place to enable a planned and timely move.

Young people leaving care

22. It is important that, wherever possible, the housing needs of care leavers are addressed before they leave care. All care leavers must have a pathway plan prepared by appropriate staff of the authority responsible for their care, setting out the support they will be provided with to enable them make a successful transition to a more independent lifestyle. Making arrangements for accommodation and ensuring that, where necessary, care leavers are provided with suitable housing support will be an essential aspect of the pathway plan. Where care leavers may require social housing, their housing and related support needs should be discussed with the appropriate agencies. Where necessary, arrangements will need to be made for joint assessment between social services and housing authorities, as part of a multi-agency assessment necessary to inform the pathway plan of individual young people.

23. Consideration of an individual care leaver's housing needs should take account of their need for support and reasonable access to places of education, employment, training and health care. As far as possible, pathway plans should include contingency plans in the event of any breakdown in the young person's accommodation arrangements. It is recommended that housing and social services authorities (and relevant departments within unitary authorities) develop joint protocols for meeting the needs of care leavers to ensure that each agency (or department) plays a full role in providing support to – and building trust with – this client group.

Custody or detention

24. Around a third of prisoners lose their housing on imprisonment, so it is important that prisoners receive effective advice and assistance about housing options, either prior to or when being remanded or sentenced to custody. Assessing an offender's housing needs at this point will help to identify those prisoners who may require assistance to bring to an end, sustain or transfer an existing tenancy, make a claim for Housing Benefit to meet rent costs while in prison, or to help a prisoner transfer or close down an existing tenancy appropriately. Local authorities are advised to assist the Prison Service in providing advice to prisoners and taking action to ensure they can sustain their accommodation while in custody.

25. It is recommended that housing advice be made available to offenders throughout the period of custody or detention to ensure that any housing needs are addressed. It is important that early planning takes place between prison staff and housing providers to identify housing options on release, to prevent homelessness and enable them to make a smooth transition from prison, or remand, to independent living.

26.   All prisoners in local prisons and Category C prisons have access to housing advice. And, from April 2005 all local prisons have been required to carry out a housing needs assessment for every new prisoner, including those serving short sentences. Local authorities are advised to assist the Prison Service in delivering these services.

27.   All Youth Offending Teams (YOTs) now have named accommodation officers. YOTs can offer both practical support to children, young people and their families and can increasingly play a key strategic role in ensuring that young offenders are effectively resettled through accessing mainstream provision and services.

28.   Joint working between the National Offender Management Service/Youth Offending Teams and their local housing authorities is essential to help prevent homelessness amongst offenders, ex-offenders and others who have experience of the criminal justice system. Options might include:

- having a single contact point within the housing authority to provide housing advice and assistance for those who have experience of the criminal justice system;
- Probation staff offering information on securing or terminating tenancies prior to custody;
- running housing advice sessions in local prisons to further enable prisoners to access advice on housing options prior to their release;
- prisons granting prisoners Release On Temporary Licence to attend housing interviews with landlords;
- developing tenancy support services for those who have experienced the criminal justice system.

Armed forces

29.   Members of Her Majesty's regular naval, military and air forces are generally provided with accommodation by the Ministry of Defence (MOD), but are required to leave this when they are discharged from the service. The principal responsibility for providing housing information and advice to Service personnel lies with the armed forces up to the point of discharge and these services are delivered through the Joint Service Housing Advice Office (telephone: 01722 436575). Some people, who have served in the armed forces for a long period, and those who are medically discharged, may be offered assistance with resettlement by Ministry of Defence (MOD) resettlement staff. The MOD issues a *Certificate of Cessation of Entitlement to Occupy Service Living Accommodation* (see examples at Annexes 14 and 15) six months before discharge.

30.   Housing authorities that have a significant number of service personnel stationed in their area will need to work closely with relevant partners, such as the Joint Service Housing Advice Office and MOD's resettlement services, to ascertain likely levels of need for housing assistance amongst people leaving the forces and plan their services accordingly. In particular, housing authorities are advised to take advantage of the six-month period of notice of discharge to ensure that service personnel receive timely and comprehensive advice on the housing options available to them when they leave the armed forces. Authorities may also wish to consider creating links with the employment and business communities to assist people leaving the armed forces to find work or meaningful occupation, enabling them further to make a successful transition to independent living in the community.

31. The Veterans Agency should be the first point of contact for all former armed forces personnel who require information about housing issues. The agency provide a free help line (telephone: 0800 169 2277) which offers former armed forces personnel advice and signposting to ex-Service benevolent organisations who may be able to offer assistance with housing matters.

Hospital

32. Some people who are admitted to hospital – even for a short time – may be in housing need or at risk of homelessness. And some people who may not be in housing need when they are admitted may become at risk of losing their home during a protracted stay in hospital, for example, if they are unable to maintain their rent or mortgage payments. This can apply, in particular, to people admitted to hospital for mental health reasons and for whom family, tenancy or mortgage breakdown is an accompanying factor to the admission to hospital.

33. Housing authorities are advised to work closely with social services and NHS Trusts in order to establish good procedures for the discharge of patients, and to ensure that former patients are not homeless or at risk of homelessness on leaving hospital. This could involve agreeing joint protocols for hospital admissions and discharge of patients to ensure that the housing and support needs of inpatients are identified as early as possible after admission, and that arrangements are put in place to meet the needs of patients in good time prior to discharge. Measures might include, for example, setting up a multi-agency discharge team as part of the homelessness strategy action plan or funding a dedicated post to support patients who may be at risk of homelessness when discharged from hospital.

34. Further guidance is provided in Department of Health publications on *Achieving timely simple discharge from hospital: A toolkit for the multi-disciplinary team (2004)* and *Discharge from hospital: pathway, process and practice (2003)*.

Accommodation provided by National Asylum Support Service (NASS)

35. Asylum seekers who receive leave to remain in the UK must move on from their NASS accommodation within 28 days of the decision on their case.

Former asylum seekers will therefore have little time to find alternative accommodation and are unlikely to have had any experience of renting or buying accommodation in the UK, or experience of related matters such as claiming benefits or arranging essential services such as gas, water and electricity. These difficulties are likely to be compounded by the fact that many former asylum seekers may face cultural barriers such as language.

36. In order to prevent these factors leading to homelessness amongst former asylum seekers, housing authorities are advised to develop protocols with NASS accommodation providers, refugee support services and NASS regional managers to ensure that, where possible, a planned and timely move to alternative accommodation or the sustainment of existing accommodation can take place. Housing benefit, rent deposits, homeless prevention loans and discretionary housing benefit payments can all help to fund temporary extensions of the NASS notice period or longer-term tenancy conversion through the establishment of assured shorthold tenancies.

37. Former asylum seekers will need effective and timely advice on the range of housing options available. It is vital that housing authorities ensure that this advice and information can be readily translated into community languages and delivered in locations accessible to asylum seekers and refugees. Authorities are also advised to consider whether there may be a need for ongoing resettlement support in order to maximise the chances of tenancy sustainment. As standard, authorities are advised to ensure that new refugees are made fully aware of the steps that they need to take to maintain a UK tenancy.

38. Authorities may wish to refer to *Housing and Support Services for asylum seekers and refugees: a good practice guide (2005)* published by the Chartered Institute of Housing.

Ethnic minority populations

39. Statistics provided by local authorities show that people from ethnic minority backgrounds are around three times more likely to be accepted as owed a main homelessness duty than their White counterparts. This pattern is found across all regions in England and the reasons are varied and complex. It is therefore critical that housing authorities and their partner agencies develop comprehensive strategies to better prevent and respond to homelessness among people from ethnic minority communities.

40. ODPM published *Tackling homelessness amongst ethnic minority households – a development guide (2005)* to assist local authorities and their partner agencies in the development of inclusive, evidence-based and cost-effective homelessness services for their local ethnic minority populations.

Drug Users

41. Drug use can both precede and occur as a result of homelessness. Between half and three quarters of single homeless people have in the past been problematic drug misusers. Many have a wide range of support needs, which reinforce each other and heighten the risk of drug use and homelessness. For those who are engaging in drug treatment, or have stabilised their use, homelessness increases their chances of relapse and continued problematic drug use. Housing authorities are advised to work closely with Drug Action Teams (multi-agency partnerships who co-ordinate the drug strategy at the local level) to ensure that housing and homelessness strategies are aligned with DAT treatment plans and Supporting People strategies help address the needs of homeless drug users as a shared client group.

ANNEX 8
HOW TO CONTACT THE HOME OFFICE IMMIGRATION AND NATIONALITY DIRECTORATE

1. The Home Office's Immigration and Nationality Directorate (IND) will exchange information with housing authorities subject to relevant data protection and disclosure policy requirements being met and properly managed, provided that the information is required to assist with the carrying out of statutory functions or prevention and detection of fraud.

2. The Evidence and Enquiries Unit (EEU) will provide a service to housing authorities to confirm the immigration status of an applicant from abroad (Non-Asylum Seekers). In order to take advantage of the service, housing authorities first need to register with the Evidence and Enquiries Unit, Immigration and Nationality Directorate, 12th Floor Lunar House, Croydon, CR9 2BY either by letter or Fax: 020 8196 3049.

3. Registration details required by the EEU's Local Authorities' Team are:

    (a) Name of enquiring housing authority on headed paper;
    (b) Job title/status of officer registering on behalf of the local housing authority; and
    (c) Names of housing authority staff and their respective job titles/status who will be making enquiries on behalf of the housing authority.

4. Once the housing authority is registered with the EEU, and this has been confirmed, then the authorised personnel can make individual enquiries by letter or fax, but replies will be returned by post.

5. The EEU will not usually indicate that someone is an asylum seeker unless the applicant has signed a disclaimer and it is attached to the enquiry or if the enquirer has specifically asked about asylum.

6. If a response indicates that the applicant has an outstanding asylum claim, or there are any queries regarding an ongoing asylum case, enquiries should be made to NASS LA Comms on 020 8760 4527. Local authorities will also need to be registered with this team before any information can be provided.

7. The Home Office (IND) can only advise whether an EEA/foreign national has a right of residence in the United Kingdom. IND does not decide whether an EEA/Foreign national qualifies for benefits or for local authority housing.

ANNEX 9
ASYLUM SEEKERS

Overview

1. Generally, asylum seekers can be expected to be *persons subject to immigration control* who have been given *temporary admission* but have not been granted leave to enter or remain in the UK.

2. Asylum seekers who are *persons subject to immigration control* and whose claim for asylum was made <u>after 2 April 2000</u> are not eligible for assistance under Part 7. However, some asylum seekers who are *persons subject to immigration control* and whose claim for asylum was made before 3 April 2000 may be eligible (see below).

3. Broadly speaking, an asylum seeker is a person claiming to have a well-founded fear of being persecuted for reasons of race, religion, nationality, membership of a particular social group, or political opinion, and who is unable or unwilling to avail him or her self of the protection of the authorities in his or her own country.

4. A person only becomes an asylum seeker when his or her claim for asylum has been recorded by the Home Secretary, and he or she remains an asylum seeker until such time as that application has been finally resolved (including the resolution of any appeal). The recording, consideration and resolution of such claims is a matter for the Home Office Immigration and Nationality Directorate (IND).

5. If there is any uncertainty about an applicant's immigration or asylum status, housing authorities should contact the Home Office Immigration and Nationality Directorate, using the procedures set out in Annex 8. Before doing so, the applicant should be advised that an inquiry will be made: if at this stage the applicant prefers to withdraw his or her application, no further action will be required.

Asylum seekers who are eligible for Part 7 assistance

6. The *Allocation of Housing and Homelessness (Eligibility) (England) Regulations 2006* (SI 2006 No 1294) ('the Eligibility Regulations') provide that asylum seekers who are *persons subject to immigration control* and who claimed asylum before 3 April 2000 are eligible for assistance under Part 7 in certain circumstances (set out below). However, by virtue of s 186(1), an asylum seeker is not eligible for Part 7 assistance if he or she has any accommodation in the UK – however temporary – available for his or her occupation. This would include a place in a hostel or bed and breakfast hotel.

7. Subject to s 186(1), such asylum seekers are eligible for assistance under Part 7, if they claimed asylum <u>before 3 April 2000</u>, and:

    i)   the claim for asylum was made at the port on initial arrival in the UK (but not on re-entry) from a country outside the United Kingdom, the Channel Islands, the Isle of Man or the Republic of Ireland; **or**

ii)   the claim for asylum was made within 3 months of a declaration by the Secretary of State that he would not normally order the return of a person to the country of which he or she is a national because of a fundamental change of circumstances in that country, and the asylum seeker was present in Great Britain on the date the declaration was made; **or**

iii)   the claim for asylum was made on or before 4 February 1996 and the applicant was entitled to housing benefit on 4 February 1996 under regulation 7A of the *Housing Benefit (General) Regulations 1987*.

8.   Generally, a person ceases to be an asylum seeker for the purposes of the Eligibility Regulations when his claim for asylum is recorded by the Secretary of State as having been decided (other than on appeal) or abandoned. However, a person does not cease to be an asylum seeker in these circumstances for the purposes of paragraph 7(iii) if he continues to be eligible for housing benefit by virtue of:

–   regulation 10(6) of the *Housing Benefit Regulations 2006* (SI 2006 No 213), or

–   regulation 10(6) of the *Housing Benefit (persons who have attained the qualifying age for state pension credit) Regulations 2006* (SI 2006 No 214).

as amended by the *Housing Benefit and Council Tax Benefit (Consequential Provisions) Regulations 2006* (SI 2006 No 217).

Former asylum seekers

9.   Where an asylum claim is successful – either initially or following an appeal – the claimant will normally be granted refugee status. If a claim is unsuccessful, leave to remain in the UK may still be granted, in accordance with published policies on Humanitarian Protection and Discretionary Leave. Former asylum seekers granted refugee status, or those granted Humanitarian Protection or Discretionary Leave which is not subject to a condition requiring him to maintain and accommodate himself without recourse to public funds will be eligible for homelessness assistance.

10.   Prior to April 2003, Exceptional Leave to Remain was granted rather than Humanitarian Protection or Discretionary Leave. Those with Exceptional Leave to Remain which is not subject to a condition requiring him to maintain and accommodate himself without recourse to public funds will also be eligible for homelessness assistance.

Information

11.   Under s 187 of the *Housing Act 1996*, the Home Office Immigration and Nationality Directorate (IND) will, on request, provide local housing authorities with the information necessary to determine whether a particular housing applicant is an asylum seeker, or a dependant of an asylum seeker, and whether he or she is eligible for assistance under Part 7. In cases where it is confirmed that a housing applicant is an asylum seeker, or the dependant of an asylum seeker, any subsequent change in circumstances which affect the applicant's housing status (eg a decision on the asylum claim) will be notified to the authority by the IND. The procedures for contacting the IND are set out in Annex 8.

ANNEX 10
THE HABITUAL RESIDENCE TEST

1.   In practice, when considering housing applications from persons who are subject to the habitual residence test, it is only necessary to investigate habitual residence if the applicant has arrived or returned to live in the UK during the two year period prior to making the application.

Definition of habitually resident

2.   The term 'habitually resident' is not defined in legislation. Local authorities should always consider the overall circumstances of a case to determine whether someone is habitually resident in the UK, the Channel Islands, the Isle of Man or the Republic of Ireland.

General principles

3.   When deciding whether a person is habitually resident in a place, consideration must be given to all the facts of each case in a common sense way. It should be remembered that:

- the test focuses on the fact and nature of residence;
- a person who is not resident somewhere cannot be habitually resident there. Residence is a more settled state than mere physical presence in a country. To be resident a person must be seen to be making a home. It need not be the only home or a permanent home but it must be a genuine home for the time being. For example, a short stay visitor or a person receiving short term medical treatment is not resident;
- the most important factors for habitual residence are the length, continuity and general nature of actual residence rather than intention;
- the practicality of a person's arrangements for residence is a necessary part of determining whether it can be described as settled and habitual;
- established habitual residents who have periods of temporary or occasional absence of long or short duration may still be habitually resident during such absences.

Action on receipt of an application

Applicant came to live in the UK during the previous two years

4. If it appears that the applicant came to live in the UK during the previous two years, authorities should make further enquiries to decide if the applicant is habitually resident, or can be treated as such.

Factors to consider

5. The applicant's stated reasons and intentions for coming to the UK will be relevant to the question of whether he or she is habitually resident. If the applicant's stated intention is to live in the UK, and not return to the country from which they came, that intention must be consistent with their actions.

6. To decide whether an applicant is habitually resident in the UK, authorities should consider the factors set out below. However, these do not provide an exhaustive check list of the questions or factors that need to be considered. Further enquiries may be needed. The circumstances of each case will dictate what information is needed, and all relevant factors should be taken into account.

Why has the applicant come to the UK?

7. If the applicant is returning to the UK after a period spent abroad, and it can be established that the applicant was previously habitually resident in the UK and is returning to resume his or her former period of habitual residence, **he or she will be immediately habitually resident**.

8. In determining whether an applicant is returning to resume a former period of habitual residence authorities should consider:

- when did the applicant leave the UK?
- how long did the applicant live in the UK before leaving?
- why did the applicant leave the UK?
- how long did the applicant intend to remain abroad?
- why did the applicant return?
- did the applicant's partner and children, if any, also leave the UK?
- did the applicant keep accommodation in the UK?
- if the applicant owned property, was it let, and was the lease timed to coincide with the applicant's return to the UK?
- what links did the applicant keep with the UK?
- have there been other brief absences? If yes, obtain details.
- why has the applicant come to the UK?

9. If the applicant has arrived in the UK within the previous two years and is not resuming a period of habitual residence, consideration should be given to his or her reasons for coming to the UK, and in particular to the factors set out below.

Applicant is joining family or friends

10. If the applicant has come to the UK to join or rejoin family or friends, authorities should consider:

- has the applicant sold or given up any property abroad?
- has the applicant bought or rented accommodation or is he or she staying with friends?
- is the move to the UK intended to be permanent?

Applicant's plans

11. Authorities should consider the applicant's plans, eg:

- if the applicant plans to remain in the UK, is the applicant's stated plan consistent with his or her actions?
- were any arrangements made for employment and accommodation (even if unsuccessful) before the applicant arrived in the UK?
- did the applicant buy a one-way ticket?
- did the applicant bring all his or her belongings?
- is there any evidence of links with the UK, eg membership of clubs?

12. The fact that a person may intend to live in the UK for the foreseeable future does not, of itself, mean that habitual residence has been established. However, the applicant's intentions along with other factors, for example the disposal of property abroad, may indicate that the applicant is habitually resident in the UK.

13. An applicant who intends to reside in the UK for only a short period, for example for a holiday or to visit friends is unlikely to be habitually resident in the UK.

Length of residence in another country

14. Authorities should consider the length and continuity of an applicant's residence in another country:

- how long did the applicant live in the previous country?
- does the applicant have any remaining ties with his or her former country of residence?
- has the applicant stayed in different countries outside the UK?

15. It is possible that a person may own a property abroad but still be habitually resident in the UK. A person who has a home or close family in another country would normally retain habitual residence in that country. A person who has previously lived in several different countries but has now moved permanently to the UK may be habitually resident here.

Appendix 2
England: Homelessness

Centre of interest

16. An applicant is likely to be habitually resident in the UK, the Channel Islands, the Isle of Man or the Republic of Ireland, despite spending time abroad, if his or her centre of interest is located in one of these places.

17. People who maintain their centre of interest in the UK, the Channel Islands, the Isle of Man or the Republic of Ireland, for example a home, a job, friends, membership of clubs, are likely to be habitually resident there. People who have retained their centre of interest in another country and have no particular ties with the UK, the Channel Islands, the Isle of Man or the Republic of Ireland, are unlikely to be habitually resident in the UK, the Channel Islands, the Isle of Man or the Republic of Ireland.

18. Authorities should take the following into account when deciding the centre of interest:

- home;
- family ties;
- club memberships;
- finance accounts.

19. If the centre of interest appears to be in the UK, the Channel Islands, the Isle of Man or the Republic of Ireland but the applicant has a home somewhere else, authorities should consider the applicant's intentions regarding the property.

20. In certain cultures, e g the Asian culture, it is quite common for a person to live in one country but have property abroad that they do not intend to sell. Where such a person has lived in the UK, the Channel Islands, the Isle of Man or the Republic of Ireland for many years, the fact that they have property elsewhere does not necessarily mean that they intend to leave, or that the applicant's centre of interest is elsewhere.

ANNEX 11
EUROPEAN GROUPINGS (EU, A8, EEA, SWITZERLAND)

The European Union (EU)

Austria, Belgium, Cyprus, the Czech Republic, Denmark, Estonia, Finland, France, Germany, Greece, Hungary, Ireland, Italy, Latvia, Lithuania, Luxembourg, Malta, the Netherlands, Poland, Portugal, Slovakia, Slovenia, Spain, Sweden, the United Kingdom and the A8 or Accession States.

The 'A8' or 'Accession States'

The 8 eastern European States that acceded to the EU in 2004 (and whose nationals may be subject to the UK Worker Registration Scheme for a transitional period): the Czech Republic, Estonia, Hungary, Latvia, Lithuania, Poland, Slovakia and Slovenia.

The European Economic Area (EEA)

All EU countries, plus: Iceland, Norway and Liechtenstein.

Switzerland

Note: Although not an EEA State, Switzerland should be treated as an EEA State for the purpose of this guidance. (See the *Immigration (European Economic Area) Regulations 2006* (SI 2006 No 1003), regulation 2(1).)

ANNEX 12
RIGHTS TO RESIDE IN THE UK DERIVED FROM EC LAW

1. EEA nationals and their family members who have a right to reside in the UK that derives from EC law are not persons subject to immigration control. This means that they will be eligible for assistance under Part 7 of the *Housing Act 1996* ('housing assistance') unless they fall within one of the categories of persons to be treated as a person from abroad who is ineligible for assistance by virtue of regulation 6 of the *Allocation of Housing and Homelessness (Eligibility) (England) Regulations 2006* ('the Eligibility Regulations').

General

Nationals of EU countries

2. Nationals of EU countries enjoy a number of different rights to reside in other Member States, including the UK. These rights derive from the EC Treaty, EC secondary legislation (in particular *Directive 2004/38/EC*), and the case law of the European Court of Justice.

3. Whether an individual EU national has a right to reside in the UK will depend on his or her circumstances, particularly his or her economic status (eg whether employed, self-employed, seeking work, a student, or economically inactive etc).

The accession states

4. A slightly different regime applies to EU nationals who are nationals of the accession states. For the purposes of this guidance, 'the accession states' are the 8 eastern European countries that acceded to the EU on 1 May 2004: Poland, Lithuania, Estonia, Latvia, Slovenia, Slovakia, Hungary and the Czech Republic.

The Immigration (European Economic Area) Regulations 2006

5. The *Immigration (European Economic Area) Regulations 2006* ('the EEA Regulations') implement into UK domestic law EC legislation conferring rights of residence on EU nationals. Broadly, the EEA Regulations provide that EU nationals have the right to reside in the UK without the requirement for leave to remain under the *Immigration Act 1971* for the first 3 months of their residence, and for longer, if they are a 'qualified person' or they have acquired a permanent right of residence.

Nationals of Iceland, Liechtenstein and Norway.

6. The EEA Regulations extend the same rights to reside in the UK to nationals of Iceland, Liechtenstein and Norway as those afforded to EU nationals (The EU countries plus Iceland, Liechtenstein and Norway together comprise the EEA.)

Nationals of Switzerland

7. The EEA Regulations also extend the same rights to reside in the UK to nationals of Switzerland.

8. For the purposes of this guidance, 'EEA nationals' means nationals of any of the EU member states (excluding the UK), and nationals of Iceland, Norway, Liechtenstein and Switzerland.

Initial 3 months of residence

9. Regulation 13 of the EEA Regulations provides that EEA nationals have the right to reside in the UK for a period of up to 3 months without any conditions or formalities other than holding a valid identity card or passport. Therefore, during their first 3 months of residence in the UK, EEA nationals will not be subject to immigration control (unless the right to reside is lost following a decision by an immigration officer in accordance with regulation 13(3) of the EEA Regulations).

10. However, regulations 6(1)(b)(i) and (c) of the Eligibility Regulations provide that a person who is not subject to immigration control is not eligible for housing assistance if:

    (i)   his or her **only** right to reside in the UK is an initial right to reside for a period not exceeding 3 months under regulation 13 of the EEA Regulations, or

    (ii)   his or her **only** right to reside in the Channel Islands, the Isle of Man or the Republic of Ireland is a right equivalent to the right mentioned in (i) above which is derived from the Treaty establishing the European Community.

On (ii), article 6 of *Directive 2004/38/EC* provides that EU citizens have the right of residence in the territory of another Member State (eg the Republic of Ireland) for a period of up to 3 months without any conditions or formalities other than holding a valid identity card or passport.

Rights of residence for 'qualified persons'

11.   Regulation 14 of the EEA Regulations provides that 'qualified persons' have the right to reside in the UK so long as they remain a qualified person. Under regulation 6 of the EEA Regulations, 'qualified person' means:

a)   a jobseeker,
b)   a worker,
c)   a self-employed person,
d)   a self-sufficient person,
e)   a student.

Jobseekers

12.   For the purposes of regulation 6(1)(a) of the EEA Regulations, 'jobseeker' means a person who enters the UK in order to seek employment and can provide evidence that he or she is seeking employment and has a genuine chance of being employed.

13.   Accession state nationals who need to register to work (see paragraph 20 below) do not have a right to reside in the UK as a jobseeker (see regulation 5(2) of the Accession Regulations, as amended). However, accession state nationals seeking work may have a right to reside by virtue of another status, eg as a self-sufficient person.

14.   Although a person who is a jobseeker for the purposes of the definition of 'qualified person' in regulation 6(1)(a) of the EEA Regulations is not subject to immigration control, regulation 6 of the Eligibility Regulations provides that a person is not eligible for housing assistance if:

(i)   his or her only right to reside in the UK is derived from his status as a jobseeker or the family member of a jobseeker, or

(ii)   his or her only right to reside in the Channel Islands, the Isle of Man or the Republic of Ireland is a right equivalent to the right mentioned in (i) above which is derived from the Treaty establishing the European Community.

Workers

15.   In order to be a worker for the purposes of the EEA Regulations, a person must be employed, that is, the person is obliged to provide services for another person in return for monetary reward and who is subject to the control of that other person as regards the way in which the work is to be done.

16.   Activity as an employed person may include part-time work, seasonal work and cross-border work (ie where a worker is established in another Member State and travels to work in the UK). However, the case law provides that the employment must be effective and genuine economic activity, and not on such a small scale as to be regarded as purely marginal and ancillary.

17. Provided the employment is effective and genuine economic activity, the fact that a person's level of remuneration may be below the level of subsistence or below the national minimum wage, or the fact that a person may be receiving financial assistance from public benefits, would not exclude that person from being a 'worker'. Housing authorities should note that surprisingly small amounts of work can be regarded as effective and genuine economic activity.

18. Applicants in the labour market should be able to confirm that they are, or have been, working in the UK by providing, for example:

- payslips,
- a contract of employment, or
- a letter of employment.

Retention of worker status

19. A person who is no longer working does not cease to be treated as a 'worker' for the purpose of regulation 6(1)(b) of the EEA Regulations, if he or she:

   (a)   is temporarily unable to work as the result of an illness or accident; or

   (b)   is recorded as involuntarily unemployed after having being employed in the UK, provided that he or she has registered as a jobseeker with the relevant employment office, and:

      (i)   was employed for one year or more before becoming unemployed, or

      (ii)   has been unemployed for no more than 6 months, or

      (iii)   can provide evidence that he or she is seeking employment in the UK and has a genuine chance of being engaged; or

   (c)   is involuntarily unemployed and has embarked on vocational training; or

   (d)   has voluntarily ceased working and embarked on vocational training that is related to his or her previous employment.

Accession state workers requiring registration who are treated as workers

20. By virtue of the *Accession (Immigration and Worker Registration) Regulations 2004* (SI 2004/1219) ('the Accession Regulations'), accession state nationals (with certain exceptions) are required to register their employment in the UK until they have accrued a period of 12 months' continuous employment. The exceptions are set out in Annex 13.

21. An accession state national requiring registration is only treated as a worker if he or she is actually working and:

   (a)   has registered his or her employment and is working in the UK for an authorised employer (see regulation 5(2) of the Accession Regulations, as amended), or

   (b)   is not registered for employment, but has been working for an employer for less than one month (regulation 7(3) of the Accession Regulations), or

(c)   has applied to register under the Worker Registration Scheme and is working for the employer with whom he or she has applied to register (regulation 7(2)(b) of the Accession Regulations).

22. To demonstrate eligibility for housing assistance, accession state workers requiring registration should be able to:

(a)   provide a valid worker registration card, and a valid worker registration certificate showing their current employer (see Annex 13 for specimens of these documents), or

(b)   (where the accession state worker has applied to register but not yet received the registration certificate) provide a copy of their application to register, or

(c)   show they have been working for their current employer for less than one month.

23. Authorities may need to contact the employer named in the registration certificate, to confirm that the applicant continues to be employed.

24. See Annex 13 for guidance on the Worker Registration Scheme.

25. A person who is a 'worker' for the purposes of the definition of a qualified person in regulation 6(1) of the EEA Regulations is not subject to immigration control, and is eligible for housing assistance whether or not he or she is habitually resident in the UK, the Channel Islands, the Isle of Man or the Republic of Ireland.

Self-employed persons

26. 'Self-employed person' means a person who establishes himself in the UK in order to pursue activity as a self-employed person in accordance with Article 43 of the Treaty establishing the European Union.

27. A self-employed person should be able to confirm that he or she is pursuing activity as a self-employed person by providing documents relating to their business such as:

a)   invoices,
b)   tax accounts, or
c)   utility bills.

28. A person who is no longer in self-employment does not cease to be treated as a self-employed person for the purposes of regulation 6(1)(c) of the EEA regulations, if he or she is temporarily unable to pursue his or her activity as a self-employed person as the result of an illness or accident.

29. Accession state nationals are not required to register in order to establish themselves in the UK as a self-employed person.

30. A person who is a self-employed person for the purposes of the definition of a qualified person in regulation 6(1) of the EEA Regulations is not subject to immigration control, and is eligible for housing assistance whether or not he or she is habitually resident in the UK, the Channel Islands, the Isle of Man or the Republic of Ireland.

Self-sufficient persons

31. Regulation 4(1)(c) of the EEA regulations defines 'self-sufficient person' as a person who has:

    (i)   sufficient resources not to become a burden on the social assistance system of the UK during his or her period of residence, and

    (ii) comprehensive sickness insurance cover in the UK.

32. By regulation 4(4) of the EEA Regulations, the resources of a person who is a self-sufficient person or a student (see below), and where applicable, any family members, are to be regarded as sufficient if they exceed the maximum level of resources which a UK national and his or her family members may possess if he or she is to become eligible for social assistance under the UK benefit system.

33. Where an EEA national applies for housing assistance as a self-sufficient person and does not appear to meet the conditions of regulation 4(1)(c), the housing authority will need to consider whether he or she may have some other right to reside in the UK.

34. Where the applicant does not meet the conditions of regulation 4(1)(c) but has previously done so during his or her residence in the UK, the case should be referred to the Home Office for clarification of their status.

35. A person who is a self-sufficient person for the purposes of the definition of a qualified person in regulation 6(1) of the EEA Regulations is not subject to immigration control, but must be habitually resident in the UK, the Channel Islands, the Isle of Man or the Republic of Ireland to be eligible for housing assistance.

Students

36. Regulation 4(1)(d) of the EEA regulations defines 'student' as a person who:

    (a)   is enrolled at a private or public establishment included on the Department of Education and Skills' Register of Education and Training Providers, or is financed from public funds, for the principal purpose of following a course of study, including vocational training, and

    (b)   has comprehensive sickness insurance cover in the UK, and

    (c)   assures the Secretary of State, by means of a declaration or such equivalent means as the person may choose, that he or she (and if applicable his or her family members) has sufficient resources not to become a burden on the social assistance system of the UK during his or her period of residence.

37.   A person who is a student for the purposes of the definition of a qualified person in regulation 6(1) of the EEA Regulations is not subject to immigration control. The eligibility of such a person for housing assistance should therefore be considered in accordance with regulation 6 of the Eligibility Regulations.

Permanent right of residence

38.   Regulation 15 of the EEA Regulations provides that the following persons shall acquire the right to reside in the UK permanently:

(a)   an EEA national who has resided in the UK in accordance with the EEA regulations for a continuous period of 5 years;

(b)   a non-EEA national who is a family member of an EEA national and who has resided in the UK with the EEA national in accordance with the EEA regulations for a continuous period of 5 years;

(c)   a worker or self-employed person who has ceased activity (see regulation 5 of the EEA Regulations for the definition of worker or self-employed person who has ceased activity);

(d)   the family member of a worker or self-employed person who has ceased activity;

(e)   a person who was the family member of a worker or self-employed person who has died, where the family member resided with the worker or self-employed person immediately before the death and the worker or self-employed person had resided continuously in the UK for at least 2 years before the death (or the death was the result of an accident at work or an occupational disease);

(f)   a person who has resided in the UK in accordance with the EEA regulations for a continuous period of 5 years, and at the end of that period was a family member who has retained the right of residence (see regulation 10 of the EEA Regulations for the definition of a family member who has retained the right of residence).

Once acquired, the right of permanent residence can be lost through absence from the UK for a period exceeding two consecutive years.

39.   A person with a right to reside permanently in the UK arising from (c), (d) or (e) above is eligible for housing assistance whether or not he or she is habitually resident in the UK, the Channel Islands, the Isle of Man or the Republic of Ireland. Persons with a permanent right to reside by virtue of (a), (b), or (f) must be habitually resident to be eligible.

Rights of residence for certain family members

The right to reside

40.   Regulation 14 of the EEA Regulations provides that the following family members are entitled to reside in the UK:

(i)   a family member of a qualified person residing in the UK;

Appendix 2
England: Homelessness

(ii)   a family member of an EEA national with a permanent right of residence under regulation 15; and

(iii)   a family member who has retained the right of residence (see regulation 10 of the EEA Regulations for the definition).

41.   A person who has a right to reside in the UK as the family member of an EEA national under the EEA Regulations will not be subject to immigration control. The eligibility of such a person for housing assistance should therefore be considered in accordance with regulation 6 of the Eligibility Regulations.

42.   When considering the eligibility of a family member, local authorities should consider whether the person has acquired a right to reside in their own right, for example a permanent right to reside under regulation 15 of the EEA Regulations (see paragraph 38 above).

Who is a 'family member'?

43.   Regulation 7 of the EEA regulations provides that the following persons are treated as the family members of another person (with certain exceptions for students – see below):

(a)   the spouse of the person;

(b)   the civil partner of the person (part of a registered partnership equivalent to marriage);

(c)   a direct descendant of the person, or of the person's spouse or civil partner, who is under the age of 21;

(d)   a direct descendant of the person, or of the person's spouse or civil partner, who is over 21 and dependent on the person, or the spouse or civil partner;

(e)   an ascendant relative of the person, or of the person's spouse or civil partner, who is dependent on the person or the spouse or civil partner.

(f)   a person who is an extended family member and is treated as a family member by virtue of regulation 7(3) of the EEA regulations (see below).

Family members of students

44.   Regulation 7(2) of the EEA regulations provides that a person who falls within (c), (d) or (e) above shall not be treated as a family member of a student residing in the UK after the period of 3 months beginning on the date the student is admitted to the UK unless:

(i)   in the case of paragraph 43 (c) and (d) above, the person is the dependent child of the student, or of the spouse or civil partner, or

(ii)   the student is also a qualified person (for the purposes of regulation 6(1) of the EEA regulations) other than as a student.

Extended family members

45.   Broadly, extended family members will be persons who:

(a)   do not fall within any of the categories (a) to (e) in paragraph 43 above, and

(b)   are either a relative of an EEA national (or of the EEA national's spouse or civil partner) or the partner of an EEA national, and

(c)   have been issued with an EEA family permit, a registration certificate or a residence card which is valid and has not been revoked.

Family members' eligibility for housing assistance

Relationship with other rights to reside

46.   This section concerns the eligibility of an applicant for housing assistance whose right to reside is derived from his or her status as the family member of an EEA national with a right to reside. In some cases, a family member will have acquired a right to reside in his or her own right. In particular, a person who arrived in the UK as the family member of an EEA national may have subsequently acquired a permanent right of residence under regulation 15 of the EEA Regulations, as outlined in paragraph 38(a)–(f) above. The eligibility for housing assistance of those with a permanent right of residence is discussed at paragraph 39.

Family members who must be habitually resident

47.   For family members with a right to reside under regulation 14 of the EEA Regulations, the following categories of persons must be habitually resident in the UK, the Channel Islands, the Isle of Man or the Republic of Ireland in order to be eligible for housing assistance:

a)   a person whose right to reside derives from their status as a family member of an EEA national who is a self-sufficient person for the purposes of regulation 6(1)(d) of the EEA regulations;

b)   a person whose right to reside derives from their status as a family member of an EEA national who is a student for the purposes of regulation 6(1)(e) of the EEA regulations;

c)   a person whose right to reside is dependent on their status as a family member of an EEA national with a permanent right to reside;

d)   a person whose right to reside is dependent on their status as a family member who has retained the right of residence.

Family members who are exempt from the habitual residence requirement

48.   A person with a right to reside under regulation 14 as a family member of an EEA national who is a worker or a self-employed person for the purposes of regulation 6(1) of the EEA regulations is exempted from the requirement to be habitually resident by regulation 6(2)(d) of the Eligibility Regulations. However, authorities should note that an extended family member (see above) is not counted as a family member for the purposes of regulation 6(2)(d) of the Eligibility Regulations (see regulation 2(3) of the Eligibility Regulations).

Family members of UK nationals exercising rights under the EC Treaty

49.   There are some limited cases in which the non-EEA family member of a UK national may have a right to reside under EU law. Under regulation 9 of the EEA Regulations, the family member of a UK national should be treated as an EEA family member where the following conditions are met:

(i)   the UK national is residing in an EEA State as a worker or self-employed person, or was so residing before returning to the UK; and

(ii)   if the family member of the UK national is his spouse or civil partner, the parties are living together in the EEA State, or had entered into a marriage or civil partnership and were living together in that State before the UK national returned to the UK.

50.   Where the family member of a UK national is to be treated as an EEA family member by virtue of regulation 9 of the EEA Regulations, that person is not subject to immigration control, and his or her eligibility for housing assistance should therefore be determined in accordance with regulation 6 of the Eligibility Regulations.

ANNEX 13
WORKER REGISTRATION SCHEME

Introduction

1.   On 1 May 2004, 10 new countries acceded to the European Union: Cyprus, Malta, Poland, Lithuania, Estonia, Latvia, Slovenia, Slovakia, Hungary and the Czech Republic.

2.   Nationals of all of these countries have the right to move freely among all member states. Nationals of 2 of the Accession countries – Malta and Cyprus – enjoyed full EU Treaty rights from 1 May 2004. These include the right to seek work and take up employment in another Member State.

3.   However, under the EU Accession Treaties that apply to the other 8 Accession states ('the A8 Member States'), existing Member States can impose limitations on the rights of nationals of the A8 Member States to access their labour markets (and the associated rights of residence), for a transitional period. (The EU Accession Treaties do not allow existing Member States to restrict access to their labour markets by nationals of Malta or Cyprus.)

4.   Under the *Accession (Immigration and Worker Registration) Regulations 2004* (SI 2004/1219) as amended ('the Accession Regulations'), nationals of the A8 Member States (with certain exceptions) are required to register with the Home Office if they work in the UK during the transitional period. While looking for work (or between jobs) their right to reside will be conditional on them being self-sufficient and not imposing an unreasonable burden on the UK social assistance system. These conditions cease to apply once they have worked in the UK continuously for 12 months.

The Accession (Immigration and Worker Registration) Regulations 2004

5. The *Accession (Immigration and Worker Registration) Regulations 2004* provide that, from 1 May 2004, nationals of the A8 Member States can take up employment in the UK provided they are authorised to work for their employer under the Worker Registration scheme.

6. The Accession Regulations also give workers from the A8 Member States the right to reside in the UK. Workers from the A8 Member States who are working lawfully have the same right to equal treatment as other EEA workers while they are working.

The Worker Registration scheme

7. The Worker Registration scheme applies only to nationals of: Poland, Lithuania, Estonia, Latvia, Slovenia, Slovakia, Hungary and the Czech Republic (the A8 Member States). It is a transitional scheme under which the UK Government allows nationals of the A8 Member States access to the UK labour market provided they comply with the registration scheme.

8. The derogation from EC law allowed by the Treaties of Accession does not apply to nationals of existing EEA states. Workers from those states, therefore, have an EC right to work and reside in the UK.

9. The Worker Registration scheme is a transitional measure. The *Accession (Immigration and Worker Registration) Regulations 2004* provide for the registration scheme to operate for up to five years from 1 May 2004 (ie until 30 April 2009). The Government reviewed the scheme within its first two years of operation and decided that the scheme will continue beyond 1 May 2006, and may continue throughout the second phase of the transitional arrangements. However, the need to retain the scheme during the whole of the second phase will be kept under review.

10. Nationals of A8 Member States who are self-employed are not required to register. (Under the Accession Treaties, there is no derogation from the right of EU citizens to establish themselves in another Member State (including the UK) as self-employed persons.) However, nationals of A8 Member States who are self-employed cannot take paid employment unless they register (unless they are exempt from registration, see below).

Registration under the scheme

11. Nationals of A8 Member States (except those who are exempt from the scheme, see below) must apply to register with the Home Office as soon as they start work in the UK, and within one month of taking up employment at the very latest. They will be issued with a **worker registration card** and a **worker registration certificate**, authorising them to work for the employer concerned.

12. If they change employers they will have to apply to for a new **registration certificate** authorising them to work for their new employer. They will then be provided with a new certificate for that employer. If they change employer or have a break in employment and resume working for the same employer, they must apply for a new registration certificate.

13. Workers from the A8 Member States have the same right to equal treatment as other EEA workers while they are working.

14. After 12 months' uninterrupted work in the UK, a worker from an A8 Member State will acquire full EU Treaty rights, and will be free from the requirement to register to work. At that stage, they will be able to apply to the Home Office for an EEA residence permit to confirm their right to equal treatment on the same basis as other EEA nationals.

15. The Worker Registration Team issues applicants with a secure **worker registration card** containing:

- Name;
- Date of Birth;
- Nationality;
- Date of issue;
- Unique identification number;
- A facial identifier (photograph);

and a **certificate** (on secure paper) which states:

- Worker's name;
- Worker's Date of Birth;
- Nationality;
- Worker's unique identification number;
- Name and address (head or main office) of employer;
- Job title;
- Start date;
- Date of issue.

16. The **registration card** is a secure document that provides applicants with a unique identification reference number. This is valid for as long as the applicant requires registration under the scheme.

17. The **registration certificate** is specific to a particular employer. The certificate expires as soon as the person stops working for that employer. If the person changes employers or has a break in employment and resumes working for the same employer, he or she must apply for a new registration certificate.

18. Specimen copies of the registration card and registration certificate are provided at the end of this annex.

12 months' uninterrupted work

19. A worker from an A8 Member State (who is subject to the registration scheme) must not be out of work more than a total of 30 days in a 12-month period, in order to establish '12 months' uninterrupted work'.

20. If a national of an A8 Member State has worked for a period of less than 12 months when the employment comes to an end, he or she will need to find another job within 30 days to be able to count the first period of work towards accruing a period of 12 months' uninterrupted employment.

21. If the worker's second (or subsequent) employment comes to an end before he or she has accrued a period of 12 months' uninterrupted employment, he or she must ensure that there has been no more than a total of 30 days between all of the periods of employment. If more than 30 days between periods of employment occur before a 12-month period of uninterrupted employment is established, a fresh period of 12 months' uninterrupted employment would need to commence from that point.

22. The Worker Registration scheme is based on continuity of employment – there is no restriction on the number of different jobs (or employers) that a worker can have during a 12-month period of continuous employment.

23. When an A8 Member State worker has worked for 12 months without interruption he or she can apply to the Home Office for an EEA residence permit. Evidence of 12 months' uninterrupted employment would include the worker registration card, registration certificates for each of the jobs they have undertaken, letters from employers and pay slips.

A8 nationals who must register

24. The Worker Registration Scheme applies to nationals of the following accession states: Poland; Lithuania; Estonia; Latvia; Slovenia; Slovakia; Hungary; and the Czech Republic.

25. Nationals of A8 Member States need to apply for a registration certificate under the Worker Registration Scheme, if they are a citizen of one of the countries listed above and they:

- start a new job on or after 1 May 2004;
- have been working in the UK before 1 May 2004 without authorisation or in breach of their immigration conditions;
- are working on a short-term or temporary basis; or
- are a student who is also working.

A8 nationals exempt from registration

26. The following are the categories of nationals of an A8 Member State who are not required to register under the Worker Registration Scheme:

- those working in a self-employed capacity;
- those who have been working with permission in the UK for 12 months or more without interruption;

- those who have been working with permission in the UK for their current employer since before 1 May 2004;
- those who have leave to enter the UK under the *Immigration Act 1971* on 30 April 2004 and their leave was not subject to any condition restricting their employment; established in the UK;
- those who are a citizen of the UK, another EEA state (other than an A8 state) or Switzerland;
- those who are a family member (spouse, civil partner, or child under the age of 21 or dependant) of a Swiss or EEA national (other than an A8 national) who is working in the UK;
- those who are a family member (spouse, civil partner or dependent child) of a Swiss or EEA national who is in the UK and is a student, self-employed, retired, or self-sufficient.

Home Office
BUILDING A SAFE, JUST
AND TOLERANT SOCIETY

[First Name] [Surname] [House Number] [Street Name] [Town] [County] [Post Code]	DATE OF ISSUE : [Issue Date] REFERENCE No : [URN] WORK CARD SERIAL No : ▮▮▮▮▮▮ TELEPHONE : 0114 207 6022

Accession State Worker Registration Scheme

Thank you for your application to register on the Accession State Worker Registration scheme. I am pleased to inform you that we have approved your application and that you are now registered.

Your worker registration card is attached below. If you have any queries about this document, then please contact Work Permits (UK) on the telephone number above.

- -

Accession State Worker Registration Scheme
Registration Card

SURNAME	:	[Surname]
FORENAME(S)	:	[First Name]
DATE OF BIRTH	:	[Date of Birth]
NATIONALITY	:	[Nationality]
REFERENCE No	:	[URN]
DATE OF ISSUE	:	[Issue Date]

Photo
Here

This worker registration card should be retained as evidence of your registration with the Accession State Worker Registration Scheme.

PLEASE DO NOT LOSE - REPLACEMENTS MAY NOT BE ISSUED

WORK CARD SERIAL No

Home Office
BUILDING A SAFE, JUST
AND TOLERANT SOCIETY

Managed Migration
Home Office
PO Box 3468
Sheffield S3 8WA

www.workingintheuk.gov.uk

[First Name] [Surname]
[House Number] [Street]
[Town]
[County]
[Post Code]

Date of Issue: [Issue Date]

ACCESSION STATE WORKER REGISTRATION SCHEME
REGISTRATION CERTIFICATE

Thank you for your application to register on the Accession State Worker Registration Scheme. I am pleased to inform you that we have approved your application.

This is your worker registration certificate. It authorises you to work for the employer specified in this certificate.

This certificate ceases to be valid if you are no longer working for the employer specified in this certificate on the date on which it is issued.

This certificate expires on the date you cease working for the specified employer.

This certificate should be retained with your worker registration card.

Name	: [First Name] [Surname]
Date of Birth	: [Date of Birth]
Nationality	: [Nationality]
Unique Reference Number	: [URN]
Job start date	: [Date Started Employment]
Employer's Name	: [Employer Name]
Employer's Address	: [Unit Number] [Street Name] [Town] [County] [Post Code]

ANNEX 14
MOD CERTIFICATE: CERTIFICATE OF CESSATION OF ENTITLEMENT FOR SINGLE PERSONNEL TO OCCUPY SERVICE LIVING ACCOMMODATION

		MOD Form 1166
	MINISTRY OF DEFENCE	*Introduced 5/97* *Revised 4/03*

CERTIFICATE OF CESSATION OF ENTITLEMENT FOR SINGLE PERSONNEL TO OCCUPY SERVICE LIVING ACCOMMODATION

I certify that   (Name)

(Rank & Number)

Of   (Unit)

Will cease to be entitled   (Address)
to occupy Service Living
Accommodation

(Date)
From

By reason of

An application for housing was made to ....Housing

Authority/Housing Association on .... (copy of letter attached)

The person has the following special circumstances ....

....

Signed	UNIT STAMP
Name	
Position	
Date	

1. This certificate provides evidence of cessation of entitlement to occupy Service Living Accommodation.

2. The certificate should be completed by the unit admin authority and sent at the earliest possible date to the Housing Authority/Association to which application for accommodation has been made, preferably as soon as it is known that entitlement to occupy Service Living Accommodation will cease.

3. Copies of this form are published in the Homelessness Code of Guidance For Local Authorities issued by DCLG, and in guidance issued by the Welsh Assembly and Scottish Executive.

Appendix 2
England: Homelessness

ANNEX 15
CERTIFICATE OF CESSATION OF ENTITLEMENT TO OCCUPY SERVICE FAMILIES ACCOMMODATION OR SUBSTITUTE SERVICE FAMILIES ACCOMMODATION (SFA/SSFA)

MINISTRY OF DEFENCE	MOD Form *Introduced 4/03*

CERTIFICATE OF CESSATION OF ENTITLEMENT TO OCCUPY SERVICE FAMILIES ACCOMMODATION OR SUBSTITUTE SERVICE FAMILIES ACCOMMODATION(SFA/SSFA)

I certify that   (Name)

(Rank & Number) #

Of   (Unit) #
(# Omit if only family involved)

Will cease to be entitled   (Address of SFA or
to occupy   SSFA)

From   (Date)
By reason of loss of entitlement to occupy Service Families Accommodation.

An application for housing was made to ....Housing Authority/
Housing Association on .... (copy of letter attached)

The following special circumstances apply ....
....

The household is as follows ....
....
....

	DHE STAMP
Signed	
Name	
Designation	
Date	

1. **This certificate provides evidence of cessation of entitlement to occupy Service Families Accommodation or Substitute Service Families Accommodation. Authorities should not insist on a Court Order for possession to establish a threat of homelessness.**

2. The certificate should be completed by the Licences Officer of the Defence Housing Executive and sent at the earliest possible date to the Housing Authority/Association to which application for accommodation has been made, preferably as soon as it is known that entitlement to occupy Service Families Accommodation will cease.

3. A period of at least six months notice should normally be allowed so that the appropriate arrangements can be made.

4. Copies of this form are published in the Homelessness Code of Guidance For Local Authorities issued by DCLG, and in guidance issued by the Welsh Assembly and Scottish Executive.

ANNEX 16
DEFINITION OF OVERCROWDING

Under s 324 of the *Housing Act 1985* a dwelling is overcrowded when the number of persons sleeping in the dwelling is such as to contravene –

(a)   the standard specified in s 325 (the room standard), or
(b)   the standard specified in s 326 (the space standard).

a)   The room standard

(1)   The room standard is contravened when the number of persons sleeping in a dwelling and the number of rooms available as sleeping accommodation is such that two persons of opposite sexes who are not living together as husband and wife must sleep in the same room.
(2)   For this purpose –
    (a)   children under the age of ten shall be left out of account, and
    (b)   a room is available as sleeping accommodation if it is of a type normally used in the locality either as a bedroom or as a living room.

b)   The space standard

(1)   The space standard is contravened when the number of persons sleeping in a dwelling is in excess of the permitted number, having regard to the number and floor area of the rooms of the dwelling available as sleeping accommodation.
(2)   For this purpose –
    (a)   no account shall be taken of a child under the age of one and a child aged one or over but under ten shall be reckoned as one-half of a unit, and
    (b)   a room is available as sleeping accommodation if it is of a type normally used in the locality either as a living room or as a bedroom.
(3)   The permitted number of persons in relation to a dwelling is whichever is the less of –
    (a)   the number specified in Table I in relation to the number of rooms in the dwelling available as sleeping accommodation, and
    (b)   the aggregate for all such rooms in the dwelling of the numbers specified in column 2 of Table II in relation to each room of the floor area specified in column 1.

No account shall be taken for the purposes of either Table of a room having a floor area of less than 50 square feet.

Appendix 2
England: Homelessness

Table I	
Number of rooms	*Number of persons*
1	2
2	3
3	5
4	7½
5 or more	2 for each room

Table II	
Floor area of room	*Number of persons*
110 sq ft or more	2
90 sq ft or more but less than 110 sq ft	1½
70 sq ft or more but less than 90 sq ft	1
50 sq ft or more but less than 70 sq ft	½

(4)   The Secretary of State may by regulations prescribe the manner in which the floor area of a room is to be ascertained for the purposes of this section; and the regulations may provide for the exclusion from computation, or the bringing into computation at a reduced figure, of floor space in a part of the room which is of less than a specified height not exceeding eight feet.

(5)   Regulations under subsection (4) shall be made by statutory instrument which shall be subject to annulment in pursuance of a resolution of either House of Parliament.

(6)   A certificate of the local housing authority stating the number and floor areas of the rooms in dwelling, and that the floor areas have been ascertained in the prescribed manner, is prima facie evidence for the purposes of legal proceedings of the facts stated in it.

ANNEX 17
RECOMMENDED MINIMUM STANDARDS FOR BED AND BREAKFAST ACCOMMODATION

The Secretary of State recommends that housing authorities apply the standards set out below as minimum standards in deciding whether Bed and

Breakfast accommodation is suitable for an applicant for the purposes of Part 7 of the *Housing Act 1996* ('the homelessness leglislation') in the very limited circumstances where an authority may use such accommodation for this purpose.

Space Standards for Sleeping Accommodation

1. *Room sizes where cooking facilities provided in a separate room/kitchen*

Floor Area of Room	Maximum No of Persons
Less than 70 sq ft (6.5 m^2)	Nil persons
Not less than 70 sq ft (6.5 m^2)	1 person
Not less than 110 sq ft (10.2 m^2)	2 persons
Not less than 160 sq ft (14.9 m^2)	3 persons
Not less than 210 sq ft (19.6 m^2)	4 persons
Not less than 260 sq ft (24.2 m^2)	5 persons

Room sizes where cooking facilities provided within the room

Floor Area of Room	Maximum No of Persons
Less than 110 sq ft (10.2 m^2)	Nil persons
Not less than 110 sq ft (10.2 m^2)	1 person
Not less than 150 sq ft (13.9 m^2)	2 persons
Not less than 200 sq ft (18.6 m^2)	3 persons
Not less than 250 sq ft (23.2 m^2)	4 persons
Not less than 300 sq ft (27.9 m^2)	5 persons

2. In no case should a room be occupied by more than 5 persons. The standard is to be applied irrespective of the age of the occupants. The sharing of rooms in bed and breakfast accommodation is not desirable, but it is accepted that where accommodation is not self-contained families may find it preferable to share.

3. No persons of the opposite sex who are aged 12 and over should have to share a room unless they are living together as partners and both are above the age of consent or are lawfully married.

4. All rooms must have a minimum floor to ceiling height of at least 7 feet (2.14 metres) over not less than 75% of the room area. Any floor area where the ceiling height is less than 5 feet (1.53 metres) should be disregarded.

5. Separate kitchens, bathrooms, toilets, shower rooms, communal rooms and en-suite rooms are deemed unsuitable for sleeping accommodation.

Appendix 2
England: Homelessness

Installation for Heating

6. The premises should have adequate provision for heating. All habitable rooms and baths or shower rooms should be provided with a fixed space-heating appliance. The appliance must be capable of efficiently maintaining the room at a minimum temperature of 18°C when the outside temperature is –1°C. 'Fixed space heating appliance' means fixed gas appliance, fixed electrical appliance or an adequate system of central heating, operable at all times.

Facilities for the Storage, Preparation and Cooking of Food and Disposal of Waste Water

7. Wherever practicable, each household should have exclusive use of a full set of kitchen facilities including:

- cooking facilities – a gas or electric cooker with a four-burner hob, oven and grill. In single person lettings, a cooker with a minimum of two burners, oven and grill is permissible. Where the establishment caters for fewer than 6 persons, a small guest house for example, a microwave may be substituted for a gas or electric cooker for periods of stay not exceeding 6 weeks for any homeless household;
- sink and integral drainer – with a constant supply of hot and cold water and properly connected to the drainage system;
- storage cupboard, minimum capacity 0.4 m³ (400 litres/15 ft³). This provision is in addition to any base unit cupboards provided below the sink/drainer;
- refrigerator – minimum capacity 0.14 m³ (140 litres/5 ft³);
- electrical power sockets – minimum of two double 13 amp sockets situated at worktop height. These are in addition to electrical power sockets provided elsewhere in the letting;
- worktop – minimum surface area 1000 mm x 600 mm.

8. There may be circumstances where the housing authority is satisfied that the provision of kitchen facilities for exclusive use is not practicable or appropriate. These circumstances could, for example, include where a property is very small, no more than two or three letting rooms, or where the overall standard of the property is considered reasonable in all other respects and the costs of provision of exclusive use kitchens would be prohibitive or detrimentally affect the remaining amenity space. In circumstances such as these, the following standards for communal kitchens may be applied.

9. Kitchen facilities may be provided in the ratio of no less than one set for every 10 persons, irrespective of age. Such kitchen facilities should comprise a minimum of shared:

- gas or electric cooker with four burners, oven and grill. Where the establishment caters for fewer than 6 persons, a small guest house for example, a microwave may be substituted for a gas or electric cooker for periods of stay not exceeding 6 weeks for any homeless household;

- sink and integral drainer – with a constant supply of hot and cold water and properly connected to the drainage system;
- storage cupboard, minimum capacity 0.4 m³ (400 litres/15 ft³). This provision is in addition to any base unit cupboards provided below the sink/drainer;
- electrical power sockets – minimum of two double 13 amp sockets situated at worktop height. These are in addition to electrical power sockets provided elsewhere in the letting;
- worktop – minimum surface area 1000 mm x 600 mm;
- lockable storage cupboards, minimum capacity 0.14 m³ (140 litres/5 ft³) for each bedroom whose occupants use the kitchen. In calculating the required provision of storage cupboards, base unit cupboards below sinks/drainers should be discounted.

10. In addition, the following facilities should be provided within each bedroom, or within the total accommodation occupied exclusively by each household:

- worktop – minimum surface area 1000 mm x 600 mm;
- refrigerator – minimum capacity 0.14 m³ (140 litres/5 ft³);
- storage cupboard – minimum capacity 0.4 m³ (400 litres/15 ft³).

11. The kitchen used by management to provide breakfast may be included when calculating the one in ten ratio, unless it is not available, does not meet the conditions above or is deemed unsuitable for use by residents because:

- of the size of the kitchen and the equipment provided in it. In a commercial kitchen some equipment may be dangerous or unsatisfactory for use by residents; or
- the unsatisfactory location of the kitchen in relation to the accommodation it is supposed to serve.

12. In schemes providing a mix of kitchens for shared and exclusive use, one set of kitchen facilities should be provided for every 10 persons sharing. The number of persons who have kitchen facilities provided for their exclusive use should not be included in the calculations. Again, the kitchen used by management to provide breakfast may be included in the one in ten calculation subject to the above conditions.

13. Cooking facilities which are provided should be reasonably located in relation to the room(s) occupied by the person(s) for whom they are provided and in any event not more than one floor distant from these rooms. Please note the exception for smaller establishments described below.

14. In smaller establishments of not more than three storeys and not more than 30 bed spaces, communal cooking facilities may be provided in one area of the premises more than one floor distant from some bedrooms. In such cases, these kitchens must be provided in association with a suitable dining room or dining rooms of adequate size calculated on the basis of 1 m² per bed space. This should include one area of at least 15 m². Only effective usable space will be considered when calculating the areas for the purpose of this requirement. Dining room facilities should be provided with adequate seating provision.

Appendix 2
England: Homelessness

15. Kitchen facilities should be made available for use 24 hours per day, subject to any representation from the owner/manager, which must be agreed by the receiving and placing authorities.

Toilet and personal washing facilities

16. One internal water closet should be provided for every five persons irrespective of age. The water closet must be within a reasonable distance from its users and not more than one floor distant and, where practicable, a water closet should not be situated within a bathroom. At least 50% of the water closets that are required to be provided should be situated in separate accommodation. The number of persons occupying a bedroom where this facility is provided for their exclusive use should not be included in the calculations.

17. A suitable wash hand basin (minimum dimensions 500 mm x 400 mm) with constant hot and cold water supplies, should be provided in every bedroom, except where an en suite bathroom is available, when the wash hand basin may be provided in that bathroom.

18. Each separate water closet compartment and bathroom should be provided with a suitable wash hand basin (minimum dimensions 500 mm x 400 mm), together with constant supplies of hot and cold running water. A tiled splashback (minimum 300 mm high) is to be provided to each wash hand basin.

19. One bath (minimum dimensions 1700 mm x 700 mm) or one shower (minimum dimensions 800 mm x 800 mm) should be provided for every eight persons, irrespective of age. These facilities must be within a reasonable distance of each user and not more than one floor distant. The number of persons having the exclusive use of a bath or shower should not be included in the calculations.

20. Where the operator chooses to provide showers for the exclusive use of each separate household or the majority of households, a minimum provision of baths, rather than showers will always be required. In such circumstances a minimum of one communal bath should be provided for every 20 persons, irrespective of age, with a minimum of one bath per property. These facilities must be within a reasonable distance of each user and ideally no more than one floor distant.

Other facilities

21. In the case of families with young children, the facilities should include a safe play area(s) that is located away from sleeping accommodation and cooking areas.

Management Standards

22. In any B&B accommodation, suitability for the purposes of Part 7 will depend upon the management standards operated within an establishment as well as the adequate provision of basic amenities. The minimum management standards set out below should apply and it is the responsibility of the housing authority to monitor the management of the property.

- Operators are required to ensure the property complies with all relevant statutory and regulatory requirements especially in relation to fire, gas and electrical safety. The supply of gas or electricity to any resident should never be interfered with.
- A clear emergency evacuation plan should be in place setting out action upon hearing the fire alarm, escape routes and safe assembly points. The manager must ensure that each person newly arriving at the premises is told what to do in the event of a fire and about the fire precautions provided.
- Residents should have access to their rooms at all times except when rooms are being cleaned. Provision should be made to accommodate residents at these times.
- Refuse and litter should be cleared from the property and not allowed to accumulate in, or in the curtilage, of the property, except in adequately sized and suitable bulk refuse container(s).
- All communal areas (including, hallways, kitchens, bathrooms/ showers, WCs, dining areas, lounges if provided) should be regularly cleaned.
- Appropriate officers of the authority in whose area the premises are situated should have access to inspect the premises as and when they consider necessary, to ensure that the requirements are being complied with. The manager should allow such inspections to take place, if necessary without notice.
- Officers of the health authority, local authority and authorised community workers for the area in which the premises are situated should have acess to visit the occupiers of the premises and interview them in private in the room(s) they occupy.
- A manager with adequate day to day responsibility to ensure the good management of the property should be contactable at all times. A notice giving the name, address and telephone number of the manager should be displayed in a readily visible position in the property.
- Procedures should be in place to deal with any complaints relating to harassment on racial, sexual or other discriminatory grounds by either residents or staff.
- There should be a clear complaints procedure for the resolution of disputes between residents and/or staff.
- There should be available within the premises a working telephone available for use by the occupiers and a notice should be displayed by the telephone with information on the address and telephone numbers of: the local Environmental Health Department, Fire Brigade, Gas Company, Electricity Company, Police Station and local doctors.

Appendix 2
England: Homelessness

ANNEX 18[7]
PROCEDURES FOR REFERRALS OF HOMELESS APPLICANTS ON THE GROUNDS OF LOCAL CONNECTION WITH ANOTHER LOCAL AUTHORITY

GUIDELINES FOR LOCAL AUTHORITIES AND REFEREES

Agreed by

> ASSOCIATION OF LONDON GOVERNMENT (ALG)
> CONVENTION OF SCOTTISH LOCAL AUTHORITIES (CoSLA)
> LOCAL GOVERNMENT ASSOCIATION (LGA)
> WELSH LOCAL GOVERNMENT ASSOCIATION (WLGA)
> (*'the local authority associations'*)

Index

---

[7] This is not guidance issued by the Secretaries of State.

Standard notification form

Procedures for referrals of homeless applicants on the grounds of local connection with another local authority

Guidelines for local authorities on procedures for referral

Agreed by

ASSOCIATION OF LONDON GOVERNMENT (ALG) CONVENTION OF SCOTTISH LOCAL AUTHORITIES (CoSLA) LOCAL GOVERNMENT ASSOCIATION (LGA) WELSH LOCAL GOVERNMENT ASSOCIATION (WLGA) (*'the local authority associations'*)

This procedure concerns the situation where, under Part 7 of the *Housing Act 1996*, a housing authority is satisfied that a housing applicant is eligible for assistance, homeless and has a priority need for accommodation, is not satisfied that the applicant is homeless intentionally and the authority consider that the conditions for referral of the case to another housing authority are met, and notifies the other housing authority of its opinion. Referrals are discretionary only. Housing authorities are not required to make inquiries as to whether an applicant has a local connection with another district, and where they decide to do so, there is no requirement to refer applicants to another authority, if the conditions for referral are met. Authorities may have a policy about how they may exercise their discretion. However, they cannot decide in advance that a referral will be made in all cases where an applicant who is eligible for assistance, unintentionally homeless and in priority need may have a local connection with another district.

Appendix 2
England: Homelessness

1   Purpose of the guidelines

1.1   For English and Welsh authorities s 198 of the *Housing Act 1996* provides that:

'(5)   The question whether the conditions for referral of a case are satisfied shall be determined by agreement between the notifying authority and the notified authority or, in default of agreement, in accordance with such arrangements as the Secretary of State may direct by order.

(6)   An order may direct that the arrangements shall be:

(a)   those agreed by any relevant authorities or associations of relevant authorities, or
(b)   in default of such agreement, such arrangements as appear to the Secretary of State to be suitable, after consultation with such associations representing relevant authorities, and such other persons, as he thinks appropriate.'

1.2 Subsections 33(4) and (5) of the *Housing (Scotland) Act 1987* make the same provision for Scotland. However, s 8 of the *Homelessness (Scotland) Act 2003* gives Scottish ministers the power to suspend or vary the circumstances under which a homeless applicant may be referred by a Scottish local authority to another authority in Scotland. Please note any future orders made will need to be taken into account.

1.3 The ALG, CoSLA, LGA and the WLGA, the local authority associations in England, Scotland and Wales, have agreed guidelines for referrals which they recommend to local housing authorities. Section 198 *Housing Act 1996* and s 33 *Housing (Scotland) Act 1987* lay down the general procedures to be followed where it appears that s 192(2) (England and Wales) or s 31 (Scotland) applies to the applicant and the applicant does not have a local connection with the area of the authority receiving the housing application but does have one with another area in England, Scotland or Wales. There are, however, considerable areas of possible disagreement and dispute in determining whether the conditions of referral are met in any particular case. Although, in the last resort, disagreements can only be resolved by the courts, the associations are anxious to avoid, as far as possible, legal disputes between local authorities. The associations therefore issue these agreed guidelines on the procedures and criteria to be followed, and recommend them for general adoption by all their members. **These Guidelines are without prejudice to the duty of local authorities to treat each case on its merits and to take into account existing and future case law.** Furthermore, these Guidelines only apply to the issues of local connection and whether the conditions for referral are met for the purposes of Part 7 of the *Housing Act 1996* (England and Wales) and s 33 of the *Housing (Scotland) Act 1987*.

1.4 *In Re Betts (1983) the House of Lords considered the application of the referral arrangements agreed between the local authority associations. Their Lordships decided that a rigid application of the arrangements would constitute a fetter on an authority's discretion. The agreement could be taken into account, and applied as a guideline, provided its application to each case is given individual consideration.*

2 Definitions

2.1 All references in this agreement to an 'applicant' are to be taken as references to a housing applicant to whom s 193 of the *Housing Act 1996* (England and Wales) or s 28 *Housing (Scotland) Act 1987* or s 31 *Housing (Scotland) Act 1987* would apply but for the decision to refer the case to another authority. For the purposes of this agreement the 1996 Act and 1987 (Scotland) Act definitions apply.

2.2 The authority to whom the applicant applies for accommodation or assistance (for the purposes of s 183 *Housing Act 1996* or s 28 *Housing (Scotland) Act 1987*) and which decides to refer the case to another authority is the *'notifying authority'*.

2.3   Where the notifying authority consider that neither the applicant nor any person who might reasonably reside with the applicant, has a local connection with its district but does have one with another local authority district and notifies the other local authority of its opinion, the authority which they notify is known as the *'notified authority'*.

2.4   Section 199 *Housing Act 1996* and s 27 *Housing (Scotland) Act 1987* set out the circumstances when a person may have a 'local connection' with a district. These guidelines provide a framework within which the local connection referral procedures may be applied.

3   Criteria for notification

3.1   Before a local authority can consider referring an applicant to another local authority it must first be satisfied that the applicant is:

  (i)   eligible for assistance
  (ii)   homeless, and
  (iii) in priority need,
  (iv)   not homeless intentionally.

3.2   Before making a referral the notifying authority must be satisfied that the conditions of referral are met. Broadly, the conditions for referral will be met if:

  (a)   neither the applicant nor any person who might reasonably be expected to reside with the applicant has a local connection with the district of the authority receiving the application,
  (b)   either the applicant or any person who might reasonably be expected to reside with the applicant has a local connection with the district of another authority in England, Scotland or Wales,
  (c)   neither the applicant nor any person who might reasonably be expected to reside with the applicant would run the risk of domestic violence/domestic abuse (Scotland) or face a probability of other violence in the district of the other authority (Refer to s 198 of the 1996 Act as amended by s 10 subsection (2&3) *Homelessness Act 2002* (England and Wales)). However, there are exceptions to these conditions, for example, where an applicant applies to an English or Welsh authority for assistance and has been provided with NASS support in Scotland.
  (d)   **For Welsh authorities only**, the conditions for referral to another authority will also be met if the applicant was placed in accommodation in the district of the notifying authority by the other authority as a discharge of a duty to secure accommodation under Part 7 of the 1996 Act following an application to the other authority made within the last five years. (The period of 5 years is prescribed by the *Homelessness (Wales) Regulations 2000 SI 2000 No 1079*.)

3.3   3.2(a)(b) and (c) above apply to Scottish authorities. 3.2(d) above does not apply in Scotland.

3.4   In deciding whether or not to make a referral authorities should also consider the court judgment in the case of *R v LB Newham ex parte LB Tower Hamlets* (1990). The notifying authority should have regard to any decisions made by the notified authority that may have a bearing on the case in question (eg a previous decision that the applicant was intentionally homeless) as well as any other material considerations, which should include the general housing circumstances prevailing in the district of the notifying authority and in the district of the notified authority. The notifying authority should also consider whether it is in the public interest to accept a duty to secure accommodation under s 193(2) (England and Wales).

3.5   Should a local authority wish to accept a duty to secure accommodation for an applicant who does not have a local connection with its district, nothing in this agreement shall prevent the authority from providing such assistance. The decision to make a referral is discretionary and could be challenged if the discretion was considered to have been exercised unreasonably.

3.6   Under s 202 of the 1996 Act, housing applicants in England and Wales have the right to request a review of certain decisions made by the local authority about their application, including a decision to notify another authority under s 198 and a decision that the conditions are met for referral of the case. The equivalent right to review in Scotland is set out in s 4 of the *Housing (Scotland) Act 2001*.

4   Local connection

4.1   The relevant date for deciding whether or not a local connection has been established is not the date when the application for housing assistance was made but the date of the decision or, if there is a review, the date of the review decision (cf House of Lords' judgment in *Mohamed v Hammersmith and Fulham London Borough Council 2001*). Moreover, if inquiries prior to a decision have been prolonged, the notifying authority should also consider whether there may have been any material change in circumstances that might affect the question of whether a local connection has been established. A local connection may be established where the following grounds apply, subject to the exceptions outlined in paragraph 4.2:

  (i)   the applicant or a person who might reasonably be expected to reside with the applicant is, or in the past was, normally resident in the district. It is suggested that a working definition of 'normal residence' should be residence for at least 6 months in the area during the previous 12 months, or for not less than 3 years during the previous 5 year period. The period taken into account should be up to the date of the authority's decision. This should include any periods living in temporary accommodation secured by the authority under s 188 (interim duty pending inquiries);

  (ii)   the applicant or a person who might reasonably be expected to reside with the applicant is at present employed in the district. The local authority should obtain confirmation from the employer that the person is in employment and that the employment is not of a casual nature;

(iii) the applicant or a person who might reasonably be expected to reside with the applicant has family associations in the district. Family associations normally arise where an applicant or a person who might reasonably be expected to reside with the applicant has parents, adult children or brothers or sisters who have been resident in the district for a period of at least 5 years at the date of the decision, and the applicant indicates a wish to be near them. Only in exceptional circumstances would the residence of relatives other than those listed above be taken to establish a local connection. The residence of dependent children in a different district from their parents would not be residence of their own choice and therefore would not establish a local connection with that district. However, a referral should not be made to another local authority on the grounds of a local connection because of family associations if the applicant objects to those grounds. **NB:** A Scottish authority, when considering the application of this clause, is advised to bear in mind the definition of 'family' in s 83 of the *Housing (Scotland) Act 1987* as amended;

(iv) there are special circumstances which the authority considers establish a local connection with the district. This may be particularly relevant where the applicant has been in prison or hospital and his or her circumstances do not conform to the criteria in (i)–(iii) above. Where, for example, an applicant seeks to return to a district where he or she was brought up or lived for a considerable length of time in the past, there may be grounds for considering that the applicant has a local connection with that district because of special circumstances. An authority must exercise its discretion when considering whether special circumstances apply.

4.2 A notifying authority should not refer an applicant to another authority on grounds of a local connection because of special circumstances without the prior consent of the notified authority. Alternatively, authorities may come to an informal arrangement in such cases on a reciprocal basis, subject to the agreement of the applicants.

4.3 There are certain circumstances where a local connection is not established because of residence or employment in a district. For these purposes:

(i) a person is not employed in a district if he or she is serving in the Regular Armed Forces of the Crown; and

(ii) residence in a district is not of a person's own choice if he or she (or anyone who might reasonably be expected to reside with them) becomes resident there because he or she is serving in the Regular Armed Forces of the Crown or is detained under the authority of any Act of Parliament (eg held in prison, or a secure hospital).

4.4   For Welsh authorities only the conditions for referral to another authority are met if the applicant was placed in accommodation in the district of the notifying authority by the other authority as a discharge of a duty to secure accommodation under Part 7 of the 1996 Act following an application to the other authority made within the last five years. This is without prejudice to whether or not the applicant may have established a local connection with a particular district.

4.5   Former asylum seekers (England and Wales). Broadly, s 199(6) of the 1996 Act (inserted by s 11 of the *Asylum and Immigration (Treatment of Claimants, etc) Act 2004* ('the 2004 Act')) (England and Wales) provides that a person has a local connection with the district of a local housing authority if that person was provided with accommodation there under s 95 of the *Immigration and Asylum Act 1999* (NASS accommodation). Where a person has been provided with NASS accommodation in more than one area, the local connection is with the area where accommodation was last provided. A local connection with a district by virtue of s 199(6) does not override a local connection by virtue of s 199(1). So, a former asylum seeker who has a local connection with a district because he or she was provided with NASS accommodation there could also have a local connection elsewhere for some other reason, for example, because of employment or family associations.

4.6   Former asylum seekers (Scotland). Under s 27(2)(a)(iii) of the *Housing (Scotland) Act 2001*, as inserted by s 7 of the *Homelessness etc (Scotland) Act 2003*, residence in accommodation provided in pursuance of s 95 of the *Immigration and Asylum Act 1999* does not constitute a local connection as it is deemed to be residence which is not of the applicant's own choice. A local connection could be formed for other reasons, such as family association.

4.7   Former asylum seekers (cross-border arrangements). If a former asylum seeker who was provided with asylum support in England or Wales seeks homelessness assistance in Scotland the Scottish local authority could refer the application to another area where a local connection is established, if there was no local connection with the authority applied to. However under Scottish legislation, a local connection would not be formed by virtue of residence in accommodation provided in pursuance of s 95 of the *Immigration and Asylum Act 1999*.

4.8   This paragraph explains the position where a former asylum seeker who was provided with asylum support in Scotland seeks homelessness assistance in England or Wales. The provisions of s 11(2) and (3) of the 2004 Act provide that where a local housing authority in England or Wales are satisfied that an applicant is eligible for assistance, unintentionally homeless and in priority need, the s 193 duty to secure accommodation does not apply if the authority are satisfied that the applicant: has been provided with s 95 accommodation in Scotland at any time and does not have a local connection anywhere in England and Wales (within the meaning of s 199(1) of the 1996 Act) or anywhere in Scotland (within the meaning of s 27 of the *Housing (Scotland) Act 1987*). However, the authority may secure that accommodation is available for the applicant for a period giving him a reasonable opportunity of securing accommodation for himself, and provide the applicant (or secure that he is provided with) advice and assistance in any attempts he may make to secure accommodation for himself.

4.9   Subject to paragraphs 4.6 to 4.9 above (former asylum seekers), once the local authority is satisfied that the applicant is eligible, unintentionally homeless, falls within a priority need category, and does not have a local connection with the district, the authority may notify another authority under s 198 *Housing Act 1996* or s 33 *Housing (Scotland) Act 1987*, provided it is satisfied that all the conditions for referral set out in paragraph 3.3 above are met.

4.10   Once the local authority has established that the applicant is eligible, homeless, in a priority need category, not intentionally homeless and does not have any local connection in its own area it may notify another authority under s 198 *Housing Act 1996* or s 33 *Housing (Scotland) Act 1987*, provided it has satisfied itself that a local connection with the notified authority exists and that no member of the household would be at risk of domestic violence or threat of domestic violence in returning to that area. In determining whether or not there is such a risk authorities should have regard, where relevant, to the advice in the Homelessness Code of Guidance.

4.11   The notifying authority must consider that neither the applicant nor any person who might reasonably be expected to reside with the applicant has **any** local connection with its own district but **does** have a local connection with another local authority district in England, Scotland or Wales, in accordance with the criteria and exceptions listed above. The strength of local connection is irrelevant except where an applicant has no local connection with the notifying authority's district but has a local connection with more than one other local authority district. In such a scenario, the notifying authority must weigh up all the relevant factors in deciding to which authority it would be appropriate to refer the applicant.

4.12   Any relevant changes in an applicant's circumstances, eg obtaining employment, will need to be taken into account in determining whether the applicant has a local connection. Authorities should always consider whether special circumstances may apply.

5   Procedures prior to making a referral

5.1   If an authority considers that the conditions for referral s 198 *Housing Act 1996* or s 33 *Housing (Scotland) Act 1987* are likely to be met in a particular case it should make any necessary enquiries in the area/s where there may be a local connection. This should be undertaken as soon as possible. An authority that is considering making a referral must investigate all the circumstances of the case with the same thoroughness as if it were not considering a referral.

5.2   The notifying authority has a duty under s 200(1) (England and Wales) or s 34 *Housing (Scotland) Act 1987* to ensure that suitable accommodation is available for occupation by the applicant until the question of whether the conditions for referral are met have been decided.

5.3 Under section 184(4) *Housing Act 1996* or s 34 *Housing (Scotland) Act 1987*, if a housing authority notify, or intend to notify another authority that they consider that the conditions for referral of a case are met, the authority must notify the applicant of this decision, and the reasons for it, at the same time. For English and Welsh authorities, under s 184(5) of the 1996 Act, the notice must also inform the applicant of his right, under s 202, to request a review of the decision and that any request must be made within 21 days (or such longer period as the authority allows in writing). Regulations made under s 203 of the 1996 Act set out the procedure to be followed when making a review and the period within which a request for review must be carried out and the decision made. The *Allocation of Housing and Homelessness (Review Procedures) Regulations 1999 (SI 1999 No 71)* establishes for England and Wales the period within which the review must be carried out and the decision made. For England and Wales s 204 of the 1996 Act gives applicants the right to appeal to the county court on a point of law if dissatisfied with the decision on the review (or the initial decision, if a review decision is not made within the prescribed time limit).

5.4 Scottish local authorities have a duty to review homelessness decisions under s 35A of the *Housing (Scotland) Act 1987* as amended by s 4 of the *Housing (Scotland) Act 2001*. This process does not affect the rights of a homeless applicant to seek judicial review or to seek the redress of the Scottish Public Services Ombudsman.

5.5 Once the notifying authority is has decided that the applicant is eligible, unintentionally homeless, and in priority need, there is no provision for the notified authority to challenge the decision other than judicial review in the High Court. The local authority associations' disputes procedure should be used only where there is a disagreement over the question of whether the conditions for referral are met and not for resolving disagreement on any other matter.

6   Making the notification

6.1 All notifications and arrangements concerning an applicant should be made by telephone and then confirmed in writing. A specimen standard notification form is attached, which authorities are advised to use. If telephone contact cannot be made a fax or e-mail should be sent. Where the notified authority accepts the conditions for referral are met, it should not wait for the receipt of written confirmation of notification before making appropriate arrangements to secure accommodation for the applicant and his or her household.

6.2 Each authority should nominate an officer responsible for making decisions about applications notified by another authority. Appropriate arrangements should also be put in place to ensure cover during any absences of the designated officer.

6.3 The notified authority should normally accept the facts of the case relating to residence, employment, family associations etc, as stated by the notifying authority, unless they have clear evidence to the contrary. It is the notifying authority's duty to make inquiries into the circumstances of homelessness with the same degree of care and thoroughness before referring a case to another authority as it would for any other case.

6.4 Local authorities should try to avoid causing undue disruption to the applicant which could arise from the operation of the criteria and procedures set out above. For instance, where it is agreed that the conditions for referral are met two authorities involved could agree, subject to the applicants' consent, to enter into a reciprocal arrangement so as to avoid having to move a household which may already have made arrangements within the notifying authority's area for schooling, medical treatment etc. Such arrangements could involve provision via nominations to other social housing providers such as registered social landlords. Authorities are reminded that there is no requirement to refer applicants to another authority even where it is agreed that the conditions for referral are met.

6.5 Once written confirmation of notification has been received the notified authority should, within 10 days, reply to the notifying authority. If, despite reminders, there is an unreasonable delay by the notified authority in formally responding to the notification, the notifying authority may ask its local authority association to intercede on its behalf.

7 *Arrangements for securing accommodation*

7.1 As soon as the notifying authority has advised the applicant that it intends to notify, or has already notified, another authority that it considers that the conditions for referral are met, the notifying authority has a duty (under s 200 (1) of the 1996 Act) (England and Wales) and s 34 *Housing (Scotland) Act 1987* to secure accommodation until the applicant is informed of the decision whether the conditions for referral are met. During this period, the notifying authority also has a duty (under s 211) (England and Wales) and s 36 of the *Housing (Scotland) Act 1987* to take reasonable steps for the protection of property belonging to the applicant or anyone who might reasonably be expected to reside with the applicant.

7.2.1 When it has been decided whether the conditions for referral are met the notifying authority must inform the applicant of the decision and the reason for it (s 200(2), England and Wales or s 34 of the *Housing (Scotland) Act 1987*). The applicant must also be informed of his right to ask for a review of the decision and that any request must be made within 21 days or such longer period as the authority may allow in writing.

7.2.2 If it is decided that the conditions for referral are not met, under s 200(3) England and Wales or s 34(2) of the *Housing (Scotland) Act 1987* the notifying authority will be subject to the s 193 duty (England and Wales) or s 31 of the *Housing (Scotland) Act 1987* and must ensure that suitable accommodation is available for the applicant.

7.2.3 If it is decided that the conditions for referral are met, under s 200(4) or s 34(2) of the *Housing (Scotland) Act 1987*, the notified authority will be subject to the s 193 duty (England and Wales) s 31 of the *Housing (Scotland) Act 1987* and must ensure that suitable accommodation is available for the applicant.

7.3 The local authority associations recommend that once a notified authority has accepted that the conditions of referral are met it shall reimburse the notifying authority for any expenses which may reasonably have been incurred in providing temporary accommodation, including protection of property. If the notifying authority unduly delays advising an authority of its intention to refer an applicant then the notified authority shall only be responsible for expenses incurred after the receipt of notification. In normal circumstances a period of more than 30 working days, commencing from the date when the notifying authority had reason to believe that the applicant may be homeless or threatened with homelessness and commenced inquiries under s 184, (England & Wales), s 28 of the *Housing (Scotland) Act 1987*, should be considered as constituting undue delay.

8   Right of review of referral decisions (England and Wales)

8.1   Under s 202(1)(c) *Housing Act 1996*, applicants in England and Wales have the right to request a review of any decision by the authority to notify another authority of its opinion that the conditions for referral are met. And, under s 202(1)(d), applicants in England and Wales have the right to request a review of any decision whether the conditions for referral are met. In Scotland (under s 34(3A) and s 35A(2)(b) of the *Housing (Scotland) Act 1987*) as inserted by s 4 of the *Housing Scotland Act 2001* the applicant must be notified that they can request a review of any decision to refer their case to another authority, any determination reached following referral and the time within which this request should be made – the authority should also notify the applicant of advice and assistance available to him in connection with this review. In both cases the request for review will be made to the notifying authority.

9   Statutory procedure on review

9.1   **Review procedure for England** – The procedural requirements for a review are set out in the *Allocation of Housing and Homelessness (Review Procedures) Regulations 1999* (SI 1999 No 71).

9.2   The notifying authority shall notify the applicant:

   (i)   that the applicant, or someone acting on the applicant's behalf, may make written representations,

   (ii)   of the review procedures.

9.3   If the reviewer acting for the notifying authority considers that there is an irregularity in the original decision, or in the manner in which it was made, but is nevertheless minded to make a decision which is against the interests of the applicant, the reviewer shall notify the applicant:

(i)   that the reviewer is so minded, and the reasons why,
(ii) that the applicant, or someone acting on the applicant's behalf, may make further written or oral representations.

9.4 In carrying out a review the reviewer shall:

(i)   consider any representations made by, or on behalf of, the applicant,
(ii) consider any further written or oral representations made by, or on behalf of, the applicant in response to a notification referred to in paragraph 9.2 (b) above,
(iii) make a decision on the basis of the facts known at the date of the review.

9.5 The applicant should be notified of the decision on a review within: eight weeks from the date on which a request for review was made under s 202(1)(c), ten weeks from the date on which a request for review was made under s 202(1)(d), or such longer period as the applicant may agree in writing.

9.6 Review procedure for Scotland – Procedures are set out in s 35A and s 35B of the *Housing (Scotland) Act 1987*. Good practice guidance on the procedures is set out in Chapter 11 of the Code of Guidance on Homelessness.

9.7 Review Procedure for Wales. The procedures are set out in *The Allocation of Housing and Homelessness (Review Procedures) Regulations 1999* (SI 1999 No 71).

9.8 Where the decision under review is a joint decision by the notifying housing authority and the notified housing authority s 202(4) requires that the review should be carried out jointly by the two housing authorities.

9.9 The notifying authority shall notify the applicant:

(i)   that the applicant, or someone acting on the applicant's behalf, may make written representations,
(ii) of the review procedures.

9.10 If the reviewer acting for the notifying authority considers that there is an irregularity in the original decision, or in the manner in which it was made, but is nevertheless minded to make a decision which is against the interests of the applicant, the reviewer shall notify the applicant:

(i)   that the reviewer is so minded, and the reasons why,
(ii) that the applicant, or someone acting on the applicant's behalf, may make further written and/or oral representations.

9.11 In carrying out a review the reviewer shall:

(i)   consider any representations made by, or on behalf of, the applicant,
(ii) consider any further written or oral representations made by, or on behalf of, the applicant in response to a notification referred to in paragraph 9.9(ii) above,

Appendix 2
England: Homelessness

(iii) make a decision on the basis of the facts known at the date of the review.

9.12 The applicant should be notified of the decision on a review within:

(i) eight weeks from the date on which a request for review, where the original decision was made by the housing authority,

(ii) ten weeks from the date on which a request for review was made where the decision was made jointly by two housing authorities,

(iii) twelve weeks, where the decision is taken by a person appointed pursuant to the Schedule to the *Homelessness (Decisions on Referrals) Order 1998* (SI 1998 No 1578).

In all these cases it is open to the reviewer to seek the applicant's agreement to an extension of the proscribed period; any such agreement must be given in writing.

10 Disputes between authorities

10.1 The *Homelessness (Decisions on Referrals) (Scotland) Order 1998* and the *Homelessness (Decisions on Referrals) Order 1998* (SI 1998 No 1578) (England and Wales) set out the arrangements for determining whether the conditions for referral are met, should the notifying and the notified authority fail to agree. These arrangements allow the question to be decided either by a person agreed between the two authorities concerned or, in default of such agreement, by a person appointed from a panel established by the LGA.

10.2 Where a notified authority considers the conditions for referral are not met it should write to the notifying authority giving its reasons in full, within 10 days. The letter should contain all the reasons for its opinion, to avoid delaying the appointment of a referee and to minimise any inconvenience for the applicant.

10.3 Where two authorities cannot reach agreement on whether the conditions for referral are met they must seek to agree on a referee who will make the decision. CoSLA and the LGA have jointly established an independent panel of referees for this purpose. A referee should be appointed within 21 days of the notified authority receiving the notification.

10.4 Authorities invoking the disputes procedure should, having first agreed on the proposed referee, establish that he or she is available and willing to accept the case. Each authority is then responsible for providing the referee with such information as he or she requires to reach a decision, making copies of the submission available to the applicant and ensuring prompt payment of fees and expenses. Sections 10–19 (Guidelines for Invoking the Disputes Procedure) set out in greater detail the requirements and timescale for the disputes procedure.

10.5 Authorities invoking the disputes procedure should be bound by the decision of the referee, including the apportionment of fees and expenses, subject to a further decision by a referee where the applicant asks for a review of the initial decision.

10.6 If the authorities are unable to agree on the choice of a referee, they must jointly request that CoSLA (for Scottish authorities) or the LGA (for English or Welsh authorities) appoint a referee on their behalf as outlined in paragraph 10.8 below.

10.7 If a referee has not been appointed within six weeks of the notified authority receiving the referral the notifying authority may request CoSLA or the LGA, as appropriate, to appoint a referee as outlined in paragraph 10.8 below.

10.8 Where two authorities fail to agree on the appointment of a referee CoSLA (if the dispute is between Scottish authorities) or the LGA (if the dispute is between English or Welsh authorities) may appoint a referee from the panel. Where the **notified** authority is Scottish then the local authority association responsible for appointing a referee will be CoSLA, even if the notifying authority is in England or Wales. The LGA will be the responsible association if the notified authority is English or Welsh.

10.9 The local authority associations should only be involved in the direct appointment of referees as a last resort. Under normal circumstances authorities should jointly agree the arrangements between themselves in accordance with the Guidelines for Invoking the Disputes Procedure.

Procedures for referrals of homeless applicants on the grounds of local connection with another local authority

Guidelines for invoking the disputes procedure

Agreed by

> ASSOCIATION OF LONDON GOVERNMENT (ALG)
> CONVENTION OF SCOTTISH LOCAL AUTHORITIES (CoSLA)
> LOCAL GOVERNMENT ASSOCIATION (LGA)
> WELSH LOCAL GOVERNMENT ASSOCIATION (WLGA)
> (*'the local authority associations'*)

11 Determining disputes

11.1 The local authority associations have been concerned to establish an inexpensive, simple, speedy, fair and consistent way of resolving disputes between authorities arising from the referral of homeless applicants under s 198 *Housing Act 1996* (England and Wales). In Scotland the provisions of s 33 *Housing (Scotland) Act 1987* apply.

11.2 For the purpose of this Disputes procedure, arbitrators are referred to as 'referees'. Referees will not normally be entitled to apply the criteria set out in

Appendix 2
England: Homelessness

this agreed procedure without the consent of the local authorities involved in the dispute. Where the issues in the case are evenly balanced, referees may have regard to the wishes of the applicant.

11.3   In determining disputes referees will need to have regard to:

a)   for English and Welsh authorities

- Part VII *Housing Act 1996*
- regulation 6 of the *Homelessness Regulations1996* (SI 1996 No 2754) for Wales
- the *Homelessness (Decisions on Referrals) Order 1998* (SI 1998 No 1578)
- the *Allocation of Housing and Homelessness (Review Procedures) Regulations 1999* (SI 1999 No 71)
- *Code of Guidance for Local Authorities on Allocation of Accommodation and Homelessness 2003 (Wales)* – currently under review
- *Homelessness Code of Guidance for Local Authorities 2006 (England)*

b)   for Scottish authorities

- *Housing (Scotland) Act 1987*
- the *Homelessness (Decisions on Referrals) (Scotland) Order 1998*
- the *Persons subject to Immigration Control (Housing Authority Accommodation and Homelessness) Order 2000* (SI 2000 No 706)
- *Homelessness etc (Scotland) Act 2003*
- *Code of Guidance on Homelessness: Guidance on legislation, policies and practices to prevent and resolve homelessness 2005 (Scotland)*

c)   for all authorities

- the *Procedures for s 198 (Local Connection) Homeless Referrals: Guidelines for Local Authorities and Referees* produced by the local authority associations
- *Asylum and Immigration (Treatment of Claimants, etc) Act 2004*

11.4   Where there is a cross border dispute between a Scottish authority and an English or Welsh authority then the legislation relevant to the location of the notified authority should be applied in determining whether the conditions for referral are met.

11.5   Scottish authorities need to be aware of any orders exercised by s 8 of the *Homelessness (Scotland) Act 2003* that may effect referrals between Scottish authorities in the future.

12   *Arrangements for appointing referees*

12.1   Referees will be approached by the authorities in dispute, both of which must agree that the referee should be invited to accept the appointment, to establish whether they are willing and able to act in a particular dispute. The referee should be appointed within 21 days of the notified authority receiving the referral. If the local authorities are unable to agree on the choice of referee they should contact CoSLA or the LGA, as appropriate, in accordance with section 10 of the Guidelines for Local Authorities on Procedures for Referral.

12.2 A referee will be given an initial indication of the reason for the dispute by the relevant authorities or the local authority association. The referee's jurisdiction is limited to the issue of whether the conditions for referral are met.

12.3 A referee must not have any personal interest in the outcome of the dispute and should not accept the appointment if he or she is, or was, employed by, or is a council tax payer in, one of the disputing local authorities, or if he or she has any connection with the applicant.

13 Procedures for determining the dispute

13.1 The general procedures to be followed by a referee in determining a dispute are outlined in the Schedule to the *Homelessness (Decisions on Referrals) Order 1998* (SI 1998 No 1578). (England and Wales) and SI 1998 No 1603 (Scotland). It is recommended that the following, more detailed, procedures are applied to *all* cases.

13.2 Following appointment, the referee shall invite the notifying and notified authorities to submit written representations within a period of *fourteen* working days, specifying the closing date, and requiring them to send copies of their submission to the applicant and to the other authority involved in the dispute. Authorities must have the opportunity to see each other's written statements, and should be allowed a further period of *ten* working days to comment thereon before the referee proceeds to determine the issue. The referee may also invite further written representations from the authorities, if considered necessary.

13.3 The homeless applicant to whom the dispute relates is not a direct party to the dispute but the referee may invite written or oral representations from the applicant, or any other person, which is proper and relevant to the issue. Where the referee invites representations from a person they may be made by another person acting on the person's behalf, whether or not the other person is legally qualified.

13.4 The disputing authorities should make copies of their submissions available to the applicant. The authorities should have the opportunity to comment on any information from the applicant (or any other source) upon which the referee intends to rely in reaching his/her decision.

13.5 Since the applicant's place of abode is in question, and temporary accommodation and property storage charges may be involved, it is important that a decision should be reached as quickly as possible – normally within *a month* of the receipt of the written representations and comments from the notifying and notified authority. This period will commence at the end of the process described in point 13.2. In the last resort, a referee may determine a dispute on the facts before him/her if one authority has, after reminders, failed to present its case without reasonable cause.

14   Oral hearings

14.1   Where an oral hearing is necessary or more convenient (eg where the applicant is illiterate, English is not his/her first language or further information is necessary to resolve issues in dispute), it is suggested that the notifying authority should be invited to present its case first, followed by the notified authority and any other persons whom the referee wishes to hear. The applicant may be invited to provide information on relevant matters. The authorities should then be given a right to reply to earlier submissions.

14.2   The referee's determination must be in writing even when there is an oral hearing. The referee will have to arrange the venue for the hearing and it is suggested that the offices of the notifying authority would often be the most convenient location.

14.3   Where a person has made oral representations the referee may direct either or both authorities to pay reasonable travelling expenses. The notifying and notified authorities will pay their own costs.

15   Notification of determination

15.1   The written decision of the referee should set out:

(a)   the issue(s) which he has been asked to determine
(b)   the findings of fact which are relevant to the question(s) in issue
(c)   the decision
(d)   the reasons for the decision.

The referee's determination is binding upon the participating local authorities, subject to the applicant's right to ask for a review of the decision under s 202 of the 1996 Act (and possible right of appeal to the county court on a point of law under s 204). The statutory right to review does not apply to Scottish legislation.

16   Costs of determination

16.1   Referees will be expected to provide their own secretarial services and to obtain their own advice on points of law. The cost of so doing, however, will be costs of the determination and recoverable as such.

17   Circulation of determination

17.1   Referees should send copies of the determination to both disputing authorities and to the LGA. The LGA will circulate copies to other members of the Panel of Referees as an aid to settling future disputes and promoting consistency in decisions.

17.2   The notifying authority should inform the applicant of the outcome promptly.

18 Payment of fees and costs

18.1 The local authority associations recommend a flat rate fee of **£500** per determination (including determinations made on a review) which should be paid in full and as speedily as possible after the determination has been received. However, in exceptional cases where a dispute takes a disproportionate time to resolve, a referee may negotiate a higher fee. In addition, the referee may claim the actual cost of any travelling, secretarial or other incidental expenses which s/he has incurred, including any additional costs arising from the right of review or the right of appeal to a county court on a point of law.

18.2 The LGA will determine such additional fees as may be appropriate for any additional work which may subsequently arise should there be a further dispute or appeal after the initial determination has been made or should a referee be party to an appeal, under s 204 *Housing Act 1996*, to the county court on a point of law.

18.3 The referee's fees and expenses, and any third party costs, would normally be recovered from the unsuccessful party to the dispute, although a referee may choose to apportion expenses between the disputing authorities if he considers it warranted. Referees are advised, when issuing invoices to local authorities, to stipulate that payment be made within **28 days**.

19 Reopening a dispute

19.1 Once a determination on a dispute is made, a referee is not permitted to reopen the case, even though new facts may be presented to him or her, unless a fresh determination is required to rectify an error arising from a mistake or omission.

20 Right of review of referee's decision

20.1 Section 202(1)(d) *Housing Act 1996* gives an applicant the right to request a review of any decision made under these procedures. The right to review does not apply to Scottish legislation.

20.2 If an applicant asks for a review of a referee's decision the notifying and notified authority must, within five working days, appoint another referee ('the reviewer') from the panel. This applies even if the original referee was appointed by the LGA. The reviewer must be a different referee from the referee who made the initial decision. If the two authorities fail to appoint a reviewer within this period then the notifying authority must, within five working days, request the LGA to appoint a reviewer and the LGA must do so within seven days of the request.

20.3 The authorities are required to provide the reviewer with the reasons for the initial decision, and the information on which the decision is based, within five working days of his or her appointment. The two authorities should decide between them who will be responsible for notifying the applicant of the reviewer's decision, once received.

Appendix 2
England: Homelessness

21 Statutory procedure on review

21.1 The procedural requirements for a review are set out in the *Allocation of Housing and Homelessness (Review Procedures) Regulations 1999* (SI 1999 No 71).

21.2 The reviewer is required to:

(i) notify the applicant that he or she, or someone acting on his or her behalf, may make written representations,

(ii) notify the applicant of the review procedures, and

(iii) send copies of the applicant's representations to the two authorities and invite them to respond.

21.3 If the reviewer considers that there is an irregularity in the original decision, or in the manner in which it was made, but is nevertheless minded to make a decision which is against the interests of the applicant, the reviewer shall notify the applicant:

(a) that the reviewer is so minded and the reasons why, and

(b) that the applicant, or someone acting on his behalf, may make further written or oral representations.

21.4 In carrying out a review, the reviewer is required to:

(i) consider any representations made by, or on behalf of, the applicant,

(ii) consider any responses to (i) above,

(iii) consider any further written or oral representations made by, or on behalf of, the applicant in response to a notification referred to in paragraph 21.3(b), and

(iv) make a decision on the basis of the facts known at the date of the review.

21.5 The applicant should be notified of the decision on a review within twelve weeks from the date on which the request for the review was made, or such longer period as the applicant may agree in writing. The two authorities should be advised in writing of the decision on the review, and the reasons for it, **at least a week before the end of the period** in order to allow them adequate time to notify the applicant. Copies of the decision should also be sent to the LGA.

Procedures for referrals of homeless applicants on the grounds of local connection with another local authority

Standard notification form

Agreed by

> ASSOCIATION OF LONDON GOVERNMENT (ALG)
> CONVENTION OF SCOTTISH LOCAL AUTHORITIES (CoSLA)
> LOCAL GOVERNMENT ASSOCIATION (LGA)
> WELSH LOCAL GOVERNMENT ASSOCIATION (WLGA)
> (*'the local authority associations'*)

A   NOTIFYING AUTHORITY DETAILS

Contact Name _____

Authority _____

Telephone Number _____ Fax Number _____

E-mail _____

Address for Correspondence _____

_____

B   APPLICANT DETAILS

Name of Main Applicant _____ Date of Birth _____

Current Address _____

_____

_____

_____

_____

Appendix 2
England: Homelessness

C FAMILY MEMBERS

Name   Relationship   Date of Birth

_____   _____   _____

_____   _____   _____

_____   _____   _____

_____   _____   _____

_____   _____   _____

_____   _____   _____

_____   _____   _____

_____   _____   _____

D ADDRESSES IN LAST 5 YEARS (include dates and type of tenure)

_____

_____

_____

_____

_____

_____

_____

_____

E   PRESENT/PREVIOUS EMPLOYMENT DETAILS

Employer _____ Tel No _____

Address _____

Contact Name _____ Job Title _____

Previous Employer _____

Date from _____ Date to _____

Address _____

F   REASONS FOR HOMELESSNESS

_____

_____

_____

_____

_____

H   PRIORITY NEED CATEGORY

_____

_____

I   LOCAL CONNECTION DETAILS

_____

_____

_____

_____

_____

_____

Appendix 2
England: Homelessness

J   WISHES OF THE APPLICANT(S) (in the context of the referral)

_____

_____

_____

_____

_____

_____

K   THE NOTIFYING AUTHORITY CONSIDER THE CONDITIONS FOR REFERRAL ARE MET BECAUSE:

_____

_____

_____

_____

_____

_____

L   ANY SUPPLEMENTARY INFORMATION
        (attach supporting documentation if relevant)

I confirm that, in accordance with s.198 *Housing Act 1996*, this authority considers that neither the applicant nor any person who might reasonably be expected to reside with the applicant would run the risk of domestic violence or face a probability of other violence in the district of your authority, if this referral is made.

Signed _____ Date _____

Homelessness Code of Guidance for Local Authorities Supplementary Guidance on Intentional Homelessness

APPLICANTS WHO FACE HOMELESSNESS FOLLOWING DIFFICULTIES IN MEETING MORTGAGE COMMITMENTS

In response to the current economic climate, and the robust framework of financial support the Government has put in place to help homeowners in financial difficulty,[8] this note provides guidance on how local housing authorities should exercise their homelessness functions, and apply the various statutory criteria,when considering whether applicants who are homeless having lost their home because of difficulties in meeting mortgage commitments are intentionally or unintentionally homeless.

Introduction

1. This guidance is issued by the Secretary of State under s 182 of the Housing Act 1996 ('the 1996 Act'). Under s 182(1) of the 1996 Act, housing authorities are required to have regard to this guidance in exercising their functions under Part 7 of the 1996 Act.

2. This statutory guidance supplements Chapter 11 of the *Homelessness Code of Guidance for Local Authorities* issued in July 2006 ('the 2006 Code'), and should be read in conjunction with that chapter.

Homelessness following mortgage difficulties

3. Homeowners may be at risk of homelessness if they experience difficulties in meeting their mortgage commitments, for example, because a member of the household loses their employment or suffers an income shock. Individual homeowners may respond in different ways when faced with such difficult circumstances.

4. Some homeowners may voluntarily give up possession of the property (hand back the keys to the lender). Some homeowners may decide to sell the property. Others may seek help to remain in their home, including help under the Mortgage Rescue Scheme (MMRS) or Homeowner Mortgage Support (HHMS), but decide – if found eligible for the scheme – not to accept an offer because they consider that continuing with home ownership would be unsustainable or would entail unacceptable financial risk. Where homeowners who have experienced such circumstances become homeless or threatened with

---

[8] The Mortgage Rescue Scheme and Homeowner Mortgage Support.

Appendix 2
England: Homelessness

homelessness and apply to a local housing authority for assistance, the authority will need to give careful consideration to the substantive cause(s) of homelessness before coming to a decision on intentionality.

Definition of intentional homelessness

5. Authorities are reminded that by sections 191(1) and 196(1) of the 1996 Act, a person becomes homeless intentionally or threatened with homelessness intentionally, if:

i) the person deliberately does or fails to do anything in consequence of which the person ceases to occupy accommodation (or the likely result of which is that the person will be forced to leave accommodation);

ii) the accommodation is available for the person's occupation; and

iii) it would have been reasonable for the person to continue to occupy the accommodation.

However, an act or omission made in good faith by someone who was unaware of any relevant fact must not be treated as deliberate.

6. Authorities are also reminded that they must not adopt general policies that seek to pre-define circumstances that do or do not amount to intentional homelessness or threatened homelessness (see paragraph 11.55 of the *Homelessness Code of Guidance for Local Authorities*).

Principles established by case law

7. The broad thrust of section 191 is to ascribe intentional homelessness to a person who on the facts is responsible for his homelessness by virtue of his own act or omission. Whilst it is not part of the purpose of the legislation to require local authorities to house people whose homelessness is brought upon them by their own fault, equally, it is not part of the legislation that authorities should refuse to accommodate people whose homelessness has been brought upon them without fault on their part, for example, by an inability to make ends meet.

8. Nobody may be presumed to be intentionally homeless; the local housing authority must be satisfied of intentionality and must ask and answer the questions set out in the legislation. The decision maker in the local authority must look for the substantive cause of the homelessness and the effective cause will not always be the most immediate proximate cause.

9. Intentionality does not depend on whether applicants have behaved wisely or prudently or reasonably. Where an applicant's failure to seek help may have been foolish, imprudent or even unreasonable, this would not necessarily mean his or her conduct was not in good faith.

Some possible scenarios

10.　As mentioned above, some former homeowners may seek housing assistance from a local housing authority having lost their home in one of the following circumstances:

i)　having voluntarily surrendered the property (handed the keys back);

ii)　having sold the property;

iii)　where the property was repossessed after the applicant refused an offer under the MRS;

iv)　where the property was repossessed after the applicant refused an offer of HMS;

v)　where the property was repossessed and the applicant had not sought help.

There should be no general presumption that a homeowner will have brought homelessness on him or herself in any of the above scenarios. A person cannot be found to have become intentionally homeless from a property where he or she was already statutorily homeless: eg because it was not reasonable for him to continue to occupy the property (see paragraph 8.18 et seq of the *Homelessness Code of Guidance for Local Authorities*). Consequently, where someone was already homeless before surrendering or selling their home or refusing an offer under MRS or HMS, the 'acts' of surrender or sale, and the 'omission' of refusing an offer of MRS or HMS cannot be treated as the cause of homelessness.

11.　In particular, authorities will need to satisfy themselves on two questions as applied at the point in time immediately before the applicant ceased to occupy accommodation (ie prior to the surrender, sale or refusal of help). First, was the applicant's home available as accommodation for the applicant, any other person who normally resides with him as a member of his family and any person who might reasonably be expected to reside with him? Second, did the applicant's home constitute accommodation that it would have been reasonable for him or her to continue to occupy? It would not have been reasonable for the applicant to continue to occupy his or her home, for example, if the home was not affordable, for example, because the applicant could not meet the cost of his or her mortgage commitments.

12.　If the answer to either of the two questions above is in the negative, the applicant will have been homeless prior to the surrender or sale of the property or refusal of an offer of assistance under the MRS or HMS. In such a case, the authority may still consider whether the applicant's homelessness was intentional but will need to look at the substantive causes of that homelessness prior to surrender or sale of the property or refusal of an offer of assistance under the MRS or HMS.

Homelessness (Suitability of Accommodation) Order 1996

SI 1996/3204

Made	*19th December 1996*
Laid before Parliament	*23rd December 1996*
Coming into force	*20th January 1997*

The Secretary of State for the Environment, as respects England, and the Secretary of State for Wales, as respects Wales, in exercise of the powers conferred on them by sections 177(3)(b) and 210(2)(b) of the Housing Act 1996, and of all other powers enabling them in that behalf, hereby make the following Order:

1 Citation and commencement

This Order may be cited as the Homelessness (Suitability of Accommodation) Order 1996 and shall come into force on 20th January 1997.

2 Matters to be taken into account

In determining whether it would be, or would have been, reasonable for a person to continue to occupy accommodation and in determining whether accommodation is suitable for a person there shall be taken into account whether or not the accommodation is affordable for that person and, in particular, the following matters –

(a) the financial resources available to that person, including, but not limited to –
  (i) salary, fees and other remuneration;
  (ii) social security benefits;
  (iii) payments due under a court order for the making of periodical payments to a spouse or a former spouse, or to, or for the benefit of, a child;
  (iv) payments of child support maintenance due under the Child Support Act 1991;
  (v) pensions;
  (vi) contributions to the costs in respect of the accommodation which are or were made or which might reasonably be expected to be, or have been, made by other members of his household;
  (vii) financial assistance towards the costs in respect of the accommodation, including loans, provided by a local authority, voluntary organisation or other body;
  (viii) benefits derived from a policy of insurance;
  (ix) savings and other capital sums;
(b) the costs in respect of the accommodation, including, but not limited to –

      (i)   payments of, or by way of, rent;
      (ii)   payments in respect of a licence or permission to occupy the accommodation;
      (iii) mortgage costs;
      (iv) payments of, or by way of, service charges;
      (v)   mooring charges payable for a houseboat;
      (vi) where the accommodation is a caravan or a mobile home, payments in respect of the site on which it stands;
      (vii) the amount of council tax payable in respect of the accommodation;
      (viii) payments by way of deposit or security in respect of the accommodation;
      (ix) payments required by an accommodation agency;
  (c)   payments which that person is required to make under a court order for the making of periodical payments to a spouse or a former spouse, or to, or for the benefit of, a child and payments of child support maintenance required to be made under the Child Support Act 1991;
  (d)   that person's other reasonable living expenses.

[3 Circumstances in which accommodation is not to be regarded as suitable

For the purposes of section 197(1) of the Housing Act 1996 (duty where other suitable accommodation available), accommodation shall not be regarded as suitable unless the local housing authority are satisfied that it will be available for occupation by the applicant for at least two years beginning with the date on which he secures it.][1]

AMENDMENT

[1] Article inserted: SI 1997/1741, art 2.

LOCAL AUTHORITIES (CONTRACTING OUT OF ALLOCATION OF HOUSING AND HOMELESSNESS FUNCTIONS) ORDER 1996, SI 1996/3205

See Appendix 1, p 1105

Homelessness (Isles of Scilly) Order 1997

SI 1997/797

Made	*12th March 1997*
Laid before Parliament	*13th March 1997*
Coming into force	*3rd April 1997*

The Secretary of State, in exercise of the powers conferred on him by section 225(1) of the Housing Act 1996, and of all other powers enabling him in that behalf, hereby makes the following Order:

1 Citation, commencement and interpretation

(1) This Order may be cited as the Homelessness (Isles of Scilly) Order 1997 and shall come into force on 3rd April 1997.

(2) In this Order –

'the Act' means the Housing Act 1996;
'the Council' means the Council of the Isles of Scilly.

2 Eligibility for assistance by the Council and local connection with the district of the Council

(1) Where –

(a) a person applies to the Council for assistance under Part 7 of the Act (homelessness); or

(b) a person applies to a local housing authority other than the Council for such assistance and, but for the provisions of paragraphs (2) and (3), the conditions specified in section 198(2) of the Act (referral of case to another authority) for referral of the case to the Council are satisfied,

sections 183 to 218 of the Act shall be subject to the following provisions of this article.

(2) A person is not eligible for assistance by the Council if he has not been resident in the district of the Council for a period of two years and six months during the period of three years immediately prior to his application.

(3) Where a person is not excluded from assistance by the Council by paragraph (2) –

(a) he has a local connection with the district of the Council; and

(b) section 199 of the Act (local connection) shall not apply for the purpose of determining whether he has a local connection with the district of the Council.

Homelessness (Decisions on Referrals) Order 1998

SI 1998/1578

Made	*25th June 1998*
Coming into force	*20th June 1998*

The Secretary of State for the Environment, Transport and the Regions, as respects England, and the Secretary of State for Wales, as respects Wales, in exercise of the powers conferred on them by section 198(5) and (6)(a) of the Housing Act 1996 and of all other powers enabling them in that behalf, hereby make the following Order, a draft of which has been laid before and approved by resolution of each House of Parliament:

1 Citation and commencement

This Order may be cited as the Homelessness (Decisions on Referrals) Order 1998 and shall come into force on the twenty-eighth day after the day on which it is approved by resolution of each House of Parliament.

2 Arrangements for deciding whether conditions for referral are satisfied

The arrangements set out in the Schedule to this Order are those agreed by the Local Government Association, the Welsh Local Government Association, the Association of London Government and the Convention of Scottish Local Authorities, and shall be the arrangements for the purposes of section 198(5) and (6)(a) of the Housing Act 1996.

3 Revocation of order

(1) Subject to paragraph (2), the Housing (Homeless Persons) (Appropriate Arrangements) Order 1978 ('the 1978 Order') is hereby revoked.

(2) The 1978 Order shall remain in force for any case where a notified authority has received a notification under section 67(1) of the Housing Act 1985 or section 198(1) of the Housing Act 1996 (referral to another local housing authority) prior to the date on which this Order comes into force.

Schedule

Article 2

The Arrangements

1 Appointment of person by agreement between notifying authority and notified authority

Where the question whether the conditions for referral of a case are satisfied has not been decided by agreement between the notifying authority and the notified authority, the question shall be decided by a person appointed by those authorities.

2 Appointment of person other than by agreement between notifying authority and notified authority

If within a period of 21 days commencing on the day on which the notified authority receives a notification under section 198(1) of the Housing Act 1996 a person has not been appointed in accordance with paragraph 1, the question shall be decided by a person –

    (a)   from the panel constituted in accordance with paragraph 3, and
    (b)   appointed in accordance with paragraph 4.

3

(1) Subject to sub-paragraph (2), the Local Government Association shall establish and maintain a panel of persons from which a person may be appointed to decide the question whether the conditions for referral of a case are satisfied.

(2) The Local Government Association shall consult such other associations of relevant authorities as they think appropriate before –

    (a)   establishing the panel,
    (b)   inviting a person to join the panel after it has been established, and
    (c)   removing a person from the panel.

4

(1) The notifying authority and the notified authority shall jointly request the Chairman of the Local Government Association or his nominee ('the proper officer') to appoint a person from the panel.

(2) If within a period of six weeks commencing on the day on which the notified authority receives a notification under section 198(1) of the Housing Act 1996 a person has not been appointed, the notifying authority shall request the proper officer to appoint a person from the panel.

5 Procedural requirements

(1) Subject to the following provisions of this paragraph, the procedure for deciding whether the conditions for referral of a case are satisfied shall be determined by the appointed person.

(2) The appointed person shall invite written representations from the notifying authority and the notified authority.

(3) The appointed person may also invite –

    (a)   further written representations from the notifying authority and the notified authority,

    (b)   written representations from any other person, and

    (c)   oral representations from any person.

(4) If the appointed person invites representations from any person, those representations may be made by a person acting on his behalf, whether or not legally qualified.

6 Notification of decision

The appointed person shall notify his decision, and his reasons for it, in writing to the notifying authority and the notified authority.

7 Costs

(1) The notifying authority and the notified authority shall pay their own costs incurred in connection with the arrangements set out in this Schedule.

(2) Where a person has made oral representations, the appointed person may give directions as to the payment by the notifying authority or the notified authority or both authorities of any travelling expenses reasonably incurred by that person.

8 Meaning of 'appointed person'

In this Schedule 'appointed person' means a person appointed in accordance with paragraph 1 or 4.

Allocation of Housing and Homelessness (Review Procedures) Regulations 1999

SI 1999/71

Made	*14th January 1999*
Laid before Parliament	*21st January 1999*
Coming into force	*11th February 1999*

The Secretary of State for the Environment, Transport and the Regions, as respects England, and the Secretary of State for Wales, as respects Wales, in exercise of the powers conferred on them by sections 165(1), (2) and (5) and 203(1), (2) and (7) of the Housing Act 1996 and of all other powers enabling them in that behalf, hereby make the following Regulations:

PART I
GENERAL

1 Citation, commencement and interpretation

(1) These Regulations may be cited as the Allocation of Housing and Homelessness (Review Procedures) Regulations 1999 and shall come into force on 11th February 1999.

(2) In these Regulations –

'the authority' means the local housing authority which has made the decision whose review under section 164 or 202 has been requested;

'the Decisions on Referrals Order' means the Homelessness (Decisions on Referrals) Order 1998;

'the reviewer' means –

    (a) where the original decision falls within section 202(1)(a), (b), (c), (e) or (f), the authority;

    (b) where the original decision falls within section 202(1)(d) (a decision under section 198(5) whether the conditions are met for referral of a case) –

        (i) the notifying authority and the notified authority, where the review is carried out by those authorities;

        (ii) the person appointed to carry out the review in accordance with regulation 7, where the case falls within that regulation.

(3) In these Regulations, references to sections are references to sections of the Housing Act 1996.

2 Who is to make the decision on the review

Where the decision of the authority on a review of an original decision made by an officer of the authority is also to be made by an officer, that officer shall be someone who was not involved in the original decision and who is senior to the officer who made the original decision.

PART II
THE HOUSING REGISTER

3 Notification of review procedure

Following a duly made request for a review under section 164, the authority shall –

    (a)   notify the person concerned that he, or someone acting on his behalf, may make representations in writing to the authority in connection with the review; and

    (b)   if they have not already done so, notify the person concerned of the procedure to be followed in connection with the review.

4 Procedure on a review

The authority shall, subject to compliance with the provisions of regulation 5, consider any representations made under regulation 3.

5 Notification of the decision on a review

The period within which the authority shall notify the person concerned of the decision on a review under section 164 is eight weeks from the day on which the request for a review is made to the authority or such longer period as the authority and the person concerned may agree in writing.

PART III
HOMELESSNESS

6 Request for a review and notification of review procedure

(1) A request for a review under section 202 shall be made –

    (a)   to the authority, where the original decision falls within section 202(1)(a), (b), (c), (e) or (f);

    (b)   to the notifying authority, where the original decision falls within section 202(1)(d) (a decision under section 198(5) whether the conditions are met for referral of a case).

(2) Except where a case falls within regulation 7, the authority to whom a request for a review under section 202 has been made shall –

    (a)   notify the applicant that he, or someone acting on his behalf, may make representations in writing to the authority in connection with the review; and

    (b)   if they have not already done so, notify the applicant of the procedure to be followed in connection with the review.

(3) Where a case falls within regulation 7, the person appointed in accordance with that regulation shall –

Appendix 2
England: Homelessness

(a)   notify the applicant that he, or someone acting on his behalf, may make representations in writing to that person in connection with the review; and

(b)   notify the applicant of the procedure to be followed in connection with the review.

7 Initial procedure where the original decision was made under the Decisions on Referrals Order

(1) Where the original decision under section 198(5) (whether the conditions are met for the referral of the case) was made under the Decisions on Referrals Order, a review of that decision shall, subject to paragraph (2), be carried out by a person appointed by the notifying authority and the notified authority.

(2) If a person is not appointed in accordance with paragraph (1) within five working days from the day on which the request for a review is made, the review shall be carried out by a person –

(a)   from the panel constituted in accordance with paragraph 3 of the Schedule to the Decisions on Referrals Order ('the panel'), and

(b)   appointed in accordance with paragraph (3) below.

(3) The notifying authority shall within five working days from the end of the period specified in paragraph (2) request the chairman of the Local Government Association or his nominee ('the proper officer') to appoint a person from the panel and the proper officer shall do so within seven days of the request.

(4) The notifying authority and the notified authority shall within five working days of the appointment of the person appointed ('the appointed person') provide him with the reasons for the original decision and the information and evidence on which that decision was based.

(5) The appointed person shall –

(a)   send to the notifying authority and the notified authority any representations made under regulation 6; and

(b)   invite those authorities to respond to those representations.

(6) The appointed person shall not be the same person as the person who made the original decision.

(7) For the purposes of this regulation a working day is a day other than Saturday, Sunday, Christmas Day, Good Friday or a bank holiday.

8 Procedure on a review

(1) The reviewer shall, subject to compliance with the provisions of regulation 9, consider –

(a)   any representations made under regulation 6 and, in a case falling within regulation 7, any responses to them; and

(b)   any representations made under paragraph (2) below.

(2) If the reviewer considers that there is a deficiency or irregularity in the original decision, or in the manner in which it was made, but is minded nonetheless to make a decision which is against the interests of the applicant on one or more issues, the reviewer shall notify the applicant –

(a)   that the reviewer is so minded and the reasons why; and
(b)   that the applicant, or someone acting on his behalf, may make representations to the reviewer orally or in writing or both orally and in writing.

9 Notification of the decision on a review

(1) The period within which notice of the decision on a review under section 202 shall be given under section 203(3) to the applicant shall be –

(a)   eight weeks from the day on which the request for the review is made, where the original decision falls within section 202(1)(a), (b), (c), (e) or (f);
(b)   ten weeks from the day on which the request for the review is made, where the original decision falls within section 202(1)(d) and the review is carried out by the notifying authority and the notified authority;
(c)   twelve weeks from the day on which the request for the review is made in a case falling within regulation 7.

(2) The period specified in paragraph (1) may be such longer period as the applicant and the reviewer may agree in writing.

(3) In a case falling within paragraph (1)(c), the appointed person shall notify his decision on the review, and his reasons for it, in writing to the notifying authority and the notified authority within a period of eleven weeks from the day on which the request for the review is made, or within a period commencing on that day which is one week shorter than that agreed in accordance with paragraph (2).

PART IV
REVOCATION

10 Revocation and transitional provisions

(1) Subject to paragraph (2), the following provisions are hereby revoked –

(a)   regulations 2 to 8 of the Allocation of Housing and Homelessness (Review Procedures and Amendment) Regulations 1996;
(b)   the definition of 'the Review Regulations' in regulation 1(3) of the Allocation of Housing and Homelessness (Amendment) Regulations 1997 and regulation 6 of those Regulations.

(2) The provisions revoked by paragraph (1) shall continue in force in any case where a request for a review under section 164 or 202 is made prior to the date these Regulations come into force.

Homelessness (Priority Need for Accommodation) (England) Order 2002

SI 2002/2051

Made	*30th July 2002*
Coming into force	*31st July 2002*

The Secretary of State for Transport, Local Government and the Regions, in exercise of the powers conferred on him by section 189(2) of the Housing Act 1996, having consulted such associations representing relevant authorities, and such other persons as he considers appropriate, in accordance with section 189(3) of that Act, hereby makes the following Order –

1 Citation, commencement and interpretation

(1) This Order may be cited as the Homelessness (Priority Need for Accommodation) (England) Order 2002 and shall come into force on the day after the day on which it is made.

(2) This Order extends to England only.

(3) In this Order –

'looked after, accommodated or fostered' has the meaning given by section 24(2) of the Children Act 1989; and
'relevant student' means a person to whom section 24B(3) of that Act applies –
    (a)   who is in full-time further or higher education; and
    (b)   whose term-time accommodation is not available to him during a vacation.

2 Priority need for accommodation

The descriptions of person specified in the following articles have a priority need for accommodation for the purposes of Part 7 of the Housing Act 1996.

3 Children aged 16 or 17

(1) A person (other than a person to whom paragraph (2) below applies) aged sixteen or seventeen who is not a relevant child for the purposes of section 23A of the Children Act 1989.

(2) This paragraph applies to a person to whom a local authority owe a duty to provide accommodation under section 20 of that Act (provision of accommodation for children in need).

4 Young people under 21

(1) A person (other than a relevant student) who –

(a) is under twenty-one; and

(b) at any time after reaching the age of sixteen, but while still under eighteen, was, but is no longer, looked after, accommodated or fostered.

5 Vulnerability: institutional backgrounds

(1) A person (other than a relevant student) who has reached the age of twenty-one and who is vulnerable as a result of having been looked after, accommodated or fostered.

(2) A person who is vulnerable as a result of having been a member of Her Majesty's regular naval, military or air forces.

(3) A person who is vulnerable as a result of –

(a) having served a custodial sentence (within the meaning of section 76 of the Powers of Criminal Courts (Sentencing) Act 2000);

(b) having been committed for contempt of court or any other kindred offence;

(c) having been remanded in custody (within the meaning of paragraph (b), (c) or (d) of section 88(1) of that Act).

6 Vulnerability: fleeing violence or threats of violence

A person who is vulnerable as a result of ceasing to occupy accommodation by reason of violence from another person or threats of violence from another person which are likely to be carried out.

Homelessness (Suitability of Accommodation) (England) Order 2003

SI 2003/3326

Made	*19th December 2003*
Laid before Parliament	*23rd December 2003*
Coming into force	*1st April 2004*

The First Secretary of State, in exercise of the powers conferred upon him by sections 210(2)(a) and 215(2) of the Housing Act 1996 hereby makes the following Order:

1 Citation, commencement and application

(1) This Order may be cited as the Homelessness (Suitability of Accommodation) (England) Order 2003 and shall come into force on 1st April 2004.

(2) This Order applies in relation to the duties of local housing authorities in England to make accommodation available for occupation by applicants under Part 7 of the Housing Act 1996.

2 Interpretation

In this Order –

   'applicant with family commitments' means an applicant –
   (a)   who is pregnant;
   (b)   with whom a pregnant woman resides or might reasonably be expected to reside; or
   (c)   with whom dependent children reside or might reasonably be expected to reside;

   'B&B accommodation' means accommodation (whether or not breakfast is included) –
   (a)   which is not separate and self-contained premises; and
   (b)   in which any one of the following amenities is shared by more than one household –
   (i)   a toilet;
   (ii)   personal washing facilities;
   (iii)   cooking facilities,

   but does not include accommodation which is owned or managed by a local housing authority, [a non-profit registered provider of social housing]¹ or a voluntary organisation as defined in section 180(3) of the Housing Act 1996; and
any reference to a numbered section is a reference to a section of the Housing Act 1996.

AMENDMENT

[1] Words substituted: Housing and Regeneration Act 2008 (Consequential Provisions) (No 2) Order 2010, SI 2010/671, art 4, Sch 1, para 39, with effect from 1 April 2010.

3 Accommodation unsuitable where there is a family commitment

Subject to the exceptions contained in article 4, B&B accommodation is not to be regarded as suitable for an applicant with family commitments where accommodation is made available for occupation –

    (a)   under section 188(1), 190(2), 193(2) or 200(1); or

    (b)   under section 195(2), where the accommodation is other than that occupied by the applicant at the time of making his application.

4 Exceptions

(1) Article 3 does not apply –

    (a)   where no accommodation other than B&B accommodation is available for occupation by an applicant with family commitments; and

    (b)   the applicant occupies B&B accommodation for a period, or a total of periods, which does not exceed 6 weeks.

(2) In calculating the period, or total period, of an applicant's occupation of B&B accommodation for the purposes of paragraph (1)(b), there shall be disregarded –

    (a)   any period before 1st April 2004; and

    (b)   where a local housing authority is subject to the duty under section 193 by virtue of section 200(4), any period before that authority became subject to that duty.

Appendix 2
England: Homelessness

The Immigration (European Economic Area) Regulations 2006

SI 2006/1003

Made	*30th March 2006*
Laid before Parliament	*4th April 2006*
Coming into force	*30th April 2006*

The Secretary of State, being a Minister designated for the purposes of section 2(2) of the European Communities Act 1972 in relation to measures relating to rights of entry into, and residence in, the United Kingdom, in exercise of the powers conferred upon him by that section, and of the powers conferred on him by section 109 of the Nationality, Immigration and Asylum Act 2002, makes the following Regulations:

PART 1
INTERPRETATION ETC

1 Citation and commencement

These Regulations may be cited as the Immigration (European Economic Area) Regulations 2006 and shall come into force on 30th April 2006.

2 General interpretation

(1) In these Regulations –

'the 1971 Act' means the Immigration Act 1971;
'the 1999 Act' means the Immigration and Asylum Act 1999;
'the 2002 Act' means the Nationality, Immigration and Asylum Act 2002;
['the Accession Regulations' means the Accession (Immigration and Worker Registration) Regulations 2004;][4]
['civil partner' does not include –
    (a)   a party to a civil partnership of convenience; or
    (b)   the civil partner ('C') of a person ('P') where a spouse, civil partner or durable partner of C or P is already present in the United Kingdom;][7]

'decision maker' means the Secretary of State, an immigration officer or an entry clearance officer (as the case may be);
['deportation order' means an order made pursuant to regulation 24(3);][1]
['derivative residence card' means a card issued to a person, in accordance with regulation 18A, as proof of the holder's derivative right to reside in the United Kingdom as at the date of issue;][5]
'document certifying permanent residence' means a document issued to an EEA national, in accordance with regulation 18, as proof of the holder's permanent right of residence under regulation 15 as at the date of issue;

['durable partner' does not include the durable partner ('D') of a person ('P') where a spouse, civil partner or durable partner of D or P is already present in the United Kingdom and where that marriage, civil partnership or durable partnership is subsisting;][6]

['EEA decision' means a decision under these Regulations that concerns –

(a)   a person's entitlement to be admitted to the United Kingdom;

(b)   a person's entitlement to be issued with or have renewed, or not to have revoked, a registration certificate, residence card, derivative residence card, document certifying permanent residence or permanent residence card;

(c)   a person's removal from the United Kingdom; or

(d)   the cancellation, pursuant to regulation 20A, of a person's right to reside in the United Kingdom;][8]

'EEA family permit' means a document issued to a person, in accordance with regulation 12, in connection with his admission to the United Kingdom;

'EEA national' means a national of an EEA State [who is not also a [British citizen][12]][9];

'EEA State' means –

(a)   a member State, other than the United Kingdom;

(b)   Norway, Iceland or Liechtenstein; or

(c)   Switzerland;

'entry clearance' has the meaning given in section 33(1) of the 1971 Act;

'entry clearance officer' means a person responsible for the grant or refusal of entry clearance;

['exclusion order' means an order made under regulation 19(1B);][2]

'immigration rules' has the meaning given in section 33(1) of the 1971 Act;

'military service' means service in the armed forces of an EEA State;

'permanent residence card' means a card issued to a person who is not an EEA national, in accordance with regulation 18, as proof of the holder's permanent right of residence under regulation 15 as at the date of issue;

'registration certificate' means a certificate issued to an EEA national, in accordance with regulation 16, as proof of the holder's right of residence in the United Kingdom as at the date of issue;

'relevant EEA national' in relation to an extended family member has the meaning given in regulation 8(6);

'residence card' means a card issued to a person who is not an EEA national, in accordance with regulation 17, as proof of the holder's right of residence in the United Kingdom as at the date of issue;

['spouse' does not include –

(a)   a party to a marriage of convenience; or

(b)   the spouse ('S') of a person ('P') where a spouse, civil partner or durable partner of S or P is already present in the United Kingdom;][10]

...[11]

(2) Paragraph (1) is subject to paragraph 1(a) of Schedule 4 (transitional provisions).

[(3) Section 11 of the 1971 Act (construction of references to entry) shall apply for the purpose of determining whether a person has entered the United Kingdom for the purpose of these Regulations as it applies for the purpose of determining whether a person has entered the United Kingdom for the purpose of that Act.][3]

AMENDMENT

[1] Definition inserted: SI 2009/1117, reg 2, Sch 1, para 1(a)(i).

[2] Definition inserted: SI 2009/1117, reg 2, Sch 1, para 1(a)(ii).

[3] Paragraph inserted: SI 2009/1117, reg 2, Sch 1, para 1(b).

[4] Definition inserted: Accession (Immigration and Worker Registration) (Revocation, Savings and Consequential Provisions) Regulations 2011, SI 2011/544, reg 5, Sch 2, para 1, with effect from 1 May 2011.

[5] Definition inserted: Immigration (European Economic Area) (Amendment) Regulations 2012, SI 2012/1547, reg 3, Sch 1, para 1(a), with effect from 16 July 2012.

[6] Definition inserted: Immigration (European Economic Area) (Amendment) Regulations 2012, SI 2012/1547, reg 3, Sch 1, para 1(a), with effect from 16 July 2012.

[7] Definition substituted: Immigration (European Economic Area) (Amendment) Regulations 2012, SI 2012/1547, reg 3, Sch 1, para 1(b), with effect from 16 July 2012.

[8] Definition substituted: Immigration (European Economic Area) (Amendment) Regulations 2012, SI 2012/1547, reg 3, Sch 1, para 1(c), with effect from 16 July 2012.

[9] Words inserted: Immigration (European Economic Area) (Amendment) Regulations 2012, SI 2012/1547, reg 3, Sch 1, para 1(d), with effect from 16 October 2012, for transitional provisions see Sch 3.

[10] Definition substituted: Immigration (European Economic Area) (Amendment) Regulations 2012, SI 2012/1547, reg 3, Sch 1, para 1(e), with effect from 16 July 2012.

[11] Definition 'United Kingdom National' repealed: Immigration (European Economic Area) (Amendment) (No 2) Regulations 2012, SI 2012/2560, regs 1, 2, Sch, para 7(1), with effect from 8 November 2012.

[12] Words substituted: Immigration (European Economic Area) (Amendment) (No 2) Regulations 2012, SI 2012/2560, regs 1, 2, Sch, para 7(2), with effect from 8 November 2012.

3 Continuity of residence

(1) This regulation applies for the purpose of calculating periods of continuous residence in the United Kingdom under regulation 5(1) and regulation 15.

(2) Continuity of residence is not affected by –

    (a)   periods of absence from the United Kingdom which do not exceed six months in total in any year;

    (b)   periods of absence from the United Kingdom on military service; or

(c)   any one absence from the United Kingdom not exceeding twelve months for an important reason such as pregnancy and childbirth, serious illness, study or vocational training or an overseas posting.

(3) But continuity of residence is broken if a person is removed from the United Kingdom under [these regulations].[1]

AMENDMENT

[1] Words substituted: SI 2009/1117, reg 2, Sch 1, para 2.

4 'Worker', 'self-employed person', 'self-sufficient person' and 'student'

(1) In these Regulations –

(a)'worker' means a worker within the meaning of [Article 45 of the Treaty on the Functioning of the European Union][4];

(b)'self-employed person' means a person who establishes himself in order to pursue activity as a self-employed person in accordance with [Article 49 of the Treaty on the Functioning of the European Union][5];

(c)'self-sufficient person' means a person who has –

(i)   sufficient resources not to become a burden on the social assistance system of the United Kingdom during his period of residence; and

(ii)   comprehensive sickness insurance cover in the United Kingdom;

(d)'student' means a person who –

[(i)   is enrolled, for the principal purpose of following a course of study (including vocational training), at a public or private establishment which is –

(aa) financed from public funds; or

(bb) otherwise recognised by the Secretary of State as an establishment which has been accredited for the purpose of providing such courses or training within the law or administrative practice of the part of the United Kingdom in which the establishment is located;][1]

(ii)   has comprehensive sickness insurance cover in the United Kingdom; and

(iii)   assures the Secretary of State, by means of a declaration, or by such equivalent means as the person may choose, that he has sufficient resources not to become a burden on the social assistance system of the United Kingdom during his period of residence.

(2) For the purposes of paragraph (1)(c), where family members of the person concerned reside in the United Kingdom and their right to reside is dependent upon their being family members of that person –

(a)   the requirement for that person to have sufficient resources not to become a burden on the social assistance system of the United Kingdom during his period of residence shall only be satisfied if his

**Appendix 2
England: Homelessness**

resources and those of the family members are sufficient to avoid him
and the family members becoming such a burden;

(b) the requirement for that person to have comprehensive sickness
insurance cover in the United Kingdom shall only be satisfied if he and
his family members have such cover.

(3) For the purposes of paragraph (1)(d), where family members of the person
concerned reside in the United Kingdom and their right to reside is dependent
upon their being family members of that person, the requirement for that
person to assure the Secretary of State that he has sufficient resources not to
become a burden on the social assistance system of the United Kingdom
during his period of residence shall only be satisfied if he assures the Secretary
of State that his resources and those of the family members are sufficient to
avoid him and the family members becoming such a burden.

[(4) For the purposes of paragraphs (1)(c) and (d) and paragraphs (2) and (3),
the resources of the person concerned and, where applicable, any family
members, are to be regarded as sufficient if –

(a) they exceed the maximum level of resources which a [British citizen][6]
and his family members may possess if he is to become eligible for
social assistance under the United Kingdom benefit system; or

(b) paragraph (a) does not apply but, taking into account the personal
situation of the person concerned and, where applicable, any family
members, it appears to the decision maker that the resources of the
person or persons concerned should be regarded as sufficient.][2]

[(5) For the purpose of regulation 15A(2) references in this regulation to
'family members' includes a 'primary carer' as defined in regulation 15A(7).][3]

AMENDMENT

[1] Sub-paragraph substituted: Immigration (European Economic Area) (Amendment) Regulations 2012, SI 2012/1547, reg 3, Sch 1, para 2(a), with effect from 16 July 2012.

[2] Sub-paragraph substituted: Immigration (European Economic Area) (Amendment) Regulations 2011, SI 2011/1247, reg 2(1), (2), with effect from 2 June 2011.

[3] Paragraph inserted: Immigration (European Economic Area) (Amendment) Regulations 2012,
SI 2012/1547, reg 3, Sch 1, para 2(b), with effect from 16 July 2012.

[4] Words in paragraph 1(a) substituted (for Article 39 of the Treaty establishing the European
Community): Treaty of Lisbon (Changes in Terminology or Numbering) Order 2012, SI 2012/1809,
arts 2, 3(1), Sch, Pt 2 with effect from 1 August 2012 (except where affecting action before 1
December 2009, when the Treaty of Lisbon came into force).

[5] Words in paragraph 1(b) substituted (for Article 43 of the Treaty establishing the European
Community): Treaty of Lisbon (Changes in Terminology or Numbering) Order 2012, SI 2012/1809,
arts 2, 3(1), Sch, Pt 2 with effect from 1 August 2012 (except where affecting action before 1
December 2009, when the Treaty of Lisbon came into force).

[6] Words substituted: Immigration (European Economic Area) (Amendment) (No 2)
Regulations 2012, SI 2012/2560, regs 1, 2, Sch, para 7(2), with effect from 8 November 2012.

5 'Worker or self-employed person who has ceased activity'

(1) In these Regulations, 'worker or self-employed person who has ceased activity' means an EEA national who satisfies the conditions in paragraph (2), (3), (4) or (5).

(2) A person satisfies the conditions in this paragraph if he –

- (a) terminates his activity as a worker or self-employed person and –
  - (i) has reached the age at which he is entitled to a state pension on the date on which he terminates his activity; or
  - (ii) in the case of a worker, ceases working to take early retirement;
- (b) pursued his activity as a worker or self-employed person in the United Kingdom for at least twelve months prior to the termination; and
- (c) resided in the United Kingdom continuously for more than three years prior to the termination.

(3) A person satisfies the conditions in this paragraph if –

- (a) he terminates his activity in the United Kingdom as a worker or self-employed person as a result of a permanent incapacity to work; and
- (b) either –
  - (i) he resided in the United Kingdom continuously for more than two years prior to the termination; or
  - (ii) the incapacity is the result of an accident at work or an occupational disease that entitles him to a pension payable in full or in part by an institution in the United Kingdom.

(4) A person satisfies the conditions in this paragraph if –

- (a) he is active as a worker or self-employed person in an EEA State but retains his place of residence in the United Kingdom, to which he returns as a rule at least once a week; and
- (b) prior to becoming so active in that EEA State, he had been continuously resident and continuously active as a worker or self-employed person in the United Kingdom for at least three years.

(5) A person who satisfies the condition in paragraph (4)(a) but not the condition in paragraph (4)(b) shall, for the purposes of paragraphs (2) and (3), be treated as being active and resident in the United Kingdom during any period in which he is working or self-employed in the EEA State.

(6) The conditions in paragraphs (2) and (3) as to length of residence and activity as a worker or self-employed person shall not apply in relation to a person whose spouse or civil partner is a [British citizen].[2]

(7) [Subject to regulation 7A(3), for the purposes of this regulation –][1]

- (a) periods of inactivity for reasons not of the person's own making;
- (b) periods of inactivity due to illness or accident; and
- (c) in the case of a worker, periods of involuntary unemployment duly recorded by the relevant employment office,

Appendix 2
England: Homelessness

shall be treated as periods of activity as a worker or self-employed person, as the case may be.

AMENDMENT

[1] Words substituted: Accession (Immigration and Worker Registration) (Revocation, Savings and Consequential Provisions) Regulations 2011, SI 2011/544, reg 5, Sch 2, para 2, with effect from 1 May 2011.

[2] Words substituted: Immigration (European Economic Area) (Amendment) (No 2) Regulations 2012, SI 2012/2560, regs 1, 2, Sch, para 7(2), with effect from 8 November 2012.

6 'Qualified person'

(1) In these Regulations, 'qualified person' means a person who is an EEA national and in the United Kingdom as –

    (a)   a jobseeker;

    (b)   a worker;

    (c)   a self-employed person;

    (d)   a self-sufficient person; or

    (e)   a student.

(2) [Subject to regulation 7A(4), a person who is no longer working shall not cease to be treated as a worker for the purpose of paragraph (1)(b) if –][1]

    (a)   he is temporarily unable to work as the result of an illness or accident;

    (b)   he is in duly recorded involuntary unemployment after having been employed in the United Kingdom, provided that he has registered as a jobseeker with the relevant employment office and –

        (i)   he was employed for one year or more before becoming unemployed;

        (ii)   he has been unemployed for no more than six months; or

        (iii)   he can provide evidence that he is seeking employment in the United Kingdom and has a genuine chance of being engaged;

    (c)   he is involuntarily unemployed and has embarked on vocational training; or

    (d)   he has voluntarily ceased working and embarked on vocational training that is related to his previous employment.

(3) A person who is no longer in self-employment shall not cease to be treated as a self-employed person for the purpose of paragraph (1)(c) if he is temporarily unable to pursue his activity as a self-employed person as the result of an illness or accident.

(4) For the purpose of paragraph (1)(a), 'jobseeker' means a person who enters the United Kingdom in order to seek employment and can provide evidence that he is seeking employment and has a genuine chance of being engaged.

AMENDMENT

[1] Words substituted: Accession (Immigration and Worker Registration) (Revocation, Savings and Consequential Provisions) Regulations 2011, SI 2011/544, reg 5, Sch 2, para 3, with effect from 1 May 2011.

7 Family member

(1) Subject to paragraph (2), for the purposes of these Regulations the following persons shall be treated as the family members of another person –

(a)   his spouse or his civil partner;
(b)   direct descendants of his, his spouse or his civil partner who are –
   (i)   under 21; or
   (ii)   dependants of his, his spouse or his civil partner;
(c)   dependent direct relatives in his ascending line or that of his spouse or his civil partner;
(d)   a person who is to be treated as the family member of that other person under paragraph (3).

(2) A person shall not be treated under paragraph (1)(b) or (c) as the family member of a student residing in the United Kingdom after the period of three months beginning on the date on which the student is admitted to the United Kingdom unless –

(a)   in the case of paragraph (b), the person is the dependent child of the student or of his spouse or civil partner; or
(b)   the student also falls within one of the other categories of qualified persons mentioned in regulation 6(1).

(3) Subject to paragraph (4), a person who is an extended family member and has been issued with an EEA family permit, a registration certificate or a residence card shall be treated as the family member of the relevant EEA national for as long as he continues to satisfy the conditions in regulation 8(2), (3), (4) or (5) in relation to that EEA national and the permit, certificate or card has not ceased to be valid or been revoked.

(4) Where the relevant EEA national is a student, the extended family member shall only be treated as the family member of that national under paragraph (3) if either the EEA family permit was issued under regulation 12(2), the registration certificate was issued under regulation 16(5) or the residence card was issued under regulation 17(4).

[7A Application of the Accession Regulations

(1) This regulation applies to an EEA national who was an accession State worker requiring registration on 30th April 2011 ('an accession worker').

(2) In this regulation –

'accession State worker requiring registration' has the same meaning as in regulation 1(2)(d) of the Accession Regulations;
'legally working' has the same meaning as in regulation 2(7) of the Accession Regulations.

(3) In regulation 5(7)(c), where the worker is an accession worker, periods of involuntary unemployment duly recorded by the relevant employment office shall be treated only as periods of activity as a worker –

    (a)   during any period in which regulation 5(4) of the Accession Regulations applied to that person; or

    (b)   when the unemployment began on or after 1st May 2011.

(4) Regulation 6(2) applies to an accession worker where he –

    (a)   was a person to whom regulation 5(4) of the Accession Regulations applied on 30th April 2011; or

    (b)   became unable to work, became unemployed or ceased to work, as the case maybe, on or after 1st May 2011.

(5) For the purposes of regulation 15, an accession worker shall be treated as having resided in accordance with these Regulations during any period before 1st May 2011 in which the accession worker –

    (a)   was legally working in the United Kingdom; or

    (b)   was a person to whom regulation 5(4) of the Accession Regulations applied.

(6) Subject to paragraph (7), a registration certificate issued to an accession worker under regulation 8 of the Accession Regulations shall, from 1st May 2011, be treated as if it was a registration certificate issued under these Regulations where the accession worker was legally working in the United Kingdom for the employer specified in that certificate on –

    (a)   30th April 2011; or

    (b)   the date on which the certificate is issued where it is issued after 30th April 2011.

(7) Paragraph (6) does not apply –

    (a)   if the Secretary of State issues a registration certificate in accordance with regulation 16 to an accession worker on or after 1st May 2011; and

    (b)   from the date of registration stated on that certificate.][1]

AMENDMENT

[1] Regulation inserted: Accession (Immigration and Worker Registration) (Revocation, Savings and Consequential Provisions) Regulations 2011, SI 2011/544, reg 5, Sch 2, para 4, with effect from 1 May 2011.

8 'Extended family member'

(1) In these Regulations 'extended family member' means a person who is not a family member of an EEA national under regulation 7(1)(a), (b) or (c) and who satisfies the conditions in paragraph (2), (3), (4) or (5).

(2) A person satisfies the condition in this paragraph if the person is a relative of an EEA national, his spouse or his civil partner and –

    (a)   the person is residing in [a country other than the United Kingdom][1] ...[2] and is dependent upon the EEA national or is a member of his household;

(b)   the person satisfied the condition in paragraph (a) and is accompanying the EEA national to the United Kingdom or wishes to join him there; or

(c)   the person satisfied the condition in paragraph (a), has joined the EEA national in the United Kingdom and continues to be dependent upon him or to be a member of his household.

(3) A person satisfies the condition in this paragraph if the person is a relative of an EEA national or his spouse or his civil partner and, on serious health grounds, strictly requires the personal care of the EEA national, his spouse or his civil partner.

(4) A person satisfies the condition in this paragraph if the person is a relative of an EEA national and would meet the requirements in the immigration rules (other than those relating to entry clearance) for indefinite leave to enter or remain in the United Kingdom as a dependent relative of the EEA national were the EEA national a person present and settled in the United Kingdom.

(5) A person satisfies the condition in this paragraph if the person is the partner of an EEA national (other than a civil partner) and can prove to the decision maker that he is in a durable relationship with the EEA national.

(6) In these Regulations 'relevant EEA national' means, in relation to an extended family member, the EEA national who is or whose spouse or civil partner is the relative of the extended family member for the purpose of paragraph (2), (3) or (4) or the EEA national who is the partner of the extended family member for the purpose of paragraph (5).

AMENDMENT

[1] Words substituted: Immigration (European Economic Area) (Amendment) Regulations 2011, SI 2011/1247, reg 2(1), (3), with effect from 2 June 2011.

[2] Words repealed: Immigration (European Economic Area) (Amendment) (No 2) Regulations 2012, SI 2012/2560, regs 1, 2, Sch, para 1, with effect from 8 November 2012.

9 Family members of [British citizens][1]

(1) If the conditions in paragraph (2) are satisfied, these Regulations apply to a person who is the family member of a [British citizen][1] as if the [British citizen][1] were an EEA national.

(2) The conditions are that –

(a)   the [British citizen][1] is residing in an EEA State as a worker or self-employed person or was so residing before returning to the United Kingdom; and

(b)   if the family member of the [British citizen][1] is his spouse or civil partner, the parties are living together in the EEA State or had entered into the marriage or civil partnership and were living together in that State before the [British citizen][1] returned to the United Kingdom.

(3) Where these Regulations apply to the family member of a [British citizen]¹ the [British citizen]¹ shall be treated as holding a valid passport issued by an EEA State for the purpose of the application of regulation 13 to that family member.

¹ Words substituted: Immigration (European Economic Area) (Amendment) (No 2) Regulations 2012, SI 2012/2560, regs 1, 2, Sch, para 7(2), with effect from 8 November 2012.

10 'Family member who has retained the right of residence'

(1) In these Regulations, 'family member who has retained the right of residence' means, subject to paragraph (8), a person who satisfies the conditions in paragraph (2), (3), (4) or (5).

(2) A person satisfies the conditions in this paragraph if –

    [(a) he was a family member of a qualified person or of an EEA national with a permanent right of residence when that person died;]¹

    (b) he resided in the United Kingdom in accordance with these Regulations for at least the year immediately before the death of [the qualified person or the EEA national with a permanent right of residence]⁴; and

    (c) he satisfies the condition in paragraph (6).

(3) A person satisfies the conditions in this paragraph if –

    (a) he is the direct descendant of –

        (i) [a qualified person or an EEA national with a permanent right of residence]⁵ who has died;

        (ii) a person who ceased to be a qualified person on ceasing to reside in the United Kingdom; or

        (iii) the person who was the spouse or civil partner of [the qualified person or the EEA national with a permanent right of residence]⁴ mentioned in sub-paragraph (i) when he died or is the spouse or civil partner of the person mentioned in sub-paragraph (ii); and

    (b) he was attending an educational course in the United Kingdom immediately before [the qualified person or the EEA national with a permanent right of residence]⁴ died or ceased to be a qualified person and continues to attend such a course.

(4) A person satisfies the conditions in this paragraph if the person is the parent with actual custody of a child who satisfies the condition in paragraph (3).

(5) A person satisfies the conditions in this paragraph if –

    [(a) he ceased to be a family member of a qualified person or of an EEA national with a permanent right of residence on the termination of the marriage or civil partnership of that person;]²

    (b) he was residing in the United Kingdom in accordance with these Regulations at the date of the termination;

    (c) he satisfies the condition in paragraph (6); and

(d) either –

    (i) prior to the initiation of the proceedings for the termination of the marriage or the civil partnership the marriage or civil partnership had lasted for at least three years and the parties to the marriage or civil partnership had resided in the United Kingdom for at least one year during its duration;

    (ii) the former spouse or civil partner of [the qualified person or the EEA national with a permanent right of residence][4] has custody of a child of the qualified person;

    [(iii) the former spouse or civil partner of the qualified person or the EEA national with a permanent right of residence has the right of access to a child of the qualified person or the EEA national with a permanent right of residence, where the child is under the age of 18 and where a court has ordered that such access must take place in the United Kingdom; or][3]

    (iv) the continued right of residence in the United Kingdom of the person is warranted by particularly difficult circumstances, such as he or another family member having been a victim of domestic violence while the marriage or civil partnership was subsisting.

(6) The condition in this paragraph is that the person –

(a) is not an EEA national but would, if he were an EEA national, be a worker, a self-employed person or a self-sufficient person under regulation 6; or

(b) is the family member of a person who falls within paragraph (a).

(7) In this regulation, 'educational course' means a course within the scope of Article 12 of Council Regulation (EEC) No 1612/68 on freedom of movement for workers.

(8) A person with a permanent right of residence under regulation 15 shall not become a family member who has retained the right of residence on the death or departure from the United Kingdom of [the qualified person or the EEA national with a permanent right of residence][4] or the termination of the marriage or civil partnership, as the case may be, and a family member who has retained the right of residence shall cease to have that status on acquiring a permanent right of residence under regulation 15.

AMENDMENT

[1] Sub-paragraph substituted: Immigration (European Economic Area) (Amendment) Regulations 2012, SI 2012/1547, reg 3, Sch 1, para 3(a), with effect from 16 July 2012.

[2] Sub-paragraph substituted: Immigration (European Economic Area) (Amendment) Regulations 2012, SI 2012/1547, reg 3, Sch 1, para 3(b), with effect from 16 July 2012.

[3] Sub-paragraph substituted: Immigration (European Economic Area) (Amendment) Regulations 2012, SI 2012/1547, reg 3, Sch 1, para 3(c), with effect from 16 July 2012.

[4] Words substituted: Immigration (European Economic Area) (Amendment) Regulations 2012, SI 2012/1547, reg 3, Sch 1, para 3(d), with effect from 16 July 2012.

Appendix 2
England: Homelessness

[5] Words substituted: Immigration (European Economic Area) (Amendment) Regulations 2012, SI 2012/1547, reg 3, Sch 1, para 3(e), with effect from 16 July 2012.

PART 2
EEA RIGHTS

11 Right of admission to the United Kingdom

(1) An EEA national must be admitted to the United Kingdom if he produces on arrival a valid national identity card or passport issued by an EEA State.

(2) A person who is not an EEA national must be admitted to the United Kingdom if he is a family member of an EEA national, a family member who has retained the right of residence[, a person who meets the criteria in paragraph (5)][1] or a person with a permanent right of residence under regulation 15 and produces on arrival –

(a) a valid passport; and
(b) an EEA family permit, a residence card[, a derivative residence card][2] or a permanent residence card.

(3) An immigration officer may not place a stamp in the passport of a person admitted to the United Kingdom under this regulation who is not an EEA national if the person produces a residence card[, a derivative residence card][3] or permanent residence card.

(4) Before an immigration officer refuses admission to the United Kingdom to a person under this regulation because the person does not produce on arrival a document mentioned in paragraph (1) or (2), the immigration officer must give the person every reasonable opportunity to obtain the document or have it brought to him within a reasonable period of time or to prove by other means that he is –

(a) an EEA national;
(b) a family member of an EEA national with a right to accompany that national or join him in the United Kingdom; ...[4]
[(ba) a person who meets the criteria in paragraph (5); or][5]
(c) a family member who has retained the right of residence or a person with a permanent right of residence under regulation 15.

[(5) A person ('P') meets the criteria in this paragraph where –

(a) P previously resided in the United Kingdom pursuant to regulation 15A(3) and would be entitled to reside in the United Kingdom pursuant to that regulation were P in the country;
(b) P is accompanying an EEA national to, or joining an EEA national in, the United Kingdom and P would be entitled to reside in the United Kingdom pursuant to regulation 15A(2) were P and the EEA national both in the United Kingdom;
(c) P is accompanying a person ('the relevant person') to, or joining the relevant person in, the United Kingdom and –

(i) the relevant person is residing, or has resided, in the United Kingdom pursuant to regulation 15A(3); and

(ii) P would be entitled to reside in the United Kingdom pursuant to regulation 15A(4) were P and the relevant person both in the [United Kingdom;][8]

(d) P is accompanying a person who meets the criteria in (b) or (c) ('the relevant person') to the United Kingdom and –

(i) P and the relevant person are both –

(aa) seeking admission to the United Kingdom in reliance on this paragraph for the first time; or

(bb) returning to the United Kingdom having previously resided there pursuant to the same provisions of regulation 15A in reliance on which they now base their claim to admission; and

(ii) P would be entitled to reside in the United Kingdom pursuant to regulation 15A(5) were P and the relevant [person there; or][9]

[(e) P is accompanying a British citizen to, or joining a British citizen in, the United Kingdom and P would be entitled to reside in the United Kingdom pursuant to regulation 15A(4A) were P and the British citizen both in the United Kingdom.][9]

(6) Paragraph (7) applies where –

(a) a person ('P') seeks admission to the United Kingdom in reliance on [paragraph (5)(b), (c) or (e)][10]; and

(b) if P were in the United Kingdom, P would have a derived right of residence by virtue of regulation 15A(7)(b)(ii).

(7) Where this paragraph applies a person ('P') will only be regarded as meeting the criteria in [paragraph (5)(b), (c) or (e)][10] where P –

(a) is accompanying the person with whom P would on admission to the United Kingdom jointly share care responsibility for the purpose of regulation 15A(7)(b)(ii); or

(b) has previously resided in the United Kingdom pursuant to [regulation 15A(2), (4) or (4A)][10] as a joint primary carer and seeks admission to the United Kingdom in order to reside there again on the same basis.][6]

[(8)][7] But this regulation is subject to regulations 19(1) and (2).

AMENDMENT

[1] Words inserted: Immigration (European Economic Area) (Amendment) Regulations 2012, SI 2012/1547, reg 3, Sch 1, para 4(a)(i), with effect from 16 July 2012.

[2] Words inserted: Immigration (European Economic Area) (Amendment) Regulations 2012, SI 2012/1547, reg 3, Sch 1, para 4(a)(ii), with effect from 16 July 2012.

[3] Words inserted: Immigration (European Economic Area) (Amendment) Regulations 2012, SI 2012/1547, reg 3, Sch 1, para 4(b), with effect from 16 July 2012.

[4] Word omitted: Immigration (European Economic Area) (Amendment) Regulations 2012, SI 2012/1547, reg 3, Sch 1, para 4(c)(i), with effect from 16 July 2012.

Appendix 2
England: Homelessness

[5] Sub-paragraph inserted: Immigration (European Economic Area) (Amendment) Regulations 2012, SI 2012/1547, reg 3, Sch 1, para 4(c)(ii), with effect from 16 July 2012.

[6] Paragraphs inserted: Immigration (European Economic Area) (Amendment) Regulations 2012, SI 2012/1547, reg 3, Sch 1, para 4(d), with effect from 16 July 2012.

[7] Paragraph renumbered (8): Immigration (European Economic Area) (Amendment) Regulations 2012, SI 2012/1547, reg 3, Sch 1, para 4(d), with effect from 16 July 2012.

[8] Words substituted: Immigration (European Economic Area) (Amendment) (No 2) Regulations 2012, SI 2012/2560, regs 1, 2, Sch, para 2(a), with effect from 8 November 2012.

[9] Words substituted and sub-paragraph inserted: Immigration (European Economic Area) (Amendment) (No 2) Regulations 2012, SI 2012/2560, regs 1, 2, Sch, para 2(b), with effect from 8 November 2012.

[10] Words substituted: Immigration (European Economic Area) (Amendment) (No 2) Regulations 2012, SI 2012/2560, regs 1, 2, Sch, para 2(c), (d), with effect from 8 November 2012.

12 Issue of EEA family permit

(1) An entry clearance officer must issue an EEA family permit to a person who applies for one if the person is a family member of an EEA national and –

    (a)   the EEA national –
        (i)   is residing in the UK in accordance with these Regulations; or
        (ii)   will be travelling to the United Kingdom within six months of the date of the application and will be an EEA national residing in the United Kingdom in accordance with these Regulations on arrival in the United Kingdom; and
    [(b)   the family member will be accompanying the EEA national to the United Kingdom or joining the EEA national there.][1]

[(1A) An entry clearance officer must issue an EEA family permit to a person who applies and provides proof that, at the time at which he first intends to use the EEA family permit, he –

    (a)   would be entitled to be admitted to the United Kingdom by virtue of regulation 11(5); and
    (b)   will (save in the case of a person who would be entitled to be admitted to the United Kingdom by virtue of regulation 11(5)(a)) be accompanying to, or joining in, the United Kingdom any person from whom his right to be admitted to the United Kingdom under regulation 11(5) will be derived.

(1B) An entry clearance officer must issue an EEA family permit to a family member who has retained the right of residence.][2]

(2) An entry clearance officer may issue an EEA family permit to an extended family member of an EEA national who applies for one if –

    (a)   the relevant EEA national satisfies the condition in paragraph (1)(a);
    (b)   the extended family member wishes to accompany the relevant EEA national to the United Kingdom or to join him there; and

(c)   in all the circumstances, it appears to the entry clearance officer appropriate to issue the EEA family permit.

(3) Where an entry clearance officer receives an application under paragraph (2) he shall undertake an extensive examination of the personal circumstances of the applicant and if he refuses the application shall give reasons justifying the refusal unless this is contrary to the interests of national security.

(4) An EEA family permit issued under this regulation shall be issued free of charge and as soon as possible.

(5) But an EEA family permit shall not be issued under this regulation if the applicant or the EEA national concerned [is not entitled to be admitted to the United Kingdom as a result of regulation 19(1A) or falls to be excluded in accordance with regulation 19(1B)][3].

[(6) An EEA family permit will not be issued under this regulation to a person ('A') who is the spouse, civil partner or durable partner of a person ('B') where a spouse, civil partner or durable partner of A or B holds a valid EEA family permit.][4]

AMENDMENT

[1] Sub-paragraph substituted: Immigration (European Economic Area) (Amendment) Regulations 2011, SI 2011/1247, reg 2(1), (4), with effect from 2 June 2011.

[2] Paragraphs inserted: Immigration (European Economic Area) (Amendment) Regulations 2012, SI 2012/1547, reg 3, Sch 1, para 5(a), with effect from 16 July 2012.

[3] Words substituted: Immigration (European Economic Area) (Amendment) Regulations 2012, SI 2012/1547, reg 3, Sch 1, para 5(b), with effect from 16 July 2012.

[4] Paragraph inserted: Immigration (European Economic Area) (Amendment) Regulations 2012, SI 2012/1547, reg 3, Sch 1, para 5(c), with effect from 16 July 2012.

13 Initial right of residence

(1) An EEA national is entitled to reside in the United Kingdom for a period not exceeding three months beginning on the date on which he is admitted to the United Kingdom provided that he holds a valid national identity card or passport issued by an EEA State.

(2) A family member of an EEA national [or a family member who has retained the right of residence who is][1] residing in the United Kingdom under paragraph (1) who is not himself an EEA national is entitled to reside in the United Kingdom provided that he holds a valid passport.

[(3) An EEA national or his family member who becomes an unreasonable burden on the social assistance system of the United Kingdom will cease to have a right to reside under this regulation.

(4) A person who otherwise satisfies the criteria in this regulation will not be entitled to reside in the United Kingdom under this regulation where the Secretary of State has made a decision under regulation 19(3)(b), 20(1) or 20A(1).][2]

AMENDMENT

[1] Words inserted: Immigration (European Economic Area) (Amendment) Regulations 2012, SI 2012/1547, reg 3, Sch 1, para 6(a), with effect from 16 July 2012.

[2] Paragraphs (3) and (4) substituted for paragraph (3): Immigration (European Economic Area) (Amendment) Regulations 2012, SI 2012/1547, reg 3, Sch 1, para 6(b), with effect from 16 July 2012.

14 Extended right of residence

(1) A qualified person is entitled to reside in the United Kingdom for so long as he remains a qualified person.

(2) A family member of a qualified person residing in the United Kingdom under paragraph (1) or of an EEA national with a permanent right of residence under regulation 15 is entitled to reside in the United Kingdom for so long as he remains the family member of the qualified person or EEA national.

(3) A family member who has retained the right of residence is entitled to reside in the United Kingdom for so long as he remains a family member who has retained the right of residence.

(4) A right to reside under this regulation is in addition to any right a person may have to reside in the United Kingdom under regulation 13 or 15.

[(5) A person who otherwise satisfies the criteria in this regulation will not be entitled to a right to reside in the United Kingdom under this regulation where the Secretary of State has made a decision under regulation 19(3)(b), 20(1) or 20A(1).][1]

AMENDMENT

[1] Paragraph substituted: Immigration (European Economic Area) (Amendment) Regulations 2012, SI 2012/1547, reg 3, Sch 1, para 7, with effect from 16 July 2012.

15 Permanent right of residence

(1) The following persons shall acquire the right to reside in the United Kingdom permanently –

  (a) an EEA national who has resided in the United Kingdom in accordance with these Regulations for a continuous period of five years;
  (b) a family member of an EEA national who is not himself an EEA national but who has resided in the United Kingdom with the EEA national in accordance with these Regulations for a continuous period of five years;
  (c) a worker or self-employed person who has ceased activity;
  (d) the family member of a worker or self-employed person who has ceased activity;
  (e) a person who was the family member of a worker or self-employed person where –
       (i)   the worker or self-employed person has died;

   (ii)   the family member resided with him immediately before his death; and

   (iii) the worker or self-employed person had resided continuously in the United Kingdom for at least the two years immediately before his death or the death was the result of an accident at work or an occupational disease;

(f)   a person who –

   (i)   has resided in the United Kingdom in accordance with these Regulations for a continuous period of five years; and

   (ii)   was, at the end of that period, a family member who has retained the right of residence.

[(1A) Residence in the United Kingdom as a result of a derivative right of residence does not constitute residence for the purpose of this regulation.][1]

(2) [The][2] right of permanent residence under this regulation shall be lost only through absence from the United Kingdom for a period exceeding two consecutive years.

[(3) A person who satisfies the criteria in this regulation will not be entitled to a permanent right to reside in the United Kingdom where the Secretary of State has made a decision under regulation 19(3)(b), 20(1) or 20A(1).][3]

AMENDMENT

[1] Paragraph inserted: Immigration (European Economic Area) (Amendment) Regulations 2012, SI 2012/1547, reg 3, Sch 1, para 8(a), with effect from 16 July 2012.

[2] Word substituted: Immigration (European Economic Area) (Amendment) Regulations 2012, SI 2012/1547, reg 3, Sch 1, para 8(b), with effect from 16 July 2012.

[3] Paragraph substituted: Immigration (European Economic Area) (Amendment) Regulations 2012, SI 2012/1547, reg 3, Sch 1, para 8(c), with effect from 16 July 2012.

[15A Derivative right of residence

(1) A person ('P') who is not [an exempt person][2] and who satisfies the criteria in paragraph (2), (3), (4)[, (4A)][3] or (5) of this regulation is entitled to a derivative right to reside in the United Kingdom for as long as P satisfies the relevant criteria.

(2) P satisfies the criteria in this paragraph if –

(a)   P is the primary carer of an EEA national ('the relevant EEA national'); and

(b)   the relevant EEA national –

   (i)   is under the age of 18;

   (ii)   is residing in the United Kingdom as a self-sufficient person; and

   (iii) would be unable to remain in the United Kingdom if P were required to leave.

(3) P satisfies the criteria in this paragraph if –

(a)   P is the child of an EEA national ('the EEA national parent');

(b)   P resided in the United Kingdom at a time when the EEA national parent was residing in the United Kingdom as a worker; and

(c)   P is in education in the United Kingdom and was in education there at a time when the EEA national parent was in the United Kingdom.

(4) P satisfies the criteria in this paragraph if –

(a)   P is the primary carer of a person meeting the criteria in paragraph (3) ('the relevant person'); and

(b)   the relevant person would be unable to continue to be educated in the United Kingdom if P were required to leave.

[(4A) P satisfies the criteria in this paragraph if –

(a)   P is the primary carer of a British citizen ('the relevant British citizen');

(b)   the relevant British citizen is residing in the United Kingdom; and

(c)   the relevant British citizen would be unable to reside in the UK or in another EEA State if P were required to leave.]⁴

(5) P satisfies the criteria in this paragraph if –

(a)   P is under the age of 18;

(b)   P's primary carer is entitled to a derivative right to reside in the United Kingdom by virtue of paragraph (2) or (4);

(c)   P does not have leave to enter, or remain in, the United Kingdom; and

(d)   requiring P to leave the United Kingdom would prevent P's primary carer from residing in the United Kingdom.

(6) For the purpose of this regulation –

(a)   'education' excludes nursery education; ...⁵

(b)   'worker' does not include a jobseeker or a person who falls to be regarded as a worker by virtue of [regulation 6(2); and]⁵.

[(c)   'an exempt person' is a person –
   (i)   who has a right to reside in the United Kingdom as a result of any other provision of these Regulations;
   (ii)   who has a right of abode in the United Kingdom by virtue of section 2 of the 1971 Act;
   (iii)   to whom section 8 of the 1971 Act, or any order made under subsection (2) of that provision, applies; or
   (iv)   who has indefinite leave to enter or remain in the United Kingdom.]⁵

(7) P is to be regarded as a 'primary carer' of another person if –

(a)   P is a direct relative or a legal guardian of that person; and

(b)   P –
   (i)   is the person who has primary responsibility for that person's care; or
   [(ii)   shares equally the responsibility for that person's care with one other person who is not an exempt person.]⁶

(7A) Where P is to be regarded as a primary carer of another person by virtue of paragraph (7)(b)(ii) the criteria in paragraphs (2)(b)(iii), (4)(b) and (4A)(c) shall be considered on the basis that both P and the person with whom care responsibility is shared would be required to leave the United Kingdom.

(7B) Paragraph (7A) does not apply if the person with whom care responsibility is shared acquired a derivative right to reside in the United Kingdom as a result of this regulation prior to P assuming equal care responsibility.

(8) P will not be regarded as having responsibility for a person's care for the purpose of paragraph (7) on the sole basis of a financial contribution towards that person's care.

(9) A person who otherwise satisfies the criteria in paragraph (2), (3), (4)[, (4A)]⁶ or (5) will not be entitled to a derivative right to reside in the United Kingdom where the Secretary of State has made a decision under regulation 19(3)(b), 20(1) or 20A(1).]¹

AMENDMENT

¹ Regulation inserted: Immigration (European Economic Area) (Amendment) Regulations 2012, SI 2012/1547, reg 3, Sch 1, para 9, with effect from 16 July 2012.

² Words substituted: Immigration (European Economic Area) (Amendment) (No 2) Regulations 2012, SI 2012/2560, regs 1, 2, Sch, para 3(a)(i), with effect from 8 November 2012.

³ Paragraph number inserted: Immigration (European Economic Area) (Amendment) (No 2) Regulations 2012, SI 2012/2560, regs 1, 2, Sch, para 3(a)(ii), with effect from 8 November 2012.

⁴ Paragraph inserted: Immigration (European Economic Area) (Amendment) (No 2) Regulations 2012, SI 2012/2560, regs 1, 2, Sch, para 3(b), with effect from 8 November 2012.

⁵ Word repealed, words substituted and sub-paragraph inserted: Immigration (European Economic Area) (Amendment) (No 2) Regulations 2012, SI 2012/2560, regs 1, 2, Sch, para 3(c)(i), (ii), with effect from 8 November 2012.

⁶ Sub-paragraph substituted, paragraphs inserted and paragraph number inserted: Immigration (European Economic Area) (Amendment) (No 2) Regulations 2012, SI 2012/2560, regs 1, 2, Sch, para 3(d)–(f), with effect from 8 November 2012.

[15B Continuation of a right of residence

(1) This regulation applies during any period in which, but for the effect of regulation 13(4), 14(5), 15(3) or 15A(9), a person ('P') who is in the United Kingdom would be entitled to reside here pursuant to these Regulations.

(2) Where this regulation applies, any right of residence will (notwithstanding the effect of regulation 13(4), 14(5), 15(3) or 15A(9)) be deemed to continue during any period in which –

    (a)   an appeal under regulation 26 could be brought, while P is in the United Kingdom, against a relevant decision (ignoring any possibility of an appeal out of time with permission); or

    (b)   an appeal under regulation 26 against a relevant decision, brought while P is in the United Kingdom, is pending (within the meaning of section 104 of the 2002 Act).

(3) Periods during which residence pursuant to regulation 14 is deemed to continue as a result of paragraph (2) will not constitute residence for the purpose of regulation 15 unless and until –

(a)   a relevant decision is withdrawn by the Secretary of State; or
(b)   an appeal against a relevant decision is allowed and that appeal is finally determined (within the meaning of section 104 of the 2002 Act).

(4) Periods during which residence is deemed to continue as a result of paragraph (2) will not constitute residence for the purpose of regulation 21(4)(a) unless and until –

(a)   a relevant decision is withdrawn by the Secretary of State; or
(b)   an appeal against a relevant decision is allowed and that appeal is finally determined (within the meaning of section 104 of the 2002 Act).

(5) A 'relevant decision' for the purpose of this regulation means a decision pursuant to regulation 19(3)(b), 20(1) or 20A(1) which would, but for the effect of paragraph (2), prevent P from residing in the United Kingdom pursuant to these Regulations.][1]

AMENDMENT

[1] Regulation inserted: Immigration (European Economic Area) (Amendment) Regulations 2012, SI 2012/1547, reg 3, Sch 1, para 10, with effect from 16 July 2012.

*****

Allocation of Housing and Homelessness (Eligibility) (England) Regulations 2006

SI 2006/1294

Made	*11th May 2006*
Laid before Parliament	*11th May 2006*
Coming into force	*1st June 2006*

The Secretary of State, in exercise of the powers conferred by sections 160A(3) and (5), 172(4), 185(2) and (3) and 215(2) of the Housing Act 1996 makes the following Regulations:

1 Citation, commencement and application

(1) These Regulations may be cited as the Allocation of Housing and Homelessness (Eligibility) (England) Regulations 2006 and shall come into force on 1st June 2006.

(2) These Regulations apply to England only.

2 Interpretation

(1) In these Regulations –

'the 1996 Act' means the Housing Act 1996;
['the Accession Regulations 2004' means the Accession (Immigration and Worker Registration) Regulations 2004;
'the Accession Regulations 2006' means the Accession (Immigration and Worker Registration) Regulations 2006;][1]
'the EEA Regulations' means the Immigration (European Economic Area) Regulations 2006;
'the Immigration Rules' means the rules laid down as mentioned in section 3(2) of the Immigration Act 1971 (general provisions for regulation and control);
'the Refugee Convention' means the Convention relating to the Status of Refugees done at Geneva on 28th July 1951, as extended by Article 1(2) of the Protocol relating to the Status of Refugees done at New York on 31st January 1967; and
'sponsor' means a person who has given an undertaking in writing for the purposes of the Immigration Rules to be responsible for the maintenance and accommodation of another person.

(2) For the purposes of these Regulations –

(a) 'jobseeker', 'self-employed person', and 'worker' have the same meaning as for the purposes of the definition of a 'qualified person' in regulation 6(1) of the EEA Regulations; and

(b)   subject to paragraph (3), references to the family member of a jobseeker, self-employed person or worker shall be construed in accordance with regulation 7 of those Regulations.

(3) For the purposes of regulations 4(2)(d) and 6(2)(d) 'family member' does not include a person who is treated as a family member by virtue of regulation 7(3) of the EEA Regulations.

[(4) For the purposes of regulations 4(2)(h) and 6(2)(h), 'the relevant period' means the period beginning at 4 p.m. on 25th July 2006 and ending on 31st January 2007.][2]

AMENDMENT

[1] Words substituted: Allocation of Housing and Homelessness (Eligibility) (England) (Amendment) (No 2) Regulations 2006, SI 2006/3340, reg 2(1), (2).

[2] Paragraph inserted: The Allocation of Housing and Homelessness (Eligibility) (England) (Amendment) Regulations 2006, SI 2006/2007, reg 2(1), (2).

3 Persons subject to immigration control who are eligible for an allocation of housing accommodation

The following classes of persons subject to immigration control are persons who are eligible for an allocation of housing accommodation under Part 6 of the 1996 Act –

(a)   Class A – a person who is recorded by the Secretary of State as a refugee within the definition in Article 1 of the Refugee Convention and who has leave to enter or remain in the United Kingdom;

(b)   Class B – a person –

    (i)   who has exceptional leave to enter or remain in the United Kingdom granted outside the provisions of the Immigration Rules; and

    (ii)   who is not subject to a condition requiring him to maintain and accommodate himself, and any person who is dependent on him, without recourse to public funds;

(c)   Class C – a person who is habitually resident in the United Kingdom, the Channel Islands, the Isle of Man or the Republic of Ireland and whose leave to enter or remain in the United Kingdom is not subject to any limitation or condition, other than a person –

    (i)   who has been given leave to enter or remain in the United Kingdom upon an undertaking given by his sponsor;

    (ii)   who has been resident in the United Kingdom, the Channel Islands, the Isle of Man or the Republic of Ireland for less than five years beginning on the date of entry or the date on which his sponsor gave the undertaking in respect of him, whichever date is the later; and

    (iii)   whose sponsor or, where there is more than one sponsor, at least one of whose sponsors, is still alive; and

[(d)   Class D – a person who has humanitarian protection granted under the Immigration Rules].[1]

AMENDMENT

[1] Paragraph substituted: Allocation of Housing and Homelessness (Miscellaneous Provisions) (England) Regulations 2006, SI 2006/2527, reg 2(1), (2).

4 Other persons from abroad who are ineligible for an allocation of housing accommodation

(1) A person who is not subject to immigration control is to be treated as a person from abroad who is ineligible for an allocation of housing accommodation under Part 6 of the 1996 Act if –

    (a)   subject to paragraph (2), he is not habitually resident in the United Kingdom, the Channel Islands, the Isle of Man, or the Republic of Ireland;

    (b)   his only right to reside in the United Kingdom –
        (i)   is derived from his status as a jobseeker or the family member of a jobseeker; or
        (ii)   is an initial right to reside for a period not exceeding three months under regulation 13 of the EEA Regulations; or
        [(iii)   is a derivative right to reside to which he is entitled under regulation 15A(1) of the EEA Regulations, but only in a case where the right exists under that regulation because the applicant satisfies the criteria in regulation 15A(4A) of those Regulations; or
        (iv)   is derived from Article 20 of the Treaty on the Functioning of the European Union, in a case where the right to reside arises because a British citizen would otherwise be deprived of the genuine enjoyment of the substance of their rights as a European Union citizen; or][6]

    [(c)   his only right to reside in the Channel Islands, the Isle of Man or the Republic of Ireland –
        (i)   is a right equivalent to one of those mentioned in sub-paragraphs (b)(i), (ii) or (iii) which is derived from the Treaty on the Functioning of the European Union; or
        (ii)   is derived from Article 20 of the Treaty on the Functioning of the European Union, in a case where the right to reside –
            (a)   in the Republic of Ireland arises because an Irish citizen, or
            (b)   in the Channel Islands or the Isle of Man arises because a British citizen also entitled to reside there
    would otherwise be deprived of the genuine enjoyment of the substance of their rights as a European Union citizen.][6]

(2) The following are not to be treated as persons from abroad who are ineligible for an allocation of housing accommodation pursuant to paragraph (1)(a) –

    (a)   a worker;
    (b)   a self-employed person;

[(c)   a person who is treated as a worker for the purpose of the definition of 'qualified person' in regulation 6(1) of the EEA Regulations pursuant to either –

    (i)   regulation 5 of the Accession Regulations 2004 (application of the 2006 Regulations in relation to accession State worker requiring registration), or

    (ii)   regulation 6 of the Accession Regulations 2006 (right of residence of an accession State national subject to worker authorisation);][1]

(d)   a person who is the family member of a person specified in sub-paragraphs (a)–(c);

(e)   a person with a right to reside permanently in the United Kingdom by virtue of regulation 15(c), (d) or (e) of the EEA Regulations;

(f)   a person who left the territory of Montserrat after 1st November 1995 because of the effect on that territory of a volcanic eruption; ...[2]

(g)   a person who is in the United Kingdom as a result of his deportation, expulsion or other removal by compulsion of law from another country to the United Kingdom[; ...][3]

[(h)   during the relevant period, a person who left Lebanon on or after 12th July 2006 because of the armed conflict there.][4]; [and

(i)   a person who –

    (i)   arrived in Great Britain on or after 28th February 2009 but before 18th March 2011;

    (ii)   immediately before arriving in Great Britain had been resident in Zimbabwe; and

    (iii)   before leaving Zimbabwe, had accepted an offer, made by Her Majesty's Government, to assist that person to settle in the United Kingdom].[5]

AMENDMENTS

[1] Paragraph substituted: Allocation of Housing and Homelessness (Eligibility) (England) (Amendment) (No 2) Regulations 2006, SI 2006/3340, reg 2(1), (3).

[2] Word omitted: The Allocation of Housing and Homelessness (Eligibility) (England) (Amendment) Regulations 2006, SI 2006/2007, reg 2(1), (3).

[3] Word omitted: The Allocation of Housing and Homelessness (Eligibility) (England) (Amendment) Regulations 2006, SI 2006/2007, reg 2(1), (4); word omitted revoked: SI 2009/358, reg 2(1), (2).

[4] Sub-paragraph inserted: The Allocation of Housing and Homelessness (Eligibility) (England) (Amendment) Regulations 2006, SI 2006/2007, reg 2(1), (5).

[5] Paragraph inserted: Allocation of Housing and Homelessness (Eligibility) (England) (Amendment) Regulations 2009, SI 2009/358, reg 2(1), (3).

[6] Sub-paragraphs (1)(b)(iii), (iv) inserted and paragraph (1)(c) substituted: Allocation of Housing and Homelessness (Eligibility) (England) (Amendment) Regulations 2012, SI 2012/2588, art 2(1)–(3).

5 Persons subject to immigration control who are eligible for housing assistance

(1) The following classes of persons subject to immigration control are persons who are eligible for housing assistance under Part 7 of the 1996 Act –

- (a) Class A – a person who is recorded by the Secretary of State as a refugee within the definition in Article 1 of the Refugee Convention and who has leave to enter or remain in the United Kingdom;
- (b) Class B – a person –
  - (i) who has exceptional leave to enter or remain in the United Kingdom granted outside the provisions of the Immigration Rules; and
  - (ii) whose leave to enter or remain is not subject to a condition requiring him to maintain and accommodate himself, and any person who is dependent on him, without recourse to public funds;
- (c) Class C – a person who is habitually resident in the United Kingdom, the Channel Islands, the Isle of Man or the Republic of Ireland and whose leave to enter or remain in the United Kingdom is not subject to any limitation or condition, other than a person –
  - (i) who has been given leave to enter or remain in the United Kingdom upon an undertaking given by his sponsor;
  - (ii) who has been resident in the United Kingdom, the Channel Islands, the Isle of Man or the Republic of Ireland for less than five years beginning on the date of entry or the date on which his sponsor gave the undertaking in respect of him, whichever date is the later; and
  - (iii) whose sponsor or, where there is more than one sponsor, at least one of whose sponsors, is still alive;
- [(d) Class D – a person who has humanitarian protection granted under the Immigration Rules; and][1]
- (e) Class E – a person who is an asylum-seeker whose claim for asylum is recorded by the Secretary of State as having been made before 3rd April 2000 and in the circumstances mentioned in one of the following paragraphs –
  - (i) on arrival (other than on his re-entry) in the United Kingdom from a country outside the United Kingdom, the Channel Islands, the Isle of Man or the Republic of Ireland;
  - (ii) within three months from the day on which the Secretary of State made a relevant declaration, and the applicant was in Great Britain on the day on which the declaration was made; or
  - (iii) on or before 4th February 1996 by an applicant who was on 4th February 1996 entitled to benefit under regulation 7A of the Housing Benefit (General) Regulations 1987 (persons from abroad).

(2) For the purpose of paragraph (1)(e) –

- (a) 'asylum-seeker' means a person who is at least 18 years old, who is in the United Kingdom, and who has made a claim for asylum;

(b) 'claim for asylum' means a claim that it would be contrary to the United Kingdom's obligations under the Refugee Convention for the claimant to be removed from, or required to leave, the United Kingdom;

(c) 'relevant declaration' means a declaration to the effect that the country of which the applicant is a national is subject to such a fundamental change of circumstances that the Secretary of State would not normally order the return of a person to that country; and

(d) subject to paragraph (3), a person ceases to be an asylum-seeker when his claim for asylum is recorded by the Secretary of State as having been decided (other than on appeal) or abandoned.

(3) For the purposes of paragraph (1)(e)(iii), a person does not cease to be an asylum-seeker as mentioned in paragraph (2)(d) while he is eligible for housing benefit by virtue of –

(a) regulation 10(6) of the Housing Benefit Regulations 2006; or

(b) regulation 10(6) of the Housing Benefit (Persons who have attained the qualifying age for state pension credit) Regulations 2006,

as modified in both cases by paragraph 6 of Schedule 3 to the Housing Benefit and Council Tax Benefit (Consequential Provisions) Regulations 2006.

AMENDMENT

[1] Sub-paragraph substituted: Allocation of Housing and Homelessness (Miscellaneous Provisions) (England) Regulations 2006, SI 2006/2527, reg 2(1), (3).

6 Other persons from abroad who are ineligible for housing assistance

(1) A person who is not subject to immigration control is to be treated as a person from abroad who is ineligible for housing assistance under Part 7 of the 1996 Act if –

(a) subject to paragraph (2), he is not habitually resident in the United Kingdom, the Channel Islands, the Isle of Man, or the Republic of Ireland;

(b) his only right to reside in the United Kingdom –
 (i) is derived from his status as a jobseeker or the family member of a jobseeker; or
 (ii) is an initial right to reside for a period not exceeding three months under regulation 13 of the EEA Regulations; or
 [(iii) is a derivative right to reside to which he is entitled under regulation 15A(1) of the EEA Regulations, but only in a case where the right exists under that regulation because the applicant satisfies the criteria in regulation 15A(4A) of those Regulations; or
 (iv) is derived from Article 20 of the Treaty on the Functioning of the European Union in a case where the right to reside arises because a British citizen would otherwise be deprived of the genuine enjoyment of the substance of the rights attaching to the status of European Union citizen; or][6]

[(c)   his only right to reside in the Channel Islands, the Isle of Man or the Republic of Ireland –

(i)   is a right equivalent to one of those mentioned in sub-paragraph (b)(i),(ii) or (iii) which is derived from the Treaty on the Functioning of the European Union; or

(ii)   is derived from Article 20 of the Treaty on the Functioning of the European Union, in a case where the right to reside –

(a)   in the Republic of Ireland arises because an Irish citizen, or

(b)   in the Channel Islands or the Isle of Man arises because a British citizen also entitled to reside there

would otherwise be deprived of the genuine enjoyment of the substance of their rights as a European Union citizen.][6]

(2) The following are not to be treated as persons from abroad who are ineligible for housing assistance pursuant to paragraph (1)(a) –

(a)   a worker;

(b)   a self-employed person;

[(c)   a person who is treated as a worker for the purpose of the definition of 'qualified person' in regulation 6(1) of the EEA Regulations pursuant to either –

(i)   regulation 5 of the Accession Regulations 2004 (application of the 2006 Regulations in relation to accession State worker requiring registration), or

(ii)   regulation 6 of the Accession Regulations 2006 (right of residence of an accession State national subject to worker authorisation);][1]

(d)   a person who is the family member of a person specified in sub-paragraphs (a)–(c);

(e)   a person with a right to reside permanently in the United Kingdom by virtue of regulation 15(c), (d) or (e) of the EEA Regulations;

(f)   a person who left the territory of Montserrat after 1st November 1995 because of the effect on that territory of a volcanic eruption; ...[2]

(g)   a person who is in the United Kingdom as a result of his deportation, expulsion or other removal by compulsion of law from another country to the United Kingdom[; ...][3]

[(h)   during the relevant period, a person who left Lebanon on or after 12th July 2006 because of the armed conflict there.][4];[and

(i)   a person who –

(i)   arrived in Great Britain on or after 28th February 2009 but before 18th March 2011;

(ii)   immediately before arriving in Great Britain had been resident in Zimbabwe; and

(iii)   before leaving Zimbabwe, had accepted an offer, made by Her Majesty's Government, to assist that person to settle in the United Kingdom].[5]

AMENDMENTS

[1] Paragraph substituted: Allocation of Housing and Homelessness (Eligibility) (England) (Amendment) (No 2) Regulations 2006, SI 2006/3340, reg 2(1), (4).

Appendix 2
England: Homelessness

[2] Word omitted: The Allocation of Housing and Homelessness (Eligibility) (England) (Amendment) Regulations 2006, SI 2006/2007, reg 2(1), (6).

[3] Word omitted inserted: The Allocation of Housing and Homelessness (Eligibility) (England) (Amendment) Regulations 2006, SI 2006/2007, reg 2(1), (7); word omitted revoked: SI 2009/358, reg 2(1), (4).

[4] Sub-paragraph inserted: The Allocation of Housing and Homelessness (Eligibility) (England) (Amendment) Regulations 2006, SI 2006/2007, reg 2(1), (8).

[5] Sub-paragraph inserted: Allocation of Housing and Homelessness (Eligibility) (England) (Amendment) Regulations 2009, SI 2009/358, reg 2(1), (5).

[6] Sub-paragraphs (1)(b)(iii), (iv) inserted and paragraph (1)(c) substituted: Allocation of Housing and Homelessness (Eligibility) (England) (Amendment) Regulations 2012, SI 2012/2588, art 2(1), (4), (5).

7 Revocation

Subject to regulation 8, the Regulations specified in column (1) of the Schedule are revoked to the extent mentioned in column (3) of the Schedule.

8 Transitional provisions

The revocations made by these Regulations shall not have effect in relation to an applicant whose application for –

(a)   an allocation of housing accommodation under Part 6 of the 1996 Act; or

(b)   housing assistance under Part 7 of the 1996 Act,

was made before 1st June 2006.

Schedule

Regulation 7

Revocation schedule

(1)	(2)	(3)
Regulations Revoked	*References*	*Extent of revocation*
The Homelessness (England) Regulations 2000	SI 2000/701	The whole Regulations
The Allocation of Housing (England) Regulations 2002	SI 2002/3264	Regulations 4 and 5
The Allocation of Housing and Homelessness (Amendment) (England) Regulations 2004	SI 2004/1235	The whole Regulations

Revocation schedule

(1)	(2)	(3)
Regulations Revoked	*References*	*Extent of revocation*
The Allocation of Housing and Homelessness (Amendment) (England) Regulations 2006	SI 2006/1093	The whole Regulations

Allocation of Housing and Homelessness (Miscellaneous Provisions) (England) Regulations 2006

SI 2006/2527

Made	*14th September 2006*
Laid before Parliament	*18th September 2006*
Coming into force	*9th October 2006*

The Secretary of State, in exercise of the powers conferred by sections 160A(3), 172(4), 185(2), 198(4) and 215(2) of the Housing Act 1996, makes the following Regulations:

1 Citation, commencement, interpretation and application

(1) These Regulations may be cited as the Allocation of Housing and Homelessness (Miscellaneous Provisions) (England) Regulations 2006 and shall come into force on 9th October 2006.

(2) In these Regulations, 'the 1996 Act' means the Housing Act 1996.

(3) These Regulations apply to England only.

2 Amendment of the classes of person from abroad who are eligible for an allocation of accommodation and for housing assistance

(1) The Allocation of Housing and Homelessness (Eligibility) (England) Regulations 2006 are amended as follows.

(2) For regulation 3(d), substitute –

> '(d) Class D – a person who has humanitarian protection granted under the Immigration Rules.'.

(3) For regulation 5(1)(d), substitute –

> '(d) Class D – a person who has humanitarian protection granted under the Immigration Rules; and'.

3 Prescribed period for referral of case to another local housing authority

For the purposes of section 198(4)(b) of the 1996 Act (referral of case to another local housing authority), the prescribed period is the aggregate of –

    (a)   five years; and

    (b)   the period beginning on the date of the previous application and ending on the date on which the applicant was first placed in pursuance of that application in accommodation in the district of the authority to whom the application is now made.

4 Transitional provisions

The amendments made by these Regulations shall not have effect in relation to an applicant whose application for –

(a)   an allocation of housing accommodation under Part 6 of the 1996 Act; or

(b)   housing assistance under Part 7 of the 1996 Act,

was made before 9th October 2006.

The Localism Act 2011 (Commencement No 2 and Transitional Provisions) (England) Order 2012

SI 2012/2599

Made   *11th October 2012*

The Secretary of State, in exercise of the power conferred by section 240(2) and (7) of the Localism Act 2011(1), makes the following Order:

1 Citation and interpretation

(1) This Order may be cited as the Localism Act 2011 (Commencement No. 2 and Transitional Provisions) (England) Order 2012.

(2) In this Order–

"the Act" means the Localism Act 2011;
"the 1996 Act" means the Housing Act 1996(2); and
"commencement date" means 9th November 2012.

2 Commencement of provisions regarding duties to homeless persons

Sections 148 and 149 of the Act shall come into force for England only on the commencement date.

3 Transitional provisions

The amendments made by sections 148 and 149 of the Act do not apply to a case where–

(a)   a person ("the applicant") has applied to a local housing authority for accommodation, or for assistance in obtaining accommodation, under Part 7 of the 1996 Act; and

(b)   a duty of the local housing authority to secure that accommodation is available for the applicant's occupation under Part 7 of the 1996 Act(3) including on an interim or temporary basis has arisen and has not ceased,

before the commencement date.

Homelessness (Suitability of Accommodation) (England) Order 2012

SI 2012/2601

Made	*11th October 2012*
Laid before Parliament	*17th October 2012*
Coming into force	*9th November 2012*

The Secretary of State in exercise of the powers conferred by sections 210(2)(a), (2)(b) and 215(2) of the Housing Act 1996, makes the following Order:

1 Citation, commencement and application

(1) This Order may be cited as the Homelessness (Suitability of Accommodation) (England) Order 2012 and comes into force on 9th November 2012.

(2) This Order applies in relation to England only.

2 Matters to be taken into account in determining whether accommodation is suitable for a person

In determining whether accommodation is suitable for a person, the local housing authority must take into account the location of the accommodation, including –

(a) where the accommodation is situated outside the district of the local housing authority, the distance of the accommodation from the district of the authority;

(b) the significance of any disruption which would be caused by the location of the accommodation to the employment, caring responsibilities or education of the person or members of the person's household;

(c) the proximity and accessibility of the accommodation to medical facilities and other support which –

  (i) are currently used by or provided to the person or members of the person's household; and

  (ii) are essential to the well-being of the person or members of the person's household; and

(d) the proximity and accessibility of the accommodation to local services, amenities and transport.

3 Circumstances in which accommodation is not to be regarded as suitable for a person

For the purposes of a private rented sector offer under section 193(7F) of the Housing Act 1996 accommodation shall not be regarded as suitable where one or more of the following apply –

Appendix 2
England: Homelessness

(a)   the local housing authority are of the view the accommodation is not in a reasonable physical condition; or

(b)   the local housing authority are of the view that any electrical equipment supplied with the accommodation does not meet the requirements of regulations 5 and 7 of the Electrical Equipment (Safety) Regulations 1994; or

(c)   the local housing authority are of the view the landlord has not taken reasonable fire safety precautions with the accommodation and any furnishings supplied with it;

(d)   the local housing authority are of the view the landlord has not taken reasonable precautions to prevent the possibility of carbon monoxide poisoning in the accommodation;

(e)   the local housing authority are of the view the landlord is not a fit and proper person to act in the capacity of landlord, having considered if the person has –

   (i)   committed any offence involving fraud or other dishonesty, or violence or illegal drugs, or any offence listed in Schedule 3 to the Sexual Offences Act 2003 (offences attracting notification requirements);

   (ii)   practised unlawful discrimination on grounds of sex, race, age, disability, marriage or civil partnership, pregnancy or maternity, religion or belief, sexual orientation, gender identity or gender reassignment in, or in connection with, the carrying out of any business;

   (iii)   contravened any provision of the law relating to housing (including landlord or tenant law); or,

   (iv)   acted otherwise than in accordance with any applicable code of practice for the management of a house in multiple occupation, approved under section 233 of the Housing Act 2004;

(f)   the accommodation is a house in multiple occupation subject to licensing under section 55 of the Housing Act 2004 and is not licensed;

(g)   the accommodation is a house in multiple occupation subject to additional licensing under section 56 of the Housing Act 2004 and is not licensed;

(h)   the accommodation is or forms part of residential property which does not have a valid energy performance certificate as required by the Energy Performance of Buildings (Certificates and Inspections) (England and Wales) Regulations 2007;

(i)   the accommodation is or forms part of relevant premises which do not have a current gas safety record in accordance with regulation 36 of the Gas Safety (Installation and Use) Regulations 1998; or

(j)   the landlord has not provided to the local housing authority a written tenancy agreement, which the landlord proposes to use for the purposes of a private rented sector offer, and which the local housing authority considers to be adequate.

Appendix 3

WALES: ALLOCATION
AND HOMELESSNESS

HOUSING ACT 1996
1996 C 52

Part 6

Allocation of Housing Accommodation

See Appendix 1, p 1045

HOUSING ACT 1996
1996 C 52

Part 7

Homelessness

See Appendix 2, p 1115

HOMELESSNESS ACT 2002
2002 C 7

Sections 1–4 and 17–21

See Appendix 2, p 1157

CODE OF GUIDANCE FOR LOCAL AUTHORITIES ON ALLOCATION OF ACCOMMODATION AND HOMELESSNESS (WELSH GOVERNMENT, AUGUST 2012)

See CD-ROM

HOMELESSNESS (SUITABILITY OF ACCOMMODATION) ORDER 1996
SI 1996/3204

See Appendix 2, p 1402

LOCAL AUTHORITIES (CONTRACTING OUT OF ALLOCATION OF HOUSING AND HOMELESSNESS FUNCTIONS) ORDER 1996
SI 1996/3205

See Appendix 1, p 1105

Appendix 3
Wales: Allocation and Homelessness

Local Housing Authorities (Prescribed Principles for Allocation Schemes) (Wales) Regulations 1997

SI 1997/45

Made	*13th January 1997*
Laid before Parliament	*16th January 1997*
Coming into force	*7th February 1997*

The Secretary of State for Wales, in exercise of the powers conferred on him by sections 167(5) and 172(4) of the Housing Act 1996 and of all other powers enabling him in that behalf, hereby makes the following Regulations:

1 Citation, commencement and application

These Regulations may be cited as the Local Housing Authorities (Prescribed Principles for Allocation Schemes) (Wales) Regulations 1997 and shall come into force on 7th February 1997. They apply to Wales only.

2 Interpretation

In these Regulations –

'the Act' means the Housing Act 1996;
'allocation decision' means a decision to allocate housing accommodation;
'allocation scheme' means an allocation scheme within the meaning of section 167(1) of the Act;
'authority' means a Welsh local housing authority;
'delegation arrangements' means arrangements made under section 101(1) or (2) of the Local Government Act 1972 for the discharge of an authority's function of making allocation decisions;
'officer delegation arrangements' means delegation arrangements which arrange for the discharge (in whole or in part) of an authority's function of making allocation decisions, by an officer or a description of officers of the authority; and
'qualifying person', in relation to an authority, means a person who is qualified to be allocated housing accommodation by that authority.

3 Allocation scheme principles

As regards the procedure to be followed in allocating housing accommodation, the principles set out in the Schedule are prescribed as principles in accordance with which an authority's allocation scheme shall be framed.

Schedule
Allocation Scheme Principles

Regulation 3

(1) In relation to an allocation decision where either –

(a)   the housing accommodation in question is situated in the electoral division for which a member is elected, or

(b)   the qualifying person in question has his sole or main residence in the electoral division for which a member is elected,

that member shall not be included in the persons or descriptions of persons by whom the allocation decision is to be taken.

(2) An officer or a description of officers of the authority shall be included in the persons or descriptions of persons by whom allocation decisions, or descriptions of allocation decisions, may be taken, except where the authority or a committee or sub-committee of the authority, as the case may be, has determined that no officer delegation arrangements shall be made.

HOMELESSNESS (DECISIONS ON REFERRALS) ORDER 1998
SI 1998/1578

See Appendix 2, p 1405

ALLOCATION OF HOUSING AND HOMELESSNESS (REVIEW PROCEDURES) REGULATIONS 1999
SI 1999/71

See Appendix 2, p 1408

Homeless Persons (Priority Need) (Wales) Order 2001

SI 2001/607

Made	*27th February 2001*
Coming into force	*St David's Day 1st March 2001*

The National Assembly for Wales makes the following Order in exercise of the power conferred on the Secretary of State by section 189(2) of the Housing Act 1996 which is now exercisable by it in relation to Wales; after consultation with such associations representing relevant authorities and such other persons as it considers appropriate in accordance with section 189(3):

1 Name, commencement and application

(1) The name of this Order is the Homeless Persons (Priority Need) (Wales) Order 2001 and it shall come into force on St David's Day, March 1st 2001.

(2) This Order applies to Wales only.

2 Persons with priority need for accommodation

The descriptions of person specified in articles 3 to 7 have priority need for accommodation under section 189 of the Housing Act 1996.

3 A care leaver or person at particular risk of sexual or financial exploitation, 18 years or over but under the age of 21

(1) A person who

(a) is 18 years old or older but under the age of 21; and

(b) at any time while still a child was, but is no longer, looked after, accommodated or fostered; or

(c) is at particular risk of sexual or financial exploitation.

(2) In paragraph (1)(b) above 'looked after, accommodated or fostered' means:

(a) looked after by a local authority;

(b) accommodated by or on behalf of a voluntary organisation;

(c) accommodated in a private children's home;

(d) accommodated for a consecutive period of at least three months –

(i) by any health authority, special health authority or [local authority]², or

(ii) in any residential care home, nursing home or mental nursing home or in any accommodation provided by a National Health Service Trust [or NHS foundation trust]¹; or

(e) privately fostered.

AMENDMENT

[1] Words inserted: Health and Social Care (Community Health and Standards) Act 2003 (Supplementary and Consequential Provision) (NHS Foundation Trusts) Order 2004, SI 2004/696, art 3(2), Sch 2.

[2] Words substituted: Local Education Authorities and Children's Services Authorities (Integration of Functions) (Subordinate Legislation) (Wales) Order 2010, SI 2010/1142, art 3, Sch 2, para 3.

4 A 16 or 17 year old

A person who is 16 or 17 years old.

5 A person fleeing domestic violence or threatened domestic violence

A person without dependant children who has been subject to domestic violence or is at risk of such violence, or if he or she returns home is at risk of domestic violence.

6 A person homeless after leaving the armed forces

(1) A person formerly serving in the regular armed forces of the Crown who has been homeless since leaving those forces.

(2) In paragraph (1) above the expression 'regular armed forces of the Crown' has the meaning given to it in section 199(4) of the Housing Act 1996.

7 A former prisoner homeless after being released from custody

(1) A former prisoner who has been homeless since leaving custody and who has a local connection with the area of the local housing authority.

(2) A 'prisoner' means any person for the time being detained in lawful custody as the result of a requirement imposed by a court that he or she be detained.

Allocation of Housing (Wales) Regulations 2003

SI 2003/239

Made	*28th January 2003*
Coming into force	*29th January 2003*

The National Assembly for Wales makes the following Regulations in exercise of the powers given to the Secretary of State by sections 160(4), 160A(3) and (5) and 215(2) of the Housing Act 1996 which powers are now vested in the National Assembly for Wales so far as exercisable in relation to Wales:

1 Citation, commencement and application

(1) These Regulations may be cited as the Allocation of Housing (Wales) Regulations 2003 and shall come into force on 29 January 2003.

(2) These Regulations apply to Wales only.

2 Interpretation

In these Regulations –

  'the Act' ('*y Ddeddf*') means the Housing Act 1996;
  'the Common Travel Area' ('*Ardal Deithio Gyffredin*') means the United Kingdom, the Channel Islands, the Isle of Man and the Republic of Ireland collectively; and
  'the immigration rules' ('*y rheolau mewnfudo*') mean the rules laid down as mentioned in section 3(2) of the Immigration Act 1971 (general provisions for regulation and control).

3 Cases where the provisions of Part 6 of the Act do not apply

The provisions of Part 6 of the Act about the allocation of housing accommodation do not apply in the following cases –

  (a)   where a local housing authority secures the provision of suitable alternative accommodation under section 39 of the Land Compensation Act 1973 (duty to rehouse residential occupiers);
  (b)   in relation to the grant of a secure tenancy under section 554 and 555 of the Housing Act 1985 (grant of tenancy to former owner-occupier or statutory tenant of defective dwelling-house).

4 Classes prescribed under section 160A(3) who are eligible persons

The following are classes of persons subject to immigration control prescribed for the purposes of section 160A(3) of the Act (persons prescribed as eligible for an allocation of housing accommodation by a local housing authority) –

  (a)   Class A – a person recorded by the Secretary of State as a refugee within the definition in Article 1 of the Convention relating to the

Status of Refugees done at Geneva on 28th July 1951 as extended by Article 1(2) of the Protocol relating to the Status of Refugees done at New York on 31st January 1967;

(b) Class B – a person –

    (i) who has been granted by the Secretary of State exceptional leave to enter or remain in the United Kingdom outside the provisions of the immigration rules; and

    (ii) whose leave is not subject to a condition requiring them to maintain and accommodate themselves, and any person who is dependent on them, without recourse to public funds;

(c) Class C – a person who has current leave to enter or remain in the United Kingdom which is not subject to any limitation or condition and who is habitually resident in the Common Travel Area other than a person –

    (i) who has been given leave to enter or remain in the United Kingdom upon an undertaking given by another person (that person's 'sponsor') in writing in pursuance of the immigration rules to be responsible for that person's maintenance and accommodation;

    (ii) who has been resident in the United Kingdom for less than five years beginning on the date of entry or the date on which the above-mentioned undertaking was given in respect of that person, whichever date is the later; and

    (iii) whose sponsor or, where there is more than one sponsor, at least one of whose sponsors, is still alive;

(d) Class D – a person who is habitually resident in the Common Travel Area and who –

    (i) is a national of a state which has ratified the European Convention on Social and Medical Assistance done at Paris on 11th December 1953 or a state which has ratified the European Social Charter done at Turin on 18th October 1961 and is lawfully present in the United Kingdom; or

    (ii) before 3rd April 2000 was owed a duty by a housing authority under Part III of the Housing Act 1985 (housing the homeless) or Part 7 of the Act (homelessness) which is extant, and who is a national of a state which is a signatory to the European Convention on Social and Medical Assistance done at Paris on 11th December 1953 or a state which is a signatory to the European Social Charter done at Turin on 18th October 1961[;][1]

[(e) Class D1 – a person who has humanitarian protection granted under the Immigration Rules.]

AMENDMENT

[1] Words inserted: Allocation of Housing (Wales) (Amendment) Regulations 2006, SI 2006/2645, reg 2(1), 2(a).

[2] Paragraph inserted: Allocation of Housing (Wales) (Amendment) Regulations 2006, SI 2006/2645, reg 2(1), 2(b).

5 Classes prescribed under section 160A(5) who are not eligible persons

The following is a class of persons, not being persons subject to immigration control, prescribed for the purposes of section 160A(5) of the Act (persons prescribed as ineligible for an allocation of housing accommodation) –

Class E – a person who is not habitually resident in the Common Travel Area other than –

(a) a worker for the purposes of Council Regulation (EEC) No 1612/68 or (EEC) No 1251/70;

(b) a person with a right to reside in the United Kingdom pursuant to the Immigration (European Economic Area) Order 2000 and derived from Council Directive No 68/360/EEC or No 73/148/EEC;

(c) a person who left the territory of Montserrat after 1st November 1995 because of the effect on that territory of a volcanic eruption[;

(d) a person who –

   (i) arrived in Great Britain on or after 28th February 2009 but before 18th March 2011;

   (ii) immediately before arriving in Great Britain had been resident in Zimbabwe; and

   (iii) before leaving Zimbabwe, had accepted an offer, made by Her Majesty's Government, to assist that person to settle in the United Kingdom].[1]

AMENDMENT

[1] Sub-paragraph inserted: Allocation of Housing and Homelessness (Eligibility) (Wales) Regulations 2009, SI 2009/393, reg 2.

6 Revocation

The Allocation of Housing (Wales) Regulations 2000 are revoked.

Homelessness (Suitability of Accommodation) (Wales) Order 2006

SI 2006/650

Made	*8 March 2006*
Coming into force	
Articles 1–3	*3 April 2006*
Articles 4–6	*2 April 2007*
Articles 7–10	*7 April 2008*

The National Assembly for Wales, in exercise of the powers conferred on the Secretary of State by sections 210(2) and 215(2) of the Housing Act 1996, and now vested in the National Assembly for Wales, hereby makes the following Order:

1 Title, commencement and application

(1) The title of this Order is the Homelessness (Suitability of Accommodation) (Wales) Order 2006.

(2) Save as provided in paragraphs (3) and (4) of this Article, this Order comes into force on 3 April 2006.

(3) Articles 4, 5 and 6 of, and the Schedule to this Order come into force on 2 April 2007.

(4) Articles 7, 8, 9 and 10 of this Order come into force on 7 April 2008.

(5) This Order applies in relation to the duties of local housing authorities in Wales under Part 7 of the Housing Act 1996 (homelessness).

2 Interpretation

In this Order –

'the 1996 Act' ('*Deddf 1996*') means the Housing Act 1996; and any reference to a numbered section is a reference to a section of the Housing Act 1996;

'B&B accommodation' ('*llety Gwely a Brecwast*') means commercially provided accommodation (whether or not breakfast is included) –

(a) which is not separate and self-contained premises;

(b) in which any of the following amenities is not available to the applicant or is shared by more than one household –

(i) a toilet;

(ii) personal washing facilities;

(iii) cooking facilities;

    (c)   which is not accommodation which is owned or managed by a local housing authority, a registered social landlord or a voluntary organisation as defined in section 180(3) of the Housing Act 1996; or

    (d)   which is not an establishment registered under the provisions of the Care Standards Act 2000;

and 'B&B' ('*Gwely a Brecwast*') is to be construed accordingly;

'basic standard accommodation' ('*lletty o safon sylfaenol*') means accommodation that –

    (a)   complies with all statutory requirements (such as requirements relating to fire and gas safety, planning and licences for houses in multiple occupation, where applicable); and

    (b)   has a manager deemed by the local housing authority to be a fit and proper person with the ability to manage B&B accommodation;

and 'basic standard' ('*safon sylfaenol*') is to be construed accordingly;

'higher standard accommodation' ('*lletty o safon uwch*') means accommodation that meets –

    (a)   the basic standard; and

    (b)   the standards contained in the Schedule to this Order,

and 'higher standard' ('*safon uwch*') is to be construed accordingly;

'shared accommodation' ('*lletty a rennir*') means accommodation –

    (a)   which is not separate and self-contained premises; or

    (b)   in which any of the following amenities is not available to the applicant or is shared by more than one household –

        (i)   a toilet;

        (ii)   personal washing facilities;

        (iii) cooking facilities; or

    (c)   which is not an establishment registered under the provisions of the Care Standards Act 2000;

'small B&B' ('*lletty Gwely a Brecwast bach*') means –

B&B accommodation –

        (i)   where the manager resides on the premises; and

        (ii)   which has fewer than 7 bedrooms available for letting.

PART 1
ADDITIONAL MATTERS TO BE TAKEN INTO ACCOUNT IN DETERMINING SUITABILITY

3

In determining for the purposes of Part 7 of the 1996 Act whether accommodation is suitable for a person in priority need there must be taken into account the following matters –

    (a)   the specific health needs of the person;

    (b)   the proximity and accessibility of social services;

(c) the proximity and accessibility of the support of the family or other support services; or

(d) any disability of the person.

PART 2
CIRCUMSTANCES APPLYING FROM 2 APRIL 2007 IN WHICH ACCOMMODATION IS NOT TO BE REGARDED AS SUITABLE

4 B&B accommodation used for housing a homeless person to meet the basic standard

For the purposes of Part 7 of the 1996 Act, B&B accommodation is not to be regarded as suitable unless it meets at least the basic standard.

5 B&B accommodation not to be regarded as suitable for a minor or a pregnant woman

For the purposes of Part 7 of the 1996 Act and subject to the exceptions contained in article 6, B&B accommodation is not to be regarded as suitable for a person who is a minor or a pregnant woman.

6 Exceptions

(1) Article 5 does not apply where –

(a) the person occupies a basic standard B&B for a period, or a total of periods, which does not exceed 2 weeks;

(b) the person occupies a higher standard B&B for a period or a total of periods which does not exceed 6 weeks;

(c) the person occupies a basic standard small B&B for a period or a total of periods which does not exceed 6 weeks, and the local housing authority has, before the expiry of the two-week period referred to in sub-paragraph (a), offered suitable alternative accommodation, but the person has chosen to remain in the said B&B;

(d) the person occupies a basic standard small B&B after exercising the choice referred to in sub-paragraph (c) above, and the local housing authority has offered suitable alternative accommodation before the end of the six-week period referred to in sub-paragraph (c) above, but the person has chosen to remain in the said B&B; or

(e) the person occupies a higher standard small B&B, and the local housing authority has offered suitable alternative accommodation, before the expiry of the six-week period referred to in sub-paragraph (b) above, but the person has chosen to remain in the said B&B.

(2) If the suitable alternative accommodation offered for the purposes of paragraph (1) is shared, it must meet the higher standard.

(3) In the case of households with dependent children or a pregnant woman, the offer made under sub-paragraphs (d) or (e) must be of suitable self-contained accommodation. In the case of an applicant who is a minor, the offer must be of suitable accommodation with support.

Appendix 3
Wales: Allocation and Homelessness

(4) In calculating a period, or total period, of a person's occupation of B&B accommodation for the purposes of paragraph (1), there must be disregarded –

- (a) any period before 2 April 2007; and
- (b) where a local housing authority is subject to the duty under section 193 by virtue of section 200(4), any period before that authority became subject to that duty.

PART 3
EXTENSION FROM 7 APRIL 2008 TO ALL ACCOMMODATION PROVIDED IN DISCHARGE OF HOMELESSNESS FUNCTIONS

7 B&B accommodation not to be regarded as suitable for a homeless person in priority need

For the purposes of Part 7 of the 1996 Act and subject to the exceptions contained in article 9, B&B accommodation is not to be regarded as suitable for a person who is in priority need.

8 Shared accommodation to meet the higher standard

For the purposes of Part 7 of the 1996 Act and subject to the exceptions contained in articles 9 and 10, shared accommodation is not to be regarded as suitable for a person who is in priority need unless it meets the higher standard.

9 Exceptions

(1) Articles 7 and 8 do not apply where –

- (a) the person occupies basic standard B&B for a period, or a total of periods, which does not exceed 2 weeks;
- (b) the person occupies a higher standard B&B for a period or a total of periods which does not exceed 6 weeks;
- (c) the person occupies a basic standard small B&B for a period or a total of periods which does not exceed 6 weeks, and the local housing authority has, before the expiry of the two-week period referred to in sub-paragraph (a), offered suitable alternative accommodation, but the person has chosen to remain in the said B&B;
- (d) the person occupies a basic standard small B&B after exercising the choice referred to in sub-paragraph (c), and the local housing authority has offered suitable alternative accommodation before the end of the six-week period referred to in sub-paragraph (c) above, but the person has chosen to remain in the said B&B;
- (e) the person occupies a higher standard small B&B, the local housing authority has offered suitable alternative accommodation, before the expiry of the six-week period referred to in sub-paragraph (b), but the person has chosen to remain in the said B&B; or
- (f) the person occupies basic standard shared accommodation for a period, or a total of periods, which does not exceed 2 weeks;
- (g) the person occupies, for a period or a total of periods which does not exceed 6 weeks, basic standard shared accommodation owned by a

local housing authority or registered social landlord, and the local housing authority has offered suitable alternative accommodation before the expiry of the two-week period referred to in sub-paragraph (f), but the person has chosen to remain in the said accommodation.

(2) If the suitable alternative accommodation offered for the purposes of paragraph (1) is shared, it must meet the higher standard.

(3) In the case of households with dependent children or a pregnant woman, the offer made under sub-paragraphs (d) or (e) must be of suitable self-contained accommodation. In the case of an applicant who is a minor, the offer must be of suitable accommodation with support.

(4) In calculating a period, or total period, of a person's occupation of shared accommodation for the purposes of paragraph (1), there must be disregarded –

(a) any period before 7 April 2008; and
(b) where a local housing authority is subject to the duty under section 193 by virtue of section 200(4), any period before that authority became subject to that duty.

10 Delayed application to Social Housing

Article 7 is not to apply until 4 April 2011 to any property owned or managed by a local authority or registered social landlord and used for the purposes of Part 7 of the 1996 Act on 7 April 2008.

Higher Standard

Schedule

1 Minimum Space Standards

SPACE STANDARDS FOR SLEEPING ACCOMMODATION

Room sizes where cooking facilities provided in a separate room or kitchen

Floor Area of Room	Maximum No of Persons
Not less than 6.5 square metres	1 person
Not less than 10.2 square metres	2 persons
Not less than 14.9 square metres	3 persons
Not less than 19.6 square metres	4 persons

Room sizes where cooking facilities provided within the room

Floor Area of Room	Maximum No of Persons
Not less than 10.2 square metres	1 person
Not less than 13.9 square metres	2 persons

Floor Area of Room	**Maximum No of Persons**
Not less than 18.6 square metres	3 persons
Not less than 23.2 square metres	4 persons

For the purposes of the room size calculations above, a child less than 10 years old is treated as a half person.

- (a) No room to be occupied by more than 4 persons, except where the occupants consent.
- (b) No sharing of rooms for those of opposite genders, aged 10 or above unless they are living together as partners and both are over the age of consent, or where a parent or guardian elects to share with an older child.
- (c) All rooms must have a floor to ceiling height of at least 2.1 metres over not less than 75% of the room area. Any part of the room where the ceiling height is less than 1.5 metres must be disregarded when calculating the floor area.
- (d) Separate kitchens and bathrooms are unsuitable for sleeping accommodation.

2 Installation for heating

The premises must have adequate provision for heating. All habitable rooms and bath- or shower-rooms must have a heating system capable of maintaining the room at a minimum temperature of 18°C when the outside temperature is minus 1°C.

3 Facilities for the storage, preparation and cooking of food within the unit

(1) In a unit of accommodation accommodating more than one person, the food preparation area provided within the unit must include the following facilities:

- (a) four burners or hobs, conventional oven and grill, or two burners or hobs and a microwave with a built in oven and grill,
- (b) a sink and integral drainer, with a constant supply of hot water and cold drinking water,
- (c) a storage cupboard of a minimum capacity 0.2 cubic metres excluding storage beneath the sink,
- (d) a refrigerator,
- (e) a minimum of four 13-amp sockets (single or double) situated over the worktop,
- (f) a worktop for food preparation of minimum dimensions 1 metre x 0.6 metre, and
- (g) a minimum of 1 metre circulation space from facilities to other furniture in the room.

(2) In a unit of accommodation accommodating one person, the food preparation area provided within the unit of accommodation must include the following facilities:

As (a)–(g) above but (a) to have a minimum of two burners or hobs.

4 Storage, preparation and cooking of food in a shared facility

(1) Where food preparation areas are shared between more than one household there must be one set of kitchen facilities for:

(a) every 3 family households or fewer;

(b) every 5 single-person households or fewer. (For between 6 and 9 single-person households an additional oven or microwave is required.)

(c) every 10 persons or fewer where there is a mixture of family and single-person households within the same premises.

(2) Each set of shared facilities must provide the following facilities:

(a) as for unit accommodating more than one person except that cooking facilities must consist of 4 burners or hobs, conventional oven, grill and microwave,

(b) an electric kettle,

(c) a toaster.

The food preparation area used by the management may be included when calculating the ratio, provided it meets the criteria for storage, preparation and cooking of food in a shared facility.

Where residents have no access to kitchen facilities and the proprietor provides at least a breakfast and evening-meal for residents, the requirements for shared kitchen facilities will be deemed to have been met.

Additional facilities to be provided in each bedroom or within the total accommodation occupied exclusively by each household must include:

(a) a refrigerator; and

(b) lockable storage.

Alternatively, these may be provided elsewhere within the building.

5 Toilet and washing facilities

(1) Facilities for the exclusive use of the occupant or household must include:

(a) bath or shower,

(b) a wash hand basin with a constant supply of hot and cold water, and

(c) a water-closet either en-suite or in a separate room reserved for the exclusive use of individuals or households.

(2) Shared facilities must include:

(a) One water closet and wash hand basin with a constant supply of hot and cold water within the building for every five households or fewer. This must be located not more than one floor away from the intended users. For the first five households the water closet and wash hand basin may be in the shower or bathroom. All additional water closets and wash hand basins for occupancies of six households or more must be in a separate compartment.

(b)   One bathroom or shower-room to be provided for every five persons. This must be located not more than one floor away from the intended users.

(c)   In premises accommodating children under the age of 10, at least half of the bathing facilities must contain baths suitable for children.

The number of persons occupying a unit of accommodation with a water closet facility provided for their exclusive use is not to be included in the calculation for shared water closets.

6 Security

The entrance door to each unit of accommodation must be lockable and be capable of being unlocked from inside without the use of a key.

7 Common Room(s)

Every premises must have a common room of at least 12 square metres unless all households have a living area separate from their sleeping area that is available for their exclusive use or the premises are for single person households only.

8 Management Standard

(a) Each household must be issued with written 'house rules' which include details as to how sanctions will be applied. This document is to be approved by the local authority placing homeless households in the premises.

(b) Each household must be issued with written information relating to the premises including how to operate all installations, for example heating and hot water appliances and fire fighting equipment.

(c) Written information must be made available to residents relating to the local area including the location or contact details of local facilities, laundrettes, doctors' surgeries and schools.

(d) Residents must have access to their rooms at all times except when rooms are being cleaned or otherwise maintained. Provision must be made to accommodate residents at these times.

(e) Access is allowed for the appropriate officers of the local housing authority in whose area the premises are situated, and officers of any authority placing homeless households in the premises, to inspect the premises as and when they consider necessary, to ensure that the requirements are being complied with; and that the manager will allow such inspections to take place, if necessary without notice.

(f) Access is allowed for the officers of the local authority and authorised health and community workers for the area in which the premises are situated, to visit the occupiers of the premises and interview them in private in the room(s) they occupy.

(g) A manager with adequate day to day responsibility to ensure the good management of the property can be contacted at all times and that a notice giving the name, address and telephone number of the manager must be displayed in a readily visible position in the property.

(h) A clear emergency evacuation plan is in place setting out action upon hearing the fire alarm, escape routes and safe assembly points. The managers must ensure that each person newly arriving at the premises is told what to do in the event of a fire and about fire precautions provided.

(i) Each household must be issued with a complaints procedure which specifies how a complaint can be made. This information must also include where the complainant can obtain further advice and assistance.

Homelessness (Wales) Regulations 2006

SI 2006/2646

Made	*3 October 2006*
Coming into force	*9 October 2006*

The National Assembly for Wales makes the following Regulations in exercise of the powers conferred upon the Secretary of State by sections 185(2) and (3) of the Housing Act 1996 which are now vested in the National Assembly so far as exercisable in Wales.

1 Title, commencement and application

(1) The title of these Regulations is the Homelessness (Wales) Regulations 2006 and they come into force on 9 October 2006.

(2) These Regulations apply to Wales.

2 Interpretation

(1) In these Regulations

'the 1971 Act' (*'Deddf 1971'*) means the Immigration Act 1971;

'the 1995 Act' (*'Deddf 1995'*) means the Jobseekers Act 1995;

'the 1996 Act' (*'Deddf 1996'*) means the Housing Act 1996;

'asylum-seeker' (*'ceisydd lloches'*) means a person who is not under 18 and who made a claim for asylum which is recorded by the Secretary of State as having been made before 3 April 2000 but which has not been determined;

'claim for asylum' (*'hawliad lloches'*) means a claim that it would be contrary to the United Kingdom's obligations under the Refugee Convention for the claimant to be removed from, or required to leave, the United Kingdom;

'the Common Travel Area' (*'Ardal Deithio Gyffredin'*) means the United Kingdom, the Channel Islands, the Isle of Man and the Republic of Ireland collectively;

'the immigration rules' (*'y rheolau mewnfudo'*) means the rules laid down as mentioned in section 3(2) of the 1971 Act (general provisions for regulation and control);

'limited leave' (*'caniatâd cyfyngedig'*) means leave under the 1971 Act to enter or remain in the United Kingdom which is limited as to duration; and

'the Refugee Convention' (*'y Confensiwn ynglyn â Ffoaduriaid'*) means the Convention relating to the Status of Refugees done at Geneva on 28 July 1951, as extended by Article 1(2) of the Protocol relating to the Status of Refugees done at New York on 31 January 1967.

(2) For the purposes of the definition of 'asylum-seeker', a claim for asylum is determined at the end of such period beginning –

(a) on the day on which the Secretary of State notifies the claimant of the decision on the claim; or

(b) if the claimant has appealed against the Secretary of State's decision, on the day on which the appeal is disposed of,

as may be prescribed under section 94(3) of the Immigration and Asylum Act 1999.

(3) For the purposes of regulations 3(1)(i) (Class I) –

(a) 'an income-based jobseeker's allowance' (*'lwfans ceisio gwaith ar sail incwm'*) means a jobseeker's allowance, payable under the 1995 Act, entitlement to which is based on the claimant satisfying conditions which include those set out in section 3 of the 1995 Act (the income-based conditions);

(b) 'income support' (*'cymhorthdal incwm'*) has the same meaning as in section 124 of the Social Security Contributions and Benefits Act 1992 (income support); ...[1]

(c) a person is on an income-based jobseeker's allowance on any day in respect of which an income-based jobseeker's allowance is payable to that person and on any day –

    (i) in respect of which that person satisfies the conditions for entitlement to an income-based jobseeker's allowance but where the allowance is not paid in accordance with section 19 of the 1995 Act (circumstances in which jobseeker's allowance is not payable); or

    (ii) which is a waiting day for the purposes of paragraph 4 of Schedule 1 to the 1995 Act (waiting days) and which falls immediately before a day in respect of which an income-based jobseeker's allowance is payable to that person or would be payable to that person but for section 19 of the 1995 Act; [and

(d) 'an income-related employment and support allowance' means an employment and support allowance payable under Part 1 of the Welfare Reform Act 2007 entitlement to which is based on the claimant satisfying conditions which include those set out in Part 2 of Schedule 1 to that Act][2].

AMENDMENT

[1] Word revoked: Employment and Support Allowance (Consequential Provisions) (No 3) Regulations 2008, SI 2008/1879, reg 31(1), (2)(a).

[2] Sub-paragraph inserted: Employment and Support Allowance (Consequential Provisions) (No 3) Regulations 2008, SI 2008/1879, reg 31(1), (2)(b).

3 Classes of persons subject to immigration control who are eligible for housing assistance

(1) The following are classes of persons prescribed for the purposes of section 185(2) of the 1996 Act (persons subject to immigration control who are eligible for housing assistance) –

(a) Class A – a person recorded by the Secretary of State as a refugee within the definition in Article 1 of the Refugee Convention;

(b) Class B – a person –

   (i) who has been granted by the Secretary of State exceptional leave to enter or remain in the United Kingdom outside the provisions of the immigration rules; and

   (ii) whose leave is not subject to a condition requiring that person to maintain and accommodate themselves, and any person who is dependent on that person, without recourse to public funds;

(c) Class C – a person who has current leave to enter or remain in the United Kingdom which is not subject to any limitation or condition and who is habitually resident in the Common Travel Area other than a person –

   (i) who has been given leave to enter or remain in the United Kingdom upon an undertaking given by another person (that person's 'sponsor') in writing in pursuance of the immigration rules to be responsible for that person's maintenance and accommodation;

   (ii) who has been resident in the United Kingdom for less than five years beginning on the date of entry or the date on which the undertaking was given in respect of that person, whichever date is the later; and

   (iii) whose sponsor or, where there is more than one sponsor, at least one of whose sponsors, is still alive;

(d) Class D – a person who left the territory of Montserrat after 1 November 1995 because of the effect on that territory of a volcanic eruption;

(e) Class E – a person who is habitually resident in the Common Travel Area and who –

   (i) is a national of a state which has ratified the European Convention on Social and Medical Assistance done at Paris on 11 December 1953 or a state which has ratified the European Social Charter done at Turin on 18 October 1961 and is lawfully present in the United Kingdom; or

   (ii) before 3 April 2000 was owed a duty by a housing authority under Part III of the Housing Act 1985 (housing and homeless) or Part VII of the 1996 Act (homelessness) which is extant, and who is a national of a state which is a signatory to the European Convention on Social and Medical Assistance done at Paris on 11 December 1953 or a state which is a signatory to the European Social Charter done at Turin on 18 October 1961;

(f) Class F – a person who is an asylum-seeker and who made a claim for asylum –

   (i) which is recorded by the Secretary of State as having been made on his arrival (other than on his re-entry) in the United Kingdom from a country outside the Common Travel Area; and

   (ii) which has not been recorded by the Secretary of State as having been either decided (other than on appeal) or abandoned;

   (g)   Class G – a person who is an asylum-seeker and –

      (i)   who was in Great Britain when the Secretary of State made a declaration to the effect that the country of which that person is a national is subject to such a fundamental change in circumstances that the Secretary of State would not normally order the return of a person to that country;

      (ii) who made a claim for asylum which is recorded by the Secretary of State as having been made within a period of three months from the day on which that declaration was made; and

      (iii) whose claim for asylum has not been recorded by the Secretary of State as having been either decided (other than on appeal) or abandoned;

   (h)   Class H – a person who is an asylum-seeker and –

      (i)   who made a relevant claim for asylum on or before 4 February 1996; and

      (ii) who was, on 4 February 1996, entitled to benefit under regulation 7A of the Housing Benefit (General) Regulations 1987 (persons from abroad);

   (i)   Class I – a person who is on an income-based jobseeker's allowance[, an income-related employment and support allowance][1] or in receipt of income support and is eligible for that benefit other than because –

      (i)   that person has limited leave to enter or remain in the United Kingdom which was given in accordance with the relevant immigration rules and that person is temporarily without funds because remittances to that person from abroad have been disrupted; or

      (ii) that person has been deemed by regulation 3 of the Displaced Persons (Temporary Protection) Regulations 2005 to have been granted leave to enter or remain in the United Kingdom exceptionally for the purposes of the provision of means of subsistence; and

   (j)   Class J – a person who has humanitarian protection granted under the Immigration Rules.

(2) In paragraph (1)(h)(i) (Class H), a relevant claim for asylum is a claim for asylum which –

   (a)   has not been recorded by the Secretary of State as having been either decided (other than on appeal) or abandoned; or

   (b)   has been recorded as having been decided (other than on appeal) on or before 4 February 1996 and in respect of which an appeal is pending which –

      (i)   was pending on 5 February 1996; or

      (ii) was made within the time limits specified in the rules of procedure made under section 22 of the 1971 Act (procedure).

(3) In paragraph (1)(i)(i) (Class I), 'relevant immigration rules' ('*rheolau mewnfudo perthnasol*') means the immigration rules relating to –

   (a)   there being or there needing to be no recourse

(b)   there being no charge on public funds.

(4) In paragraph (1)(i) (Class I), 'means of subsistence' (*'moddion byw'*) has the same meaning as in regulation 4 of the Displaced Persons (Temporary Protection) Regulations 2005.

AMENDMENT

[1] Words inserted: Employment and Support Allowance (Consequential Provisions) (No 3) Regulations 2008, SI 2008/1879, reg 31(1), (3).

4 Description of persons who are to be treated as persons from abroad ineligible for housing assistance

(1) The following are descriptions of persons, other than persons who are subject to immigration control, who are to be treated for the purposes of Part VII of the 1996 Act (homelessness) as persons from abroad who are ineligible for housing assistance –

(a)   subject to paragraphs (2) and (3), a person who is not habitually resident in the United Kingdom, the Channel Islands, the Isle of Man or the Republic of Ireland;

(b)   a person whose right to reside in the United Kingdom, the Channel Islands, the Isle of Man or the Republic of Ireland is derived solely from Council Directive No 90/364/EEC or Council Directive No 90/365/EEC.

(2) The following persons will not, however, be treated as persons from abroad who are ineligible pursuant to paragraph (1)(a) –

(a)   a person who is a worker for the purposes of Council Regulation (EEC) No 1612/68 or (EEC) No 1251/70;

(b)   a person who is an accession state worker requiring registration who is treated as a worker for the purpose of the definition of 'qualified person' in regulation 6 of the Immigration (European Economic Area) Regulations 2006 pursuant to regulation 5 of the Accession (Immigration and Worker Registration) Regulations 2004;

(c)   a person with a right to reside pursuant to the Immigration (European Economic Area) Regulations 2006, which is derived from Council Directive No 68/360/EEC, No 73/148/EEC or No 75/34/EEC;

(d)   a person who left the territory of Montserrat after 1 November 1995 because of the effect on that territory of a volcanic eruption[;

(e)   a person who –
   (i)   arrived in Great Britain on or after 28 February 2009 but before 18 March 2011;
   (ii) immediately before arriving in Great Britain had been resident in Zimbabwe; and
   (iii) before leaving Zimbabwe, had accepted an offer, made by Her Majesty's Government, to assist that person to settle in the United Kingdom].[1]

(3) A person will not be treated as habitually resident in the United Kingdom, the Channel Islands, the Isle of Man or the Republic of Ireland for the

purposes of paragraph (1)(a) if he does not have a right to reside in the United Kingdom, the Channel Islands, the Isle of Man or the Republic of Ireland.

AMENDMENT

[1] Sub-paragraph inserted: Allocation of Housing and Homelessness (Eligibility) (Wales) Regulations 2009, SI 2009/393, reg 3.

5 Transitional Provisions

The amendments made by these Regulations do not have effect in relation to an applicant whose application for housing assistance under Part VII of the 1996 Act was made before 9 October 2006.

6 Revocation

The Homelessness (Wales) Regulations 2000 are hereby revoked.

Allocation of Housing (Wales) (Amendment) Regulations 2006

SI 2006/2645

Made	*3rd October 2006*
Coming into force	*9th October 2006*

1 Title, commencement, interpretation and application

(1) The title of these Regulations is The Allocation of Housing (Wales) (Amendment) Regulations 2006 and they come into force on 9 October 2006.

(2) In these Regulations –

'the 1996 Act' ('Deddf 1996') means the Housing Act 1996; and
'the Immigration Rules' ('y Rheolau Mewnfudo') means the rules laid down as mentioned in section 3(2) of the Immigration Act 1971 (General provisions for regulation and control).

(3) These Regulations apply in relation to Wales.

2 Amendment of the classes of persons prescribed under section 160A(3) who are eligible persons

(1) The Allocation of Housing (Wales) Regulations 2003 are amended as follows.

(2) In regulation 4 (Classes prescribed under section 160A(3) who are eligible persons) –

    (a)   at the end of paragraph (d)(ii), after '1961', omit '.' and substitute ';'; and

    (b)   after paragraph (d), insert –

        '(e)Class D1—a person who has humanitarian protection granted under the Immigration Rules.'

3 Transitional provisions

The amendment made by these Regulations does not have effect in relation to an applicant whose application for an allocation of housing accommodation under Part 6 of the 1996 Act was made before 9 October 2006.

Allocation of Housing and Homelessness (Eligibility) (Wales) Regulations 2009

SI 2009/393

Made	*26th February 2009*
Coming into force	*27th February 2009*

1 Title, commencement and application

(1) The title of these Regulations is the Allocation of Housing and Homelessness (Eligibility) (Wales) Regulations 2009 and they come into force on 20 March 2009.

(2) These Regulations apply in relation to Wales.

2 Persons who have left Zimbabwe

(1) The Allocation of Housing (Wales) Regulations 2003 are amended as follows –

(2) In regulation 5(c) for '.' substitute ';'.

(3) After regulation 5(c) insert –

'(d)   a person who –
    (i)   arrived in Great Britain on or after 28 February 2009 but before 18 March 2011;
    (ii)   immediately before arriving in Great Britain had been resident in Zimbabwe; and
    (iii)   before leaving Zimbabwe, had accepted an offer, made by Her Majesty's Government, to assist that person to settle in the United Kingdom.'.

3

(1) The Homelessness (Wales) Regulations 2006 are amended as follows –

(2) In regulation 4(2)(d) for '.' substitute ';'.

(3) After regulation 4(2)(d) insert –

'(e)   a person who –
    (i)   arrived in Great Britain on or after 28 February 2009 but before 18 March 2011;
    (ii)   immediately before arriving in Great Britain had been resident in Zimbabwe; and
    (iii)   before leaving Zimbabwe, had accepted an offer, made by Her Majesty's Government, to assist that person to settle in the United Kingdom.'.

Appendix 3

Wales: Allocation and Homelessness

Appendix 4

STOP PRESS ITEMS: NEW GUIDANCE

Letter from the Department of Communities and Local Government to all Chief Housing Officers (England) concerning new eligibility regulations (17 October 2012)

DEPARTMENT FOR COMMUNTIES AND LOCAL GOVERNMENT

To: Chief Housing Officers of Local   17 October 2012
Authorities in England

Dear Chief Housing Officer

This letter notifies local housing authorities that **The Allocation of Housing and Homelessness (Eligibility) (England) (Amendment) Regulations 2012** *(SI 2012/ 2588) will come into force on 8 November 2012.*

These regulations (the Eligibility Amendment Regulations) are made by the Secretary of State under sections 160ZA(4), 172(4), 185(3) and 215(2) of the Housing Act 1996 (the 1996 Act) and were laid in Parliament today.

They amend regulations 4 and 6 of *The Allocation of Housing and Homelessness (Eligibility) (England) Regulations 2006* (SI 2006 No. 1294) (the Eligibility Regulations). Regulations 4 and 6 prescribe the classes of persons who are not subject to immigration control but who are to be treated as persons from abroad who are ineligible for an allocation of housing accommodation or for homelessness assistance under Parts 6 and 7 of the 1996 Act respectively.

Specifically, the Eligibility Amendment Regulations amend regulations 4 and 6 of the Eligibility Regulations to provide that the following persons are ineligible for an allocation of housing accommodation or homelessness assistance:

- Persons who have rights of residence in the UK as a result of regulation 15A(1) and (4A) of the Immigration (European Economic Area) (Amendment) (No 2) Regulations 2012 (the EEA Amendment Regulations)

- Persons who have a right derived from Article 20 of the Treaty on the Functioning of the European Union, in a case where rights of residence arise because a British citizen would otherwise be deprived of the genuine enjoyment of the substance of their rights as a European Union citizen

The Eligibility Amendment Regulations also make provision for persons who have equivalent rights of residence in the Channel Islands, the Isle of Man or the Republic of Ireland (the Common Travel Area).

The Government is making these amendments to the Eligibility Regulations following the ruling of the Court of Justice of the European Union in the case known as *Zambrano* (C-34/09 *Gerardo Ruiz Zambrano v Office national de l'emploi (ONEm)*). In that case, the Court ruled that a third country national (Mr Zambrano), who had been living and working in Belgium without a work permit, had a right of residence and right to work so that his Belgian national children were not forced to leave the EU and thereby prevented from exercising their rights as EU citizens.

Regulation 15A(1) and (4A) of the EEA Amending Regulations give effect to the *Zambrano* right by providing for a national from a non EEA country, who is resident in the UK and is the primary carer of a British citizen, to be granted a right of residence in the UK where not doing so would mean that the British citizen would have to leave the European Union.

The effect of the Eligibility Amendment Regulations is to maintain the Government's policy that non EEA nationals who are normally subject to immigration control should only have access to social housing or homelessness assistance if it accords with the Government's immigration and asylum policy, which broadly means only if they have been granted leave to enter or remain in the UK and this leave is not conditional on the person having no recourse to public funds.

The Department for Work and Pensions and HM Revenue and Customs are making similar amendments to regulations governing income-related benefits and tax credits which also come into force on 8 November.

The Eligibility Amendment Regulations are published by the Stationery Office and are available on the OPSI website at:

http://www.legislation.gov.uk/2012/2588.

Inquiries about the Eligibility Amendment Regulations should be addressed to Frances Walker, by telephone on 0303 444 3655 or by e-mail to: frances.walker@communities.gsi.gov.uk

A copy of this letter and the draft regulations is also being sent, by e-mail, to the homelessness strategy contact in each authority.

Yours sincerely,

Frances Walker   **John Bentham**

Appendix 4

Stop Press Items: New Guidance

Supplementary Guidance on the homelessness changes in the Localism Act 2011 and on the Homelessness (Suitability of Accommodation) (England) Order 2012 (8 November 2012)

Department for Communities and Local Government

November, 2012

Introduction

1. This supplementary guidance explains the changes sections 148 and 149 of the Localism Act make to the homelessness legislation. It explains in practice how the new power, that allows private rented sector offers to be made to end the main homelessness duty, should work and what local authorities should do as a consequence of the new power's introduction.

2. This guidance also explains the requirements of the Homelessness (Suitability of Accommodation) (England) Order 2012. The Order requires local authorities to put in place arrangements to ensure that private rented sector offer accommodation is suitable. The location requirements of the Order also extend to any accommodation secured under Part VII of the Housing Act 1996 (including temporary accommodation).

3. Sections 148 and 149 of the Localism Act 2011 amend Part 7 of the Housing Act 1996 ("the 1996 Act"). These sections as well as the Homelessness (Suitability of Accommodation) (England) Order 2012 come into force on 9th November 2012.

4. This guidance is issued by the Secretary of State under section 182 of the the1996 Act. Under section 182(1) of the 1996 Act, local housing authorities are required to have regard to this guidance in exercising their functions under Part 7 of the 1996 Act, as amended.

5. This statutory guidance supplements the relevant sections of the Homelessness Code of Guidance for Local Authorities issued in July 2006 ("the 2006 Code"), which deal with qualifying offers and reasonable to accept an offer. This guidance should be read in conjunction with the Homelessness Code of Guidance.

Overview

Localism Act 2011

6. The principal effect of the legislative changes is to amend the way in which the duty on authorities to secure accommodation under

section 193(2) of the 1996 Act can be brought to an end with an offer of suitable accommodation in the private rented sector.

7.   These changes will allow local authorities to end the main homelessness duty with a private rented sector offer, without the applicant's consent. The duty can only be ended in the private rented sector in this way with a minimum 12 month assured shorthold tenancy. If the household becomes unintentionally homeless within two years of taking the tenancy then the reapplication duty (section195A(1)) applies.

The Homelessness (Suitability of Accommodation) (England) Order 2012

8.   When ending the duty using the Localism Act power, local authorities are also subject to the provisions of the Homelessness (Suitability of Accommodation) (England) Order 2012. The order consists of two parts. The first part deals with the suitability of <u>location</u> of accommodation and applies to all accommodation secured under Part 7 of the 1996 Act (including temporary accommodation). The second part is concerned with those circumstances in which accommodation is not to be regarded as suitable for a person for the purposes of a private rented sector offer under section 193(7F) of the Housing Act 1996 only.

The changes

9.   Under the legislation as it stood prior to the amendments made by the Localism Act 2011, the authority could arrange an offer of a fixed term assured shorthold tenancy, which was a *"qualifying offer"*, and the section 193(2) main homelessness duty would have ended only if the offer was accepted, but not if refused – this is discussed in more detail below.

10. In a restricted case, local housing authorities were required to end the section 193(2) duty with a *private accommodation offer*, so far as reasonably practicable. A *private accommodation offer* must be a fixed term assured shorthold tenancy for a period of at least 12 months.

11. The provisions on *qualifying offers* (s193(7B) to (7E)) are repealed. This means a local authority will no longer be able to end the section 193(2) duty with a qualifying offer of 6 months by consent for new applicants.

12. The provisions on *private accommodation offers* are amended so that they are now referred to as *private rented sector offers* and authorities can consider bringing the duty to an end in this way for all cases, not just in a restricted case. However, in a restricted case, authorities **must** bring the section 193(2) main homelessness duty to an end with a *private rented sector offer*, so far as reasonably possible; in any other case it is at the authority's discretion whether to arrange a *private rented sector offer*.

Transitional arrangements

13. The amendments made by sections 148 and 149 of the Localism Act 2011 do not apply to a case where:

    (a) a person ("the applicant") has applied to a local housing authority for accommodation, or for assistance in obtaining accommodation, under Part 7 of the 1996 Act; and

    (b) a duty of the local housing authority to secure that accommodation is available for the applicant's occupation under Part 7 of the 1996 Act (including on an interim or temporary basis) has arisen and not ceased, before the commencement date of 9th November 2012.

Power not a duty

14. Authorities are reminded that the discretion to arrange a private rented sector offer is a power, not a duty, and as such, authorities should not seek to rely on the power in all cases. Authorities should consider whether to arrange a private rented sector based on the individual circumstances of the household and undertake to develop clear policies around its use.

Detailed changes to section 193 of the 1996 Act

15. Section 148 of the Localism Act 2011 makes a number of other changes to section 193 of the 1996 Act.

Statement of policy on offering choice to people under Part 6

16. Section 193(3A) is repealed. This means that authorities will no longer be required to give applicants owed the section 193(2) main homelessness duty a copy of their statement about their policy on offering choice to people allocated housing accommodation under Part 6 of the 1996 Act. This recognises that there will no longer be a presumption that most applicants owed the section 193 duty will have the duty ended with an offer of accommodation under Part 6.

17. The requirement to provide a copy of the statement (about the policy on offering choice under Part 6) to applicants owed the section 195(2) duty (eligible applicants in priority need threatened with homelessness) is similarly repealed.

Refusal of offer of suitable temporary accommodation

18. Section 148 of the Localism Act 2011 also substitutes a new section 193(5). This clarifies the position where an applicant is offered

"temporary accommodation" (i.e. offers of accommodation that, when accepted, do not have the effect of bringing the section 193(2) duty to an end).

19. Under the revised section 193(5), where an offer of accommodation is made which is neither a *Part 6 offer* nor a *private rented sector offer* (i.e. what is being offered is 'temporary accommodation' that would not otherwise bring the duty to an end if accepted), the section 193(2) duty may end if the applicant refuses the offer, but only if:
    (a) the applicant has been notified **in writing** of the possible consequences of refusal or acceptance,
    (b) the applicant has been notified in writing of the right to request a review of the suitability of the accommodation,
    (c) the authority are satisfied that the accommodation is suitable, and
    (d) the authority notify in writing the applicant that they regard themselves as ceasing to be subject to the section 193(2) duty.

Obligations in respect of existing accommodation

20. Sections 193(7F) and (8) of the 1996 Act are amended, such that local housing authorities shall not make a final offer of accommodation under Part 6 or approve a *private rented sector offer* unless they are satisfied that:
    (a) the accommodation is suitable for the applicant, and that
    (b) if the applicant is under contractual or other obligations in respect of the applicant's existing accommodation, the applicant is able to bring those obligations to an end before being required to take up the offer.

21. The previous requirement (in section 193(7F)) that authorities must be satisfied that it is reasonable for the applicant to accept the offer has been amended so that no factors, other than contractual or other obligations in respect of existing accommodation, are to be taken into account in determining whether it is reasonable to accept the offer. Where an applicant has contractual or other obligations in respect of their existing accommodation (e.g. a tenancy agreement or lease), the housing authority can reasonably expect the offer to be taken up only if the applicant is able to bring those obligations to an end before he is required to take up the offer.

22. This change **does not mean** that those subjective suitability issues which have become associated with 'reasonable to accept', such as those discussed in *Ravichandran and another v LB Lewisham*[1] or *Slater v LB Lewisham*[2] are not to be taken into account. The intention is that these factors as already highlighted in paragraph 17.6 of the Homelessness Code of Guidance for Local Authorities (for example, fear of racial

---

[1] [2010] EWCA Civ 755.
[2] [2006] EWCA Civ 394.

harassment; risk of violence from ex-partner's associates) continue to be part of those factors/elements an authority consider in determining suitability of accommodation.

Power to amend minimum fixed term for private rented sector offers

23.   Section 148 of the Localism Act 2011 inserts new sections 193(10), (11) and (12) into the 1996 Act. Section 193(10) provides a power for the appropriate authority to amend by regulations the minimum fixed term period for private rented sector offers specified in section 193(7AC)(c). Section 193(12) provides that the appropriate authority in England is the Secretary of State.

24.   However, section 193(11) provides that regulations made under section 193(10) may not:
      (a)   specify a period of less than 12 months, or
      (b)   apply to restricted cases.

25.   The Secretary of State recommends that a local private rented sector offer policy should take account of individual household circumstances, and be developed with regard to prevailing housing demand and supply pressures in the local area in order to support the best use of available housing stock locally.

Ending the duty using the new power

26.   Under section 193(7A) (duties to persons with priority need and who are not homeless intentionally) a local authority shall cease to be subject to the main homelessness duty, if the applicant, having been informed of the matters mentioned in section 193(7AB), accepts or refuses a private rented sector offer.

27.   A *private rented sector offer* is defined by section 193(7AC) as an offer of an assured shorthold tenancy made by a private landlord to an applicant in relation to any accommodation which:
      (a)   has been made available for the applicant's occupation by arrangements made by the local authority with a private landlord or
      (b)   is made with the approval of the authority, in pursuance of arrangements made by the authority with the landlord with a view to bringing the section 193(2) duty to an end, and
      (c)   is a fixed term Assured Shorthold Tenancy for a period of at least 12 months.

28.   The applicant must be informed in writing of the following matters (as mentioned in section 193(7AB)):
      (a)   the possible consequence of refusal or acceptance of the offer,

(b)   that the applicant has the right to request a review of the suitability of the accommodation, and

(c)   the effect under new section 195A of a further application to the authority within two years of acceptance of the offer (the 'reapplication duty').

29.   Applicants can continue to request a review of the housing authority's decision that the accommodation offered to them is suitable under section 202(1)(f).

Re-application within two years of acceptance of a private rented sector offer

30.   Under new section 195A(1) (re-application after private rented sector offer), the section 193(2) duty will apply regardless of whether the applicant has a priority need where:

(a)   a person makes a re-application for assistance within two years of accepting a private rented sector offer, and

(b)   the applicant is eligible for assistance and has become homeless unintentionally.

31.   Similarly under section 195A(3), the section 195(2) duty (owed to eligible applicants in priority need and threatened with homelessness) will apply regardless of whether the applicant has a priority need where:

(a)   a person makes a re-application for assistance within two years of accepting a private rented sector offer, and

(b)   the applicant is eligible for assistance and is threatened with homelessness unintentionally.

32.   Authorities should be aware that if, following the expiry of the initial 12 month assured shorthold tenancy, an applicant secures their own accommodation and then subsequently becomes homeless within two years of the original private rented sector offer then the re-application duty will still apply.

33.   Given the two year re-application duty, authorities are advised to keep the household circumstances under review as they approach the expiry of the 12 month tenancy so they can help actively manage cases where the tenancy may end unnecessarily. Please see the section below referring to section 21 notices.

Referrals to another local housing authority

34.   Authorities should note that the section 193(2) duty on re-application will apply regardless of whether or not the housing authority receiving the re-application is the same authority that arranged the *private rented sector offer*. This means that the authority receiving the re-application cannot

simply refer the applicant to the authority which made the private rented sector offer but must first carry out investigations to determine whether the applicant is homeless through no fault of their own, under section 195A. It is for the receiving authority to establish whether the applicant has become homeless unintentionally. Once established, this matter cannot be reopened.

35. Once the receiving authority has established that the applicant is unintentionally homeless and eligible for assistance, the receiving authority may refer the applicant to the authority that made the private rented sector offer (provided the conditions of section 198 which refer to the referral of a case to another local housing authority are met – explored further in the 'Referrals to another local housing authority' section below). The conditions for referral of the case to the other authority are met once it has been established that the re-application has been made within two years. The authority which made the private rented sector offer will owe the reapplication duty and it will be their responsibility to secure accommodation is available for occupation by the applicant. We would expect authorities to respond quickly to referrals. Here section 200 (which refers to referral and notification) continue to apply. This is supported by paragraphs 18.26 – 18.37 of the Homelessness Code of Guidance.

36. Similarly, authorities should note that the section 195(2) duty owed to those threatened with homelessness will apply regardless of whether the housing authority receiving the re-application is the same authority that arranged the *private rented sector offer*. (Under section 195(2), a local housing authority must take reasonable steps to secure that accommodation does not cease to be available for occupation by eligible applicants who have priority need and are threatened with homelessness.).

Section 21 Notices

37. As a consequence of the introduction of the re-application duty, an authority is required to treat section 21 notices differently.

38. Section 195(4) provides that, for the purpose of section 195A(3), where an applicant has been given a notice under section 21 of the *Housing Act 1988*, the applicant **must be treated as threatened with homelessness** from the date the notice is issued. This means that the authority must take reasonable steps to secure that accommodation does not cease to be available for their occupancy.

39. Section 195A(2) provides that, for the purpose of section 195A(1), where an applicant has been given a notice under section 21 of the Housing Act 1988, the applicant must be treated as homeless from the date the notice expires. It is not necessary for a possession order to have been sought by the landlord for the applicant to be considered homeless.

Referrals to another authority and risk of violence

40. Section 149 of the Localism Act 2011 also amends section 198 of the 1996 Act (*referrals to another local housing authority*). Section 149 (6) inserts new section 198(2ZA). Under section 198(2ZA), the conditions for referral of a case to another local housing authority are met if:
    (a) the application is made within 2 years of the date they applicant takes the tenancy of a *private rented sector offer* made by the other authority, and
    (b) there would be no risk of domestic violence to either the applicant, or anyone who might reasonably be expected to reside with the applicant, in the district of the other authority.

41. Section 149(7) and (8) make further amendments to section198 which mean that the new conditions for referral in section 198(2ZA) are not met if the applicant, or anyone who might reasonably be expected to reside with the applicant, has suffered violence (not limited to domestic violence) in the district of the other authority and it is probable that return to that district would lead to further violence against them.

42. Referrals regarding re-applications are not subject to any consideration of local connection. Section 200 on referrals continues to apply to these cases. Annex 18 of the Homelessness Code of Guidance for Local Authorities sets out the procedures for referrals of homeless applicants on the grounds of local connection with another local authority as well as guidelines for invoking the disputes procedure. The LGA have recently updated this guidance and it is available on their website.[3]

When re-application does not apply

43. The provisions in section 195A(1) to (4), which apply to the re-application duty, do not apply in a restricted case. Additionally, these provisions do not apply in a case where the applicant has previously made a re-application which resulted in their being owed the duty under section 193(2) or 195(2) by virtue of section 195A(1) or (3). This effectively means that an applicant can only be owed the re-application duty once following each private rented sector offer. If an applicant becomes become unintentionally homeless again within the two year limit and have already been assisted under the re-application duty, then they must make a fresh homelessness application.

---

[3] http://www.local.gov.uk/web/guest/housing/-/journal_content/56/10171/3479463/ARTICLE-TEMPLATE.

Interim duty to accommodate

44. Section 149 of the Localism Act 2011 inserts a new section 188(1A) in the 1996 Act. Under section 188(1A), any local housing authority in England that the applicant has applied to must secure accommodation for them (pending a decision as to what duty, if any, is owed to the applicant under Part 7) regardless of whether the applicant has priority need, if the authority have reason to believe that the duty under section 193(2) may apply in the circumstances mentioned in section 195A(1) (that is a re-application within 2 years of acceptance of a *private rented sector offer*).

45. Authorities should note that the duty under section 188(1A) will apply regardless of whether the housing authority receiving the re-application is the same authority that arranged the *private rented sector offer.*

Homelessness (Suitability of Accommodation) (England) Order 2012

46. The Homelessness (Suitability of Accommodation) (England) Order 2012 consists of two parts. The first deals with the suitability of location of accommodation and applies to **all accommodation secured under Part VII** of the Housing Act 1996 (including temporary accommodation). The second deals with those circumstances in which accommodation is not to be regarded as suitable for a person for the purposes of a private rented sector offer under section 193(7F) of the Housing Act 1996 only.

Location

47. Location of accommodation is relevant to suitability. Existing guidance on this aspect is set out at paragraph 17.41 of the Homelessness Code of Guidance offers. The suitability of the location for all the members of the household must be considered by the authority. Section 208(1) of the 1996 Act requires that authorities shall, in discharging their housing functions under Part 7 of the 1996 Act, in so far as is reasonably practicable, secure accommodation within the authority's own district.

48. Where it is not possible to secure accommodation within district and an authority has secured accommodation outside their district, the authority is required to take into account the distance of that accommodation from the district of the authority. Where accommodation which is otherwise suitable and affordable is available nearer to the authority's district than the accommodation which it has secured, the accommodation which it has secured is not likely to be suitable unless the authority has a justifiable reason or the applicant has specified a preference.

49. Generally, where possible, authorities should try to secure accommoda-tion that is as close as possible to where an applicant was previously

living. Securing accommodation for an applicant in a different location can cause difficulties for some applicants. Local authorities are required to take into account the significance of any disruption with specific regard to employment, caring responsibilities or education of the applicant or members of their household. Where possible the authority should seek to retain established links with schools, doctors, social workers and other key services and support.

50. In assessing the significance of disruption to **employment**, account will need to be taken of their need to reach their normal workplace from the accommodation secured.

51. In assessing the significance of disruption to **caring responsibilities**, account should be taken of the type and importance of the care household members provide and the likely impact the withdrawal would cause. Authorities may want to consider the cost implications of providing care where an existing care arrangement becomes unsustainable due to a change of location.

52. Authorities should also take into account the need to minimise disruption to the **education** of young people, particularly at critical points in time such as leading up to taking GCSE (or their equivalent) examinations.

53. Account should also be taken of medical facilities and other support currently provided for the applicant and their household. Housing authorities should consider the potential impact on the health and well being of an applicant or any person reasonably expected to reside with them, were such support removed or medical facilities were no longer accessible. They should also consider whether similar facilities are accessible and available near the accommodation being offered and whether there would be any specific difficulties in the applicant or person residing with them using those essential facilities, compared to the support they are currently receiving. Examples of other support might include support from particular individuals, groups or organisations located in the area where the applicant currently resides: for example essential support from relatives or support groups which would be difficult to replicate in another location

54. Housing authorities should avoid placing applicants in isolated accommodation away from public transport, shops and other facilities, where possible.

55. Whilst authorities should, as far as is practicable, aim to secure accommodation within their own district, they should also recognise that there can be clear benefits for some applicants to be accommodated outside of the district. This could occur, for example, where the applicant, and/or a member of his or her household, would be at risk of domestic or other violence in the district and need to be accommodated elsewhere to

reduce the risk of further contact with the perpetrator(s) or where ex-offenders or drug/alcohol users would benefit from being accommodated outside the district to help break links with previous contacts which could exert a negative influence. Any risk of violence or racial harassment in a particular locality must also be taken into account. Where domestic violence is involved and the applicant is not able to stay in the current home, housing authorities may need to consider the need for alternative accommodation whose location can be kept a secret and which has security measures and staffing to protect the occupants.

56. Similarly there may also be advantages in enabling some applicants to access employment opportunities outside of their current district. The availability, or otherwise, of employment opportunities in the new area may help to determine if that area is suitable for the applicant.

57. Where it is not reasonably practicable for the applicant to be placed in accommodation within the housing authority's district, and the housing authority places the applicant in accommodation in another district, section 208(2) **requires the housing authority to notify in writing within 14 days of the accommodation being made available to the applicant the housing authority in whose district the accommodation is situated.**

58. Local authorities are reminded that in determining the suitability of accommodation, affordability must be taken into account. This aspect of suitability must continue to form part of your assessment when considering the location of accommodation.

Circumstances in which accommodation secured under section 193(7F) is not to be regarded as suitable for a person

59. This part of the Order sets out those circumstances in which accommodation is not to be regarded as suitable for a person. It applies only to accommodation secured under s193(7F). The requirements can be grouped under five broad headings.

Physical condition of the property

60. Local housing authorities are obliged under section 3 of the Housing Act 2004 to keep the housing conditions in their area under review with a view to identifying any action that may need to be taken by them under the Household Health and Safety Ratings System legislation. The local housing authority is also required to keep the housing conditions in their area under review in relation to other powers/duties such as licensing of HMOs.

61. Section 4 of the 2004 Act provides that an authority must arrange for an inspection of residential premises in its district with a view to determining

whether any category 1 or 2 hazard exists on those premises. Such an inspection is only required if the authority considers that it would be appropriate for them to be inspected, as a result of any matters of which they have become aware in carrying out their duty under section 3, or for any other reason.

62. Authorities should secure accommodation that is in reasonable physical condition. Authorities should ensure that the property has been visited by either a local authority officer or someone acting on their behalf to determine its suitability before an applicant moves in. Existing aspects of suitability such as space and arrangement set out in statutory guidance will continue to apply.

63. In determining whether the property is in reasonable physical condition attentions should be paid to signs of damp, mould, indications that the property would be cold, for example cracked windows, and any other physical signs that would indicate the property is not in good physical condition.

Health and safety matters

64. Landlords are by law required to ensure that all electrical equipment in a property is safe. The local authority are required to satisfy themselves that any electrical equipment provided in the property meets the requirements of regulations 5 and 7 of the Electrical Equipment (Safety) Regulations 1994. Generally speaking, it is likely that a visual inspection of the property, by a person authorised to act on behalf of the local authority, that checks for obvious signs of loose wiring, cracked or broken electrical sockets, light switches that do not work and evidence of Portable Appliance Testing will be indicative that the specific regulations have been applied.

65. The Fire Safety Order[4] applies to the common or shared parts of multi-occupied residential buildings. As such landlords, owners or managing agents will need to carry out a fire risk assessment of the common parts and implement and maintain appropriate and adequate fire safety measures. As part of their responsibilities, landlords should put in place appropriate management and maintenance systems to ensure any fire safety equipment or equipment which may represent a fire hazard, is maintained in good working order, and in accordance with the manufacturers instructions. Landlords are also required to ensure that furniture and furnishings supplied must comply with the Furniture and Furnishings (Fire) (Safety) Regulations 1988 (as amended).

66. Local authorities and fire and rescue authorities should work together to ensure the safety of domestic premises including the provision of fire

[4] Regulatory Reform (Fire Safety) Order 2005.

safety advice to households (such as the benefits of a working smoke alarm). Local authorities will need to satisfy themselves that these regulations have been adhered to.

67. Local authorities are asked to satisfy themselves that the landlord has taken reasonable precautions to prevent the possibility of carbon monoxide poisoning in the accommodation, where such a risk exists. Taken together with a valid gas Safety Record, the installation of a carbon monoxide alarm would constitute reasonable precaution to prevent the possibility of carbon monoxide poisoning, where such a risk exists.

68. If the accommodation is or forms part of residential property which does not have a valid energy performance certificate as required by the Energy Performance of Buildings (Certificates and Inspections) (England and Wales) Regulations 2007, then it will not be regarded as suitable. Local authorities should ensure they have had sight of a current certificate to ensure that this requirement has been met.

69. Housing authorities should satisfy themselves that accommodation that is or forms part of relevant premises in accordance with regulation 36 of the Gas Safety (Installation and Use) Regulations 1994 has a current gas safety certificate. A local authority can do this by requesting sight of the valid Gas Safety certificate.

Licensing for Houses in Multiple Occupation

70. Accommodation that is in a house of multiple occupation which is subject to licensing under section 55 of the Housing Act 2004 and is not licensed is unsuitable. Accommodation in a house of multiple occupation that is subject to additional licensing under section 56 of the Housing Act 2004 and is not licensed is unsuitable.

Landlord behaviour

71. Authorities should satisfy themselves that landlords of accommodation secured under s 193(7F) are fit and proper persons to act in the capacity of a landlord. Local authorities are required to consider any convictions in relation to landlord and tenant law, fraud or other dishonesty, violence or drugs as well as any discrimination and/or sexual offences as set out in the legislation. Most local authorities currently do this for Houses in Multiple Occupancy and they can also check their own records for any prosecutions for offences of harassment and illegal eviction brought by the local authority. If their record checking does not satisfy them that the landlord is a fit and proper person to act in the capacity of a landlord then the local authority can require the landlord to carry out a Criminal Records Bureau check, but they are not required to do this in every case.

The Secretary of State recommends that when placing households outside of their district that the authority liaise with the receiving district to check whether that authority has taken any enforcement activity against the landlord.

Elements of good management

72. The local authority should ensure that the landlord has provided to them a written tenancy agreement which they propose to use for the purposes of a private rented sector offer and which the local authority considers to be adequate. It is expected that the local authority should review the tenancy agreement to ensure that it sets out, ideally in a clear and comprehensible way, the tenant's obligations, for example a clear statement of the rent and other charges, and the responsibilities of the landlord, but does not contain unfair or unreasonable terms, such as call-out charges for repairs or professional cleaning at the end of the tenancy.

Tenancy Deposit Scheme

73. Whilst a local authority will not be able to check that a tenant's deposit has been placed in a tenancy deposit protection scheme prior to them taking the tenancy we recommend that local authorities remind prospective landlords and tenants of their responsibilities in this area.

74. Tenancy deposit protection schemes guarantee that tenants will get their deposits back at the end of the tenancy, if they meet the terms of the tenancy agreement and do not damage the property. Landlords must protect their tenants' deposits using a TDP scheme if they have let the property on an assured shorthold tenancy (AST) which started on or after 6 April 2007.

INDEX

References are to paragraph numbers.